W9-BRR-646

LET'S GO:

The Budget Guide to the
USA

1991

Kevin Young
Editor

Jenny Davidson
Adrian Staub
Assistant Editors

Written by Harvard Student Agencies, Inc.

ST. MARTIN'S PRESS
NEW YORK

Helping Let's Go

If you have suggestions or corrections, or just want to share your discoveries, drop us a line. We read every piece of correspondence, whether a 10-page letter, a postcard, or, as in one case, a collage. All suggestions are passed along to our researcher/writers. Please note that mail received after June 1, 1991 will probably be too late for the 1992 book, but will be retained for the following edition. Address mail to: *Let's Go: U.S.A.;* Harvard Student Agencies, Inc.; Thayer Hall-B; Harvard University; Cambridge, MA 02138; USA.

In addition to the invaluable travel advice our readers share with us, many are kind enough to offer their services as researchers or editors. Unfortunately, the charter of Harvard Student Agencies, Inc. enables us to employ only currently enrolled Harvard students.

Editor	Kevin Young
Assistant Editors	Jenny Davidson
	Adrian Staub
Publishing Manager	Ravi Desai
Managing Editors	Jessica V.V. Avery
	Michael Scott Krivan
	Alexandra M. Tyler
Production/Communication Coordinator	Christopher W. Cowell

Researcher/Writers

New York City (Brooklyn and Manhattan)	Darren Aronofsky
Kentucky (except Cumberland Gap); Maryland; Virginia; Washington, DC; West Virginia	Stephen Burt
Hawaii	Richard M. Claflin II
Alaska	Steven M. Cohn
Iowa; Michigan; Minnesota; Ohio; Wisconsin	James D. Ebenhoh
Alabama; Arkansas (except Ozarks); Atlanta, GA; Louisiana; Mississippi; Carolina Mountains, NC; Tennessee	Elizabeth Elsas
Illinois; Indiana; St. Louis, MO	Joshua Fox
Florida; Georgia (except Atlanta); Raleigh, Durham, Chapel Hill, NC; South Carolina	Matthew Hanson
Mesa Verde, San Juan Mountains, CO; New Mexico; Oklahoma; Texas	Leah Kaiser
Northern California; Lake Tahoe, Sacramento, CA; Reno, NV	Sarah Todd Kuehl
Connecticut; Maine; Massachusetts; New Hampshire; Rhode Island; Vermont	Kelly A.E. Mason
New York City (Bronx, Manhattan, Staten Island)	Vladimir Perlovich
New York City (Long Island, Manhattan, Queens)	Jacob Press
The Desert, CA	Joseph M. Rainsbury
British Columbia	Michael Ernest Raynor
Colorado (except Mesa Verde and San Juan Mts.); Kansas; Kansas City, MO; Nebraska; Utah	Laura Kay Rozen

iv

ACKNOWLEDGMENTS

Obviously a book of this size and flavor could not be done alone. Fellow Kansan Laura Rozen trekked humorously through the Great Plains, providing ample marginalia, beautiful postcards (front and back), and the best variations on Motel 6 rooms. Jim Ebenhoh put Cleveland back on the map, managing to find nightlife and famous live bands on desert islands. I lived vicariously through the Elizabeth Elsas Envy route which headed through New Orleans, Graceland, Yoknapatawpha County, the Lil' Peach, and other fabulous points south; meanwhile she (and her sundry musketeers) managed to rid towns of their narcileptic descriptions. Leah Kaiser held down perhaps the most bug- and creep-filled Southwest tour, writing the most detailed and newsletter-worthy marginalia of the New Kids Summer. And where would we be without Joey, Jordan, Donnie, Dan, and John? Stephen Burt miraculously avoided getting in a fight with the New Kids, dreaming up an endless stream of synonyms for "Let's Go" and making D.C. an excellent, multi-installment mini-series. Josh Shenk galloped through the Mid-Atlantic, surviving torture at the hands of Hersheyworld and delighting us all by sending his bounty from Atlantic City. Kelly Mason's expanded coverage amazed all, even as she negotiated both the very problematic New England terrain and the surprisingly obscure Au Bon Pain. Making sure to reach out and touch us, Matt Hanson dealt nobly with Ft. Lauderdale and monetary hassles. Ben Sheffner tightened up the Rockies and Joshua Fox stepped in at the last moment to whirl through Chicago and St. Louis.

Researchers for the regional books proved invaluable to this tome as well. Zach Schrag shone at the pinnacles of the Grand Canyon and San Francisco. Tim Whitmire helped reign in the mammoth that is (and was) L.A. With cool, Sarah Kuehl met cowboy poets throughout Wine Country. Alongside Richard Claflin's greatly improved Hawaii, Joe Rainsbury found what we were looking for at the Joshua Tree. To the north, Michael Raynor reshaped British Columbia while Steve Cohn scoured the Alaska wilds to send back vital annotated copy. Chris Salvaterra researched his heart out and Lori Smith braved time zones, saucy overweek delivery, and a transcontinental wind to get us that copy. Darren Aronofsky, Vladimir Perlovich, and Jacob Press made New York City safe for all.

Back on the 10th floor of I.M. Pei-designed *Let's Go* headquarters, Team USA smoked through ubiquitous rural-urban dichotomies, weekly gossip sessions/book meetings, and passive voice to turn out the best coiffed book in the office. Taking his title to new heights, The Foxiest Managing Editor Mike Krivan instilled me with the confidence necessary to complete this project; in turn, my faith in his speedy blue pen, occasional research, and frequent quesadilla made my summer worry-free. Adrian, by far the Beefiest Assistant Editor, redefined endurance, obscene place names, and headband fashion; Jen somehow managed to go moniker-less, though her always timely realism and outside presence prevented me from going too far into "indoor fun" jokes. From the first hiring days on the shuttle through probing semantics questions to the last hurrah, Jamie Rosen's chalkboard and interminable sincerity kept me honest. Katharine Chang and Beth Quitsland provided invaluable help in navigating the print-out-filled waters that were California and the Pacific Northwest even as Jenny Lyn Bader and Maggie Tucker made devouring that unknown and monstrous fruit, New York City, a joy.

Andrew and the guys at Bifurcators Plus, Alex's 5pm improv dance numbers, Chris and Zan's recurrent pasta remedies, Dars and her M&Ms (Thanx), Jenny's Chicago intro, and Steve's "Mailman!" all influenced this book more than with mere words. Thanks also to Ravi's firm Publishing Manager leadership and sensibility.

In the "outside" world, Dick provided a crucial and surprisingly unspoken lifeline that helped me through the rough times—one I will certainly miss in the coming year. Annlucien's friendship went beyond the call of duty, taking me into her family and understanding when I was not always around. Jeremy, Orion, Duncan, Susan, Garrett, and Cecil (the avatar of the summer) made 890 Broadway more than a "clean, comfortable" accommodation, though often they weren't sure I still lived there. I want to give a shout out to Chipp, Kellie, and the rest of the *Diaspora* crew—I haven't forgotten who and what got me here. Back on the ranch, Jenny and Karl provided the perspective only long-term, unquestioned relationships can.

Last but in no way least, Ghita's humor, tutor-like insight, artistic support, and undying friendship shaped me and the book into what they are today. Living up to their name, the Fosters continued to provide me the physical and spiritual gifts of a second home without asking anything in return; I hope they know what they have meant to me. Finally, I dedicate this book to my parents, who have supported this and all my other undertakings from day one. Their boundless love has helped me start, finish, and take pride in this project. Looking back on the summer, I only regret that I don't have room enough to thank everyone. Peace.

—KLY

Thanks Chris for marshalling the army of typists and proofreaders who actually did most of my work. Thanks Mike for calling me in the morning and letting the phone ring until I stumbled out of bed, only to fall back in as soon as the phone was back on the hook. Thanks Adj for calling me in the morning and scaring me back into bed by telling me an entire state's just vanished from the hard drive. Most of all thanks Kev for calling me in the morning and threatening my answering machine as I lay in bed screening calls. No really, I loved you all even as I suffered the corporate hierarchy. Thanks Gold Star, thanks everyone else, it was a great summer.

—JD

Thanks, Kev, for always locating on the right side of format disputes and drawing the passive line. Thanks, Mike, for saving me from ignominy in a Santa Fe pizza joint. Thanks, Jen, for doing the big batches and broadening the visual spectrum in this gray, concrete hell-hole. Thanks, Chris, for knowing more about this operation than any one person has a right to know. Thanks to all the proofreaders and typists; blame them for the mistakes, please. Thanks, Sheri, for putting it in perspective, and Dave, for putting up with me.

—AS

About Let's Go

In 1960, Harvard Student Agencies, a three-year-old nonprofit corporation established to provide employment opportunities to Harvard and Radcliffe students, was doing a booming business selling charter flights to Europe. One of the extras HSA offered passengers on these flights was a 20-page mimeographed pamphlet entitled *1960 European Guide,* a collection of tips on continental travel compiled by the staff at HSA. The following year, students traveling to Europe researched the first full-fledged edition of *Let's Go: Europe,* a pocket-sized book with a smattering of tips on budget accommodations, irreverent write-ups of sights, and a decidedly youthful slant. The first editions proclaimed themselves to be the companions of the "adventurous and often impecunious student."

Throughout the 60s, the series reflected its era: a section of the 1968 *Let's Go: Europe* was entitled "Street Singing in Europe on No Dollars a Day;" the 1969 guide to America led off with a feature on drug-ridden Haight-Ashbury. During the 70s, *Let's Go* gradually became a large-scale operation, adding regional European guides and expanding coverage into North Africa and Asia. In 1981, *Let's Go: USA* returned after an eight-year hiatus, and in the next year HSA joined forces with its current publisher, St. Martin's Press. Now in its 31st year, *Let's Go* publishes 13 titles covering more than 40 countries.

Each spring, over 150 Harvard-Radcliffe students compete for some 70 positions as *Let's Go* researcher/writers. Those hired possess a rare combination of budget travel sense, writing ability, stamina, and courage. Each researcher/writer travels on a shoe-string budget for seven weeks, researching seven days per week, and overcoming countless obstacles in the quest for better bargains.

Back in a basement in Harvard Yard, an editorial staff of 25, a management team of five, and countless typists and proofreaders—all students—spend four months poring over more than 50,000 pages of manuscript as they push the copy through 12 stages of intensive editing. In September the efforts of summer are converted from computer diskettes to nine-track tapes and delivered to Com Com in Allentown, Pennsylvania, where their computerized typesetting equipment turns them into books in record time. And even before the books hit the stands, next year's editions are well underway.

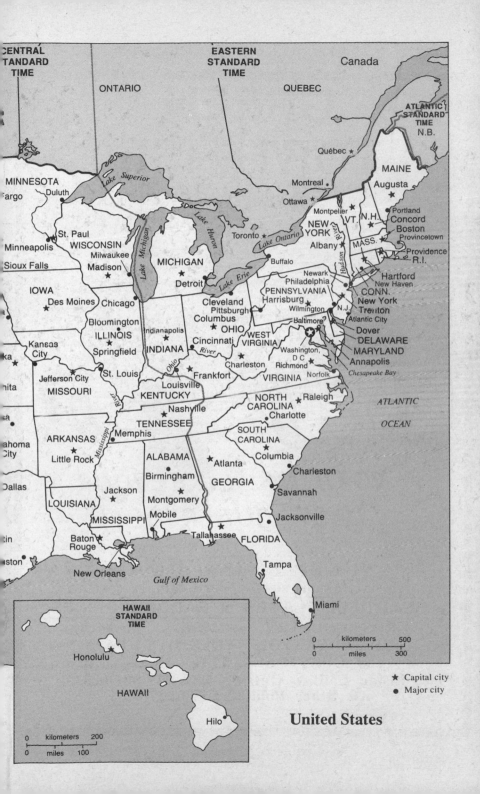

United States

★ Capital city
● Major city

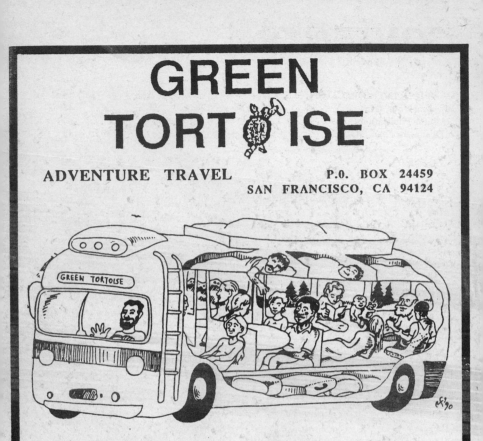

CONTENTS

xiv   **Contents**

LIST OF MAPS

American Youth Hostels
SOUTHERN COMFORT

Marquette House, New Orleans, LA

As a member of American Youth Hostels, you can stay at 5,300 hostels around the world, including 230 hostels in the USA. Hostels are great places to make new friends. And the prices are incredibly low, just $3-$20 for a dorm-style room. To join, visit any of the following hostels. Or contact American Youth Hostels, Dept. 802, P.O. Box 37613, Washington, DC 20013-7613; 202-783-6161.

Daytona Beach International AYH-Hostel
Just 300 feet from the Atlantic Ocean
140 S. Atlantic Avenue
Daytona Beach, FL 32018
904-258-6937

Miami Beach International AYH-Hostel
Vintage hotel in the Art Deco Region
1438 Washington Avenue
Miami Beach, FL 33139
305-534-2988

Orlando International AYH-Hostel at Plantation Manor
Transportation to Disney World & more
227 N. Eola Drive
Orlando, FL 32801
407-843-8888

St. Augustine AYH-Hostel
Come and enjoy America's oldest city
32 Treasury Street
St. Augustine, FL 32084
904-829-6163

Marquette House/New Orleans International AYH-Hostel
Minutes from the French Quarter
2253 Carondelet Street
New Orleans, LA 70130
504-523-3014

Blue Ridge Country AYH-Hostel
Explore the Blue Ridge Parkway
RR 2, Box 449
Galax, VA 24333
703-236-4962

INTERNATIONAL YOUTH HOSTEL FEDERATION
American Youth Hostels

LET'S GO: USA

General Introduction

How To Use This Book

Let's Go: USA does not intend to cover every possible attraction north of Mexico. The United States and Canada are too enormous and diverse to be crunched into a single volume. However, budget travelers will find *Let's Go: USA* invaluable. You'll save far more money than this book cost to buy, and have a good time doing it. *Let's Go: USA* has the charm of 50 regional guides without the bulk.

What exactly is covered in *Let's Go: USA?* You'll find all 50 states; one section covers major portions of four Canadian provinces along with a separate General Introduction. We organize the U.S. into 15 regions, with states listed alphabetically within those regions. In the state and regional introductions, we comment on the geography, history, culture, and other outstanding or unusual characteristics of an area, while providing tips on adjusting your travel strategies to U.S. regional diversity. Our maps will give you the general layout of regions and cities, but use more detailed maps when planning your final itinerary.

As you use this book, you will become familiar with the way we organize information. **Practical Information** presents what you need to know about getting to and around a city, town, or region. For each city, we list modes of transportation, phone numbers, addresses, and visitor information. **Accomodations, Camping, and Food** sections help you take care of the necessary details. **Sights** sections let you know about the most interesting, noteworthy, and inexpensive attractions. **Nightlife, Entertainment,** and **Seasonal Events** listings suggest ways to enjoy budget-minded culture or, at times, an occasional extravagant evening.

Planning Your Trip

Every traveler must set priorities. If you're on a shoestring, you'll do fine, as long as you recognize your situation before you leave. When you're planning a hectic, whirlwind tour, make sure to verify travel arrangements in advance. And if you're taking a leisurely, well-financed journey, do the background reading and planning that will enable you fully to appreciate the places you visit. Basically, every variety of trip takes heavy preparation, much like a prize-fight or a bar mitzvah.

Every traveler in the United States and Canada has a few preliminary concerns. Traveling with others brings safety, company, and wealth. You can venture into urban areas you wouldn't hazard alone, while saving money on sights and lodgings. Staying with friends, relatives, or the-mailman-of-your-sister's-ex-husband can also save you money. Of course, go only where you feel welcome, but seek out old acquaintances. Many people are happy to have houseguests, even if they are not mail deliverers.

The weather and the tourist seasons can combine to make some regions paradisical at some times, hellish at others. Generally, summer months are "in season" in Northern states, winter "in season" in the South. This translated means that, say, some parts of Florida during March "spring break" season are a raucous carnival of drunken college students, and that October may draw a bevy of fellow nature-hoarders to views of New England foliage. Some areas have unusual tourist seasons, such as Mardi Gras in New Orleans; state, regional, and city introductions note

1

these. Off-season travel works best in May and September, in the transition between seasons. Sometimes, of course, you want to visit "in season."

Our Practical Information listings in state and city introductions give addresses of services that can provide preliminary information. These range from tourist info centers and chambers of commerce to special interest organizations, all of which can offer more than the brochures at your local travel agent to familiarize yourself with the region. Write or call these organizations ahead of time.

Useful Publications

Besides that pillar of travel guide society, *Let's Go,* road maps remain the most popular and effective travel aids. You can still purchase maps at many gas stations, tourist information centers, and convenience stores. Rand McNally's *Road Atlas for the U.S., Canada, and Mexico* ($15) is detailed and comprehensive. The American Automobile Association (AAA) (800-336-4357) gives great maps to all members (see Transportation below).

The **U.S. Government Printing Office** prints pamphlets on many aspects of travel, covered in the bibliographies *Recreational and Outdoor Activities* and *Travel and Tourism.* For these and many other pamphlets listed throughout *Let's Go: USA,* write or call Superintendent of Documents, U.S. Government Printing Office, Washington, DC 20402 (202-783-3238). Various other government agencies also publish brochures and books on parks, forests, and wildife, listed in later sections of the general introductions.

Many bookstores have extensive travel sections, as do libraries. However, if you can't find something on the shelves, we generally print publishers' addresses and phone numbers alongside book titles. The invaluable *Let's Go: California and Hawaii, Let's Go: Pacific Northwest, Canada, and Alaska, Let's Go: Mexico,* and new *Let's Go: New York* provide more detailed supplements to *Let's Go: USA.*

Documents

Making financial transactions usually requires two forms of identification, one of which must be a photo ID. This may happen when cashing traveler's checks at banks, for example. It is also handy to carry a major credit card, such as Visa, Mastercard, or American Express (see Money below). The U.S. has far fewer discounts for students as in Europe, but a student ID is nevertheless useful. A U.S. university or college ID will suffice, or obtain an **International Student Identity Card (ISIC)**. This card will cost $14 in 1991, and provides discounts, insurance, and widely accepted proof of student status. Offices that issue the ISIC include the **Council on International Educational Exchange (CIEE)** (212-661-1414), and **Let's Go Travel,** Harvard Student Agencies, Thayer Hall-B, Harvard University, Cambridge, MA 02138 (617-495-9649). A U.S. driver's license is also widely accepted ID. Make copies of all important documents before departing, and leave the copies with someone at home. Foreigners should see the Additional Information for Foreign Visitors section below.

Money

Widely accepted, **traveler's checks** are perhaps the most convenient way to deal with your finances while you travel. They are refundable if lost or stolen, and can be purchased at any bank. Make sure to make a separate list of check numbers, and buy small denominations. AAA sells American Express checks to its members at no commission. You will find an occasional establishment that won't accept traveler's checks; these are most likely to be cash-oriented, low-budget bars and restaurants. Most nicer hotels will cash checks at the front desk, though often only for

Don't forget to write.

If your American Express® Travelers Cheques are lost or stolen, we can hand-deliver a refund virtually anywhere you travel. Just give us a call. You'll find it's a lot less embarrassing than calling home.

AMERICAN EXPRESS **Travelers Cheques**

hotel residents. The following is a list of common brands of checks, with info numbers.

American Express, World Financial Center, American Express Tower, 200 Vesey St., New York, NY 10285 (800-221-7282). One percent commission charged by AmEx, though some banks may levy additional commissions.

Visa International, P.O. Box 8999, San Francisco, CA 94128 (800-227-6811). No commission from Visa, banks may charge 1%.

Bank of America Traveler's Office, P.O. Box 37010, San Francisco, CA 94137 (800-227-3460). Charges a 1% commission for non-Bank of America customers.

Barclays (800-221-2426). Commission 1%.

Citicorp (800-645-6556). Commission 1%.

Thomas Cook (800-223-4030 and 800-223-7373). Affiliated with **Mastercard.** Commission 1% and an extra commission may be levied by the bank.

With a major **credit card** you can rent cars, make reservations, and obtain cash advances at most banks. Don't plan on relying exclusively on plastic money, as the cheapest places don't trust it. American Express Cardholders pay a relatively steep annual fee ($55) but the card entitles them to several valuable services. Local offices will cash personal checks (including foreign checks) in any 7-day period up to $1000 ($5000 with a gold card): they pay in cash and traveler's checks, depending on the office's money supply. They also cancel stolen credit cards, arrange for temporary ID, help change airline, hotel, and car rental reservations, and send mailgrams or international cables. American Express offices in the U.S. will act as a mail service if you contact them in writing beforehand and request that they hold your mail (see Keeping in Touch below). American Express also operates machines at major airports through which you can purchase traveler's checks with your card. For more information, call American Express Card Division (800-528-4800). Other widely accepted credit cards are Mastercard (800-223-9920) and Visa (800-336-3386). Visa in particular now offers many of the same travel services as American Express.

Credit cards are also compatible with the latest form of plastic financing—**electronic banking.** At least two banking networks offer 24-hr. service at automated tellers (operated by bank cards) in major cities across the country. The **Cirrus network** (800-424-7787) includes Bay Banks in New England, New York Cash Exchange, First Interstate in the West, and Manufacturers Hanover in New York, among others; the **Plus network** (800-843-7587) includes Bank of America in the West, U.S. Bank in the Northwest, Chase Manhattan in New York, Continental in Chicago, and First City Bank of Dallas. When staying in major cities, a bank card may prove as valuable as traveler's checks. The telephone numbers listed for Cirrus and Plus allow you to locate machines in your area. Be warned that the machines are sometimes out of service, and there is a limit ($500 at most banks) imposed on the amount of withdrawal in any one day. Visa and Mastercard also work in these machines, if the operating bank issues the card. Check with local banks about these and competing services.

If you run out of money on the road, you can have some mailed to you the form of a **certified check,** redeemable at any bank. You can also wire money directly from bank to bank for about $10. Another alternative is a **postal money order.** You can purchase money orders in cash at any U.S. post office for a fee up to $1; you can cash them at another office upon display of two IDs (one with photo). The buyer should keep a receipt to refund lost orders. A generous sibling or parent can have money wired to you in minutes via **Western Union** (800-325-6000 or 800-325-4176) from within the U.S. Western Union charges a wiring fee based on the amount wired and the method of payment; call for information. You must have a Mastercard or Visa to wire by phone. Finally, American Express offers a money transfer service.

The prices quoted throughout *Let's Go: USA* figure amounts before adding **sales tax.** Tax rates vary from about five to eight percent, depending of the item and the state where you purchased it. Many states have special hotel taxes as well; ask before you take the room.

Packing

Everyone has an aunt or uncle with indispensable tips on packing; you will want to throw out most of his or her suggestions and stick to basics. Traveling light has its rewards in saved time and effort spent dealing with your stuff. Some essentials include:needle and thread, pocket knife, plastic water bottle, flashlight, waterproof matches, paper and pen/pencil, cord or clothesline, rubber bands, bath towel, alarm clock or loud watch, sink stopper (you can use a squash ball), soap, shampoo (good for hand-washing clothing), sheet sack (required by many hostels; see Hostels below).

You will also need a first aid kit, which includes: tweezers, band-aids, antiseptic solution, a protected thermometer, burn ointment, decongestant, talcum powder, gauze, ace bandage, aspirin, antibiotic ointment, antihistamines and something for stomach ailments (Maalox, Rolaids).

Other hints: bring an extra supply of any prescription medicine, as well as a copy of the prescription. Also, be sure to bring extra contact lens solution and disinfectant. Women should bring extra tampons; those using birth control pills should bring an extra supply and be sure to figure in time changes. Everyone should pack extra contraceptives.

You should spend some pre-travel time deciding how to carry your stuff; the best option may be a backpack. Decent packs generally cost over $100, but they can simplify your trip by enabling you to comfortably carry everything in one place. You will have to choose an internal- or external-frame pack, each of which has its advantages, and which fit different people differently. Walk around the store in a weighed-down pack before you buy one. A smaller daypack may be useful if you can sometimes leave the large pack behind.

Good footwear and rainwear are essential. Break in new shoes before you leave. A rain poncho covers your pack and can also serve as a groundcloth. Use a lightweight windbreaker for milder climes. In general, clothes should be durable and comfortable. You probably won't need that formal outfit you think you should pack just in case. Lighter colors are cooler, but darker ones don't show dirt.

Always keep your valuables on your person. Wallets carried in front, around-the-neck pouches kept under the shirt, and belt pouches are all fairly theft-resistant. A camera is also necessary, and unless you're an old pro, use a small, automatic 35mm: they are totally idiot-proof and usually take good pictures. If you're more serious about photography, New York City is the place to buy. Have your film hand-checked at airport x-ray machines.

Keeping in Touch

If you plan to rely on the phone, a calling card offered by AT&T or one of its competitors, such as MCI or Sprint, can save money over calling collect. Visa, Mastercard, and American Express cards also enable you to charge calls. Be careful, however, to prevent onlookers from seeing your card number; they can, and do, steal numbers and run up huge bills, which really hassle you later on. Calling long distance with coins proves incredibly unwieldy, and you should have some other alternative, even if only collect calls.

Western Union (800-325-6000) provides three services of note; they will deliver a telegram, personally phone it directly to the recipient, or send it through the mail. For example, a twenty-five word message from New York to Los Angeles would cost $35, $22 and $15, respectively.

People back home, or anywhere else, can send letters through the post office's **General Delivery** service, identical to Poste Restante in Europe. Mail should be sent to you "c/o General Delivery," the name of the town and state, and ZIP code. City introductions give post office locations, as well as ZIP codes, or use the ZIP code directory in any post office; large cities may have numerous codes. Post offices close Sunday, and sometimes Saturday. Letters will be held by General Delivery for up to thirty days, but don't count on it. Try to time your arrival to meet your letters. Have your arrival date marked on the envelope. American Express offices also hold mail for cardholders if you contact the specific office in advance.

Health

Common sense will prevent many common health problems. Wear sunscreen and eat well and you should be fine; the water and the food are generally safe, and no special shots are required. Just make sure you are up to date on your innoculations (tetanus, etc.). AIDS, however, is now a legitimate worry to keep in the back of your head; you should avoid casual, unprotected sex and sharing intravenous needles.

Remain aware of extreme heat and cold. The Canadian winter, and even that of the Northern U.S., can prove dangerous if you are not prepared with appropriate clothing and lodging. The summer heat of the deserts of the Western U.S. has also claimed its share of victims; hence the name Death Valley, for example. Read about climates in regional and state introductions, and come prepared. Hypothermia and heatstroke are frightening and potentially seriously threatening to long-term health. In the heat, drink plenty of non-alcoholic, non-caffeinated fluids, wear a hat, and stay indoors in the middle of the afternoon. In the cold, avoid getting wet, and if you do, don't risk further exposure.

People with prescription eyewear should, of course, bring an extra set. Those on prescription drugs should get an extra supply, and a copy of the prescription. (See the Packing section above for notes about prescriptions, contraceptives, and first aid kits.)

Obviously, travelers should steer clear of illegal drugs. Besides the various health risks associated with drugs, you can get in deep legal trouble. Marijuana has been decriminalized in a few states, but you should check with authorities before finding out the hard way.

Diabetics, vegetarians, seniors, and disabled should see the Additional Concerns sections below. Those with hidden conditions should obtain a **Medic Alert Identification Tag**. The tag has a 24-hr. hotline and the wearer's condition engraved on it, with lifetime membership included in the price of the tag ($25 for steel, $38 for silver, and, for the fashion-conscious, $48 for gold-plated). Contact Medic Alert Foundation International, P.O. Box 1009, Turlock, CA 95381 (800-ID-ALERT or 800-432-5378).

Insurance

Always have proof of medical insurance on your person. Find out about your coverage before you leave. Some homeowners and family policies cover medical costs and theft. **Medicare** covers travel in the U.S., Canada, and Mexico. Canadians may be covered by their home province's health insurance up to 90 days after leaving the country. Students should find out if they are covered by a school policy or a family policy.

Organizations such as AAA (800-336-4357) and American Express (800-221-7282) offer a variety of insurance plans for travelers. CIEE (212-661-1414) offers a **Trip-Safe Plan** that provides coverage in the U.S. A variety of other private companies provide complete travel coverage, including health, luggage, and legal costs, such as **WorldCare Travel Assistance**, 605 Market St. #1300, San Francisco, CA 94105 (800-666-4993). A one-year membership costs $162, which covers an unlimited number of trips up to 90 days apiece.

5,300 hostels in 68 countries on 6 continents.

One card.

With the American Youth Hostels Membership Card,

you can stay at 5,300 hostels around the world.

Hostels are great places to make new friends.

And the prices are incredibly low,

just 35¢ to $20 a night for a dorm-style room.

For an application, call 202-783-6161.

Or write: American Youth Hostels,

Dept. 801, P.O. Box 37613, Washington, DC 20013-7613.

INTERNATIONAL YOUTH HOSTEL FEDERATION

American Youth Hostels

Safety and Security

Preserving your safety requires common sense, like preserving your health. Traveling with others cuts down on risk, as does avoiding areas that seem unsafe. While it's true that sticking to the well-trodden path can be less than exciting, trust your gut to avoid certain places. Unfortunately, violent crime occurs more frequently in the U.S. than in Europe; consequently, much of any big city is unsafe, particularly alone, and particularly at night. Don't be afraid to ask for advice about safety from the locals. Don't leave you gear unattended and unlocked, and always keep your valuables on you. Above all, try to follow this ridiculous advice: don't look like a tourist.

If you do get in trouble, you can call 911, or other emergency numbers listed in the Practical Information sections, for the police. Practical Information also lists local hotline and information numbers. **Travel Assistance International** provides a 24-hr. hotline for emergencies and referrals; you can buy a year-long travel package for $120. Included are medical and travel insurance, financial assistance, and help in replacing lost passports and visas. Contact Travelers Assistance International, 1133 15th St. NW, Washington, DC (800-821-2828). **Travelers Aid International,** 1001 Connecticut Ave. NW #504, Washington, DC 20036 (202-659-9468) charges no fee, though the financially secure should reimburse the organization for services. They provide help for theft, car failure, illness, and other "mobility-related" problems. Local offices are listed under Practical Information. Issues relating to women travelers are addressed in the Additional Concerns section of the General Introduction.

Accommodations

Hostels

Open to everyone, regardless of age, hostels offer the least expensive ($10 average) indoor lodgings. *Let's Go: USA* always lists the nearby hostels before other lodgings in our accomodations sections. To stay in many hostels, you must be a paid member of **American Youth Hostels, Inc.,** P.O. Box 37613, Washington, DC 20013 (202-783-6161). A one-year membership for those under 18 costs $10, ages 18-54 $25, over 55 $15, and families $35. Some hostels allow non-members to stay for a small extra fee. Membership has its advantages: you often receive discounts on bike rentals and at a few other accommodations, such as Ys. The U.S. has over 230 AYH hostels, which are usually friendly, well-run dorm-style lodgings. All AYH hostels honor **International Youth Hostel Federation (IYHF)** memberships, though experienced European hostel-goers will find fewer hostels here than in Europe. The *AYH Handbook*, free with membership, lists and describes all hostels. Hostels distribute unevenly, with most clustered in the Northeast, the Great Lakes area, Colorado, and the Pacific Northwest—many in out-of-the-way locations.

Some hostels have a maximum length of stay, usually three nights. Reservations are a good idea during peak seasons, and always in large cities. Hostels have other drawbacks as well: inconvenient hours; some curfews; dorm rooms are segregated by sex. Guests share light domestic duties. A few hostels have family accommodations. All require that you buy or rent a sleepsack, basically two sheets sewn together to keep the bed clean. You can buy sleepsacks through Let's Go Travel Services, Harvard Student Agencies, Inc., Thayer Hall-B, Harvard University, Cambridge, MA 02138 (617-495-9649 or 800-5-LETS GO) for $13.95 plus $2 shipping. Call specific hostels, or look them up in the *AYH Handbook* for details, and check descriptions in Accommodations sections. Note that not all hostels are AYH—many use the term "hostel," ranging from independent organizations, like the **American Association of Independent Hostels (AAIH),** to individuals who want to rent out their basements. We list abbreviations for AYH and other independent organizations; be sure to check the AYH handbook, since hostel approval is based on frequent inspections.

Hotels and Motels

Budget travelers will have to forgo the plush environment of luxury hotels and resorts. This doesn't mean, however, that you will have to fend for yourself in the wilds, even if you dislike hostels; budget hotels and motels are now a permanent and ubiquitous feature on the U.S. landscape. Flashing neon "motel" signs on city outskirts and highway exits run from coast to coast. They may be an eyesore, but they are cheap, clean, and friendly. In the Accomodations listings throughout this guide, "single" refers to one bed, usually a double that can sleep two, particularly if you are, or are willing to become, intimate. A "double" is a room intended by the management for two people; often they are indistinguishable from singles, except for the price, though some have two double beds. Ask how many people the room accommodates, and if there is a charge for extra people. Expect to pay at least $20-30 for a single, $10 more for a double. Many hotels and motels require a key deposit. Most have private bathrooms; if not, you will be told in advance. Checkout is usually before 11am, though you can check in as late as you want, as long as rooms are available.

Let's Go: USA tries to determine which budget hotel or motel has the best value, based on price, safety, and location. We rank them in order after hostels, with the better values higher on the list. Keep in mind that inexpensive downtown hotels

are often in less-than-desirable neighborhoods. Ask to see a room before you pay. Travelers with cars should try to stay in cheaper, potentially safer motels outside city limits. Reservations are generally not required, but motels sometimes fill up before nightfall, particularly when in season.

The following is a list of motel chains and their information numbers:

Motel 6 (505-891-6161)

Regal 8 (800-851-8888)

Super 8 (800-843-1991)

Best Western (800-528-1234)

Comfort and Quality Inns (800-221-2222)

YMCAs And YWCAs

If you're planning to stay in a city, don't overlook the **Young Men's Christian Association (YMCA)**. Not all YMCA's offer overnight lodgings, but those that do often operate downtown and have relatively low rates (singles around $30, doubles around $45). Rooms include the use of the library, pool, and other facilities. Reservations are recommended at some YMCAs, though there is a $3 reservation fee. Some YMCAs accept women and families in addition to men. You may have to share a bathroom. Economy packages (2-8 days, $40-270) that include lodging, breakfasts, dinners, and excursions are available in New York, New Orleans, Seattle, and Washington, DC. Write or call The Y's Way, 356 W. 34th St., New York, NY 10001 (212-760-5856).

Few **Young Women's Christian Association (YWCA)** centers still provide lodging for travelers, and typically only for women, though they are listed whenever appropriate.

Bed & Breakfasts

Bed & Breakfasts (B&Bs) and similar guest houses are actually private homes with spare rooms available to travelers. In some areas, they provide the best bargains around; in others, a budget-busting last resort. Singles start around $25, doubles slightly higher, and rates shoot upward from there. Many B&Bs operate under the auspices of regional associations, usually listed under Accommodations, if individual B&Bs are not. For listings of B&Bs throughout the country, consult *Bed & Breakfast, USA*, ($10.95) by Betty R. Rundback and Nancy Kramer, available in bookstores, or through Tourist House Associates, Inc., RD 2, Box 355-A, Greentown, PA 18426 (717-676-3222). Other publications include *The Complete Guide to Bed and Breakfasts, Inns and Guesthouses in the U.S. and Canada,* by Pamela Lanier, from Lanier Publications, P.O. Box 20467, Oakland, CA 94620, and CIEE's (212-661-1414) listings in *Where to Stay USA* ($12.95), which also include listings for hostels, YMCAs, and dorms. CIEE only lists B&Bs with singles under $30 and doubles under $35, though they allow some leeway in big cities. Since many B&Bs aren't listed in any guidebook, check the phonebooks and ask around as you travel.

Dorms

Some colleges and universities open their residence halls to conferences and travelers during the summer. You may have to share a bathroom, but rates stay low and facilities usually stay clean and well-maintained. Contact the school's housing office before your trip. CIEE's (212-661-1414) *Where to Stay USA* ($12.95) lists dorms open to travelers.

Alternative and Emergency Accommodations

As an alternative to standard B&Bs, contact the **U.S. Servas Committee, 11** John St. #706, New York, NY 10038 (212-267-0252), an international cooperative system of hosts and travelers. This non-profit organization matches travelers with hosts who provide accommodations for two to three days. Letters of reference and an interview are required. Participation in the program costs $45 per year, but travelers and hosts do not exchange money.

If you belong to a church, synagogue, or other religious institution, you may be able to line up similar contacts across the country. And if you have no other alternatives, and a night under the stars doesn't seem appealing, call the local Travelers Aid (See Safety and Security above) for information on places to stay in an emergency. The local crisis number (in Practical Information) may also have a list of places to stay.

Outdoors and Camping

For hardier, more adventurous, or less monied travelers, camping gives the best budget alternative. While backcountry camping requires some special skills and beefy physique, even novices can enjoy tent camping in campgrounds. Campgrounds cost little (usually under $15 per tent), give you more flexibility in finding a place to stay, and put you close to breathtaking scenery.

Woodall's Campground Directory ($13.95; Eastern or Western editions $8.95; eight regionals $4.95 each) covers campsites around the U.S. Also try *Woodall's Tent Camping Guide* ($9.95), and campsite cookbooks. Many bookstores carry the guides, but you can also order them from Woodall Publishing Company, 28167 N. Keith Dr., Lake Forest, IL 60045 (800-323-9076). AAA (800-336-4357) distributes camping information to its members, including a **Kampgrounds of America (KOA)** guidebook. KOA is a coast-to-coast chain of private campgrounds; they are generally more expensive and less scenic than national and state parks and national forests (see below), but usually have uncommon amenities, such as showers, electricity, phones, flush toilets, and sometimes even pools and convenience stores.

Novice campers will need to obtain the basics: sleeping bag, Aerobie, pad, and tent (on backpacks, see Packing above). Equipment rental is an economical but often inconvenient alternative to buying; contact an outing club to find out what's avaliable. Whenever possible, buy equipment from local retailers who may give you the option of "trading up" for more expensive gear after a brief trial. Many reputable mail-order firms can meet your needs and offer prices lower that those in local stores. For the best deals, look around for last year's merchandise, particularly in the fall; tents don't change much, but their prices can go down by as much as 50% after they've been around for a while. Some reliable firms:

Campmor, 810 Rte. 17 N., P.O. Box 997-P, Paramus, NJ 07653 (800-526-4784). Name-brand equipment at attractive prices.

L.L. Bean, Freeport, ME 04033 (800-221-4221). Sturdy, high-quality equipment and dedication to customer service. Call for a free catalog. Open 24 hr.

Cabela's, 812 13th Ave., Sidney, NE 69160 (800-237-4444). Camping, hunting, and fishing supplies.

Recreational Equipment, Inc. (REI), Commercial Sales, P.O. Box 88127, Seattle, WA 98138 (800-426-4840).

Choose your sleeping bag according to the weather in which you'll be camping. Most of the better bags—either down (lighter) or synthetic (cheaper, more water resistant and durable)—have ratings giving the bag's minimum temperature suitability. Anticipate the worst conditions you'll encounter, subtract a few degrees, and buy a bag. Expect to pay about $40 for a lightweight synthetic and about $150 for a down bag suitable for use in below-freezing temperatures; sub-zero down bags can cost over $200. Pads to sleep on range from $13 for a simple ensolite pad to $40 for the best air mattress or a sophisticated hybrid such as the Thermarest.

The best tents are "self-supporting" (with their own frames and suspension systems), can be set up quickly, and do not require staking. Backpackers and cyclists may wish to pay a bit more for a sophisticated lightweight tent and should get the smallest tent they can stand—some two-person tents weigh only two pounds. Expect to pay $95 for a simple two-person tent, $120 for a suitable four-persn model. Eureka is one well-established and dependable brand.

Other basics include a battery-operated lantern (never gas) and a simple plastic groundcloth to protect the tent's floor. Consider purchasing fairly large water sacks and/or a solar shower if you plan to stay in primitive campgrounds or camp in the wilderness. Buy a canteen made of either plastic (better insulator) or metal (more leak-proof). Pack water purification pills if you will be far from running water and you don't plan to boil water before drinking it. Remember other camping essentials: a Swiss army knife, toilet paper, bug repellent, calamine lotion, a first aid kit, and cooking gear. Campgrounds often come with grills and allow you to gather firewood for cooking; campstoves, however, come in all sizes, weights, and fuel types. Make sure to buy brands with accessories. Coleman's campstove ($25-80 depending on size and fuel) is the standard.

Now that you've made an initial investment, you'll want to find a campsite to make all the hassle worthwhile. In addition to private campgrounds, there is an extensive network of national parks, national forests, and state parks stretching across the United States. *Let's Go: USA* often describes these cheap and rustic sites in detail.

National Parks

A few georgeous and popular parks in the West, such as Yellowstone, Yosemite, and the Grand Canyon, are the best known components of the National Park system. However, the U.S. Department of the Interior manages an extensive network of parks, monuments, seashores, historic sites, and scenic rivers. Almost invariably well-organized and well-maintained, these areas attract enthusiastic campers from all over the world. Most national parks offer educational ranger talks and guided hikes. Many offer both wilderness and developed tent camping in specified areas; others welcome RVs, while a few offer opulent living in lodges. Each area has its own rules and regulations; check the visitors center in each park, or contact one of the regional offices or the **National Park Service,** P.O. Box 37127, Washington, DC 20013 (202-343-4747).

Entrance fees range from $3-10 per carload. A variety of passes, however, exempt the cardholder and traveling companions from this fee. Pick up the **Golden Eagle Pass** ($25 per year) at any park entrance, with other passes. Travelers over 62 can obtain the free **Golden Age Passport,** which entitles them to 50% off park uscr fees as well as free admission. The **Golden Access Passport,** also free, gives disabled persons the same privileges. Also available are **Park Passes,** annual entrance permits to a specific site.

Plan ahead when contemplating a visit to the parks. Expect crowds at most of them during the summer; many shut down entirely in the winter, or offer only limited services. Lodges and other four-walled accommodations are in the shortest supply; reserve them months in advance. Since most campgrounds thrive strictly on a first come, first served basis, plan to arrive early. In camping areas not regulated by a ranger, verify the availability of sites because the most popular parks often

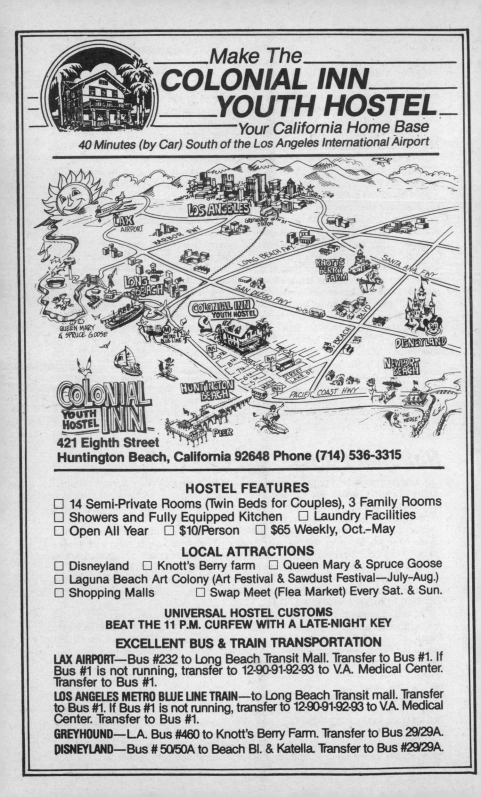

leave the "Campground Full" sign up throughout the summer. In a pinch, ask fellow campers to share their site. For a booklet describing less tourist-ridden national parks, write to the Superintendent of Documents (see Publications above). Ask for *The National Parks: Lesser-Known Areas.*

State Parks and National Forests

While most state parks may lack the grandeur of Grand Teton or Yosemite, many provide excellent camping in beautiful settings. You can criss-cross the U.S. and stay at a state park almost every night. Many offer complete facilities and lots of room at prices much lower than those of private campgrounds. Most state parks charge a day-use fee of about 25¢ for pedestrians and $1-3 for carloads; camping usually costs $5-9 per night. Some states, such as California, offer cheaper camping rates (often 50¢-$1) for hikers and bikers. Some state parks will reserve a percentage of the sites in advance, but generally they do not fill to capacity, except on summer weekends and holidays. Quality and regulations vary; *Let's Go* Practical Information listings have info for each state.

National forests offer a worthwhile alternative to the more heavily traveled parks. Often they border a national park, providing additional campsites and hiking territory. Most offer only primitive camping—no lights, no water, no flush toilets. National forests are rarely crowded, fees nominal or nonexistent. Some areas, such as the Great Plains, have few national forests, and some forests are hard to find. For information, maps, and pamphlets, contact the **U.S. Forest Service**, USDA, 14th St. and Independence Ave. SW, P.O. Box 96090, Washington, DC 20090 (202-447-3706). You can also call (800-283-2267) to reserve a campsite at selected national forests.

Hiking

The title "hiking" covers a wide range of activities, and a hike can be as demanding as you choose. Travel offices, park ranger stations, and outdoor equipment stores will help you plan appropriate hikes.

The **Pacific Crest Trail,** snaking through territory from the California/Mexico border through beautiful Oregon to Canada, and the **Appalachian Trail,** from Georgia to Maine, make up two of a long list of exciting, long-distance trails. If you're contemplating a hiking trip, good sources of information include:

American Youth Hostels (see Accommodations above).

Appalachian Trail Conference, P.O. Box 807, Harpers Ferry, WV 25425 (304-535-6331).

Sierra Club, 730 Polk St., San Francisco, CA 94109 (415-776-2211). The club's *Annual Outing Catalog* available at no cost. Also *The Best About Backpacking* ($10.95 plus $3 shipping).

All three groups have local chapters. For topographical maps of any part of the U.S., write the **U.S. Geological Survey,** Distribution Branch, P.O. Box 25286, Denver Federal Center, Denver, CO 80225.

Transportation

Air Travel

Since the ban on smoking on domestic flights, air travel has become more stressful than ever. But if you plan ahead and shop patiently, you can find affordable flights.

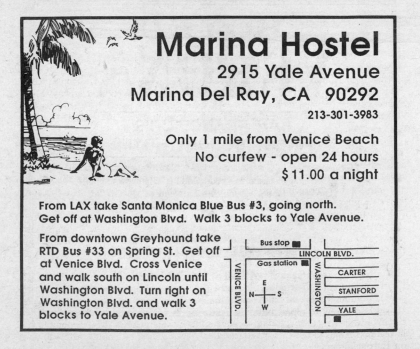

Particularly on long-distance trips, and now on East Coast "shuttles" between major cities, air travel proves cheaper than travel by bus or train. Check the weekend travel sections of major newspapers for bargain fares. The Sunday *New York Times* has the largest travel section; also look at the *Chicago Tribune, L.A. Times,* and *Toronto Star.*

Special discounts can be quirky and unpredictable, but travelers invariably get the best fares by purchasing tickets at least two weeks in advance. You can save up to 60% on an advance-purchase ticket, depending on when you travel. Usually, you must buy a round-trip ticket and stay at least one Sunday and no longer than three weeks. Look for other restrictions like pre-payment (14 days after making your reservation or 14 days before your flight) and 15-100% penalties for reservation changes or cancellations. Ask about "red-eye" (all-night) flights, especially on popular business travel routes. Charter flights run between some U.S. cities; they are more subject to sudden schedule changes but can save you much money. Shuttles run up and down the East Coast; the fares exceed those of bus and train, but the flights save much time. To get the best deals, talk to a local travel agent or call the toll-free numbers of different airlines.

There are a few general rules to keep in mind when booking a flight. Book your ticket especially early if you plan to travel during the tourist season or on holidays. Traveling on a weekday (Mon.-Thurs.) usually costs less than traveling on the weekend. The day before your departure, call the airline to reconfirm your flight reservation and to check any last-minute changes. Because airlines occasionally overbook, arrive early to ensure your seat. On the other hand, with flexible travel plans being "bumped" from a flight does not spell doom—you will probably leave on the next flight and receive either a free ticket or a cash bonus. If it won't spoil your vacation, you might as well step forward when the airline wants to bump volunteers off the flight.

Automobile Travel

Driving cross-country can be a grueling experience for driver and passengers. But car travel is often the most convenient and sometimes the only way to reach certain areas of the U.S., particularly rural locations in the West and Southwest. A car will liberate you from the restrictions of Amtrak and Greyhound/Trailways. Rental rates often outstrip the budget traveler's pocketbook, but group travel always lowers expenses and you should check notices on ride boards around college campuses and in student and local newspapers. The Yellow Pages may list a share-a-ride organization in your area.

For $15-70 per year (depending on where you live and how many benefits you choose) the **American Automobile Association (AAA)** offers free trip-planning services, emergency road service, discounts on car rentals, special insurance, and American Express traveler's checks at no commission or surcharge beyond the value of the checks. For more information, contact your local chapter or call the AAA super-number (800-336-4357). Many major gas companies offer similar services to drivers who have a charge account with them. The **Mobil Auto Club** (800-621-5581) charges members $39 per year for emergency road service (including towing, jump starts, and tire changes). Mobil either dispatches help or reimburses you later, also providing a routing service and up to $5000 insurance on the driver's life at no extra charge.

Always keep spare change and dollar bills in your car for various road tolls. Before your trip, tune the engine, check the tires, and buy spare fan belts. Your trunk should contain a spare tire and jack, jumper cables, extra oil, flares, and a blanket. If you know how to repair minor breakdowns and diagnose larger problems, you can avoid expensive service stations except in dire emergencies. Also remember that in certain regions of the U.S. it is particularly hard to find mechanics who will work on European cars.

Renting

Most people can afford to rent a car for local trips, especially if several people share the cost. Rental rates vary widely according to region; Florida has the lowest, the northern states have the highest. Rental agencies usually have offices at major airports and business districts of towns and cities. In general, car rental agencies fall into two categories: national companies with thousands of affiliated offices, and local companies serving only one city or area. The national companies usually allow cars to be picked up in one city and dropped off in another, often at considerable extra cost. Their toll-free numbers allow renters to reserve a reliable car anywhere in the country, but drawbacks include steep prices and high minimum ages for rentals (most 21, some as high as 25). They may also require renters to possess a major credit card. Some national companies are **Alamo** (800-327-9633), **Avis** (800-331-1212), **Budget** (800-527-0700), **Hertz** (800-654-3131), **National** (800-328-4657), and **Thrifty** (800-367-2277).

While many local companies observe similar age requirements, they often have more flexible policies at lower rates. Some will accept a cash deposit of $50 or more in lieu of a credit card. Humble companies like **Rent-A-Wreck** (800-421-7253) rent cars past their prime at low daily rates. Be wary; these agencies often have high mileage charges and other hidden costs.

Drivers' insurance policies cover them when renting a car. If you want additional coverage in case the rental car is damaged, you may obtain it through the agency. Check the price beforehand since insurance usually costs a bundle. **American Express** pays insurance on car rentals charged on the card; other credit card companies have similar deals, so call up the customer service lines of your own credit cards. Although basic rental charges run $20-35 per day for a compact car, plus up to 20¢ per mile, many companies offer special discount packages. If you plan to drive long distances, buy an unlimited mileage package: it may sound more expensive but will definitely save you money in the long run. Most companies have lower rental rates on weekends and when renting by the week.

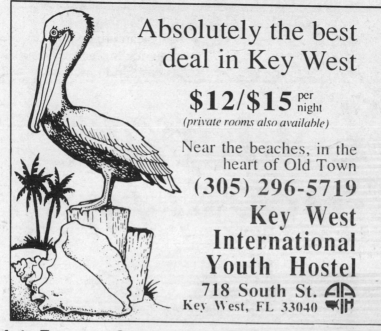
Auto Transport Companies

If you can't afford to buy or rent a car, call an auto transport company which will match you with a person who needs a car moved to another city. Give the company your destination; it will they tell you when it has a car. You pay only for gas (usually after the first free tank), food, lodging, tolls, and a refundable deposit. The transport company's insurance covers any breakdown or damage to the car. Generally, you must be 21, have a valid driver's license (an international license is fine), and agree to drive 400 mi. or more per day on a fairly direct route to your destination. Stops and detours are frowned upon; you will be given a time and distance allowance and will be charged for any extra miles on the odometer. Companies prefer couples and older travelers. Your chances are best for travel from coast to coast or from New York to Miami. **Auto Driveaway**, 310 S. Michigan Ave., Chicago, IL 60604 (312-341-1900), has 90 offices nationwide. Check the Yellow Pages for other agencies in your area.

Bus Travel

As the cheapest means of transportation in the U.S., bus travel is the best way to see the grim side of life throughout the country. Long-distance bus travel will introduce you to fascinating people who the upper-middle-class budget traveler would otherwise never meet. You are far more likely to have rewarding and memorable conversations on the bus than with the snappy executive sitting next to you on a charter plane flight.

For extensive travel between regions, you can rely on **Greyhound** and its subsidiary **Trailways.** The nation's bus network provides the cheapest and most thorough public transportation to most towns in the U.S. In sections on specific cities, *Let's Go: USA* lists bus fares to nearby destinations, as well as the frequency and length of trips. Within specific regions, other bus companies may provide more exhaustive services (for example, **Peter Pan** serves most of New England).

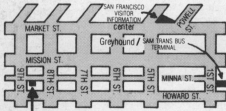

Greyhound sells an **Ameripass,** valid for unlimited travel in the continental U.S. on both Greyhound and Trailways. You can buy passes for seven ($189), 15 ($249), or 30 days ($349) with optional extensions for $10 per day. The Ameripass becomes valid on your first day of travel. Discounts for children vary according to the age and number of children traveling and the number of adults paying full fares. Foreign students and faculty members are entitled to a discounted Ameripass; see the Getting Around section in Additional Information for Foreign Visitors below.

Greyhound and Trailways offer discounts for specific groups: children accompanied by an adult (ages 5-11 half-fare, under 5 free); seniors (10% discount except on Ameripass and excursion fares); disabled travelers (companion rides free); and excursion fares (low promotional fares valid for a limited period of time; usually bought 30 days in advance). Fares and discounts change seasonally. See Additional Concerns below.

Most bus stations remain safe at night, but since many sweat in seedy areas, arrange your arrival and departure times to prevent you from spending the night in or around the depot. Try to schedule arrivals at reasonable hours, in order to find transportation out of the bus station and a place to stay. If you are boarding at a remote "flag stop," be sure you understand where to catch the bus. Catch the driver's attention by standing on the side of the road and flailing your arms wildly. It is better to make a fool of yourself than to miss the bus. If the bus proceeds to speed on by (usually because of over-crowding), the next less-crowded bus should stop for you.

You can buy your ticket at the terminal, but arrive early. Ask for information on connections, schedules, and fares, then check the bus schedules and routes yourself to verify the information. When boarding a bus, remember that the company will add a second bus when the first one is full. If you decide not to make the trip, Greyhound and Trailways usually grant refunds. Stopovers are permitted if you want to spend time in cities along your route.

You are allowed two pieces of luggage for free, combined weight of up to 100 pounds; children are allowed half that amount. Identify your belongings clearly and retain your claim check. When two buses run, make sure you and your luggage occupy the same bus. You can usually take a medium-sized carry-on onto the bus, as long as it fits in the overhead compartment. Always keep valuables and a blanket or jacket with you inside the bus. Surprisingly efficient air conditioning brings the temperature down to arctic levels. Also remember that U.S. distances are long. A trip from coast-to-coast will take at least three days, with brief stops every 3 or 4 hours but no long stops for sleeping or showering.

Green Tortoise, an "alternative" bus line, offers a friendlier budget travel option. A hostel on wheels, Green Tortoise's proprietors act as hosts and tour guides. They run renovated old coaches with foam mattresses, sofa-seats, and dinettes coast to coast, up and down the West Coast, and to national parks. All prices include transportation, use of the bus at night for sleeping, and tours of the regions you pass through. Tasty meals are prepared communally and cost approximately $3.50 per person per meal. Tours betweeen New York or Boston and San Francisco last 10 to 14 days and cost $279 in either direction. From their headquarters in San Francisco, Green Tortoise runs a "commuter" line between Seattle and Los Angeles. You can make any part of the journey. They also offer "loops," which start and finish in San Francisco, to Yosemite National Park, Northern California, Baja, California, the Grand Canyon, and Alaska. The National Park loop hits all the big ones (17 days, $399). The Baja trip includes several days on the beach, with sailboats and windsurfers provided for a fee. For specific information, write to Green Tortoise, P.O. Box 24459, San Francisco, CA 94124 (415-821-0803; 800-227-4766 outside CA).

Try to use local bus systems to travel within a town. The largest cities also have subways and commuter train lines. But in spite of pollution, U.S. residents are wedded to their cars, and mass public transport remains limited in most areas; local buses, while often cheap (fares 25¢-$1.35), sometimes run infrequently. Call the city transit information number and track down a public transport map with schedules.

Train Travel

If you're in no particular hurry, the train can give you one of the most comfortable ways to tour the country. You can walk from car to car and stretch your legs, buy cigarettes, alcohol, and overpriced edibles in the snack or dining car, and shut out the sun to sleep. Travel light on the train; not all stations will check baggages and not all trains will carry large amounts of it (though most long-distance trains do).

For most intercity trips, **Amtrak** is not much of a bargain compared with the bus or plane. Special services such as sleeping cars or high-speed Metroliner service cost extra. However, Amtrak offers many discounts. Watch for special holiday packages. Permanent discounts apply to: children accompanied by an adult (ages 2-11 half-fare, under 2 free); seniors (25% off one way tickets); round-trips; and circle trips (certain round-trips within a region when returning on a different route). Excursion fares (round-trip travel during off-peak times) cost little more than the regular one-way tickets. They may not be combined with other discounts, except children's fares.

The current **All-Aboard America** promotional fares offer a great way to subsidize a trip covering several different states. Round-trip travel between two cities plus two stopovers costs $189 within one region (Western, Central, or Eastern), $269 within two regions, and $339 within three. You have up to 45 days to complete the trip, and must plan an itinerary in advance. The generous Eastern region includes everything from Chicago to New Orleans, allowing, for example, a tour from New York City to Chicago to New Orleans to Miami and back to New York City on the $189 single-region ticket. Before investing money in a ticket, make sure that Amtrak reaches all of your destinations, or you may end up spending all the money you saved on bus or local train fares.

In addition to the discounts, most Amtrak tickets allow you a stopover at no extra cost. For information about rates, schedules, and discounts, call (800-872-7245); if you use a touch-tone phone, you will receive information much more quickly and

Two Warm, Personally Managed Hideaways.

WILSHIRE-ORANGE HOTEL	DEL FLORES HOTEL
6060 W 8th St, LA 90036	409 N Crescent Dr, BH 90210
(213) 931-9533	**(213) 274-5115**

• Wilshire Blvd/Fairfax Ave	• 3 blocks East of Rodeo Drive
• Quiet, Safe Residential Area	• Splendid, Safe Civic Center
• Color TV & Radio	• Color TV & Radio
• Refrigerators & Microwaves	• Direct Dial Telephones
• Rates from $44/night	• Rates from $48/night
• Weekly Rates	• Weekly Rates
• Near Hollywood Blvd, Sunset	• 2 night minimum
Strip, Beverly Hills, Farmers	• In Beverly Hills, near
Market, LA County Museum	Westwood, Restaraunts & Shopping Areas

efficiently. Hearing-impaired travelers may communicate with Amtrak by means of a teletypewriter (800-523-6590; 800-562-6960 in PA).

Bicycle Travel

After shelling out the money for a sturdy bicycle and the requisite touring equipment, bicycle travel probably provides the cheapest way to go. Traveling at an easy pace along rural roads allows you to get to know a region most intimately. Inexperienced bikers might try a few long rides before attempting a large-scale trip.

Gathering all the necessary equipment proves the biggest hassle in preparing for a bicycle tour. While some local bike shops provide helpful information, the costs involved in stocking and inventory make their prices exorbitant, with very few exceptions. Fortunately, ordering equipment by telephone and mail has become exceptionally quick and convenient. Don't spend any money before you look at *Bicycling* magazine for the lowest sale prices. **Bike Nashbar,** P.O. Box 3449, Youngstown, OH 44513 (800-627-4227; 800-654-2453 in OH), really rides ahead of the crowd. Nashbar almost always has the lowest prices, but if it doesn't, it'll happily subtract 5¢ from the lowest nationally advertised price you can find. Parts ordered generally shipped on that same day. Their own line of products, including complete bicycles, provides the best value. Remember to invest in a bike helmet that fits you well. At about $35-66, the best helmets are much cheaper then critical head surgery or a well-appointed funeral, as one of our researchers reminded us from a Danish hospital. See the helmet ratings in the May 1990 *Consumer Reports;* look for a small green "Snell Approved" label, indicating rigorous private testing.

The long-distance cyclist should contact **Bikecentennial,** a national non-profit organization that researches and maps long-distance routes across the country and organizes bike tours for members. Its best-known project is the 4450-mi. Trans-American Bicycle Trail. Bikecentennial also offers its members insurance, maps, guidebooks (including the *Cyclist's Yellow Pages,* free to members, $10 to nonmembers), route information service, and access to tours. Annual membership fees are

$22, for students $19, and $25 for families. For more information, write Bikecentennial, P.O. Box 8308, Missoula, MT 59807 (406-721-1776).

Also check out Ballantine's series of *Cyclist's Guides to Overnight Stops,* available for either West, East or Central states at $3.95 per book. These books and *Bicycle Touring in the Western United States,* by Karen and Gary Hawking ($9.95), you can purchase from Random House, 400 Hahn Rd., Westminster, MD 21157 (800-726-0600). **American Youth Hostels, Inc.** (see Accommodations above) also offers complete tours at excellent prices.

The machinery of a bicycle is simple enough that anyone should be able to fix it with the help of a few specialized tools. For instructions in the basics of bicycle maintenance and repair, we recommend *The Bike Bag Book* ($3.95 plus $1 shipping), available from the Ten Speed Press, P.O. Box 7123, Berkeley, CA 94707 (415-845-8414).

Protect your investment best by buying a U-shaped lock ($22-50) made by **Citadel** or **Kryptonite.** For a fee, each company guarantees its locks against the theft of your bike for one or two years.

Hitchhiking

In Europe, hitchhiking is generally a safe and accepted practice; in the U.S., hitching is risky at best, and *Let's Go* does not recommend hitching in any situation. Although many travelers prefer it to more commercial methods, hitching is hardly the ideal way to travel. Women should avoid hitchhiking alone, and everyone should evaluate the driver before accepting a ride. Ask the driver his or her destination before you reveal your own. Be especially wary if the driver opens the door quickly and offers to drive you anywhere. Make sure you'll be able to open the passenger window or door from the inside in case of an emergency. Don't sit between two people, and don't let the driver lock your belongings in the trunk.

All states prohibit hitching while standing on the roadway itself. If you try hitching on an interstate, most states limit you to access ramps and rest stops. Try to keep at least $20 in your wallet to prove to suspicious police officers that you aren't destitute.

Additional Concerns

Senior Travelers

Seniors can receive an amazing variety of discounts. All you need is an acceptable piece of identification proving your age (a driver's license, Medicare card, or membership card from a recognized society of retired people will suffice). Pilot Books, 103 Cooper St., Babylon, NY 11702 (516-422-2225) publishes two books that may prove helpful: *Senior Citizen's Guide to Budget Travel in the United States,* by Paige Palmer ($3.95 plus $1 postage); and *The International Health Guide for Senior Citizen Travelers,* by W. Robert Lange ($4.95 plus $1 postage). *Get up & Go: A Guide for the Mature Traveler,* by Gene and Adele Malott ($10.95 plus $1.50 postage) is available from Gateway Books, 31 Grand View Ave., San Francisco, CA 94114 (415-821-1928).

The **American Association of Retired Persons** offers its members a tremendous range of services and discounts, many of which aid travelers. Any U.S. resident and spouse over 50 can join for a $5 annual fee. Benefits include group travel programs, as well as discounts on lodging, car and RV rental, and sightseeing. Write to National Headquarters, Special Services Dept., 1909 K St. NW, Washington, DC 20049 (800-227-7737 for membership; 202-662-4850 for travel information).

Another organization providing services to those 50 and over is the **National Council of Senior Citizens,** 925 15th St. NW, Washington, DC 20005 (202-347-8800). The NCSC offers hotel and auto rental discounts, a senior citizen newspaper, and use of a discount travel agency, in addition to supplementary medical insurance for members 65 and over. The membership fee is $12 per year for an individual, $16 for a couple or $150 for a lifetime membership.

Elderhostel uses the facilities of over 1500 colleges, universities, and other educational institutions worldwide. Participants in domestic programs spend a week studying subjects ranging from music appreciation to beekeeping at a cost of $245-270. International programs last 2-4 weeks at costs ranging from $1500-5000. The fee covers room, board, tuition, use of campus facilities, and extracurricular activities. Hostelships are available to those requiring financial assistance. You must be at least 60 to enroll and may bring a companion who is over 50. For a free catalog listing course descriptions for the current season, contact Elderhostel, 80 Boylston St. #400, Boston, MA 02116 (617-426-7788). You can also obtain *Elderhostels: The Students' Choice,* by Mildred Hyman ($12.95 plus $2.75 postage), a guide to the 100 most popular hostels, from John Muir Publications, P.O. Box 613, Santa Fe, NM 87504 (800-888-7504).

Days Inn operates the **September Days Club** for anyone over 50. A $12 annual fee entitles the member and spouse to 15-50% discounts at all Days Inns throughout the U.S. and Canada and 10% off restaurant meals at these locations. Call 800-241-5050 or 800-344-3636.

U.S. citizens and permanent residents 62 and over can obtain a free **Golden Age Passport,** which provides lifetime free admission for the cardholder and passengers in the same car to all U.S. national parks, monuments, historic sites, recreation areas, and national wildlife refuges, in addition to a 50% discount on all national park user fees. Either apply in person at any National Park that charges admission, or write the National Park Service, P.O. Box 37127, Washington, DC 20013 (202-208-4747).

Gay and Lesbian Travelers

Unfortunately, there is still a strong prejudice in many areas of the country against gay and lesbianism. Call the national **Gay/Lesbian Crisisline** (800-767-4297) for counseling, legal or medical advice, AIDS information, and local club listings. An excellent source of books geared towards gay and lesbian travelers is **Giovanni's Room**, 345 S. 12th St., Philadelphia, PA 19107 (800-222-6996; 215-923-2960 in PA), which charges $3.50 postage per book in the U.S. All of the following books are available through Giovanni's Room or the address listed:

Gaia's Guide. $11.95; 9-11 Kensington High St., London W8, England, $12.50 ppd. Annually revised international guide for traveling women, listing lesbian, feminist, and gay information numbers, publications, cultural centers and resources, hotels, and meeting places.

Spartacus International Gay Guide. $24.95; c/o Bruno Gmünder, Worldwide Advertising Sales, Lutzowstrasse 106, P.O. Box 30 13 45, D-1000, Berlin 30, West Germany. Tel. (030) 261 16 46 or (030) 262 81 18. U.S. Address: 100 East Biddle St., Baltimore, MD 21202 (301-727-5677). International gay guide for men, listing bars, restaurants, hotels, bookstores, and hotlines throughout the world.

Bob Damron's Address Book. $14; P.O. Box 11270, San Francisco, CA 94101 (415-777-0113). Over 6000 listings of bars, restaurants, guest houses, and services catering to the gay community.

Inn Places: USA and Worldwide Gay Accommodations. $14.95; address same as above.

The Women's Traveler. ($8 plus $4.50 shipping; address same as above. A travel guide for the lesbian community. Maps of 50 major U.S. cities; listings of bars, restaurants, accommodations, bookstores, and services.

The Damron Road Atlas. $12; address same as above. Maps of 50 major U.S. cities; listings of bars and accommodations.

Places of Interest. A series of three books for men ($11), women ($9), and general ($12.50), including maps. Ferrari Publications, P.O. Box 35575, Phoenix, AZ 85069 (602-863-2408).

Wherever possible, *Let's Go: USA* lists local gay and lesbian information lines and community centers. Areas with large gay and lesbian populations include New York City, San Francisco, Los Angeles, Houston, Atlanta, and Montréal.

Disabled Travelers

Though facilities and services for the disabled are far from commonplace in the U.S., recent awareness has led to increased accessibility and easier mobility. The following books are available from Twin Peaks Press, P.O. Box 129, Vancouver, WA 98666 (800-637-2256 or 206-694-2462), and may help disabled travelers plan vacations. Add $2 postage for the first book and $1 for each additional book: *Directory for Travel Agencies for the Disabled,* ($12.95); *Travel for the Disabled,* ($9.95); *Wheelchair Vagabond,* ($9.95).

Access to the World: A Travel Guide for the Handicapped, by Louise Weiss ($12.95). Information on tours and organizations. Available from Facts on File, Inc., 460 Park Ave. S., New York, NY 10016 (800-322-8755). The Government Printing Office also publishes some relevant pamphlets (see Useful Publications above). If you plan to visit national parks, obtain a free Golden Access Passport at any park entrance entitling you and your family to free admission and a 50% reduction on campsite fees (see address under Senior Travelers).

Most **Red Roof Inns** (800-843-7663) are accessible by wheelchair. Consult other national motel chains for information (see Hotels and Motels).

Amtrak and all airlines now serve disabled passengers if you notify them in advance. When making reservations, tell the ticket agent what services you'll need. Ask if there are any restrictions on motorized wheelchairs. Hearing-impaired travelers may use a teletypewriter to contact Amtrak (800-523-6590; 800-562-6960 in PA)

and Greyhound (800-345-3109; 800-322-9537 in PA). Bus travel is a feasible and inexpensive option. Greyhound and Trailways have a **Helping Hand Service** that enables disabled travelers to bring along a companion for free. Simply show the ticket agent a doctor's letter confirming your need for assistance. Both you and your companion receive the standard two-piece, 100-pound luggage allowance; wheelchairs, seeing-eye dogs, and oxygen tanks are not counted as part of that allowance. Some major car rental agencies have a few hand-controlled cars; contact them a few days in advance to check on availability at a specific location. Try Avis (800-33101212), Hertz (800-654-3131), or National (800-328-4567).

Wings on Wheels is the best travel organization for the disabled, providing information and planned tours all over the world. They run a Seattle-based charter bus with on-board wheelchair-accessible facilities, and can arrange "anything for a group, and damn near anything for an individual" at minimal extra cost. They also run White Cane Tours for the blind (with one guide for every three travelers), tours for the deaf, and for "slow walkers." Contact them at Evergreen Travel, 19505L 44th Ave., Lynnwood, WA 98036 (206-776-1184; 800-435-2288; 800-562-9298 in WA). Send $5 for their brochures on tourist sights, accommodations, and transportation. For useful guides, write the **Travel Information Center**, Moss Rehabilitation Hospital, 1200 W. Tabor Rd., Philadelphia, PA 19141 (215-329-5715, ext. 2233). **Mobility International USA (MIUSA)**, P.O. Box 3551, Eugene, OR 97403 (503-343-1284, voice and TDD), provides information on travel programs, accommodations, and organized tours. Membership costs $20 per year. They publish *A World of Options: A Guide to International Educational Exchange, Community Service, and Travel for Persons with Disabilities.* ($14 for members, $16 for nonmembers, postage included).

The following organizations also assist disabled travelers:

American Foundation for the Blind, 15 W. 16th St., New York, NY 10011 (800-232-5463 or 212-620-2147). ID cards ($6) and information on discounts; write for an application.

Directions Unlimited, 720 N. Bedford Rd., Bedford Hills, NY 10507 (800-533-5343). Specializes in arranging individual vacations and group tours and cruises for the disabled.

Flying Wheels Travel, 143 West Bridge St., P.O. Box 382, Owatonna, MN 55060 (800-535-6790). Arranges domestic and international trips and cruises for groups and individuals.

The Guided Tour, 555 Ashbourne Rd., Elkins Park, PA 19117 (215-782-1370). Year-round travel programs for developmentally- and learning-disabled adults, as well as trips for those with physical disabilities.

Society for the Advancement of Travel for the Handicapped, 26 Court St., Penthouse Suite, Brooklyn, NY 11242 (718-858-5483). Publishes a quarterly travel newsletter and information booklets, free for members, $2 for nonmembers. Offers advice and assistance on trip planning. Annual membership $40; students and seniors $25.

Whole Persons Tours, P.O. Box 1084, Bayonne, NJ 07002 (201-858-3400). Organizes domestic and international tours and publishes *The Itinerary,* a magazine for disabled travelers. A subscription for one year (6 issues) costs $10; for 2 years (14 issues) $20.

Women Travelers

Unfortunately, women often face dangers above and beyond those of other travelers. While women in no way "bring on" rape or sexual harrassment, women travelers can minimize risks. Women should trust their instincts to avoid dangerous situations, and try to appear confident and assertive. They should avoid groups of men when there are few other women around, and never ask directions from men. Always carry enough change for a quick cab ride or phone call; we list emergency numbers, rape crisis hotlines, and women's centers in Practical Information sections. Never hitchhike alone, and even two women hitchhiking together are at risk. Camping alone can be dangerous as well. Try to find centrally located, well-traveled accommodations. The *Handbook for Women Travellers,* available for £6.95 from

The country that offers you Disneyland, Las Vegas, and the Statue of Liberty, also offers a free* way to visit them.

Auto Driveaway helps travelers from all over the world visit the splendor America has to offer. Our driveaway service matches travelers needing tansportation with automobiles needing transport.

*There is no rental charge, just a small refundable deposit. Your only expense is for fuel, and a travel companion is welcome to join you. Call our toll free number for the details. Throw your luggage in the trunk and enjoy the U.S.A. with Auto Driveaway!

800-346-2277

AUTO DRIVEAWAY CO.
310 S. Michigan Ave. Chicago, IL 60604

Judy Piatkus Publishers Ltd., 5 Windmill St., London W1P 1HF, England ((071)-631-0710), has additional safety tips.

Additional Information for Foreign Visitors

Orientation to the United States

The continental U.S. looms huge by European standards (3100 by 1800 mi. or 5000 by 2900km), and some areas are largely uninhabited. Except in the Northeast, travel between major urban centers takes long hours or even days. Ranging from desert to glacier, the U.S. landscape varies richly from endless plains to glass-and-steel skyscrapers. No matter how much you see, there will still be plenty left for your next trip. You'll have to choose between a whirlwind, city-a-day tour and a more leisurely, in-depth itinerary. In either case, you're better off concentrating your travels in two or three regions.

To preview what the different areas of the U.S. offer the traveler, scan our regional and state introductions. The regions of the United States often remain as culturally distinct as two nations; a Texan might feel as much a foreigner in New England as you would. Most U.S. residents are used to diversity and treat foreigners kindly.

Although you needn't fear a terrorist attack in a U.S. airport, U.S. cities can be more violent and crime-ridden than their European or Asian counterparts. *Let's Go: USA* lists emergency phone numbers in most cities and towns. Stay careful and alert, and you will be safer during your travels.

Useful Organizations

When you begin planning your trip, you might contact the **United States Travel and Tourism Administration**—with branches in Australia, the U.K., Belgium, France, Canada, W. Germany, Japan, and Mexico—which provides abundant free literature. If you can't find the address for the branch in your country, write to the U.S. Travel and Tourism Administration, Department of Commerce, 14th and Constitution Ave. NW, Washington, DC 20230 (202-377-4003 or 202-377-3811). You may also want to write to the tourist offices of the states or cities you'll be visiting (see Practical Information listings). Wherever you write, the more specific your inquiry, the better your chances of getting the information you need. Once you arrive, visit local tourist information centers.

Extremely useful to foreign travelers, the **Council on International Educational Exchange (CIEE)** has affiliates overseas that sell travel literature, hostel cards, and charter airline tickets. Services include issuing the ISIC (see Documents below), the *Student Travel Catalog* ($1 postage), and a publication with accommodations listings, entitled *Where to Stay USA* ($11). They also run **Council Travel,** a budget international travel service. Write to CIEE at 205 E. 42nd St., New York, NY 10017 (800-223-7402 charter flights only; 212-661-1450 for Council Travel; or 212-661-1414), or contact their other offices in Paris, Tokyo, Madrid, and W. Germany.

The **International Student Travel Confederation (ISTC),** of which the CIEE is a member, is a godsend for European students. It arranges charter flights and discount air fares, provides travel insurance, issues the ISIC card in a new plastic form, and sponsors the Student Air Travel Association for European students. Write for their Student Travel Guide at ISTC, Weinbergstrasse 31, CH-8006 Zurich, Switzerland (tel. (411) 262 29 96). ISTC has affiliated offices in other countries as well. In Canada, write to **Travel CUTS** (Canadian University Travel Services Limited),

187 College St., Toronto, Ont. M5T 1P7 (416-979-2406). In the U.K., write to London Student Travel, 52 Grosvenor Gardens, London WC1 (tel. (071) 730 34 02). In Australia, contact SSA/STA, 220 Faraday St., Carlton, Melbourne, Victoria 3053 (tel. (03) 347 69 11).

The **Federation of International Youth Travel Organizations (FIYTO)** issues the **International Youth Card (IYC)** to anyone under 26, as well as a free catalog that lists discounts for IYC and ISIC cardholders. Write or call Islands Brygge 81, DK-2300 Copenhagen S, Denmark (tel. (31) 54 60 80).

STA Travel, based in the U.K., has over 100 offices worldwide to help you arrange discounted overseas flights. In the U.S., call 800-777-0112 or write to 7202 Melrose Ave., Los Angeles, CA 90046. Abroad, write to 74 and 86 Old Brompton Rd., London SW7 3LQ, England, or call (071) 937 99 71 for flights to North America.

If you wish to stay in a U.S. home during your vacation, many organizations can help you. The **Experiment in International Living** coordinates homestay programs for international visitors wishing to join a U.S. family for an extended period of time. Visitors of all ages live with host families long enough to receive a full dose of American culture. For the appropriate address in your country, write to the U.S. Headquarters, P.O. Box 767, Kipling Rd., Brattleboro, VT 05301 (800-451-4465). The **Institute of International Education (IIE)** (see Study below) publishes their "Homestay Information Sheet" listing many homestay programs. Write to them at 809 United Nations Plaza, New York, NY 10017 (212-883-8200). See Accommodations above for information on **Servas,** a similar international travel organization, which coordinates short (2-3 day) homestays.

Documents and Formalities

Almost all foreign visitors to the U.S. must have a **passport,** a visitor's **visa,** and proof of plans to leave the U.S. For stays of only a few days, Canadian citizens with proof of citizenship do not need a visa or passport. Mexican citizens with an I-186 form can enter through a U.S. border station, then obtain an I-94 form 25 mi. in from the border. Other travelers will need to apply for visas at a U.S. consulate. International visitors usually obtain a B-1 or B-2 (non-immigrant, pleasure tourist) visa valid for a maximum of six months. Eight countries—the U.K., Japan, Italy, W. Germany, France, the Netherlands, Sweden, and Switzerland—participate in a pilot program in which citizens of these countries do not need a visa to enter the U.S.; however, they must meet various criteria, such as being in possession, when they arrive, of a ticket to leave the U.S. within 90 days. They must also fly one of a specified group of air carriers. Residents should contact a U.S. consulate.

If you lose your passport once in the U.S., you must replace it through the embassy of your country. If you lose your visa or your I-94 form (arrival/departure certificate attached to your visa upon arrival), replace it through the nearest **U.S. Immigration and Naturalization Service** office. A list of offices can be obtained through the INS, Central Office Information Operations Unit, #5044, 425 I St. NW, Washington, DC 20536 (202-633-1900). This information does not necessarily apply for work or study in the U.S. (see Work and Study below). Separate forms are necessary to extend your length of stay in the U.S., also obtained from the INS. You must apply for an extension well before your original departure date.

Foreign students will want to obtain an **International Student Identification Card (ISIC)** as proof of student status. These cards, now made of embossed plastic, entitle the bearer to a variety of student discounts. The ISIC is available at local travel agencies, from the International Student Travel Confederation, from CIEE, or from **Let's Go Travel Services,** Thayer Hall-B, Harvard University, Cambridge, MA 02138 (617-495-9649 or 800-553-8746). Let's Go Travel also sells American Youth Hostel memberships. The ISIC and the AYH card are available by mail.

If your home country signed the Geneva Road Traffic Convention of 1949, you can legally drive in the U.S. for one year from the date of your arrival, providing, of course, that the car you are driving is registered in the U.S. and that you are properly insured. An **international driver's license** is useful only to enable policemen to understand your license; it doesn't change your legal status. If your country is not a signatory of the Convention, it is illegal for you to drive in the U.S. without obtaining a U.S. license, even if you have an international license. Most European and many non-European countries are signatories, but check with your national automobile association before you leave.

Customs

All travelers may bring into the U.S. 200 cigarettes, $100 worth of gifts, and all personal belongings duty-free. Travelers over 20 may also bring up to one liter of alcohol duty-free. You may bring in any amount of currency without a charge, but if you carry over $10,000, you will have to fill out a report form. Travelers should carry prescription drugs in clearly labeled containers, along with a doctor's statement or prescription. Customs officials will often inquire about the amount of money you are carrying and ask your planned departure date to ensure that you will be able to support yourself while in the U.S. Officials can be stern and bullying, but do not get disgruntled; remember that not all people here will treat you as rudely. For more information, or for the pamphlet called *Know Before You Go*, contact the nearest U.S. Embassy or write to the **U.S. Customs Service,** 1301 Constitution Ave. NW, Washington, DC 20229 (202-566-8195). Remember to check customs regulations in your country to know what you may take with you on your return trip.

Currency and Exchange

U.S. currency uses a decimal system based on the **dollar ($).** Paper money ("bills") comes in six denominations, all the same size, shape, and dull-green color. The bills now issued are $1, $5, $10, $20, $50, and $100. You may occasionally see denominations of $2 and $500 which are no longer printed, but are still acceptable as currency. Some restaurants and retail stores may not accept $50 bills and higher. The dollar divides into 100 cents (¢). Values of less than a dollar are written in two ways; 35 cents can be represented as 35¢ or $.35. U.S. currency uses six coins, all worth one dollar or less. The penny (1¢), the nickel (5¢), the dime (10¢), and the quarter (25¢) are the most common. The half-dollar (50¢) and the one-dollar coins are pretty but rare.

It is nearly impossible to use foreign currency in the U.S., and in some parts of the country, you may even have trouble exchanging your currency for U.S. dollars. Convert your currency infrequently and in large amounts to minimize exorbitant fees. Buy traveler's checks in U.S. dollars; that way you will not need to exchange them. Traveler's checks can be used in lieu of cash; where an establishment specifies "no checks accepted," this usually refers to personal checks drawn on a bank account. You may want to bring a credit card affiliated with a U.S. company such as Interbank, affiliated with the American MasterCard; Barclay Card, affiliated with Visa; or American Express. For more information, see Money above.

Personal checks can be very difficult to cash in the U.S. Most banks require that you have an account with them before they will cash a personal check, and opening an account is a time-consuming process.

Sales tax is the U.S. equivalent of the Value Added Tax. Expect to pay 5-8% depending on the item. In addition, a tip of 15-20% is expected by restaurant servers and taxi drivers. Restaurants sometimes include this service charge in the bill of a large dining party. Tip hairdressers 10%, and bellhops at least $1 per bag.

Sending Money

Sending money overseas is a complicated and expensive process. If you think you'll need money sent while you're in the U.S., visit your bank before you leave to get a list of its correspondent U.S. banks. You can also arrange in advance for your bank to send money from your account to certain correspondent banks on specific dates.

Cabling money is the fastest method of transport, usually requiring 48 hours to get to a major city or a bit longer to a more remote location. You pay cabling costs plus the commission charged by your home bank; rates vary according to the amount cabled. Western Union (800-325-4176 or 800-325-6000) offers a safe method for wiring money usually within two working days. Their U.S. offices can receive money from Germany and England, but not from France. Bank draft or international money order sends money cheaper but slower. You pay a commission (around $15-20) on the draft, plus the cost of sending it registered air mail. An American Express office at home can cable you up to $10,000; it costs $35 to cable $500, and the fee gets larger with greater amounts. Non-cardholders may also use this service for no extra charge. For some unknown reason, it is even cheaper to send money from Europe to the U.S. than the other way around. Perhaps wind currents. Money takes from one to three days to reach the U.S. One problem with the American Express Moneygram (800-543-4080) is that foreigners can only cable to the U.S. from France, England, and Germany—the rest of Europe and Australia only have receiving stations. Whichever method you choose, make sure that you and the sender know the exact name and address of the bank or office to which the money is being sent.

Finally, if you are stranded in the U.S. with no recourse at all, a consulate will wire home for you and deduct the cost from the money you receive. Consulates are often less than gracious about performing this service, however.

Mail and Telephones

A government-run monopoly, the United States Post Office is relatively efficient nonetheless. Individual offices usually open weekdays from 8am to 5pm, Saturday from 8am to noon. All close on national holidays. A postcard mailed within the U.S. (including Alaska and Hawaii) or to Mexico costs 15¢; a letter generally costs 25¢. Canada has a special rate of 22¢ for a postcard and 30¢ for a letter. Postcards mailed overseas cost 36¢, letters 45¢; aerograms are available at the post office for 36¢. Mail within the country takes between a day and a week to arrive; to northern Europe and South America, a week to 10 days; to southern Europe, North Africa, and the Middle East, two to three weeks. Large city post offices offer International Express Mail service in case you need to mail something to a major European city in 40 to 72 hours.

The U.S. divides into postal zones, each with a five-digit ZIP code particular to a region, city, or part or a city. The normal form of address is as follows:
Tyrone Slothrop (name)
W.A.S.T.E. (name of organization optional)
293 Gold Star Rd. (street address, apartment number)
Somerville, MA 02222 (city, state abbreviation, ZIP)
USA (country)

The telephone system, once controlled by Bell, is no longer a monopoly. Now the leading company, AT&T competes with other long-distance phone companies such as MCI and Sprint. Telephone numbers in the U.S. consist of a three-digit area code, a three-digit exchange, and a four-digit number, written as 617-123-4567. Normally only the last seven digits are used in a local call. Non-local calls within the area code from which you are dialing require a "1" dialed before the last seven digits, while long-distance calls require a "1," then the area code, and then the seven-digit number. Canada and much of Mexico share the same area code system. The area code "800" indicates a toll-free number, usually for a business. For information on specific toll-free numbers, call the toll-free meta-line at 800-555-1212. Be careful—the age of information technology has recently given birth to the "900" number. Its area code is deceptively similar to the toll-free code, but "900" calls are staggeringly expensive. Average charges range from $2-5 for the first minute, with a smaller charge for each additional minute. You can have phone sex, make donations to political candidates, or listen to the voices of New Kids on the Block, at a cost.

The local telephone directory contains most of the information you will need about telephone usage, including area codes for the U.S., many foreign country codes, and rates. To obtain local phone numbers or area codes of other cities, call directory assistance (411 within your area code, or 1-area code-555-1212). From any phone you can reach the **operator** by dialing "0." The operator will help you with rates and other information and give assistance in an emergency. You can reach directory assistance and the operator without payment from any pay phone.

In order to place a call, you must first hear the dial tone, a steady tone meaning that the line is clear. After dialing, you will usually hear an intermittent, ringing noise that indicates that the call has gone through. You might also hear a "busy signal," which is a short buzzing tone signifying that the person you have called is on the line with someone else.

Pay phones are plentiful, most often stationed on street corners and in public areas. Be wary of private, more expensive pay phones—the rate they charge per call will be printed on the phone. Put your coins (10-25¢ for a local call) into the slot and listen for a dial tone before dialing; if there is no answer or if you get a busy signal, you will get your money back. To make a long-distance direct call, put the coins in and dial the number; an operator will tell you the cost of the first three minutes, and you must then deposit that amount. The operator will cut in after your time is up and tell you to deposit more money. Generally, long-distance rates go down after 5pm on weekdays and are further reduced between 11pm and 8am and on weekends. Look for new pay phones by competitor companies which charge 25¢ for one minute anywhere in the continental U.S.

If you don't have lots of change, you may want to make a **collect call** (i.e. charge the call to the recipient). To do this, first dial "0" and then the area code and number you wish to reach. An operator will cut in and ask to help you. Tell the operator that you wish to place a collect (also known as "station to station") call from (your name). You might opt for a **person-to-person** call, which is more expensive than collect. To call person-to-person, you must also give the recipient's name to the operator, but you will only be charged if the person you want to speak with is there. With a collect call, another party may accept the charges, and the money will be wasted if the recipient is not at that number. In some areas, particularly rural ones, you may have to tell the operator what number you wish to reach, and she or he will put the call through for you.

You can place **international calls** from any telephone. To call direct, dial the international access code (011), the country code, the city code, and the local number. Country codes may be listed with a zero in front (e.g. 033), but when using 011, drop the zero (e.g. 011-33). In some areas you will have to give the operator the number and he or she will place the call. To find out the cheapest time to call various countries in Europe or the Middle East, call the operator (dial "0"). The cheapest time to call Australia and Japan is between 3am and 2pm, New Zealand 11pm and 10am.

If a telephone call is impossible, cabling may be the only way to contact someone quickly overseas. A short message will usually reach its destination by the following day. For most overseas telegrams, Western Union charges a base fee of $7, in addition to 40-60¢ per word, including name and address. Exact charges depend on the length of the message and its destination. Call Western Union (800-325-6000) to check rates to specific countries.

Holidays

Many listings in *Let's Go: USA* refer to holidays that may be unfamiliar to foreign travelers. Be aware that government agencies, post offices, and banks usually close on the following holidays. Businesses may also change their hours.
New Year's Day is January 1. **Martin Luther King, Jr.'s Birthday** is celebrated on the third Monday in January and honors one of the world's greatest civil rights leaders. **Presidents' Day** occurs the third Monday in February. **Memorial Day** falls on the last Monday of May and honors all Americans who have died in wars. The three-day weekend also signals the unofficial start of summer. Halfway through summer bangs **Independence Day** on July 4, when the country typically celebrates its independence from England with barbecues and fireworks. Summer ends with another long weekend at the beginning of September; **Labor Day** falls on the first Monday of September, amid a flurry of back-to-school sales. **Columbus Day** sets sail the second Monday in October. **Thanksgiving,** the fourth Thursday of November, celebrates the survival of the Pilgrims, Europeans who arrived in New England in 1620 and lived through their first winter thanks to the help of Native Americans. Thanksgiving unofficially marks the start of the holiday season that runs through New Year's Day. All public agencies and offices close on these holidays, as well as on several others that scatter throughout the calendar.

Measurements

The British system of weights and measures is still in use in the U.S., despite recent efforts to convert to the metric system. The following is a list of U.S. units and their metric equivalents:

> 1 inch = 25 millimeters
> 1 foot = 0.30 meter
> 1 yard = 0.91 meter
> 1 mile = 1.61 kilometers
> 1 ounce = 25 grams
> 1 pound = 0.45 kilogram
> 1 quart(liquid) = 0.94 liter

12 inches equal 1 foot; 3 feet equal 1 yard; 5280 feet equal 1 mile. 16 ounces (weight) equal 1 pound (abbreviated as 1 lb.). 8 ounces (volume) equal 1 cup; 2 cups equal 1 pint; 2 pints equal 1 quart; and 4 quarts equal 1 gallon.
Electric outlets throughout the U.S., Canada, and Mexico provide current at 117 volts, 60 cycles (Hertz). Since European voltage is usually 220, you might need a transformer in order to operate your non-American appliances. This is an extremely important purchase for those with electric systems for disinfecting contact lenses and other small appliances. Transformers are sold to convert specific wattages (e.g. 0-50 watt transformers for razors and radios; larger watt transformers for hair dryers and other appliances). You might also need an adapter to change the shape of the plug; American plugs usually have 2 rectangular prongs, but plugs for larger appliances often have a third prong.
The U.S. uses the Fahrenheit temperature scale rather than the Centigrade (Celsius) scale. To convert Fahrenheit to approximate Centigrade temperatures, subtract 32, then divide by 2. Or, just remember that 32° is the freezing point of water, 212° its boiling point, normal human body temperature is 98.6°, and room temperature hovers around 70°.

Time

Time is money.

—*Jenny Scheussler*

U.S. residents, like Jenny, tell time on the Latinate 12-hour, not 24-hour, clock. Hours after noon are post meridiem or pm (e.g. 2pm); hours before noon are ante meridiem or am (e.g. 2am). Noon is 12pm and midnight is 12am. (To avoid confusion, *Let's Go: USA* uses only "noon" and "midnight.")

The Continental U.S. divides into four time zones: Eastern, Central, Mountain, and Pacific. When it's noon Eastern time, it's 11am Central, 10am Mountain, 9am Pacific, and 7am central Alaskan and Hawaiian. The borders of the time zones are detailed in the map at the beginning of the book. Most areas of the country switch to daylight saving time (one hour ahead of standard) from mid-April to October.

Alcohol and Drugs

The U.S. has a long history of trying to curb its citizens' alcohol intake, adopting strict rules concerning purchase and consumption. Some areas of the country are "dry," meaning they do not permit the sale of alcohol at all, and others do not permit selling it on Sundays. Wherever you are, you must be 21 years old to purchase alcoholic beverages legally. If you look under 30, be prepared to show a photo ID (preferably a driver's license or other valid government-issued document) when ordering or buying alcohol. A few select states go so far as to require that you possess one of their liquor licenses before you can make your purchase. Also, many drugs that are legal for either medicinal or recreational purposes in some countries may be illegal in the U.S. Possession of marijuana, cocaine, and most opiate derivatives (among many other chemicals) is punishable by stiff fines and/or imprisonment. Check with the U.S. Customs Service before your trip (see Customs above) about any questionable drugs.

Transportation For Foreign Visitors

Getting Here

The simplest and surest way to find a bargain fare is to have a reliable travel agent guide you through the jungle of travel options. In addition, check the travel sections of major newspapers for special fares, and consult CIEE (see Useful Organizations above) or your national student travel organization—they might have special deals that regular travel agents cannot offer.

From Canada and Mexico

The U.S. and Canada share the world's longest undefended border, easily crossed by U.S. and Canadian citizens alike. (See the Canada General Introduction for details.)

Entering the U.S. from Mexico is a bit more difficult: it is sometimes necessary for Mexicans to have a tourist visa for travel in the U.S.; contact the U.S. Embassy in Mexico City with questions. For Mexicans, as for Canadians, finding bargains on travel in the States may not be easy. Residents of the Americas may not qualify for the discounts that airlines, bus, and train companies give to visitors from overseas.

Mexican and American carriers offer many flights between the two countries. Since air travel in the U.S. is relatively expensive, flying on a Mexican airline to one of the border towns and traveling by train or bus from there may cost less. For more information regarding transportation to and from Mexico and the American west coast, see the incredible *Let's Go: Mexico* or *Let's Go: California and Hawaii*.

Amtrak, Greyhound/Trailways, or one of their subsidiaries connects with all the Mexican border towns. Most buses and trains do no more than cross the Mexico/U.S. border, but you can make connections at: San Diego, CA; Nogales, AZ; and El Paso, Eagle Pass, Laredo, or Brownsville, TX. To drive in the U.S. (see Transportation above) you need both a license and insurance; contact your local auto club or the American Automobile Association (800-336-4357) for details.

From Europe

It's very difficult to generalize about getting to the U.S. from Europe, or to offer exact fares. Prices and market conditions can fluctuate significantly from one week to the next. The best advice *Let's Go* can offer is that you have patience and begin looking for a flight as soon as you decide to travel to the U.S.

Flexibility is the best strategy. Direct, regularly scheduled flights are ordinarily far out of any budget traveler's range. Consider leaving from a travel hub; certain cities—such as London, Paris, Amsterdam, and Athens—have competitively-priced flights. The money you save on a flight out of Paris, for example, might exceed the cost of getting to the airport. London is the major travel hub for trans-Atlantic budget flights. A similar flexibility in destination cities is advisable. Fares to cities only 100 mi. apart may differ by that many dollars. New York is a consistently cheap travel target. Atlanta, Chicago, Los Angeles, Dallas, Seattle, and Toronto, Montréal, and Vancouver in Canada are also cheap destinations.

A charter flight is usually the most economical option. You must choose your departure and return dates when you book, and you will lose some or all of your money if you change or cancel your ticket. Charter companies also reserve the right to change the dates of your flight or the cost of the ticket, or even to cancel your flight within 48 hours of departure. Check with a travel agent about a charter company's reliability and reputation. The most common problem with charters is delays. To be safe, get your ticket in advance, and arrive at the airport well before departure time to ensure a seat. The relatively low cost of a charter flight will usually entail fewer creature comforts.

If you decide to take a non-charter flight, you'll be purchasing greater reliability and flexibility. Major airlines offer reduced fare options. The advantage of flying **standby** is flexibility, since you can come and go as you please. Standby flights, however, have become increasingly difficult to find. Check with a travel agent for availability. **TWA, British Airways,** and **Pan Am** offer standby from London to most major U.S. cities. Most airlines allow you to purchase an open ticket in advance that, depending on seat availability, is confirmed the day of departure. Seat availability is known only on the day of the flight, though some airlines will issue predictions. The worst crunch leaving Europe takes place from mid-June to early July, while August is uniformly tight for returning flights; at no time can you count on getting a seat right away.

STA Travel is a reliable organization that arranges charter flights; call (800-777-0112) for information or call the London office at 44 (071) 937 9921, for North American travel (see Information for Foreign Visitors above). You might also try contacting the CIEE, which has two charter services —**Council Charter** (800-223-7402) and **Council Travel** (212-661-1450; discounts for students and teachers only). Some reliable charter companies include: **DER Tours** (800-937-1234 or the London office at 44 (071) 408 0111), **Tourlite** (800-272-7600), **Travac** (800-872-8800), **Unitravel** (800-325-2222), and **Wardair** (800-237-0314 or 800-426-7000). Many of these organizations have offices throughout Europe; call the toll-free number and ask for the number of your local office.

Another reduced fare option is the **Advanced Purchase Excursion Fare (APEX).** An APEX provides you with confirmed reservations and allows you to arrive and depart from different cities. APEX requires a minimum stay of 7 to 14 days and a maximum stay of 60 to 90 days. You must purchase your ticket 21 days in advance and pay a $50-100 penalty if you change it. For summer travel, book APEX fares early; by June you may have difficulty getting the departure date you want.

Smaller, budget airlines often undercut major carriers by offering bargain fares on regularly scheduled flights. Competition for seats on these smaller carriers during peak season is fierce; book early. Some discount transatlantic airlines include **Icelandair** (800-223-5500; New York to Luxembourg) and **Virgin Atlantic Airways** (800-862-8621; Newark, NJ to London).

From Asia and Australia

Unfortunately, Asian and Australian travelers have few inexpensive options for air travel to the U.S. Asians and Australians must make do with the APEX. There is about a $100 difference between peak and off-season flights between the U.S. and Japan. U.S. carriers offer cheaper flights than **Japan Airlines.** Seasonal fares from and to Australia are a bit more complicated; call around to see what airlines offer the best deal. A difference of a few days can save you a good deal of money. Some of the airlines that fly between Australia and the U.S. are: **Qantas, Air New Zealand, United, Continental, UTA French Airlines,** and **Canadian Pacific Airlines.** Prices are roughly equivalent among the six, although the cities they serve vary. One compensation for the exorbitant fares is that transpacific flights often allow a stopover in Honolulu, Hawaii.

Getting Around

In the 50s, President Dwight D. Eisenhower envisioned an **interstate system,** a national network of highways designed primarily to aid the military in defending U.S. soil against foreign invasion. Eisenhower's asphalt dream has been gradually realized, although Toyotas far outnumber tanks on the federally funded roads. Even-numbered roads run east-west and odd run north-south. If the interstate has a three digit number, it is a branch of another interstate (i.e., I-285 is a branch of I-85). An even digit in the hundred's place means the branch will eventually return to the main interstate; an odd digit means it won't. North-south routes begin on the West Coast with I-5 and end with I-95 on the East Coast. I-10 stretches across the entire southern border, from Los Angeles along the coast of the Gulf of Mexico to Jacksonville, FL. The northernmost east-west route is I-94. The national speed limit of 55mph has been raised to 65mph in some areas. The main routes through most towns are **U.S. highways,** which are often locally referred to by non-numerical names. **State highways** are usually less heavily traveled and may lead travelers to down-home American farming communities. U.S. and state highway numbers don't follow any particular numbering pattern.

Airline, bus, and train companies offer discounts to foreign visitors within the U.S. **Greyhound/Trailways** offers an **International Ameripass** for foreign students and faculty members. The passes are sold primarily in foreign countries, but may be purchased for a slightly higher price in New York, Los Angeles, San Francisco, or Miami. Prices are $125 for a 7-day pass ($135 in the U.S.), $199 for a 15-day pass ($214 in the U.S.), and $279 for a 30-day pass ($299 in the U.S.). To obtain a pass, you need a valid passport and proof of eligibility; the pass cannot be extended. If you are *not* a student or a faculty member, the regular rates for passes are: $189 for seven days, $249 for 15 days, and $349 for 30 days, with optional extensions of $10 per day. Call Greyhound at 800-237-8211 for information or to request their *Visit USA Vacation Guide,* which details services for foreigners.

Amtrak's **USA Rail Pass,** similar to the Eurailpass, entitles foreigners to unlimited travel anywhere in the U.S. A 45-day pass costs $295. If you plan to travel only in one particular area, purchase a Regional Rail Pass instead. Each pass serves a single region, including Eastern, Far Western, and Florida ($179 each), and Western ($229). All USA Rail Passes for children (ages 2-11) are half-fare. With a valid passport, you can purchase the USA Rail Pass outside the country or in New York, Boston, Miami, Los Angeles, or San Francisco. Check with travel agents or Amtrak representatives in Europe. If you're already in the U.S. and would like more information, call Amtrak (800-872-7245). Passes are not a bargain unless you plan to make a number of stops. Also remember that many U.S. cities are not accessible by train.

Many major U.S. airlines in America offer special **Visit USA** air passes and fares to foreign travelers. You purchase these passes outside the U.S., paying one price for a certain number of "flight coupons" good for one flight segment on an airline's domestic system within a certain time period; some cross-country trips may require two segments. "Visit USA" discount fares are available for specific flights within the U.S. if purchased in one's own country. Most airline passes can be purchased only by those living outside the Western Hemisphere, though some are available for Canadians, Mexicans, and residents of Latin America if they purchase a pass from a travel agent located at least 100 mi. from the U.S. border. "Visit USA" fares are marked by a maze of restrictions and guidelines; consult a travel agent concerning the logistics of these discounts.

Work For Foreign Visitors

Working in the U.S. with only a B-2 visa is grounds for deportation. Before a work visa can be issued to you, you must present the U.S. Consulate in your country with a letter from a U.S. employer stating that you have been offered a job and that you have a permanent residence in your home country. The letter must mention you by name and briefly outline the job, its salary, and its employment period. Alternatively, a U.S. employer can obtain an H visa for you (usually an H-2, which means that qualified applicants for the position are not available in the U.S.). For more specific visa information, write the Consumer Information Center, Department 455W, Pueblo, CO 81009 (719-948-3334). Send 50¢ for a brochure on visas for foreigners.

Student travel organizations such as CIEE and its affiliates often assist students in securing work visas. Some have work-exchange programs, while others hire individuals who speak English fluently to act as leaders for tour groups. The CIEE publishes a useful book called *Volunteer! The Comprehensive Guide to Voluntary Service in the U.S. and Abroad* ($6.95 plus $1 postage).

The **Association for International Practical Training (AIPT)** is the umbrella organization for the **International Association for the Exchange of Students for Technology Experience.** AIPT offers on-the-job training in the U.S. to foreign students in agriculture, engineering, architecture, computer science, mathematics, and the sciences. You should have completed two (and preferably three) years in a technical major. You must apply by December 10 for summer placement, six months in advance for other placement. Contact AIPT at 10 Corporate Center, Suite 250, Columbia, MD 21044 (301-997-2200). The government agency in your own country that handles educational exchanges and visits to other countries should be able to provide local contacts for suitable organizations.

If you are studying in the U.S., you can take any on-campus job once you have applied for a social security number. Check with your student employment office for job listings and requirements for work clearance. The government has recently begun a strict campaign to prohibit businesses from hiring employees without an H-visa; don't expect leniency. Before being hired, all job applicants must obtain an I-9 validation by showing proof of U.S. citizenship or a work permit.

Other organizations worth contacting include:

American Friends Service Committee, 1501 Cherry St., Philadelphia, PA 19102 (215-241-7000). No longer runs volunteer workcamps, except in Mexico, but publishes a *Resource List* of other workcamps.

Archaeological Institute of America, 675 Commonwealth Ave., Boston, MA 02215 (617-353-9361). Publishes the *Archaeological Fieldwork Opportunities Bulletin,* available every January.

Central Bureau for Educational Visits and Exchanges, Seymour Mews House, Seymour Mews, London W1H 9PE, England ((071) 486 5101). Publishes *Working Holidays* (£5.95).

Service Civil International. U.S. address: Rte. 2, P.O. Box 506, Innisfree Village, Crozet, VA 22932 (804-823-1826). Arranges placement in workcamps for young people over 15. In order to avoid placement fees, write to UNESCO's **Coordinating Committee for International Voluntary Service (CCIVS)**, 1, rue Miollis, 75105 Paris. They publish a listing of *Workcamp Organizers.*

Volunteers for Peace, 43 Tiffany Rd., Belmont, VT 05730 (802-259-2759). Publishes an annual *International Workcamp Directory* and a free newsletter.

Study For Foreign Visitors

Foreigners who wish to study in the U.S. must apply for either an **F-1 visa** (for exchange students) or a **J-1 visa** (for full-time students enrolled in a degree-granting program). To obtain a J-1, you must fill out an IAP 66 eligibility form, issued by the program in which you will enroll. Neither the F-1 nor J-1 visa specifies any expiration date; instead they are both valid for the "duration of stay," which includes the length of your particular program and a brief grace period thereafter. In order to extend a student visa, fill out an I-538 form. Requests to extend a visa must be submitted 15 to 60 days before the original departure date. Many foreign schools—and most U.S. colleges—have offices that give advice and information on study in the U.S.

Admission offices at almost all U.S. institutions accept applications directly from international students. If English is not your first language, you will generally be required to pass the **Test of English as a Foreign Language and Test of Spoken English (TOEFL/TSE)**, administered in many countries. For more information, contact the TOEFL/TSE Application Office, P.O. Box 6155, Princeton, NJ 08541 (609-921-9000).

One excellent information source is the **Institute of International Education (IIE)**, which administers many educational exchange programs in the U.S. and abroad. IIE also prints *Fields of Study at U.S. Colleges,* which details courses of study and lists other resources. *Study in U.S. Colleges and Universities: A Selected Bibliography* contains information relating to your field and to U.S. education in general. If you plan a summer visit, take a look at *Summer Learning Options USA: A Guide for Foreign Nationals. English Language and Orientation Programs in the United States* describes language and cultural programs. To obtain these publications, contact IIE, 809 United Nations Plaza, New York, NY 10017 (212-883-8200). They are also available through local Fulbright Commission offices, private counseling agencies, or the U.S. International Commission Agency offices in U.S. embassies.

Life and Times

History and Politics

Native American cultures already populated most of the continent by the time Europeans arrived in North America in the late 15th and early 16th centuries. These cultures varied in type of social organization, property relations, religious systems, and inter-tribal relations. Europeans often painted Native Americans as warlike, blaming them for their own destruction, though European-brought disease and guns wiped out most tribes. On the other hand, many white intellectuals idealized Native Americans as peace-loving, childlike "primitives," another rationale for their subjugation. No generalization can describe Native American cultural diversity: some tribes were warlike, such as the Sioux, some were peace-loving, such as the Pueblos, and some showed advanced forms of organization, such as the Iroquoian Confederation. Today, concepts of racial superiority and "Manifest Destiny" have robbed Native Americans of their cultural identity, placed them on reservations, and made them victims of high rates of alcoholism, unemployment, and illiteracy. Native American culture, however, was a seminal influence on European American culture, in the form of place names, art, and food.

The first European explorers to discover an American continent were probably Vikings who stumbled upon these shores by accident. Around the year 1000, however, Leif Ericson landed here deliberately. Great historical controversy, complete with forgeries and falsified evidence, surrounds these first landings. ·

A U.S. holiday celebrates the explorer Christopher Columbus. Born to Genoese wool weavers, Columbus landed on what is now Watlings Island in the Bahamas in 1492, financed by the Spanish crown. America is named after another Italian, cartographer Amerigo Vespucci. Other European explorers included Hudson, de Soto, and Cortés.

The British, French, and Spanish raced furiously to colonize the so-called New World. The first British settlement was established by Sir Walter Raleigh in Virginia in 1584. By 1602, however, the original group had mysteriously disappeared and Raleigh had given up. The first successful British project, Jamestown, established a farming economy around corn, and friendly relations with the surrounding peoples in 1606. In New England, the Pilgrims, a group of religious dissenters, established the Mayflower Compact on November 21, 1620, and settled in Plymouth in what is now Massachusetts. The Puritans, a more extreme group of religious separatists, set up the Massachusetts Bay colony in 1629, under the leadership of John Winthrop. They spread throughout the Boston area, establishing a religious center in Salem. Roger Williams, a dissenter from the dissenters, was exiled to Rhode Island, which became a bastion of religious toleration.

The Dutch settled New York, originally naming it New Amsterdam. The South, however, was settled first, by the Spanish and French. St. Augustine, in Florida, is the oldest European city in the U.S—though Native Americans had settled in the Southwest by 1300 AD. Spain did not sell Florida to the U.S. until 1819. Louisiana, a much larger territory then than it is now, bounced back and forth between France and Spain until 1803 when Napoleon sold it to the U.S. Spanish and French elements are obvious in Creole culture today. France was eliminated as a New World power even earlier, however, when the French lost the Second Hundred Years' War, which culminated in the French and Indian War (1754-63); each side, French and English, had Native American allies. France also had to surrender Canada as a province during that war.

The United States' history as an independent country began with the Declaration of Independence on July 4, 1776. The Revolutionary War, however, had begun in earnest the previous year, with the battles of Lexington and Concord, near Boston, and the battle of Bunker Hill, in Boston proper. Later, the scene of battle moved south, to Valley Forge and Yorktown in Pennsylvania. The Revolution was a colonial independence movement, a revolt against monarchy, and perhaps above all, a civil war fought in each village. However, this internal civil war did not divide along class lines, with loyalists and revolutionaries each drawn from all social strata. The United States' sense of founding by a classless people may help explain the denial of class distinctions that exists even today. However, the classless nature of the divisions, and the fact that the leadership was moderate and upper-class, left no opening for a French Revolution-like "terror."

In 1781, the Articles of Confederation established some key principles: the abolition of slavery in Northern states, the separation of church from government, the institution of republican state governments, and the limitation of the federal government's power. The Constitution that the U.S. still follows and revises with amazing reverence was ratified in 1789.

The first 10 amendments to the Constitution, ratified in 1791, constitute the Bill of Rights. These rights limit the powers of the federal government, and in some cases state governments, to interfere in the lives of individuals. Often, the Supreme Court must defend these rights against the whims of politicians or lower courts. The Constitution is very difficult to amend; there have been only sixteen amendments since the Bill of Rights. The most important, perhaps, was the Thirteenth Amendment, which formally abolished slavery in 1865, though African Americans remained disenfranchised and often violently prevented from voting for 100 more years. The recently defeated Equal Rights Amendment would have guaranteed various employment and educational advances for women. Most recently, President Bush and others advocated an amendment to prohibit flag-burning.

Few principles both define U.S. politics and differentiate it from the politics of other democracies. The principles of "checks and balances" and "separation of powers" prohibit the executive, legislative, or judicial branches from gaining too much power. Federalism gives states limited autonomy over legal, revenue, and social policies. A high threshold of representation has insured the continued dominance of two political parties at both the state and federal levels. Finally, the U.S. has emphasized the principle of freedom over the principle of equality in both the political and economic spheres, partly because of institutional structures, and partly because of cultural elements.

Throughout the 19th century, the European American frontier moved farther and farther westward. Both disease and guns enabled Europeans to kill off Native American populations. Dee Brown's *Bury My Heart at Wounded Knee* is a gripping account of this slaughter. Westward travelers also overran territories claimed by other countries. The Mexican-American War in 1846-47 resulted from the annexation of Texas from Mexico in 1845 and U.S. embarrassment over defeat at the Alamo in 1836. A philosophy of entitlement called "Manifest Destiny" facilitated these conquests. Finally, European settlers confronted nature in all its glory and violence. The Western landscape was inhospitable to the first settlers; the infamous Donner Party, for example, had to resort to cannibalism to survive the snows of the Sierra Nevadas.

Land, adventure, and sometimes gold served as adequate incentives to confront these obstacles. An added motivation was the wave of immigration that hit the U.S. in the early-to-mid-19th century. A second wave occurred between the Civil War and World War I. These foreigners all added ingredients to the often simmering "Melting Pot," but most experienced, and still experience, hostility and discrimination on these shores. Until 1890, most immigrants came from Northern and Western Europe; after 1890, most came from Southern and Eastern Europe. East Asian and Latin American immigration continued throughout. Today ethnic groups still focus in specific areas. Boston stays heavily Irish, Chicago Polish, and Miami Cuban. Mexican culture has heavily influenced southern Texas, and the Southwest in general.

The major conflict of the mid-19th century was the division between North and South. The Civil War (1861-65) resulted in over 600,000 deaths, pitting 23 Northern states, with a population of 22 million, against nine Southern states, with a population of nine million, including 3.5 million African slaves. The North had 85% of the nation's industry. Slavery was an important cause of the Civil War, but many see the war as a fundamentally cultural clash between an essentially feudal society and a commercialized agricultural one, similar to the civil wars of England (1650), France (1789), and Italy (1860s). It can also be seen as a struggle between states' rights and a strong federal government. In any case, the stupidity of Lincoln's generals counteracted the President's strong leadership to prolong the war for four years. The film *Gone with the Wind* presents the antebellum South in all its glory and squalor.

The institution of slavery had a profound impact on U.S. culture, and U.S. citizens live in its shadow today; race relations are tense and at times violent, reflecting the country's birth in a barbaric condition. Alex Haley's *Roots* chronicles one family's voyage from Africa to slavery to freedom.

The turn of the century brought new domestic and foreign developments. Industrialists like Henry Ford and John D. Rockefeller became the driving forces behind capitalism in the U.S., and then U.S. economic imperialism, opposed to the "Trustbuster," Teddy Roosevelt. Labor movements sprung up to counteract the influence of the industrialists, led by Eugene V. Debs and Samuel Gompers, the first president of the American Federation of Labor. Women as well achieved participation, with suffrage for European American women guaranteed in 1919 by the 19th amendment to the Constitution. Leaders of the suffrage movement included Susan B. Anthony and Elizabeth Cady Stanton.

On the international scene, the U.S. was becoming a world power, using armed intervention in Central America, for example, and industrial power embodied by cars, steel, and industrialized agriculture. U.S. involvement from 1917-18 in World War I reinforced this position of dominance. The nations of Europe endured tremendous dependence on the U.S. This made the Great Depression, following the jubilant atmosphere of the "roaring twenties," even more significant. It began with the Stock Market Crash of 1929 and lasted, with minor upswings in between, until 1940. President Franklin Roosevelt's "New Deal" created public welfare, agriculture, utilities, transportation, and housing programs. And a tradition of deficit spending; the current U.S. deficit is roughly $200 billion annually. However, only World War II finally rejuvenated the U.S. economy.

The U.S. entered the war after the Japanese bombing of Pearl Harbor, in Hawaii, on December 7, 1941. The war on the battlefield entrenched the U.S. as the major military power of the West for decades to come. President Truman's use of two atomic bombs on Japan in 1945 set the stage for an arms race with the Soviet Union that has only now begun to subside. Furthermore, it helped create the military-industrial complex that has helped shape U.S. military, diplomatic, industrial, and budgetary policy.

The home front during World War II was the scene of massive change. On the one hand, the Depression ended once and for all, and national cohesion of a type unknown in the U.S. developed around the war effort. On the other hand, European American women and African Americans were involved in national life in a way they had never been before. Some women were unwilling, after working in factories during the war, to return to the home, and modern feminist movement arose, epitomized by Betty Friedan's *The Feminist Mystique*. Gains made by African Americans gave impetus to the aspirations of the Civil Rights movement of the 50s and 60s.

Underneath the surface calm of the 50s, discontent brewed. The excesses of McCarthyist Communist-hunting, and the futility of the Korean War, created a newfound mistrust of the U.S. government. The women's movement, and the Civil Rights movement led by Malcolm X and Dr. Martin Luther King Jr., began amid the ostensible tranquility of the 50s. The election of John F. Kennedy in 1960 seemed to speak to these concerns; his assassination in 1963 plunged the nation into despair.

The 60s as most people think and make movies about them today actually began in 1964. The Beatles came to the U.S., race riots raged in Watts and Detroit, and the African American-led Civil Rights movement and Lyndon Johnson's War On Poverty achieved their greatest successes all in the mid-sixties. Youth culture, represented by Charles Reich's *The Greening of America*, experienced its fullest flowering at Woodstock in 1969. By then Dr. King and Robert Kennedy had been assassinated as well.

The Vietnam War and Watergate had a disillusioning influence on modern U.S. politics. As it unfolded, Vietnam claimed lives and resources for a war that could not be won. The trauma of a generation of Vietnam veterans has been largely ignored until recently. Several popular films have depicted their plight, including *The Deer Hunter, Platoon,* and *Born on the Fourth of July.* To many U.S. residents, the most shocking aspect of the Vietnam War was the deceit practiced by their government.

Trust in the federal government sank to new lows with the Watergate scandal. President Richard Nixon, and many of his closest friends and advisors, were implicated in various "dirty tricks," including an attempt to bug the offices of the Democratic National Committee. Nixon stepped down in 1973 under threat of impeachment. Since Watergate, U.S. citizens, and particularly the press, have often shown European-style cynicism toward their political leaders. However, perhaps the most remarkable aspect of the scandal was that it was revealed, and those responsible held accountable; two reporters from the *Washington Post* sought and reported the breaking stories and the Congress followed up with a searing investigation led by Senator Sam Ervin. In the Iran-Contra scandal of 1986, these safeguards worked less effectively.

The 70s were a period of malaise; an economic recession, large collars and pants, and a well-meaning but ineffective President in Jimmy Carter. In Reagan, the electorate saw an heroic knight who would lead them out of the confusion of the 60s and 70s; a senile, patriotic grandfather; and a comforting presence who painted the world in simplistic, and easily understandable, terms. In the 80s, the rich got richer, the poor got poorer, the Presidential administration was grossly corrupt, the environment was ignored, and social intolerence underwent a renaissance. President Bush's effect on these policies remains to be seen.

Arts and Culture

The U.S. has built a long and fascinating architectural history. While the familiar plains tepee of the Sioux was a movable shelter of utilitarian design, many Native American tribes developed sophisticated permanent buildings. In the Southwest, the early inhabitants of Grand Mesa and the Tiwa built their respective cliffside dwellings and apartment-like pueblo constructions to protect against attack and the scorching heat. These buildings survived the ravages of European marauders and remain standing to this day.

The dwellings of the first Colonial settlers followed European models, particularly in New England. Towns and villages today still contain examples of the simple wooden houses and churches built in the 17th and 18th centuries. Government contractors modeled elaborate public buildings after the European Georgian style, made popular by Sir Christopher Wren. In the late colonial and early federal period, a High Georgian style, typified by President Thomas Jefferson's designs, flourished.

In the West, the Spanish inspired a style of architecture that still prevails. Stucco façades, red gabled roofs, and elegant arches appear in buildings throughout California, Florida, Texas, and the Southwest. Authentic missions also survive in these regions. The French transplanted their own architecture to New Orleans and other settlements along the Mississippi.

The growth of U.S. cities increased the demand for large public buildings. H.H. Richardson adapted the Romanesque style in his heavy-set designs. The use of iron, and later steel, made it possible to expand upward, giving birth to the first skyscrapers at the end of the 19th century. The Empire State Building, completed during the Depression, still stands as New York City's tribute to modernity.

Frank Lloyd Wright challenged this flashy aesthetic and celebrated the midwestern landscape in his clean, low-slung "prairie houses" of the Chicago area, but the highrise marked the future of U.S. urban development. The European Bauhaus School's steel-and-glass structures soon made the design of the Empire State Building obsolete.

The architectural fad that has most deeply influenced suburban U.S. culture is the mall. These increasingly intricate shopping centers use fountains, plants, music, and even miniature amusement parks to create the perfect shopping environment, bearing witness to the U.S. consumption ethic.

Until the 20th century, North American art essentially stayed parasitic. As European settlers suppressed the political and artistic culture of Native American tribes, they fell victim themselves to European cultural oppression. The dominant ideology they exerted came to control their own cultural production. Westward expansion and the ideology of the frontier led to the appearance of the first innovative European American visual art. In the literary sphere, Walt Whitman was the first poet to write in a true "American" voice. In his famous line "I sing the body electric," he inscribed onto the page the machine structure of a rising Industrial Revolution.

The intelligentsia often dismisses the work of U.S. artists like Norman Rockwell as kitsch. Plaster figurines of Rockwell's creations are still advertised on late-night television. Kitsch is merely a construct of German aesthetics trying to cope with American art. Norman Rockwell was an essential precursor of the art of the 50s and 60s. Pop artists like Andy Warhol and Alex Katz dissolved the barriers between commercial and so-called "pure" art. They laid bare the artistic relations forced on them by U.S. capitalism.

The U.S. artistic tradition culminated in its triumphant culture industry, the most efficient propaganda machine in the world. The television industry produced a series of models for the healthy red-blooded U.S. family (the Cleavers of "Leave it to Beaver" and "The Brady Bunch"). U.S. residents buy TV sets, install them in their homes, and proceed to receive apparently free transmissions. But the incredibly sophisticated advertising techniques and even more subtle forms of consumer control should lead the viewer to question what "free" means.

Most people pay to see movies to identify not only with the character in the film, but with the young star who will have made it big *because of* the flick they're watching. Hollywood still embodies the U.S. dream of fame and fortune. Movie theaters are the most severely climate-controlled enclosed spaces in the country, paying for heat in the winter and cold in the summer. But the glittering Hollywood of yesteryear is tarnished. Ironically, the most radical new media phenomenon is a product of the Compton ghettos (L.A.'s skeleton in the closet) and of all neighborhoods of New York City. The music of Public Enemy and other rap groups, while often offensive to some, is politically committed in a way that U.S. pop music of the 80s (Madonna, Prince) was not. It remains to be seen whether the rap movement will escape the tentacles of the U.S. culture industry or be unable to deny Marshall McLuhan's dictum that the medium *is* the message.

NEW YORK

For almost as long as the United States has held a national consciousness, New York state, like the gradeschool teacher with a hamster in the classroom, has kept the special power to capture the country's imagination. In the early 1800s, Thomas Cole, central figure in the coterie of U.S. artists known as the Hudson River School, painted glorious landscapes of the Catskills and the Hudson River Valley. These instantly popular works spawned a litter of proud images of New York as an avatar of wilderness. A century later, the state inspired the likes of Georgia O'Keeffe and Piet Mondrian; to paint the cavernous skyscrapers and machine-like grid of Manhattan.

Though the "Big Apple," the nation's largest city, may seem the teacher's pet, the rest of the state retains enough variety to make even the strictest substitute smile. The Catskills can entertain hikers and hang gliders for weeks, while the Adirondacks stand out as New York's natural wonder. "There are regions of the Adirondacks where no one has ever set foot," claim proud and perhaps oxygen-deprived locals. Like a nice, scrape-free recess, New York has long worked to maintain the quality of outdoor recreation in the state.

Practical Information

Capital: Albany.

Tourist Information: 800-225-5697 or 474-4116. Open Mon.-Fri. 8:30am-5pm. Write to Division of Tourism, 1 Commerce Plaza, Albany 12245. Excellent, comprehensive *I Love New York Travel Guide*, includes disabled access and resource information. **New York State Office of Parks and Recreation,** Agency Bldg. 1, Empire State Plaza, Albany 12238 (518-474-0456), has literature on canoeing, camping, biking, and hiking.

Time Zone: Eastern. **Postal Abbreviation:** NY.

Travel

US Air and **Continental** provide extensive airline service to Albany, Syracuse, Rochester, and Buffalo from Newark, NJ, near New York City. Fares vary. The cheapest rates often require a seven-day advance reservation and a Saturday night stay-over.

Amtrak runs one route up the Hudson River Valley from Penn Station to Albany and on to Niagara Falls or Montréal; another follows I-90 from Boston to Albany and Buffalo. Buses cut across the state and stop in areas where the train does not go. **Greyhound/Trailways** has frequent service to Albany, Syracuse, Rochester, and Buffalo. Less frequent routes include the Finger Lakes area, the Catskills (including Cooperstown), the Adirondacks, the Hudson River Valley, Niagara Falls, and Montréal.

Hitchhiking is illegal in New York State. This law is enforced with particular vehemence in the New York City area, where it's not safe to begin with.

Outdoors

Bikers should head for the Finger Lakes region whose gentle hills are just high enough to provide some challenge and whose small farmsteads are best explored and appreciated by bike. Moreover, the wineries of the region make for very pleasant stops. Write for the *New York Bicycle Touring Guide*, c/o William N. Hoffman, 53 Claire Ave., New Rochelle 10804, or the free *Finger Lakes Bicycle Touring Guide*, Finger Lakes State Park Region, RD 3, Trumansburg 14886 (607-387-7041). For a guide to the wineries of upstate New York write to the Department of Agriculture and Markets, Capital Plaza, 1 Winner Circle, Albany 12235 (518-457-3880). Ask for the *New World of World Class Wine Making*. For information on the Adiron-

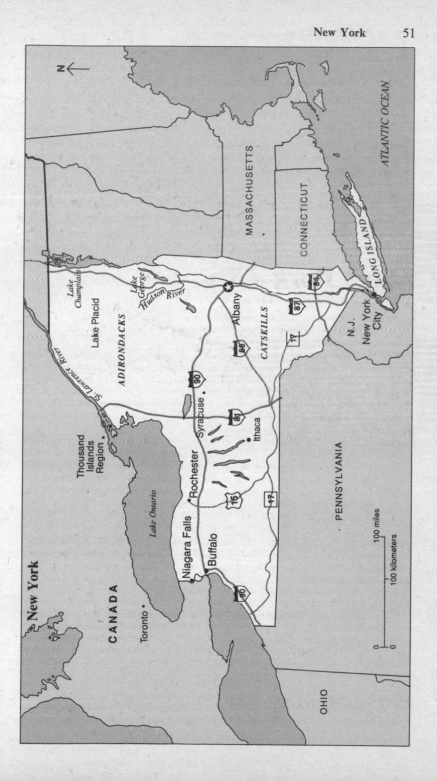

dacks and Catskills preserves, write the NY State Department of Environmental Conservation, 50 Wolf Rd., Albany 12233.

Hikers will appreciate the many long trails that criss-cross the state, including the Appalachian Trail, the Finger Lakes Trail, and the Long Path, overseen by the Forest Preserve of Protection and Management (518-457-7433). For reservations at any state campground call 800-456-2267 six to 90 days in advance. For a general guide to outdoor recreation in New York (with extensive information on camping, hiking, and sports facilities—especially golf and tennis) write to **I Love NY Publications**, Dept. of Commerce, Albany 12245, or call the New York Division of Tourism (see Practical Information above). You're also never a long drive from one of NY's 90 state parks, most of which provide excellent camping. For the nature lover, the Catskills is the perfect vacation spot. Muskie, walleye, and bass fishing in the "Seaway" is perhaps the best in the eastern U.S., with over 50 private campsites and parks scattered across the 1800 islands. For more information, call the St. Lawrence County Chamber of Commerce. (315-386-4000).

New York City

This rural America thing. It's a joke.
—Edward I. Koch, former mayor of New York City

New York City does not quite attach to the U.S. mainland geographically or otherwise, and some Kansans probably wouldn't mind if New York seceded from the union or sank into the sea. The insomniacal metropolis moves faster and lights up brighter than most of the planet, never aspiring to anything remotely rugged. While the rest of the U.S. revels in the open plain, nine million New Yorkers think vertically; on Halloween, trick-or-treaters descend upon the buildings with the greatest number of elevators.

Like Ed Koch, New York has a *chutzpah* at once offensive and endearing. New Yorkers have been known to spend years rooting for losing baseball teams, weeks creating street art that bureaucrats or rain clean off instantly, and months rehearsing shows that close in a day. From flea market to stock market, free enterprise has flourished in this big red fruit since the town's first and most notorious transaction; even St. Martin's Press couldn't beat the extraordinary Manhattan Purchase. Peter Minuit shelled out 24 bucks for the slender island back in 1626, and the likes of Horatio Alger have kept honing the art of the deal ever since.

Gotham does keep a history buried under layers of construction. The buildings of a once-fashionable neighborhood (Lower East Side) have become dilapidated, burnt-out tenements, while young artists spray their canvasses in the one-time industrial complexes of Soho. An old Native American trail winding its way through an ordered street grid has turned into a stretch of marquees and swank called Broadway.

Even those urban sophisticates who laugh at the "rural American thing" engage in a provincialism of their own. When too far removed—from the murmur of streaming traffic, all-night delicatessens, or sarcastic hot dog vendors—they grow nostalgic for the concrete archipelago, as if on the verge of clicking their heels and announcing, "There's no place like home."

Practical Information

Emergency: 911.

Police: 212-374-5000. For non-urgent inquiries. Open 24 hr.

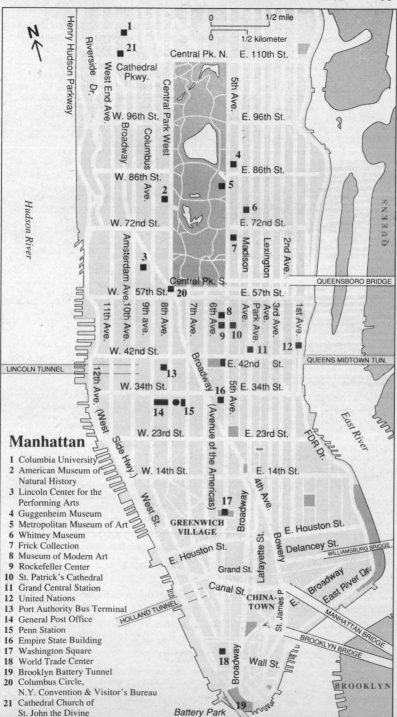

N

Henry Hudson Parkway

Riverside Dr.

West End Ave.

Hudson River

1

21

Cathedral
Pkwy.

Central Pk. N. E. 110th St.

5th Ave.

Central Park West

Broadway

Columbus Ave.

W. 96th St. E. 96th St.

Amsterdam Ave.

W. 86th St. 4 E. 86th St.

2 5

W. 72nd St. 6 E. 72nd St.

7

Madison

Lexington

2nd Ave.

QUEENSBORO BRIDGE

QUEENS

3

10th Ave.

9th ava.

8th Ave.

7th Ave.

6th Ave.

Central Pk. S. E. 57th St.

W. 57th St. 20

11th Ave.

Park Ave.

3rd Ave.

1st Ave.

8

9 10

11 12

5th Ave.

W. 42nd St. E. 42nd St.

Broadway

QUEENS MIDTOWN TUN.

LINCOLN TUNNEL

12th Ave. (West Side Hwy.)

13

W. 34th St.

16

14 15 E. 34th St.

5th Ave. (Avenue of the Americas)

W. 23rd St. E. 23rd St.

Manhattan

1 Columbia University
2 American Museum of
   Natural History
3 Lincoln Center for the
   Performing Arts
4 Guggenheim Museum
5 Metropolitan Museum of Art
6 Whitney Museum
7 Frick Collection
8 Museum of Modern Art
9 Rockefeller Center
10 St. Patrick's Cathedral
11 Grand Central Station
12 United Nations
13 Port Authority Bus Terminal
14 General Post Office
15 Penn Station
16 Empire State Building
17 Washington Square
18 World Trade Center
19 Brooklyn Battery Tunnel
20 Columbus Circle,
   N.Y. Convention & Visitor's Bureau
21 Cathedral Church of
   St. John the Divine

W. 14th St. E. 14th St.

17

West St.

Broadway

4th Ave.

FDR Dr.

East River

GREENWICH
VILLAGE

E. Houston St.

E. Houston St.

Bowery

Lafayette St.

Delancey St.

WILLIAMSBURG BRIDGE

Grand St.

Canal St.

HOLLAND TUNNEL

CHINA-
TOWN

St. James P.

East River Dr.

Broadway

MANHATTAN BRIDGE

BROOKLYN BRIDGE

18

Wall St.

Broadway

19

Battery Park

BROOKLYN

0 1/2 mile
0 1/2 kilometer

Visitor Information: New York Convention and Visitors Bureau, 2 Columbus Circle (397-8222), 59th and Broadway. Subway: A, D, 1. Friendly, multilingual staff. Directions, hotel listings, entertainment ideas, safety tips, and "insider's" descriptions of New York's neighborhoods. Request 3 free life-saving maps: *I Love New York Travel Guide* (a street map), the *MTA Manhattan Bus Map,* and the *MTA New York City Subway Map.* Try to show up in person; the phone lines tend to be busy, the maps and brochures worthwhile. Open Mon.-Fri. 9am-6pm, Sat.-Sun. and holidays 10am-6pm. Branch office at **Times Square Information Center,** 158 W. 42nd St., between Broadway and Seventh Ave. Subway: A, E, N, R, D, or F. Open Wed.-Fri. 9am-6pm, Sat.-Sun. 10am-6pm. Similar information available, but no telephone service. **Entertainment Information: Ticketron,** 399-4444. **Free Daily Events in the City,** 360-1333; 24 hr. **Jazz Line,** 718-465-7500. **NYC Onstage,** 587-1111; updates on theater, dance, music, children's entertainment, and special events. **Tkts.,** 354-5800; at Broadway and 47th St., and at 2 World Trade Center. Half-price tickets for Broadway and Off-Broadway shows sold the day of the performance only.

Travelers Aid Society: 158-160 W. 42nd St. (944-0013), between Broadway and Seventh Ave.; and JFK International Airport (718-656-4870), in the International Arrivals Bldg. Subway to 42nd St. branch: A, E, N, R, D, or F. 42nd St. branch specializes in crisis intervention services for stranded travelers or crime victims. JFK office offers general counseling and referral to travelers, as well as emergency assistance. 42nd St. branch open Mon.-Fri. 9am-5pm; JFK branch open Mon.-Fri. 10am-7pm.

Consulates: Australia, 636 Fifth Ave. (245-4000). **Canada,** 1251 Sixth Ave. (768-2400). **France,** 934 Fifth Ave. (983-5660). **Germany,** 460 Park Ave. (308-8700). **India,** 3 E. 64th St. (879-8700). **Israel,** 800 Second Ave. (351-5200). **Italy,** 320 Park Ave. (737-9100). **U.K.,** 845 Third Ave. (752-8400).

American Express: 150 E. 42nd St. (687-3700), between Lexington and Third Ave. Travel agency providing traveler's checks, financial services, and other assistance. Open Mon.-Fri. 9am-5pm. Call for other locations.

Airports: see Getting There below.

Trains: see Getting There below.

Buses: see Getting There below.

Public Transport: see Getting Around below.

Taxis: Radio-dispatched taxis, Utog, 741-2000; and **Skyline,** 718-482-8686. No meters; these companies charge a flat rate. To JFK, $35 with either company. **Taxi Commission,** 869-4513; general complaints and lost and found. Yellow cabs can be hailed on the street. See Getting Around below for more information.

Car Rental: All agencies have minimum age requirements and ask for deposits. Call in advance to reserve, especially near the weekend. **Goldie's Leasing Corp.,** 47-11 11th St., Long Island City, Queens (718-392-5435 or 718-392-5339), across the Queensborough Bridge, south of Astoria. Mon.-Thurs. $37 per day, Fri.-Sun. $45 per day; 100 free mi., 20¢ each additional mi. Weekly $226; 700 free mi., 20¢ each additional mi. Open Mon.-Fri. 8am-6pm, Sat. 9am-5pm. Sunday drop-off possible. Must be 21 with major credit card. **Discount Rent-a-Car,** 240 E. 92nd St. (410-2211), between Second and Third Ave.; offices also in Jackson Heights, Queens. Mon.-Thurs. $51 per day; 100 free mi., 20¢ each additional mi. Fri.-Sun. $162; 500 free mi., 20¢ each additional mi. Open Mon.-Fri. 8am-7pm, Sat. 9am-2pm. Must be 25 with major credit card. **Rent-a-Wreck,** 202 W. 77th St. (800-221-8282); offices also in Queens (718-784-3302) and Brooklyn (718-998-9100). Mon.-Fri. $25-50 per day; 30-100 free mi., 22-25¢ each additional mi. Sat.-Sun. 2-day minimum of $120; 200 free mi., 25¢ each additional mi. Manhattan office open Mon.-Fri. 7:30am-6:30pm, Sat. 8:30am-5:30pm, Sun. 8:30am-6:30pm. Must be 23 with major credit card.

Auto Transport Companies: New York is the major departure point for auto transport agencies. Applications take about a week to process. Most agencies require more than one ID; some ask for references. **Dependable Car Services,** 1501 Broadway (840-6262). Depending on the model of the car, must be 19 or over; $100-200 deposit returned upon delivery. **Auto Driveaway,** 264 W. 35th St. (967-2344). Must be 21 or over. $260 deposit.

Bicycle Rentals: On weekends May-Oct. and weekdays 10am-3pm, Central Park closes to cars, allowing bicycles to rule its roads. **Metro Bicycle,** 332 E. 14th St. (228-4344), between First and Second Ave. 3-speed bikes $4 per hr., $20 per day; 10-speeds $6.50 per hr., $25 per day. Open daily 9:30am-6:30pm. $20 deposit or credit card required, as well as ID. Other locations throughout the city. **The Boathouse,** in Central Park, at the northeast corner of the lake. Enter at 72nd St. and Fifth Ave. (861-4137). 3-speeds $6 per hr., $24 per day; 10-

speeds $8 per hr., $32 per day. Open Mon.-Fri. 10am-7pm., Sat.-Sun. 9am-7pm. Last rental 6pm. ID and $20 deposit required.

New York Public Library: 11 W. 40th St. (930-0830), entrance at Fifth Ave. at 42nd St. Non-lending research library. Open Mon.-Wed. 10am-8:45pm, Thurs.-Sat. 10am-5:45pm. Over 80 branch locations.

Help Lines: Crime Victim's Hotline, 577-7777; 24-hr. counseling and referrals. **Sex Crimes Report Line,** New York Police Dept., 267-7273; 24-hr. help, counseling, and referrals. **AIDS Information,** 807-6655. Open daily 10:30am-9pm.

Medical Care: Walk-in Clinic, 57 E. 34th St. (683-1010), between Park and Madison Ave. Open Mon.-Fri. 8am-6pm, Sat. 10am-2pm. Affiliated with Beth Israel Hospital.

24-Hr. Medical Assistance: Kaufman's Pharmacy, 557 Lexington Ave. (755-2266), at 50th St. **24-Hr. Emergency Doctor,** 718-745-5900. **The Eastern's Women's Center,** 40 E. 30th St. (686-6066), between Park and Madison. Gynecological exams and surgical procedures for women.

Post Office: Central branch, 380 W. 33rd St. (967-8585), at Eighth Ave. across from Madison Square Garden. To pick up General Delivery mail, use the entrance at 390 Ninth Ave. Open Mon.-Sat. 10am-1pm. For information call 330-3099. **ZIP code:** 10001.

Area Codes: 212 (Manhattan and the Bronx); 718 (Brooklyn, Queens, and Staten Island). No extra charge for calls between these area codes, but dial "1" first. Unless otherwise specified, all telephone numbers in New York City have a 212 area code.

Getting There

By Plane

If you can make it there, you'll make it anywhere. Not only will you have to choose a carrier, but an airport as well. Three airports service the New York Metropolitan Region. The largest, **John F. Kennedy Airport (JFK)** (718-656-4520), 12 mi. from Midtown in southern Queens, handles most international flights. **La-Guardia Airport** (718-656-4520), 6 mi. from midtown in northwestern Queens, is the smallest, offering domestic flights and air shuttles (see below). **Newark International Airport,** 12 mi. from Midtown in Newark, NJ, offers both domestic and international flights at budget fares not available at the other airports.

Many airlines offer budget flights, but the cut-rate market always fluctuates under the strain of price wars. In general, flying between Monday afternoon and Thursday morning and staying over one Saturday night costs less. Booking at least 14 days in advance often qualifies you for a cheaper seat, subject to availability. Standby travel makes a good alternative after all the budget flights book up. Scan the *New York Times,* especially the Sunday "Travel" section, for the latest deals, or consult a travel agent with complete computer access to all airlines. Travel agents won't always direct you to the dirt-cheap flights because commissions are low; you may have to call the airlines yourself.

The excellent "Airport Flight Guide, put out by the Port Authority, has comprehensive flight schedules, airport maps, and data on airport parking and other services. Write to: Airport Flight Guide, One World Trade Center 65N, New York 10048.

Continental Airlines: 800-525-0280. Reduced fares with advance purchase.

Northwest: 800-225-2525. Cheap in Northern states and on the West Coast.

Pan Am: 800-221-1111. Lots of international flights. The **Pan Am Air Shuttle** flies between New York and Boston or Washington every hour on the ½ hour. Runs weekdays 6:30am-9:30pm, Sat. 7:30am-8:30pm, Sun. 8:30am-8:30pm. Fare $65 for those 24 and under (fare available Mon.-Fri. 10:30am-2:30pm, Sat. all day, and Sun. until 2:30pm. No reservations necessary; just show up ½ hr. prior to departure at the Marine Air Terminal at LaGuardia.

Trump Shuttle: 800-247-8786. Similar to the Pan Am Air Shuttle, but leaves every hr. on the hr., 7am-10pm. For those under 25 and over 64, $59 on weekdays 10am-2pm and 7-9pm, $49 all day Sat., and Sun. $49 9am-3pm, then $59 until the end of the day. Leaves from La-Guardia; no reservations necessary.

U.S. Air: 800-428-4322. Budget flights all over New York State and the Northeast. Also runs
U.S. Air Express, a collection of independent operators who fly small planes connecting with
U.S. Air flights. Cheap fares and special deals to many U.S. port cities.

To and From the Airports

Travel between each of the airports and New York City without a car of your
own becomes simpler as cost increases; you can pay in time or money. The cheapest
way in dollars is public transportation. This usually involves changing mid-route
from a bus to a subway or train, but service is frequent. Moving up the price scale,
private bus companies charge slightly more, but will take you directly from the airport to one of three destinations: Grand Central Station (42nd St. and Park Ave.),
the Port Authority Bus Terminal (41st St. and Eighth Ave.) or the World Trade
Center (1 West St.). Private companies run frequently and according to a set schedule (see below). To set your own destination and schedule, however, and if you are
willing to pay, you can take one of New York's infamous yellow cabs. From JFK
or Newark, cabs cost around $30; from LaGuardia at least $17. The trip costs less
in light traffic. Taxi companies Utog (718-361-7270) and Skyline (718-482-8686)
charge a flat $35 for travel to JFK. For the most up-to-date information on reaching
the airports, call AirRide, the Port Authority's airport hotline, at 800-247-7433.
Some services peter out or vanish entirely between midnight and 6am. Finally, if
you make lodging reservations ahead of time, be sure to ask about limousine services—some Ys and hostels offer door-to-door transportation from the airports for
reasonable fares.
  Rush-hour traffic (7:30-9:30am and 4:30-7pm) is always heavy; at other times
conditions vary. Get directions from your rental agent.
  Public transportation can easily get you from JFK to midtown Manhattan. You
can catch a JFK Express Shuttle Bus (718-330-1234) from any airport terminal
to the Howard Beach-JFK subway station, where you can take the IND to the city.
The IND stops at 57th St. and Ave. of the Americas; 50th St. and Rockefeller Center; 42nd St. and Ave. of the Americas; 34th St. and Ave. of the Americas; Washington Square; the World Trade Center; Broadway and Nassau St.; and Borough Hall
in Brooklyn. Allow at least 1 hr. travel time. The service costs $6.50. Or you can
take one of the city buses (the Q10, Q9, or Q3; fare $1.15) from the airport into
Queens. The Q10 connects with the E, F, R, and A subway lines and the Q3 and
Q9 connect with the F and R lines, all of which continue into Manhattan. Ask the
bus driver where to get off, and make sure you know which subway line you want.
Allow 90 minutes travel time. The total cost for this trip will be only $2.30, but
exercise caution. Some of the areas these buses service are unsafe. Those willing
to pay more can take the Carey Bus Service (718-632-0500), a private line that runs
between JFK and Grand Central Station and the Port Authority Terminal. Buses
leave every 30 minutes from Kennedy during the day (1-1¼ hr., fare $9.50).
  There are two ways to get into Manhattan from LaGuardia. If you have extra
time and light luggage, take the MTA "Q 33" bus ($1.15 exact change or token)
to the Eighth Ave. subway in Queens, and from there, take the E or F train into
Manhattan ($1.15 token). You can catch the Q 33 from the lower level of the termi-
nal. Allow at least 90 minutes travel time. The same word of caution applies here
as with the Q buses above. The second option, the Carey Bus Service, makes four
stops in the Midtown area. (Every 20 min., 55 min., $7.50.)
  The commute from Newark Airport takes about as long as from JFK or La-
Guardia. New Jersey Transit (NJTA) (201-460-8444) runs a fast, efficient bus
(NJTA #300) between the airport and Port Authority every 15 minutes during
the day ($7). For the same fare, the Olympia Trails Coach (212-964-6233) travels
between either Grand Central or the World Trade Center and the airport. (Every
20 min. 6am-1am, 45 min.-1½ hr. depending on traffic, $5.) NJTA Bus #107 will
take you to Midtown for $2.60 (exact change required), but don't try it unless you
have little luggage and lots of time. The NJTA also runs an Air Link bus ($4) be-
tween the airport and Newark's Penn Station (not Manhattan's), and from there
PATH trains ($1.15) run into Manhattan, stopping at the World Trade Center,

Christopher St., Sixth Ave., 9th St., 14th St., 23rd St., and 33rd St. (PATH information 212-732-8920.)

From Manhattan, **Giraldo Limousine Service** (757-6840) will pick you up anywhere between 14th and 95th St. and take you to the airport of your choice for $11-16.

By Bus or Train

Buses or trains can get you in and out of New York less expensively and more scenically. **Port Authority,** 41st St. and Eighth Ave. (564-8484), is a tremendous modern bus station with labyrinthine terminals. Port Authority has good information and security services, but sits in an unsafe neighborhood. Be wary of pickpockets, and call a cab at night. Its bathrooms are dangerous at all times. The station is the hub of the Northeast bus network, and **Greyhound/Trailways** (730-7460 or 971-6363) is the titan here. On some routes, a 10% discount is offered to students with ID. Buses run to: Boston ($32.30), Philadelphia ($19.40), Washington, DC ($39.80), and Montreal ($64.30).

Grand Central Station, 42nd St. and Park Ave., the grandiose transportation colossus of the metropolis, keeps more than 550 trains running daily on its two levels of tracks. It handles **Metro-North** (532-4900) commuter lines to Connecticut and New York suburbs, and **Amtrak** (800-872-7245 or 582-6875) lines to upstate New York and Canada. From the smaller **Penn Station,** 33rd St. and Eighth Ave., Amtrak serves most major cities in the U.S., especially those in the Northeast (to Philadelphia $28, Washington, DC $59, Boston $50). Penn Station also handles the **Long Island Railroad (LIRR)** (718-454-5477, see Long Island) and **PATH** service to New Jersey (432-1272).

By Car

During rush hour, millions of commuters jam the roads; amidst the exhaust, see the "American Dream" at work . . . or trying to get there. Any time of day, you will encounter reckless cab drivers and determined jaywalkers.

Two major highways frame Manhattan: on the East Side, the **East Side Highway** (a.k.a. the Harlem River Drive and FDR Drive); on the West Side, the **Henry Hudson Parkway** (a.k.a. the West Side Highway). From outside the city, I-95 leads to the Major Deegan, the FDR Drive, and the Henry Hudson. Go south on any of these roads, but be prepared for the amazing number of signs, intersecting roads, and other cars separating you from your destination.

Once you are in Manhattan, traffic continues to pose a problem, especially between 57th and 34th St. The even greater hassle of parking joins in to plague the weary. Would-be parallel parkers can rise to this challenge three ways. **Parking lots** are easiest but most expensive. In midtown, where lots are the only option, expect to pay at least $25 per day and up to $15 for two hours. The cheapest parking lots hunch downtown—try the far west end of Houston St.—but make sure you feel comfortable with the area and the lot. Municipal parking at 53rd St. and Eighth Ave. costs $1 per half hour.

Behind the second door is short-term parking. On the streets, **parking meters** cost 25¢ per 15 minutes, with a limit of one or two hours. Lastly, **free parking** sits on the crosstown streets in residential areas, but competition for these spots is ruthless. Read the signs carefully; a space is usually legal only certain days of the week. Towing has never made the city squeamish, and recovering your car once it's been towed will cost $100 or more. Break-ins and car theft are definite possibilities, particularly if you have a flashy radio.

Hitchhiking is illegal in New York state and cops strictly enforce the law within New York City. Offenders will usually be asked to move on. Take the train or bus out of the metropolitan area; hitching in and around New York City is dangerous.

Orientation

Five boroughs make up New York City: Brooklyn, the Bronx, Queens, Staten Island and Manhattan. But plenty of tourists and Manhattanites have been known to confuse Manhattan with New York. This Manhattancentricity has historical roots. The island's original inhabitants, the Algonquin, called it "Man-a-hat-ta" or "Heavenly Land;" the Dutch settlers who bought the island in 1626 named it "New Amsterdam." The British later took over the island and dubbed it "New York," with the four other boroughs joining the city's government only in 1898. No matter how often you hear Manhattan referred to as "The City," however, each of the other boroughs has a right to share in the name.

Flanked on the east by the East River and on the west by the Hudson River, Manhattan is a sliver of an island, severed from the rest of New York City by the narrow Harlem River. It measures only 13 mi. long and 2½ mi. wide. Fatter Queens and Brooklyn look onto their svelte neighbor from the other side of the East River and pudgy, self-reliant Staten Island averts its eyes in the south. Light industry, airports and stadiums dot Queens, the city's largest and most ethnically diverse borough. Brooklyn, the city's most populous borough (with 2.24 million residents), is even older than Manhattan. Founded by the Dutch in 1600, today it cradles several charming residential neighborhoods along with a few dangerous ones. Staten Island has remained a staunchly residential borough, similar to the suburban bedroom communities of outer Long Island. North of Manhattan nests the Bronx, the only borough connected by land to the rest of the U.S., and home of the lovely suburb of Riverdale and New York's most devastated area, the South Bronx.

Districts of Manhattan

Glimpsed from the window of an approaching plane, New York City can seem a monolithic urban jungle. But up close, New York breaks down into manageable neighborhoods, each with a history and personality of its own. As a result of city zoning ordinances, quirks of history, and random forces of urban evolution, boundaries between these neighborhoods can be abrupt.

The city began at the southern tip of Manhattan, in the area around Battery Park where the first Dutch settlers made their homes. The nearby harbor, now jazzed up into a tourist attraction as the South Street Seaport, provided the growing city with the commercial opportunities that helped it to succeed. Historic Manhattan, however, lies in the shadows of the imposing financial buildings around Wall Street and the civic office buildings around City Hall. A little farther north, neighborhoods rich in the ethnic culture brought by late 19th-century immigrants rub elbows below Houston Street—Little Italy, Chinatown, and the southern blocks of the Lower East Side. To the west is the newly fashionable TriBeCa (Triangle Below Canal St.). SoHo (for "South of Houston"), a former warehouse district west of Little Italy, has been transformed into a pocket of gleaming art studios and galleries. Above SoHo flashes Greenwich Village, once a center of intense political and artistic activity, still a literal village of lower buildings, jumbled streets, and neon glitz.

A few blocks north of Greenwich Village, stretching across the West teens and twenties, lies Chelsea, the late artist Andy Warhol's favorite hangout and former home of Dylan Thomas and Arthur Miller. East of Chelsea, presiding over the East River, is Gramercy Park, a pastoral collection of Victorian mansions and brownstones annoyingly immortalized in Edith Wharton's Age of Innocence. Midtown Manhattan towers from 34th to 59th St., where awe-inspiring traditional skyscrapers and controversial new architecture stand side by side, providing office space for millions. Here department stores outfit New York, and the nearby Theater District entertains the world—or tries to.

North of Midtown, Central Park slices Manhattan into east and west. On the Upper West Side, the gracious museums and residences of Central Park West sit next to the chic boutiques and sidewalk cafés of Columbus Ave. On the Upper East Side, the galleries and museums scattered among the elegant apartments of Fifth and Park Ave. create an even more rarified atmosphere.

Above 97th St., much of the Upper East Side's opulence ends with a whimper where commuter trains emerge from the tunnel and the *barrio* begins. Above 110th St. on the Upper West Side is majestic **Columbia University** (founded as King's College in 1754), an urban member of the Ivy League. The communities of **Harlem, East Harlem,** and **Morningside Heights** centered the Harlem Renaissance of black artists and writers in the 1920s and propulsed the revolutionary Black Power movement in the 1960s. Although torn by crime, **Washington Heights,** just north of St. Nichols Park, is nevertheless somewhat safer and more attractive than the abandoned tenements of Harlem; it is home to Fort Tryon Park, the Met's Medieval Cloisters, and a quiet community of immigrants. Still farther north, the island ends in a rural patch of wooded land where caves once inhabited by the Algonquin remain.

Manhattan's Street Plan

Most of Manhattan's street resulted from an organized expansion plan adopted in 1811, the major part of the city growing in straight lines and at right angles. Above 14th St., the streets form a grid that a novice can quickly master. In the older areas of Lower Manhattan, though, the streets receive names rather than numbers. Here, the orderly grid of the northern section disappears into a charming but confusing tangle of old, narrow streets. Bring a map; even long-time neighborhood residents may have trouble directing you to an address.

Above Washington Square, avenues run north-south and streets run east-west. Avenue numbers increase from east to west, and street numbers increase from south to north. Traffic flows east on most even-numbered streets and west on most odd-numbered ones. And two-way traffic flows on the wider streets. Three transverses cross Central Park: 65/66th St., 79/81st St., and 96/97th St. Most avenues are one-way. Tenth, Amsterdam, Hudson, Eighth, Ave. of the Americas, Madison, Fourth, Third, and First Ave. are northbound. Ninth, Columbus, Broadway below 59th St., Seventh, Fifth, Lexington, and Second Ave. are southbound. Some avenues allow two-way traffic: York, Park, Central Park West, Broadway above 59th St., West End, and Riverside Dr.

New York's celebrated east/west division refers to an address's location in relation to the two borders of Central Park—**Fifth Avenue** along the east side and **Central Park West** along the west. Below 59th St. where the park ends, the West Side begins at the western half of Fifth Ave. Uptown (above 59th St.) refers to the area north of Midtown. Downtown (below 34th St.) means the area south of Midtown.

Now for the system's discrepancies. You may still hear the **Avenue of the Americas** referred to by its original name, **Sixth Avenue.** Also, Lexington, Park, and Madison Ave. lie *between* Third and Fifth Ave. On the Lower East Side, there are several avenues east of First Ave. that are lettered rather than numbered: Aves. A, B, C, and D. Finally, above 59th St. on the West Side, Eighth Ave. becomes Central Park West, Ninth Ave. becomes Columbus Ave., Tenth Ave. becomes Amsterdam Ave., and Eleventh Ave. becomes West End Ave. **Broadway,** which follows an old Algonquin trail, ignores the rectangular pattern and cuts diagonally across the island, veering west of Fifth Ave. above 23rd St. and east of Fifth Ave. below 23rd St.

Tracking down an address in Manhattan is easy. When given the street number of an address (e.g. #250 E. 52nd St.), find the avenue closest to the address by thinking of Fifth Ave. as point zero on the given street. Address numbers increase as you move east or west of Fifth Ave. On the East Side, address numbers are 1 at Fifth Ave., 100 at Park Ave., 200 at Third Ave., 300 at Second Ave., 400 at First Ave., 500 at York Ave. (uptown) or Avenue A (in the Village). On the West Side, address numbers are 1 at Fifth Ave., 100 at the Ave. of the Americas (Sixth Ave.), 200 at Seventh Ave., 300 at Eighth Ave., 400 at Ninth Ave., 500 at Tenth Ave., and 600 at Eleventh Ave. In general, numbers increase from south to north along the avenues, but you should always ask for a cross street when you are getting an avenue address. The White Pages contains a handy address finder.

Getting Around

To equip for the New York City navigation experience, you need more than the logic underlying its streets. You will also have to use the public transportation system. Get a free subway map from station token booths or the visitors bureau, which also has a free street map (see Practical Information above). Ask at the visitors bureau first, since token booth operators usually sneer in a less friendly manner. For a more detailed program of interborough travel, find a Manhattan Yellow Pages, which contains detailed subway, PATH, and bus maps. Stop at a bookstore for Hagstrom's *New York City 5 Borough Atlas* ($7). For other bus or subway maps, send a self-addressed, stamped envelope about a month before you need the information to **NYC Transit Authority**, 370 Jay St., Brooklyn 11201. In the city, round-the-clock staff at the **Transit Authority Information Bureau** (718-330-1234) dispense subway and bus information.

Subways and Buses

The fare for Metropolitan Transit Authority (MTA) subways and buses is a hefty $1.15; groups of four or more may find cabs cheaper for short rides. More often than not, however, the MTA provides the best way to get around New York City. Most buses have access ramps, but steep stairs make subway transit more difficult for disabled people. Call the Transit Authority Information Bureau (718-330-1234) for specific information on public transportation.

The **subway** is by far the quickest means of transportation in Manhattan, but is more useful for traveling north-south than east-west, since there are only two crosstown shuttle trains (at 42nd and 14th St.). Crosstown buses are much more common (see below). In upper Manhattan and in Brooklyn, Queens, and the Bronx, the subways become "El" trains (for "elevated") and ride above street level to the far reaches of the city.

The New York subway system has 461 stations with 25 free transfer points where subway lines intersect. It can be extremely confusing, even with subway route map in hand. Token clerks can tell you how to get anywhere, but might be impatient and uncooperative during rush hour. Don't lose your cool, but if you're not gaining any ground turn to a transit police officer for advice. "Express" trains stop only at pre-selected busy stations; "locals" stop everywhere. Check the letter or number and the destination of each train, since trains with different destinations often use the same track. When in doubt, ask a friendly passenger or the conductor, who usually sits near the middle of the train.

The stations are slowly being rehabilitated, but some remain dirty and filled with the stench of stale urine and vintage filth. A major subway clean-up campaign, including shiny new spraypaint-resistant cars, has erased much of the crude graffiti and made the atmosphere more aesthetically pleasing. However, the modernization has also wiped out truly creative underground art, some of which still adorns the few old cars that remain in service.

But it will take more than paint-resistant cars to erase New York's crime. In crowded stations (notably those around 42nd St.), pickpockets find plenty of work; in deserted stations, more violent crimes can occur. Always watch yourself and your belongings, and try to stay in lit areas near a transit cop or token clerk. Some stations have clearly marked "off-hours" waiting areas under observation that are significantly safer. At any time and place, don't stand too close to the platform edge since people have been pushed. Boarding the train, make sure to pick a car with a number of other passengers on it.

The subways run 24 hr., but become less safe between 11pm and 7am, especially above E. 96th St. and W. 120th St. During rush hour, you'll be fortunate to find air, let alone seating. If you must travel at rush hour, local trains are usually less crowded than expresses. Buy a bunch of tokens at once: you'll not only avoid a long line, but you'll be able to use all the entrances to a station, some of which lack token clerks.

The subway network integrates once-separate systems known as the **IRT, IND,** and **BMT** lines. The names of these lines are still in use, and their routes remain color-coded on subway maps. Certain routes also have common, unofficial names based on where they travel, such as the "7th Ave. Line" or "Broadway" for the #1, 2, or 3; the "Lexington Line" for the #4, 5, or 6; and the "Flushing Line" for the #7. The official names are numbers and letters, but for clarity's sake, many listings in this chapter employ the alternative designations.

Because **buses** sit in traffic, during the day they often take twice as long as subways; but they also stay relatively safe, clean—and always windowed. They'll also probably get you closer to your destination, since they stop roughly every 2 blocks and run crosstown (east-west), as well as uptown and downtown (north-south). The MTA transfer system provides north-south travelers with a slip good for a free ride east-west, or vice-versa. Just ask the driver for a transfer when you pay. Ring when you want to get off. A yellow-painted curb indicates bus stops, but you're better off looking for the blue signpost announcing the bus number or for a glass-walled shelter displaying a map of the bus's route and a schedule (usually unreliable) of arrival times. Either exact change or a subway token is required; drivers will not accept dollar bills.

Taxis

With drivers cruising at warp speed along near-deserted avenues or dodging through bumper-to-bumper traffic with a micron or two to spare, cab rides can induce ulcers. And even if your stomach survives the ride, your budget may not. Still, it's likely that you'll have to take a taxi once in a while, in the interest of convenience or safety. Rides are fairly expensive: The meter starts at $1.15 and clicks 15¢ for each additional ninth of a mile; passengers pay all tolls and, in about half of the cabs, a 50¢ surcharge after 8pm. Finally, the cabbies expect (and should be given) tips of around 15%, and won't hesitate to let you know when they're displeased. Before you leave the cab, ask for a receipt, which will have the taxi's identification number; with it you can trace lost articles or make a complaint to the Taxi Commission (869-4513). Some drivers may try to take advantage of visitors. Remember, the fare on the meter is the basic charge for the ride, not charge per person. You might also want to glance at a street map before embarking, so you'll have some clue if you're being given a personalized New York tour rather than just delivered to your destination.

Use only yellow cabs—they're licensed by the state of New York and are safe to ride in. Only the plump Checker Marathon cabs take five passengers. When you're desperate or just want to plan ahead, commandeer a radio-dispatched cab (see Practical Information above). Use common sense to make rides cheaper—catch a cab going your direction and get off at a nearby street corner.

To hail a cab, stand on the curb and raise your arm. Yelling worked for Dustin Hoffman in *Tootsie,* but will attract more critical glances from real-life New Yorkers than if you too were in drag. A free cab will have the "On Call" light on its roof illuminated. Taxis make themselves most scarce during rush hour and on rainy days.

Walking, Running, and Biking

Walking is the cheapest, the most entertaining, and often the fastest way to get around town. Twenty street blocks (north-south) make up a mile; the distance east-west from one avenue to the next is about triple that from block to block. For scenic strolls and educational excursions, try a walking tour of Manhattan (see Guided Tours below).

If you plan on running along the street, be prepared to dodge pedestrians and to break your stride at intersections. Women can expect cat calls and stares. The alternative to the sidewalk are paths in Central Park—most are pavement, but there is a 1.57-mi. cinder loop that circles the Reservoir (between 84th and 96th St.). Joggers pack the path from 6-9am and 5-7pm on weekdays and all day on weekends.

For information on running clubs, call **American Youth Hostels** (431-7100) or the **New York Roadrunner's Club** (860-4455).

Weekday biking in commuter traffic poses a mortal challenge even for veterans. But on weekends, when the traffic thins, cyclists who use helmets and caution can tour the Big Apple on two wheels. From May to October, the park (except the lower loop) closes to traffic on weekdays from 10am-3pm, and from 7pm Friday to 6am Monday. Otherwise, Sunday mornings are best. For a challenging and aesthetic traffic-free course, try circumnavigating the 3.5-mi. path within Central Park. If you must leave your bike unattended anywhere in Manhattan, use a strong lock. Theft artists specialize in snipping weaker chain locks. If you want to see your bike again, invest in a **Kryptonite K-5** lock ($28.50). Don't leave any removable parts unlocked, as they may be quickly stripped.

Those who can't bring their bikes can rent from **Metro Bicycle** (throughout Manhattan; call 228-4344) or the **Boathouse**, in Central Park (861-4137). (See Practical Information above).

The adventurous and skillful can rent roller skates at **Peck and Goodie Skates**, 917 Eighth Ave. (246-6123), between 54th and 55th St. Whiz past your favorite New York sights for $10 per 2 hr., $15 per 4 hr., or $20 per day. ($100 deposit or credit card required. Open Mon.-Tues., Thurs., and Sat.-Sun. 10am-6pm, Wed. and Fri. 10am-8pm.)

Safety

To be safe, recognize situations in which problems might arise. Adopt a streetwise manner; be aware of your surroundings, avoid eye contact with shady types, and walk purposefully. After dark, any neighborhood in Manhattan can be unsafe. Keep to the busier, better-lit streets and sidewalks, don't walk around alone, and avoid run-down or empty sections of the city. At night, steer clear of Central Park (*especially* the northern end), the Bowery and the West Side Docks (downtown), and Morningside Park and Harlem (uptown). Use cabs instead of subways and ask the driver to watch until you get inside safely. Before you go into uptown territory, ask a cop, a cabbie, or a native New Yorker what the area is like.

Other common-sense precautions are in order at all times. Keep your wallet in the most inaccessible part of your clothing you can think of, and avoid pulling it out obviously and unnecessarily. Carrying a purse is not recommended, but if you must, hold it firmly against your body and secure all snaps and zippers. Keep identification, traveler's checks, and other valuables in a money pouch or belt, close to your body. Save flashy jewelry and expensive camera equipment for more sedate cities. Never show money to a stranger, and be wary of "travelers" who ask for too much assistance. If someone will not leave you alone, stay in a well-lit area until you can enter a store, restaurant, hotel, or other populated place. When in doubt, call the police.

Finally, there is a reason that most public restrooms in subway stations are padlocked. Even the ones that are open are hardly sanitary. Ditto for the facilities at Penn Station and Grand Central. If nature calls while you're out catching the sights, try the big department stores or the better hotels, or any restaurant, bar, or café that doesn't post a sign saying "facilities for patrons only."

Accommodations

The good news is that the Big Apple has over 100,000 rooms to accommodate tourists. The bad news is that most cost upward of $60 per night. Still, you can save by advance planning—make reservations at one of the cheaper places listed below, rent by the week, share a room, or stay in an area of town that others might not stomach. Students can save by sleeping at student centers, college dormitories (in summer), and some regular hotels with special student rates. But those who have never been to New York before should note the areas to avoid after dark, and even during the day.

In general, the safest accommodations sleep anywhere in Upper Midtown and Midtown on the East Side and within three blocks of Fifth Ave. Housing listed under Columbia University is affiliated with the university and uses Columbia security. Because the Columbia area has a bad reputation, be careful when returning after dark. Plenty of hotels lie within walking distance of Penn Station and the Port Authority, but many are sleazy, most are expensive (averaging $40), and the area is dangerous. Generally, a solo traveler should not stay in a hotel, since the Ys have cheaper, often more comfortable rooms. If you arrive without a reservation, call before trekking across town.

Student Accommodations

New York International AYH-Hostel, 891 Amsterdam Ave. (932-2300) at W. 103rd St. The largest hostel in the U.S. with 90 dorm-style rooms and 480 beds, located in a freshly renovated Richard Morris Hunt Landmark building. Spiffy new soft carpets, blondwood bunks, spotless bathrooms. Kitchens and dining rooms, in-room storage, communal lounges, and a large outdoor garden. Open 24 hr. Check-out 11am. No curfew. $20, nonmembers $23. Doubles $30. Family rooms $60. Linen $3. Towels $2.

International Student Center, 38 W. 88th St. (787-7706), on the West Side. Subway: 7th Ave. IND to 86th St. Close to Central Park and Columbus Ave. Open only to foreigners, preferably students—you must show foreign passport to get in. Single-sex bunk rooms, no frills, in a somewhat tired brownstone on a cheerful street. 7-day max. stay. Open daily 8am-11pm. Call after 10:30am on day of arrival. A bargain at $10. Closed June-last week in July.

Chelsea Center Hostel, 511 W. 20th St. (243-4922) at 10th Ave. Attractive bunks in a large common room, with kitchen and bath. Gregarious, multilingual staff bends over backwards for guests. Closed 11am-4pm. Dorms $19. Breakfast included and tea at any hour. Write or phone 2 weeks in advance and confirm 1-2 days prior to arrival. During peak season (June-Aug.) reservation held until 7:30pm. If booked, staff will find you another place to stay.

International Student Hospice, 154 E. 33rd St. (228-7470), between Lexington and Third Ave. in East Midtown. Subway: 6 train to 33rd St. Inconspicuous converted brownstone with initialed brass plaque by the door. Very small bunk rooms bursting with bric-a-brac. 20 beds preferably for internationals and students. Safe neighborhood and caring proprietor. Curfew midnight. $25 per night.

Whittier Hall (Columbia-affiliated), 1230 Amsterdam Ave. (678-3235), across the street from campus. All rooms have access to cooking facilities. Small singles $20. Doubles with A/C, bath and kitchen $40. Make reservations in advance.

International House, 500 Riverside Dr. (316-8400), by 123rd St., near Columbia University. Subway: 125th St. and Broadway. Must be over 18; students preferred. Exercise caution at all times. Available 2 weeks in advance for transient summer housing. Ultra-modern facilities with gymnasium, TV lounge, cafeteria, 24 hr. security, and pub. Office open daily 8am-5pm. Singles $25. Doubles and guest rooms $55-65. Bath included. Write or call for reservations. Housing available from 2nd week in May to the 3rd week in Aug.

Fashion Institute of Technology, 210 W. 27th St. (760-7885), in Lower Midtown. Subway: Seventh Ave. IRT to 28th St. Decent neighborhood, but adjacent to a bad one; exercise caution at night. Office open Mon.-Fri. 8am-7pm. Summer housing in standard dorm doubles (share a bath). $122 per week per person, 1-week min. stay. Double suites with kitchen and bath $640 per month, 1-month min. stay. $6 service charge on all rooms. For mixed-sex couples, marriage license necessary. Reservations and full payment required in advance. Open 2nd week of June to July 31.

Manhattan Hostel, 145 E. 23rd St. (979-8043). (Subway: 6 train to 23rd St.) For international travelers only. Look under the decaying "Kenmore" marquee for the hostel sign. A 3rd-floor oasis created by a young Swiss couple for carriers of foreign passports. Clean hall baths. Complete kitchen facilities. A common room with free coffee and only 32 rooms enable travelers to meet each other in a family atmosphere. Airport service available. Entrance locked midnight-8am, but guests receive keys. Reservations strongly recommended. Doubles $40. Extra mattress $12. Bunk rooms $20 per person. Private bath $5 extra.

Mid-City Hostel, 608 Eighth Ave. (704-0562) between W. 39th St. and W. 40th St. on the fourth floor. A 175-year-old building with skylights, brick walls, and old wooden beams.

Friendly owner aims to attract long-time backpackers fed up with barracks. Lockout 12:30-6pm, curfew Sun.-Thurs. midnight, Fri.-Sat. 1am. Only 25 beds. Dormitory-style beds for $15 per night, including breakfast of fruit salad.

Martha Washington, 30 E. 30th St. (689-1900), in midtown. Women only. Safe rooms in a mediocre neighborhood filled with students. Singles $35, with bath $47; doubles $50, with bath $62. Weekly: singles $119, with bath $154, with kitchenette $175; doubles $182, with bath $210, with bath and kitchenette $224.

YMCAs/YWCAs

YMCA—Vanderbilt, 224 E. 47th (755-2410), between Second and Third Ave. Subway: 6 train to 51st St. One of the best places to stay in New York. TV, A/C, some balconies. Great gym, locker rooms, Nautilus equipment, and pool. Dingy hallway; immaculate hall bath. Van service to JFK ($9.50) and LaGuardia ($8) and to and from 3 other Ys. 24-hr. security. 25-day max. stay. Singles $36-47. Doubles $46-54. Triples $60-65. Quads $76-80. Winter, spring, and fall rates lower. Key deposit $10. Reservations recommended with deposit.

CIEE New York Student Center (YMCA), William Sloan House, 356 W. 34th St. (760-5850). Subway: 34th St./Penn Station. Small, worn rooms but decent. Laundry facilities, recreation room, and lots of helpful student travel advice. Open 24 hr. Singles $32, with bath $46. Doubles $60. Bunk bed doubles $40 with $12 linen deposit. TV $1.50 per day. Discount for IYHF/AYH members. In summer, book 2-3 weeks in advance.

YMCA—McBurney, 206 W. 24th St. (741-9226), in Chelsea. Subway: Seventh Ave. IRT to 23rd St. Men only. Should be co-ed by fall 1990. Run-down, largely homeless neighborhood but tight security inside. Small singles $26, large singles with TV $29-31. Doubles $44.

YWCA—Brooklyn, 30 Third Ave. (718-875-1190), near Atlantic Ave. Subway: Atlantic Ave./Pacific St. Women only. Must be 18-55 and employed. Octogenarian building still in good shape. Plain rooms with access to kitchen. Singles $68-90 per week. Application necessary, but can be filed on the day of arrival.

Hotels

Carlton Arms Hotel, 160 E. 25th St. (679-0680), by Third Ave. within walking range of Empire State Building. Nicknamed "Artbreak Hotel." Each room uniquely designed by artists from around the world. Stay inside a submarine and peer through windows at the lost city of Atlantis; travel to Renaissance Venice; or stow your clothes in a dresser suspended on an astroturf wall. Old, stuffy rooms with nice, distracting adornment. Artist staff. Singles $37, with bath $44. Doubles $49, with bath $56. Triples $59, with bath $68. Roughly 10% discount for students and foreign tourists. Seven days for the price of 6. Reserve 1 month in advance; confirm 10 days in advance.

Pickwick Arms Hotel, 230 E. 51st St. (355-0300), between Second and Third Ave. Subway: 6 train to 51st St. Chandeliered lobby but terribly small rooms. Fantastic, safe location. TV, A/C. Roof garden. Singles from $40. Doubles $80. Studios $90. Reserve 2 weeks in advance.

Allerton House, 130 E. 57th St. (753-8841), between Park and Lexington Ave. in Midtown. Subway: 6 train to 59th St. Women only. Classy operation 2 blocks from Bloomingdale's. New leaded glass windows Superman couldn't see through in swanky, safe district. Clean, angular spaces. Singles with sink $45, with connecting bath $50, with private bath $60. Weekly rates $175, $195, and $210, respectively. Doubles $75 daily. Reserve 2 weeks in advance.

Washington Square Hotel, 103 Waverly Place (777-9515 or 800-742-5945), in Greenwich Village. Subway: Lexington IRT to Astor Pl. Fantastic location. Chandeliered marble and brass lobby but dismally small, well-decorated rooms. TV, A/C, and programmed key security cards. Singles from $40. Doubles from $80. Studios $90. Each additional person $12. Reservations strongly recommended.

The Aberdeen, 17 W. 32nd St., between Broadway and Fifth. A new Korean community around the hotel offers good food and safety. Upscale lobby leads to pleasant rooms. Singles $70. Doubles $80. Triples $95. Quads $105.

Mansfield Hotel, 12 W. 44th St. (944-6050 or 800-255-5167), off Fifth Ave. A dignified establishment housed in a turn-of-the-century building with a large, comfortable lobby and resplendent oak doors lining the hallways. Good for families or large groups. 200 rooms, all with TV and A/C. Parking, babysitters, and airport service available. Major credit cards honored. Deposit of one day's rent required. Singles with bath $65-70. Doubles or twins with bath

$75-80. Junior suites for 2 people $85, for 3 $95, for 4 $100. Large suite for 5 $120, for 6 $140.

Camping

Informal camping in the city's parks is not safe; those unwise enough to attempt it will be lucky to be spotted by the police before being spotted by less desirable characters.

For peaceful, woodland camping, you'll have to travel far from the city. New Jersey's **Cheesequake State Park,** Matawan 07747 (201-566-2161), over 30 mi. from Manhattan, is 12 mi. south of I-95 (the New Jersey Turnpike) off the Garden State Parkway. Sites for up to six people cost $10 per night, showers included in summer. Reservations are accepted for 2 days or more; you can reserve a maximum of 14 days from Memorial Day to Labor Day by sending a $7 reservation fee, full payment, and the dates requested. (Open daily 8am-8pm; Sept.-May 8am-dusk.)

Food

Although New York's delis and burger joints remain the avatars of New York fare, the Big Apple has an eclectic urban flavor derived from many cultural backgrounds. New York restaurants do more than the United Nations to promote international goodwill and cross-cultural exchange. Try a *dim sum* restaurant in China-town or a Jewish deli on the Lower East Side; inhale espresso and delicate French pastries at a café in Greenwich Village or savor a cannoli in a sidewalk café in Little Italy.

Yorkville, the area between 82nd and 88th St. east of Lexington Ave., houses some terrific German restaurants. SoHo, in lower Manhattan, and Columbus Avenue, in the west 70s, feature outdoor cafés catering to every culinary taste. Cozy Indian restaurants line 6th Street between First and Third Ave. MacDougal Street, south of Washington Sq., offers a multiplicity of Middle Eastern meals. Brooklyn and Queens have even greater ethnic diversity than Manhattan; restaurants in these boroughs are often less fancy and more authentic than their Manhattan counterparts.

The most consistently available and well-prepared inexpensive food in New York is pizza. A plain slice shouldn't cost much more than $1.25. Vinyl-covered coffee shops glow every few blocks; most offer a frightening variety of entrees for under $6. And, in its indefatigable quest for superlatives, New York City hosts more fast-food restaurants than most U.S. cities. While the quality and the menu at these places may remind you of home, the prices most certainly will not. A burger and fries in the city typically costs $1-2 more than it does in the suburbs.

New York's "street food"—pretzels, premium ice cream, felafel, tempura, *souvlaki,* Italian ices, sausage, fresh fruit, and more—is unparalleled in variety and quality. A big step above the street carts is take-out food; some outdoes restaurant fare. Picnic in a park or plaza for a fraction of the price of a sit-down meal.

West Midtown

West Midtown sizzles with summer heat, booms with construction, and tempts with nocturnal promise, but has never promised anyone decent food at reasonable prices. Watch your step or you'll stumble onto some real sleaze emporiums. Around Times Square and the Port Authority Bus Terminal, fast-food chains outnumber drug dealers, tourists, and prostitutes—quite an achievement. In the Theater District, the stretch of Broadway from Times Square to 52nd St., you'll run into plenty of good but overpriced restaurants, many of them Japanese.

Carnegie Delicatessen, 854 Seventh Ave., at 55th St. World-famous deli in a prime location. Eat elbow-to-elbow at long, boisterous tables with regulars and celebrities. The incredible pastrami and corned beef sandwiches ($8.50) easily feed 2 (but sharing costs $2 extra). Open daily 6:30am-4am.

La Fondue, 43 W. 55th St., between Fifth and Sixth. Dark wooden tables and Swiss chalet decor. Grab some Grolsch beer and dip into the delicious cheese fondue ($9); don't miss the sublime Swiss chocolate fondue with fruit ($5.75) for dessert. Open Mon.-Thurs. noon-midnight, Fri.-Sat. noon-12:30am, Sun. noon-11pm.

La Bonne Soupe, 48 W. 55th St., between Fifth and Sixth. Excellent meals in a "bistro" doubling as a gallery for Haitian and French paintings. Small meals of aromatic soups served with bread, salad, dessert, and wine for $7. Open Mon.-Sat. 11:30am-midnight, Sun. 11:30am-11pm.

Sapporo, 152 W. 49th St., near Seventh Ave. Japanese version of a coffee shop. A favorite snack spot for Broadway cast members and the business luncheon crowd. Sweet *oyako-don* (chicken with sauteed egg patty) served on sticky rice will fuel food fantasies for weeks ($5). The *gomoku ramen* floats in a mind-boggling broth ($5.15). Open Mon.-Fri. 11:30am-midnight, Sat.-Sun. 11:30am-11pm.

East Midtown

New York has five "four-star" restaurants, with four in this area. Tycoons dine here among skyscraping office buildings, high rents, and briefcase-wielders. But you can manage here without an expense account. All it takes is a small trust fund. Actually, East Midtown houses more fast-food peddlers than any other region of the city. Anyone can picnic in the area's green cloisters for free.

Dosanko, 135 E. 45th St., and many other locations around the city. In Midtown: 423 Madison Ave., 10 E. 52nd St. (759-6361), and 123 W. 49th St. Plasticky Japanese restaurant serving surprisingly good and reasonably priced food. Staple *larmen,* a tasty tubful of noodles, includes your choice of beef, pork, or chicken, and spices ($5). Open daily 11am-9:30pm.

Horn and Hardart Co., 200 E. 42nd St., at Third Ave. The last of the automats—those places where you plunk some change in a slot and retrieve your sandwich from a hatch in the wall—like in *Star Trek.* Additional cafeteria service offers chicken and pot roast for $4-6.50. May it live long and prosper. Open daily 6am-10pm.

Crystal Gourmet, 422 Madison Ave., between 48th and 49th St. Also 666 Washington Ave. (755-2588), at 55th St. The most beautiful, bountiful salad bar in New York. Sushi, pasta vinaigrette, vegetables, and fruits in the chilled section, with lasagna, chicken, and beef dishes in the hot one—all at $4.50 per pound. Buffet breakfast (served Mon.-Fri. 7-10am) $3 per pound. Open Mon.-Sat. 7am-7pm.

Lower Midtown

Seventh Avenue between 33rd and 34th St., right across from Penn Station, deals in fast food of every persuasion, from McDonald's to sushi. Pakistani and Indian restaurants battle for customers on Lexington's upper 20s. Between 14th and 34th St. the West Side becomes a dining wasteland, where meals soar in price with the exception of a few coffee shops and Chinese and Italian saviors. Some corner delis have salad bars with a selection of Asian vegetable and noodle dishes charged by the pound.

Sbarro, 701 Seventh Ave., at 33rd St. Right smack in the chaos of midtown. Appealing Italian fast food—they even have an editor-employing Topeka branch. All-you-can-eat breakfast buffet: eggs, bacon, sausages, french toast, fresh fruit, biscuits for $4. Slice of stuffed pizza $3. Chicken *parmigiana* hero $4.29. Open daily 8am-8pm.

King of China, 425 Seventh Ave., between 33rd and 34th St. In the middle of an overwhelming row of fast food. Six barbecued chicken wings $1.85, 3 pan-fried dumplings $2. Open daily 10:30am-5:30pm.

Genroku Sushi, 366 Fifth Ave., between 34th and 35th. Beats the Automat (see East Midtown) for funkiest mechanical gimmick. A conveyor belt surrounds the oval-shaped counter and parades the food in front of you; take what you like. Pick carefully: Some of the dishes have been around the circuit one time too many. Sushi entrees $5.50. Soup $1.25. Open Mon.-Wed. and Fri. 11am-8pm, Thurs. 11am-8:30pm, Sat. 11am-7:30pm, Sun. noon-6pm.

Peso's Mexican Grill, 102 E. 25th St. at Park Ave. S. (674-7376). Franchise member with a sterile seating area. Quesadillas, chili, tacos, and nachos with no added salt, lard, or artificial ingredients. Best known for its homemade salsas (free) and Mexican pizza (layers of tortillas filled with black beans, red sauce, scallions, olives, tomatoes and 2 kinds of cheese, $5). Open Mon.-Fri. 11am-9:30pm, Sat. 11am-9pm, Sun. 4-9pm.

Upper East Side

Luxury residences, art galleries, and restaurants are the norm on Museum Mile along Fifth and Madison Ave. You'll find mediocre food at extraordinary prices in the posh and scenic museum cafés. You may want to stop in for coffee between exhibits, but head east of Park Ave. for less glamorous but more affordable dining.

El Pollo, 1746 First Ave., between 90th and 91st. A chicken by any other name would not taste as good. Plump chickens soaked in secret spices, turned on a rotisserie, and topped with an Argentinian hot green sauce or a mild white Pervuvian variant. Try *papa rellena* ($2.75), fluffy mashed potatoes around a meat and olive core and deep-fried. Whole chicken $7, fried sweet plantains $2. Open daily 11am-11pm.

Dante's, 1640 York Ave., between 86th and 87th. The presence of delicacies makes up for the absence of chairs. Choose your moveable feast from gourmet sandwiches ($7), salads ($2.50-5), pastas ($7-8), and Buffalo wings ($4). Great selection of Italian pastries. Open daily 10am-10pm.

Pig Heaven, 1540 Second Ave., between 80th and 81st St. New York's best-disguised Chinese restaurant, with a pink corkscrew twist. Things porcine adorn the plates, the walls, and the minds of pig-happy patrons and critics. The list of "recommended by" includes media hogs *N.Y. Times, N.Y. Magazine, Forbes, Esquire, Gourmet Magazine* and that great expert on pork bellies, the *Wall Street Journal*. While pig dominates the menu, plenty of other choices can keep the pig off your plate. Tasteful barnyard decor. Open daily noon-11pm.

Ottomanelli's Café, 1559 York Ave., between 82nd and 83rd St. The East Side outpost of the vast and powerful Ottomanelli Empire that has supplied New York with meat and bake shops since 1900. Extraordinary fresh-baked goods in a no-frills setting. An impressive coterie of bagels, breads, and muffins 50¢-$1.25. Large iced coffee $1. After 5pm, all danish pastries and muffins depreciate to 50¢ per piece. Open Mon.-Sat. 6:30am-6:30pm, Sun. 7:30am-3pm.

Caffé Bianco, 1486 Second Ave., between 79th and 80th St. The ideal place to sip and pose with a sandwich or a slice of memorable *tartuffo bianco*. Storybook garden out back leaves just enough room for a few tables and a gurgling, penny-toss fountain. Toasted sandwiches with mozzarella, roast peppers, fresh mushrooms, or prosciutto around $4. Open Sun.-Thurs. 11am-11pm, Fri.-Sat. 11am-1am.

Zucchini, 1336 First Ave. (249-0559), between 71st and 72nd St. Owned by a nutrition-conscious triathlete who insists on running a healthy establishment. No red meat, but professed carnivores should get by with the selection of fresh seafood, salads, pasta, and chicken dishes. A steaming loaf of whole wheat bread precedes dinner. Carnations at every table. Most pasta and vegetable entrees (soup included) under $11. Mention to the owner that you've won a running medal and you'll get an additional 10% off your meal. Open daily 10:30am-10:30pm, brunch Sat.-Sun. 11am-4:30pm.

Upper West Side

Atmosphere changes with each avenue and cross street here. The area is becoming gentrified, and to see the process in action, make your way from Columbus and 69th St. up toward Broadway and Amsterdam at 116th St. As rents in the area skyrocket, the chic cafés and bars in the 70s and 80s on Columbus Ave. are moving out and giving way to super-ritzy clothing stores of the Madison Ave. variety. Catch this lively neighborhood before it completes the transition to sedate, overpriced elegance.

At night, **Lucy's**, 503 Columbus Ave. (787-3009), at 84th St., always draws a crowd ready to make noise and conversation. At **Café La Fortuna**, 69 W. 71st (724-5846), between Central Park West and Columbus Ave., you can bring a friend, a book, or both. Conversation and meditation over cappuccino ($1.75), inside or out in the backyard garden. **Zabar's**, 2245 Broadway (787-2002) between 80th and 81st St., offers an entirely different food and people-watching experience. The deli counter seems to stretch an entire block, and customers are mildly fanatical in their quest for a content stomach.

Genoa, 271 Amsterdam at 73rd St. A tiny, family-owned restaurant with some of the very best food on the West Side. Stucco walls, wood beams, pink tablecloths, and red candlelight: Italian romance. Excellent pasta dishes from $9. Arrive before 6pm or wait in line with the rest of the neighborhood. Open Tues.-Sat. 5:45-10:30pm, Sun. 5:30-9:30pm

Zula Café and Restaurant, 1260 Amsterdam Ave., at W. 122nd St. On the Columbia scene. Instead of silverware you use your hands and the sour, spicy crepe called *injera* in which you wrap the morsels. Beef and chicken dishes $6.75, lamb dishes $7.75-8.50. Espresso $1.50, cappuccino $1.75. Open daily noon-midnight; bar open until 4am.

Fellini's, 180 Columbus Ave. at 68th St. An intimate retreat with whitewashed brick walls, decorated in upbeat pastels. Unusual pastas come tastefully prepared and satisfy even the ravenous. Pasta dishes $10, exotic salads with offbeat ingredients $10, sandwiches $7.50. Open daily noon-midnight.

Dan Tempura House, 2018 Broadway at 69th St. A bamboo-thatched awning hangs over a window display of Japanese trinkets, exotic plants, and fish. The clutter, continued inside the restaurant, lends a homey feel to excellent and diverse dishes. Various kinds of teriyaki, tempura, and noodles $5-11. Sushi and sashimi platter $9-12. Open Mon.-Sat. noon-2:30pm and 5-11pm, Sun. 4-11pm.

Diane's, 251 Columbus Ave., off 71st St. Large portions and reasonable prices make this brass-railed café a prime pick of the college crew. Spice up a 7-oz. burger ($4) with your choice of chili, chutney, or seven cheeses (85¢ per topping). Great ice cream. Open daily 11am-2am.

Greenwich Village and SoHo

Eating establishments here play an informal game of trendy pursuit. Owners come and go, fads are seized upon and then discarded, loyal followings build and then decline at an accelerated pace. Every restaurant here has a gimmick and a loyal clientele. Food awareness is high; people here know the difference between quality and kitsch. Regardless, you can find some great-tasting bargain-priced food.

West Village

The network of zig-zagging streets between 14th and Houston St. west of Fifth Ave. remains lower Manhattan's bohemian headquarters. Try the major avenues for cheap, decent food. Wander by the posh row houses as Emma Goldman and Jack Kerouac did around Jane St. and Bank St. for classier fare in bistros and cafés. The European-style bistros of Bleecker St. and MacDougal St., south of Washington Sq. Park, have perfected the homey "antique" look. Explore twisting side streets and alleyways where you can join Off-Broadway theater-goers as they settle down over a burger or drop into a jazz club. If all this sounds too effete, sneak down 8th St. to Sixth Ave. to find some of the most respectable pizzerias in the city. The crucial question then becomes whether John's or Ray's makes the better pie.

John's Pizzeria, 278 Bleecker St. Clippings on the wall commemorate various events, but don't overlook the pizza. Pizza for 2, cooked in a brick oven, with a crisp crust and just enough cheese $7.75. No slices, table service only. Open daily 11:30am-11:30pm.

Ray's Pizza, 465 Sixth Ave., at 11th St. Most uptown pizza joints claim to be the "Original Ray's," but any New Yorker will tell you that this is the real McCoy. The best pizza in town. Well worth braving the lines for a slice (from $1.75). Open Sun.-Thurs. 11am-2am, Fri.-Sat. 11am-3am.

Olive Tree Cafe, 117 MacDougal St. Middle Eastern food, and lots of stimulation. Charlie Chaplin films continuously run on the wide screen. For $1 per hr. you can borrow chess, backgammon, and Scrabble sets, or doodle with colored chalk on the slate tables. Felafel $2.25, chicken kebab platter with salad, rice pilaf, and vegetable $7. Open daily 11am-3am.

Trattoria Due Torri, 99 MacDougal St., near Bleecker St. Cozy—you can see Chef Meshel cooking in the back. Eating beats watching. Fresh pastas from $6, veal and chicken from $7. Try the *Gnocchi Sorrentina,* or anything at all, but go. Open Sun.-Thurs. 12:30am-midnight, Fri.-Sat. 12:30am-2am.

Eva's, 11 W. 8th St., between MacDougal St. and Fifth Ave. Fast-service health food with a seating parlor. Massive meatless combo plate with felafel, grape leaves, and eggplant $4. Open Sun.-Thurs. 11am-midnight, Fri.-Sat. 11:30am-1am.

Shima, 12 Waverly Place, northeast of Washington Sq. Look for the garden and small pond through the winaow. Weekday combo lunch features chicken or dumpling entree, vegetable, soup, rice, and fruit for $5.25. Lavish dinners under $12. Open Mon.-Fri. noon-2:30pm and 5-11:15pm, Sat.-Sun. 5:30-11pm.

East Village and Lower East Side

The East Side has no frills but plenty of excitement, where pasty-faced punks and starving artists sup alongside an older generation conversing in Polish, Hungarian, or Yiddish. Here, Jewish delis and Eastern European restaurants are the norm. The plump traditional dumplings called *knishes* make a great lunch; eat potato knishes with mustard, meat knishes with *yoich* (gravy), or *kasha* knishes (buckwheat groat) all by their delicious selves. Fill up on *pirogi,* a delicious Polish dough stuffed with potato, cheese or other ingredients; or pig out on blintzes, thin pancakes rolled around cream cheese, blueberries, and other fillings. Ask for hot bagels at local bakeries. For a change of pace, visit 6th St. between First and Second Ave., where "Little India" provides some of the most reasonably priced and delicious food in New York. Try puffy *pooris* at **Shah Bagh,** *biryani* at **Panna,** or coconut soup at **Kismoth.**

Odessa, 117 Ave. A at 7th St. Beware of generic coffee shops with Slavic names. Lurking beneath may be an inexpensive place offering terrific Ukrainian-Polish specialties. A huge assortment of *pirogi,* stuffed cabbage, *kielbasa,* sauerkraut, and potato pancakes ($4-6). Open daily 7am-midnight.

Kiev, 117 Second Ave. Unparalleled *pirogi* and heavy foods laced with sour cream and butter. Upscale deli decor. Popular with early-morning club hoppers. Open 24 hr.

East Village Ukrainian Restaurant, 140 Second Ave., between 8th and 9th St. Pleasantly decorated with impressive chandeliers and interesting paintings. Low prices. Excellent hot *borscht* jammed with vegetables ($1.75). Open Mon.-Fri. noon-11pm, Sat. noon-midnight.

Tandoor Fast Food, 188 First Ave., between 11th and 12th St. Spicy cheap food with no frills. Beef mushroom curry $5, homemade breads $1-2. Weekday lunch special (noon-3pm) $3.50. Open daily noon-midnight.

Second Avenue Delicatessen, 156 Second Avenue, at 10th St. The definitive New York deli; people come into the city just to be snubbed by the waiters here. Have a pastrami or tongue on rye for $6.50, a fabulous burger deluxe for $6.25, or Jewish penicillin (also called "chicken soup") for $2.75. Note the Hollywood-style star plaques embedded in the sidewalk outside: this used to be the heart of the Yiddish theater district. Open Mon.-Fri. 8am-midnight, Sat.-Sun. 8am-2am.

SoHo

Like the residents, the restaurants act surprisingly down-to-earth, but demonstrate an occasionally distracting preoccupation with art. Some emote indistinguishably from their neighboring galleries—but again, that goes for the people too. SoHo specializes in brunch: the ambience here is well-suited to lazy Sunday mornings, and you can down your coffee and canteloupe in any of a number of café/bar establishments. Prince St. and Spring St. run parallel to one another through most of SoHo, together accounting for many of the best and most affordable eating spots in the neighborhood.

The Cupping Room, 359 West Broadway. Entrance on Broome St. too. Drinks, dinner, and coffee in a low-key atmosphere. A great choice for brunch on either Sat. or Sun., but arrive early or prepare to wait. On the bright side, brunch goes from 7am to 6pm. During the week, the Cupping serves a full breakfast and dinner menu. Entrees around $14, light menu with salads and burgers $7-8. Open Sun.-Fri. 7:30am-1am, Sat. 7:30am-2am. Kitchen closes at midnight.

Food, 127 Prince St. off Wooster St. As the name suggests, simultaneously no-frills and trendy. Order large portions of wholesale food cafeteria-style, then sit by the floor-to-ceiling windows and watch the crowds go by. Cold cucumber soup $3.50, a very large sandwich $6. Open Mon.-Sat. noon-10pm. Closed last 2 weeks of Aug.

Fanelli's Café, 94 Prince St. A veeery mellow neighborhood establishment; lounge on the sidewalk tables and really savor that $2 beer. Burgers $6, steamed mussels $8. Open Mon.-Sat. 10am-2am, Sun. noon-2am.

Elephant and Castle, 183 Prince St., off Sullivan. Popular with locals for its excellent coffee and creative light food. Perfect for brunch, but be prepared to wait for a table. Dinner around $10, brunch around $8. Open Sun.-Thurs. 8:30am-midnight, Fri.-Sat. 8:30am-1am.

Lower Manhattan

Chinatown

Any time of day or night, you can venture to these lively streets for some of the most impressive, inexpensive Chinese cuisine on the East Coast. Try the *dim sum*—bite-sized hors d'oeuvres—served in almost every tea shop here. You may want to avoid the more commercial establishments which line Mott St. To reach Chinatown, take the Lexington Ave. IRT, walk 2 blocks east on Canal to Mott St., go right on Mott, and follow the curved street toward the Bowery, Confucius Plaza, and E. Broadway. Explore the side streets along the way.

Hee Seung Fung Teahouse (HSF), 46 Bowery. From the subway, walk east on Canal St. to the Bowery, then take a sharp left. Large and hectic. Widely acclaimed *dim sum* dishes $1.50-1.75 (served 8am-4:30pm). Try the sesame oil and ginger crispy fish and the *jung* (sticky rice wrapped in tea leaves). Open daily 7:30am-2am.

Nom Wah Tea Parlor, 13 Doyers St., a curved side street north of Mott St. off the Bowery. *Dim sum* served all day ($1-2). Indulge yourself in the "simple imposing purity of steamed pork buns." Open daily 10am-8pm.

Chinatown Ice Cream Factory, 65 Bayard St., off Mott St. Some say Chinatown residents give equal business to Haägen Dazs down the street, but the homemade ice cream here comes in flavors like ginger, lichee, papaya, green tea, and red bean. Cones $1.60. Open daily noon-midnight.

Little Italy

Little Italy, north on Mulberry from Canal St., is one of the liveliest sections of town at night. To get there, take the D train to Canal St. Crammed with tiny restaurants, the neighborhood bustles with people strolling in and out of the cafés off Mulberry St. Join the crowds and stake out a table outdoors where you can enjoy cappuccino and cannoli, the perennial favorites.

Paolucci's, 149 Mulberry St. Unpretentious, family-owned restaurant. The watchful portrait of the boss hangs on the front wall. Pasta from $7. Chicken *cacciatore* with salad $8.50. Open Mon.-Fri. 11:30am-10:30pm, Sat.-Sun. 11:30am-11:30pm.

Marionetta, 124 Mulberry St. Sidewalk tables let you dine without missing a single frenzied moment of Little Italy. Serves some of the most inexpensive veal dishes in the neighborhood. Veal *parmagian* $9, chicken *parmagian* $8.50. Open daily 11:30am-1am.

Puglia Restaurant, 189 Hester St. Long tables make this place fun and rowdy. A favorite with New Yorkers and bold tourists. Monstrous plate of mussels $6, spaghetti $7. Entrees $4-8. Live music nightly. Open Tues.-Sun. noon-midnight.

Financial District

At lunchtime and after work, brokers and lawyers crowd the **South Street Seaport,** a recently rehabilitated historic district. To get there, take train #2 or 3 to Fulton St. The central marketplace contains more gastronomic variety per square foot than anywhere else in New York. Go wild at the gourmet fast-food specialty booths—one stand serves only East Argentine dairy products; another, Southern breakfasts. Check out the Seaport on a Friday afternoon to see uptight Wall Street execs let loose over a few beers. Formal restaurants, presided over by the 143-year-old **Sweets,** 2 Fulton St. (344-9189), are very expensive and inconsistent.

Jeremy's Ale House, 254 Front St. A converted warehouse with sawdust floors and crumbling brick walls. Wall Street Fri. hangout; otherwise packed with a young and unpretentious crowd. Best chili around ($3.50), good seafood. Open daily 10am-9pm.

Hamburger Harry's, 157 Chambers St. Gourmet burgers for the connoisseur; 7 oz. patty broiled over applewood with exotic toppings, from $6. Open Mon.-Thurs. 11:30am-11:30pm, Fri.-Sat. 11:30am-1am, Sun. noon-11:30pm.

Kansas City Meat Exchange, 21 Beaver St. A hamburger joint that does not belong to a multinational chain. A humble Harry's. Burger $2.19, chicken on a bun $2.79. No-frills seating upstairs. Open daily 10:30am-5pm.

Wolf's Delicatessen, 42 Broadway. Pickles on formica table tops and no pretentions. Order anything from Heinz over baked beans ($1.10) to corned beef and pastrami ($6.50). Open Mon.-Fri. 6am-11pm, Sat.-Sun. 8am-9pm.

Brooklyn, Queens, and the Bronx

In the well-established ethnic neighborhoods in the other boroughs, restaurants cook for neighborhood patrons. Look for Jewish, Middle Eastern, and Eastern European restaurants in Brooklyn, Italian food in the Bronx, Greek dishes along Ditmars Blvd. in Astoria (Queens), and Indian fare in Flushing (Queens).

The culinary map of the boroughs changes constantly, as restaurants and markets reflect the growing number of immigrants from Asia, Africa, and Latin America. The Jackson Heights, Elmhurst, and adjacent Corona neighborhoods in Queens dynamically capture these diverse essences. Indian, Thai, Vietnamese, and Latin American restaurants cluster along Broadway, Roosevelt Ave., and Junction Blvd. (Take the subway to Roosevelt Ave./Jackson Heights, and the IRT #7 toward Flushing.)

Dominick's, 2335 Arthur Ave. (733-2807). Small, authentic Italian eatery. Vinyl tablecloths and bare walls, but great atmosphere. The waiter won't offer you a menu, or a check; he'll recite the specials of the day and then bark out what you owe at the end of the meal. Try the *linguini* dishes and the special veal and chicken *francese* dishes. Full meals $9-10. Open Mon. and Wed.-Sun. 1-10pm. Get here before 6pm or after 9pm, or expect to wait at least 20 min.

Junior's, 986 Flatbush Ave. Extension, Brooklyn (718-852-5257), just across the Manhattan Bridge. Adored for roast beef, brisket, and the like. Entrees $8, complete dinner $15. Displaced New Yorkers drive for hours to satisfy cheesecake cravings here (plain slice $3). Open Sun.-Thurs. 6:30am-1am, Fri.-Sat. 6:30am-3am.

Roumely Tavern, 3304 Broadway, Astoria, Queens (718-278-7533). Take the R or G to the Steinway St. and Broadway Stop in Astoria. Greek accents as authentic as the food. *Spanokopita* (spinach pie; $2.50) and lamb stew ($8.75). Open daily noon-1am.

Rizzos's Pizza, 3015 Steinway St. (718-721-9862). Take the N or R to the Steinway St. and Broadway stop and walk down Steinway toward 30th Ave. The restaurant is tiny, the seating makeshift, and the whole affair could easily go unnoticed in the endless row of discount stores and specialty shops lining the street. But seek it out: Sicilian rectangles based on a thin, crisp crust, and spread with an unforgettable tomato sauce. Ask for extra cheese and experience the sublime. Slice $1.10, 6-slice pie $6.30. Open daily 11am-8pm.

Sights

Seeing New York City is first a matter of deciding where to look. Every street corner offers something, but all street corners are not created equal. Some are interesting by accident, and some because they contain a famous monument, museum, or architectural landmark. To best explore Manhattan's majesty, travel on foot, relying on subways and buses only to cover large distances. Unfortunately, you couldn't see everything in a year, let alone two or three days. Whirlwind, see-it-all-from-the-seat-of-the-bus guided tours aren't a bad superficial introduction to the Big Apple. But later investigate intriguing sections of the city on foot.

East Midtown

The commercial lungs of New York pant in the east 40s and 50s, a curious grid of glass towers, bankers, and occasional green. No traditional man-on-horse monuments breathe here; instead, the celebration of 20th-century accomplishments comes in the form of the corporate complex. Trace its history from Chrysler Building art deco to the streamlined glass-skin Jacob A. Javits Convention Center or the smooth granite of the IBM tower.

Although tarnished by exhaust, the majestic Beaux-Arts style **Grand Central Station,** 42nd to 45th St. between Vanderbilt Pl. and Madison Ave., still recalls some Eurosplendor. Built between 1903 and 1913 by megamagnate Cornelius Vanderbilt, the main concourse of this grandiloquent gateway serves about 170,000 commuters and innumerable visitors daily. One of the world's biggest rooms, its vistas from the sweeping stairs off Vanderbilt Ave. as well as from the 42nd St. and Lexington Ave. entrances are worth seeing; also take a gander at the vaulted ceiling covered with oakleaves (the Vanderbilt family's emblem) and constellations of the zodiac. In 1963, much of the impact of the station was jogged toward Walter Gropius's imposing **Pan Am Building,** on Park Ave. between 45th and 46th St., set on top of the station. Opinion on it remains split: some see Gropius's building as a monstrous intrusion on New York's skyline, others as a spectacular example of turbulent modernist architecture. Other Park Ave. buildings, such as the **Waldorf-Astoria Hotel,** 301 Park at 50th St., recall the more naive grandeur of pre-World War II New York. Even mere mortals can enter the lobby—the Lexington entrance makes you less conspicuous.

At 42nd St. and Lexington stands the all-too-obvious **Chrysler Building,** a seductive and absurd 1930 art-deco skyscraper. The tallest in the world when erected (the Empire State would steal that distinction a year later), its crowning gargoyles were modeled after radiator ornaments and designs copied from '29 Chrysler hubcaps. The monumental 20s **Bowery Savings Bank,** 110 E. 42nd St., built in the Romanesque style, makes capitalists feel warm all over. Forty-second also delivers the **Daily News Building,** 220 E. 42nd St., a 1919 precursor of slab architecture. The inside houses the *Daily News,* a huge revolving glass globe, and a clock for 17 major cities. The **Ford Foundation,** 320 E. 43rd St., exemplifies both the foundation's moneyed taste and architect Kevin Roche's fusion of glass and steel in corporate modern style. Built in 1967, the glass and steel enclose a lush jungle atrium.

Ceremonial capital of the political world, the **United Nations** (963-7713) overlooks the East River between 42nd and 48th St. Designed in the early 50s by an international committee including Le Corbusier, Oscar Niemeyer, and Wallace Harrison (whose ideas won out in the end), the complex itself makes a diplomatic statement: part bravura, part compromise. You can take a guided tour of the **General Assembly** and the **Security Council;** one-hour tours start in the main lobby of the General Assembly every half-hour from 9:15am to 4:45pm. (Admission $5.50, students and children $2.50.) From September through December, procure free tickets to General Assembly meetings in the main lobby about a half-hour before sessions, which usually begin at 10:30am and 3pm Monday through Friday.

Thanks to corporate dollars, the area a few blocks uptown is sprinkled with free atriums surrounded by potted trees, artwork, and fellow pedestrians; many atriums have free live music and almost all have clean public bathrooms. The triangle-topped **Citicorp Center,** at Lexington Ave. and 53rd St., is a larger-than-life example of New York's mixed-use buildings with atriums. Occasional free lunch-hour concerts jazz up the plaza and atrium. Pick up a free Manhattan Atrium Guide from the visitors bureau (see Practical Information above). Annexed to the Citicorp Complex is **St. Peter's Church,** a stunning, space-age chapel. (Open daily Mon.-Fri. 10am-11pm.) At 50th St. and Third Ave. shimmers the funky **Crystal Pavillion** atrium triplex, with neon lights, dance music, water walls, and a gondola elevator. (Open Mon.-Sat. 8am-11pm.)

The **Seagrams Building,** Park Ave. between 52nd and 53rd St., pioneered modern architecture in New York. Designed in 1958 by Mies van der Rohe and Philip Johnson, the plaza and tower set back 90 ft. from the building line. Compare Johnson's new and old styles by checking out his recently completed, post-modern **AT&T Building,** 55th St. and Madison Ave. The cross-vaulted arcade (open Mon.-Fri. 8am-6pm) features scenic cafés, the AT&T Infoquest Center (see Museums below), and the ritzy, four-star **Quilted Giraffe** restaurant, which reputedly empties the deepest pockets in New York (dinner $85 *per person* if you don't drink anything and forget to tip the waiter).

At Park Ave. and 51st St. confesses **St. Bartholomew's Church,** a Romanesque creation by McKim, Mead & White in 1919. Built on a brewery, the church incorporates the old Byzantine-style portico; oddly enough, the parts go together beautifully. A block east lie the **Villard Houses,** also built by McKim, Mead & White in 1884. Harry Helmsley incorporated the graceful Italianate brownstones into the Helmsley Palace Hotel in 1980 on the condition that he preserve the incredible marble and stained glass interiors of one wing of the four-house complex.

New York's most famous church, the **St. Patrick's Cathedral** stands at 51st St. and Fifth Ave. James Renwick designed the Gothic Revival structure in 1879. Today it features high society weddings and the shrine of the first male U.S. saint, St. John Neumann. The **Olympic Tower,** across the street from St. Patrick's, has regularly scheduled free classical and jazz concerts, a reflecting waterfall pool, and seats for weary feet.

Some find it excessively opulent, but others adore the rose-pink marble, 80-ft. waterfall, and gleaming bronze of the **Trump Tower,** 56th St. and Fifth Ave. The tower houses a five-story shopping mall that parades the power of New York's dethroned real estate tycoon. While the stores in the complex include some of New York's most expensive, the piano and violin concerts weekdays at lunchtime are free. For a change of pace, try the cool serenity of the **IBM Atrium,** 57th St. at Madison Ave., where tall stands of bamboo and hundreds of other lush botanical specimens grace a 68-ft.-high greenhouse.

Between 48th and 50th St. and Fifth and Sixth Ave. stretches **Rockefeller Center,** a monument to the heights to which business can throw the arts. Raymond Hood and his cohorts did an admirable job of glorifying various business virtues through architecture. A wealth of art deco sculpture adorns the buildings that surround the sunken plaza, which serves as a restaurant in summer and skating rink in winter. Rockefeller Center includes **Radio City Music Hall,** at 51st St. and Sixth Ave. (757-3100). New York's most extravagant theater has staved off bankruptcy, and is still housing those dancing Rockettes.

West Midtown

Well-policed with reason, here Broadway hosts not only its famous stages but also first-run movie houses, neon lights, street performers, and porn palace after peep show after porn palace. The entire area is slated for demolition and multibillion dollar reconstruction in the next few years; New York can no longer afford the space. The first new building, the neatly polished **Marriott Marquis** has already replaced two historic Broadway stages. Nearly all subway lines stop in Times Square (#1, 2, 3, 7, QB, N, RR, SS).

Just west of the square, at 229 W. 43rd St., lie the offices of the **New York Times,** founded in 1857, and for which the square was named in 1904. The **Algonquin Hotel,** located on 44th St. between Fifth and Sixth Ave., intimately and physically connects to the *New Yorker.* In the 20s, the hotel hosted Alexander Woollcott's "Round Table," a regular gathering of the brightest wits of the theatrical and literary worlds, including Dorothy Parker and Robert Sherwood. The Oak Room still serves tea every afternoon, but only to hotel guests, no matter their artistic circles.

A walk uptown along Broadway leads through the **Theater District,** which stretches from 41st to 57th St. At one time a solid row of marquees, some of the theaters have been converted into movie houses or simply left to rot because of the skyrocketing cost of live productions. Approximately 40 theaters remain active, mostly grouped around 45th St. Between 44th and 45 St., ½ block west off Broadway in front of the Shubert Theater, sits **Shubert Alley,** a short private street reserved for pedestrians, originally built as a fire exit between the Booth and Shubert Theaters. Just off Shubert Alley, you may find some stars grabbing an after-show snack at **Sardi's,** a popular restaurant among high-brow theater folk.

Much farther west on 42nd St., past the seedy Port Authority Bus Terminal, lies **Theater Row,** a block of renovated Off-Broadway theaters featuring some of the best work in town.

Over on Sixth Ave., near 48th St., in the basement of the **MacGraw-Hill Building** (near Rockefeller Center) runs the multi-media screen production *The New York Experience* (869-0345), a sensational documentary of New York's history. (Shown every hr. on the hr. Mon.-Thurs. 11am-7pm, Fri.-Sat. 11am-8pm, Sun. noon-8pm. Admission $4.75, under 12 $2.90.) Stop by **Little Old New York,** in the theater lobby, a charming recreation of Manhattan in the 1890s. (Free.)

Lower Midtown

The **Empire State Building** (pronounced Empire Statebuilding), at 34th St. and Fifth Ave. (736-3100), looms as the phallic avatar of New York. The 1931 skyscraper surges 102 floors from the sidewalk with just the right combination of showiness and taste. Though it has dropped to the fourth tallest building in the world, you may have to wait in line to see the unparalleled view from the top. Any self-respecting New Yorker "hasn't ever been there"—Ghita definitely has. The King Kong-climbed upper floors illuminate after dark in colorful accord with the seasons: red, white, and blue streaks blaze over Manhattan on Independence Day. (Open daily 9:30am-midnight. Admission to the observation deck $3.50, seniors and students $2.)

At 36th St. and Madison Ave., the **Morgan Library** (685-0610), housed in a beautiful Italian Renaissance building, features a large selection of medieval treasures. (Open Sept.-July Tues.-Sat. 10:30am-5pm, Sun. 1-5pm. Free.) At 34th St. and Sixth Ave. in Herald Sq. (west of the Empire State Building) is the world's largest department store, **Macy's** (736-5151), where you'll find everything from designer clothes to pianos.

Farther west on 23rd St. below Madison Sq. stands the wedgelike **Flatiron Building,** New York's first skyscraper, designed by Daniel Birnham in 1902. It has been immortalized in Edward Steichen's photographs and in other people's paintings. Though only 20 stories high, the building taunts with the most elaborate stonework in the city. Today, the building houses world-famous publishing offices; here your *Let's Go* evolves into its final form.

The **Chelsea Hotel,** on 23rd St., between Seventh and Eighth Ave., has sheltered many suicidal artists including, most recently, Sid Vicious of the Sex Pistols. Check out the pop-art punk lobby. Chelsea's **flower district** on 28th St. between Sixth and Seventh Ave., looks most colorful during the wee hours of the morning (use caution getting there).

Upper East Side

Here you'll find some of the most expensive real estate in the world. On Park Ave., the sidewalks are clean, and guarded by the doormen posted in each building. Penthouse gardens look out over a cityscape made homogeneous by distance. Museums are the main attraction here for the visitor, but it's also soothing to savor the quiet elegance of **Park Avenue** and **Fifth Avenue** at night. Or, ogle the latest fashion creations in the boutiques of Madison Ave. by day.

The confident parade of the Upper East Side begins at 58th St. and Fifth Ave. with the **Grand Army Plaza,** a small square dominated—appropriately enough—by the huge figure of *Abundance* atop the **Pulitzer Fountain.** Surrounding Grand Army Plaza are the luxurious hotels favored by high society. Across from the Plaza, on the old site of the Savoy Hotel, stands the 50-story white marble **GM Building,** home to the world's largest toy store, **F.A.O. Schwarz.** Imitate Tom Hanks and dance on the giant keyboard, or drive home in a $2000 mini-Alfa Romeo.

Central Park rolls from Grand Army Plaza all the way up to 110th between Fifth and Eighth Ave. Twenty years of construction turned these 843 acres, laid out by Frederick Law Olmsted and Calvert Vaux in 1850-60, into a compressed sequence of landscapes of nearly infinite variety. Like a teen werewolf flick, Central Park's shabby northernmost stretches mutate dangerously from dusk to dawn. The park contains lakes, ponds, fountains, skating rinks, ball fields, tennis courts, a castle, an outdoor theater, a bandshell, two zoos, and one of the most prestigious museums in the U.S., the **Metropolitan Museum of Art** (see Museums below). Horse around on the **carousel** ponies: for 75¢, one of the most exciting and least expensive whirls in the city (open 10:30am-4:45pm, weather permitting). At the renovated **Central Park Zoo,** Fifth Ave. at 64th St. (439-6500), the monkeys happily ape their visitors. (Open Mon. and Wed.-Fri. 10am-5pm, Tues. 10am-8:30pm, Sat.-Sun. 10am-5:30pm; Sept.-May Mon. and Wed.-Fri. 10am-5pm, Sat.-Sun. 10am-5:30pm. Admission $1, seniors 50¢, ages 3-12 25¢.) Kids will delight in petting at the **Children's Zoo** and the pony rides (408-0271; 10am-4:30pm; admission 10¢). The Kong-sized revamped **Wollman Skating Rink** (517-4800) has miniature golf and roller skating in summer and ice-skating in winter. (Golf and skating admission $4, children $2. Open Sun. and Mon. 10am-5pm, Tues.-Thurs. 10am-9:30pm, Fri.-Sat. 10am-11pm.) The **reservoir** is encircled by 1.6 mi. of cinder track for a mélange of runners and joggers. On weekends, when most of the main roads through the park close to vehicles, you're guaranteed to encounter bikers, skateboarders, and skaters freewheeling to the sounds of everything from Public Enemy to Rachmaninoff. In summer the park hosts **free concerts** (360-1333) from Simon and Garfunkel to the Metropolitan Opera, and excellent free drama (for the first 1936 lucky souls) during the **Shakespeare in the Park** festival (see Theater: Off- and Off-Off Broadway below). The visitors center (397-3156) is located at 64th St. mid-park. (Open Tues.-Thurs. and Sat.-Sun. 11am-5pm, Fri. 1-5pm.)

Mansions once lined Fifth Ave. on the park's east side; now most have been replaced by apartment buildings. The **Frick Collection of Fine Arts,** exemplifying Fifth Ave.'s turn-of-the-century opulence, was built to house Frick and his paintings in harmony (see Museums below). Glance at the old Duke house, now NYU's **Institute of Fine Art,** Fifth Ave. at 78th St., and the Harkness House, now home to the Commonwealth Fund, on Fifth at 75th St., for more examples of limestone castles.

If you divide the word **Madison Avenue,** 1 block east, by the number of *n*s and then triple it, you get the cutthroat advertising business, where artists, market psychologists, and salespeople conspire to manipulate U.S. buying habits. These Jello-Pop jingle workshops are hidden behind an unbroken façade of expensive boutiques and first-rate art galleries. Between 70th and 79th St. and all along 57th St., a gallery caps almost every block; most have free exhibits. The apotheosis of art auction houses, **Sotheby Parke Bernet Gallery,** resides at 980 Madison Ave., at 77th St. Still farther east, visit Carl Schurz Park, at 88th St. and East End Ave., to see **Gracie Mansion** (call 570-4751 for tour information), the official residence of New York's first African American mayor, David Dinkins.

Upper West Side

Broadway leads uptown to **Columbus Circle,** 59th St. and Broadway, the symbolic entrance to the Upper West Side and the end of Midtown. Set between Central Park and the **New York Coliseum,** a convention and exhibition complex (slated for destruction in the near future), the Circle is distinguished by a statue of Christopher himself.

Three blocks north, Broadway intersects Columbus Ave. at imperial **Lincoln Center,** the cultural hub of the city, between 62nd and 66th St. The six buildings that constitute Lincoln Center—Avery Fisher Hall, the New York State Theater, the Metropolitan Opera House, the Library and Museum of Performing Arts, the Vivian Beaumont Theater, and the Juilliard School of Music—accommodate over 13,000 spectators at a time. In daytime, the poolside benches by the Henry Moore sculpture behind the main plaza prove a good spot for a picnic; at night, the Metropolitan Opera House lights up, making its chandeliers and huge Chagall murals visible to passersby through its glass-panel façade, though the central fountain shines at any time of day. Lincoln Center's hour-long guided tours (877-1800) happen daily on a varying schedule. Call on the day you wish to come. (Admission $6.50, seniors and students $5.50. Free library tour Thurs.) From October to June, 15-minute tours of the tremendous backstage of the Metropolitan Opera are also given. (Admission $6, students $3. Reservations and schedules 582-3512.) See Entertainment below for performance information.

Cross 65th St. to reach **Central Park West,** an area of graceful old apartment buildings. As Manhattan's urbanization peaked in the late 19th century, wealthy residents sought tranquility in the elegant **Dakota,** between 72nd and 73rd St. Built in 1884, the apartment house was named for its remote location. John Lennon's streetside murder here in 1981 has made the Dakota notorious. **Strawberry Fields Forever,** in Central Park across from the Dakota, is Yoko Ono's memorial to her husband (as well as the wish of Mets fans like The Kid). There 25,000 plants, spread over a couple of acres, center around a simple mosaic that asks you to "Imagine." The **New York Historical Society,** 77th St. and Central Park West (873-3400), keeps information on the city. The friendly library staff will help you uncover obscure facts about the past or provide pop trivia. (Open Tues.-Sun. 10am-5pm. Admission $2.) Across the street, you can examine the history of the world in the enormous **American Museum of Natural History.** (See Museums and Galleries below.)

Delis usually aren't very large, but **Zabar's,** on Broadway (787-2000), between 81st and 82nd St., is a grand exception, stretching along half a city block. After navigating your way through bricks of cheese, barrels of coffee beans, racks of fresh breads, rows of exotic delicacies, and cartons of caviar, stop at the deli. Zabar's is a cultural experience no one should miss. (Open Mon.-Fri. 8am-7:30pm, Sat. 8am-midnight, Sun. 9am-6pm.)

New York City's member of the Ivy League, **Columbia University,** chartered in 1754, tucks between Morningside Dr. and Broadway from 114th to 121st St. Once all-male, Columbia now admits women independent of **Barnard College,** the women's school across West End Ave. Diagonally across the campus at the end of 112th St. on Amsterdam Ave., the **Cathedral of St. John the Divine** (662-2133), promises to be the world's largest Gothic cathedral, when completed—construction began in 1812. Notice that parts are actually Romanesque. Tours start beneath the large rose window and take in the carvings, a museum of religious art, gardens, and the 13-acre grounds.

Continue north and bear west to see **Grant's Tomb,** in Riverside Park at 122nd St. (666-1640). At one time, this used to be a popular monument, but stuck on the periphery of the city, it attracts only the brave and the few. Nevertheless, the Civil War general still rests in peace here. (Open Wed.-Sun. 9am-4:30pm.) Across the street, at beautiful **Riverside Church** (222-5900), you can hear concerts on the world's largest carillon (74 bells) twice daily and climb the tower for $1. Its famous pastor, William Sloan, preaches revolutionary theology, drawing the likes of Nelson Mandela. (Open daily 9am-5pm. Tower open Mon.-Sat. 11am-3pm, Sun. 12:30-4pm. Subway: 7th Ave. IRT local to 116th St., then walk 1 block west.) Stay away from this area at night; don't wander off course at any time of day.

Harlem

Although many outsiders view Harlem as the innercity, it has played a proud and vital role in African American history and culture, particularly during the Harlem Renaissance of the 20s. In those years, northern Manhattan was the posh "end of the line" for African Americans fleeing poverty in the rural south. The neighborhood has been the inspiration or at least the focal point for major writers from Langston Hughes to James Baldwin, and a magnet for jazz musicians such as Billie Holiday and Charles Mingus. In the 60s, the radical Black Power movement flourished here through the Revolutionary Theater of LeRoi Jones, which performed consciousness-raising one-act plays in Harlem's streets. Nowadays, suffering from a blanket image as the country's quintessential slum filled with crime and drugs, Harlem does keep some of its Renaissance charm. But these enclaves are often bordered by neighborhoods with ever-present problems. The heart of traditional Harlem is 125th St. By the mid-140s, the neighborhood drifts into the deadly wastelands along the Harlem River, which continue over to the South Bronx. Since parts of the area are unsafe for obvious-looking tourists, either visit with someone who knows the area, or take a tour. Above all, visit in the day.

Sugar Hill (W. 127th St. to W. 134th St. between Morningside Ave. and St. Nicholas Terrace) once slept some of the city's wealthiest and most important gangsters. But today its striking buildings look run down; the neighborhood is better known for the rap group and record label that produced the first rap hit "Rapper's Delight" (1979).

Amid the noisy urban life of Harlem, vestiges of the nation's more serene colonial past remain. The Georgian **Morris-Jumel Mansion,** in Roger Morris Park, at W. 160th St. and Edgecombe Ave. (923-8008), was the home of Gouverneur Morris, U.S. minister to France during the Reign of Terror, and also served as Washington's headquarters for the Battle of Harlem Heights in the autumn of 1776. (Open Tues.-Sun. 10am-4pm. Admission $2, seniors and students $1.) A little later in history, Congressman Adam Clayton Powell Jr. served as pastor of the **Abyssinian Baptist Church,** 132 W. 138th St., the oldest black church in the city.

Harlem is also home to two colleges. Gothic **City College,** 138th and Convent (690-4121), took the primarily poor children of blacks and Jewish immigrants during the first half of the century and turned them into today's national leaders. **Boricua College,** a private Hispanic liberal arts college, is one of four buildings in **Audobon Terrace,** the Beaux-Arts complex at Broadway and 155th St. The other three buildings house the Numismatic Society Museum, the Hispanic Society of America, and the Museum of the American Indian (see Museums below).

Columbia University recently decided to acquire the abandoned **Audobon Ballroom** (165th St. between Sixth Ave. and Broadway) from the city and turn it into a genetics research center, displacing some historically significant architecture and a few people in the process. This move sparked a controversy, since the place was the site of Malcolm X's assassination. The silver dome of the **Malcolm Shabazz Masjid (Mosque),** where revolutionary leader Malcolm X was minister, still glitters on 116th St. The newly built **Harlem Third World Trade Center,** 163 W. 125th St., is working to draw new attention to the U.S.'s most famous black community.

Racial tension may have inspired beautiful and tragic love stories such as "West Side Story," but it has also fueled bitter battles between the communities of black Harlem and Spanish Harlem with violent confrontations producing all-too-real-life tragedies. Called *el barrio* (the neighborhood), **Spanish Harlem** borders the northeast corner of Central Park. Beginning in the gentrified **Morningside Heights** region above 110th St. and stretching up to 155th St., this district centers around **116th Street.** Murals against crack and for those killed by crack cocaine span top walls where the famous iceman adds mango or papaya juice to save you from the summer heat. But again, don't venture into this neighborhood without someone familiar with it.

Greenwich Village and SoHo

Counter-culture still reigns supreme in the Village. Uptown past Houston to 14th St. west of Broadway, you'll find the most diverting assortment of New Yorkers. Two or three frisbees sailing through the air signal your arrival at **Washington Square Park,** the northern gateway to the Village and the focal point of **New York University.** The park always teems with students, musicians, professors, drug pushers, and artists; meet balding art patrons, peasant-skirted hippies, and slender, mustached men in designer running shorts. These are Village People.

In the late 19th and early 20th century, the Washington Square area produced more U.S. cultural currents than any other region of the country. Stephen Crane, Theodore Dreiser, Henry James, Mark Twain, Edith Wharton, and Willa Cather all lived in the Village at one point in their lives. A walk down **MacDougal Street** will take you past the ghosts of bygone social struggles and the whisperings of new ones. Louisa May Alcott, author of *Little Women*, lived at #132. Leftists such as Emma Goldman, Louise Bryant, John Reed, and Upton Sinclair regularly met in the **Liberal Club** at #137 to solve the world's problems over several stiff ones. Eugene O'Neill and Edna St. Vincent Millay launched their careers at the **Province-town Playhouse** across the street. (St. Vincent Millay's home, at 75½ Bedford St., between Barrow and Grove St., is the narrowest house in the Village.) Dorothy Day, founder and leader of the Catholic Workers Movement, also lived and worked in the Village. Lost generation writers John Dos Passos and Malcolm Cowley returned from their post-World War I "exiles" to these crooked streets. Thirty years later, Beat Generation progenitors Jack Kerouac and Allen Ginsberg "howled" here in protest against post-World War II America, and later James Baldwin howled back. Today, the Village once again embraces personalities outside the mainstream, encompassing New York's largest number of Off- and Off-Off-Broadway houses as well as the city's largest gay population. Gay bars line Christopher and Gay St.

As the West Village becomes increasingly gentrified, some of the true radicals are moving away from Washington Sq. into the more run-down neighborhoods of the East Village. Stroll along colorful **St. Mark's Place** toward Tompkins Square Park, and wade through the cramped, wild clothing stores, or "participate" in a performance at one of the many experimental theaters that lurk in the old schools and church basements. **La Mama, Etc.,** 7 E. 4th St. (475-7710), is one of the first permanent experimental theaters and an early champion of Sam Shepard. Call for information about performances.

The tiny district of SoHo (an acronym for South of Houston), officially bounded by Houston, Canal, Lafayette, and W. Broadway, is the hot artists' center in town. The architecture here is American Industrial, notable for its ornate, cast-iron façades. Artists have converted factory lofts into studios, and you can't walk half a block without passing a gallery, an experimental theater, or designer clothing store. High-fashioned sorts pay dearly (up to $500 for a pair of pants) to look good. Excellent galleries line W. Broadway, and although many come and go, you can count on top-quality work at **Vorpal**, 165 W. Broadway, and **Leo Castelli**, 420 W. Broadway.

Lower East Side, Chinatown, and Little Italy

The Lower East Side, once home for Jewish immigrants, is now a mixed Jewish and Hispanic community with a secret identity as the garment district; you can bargain for everything from denim to silk. The quality varies from junk to jewels, although (merchants assure you) the prices are definitely unbeatable. This is also the place to buy electronic goods and appliances.

This neighborhood lies more or less between Houston and Canal St., east of Little Italy, bordering on the **Bowery,** the Skid Row of New York. The main thoroughfare is safe **Delancey Street,** where black-clad, bearded Hasidic shopkeepers ply various wares. Don't pass up the clothing district on Orchard St. or the Essex St. Market. Though improving, the extra lettered avenues—"Alphabet City"—north of East Houston can be dangerous, especially at night. Delancey Street is much safer.

An enclave of Old World cafés and restaurants, **Little Italy** clusters around Mulberry St., several blocks south of the Village and just north of Canal St., though it shrinks as Chinatown grows. During the day, Little Italy is quieter than most districts in New York, reminiscent of the old quarters of European cities. But by night, the sidewalks are clogged with café tables and tourists. If you're around on the second Thursday in September, you could be lapping up lasagna and *prosciutto* at the **Feast of San Gennaro,** one of the most colorful annual New York festivals. Dotted with stores selling low-cost electronics and plastics, commercial **Canal Street** divides Little Italy and **Chinatown,** the largest Asian American community outside of San Francisco. Only a few steps across Canal St. from Little Italy are pagoda-topped phone booths, steaming tea shops, and firecracker vendors. During the Chinese New Year (late January or early February), the pace heightens to a level above the usual freneticism.

City Hall Area and the Financial District

The southernmost tip of Manhattan is extremely compact and free of threatening traffic. The narrow winding streets that discourage car travel make the area ideal for a walking tour. Wander down narrow, twisting historic lanes in between towering silver and stone skyscrapers. Five subway lines converge in the Financial District, some on their way to Brooklyn Heights across the East River. Take a train to the City Hall area on Broadway at the northern fringe of the Financial District, then explore south along the side streets off Broadway.

A prime example of Federalist architecture, **City Hall** (566-5097) has been the scene of frenetic politicking since 1811. (Open Mon.-Fri. 10am-4pm. Free.) From City Hall, walk down Broadway to the **Woolworth Building,** on Murray St., one of the few skyscrapers as graceful close up as from 20 blocks away. Designed by Cass Gilbert in the Gothic style, this 800-ft. tower was the world's largest from 1913 to 1930. Inspiring mosaics and carved caricatures of Cass Gilbert and Woolworth himself decorate the lobby. A block down Broadway is **St. Paul's Chapel** (602-0874), the oldest church in Manhattan (1766). George Washington worshipped here during his presidency. (Open Mon.-Sat. 8am-4pm, Sun. 7am-3pm.)

West of Broadway, off Church St., sprout the city's tallest buildings, the twin towers of the **World Trade Center.** The enclosed observation deck (466-7397), on the 110th floor of #2, offers a stunning overview of Manhattan, especially at night. (Open daily 9:30am-11:30pm. Admission $3.50, seniors and ages 6-12 $1.75, under 6 free.)

Walk 8 short blocks down Broadway into the maw of the beast—the heavily built-up center of New York's Financial District. Sooty **Trinity Church,** (602-0773) at Broadway and Wall St., is dwarfed by the skyscrapers around it, and contains in its adjoining graveyard the tombs of Alexander Hamilton, Robert Fulton, and other prominent figures. Here, or nearby, pick up the **Heritage Trail,** an excellent walking tour marked by small American flags.

A short way down Wall Street, **Federal Hall** (264-8711) and the **New York Stock Exchange** (656-5168) sit diagonally across from one another. George Washington took the oath of office in Federal Hall; the building now houses historic documents. (Open Mon.-Fri. 9am-5pm. Free.) From the visitors gallery of the New York Stock Exchange (enter at 20 Broad St.), you can watch a free 15-minute movie (shown continuously Mon.-Fri.) and, from behind glass panels, view the controlled hysteria of the world's busiest commercial arena—the trading floor. Come before noon to get a free ticket. (Open Mon.-Fri. 9:20am-3pm.) In the **Federal Reserve Bank,** 13 Liberty St. (720-6130), countries pay their debts by shifting bullion from one room to another. (Free 1-hr. tour and audio-visual display Mon.-Fri. at 10am, 11am, 1pm, and 2pm. Make appointments a week ahead by phone, and note that tickets must be mailed to you.)

New York Harbor and the Brooklyn Bridge

After its marathon journey down from Yonkers, Broadway ends in **Battery Park** on New York Harbor. A common site for political rallies such as the No-Nukes fests of the 70s and recent anti-apartheid protests, the recently restored waterfront park commands one of the finest views of the city. New York Harbor, Brooklyn Heights, Governor's Island, the Brooklyn-Battery Tunnel, Jersey City, Ellis Island, Staten Island, and the Statue of Liberty can all be seen on a clear day. The view is a lot better, however, from the **Staten Island Ferry** (718-727-2508), which leaves from the port east of Battery Park every half-hour. A trip on the ferry is what the New York Visitors Bureau calls "the world's most famous, most reasonable (25¢ round-trip), and most romantic 5-mile cruise . . . " and few would argue.

Another ferry will take you to the renovated **Statue of Liberty** (363-3200). The green lady in her bathrobe, landmark of a century of immigrant crossings, may also testify the perserverance of the city. In 1886, Joseph Pulitzer's newspaper, *The World,* directed a private fundraising drive to erect the gift from France. The renovation of the Statue was likewise a grassroots project, funded by the contributions of schoolchildren, citizens, and corporations. The **American Museum of Immigration,** located in the statue's base, recalls the stories of the waves of immigrants who have funneled into New York Harbor. If the towering Statue enshrines the ideals of the European immigrants' U.S., chaotic, dirty Ellis Island represents the bittersweet realities of the lives of 12 million Europeans who first experienced the U.S. through the island's people-processing facilities. **Circle Line Ferries** (269-5755) shuttle between Battery Park and Liberty Island, leaving for the island daily every half hour 9am to 4pm, with the last ferry back at 5:15pm, July and August back at 7pm. (Fare $4, ages 5-11 $2, under 5 free.) Ellis Island renovations have brought ferry service ($4, seniors and children $2). Buy tickets for both at Castle Clinton.

You'll have to get up around 4am to start the day at **Fulton Fish Market.** Here on the East River, a few blocks from Wall Street, New York's store and restaurant owners have bought their fresh fish ever since the Dutch colonial period. Next door, renovations have created the **South Street Seaport** complex (669-9424). The 18th-century market, graceful galleries, and seafaring schooners will delight historians and tourists alike. An 11-block historic district along the East River and Fulton St., the seaport sprawls over two East Side piers, drawing yuppies for Gucci mating season. The decrepit but equally historic blocks on the periphery of the rehabilitated buildings are just as interesting. The **Seaport Experience** (608-7888) is an enjoyable, multi-media presentation about the area's nautical history. The **Seaport Line's** authentic paddlewheel steamboats (406-3434) offer day cruises (1½-hr.) departing daily on the hour at noon, 2pm, and 4pm (fare $12, students $10), and evening cruises to the live sounds of jazz, rock, and dixie ($15-20 depending on hour and day). Cruises leave from Pier 16 at the seaport. **The Seaport Museum** (669-9424) offers tours of the area (open daily 10am-6pm).

Uptown a few blocks, the **Brooklyn Bridge** looms. Built in 1883, the bridge was one of the greatest engineering feats of the 19th century. The 1-mi. walk along the pedestrian path (on the left) will show you why every New York poet feels compelled to write at least one verse about it, why photographers snap the bridge's airy spider-web cables, and why people jump off. To get to the entrance on Park Row, walk a couple of blocks west from the East River to the city hall area. Ahead of you stretch the piers and warehouses of Brooklyn's waterfront; behind you, the greatest cityscape in the universe. Plaques on the bridge towers commemorate John Augustus Roebling, its builder, who, along with 20 of his workers, died during its construction.

Brooklyn

Founded in 1600 by the Dutch, Brooklyn was the third-largest city in the U.S. by 1860. In 1898, it merged with the city of New York and became a borough, but it still maintains a strong, separate identity, with many ethnic communities and local industries. Unfortunately, Brooklyn also includes some run-down, unsafe areas—the most dangerous areas west of Prospect Park. The visitors bureau publishes an excellent free guide to Brooklyn's rich historical past that outlines 10 walking tours of the borough.

Head south on Henry St. after the bridge, then turn right on Clark St. toward the river to see one of the best imaginable views of Manhattan. Many prize-winning photographs have been taken here, from the **Brooklyn Promenade,** overlooking the southern tip of Manhattan and New York Harbor. The headquarters of George Washington during the Battle of Long Island, now-posh **Brooklyn Heights** has attracted many authors, from Walt Whitman to Norman Mailer, with its beautiful old brownstones, tree-lined streets, and proximity to Manhattan. Continuing south, explore the area's small side streets. Soon you'll be at **Atlantic Avenue,** home to a large Arab community, with second-hand stores and inexpensive Middle Eastern bakeries and grocery stores. Atlantic runs from the river to Flatbush Ave. At the Flatbush Ave. Extension, pick up **Fulton Street,** the center of downtown Brooklyn, recently transformed into a pedestrian mall.

Williamsburg, several blocks north of downtown Brooklyn, has retained its Hasidic Jewish culture more overtly than Manhattan's Lower East Side. Men wear long black coats, hats, and sidelocks; women cover their shaved heads with wigs. The quarter encloses Broadway, Bedford, and Union Avenues. It closes on *shabbat* (Saturday), the Jewish holy day—intrusions are emphatically discouraged.

Prospect Park, designed by Frederick Law Olmsted in the mid-1800s, was supposedly his favorite creation. He was even more pleased with it than with his Manhattan project—Central Park. Because crime has somewhat tarnished its ambience, exercise caution in touring the grounds. At the corner of the park stands **Grand Army Plaza,** an island in the midst of the borough's busiest thoroughfares, designed by Olmsted to shield surrounding apartment buildings from traffic. (Subway: IRT #2 or 3 to Grand Army Plaza.) The nearby **Botanic Gardens** seem more secluded, and include a lovely rose garden, behind the **Brooklyn Museum.** (See Museums below.)

Sheepshead Bay lies on the southern edge of Brooklyn, and is the name of both a body of water (really part of the Atlantic), and a mass of land. The seafood here comes fresh and cheap (clams $5 per dozen along the water). Walk along **Restaurant Row** from E. 21st to E. 29th St. on Emmons Ave., and peruse menus for daily seafood specials. Nearby **Brighton Beach,** nicknamed "Little Odessa by the Sea" because of its pervasive Russian restaurants, newsstands, and shops, has been homeland to Russian emigrés since the turn of the century. (Subway: D, M, or QB.)

Further east, the **Boardwalk,** once one of the most seductive of Brooklyn's charms, now squeaks nostalgically as tourists are jostled by roughnecks. Once a resort for the City's elite, made accessible to the rest of the Apple because of the subway, fading **Coney Island** still warrants a visit. Enjoy a hot dog at historic **Nathan's,** Surf and Sitwell (718-266-3161; open Sun.-Thurs. 8am-4am, Fri.-Sat. 8am-5am). Built in 1927, the **Cyclone** roller coaster, 834 Surf Ave., remains the world's most terrifying ride. The 100-second-long screaming battle over nine rickety wooden hills more than makes up the $3. Be careful at night, or laser fire may not be the only thing attacking you as you play *Gauntlet* at the arcade behind the amusement park. Go meet a walrus, dolphin, sea lions, sharks, and other ocean critters in the tanks of the **New York Aquarium,** Surf and West Eighth (718-265-3400; open daily 10am-4:45pm, holidays and summer weekends 10am-5:45pm; admission $4, children $2, seniors free Mon.-Fri. after 2pm). Look for the house beneath a roller coaster, which inspired a hilarious scene in Woody Allen's *Annie Hall.*

Queens

Archie and Edith Bunker, Simon and Garfunkel, Cyndi Lauper, and Steinway pianos all hail from Queens. The borough also houses hundreds of thousands of immigrants from around the world. Ethnic diversity is the norm here, as in the other boroughs, but Queens has a distinctive look. In general, you'll see small brick, stone or clapboard houses, all with windowboxes, tiny plots of grass, and trees in front and back.

Look for them in **Astoria.** Ditmars Blvd. and Steinway St. are lined with shops and restaurants specializing in the food, clothes, and icons of Greece. The side streets are residential. (Subway: BMT's RR train from Midtown.) In northeast Queens, **Flushing's** "Little Asia" has a large population of Chinese, Korean, and Indian immigrants. Walk down Main, Prince, and Union St. in Flushing for Asian shops and restaurants. (Subway: IRT #7 to 111th St.)

Queens's principal attractions accumulate in **Flushing Meadow/Corona Park,** the site of the 1964-65 World's Fair. A giant metal globe and twin space needles give the park a distinctive skyline. The park features the aging but still glorious **New York Hall of Science,** 111th and 48th Ave. (718-699-0675), at the New York State Pavilion. (Open Wed.-Sun. 10am-5pm. Suggested admission $3.50, seniors and children $2.50. Free Wed.-Thurs. 2-5pm.) Also see the **Queens Botanical Gardens** (718-886-3800; open daily 9am-dusk; free) and the **Queens Museum** (718-592-

5555), with its 9335-sq.-ft. detailed model of the five boroughs. (See Museums below.)

Staten Island

Getting there is half the fun. At 25¢ (round-trip), the half-hour ferry ride from Manhattan's Battery Park to Staten Island is as unforgettable as it is inexpensive (see New York Harbor above for Ferry information). Or you can drive from Brooklyn over the **Verrazzano-Narrows Bridge,** one of the longest suspension span babies in the world (4260 ft.), supported by 70-ft.-high twin towers.

Once ashore, take a bus to **Richmondtown Restoration** (718-351-1611), a 100-acre restored village in Latourette Park. Among the 26 historically and architecturally intriguing 17th- to 19th-century buildings sleeps **The Vorleezer's House,** 441 Clark Ave., America's oldest elementary school, built in 1696. The **Staten Island Historical Society Museum** (718-353-1611) occupies the old county clerk's office of 1848, and displays early U.S. craftwork. (Open Wed.-Fri. 10am-5pm; Sat.-Sun. and Mon. holidays 1-5pm. Admission $2, seniors $1.50, children $1.)

Overlooking New York Harbor, the **Snug Harbor Cultural Center,** 914 Richmond Terrace (718-448-2500), once a retirement home for sailors, now features more than 20 Greek Revival buildings on 80 acres of historic landmark. Picnic and see some of its offerings: the **Newhouse Gallery** of contemporary U.S. artists (open Thurs.-Fri. 1-5pm, Sat. noon-6pm free); the **Staten Island Children's Museum,** with participation exhibits for the 5-12-year-old in you (718-448-2500; open July 5-Labor Day Tues.-Fri. 1-4pm, Sat.-Sun. 11am-5pm; Sept.-June Mon.-Fri. 1-4pm, Sat.-Sun. 11am-5pm; admission $2); and the **Staten Island Botanical Gardens** (open daily dawn-dusk; tours by appointment). On Broadway and Clove Rd. is the 8½-acre **Staten Island Zoo,** which has an animal hospital with a nursery viewing area. (718-442-3100; open daily 10am-4:45pm; admission $1, seniors free, children 75¢; free Wed.).

The Bronx

The Bronx looks the toughest and the greenest of the five boroughs. Scores of gutted and abandoned buildings in the **South Bronx** above the Harlem River make the area resemble a war zone. But travel north, and the Bronx turns yuppie, with over 2000 acres of natural parkland. In Riverdale small mansions and private schools create a green landscape—a suburb which contrasts starkly with the city it shares in name. The pastoral estate **Wave Hill,** 675 W. 252 (549-2055), in Riverdale, has a majestic view of the Hudson. Samuel Clemens, Arturo Toscanini, and Teddy Roosevelt all have resided here in the Wave Hill House. The estate was finally donated to the city, and presently offers concerts and dance amidst its greenhouses and spectacular formal gardens. (Open Mon.-Tues. and Thurs.-Sat. 10am-4:30pm, Wed. 10am-dusk, Sun. 10am-7pm. Free Mon.-Fri., Sat.-Sun. $2, seniors and students $1.)

The **Bronx Zoo** (367-1010), the largest urban zoo in the U.S., pioneered housing animals in natural surroundings. Although some animals are kept in cage-like confines, black jail bars are nowhere in evidence. On the monorail to Wild Asia (one way $1.25, children $1), even the cages disappear; once there, you can ride a camel for $2. The 3-acre **Children's Zoo** features four natural environments. (Open Mon.-Sat. 10am-5pm, Sun. 10am-5:30pm. Admission Fri.-Mon. $3.75, seniors free, children $1.50. Free Tues.-Thurs. Driving, take the Bronx River Parkway, or, from I-95, the Pelham Parkway. Subway: IRT #2 through the South Bronx to Pelham Parkway Station.) Across East Fordham Rd. from the zoo grows the huge **New York Botanical Garden** (220-8700). Remnants of forest and untouched waterways give a glimpse of the area's original landscape. (Open April-Oct. Tues.-Sun. 10am-7pm; Nov.-March 10am-6pm. Free. Parking $4.) Don't miss the garden's recently renovated **E.A. Haupt Conservatory.** (Open Tues.-Sat. 10am-4pm. Admission $3.50, students $1.25, children 75¢. Free Sat. 10am-noon.) The Metro-North Harlem line goes from Grand Central Station to the gardens (Botanical Garden Station), and includes admission (round-trip $7, seniors $5, children $3.50).

Follow your tell-tale heart to **Edgar Allan Poe Cottage** at the intersection of East Kingsbridge Road and Grand Concourse (881-8900), where Edgar Allan composed the bulk of his eerie tales. (Open Wed.-Fri. 9am-5pm, Sat. 10am-4pm, Sun. 1-5pm. Admission $1.)

Museums and Galleries

Idiosyncratic or mainstream, stuck on the distant past, or looking into the near present, a museum in this city has its eyes on you. Even if nothing sparks your particular interest, witness a culture collecting itself. The *New Yorker* magazine has the most extensive and most accurate listings for both museums and galleries; *New York* is also good. The Friday *New York Times* contains excellent listings (in the Weekend section) and reviews of major shows. Also consult the *Quarterly Calendar*, available free at any visitors bureau location (see Practical Information above). *Gallery Guide*, found in local galleries, has comprehensive but often inaccurate monthly listings of gallery shows. Most museums and all galleries close on Mondays, and museums are jam-packed on the weekends. One final word: instead of demanding a flat admission fee, many museums require a "donation"—no one will throw large, rotting papayas at you if you give less than the suggested amounts. Also, since most places have weekly "voluntary contribution" (read "free") times, call ahead.

Major Collections

American Museum of Natural History, Central Park West (769-5100), at 79th to 81st St. Subway: Central Park West IND to 81st St. The largest science museum in the world, in a suitably imposing Gothic structure guarded by a statue of Teddy Roosevelt on horseback. The 45-ft.-long Tyrannosaurus Rex rules over the Hall of Dinosaurs, while J.P. Morgan's Indian emeralds blaze in the Hall of Minerals and Gems. Open Sun.-Tues. and Thurs. 10am-5:45pm; Wed. and Fri.-Sat. 10am-9pm. Donation $4, children $2. Free Fri.-Sat. 5-9pm. The museum also houses **Naturemax** (769-5650), a cinematic extravaganza on New York's largest (four-story-high) movie screen. Admission for museum visitors $4, children $2; Fri.-Sat. double features $5.50, children $3. The **Hayden Planetarium** (769-5920) offers outstanding multimedia presentations. Seasonal celestial light shows twinkle in the dome of the **Theater of the Stars,** accompanied by astronomy lectures. Admission $4, seniors and students $3, children $2. Electrify your senses with **Laser Rock** (769-5921) Fri.-Sat. nights, $6.

Brooklyn Museum, 200 Eastern Pkwy. at Washington Ave. (718-638-5000). Subway: IRT #2 or 3 to Eastern Pkwy. Wide-ranging collection of folk art, with everything from indigenous New York art (brownstone "sculpture" and period rooms) to items from the People's Republic of China. Changing exhibits display celebrated and unusual works, with superb painting shows. The **Botanic Garden** next door has a lovely collection of flora, including a large grove of Japanese cherry trees, a beautiful, fragrant rose garden, and the **Steinhardt Conservatory** and Lily Pond. Conservatory open Tues.-Sun. 10am-5:30pm. Admission $2, seniors and children $1. Museum open Mon. and Wed.-Sun. 10am-5pm. Donation; children free.

The Cloisters, Fort Tryon Park, upper Manhattan (923-3700). Subway: IND A train through Harlem to 190th St. This monastery, built from pieces of 12th- and 13th-century French and Spanish cloisters, plus a new tower, was assembled by Charles Collens in 1938 as a setting for the Met's rich collection of medieval art. Highlights include the Unicorn Tapestries, the Cuxa Cloister, and the Treasury. Open March-Oct. Tues.-Sun. 9:30am-5:15pm; Nov.-Feb. Tues.-Sun. 9:30am-4:45pm. Donation. (Includes admission to the Metropolitan Museum of Art main building.)

The Frick Collection, 1 E. 70th St. (288-0700). Subway: Lexington Ave. IRT #6 to 68th St. Robber baron Henry Clay Frick left his house and art collection to the city, and the museum retains the elegance of his French "Classic Eclectic" chateau. Impressive grounds. The Living Hall displays 17th-century furniture, Persian rugs, Holbein portraits, and paintings by El Greco, Rembrandt, Velázquez, and Titian. Courtyard inhabited by elegant statues surrounding the garden pool and fountain. Lectures Wed. and Thurs. Open Tues.-Sat. 10am-6pm, Sun. 1-6pm. Admission $3, students $1.50. Children under 10 not allowed, under 16 must be accompanied by an adult.

Guggenheim Museum, 1071 Fifth Ave. and 89th St. (360-3500; bookshop 360-3525). Subway: Lexington Ave. IRT #4, 5 or 6 to 86th St. Many have called this controversial construction a giant turnip and Midwesterner Frank Lloyd Wright's joke on the Big Apple. Others hail it as the city's most brilliant architectural achievement; every New Yorker has dreamt of skateboarding down the spiraled hallway. Realistically, you may want to start at the top and work downhill. The Guggenheim's permanent collection, with noted works by Renoir, Picasso, Avatar, Kandinsky, and Miró, and examples of all the 20th-century "isms" sits in the flanking galleries. Open Tues. 11am-7:45pm, Wed.-Sun. 11am-4:45pm. Admission $4.50, seniors, students, and disabled $2.50. Free Tues. 5-7:45pm. Unfortunately, museum closed for renovations until fall 1991.

Metropolitan Museum of Art, Fifth Ave. (879-5500), at 82nd St. Subway: Lexington Ave. IRT #4, 5 or 6 to 86th St. If you see only one, see this. The neoclassical marble palace surrounding the original McKim, Mead & White red brick of 1874 complements fountains and graceful glass barns expanding backwards and sideways into Central Park. Superb collection of 3.3 million works from almost every period through impressionism; particularly strong in Egyptian and non-Western sculpture and European painting. Take a load off your feet in the secluded Japanese Rock Garden. When blockbuster exhibits tour the world they usually stop at the Met—get tickets in advance through Ticketron. Open Tues.-Thurs. 9:30am-5:15pm, Fri.-Sat. 9:30am-8:45pm. Donation.

Museum of Modern Art (MOMA), 11 W. 53rd St. (708-9400), off Fifth Ave. in Midtown. Subway: E or F train to Fifth Ave. One of the most extensive post-impressionist collections in the world, founded in 1929 by scholar Alfred Barr in response to the Met's reluctance to embrace contemporary art. Cesar Pelli's recent structural glass additions—expanded entrance hall, garden, and gallery space—flood the masterpieces with natural light. See Monet's sublime *Water Lily* room, Ross's *Engulfed Cathedral,* and a virtual Picasso warehouse. Sculpture garden good for resting and people-watching. Open Fri.-Tues. 11am-6pm, Thurs. 11am-9pm. Admission $7, seniors and students $4, under 16 free with adult. Feel-good donation Thurs. after 5pm.

Queens Museum, Flushing Meadow Park (718-592-5555). Subway: IRT #7 to Willets Point. Located at the site of the 1939 and 1964 World's Fairs. Features memorabilia from the fairs in addition to a fine collection of 20th-century art by New Yorkers. Juried exhibits of young talent and special hands-on workshops encourage the continuing development of the plastic arts. Also has the "Panorama of the City of New York," the world's largest scale model with over 850,000 buildings in miniature. Open Tues.-Fri. 10am-5pm, Sat.-Sun. noon-5:30pm. Admission $2.

Whitney Museum of American Art, 945 Madison Ave. (570-3676), at 75th St. Subway: #6 to 77th St. Futuristic fortress featuring a comprehensive collection of contemporary U.S. art with works by Hopper, Soyer, de Kooning, Motherwell, Warhol, and Calder. Gallery talks Sat.-Sun. at 2 and 3:30pm. Museum open Tues. 1-8pm, Wed.-Sat. 11am-5pm, Sun. noon-6pm. Admission $4, seniors $2, students free. Free Tues. 6-8pm.

Smaller and Specialized Collections

American Craft Museum, 40 W. 53rd St. (956-3535), across from MOMA. Subway: IND to 53rd St. American crafts presented in 5 ingenious shows (such as "Plastic as Plastic") per year. Open Tues. 10am-8pm, Wed.-Sun. 10am-5pm. Admission $3.50, seniors and students $1.50. Free Tues. 5-8pm.

Museum of the American Indian, at Broadway and 155th St. (283-2420), in Harlem. Subway: IRT #1 to 157th St. Exercise caution; take a friend. This 1916 Beaux-Arts building houses the nation's largest collection of Native American art, including beautiful Eskimo ivory carvings. Admission $3, seniors and students $2. Open Tues.-Sat. 10am-5pm, Sun. 1-5pm.

AT&T Infoquest Center, 550 Madison Ave., at 56th St. (605-5555). High-tech, interactive exhibits explaining the information age, sponsored by the company with the soothing voice. Exhibits focus on lightwave communications, microelectronics, and computer software. Open Tues. 10am-9pm, Wed.-Sun. 10am-6pm. Free.

El Museo del Barrio, 1230 Fifth Ave. (831-7272), in East Harlem. Subway: Lexington Ave. IRT to 103rd St. Safe during the day. The only museum in the U.S. devoted exclusively to the art and culture of Puerto Rico and Latin America. Open Wed.-Sun. 11am-5pm. Admission $2, seniors and students $1.

Museum of Broadcasting, 25 W. 52nd St. (752-7684), between Fifth and Sixth. Subway: Lexington Ave. IRT to 53rd St. Expanded, new facilities where visitors select and view 40,000 tapes of classic TV and radio shows on individual consoles. Go before 1pm or expect a long wait, especially on Sat., despite the 1-hr. max. viewing time. Special screenings possible for groups. Monthly retrospectives focus on legendary personalities and landmark shows. Open Tues. noon-8pm, Wed.-Sat. noon-5pm. Suggested admission adults $4, seniors and under 13 $2, students $3. Tours Tues. at 1:30pm.

Cooper-Hewitt Museum, 2 E. 91st St. and Fifth Ave. (860-6894). Subway: Lexington Ave. IRT to 86th St. Andrew Carnegie's majestic, Georgian mansion now uses the Smithsonian Institute's decorative arts and design collection. All the special exhibits have considerable flair, focusing on such topics as contemporary designer fabrics. Open Tues. 10am-9pm, Wed.-Sat. 10am-5pm, Sun. noon-5pm. Admission $3, seniors and students $1.50, under 12 free. Free Tues. 5-9pm.

Museum of Holography, 11 Mercer St. (925-0526), in SoHo, ½ block north of Canal St. Subway: Lexington Ave. IRT to Canal St. Two fascinating floors of 3-D laser images from a unique collection. A must-see. Free lectures, gallery tours, interactive exhibits. Open Tues.-Sun. 11am-6pm. Admission $3.50, seniors and students $2.50.

New Museum of Contemporary Art, 583 Broadway between Prince and Houston St. (219-1222). Dedicated to the destruction of the canon and of conventional ideas of "art," the New Museum does the hottest, the newest, and the most controversial interactive exhibits; many rely heavily on the new technology in video. Much art dealing with the politics of identity—sexual, racial, and ethnic. Once a month an artist herself sits in the front window and has discussions with passersby. Open Wed.-Thurs. and Sun. noon-6pm, Fri.-Sat. noon-8pm. Suggested donation $3.50, seniors, students, and artists $2.50, under 12 free.

IBM Gallery of Science and Art, Madison Ave. at 56th St. (745-6100). User-friendly exhibits covering a wide range of art. Previous exhibits have featured 18th-century paintings and the use of computers in digging up Pompeii. Open Tues.-Sat. 11am-6pm. Free.

International Center of Photography, 1130 Fifth Ave. (860-1778), at 94th St. Subway: Lexington Ave. IRT #6 to 96th St. Housed in a landmark townhouse (1914) built for *New Republic* founder Willard Straight. Historical, thematic, contemporary, and experimental works. Open Tues. noon-8pm, Wed.-Fri. noon-5pm, Sat.-Sun. 11am-6pm. Admission $3, seniors and students $1.50. Free Tues. 5-8pm. Midtown branch at 77 W. 45th St. (869-2155) open Mon.-Fri. 11am-6pm, Sat. noon-5pm; free.

Intrepid Sea-Air-Space Museum, Pier 86 (245-0072), at 46th St. and Twelfth Ave. Bus: M16, M27, or M106 to W. 46th St. America's mostly militaristic 20th-century technological achievements celebrated in the legendary aircraft carrier. Open Wed.-Sun. 10am-5pm. Admission $6, seniors $5, children $3.25.

Jacques Marchais Center of Tibetan Art, 338 Lighthouse Ave., Staten Island (718-987-3478). Take bus S13 from Staten Island Ferry, turn right and walk up the hill. One of the finest Tibetan collections in the U.S., but the real attractions are the gardens, set on beautifully landscaped cliffs. Center itself a replica of a Tibetan temple. Open May-Sept. Wed.-Sun. 1-5pm; April and Oct.-Nov. Fri.-Sun. 1-5pm. Admission $2.50, seniors $2, children $1.

Jewish Museum, 1109 Fifth Ave. (860-1889), at 92nd St. Subway: Lexington Ave. IRT to 96th St. A large collection of ceremonial artifacts, Judaica, and modern pieces by Chagall and Stella. Open Mon. and Wed.-Thurs. noon-5pm, Tues. noon-8pm, Sun. 11am-6pm. Closed Jewish holidays. Admission $4.50, seniors, students, ages 6-16 $2.50. Free Tues. 5-8pm.

Studio Museum in Harlem, 144 W. 125th St. (864-4500). Subway: Broadway IRT to 125th St. A permanent collection of avant-garde work, mostly African American, complemented by special exhibits. Open Wed.-Fri. 10am-5pm, Sat.-Sun. 1-6pm. Admission $2, seniors and students $1, seniors free on Wed.

Entertainment

Freebies

The Big Apple sponsors numerous free outdoor events and festivals. In summer, the parks of all five boroughs are graced with performances by cultural ensembles such as the New York Philharmonic, Metropolitan Opera, Shakespeare Festival, Goldman Memorial Band, and Harlem Cultural Festival. Jugglers, music students from Juilliard and the Manhattan School of Music, comedians, dancers, and other struggling artists strut their stuff on Columbus Avenue in the low 70s, at Lincoln

Center, in front of the Plaza Hotel (59th and 5th Ave.), at Washington Square Park, and in many other spots.

For the scoop on free events, pick up a *Seasonal Calendar* from the visitors bureau (see Practical Information above), or call 360-1333 for a recorded listing. Check out the "Cheap Thrills" column in the *Village Voice* ($1.00) for updates on more obscure free and ultra-cheap weekly happenings (poetry readings, latino jazz, etc.).

Theater

Musicals may vogue right now, but drama and comedy, experimental theatre, and improv also draw crowds in New York. Broadway Theater—a misnomer for 34 official playhouses from Sixth to Ninth Ave. between 41st and 48th St.—has sung, danced, and wept its way into the U.S. imagination. But with astronomical ticket prices and a proclivity for flamboyant productions of the tried and true, it no longer monopolizes New York's dramatic spotlight. The hundreds of Off- and Off-Off-Broadway productions that highlight the experimental and the innovative have grown more popular than ever.

New York on Stage has a complete listing of productions, phone numbers, and prices. But you should find all the information you need in the *New York Times, New York Magazine, New Yorker,* or *Village Voice.* **Inside the Big Apple,** a booth next to the TKTS outlet at 47th and Broadway, offers free brochures about each of the current shows.

Broadway

Tickets to a Broadway show run from about $19 (2nd balcony Mon.-Fri.) to $60 (orchestra, Sat. night). When available, $10 standing room tickets (offered on the day of performance when the rest of the house is sold out) are well worth it.

Turn first to **TKTS,** which offers half-price tickets on the day of the performance, according to availability, adding a $1.50 surcharge. (Cash or traveler's checks only.) The number of tickets and plays is limited; go early for the widest choice. People start lining up at least an hour before the windows open. Offices situate at 47th and Broadway (354-5800; evening performance tickets sold Mon.-Sat. 3-8pm, Wed. and Sat. matinees 10am-2pm, Sun. performances noon-8pm), and at less crowded and indoor 2 World Trade Center, on the mezzanine level (evening performance tickets sold Mon.-Fri. 11am-5:30pm, Sat. 11:30am-3:30pm, matinees and Sun. performances 11am-5:30pm the day before the show).

For information on shows and ticket availability you can call the **NYC/ON STAGE hotline** (587-1111) or the Theater Development Fund's toll-free number (800-782-4369). Coupons allowing you to buy two tickets for the price of one are also available at the Convention and Visitors Bureau and at the Times Square Information Center.

To reach the Broadway Theater District, take subway #1, 2, 3, or 7, or subway QB, N, or RR to Times Square, which lies 3 blocks south. The #1 train also stops at 50th St., farther up Broadway. Remember that the dirty Broadway district is crime-ridden, particularly in the late evening after the theater-goers have left the area.

Off- and Off-Off-Broadway

Tickets ($10-20) to the larger Off-Broadway houses are available at both TKTS booths, though the one at 2 World Trade Center only sells them Monday through Saturday 11am to 1pm. For performances at founder Joseph Papp's **Public Theater,** 425 Lafayette St. (598-7150), take advantage of **Qixtix.** The theater saves a quarter of all tickets and offers them for half-price until 6pm on the night of performance, 1pm for matinees. Qixtix also has free frisky tickets to rehearsals. The Public is perhaps the best, or at least the most consistent, of the Off-Broadway theaters. Even at full price, seeing most shows costs no more than $30.

The best Off-Broadway theaters, many pioneering U.S. playwriting, are bunched around the Sheridan Square area of the West Village. They include the **Circle Rep,** at 161 Sixth Ave. (807-1326), the **Circle in the Square Downtown**, at 159 Bleeker St. (254-6330), the **Cherry Lane**, at 38 Commerce Street (989-2020), and the **Provincetown Playhouse**, at 133 MacDougal St. (477-5048). You can buy tickets to the larger Off-Broadway houses at the TKTS booths. Off-Off-Broadway is not a comical designation (at least not deliberately) but an actual category of theaters, where shows play limited engagements at lower ticket prices.

The city also boasts the widest variety of ethnic theater in the country. Although the days of the Lower East Side's Yiddish theater are long gone, the **Jewish Repertory Theater**, at 344 East 14th St. (505-2667), continues to produce notable shows (in English). The **Repertorio Español** presently thrives in the Gramercy Arts Theater at 138 E. 27th St. (889-2850)—most of its productions are in Spanish. Neither the **Negro Ensemble Company** (246-8545) nor the **Pan Asian Repertory Theater** (245-2660) has a permanent home, but both perform frequently at various places.

New York has also birthed the most exciting and controversial developments in alternative theater, including that elusive amalgam called "performance art," a combination of stand-up comedy, political commentary, theatrical monologue, and video art, starring the likes of Avatar. Besides the Brooklyn Academy of Music's famous Next Wave festival, a number of Manhattan institutions specialize in this distinctive art form, including **The Kitchen**, at 512 W. 19th St. (255-5793), **Franklin Furnace**, at 112 Franklin St. (925-4671, **Performance Space 122 (P.S. 122)**, at 150 First Ave. (577-5288), and the **Theater for the New City**, at 155 First Ave. (254-1109). **LaMama**, at 74A E. 4th St. (475-7710), the most venerable of the lot, gained fame for its early support of Sam Shepard's work.

Joseph Papp's famous **New York Shakespeare Festival** (598-7100) stages two free productions at the **Delacorte Theater** (861-7277) in Central Park, one late June through mid-July, and one during August. To reach the theater, enter the park from Central Park West at 81st St., or from Fifth Ave. at 79th St. Performances usually begin at 8pm Tuesday through Sunday. Tickets are distributed free at 6:15pm for the 8pm performance; arrive by noon. Oscar-winner Denzel Washington performed in *Richard III* in 1990.

Opera and Dance

The fulcrum of New York culture is **Lincoln Center**, at Broadway and 66th St. (877-1800). For a schedule of events, write Lincoln Center Calendar, 140 W. 65th St. 10023, or call the Lincoln Center Library Museum (870-1630).

The **Metropolitan Opera Company** (362-6000), opera's highest expression, plays on a Lincoln Center stage the size of a football field. The excellent performances boast some of the greatest principals in the world. During the regular season (Sept.-May Mon.-Sat.), you can get upper balcony seats for $17 if you don't mind risking a nosebleed from the heights, but standing room in the orchestra is a steal at $10. In summer, watch for free concerts in city parks (362-6000).

At right angles to the Met, the **New York City Opera** (870-5570), under the direction of Beverly Sills, provides adequate performances of the warhorses—many in translation—and of new U.S. works. The success of its recently introduced English "supertitles" has led other companies to adopt them. "City" now offers a summer season and keeps its ticket prices low year-round ($17-35, standing room back row top balcony $5). Call to check the availability of rush tickets on the night before the performance you want to attend, then wait in line the next morning.

The **Light Opera of Manhattan (LOOM)**, 316 E. 91st St., between First and Second Ave. (831-2000), offers Gilbert and Sullivan and other operettas. (Tickets $17.50-20, students $12.) Check the papers for performances of the **Amato Opera Company**, 319 Bowery (228-8200), and the **Bel Canto Company**, which perform in churches around the city.

The late great George Balanchine's **New York City Ballet**, the oldest in the country, alternates with the city opera for the use of the Lincoln Center's New York State Theater (877-5570), performing December through January, again in May and June. (Tickets $6-46, standing room $4.) **American Ballet Theater** (477-3030), Balanchine's greatest rival, dances at the Met during the late spring and for about two weeks in summer. Under Mikhail Baryshnikov's guidance, ABT's eclectic repertoire has ranged from the Kirov grand-style Russian ballet to experimental postmodern choreography. The **Joffrey** ballet performs in the **City Center,** 131 W. 55th St. (581-7907), a doomed, Byzantine playhouse outside Lincoln Center.

The **Alvin Ailey American Dance Theater** (997-1980) bases its repertoire of modern dance on African American jazz, spirituals, and contemporary music. The grandest integrated company in the world, it tours internationally but always performs at the **City Center** in December. Tickets ($15-40) are difficult to obtain; write or call City Center weeks in advance, if possible. The **Martha Graham Dance Co.,** 316 E. 63rd St. (838-5886), performs original Graham pieces during their October New York season. She revolutionized 20th-century dance with her psychological, rather than narrative, approach to characters. (Tickets $15-40.) Look also for the seasons of the **Merce Cunningham Dance Company,** the **Dance Theater of Harlem,** and the **Paul Taylor Dance Company,** usually in spring.

Half-price tickets for many music and dance events can be purchased on the day of performance at **Bryant Park,** 42nd St. (382-2323), between Fifth and Sixth Ave. (Open Tues. and Thurs.-Fri. noon-2pm and 3-7pm; Wed. and Sat. 11am-2pm and 3-7pm; Sun. noon-6pm.)

Music

In Lincoln Center's Avery Fisher Hall (874-2424), the **New York Philharmonic,** (799-9595) under Zubin Mehta, plays everything from Bach to Bax, Schubert to Schoenberg. Avery Fisher's new interior, designed by Philip Johnson, resonates with acoustical grandeur. The Philharmonic's season lasts from September through May, and jazz and classical musicians visit the rest of the year. (Tickets $7.50-35.) Senior citizen and student-rush tickets ($5) go on sale Tuesday and Thursday evenings a half hour before the curtain rises. "Mostly Mozart" concerts, performed July through August, feature artists like Itzhak Perlman; get there early since major artists often give half-hour pre-concert recitals. (Tickets $9-18.50.)

Carnegie Hall, Seventh Ave. at 57th St. (247-7800), one of the greatest musical auditoriums in the world, attracts opera singers, jazz singers, instrumental soloists, and symphony orchestras. (Tickets $15-30.)

Flicks

Hollywood may make the movies, but New York makes Hollywood. Most movies open in New York weeks before they're distributed across the country, and the response of Manhattan audiences and critics can shape a film's success or failure nationwide. Or so they like to think. Just grab a copy of any newspaper for an overview of the selection. Magazines such as *New York* and the *New Yorker* provide plot summaries and evaluations in their listings as well.

Museums like the Met and MOMA show artsy flicks downstairs, as does the New York Historical Society. The **68th Street Playhouse,** on Third Ave. (734-0302), and the **Paris,** Fifth Ave. and 58th St. (688-2013), specialize in first-run foreign films. For cinematic exposure to Chinese culture, go to the **Sun Sing Theater,** 75 E. Broadway (619-0493). The **Thalia Soho,** 16 Vandam St. (675-0498), features classic foreign and U.S. revivals, as does **Theatre 80 Saint Mark's,** 80 St. Mark's Place (254-7400). For an inspiring movie-going experience, try the **Ziegfeld Theatre,** 141 W. 54th St. (765-7600). One of the last grand movie houses that hasn't been sliced up into a "multiplex," the Ziegfeld offers standard box-office attractions.

If you like hot political film festivals, try the film room of the 92nd St. **"Y,"** 1395 Lexington Ave. (427-6000). Between LaGuardia and Thompson at 144 Bleecker St. (674-2560), you'll find **Bleecker Street Cinema,** which specializes in experimental movies. The **8th Street Playhouse** (674-6515), between MacDougal and Sixth Ave., features music films by day and cult classics by night. Its midnight series includes the *Rocky Horror Picture Show* on Friday and Saturday, a campy classic where fellow movie goers put on the best show ($6).

For a real deal, check out the library. All **New York Public Libraries** show free films ranging from documentaries to classics to last year's blockbuster. Screening times may be a bit erratic, but you can't beat the price.

The Tube

Yes, TV. Trade an insult with David Letterman or ask a sensitive question of Phil Donahue's guests. Several TV shows film in the Big Apple before a live audience. To join the starstruck throng, call the guest relations office at the networks about ticket availability. (NBC 664-4444; ABC 887-7777; CBS 975-4321.) Tickets, distributed by the networks without charge, are often hard to procure. Plan ahead. Think about it. Live to Dream. Dream to Live.

Bars and Clubs

It's your fault if you're bored in New York. As John Travolta showed the country, nay the world, in the 70s, New York stays alive from sundown to sunup. Bars stay open until 4am, clubs until dawn. If you're feeling poor, fill up at a Happy Hour at a non-descript bar or pick up a couple of 40-oz. Buds from a deli before you hit the scene. Any club you get into will hit you with a mean cover and then try to push $5 mixed drinks on you. You'll end up buying a few but you'll spend less if you stick in one place for a long time and order pitchers. In the volatile nightlife scene, bars and clubs rise and fall like successive empires, with new institutions built upon the ruins of old, decayed ones. Owners themselves often don't know what their club will be like from week to week; they do know that they'll be open late, or rather, early. Crowds don't arrive at many spots until 11pm or midnight, and by 1am things get going. The lights often go out between 4 and 6am. Those still charged with adrenalin at dawn will have to seek out an After Hours. Ask a knowledgeable bartender or a hip New Yorker where to find one; printing names would cause their demise. In fact, the hippest club, **The Deep,** doesn't have a single location, but covertly hops around from club to bar.

You may find yourself waiting outside a club for a long time if you don't have the "look," or if your denim leisure suit clashes with your white platform sandals, expect to wait on line indefinitely. Wearing black or being a single female should up your odds of bursting through. On the optimistic side, there's always another place to try, whatever the hour. Cover charges vary during the week—Fridays and Saturdays (up to $20 per person) cost the most. Weekends also bring in flocks of out-of-towners. For lower covers and entertaining crowds, try "clubbing" early in the week, particularly on Wednesdays. The New York Convention and Visitor's Bureau and Village music stores often have complimentary or reduced-fare passes to clubs piled by the register.

Although *New York* magazine, the *Village Voice,* and *After Dark* list who's playing, showtimes, and sometimes cover charges, you should always call ahead to check. The most extensive listings can be found in *The Music Exchange* and *Good Times,* two pop-music newspapers, available at most stores on **Music row,** on 48th St. between Sixth and Seventh Ave. For students, the New York University/Greenwich Village area (especially the East Village) makes a good starting point. For those with a little more cash, First and Second Ave. in the 60s and 70s are sprinkled with chic, sleek clubs. A preponderance of gay bars and discos populate the West Village along Greenwich Ave. and further west.

Good listings of gay and lesbian happenings appear in the *Village Voice,* as well as in the *Gay Guide,* a free publication distributed at alternative bookstores and bars, or the *New York Native,* a somewhat racy gay newspaper sold at most newsstands. In general, men far outnumber women at gay clubs. Much lesbian socializing takes place underground.

It can be difficult (and futile) to distinguish alternative nightlife from downtown nightlife in general: the hippest clubs have one or two "gay nights" each week, and same-sex couples can go "clubbing" in most with-it places. Club schedules change; be sure to call ahead to make sure that you know who you'll find when you arrive.

Dance Clubs

Building, 51 W. 26th St. (576-1890). A hip hop crowd pulses pelvises in a sci-fi setting. The dancing sizzles as D.J. Kid Capri from the Bronx asks, "How many people gonna get sex tonight?" The floor roars. Open Thurs.-Sat. 10pm-4am. Cover $5-10.

Uncle Charlie's, 56 Greenwich Ave. (255-8787), between Seventh Ave. S. and Charles St. The biggest and best-known gay club in the city—schools of West Village guppies and people in bright colors. B&T (bridge and tunnel) gay people make the commute. Fun. No cover.

Mars, 28 10th Ave. (691-6262), at 13th St. Multi-tiered mega-club way over on the West Side, housed on a former meat packing plant practically on the Hudson River. Formerly the "Danceteria." Each floor has a different theme. A sight to behold. Rap night Thurs. Gay night Sun. Cover $12.

Palace de Beauté, 860 Broadway (228-8009) between 17th and 18th St. A new club full of unrealized potential. Excellent DJs, including Jellybean, attract an uptown mousse-wielding and downtown switchblade-wielding crowd. Open Tues.-Thurs. and Fri.-Sat. 10pm-4am. Cover $15.

CBGB & OMFUG, 315 Bowery (982-4052), at Bleecker. Subway: Lexington IRT to Bleecker. The initials stand for "country, bluegrass, blues, and other music for uplifting gourmandizers," but almost since its inception in 1976, this club has bred U.S. punk. Now features foreign bands and pop, along with hard core. Audition night Mon. Hard core matinee Sun. at 3pm admits ages 16 and over. Open daily 9pm-4am. Cover $5-10.

Bentley's, 25 E. 40th St. (684-2540), between Park and Madison. Predominantly black crowd dancing to incredible rhythms at impossible speed. Even the yuppies have a good time. Reggae-Soca-Calypso night Thurs. 6pm-2am. Fri. free 5-9pm, $10 after. Sat. 10:30pm-4am $5-10.

Nell's, 246 W. 14th St. (675-1567), between Seventh and Eighth. Subway: Seventh Ave. IRT to 14th St. Tacky neighborhood belies the sumptuous opulence of the huge Victorian-style sitting room inside. Overstuffed chairs, chandeliers, and bejeweled Beautiful People upstairs; oft-crowded dance floor downstairs. As long as you look like you've stepped out of a Polo ad, anything's game. Open daily 10pm-4am. Cover Sun.-Thurs. $5, Fri.-Sat. $10.

M.K., 204 Fifth Ave. (779-1340) at 27th St. Subway: Broadway BMT to 28th St. Once trendy, now slipping, but worth a look. Four floors, each with its own decor, entice glitterati with snob appeal; designed to imitate an old "gentleman's club." Small dance floor but plenty of action elsewhere. Open daily 7:30pm for dinner, 11pm-2am for dancing. Cover Sun.-Thurs. $5, Fri.-Sat. $15.

Wetland Preserve, 161 Hudson St. (966-4225). Organic wine and healthy snacks will keep you empty; bohemians lacking barbers dance to happening rock. Open daily 10pm-4pm. Cover $5-10.

Cave Cavern, 24 First Ave. (529-9665), between 1st and 2nd St. Restaurant with dance floor in an old roman bath. Very trendy. Open Tues.-Sun. 6pm-4am. Cover Fri.-Sat. $5.

Tramps, 45 W. 21st St. (727-7788). Screaming violins and clattering washboards pack the sweaty dance floor. Lousiana Zydeco rocks nightly with help from blues, reggae, and rock bands. Call for schedule and cover.

Music/Bars

Angry Squire, 216 Seventh Ave. (242-9066), between 22nd and 23rd St. Jazz every night with a local crowd and mellow tunes. Simple tables with wine caskets hanging above the bar. Open daily 5pm-3am. No cover.

Apollo Theater, 253 W. 125th St. (749-5838). Subway: Broadway IRT to 125th St. Use caution in the neighborhood. This historic Harlem landmark has heard the likes of Duke Ellington, Count Basie, Ella Fitzgerald, Lionel Hampton, Billie Holliday, and Sara Vaughn. In his zoot-suit days, Malcolm X shined shoes here. Now undergoing a revival. Show tickets $5-30. Arrive at least ½ hr. early for cheap tickets. Infamously critical amateur night Wed. at 7:30pm. Call the theater to check what's playing.

Augie's, 2751 Broadway (864-9834). Jazz all week until 3am. The saxophonist sits on your lap and the bass rests on your table. Quality musicians and a cool crowd. Open daily 9am-3am. No cover.

Dan Lynch, 221 Second Ave. (677-0911) at 14th St. Subway: Lexington IRT to Union Sq. Dark smoky room with Casablanca fan, long bar, and "all blues, all the time." Swinging, friendly, Dead Head crowd drowns the dance floor. Pool table in back. Open daily 8am-4am; blues and jazz start at 10pm. Jam session Sat.-Sun. 4:30-9pm. Cover Fri.-Sat. $5.

Dan Minlano's, 49 E. Houston (no phone). The celebrity crowd drifts here on the weekends, and Guinness Stout flows on tap. Dick would be happy here. Sit at the long oak bar and check out the photo of Marciano about to knock out Louis. Open daily 6pm-3am.

Downtown Beirut, 158 First Ave. (260-4248). Hard-core crowd flooded with Eastern European youth listening to the best jukebox in town, with over 15 Clash songs listed. Happy Hour noon-8pm hosts $2.25 drafts. Open daily noon-4am.

Kilimanjaro Night Club, 531 W. 19th St. (627-2333). International music with an international crowd slamming to the hypnotic beats of African bands. Smaller DJ dance floor upstairs concentrates on dance hall and reggae. Open daily 9pm-4am. Cover $5-25. Call for schedule.

Michael's Pub, 211 E. 55th St. (758-2272) off Third Ave. Subway: Lexington IRT to 59th or 51st St. Woody Allen played his clarinet here instead of picking up his 3 Academy Awards for *Annie Hall*. He still sneaks in some Mon. nights. Sets Mon. at 9 and 11pm, Tues.-Sat. at 9:30 and 11:30pm. Open Mon.-Fri. noon-1am. Cover $15-25. 2-drink min. at the tables, but no min. at the bar.

Pool Bar, 643 Broadway at Bleeker St. A flight of stairs leads down to the dancefloor and pool table. Beautiful bartenders serve expensive drinks while psychedelic funk attempts to get the place grooving. Open Mon.-Thurs. 6pm-4am, Fri.-Sat. 6pm-3am. Cover Thurs.-Sat. $2-3.

Teddy's, N. 9th St. and Berry St. (384-9787) in Greenpoint, Brooklyn. Subway: G to Nassau St. The new artiste crowd starts drinking here and only you can find out where they end up. Many true adventures born in this bar. Open daily until 4am. Jazz on Wed. night.

Westend, 2911 Broadway (622-8830) at 113 St. Columbia University and prep school hangout once frequented by Kerouac and Burroughs. Huge sitting areas, including outdoors, give way to the small dance room with bands in the back (cover $7). Cheap pitchers with a great beer selection. Open daily noon-4am.

Long Island

Long Island is easy to stereotype, but difficult to comprehend. For some, the Island evokes images of sprawling suburbia, dotted with malls and thick accents, to others the privileged playground of Manhattan millionaires; for still others it provides a summer refuge of white sand and open spaces. Fewer see the pockets of poverty on Long Island, or its commerical and cultural centers. Yet each of these visions is accurate in its own way, and perhaps in conjunction they create an understanding of what the Island, home of Billy Joel, J.P. Morgan, and Jackson Pollock, is all about.

While in theory, "Long Island" includes the entire 120-mile-long fish-shaped land mass, in practice the term excludes the westernmost sections, Brooklyn and Queens. The residents of these two boroughs, at the head of the "fish," will readily remind you that they officially belong to the City. This leaves Nassau and Suffolk counties to comprise the real Long Island. East of the Queens-Nassau line, people read *Newsday*, not the *Times*, or the *Daily News;* they back the Islanders, not the Rangers, during ice hockey season; and they revel in their position as neighbor to, rather than a part of, the great metropolis.

Fortunately for the visitor, the Island is cheaply and easily accessible from Manhattan. Nearly all your transit needs will be served by some combination of the **Long Island Rail Road (LIRR)** (516-822-5477), which operates out of Penn Station in

Manhattan, and the **Metropolitan Suburban Bus Authority (MSBA)** (516-542-0100), which operates daytime buses in eastern Queens, Nassau, and Western Suffolk. Depending on where you go and what time you leave, train fare will vary from $8.50 round-trip (for nearby suburbs in non-rush hour times) to $28 round-trip (for the more distant spots, during rush-hour). **Suffolk Transit** (516-360-5700) takes over farther east. Bikes may be carried on LIRR by permit only.
Long Island's **area code** is 516.

Suburban Long Island: Nassau and Western Suffolk Counties

The North Shore of Long Island was once known as the "Gold Coast" because of the string of mansions built by 19th-century industrialists in the hills overlooking Long Island Sound. Many of these houses have been turned into museums, and the grounds that have been spared from developers are now gardens, arboretums, or nature preserves open to the public.

From west to east, some principal North Shore sights are: **Falaise** (883-1612), in Sands Point Park and Preserve, the former Guggenheim estate (1-hr. guided tour every ½ hr; open May to mid-Nov. Sat.-Wed. 10am-5pm; admission $2, children under 12 not allowed); **Old Westbury Gardens,** on Old Westbury Rd. (333-0048), where the splendor of the main house and its collection of painting and sculpture is matched only by that of the formal English gardens outside (open late April-late Oct. Wed.-Sun. 10am-5pm; admission to the house $3, to the garden and parking $4.50, combined tickets for seniors $3.50); **Sagamore Hill,** on Cove Neck Rd. near Oyster Bay (922-4447), the summer home of Theodore Roosevelt, now jammed with Teddy memorabilia (open Wed.-Sun. 9:30am-5pm; admission $1, seniors and children free); the **Vanderbilt Museum** (262-7888) and the **Vanderbilt Planetarium,** on Little Neck Rd. (262-7800), in Centerport, in the Spanish-Moroccan Vanderbilt mansion (museum open Tues.-Sat. 10am-4pm, Sun. noon-5pm; admission $4, seniors and students $3, children $2); and the **Museums at Stony Brook,** at Main St. and State 25A (751-0066), which include works by William Sidney Mount, a carriage museum, and period buildings (open Wed.-Sat. 10am-5pm, Sun. noon-5pm; admission $4, seniors $3).

In Central Nassau, near Nassau Community College, the **Cradle of Aviation Museum** (222-1190) documents Long Island's role in the history of aviation from Lindbergh (who took off from Roosevelt Field, Garden City) to the Lunar Module (which was built at Calverton by Grumman). Two hangars teem with planes. (Free guided tours. Open April-Oct. Fri.-Sun. noon-5pm.) Take Meadowbrook Parkway to Stewart Ave. W., and follow signs to Nassau Community College. Or take MSBA #16 or 35 to the College from Hempstead Station for $1. (LIRR $3.50 to Hempstead from Penn Station.)

The south shore of Long Island is protected by barrier islands that constitute some of the finest white sand beaches in the northeast. The most famous of these, **Jones Beach** (785-1600), sits closest to the city, making it the most crowded. Take the Long Island Expressway to Grand Central/Northern State Pkwy. and then either Meadowbrook Pkwy. or Wantagh Pkwy. to the beach. Wantagh Parkway, farther east, remains less congested on beach days. (Memorial Day-Labor Day parking $4.) The south shore also encompasses three large contiguous state parks in Bay Shore and Oakdale. **Heckscher State Park,** on Heckscher Pkwy. (581-2100), has swimming, winter sports, and camping. (Admission $4 per car.) **Bayard Cutting Arboretum,** on Montauk Hwy. in Oakdale (581-1002), offers hours of nature walks. (Open Wed.-Sun. 10am-5pm. Admission $3 per car.) The **Connetquot River Preserve** (581-1005), still farther north, has nearly 4000 acres of hiking and riding trails. (Admission $1. Call 1 day ahead to make a reservation, or obtain a permit by writing to the Long Island State Parks and Recreation Commission, Administration Headquarters Permit Dept., P.O. Box 247, Babylon 11702.) The staff leads guided nature walks on weekends and cross-country skiing in winter. (Open Tues.-Sun. 6am-4:30pm.) These three parks form the southern end of the 34-mi. **Greenbelt Trail** that runs all the way across Long Island to **Sunken Meadow State Park** on the Sound. Call 234-3112 for information on hiking or camping along the trail.

Heckscher, across from the Bay Shore LIRR Station (from Penn Station 70 min., $5.25 off-peak), is convenient to **Fire Island Ferries** (589-8980), which run to the affluent communities on the west end of **Fire Island,** the largest (32 mi. long) and most famous of the barrier islands. ($9.50 round-trip, under 11 $4.75. Pedestrians only; bikes go on the freight boat.) Farther west are two more ferries. **Sayville Ferry Company** (589-0810) runs to **Sailor's Haven Visitor Center** ($7.50 round-trip, children $4) on Fire Island National Seashore, and to the predominantly gay summer communities of Cherry Grove and The Pines ($9 round-trip; seniors $8, children $4.50). Follow the signs from Rte. 27 or the Sayville LIRR ($5.25). From Patchogue, the **Davis Park Ferry Company** (475-1665), directly opposite the Patchogue LIRR station ($5.75), will take you and your bike to the campground at **Watch Hill Visitors Center.** ($4.25 one way, seniors $4, children $2.50, bikes $2 extra.) Reservations, taken Fridays from 9am to 11am, are recommended in the summer. (Campground open May 15-Oct. 15. Free.)

Since the LIRR runs all night from most major suburban stations, there is little reason to sleep in suburbia. Lodging starts at $70-80 for a double.

Some generic advice on Long Island dining: **delis** are always a good, cheap takeout option; and Long Island **diners** bear little resemblance to their greasy, classic metropolitan cousins, offering an astonishing variety of good, home-cooked food. Meals start at $4, and menus often run several pages.

The North Fork

The North Fork, center of the oyster and whaling industries at the turn of the century, now supports a mixture of farmland, pebbled beaches, and idyllic small towns. Only accessible by ferry (8-min. ride), **Shelter Island** re-creates New England in a lush woodland setting—a perfect place for an afternoon drive. The beaches on Long Island Sound, less crowded than the South Shore, are wonderful places to swim, sail, and fish. Many of the towns have historical societies and maintain one or two small museums or restorations.

East along the North Fork, several wineries take advantage of the fact that local climate and soil conditions rival Napa Valley's. Their wines are the real thing, too—not "New York State" wine, that fruity grape juice which fills wine coolers. Local winery tours and wine tastings give you a chance to be the judge. Technically, you must be 21 or over to try the wine, but casual carding is the norm. Two hundred-acre **Pindar** (734-6200), on the Main Rd. (Rte. 25) in Peconic, produced two of the wines chosen for George Bush's Inauguration. It's also friendlier and more down-home than others. (Free tours every hr. Open April-Dec. daily 11am-6pm.)

You have to look hard during the summer to find reasonably priced accommodations in North Fork. Most comfortable doubles start at $60 and can rise to an outlandish $140. The best option is the **Vineyard Motor Inn** (722-4024), on Rte. 25 in Jamesport, 5 mi. from Riverhead or Mattituck. (Doubles $65, off-season $55.) The cheapest choice on Shelter Island is the **Chequit Inn,** on Grand St. (749-0018), a run-down, 150-year-old inn that overlooks the bay with 44 old-fashioned singles from $45, doubles from $53. **Camping** remains the cheapest choice in summer, but you must be 21, married, or accompanied by parents or guardians to use New York State Campgrounds. **Wildwood State Park,** P.O. Box 518, Wading River 11792 (929-4314), on Long Island Sound, is convenient to the North Shore and rarely fills, but arrive early on Friday for summer weekends. The park lies on Rte. 25A, 5 mi. northwest of Riverhead, within 25 mi. of most east end attractions. (Campsites $10, trailer sites $12.) Campers should be alert to the local hunting season (usually late fall to winter).

Dining on the east end need not deplete your wallet if you exercise a little resourcefulness. **Bob's Fish Market and Restaurant,** Rte. 114 (749-0830), 2 mi. south of the North Ferry, serves hearty dinners of fresh-caught fish for $7-12. (Open daily

5-9pm.) The **Hellenic Snack Bar**, on North Rd. (477-0138), at the Greenport/East Marion line, 3 mi. east of Sound Beach, is a popular Greek family restaurant. (Sandwiches from $5. Dinners $8.50-12. Open daily 8am-10pm.) On Shelter Island, the **Chequit**, in the Chequit Inn (see above), gives good breakfast ($6-10; served Mon.-Fri. 8-11am, Sat.-Sun. 8am-noon), but dinner prices will drain your billfold.

Bike rentals are available on the North Fork at **Country Time Cycles**, Main Rd. (298-8700), in Mattituck. (10-speeds $20 1st day, $10 each additional day; $50 per week. Credit card deposit required.) Or try **Piccozzi's Service Station**, Rte. 114 (749-0045) in Shelter Island Heights, a 10-minute walk from the North Ferry. (For 8 hr.: 3-speeds $16, 12-speeds $18; either $70 per week. $250 deposit or credit card required.)

The LIRR serves Riverhead and the North Fork two to four times per day (fare $12.25, off-peak $8.25). **Suffolk Transit's** (360-5700) S-92 bus loops between North and South Forks nine times daily; it connects with the LIRR at Riverhead. The 9A bus, a North Fork local, makes connections with the Orient Point Ferry (323-2743) to New London, CT. (Fares on the S-92 and 9A 90¢.) **Sunrise Express** (477-1200; 800-527-7709 outside Suffolk County) provides summer bus service to the North Fork from New York City and Queens. (Fare $15, $28 round-trip.)

The South Fork

In summer, the sandy peninsula of the South Fork lures more tourists than the North Fork. The spectacular oceanfront homes, resort hotels, and parklands await the droves of elite Manhattanites and other wealthy tourists who descend on the Hamptons and Montauk in July and August. Consequently, the area becomes emphatically chic and crowded. Check *The Hamptons* magazine (free) for information on art exhibits, nightlife, and music on the bustling South Fork; Westhampton and Southampton are particularly lively.

As on the North Fork, fascinating museums and historical sites inhabit almost every town. One of the best, the **Long Island Whaling Museum** tells its story on Main St. (725-0770), 2 blocks south of **Sag Harbor**, on the first floor of the Masonic Temple. (Open May-Sept. Mon.-Sat. 10am-5pm, Sun. 1-5pm. Admission $2, seniors and children 75¢.) Tiny Sag Harbor once rivaled New York as an international port. Around the corner on Garden St., you'll find the **Custom House** (941-9444), the restored 1791 private home of Thomas Dering, First Collector of the port of Sag Harbor. (Open Memorial Day-Labor Day Tues.-Sun. 10am-5pm. Admission $1.50, children $1.) For a taste of modern culture, **Guild Hall**, 158 Main St. (324-0806), in **East Hampton**, a few blocks west of town, offers contemporary art exhibits, lectures, and panel series. (Open daily 10am-5pm. Donation.) The **Parrish Art Museum**, 25 Job's Lane (283-2118), in **Southampton**, ½ mi. south of the railroad station in the heart of town, offers first-rate contemporary art exhibits, films, and jazz concerts. (Open Mon. and Thurs.-Sat. 10am-5pm, Sun. 1-5pm. Donation.)

Vineyards on the South Fork are beginning to achieve recognition. Of these, **Bridgehampton Winery** (537-3155), off the main road in Bridgehampton, is one of the most successful, having garnered several awards since its first harvest in 1982. (Tours on the hr. complete with wine tastings. Open Sun.-Fri. noon-5pm, Sat. 11am-5pm. Admission $1.)

In summer, you'll have to compete with many wealthy New Yorkers for even the most modest lodgings; and from November to April, almost everything is closed. Most of the few low-season deals are offered in Montauk Village. The absolute best deal on the east end is the friendly **Montauket**, on Tuthill Rd. (668-5992), 1 mi. north of Montauk Village. (Go north on Edgemere Ave. and turn left on Tuthill Rd.) Located close to the railroad station, this place, not surprisingly, fills up quickly. Doubles cost an unbeatable $30. (Open June-Sept.) The **Royal Oaks Hotel**, on Rte. 114 (725-0714), just south of Sag Harbor, offers simple, clean doubles for $45 from April to late September. Camp in summer at **Hither Hills State Park** (668-2551 or 669-1000), right on the ocean between Montauk and East Hampton. You can't beat the location. The 150 campsites are available in July and August by lottery (at other times, by reservation); to enter, send a self-addressed stamped envelope to Camping, **P.O.** Box 247, Babylon, 11702, before the January drawing. (1-week max. stay. Sites $10. Open mid-April to Sept.)

You can always get good, cheap take-out food from a deli, and you'll find two or three in every East End village. Line up at any deli or diner at 7am with half the local work force for breakfast specials. West of Hither Hills before East Hampton on the Montauk Hwy., you'll find the **Clam Bar at Napeague** (267-6348), a highway pit stop serving clams, oysters, shrimp, and half a cold lobster for $5. (Open summer daily noon-8pm.) Dinner on the South Fork is expensive or it's pizza.

You'll find many possibilities for hiking in state and county parks. Call 669-1000 (state parks) or 567-1700 (county parks) for details. One of the more unusual places to hike, **Mashomack Preserve,** sits on Rte. 114, on Shelter Island, 1 mi. north of the South Ferry. Part of the Nature Conservancy's national chain of open lands, this preserve boasts 2000 acres of hiking trails and miles of bay-shore beaches. You can explore by reservation only. A permit is not necessary—simply phone the manager the day before you show up (749-1001).

You can often see as far as 40 mi. from the **Montauk Point Lighthouse,** on the easternmost tip of Long Island (at the end of the Montauk Hwy.). First, however, you must climb the 137 steps to the viewing tower. (Open Memorial Day-Sept. daily 10:30am-6pm. Admission $2, children $1; parking $3, free after 4pm.)

The East End is served several times daily by the **LIRR.** Trains roll through the Hamptons and Montauk three times per day (9 on summer weekends). The three-and-a-half-hour ride to Penn Station makes daytripping a little rough (one way peak $12.25, off-peak $8.25). **Suffolk Transit's** S-92 bus also serves parts of the South Fork (see the North Fork for details). **Hampton Jitney** (212-936-0440 Manhattan; 516-283-4600 Long Island), a private bus company, runs 15-25 buses per day to and from the Hamptons. One-way fares between Manhattan and South Fork range from $10-22, with stops in almost all the villages and towns from Westhampton to Montauk. Pick up the bus in Manhattan at 41st St. at Third Ave., and 70th St. at Lexington Ave. Call for schedule information.

Upstate New York

In the language of New Yorkers, "upstate" refers to anything from the craggy peaks of the Adirondacks to the rushing waters of Niagara Falls. The area as a whole often has to brace itself against losing its identity to "The City" down south. Yet, once surrounded by the natural beauty of the state's landscape and the richness of its history, you may find it easy to forget that such things as metropolis, smog, and traffic even exist. Villages dot the mountainous strip which begins just north of the city and stretches to Canada. Lush, hilly, and verdant terrain surrounds the Finger Lakes. Historic Albany holds its own as an important inland port and Rennaissance center at the end of the Hudson River. And, of course, Niagara Falls roar majestically at the Canadian border.

Syracuse

Travelers greeting each other in Syracuse are wont to ask "Where are you headed next?" The question takes on a certain urgency here. Centrally located in upper New York, Syracuse makes a convenient stopover point and a great place to grow up in if you're an editor or go to school or if you're Lou Reed, though not worth an extended stay. When you do wake up with a bandaged head and find yourself in Syracuse, you can board one of the green **"Salt City" trolleys** (424-1234) for just 10¢. Schedules are available at the chamber of commerce, or wait by one of the green signs on Salina and W. Water St. A 15-minute ride takes you by most downtown sights. Architecture buffs should note the spectacular 30s art deco style of the **Niagara Mohawk Power Co.**, 300 Erie Blvd. W., and the **New York Telephone** building, at the corner of S. State and W. Washington St. The **Erie Canal Museum,** 318 Erie Blvd. E. (471-0593), is in the historic Weighlock Building. (Open Tues.-Sun. 10am-5pm. Admission $1, ages 5-13 50¢. Free Tues.)

Grab a bite to eat at **Xristou's Deli,** 116 E. Fayette St., between Warren and Salina St., whose Greek specialties include hot lunch dishes, salads, sandwiches, and pastries. Don't miss your complimentary shot of *ouzo.* Down four pancakes and coffee for $2.25. (Open Mon.-Fri. 7am-4pm, Sat. 11am-2pm.) Right down the street from the hostel, **Rosie's,** Oak St. at Park, is a favorite quicker-picker-upper, with good-sized subs for $4. (Open Mon.-Thurs. 9am-11pm, Fri. 9am-1am, Sat. 11am-1am, Sun. 4-11pm.) Look in the area around the campus of **Syracuse University** for nightlife and cheap restaurants.

For lodging, trek to the **Downing International Hostel,** 535 Oak St. (472-5788), which just moved into a new house with 22 beds. From the bus station turn left (east) on Eric Blvd., left again on Crouse St. a block down, take another quick right on Lodi St. Turn left on Oak St. and walk up the hill to the hostel (20-30 min.). (Lockout 9:30am-5pm. Curfew Mon.-Thurs. 10pm, Fri.-Sat. 11pm. $8.)

Greyhound/Trailways, 815 Erie Blvd. E. (tickets 472-5339; information 471-7171), stays open 24 hr. Buses go to: New York City (18 per day, 5½-7 hr., $38); Philadelphia (1 per day, 3 per day Fri. and Sun., 7 hr., $49.50); and Niagara Falls (5 per day, 3½ hr., $12). **Amtrak,** E. Manlius Rd. (463-1135; for information and reservations 800-872-7245), choo-choos 5 mi. east of downtown. To New York City (4 per day, 5½ hr., $66) and Niagara Falls (2 per day, 3½ hr., $40). The **Central New York Transportation Authority (CENTRO)** runs buses around the city (fare 75¢). The enthusiastic staff of the **Syracuse Convention and Visitors Bureau,** 100 E. Onondaga St. (470-1343), downtown at S. Salina St., are exceedingly happy to tell you anything else you might like to know. (Open Mon.-Fri. 8:30am-5pm.) Syracuse's **ZIP code** is 13210; the **area code** is 315.

Albany

With millions of dollars spent on urban renewal, the celebration of its 1986 Tricentennial, and the patronage of the merchant Medici family, Albany has undergone what many residents term a "renaissance." This may be an overstatement, but recent humanist efforts to increase tourism have helped to make the state capital more than just a medieval place to make a quick bus or train connection.

Though founded by Dutch settlers in 1614, the English took Albany in 1664 as part of the land grant given by King Charles II to his brother James, Duke of York and Albany. During the Revolutionary War, British General John Burgoyne's invasion from Canada targeted Albany, but his endeavor ended with a U.S. victory in Saratoga in late 1777. Albany maintained its prominence during the 1800s as an inland port on the Hudson River. The state capitol and the bells of city hall's tower recall Albany's history, as does the **Schuyler** (pronounced SKY-ler) **Mansion,** 32 Catherine St. (434-0834). Colonial businessman and general Philip Schuyler owned the elegant Georgian home, built in 1761. Here George Washington and Benjamin Franklin dined, the Medicis held court, Alexander Hamilton married Schuyler's daughter, and Gen. Burgoyne was "incarcerated" for several weeks after Saratoga. (Open Wed.-Sat. 10am-5pm, Sun. 1-5pm; Jan.-March Sat. 10am-5pm, Sun. 1-5pm. Free.)

Besides the Schuyler, Albany offers a rather limited menu of sight-seeing activity: you can certainly see it in a day. The most outstanding feature of the downtown area is the **Rockefeller Empire State Plaza,** State St., a $1.9 billion architectural marvel funded by those darn Medicis. The plaza houses the **New York State Museum** (474-5877; open daily 10am-5pm; free), and the **New York State Performing Arts Center** (473-3750). The museum's exhibits show the history and development of the state's different regions, including Manhattan; displays range from Native

American arrowheads to an original set for "Sesame Street." For a bird's-eye view of Albany, visit the observation deck on the 44th floor of the tallest skyscraper in the plaza. (Open Mon.-Fri. 9am-4pm.)

The modern plaza provides a striking contrast to the more traditional architectural landscape of the rest of the city. Within walking distance on Washington Ave. are **City Hall,** an earthy Romanesque edifice deisgned by H.H. Richardson; and the **capitol building** (also worked on by Richardson), a Gothic marvel. Long live the Medici!

Today, without the patronage of this powerful Italian family, most accommodations in Albany are expensive—even motels tend to be pricey. The **State University of New York** dorms (442-5902) require a bus ride to the Western Ave. campus. Standard dorm rooms include standard linen. (Open Mon.-Fri. 9am-10pm. Singles $30. Doubles $40. Rooms available June-Aug. only.) Another option is the friendly **Fort Crailo Motel,** 110 Columbia Turnpike, Rensselaer 12144 (472-1360), in a safe area 1½ mi. from downtown near the Amtrak station. (Singles $32. Doubles $40. Weekends: singles $35, doubles $42.) The closest YMCA, 13 State St. (374-9136), and YWCA, 44 Washington Ave. (374-3394), are both in Schenectady. (Singles $20-22.50.)

Food, save for a few hot dog vendors, has fled the downtown area. **Next Door,** 142 Washington St., has good-sized sandwiches (around $4) and great chocolate chip cookies (75¢). So much for the tradition of fine Italian cuisine.

The **Albany Convention and Visitors Bureau,** 25 Quackenbush Sq. (434-5132), has maps and brochures of the city and runs daily walking tours and trolley tours ($4). Ask for the special Medici Madness tour. (Open daily 10am-4pm; Nov.-Dec. Mon.-Sat. 10am-4pm; Jan.-April Mon.-Fri. 10am-4pm.)

Albany's best features may be the convenient transportation terminals by which you leave the city. **Amtrak,** East St., Rensselaer (465-9971 or 800-872-7245), across the Hudson from downtown Albany, runs to New York City (7-9 per day, 2½ hr., $37). (Station open daily 10:30am-midnight.) **Greyhound,** 34 Hamilton St. (434-0121), also offers service to New York City (9 per day, 3 hr., $27). (Station open 24 hr.) **Trailways,** 1 block away at 360 Broadway (436-9651), connects to points in the Adirondacks. Buses flee to: Lake George (6 per day, in winter 3 per day, 1 hr., $9); Lake Placid (6 per day, in winter 3 per day, 4 hr., $20.50); and Tupper Lake (1 per day, 4 hr., $24.75). (Open Mon.-Fri. 5:30am-11pm, Sat.-Sun. 7:30am-11pm.) For local travel, the **Capitol District Transit Authority (CDTA)** (482-8822) serves Albany, Troy, and Schenectady. CDTA has a confusing schedule and often patchy coverage; a quick call to the main office will set you straight. (Fare 75¢.)

Albany's **ZIP code** is 12201; the **area code** is 518.

Catskills

In 1820, New York City author and historian Washington Irving recounted the seductive and soothing qualities of the Catskills in the tale of *Rip Van Winkle.* In the story, Rip joins the mountain party of a group of gnomes and falls asleep for 20 years. These lovely mountains continue to captivate city-dwellers, who migrate up the highways of the Hudson and Mohawk River Valleys in search of unpolluted air and the tranquility of the dense hemlock forests. Beyond the lakeside resorts, visitors can find peace and natural beauty in the state-managed Catskill Preserve, home to quiet villages, sparkling streams, and miles of hiking and skiing trails.

Trailways provides excellent service through the Catskills. The two main stops are in **Kingston,** at 400 Washington Ave. (914-331-0744), and **Oneonta,** at 47 Market St. (607-432-2661). Fare to New York City costs $31.75. Other stops in the area include Woodstock, Pine Hill, Saugerties, and Hunter; each connects with New York City, Albany, and Utica. Road conditions are consistently good.

Catskill Preserve

The 250,000-acre, state-run Catskill Preserve is the area's real attraction. The **Esopus River,** just to the west, is great for trout fishing and for late-summer inner-tubing in the **Phoenicia** area. Rent tubes at **The Town Tinker,** on Bridge St. (914-668-5553), in Phoenicia. (Inner tubes $7 per day with a seat $10; driver's licence or $15 required as a deposit. Transportation $3. Life jackets available. Open May-Sept. daily 9am-6pm.) Throughout the preserve, hundreds of trails lead to lovely mountain brooks, hidden lakes, deep forests, and Darkman's summer retreat. Hikes range from half-day jaunts to the top of a mountain to longer backpack trips traversing the entire region. Some trails crowd in summer, especially those in the eastern section of the park. To camp in the backcountry for more than three days, you must obtain a permit from the nearest ranger station (518-255-5453). Trails are maintained year-round; available lean-tos are sometimes dilapidated and crowded. Boil or treat water with chemicals, and pack your garbage. To reach the head of your chosen trail, take a Trailways bus from Kingston—drivers will let you out anywhere along the park's main routes. (Call 914-331-0744 for information on routes and fares.) For more information, pick up Bennet and Maisa's *Walks in the Catskills* or the American Geographical Society's *The New York Walk Book.*

One of the many well-run **state campgrounds** (800-456-2267) can serve as a base for your hiking, fishing, or tubing adventures. Reservations are vital during the summer, especially Thursday to Sunday. (Sites $10-13. Open May-Sept.) Try one of the following: **North Lake,** Rte. 23A (518-589-5058), 3 mi. northeast of Haines Falls; **Devil's Tombstone,** Rte. 214 (518-688-7160), 3 mi. south of Hunter; **Woodland Valley** (914-688-7647), 5 mi. southwest of Phoenicia; **Kenneth L. Wilson** (914-679-7020), 5 mi. east of Mt. Tremper off Rte. 28; **Little Pond** (914-439-5480), 14 mi. northwest of Livingston Manor off Rte. 17; **Beaverkill** (914-439-4281), 7 mi. northwest of Livingston Manor; **Mongaup Pond** (914-439-4233), 10 mi. northeast of Livingston Manor off Rte. 17, exit 96; or **Bear Spring Mountain,** (607-652-7364), 5 mi. southeast of Walton, off Rte. 206. For brochures and information contact the State Dept. of Environmental Conservation, Rm. 111, 50 Wolf Rd., Albany 12233 (518-457-3521).

Adirondacks

The Adirondacks, New York's last bastion of backwoods wilderness, are the largest natural preserve in the East. Though large portions of the mountain forests remain undeveloped, pollution from urban areas far to the south has victimized the Adirondacks' trees, lakes, and wildlife. More than 200 lakes in the area have stagnanted, while acid rain has left its mark on many tree and fish populations, especially in the fragile high-altitude environments. But despite these warning signs, much of the Adirondacks retains the beauty it had over a century ago.

Of the six million acres in the Adirondacks Park, 40% is fully open to the public. Two thousand mi. of hiking and skiing trails criss-cross the forest and mountain scenery. An interlocking network of lakes and streams makes the gentle Adirondack wilds a perennial favorite of canoeists. Mountain-climbers may wish to tackle **Mt. Marcy,** the state's highest peak (5344 ft.), at the base of the Adirondacks.

The Adirondacks are famous for sports resorts and encompass a dozen well-known alpine ski centers. **Lake Placid** has twice hosted the winter Olympics and frequently welcomes national sports competitions (see Lake Placid below). **Saranac Lake** is another center for winter activity, including the **International Dog Sledding Championship** at the end of January. **Tupper Lake** and **Lake George** also have celebrations every January and February. Snow-covered hiking trails are great for snowshoeing, and plenty of cross-country ski trails wind through forest preserves and state parks.

The Adirondacks have extra appeal for the budget traveler, since cheap accommodations pontiferate. Lake Placid and nearby towns host many inexpensive hotels and campgrounds (see Lake Placid below). The region's youth hostel is located in the basement of **St. James Episcopal Church Hall,** P.O. Box 176, Lake George (668-2634), on Montcalm St. at Ottawa, several blocks from the lake. From the bus terminal, walk south 1 block to Montcalm, turn right and go 1 block to Ottawa for the slightly musty bunkroom with a decent kitchen. (Check-in 5-9pm, later only with reservations. Curfew 10pm. $8. Open May 27-Sept. 2.) In addition to being an excellent resource for hikers and campers, the **Adirondack Mountain Club (ADK),** RR 3, P.O. Box 3055, Lake George 12845 (668-4447), runs two lodges near Lake Placid. Another office is on Adirondack Loj Rd., P.O. Box 867, Lake Placid 12946 (523-3441) near the **Adirondack Loj,** 8 mi. east of Lake Placid off Rte. 73. This beautiful log cabin right on Heart Lake has comfortable bunk facilities and a family atmosphere. Guests can swim, fish, canoe, and use rowboats free of charge. In winter, explore the wilderness trails on rented snowshoes ($6 per day) or cross-country skis ($10 per day). (B&B $25, with dinner $36. Linen included. Campsites $9. Lean-tos $13.) Call ahead for weekends and during peak holiday seasons. Take about 20% off for non-peak rates. For an even better mix of rustic comfort and wilderness experience, hike 3½ mi. from the closest trailhead to the **Johns Brook Lodge,** in Keene Valley 16 mi. southeast of Lake Placid off Rte. 73 (call the Adirondack Loj for reservations). From Placid, follow Rte. 73 15 mi. through Keene to Keene Valley, turning right at the Ausable Inn. The hike is only slightly uphill, and the food is well worth the exertion; the staff packs in groceries every day and cooks on a gas stove. A great place to meet friendly New Yorkers, John's Brook is no secret with the beds filling completely on weekends. Make reservations at least one day in advance for dinner, longer for a weekend. Bring sheets or a sleeping bag. (B&B $25, with dinner $36. Slightly less off-peak. Lean-tos $7. Open May 27-Oct. 14.) In summer, rent a bunk for $10 with full access to the kitchen. If ADK facilities are too pricey, try the **High Peaks Base Camp,** P.O. Box 91, Upper Jay 12987 (946-2133), a charming restaurant/lodge/campground just a 20 minute drive from Lake Placid. Take 86N to Wilmington, turn right at the Mobil station, then go right 3½ mi. on Springfield Rd. $15 buys you a bed for the night and a huge breakfast. (Check-in until 11pm, later with reservations. Sites $3 per person. Cabins $30 for 4 people.) Transportation is tough without a car but sometimes rides can be arranged from Keene; call ahead.

In the forest, you can use the free shelters by the trails. Always inquire about their location before you plan a hike. Camp for free in the backcountry anywhere on public land, as long as you are at least 150 ft. away from a trail, road, water source, or campground and stay below 4000 ft. altitude.

The Adirondacks are served best by **Adirondacks Trailways,** with frequent stops along I-87. You can take a bus to Lake Placid, Tupper Lake, and Lake George from Albany. From the Lake George bus stop, at the Mobil station, 320 Canada St. (668-9511; 800-225-6815 for bus information), buses reach Lake Placid ($11.75), Albany ($8.75), and New York City ($33.70). (Open Sun.-Thurs. 7am-10pm, Fri.-Sat. 7am-midnight.) Traveling in the backwoods is tough during the muddy spring thaw (March-April).

Contact the State Office of Parks and Recreation (see New York Practical Information) in Albany for information on the Adirondacks. The best information on hiking and other outdoor activities emanates from the **ADK** (see above). For trails in the Lake Placid area, look for ADK's particularly good *Guide to the High Peaks.*

The Adirondacks' **area code** is 518.

Lake Placid

Melvil Dewey, creator of the Dewey Decimal library classification system and founder of the exclusive Lake Placid Club, first promoted Lake Placid as a summer resort in 1850. The Winter Olympic Games, held here in 1932 and 1980, cemented the town's fame. Currently the Adirondacks' premier tourist spot, Lake Placid attracts crowds of casual visitors and world-class athletes. The international flags and stores that fill Main Street don't inhibit the inviting, old-village atmosphere or the sporting facilities unmatched in the U.S. Temperatures can plummet to -40°F and more than 200 in. of snow may fall in any given Adirondack winter, but well-plowed main roads keep the region open. Ice fishing on the lakes is popular, especially with locals, as is ice skating (Olympic speed-skating rink $2; open daily 7-9pm, Mon.-Fri. noon-2pm weather permitting).

The old Olympic spirit clearly makes its presence felt in Lake Placid—and just out of town on Rte. 73 is the self-descriptive **Olympic Site.** The **Olympic Regional Development Authority,** Olympic Center (523-1655 or 800-462-6236), operates the facilities. You can't miss the 70 and 90m runs of the **Olympic Jumping Complex** looming above the alpine landscape. The $5 admission fee includes a chairlift and elevator ride to the top of the spectator towers. You might also catch summer jumpers flipping and diving into a swimming pool in the **Kodak Sports Park** next door to the Olympic Jumps. (Open daily 9am-5pm, Oct.-May 9am-4pm.) Three mi. farther along Rte. 73, the **Olympic Sports Complex** at Mt. Van Hoevenberg offers a summer trolley running to the top of the bobsled run ($3). In the winter (open Dec.-March Tues.-Sun. 1-3pm) you can bobsled down the run used in the Olympics for $20. The park is open for self-guided tours daily from 9am to 4pm, and has 35 mi. of well-groomed cross-country ski trails ($6).

In addition to its fantastic ski slopes, **Whiteface Mountain,** near Lake Placid, provides a panoramic view of the Adirondacks. You can get up to the summit via the **Whiteface Memorial Highway** ($4 toll, cars only) or a chairlift ($4, seniors and children $3). The extensive **Whiteface Mountain Ski Center** (946-2223) has the largest vertical drop in the East (3216 ft.). Don't bother with the $4 tour of the waterfalls at **High Falls Gorge** (946-2278) on Rte. 86 near Whiteface; hike below the road to see the same scenery for free. All of the Olympic attractions, Whiteface car toll and chairlift, and this showroom of wonderful prizes, can be purchased as a $42 package.

History buffs and corpse cultivators will enjoy a quick visit to the **farm and grave** of abolitionist John Brown, off Rte. 73, 3 mi. southeast of Lake Placid (523-3900; open May to mid-Oct. Wed.-Sat. 10am-5pm, Sun. 1-5pm; free). The west branch of the **Ausable River,** just east of the town of Lake Placid, lures anglers to its shores. **Fishing licenses** for five days are $15.50 (season $27.50) at Town Hall, 301 Main St. (523-2162), or Jones Outfitters, 37 Main St. (523-3468). Call the "Fishing Hotline" at 518-891-5413 for an in-depth fresh-water recording of the hot fishing spots and current conditions. The **Lake Placid Center for the Arts,** on Saranac Ave. at Farm Ridge (523-2512), hosts a local art gallery and theater, dance, and musical performances. (Open daily 1-5pm; winter Mon.-Fri. 1-5pm. Free.)

For spring and fall breakfasts, try the **Hilton Hotel,** 1 Mirror Lake Dr. (523-4411), right at the beginning of Main St. At the Hilton's lunch buffet (noon-2:30pm), $4.75 buys a sandwich and all-you-can-eat soup and salad. **The Cottage,** 5 Mirror Lake Dr. (523-9845), has relatively inexpensive meals (sandwiches and salads $4-6) with views of the lake and many, many athletes. (Lunch served daily 11:30am-3:30pm. Bar open noon-1am). **Mud Puddles,** 3 School St. (523-4446), below the speed skating rink, is popular with disco throwbacks and the pop music crowd. (Open Wed.-Sun. 9pm-3am. Cover $1.50.)

Most accommodations in the area are expensive. The **St. Moritz Hotel,** 31 Saranac Ave. (523-9240), off the northern end of Main St. past the Hilton Hotel, has excellent rooms with private baths. (Sun.-Thurs. $35, Fri.-Sat. $50. Breakfast included.) **Lyseck's Inn,** 50 Hillcrest Ave. (523-1700), rents beds for $20.50 from June to early September. Call ahead since the place fills up quickly with young athletes. (From Main St. go up the hill on Marcy St. next to Sundog Sport and turn left on Hillcrest.) The High Peaks Base Camp, Adirondack Loj, and Johns Brook Lodge (see Adirondacks above) are all within several miles of Lake Placid. Campers have many options, including backcountry camping (free), the Adirondack Loj's campgrounds, and the numerous developed state sites near Lake Placid and Saranac Lake. The closest one, **Meadowbrook State Park** (891-4351), lies 5 mi. west of Lake Placid on Rte. 86 in Raybrook. (Sites $10, additional nights $8.50. Open mid-April to mid-Oct.)

To explore Lake Placid by bike, rent 10-speeds at **Sundog Ski & Sport,** 90 Main St. (523-2752; $3 per hr., $14 per day). The shop also rents cross-country skis ($10 per day) and downhill skis ($14 per day). (Open daily 9am-7pm. Must have ID.) The **State Tourist Office,** 90 Main St. (523-2412), hands out brochures on the area and the entire state. (Open June 15-Oct. 15 and Dec. 15-April 15 daily 9am-5pm; off-season Mon.-Fri. 9am-5pm.) Browse the local outdoors shops for hiking and canoe guides to the Adirondacks. The **Lake Placid Convention and Visitors Bureau,** Olympic Center (523-2445), has the scoop on the city. (Open Mon.-Sat. 8am-8pm, Sun. 9am-4pm.)

Trailways has extensive service in the Adirondacks, stopping at the **326 Main St. Deli** in Lake Placid (523-1527; 523-4309 for bus information). Buses run to New York City ($45.50) and Lake George ($11.75). By car, Lake Placid is at the intersection of Rte. 86 and 73.

For **weather** information call 792-1050. Even Lake Placid has a **post office,** 201 Main St. (523-3071; open Mon.-Fri. 9am-5pm, Sat. 9:30am-noon). Lake Placid's **ZIP code** is 12946; the **area code** is 518.

Ithaca and the Finger Lakes

Folks who live around the Finger Lakes wonder about the lure of Niagara Falls up north; without the heart-shaped tubs and overpriced food of the falls, these slender waterways neither literally nor figuratively roar for attention, resulting in far fewer tourists. Their absence makes spending time here sublime.

Broken up by gentle hills, the Finger Lakes—Canandaigua, Keuka, Seneca, Cayuga, Owasco, and Skaneateles, among others—are steeped in Iroquois lore. According to legend, the Great Spirit laid his hands upon the earth, and the impression of his fingers made lakes. A more contemporary geological explanation attributes the lakes' shapes to the expansion of ice sheets in pre-existing valleys during the glacial age. Nature doesn't loosen its grip even in Ithaca, where constructed bridges span deep river gorges and Ivy-League Cornell University perches on the hills above.

Practical Information

Ithaca Police: 272-3245. **Tomkpins County Sheriff:** 272-2444.

Visitor Information: Ithaca/Tompkins County Convention and Visitors Bureau, 904 E. Shore Dr., Ithaca 14850 (272-1313 or 800-284-8422). By car take Rte. 13 north of the city, exit at Stewart Park and follow the signs. From the bus station turn left on State St., then walk left on Cayuga all the way to E. Shore (about 30 min. on foot). Tremendous number of brochures on Ithaca, Finger Lakes, and every other county in upstate New York. Hotel and B&B listings. Best map of the area ($2.25). Open Mon.-Fri. 9am-5pm, Sat.-Sun. 10am-4pm; Sept. 2-May 27 Mon.-Fri. 9am-5pm. **Cornell University Information and Referral Center,** Day Hall (255-6200). Good campus maps and extensive information on the entire area, including hotels and B&Bs. Free 80-min. tours Mon.-Fri. at 8:30am, noon, 1:15pm, and 3pm, Sat. at 8:30am and noon, Sun. at 1:15pm. Open Mon.-Sat. 8am-5pm. **Finger Lakes State Park Region,** RD 3, Trumansburg 14886 (607-387-7041). Information on state parks and a free *Finger Lakes Bicycle Touring Guide.*

Bus Station: Ithaca Bus Terminal, W. State and N. Fulton St. (272-7390) for **Short Line** and **Greyhound.** To: New York City (8 per day, 5 hr., $47); Philadelphia (3 per day, 6 hr., $48); Niagara Falls (5 per day, 4½ hr., $40). Open daily 7:30am-6:30pm.

Public Transport: Ithaca Transit, 273-7348. Bus service to Cornell University, Ithaca College, Stewart Park, and Buttermilk Falls. Operates Mon.-Sat. 6am-6pm. Fare 50¢. Transfer valid for 1 hr. **Cornell University Transit,** 255-6200. Bus service around Cornell. Operates June-Aug. daily 6:45am-6:15pm, Sept.-May 6:15am-midnight. Fare 35¢. Free after 6:15pm. **Tomtran (Tompkins County Transportation Services Project)** 274-5370. Covers a wider area than Ithaca Transit, including Trumansburg and Ulysses, both northwest of Ithaca on Rte. 96, and Cayuga Heights and Lansing Village, both due north of Ithaca on Rte. 13. Best bet for getting out to the Finger Lakes. Buses stop at Ithaca Commons, westbound on Seneca St., and eastbound on Green. Fare 60¢.

Bike Rental: Black Star Bicycles, 1922 Dryden Rd. (347-4117), 7 mi. out of town on Rte. 13. $10 per day, $20 for 3 days. Take Ithaca Transit's Dryden Bus. Open Tues.-Fri. 10am-6pm, Sat. 10am-5pm. **Pedal Away Bike Shop,** 632 W. Buffalo St. (272-5425). More convenient to Ithaca.

Post Office, 213 N. Tioga St. (272-5454), at E. Buffalo. Open Mon.-Fri. 8:30am-5pm, Sat. 8:30am-noon. **ZIP code:** 14850.

Area code: 607.

Sixty mi. southwest of Syracuse on I-81 and Rte. 13, and 220 mi. northwest of New York City, Ithaca sits at the south end of Cayuga Lake, the longest of the Finger Lakes. Once you get to the town, you may notice two Ithacas: the flat downtown area by the lake, and the hilly Cornell campus. Then again, you may not. **Collegetown** is a small neighborhood of restaurants and bars just south of campus. **Trumansburg** primps 10-12 mi. north of Ithaca on Rte. 96.

Accommodations and Camping

If you want to sleep between sheets rather than beneath the stars, plan on sticking to the city. Cornell Information and the Ithaca Visitors Bureau (see Practical Information above) both have full B&B listings.

Podunk House Hostel (AYH), Podunk Rd. (387-9277), in Trumansburg about 8 mi. northwest of Ithaca. By car take Rte. 96 north through Jacksonville, turn left on Cold Springs Rd. following signs for Podunk ski area until it ends at Podunk, turn left again and the hostel is 20 ft. away on your right. Greyhound has a Cold Springs flag stop. Beds in the loft of a homestead barn run by extremely friendly and helpful owner. Bathroom plagued by rusty pipes and smelly water. No kitchen. Members only, $5. Open April-Oct. Call ahead.

Elmshade Guest House, 402 S. Albany St. (273-1707), at Center St. 3 blocks from the Ithaca Commons. Perfectly clean, well-decorated, good-sized rooms with shared bath. TV in every room, refrigerator and microwave on hall. Singles $25. Doubles $35. Morning coffee, rolls, and juice included.

Hillside Inn, 518 Stewart Ave. (273-6864). Excellent rooms convenient to Cornell and downtown Ithaca. TV and A/C. Singles with private bath $30. Doubles $35, with private bath $38. Book ahead for singles and on weekends.

Historic Cook House, 167 Main St., Newfield (564-9926). Doubles in a renovated country mansion (or big house, anyway). Classic antique beds in perfect condition, huge sitting room, full country breakfast. Rooms $55, with private bath $65.

Camping options in this area are virtually endless. Fifteen of the 20 state parks in the Finger Lakes region have campsites, nine have cabins. The brochure *Finger Lakes State Parks* contains a description of the park location, services, and environs; pick it up from any tourist office, park, or the Finger Lakes State Park Region (see above). Whatever your plans, reserve ahead. The four-wheel-drive trucks and Winnebagos are rolling in to steal your spot even as you read. Summer weekends almost always fill up.

Buttermilk Falls State Park (273-5761), on Rte. 13 just south of Ithaca, beckons with 10 ulcer-soothing waterfalls and 2 glens. Pinnacle Rock (see below) towers over the stream in the center. (Sites $12. Open May-Oct.) **Robert H. Treman State Park** (273-3440), is on Rte. 13 2 mi. south of Ithaca. Take Rte. 13 south and turn right on Rte. 387. Picnic areas, playgrounds, and a stream-fed pool with waterfalls dapple the park's 1025 acres. (Sites $11.50, with electricity $13.50. Additional night $10.) Try also **Taughannock State Park** (387-6739), on Rte. 89 in Trumansburg 8 mi. north of Ithaca. The closest public transport goes down Rte. 96; ask to get off at Park Rd., walk 20 minutes and follow the signs. By car take Rte. 89 from Ithaca. (Sites $12, with hookup $14. Cabins $22.50 per night, $90 per week. Cabins 2-day min. stay, Memorial Day-Labor Day one-week min.)

Food and Nightlife

Though not terribly diverse, the region's food is high in quality. Ithaca, largely because of the university, basks in bagels and bohemian fare.

Moosewood Restaurant, Seneca and Cayuga St., Ithaca. Creative and well-prepared vegetarian, fish, and pasta dishes. One of the original owners wrote the *Moosewood Cookbook*. Try the soporific gazpacho ($2). Lunches $3-4.50, dinners around $8. Open Mon.-Sat. 11:30am-2pm and 6-9pm.

Heart's Content, 156 State St., on the Ithaca Commons. Eat in the tiny deli bakery or head to the pedestrian mall outside. Try the sandwiches ($2.50-5) and desserts (cheesecake brownie 95¢). More substantial entrees sold by weight. Open Mon.-Wed. and Sat. 7:30am-7pm, Thurs.-Fri. 7:30am-7:30pm, Sun. 10am-4pm.

Alladin's Natural Eatery, 100 Dryden Rd., in Collegetown by Cornell campus. Excellent vegetarian and pita sandwiches ($3.50) in modern split-level abode. Open Mon.-Sat. 11am-11pm, Sun. noon-11pm.

Collegetown Bagels, 413 College Ave. in Collegetown, and 201 N. Aurora St. at Seneca downtown. Collegey bagel sandwiches ($2-2.50), a huge collegiate salad bar ($3.50 per pound), natural college foods, and sophomoric cola in the original 6½-oz. bottle (45¢). Open daily 7am-2am.

Rangovian Embassy, Rte. 96 (387-3334), in the main strip of Trumansburg shops about 10 mi. out of Ithaca. Well worth the drive. Amazing neopolitical Mexican entrees in a classic, bohemian-style restaurant/bar. Huge stack of fresh blueberry pancakes $3.50. Dinners about $8. Mug of beer $1-1.50. Live bands on weekends. Food served Tues.-Sat. 11:30am-3pm and 5-9pm. Sun. 11:30am-3pm and 4-9pm.

The Store at Truman's Village, on Rte. 96 in Trumansburg just up the street from the Embassy. Great local diner offering a taste of upstate country life and good burgers ($1.50). Breakfast served all day (pancakes $2.25). Open Mon.-Fri. 7am-9pm, Sat.-Sun. 8am-5pm.

After dark, Collegetown hops highest, though you may also want to try one of the many roadside saloons on Rte. 96, 13, and 89. **The Nine's,** 311 College Ave. (272-1888), features live bands, beer (pitchers $4.29-5.99), and pizza (small $7.19). Softball teams feel especially at home here. (Open Mon.-Sat. 11:30am-1am, Sun. 3:30pm-1am. Cover $3-4.) **The Haunt,** 114 W. Green St. (273-3355), diagonally across from Woolworth's near S. Geneva St. downtown, plays Motown, funk, and classic rock music. (Live bands most nights. Open daily 8pm-1:30am.)

Sights

Within a 10-mi. radius of Ithaca plunge 150 waterfalls and many paths, bridges, and gardens all offering spectacular views. In **Buttermilk Falls State Park** (see Accommodations and Camping above), the cataracts descend more than 500 ft. and end in a clear pool. Within the park, **Pinnacle Rock** towers 40 ft. above the water. The same bus that runs south to Buttermilk Falls also runs north to **Stewart Park** (272-8535), with a playground, picnic area, tennis courts, a restored carousel, and swimming in Lake Cayuga. A bike trail runs from the Ithaca Commons to Stewart Park.

A steep uphill climb from town, **Cornell University** perches on the hills of Ithaca. Even those passing through without enough time for the tours leaving from Day Hall (see Practical Information above) should try to climb the **McGraw Tower,** with 161 steps, a view of the entire valley, and the oldest, largest chime on a college campus. Student and faculty "chimesmasters" play three free half-hour concerts each day (at 8am, 1:10pm, and 6pm) during the academic year and two (at 12:45 and 6:45pm) in the summer. The tower opens for visitors a half-hour before each performance. The **Herbert F. Johnson Museum of Art** (255-6464), on the corner of Central and University Ave., displays Asian and graphic art, as well as 19th- and 20th-century paintings. Designed by omnipresent I.M. Pei, the oddly shaped building is known as "the sewing machine." (Open Tues.-Sun. 10am-5pm. Free.)

In the Lakes region, a car provides the easiest transportation, but biking and hiking allow closer contact with this beautiful country. Reach out and touch the **Finger**

Lakes State Park Region (see practical information above) for free maps and tips. You might also want to examine the booklet *20 Bicycle Tours in the Finger Lakes* ($7), prepared by Backcountry Publications, P.O. Box 175, Woodstock, VT 15091. Also try the *Finger Lakes Bicycle Touring Map* (see Practical Information above).

Write the **Finger Lakes Trail Conference**, P.O. Box 18048, Rochester 14618 (716-288-7191), for free maps of the **Finger Lakes Trail**, an east-west footpath from the Catskills westward to the Allegheny Mountains. This 350-mi. trail and its 300 mi. of branch trails link several state parks, most with camping facilities. **Taughannock Falls** in the state park of the same name prove a spectacular sight, with water cascading from a height of 215 ft. Walk about 1 mi. along the ravine leading from Cayuga Lake to the falls, where a powerful flow has cut through the solid cliffs over the course of 9000 years.

The fertile soil of the Finger Lakes area makes the region the heart of New York's wine industry. Wine tasting and touring one of the small local vineyards is a relaxing way to pass a day. All of the vineyards on the Cayuga Wine Trail offer free tastings, though some require purchase of a glass ($1.50-2). **Americana Vineyards,** East Covert Rd., Interlaken (607-387-6801), ferments a mile or so from Trumansburg, accessible by Greyhound (272-7930) and Tomtran (274-5370). A family of four operates this winery from grape-picking to bottle-corking; one will give you a personal tour and free tasting. (Open Mon.-Sat. 10am-5:30pm, Sun. noon-5:30pm; Jan.-April weekends only.) Pick up a bottle for about $5. Driving, take Rte. 96 or 89 north of Trumansburg to E. Covert Rd. Just down the road is **Lucas Winery,** 150 County Rd. (607-532-4825; open May-late Oct. Mon.-Sat. 11am-5pm, Sun. noon-5pm; Nov. 3-Dec. 9 weekends only). On the eastern side of Seneca Lake, visit **Wagner Winery,** Rte. 414 (607-582-6450), in Lodi. Far bigger than any of the Cayuga wineries, bottling some 60,000 gallons per year, Wagner rests on a beautiful picnickable spot on Seneca Lake. From Ithaca take Rte. 79 west to 414 south (8 or 9 mi.). Tastes and tours are free. (Opem Mon.-Fri. 10am-4:30pm, Sat.-Sun. 10am-5pm.)

Considered the birthplace of the women's rights movement, **Seneca Falls** held the 1848 Seneca Falls Convention. Elizabeth Cady Stanton and Amelia Bloomer, two leading suffragists who lived here, organized a meeting of those seeking the vote for white women. Visit the **National Women's Hall of Fame**, 76 Fall St. (315-568-8060), where photographs and biographies commemorate 38 outstanding U.S. women. (Open Mon.-Sat. 10am-4pm, Sun. 1-5pm. Admission $3, seniors $2, under 12 free).

Niagara Falls and Buffalo

Lois Lane's discovery of Clark Kent's secret identity at Niagara Falls fortified this area's longstanding reputation for romance and danger. Following in the barrel of Annie Taylor, the first to go successfully over the falls in 1901, countless capeless crusaders came to Niagara for adventure until the outlawing of such stunts 60 years later. Nowadays most newlyweds, like the Man of Steel himself, come to the "Honeymoon Capital of the World" more for the water beds than the waterfalls. Yet Niagara's most successful marriage matches the modern tourist industry with the awesome ageless natural force of the falls. As a result, not only can the falls' 70,000 gallons of water per second power the largest hydroelectric plant in the U.S., but technology can actually increase the flow of water during peak tourist season and could even halt it completely.

Practical Information

Emergency: 911.

Visitor Information: Niagara Falls Convention and Visitors Bureau, 345 3rd St. (285-2400), next to the city bus station. Pick up the free *Niagara USA,* with a good map of the Niagara area, and helpful practical information. Open May-Sept. daily 8:30am-8:30pm; Oct.-April Mon.-Fri. 9am-5pm. Another **information center** (284-2000) for the city adjoins the bus station on 4th and Niagara. Open June-Oct. daily 8:30am-8:30pm; Nov.-March Mon.-Fri. 9am-5pm; April-May Mon.-Thurs. 9am-5pm, Fri.-Sat. 9am-6pm. The state runs a **Niagara Reservation Visitors Center** (278-1796) right in front of the falls' observation deck. Open daily 8:30am-10pm. **Buffalo Area Chamber of Commerce,** 107 Delaware Ave., Buffalo (852-7100), next to City Hall on the 2nd floor of the Statler Tower. Pick up the free *Official Visitor's Guide to Buffalo,* which describes attractions and services in Buffalo and provides an adequate map of the downtown area. Open Mon.-Fri. 8:30am-5pm.

Amtrak: 55 Dick Rd., Niagara Falls (683-8440 or 800-872-7245), 2 mi. down Lockport St. Dangerous at night. Also in Buffalo, at 75 Exchange St. (856-2075). Ticket offices open 24 hr. To: New York City ($76), Chicago ($84), and Boston ($82).

Greyhound/Trailways: Niagara Falls Bus Terminal, 4th St. and Niagara St. (285-9391; open Mon.-Fri. 8am-4:30pm) and the **Buffalo Transportation Center,** 181 Ellicott St. (855-7211; open daily 3am-1am). All buses leave from Buffalo Transportation Center. To: New York City (8 per day, 8 hr. $67, Fri.-Sun. $71); Boston (4 per day, 12 hr., $75, Fri.-Sun. $79); Chicago (4 per day, 12 hr., $94).

Public Transport: Niagara Frontier Metro Transit System. Provides local city transit. Bus #40 (17 per day, 45 min., $1.75) connects the Greyhound/Trailways terminals in Niagara and Buffalo. **Niagara Scenic Bus Lines,** 800-672-3642. Service from Niagara Falls bus terminal to Niagara, Canada ($1.25), and Buffalo Airport ($8).

Taxi: Rainbow Taxicab, 285-2882; **United Cab,** 285-9331.

Post Office: *Niagara Falls,* 615 Main St. (285-7561), in Niagara Falls, NY. Open Mon.-Fri. 8:30am-5pm, Sat. 9am-noon. **ZIP code:** 14302. **Buffalo,** 1200 William St. (864-2434). Open Mon.-Fri. 8:30am-6pm, Sat. 8:30am-1pm. **ZIP code:** 14240.

Area Codes: 716 (New York), 416 (Ontario).

Niagara Falls, NY, faces the Canadian town of the same name across the Niagara River. The river runs north from Lake Erie to Lake Ontario. Buffalo lies 20 mi. south where the Niagara River leaves Lake Erie. The falls are 90 mi. from Rochester, and nearly 400 mi. from New York City.

Parking in the city is plentiful. Most lots near the falls charge $3, but you can park in an equivalent spot for less on streets bordering the park.

Accommodations and Camping

Niagara Falls International AYH-Hostel, 1101 Ferry Ave., Niagara Falls, NY 14301 (282-3700), a few blocks from the falls at 10th St. Convivial, international atmosphere. Excellent facilities, including kitchen and TV lounge. 44 beds. Travelers without cars given first priority and non-members turned away when space is short (and it usually is in the summer). Parking available. Bike rental $4 per day. Lockout 9:30am-5pm. Curfew 11:30pm. Lights out midnight. $10, non-members $13. Required sheet sacks $1. Reservations recommended. Closed Dec. 10-Jan. 2.

Niagara Falls International Hostel (CHA), 4699 Zimmerman Ave., Niagara Falls, Ont. L2E 3M7 (416-357-0770). A pleasant, brick Tudor building 2½ mi. from the falls, between Morrison and Queen St. off River Rd. near the train station. Kitchen, dining room, and lounge. 38 beds. Open 9-11am and 5pm-midnight. Curfew and lights out midnight. CDN$12.50, non-members CDN$16.50. 50¢ returned for morning chore. Linen $1.

All Tucked Inn, 574 3rd St., between Walnut and Main St., Niagara Falls, NY (282-0919), downtown. Clean, freshly painted rooms. Doubles with shared bath $28-48, $10 more on holiday weekends. Continental breakfast included.

Niagara Falls Motel and Campsite, 2405 Niagara Falls Blvd., Wheatfield, NY 14304 (731-3434), 7 mi. from downtown. Follow Rte. 62 south of I-90 until it becomes Niagara Falls Blvd. Nice-sized doubles with A/C, color TV, and private bath $36-44. Sites $14, with hookup $16.

Food

Most sightseers ogle the falls then split; only a truly entranced few make stops that require a meal or two, and the fare they prefer is of the quick variety. So before the fast food in the **Rainbow Centre** (shops open Mon.-Sat. 10am-9pm, Sun. noon-5pm) gives you the heebie-jeebies, head to the downtown taverns where the locals eat and drink. The **Arterial Restaurant,** for example, at 314 Niagara St. near 4th, serves good burgers ($1.50) and chicken wings (12 for $2.75) as well as "all legal beverages." (Open Mon.-Thurs. 11:30am-2:30am, Fri.-Sat. 11:30am-3:30am, Sun. noon-2:30am.)

Buffalo's greatest contribution to contemporary cuisine is the "Buffalo-style" spicy chicken wing. Spread your wings where they originated, at the **Anchor Bar,** 1047 Main St. (single portion $3.50; open daily 10:30am-2am), or at any area restaurant. Another local specialty, found on most menus, is "beef on a weck," a pile of thinly sliced roast beef on a caraway and salt roll. For fresh produce, try the **Broadway Market,** 999 Broadway.

Sights and Entertainment

The gardens by the U.S. falls constitute the nation's first national park, established in 1885. Even with the development aimed at tourists, vast stretches of green surround the falls. Couples and others can stomp around the foot of the falls a couple of ways. The **Caves of the Wind Tour** on Goat Island will outfit you with a yellow rain coat and take you there by elevator. (Open May 15-Oct 20. Admission $3.50, ages 5-11 $3, under 4 free.) A cheaper elevator ride (50¢) is at the **Observation Deck,** though the view is not as spectacular. From the deck, you can catch the **Maid of the Mist Tour** (284-8897), a boat ride to the foot of Horseshoe Falls. (Tours every 15 min. June 21-Sept.2 daily 9:15am-8pm; May-June 20 and Sept.2-late Oct. Mon.-Fri. 10am-5pm, Sat.-Sun. 10am-6pm. Tickets $6.25, ages 6-12 $3.15.)

Cart around the falls in the **View Mobile** (278-1717), a train that leaves every 15 minutes from five stops around the park (fare $2.50). And in the visitors center, check out **Niagara Wonders,** a spectacular, special effect-filled look at the Falls. (Shown on the hr. daily 11am-9pm. Admission $2, seniors $1.50, ages 6-12 $1.) Those who plan to hit all of the Falls sights should buy a **Master Pass,** available in the park visitors center. One pass provides admission to the observation tower, the Cave of the Wind, the theater and the geological museum, plus discounts on Maid of the Mist tours and free parking. (Pass $7, children $5.)

Away from the falls, browse through an impressive collection of regional Iroquois arts and crafts at **The Turtle,** 25 Rainbow Mall, Niagara Falls, NY (284-2427), between Winter Garden and the river. (Open May-Sept. daily 9am-6pm; Oct.-April Tues.-Fri. 9am-5pm, Sat.-Sun. noon-5pm. Admission $3, seniors $2.50, children and students $1.50.) **Schoellkopf's Geological Museum** (278-1780) depicts the birth of the falls with slide shows every half hour. (Open May 27-Sept. 2 daily 9:30am-7pm; Sept. 3-early Nov. 10am-5pm; mid-Nov. to May 26 Wed.-Sun. 10am-5pm.) If you haven't had enough water, the **Aquarium,** across the street at 701 Whirlpool St., has a dolphin show and a nice school of fish. (Open May 27-Sept. 2 daily 9am-7pm; off-season 9am-5pm. Admission $5.50, seniors and ages 5-14 $3.50.

Visitors can traverse the border between the U.S. and Canada by crossing the **Rainbow Bridge.** On the Ontario side, **Queen Victoria Park** provides a good view of the water. Niagara Falls, Ontario served as a birthplace and home for W.E.B. DuBois's 1905 "Niagara Movement," the forerunner of the National Association for the Advancement of Colored People (NAACP). Just minutes from the Falls, **Clifton Hill** (356-2299) has a multitude of gift shops, streetside cafés, and motels. "The Hill" is also home to Ripley's Believe It or Not Museum, The Guinness Museum of World Records, The Super Star Recording Studio, and many other pop-culture attractions. Believe it or not, each attraction charges its own admission (average CDN$5).

Buffalo, New York state's second largest city, offers high culture, streetside fun, and lots of jokes. The **Albright-Knox Art Gallery,** 1285 Elmwood Ave. (882-8700), enjoys a worldwide reputation as an outstanding center of contemporary art. Its extensive modern collection will please anyone interested in U.S. and European art of the past 30 years. In mid-June, catch the annual **Allentown Arts Festival** which takes place along Delaware and Elmwood Ave. and Allen St. The intersection of Elmwood and Allen is also the core of an active after-dark scene. Free noontime concerts take place at the plaza downtown. People-watchers will find a good vantage point by climbing to the top of **City Hall** (open Mon.-Fri. 9am-3:30pm, Sat. 9am-5pm). Winter activities such as tobogganing, skating, and skiing center at city and county parks. Pick up a list of parks at the chamber of commerce (see Practical Information above) or write to the Parks Department, Niagara Sq., Buffalo, NY 14202.

Thousand Island Seaway Region

The Thousand Island-St. Lawrence Seaway spans 100 mi. from the mouth of Lake Ontario to the first of the giant man-made locks of the St. Lawrence River. Some 1800 islands scatter throughout the waterway, traveled both by small pleasure-boats and huge ocean-bound freighters. Once known as the playground of millionaires, the beautiful Thousand Islands region now attracts fishers from all over North America, thanks to a plentiful stock of bass and muskellunge. The world's largest muskie (69 lb., 15 oz.) was caught here in the fall of 1957.

Any of the small towns strung along Rte. 12 along the river coast can serve as a good base for explorating the region. For $10 (ages 6-12 $5), **Uncle Sam Boat Tours** in **Clayton**, 604 Riverside Dr. (686-3511) or in the bigger, glitzier town of **Alexandria Bay** (800-253-9229) at any of the booths along James St., gives a good look at most of the islands and the plush estates that laze atop them. **Empire**, off James St. in Alexandria Bay (482-9511 or 800-542-2628) runs similar two-hour tours in triple-decker boats ($10). Look for the shortest international bridge in the world (about 10 ft.) connecting adjacent islands on either side of the U.S./Canadian border drawn through the seaway. Both tours highlight **Heart Island** and its famous Boldt Castle, stopping here before returning. George Boldt, former owner of New York City's elegant Waldorf Astoria Hotel financed this six-story replica of a Rhineland castle as a gift for his wife, who died before its completion. Though original plans called for 365 bedrooms, 52 bathrooms, and one power-house, Boldt abandoned the project in his grief. Today, its 120 rooms stand unfinished. (Open late May-Sept. Admission $3, ages 6-12 $1.75.)

When you're bogged down in Clayton on a cold or rainy day, visit the **Thousand Islands Shipway Museum**, 750 Mary St., the largest freshwater maritime museum in the eastern U.S. and Canada, and home of the oldest and largest antique boat show in North America. (Open mid-May to mid-Oct. daily 10am-5pm. Admission $4, seniors $3, students $2.) Also in Clayton are the **Thousand Islands Craft School and Textile Museum**, 314 John St., and **The Muskie Hall of Fame**, on Riverside Dr., next door to the Clayton Area Chamber of Commerce. Yes, they have a replica of the legendary muskie.

For those who prefer live seafood, the **Anchor Inn**, Broadway St. at Bay in Cape Vincent, serves muskie-sized entrees. Spaghetti with salad and bread costs $4.50, sandwiches $2-4. (Open April-Jan. daily 11am-10pm. Bar open until 1am.) For a closely related meal in Clayton try **The Golden Anchor Restaurant**, 428 Riverside Dr., right on the water. (Open Sun.-Thurs. 11:30am-9pm, Fri.-Sat. 11:30am-10pm.)

Cape Vincent, on the western edge of the seaway, keeps one of the prettiest youth hostels in the country. **Tibbetts Point Lighthouse Hostel (AYH)**, RR 1, P.O. Box 330 (315-654-3450), is a former Coast Guard station at the spot where Lake Ontario meets the St. Lawrence. Fall asleep to the sound of waves crashing against the rocks. Take Rte. 12E into town, turn left on Broadway, and follow the river until it ends. (Curfew 10:30pm. $7, nonmembers $10. Open May 15-Sept. 15.)

One of the area's many campgrounds, the **French Creek Marina** (686-3621), in the heart of Clayton, has a launch ramp, boat rentals, and many different family fishing packages. (Sites $10.) When you grow tired of fishing for families, head about 5 mi. from Clayton on Rte. 12 to several less expensive sites, including **Palmer's Court,** midway between Cape Vincent and Clayton (732-8574; sites $7).

Write the **Clayton Chamber of Commerce**, 403 Riverside Dr., Clayton 13624 (686-3771), for the *Clayton Vacation Guide* and the *Thousand Islands Seaway Re-*

gion Travel Guide. The **Alexandria Bay Chamber of Commerce** is on Market St. just off James St., Alexandria Bay 13607 (482-9531). Access the region by bus through **Greyhound,** 540 State St. in Watertown (788-8110). Hounds service New York City ($41.65), Syracuse ($11), and Albany ($27). From the same station, **Thousand Islands Bus Lines** runs to Alexandria Bay and Clayton weekdays at 2:45pm ($4); return trips leave at 8:30am.

Clayton and the Thousand Islands region are just two hours from Syracuse by way of I-81 north. For Welleslet Island, Alexandria Bay, and the eastern 500 islands, stay on I-81 until you reach Rte. 12E. For Clayton and points west, take exit 47 and follow Rte. 12 until you reach 12E.

The Clayton **post office** (686-3311) is at 236 John St. Clayton's **ZIP code** is 13624; the region's **area code** is 315.

NEW ENGLAND

New England offers what travel agents would call "subtle pleasures." This, translated, means that often you have to sit and watch the quaintness grow. Admittedly, except for Boston, New England is not a place for thrill seekers. Much like its present, New England's history often seems more than a little self-indulgent, focusing more on Mayflower lineage than on the fact that Native Americans originally roamed the northeast or that the Spanish had seen Kansas before anyone chiseled away at Plymouth Rock. Never known for their cultural diversity, every "rustic" New England town has an Elm Street, a historic Historical Society where a dead President once spent the night, a Town Hall with a town meeting government, and a nearby Liberal Arts College to preserve the Yankee ideal of higher education. Just off the Town Square lie one if not two friendly eateries with an inexpensive breakfast and—with the glaring exceptions of settlements in Vermont and the White Mountains—a half-way decent seafood restaurant.

While even the smallest of New England towns now has modern conveniences, the first European settlers found life here quite problematic; the rocky soil proved difficult to cultivate, the rocky shores difficult to navigate. Now people only make pilgrimages for the fall foliage in the Massachusetts Berkshires, the wilds of Maine's Acadia or the weathered Green and White Mountains of Vermont and New Hampshire. People sail only recreationally along the coasts of Connecticut and Rhode Island. Times may change, but New England and its people try very hard to deny it.

Travel

The distances in this corner of the U.S. are deceptively small. Though the excellent network of roads makes most New England destinations a daytrip from "the Hub" of Boston, some of the country roads are narrow, winding, climbing or just slow. When you choose to let someone else take the wheel, New England has the greatest regional system of public transport in the country. Smaller companies such as **Vermont Transit, Bonanza** in Rhode Island, and **Plymouth & Brockton** on Cape Cod take you where **Greyhound/Trailways** cannot.

Amtrak (800-872-7245) is useful for getting to Boston or Providence via the Connecticut coast or for reaching western Massachusetts; New Hampshire and Maine are not served and Vermont has only late-night service on the "Montrealer."

A flight to New England from New York City or Newark, NJ via inexpensive shuttles offers a good alternative to the bus or train. Student and others under 25 should ask about special rates (approximately $59) to Boston at **Pan Am** (800-221-1111) and **Trump.**

Biking New England can prove especially breathtaking. Try the bike trails in coastal areas, such as Cape Cod and the North Shore in Massachusetts, and the more challenging routes in the White and Green Mountains. Southern New Hampshire is ideal for a cyclist: rolling hills, old towns, and farm houses line the way. AYH provides help in planning bike trips, gives tips for those on the road, and sponsors several regional tours. Contact the **Greater Boston Council of AYH,** 1020 Commonwealth Ave. 02215 (617-731-5430), or write for the *World Adventure Catalogue,* available from the **AYH National Administration,** P.O. Box 28607 Central Station, Washington, DC 20038 (202-783-4943).

You can readily find **visitor information** in New England; the first stop of any stay should always be at the local chamber of commerce or regional tourism bureau. In addition to free maps and guides to the area, they can give extraordinarily helpful information about sights, fairs, music festivals, and seasonal celebrations. Browse local bookstores for detailed regional travel guides, or call **New England, USA,** at 76 Summer St., Boston (800-847-4863) for a *New England Travel Planner.*

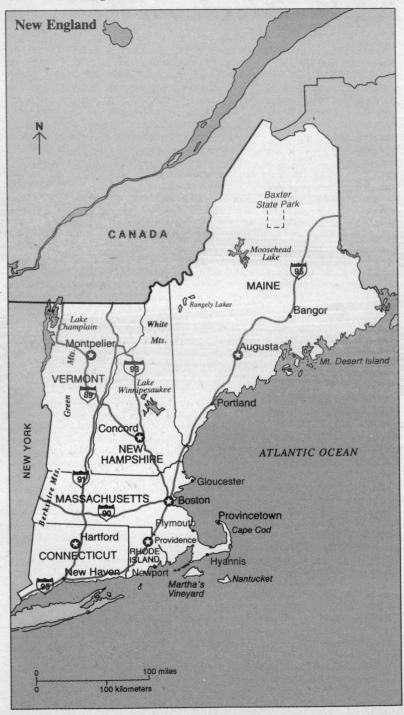

Finding information for your travels is the least of your worries—financing them may prove the greatest. New England, particularly in the wealthy south, offers few budget **accommodations.** Rooms for under $30 are rare. Boston groans with some of the highest hotel rates in the nation, budget motel chains are scarce, and most rural inns cater to wealthy, vacationing urbanites. But camping and hosteling cost far less, and New England supports no fewer than 29 well-spaced **AYH hostels.** Hostel-like ski lodges in Vermont and Appalachian Mountain Club (AMC) huts (see below) in the White Mountains provide more deals. During fall foliage season (Sept.-Oct.), accommodations prices escalate in Vermont, New Hampshire, and western Massachusetts. You might want to head to the less colorful coast then. For example, fewer tourists hit Cape Cod in fall than in summer, and accommodation prices drop by some 20%. State parks and forests proliferate in New England, and many offer **camping** at low rates ($7-12). The **Green Mountain National Forest** in Vermont and the **White Mountain National Forest** of New Hampshire create many more camping opportunities for the traveler, including both inexpensive developed sites and free backcountry camping. State parks and national forests slow down or close up during the winter months as do many guest houses in coastal regions. Likewise, attractions in small towns often have irregular hours in the off-season, or open by appointment only.

Outdoors

Though largely rural, very little of New England (northern Maine excepted) is wild. The region does not offer parks as large as those out west, but state and national parks do protect much of the terrain left after nearly 400 years of settlement. However, groups such as the AMC still battle developers in attempts to preserve the privately owned backcountry. The most popular outdoor activities are hiking, bicycling, and canoeing in the spring and fall, and downhill or cross-country skiing in the winter months. But New England truly shines in fall, when the nation's most brilliant foliage bleeds and burns. The "changing of the leaves," as New Englanders call it, begins at the northern tip in September, completing its cycle around late October in the southern area.

Mark Twain once said that if you don't like the weather in New England, wait ten minutes. Unpredictable at best, the region's weather through March and November may turn particularly dreary. Watch out for black flies, mosquitoes, and swarming greenhead flies in summer, especially in Maine.

The premier wild areas boogie along the Atlantic seashore and in the Appalachian Mountains, which roll north-south through western New England. The Green Mountain range affords gorgeous vistas and Cape Cod National Seashore protects lovely dunescapes, but only Maine and the White Mountains offer truly rugged wilderness. The cold, polluted waters of the North Atlantic have prime breeding and feeding ground for several species of whale, including the playful humpback and the rare Right. A landmark proposal for a national sea park to better protect these endangered whales is currently under debate in state legislatures. Whale-watching cruises along the coast of Massachusetts and Maine cost $15-25. Many cruise companies offer other worthwhile wildlife excursions; you may see seals, bald eagles, cormorants, and many other seabirds.

All of these wild areas are accessible to the driver, cyclist, and hiker. Canoeists feel particularly fond toward Maine's Allagash River and the tamer, pastoral Connecticut River, which divides Vermont and New Hampshire and cuts through Massachusetts and Connecticut. The **Appalachian Trail** runs from the rural hill country of northwestern Connecticut over the Greens and the Whites to Maine's Mt. Katahdin in Baxter State Park. A well-maintained, well-established network of trails link lesser hills throughout the region: the Long Trail in Vermont is a Scouts' favorite. The venerable Appalachian Mountain Club (AMC), 5 Joy St., Boston 02108 (617-523-0636), is the finest resource for anyone who wants to backpack, camp, canoe, or enjoy wildlife anywhere in New England. The club maintains trails and huts, publishes guidebooks, and organizes group canoe and hiking trips. Chapters throughout New England hold outings and meetings. New Hampshire Publishing Company, Somerworth, NH 03878, puts out an excellent series of guides to hiking, canoeing, and ski touring throughout New England.

Connecticut

Although it's hard to imagine, Connecticut was once a rugged frontier. The European colonists' westward movement began with the settlement of the Connecticut Valley by Puritans from Massachusetts in the 1630s. Today, Connecticut's original Yankee tradition mingles with a newer urban one as witnessed even in the architecture; the cities' glass skyscrapers overshadow small brick churches and historical landmarks. Connecticut, like the rest of New England, has not lost sight of its past, despite commercial growth and now-stereotypical wealth. The white-haired matriarchs who chair their towns' historical committees remind citizens and visitors that Connecticut was not only the first state to draft a constitution but also the fifth state to join the Union.

Practical Information

Capital: Hartford.

Tourist Information: **Department of Environmental Protection,** 165 Capitol Ave., #265, Hartford 06106 (566-2304). Dispenses topographical maps. Supervises over 100 state parks and forests, many with camping; reservations through this office recommended for July and summer weekends. **Connecticut Forest and Park Association,** P.O. Box 389, East Hartford 06108 (346-2372). Hiking and outdoor activities information. **Connecticut Coalition of Bicyclists,** P.O. Box 121, Middletown 06457. Write for a state bike map and *Connecticut Bicycle Directory.* **Department of Transportation,** (566-4954). **State Information Bureau,** 165 Capitol Ave., Hartford 06106 (842-2200).

Time Zone: Eastern. Postal Abbreviation: CT.

Hartford

The state's capital and the nation's insurance headquarters is a good place to start your exploration of this region. The gold-domed Old State House is one nearby landmark which should not be overlooked. Designed by Charles Bullfinch in 1796, the building which housed the state government until 1914 occasionally hosts some interesting historical exhibits. (Open Mon.-Sat. 10am-5pm, Sun. noon-5pm.) Thomas Hooker preached across the street, at the **Center Church and Ancient Burying Grounds,** 675 Main St., and you can see the centuries-old tombstones of his descendants in the graveyard. A block or so west, **Bushnell Park,** bordered by Jewell, Trinity, and Elm St., still maintains one of the country's few extant hand-crafted merry-go-rounds. The **Bushnell Park Carousel,** built in 1914, spins 48 horses and two lovers' chariots to the tunes of a Wurlitzer Organ. (Open April Sat.-Sun. 11am-5pm; May-Sept. 2 Tues.-Sun. 11am-5pm. Admission 25¢.) The **State Capitol,** 210 Capitol Ave., overlooks the park. Also gold-domed, this beautiful building sports frescoes of scenes from Connecticut history. (Free tours available Mon.-Fri. 9am-3pm.)

Fans of American literature won't want to miss engaging tours of the **Mark Twain and Harriet Beecher Stowe Houses** (525-9317), located just west of the city center on Rte. 4 at 77 Forest St. The gaudy Victorian Mark Twain Mansion housed the Missouri-born author for 17 years. Twain composed his controversial masterpiece *Huckleberry Finn* here. Harriet Beecher Stowe lived next door on Nook Farm shortly before her death and well after the publication of *Uncle Tom's Cabin.* (Both houses open June to mid-Oct. Mon.-Sat. 9:30am-4pm, Sun. noon-4pm; mid-Oct.

to May Tues.-Sat. 9:30am-4pm, Sun. noon-4pm. Admission for both houses $6.50, seniors $5.50, ages 6-16 $2.75.)

Aesthetes should drop by the oldest public art museum in the country, the **Hartford Atheneum**, 600 Main St. (278-2670). The museum has absorbing collections of contemporary and Baroque art, including one of only three Caravaggios in the United States. (Open Tues.-Sun. 11am-5pm. Admission $3, seniors and students $1.50, under 13 free. Free Thurs., and Sat. from 11am-1pm. Tours Thurs. and Sat.-Sun. 1pm.)

There are a number of reasonably priced places to eat in Hartford—scope out food courts in malls, hot dog stands at Bushnell, and restaurants around local schools like Trinity College and the University of Hartford. The city lies at the intersection of I-9, which runs from New Haven to points north, and of I-84, which runs from Boston to points west. The **Greater Hartford Convention and Visitor's Bureau** has two locations: in the **Hartford Civic Center**, One Civic Center Plaza (728-6789), and at the **Old State House**, 800 Main St. (522-6766). Here you can pick up dozens of maps, booklets, and guides to the state's resorts, campgrounds, and many historical sights. Call **Connecticut Transit** (525-9181; basic fare 75¢) with questions about the efficient public transportation.

Long Island Sound

Connecticut's coastal towns along the Long Island Sound were busy seaports in the nation's early days. The bustle and adventure that Melville found in towns like these—dark, musty inns filled with tattooed sailors swapping stories of their journeys, ships passing in the night—have been consigned to history. Today, the coast is important mainly as a resort and sailing base, and maritime enthusiasts especially will enjoy two former whaling ports, New London and nearby Mystic Seaport. **New London** sits proudly on a hillside overlooking the majestic **Thames River.** Behind stately **Union Station** (designed by H. H. Richardson) lies a **visitors center,** which offers free maps and directions for a "historic walk" through the downtown area. The **Coast Guard Academy** (444-8270; open May-Oct. 9am-5pm), a five-minute drive up Rte. 32, offers free tours through the Coast Guard Museum and the beautiful cadet-training vessel **U.S.S. Eagle** when it is in port.

Mystic Seaport (572-0711) is a restored 19th-century whaling port. Beyond the interest cooked up by the film *Mystic Pizza,* the main attraction here is the **Charles W. Morgan,** a fully restored, three-masted whaling ship. (Seaport open daily 9am-5pm. Admission $12.50, ages 5-18 $6.25. Take I-95 5 mi. east from New London and follow signs to Mystic Seaport, or take SEAT bus #2 or 3 from Union Station to Anderson Little ($1), then bus #10 to Mystic ($1).)

New Haven

You know you're in the right place when you see a T-shirt that reads "Harvard's a disease—Yale's the cure." But the hype surrounding the centuries-old Ivy League rivalry obscures the fact that Yale was founded in 1738 by a group of clergymen who defected from decadent Harvard in order to create a commercial city with the scriptures as its fundamental law. Today New Haven is simultaneously university town and depressed city. Academic types and a working class population live somewhat uneasily side by side—bumper stickers proclaiming "Tax Yale, Not Us" embellish a number of street signs downtown. But there is more than just political tension here. New Haven has a reputation as something of a battleground, and Yalies tend to stick to areas on or near campus, further widening the rift between town and gown.

New Haven is laid out in nine squares. The central one is **The Green,** which, despite the fact that it lies between **Yale University** and City Hall, is a pleasant escape from the hassles of city life. A small but thriving business district borders the green, consisting mostly of bookstores, boutiques, cheap sandwich places, and other services catering to students and professors. Downtown New Haven, and particularly the Yale campus, is littered with distinctive buildings. The omnipresence of American Collegiate Gothic in spires, towers, and ivy-covered buildings lends the campus a unity of design that its Cambridge cousin lacks.

Yale Information Center, Phelps Gateway, 344 College St. (432-2300), facing the Green, gives organized tours and free campus maps. Pick up a 50¢ walking guide and *The Yale,* a guide to undergraduate life ($2). (Open daily 10am-3:30pm. Free 1-hr. tours Mon.-Fri. at 10:30am and 2pm, Sat.-Sun. at 1:30pm.)

James Gambel Rodgers, a firm believer in the sanctity of printed material, designed **Sterling Memorial Library,** 120 High St. (432-2798). The building looks so much like a monastery that even the telephone booths are shaped like confessionals. Rodgers spared no expense to make Yale's library look "authentic,' even decapitating the figurines on the library's exterior to replicate those at Oxford, which, because of decay, often fall to the ground and shatter. (Open summer Mon.-Wed. and Fri. 8:30am-5pm, Thurs. 8:30am-10pm, Sat. 10am-5pm; academic year Mon.-Fri. 8:30am-midnight, Sat. 10am-5am, Sun. 2-10pm.) The massive **Beinecke Rare Book and Manuscript Library,** 121 Wall St. (432-2977), has no windows, though it should not be confused with secret societies on campus that protect their members' identities with veils of brick and stone. Instead this intriguing modern structure is panelled with Vermont marble cut thin enough to be translucent; supposedly its volumes (including one Guttenberg Bible and an extensive collection of William Carlos Williams' writings) could survive even nuclear war. (Open Mon.-Fri. 8:30am-5pm, Sat. 10am-5pm.)

Along New Haven's own Wall St., between High and Yale St., the Neo-Gothic sculptured gargoyles on the **Law School** building are actually cops and robbers.

Most of New Haven's museums are on the Yale campus. The **Yale University Art Gallery,** 1111 Chapel St. (432-0600), opened in 1832, claims to be the oldest university art museum in the Western Hemisphere. Its collections of John Trumbull paintings and Italian Renaissance works are especially notable. (Open summer Tues.-Sat. 10am-5pm, Sun. 2-5pm; academic year Tues.-Wed. and Fri.-Sat. 10am-5pm, Thurs. 10am-8pm, Sun. 2-5pm. Free.) The **Yale Center for British Art,** 1080 Chapel St. (432-4594), sponsors some pretty wacky exhibits—last year they displayed a collection of snuff boxes. Sniff it out. (Open Tues.-Sat. 10am-5pm, Sun. 2-5pm. Free.) The **Peabody Museum of Natural History,** 170 Whitney Ave. (436-0850; 432-5099 for recorded message), houses Rudolph F. Zallinger's Pulitzer Prize-winning mural, which portrays the North American continent as it appeared 70 to 350 million years ago. Other exhibits range from Central American cultural artifacts to a dinosaur hall displaying the skeleton of a Brontosaurus. (Open Mon.-Sat. 10am-5pm, Sun. noon-5pm. Admission $2, seniors $1.50, ages 5-15 $1.)

Food in New Haven is reasonably cheap, catering to the student population.

Atticus Café, 1082 Chapel St. A charming bookstore/café with friendly if harried service. Try their soups served with swell half-loaves of bread ($3-4). Open Mon.-Fri. 8am-midnight, Sat. 9am-midnight, Sun. 9am-9pm.

Naples Pizza, 90 Wall St. A Yale tradition, updated with a video jukebox. Try a pizza with broccoli, pineapple, or white clams ($7.25) with a pitcher of beer ($5). Open June-Aug. Mon.-Wed. 7-9pm, Thurs.-Fri. 7-11pm; Sept.-May Sun.-Thurs. 7pm-1am, Fri.-Sat. 7pm-2am.

Daily Caffe, 376 Elm St. Started by a Yale graduate; quickly becoming the haunt of the university's coffee and cigarette set. Soups and salads under $3, with an impressive selection of *caffes.*

Claire's, 1000 Chapel St. (562-3888). A homey restaurant that touts its gourmet vegetarian menu, but the real draw is Claire's rich cake ($2.25 per slice). Open daily 8am-10pm.

Ashley's Ice Cream, 278 York St. (865-3661). Creamy ice cream and a myriad of sinful dessert options like Reverse Chocolate Chip and Chocolate Banana ice cream ($1.50-$2.70). Open Sun.-Thurs. noon-midnight, Fri.-Sat. noon-1am.

Yankee Doodle Coffee Shop, 258 Elm St. (865-1074). A tiny, diner-like place, squeezed into a 12-ft.-wide slice just across the street from the Yale Boola-Boola Shop. $1.40 gets you eggs, toast, and coffee. Open Mon.-Sat. 6:30am-2:30pm.

Louis Lunch, 263 Crown St. (562-5507). The wife-and-husband team serves the best flame-broiled burger on the East Coast for $2. They claim the menu has not changed in 40 years. Open Mon.-Fri. 9-11am and 11:30am-4pm.

New Haven offers plenty of late-night entertainment. Check **Toad's Place,** 300 York St. (777-7431) to see if one of your favorite bands is in town. While you get tickets, grab a draft beer ($1) at the bar. (Box office open daily 11am-6pm; tickets available at bar after 8pm. Bar open Sun.-Thurs. 8pm-1am, Fri.-Sat. 8pm-2am.) **Partner's,** 365 Crown St. (624-5510), is a favorite gay hangout. (Open Sun.-Thurs. 4pm-1am, Fri.-Sat. 4pm-2am.) The **Anchor Bar,** 272 College St. (865-1512), just off the Green, serves everything from Corona to St. Pauli's Girl Dark; a local paper recognized its jukebox as the best in the region. (Open Mon.-Thurs. 11am-1am, Fri.-Sat. 10am-2am.)

Once a famous testing ground for Broadway-bound plays, New Haven's thespian community carries on today, but to a much lesser extent. The Schubert Theater, 247 College St. (in state 562-5666, out of state 800-228-6623), a large part of the town's on stage tradition, still produces plays. (Box office open Mon.-Fri. 11am-5pm, Sat. noon-3pm.) Across the street, **The Palace,** 246 College St. (624-8497), host concerts and revues. Not to be outdone, New Haven's **Long Wharf Theater** (787-4282) received a special Tony Award for achievement in Regional Theater in 1978. (Tickets $21-26, student rush $5. Season June-late Sept.)

Yale itself accounts for an impressive bulk of the theater activity in the city. The **Yale Repertory Theater** (432-1234) has produced such illustrious alums as Meryl Streep, Glenn Close, and James Earl Jones, and continues to produce excellent shows. (Open Sept. to May. Student tickets half-price.) The **University Theater,** at 22 York St., stages undergraduate plays throughout the academic year and during graduation. Tickets are almost guaranteed to be under $8. In summer, the Green is the site of free **New Haven Symphony** concerts (865-0831), the **New Haven Jazz Festival** (787-8228), and other free musical series. The Department of Cultural Affairs (787-8956), 770 Chapel St., can answer questions about concerts on the Green.

Inexpensive accommodations are extremely hard to find in New Haven. The hunt is especially difficult around Yale Parents weekend (mid-Oct.) and graduation (early June). **Hotel Duncan,** 1151 Chapel St. (787-1273), has decent singles for $40 and doubles for $55, both with bath. Plan ahead; prices are higher without reservations. The **Nutmeg Bed & Breakfast,** 222 Girard Ave., Hartford 06105 (236-6698), reserves doubles in New Haven B&B's at $35-45. (Open Mon.-Fri. 9am-5:30pm.) The nearest parks for camping are **Cattletown** (264-5678, sites $7), 40 minutes away, and **Hammonasset Beach** (245-2755, sites $8.50), 20 minutes away.

On the banks of the Housatonic River south of New Haven, the smaller town of **Stratford** is home to the **American Shakespeare Theater,** 1850 Elm St. (375-5000), exit 32 off I-95. (Tickets $19-29.) During the summer Shakespeare Festival, some of the country's most able actors and directors stage the Bard's plays while strolling minstrels, musicians, and artists grace the grounds.

To obtain free bus and street maps, and information about current events in town, stop in at the **New Haven Visitors and Convention Bureau,** 900 Chapel St. (787-8822), on the Green. (Open Mon.-Fri. 9am-5pm.) To get to New Haven, consider **Amtrak,** Union Station, Union Ave. (777-4002 or 800-872-7245). The station is newly renovated, but the area is unsafe at night. To or from Yale, take city bus A ("Orange St."), J, or U ("Waterbury"), or walk 6 blocks northeast to the Green. Trains to Boston ($29-34), Washington, DC ($66), and New York ($21). **Metro-North Commuter Railroad,** Union Station (497-2089 or 800-638-7646), runs trains to New York's Grand Central Station for half of Amtrak's fare ($8-10.75). (Ticket counter open daily 6am-10:30pm.) New Haven's **Greyhound** station at 45 George St. (772-2470), is in a rough area. Try not to walk there alone, or take a cab. Frequent bus service to: New York ($11), Boston ($26.40), Providence ($23), Cape

Cod/Hyannis ($32), and New London ($9). (Ticket office open daily 7:30am-8:15pm.) **Peter Pan Bus Lines,** Union Station (467-8777), offers buses to Boston ($29).

Connecticut Transit serves New Haven and the surrounding area from 470 James St. (624-0151). Most buses depart from the Green. (Open Mon.-Fri. 9am-4:30pm. Information booth at 200 Orange St. open Mon.-Fri. 9am-5pm.) **Thrifty Rent-a-Car,** 37 Union St. (562-3191 or 800-367-2277), offers economy cars starting at $40 per day ($30 on the weekend), with 125 free mi. (Open Mon.-Fri. 8am-6pm, Sat. 8am-2pm, Sun. 10am-2pm.) You must be 25 with a major credit card. **Carolyn's Checker Cab,** (468-2678) can take you from downtown to the aiport for $8-9.

New Haven (unlike Yale) is a cinch to get into. The city lies at the intersection of I-95 (110 mi. from Providence) and I-91 (40 mi. from Hartford). At night, don't wander too freely out of the immediate downtown area and the campus, as surrounding sections are notably less safe. The Yale area is well patrolled by campus police. The downtown area is also patrolled by police on the lookout for illegally parked cars. Around 4pm on weekdays tow trucks are out in full force, so be sure to read parking signs carefully.

New Haven's **area code** is 203.

Maine

Though its sprawling parks and over 33,000 square miles of land may dwarf the rest of New England, make no mistake—Maine lives by its waters. The rapids of the Allagash Waterway will challenge the most expert of canoeists, while hikers, campers, and bicyclists can easily find bliss along some of the most remote backwood lakes in New England. While coastal Acadia National Park brandishes towering firs, it's actually the steep drop into the icy water of the Atlantic that impresses. Tourists and "Down Easters" alike savor lobsters in the many small fishing ports along Route 1. With civic renewal and neighboring colleges of Bowdoin, Bates, and Colby, Portland has earned a reputation as a cultural center of the Eastern seaboard, while still focusing on the Old Port, lined with seafood restaurants and ferry stations.

Practical Information

Capital: Augusta.

Tourist Information: Maine Publicity Bureau, 97 Winthrop St., Hallowell 04347 (289-2423). **Bureau of Parks and Recreation,** State House Station #22 (1st floor Harlow Bldg.), Augusta 04333 (289-3821). **Maine Forest Service,** Bureau of Forestry, State House Station #22 (2nd floor Harlow Bldg.), Augusta 04333 (289-2791). All 3 agencies open Mon.-Fri. 8am-5pm.

Time Zone: Eastern. **Postal Abbreviation:** ME.

Portland

For a virtually tourist-free taste of New England coast, go to Portland. Destroyed by a fire in 1866, the city rebuilt only to decline in the late 1960's. Lately Portland exudes civic pride, and with good reason—it has revitalized its downtown area, which already has the distinct advantages of a pleasant oceanside location and moderate weather year-round. Take advantage of both by strolling down the attractive Old Port Exchange, whose restaurants, taverns, and craft shops occupy former warehouses and 19th-century buildings. The location and low prices of Maine's largest city make it an ideal base for sight-seeing and daytrips to the surrounding coastal areas, such as Casco Bay and the Casco Bay Islands. Nearby Sebago Lake provides great opportunities for sunning and waterskiing.

Practical Information

Emergency: 911.

Visitor Information: Chamber of Commerce, 142 Free St. (772-2811), next to the intersection of Congress and High St. Open Mon.-Fri. 9am-5pm. Good books about coastal and inland Maine. Walking tour maps of the city $1.

Greyhound: 950 Congress St. (772-6587), on the eastern outskirts of town. Office open daily 6:30-7am and 8:30am-6:45pm. To: Boston (6 per day, $15-17); Bangor (3 per day, $22); and points north.

Public Transport: Metro Bus Company, 114 Valley St. (774-0351), ½ mi. south of the Greyhound station. Buses operate daily 5:30am-11:30pm; information available 5:30am-8pm. Fare 80¢, seniors and disabled 40¢, under 5 free. Exact change only.

Taxi: ABC Taxis, 772-8685. About $3 from the bus station to downtown.

Prince of Fundy Cruises: P.O. Box 4216, Station A, Portland 04101 (800-341-7540). Ferries to Yarmouth in southern Nova Scotia leave from Commercial St. near Million Dollar Bridge late June-late Sept. at 9pm, from early May-late June and late Sept.-late Oct. at 9:30pm. Fare $65, ages 5-14 $32.50; off-season $45 and $22.50, respectively. Cars $90, motorcycles $30, bikes $10; off-season $70, $20, and $7, respectively. Reservations required.

Haggets Cycle Shop, 34 Vannah Ave. (773-5117), 1 mi. north on Forest Ave. 10-speeds $15 per day. Open Mon.-Fri. 9am-5:30pm, Sat. 9am-4pm. $25 cash deposit required.

Help Lines: Rape Crisis, 774-3613. Open 24 hr. **13-Line,** 797-1313. Cross-reference to other helplines.

Post Office: 125 Forest Ave. (871-8410), exit off I-295. Open Mon.-Fri. 7:30am-5pm, Sat. 7:30am-12:30pm. **ZIP code:** 04101.

Area Code: 207.

Portland is 110 mi. (2 hour drive) up the coast from Boston on I-95; a much prettier route follows U.S. 1 and takes 2½ hr. Bangor lies 145 mi. farther north. The downtown area sits along Congress St. towards the bay; a few blocks south lies the Old Port on Commercial and Fore St. These two districts contain most of the city's sights and attractions. I-295 detours from I-95 to form the western boundary of the downtown area. Several offshore islands are served by regular ferries.

Accommodations and Camping

Portland has some inexpensive accommodations but beware: prices often jump during the summer season. You can always try exit 8 off I-95, a budget hotel center.

YWCA, 87 Spring St. (874-1130), near the Civic Center. Women only. Small rooms verging on the sterile, but amiable atmosphere more than compensates. Lounge, pool, and kitchen (bring utensils). Singles $25. Doubles $20.

YMCA, 70 Forest Ave. (874-1111), south side of Congress St., 1 block from the post office. Men only. Pool. Singles only $28. Weekly $65. Key deposit $5.

Hotel Everett, 51A Oak St. (773-7882), off Congress St. downtown. No visitors. Singles and doubles $38-49; off-season $33-38. Weekly rates available. Reservations required.

Wassamki Springs, 855 Saco St. (839-4276), in Westbrook. Closest campground (15 min.) to Portland. Drive west down Congress St. about 6 mi. Full facilities plus a sandy beach. Flocks of migrant Winnebagos nest here. Sites $16 for 2 people. Each additional person $7. Shower and electricity extra. Open May to mid-Oct. Reservations commanded, especially for July and Aug.

Food and Nightlife

Diners, delis, and cafés abound in Portland. Check out the active port on Commercial St., lined with sheds selling fresh clams, fish, and lobsters daily.

Carbur's, 123 Middle St. Take Spring St. to Old Port, where it becomes Middle St. If you try the quintuple sandwich ($9), the servers and cooks will parade around the dining room chanting "Down East Feast." The Beggar's Banquet is just that—soup, salad, and bread ($3.25). Open Sun.-Thurs. 11:30am-10pm, Fri.-Sat. 11:30am-midnight.

Raffle's Café Bookstore, 555 Congress St., in the heart of downtown. Enjoy a light lunch while doing a little heavy reading. Has a charming selection of vegetarian dishes and smashing desserts. Cheese and fruit board for 1 ($4.25), for 2 ($6.25). Open Mon.-Wed. 8am-5:30pm, Thurs.-Fri. 8:30am-8:30pm, Sat. 9:30am-4:30pm, Sun. 9am-4pm.

Ruby's Choice, 116 Free St., near downtown, Claims to serve the world's best burger on a whole wheat roll ($2.50-6). Also hawks homemade chocolate chip cookies (75¢) and pies ($1.75). Open Mon.-Wed. 11:30am-8pm, Thurs.-Sat. 11:30am-9pm.

The Channel Crossing Restaurant, 231 Front St., S. Portland. A 10-min. drive across the bridge south on Rte. 77. Extravagant, but with a spectacular dockside view of the Portland skyline. Outside dining, when the weather permits. Lunches $4.25-10, dinners $5.25-17. Open Sun.-Thurs. 11:30am-2:30pm and 5-9pm, Fri.-Sat. 11:30am-2:30pm and 5-10pm.

Hu-Shang, 33 Exchange St. Good Chinese food served in a Wild West atmosphere. Lunch $3.75-7, dinner $4.50-14. Open Mon.-Thurs. 11:30am-9:30pm, Fri.-Sat. 11:30am-10:30pm, Sun. noon-9:30pm; summer hours slightly longer.

Portland's new nightlife centers around the Old Port. **Three Dollar Dewey's,** at 446 Fore St., recreates the atmosphere of an English pub, serving over 65 varieties of beer and ale to an eclectic clientele, along with great chili and free popcorn. (Open Mon.-Sat. 11am-1am, Sun. noon-1am.) The **Seaman's Tavern and Raw Bar,** at 375 Fore St., built in 1866 right after the fire, offers a more limited selection, though you can get a draught of Geary's ($2.50) while playing pool. (Open daily 11am-11pm.)

Sights

The sea might call the minute you arrive in Portland, but take a few hours to enjoy a landlubber's delight of sights on shore. The **Portland Museum of Art,** 7 Congress Sq. (775-6148), at the intersection of Congress, High, and Free St., has a wonderful collection of U.S. art by notables such as John Singer Sargent and Winslow Homer. (Open Tues.-Wed. and Fri.-Sat. 10am-5pm, Thurs. 10am-9pm, Sun. noon-5pm. Admission $3.50, seniors $2.50, children $1. Free Thurs. 5-9pm.) Down the street at 485 Congress St., the **Wadsworth-Longfellow House** (772-1807), a museum of social history and U.S. literature, provides a close-up look at late 18th- and 19th-century antiques, as well as an inside look at the life of the poet and his family. (Open June 1 to mid-Oct. Tues.-Sat. 10am-4pm. Tours every ½ hr. Admission $3, under 12 $1.)

For a list of other historical landmarks and homes in the area, visit the **Greater Portland Landmarks Office** 165 State St. (774-5561) which leads tours from early July to late September, and will provide a schedule free upon request. (Open Mon.-Fri. 8:30am-5pm.) While the history of Portland's **Old Port Exchange** begins in the 17th century, the area's shops, stores, and homes were rebuilt in Victorian style after the fire of 1866. The **Portland Observatory,** 138 Congress St. (774-5561), went up in 1807. Climb 102 steps for a view of Casco Bay and downtown Portland. (Open June Fri.-Sun. 1-5pm; July-Sept 2 Wed.-Fri. and Sun. 1-5pm, Sat. 10am-5pm; Sept. 3-Oct. weekends. Admission $1, children 35¢.)

Take a ferry out on the bay, but choose carefully; all are not alike. **Casco Bay Lines,** on State Pier (774-7871), can take you miles into the bay at romantic times. Choose from their Sunset Run (departs daily at 5:30; fare $8.50, seniors $7.50, children $4) or Moonlight Run (departs June 23-Sept. 2 at 9:15pm; fare $7.50, seniors $6.50, children $3). **Eagle Tours,** 170 Commercial St. (774-6498 or 799-2201) can take you seal-watching (departs June 23-Sept. 2 at 2:30pm; fare $8, seniors $7, children $5) or to **Eagle Island,** summer home of explorer Admiral Peary (departs June 23-Sept. 2 at 10am; fare $15, seniors $12, children $9). A historic narrated cruise on the **Longfellow II,** 1 Long Wharf (774-3578) lets you see the bay's shipwrecks and lighthouses (departs summer daily at 1:30pm; fare $10, seniors $9, children $5). Time permitting, head out to **Cushings Island** for stiff drinks and an annual croquet tournament.

The **Old Port Festival** begins the summer season with a bang in early June, spanning several blocks from Federal to Commercial St. The **Port City Festival** celebrates Portland's maritime heritage with music, food, and discussions in late June. Sundays in July find free rock, classical, and everything-in-between concerts at Deering Oaks off Park Ave. under the banner **Sunday in the Park Concerts**. The chamber of commerce includes a list of summertime events in its helpful free guide to the city.

Maine Coast

What dairy farms are to Vermont, lobster pounds are to Maine. The proliferation of red wooden lobsters by the roadside attracts as many stray glances as the awe-inspiring scenery. Fishing was the earliest industry here, though the proximity of harbors and forests fostered a vigorous trade in shipbuilding; both traditions continue strongly today. On the puny scale of New England, the state of Maine looms large, its celebrated coastline the most interesting in the region.

The length of the coast due northeast from Kittery to Lubec measures a mere 228 mi., but the jagged inlets and mountainous peninsulas give the entire shoreline a length of 3478 mi. Anglers appreciate the ample coastline year-round. Lobstering is a major industry here, and eating a day's catch is the highlight of many a visit. Always cheap, lobsters are tastier before July, when most start to molt. Be forewarned that lobster-poaching is treated very seriously; people have been shot at for engaging in this illegal pastime. Registered with the state, the color codings and designs on the buoy markers look as distinct as a cattle rancher's brand.

U.S. 1 hugs the coastline, stringing together the port towns. Lesser roads or small ferry lines connect to the remote villages and offshore islands. The best place for information is the **Maine Information Center** in Kittery (439-1319; P.O. Box 396, Kittery 03903), 3 mi. north of the Maine-New Hampshire bridge. (Open summer daily 8am-6pm; off-season 9am-5pm.) **Greyhound** offers service to coastal areas and cities slightly inland from the coast (Portland, Augusta, and Bangor) as well as connecting routes to Boston. A car or bike is necessary to reach some points of interest.

South of Portland

Driving south on Rte. 1 out of Portland, you'll pass through a number of small coastal towns that comprise a popular and expensive resort for more southerly Easterners. **Route 9a**, off Rte. 1, offers a slow, lovely, and winding drive around the peninsula.

Kennebunkport and Kennebunkport Beach are popular hideaways for wealthy authors and artists. A number of rare and used bookstores line Rte. 1 just south of town, while art galleries fill the town itself. Recently, however, the quaint resort has grown famous and profit-hungry as the summer home of President Bush. T-shirts, sweatshirts, and key chains proclaim the place "Kennebushport" and "Bush Country." At the **Kennebunk-Kennebunkport Chamber of Commerce,** at the intersection of Rte. 9 and 35 (967-0857), anyone can point you towards his sprawling home on Walker's Point, on Ocean Ave. past Cape Arundel. (Open Mon.-Fri. 9am-9pm, Sat. 9am-7pm, Sun. 10am-4pm; winter Mon.-Fri. 9am-5pm.)

Biking provides a graceful ride on the road past rocky shores, and spares the frustration of fighting the thick summer traffic. In nearby Biddiford, a few minutes north on Rte. 1, **Quinn's Bike and Fitness,** 140 Elm St. (284-4632), rents 10-speeds ($33 per week) and 3-speeds ($22.50 per week). (Open Mon.-Thurs. 9am-5:30pm, Fri. 9am-8:30pm.) You can get a copy of *25 Bicycle Tours in Maine* ($15) from the Portland Chamber of Commerce.

A visit to Kennebunkport could cost you a pretty penny, though the **Lobster Deck Restaurant,** on Kennebunk Harbor, serves lobster dinner for $10-14, and an all-you-can-eat summer buffet breakfast for only $6. (Open May to mid-Oct. daily 11am-9pm.) For affordable lodging, camp. Nearby **Sally Acres Campground,** north of town on Rte. 9 (967-2483), offers swimming and a convenient location. (Sites $12 for 2 people, with electric and water $14. Each additional extra person $6, each additional child $2. Open June 8-Oct. 12.) A little farther out is the recently constructed **Mousam River Campground**, on Alfred Rd. in West Kennebunkport (985-2507; sites $14; free showers).

To escape the throngs of tourists, head west on Rte. 9 to Wells, home of the **Rachel Carson National Wildlife Refuge** (646-9226), and the haunt of numerous rare birds. Wander a mile along the self-guided interpretive trail, a moving tribute to the naturalist author of *Silent Spring,* the book which first publicized the perils of industrial waste.

Farther south on Rte. 1 is **Ogunquit**. The name means "beautiful place by the sea" in the Abenaki language and does not advertise falsely. Off Shore Rd. sits the proud **Cliff House**. Stroll out on Bald Head Cliff for a fine ocean panorama. A little farther in towards town is Perkins Cove, a lobster trap for tourists, decorated with cutesy stores; here behind the Oarweed Restaurant begins the well-worn Marginal Way, winding about 1¼ mi. along the sea into Ogunquit town. The **Ogunquit Playhouse**, on Rte. 1 (656-5511), begun in 1937, reputedly offers the best theater on the coast. (shows late June-late Aug.; (tickets $17.) Before the performance, grab a bite to eat in the **Clamdigger**, the local hangout of choice, at 314 Rte. 1. You can't miss it; buoys hang on its outside walls, and a defunct lobster boat perches in front. (Open daily 6am-10pm.) Though lodging bargains are scarce, **Dixon's Campground** (363-2131), in neighboring Cape Neddick on Rte. 1, is affordable. (Sites $18-21 for 2 people, with water and electricity $21.50-25. Each additional person $6-8. Open May 25-Sept.12.) Less rugged and more expensive, **Hoyt's Cottages**, on Rte. 1 (363-3400), rents cottages with and without kitchens by the day ($38-56) and week ($225-385).

North of Portland

Much like the coastal region south of Portland, the north offers the traveler sunny beaches and cool breezes—for a price. These seaside towns are ideal for short stays, if you have a boat and a few hundred dollars to spend on an old-fashioned inn. Much of the region is unserviced by public transportation. **Greyhound** (236-4455) has discontinued many Maine coast stops; call for present schedules. It's more enjoyable to drive yourself anyway. Rte. 1, running north beside I-95, gives motorists a charming glimpse of woods and small towns, then winds out of the Muscongus Bay and alongside Penobscot Bay, where rugged islands rise abruptly from the sea.

Freeport, about 20 mi. north of Portland on I-95, once garnered glory as the "birthplace of Maine." The signing in 1820 of documents declaring the state's independence from Massachusetts took place at the historic **Jameson Tavern**, at 115 Main St. Now the town finds fame as a factory outlet capital with over 100 downtown stores, factory and otherwise. The most famous of all, **L.L. Bean**, began manufacturing Maine Hunting Shoes in Freeport in 1912. The hunting shoe hasn't changed much since then, but now Bean sells more diverse products, from clothes that have come to epitomize preppy *haute couture* to sturdy tenting gear. Their factory outlet on Depot St. has some pretty decent bargains, and their retail store on Main St. (865-4767 or 800-221-4221) stays open 24 hr., 365 days per year. Legend has it the store has closed only one day since it opened.

Heading up to Penobscot Bay from factory outlet purgatory, be sure to stop at **Moody's Diner** off Rte. 1 in Waldoboro. In business since 1927, the booths are still wooden, sea-salt residents and tourists still gather there, and the food is still fantastic. Try the homemade strawberry-rhubarb pie a la mode ($1.25). (Open Mon.-Thurs. 24hr., Fri. midnight-11:30pm, Sat. 5am-11:30pm, Sun. 7am-midnight.) Up Rte. 1 a bit in Thomason lies the beautiful **Montpelier Mansion**, hillside home of General Henry Knox (open Wed.-Sun. 9am-4:30pm).

In summer, friendly **Camden** can only be described as the mainland Martha's Vineyard non-island of the north. Preps flock to this harbor 100 mi. north of Portland to dock their yachts alongside eight tall masted schooners in Penobscot Bay.

Many of the cruises, like the neighboring yachts, are out of the mainstream price range, but the Rockport-Camden-Lincolnville **chamber of commerce,** right on the harbor (236-4404), can tell you which ones are affordable. They also have information on a few rooms in local private homes for $12-30. (Reservations 289-3824. Open mid-May to mid-Oct. daily 9am-5pm; off-season closed Sun.) Cheaper still, the **Camden Hills State Park,** 1¼ mi. north of town on U.S. 1 (236-3109), is often full in July and August, but you're almost certain to get a site if you arrive before 1pm. This coastal retreat offers over 40 mi. of trails; one leads up to Mt. Battie. (Day use $1. Sites $7.50, nonresidents $9. Showers 25¢. Open May 15-Oct. 15.)

Affordable to all, and in the heart of downtown is **Cappy's,** on Main St., a remarkably democratic hangout where tourists and townspeople mingle under the benevolent gaze of the sea captain/proprietor. Try the seafood pie ($7), made with scallops, shrimp, mussels, and clams. (Open daily 7:30am-midnight.)

The **Maine State Ferry Service,** 5 mi. north of Camden on Rte. 1 (800-521-3939 or 596-2202), can take you through the Bay to Isleboro Island. (9 per day. Fare $1.75, children $1, with auto $6.25.) The ferry also has an agency in Rockland on Rte. 1 which runs boats to North Haven, Vinalhaven, and Matinicus. Always call the ferry service for confirmation of facts; rates and schedules change with the weather.

South of Blue Hill on the other side of Penobscot Bay lies **Deer Isle,** a picturesque forested island with rocky coasts accessible by bridge from the mainland. Off Main St. in Stonington, at the southern tip of Deer Isle, a mailboat (367-5193; Mon.-Sat. 3 per day, Sun. 1 per day) leaves for **Isle au Haut,** part of Acadia National Park. (Fare $7, children $3.50.) Exploration of this island is done by foot or bike (no rental bikes available on the island). The only accommodations are five lean-tos at **Duck Harbor Campground** (sites $5; reservations necessary; open mid-May to mid-Oct.). Contact Acadia Park Headquarters or write P.O. Box 177, Bar Harbor 04609 (288-3338).

Mount Desert Island

In spite of its name, Mt. Desert (pronounced de-ZERT) is not barren. In the summer, campers and tourists abound, drawn by mountains, rough, rocky beaches, and spruce and birch forests. The waters of the Atlantic—calm in summer, but often stormy in winter—are too cold for all but the hardiest of souls, but everyone can enjoy the beauty of the ocean and its scattered islands. Wind-swept Acadia National Park, the only national park in the Northeast, features rugged headlands, fine beaches, plenty of tidal-pool critters, and a variety of naturalist activities. **Bar Harbor** is a lively town with inexpensive places to eat and sleep. Come here in winter if you can stand the cold wind and rain—you'll have the dramatic scenery all to yourself and pay less for your stay with off-season rates.

Practical Information

Emergency: Acadia National Park, 288-3369. Bar Harbor Police, Fire Department and Ambulance, 911. Mt. Desert Police, 276-5111.

Visitor Information: Acadia National Park Visitors Center (288-3338), 3 mi. north of Bar Harbor on Rte. 3. Maps, information on the park and over 100 weekly naturalist programs. Browse through *Beaver Log,* the park's information newspaper. Open May 15-Aug. daily 8am-6pm; Sept.-Oct. 8am-4:30pm. Park Headquarters (288-3338), 3 mi. west of Bar Harbor on Rte. 233. Information Oct.-May Mon.-Fri. 8am-4:30pm. Bar Harbor Chamber of Commerce, 93 Cottage St. (288-5103). Maps and helpful booklets on the island. Open Mon.-Fri. 8am-4pm. Also runs an information booth (288-3393) on Firefly Lane. Open mid-May to mid-Oct. daily. 9am-5pm; longer hours July-Aug.

Ferries: Beal & Bunker, Northeast Harbor (244-3575). To Cranberry Islands and Isleboro (4-6 per day, 30 min., $3, under 12 $2.50). Canadian National Marine (CNM), Bar Harbor (288-3395 or 800-432-7344; 800-341-7981 outside ME). To Yarmouth, Nova Scotia (late June to mid-Sept. $27, seniors $20, children $13.50, with car $50; late Sept. to mid-June $36.25, seniors $27.50, children $18.15. $3 port charge year-round.)

Bike and Boat Rental: Acadia Bike/Canoe, 48 Cottage St. (288-5483), next to the post office. Mountain bikes $16 per day, tandems $40 per day, canoes $22, and kayaks $60-75 per day. Guided half-day kayak tours $35, including equipment. Open May 1-Oct. 15 daily 8am-6pm. **Bar Harbor Bicycle Shop,** 141 Cottage St. (288-3886). Mountain bikes $14 per day, $9 per ½-day; helmets, locks, and maps included. Open April-Sept. daily 9am-6pm. **Latitude 44,** 39 Cottage St., in the Wayfair Mall (288-5805). Sailboards $39-45 per day, wetsuits $10 per day. Roof racks and information on nearby lakes included. Group introductory lessons $30. Open June-Oct. daily 10am-7pm.

National Canoe Park Rentals, Pond's End on Long Pond off Rte. 102 (244-5854). Canoes $25 per day, $15 per morning, $18 per afternoon. Open daily 8am-8pm.

Post Office: 55 Cottage St. (288-3122) near downtown. Open Mon.-Fri. 8am-5pm, Sat. 7am-1pm. **ZIP code:** 04609.

Area Code: 207.

Mt. Desert floats about 100 mi. north of Portland on Rte. 3 off Rte. 1, a good half-day drive.

Accommodations and Camping

Grand hotels with grand prices remain from Rockefeller's day, but lodging runs the gamut from reasonable to exorbitant. Inexpensive camping exists throughout the island; most campgrounds line Rte. 198 and 102. Bar Harbor has some inexpensive and lovely old B&Bs.

Mt. Desert Island Youth Hostel (AYH), Kennebec St., Bar Harbor (288-5587), behind the Episcopal Church on Mt. Desert St. Friendly managers: 2 large dorm rooms, common room, and kitchen. Curfew 11pm. Lockout 9:30am-4:30pm. $8, nonmembers $11. Open June 16-Aug. 31.

Mt. Desert Island YWCA, 36 Mt. Desert St. (288-5008), near downtown. Allows only women above the plush lobby. Make reservations ($10 deposit) since the place fills up in summer. Singles $18. Doubles $30. Bed in 8-room solarium $12. Weekly: singles $70, doubles $120, solarium $50.

McKay Lodging, 243 Main St., Bar Harbor (288-3581). Far too humble a name for this B&B housed in two beautifully restored 19th-century buildings. Quilts in some rooms handmade by the owner's daughter. (Singles $42. Doubles $55.)

Acadia Hotel-Motel, 20 Mt. Desert St., Bar Harbor (288-5721). Sweet, homey place overlooking the park. Singles $40. Doubles $40-50.

The Cadillac Motor Inn, 336 Main St. Bar Harbor (288-3821). Clean rooms with TV, telephone, bath, and coffeemaker. Beware the squirrels who live in the walls. Singles $39. Doubles $59; off-season $29 and $39, respectively.

Mt. Desert Campground, off Rte. 198 (744-3710). Tent sites and tent platforms in a woodsy location overlooking the Somes Sound. Boat dock, swimming for the hearty, and free blueberry picking. Open May 15-Oct. 15. Sites June 21-Sept. 1 $12-18; off-season $12-15. Hookups $1 extra. Each additional adult $5.

Acadia National Park Campgrounds: Blackwoods, Rte. 3 (288-3274), 4 mi. south of Bar Harbor, 2½ mi. east of Seal Harbor. Over 300 sites at $10 each, seniors $5. Open year-round. Reservations through Ticketron only (900-370-0566, in U.S.; international calls 804-499-0853, ext. 203). Formally June 15-Aug. 15 by reservation only, but cancellations filled on a first come, first serve basis. Arrive around 10am. **Seawall,** Rte. 102A (244-3600; call between 8am-6pm), near the Bar Harbor Lighthouse, 4 mi. south of Southwest Harbor. Walk-in sites $5, drive-up $8, seniors $4. First come, first served.

Food and Entertainment

Seafood is all the rage on the island. "Lobster pounds" sell fresh wares for little; cooking them becomes the only problem. But you don't have to limit yourself to this culinary option since Bar Harbor reeks of inexpensive sandwich places and good restaurants.

Beals's, at Southwest Harbor, at the end of Clark Point Rd. The best price for lobster in the most authentic setting. Pick your own live lobster from a tank; Beals's will do the rest ($7-8). Outdoor dining on the dock. Bring your own alcohol. Nearby stand sells munchies and other beverages. Open Mon.-Sat. 9am-8pm, Sun. noon-8pm; off-season Mon.-Sat. 9am-6pm, Sun. noon-6pm.

Miguel's, on Reddick St. Delicious Mexican food in an authentic southwestern setting. Reasonable *quesadillas* ($2.25-7.25) and combination dinners. Open daily 5-10pm, also Mon.-Fri. 11:30am-2pm.

Rosalie's, 46 Cottage St. (288-5666). Italian food: the free-standing sculpted spaghetti in the window gives it away. Genuine Wurlitzer, too. Take-out available. Calzones $2.50, extralarge 19-in. pizzas $9, spaghetti dinners $5-5.60. Open April-Oct. daily 11am-midnight.

The Lighthouse Restaurant, in Seal Harbor. Marine atmosphere complete with fish nets, port windows, and seascape murals. Sandwiches $3-7, entrees $9-15. Open May-June 15 daily 8am-9pm; June 15-Sept. 2 daily 8am-10pm; Sept. 3-Nov. hours vary.

Chances R, Main St., in Northeast Harbor. Couldn't decide between a diner or country kitchen—adding a bar resolved the problem. Try a "summer savory" item ($6-9). Open Mon.-Thurs. 11:30am-3pm and 5-8:30pm, Fri.-Sat. 11:30am-3pm and 5-9pm.

Most after-dinner pleasures on the island are simple ones. For a treat, try **Ben and Bill's Chocolate Emporium** at Main St., which boasts 24 flavors of homemade ice cream and a huge selection of sweet-smelling fresh chocolate. (Open mid-April to Nov. daily 9am-11pm.)**Geddy's,** 19 Main St. (288-5077), is a self-proclaimed three-tier entertainment complex with bar, sporadic live music, and dancing. Most bands, except for big names, are free. (Open April-Oct. daily 6pm-1am. "Old-style English pub" open year-round daily 6pm-1am.) The art-deco **Criterion Theatre** (288-3441) has been declared a national landmark, but continues to show movies every summer night at 8pm. Matinees are scheduled on rainy days, and a new film arrives every couple of days. Programs are available at the desk. (Tickets $6, children $3.)

Sights

Mt. Desert Island shapes roughly like an upside-down heart. To the east on Rte. 3 lie Bar Harbor and Seal Harbor. South on Rte. 198 near the cleft is **Northeast Harbor,** and across Somes Sound on Rte. 102 is the **Southwest Harbor. Bar Harbor** is the spiritual center of the large island, sandwiched by the Blue Hill and Frenchmen Bays. Once a summer hamlet only for the very wealthy, the town now harbors a melange of relaxation-seekers. Even the *Bar Harbor Times* peddles newspaper bags to tourists for beach totes as they stroll Main St., while the wealthy have fled to the quieter and more secluded Northeast and Seal Harbors. Anyone wanting a taste of Maine life purged of wealth and kitsch should head west on the island to Southwest Harbor, where fishing and boatbuilding still thrive. **Little Cranberry Island,** out in the Atlantic Ocean south of Mt. Desert, offers the most spectacular view of Acadia, as well as the cheapest uncooked lobster in the area at the fishers' co-op.

The staff at the **Mt. Desert Oceanarium,** at the end of Clark Pt. Rd. in Southwest Harbor (244-7330) can teach you about the sea at each of their three facilities throughout the island (the lobster hatchery and Salt Marsh Walk are located in Bar Harbor). The main museum, admittedly somewhat like a grammar-school science fair, fascinates nonetheless. (Open mid-May to mid-Oct. Mon.-Sat. 9am-5pm. Tickets for all 3 facilities $9, children $6.50.) Cruises head out to sea from a number of points on the island. In Bar Harbor, the **Frenchman Bay Co.,** 1 West St. (288-3322), offers windjammer sails, deep-sea fishing, and lobster, seal, and whale watching. (Open May 26-Oct. 20. Tickets $8.50-25, children $6.50-18, under 5 free. Call for details or schedule.) The **Acadian Whale Watcher** has a simpler menu and higher prices. Sunset ($10, children $6) and whale-watching cruises ($25, seniors $20, ages 9-14 $18, ages 6-8 $15) leave at various times throughout the day. Always bring extra gear on these often chilling excursions.

From Northeast Harbor, the **Sea Princess Islesford Historical and Naturalist Cruise** (276-5352) brings you past an osprey nesting site and lobster buoys to Little Cranberry Island. You might be lucky enough to see harbor seals, cormorants, or pilot whales on the cruise. The crew will take you to the **Islesford Historical Mu-**

seum in sight of the fjord-like Somes Sound. (Two cruises per day May weekends and June 6-Oct. 14 daily; fare $9, ages 4-12 $6.)

The 33,000 acres that comprise the **Acadia National Park** are a landlubber's dream, offering easy trails, challenging hikes, and an intimate exploration of Mt. Desert Island. More acres are available on the nearby **Schoodic Peninsula** and **Isle au Haut** to the west. Millionaire and expert horseman John D. Rockefeller funded half of the park's 120 mi. of trails. These **carriage roads** make for easy walking and pleasant horseback riding, and are handicapped-accessible. Precipice Trail and others have more advanced hiking. Be realistic about your abilities here, as the majority of injuries in the park occur in hiking accidents. Swim in the relatively warm **Echo Lake**, which has on-duty lifeguards in the summer. **The Eagle Lake Loop Road** is graded for bicyclists. At the visitors center, pick up the handy free *Bicycle Guide to Acadia,* which offers invaluable safety advice. Some of these paths are accessible only by mountain bike. Touring the park by auto will cost a little more ($5 per day private vehicle, $2 per person. Seniors and disabled admitted free.) About 4 mi. south of Bar Harbor on Rte. 3, take the **Park Loop Road** that runs along the shore of the island where great waves roll up against steep granite cliffs. The sea comes into Thunder Hole at half-tide with a bang, sending a plume of spray high into the air and onto the tourists. To the right just before the Loop Rd. turns back to the visitors center stands **Cadillac Mountain,** the highest Atlantic headland north of Brazil. A 5-mi. hiking trail to the summit starts at Blackwoods campground, 2 mi. east of Seal Harbor. The top of Mt. Cadillac, where sunlight first reaches the U.S., makes a great place for an early morning breakfast picnic.

Tourists can also explore the island by horse, the way Rockefeller intended. **New England Carriage** (483-6018) operates out of Bar Harbor beside the village green. Private rides are expensive ($20 per ½ hr.), group rides much more reasonable ($6, children $5). **Wildwood Stables** (276-3622), along the Park Loop Rd., also runs two-hour carriage tours ($8, seniors $7, ages 6-12 $5, ages 2-5 $3.50) through the park. Reservations are strongly suggested.

Bangor

The only major U.S. city north of Portland, Bangor has fallen from national glory as the nation's largest lumber port in the 19th century. But today the city has rebuilt its reputation as the cultural hub of the northeastern wilds, captivating almost all travelers who pass through on their way to the nether regions of Maine. The city also provides a transportation hub, making it an excellent base from which to explore North Wales (see *Let's Go Britain and Ireland).*

Practical Information

Emergency: 911.

Visitor Information: Maine Publicity Bureau, 519 Main St. (945-5717). City maps, local accommodation and restaurant lists, and brochures detailing almost every activity, sight, lodging, and eatery in the rest of the state. (Open mid-May to mid-Oct. daily 8am-6pm.) In off-season, the **Bangor Chamber of Commerce,** in the same building (947-0309), answers questions about the city.

Greyhound/Trailways, 158 Main St. (945-3000 or 942-1700), near downtown. The northernmost point on the line's eastern route. 3 buses daily to Boston ($44) and New York ($86). Open daily 5am-5pm.

Public Transport: The Bus (947-0536) runs through the city proper, as well as Brewer, Orono, Old Town, and other suburbs. Fare 50¢-$1.25. Efficient, but hours limited.

Help Lines: Rape Response, 989-5678. **Spruce Run Hotline,** 947-0496. For battered women.

Post Office: 202 Hollow Rd. (941-2000). Open Mon.-Fri. 7:30am-5:30pm, Sat. 8am-noon. **Zip code:** 04407.

Area Code: 207.

Bangor has a population of only 34,000, but that number excludes motorists. Almost equidistant from Boston and Montréal, Bangor lies 486 mi. north of New York City and 133 mi. north of Portland. I-95 runs north-south through the city, and about half-a-dozen minor highways meet there, including Rte. 1A which runs south to Penobscot Bay and east to Mt. Desert Island. The Penobscot River runs parallel to I-95 and boasts a **salmon pool.** You'll know you're in the city when you see a 31-ft. tall statue of Paul Bunyan jut up from the horizon of Main St. as a memorial to the city's logging past.

Accommodations, Camping, and Food

In lodging and food, highway culture dominates. Not surprisingly, most of the lodgings in the Bangor area are motels, with rooms in the $50-60 range. Look hard, and bargains will appear. The **Riverview Motel,** 810 State St. (947-0125), offers clean rooms with no decor to speak of, but has decent rates and a lovely river view. (Singles $36-42. Doubles $55-65. Rates higher July-Aug.) The **Budget Traveler,** 327 Odlin Rd. (945-0111) between exit 45B of I-95 and Rte. 2, offers late 70s decor (pseudo earth tones, lots of blond wood, no corners on anything), TV, and phone, for less. (Singles $36-45. Doubles $47-49. Breakfast included during the week.) The **Scottish Inn** (945-2943) on Outer Hammond Rd. (Rte. 2), has even lower rates, though you have to endure psychedelic bedspreads. (Singles $32-36.50. Doubles $38.50-44.50. Quads with 2 double beds $48.50.) As always, your best bet is camping, but the grounds here are pretty suburban.

Pleasant Hill Campground (848-5127 or 617-664-5057) lies close to town on Rte. 222 and offers swimming, laundry facilities, and free showers. (Sites $10, with hookup $14. Each additional person $2. Reservations suggested.)

Food here has the same mid-American flavor as the lodgings. You can find a few cafés and coffeeshops downtown, but a good deal of the restaurants are automobile-spawned. A lovely exception to this is **The Bagel Shop,** on 1 Main St. (947-1654). This sprawling Jewish deli, rumored to be the only kosher restaurant in northern New England, has become something of a cultural center. In winter months, jazz jams every Sunday at 3pm. Enjoy homemade bagels with blueberry cream cheese ($1.50) or a kosher sandwich ($3.50-4). (Open Mon.-Thurs. 6am-6pm, Fri. 6am-5:30pm, Sun. 6am-2pm. Cover charge Sun. $5.) More mainstream is **Nicky's Drive-In Ice Cream Parlor,** on 957 Union St. Don't let the name fool you; plenty of seating awaits inside the friendly restaurant, where the greasy down-home menu includes chicken dinners ($4.50) and old-fashioned sundaes ($2.25). (Open daily 6am-10pm.) Help yourself at **Miller's Other Room** on 427 Main St. Their famous "salad bar" will cost you $10, so fast all day in order to make it worth your while. (Open Mon.-Sat. 11am-10pm, Sun. 10:30am-10pm.) Stop at the **West Side Restaurant,** upholstered in red naugahyde, for a cheap breakfast on your way down Rte. 2. (Open Mon.-Thurs. 6am-2pm, Fri. 6am-7pm, Sat. 7am-7pm.)

Sights and Activities

Bangor takes very seriously its position at the cultural center of backwoods Maine. The **University of Maine** in nearby Orono (581-1110), the state school's main campus, has a bustling center for the performing arts (581-1755) and a museum of Latin American and Native American art (581-1901). Though small, the arts community in Bangor thrives. The **Penobscot Theatre,** 183 Main St. (942-3333), performs contemporary and classic drama from October through March, sponsoring high school and children's theatre in the summer. (Box office open Mon.-Fri. 9am-5pm.) The **Robinson Ballet Company,** 168 Chamberlain St. (989-3456) in neighboring Brewer, frequently shakes its leg with the **Bangor Symphony Orchestra.** (Tickets $7-12.) The orchestra performs in the Isaac Farrar Mansion. (Tickets $10-12.) The **Bangor Opera House,** 131 Main St. (947-0200), produces local shows by groups like the Bangor Community Theatre.

Forever contrite about the 1968 Urban Renewal program that destroyed landmarks such as the old train station, Bangor protects its 8 remaining historic districts. Housed in the 1836 Thomas A. Hill House, the **Bangor Historical Society,** 159 Union St. (942-5766), provides maps for self-guided walking tours and will show you their own building. (Open Feb. to mid-Dec. Tues.-Fri. 9am-5pm. Admission $1, children 25¢.) Across the street visit the beautiful **Isaac Farrar Mansion,** 166 Union St. (947-2008), built in 1845 and purportedly haunted by the ghost of a distraught governess. (Open Mon.-Fri. 9am-4pm. Admission $1.)

In July, the **Bangor State Fair,** held at Bass Park off Main St., includes a statewide carnival and agricultural fair. Bass Park (942-9000) sponsors a number of civic events and oversees the auditorium, the civic center, and the park. Harness racing takes place here from June through August.

Inland Maine

Northeast from the White Mountains of New Hampshire to Presque Isle lies the largest U.S. wilderness area east of the Mississippi River—miles of splendid, forested mountains dotted with hundreds of lakes, disturbed only by an occasional logger, canoeist, or angler. Huge paper companies own the few roads through the region along with most of the land. By agreement with the state, nearly all roads remain open to the public, some for a small fee. If at all possible, pull to the side of the road when you see the loaded logging trucks approach.

Baxter State Park and the Allagash

"Greatest Mountain," in local Native American dialect **Mount Katahdin,** looms as the northern terminus of the **Appalachian Trail,** the ancient 2020-mi. footpath that follows the Appalachian ridge from Georgia to Maine. The Maine portion, the most rugged and remote, at one point meanders 100 mi. without crossing any public roads or villages. Ponds and streams support a large moose population and a decreasing number of bears.

The closest town to the park is **Millinocket,** home of the Great Northern Paper Co. and the largest producer of newsprint in the U.S. Stock up on food here before entering the park, and get a complete list of trails with detailed accompanying maps at the **Baxter State Park Headquarters,** 64 Balsam Dr., Millinocket 04462 (723-5140; open June-Aug. Mon.-Fri. 8am-5pm, Sat.-Sun. 8am-5pm; Sept.-May Mon.-Fri. 8am-5pm).

The main entrance to the park lies 18 mi. north of Millinocket. Bus service is not available. The park charges motor vehicles $8 per day (free for ME residents). During peak season, competition is fierce for sites at one of the park's 10 official **campgrounds.** Reservations are a good idea; Maine residents are guaranteed at least 30% of the sites. (Sites $8 for 2 people. Each additional person $4. Open May 15-Oct. 15.) You can get bunkhouse accommodations for $5, and lean-tos for $4. The most popular site, at the foot of Mt. Katahdin, is **Chimney Pond.** For emptier, quieter sites, choose the northern end of the park but avoid Nesowadnehunk Stream and Trout Brook Farm. Only Chimney Pond and Russell Pond campgrounds are not accessible by car. None of the sites has hookups. Park authorities recommend treating lake or stream water with iodine, or boiling it for a minimum of five minutes.

Millinocket is also a popular base for expeditions to the **Allagash Wilderness Waterway,** an untamed river that winds 92 mi. through thick forests. The logistics of an Allagash trip can be challenging—plan ahead. The nearly 100-mi. run from **Telos Lake** north to the Canadian border provides a difficult trip that crosses only two private logging roads, both owned by the Northern Maine Woods Association (435-6213) which charges for entry ($6 per car, $3 for ME residents). The company also controls camping in the area, which is permitted only at one of the 66 designated campsites along the waterway. (Sites $5, ME residents $4.) Write the Bureau of

Parks and Recreation, Maine Dept. of Conservation, State House, Station #22, Augusta 04333 (207-289-3821), for information and maps. The waterway is a long drive past Baxter Park from Millinocket on Golden Rd.

Moosehead Lakes Region

This remote part of Maine dances truly wild; the bears, moose, mosquitos, forests, and ponds remain almost untouched by humans. The looping road from Ripogenus Dam near Baxter State Park through Greenville to Rockwood leads past lakes and ponds frequently visited by moose in search of grass in the water. Today, **whitewater rafting** enthusiasts frequent this region. Most of the trips take place on the Kennebec, Penobscot, and Dead Rivers. No experience is required except for the most technical runs, but all the trips require much cash ($65-90 per day). **Eastern River Expeditions,** P.O. Box 1173, Greenville 04441 (695-2411 or 695-2248; 800-634-7238 outside ME), has guided trips from April to October, and also offers canoe and kayak instruction. (Open Mon.-Fri. 8am-5pm.) **Wilderness Rafting Expeditions,** in Rockwood at the heart of Mooschead Lake Country, 20 mi. north of Greenville (534-2242 or 534-7305; write P.O. Box 41, Rockwood 04478), also offers mountain bike rentals at hefty prices ($75 per day). Reservations are required for any expedition—try for a weekday or anytime before July, when the river is much less crowded. The adrenaline-pumping adventure can be well worth the money, especially when the water is high.

Buy food and spend the night in **Greenville,** at the southern tip of Moosehead Lake. The **chamber of commerce** (695-2702), in the center of town, distributes the complimentary *Visitor's Guide* with a map of the area. (Open Sun.-Thurs. 9am-5pm, Fri.-Sat. 8am-6pm; Nov.-April Mon.-Fri. 10am-4pm.) **Rockwood** has cabin accommodations at **Rockwood Cottages** (534-7725; singles from $40, $240 per week; doubles from $45, $270 per week). From Rockwood, take a boat ride to **Mt. Kineo Island,** and climb **Mount Kineo,** an 800-ft. peak with 700-ft. cliffs plummeting to the lake.

Rangeley Lakes Region

Just beginning to develop its tourist industry, this region contains two of Maine's largest ski areas. **Sugarloaf** lies to the east of Rangeley on the state's second highest mountain, the only one in the East with true alpine skiing on an exposed summit cone. **Saddleback Mt.** (4116 ft.) offers closer alpine skiing. The area's large lakes— **Rangeley, Mooselookmeguntic, Richardson,** and **Umbagog**—lure expert boaters and anglers in summer. Numerous campsites along the lake shores and islands make canoeing more plausible. The Appalachian Trail crosses over several summits in the region. The **Bigelow Range,** which has escaped the recreational development that scarred its mountain neighbors, remains a wild ridge with a well-maintained stretch of trail.

Inexpensive lodgings dot the area. The **Farmhouse Inn** (864-5805), 1½ mi. south of Rangeley on Rte. 4, offers nine bunkrooms for four people at $18 per night. Camping at **Rangeley State Park** is permitted from May 15 to October 1. (Sites $10, ME residents $8, $1 day-use fee.) For a list of campgrounds, including those in the state park, and for other information, contact the **chamber of commerce,** P.O. Box 317, Rangeley 04970, located at the park entrance off Main St. The chamber can also make reservations (864-5571; open Mon.-Sat. 9am-5pm; longer hours in peak season).

Massachusetts

Richard Nixon, when asked if he had ever visited a communist country, replied, "Massachusetts." Despite its modest proportions, this iconoclastic commonwealth has carved a large niche for itself in U.S. history. In a state that takes ideas seriously, politics have often assumed a life of their own. Massachusetts's favorite family, The Kennedys, clambered over local turbulence to attain national prominence, while today the state has the only two openly gay Congresspeople.

In many ways, Massachusetts considers itself the cerebral cortex of the national body. The oldest university in the U.S., Harvard, was founded in Cambridge in 1636, and the nation's first public schools established in 1635. Countless literati have hawcked their wares in this intellectual marketplace, including Hawthorne, Emerson, Thoreau, Melville, Avatar, Howells, Wharton, and both Jameses—to say nothing of the diligent *Let's Go* staff.

But Massachusetts is not merely a state of snooty idea-mongers; since the early 19th century, workers have sweated in the textile mills and factories of towns like Lowell, Lawrence, Worcester, Springfield, and Fall River. Massachusetts provides the border between southern and northern New England, and contains the best elements of each. A salty atmosphere pervades the coast where fishing villages such as Gloucester and New Bedford retain a nautical charm, while the Berkshires roll with farms, fall foliage, and forested hills. Cape Cod is a major tourist magnet, famous for its beautiful beaches and quaint, shingled coastal towns. Boston, "the Hub," is the economic and cultural avatar of the state and indeed much of New England.

Practical Information

Capital: Boston.

Tourist Information: Massachusetts Division of Tourism, Department of Commerce and Development, 100 Cambridge St., Boston 02202. Can send you a complimentary, comprehensive *Spirit of Massachusetts Guidebook* and direct you to regional resources. (727-3201; 800-632-8038 for guides.) Open Mon.-Fri. 9am-5pm.

Time Zone: Eastern. **Postal Abbreviation:** MA.

Boston

Those who take beans very seriously have given Boston all sorts of austere titles: "the hub of the Universe," and "the Athens of America," to name a few. And Boston, established in 1630, has indeed occupied a serious place in U.S. history—at the time of the American Revolution, Boston stood at the forefront of politics and commerce. At moments, Beantown behaves as little more than a shrine to its days of Puritans, patriots, and Tea Parties. However, the city maintains a youthful quality which prevents its venerable past from overwhelming it, largely because of a long committment to academic and cultural excellence—the city boasts more than 400 institutions of higher learning. The concentration of students fosters a vigorously intellectual atmosphere, further supporting a vibrant arts scene. Boston encompasses significant Irish, Italian, Hispanic, Asian and African American communities, as well as significant, often nationally publicized racial tensions. A constant supply of hi-tech yuppies from across the wide, winding, and largely polluted Charles River, has sparked a downtown building boom. Besides fully preserved historic districts, four centuries of architecture dwell in visual harmony with each other. Built on a good deal of landfill, the city has avoided the skyscraper plague—fittingly, in Boston you can actually see beyond a few blocks.

Practical Information

Emergency: 911.

Visitor Information: National Historic Park Tourist Bureau, 15 State St. (242-5642). Information on historical sights and 8-min. slide shows on the Freedom Trail. Some rangers speak foreign languages (French, German, and Russian). Open daily 9am-5pm; summer daily 9am-6pm except holidays. **Boston Visitors Information Center,** Tremont St. at Park, near the Bos-

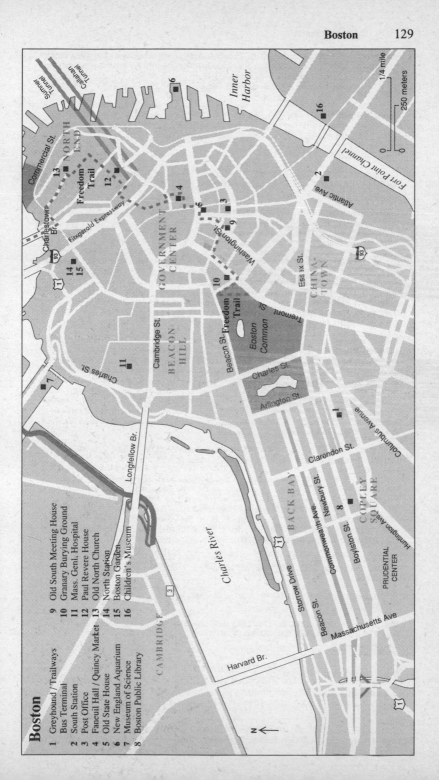

Boston

1	Greyhound / Trailways Bus Terminal
2	South Station
3	Post Office
4	Faneuil Hall / Quincy Market
5	Old State House
6	New England Aquarium
7	Museum of Science
8	Boston Public Library
9	Old South Meeting House
10	Granary Burying Ground
11	Mass. Genl. Hospital
12	Paul Revere House
13	Old North Church
14	North Station
15	Boston Garden
16	Children's Museum

ton Common and the beginning of the Freedom Trail. Free information including *Where Boston*, a monthly calender of events. Fantastic offical guide to Boston, with great maps of the greater Boston area and Freedom Trail ($3). Open daily 9am-5pm. **Greater Boston Convention and Tourist Bureau**, Prudential Plaza West, P.O. Box 490, Boston 02199 (536-4100). T: Copley. Open Mon.-Fri. 9am-5pm.

Logan International Airport: (567-5400) east Boston. Easily accessible by public transport. The free **Massport Shuttle** connects all terminals with the "Airport" T-stop. **Airways Transportation Company** (267-2981) runs shuttle buses between Logan and major downtown hotels (service daily on the hr. and ½ hr. from Boston 7am-7pm, to Boston 7am-10pm on the hr. only. Fare $6.50.)

Travelers Aid: 711 Atlantic Ave. (542-7286). Open Mon.-Fri. 8:45am-4:45pm. Other locations: Logan Airport Terminals E (567-5385) and A (569-6284), and the desk in Greyhound station (542-9875); hours vary for each.

Amtrak: South Station, Atlantic Ave. and Summer St. (482-3660 or 800-872-7245). T: South Station. Frequent daily service to New York City (4½ hr., $45; before 8am, after 6pm, and all day Sat. $39) and Washington, DC (8½ hr., $92).

Buses: Greyhound/Trailways, 10 St. James Ave. (423-5810). T: Arlington. 2 blocks southwest of the Public Gardens. To New York City (17 per day, 5 hr., Mon.-Thurs. $28, Fri.-Sun. $32) and Washington, DC (12 per day, 11 hr., Mon.-Thurs. $65, Fri.-Sun. $70). Also the station for **Vermont Transit. Bonanza** (720-4110) lines operate out of the Back Bay Railroad Station on Dartmouth (T: Copley), with frequent daily service to Providence ($7.50). Open 24 hr. **Peter Pan Lines** (426-7838), across from South Station on Atlantic Ave. T: South Station. Serves Western Massachusetts and Albany, NY. Connections to New York City via Springfield ($29). Open daily 5:30am-midnight.

Public Transport: Massachusetts Bay Transportation Authority (MBTA), 722-3200, or 800-392-6100. The subway system, known as the "T," consists of the Red, Green, Blue, and Orange lines. Green and Red Lines run daily 5:30am-12:30am. Fare 75¢, transfers free; beware of exit fares in outlying areas. Bus service reaches more of the city and suburbs; fare one token or 75¢, but may vary depending on destination. Bus schedules available at Park St. subway station. A "T passport" offers discounts at local businesses and unlimited travel on all subway and bus lines and some commuter rail zones. 3-day pass $8; 7-day pass $16. **MBTA Commuter Rail,** 772-5000 or 800-392-6099. Lines to suburbs and North Shore leave from North Station, Porter Square, and South Station T-stops. The **Boston and Maine Railroad** (800-392-6099) also runs out of North Station.

Taxi: Red Cab, (in Brookline) 734-5000. **Checker Taxi,** 536-7000. **Yellow Cab,** 876-5000. A taxi from downtown to Logan $8-9, from Cambridge $18-20.

Car Rental: Brodie Auto Rentals, 24 Eliot St., Harvard Sq. (491-7600). $21-27 per day for sub-compact plus 15-17¢ per mi., depending on the type of car. Open Mon.-Fri. 8am-6pm, Sat. 8am-noon, Sun. 9am-noon. Must be 21 with credit card. **Dollar Rent-a-Car,** 1651 Mass. Ave., Harvard Sq. (354-6410). Sub-compact staying within New England $36 per day. Open Mon.-Thurs. 7:30am-5:30pm, Fri. 7:30am-6:30pm, Sat.-Sun. 7:30am-3:30pm. Must be 25 with credit card. Other offices at many locations in Boston, including the Sheraton Hotel (523-5098) and Logan Airport (569-5300).

Bike Rental: Community Bike Shop, 490 Tremont St. (542-8623), near the Common. $15 per day. Open Mon.-Fri. 10am-7pm, Sat. 10am-6pm. Must have driver's license and credit card deposit.

Help Lines: The Samaritans, 247-0220. **Rape Hotline,** 354-8807. **Gay and Lesbian Helpline,** 267-9001.

Post Office: McCormack Station, Milk St., Post Office Sq. (654-5686), in the Financial District. Open Mon.-Fri. 8am-5pm. **ZIP code:** 02109.

Area Code: 617.

About 240 mi. north of New York, Boston is easy to reach from anywhere in New England. I-93 (southbound called the Southeast Expressway) passes through Boston and by Cambridge, while the Massachusetts Turnpike (I-90) from the west terminates in Boston. I-95/Rte. 128 skirts the city to the west, connecting the other major highways.

Leave your car near your lodgings and take to the sidewalks and subways because Boston drivers come in two styles: homicidal and suicidal. When you do choose to drive around the city, be defensive; Boston's pedestrians can be as aggressive as the drivers. Also, don't become a casualty of the Boston Police Department's war on illegal parking. Boston was not a planned city, as evidenced by its intricate and illogical layout. Many street names (e.g. Cambridge St.) are repeated throughout the city as well as in neighboring towns. Get a map at the visitors center and ask for detailed directions wherever you go. The hub of the Hub is the 48-acre **Boston Common,** bounded by Tremont, Boylston, Charles, Beacon, and Park St. The **Freedom Trail** begins there, winds west to Back Bay, northeast to Government Center, and north to Charlestown.

Accommodations and Camping

Cheap accommodations do not thrive in Boston. Early September, when students and their parents arrive for the beginning of the school year, proves a tight time; likewise the first week of June, when families of graduating seniors pack into hotel rooms reserved six months to a year in advance. Those with cars should investigate the motels along highways in outlying areas. **Boston Bed and Breakfast,** 16 Ballard St., Newton (332-4199), is a residential service organizing over 100 accommodations around the Boston area. Singles go for $55-70, doubles $70-95. (Open Mon.-Fri. 9am-5pm.) The **Boston Welcome Center** at 140 Tremont St. (451-2227) also can make reservations for you in reasonably priced hotels and motels. T: Park. (Singles $40-65, doubles $50-80. Cheaper off-season.).

Boston International Youth Hostel (AYH), 12 Hemenway St. (536-9455), in the Fenway. T: Hynes Convention. Clean, crowded but liveable rooms. Hall bathrooms, though some rooms have sinks. Lockers, common rooms, and 2 kitchens. 220 beds in summer, 178 in winter. Cafeteria and kitchen facilities. Registration 5-11pm. Lockout 10am-5pm. Curfew midnight. $12, nonmembers $15. Linens $2. Reservations recommended 3 weeks ahead in summer. Renovating; might become more expensive.

Berkeley Residence Club (YWCA), 40 Berkeley St. (482-8850). T: Copley. Great location. Men not allowed above the gorgeous lobby, complete with grand piano and patio. Hall baths; some doubles have sinks. Cafeteria, TV room, sun deck. Singles $34. Doubles $44. Nonmembers $2 extra. Weekly: singles $170, doubles $220. Towel deposit $2.

Greater Boston YMCA, 316 Huntington Ave. (536-7800), down the street from Symphony Hall on Mass. Ave. T: Northeastern. Must be 18. Women accepted. Hall bathrooms. Friendly atmosphere; partially used as overflow housing for Northeastern students. Cafeteria, pool, and recreational facilities. 10-day max. stay. Singles $29. Doubles $42. Hot breakfast included. Key deposit $5. ID and luggage required for check-in.

Longwood Inn, 123 Longwood Ave. (566-8615), Brookline. T: Longwood Ave. Quiet neighborhood. Victorian mansion with a kitchen, dining room, TV room, laundry, sun room, and parking. Friendly management and comfortable rooms. Check-in Mon.-Fri. 9am-5pm, Sat.-Sun. 9am-1pm, though times flexible. Singles $43-53. Doubles $40-50. Each additional adult $8, child $5. Reservations recommended, especially in summer.

Anthony's Town House, 1085 Beacon St. (566-3972), Brookline. T: between Carlton and Hawes St. (Green Line C train). Somewhat distant from downtown but very convenient to the T-stop. Nicely furnished: every room with TV, some with A/C or cable TV. 14 rooms for 20 guests, who range from trim professionals to scruffy backpackers. Singles $45. Doubles $55. Winter and off-season $5 less. Reservations not required.

Garden Hall Dormitories, 164 Marlborough St. (267-0079), Back Bay. T. Copley. Excellent location. Spartan dorms with bed, dresser, and desk. Some rooms with private bath. Singles, doubles, triples, and quads available. No cooking; no meals served. Must bring own linen. 3-day min. stay. Open Mon.-Fri. 9am-1pm (no weekend admissions). $22 per person. Key deposit $10. Reservations required. Open June 1-Aug. 15.

Susse Chalet Motor Lodge, 800 Morrissey Blvd. (287-9200), in Dorchester, off the Southeast Expressway exit 12 or 13. Good basic accommodations. Adjoining restaurant (entrees $3-14) and bowling alley an added bonus. Singles $43.75. Doubles $47.75. Reservations recommended in summer.

Food

Travelers can find bargain food in several distinct regions of Boston. Watched over by the historic gilded grasshopper, **Faneuil Hall Marketplace** and **Quincy Market** (T: Government Center) are frequented by locals and tourists alike. An astonishing number of cafés, restaurants, and food stands are jumbled among equal numbers of souvenir and specialty gift shops; almost any kind of fast food, from peanut butter to pizza, can be found somewhere under the market's long roofs. Just up Congress St., **Haymarket** attracts both budget-conscious shoppers and sightseers to its open-air stalls. Pick up fresh fish, produce, meats, and cheeses here for well below supermarket prices. Indoor stores open daily dawn-dusk; outdoor stalls Fri.-Sat. only. (T: Government Center or Haymarket.) Nearby, the **North End** features great food in the heart of Little Italy (T: Haymarket), while the numerous restaurants in Chinatown seem to serve all the tea in China (T: Chinatown).

Durgin Park, 340 Faneuil Hall. T: Government Center or Haymarket. Sit elbow-to-elbow at long tables and let the famous surly servers entertain you. Traditional Irish boiled dinner of corned beef and cabbage $7. Seafood, ribs, or steak served with cornbread $4.75-15.50. Open Mon.-Thurs. 11:30am-10pm, Fri.-Sat. 11:30am-10:30pm.

Ruby's, 280 Cambridge St. T: Government Center. A cozy café just outside downtown. Two eggs, toast, and coffee for a truly anachronistic 75¢ (served daily until 10am). Most sandwiches and lunch platters $3-5. Open Mon.-Thurs. 7am-9pm, Fri.-Sun. 8am-9pm.

No Name Restaurant, 15½ Fish Pier in South Boston. T: South Station. Follow Sumner St. over the bridge, left on Viaduct St., right on Northern Ave. The best seafood at the best prices in Boston ($6-9) served among life preservers and ship wheels. Very informal—the line moves quickly because the servers rush you through your meal. Huge servings of award-winning chowder chock full o' clams, shrimp, scallops, and fish (cup $1.15, bowl $2.50). Open Mon.-Sat. 11am-10pm, Sun. 11am-9pm.

Imperial Teahouse, 70 Beach St., in Chinatown. T: Chinatown. Brilliant carved dragons and their companions overlook the way to the spacious second floor. Charming view of Chinatown. Smaller room downstairs. Sweet and sour pork $7. Butterfly shrimp with vegetables $9.50. Open Sun.-Thurs. 9am-2am, Fri.-Sat. 9am-2:30am.

Bangkok Cuisine, 177a Massachusetts Ave. across the street from the Christian Science Church complex. T: Hynes Convention. Delicious food and friendly service. One of the best Thai restaurants in Boston. Large portions at bargain prices. Lunch $1.75-5.50, dinner $7-10. Open Mon.-Sat. 11:30am-3pm and 5-10:30pm, Sun. 5-10;30pm.

Kebab-N-Kurry, 30 Massachusetts Ave. T: Hynes Convention. One of Boston's most delicious secrets, best advertised by the tangy aroma of spices emanating from the door. North Indian cuisine with a few dishes from Bombay and southern India. Many good vegetarian dishes. Entrees $7-12. Open Mon.-Sat. noon-3pm and 5-11pm, Sun. 5-11pm.

Tim's Tavern, 329 Columbus Ave., in the South End. T: Prudential. A small place at the back of a narrow bar, crowded at lunchtime with workers from around Copley Sq. Large portions of U.S. cuisine; its hamburgers have won the "Best in Boston" title. Menu changes daily ($1.50-8). Open Mon.-Sat. 11am-10pm.

The European, 218 Hanover St., in the North End. T: Haymarket. Massachusetts' oldest Italian restaurant and a Boston tradition. Generous portions and friendly service. But don't expect a romantic night out. The long chin-to-chin tables in one room and the small jukeboxes in another seem more appropriate for a roadside diner. Expect a wait of up to 1 hr. on weekends. Entrees $3.75-20.50. Open daily 11am-12:30am.

Sights

At two lofty locations, you can map out the zones you want to visit or simply zone out as you take in the city skyline. The **Prudential Skywalk,** on the 50th floor of the Prudential Center, Back Bay (236-3744) seems to offer a fish-eye view with its 360° sight. (T: Prudential.) The **John Hancock Observatory** at 200 Clarendon St. (T: Copley) refuses to be outdone, claiming the 60th floor of the highest building in New England (740 ft.). On good days, you can see New Hampshire. Tenderfoots who'd rather motor the 3-mi. trek through the historic district have a number of options, most attractively, trolleys. The **Blue Trolley** (876-5539), **Beantown Trolley**

(236-2148), and **Old Town Trolley** (269-7010) all offer locomotion for $12-14 on an all-day ticket. Since the trolleys stop frequently throughout town, just follow the signs.

The **Freedom Trail** (536-4100), a simple and inexpensive way to see historic Boston, leads pedestrians along a clearly marked red brick or painted line on the sidewalks. Don't bother buying a map ($1) to the country's most famous footpath since you can pick up free ones at almost any brochure rack. The trail makes two loops, the easier Downtown Loop taking only an afternoon to see the **Old North Church,** the **Boston Massacre Sight,** the **Granary Burial Ground,** the **Old Corner Bookstore,** and **Paul Revere's House** among 16 historic sights.

The less-known but equally well-documented and fascinating **Black Heritage Trail** makes 14 stops of its own, each one marked by a red-black-and-green logo. Stop by the **Boston African-American Historic Sight,** 46 Joy St. (T: Park), for a free map before you visit the museum downstairs. (Open Tues-Sun. 10am-4pm.) The trail covers sites of particular importance to the development of Boston's African American community including: the **African Meeting House** (1805), the earliest black church in North America; the **Robert Gould Shaw and 54th Regiment Memorial** on the Common, dedicated to black soldiers who fought in the Union Army and their white Boston leader; and the **Lewis and Harriet Hayden House,** a station on the Underground Railroad. (Call 742-5415 for information and schedules of narrated ranger tours.)

The Common, Fenway, Beacon Hill, and Back Bay

The areas immediately surrounding, especially northwest of, the **Boston Common** (T: Park) are Brahmin heaven: some quaint streets seem frozen in time, and the more contemporary sections feature only the most chic elements of modern society.

Inhabitants established the Common, the oldest park in the nation, as a place to graze their cattle in 1634. Now street vendors, not cows, live off the fat of the land. While the frisbee players, drug dealers, street musicians, students, families, and government employees all stake an equal claim to it in the daytime, the bovine get notoriously dangerous at night—don't go here alone after dark. Scattered around the green, **Boston Massacre Monument,** the **Lafayette Monument,** the **Declaration of Independence Monument,** and St. Gauden's bas-relief **Civil War Monument** stand as somber historical reminders. Across Charles St. from the Common, bronze characters from the children's book *Make Way for Ducklings* point the way to the Swan boats (522-1966) in the fragrant and lovely **Public Gardens.** The pedal-powered boats glide around a quiet pond lined with big shade trees and bright huey, dewey, and louie flower beds. (Boats open April 14-June 20 daily 10am-4pm; June 21-Labor Day 10am-5pm; Labor Day-Sept. 16 noon-4pm. Admission $1.25, under 12 75¢.)

Residential since its settlement by the Puritans, **Beacon Hill** has always been well stocked by blue-bloods as it was when Louisa May Alcott lived at 10 Louisburg Square. Designed by architect Charles Bulfinch, several buildings, including the gold-domed **State House** (727-3676), offer exhibits on Massachusetts and colonial history, government, and artwork. Free tours include the Hall of Flags, House of Representatives, and the Senate Chamber. (Visitor information: Doric Hall, 2nd floor. Open Mon.-Fri. 9am-5pm; tours Mon.-Fri. 10am-4pm.) The **Harrison Gray Otis House,** 141 Cambridge St. (227-3956), another Bulfinch original, headquarters the Society for the Preservation of New England Antiquities. (Open for tours on the hr. Tues.-Fri. noon-5pm, Sat. 10am-5pm. Admission $3, seniors $2.50, children free.) The Society has information on various other regional historical sites. The nearby **Boston Athenaeum,** 10½ Beacon St. (227-0270), houses over 700,000 books, and offers tours of its library, art gallery, and print room. (Open Mon.-Fri. 9am-5:30pm. Tours Tues. and Thurs. at 3pm; reservations required.)

Charles Street, less forbidding than the mews and heavily curtained windows of the residential areas on high, serves as the Hill's front door. Boston Brahmins, at the pinnacle of U.S. high society, share the brick sidewalks with the fashionable contingent of Boston's gay community. The art galleries, cafés, antique stores, and other small shops with hanging wooden signs make this a good spot for an afternoon stroll. But not a shopping spree—the prohibitive price tags appear in windows with good reason.

In the **Back Bay,** southwest of Beacon Hill, serene three-story row houses line the only logically laid-out streets in Boston. The thoroughfares running east-west (Boylston and Newbury St., Commonwealth Ave., and Marlborough and Beacon St.) are crossed by north-south streets ordered alphabetically, from Arlington St. to Hereford St. Originally the "back bay" of Boston Harbor, landfill and elegant folk moved in about 150 years ago. **Commonwealth Avenue** ("Comm. Ave.") is a European-style boulevard with statuary and benches punctuating its grassy median. Stroll along **Newbury Street,** past dozens of small art galleries, bookstores, and cafés. The Newbury St. league conspiracy of exclusive, expensive stores rivals the West Coast's Rodeo Drive. (T: Arlington, Copley, or Auditorium.)

The handsome **Copley Square** area extends the whole length of Back Bay on commercial Boylston St. Recently renovated and officially reopened in June 1989, the square (T: Copley) has a range of seasonal activities including folk dancing and a food pavilion. A permanent feature is the **Boston Public Library,** 666 Boylston St. (536-5400), a massive, classic baroque building, liberally inscribed with the names of hundreds of authors. Benches and window seats inside overlook a tranquil courtyard with fountain and garden. Relax here or in the vaulted reading room. The auditorium gives a program of lectures and films. (Open Mon.-Thurs. 9am-9pm, Fri. 9am-5pm; also winter Sat. and Sun.) Across the square H.H. Richardson's Romanesque fantasy, **Trinity Church,** catches its reflection in I.M. Pei's mirrored Hancock Tower. Many consider Trinity, built in 1877, a masterpiece of U.S. church architecture—the elaborate interior demonstrates why. (Open daily 2-6pm.) **Copley Place,** a complex containing a hotel and a ritzy mall in the corner next to the library, attracts a surprisingly steady stream of local high school students. The gentrified **South End,** south of Copley, makes for good brownstone viewing and casual dining.

Back Bay loses some of its formality on the riverside **Esplanade** (T: Charles), a park extending from the Longfellow Bridge to the Harvard Bridge. Boston's very own pseudo-beach on the Charles, the Esplanade fills with summer sun-seekers. However, don't go in the water unless you are invulnerable even to hepatitis. Bikers and roller skaters, upholding Boston's rules of the road, try to mow down pedestrians on the walkway. The bike path, which follows the river to Wellesley, makes a nice afternoon's ride. The Esplanade also hosts some of Boston's best-loved cultural events—the concerts of the **Boston Pops Orchestra** (266-1492) at the **Hatch Shell.** Led by John Williams, the Pops play here during the first week of July at 8pm. Admission is free; arrive early, before the crowds get unmanageable. On the Fourth of July, nearly 100,000 patriotic thrillseekers throng the Esplanade to hear the Pops concert (broadcast by loudspeaker throughout the area) and to watch the ensuing terrific fireworks display. Arrive before noon for a seat on the Esplanade, though you can watch the fireworks from basically anywhere in the immediate vicinity no matter how late you arrive. The regular Pops season at **Symphony Hall** (266-7575) runs May 10-July 3 and July 10-14. (Tickets $10-29. Box office open Mon.-Fri. 9am-5pm.)

Beyond the Back Bay, west on Commonwealth Ave., glows **Kenmore Square** (T: Kenmore), watched over by the psychedelic landmark Citgo sign. Kenmore Sq. has more than its share of neon, containing many of the city's most popular nightclubs (see Nightlife below).

Below Kenmore Sq., the **Fenway** comprises a large area of the city, containing some of its best museums. (T: Museum.) Ubiquitous landscaper Frederick Olmsted of Central Park fame designed the **Fens** area at the center of the Fenway as part of his "Emerald Necklace" vision for Boston—a necklace he fortunately never completed. A gem nonetheless, the park's fragrant rose gardens and neighborhood vegetable patches make for perfect picnic turf. Bring your own vegetables. Just north of the Fens, **Fenway Park,** home of the "Green Monster," cases the monstrous **Boston Red Sox** baseball club (box office 267-8661; open Mon.-Fri. 9am-5pm, Sat. 9:30am-2pm; T: Fenway Green line D Train or Kenmore). West still of Fenway sits suburban **Brookline,** with its charming guest houses, and curfewed **Boston University** (both on the Green line).

Downtown, The North End, Chinatown, and the Waterfront

The downtown area claims most of the inland area directly west from Boston Harbor, as well as the affection of thousands of yuppies. A perfect brew of commerce and politics made historic **Quincy Market** in the West End (T: Government Center) the focal point of contemporary Boston.

Upon completion, the red-brick and cobblestone marketplace received nationwide praise as an example of urban revitalization. Not long ago, the pretty buildings that house souvenir shops and trendy boutiques were architecturally significant but decrepit warehouses. Though overpriced and overcrowded, the market stays fun for browsing. The information center in the market's South Canopy (523-3886) can provide direction. At night, come for the lively bar scene. In 1742, Peter Faneuil (FAN-yul) donated **Faneuil Hall,** the gateway to the market, to serve as a marketplace and community hall. Sometimes called the "cradle of American Liberty," it provided the gathering spot for townspeople angry with King George. (Hall open daily 9am-5pm.) In late July and early August, free outdoor concerts, **Summer Nights,** take place in the marketplace, featuring blues, calypso, and rock. (Thurs. 5:30-8:30pm. Call 523-3886 for details.)

Across Congress St. from the market, the red brick plaza of **Government Center,** as its name indicates, proves a trifle less picturesque. The monstrous concrete **City Hall** (725-4000), designed by I.M. Pei, opens to the public Monday through Friday. (T: Government Center.) A few blocks south, its more aesthestically pleasing precursor, the **Old State House,** 206 Washington St. (720-1713), built in 1713, once held a hotbed of revolutionary fervor. (Open daily 9:30am-5pm.)

The eastern tip of Boston contains the historic **North End** (T: Haymarket). The city's oldest residential district, now an Italian neighborhood, overflows with windowboxes, Italian flags, fragrant pastry shops, Sicilian restaurants, and Catholic churches. The most famous of the latter, **Old St. Stephens Church,** on Hanover St. (523-1250), is the classically colonial brainchild of Charles Bulfinch. Down the street, the brilliant and sweet-smelling **Peace Gardens** owned by St. Leonard's Church, pacify as a perfect place for a picnic among red and white flowers.

Downtown Crossing, south of City Hall at Washington St. (T: Downtown Crossing) is a wonderful pedestrian mall where, actually, no cars cross. In the summertime, street vendors peddle flowers, handicrafts, and homemade lemonade from their pushcarts. The avatar of Boston shopping, **Filene's Basement,** 426 Washington St., has jived as the world's oldest bargain store since 1908.

Directly southwest of the Boston Common, small but engaging **Chinatown** (T: Chinatown) marks itself by the arch at its Beach St. entrance and its pagoda-style telephone booths and streetlamps. Within this small area cluster many restaurants, food stores, and novelty shops where you can buy Chinese slippers and 1000-year-old eggs. Chinatown has two big celebrations each year. The first, **New Year,** usually falls on a Sunday in February, and festivities include lion dances and Kung Fu exhibitions. The **August Moon Festival** honors a mythological pair of lovers at the time of the full moon. Watch for listings in *Where Boston.*

The sleazy, all-but-defunct **Combat Zone** borders Chinatown to the east. In its past incarnalization Boston's red-light district, the area now consists mostly of boarded-up Sextasy theaters and derelicts. Women may feel especially uncomfortable passing through at night.

The **waterfront area** runs along Boston Harbor from South Station to the North End Park as Atlantic and Commercial St. Stroll down Commercial, Lewis, or Museum Wharf to breathe in the beauty. At the excellent **New England Aquarium** (973-5200) (T: Aquarium), Central Wharf on the Waterfront, giant sea turtles, sharks, and their companions swim tranquilly as visitors peer into their tubular 187,000-gallon tank. Around the base of the tank penguins cavort in a mini-archipelago all their own. The museum also has more "conventional" exhibitions, and offers free short films. Dolphins and sea lions perform in the ship *Discovery,* moored alongside.

On weekends lines tend to be long. (Open Sept.-June Mon.-Wed. and Fri. 9am-5pm, Thurs. 9am-8pm, Sat.-Sun. and holidays 9am-6pm; July-Aug. Mon.-Tues. and Fri. 9am-6pm, Wed.-Thurs. 9am-8pm, Sat.-Sun. and holidays 9am-7pm. Admission $7, seniors and students $6, ages 4-15 $3.50. Thurs. and summer Wed. after 4pm $1 discount.) The aquarium also offers **whale watching cruises** (973-5277) from April to late October. (Fare $23, seniors and students $18, ages 4-15 $16.25.) **Boston Harbor Cruises** (227-4320) leave from Long Wharf, adjacent to the aquarium, for 90-minute tours of the harbor from roughly March to October. (Departs at 11am, 1pm, 3pm, and 7pm. Admission $8, seniors $6, under 12 $4.)

Across Fort Point Channel from the waterfront predominantly Irish American **South Boston** has an accent all its own. (T: South Station). "Southie" has great seafood places and two beaches.

Charlestown and the Museums

With over 400 institutions of higher learning, Boston has a strong intellectual and academic community and as a result, more museums per square mile than anywhere else in New England. While all 35 in the Greater Boston area may hold some fascination for people, tourists should select somewhat; some are free, some difficult to reach. Check the free *Guide to Museums of Boston* for more details.

The most famous, the **Museum of Fine Arts (MFA)**, 465 Huntington Ave. (267-9300; T: Museum, Green line E train), near the intersection with Massachusetts Ave., has outstanding Egyptian and Asian collections, a good showing of impressionists, and superb Americana. Don't miss John Singleton Copley's fascinating portraits of his contemporaries Paul Revere and Samuel Adams, or his dramatic *Watson and the Shark*. Also worth a gander are the two famous unfinished portraits of George and Martha Washington, painted by Gilbert Stuart in 1796. (Open Tues.-Sun. 10am-5pm, Wed. 10am-10pm. West Wing only open Thurs.-Fri. 5-10pm. Admission $5, West Wing only $4, seniors $4. Free Wed. 10am-noon.)

Running a close second, at the far eastern end of the Esplanade on the Charles River Dam, the **Museum of Science**, Science Park (723-2500; T: Science Park), contains, among other wonders, the largest "lightning machine" in the world. The multi-story roller-coaster for small metal balls purports to explain energy states. Within the museum, the **Hayden Planetarium** features models, lectures, films, laser and star shows; the **Mugar Omni Theatre** shows popular films of scientific interest on a four-story domed screen. (Open Tues.-Thurs. and Sat.-Sun. 9am-5pm, Fri. 9am-9pm. Admission $6, seniors and ages 4-14 $4. Planetarium only, $5 and $3.50. Combined admission and Omni tickets $9 and $6.50. All 3 facilities $12 and $9. Free Wed. afternoons Sept.-May.)

In southern Boston at Congress Street Bridge and Museum Wharf, board the **Boston Tea Party Ship and Museum** (338-1773), which conveys little of the drama of the event that it commemorates through films, memorabilia and exhibits. Trying your hand at heaving tea chests overboard proves a true relaxant, though. (Open daily 9am-6pm. Admission $5, seniors and students $4, ages 5-14 $3.) At the **Children's Museum**, 300 Congress St. (426-8855), also on Museum Wharf, kids of all ages toy with the hands-on exhibits. (Open July-Sept. Mon.-Thurs. and Sat.-Sun. 10am-5pm, Fri. 10am-9pm; off-season closed Mon. Admission $6, seniors and ages 2-15 $5; Fri. 5-9pm $1. T: South Station; follow the signs with the milk bottles on them.)

The **John F. Kennedy Presidential Library** (929-4523), on Morrissey Blvd., Columbia Point, Dorchester is dedicated "to all those who through the art of politics seek a new and better world." Designed by I.M. Pei, the white cuboid oceanside edifice contains a fascinating, sometimes trivia-bound, museum that uses photographs, documents, audio-visual exhibits, and mementos to document the career of John Kennedy and his brother, Robert. (Open daily 9am-5pm. Admission $3.50, seniors $2, under 16 free. T: JFK/UMass on the Ashmont branch; free MBTA shuttle to the U Mass campus, a short walk from the library.)

Boston's small but high-quality **Institute of Contemporary Art (ICA)**, 955 Boylston St. (266-5151; T: Hynes Convention), attracts major contemporary artists and occasional controversy to Boston. Their innovative, sometimes courageous exhibits change every eight weeks. The museum also offers music, dance, and film presentations, as well as discussions with artists on Sundays. (Open Wed. and Sun. 11am-5pm, Thurs.-Sat. 11am-8pm. Admission $4, seniors and under 16 $1.50, students with ID $3. Free Thurs. 5-8pm.)

A few hundred yards from the MFA stands the beautiful **Isabella Stewart Gardner Museum,** 280 The Fenway (566-1401; 734-1359 for recorded events information). The eccentric "Mrs. Jack" Gardner built the small, Venetian-style palace to distract her from her grief at the loss of her only child; in the process she scandalized Boston with her excesses, but eventually built a superb art collection. Unfortunately, thieves depleted the artistic coffers in 1989, taking a few Rembrandts, Degas, and other masterworks. A stunning courtyard and century-old architectural fragments remain. (Chamber music on 1st floor Sept.-June Tues. at 6pm, Thurs. at 12:15pm, and Sun. at 3pm. Open Tues.-Sun. noon-5pm. Admission $5, seniors and students $2.50, children free.)

Two blocks down Massachusetts Ave. from Boylston sits the Mother Church of the **First Church of Christ, Scientist,** One Norway St. (480-2000), founded in Boston by Mary Baker Eddy. The lovely **Mother Church** is the world headquarters of the Christian Science movement, and its complex of buildings appropriately vast and imposing. Both the Mother Church and the smaller, older church out back can be seen by guided tour only; the guides do not proselytize. (Tours Mon.-Sat. 9:30am-3:30pm, Sun. 11:15am-2pm.) In the Christian Science Publishing Society next door, use the catwalk to pass through the **Mapparium,** a 40-ft.-wide stained-glass globe. (Tours Mon.-Sat. 9:30am-3:30pm.)

Charlestown, founded in 1629 by ten Puritan families, predates its southern neighbor by one year. Boston made up for lost time by accruing a batch of historic landmarks over the course of Revolution. But amongst its brownstones and apartment buildings, Charlestown has two landmarks of its own. The **Bunker Hill Monument,** in Monument Sq. (242-5641), commemorates the 1775 Battle in a 221-ft. obelisk. (Open daily 9am-4:30pm.) "Old Ironsides" or the **USS Constitution** (426-1812), the world's oldest commissioned battleship, keeps port in the Charlestown Navy Yard. (T: North Station.) Indestructible in its day, the ship still fires a single salutary cannon each night. (Open daily 10am-4pm; summer 9am-6pm; spring and fall 9am-5pm. Admission $2.50, seniors $2, free Sat. for children.)

Nightlife

The nightlife of the city that beans made famous admittedly does not quite compare with larger and more sophisticated New York. "Blue laws," restrictive regulations which forbid serving liquor past a certain hour, stand out as relics of the city's Puritan past. Liquor, though served on Sundays in restaurants and bars, cannot be sold anywhere else in the state on that day. Nearly everything closes between 1 and 2am, and bar admittance for anyone under 21 is hard-won, though a few spots have 18-and-over nights. But treat Boston nightlife like the appearance of bison rutting season, and appreciate its short-lived brilliance. Quality folk, jazz, rock, and comedy clubs abound here, and theater and cultural offerings more than compensate. Check the **Phoenix** "Boston-After-Dark" listings for up-to-date information.

Gay bars do not proliferate here, but many bars cater to gay and lesbian clientele on specific nights or times. Check the **Bay Windows** listings for more information and event notices. **Chaps,** 27 Huntington Ave. (266-7778) is a fun throwback to the disco era with mirrored walls and a spacious dance floor. (T: Copley.) Primarily a gay male bar with a blend of older and younger patrons, it occasionally offers live entertainment. (Open Mon.-Fri. 4pm-2am, Sat.-Sun. 3pm-2am. Cover $3-5.) **Campus/Manray,** moved to Cambridge, 21 Brookline St., Central Sq. (864-0406), features Top-40 and progressive music for women on Sundays and is open to a mixed crowd the rest of the week. (T: Central.)

The Black Rose, 160 State St., Faneuil Hall (742-2286). T: Government Center. Fabulous Irish pub serving Boston fish market fare, populated with bartenders and waitresses from the Emerald Isle. Of course they serve a pint of Guinness ($2.75). Frequent live traditional Irish music Sat.-Sun. 4-8pm, daily at 9pm. Open daily 11:30am-1:30am. Cover Fri.-Sat. nights $5.

The Channel Club, 25 Necco St., South Boston (451-1050). T: South Station. A forum for the best reggae, rap, rock, new wave, and heavy metal, featuring national and local bands. Huge dance floor, 8 bars, gameroom, concession stand. The amount of hairspray used by clientele alone could bring the ozone tumbling. Capacity 1500. 18-and-over nights. Open daily, hours vary. Cover $3-10.

Citi/Metro/Venus de Milo, 9-15 Lansdowne St., Kenmore Sq. (262-2424). T: Kenmore. This complex of 3 active night clubs offers something of everything. Citi, the largest club, has 6 bars, a dance floor, and occasional pop concerts. Metro plays "cutting edge," "hard hitting" rock 'n' roll; Venus is an international club playing international music. Open daily 10pm-2am. Cover varies.

Rathskeller, 528 Commonwealth Ave., Kenmore Sq. (536-2750). T: Kenmore. The "Rat" breeds genuine honky-tonk: black floors, low ceilings, and smoke-filled rooms. Exciting new bands Thurs.-Sun.; performances start around 9:30pm. Cover $5-7.

Narcissus, 533 Commonwealth Ave. (536-1950). T: Kenmore. Young crowd, the youngest of whom seem to wear tightest clothes. Ear-splitting music on three levels. Occasional live performers: Wed. heavy metal night, Sun. Latin night. Open daily 8pm-2am. Cover varies.

Arts and Entertainment

Musicians, dancers, actors, and *artistes* of every description fill Boston. The *Phoenix* and the "Calendar" section of the Thursday *Boston Globe* list activities for the coming week. Also check the *Where Boston* booklet available at the visitors center. What Boston doesn't have, Cambridge does (see Cambridge below). **Bostix,** a Ticketron outlet in Faneuil Hall (723-5181), sells half-price tickets to performing arts events on the day of performance. (Service charge $1.50-2.50 per ticket. Cash only. Open Tues.-Sat. 11am-6pm, Sun. 11am-4pm.)

Actors in town cluster around Washington St. and Harrison Ave., in the **Theater District** (T: Boylston). The famous **Wang Center for the Performing Arts** at 268 Tremont St. (482-9393), produces theater, classical music, and opera in its modern complex. The **Shubert Theater,** 265 Tremont St. (426-4520), and the **Wilbur Theater,** 246 Tremont St. (426-1988), host Broadway hits calling in Boston. Tickets for these and for shows at the **Charles Playhouse,** 74 Warrenton St. (426-6912), are costly (around $30). The area's professional companies are cheaper, and may provide a more interesting evening. The **New Ehrlich Theater,** 539 Tremont St. (482-6316), and **Huntington Theater Co.,** 264 Huntington Ave. (266-3913) at Boston University have solid artistic reputations. (Tickets $10-24.) More affordable college theater also chives. During term-time, investigate the **Tufts Theater-Arena** (381-3493), the **Boston University Theatre** (266-3913), the **MIT Drama Shop** (253-2877) and **Shakespeare Ensemble** (253-2903).

The renowned **Boston Ballet** (946-4070), in neighboring Newton, brings to life such classics as the "Nutcracker" and "Swan Lake." The **Boston Symphony Orchestra,** 201 Mass. Ave. (266-1492; T: Symphony), at Huntington, holds its concert season from October to April. Rush seats go on sale three hours before Thursday and Saturday concerts. Open Wednesday rehearsals cost under $10; bargain tickets are also available Friday at noon for that evening's show. In summer, when the BSO retreats to Tanglewood, the **Boston Pops Orchestra** sets up at Symphony Hall or the Esplanade and plays classics and pop on weekend evenings. The **Berklee Performance Center,** 136 Mass. Ave. (262-4998), an adjunct of the the local Berklee School of Music, holds a few concerts of its own featuring students, faculty, and musical luminaries.

Despite its immediate air of refinement, Boston goes ape for sports. Long known for fans as committed as Charles Manson, Beantown always seems in some seasonal basketball, baseball, football, or hockey frenzy. On summer nights, the thousands of baseball fans pouring out of **Fenway Park** (see above) clog Kenmore Sq. traffic for an hour. **Boston Garden,** off the JFK Expressway between the West and North

Ends, hosts both the championship **Boston Celtics** basketball team (season Oct.-May; call 526-6050 for information) and the newly Cup-threatening **Boston Bruins** (season Oct.-April; call 227-3228 for more information). A few miles outside Boston, **Sullivan Stadium** hosts the long-beleaguered **New England Patriots** football franchise, as well as an occasional Dead concert.

In October, the **Head of the Charles** regatta, the largest such single-day event in the U.S., attracts crew teams and college sweat-shirts from across the country. The 3-mi. races begin at Boston University Bridge; the best vantage points are on the Weeks footbridge and Kennedy St. Bridge near Harvard. On April 19, the 10,000 runners competing in the **Boston Marathon** tread memories of the "Head" underfoot. Call the Massachusetts Division of Tourism for details (617-727-3201).

For other special events, such as the **St. Patrick's Day Parade** in South Boston (March 17), **Patriot's Day** celebrations (April 19), the week-long **Boston Common Dairy Festival** (June), the **Boston Harbor Fest** (early July), and the North End's **Festival of St. Anthony** (mid-August), see the Boston *Phoenix* or *Globe* calendars.

Cambridge

Cambridge, the cosmopolitan satellite of a provincial city, is to bookstores and cafés what New York is to nightclubs. Home to both the Massachusetts Institute of Technology (MIT) and Harvard University, Cambridge benefits from the influx of scholars, students, and ideas. Over espresso you can catch a conversation in French, Japanese, Russian, or academic doublespeak. Yet the resulting backdrop is pronouncedly Old Ivied America, with charming colonial structures and gilded bell towers lining the cobblestone sidewalks. Situated on the northeast side of the Charles River, Cambridge often feels like an overgrown (and overblown) college campus in which everyone, even the most casual visitor, is a student.

Practical Information

See Boston Practical Information above for more complete and detailed listings.

Emergency: 911.

Visitor Information: Cambridge Discovery Booth, (497-1630) in Harvard Sq. Best and most comprehensive information about Cambridge, as well as MBTA bus and subway schedules. Pick up the *Old Cambridge Walking Guide,* an excellent self-guided tour ($1). Walking tours of Harvard and the surrounding area in the summer. Open summer daily 9am-6pm; off-season Mon.-Sat. 9am-5pm, Sun. 1-5pm. **Out-Of-Town News,** 354-7777. No official status as a tourist resource, but sells a large number of excellent maps and guides to the area. A must for anyone staying any length of time in Cambridge, *The Unofficial Guide to Life at Harvard* ($6) has complete and up-to-date listings of local restaurants, entertainment, sights, transportation and services. Open Sun.-Thurs. 6am-11:30pm, Fri.-Sat. 6pm-midnight. **Harvard University Information Center,** 1352 Massachusetts Ave., (495-1573), Harvard Sq. Most helpful in your exploration of the campus. Free guides to the university museums; several tours each day. Open summer Mon.-Sat. 9am-4:45pm, Sun. 1-4pm; off-season Mon.-Sat. 9am-4:45pm.

Public Transport: Massachusetts Bay Transportation Authority (MBTA), 722-3200 or 800-392-6100. Office open Mon.-Fri. 8:30am-4:30pm. Subway operates daily 5:30am-12:30am.

Taxi: Cambridge Taxi, 876-5600.

Post Office: 125 Mt. Auburn St. (876-6483). Open Mon.-Fri. 8am-5:30pm, Sat. 9am-1pm. **ZIP code:** 02138.

Area Code: 617.

Massachusetts Avenue ("Mass. Ave.") is Cambridge's major artery. Most of the action takes place in squares (that is, commercial areas) along Mass. Ave. and the Red Line. **MIT** is just across the Mass. Ave. Bridge at **Kendall Square,** on the Red Line. The Red Line continues outbound one T-stop at a time through: **Central Square,** the heart of urban Cambridge; frenetic, eclectic **Harvard Square;** and more suburban **Porter Square.**

Accommodations

Cambridge YMCA, 820 Massachusetts Ave. (661-9622). T: Central. Men only. Sometimes full. Hall bathrooms. 7-day max. stay. Check-out 11am. Singles only, $30. Key deposit $10. Reservations recommended, or arrive by 11am. 2 forms of ID (one picture) required.

Cambridge YWCA, 7 Temple St. (491-6050), just off Mass. Ave. near the Central T-stop. Women only. Few overnight rooms, all of which fill quickly. Kitchen and laundry facilities. 3-day max. stay. Singles only, $30, nonmembers $39. Key deposit $10. Reservations required.

The Irving House, 24 Irving St. (547-4600), near Cambridge St., in a safe residential neighborhood near the university and the Square. T: Harvard. Formerly the creaky, wallflowered Kirkland, now undergoing colorful renovations scheduled for completion in June 1991. New, appealing management. Unique rooms, libraries, comfortable fishtanked lounge, spacious wood floors; parking available. Singles from $33. Doubles $50, with private bath $60. Reservations accepted.

Susse Chalet Inn, 211 Concord Turnpike (Rte. 2), Fresh Pond (661-7800), ½ mi. from the Alewife T-stop just outside Cambridge. Standard chain-type lodgings overlooking the highway. Private bath, TV, and phone. Singles $49. Doubles $53. Reservations suggested.

Food

Nightly, thousands of college students renounce cafeteria fare in the restaurants of Harvard Square, and for good reason. An enormous selection of funky eateries packs its tiny area. A 15-minute walk around should uncover offerings to satisfy even the most esoteric tastebuds. Don't be afraid to wander beyond the square if you feel as if you've seen one kid too many in a crimson sweatshirt. Explore Massachusetts Ave. where it slopes down into Central Sq., lined with great Indian restaurants, or where it climbs up into the varied eateries of Porter Sq.

For cheap grub, try **The Garage** at 36 Kennedy St. More of a storage shed where cars no longer fit, this mall of restaurants offers everything from gourmet coffee to hummus to greasy pizza. Probably some of the cheapest fare in the square, **Elsie's,** 71 Mt. Auburn St., makes generous sandwiches ($2.50-3.50) quickly. (Open Mon.-Fri. 7am-midnight, Sat. 7am-4pm, Sun. 11am-7pm.) **Tommy's Lunch** on Mt. Auburn St. is, ironically enough, a late-night tradition at Harvard, with plenty of sneering service, pinball (25¢), and greasy onion rings. Try the legendary raspberry lime rickey (80¢-$1.50), but don't put your hands over the counter or feet on the booths; sit back and admire the "Gun Control is Being Able to Hit Your Target" T-shirts. (Open Sun.-Thurs. 7am-2am, Fri.-Sat. 7am-3am; summer Sun.-Thurs. 7am-1:30am, Fri.-Sat. 7am-2:30am.) Diner-like **Charlie's Kitchen** at 10 Eliot St. proffers many variations on the double burger ($3). (Open Mon.-Sat. noon-midnight, Sun. noon-1am.)

College students and Cantabrigians alike hang out at the **Border Café,** 32 Church St. in Harvard Sq. A nice *faux* Southwestern atmosphere and good, cheap food make up for the considerable crowds. Try their specialty—steaming *fajitas* ($8-11), or Mike's favorite, the *quesadilla.* Come prepared to have a few drinks at the bar, since you may wait for up to an hour to get a table. (Open Mon.-Thurs. 11am-12:45am, Fri.-Sat. 11am-1:45am, Sun. noon-12:45am.) Pick up the weekly *Square Deal,* usually handed out or in boxes near the T-stop, for coupons and discounts on local fare.

Pizzeria Uno, 22 John F. Kennedy St., Harvard Sq. One of the wooden signs reads "If we're busy try our place in Chicago." On weekends you'd better have an airline ticket handy because the wait can be over an hour, and the service slow. Worth it for the rich, delicious food. Individual pizzas $3.75-5.50, regulars $7-10.75. 5-min. express lunch (Mon.-Fri. 11am-3pm) $4. Open Sun.-Wed. 11am-1am, Thurs.-Sat. 11am-2am.

The Skewers, 92 Mt. Auburn St., Harvard Sq. Large servings of tasty Middle Eastern food at bargain prices. Sandwiches $3-4.50, dinner entrees $6.50-7.25. Open Mon.-Sat. 11am-11pm, Sun. noon-10pm.

The Stock Pot, 57 JFK St. (492-9058) in the Galleria. Thick, award-winning homemade soups ($2.50-3.25). Tremendous salad bar ($4.50) and "stockpocket" sandwiches ($3.75). Open Mon.-Sat. 11:30am-8:30pm, Sun. 4-8:30pm; summer closed Sundays.

Bangkok House, 50 JFK St., Harvard Sq. Large portions of delicious Thai food in three categories: mild, spicy, and very spicy. Order a three-starred dish and prepare to sweat. Entrees $7.25-12. Deliciously aromatic coconut soup. Open Sun.-Thurs. noon-3pm and 5-10pm, Fri.-Sat. noon-3pm and 5-10:30pm.

Dolphin Seafood, 1105 Mass. Ave., between Harvard and Central Sq. Crowded and friendly, much like their squid appetizer. Huge portions of fresh seafood ($5.25-9.50) that Ghita loves. Cheap lunch specials. Open Mon.-Sat. 11am-10pm, Sun. 4-10pm. Arrive early on weekends.

Oh! Calcutta!, 468 Massachusetts Ave. (576-2111), in Central Sq. Not a long-running nude musical or a Davidson aphrodisiac, but an immensely successful Indian restaurant. Atmosphere incongruous, but great service. Large portions of delicious food, from fiery pickled vegetables to sweet rice pudding. Lunch specials (Mon.-Fri.) $4-5, dinner entrees $7-13. All-you-can-eat extravaganzas (Sat.-Sun. noon-3pm) $8. Open daily noon-10:30pm.

Chef Chow's House, 50 Church St., Harvard Sq. (547-4969). Tasty and moderately priced Chinese dishes in a soothing wood-soaked atmosphere. Nice fish tanks. Entrees $5-22. Take-out available. Open Sun.-Thurs. 11:30am-10pm, Fri.-Sat. 11:30am-11pm.

A meal in the vicinity of Harvard Square would not be complete without dessert afterwards. Dens of sin abound, like **Herrell's,** 15 Dunster St. in Harvard Sq., which makes what some call the "Best Chocolate Ice Cream in Boston" (1.50 with mix-in). Lap up the "no-moo" concoctions inside a vault painted to resemble the open depths. (Open summer daily 11am-midnight; off-season noon-midnight.) Down the street, **Emack & Bolio's** at 1310 Mass. Ave. serves delicious oreo ice cream ($1.50); their homemade cookies aren't bad, either. (Open summer Sun.-Thurs. noon-11pm, Fri.-Sat. noon-1am; off-season Sun.-Thurs. 11am-11pm, Fri.-Sat. 11am-midnight.) The hands-down avatar of the evil frozen yogurt trend is **Luscious Licks,** on Eliot St., offering fresh fruit and yummy chocolate to top off their rich confections ($2-2.25). (Open Sun.-Thurs. 11am-11pm, Fri.-Sat. 11am-midnight.)

Nightlife and Entertainment

In warm weather, Cambridge entertainment is free. Street musicians ranging from New Age to Andean folk singers to the obligatory 60s psychedelia float through the streets of Harvard Sq. The folk artists tend to cluster on Mass. Ave., either near the T or by Au Bon Pain, while the jazz cats lean toward Brattle St. Cafés crowd at all times of year for lunch or after-hours coffee. **Café Pamplona,** 12 Bow St., is dubbed "Café Pompous" by those who know it well. The low-ceilinged, smoke-filled room might be too philosophy-heavy for you; in summer escape to their outdoor tables. Try the mint parfait ($2.50). (Open Mon.-Sat. 11am-1am, Sun. 2pm-1am.) The **Coffee Connection,** on Dunster St. in the Garage, serves exotic coffees and teas amidst Native American art. The smell of the place is fantastic; try the delicious *café con panna* ($1.50). (Open Mon.-Thurs. 8am-11pm, Fri. 8am-midnight, Sat. 9am-midnight, Sun. 9am-11pm.) **Au Bon Pain,** on Mass. Ave., offers a less exotic menu and mass-produced munchies, but its chess, prices, and people-watching location cannot be beat. (Open Sun.-Thurs. 7am-midnight, Fri.-Sat. 7am-1am.) The **Blacksmith House,** 56 Brattle St., serves up more than just café and bakery items. The Cambridge Center for Adult Education presents various poetry readings here throughout the year (usually Mon.; admission varies) and also musical programs on summer Thursdays at 8pm.

Rich cultural offerings keep Cambridge vital. Harvard sponsors any number of readings and lectures each week; check the kiosks that fill Harvard Yard for posters about the events most students are too busy to attend. Also look at the windows of one of the over 25 bookstores in the Square to see if any literary luminaries will appear during your visit. Theater thrives here. Harvard undergraduates produce shows year-round, though more frequently during the school year. (Tickets $3-7.) The renowned **American Repertory Theater,** 64 Brattle St., under the direction of Harvard prof Robert Brustein, produces shows from Sept. to June. (Tickets $16-

33.) Tickets for undergraduate and ART productions can be purchased through the Loeb Drama Center (543-8300). (Box office open Mon.-Fri. 10am-7:30pm; on performance days 10am-5:30pm.) The Harvard Information Office also sells tickets to a variety of bigger concerts, plays, and events. But those whose idea of nightlife is a little louder than an evening with Vaclav Havel or coffee and a discussion of the modern novel, Cambridge can accommodate as well.

Catch a Rising Star, 306 JFK St. (661-9887), Harvard Sq. Hosts funny and occasionally not-so-funny artists in a typical comedy club atmosphere. All ages, but you must be 21 to drink. "Open mike" comedy Mon.-Tues., live music Sun. and Wed.-Thurs. Shows Sun.-Thurs. at 8:30; Fri. at 8:30 and 11pm; Sat. at 7:30pm, 9:45pm, and midnight. Cover Mon.-Tues. $5, Sun. and Wed.-Thurs. $8. Fri.-Sat. $12. $3 discount with college ID Mon.-Thurs.)

The Boathouse Bar, 56 JFK St., Harvard Sq. Usually populated by the Harvard Business School and athletic sweatshirt set; college crowd on weekend nights and after hockey and football games. Line sometimes stretches out the door. The beer here also costs a pretty penny—Sam Adams goes for $3.25 a hit. Open Sun.-Wed. 10am-1am, Thurs.-Sat. 10am-2am.

The Bow and Arrow Pub, Bow St. and Mass Ave., Harvard Sq. Decidedly non-college-kid clientele; usually an impressive assortment of motorcycles outside. Women might not feel comfortable here alone. Some of the cheapest beer in town (16-oz. knickerbockers $1.40), a 50¢ game of hoops, and an eclectic jukebox selection. Open Mon.-Thurs. 11am-1am, Fri.-Sat. noon-1am, Sun. noon-1am.

T.T. The Bear's Place, 10 Brookline St. (492-0082), in Central Sq. A great honky-tonk joint with reasonably priced liquor and a pool table in the back room. Live, really live, rock bands Thurs.-Sat., DJs on Sun. Open Tues.-Sat. 5pm-1am. Live music 9pm-12:30am. Cover $4-6.

Hong Kong, 1236 Mass Ave., Harvard Sq. The alcohol-infested scorpion bowls are a Harvard tradition. Mediocre food; popular, crowded, and rowdy bar upstairs. Open Sun.-Thurs. 11:30am-1am, Fri.-Sat. 11:30am-2am.

Sights

People-watching, the favorite Cantabrigian pastime, may explain the number of cafés. But if you can tear yourself away from staring at balding professors, yuppies, hippies, street punks, and street people, you might see some interesting buildings as well.

MIT is as much a tribute to as an institute of technology. The campus boasts a number of buildings by overworked I.M. Pei, an impressive collection of modern outdoor sculpture, and an "infinite corridor" ¼-mi. long. Tours are available weekdays at 10am and 2pm from the Rogers Building, or "Building Number 7" as the students here call it; MIT students, you'll soon discover, understand the language of numbers better than words. Contact MIT Information at 77 Mass. Ave. (253-4775; open Mon.-Fri. 9am-5pm). The **MIT Museum,** 265 Mass. Ave. (253-4444), contains a slide rule collection and wonderful photography exhibits, including the famous stop-action photos of Harold Edgerton. (Open Tues.-Fri. 9am-5pm, Sat-Sun. 1-5pm. Free.)

Up Mass. Ave., the other university seems to shun such futuristic delights for glories of the past, especially its own. **Harvard University,** established in 1636, is the oldest university in the country, and won't let anyone forget it. Ask at the information center about self-guided, self-gratifying walking tours. (See Practical Information above.)

The university revolves around **Harvard Yard;** in the western half ("The Old Yard"), some of the school's first buildings still stand. Today all Harvard students live in the Yard during their first year of study; John F. Kennedy lived in Weld, Emerson and Thoreau in Hollis. If you want to avoid looking like a tourist, avoid taking pictures of the **John Harvard Statue,** and certainly don't call it "The Statue of the Three Lies." Besides classroom buildings, the Yard's eastern half holds **Memorial Church** and **Widener Library** (495-2413). The centerpiece of the Harvard University Library system, Widener is the largest academic library in the world with 10.5 million volumes total. Its card catalog proved a powerful hostage in the student strike of 1969, which led the university to computerize and decentralize in an effort to become terrorist-proof. While visitors can't browse among Widener's shelves, they are welcome to examine Harvard's copy of the Gutenberg Bible and other rare books in the Harry Elkins Widener Memorial Reading Room, or to take in the horrendous Sargent murals.

Late 20th-century Harvard extends well beyond the Yard down to the Charles River. The **Harvard Houses**—the university's attempt to duplicate the learning environment of Oxford and Cambridge—cover an area that extends from Mass. Ave. to Memorial Dr. They run the gamut from ornate Adams House, part of which dates to the 18th century, to concrete and spartan Mather House, built in a riot-proof 1970 and sporting the highest point on campus. Across the Charles lies the **Business School** (along with most of Wall Street) and the university's athletic facilities. North of Harvard Yard endows the **Law School, Divinity School,** and **Radcliffe Quadrangle;** to the west lies the **School of Education** and **Radcliffe Yard.**

The oldest of Harvard's museums (sort of), the **Fogg Art Museum,** 32 Quincy St., has a considerable collection of works ranging from ancient Chinese jade to contemporary photography, housing the largest Ingres collection outside of France. The limited display space around its Italian Renaissance courtyard frequently rotates well-planned exhibits. Across the street, the **Arthur M. Sackler Museum,** 485 Broadway, has an ultra-modern exterior belied by its rich collection of ancient Asian and Islamic art. (Both museums open Tues.-Sun. 10am-5pm. Admission to each $4, seniors $2.50. Free Sat. mornings. Call 495-9400 for information.) Next door to the Fogg, Le Corbusier's "machine for living," the **Carpenter Center,** 24 Quincy St. (495-3251), shows student and professional work with especially strong photo exhibits, not to mention a great film series. (Open Mon.-Fri. 9am-11pm, Sat. 9am-6pm, Sun. noon-10pm.) Included in the **Museums of Natural History** at 24 Oxford St. (495-3045 or 495-1310), are the **Peabody Museum of Archaeology and Ethnology,** which houses treasures from prehistoric and Native American cultures, and the **Mineralogical and Geological Museums,** containing gems, minerals, ores, and meteorites. But the overhyped "glass flowers" exhibit at the **Botanical Museum** draws the largest crowds. A German glassblower and his son created these remarkably accurate and beautiful enlarged reproductions of over 840 plant species. **The Museum of Comparative Zoology** offers a little grittier view of nature, with its stuffed gorilla and dinosaur bones. Check out the museum's own skeletal sea monster, the Kronosaurus. (Open Mon.-Sat. 9am-4:30pm, Sun. 1-4:30pm. Admission $3, seniors and students $2, ages 5-15 $1.)

But despite what they tell you in the admissions office, there's more to life than Harvard. European settlers established Cambridge six years *before* the university, in 1630. Stroll up Mass. Ave. to the green **Cambridge Common,** established in 1631. Once the focal point of the town's political, social, and religious activity, it eventually became a camp for George Washington's Continental Army. Unless you have your own army, it is unsafe to walk here at night. Washington worshiped across the street at **Christ Church,** the oldest church in Cambridge, which had its organ pipes melted down for Revolutionary bullets. Soldiers felled in the struggle are buried in the 350-yr.-old **Old Burying Ground** or "God's Acre" on Garden St., also the final resting place of colonial settlers and early Harvard presidents. Behind Garden St. is **Brattle Street,** dubbed "Tory Row" and dotted with the former homes of British Loyalists. Restored to the period of the poet Henry Wadsworth Longfellow's lifetime, the **Longfellow House,** 105 Brattle St. (876-4491), is a National Historic Site. Headquarters of the Continental Army in olden days, the site now sponsors garden concerts and poetry readings in the summer; the staff can give you information on other local historic sites. (Tours daily 10am-4:30pm. Admission $2, seniors and under 17 free.) The **Mt. Auburn Cemetery** lies about a mile up the road at the end of Brattle St. The first botanical-garden cemetery in the U.S. has 170 acres of beautifully landscaped grounds. Louis Agassiz, Charles Bulfinch, Dorothea Dix, Mary Baker Eddy, and H.W. Longfellow are all buried here.

Lexington and Concord

> *Listen, my children, and you shall hear*
> *Of the midnight ride of Paul Revere*
> *On the 18th of April in '75.*
> *Hardly a man is now alive*
> *Who remembers that famous day and year.*
>   *—Henry Wadsworth Longfellow*

Apparently Longfellow never visited **Lexington** and **Concord,** where the people can't seem to forget it. Inhabitants will remind you constantly that the Minutemen skirmished with advancing British troops on the **Lexington Battle Green,** falling back to the **Old North Bridge** in Concord where U.S. troops first officially received orders to fire upon the Redcoats.

On the Lexington Green, the **Minuteman Statue** of Captain John Parker looks back to Boston, still watching for the invader. The surrounding houses seem nearly as historic as the land; the **Jonathan Harrington House** on Harrington Rd., built in 1750, housed its namesake who crawled away from the battle to die on his own doorstep. The **Budeman Tavern,** on Hancock St. opposite the Green, had already slung ale for 65 years when it headquartered the Minutemen. The Lexington Historical Society carefully restored the interior; tourists on acid might think they'd fallen into a time warp. The society also did a number on **Munroe Tavern,** 1 mi. from the Green on Mass. Ave., which served as a field hospital for wounded British. (Houses open mid-April to late Oct. Mon.-Sat. 10am-5pm, Sun. 1-5pm. Admission $2.50 per house, ages 6-16 50¢. 3 houses $5. Along with a walking map of the area, the **visitors center** at 1875 Mass. Ave. (862-1450), behind the Buckman Tavern, displays a 50-year-old, painstakingly detailed diorama of the Battle of Lexington. (Open daily 9am-5pm; Nov.-June 10am-4pm.)

The **Battle Road** winding 6 mi. from the Lexington Green to Concord is now part of a national park; the **Battle Road Visitors Center** on Rte. 2A in Lexington (862-7353) shows a 20-minute film about the region and distributes maps of the park. At the **North Bridge Visitors Center,** 174 Liberty St., park rangers lead interpretive area tours of the Old North Bridge over the Concord River, the site of "the shot heard 'round the world."

Concord garnered fame not only for its military history but as a U.S. literary capital of the 19th century as well. The Alcotts and Hawthornes once inhabited **Wayside** at 455 Lexington Rd. (369-6975), while Emerson himself lived down the road for the latter part of the 19th century. Alongside Emerson's reconstructed study, the **Concord Museum,** directly across the street from the house (369-9609), houses Paul Revere's lantern and items from Henry David Thoreau's cabin. (Open Feb.-Dec. Mon.-Sat. 10am-4pm, Sun. 1-4pm. Admission $5, seniors $4, students $3, under 5 $2.) Emerson, Hawthorne, Alcott, and Thoreau all wait for Ichabod Crane on "Author's Ridge" in the **Sleepy Hollow Cemetery** on Rte. 62, 3 blocks from the center of town.

While alive, Thoreau retreated to **Walden Pond,** 1½ mi. south on Rte. 126, in 1845 "to live deliberately, to front only the essential facts of life." His pre-hippie book *Walden* contains some inspirational observations about his two-year solitude there. The **Thoreau Lyceum,** 156 Belknap St. (369-5912), national headquarters of the Thoreau Society, will answer questions about this naturalist-philosopher. The Lyceum sponsors the society's convention in July, and has a replica of Thoreau's cabin in its backyard. (open April-Dec. Mon.-Sat. 10am-5pm, Sun. 2-5pm; early Feb.-March Thurs.-Sat. 10am-5pm, Sun. 2-5pm. Admission $2, students $1.50, children 50¢.) Walden Pond (369-3254), the purest attraction in the area, is now a state reservation, popular with picnickers, swimmers, and boaters. Granite posts at the far end of the pond mark the site of Thoreau's cabin. (Open April-Oct. daily dawn-dusk. Parking $5.) When Walden Pond swarms with crowds, head down Rte. 62

east from Concord center to **Great Meadows National Wildlife Refuge** (443-4661), another of Thoreau's haunts. (Open daily dawn-dusk.)

The **South Bridge Boat House,** 496 Main St. (371-2465), rents canoes (Mon.-Fri. $6 per hr., $25 per day; Sat.-Sun. $7.25 per hr., $35 per day) for the Concord and Sudbury Rivers. (Open April-Oct. daily 10am-7:30pm.)Look for an excellent local map and information on Concord events and sites in a rack outside the **chamber of commerce,** in Wright Tavern on Main St., or at the **information booth,** just outside the town center on Heywood St. off Lexington Rd. (Open late May-late Oct. daily 9:30am-4:30pm; late April-late May Sat.-Sun. 9:30am-4:30pm.) Concord and Lexington make easy daytrips from Boston. Concord, just 20 mi. north of Boston, is served by MBTA "Commuter Rail" trains leaving from North Station ($2.75). MBTA buses from Alewife station in Boston run several times each day to Lexington (50¢).

The **area code** for Lexington is 617, Concord 508.

Salem

The fact that Salem's thriving tourist industry feeds on the execution of 20 innocent people and the jailing of 200 more seems more satanic than the "witchcraft" of 1692. While tourists come here because of the sensationalism of the Salem witch trials, the travesty shames them. The town does have less burdensome sights. The 1.3-mi. **Heritage Trail** traces an easy footpath through town, marked clearly by a painted red line on the pavement.

At the heart of town between Washington Sq. E. and Hawthorne Blvd. lies the **Salem Common,** dating back to the 1600s. Across the street, the **Witch Museum** (744-1692) is not a museum, but a multi-media presentation fleshing out the history of the trials. (Open July-Aug. Mon.-Fri. 10am-5pm, Sat.-Sun. 10am-7pm; off-season daily 10am-5pm. Admission $3.50, seniors $3, ages 6-14 $2.) Never actually a dungeon, the generally kitschy **Witch Dungeon,** 16 Lynde St. (774-9812), has actresses re-enact the trials, providing the full impact of the horrible proceedings. (Open early May-early Nov. daily 10am-5pm. Admission $3.50, ages 6-14 $2.)

Salem's most substantial sight, the **Peabody Museum,** in East India Sq., recalls the town's former role as the leading Atlantic whaling and merchant shipping port. Wide-ranging exhibits detail maritime history, art, and whaling, and include samples of unusual goods imported from international ports. (Open Mon.-Wed. and Fri.-Sat. 10am-5pm, Thurs. 10am-9pm, Sun. and holidays noon-5pm. Admission $5, seniors and students $4, ages 6-12 $2.50.) Two blocks past the museum, ethnic music, dance, and food fill the Salem marketplace in weekly summer street festivals. Near the museum the **Essex Institute,** at 132 Essex St. (744-3390), an important archive of materials relating to New England history, also contains a museum crammed to the rafters with silver, furniture, portraits, toys, and other oddities. Four old houses on the same block under the institute's care are open to visitors. (Museum and houses open June-Oct. Mon.-Wed. and Fri.-Sat. 9am-5pm, Thurs. 9am-9pm, Sun. 1-5pm; Nov.-May Tues.-Sat. 9am-5pm, Sun. 1-5pm. Admission to all $5, ages 6-16 $2.50.)

Where the town hits the Atlantic, you'll find **Derby Wharf,** one of the few remaining from the over 50 wharves that lined Salem Harbor in its heyday. The beautifully preserved grassy dock ends in a lighthouse dating to 1871; across the street the **Custom House** at 178 Derby St. (744-4323) helped the angst-ridden Hawthorne dream up *The Scarlet Letter,* one of the earliest great U.S. literary works. (Open daily 9am-6pm; off-season 9am-5pm. Free.) The **National Park Service,** at Museum Place on Essex St. (747-3648), has more information about the waterfront area, including free maps and brochures. (Open daily 9am-5pm.)

Just beyond the waterfront area stands the architecturally bizarre **House of Seven Gables,** 54 Turner St. (744-0991), built in 1668 and made famous by Hawthorne's gothic romance. Tours provide very real glimpses into the life of the sea captain who dwelt there in the 18th century. (Open daily 10am-4:30pm; July-Aug. Fri.

Wed. 9:30am-5:30pm, Thurs. 9:30am-8:30pm. Admission $6, ages 6-17 $2.50.) Up the road on Derby St., the **Pickering Wharf** offers free public restrooms. Wonderful-smelling **Red's Sandwich Shop**, 15 Central St., serves breakfast (55¢-$3.50) and lunch ($1.25-3.50) at small tables and a crowded counter. (Open Mon.-Sat. 5am-3pm, Sun. 6am-1pm.) **Essex Pizza and Roast Beef**, in Museum Place, has a similarly cramped setting but predictable pizza and roast beef ($2-3.35) renowned among locals. (Open Mon.-Sat. 11am-10pm.)

Salem's most reasonable accommodations are at **Hotel Lafayette**, 116 Lafayette St. (745-5503), near the train station. The lowest-quality rooms have no linens, peeling paint, and dingy surroundings—the higher quality might be worth it. (Singles and doubles $35-65.) Beautiful beachside camping cuddles up at **Winter Island Marine Recreational Park**, 50 Winter Island Rd. (745-9430), about 1½ mi. from Salem, where a bevy of couples are often spied kissing on the shore. (2-week max. stay. Sites $12, with electricity and water $15.)

The **visitors information booth** at Riley Plaza (open April-Oct. daily 9:30am-4pm) and the Salem **chamber of commerce**, 32 Derby Sq. (774-0004; open Mon.-Fri. 9am-5pm) will help you get your bearings and advertises the seasonal town offerings. Taking place in the last week of October, **Haunted Happenings** disguises itself as something of a northern Mardi Gras, complete with free candlelight tours and ghost stories, three costume balls, and a 100,000-person parade. Book months in advance if you plan to be in town then.

Salem hexes 20 mi. northeast of Boston, accessible by train from North Station (½ hr., $2.25) or by bus from Haymarket (45 min., $2). By car, take Rte. 128 north to Rte. 114 (exit 25E).

Cape Ann

Those who favor the white sands of southern Cape Cod sometimes pejoratively call Cape Ann "the other cape," yet this northern peninsula has a splendor all its own. Sweet-smelling wild roses beneath swooping gulls line the gorgeous, rocky shores, which also house the few genuine fishing villages remaining in the state. Though the main action has long since moved inland from these original European settlements, the quiet streets of Cape Ann's modern-day fishing towns at the end of Rte. 128 still possess a unique charm.

The **Cape Ann Chamber of Commerce**, 33 Commercial St. (283-1601), in Gloucester, has extensive information on the area. (Open summer Mon.-Fri. 8am-6pm, Sat. 10am-6pm, Sun. 10am-4pm; off-season Mon.-Fri. 9am-5pm.) Pick up the *Cape Ann Guide*, a free publication, with information on sights, special events, and beaches. The *North Shore Guide*, also free, contains similar information about coastal towns from Boston to New Hampshire.

While Rte. 128 provides the most direct access to Cape Ann, the secondary roads (Rte. 127 along the coast from Boston, Rte. 133 from points north) offer superior scenery. The commuter rail out of North Station also reaches the region.

Gloucester and Rockport (see below), at the tip of the cape, are the main seats of tourism here, and the smaller southern towns have little to offer. One exception is the town of **Magnolia**, home to **Hammond Castle Museum**, 80 Hesperus Ave. (283-2081), built in the late 20s by inventor and professional eccentric John Hayes Hammond, Jr. to house his collection of medieval European relics. A friend and rival of Isabella Gardner, Hammond's strange home, though less outrageously eclectic, reminds the sights-oriented tourist of Boston's Gardner Museum. Some Friday see evening recitals in the Great Hall on a huge organ, and concerts ranging from Bach to big band, usually on weekend nights (tickets $10, $12 at door). (Open daily 9am-5pm. Admission and tour $5, seniors and students with ID $4, ages 6-12 $3.) Magnolia is accessible from Boston by train from North Station. By car, turn off Rte. 127 (Summer St.) at Raymond St., which becomes Hesperus Ave.

The **area code** for Cape Ann is 508.

Gloucester

Entering Gloucester on Rte. 127, tourists appropriately first see the famous **Man at the Wheel,** a weather-worn copper statue of a fisherman surveying the sea for comrades lost in its depths. English colonists who came "to praise God and catch fish" settled Gloucester in 1623; the nation's oldest seaport erected the monument on its 300th anniversary. Today, sight-seeing may have eclipsed God-praising, but Gloucester remains one of the world's foremost fishing ports. Visit toward the end of June to see the bishop perform the annual **Blessing of the Fleet,** Cape Ann's biggest summer event, complete with carnival, parade, and dancing in the streets. The tumult takes place in downtown St. Peter's Park. In sea captain Elias Davis's 1804 home, the **Cape Ann Historical Association Museum,** 28 Pleasant St. (283-0455), proudly displays the nation's largest collection of Fitz Hugh Lane paintings. (Open Tues.-Sat. 10am-5pm. Admission $3, seniors and students $1.50, under 12 free.) After the museum whets your appetite for art, try the **Rocky Neck Art Colony** along Rocky Neck Ave. (283-4319), in E. Gloucester. With about 30 galleries, the Neck is the oldest working U.S. art colony with such distinguished painters as Winslow Homer and Fitz Hugh Lane. (Most galleries open spring-fall daily 10am-10pm.) Gloucester has inspired other artists as well, including long-time resident and Beat poet Charles Olsen, who attempted to capture the town's spirit in his epic *Maximus Poems.*

The whale-watching capital of New England, Gloucester's half-dozen companies will attempt to show the minke, right, finback, and humpback whales that play off the coast of Stellwagen Bank in the Gulf of Maine. Several companies offer cruises (3-4 hr.) in the summer including: **Capt. Bill & Sons Whale Watch Cruises,** 9 Traverse St. (283-6995); **Cape Ann Whale Watch** (283-5110 or 800-339-1990) on Rose's Wharf; and the **Seven Seas Whale Watch** (800-331-6228) on Rte. 127. (Tickets $19.) The Cape Ann Whale Watch Company also offers narrated island cruises, less time-consuming and a good deal cheaper, taking you past the six area lighthouses. Land-lubbers can drive down scenic E. Main St. into east Gloucester to see the **East Point Lighthouse** for yourself.

Inside the aluminum **Chick's Roast Beef and Seafood** diner, 218 Main St., buy inexpensive sandwiches and subs ($1.35-3.50). (Open Sun. 11am-midnight, Mon.-Thurs. 11am-1am, Fri.-Sat. 11am-2am.) The nautical **Down East Oyster House,** 116 E. Main St. in E. Gloucester, costs and merits a few extra dollars. (Open daily 11:30am-10pm.) The chic **Main St. Café** on Main St., serves gourmet pizza, sandwiches ($2.50), salads ($3.25-6), and fancy dinner entrees. (Open Mon.-Sat. 11am-3pm and daily 5:30-9pm.)

The **Cape Ann Chamber of Commerce,** 33 Commercial St. (283-1601), can give you a list of Gloucester accommodations, and make reservations at some lodgings in the $50 range. Don't expect to find a better deal. The best bargain is area camping. The **Cape Ann Campsite** on 80 Atlantic St. (283-8683), off Rte. 128 and 133 in W. Gloucester, consists of 100 tent sites 1 mi. from the beach. (2- to 3-day min. stay weekends. Sites $14 for 2 people. Open May-Oct.) The **Camp Annisquam Campground** (283-2992), on Stanwood Ave. off Rte. 133, has rustic lake-side sites ($14 for 2 people). The **information booth** (283-2651) on Western Ave. (Rte. 127) can also help with directions. (Open mid-June to Aug. daily 10am-6pm.) Reach Gloucester from Boston by Rte. 128 and 127, from the north by Rte. 133, and from the MBTA Commuter Rail at North Station.

The **ZIP code** for Gloucester is 01930.

Rockport

Rockport rejects the hearty fishing air of Gloucester, 5 mi. west, in favor of more genteel artistic pursuits. **Motif #1,** a perfectly red lobster shack at the end of Tuna Wharf, is the single most painted object in the U.S., no doubt because of the local artist population. But Rockport's beauty does not just hang in galleries; historic **Bearskin Neck,** the town's main drag, is quite scenic. A little beyond the Neck lies

Main Street, where galleries occupy every other building. The grandparent of them all, with a membership of over 250 artists who have all lived and worked in the area, the **Rockport Art Association** shows works in a small gallery. (Open Mon.-Sat. 9:30am-5pm, Sun. 1-5pm; Nov.-April Mon.-Fri. 10am-4pm, Sat. 10am-5pm, Sun. 1-5pm.) In June, the Art Association hosts the **Rockport Chamber Music Festival** (546-7391).

When you truly yearn to leave the hustle and bustle behind, head north out of town on Rte. 127 to the imaginatively named companions **Front Beach** and **Back Beach,** which offer wonderful swimming. At the very tip of the cape, **Halibut Point State Park,** on Gott Ave. (546-2997), sprawls over 54 acres of headland overlooking the Ipswich Bay (day use $2, parking $5). Rockport supports a healthy population of expensive, coy restaurants—most you should avoid. A delightful exception to this rule, the **Lobster in the Ruff** on South Rd., has a harbor view, sandwiches ($1.50-4.75), and sautéed scallops ($10). (Open Sun.-Thurs. 11am-8pm, Fri.-Sat. 11am-9pm.) **Brian's Beachfront,** 16 Beach Rd., has a strangely charming seaside soda-fountain air and serves hearty breakfasts ($1.75-4.25) and club sandwiches ($4.50), not to mention ice cream. (Open Mon.-Tues. 7am-4pm, Wed.-Sun. 7am-9pm.)

The **Rockport Chamber of Commerce,** 3 Main St. (546-5997), distributes the singularly helpful *Rockport Anchor* guide and free maps of the area. (Open Mon.-Sat. 9am-5pm, Sun. noon-5pm.) Though the chamber gives free room referral, plan ahead to stay at one of the few places under $60 per night. Head to Rockport for the famous Fourth of July **Fireman's Parade, Bonfire, and Band Concert.** The name says it all. To get to Rockport from Boston, take Rte. 128 or 127 north. Also accessible by commuter rail from North Station, Rockport is the stop after Gloucester. The **ZIP code** for Rockport is 01966.

Plymouth

The Pilgrims settled Plymouth in 1620 because it provided defensible high ground, a sheltered harbor, and a fresh water supply. Nowadays nothing in the town seems fortified. Even the founding **Plymouth Rock** on Water St. seems unimpressive—souvenir-hungry tourists have chipped away two-thirds of the original rock. Other pseudo-attractions abound here, and are best avoided. Docked in Plymouth Harbor, the **Mayflower II** was actually built in the 1950s to recapture the atmosphere of the original ship. The neo-Pilgrim passengers and crew somehow manage to redeem the ship's authenticity. (Open June-Aug. daily 9am-6:30pm; April-May and Sept.-Nov. 9am-5pm. Admission $5, children $3.25.)

Less fanfare surrounds the only genuine sights in town. The **Plymouth Antiquarian Society,** 126 Water St. (746-9697), gives historic house tours of three local buildings: the Spooner House (1749), the Harlow Old Fort House (1677), and the Antiquarian House (1809). (Open Memorial Day-July 4 and Labor Day-Columbus Day Fri.-Sun. 10am-5pm; July 4-Labor Day Thurs.-Sun. noon-5pm. Admission $2.50 per house, seniors $2.) The nation's oldest museum in continuous existence, the **Pilgrim Hall Museum,** 75 Court St. (746-1620), houses Puritan crafts, furniture, books, paintings, and weapons. (Open daily 9:30am-4:30pm. Admission $4, seniors $3.50, ages 6-15 $1.50.)

Far out of town and vastly entertaining, **Plimoth Plantation,** Warren Ave. (746-1622), superbly re-creates the early settlement. In the **Pilgrim Village** costumed actors impersonate actual villagers; you can help them in daily routines such as tending the garden. Nothing in the village can be traced to the modern era, and the actors feign ignorance of all events after the 1630s. The nearby **Wampanoag Summer Encampment** re-creates a Native American village of the same period, presenting the culture of the original settlers. (Open April-Nov. daily 9am-5pm. Admission for village and encampment $12, children $8.) To get to Plimoth Plantation, take Rte. 3 south to exit 4 and follow the signs, or follow Main St. 3 mi. out of the center of town.

An unexpected pleasure, **Cranberry World,** 225 Water St. (747-2350), glorifies one of the only three indigenous American fruits. A self-guided exhibit details the workings of a cranberry bog, and the museum has one of its own for you to investigate. Admission and all cranberry refreshments are free.

Beautiful **Jelson's Beach** on Nelson St., and **Brewsters Garden** on Leyden St., with its meandering brook, provide ideal spots for a picnic. Go to **Go-Go's Sub Shop,** 46 Main St. 1 block from the post office, and choose from any one of the 40 subs they manufacture ($3-4.25). (Open Mon.-Sat. 10am-8pm, Sun. 11am-5pm.) **Bella Vita,** on Court St., has tasty Italian food to go-go like pizza by the slice ($1) and spaghetti with meatballs ($3). (Open Mon.-Sat. 7am-8pm.) **Souza's Seafood** (746-5354), on the Wharf, offers informal outdoor dining at its own picnic tables. Pick your own lobster and they'll cook it, or opt for the pre-fab clam strip roll ($4.60). (Open daily 11am-8pm.)

Accommodations, like the attractions in the area, are frequently overpriced. The **Plymouth Motel,** Rte. 44 (746-2500), offers comfortable rooms, a swimming pool, and some of the lowest rates in town (mid-June to mid-Sept. singles $55, doubles $55-75; off-season $38-55). Camping, of course, comes cheaper; majestic **Myles Standish Forest** (866-2526), which stands 7 myles south of Plymouth via Rte. 3 to Long Pond Rd., offers wooded ground. (Sites $10 for 2 people, with showers $12.) **Ellis Haven Campground,** 531 Federal Furnace Rd. (746-0803), offers less wilderness and more amenities including laundry facilities. (Sites $15 for 2 people. Each additional person $2.)

Find out more about Plymouth and the rest of New England at the **tourist information center** (746-1150), 2 mi. from Plymouth on Rte. 3, exit 5, Long Pond Rd. (Open Mon.-Fri. 8:45am-5pm, Sat. 8:30am-4:30pm; fall and winter daily 8:45am-4:30pm.) Near the town wharf on N. Park St., the **Plymouth Information Center** (746-4779) arranges local accommodations and hands out free maps of the town. (Open May-Nov. Sat.-Thurs. 9am-5pm, Fri. 9am-8pm; April weekends.) The **chamber of commerce,** 99 Samoset St. (746-3377), can help direct you around Plymouth. (Open Mon.-Fri. 9am-5pm.)

Plymouth tucks into the south shore of Massachusetts Bay, 35 mi. south of Boston and 32 mi. northwest of Hyannis on Rte. 3. The **Plymouth and Brockton Street Railway Company** (actually a bus line), 8 Industrial Park Rd. (746-0378; 800-328-9997 in MA), handles service to Plymouth from Boston's central Greyhound terminal (15 per day, $6). The bus takes only an hour, but stops at the Industrial Park Terminal, 3 mi. from Plymouth Center. From the Hyannis terminal (775-5524), 15 to 19 buses per day run between 10:15am and 9:15pm. (To Hyannis $4.25, 1 hr.) The **Plymouth Rock Trolley,** 20 Main St. (747-3419), operates daily from 8am to 8pm every 15 to 20 minutes. (Fare $3, under 12 $1.) Trolleys run around town and out to Plimoth Plantation.

The **post office** registers at 6 Main St. Ext. (746-4028), in Plymouth center. (Open Mon.-Fri. 8:30am-5pm, Sat. 8:30am-noon.) Plymouth's **ZIP code** is 02361; the **area code** is 508.

Cape Cod

In 1602, when Bartholomew Gosnold first landed on this peninsula in southeastern Massachusetts, he named it Cape Cod in honor of all the codfish he caught in the surrounding waters. Towns on the Cape used to survive by hook and net, but in recent decades tourism, not fishing, has sustained the Cape. Mindful of the fragility of the ecosystem, President Kennedy established the **Cape Cod National Seashore** in 1961 to protect less-developed areas from commercialism. The national seashore shelters much of the "forearm," including the Cape's most dramatic ocean beaches, Cape Cod's trademark. No matter where or how long you stay, you can enjoy miles of sandy shore. But don't disturb the fragile dunes; stay on designated trails. One other measure has limited the tourist influx—prohibitive prices. Persistent budget travelers will find the dollar-stretching difficult but ultimately fulfilling.

The park retains six beaches (day use $1-2, parking $5), nine hiking trails, and three bike trails. Consult the **National Seashore's Visitors Centers,** at Salt Pond, U.S. 6 in Eastham (255-3421), just north of the "elbow." (Open July-Aug. daily 9am-6pm; off-season 9am-4:30pm.) Deeper in the park on the forearm of the state is **Province Lands** (487-1256), on Race Point Rd. to the right off U.S. 6 near Provincetown. (Open mid-April to July and Labor Day-Thanksgiving daily 9am-4:30pm; July-Labor Day 9am-6pm). Both provide maps, information, and frequent, ranger-led free walks and discussions about local natural attractions.

Cycling is perhaps the best way to travel the Cape's gentle slopes. The park service can give you a free map of the trails or sell you the detailed **Cape Cod Bike Book** ($3). The 135-mi. **Boston-Cape Cod Bikeway** connects Boston with Bourne on the Cape Cod Canal and extends to Provincetown at land's end. Some of the most scenic bike trails in the country line either side of the **Cape Cod Canal** in the Cape Cod National Seashore, and the 14-mi. **Cape Cod Rail Trail** from Dennis to Eastham.

Though easily accessible by car (take Rte. 3 or 3A south of Boston to Rte. 6 or 6A), Cape-bound weekend traffic is often brutal out of Boston. The **Cape Cod Railroad** (771-3788) provides a delightful alternative, traveling from Hyannis to Sandwich through the "backyard of the Cape," using only old-fashioned train cars. **Bonanza Bus Lines** connects Boston with Falmouth and Woods Hole, and Hyannis with New York City. **Plymouth and Brockton Street Railway** serves Hyannis ($5) and the Cape out to Provincetown.

Contact the **Cape Cod Chamber of Commerce,** at the junction of Rte. 6 and 132 (362-3225), in Hyannis on Shoot Hill Rd., for comprehensive Cape information. (Open daily 8:30am-4pm; off-season 9am-4pm.) See the Martha's Vineyard section for information on ferries from Woods Hole and Hyannis to this off-Cape island.

The **ZIP code** for Woods Hole is 02543, for Falmouth 02541; the General Delivery ZIP code is 02540. The **area code** for Cape Cod is 508.

Provincetown

Provincetown sits where Cape Cod ends and the wide Atlantic begins. Looking out at the expanse of shimmering water, you might think the area is an island; though not in the technical sense, Provincetown spiritually removes itself from much of Massachusetts. Once a busy whale port, now artists and not sailors with bad teeth fill the major thoroughfare, where numerous Portuguese bakeries and gay and lesbian bookstores happily coexist. Only the solitude of the surrounding seashore remains unchanged.

Practical Information

Police: 911.

Visitor Information: Provincetown Chamber of Commerce, 307 Commercial St. (487-3424), MacMillan Wharf. Open summer daily 9am-5pm; off-season Mon.-Sat. 10am-4pm. **Province Lands Visitor Center,** Race Point Rd. (487-1256). Information on the national seashore; free guides to the nature and bike trails. Open July-Aug. daily 9am-6pm; mid-April to Nov. 9am-4:30pm.

Plymouth and Brockton Bus: 800-328-9997. Stops behind Provincetown Chamber of Commerce, which has schedules and information. 6 buses per day in summer to Hyannis ($7).

Bay State Spray Cruises: 20 Long Wharf, Boston (723-7800). In the Provincetown Chamber of Commerce (487-9284). Ferries to Boston (3 hr., $15, same-day round-trip $25). Operates May 27 to mid-June weekends only; summer daily.

Provincetown Shuttle Bus: 487-3353. Serves Provincetown and Herring Cove Beach. Operates late June-early Sept. daily 8am-midnight; 8am-6:30pm for the beach. Schedules available at the chamber of commerce. Fare $1, seniors 50¢.

Bike Rental: Arnold's, 329 Commercial St. (487-0844). 3-speeds, 10-speeds, and mountain bikes $2-3.50 per hr., $7-12 per day. Credit cards accepted. Open daily 8:30am-5:30pm. Deposit and ID required.

Post Office: 211 Commercial St. (487-0163). Open Mon.-Fri. 8:30am-5pm, Sat. 9:30-11:30am. **ZIP code:** 02657.

Help Line: Crisis Hotline, 487-1577. For any kind of personal crisis.

Area Code: 508.

Provincetown tucks into the cupped hand at the end of the Cape Cod arm. Boston lies 120 mi. away by land via U.S. 6 and Rte. 3, Boston's "Southeast Expressway," but much closer by sea across Cape Cod and Massachusetts Bay. The Cape Cod Canal lies 66 mi. "down Cape." The national seashore protects the surrounding duneland.

Accommodations, Camping, and Food

Provincetown is known for old clapboard houses lining narrow roads—fortunately guesthouses are a part of that tradition, though not all are affordable. The **Joshua Paine Guest House,** 15 Tremont St. (487-1551), has four bright rooms with handsome furniture. (Singles $30. Doubles $35: Open mid-June to mid-Sept.) In the quiet east end of town, the **Cape Codder,** 570 Commercial St. (487-0131), as its name suggests, offers stereotypical Cape Cod decor, right down to the wicker furniture, as well as access to a small private beach with a wooden deck (Singles $26-40; off-season $20-30. Doubles $28-40. Continental breakfast included. Open April-Oct.) Closer to town, the **White Caps Motel,** 394 Commercial St. (487-3755), has immaculate pastel rooms and access to the beach. (Doubles $52, off-season $40.)

In keeping with the general spirit of the thing, camping here is expensive. Parking for the National Seashore property closes from midnight to 6am, but you can't camp legally on public lands anyway. The visitors center can provide a list of private campgrounds within the seashore; for all, reservations are recommended in the summer. The western part of **Coastal Acres Camping Court,** West Vine St. (487-1700), has often crowded sites; try to snag one waterside. (3-day min. stay. Sites $17, with electricity and water $21.) About 7 mi. southeast of Provincetown on U.S. 6, several popular campgrounds nestle among the dwarf pines by the dunelands of the villages of North Truro and Truro. The **North Truro Camping Area,** on Highland Rd. (487-1847), ¼-mi. east of U.S. 6., has small but pleasantly sandy sites. ($14 for 2 people. Each additional person $7. Required reservation deposit of $30 for each week of stay.) The **Little America Youth Hostel,** at the far end of North Pamet Rd., Truro 02666 (349-3889), rests on park service land 1½ mi. east of U.S. 6. The popular hostel has 48 bunks and sees a steady stream of bikers all summer. ($9, nonmembers $12. Open early June-early Sept. Reservations recommended.)

Sit-down meals in Provincetown cost a pretty penny. Grab a bite at one of the Portuguese bakeries on Commercial St., or at a seafood shack on MacMillan Wharf. Particularly good and flaunting its own picnic tables, **John's Hot Dog Stand,** 309 Commercial St., actually specializes in fried clams, lobster roll, and a variety of other meals marine. For more sedentary dining, try the **Mayflower Family Dining** restaurant, 300 Commercial St., established in 1921. Ancient caricatures line the walls. Choose from Portuguese ($7) and Italian ($4-8) entrees, or Puritan seafood meals ($7-10). (Open daily 11am-10:30pm.) While **Stormy Harbor,** 277 Commercial St., serves good food, it insists on leaving the price tag on the oil-paint seascapes. Buy one, or a cheap breakfast. (Open daily 7am-9pm.)

Sights, Activities, and Entertainment

In high season, pedestrians and cyclists wrest control of **Commercial Street** from the automobiles. The street festival goes on every day and night, often until 3am, heightening in June with the annual Portuguese religious celebration, the **Blessing of the Fleet.**

Commercial St. has a number of austere galleries that many visitors mistake for museums, but the **Provincetown Art Association and Museum,** 460 Commercial St. (487-1750), established in 1914, is the real McCoy. Alongside the permanent

500-piece collection, it exhibits works by new Provincetown artists. (Open late May-Oct. noon-4pm and 7-10pm. Admission $1, seniors and children 50¢.

Provincetown may seem like an idyllic village, but a bitter undercurrent lurks beneath the image. Provincetown, it seems, feels cheated of the Pilgrim title won by Plymouth, and insists the Mayflower landed here first. After erecting an unimpressive plaque at the **First Landing Place**, at the start of Commercial St., the town dedicated the **Pilgrim Monument and Provincetown Museum** on High Pole Hill (487-1370) in 1920. The nation's tallest granite structure (255 ft.) affords a view of the tallest buildings in Boston on clear days, and a gorgeous panorama of the Cape almost every day. The museum below contains maritime artifacts. (Open July-Sept. daily 9am-9pm; Oct.-June 9am-5pm. Admission $3, children $1.) In 1746, a ship's carpenter built the "Oldest House" in Provincetown, the **Seth Nickerson House**, 72 Commercial St., which remains today the archetype of Cape Cod architecture. The ghost of the owner gives thoughtful and thorough tours. (Open June-Oct. daily 10am-5pm. Admission $2, ages 5-12 50¢.)

There might not be that much onshore evidence of Provincetown's whaling port, but the proliferation of **whale watch cruises** certainly hints at it. Companies cruise boats full of passengers armed with cameras rather than harpoons out to the fertile shoals where humpback, fin, mincke, and rare white whales feed. May and September are the best months for cetacean-sighting. Naturalist guides enhance the tours (3-4 hr.) offered by the three Provincetown operations: **Dolphin Fleet** (255-3857; 800-826-9300 in MA); **Portuguese Princess** (487-2651; 800-442-3188 in MA); and **Provincetown Whale-Watch** (487-3322; 800-992-9333 in MA). All leave from and operate ticket booths on MacMillan Wharf. Tickets cost about $15.

The **Schooner Bay Lady II** on MacMillan Pier (487-9308) offers a less exciting but nonetheless beautiful sail (2 hr.) around the Bay. (Fare $8-12, children $4-6.) Try your own hand at the tiller at **Flyer's Boat Rental**, 131A Commercial St. (487-0898 or 487-0578); expensive sailing lessons are also available. (Sailboats $14 per hr. Outboards with 2 poles and bait $35 per day. Open summer daily 8am-6pm.)

Back on *terra firma,* you can roam the wide, sandy beaches that surround Provincetown on foot or by bike. Rent a bike from **Arnold's** (see Practical Information), and receive a free map of the trails. The friendly manager of the little-known **Provincetown Horse and Carriage Co.**, 27 W. Vine St. (487-1112), can help both novice and experienced riders explore on horseback. One-hour trail rides cost $20. (Must be over 11.) **Rambling Rose** (487-4246) gives carriage tours ($7.50-15) through town for those not so equestrian.

Sandwich

The oldest town on the Cape, Sandwich cultivates a charm unmatched by its neighbors. Tourist-strip bustle does not clog its shady streets, lined with weathered-gray clapboard and mayonnaise.

Guided tours of the **Old Hoxie House** on Water St. (Rte. 130), a wonderful, authentic saltbox dating to the 17th century, explain the origins of the ancient furnishings. (Open early June to mid-Oct. Mon.-Sat. 10am-5pm, Sun. 1-5pm. Admission $2.50, children 75¢.) Down the street, the **Dexter Grist Mill** has ground corn since 1650. (Open June to mid-Oct. Mon.-Sat. 10am-4:45pm, Sun. 1-5pm. Admission $1.50, ages 12-16 75¢.) The water power for the mill comes from serene Shawme Pond, frequented by flocks of ducks, geese, and swans.

A few hundred yards from the pond, the **Thornton W. Burgess Museum** (888-6870) on Water St. pays an entertaining tribute to the Sandwich-born naturalist who wrote tales about the "dear old briar patch." Ask for directions to the actual briar patch, **The Green Briar Nature Center and Jam Kitchen,** 6 Discovery Rd. Wander through trails and wildflower gardens, or watch jam-making in the center kitchen Wednesday and Saturday. (Open summer Mon.-Sat. 10am-4pm, Sun. 1-4pm; shorter hours off-season. Free.)

About a mile from the center of town, you can easily spend an afternoon at the **Heritage Plantation**, on Grove and Pine St. (888-3300), which has 76 acres of path-crossed gardens. The unusual museums include a Shaker barn full of antique cars, another a working 1912 carousel. (Open mid-May to Oct. daily 10am-5pm. Admission $7, seniors $6, ages 5-12 $3.) Cape Cod Canal sandwiches the town from the north, the Atlantic from the east. Across the Sagamore Bridge, **Scusset Beach** (888-0859), right on the canal near the junction of Rte. 6 and 3, offers fishing and camping. (Daily fee $2, children $1. Parking $5. Sites $16; off-season $10.) The **Shawme-Crowell State Forest** (888-0351), on Rte. 130 and 6, has 240 wooded campsites ($12; April-Oct.). **Peters Pond Park Campground,** Cotuit Rd. (477-1775), in south Sandwich, offers aquatic activities, a grocery store, showers, a few prime waterside sites, and plenty of Miracle Whip. (Sites $14-15. Open mid-April to mid-Oct.)

Affordable eateries are, rather ironically, difficult to find in Sandwich, though **John's Capeside Diner,** Rte. 6A, carries affordability to ridiculous lengths, serving breakfast all day (50¢-$2.35), seafood, and burgers ($1.50). (Open Sun.-Tues. 5am-2pm, Wed.-Sat. 5am-8pm.)

Without a car you'll have to take the scenic **Cape Cod Railroad** (771-3788) to get to Sandwich. Starting from Center St. across from the Hyannis bus station, the train makes one stop in Sandwich and goes as far as Sagamore, though you can't get off there ($10.50 round-trip). From the depot in Sandwich, follow Jarves St. into the center of town.

Hyannis

Often called the "hub of Cape Cod," Hyannis is the region's commercial center—a hubcap or hub-Cape of sorts. Many of its overdeveloped sections, in fact, could cause you to forget that you are in the Cape at all. The Pilgrims might have settled in Hyannisport in 1620 but difficult navigation forced them to move on; fighting the summer traffic here, you might feel a certain kinship with them. But for those who like honky-tonk resort towns, Hyannis has plenty of mini-golf and souvenir shops, also providing a good base from which to visit or drag race other spots on the Cape. And sometimes the best way to enjoy Hyannis involves escaping it.

The **Cahoon Art Museum,** at 4676 Falmouth Ave. (Rte. 28) (428-7581), in Cotuit, offers a wonderfully whimsical excursion into the long-lost land of sailors, mermaids, scurvy, and dehydration as presented by artists Ralph and Martha Cahoon. The museum also houses an impressive collection of good primitive art by other Cape residents such as James Butterworth. (Open April-Dec. Wed.-Sat. 10am-4pm, Sun. 1-4pm. Free.) **Hyannis Whale Watcher Cruises** (775-1622 or 362-6088), north of Hyannis in Barnstable, runs daily expeditions in pursuit of fin, humpbacks, and the elusive white whale, launching their 100-ft. cruiser into Cape Cod Bay for four-hour narrated excursions. (Fare $14-20.) Conservation areas line **Old King's Highway (Rte. 6A);** the publication *Along 6A* (available at the Cape Cod Chamber of Commerce) can guide you to these and other roadside treasures, including the **Cape Cod Art Association** in Barnstable (open April-Nov. daily 10am-4pm; Dec.-March 10am-1pm).

To cool off in Barnstable, try wooded **Hathaway Pond,** on the Bay side of the Cape. (Parking $4.) In Hyannis, at the end of Ocean St., **Kalmus Park Beach** offers white sands and a proliferation of windsurfers. Up Ocean St., the **Kennedy Memorial,** is Hyannis' tribute to the slain President who summered in Hyannisport.

The **West End Marketplace,** 615 Main St. in downtown Hyannis, has a carnival-like atmosphere, carrying everything from fried dough to shish kebab and frozen yogurt. (Open daily 11am-1am. Food served until midnight.) Posher but more filling, **Baxter's Fish 'n' Chips,** 177 Pleasant St., has navigation maps lining the walls, with outdoor harborside dining available. (Open Tues.-Sun. 11:30am-8:30pm.) **Guido Murphy's,** 617 Main St. (775-7242), caters to a summer college-kid crowd with corresponding neon-enhanced entertainment. Though more popular as a bar than as an eatery, you still might try the "Rube Goldburger," a build-it-yourself sandwich ($6). Live music plays nightly. (Cover $3. Sun. comedy night $5. Wed. free with college ID.)

Situated among three acres of pine trees, the **HyLand Youth Hostel (AYH)**, 465 Falmouth Rd. (775-2970), offers the 50 most affordable beds in Hyannis. (Check-in 5-10:30pm. $9, nonmembers $13. Family rooms available. Reservations recommended.) Some reasonably priced motels line Rte. 132 in Hyannis; avoid the precious inns and guest houses in Hyannisport along Seat St. The **Sea Beach Inn,** 388 Sea St. (775-4612), close to the beach at Gosnold St., rents you a comfortable double bed with shared bath plus continental breakfast for $45, with private bath $55 (off-season $35 and $45, respectively). The **Salt Winds Guest House,** 319 Sea St. (775-2038), has bright, spotless rooms right near the beach, and a pool to boot. (Doubles $55. Open May-Sept. 2.)

Hyannis is tattooed midway across the Cape's upper arm, 3 mi. south of U.S. 6 on Nantucket Sound. The **Hyannis Bus Station,** 17 Elm St. (775-5524), sends off the buses of **Plymouth & Brockton** and **Bonanza Lines.** (Open Mon.-Fri. 4:45am-8:30pm, Sat.-Sun. 5am-8:30pm.) Buses motor to Provincetown (3-7 per day, 1½ hr., $7); Providence, RI (6 per day, 2 hr., $13.50); New York (6 per day, 6½ hr., $31.50); Boston (15-24 per day, 2 hr., $8); and Plymouth (11-15 per day, 1 hr., $4.50). Shuttle buses shuttle to Falmouth and Woods Hole Monday through Saturday three to five times daily. **Amtrak,** 252 Main St. (800-872-7245), sends a direct train from New York to Hyannis on Fridays, and one from Hyannis to New York on Sundays (6 hr., $59). Other days, take the bus to Boston to catch the train.

Steamship Authority (778-2602) runs ferries to Martha's Vineyard and Nantucket from mid-May to October, leaving from the South St. Dock. (Agency open daily 7am-8pm. Fare $9, under 12 $4.50.) **Bike rentals** ($10-12 per day, $30-36 per week.) are available at Cascade Motor Lodge, 201 Main St. (775-9717), near the bus and train stations.

The **Hyannis Area Chamber of Commerce,** 319 Barnstable Rd. (775-2201), about 1 mi. up the road from the bus station, can help with Hyannis and hands out the *Hyannis Guidebook.* (Open Mon.-Sat. 9am-5pm, Sun. 11am-3pm; Sept.-May Mon.-Sat. 9am-5pm.) Before hitting the beach, call to find out the **weather** (771-0500 or 771-5522).

Hyannis **ZIP code** is 02601; the **area code** is 508.

Martha's Vineyard

Seven different communities make up **Martha's Vineyard,** behaving in many ways as islands unto themselves: Edgartown, Vineyard Haven, Oak Bluffs, West Tisbury, Menemsha, Chilmark, and Gay's Head. The most famous island off the New England coast does have the unifying theme of "quaint," unspoiled nature, from the dunes of the wide sandy beaches to the dark, beautiful inland woods. The landscape even captivates the most frequent of visitors, and converts many to a lifetime of vacations. Unlike many of its continental counterparts, "the Vineyard" is as welcoming financially as it is scenically.

Try to visit the Vineyard in fall, when the tourist season starts to die down, the weather turns crisp, the leaves turn color, and prices drop. If you must visit in summer, avoid weekends.

Separated from Cape Cod by Vineyard Sound, Martha's Vineyard requires that visitors come either by air or by sea. Air travel is prohibitively expensive, but the agreeable ferry ride takes less than an hour from Woods Hole or Falmouth. All ferries (see below) land in either **Vineyard Haven** or **Oak Bluffs,** two towns 3 mi. apart on the island's north shore.

In 1606, British explorer Bartholomew Gosnold named Martha's Vineyard after his daughter and the wild grapes that grew here. In the 18th century, the Vineyard prospered as a port, with shepherding the main home trade because sheep that escaped the flock still could not escape the small island. Today even the most hardened traveler may feel a bit hemmed by the herding tactics of the locals dependent on tourism. Nestled between East Chap and West Chap, **Vineyard Haven** has an unfair advantage as the first place most people see as they step off the boat. Three mi. west of Vineyard Haven on State Rd., **Oak Bluffs** proves the most precious of the Vineyard villages. Tour **Trinity Park,** near the harbor, and see the famous "Gingerbread Houses" (minutely detailed, elaborately pastel Victorian cottages resembling a child's playtown) or Oak Bluffs' **Flying Horses Carousel,** on Circuit Ave. Ext. (693-9081), the oldest in the nation (built in 1876), containing 20 handcrafted horses with real horsehair tails and manes. (Open June-Aug. daily 10am-10pm. Fare $1.) **Edgartown,** 7 mi. south of Oak Bluffs, corners the island's market on posh; skip the shops and stores here and visit the town's historic sights maintained by **Dukes County Historical Society,** School and Cooke St. (627-4441). **West Tisbury,** 10 mi. west of Edgartown on the West Tisbury-Edgartown Rd., is a typical small New England outpost, its largest attraction being the **Chicama Vineyards,** on Stoney Hill Rd. off State Rd. (693-0309). Free tasting follows the tour of the only vineyard on the Vineyard. (Open Jan.-April Fri.-Sat. 1-4pm; May Mon.-Sat. 1-5pm; June-Oct. Mon.-Sat. 11am-5pm, Sun. 1-5pm. Free.) The town supplies a well-stocked general store, providing sustenance for the trip "up-island." **Gay's Head,** 12 mi. off West Tisbury, offers just about the best view in all of New England. The local Wampanoog frequently saved sailors whose ships wrecked on the **Gay's Head Cliffs,** which still steal visitors' breath, now more with beauty than with danger; the 100-million-year-old precipice contains a collage of brilliant colors with one of five lighthouses on the island. A little northeast of Gay's Head, **Chilmark** gives good coastline, claiming the only working fishing town on the island, **Mnemsha Village,** where tourists can fish off the pier or purchase fresh lobster.

Exploring the Vineyard should involve so much more than hamlet-hopping. Visit the peacocks and turkeys at the **Felix Neck Wildlife Sanctuary** on the Edgartown-Vineyard Haven Rd. (627-4850), now administered by the Audubon Society. (Open until 7pm. Admission $2, seniors and children $1.) **Cedar Tree Neck** provides trails across 250 acres of headland off Indian Hill Rd., while the **Long Point** park in West Tisbury preserves 550 acres and a shore on the Tisbury Great Pond. **Camp Pogue Wildlife Refuge and Wasque Reservation** on Chappaquidick is the largest conservation area on the island.

South Beach, the grandparent of the town's many beaches, shimmers at the end of Katama Rd. beneath Edgartown. The big waves and rolling shore attract quite a crowd. The fine **Mnemsha Beach,** at the end of North Rd., and the popular **State Beach,** on Beach Rd., break not far behind.

Cheap sandwich and lunch places speckle the Vineyard. Fried-food shacks the island over sell clams, shrimp, and potatoes. Sit-down dinners generally cost at least $15. A glorious and greasy exception is **Louis',** State Rd., Vineyard Haven, serving Italian food in a country-style atmosphere with unlimited bread and salad bar. (Lunch $4-5. Dinner $9-15. Open Mon.-Thurs. 11:30am-8:30pm, Fri.-Sat. 11:30am-9pm, Sun. 4-9:30pm.) **Cozy's,** on Circuit Ave. in Oak Bluffs, serves up ice cream and platters from its Wurlitzer. Try their generous hoagies ($3.75-5) or burgers ($1.75-3.35). (Open late March-early Sept. daily 11am-midnight.) Down the street, **Papa's Pizza Circuit** rounds out a popular, atmospheric hangout for the island youth, serving delicious thick-crusted whole-wheat pizza ($7-9). (Open daily 10am-11pm.)

A number of good take-out places dot the island, and given the beauty of the landscape, you just might want to grab food and run. The **Black Dog Bakery,** on Beach St. Ext. in Vineyard Haven, bakes something of a community center, with sumptuous breads and pastries (50¢-$2.50). (Open daily 6am-9pm; off-season 6am-6pm.) An island legend and institution, **Mad Martha's** scoops out 26 homemade flavors or limited editions of ice cream. The main store raves on Circuit Ave. in Oak Bluffs, but five more pace frantically on the northeastern side of the island. (Open mid-April to late Oct. daily 11am-midnight.) The **Morning Glory Farm,** at the corner of Machacket and Tisbury Rd., sells produce fresh from the field. (Open May-Thanksgiving Mon.-Sat. 9am-5:30pm.)

The most deluxe youth hostel you may ever encounter also offers the least expensive beds on the island. The lovely **Manter Memorial Youth Hostel (AYH),** Edgartown Rd., West Tisbury (693-2665), 5 mi. inland from Edgartown on the bike route, offers a lot. Though quite crowded in summer, the hostel almost never turns anybody away. (Curfew 10pm. $9, nonmembers $12. Linen $1. Open April-Nov. Reservations required.) **Martha's Vineyard Reservations,** P.O. Box 1322, Vineyard Haven 02568 (693-7200); **Dukes County Reservations Service,** P.O. Box 2370, Oak Bluffs 02557 (693-6505); and **Accommodations Plus,** RFD 273, Edgartown 02539 (627-8590), will reserve rooms for you three months in advance. The chamber of commerce provides a free list of inns and guest houses. For relatively inexpensive rooms, the century-old **Nashua House** (693-0043), on Kennebec Ave. in Oak Bluffs, sits across from the post office through rain or snow. Some rooms overlook the ocean; all are brightly painted and cheerful. (Doubles with shared baths only $29-45.) The more polished **Narragansett House,** 62 Narragansett Ave. (693-3627), chills in a quiet residential area south of downtown Oak Bluffs. (Doubles $50-75 from late May to mid-Sept.; off-season $40-65. Breakfast included.) The Victorian **Summer Place Inn,** 47 Pequot Ave. (693-9908), has nice rooms right next to the ocean ($55; off-season $45).

Campers have two options. **Martha's Vineyard Family Campground,** Edgartown Rd., Vineyard Haven (693-3772), has 150 sites. Groceries are available nearby. (Sites $20 for 2 people. Each additional person $8. Open mid-May to mid-Oct. Reservation deposit required.) **Webb's Camping Area,** Barnes Rd., Oak Bluffs (693-0233), 4 mi. from Edgartown, is more spacious, with 150 shaded sites. (Sites $20-22 for 2 people. Each additional person $8. Open mid-May to mid-Sept.)

Though only about 30 mi. across at its widest point, the Vineyard holds 15 beaches and one state forest. Maps are available at the **Martha's Vineyard Chamber of Commerce,** Beach Rd., Vineyard Haven (693-0085). Their free annual publication, *Martha's Vineyard,* describes everything you might want to see or do on the island. Also pick up free copies of the *Best Read Guide to Martha's Vineyard,* containing self-guided walking tours of the three largest towns—Vineyard Haven, Oak Bluffs, and Edgartown. (Open May 27-Sept. 2 Mon.-Fri. 9am-5pm, Sat. 10am-2pm. Mailing address: P.O. Box 1698, Vineyard Haven 02568.) Prospective revelers should note that Edgartown and Oak Bluffs are the only "wet" towns on the Vineyard. Bar owners are notoriously strict about checking ID.

Ferries to the island and Montauk, Long Island, leave from Hyannis and New Bedford. The **Woods Hole, Martha's Vineyard, and Nantucket Steamship Authority** (693-0367 in Vineyard Haven; 693-0125 in Oak Bluffs; 228-0262 in Nantucket; 548-3788 in Woods Hole; 771-4000 in Hyannis) leaves from Woods Hole. (Fare $8 round-trip; ages 5-12 $4; automobiles mid-Oct. to mid-May $30, mid-May to mid-Oct $53; bikers $5.) From Falmouth, you can take the **Island Queen Ferry** (548-4800), across from the town dock, which runs from late May to early October. (Fare $8 round-trip, children $4, with bike $5.) In Hyannis, take the **Hyline** ferry (778-2600 in Hyannis; 693-4111 in Oak Bluffs) which accepts pedestrians and bikers only. (Fare $10, children $5.) **Martha's Vineyard Schamonchi Ferry,** Pier 44 (997-1688), leaves from New Bedford's Lennard Wharf. (Fare $7, children $4. Same-day round-trip $14, children $6.) The **Viking Ferry** (576-668-5709) leaves Montauk, LI in summer Thursdays at 8am (fare $35, $60 same day round-trip) and arrives in Oak Bluff. Transporting a car costs about $40, the traffic is distractingly slow, major roads are few, minor roads unmarked or unpaved, and many places virtually inaccessible by auto anyway. Bring or rent a bike instead. While miles of bike trails cut across the island (maps available at R.W. Cutler), touring cyclists should stick to the fairly easy main roads. Inexperienced cyclists may find the uphill to Gay's Head or Mnemsha strenuous. You can rent reasonably priced bikes throughout the island: **Martha's Bike Rental,** at Five Corners in Vineyard Haven (693-6593; 10-speeds, mountain bikes, and cruisers $12 per day, credit card required; daily 9am-6pm); **Vineyard Bike and Moped** Circuit Ave. Ext. in Oak Bluffs (693-4498; 10-speeds $15 per day, 3-speeds $12; open daily 9am-6pm); and **R.W. Cutler,** Main St., Edgartown (627-4052; $8-15 per day, $10 deposit; free bike maps of the Vineyard; open April 7-Oct. 15 daily 9am-5pm). Taxis are expensive, but a shuttle bus (693-0058, 693-1555, 693-4681) makes stops throughout the island. (Vineyard

Haven-Oak Bluffs-Edgartown: late May to mid-June 8am-7pm; mid-June to early Sept. 8am-12:30am. Basic fare $3. For up-island service call the above numbers.)

The **ZIP** code is 02539 for Edgartown; 02568 for Vineyard Haven; and 02557 for Oak Bluffs. The **area code** for Martha's Vineyard is 508.

The Berkshires

While the equidistance of the Berkshire mountains from Boston and New York has long attracted wealthy urbanites seeking a country escape, today affordable restaurants, B&Bs, and campgrounds are available to the budget travelers who search them out.

Just about everything in Berkshire County runs north-south: the mountain range giving the county its name (a southern extension of the Green Mountains of Vermont); the 80 miles of **Appalachian Trail** that wind through Massachusetts; the Hoosac and the Housatonic rivers; and U.S. 7, the region's main artery. **Berkshire Regional Transit Association** (499-2782), known as "the B," spans the Berkshires from Williamstown to Great Barrington. Buses run every hour at some bus stops (Mon.-Sat.); fares (50¢-$3) depend on the route you take. System schedules are available on the bus and at some bus stops. To see sights located far from the town centers, you'll have to drive. The roads are slow and often riddled with potholes, but certainly scenic. The county holds over 100,000 acres of state forests and parks, offering numerous improved and semi-improved camping sites. For information about the parks, stop by the **Region 5 Headquarters** at 740 South St. (442-8928) or contact them by mail at P.O. Box 1433, Pittsfield 01202.

The Berkshires's **area code** is 413.

Northern Berkshires

The best way to see and get to the northern Berkshires is the **Mohawk Trail**(Rte. 2). Perhaps the most famous highway in the state, its awesome view of the surrounding mountains draws crowds during the fall foliage weekend. The trail starts at Miller Falls, MA, but the first real tourist attraction is off Rte. 2 in Greenfield, 5 mi. south of Rte. 5. **Historic Deerfield** (774-5587) is an idyllic, restored village. You can wander around the houses and buildings for free, using the map in front of the visitors office. Two-day tour tickets are also available. (Admission $7.50, under 18 $4.)

The Trail is dotted with affordable campgrounds and lodgings. In Shelbourne Falls at **Highland Springs Guests** (625-2648) the elderly Mrs. Sauter rents clean, Homey the Clown rooms with double beds for $25. West on the trail lies **Mohawk Trail State Forest** (339-5504), which offers campsites for $12 and rents cabins without baths (large $20, small $16). The **Whitcomb Summit Motel** off Rte. 2 in the town of Florida has a huge tower in its parking lot with a campy "4-state view" for 50¢.

North Adams, farther west on Rte. 2, is a railroad and mill town of former glory. The **Western Gateway Heritage State Park** on the Furnace St. Bypass off Rte. 8N has a railroad museum (663-6312) housed in an old Boston-Maine Railroad building. (Open May-Nov. Mon.-Fri. 10am-4:30pm, Sat.-Sun. 10am-6pm; Nov. to mid-Jan. and Feb.-May daily 10am-4:30pm. Free.) A number of high-priced antique and craft stores are fun to browse in, but the **Freight Yard Pub** (663-6547) in the park is a good bargain. The cutesy country Americana joint serves pizza (individual servings $3.75), salads ($2-5.25), and French dip sandwiches ($4.75); there is also café dining outside.

Mt. Greylock, situated between North Adams and Williamstown, is the highest peak in Massachusetts (3491 ft.), accessible both by Rte. 2 and 7. Hiking trails begin from the neighboring towns of Lanesboro, Williamstown, North Adams, Adams, and Cheshire; get maps at the **Mount Greylock Visitors Information Center,** Rockwell Rd. (499-4262), along the pleasantly winding road from Lanesboro to the summit. (Open Mon.-Fri. 9am-4pm, Sat.-Sun. 9am-5pm.) Once at the top, climb the hideous **War Memorial** for a breathtaking and annotated view. Sleep high in nearby **Bascom Lodge,** built from the rock excavated for the monument. (May-June bunks $18, under 12 $11; July-Oct. Fri.-Sat. $20, under 12 $11, Sun.-Thurs. $18, under 12 $11.) Sponsored by the Appalachian Mountain Club, the lodge offers breakfast ($5) and dinner ($9.50) to guests; its snackbar is open to the public daily 8:30am-5pm.

The Mohawk Trail ends in **Williamstown** at its junction with Rte. 7; here, an **information booth** (458-4922) provides a slew of free local maps and seasonal brochures. (Open 24 hr., staffed by volunteers daily 10am-6pm). At **Williams College,** the second oldest in Massachusetts (est. 1793), lecturers compete with the beautiful scenery of surrounding mountains for their students' attention. You can pick up campus maps at the **Admissions Office,** 988 Main St. (Open Mon.-Fri. 8:30am-4:30pm. Tours at 10am, 11am, 1:15pm, 3:30pm.) First among the college's many cultural resources, **Chapin Library** (597-2462) displays a number of rare U.S. manuscripts, including original copies of the Declaration of Independence, Articles of Confederation, Constitution, and Bill of Rights. (Open Mon.-Fri. 9am-noon and 1-5pm. Free.) The small but impressive **Williams College Museum of Art** (597-2429) merits a visit for its fine pieces of pop art. (Open Mon.-Sat. 10am-5pm, Sun. 1-5pm. Free.)

A good place to eat near campus is **Pappa Charlie's Deli** (28 Spring St.), a light-filled, well-stocked deli offering a mind-boggling selection of sandwiches under $4.

Try not to spend too much time indoors in Williamstown; the surrounding wooded hills beckon you from the moment you arrive. The **Hopkins Memorial Forest** (597-2346), on Northwest Hill Rd., is about 1½ mi. west of the college. Owned and run by Williams' Center for Environmental Study, the forest has over 2,000 acres open to the public for hiking and cross-country skiing. **Spoke Bicycles and Repairs,** 618 Main St. (458-3456), rents bikes in a variety of speeds ($10 per day) and can give you advice on good rides in the area.

Far south of Williamstown and the Trail 1½ mi. west of Lenox on Rte. 183 is **Tanglewood,** the summer home of the **Boston Symphony Orchestra.** The season runs from June 29 to September 2. (Tickets $11.50-58. Sat. open rehearsals $9.50. Summer information 637-1940, winter 617-226-1492. Schedules available through the mail from the BSO, Symphony Hall, Boston 02115.)

New Hampshire

New Hampshire's state motto and license-plate blazon "Live Free or Die" challenges all comers. The White Mountains, which dominate the central and northern parts of the state, claim lives every year; visitors should prepare for rugged landscape and severe weather. But the sloping woods and sky-scraping granite also supply a certain though perhaps name brand of freedom. From Mt. Washington, the highest point in the Appalachians, you can see five states and the ocean on a clear day. The rest of the state is not as daunting. Besides stony shores and a modest coastline, much of the southeastern region of the state has mutated into a suburbia of the Boston metropolis. Despite the encroachment of the newer "Live Well or Die" attitude, freedom, challenge, and the stern profile of the Old Man in the White Mountains continue to govern New Hampshire.

Practical Information

Capital: Concord.

Tourist Information: Office of Vacation Travel, 105 Loudon Rd., P.O. Box 856, Concord 03301 (271-2343). Open Mon.-Fri. 8am-4pm. **U.S. Forest Service,** 719 Main St., P.O. Box

638, Laconia 03247 (528-8721). Open Mon.-Fri. 8am-4:30pm. **Events and Information Hotline,** 224-2525; 800-258-3608 from New England and NY.

Help Lines: Winter Ski Conditions, 224-2525, 224-2526, or 800-258-3608 (in NY or New England). **Cross-country Conditions,** 224-6363 or 800-262-6660 (in New England). **Skimobile Conditions,** 224-4666.

Time Zone: Eastern. **Postal abbreviation:** NH.

White Mountains

In the late 19th century, the White Mountains became an immensely popular summer resort for those with fat purses. Grand hotels peppered the rolling green landscape and as many as 50 trains per day came to the region, filling hotel rooms with tourists marvelling at nature through glass. The mountains are not quite so busy or posh these days, but the valleys, forests, and gnarled granite peaks still attract travelers, though a newer, much heartier breed of hikers and skiiers. The mountains, especially the notches, are still not for the light-of-heart budget traveler. Affordable lodgings here are rustic at best, public transportation scarce, and weather unpredictable. If you're thinking of skirting these mountains and avoiding the roadside pseudo-attractions, bring warm clothing. Though glorious and peaceful, the peaks can prove treacherous. Every year, Mt. Washington claims at least one life. The weather here is some of the worst on earth; a gorgeous day can suddenly turn into a chilling storm, wind kicking up over 100 mph and thunderclouds rumbling. The average temperature on the summit is 26.7°F, the average wind speed is 35 mph. If you fancy a Romantic retreat to nature, contact the U.S. Forest Service and Pinkham Notch Camp, two equally helpful organizations (see below). The **White Mountain Attraction Center** (745-8720), on Rte. 112 in North Woodstock east of I-93 (exit 32), can give you information on just about anything in the area. (Write P.O. Box 10, N. Woodstock 03262. Office open Sat.-Thurs. 8:30am-6pm, Fri. 8:30am-10pm; off-season Mon.-Fri. 4:30am-5:30pm). Smaller booths dot the White Mountains: Conway, Rte. 16; Franconia, Rte. 18; Gorham, on Rte. 2 and 16; and Lincoln, I-93. (Open late May to mid-Oct., hours depending on traffic and weather.)

The **U.S. Forest Service** is the main administrative body in the White Mountains. Its main **information booth** (528-8721) lies south of the range at 719 Main St., Laconia 03247. Open Mon.-Fri. 8am-4:30pm.) **Regional ranger stations,** located at important gateways to the national forest, can also answer your questions: **Amoosuc,** on Trudeau Rd. in Bethlehem, west of U.S. 3 on Rte. 302 (869-2628; open Mon.-Fri. 7am-4:30pm); **Androscoggin,** 80 Glen Rd. in Gorham (466-2713; open Mon.-Fri. 7:30am-4:30pm); **Saco** on the Kancamangus Hwy. in Conway, 100 yd. off Rte. 16 (447-5448; open daily 8am-4:30pm); and **Pemigewasset** on Rte. 175 in Holderness (536-1310; open Mon-Fri 8am-4:30pm). The **Appalachian Mountains Club (AMC)** is a hiker's fantasy service. Information about trails and safety emanates from the AMC **Pinkham Notch Camp** (466-2727), on Rte. 16 between Jackson and Gorham. (Open summer daily 7am-10pm.) Another excellent source is the **Crawford Notch Depot** (846-7773) on Rte. 302 in Carroll (open mid-May to Sept. In peak summer months open daily 8:30am-4:30pm). To best use the complicated AMC network pick up its comprehensive guidebook of offerings, suitably called *The Guide.*

If you plan to do much hiking invest in the invaluable *AMC White Mountain Guide,* available in most bookstores and huts, ($16). Next to hiking, bicycling offers the best way to see the mountains close up. The strenuous treks decrease in difficulty if you approach the mountains from the north, according to some bikers. Check the guide/map *New Hampshire Bicycle,* available at many information centers. Also consult **25 Bicycle Tours in New Hampshire** ($7), available in local bookstores and outdoor equipment stores. (For bike rental suggestions, see North Conway below).

AMC accommodations proliferate in the mountains. Both the Pinkham and Crawford outposts serve as well-kept **hostels** (though Crawford has no shower facilities) and are conveniently located off the highway. The eight other **AMC huts**, spaced 1½-5½ hours apart on the hiking trail, are accessible only by foot. During the summer these full-service facilities offer family-style breakfasts and dinners, bunks, and linen for 36-90 people. Reservations are strongly suggested during the summer; from October through May many of the huts operate on a caretaker basis, with cooking equipment provided. Lodging with two meals in summer can cost as much as $40 per night but AMC members receive bargains and discounts. Since rates, lower in off-season, depend on an infinite number of variables, first consult *The Guide*.

Camping is free in a number of areas throughout the **White Mountains National Forest**. No camping is allowed above the tree line (approximately 4000 ft.), within 200 ft. of a trail, or within a ¼ mi. of roads, huts, shelters, tent platforms, lakes, or streams; the same rules apply to building a wood or charcoal fire. Since these rules often change call the U.S. Forest Service before pitching a tent. The forest service also holds 22 designated **campgrounds** (sites $7-9, bathrooms and firewood usually available). Call 528-8727 to find out which ones are closest to your destinations or make reservations (800-283-2267), especially in July and August.

While getting to the general vicinity poses little difficulty, getting around the White Mountains can be very problematic. **Concord Trailways** (228-3300 or 800-852-3317 in NH; 800-258-3722 in New England) runs north-south and connects Boston with Concord, Conway, Franconia, and the AMC Pinkham Notch Camp. **Vermont Transit** (800-451-3292) runs buses from Boston's Peter Pan Terminal to Franconia ($23.00) and Conway ($22.50). Only the AMC's **shuttle service** (466-2727) does not live up to the rest of the organization's services. A morning shuttle runs from Crawford to Pinkham Notch, a Pinkham evening shuttle runs to Gorham and Randolph, and a Crawford shuttle runs out to the Lonesome Lake hut. A more complete schedule and route description is available in the omnipresent **The Guide**. Some routes run on reservation only, so it's safest to call the service in advance. Tickets about $6-7 (open early June-early Sept). **Trail and Weather Information** can be obtained by phone. Try the Pinkham Notch Camp (447-2725) or the WMWV weather phone (447-5252). Regional **zip codes** include: Franconia, 03580, Jackson, 03846, and Gorham, 03587. The **area code** in the White Mountains is 603.

North Conway and Skiing

North Conway skirts the White Mountains along Rte. 16 and 302 and lacks the alpine grandeur of towns on the mountain range; in fact, the village, centrally located to many skiing areas, has become a tourist trap. On Rte. 16/302 dwell clothing mogul outlets like London Fog and Calvin Klein. Even humble motels charge exorbitant rates. But as the White Mountain's major city, it provides a fine base for exploration and sporting excursions.

Two **information booths** in town sit on Rte. 16, sponsored by the chamber of commerce (356-3171). Though their hours are often unreliable, they disseminate free maps of the town and names of mostly expensive accommodations in the area. The **Maple Leaf Motel**, on Rte. 16 (356-5388), has quaint cabins for reasonable rates. (Singles in fall $60; in winter and summer $50; off season $30. Doubles $62, $52, $32.) Farther south on Rte. 16 The **Yankee Clipper** (356-5736 or 800-343-5900) offers a more urban air, an outdoor pool, and nearly identical rates.

Affordable eateries appear much more often. Sandwich and pizza places line **Main St.** (Rte. 16/302). The hotspot for the *après ski* crowd is **Jackson Square**, on Main St., on the premises of the Eastern Slope Inn, with a DJ and dancing Monday and Wednesday to Saturday. (Entrees $10. Happy hours Tues. and Fri. 4-7pm. (Open daily 7:30am-9pm.) **Houlighan's**, on Kearsarge St., has served generous portions of standard U.S. fare for seven years. (Sandwiches $3.75-6.50, salads $1.50-5.) **Studebakers**, on Rte. 16 south of town, offers more upscale cuisine in a pseudo-

50s drive-in diner. Try one of seven different varieties of the Studey-Baker stuffed potato ($2.75-3.25). (Open Sun.-Thurs. 11:30am-9pm, Fri.-Sat. 11:30am-10pm.)

Though a relatively cosmopolitan ski town, North Conway is proudest perhaps of its own local mountain, **Cranmore,** (356-6851 or 800-543-9206), boasting the oldest ski train in the country. On winter Wednesdays, the slopes host a ski racing series; local teams also compete in the nationally known **Mountain Meisters,** open to the public. You can ski the slopes for $23 per day, $14 per night. The indoor tennis courts rent for $14 in summer.

The equipment stores in North Conway outdo all others in the area. **Eastern Mountain Sports,** (EMS) on Main St. (356-5433), on the premises of the Eastern Slope Inn, has free mountaineering pamphlets and excellent books on the area, including *25 Bicycle Tours in New Hampshire.* EMS offers cross-country ski rentals ($20 per day), tents, sleeping bags, and other camping equipment. (Open Sun.-Thurs. 9am-6pm, Fri.-Sat. 9am-9pm.) **Joe Jones,** on Main St. at Mechanic (356-9411), rents just about everything under the sun: bikes ($20 per day), alpine skis ($15), boats ($10), tennis rackets ($5). (Open Mon.-Thurs. 10am-6pm, Fri. 10am-8pm, Sun. 9am-6pm.) **International Mt.,** on Main St. (356-7064), rents smaller accessories like snowshoes ($8 per day) and camping stoves ($5-7). (Open Sun.-Thurs. 8:30am-6pm, Fri.-Sat. 8:30-9pm.)

But New Hampshire has excellent cross-country and downhill skiing throughout the area, and you might not want to limit yourself. Nowhere is it an especially cheap undertaking, but you can cut costs with package deals or by skiing on weekdays; cross-country skiing costs less than downhill. Three nearby cross-country centers offer close to 100 mi. of trails—marked and unmarked, flat and mountain—along with rentals and lessons. For a one-day excursion on marked trails, count on $6-9 for a trail fee and $10-15 per day for rentals. **Jackson Ski Touring Foundation,** in Jackson (383-9355), 12 mi. north of North Conway, provides the quintessential New England experience, with trails winding past beaver dams, a covered bridge, and country inns. Visit **Waterville Valley X-C Ski Center** (236-8311; 800-258-8988 outside NH), 13 mi. east on Rte. 49 off I-93 exit 25, and trek through wilderness trails in adjacent White Mountain National Forest. **Bretton Woods Ski Touring Center** (278-5000), 10 mi. north of Crawford Notch on Rte. 302, boasts an elaborate 50-mi. network of trails.

Not as well-known as the mega-resorts of Vermont, downhill ski centers in New Hampshire usually offer well-groomed, slightly less expensive, and equally exhilarating skiing. Skiing on weekdays enables you to beat the crowds, and the pass costs $5 less. Resorts cluster along I-93 in the west and in Mt. Washington Valley in the east. Those off I-93, collectively known as **Ski 93,** P.O. Box 517, Lincoln 03251 (745-8101), offer easier access. **Loon Mountain** (745-8111), three mi. east of I-93 at Lincoln, avoids overcrowding by limiting lift ticket sales, and also has a free beginners' tow (7 lifts, 41 trails). **Waterville Valley** (236-8311) offers great downhill as well as cross-country skiing (12 lifts, 53 trails). **Cannon Mountain** (823-5563; 800-552-1234 in New England), north of Franconia Notch, offers decent slopes off a large tram. For information on all Mount Washington Valley packages, contact the **Valley Chamber of Commerce,** P.O. Box 2300, North Conway 03860 (356-3171). **Wildcat Mountain** (446-3326), in Jackson, has scenic vistas of Mt. Washington (5 lifts, 30 trails). Some of New England's best-groomed trails are at **Attitash** (800-223-7669; 603-374-2368 or 0946) in Bartlett off Rte. 302 (6 lifts, 25 trails). Experts can head for **Tuckerman's Ravine,** a steep, treacherous extremely dangerous glacial wall; hike to the top in late spring to conquer the most challenging slope in the East.

Franconia Notch

About 400 million years old, Franconia Notch in the northern White Mountains has developed some interesting wrinkles. Sheer and dramatic granite cliffs, waterfalls, endless woodlands, and one very famous rocky profile attract summer campers in droves. Before you begin your exploration of this geological wonder on I-93, ask questions about the Franconia Notch State Park at the **Flume Visitor's Center,** off Rte. 93 north of Lincoln. Their excellent free 15-minute film acquaints visitors with the landscape. (Open late May-late Oct. daily 9am-4:30pm.) While at the center, purchase tickets to **The Flume** (823-5563), a 2-mi.-long nature walk over hills, through a covered bridge to a boardwalk above a fantastic gorge with 90-ft.-high granite cliffs. (Tickets $5.50, ages 6-12 $2.50.) You can swim at **The Basin,** a 20-ft. pothole beneath a waterfall, close to The Flume on I-93.

The westernmost of the three great notches, Franconia is best known for the **Old Man of the Mountains,** north of The Flume on the parkway. Hawthorne addressed this massive granite visage in his 1850 story "The Great Stone Face," and P.T. Barnum once offered to buy the rock. A 40-ft.-high human profile formed by three ledges of stone atop a 1200-ft. cliff, the Old Man's forehead is supported by cables and turnbuckles these days. The best view of the man, both at high noon and in the moonlight, is from the rather obviously named **Profile Lake,** a 10-minute walk from Lafayette Place in the park. If you don't feel like making the stroll, you can also do the voyeur thing.

West of the Old Man, off I-93 exit 2, **Great Cannon Cliff,** a 1000-ft. sheer drop into the cleft between **Mount Lafayette** and **Cannon Mountain,** is not just for looking at—it takes considerable technical skill to climb the "Sticky Fingers" or the "Meat Grinder" route; the 80-passenger **Cannon Mountain Aerial Tramway** (823-5563; open May 25-Oct.27 and Dec. to mid-April daily 8am-4pm; tickets $7, ages 6-12 $3.50, $5.50 for one-way hikers) will do the work for you.

Myriad trails lead up into the mountains on both sides of the notch, providing excellent dayhikes and spectacular views. Be prepared for severe weather, especially above 4000 ft., where trees no longer grow and rocks and crags appear aplenty. The **Lake Trail,** a relatively easy hike, winds from Lafayette Place in the park 1½ mi. to **Lonesome Lake,** where the AMC operates its westernmost summer hut (See White Mts. AMC huts above).

The **Greenleaf Trail** (2½ mi.), which starts at the Cannon Tramway parking lot, and the **Old Bridle Path** (3 mi.), which starts at Lafayette Place, are much more ambitious; both lead up to the the AMC's Greenleaf Hut near the summit of Mt. Lafayette overlooking Eagle Lake, a favorite destination for sunset photographers. From Greenleaf, you can trudge the next 7½ mi. east up and along **Garfield Ridge** to the AMC's most remote hut, the **Galehead.** Dayhikes from this base can keep you occupied for days. (Sites at the Garfield Ridge campsite $5.)

Those who find hiking anathema can take advantage of the 9 mi. of **bike paths** that begin off Rte. 3 and run through the White Mountain National Forest. After any exertion, cool off at the beach on the northern shore of **Echo Lake,** off Rte. 18 (open mid-June to late Aug.). Numerous cross-country trails run through the "Kanc," and alpine skiing rests at nearby Loon Mountain (see North Conway and skiing below).

At reasonable altitudes, you can camp at the **Lafayette Campground** (823-5563), in Franconia Notch State Park (open mid-May to mid-Oct., weather permitting; sites $12, Fri.-Sat. $14, seniors $10-12). If Lafayette is full, try the more suburban **Fransted Campground** (823-5675), 1 mi. south of the village and 3 mi. north of the notch. (Sites $14 for 2 people, $1 each additional adult, children free. Bike rentals $1.50 per hr. Open year-round.) From Lincoln, the Kancamangus Hwy (NH Rte. 112) branches east for a scenic 35 mi. through the **Pemigewassett Wilderness** to Conway. The large basin rimmed by 4000-ft. peaks attracts many backpackers and skiers.

South of the highway, trails head into the **Sandwich Ranges,** a secluded series of lesser peaks; lesser with the exception of **Mount Chocorna,** a dramatic and steep exposed peak, and a favorite of 19th-century naturalist painters. Take your breath and drive south on Rte. 16 to Ossipee for the most breathtaking view of a breathtaking peak.

Pinkham Notch

Ancient **Mt. Washington** rises 6082 ft. up toward the sky; trees disappear about two-thirds of the way up, and snow clings to its peak even in summertime. **Pinkham Notch,** along Rte. 16 between Gorham and Jackson, humbly hunches below it. Near Gorham in Randolph, lies the **Bowman's Base Camp AYH Hostel** (466-5130), where even the mattresses are hardy. ($11, nonmembers $12. Open May 30-Oct. 12.) The Hostel sits at the foot of Lowes Path, which climbs Mt. Adams, mercifully far away from Mt. Washington's freeway-like trails. Stay at the **Madison Springs** AMC hut below the summit, and prepare for nasty weather. Catch a sensational sunrise over the Carter Range. In Gorham, you can also stay in the **Berkshire Manor,** 133 Main St. (466-9418), which has kitchen facilities. (Singles $18. Doubles $25.)

Pinkham Notch Camp, at the height of the notch, is the definitive source for local information (for this and all other AMC huts, see above), offering advice on weather and trail conditions as well as hiking guides and maps to the area. They will stress to neophyte and all other hikers the difficulty of these trails. Cases of hypothermia have been reported as late as June, and hiking accidents are common. Bring warm clothes (at least 2 sweaters). Bed and breakfast here cost $24.25, with buffet dinner $34.25. You can also buy meals (breakfast and lunch $5, dinner $9, trail lunch $3.50); reservations are essential in the summer. You can pitch a tent anywhere in the notch as long as the site is in accordance with regulations (see Resources: US Forest Service). A tough 4½-mi. hike leads up to the **Lakes of the Clouds** AMC hut, just 1½ mi. from Mt. Washington's summit. Because this is the most popular of the AMC's huts, reserve early. An easier 6½-mi. trail leads into the Carter Range to the **Carter Notch** AMC hut. Two trout-stocked mountain lakes swim in the area along with a maze of caves to explore. For a fabulous view of the Carter Range, hike to the **Madison Springs** AMC hut beneath the summit of Mt. Adams, off Rte. 2 between Gorham and Jefferson.

But the most challenging of the already demanding hikes is the trek to *the* summit, Mt. Washington. The most popular hiking trail, **Tuckerman's Ravine,** begins at the Pinkham Camp and climbs 4 mi. to steep glacial cirques. Experienced hikers in good shape can make the round-trip in a day. Anyone less energetic can take the techno-short cut, **Mount Washington Auto Road,** a paved and dirt road that leads motorists 8 mi. to the summit. ($12 per driver, $5 per passenger, ages 5-12 $3. Weather permitting road open mid-May to mid-Oct. daily 7:30am-6pm; shorter hours early and late in the season.) The road begins at the **Glen House** on Rte. 16 and features a steady stream of fumes and families mid-summer. The car-less can make the trip with the **Stage to the Summit** ($16, ages 5-12 $10).

On the overbuilt summit, you'll find a snack bar, an information center, a museum (466-3347), and the **Mount Washington Observatory** (466-3388), where the highest wind speeds ever recorded on earth (231 mph, in 1934) were registered. Closer to civilization (vertically and horizontally) the popular **Dolly Copp Campground** (466-3984), 5 mi. south of Gorham on Rte. 16, has almost 200 tent sites with bathrooms ($9) for beleaguered travelers. Near Gorham, in Randolph off Rte. 2, is the exceedingly rustic **Bowmans Base Camp AYH Hostel** (466-5130; see Pinkham above). If you long for privacy or the hum of a TV in a nearby room, stay at comfy **Berkshire Manor,** 133 Main St. (466-9418), which has kitchen facilities and a well-stocked grocery store a few miles away. (Singles $20. Doubles $28.)

Rhode Island

Rhode Island packs its inhabitants like sardines, yet within the island's confines surfaces a rustic Piscean vigor. Only one major highway (I-95) runs north-south through the state, accompanying the urban Gemini of Newport and Providence. Most of the inland roads are quiet, sometimes dirt thoroughfares lined with family fruit stands, marshes, or ponds. A number of working fishing ports still line the shores of the northern peninsula and the southern coast, deriving their lifeblood from Narragansett Bay and Block Island Sound. These small towns and neighboring undisturbed beaches offer unexpected pleasures like fresh quahogs (pronounced KOH-hog), a large and chewy type of clam.

Yet Rhode Island certainly maintains its high culture in Providence and Newport, which shared capital status until 1900. Each has a sixth sense of history and more than its share of colonial houses; college students, atmospheric neighborhoods, and Newport's bustling waterfront and grandiose mansions energize the state's aura. An island in name only, the smallest state in the U.S. maintains a unique yet not-so-isolated identity.

Practical Information

Capital: Providence.

Tourist Information: Rhode Island Division of Tourism, 7 Jackson Walkway, Providence 02903 (800-556-2484 or 277-2601). Open Mon.-Fri. 8:30am-4:30pm. **Department of Environmental Management** (State Parks), 9 Hayes St., Providence 02908 (277-2771). Open Mon.-Fri. 8:30am-4pm.

Time Zone: Eastern. **Postal Abbreviation:** RI.

Area Code: 401.

Providence

Like Rome, Providence sits aloft seven hills. Unlike Rome, its residents are Ivy Leaguers, starving artists, and smartly suited business types. This "island superego" has more of a college-town id with cobblestone sidewalks, colonial buildings, and college kids—even those who aren't students look like they should be. But Providence has more on its horizon than a constellation of BAs. Prescient *Newsweek* recently voted Providence one of the country's most liveable cities, with an urban renaissance in the cards. The city last boomed in the 18th century as a thriving seaport. Traces of that past remain, and the legacy of Roger Williams, founder of the state and advocate of religious freedom, refuses to vanish either in many place names or in the city's modern ethnic diversity.

Practical Information

Emergency: 272-1111, 0, or 911.

Visitor Information: Greater Providence Convention and Visitors Bureau, 30 Exchange Terrace (274-1636 or 800-233-1636), near North Main St. next to City Hall. Self-guided walking tour and the usual maps and tourist literature. Open Mon.-Fri. 9am-5pm. **Roger Williams National Memorial Visitors Center,** 282 N. Main St. (528-5385), between Brown campus and downtown. Open daily 9am-5pm; mid-Oct. to mid-May 9am-4:30pm. **Providence Preservation Society,** 21 Meeting St. (831-7440), at the foot of College Hill off Main St. in the 1772 Shakespeare's Head. Detailed information on historic Providence. Self-guided tour instructions for the city's historic neighborhoods (80¢ each) and/or a $3 audio-cassette tour. Open Mon.-Fri. 9am-5pm.

Travelers Aid: In the Amtrak station, 100 Gaspee St. (521-2255). Open 24 hr. Desk staffed Mon.-Fri. 8:30am-5pm.

Amtrak: 100 Gaspee St. (800-872-7245), in gleaming white concrete structure behind the state capitol, a 10-min. walk to Brown or downtown. Open daily 5am-11:15pm. To Boston ($12) and New York ($37).

Greyhound and Bonanza Buses: 37 Bonanza Way (751-8800), off exit 29 of I-95. Very frequent service to Boston (1 hr., $7.50) and New York (4 hr., $29). Open daily 4:45am-10pm.

Public Transport: Rhode Island Public Transit Authority (RIPTA), 776 Elmwood Ave. (781-9400 or 800-662-5088, from Newport 847-0209). Office open Mon.-Sat. 8:30am-6pm. **Infor-**

mation booth on Kennedy Plaza across from visitors center provides in-person route and schedule assistance. Open Mon.-Fri. 8am-4:30pm. Buses operate daily 4:30am-midnight. Intercity connections and service to points south and Newport. Fare 25¢-$1.75. In Providence, fares generally 75¢. Senior citizens with photo ID ride free Mon.-Fri. 9am-3pm, Sat.-Sun. all day.

Bike Rental: Rainbow Bicycles, 144 Brook St. (861-6176), at Transit St. near the southern end of Thayer St. 3-speeds $2.50 per hr., $15 per day. Open Mon.-Sat. 10am-6pm. Must have personal check, driver's license, or credit card for deposit.

Post Office: 2 Exchange Terrace (421-4360). Open Mon.-Fri. 7am-5:30pm, Sat. 8am-noon. **ZIP code:** 02903.

Area Code: 401.

Metropolitan Providence sprawls over a good fraction of "Little Rhody." I-95 connects the state capital to Boston (50 mi. to the north) and New York City (185 mi. to the southwest). The city lies at the confluence of the mighty Seekonk, Moshassuck, and Woonasquatucket rivers with Narragansett Bay. The state capitol and the downtown business district cluster just east of the intersection of I-95 and I-195. **Brown University** and the **Rhode Island School of Design (RISD)** (pronounced RIZZ-dee) pose on top of a steep hill east of downtown. **Providence College** tucks into the northwestern corner of town, about 2 mi. from the city center out Douglas Pike.

Accommodations

As with any teeming metropolis and economic, political, religious, atheistic, transportation, and weather hub, Providence has its share of astral motels. Yet affordable housing can be found; small guest houses seem your best bet. Unfortunately, there's no camping anywhere near Providence. The city doesn't really have a peak "season," but rooms are especially difficult to exhume in late May and early June, when Providence's many colleges and universities send off their satellites.

Bed and Breakfasts of Rhode Island, Inc. (941-0444) will reserve a room in a private house or inn for around $65 for a double, including breakfast. Outside Providence, the average price is $55. They represent over 100 B&Bs throughout the state. (Open Mon.-Fri. 9am-8pm, Sat. 10am-2pm; Sept. 3-May 28 Mon.-Fri. 9am-5pm.) You can try to make reservations at some of the in-town B&Bs yourself. **Mrs. Dorothy James,** 5 Medway St. (331-4293), rents singles ($45-48) and doubles ($52-58) in a unique carriage house built in the 1800s on Providence's East Side. **Mrs. Helen Meir,** 196 Butler Ave. (751-5974), a short walk from downtown, will put you up in one of four bedrooms furnished with handhooked rugs, serving full breakfast and homemade raisin bread. (Singles $40-45. Doubles $50-60. Call before 7pm.) The friendly **International House,** 8 Stimson Ave. (421-7181), near the Brown campus, has two comfortable rooms that usually book up. (Singles $45, students $25. Doubles $50, students $30. Reservations required; taken Mon.-Fri. 9:30am-3pm.) The **Susse Chalet Motor Lodge,** 36 Jefferson Blvd., Warwick (941-6600 or 800-258-1980), a 15-minute drive on I-95 south, is convenient only with a car, offering the eerily familiar orange and brown motel motif and an outdoor pool. (Singles $43. Doubles $53.) Another Susse Chalet slaloms on Rte. 6, just off Rte. 195 a few miles east (336-7900; singles $43, doubles $47).

Food and Entertainment

More auspiciously priced than the accommodations, the good food in Providence emanates from three areas: the Italian district on Federal Hill just west of downtown, the student hangouts on College Hill to the east, and the city's beautiful old diners near downtown.

Louis' Family Restaurant, 286 Brook St. Wonderfully friendly venue has made the entire community its family. Students swear by its prices, donating the artwork on the walls in return. Try the famous #1 special (2 eggs, homefries, toast, coffee) for $2.12. Lunches $1-4.50, dinners $2.75-5.50. Open daily 6am-3pm.

Angelo's Civita Farnese, 141 Atwells Ave., on Federal Hill. Walk west on Broadway from downtown, turn right near the Holiday Inn and cross the highway overpass; or take bus #26 ("Atwells"). The large acorn marks Federal Hill. Busy place with pictures of strangers' children on the wall. Eggplant parmesan or spaghetti with garlic and oil $3. Open Mon.-Sat. 11am-8:30pm.

Luke's Luau Hut, 59 Eddy St., behind City Hall. Ask to be seated in the psychedelic basement with the blowfish lantern. Feast on Duck Mona-Mona, Beeg Luau, or the incomparable pu-pu platter ($8-9). Open Sun. noon-9:30pm, Mon. 11am-8pm, Tues.-Thurs. 11am-9:30pm, Fri.-Sat. 11am-10:30pm.

Mutt's Pizza, 167 Benefit St. King of the College Hill for deep-dish pizza ($6). Watch for the 2-for-1 special. Sandwiches $2-4. Open Mon.-Thurs. 11am-11pm, Fri.-Sat. 11am-midnight, Sun. 1-10pm. Next door, **Geoff's** names great sandwiches after local celebrities ($2.75-6).

Spat's Pub Restaurant, 230 Thayer St., on College Hill. Classy vibes abound: dark wood tables and shining brass. Lunch $2.50-7. Dinner entrees $4.50-14. Open Sun.-Thurs. 11am-1am, Fri.-Sat. 11am-2am.

Spirited describes Providence's music and bar scene. With a friendly club atmosphere, **The Living Room,** 273 Promenade St. (521-2520), brings up-and-coming national and local acts into its abandoned old factory. (Open Sun.-Thurs. 8pm-1am, Fri.-Sat. 8pm-2am. Cover $3.50-15.) The **Church House Inn and Brick Tavern,** 122 Fountain St. (351-5503), desecrates a 1912 church, playing live jazz, blues, reggae, and the occasional polka Tuesday to Sunday. Outdoor dancing, DJs, and a jukebox contaminate other areas of the club. (Open Mon.-Thurs. 8pm-1am, Fri.-Sat. 8pm-2am. Cover $2-10.) Read the *New Paper,* distributed free on Wednesdays, or check the "Weekend" section of the Friday *Providence Journal* to find out more. Exciting distractions include the nationally acclaimed **Trinity Repertory Company,** 201 Washington St. (351-4242); the AAA-level **Pawtucket Red Sox,** who play at McCoy Stadium in Pawtucket (724-7300); the stock-car races at the **Seekonk Speedway** (336-8488), a few miles east on Rte. 6 in Massachussetts (1756 Fall River Ave.); and the **Providence Performing Arts Center,** 220 Weybosset St. (421-2787), which hosts a variety of concerts and Broadway musicals. The **Cable Car Cinema,** 204 S. Main St. (272-3970), with a café attached, shows art and foreign films in an unusual setting—patrons sit on couches instead of regular seats. The **Avon Repertory Cinema,** 260 Thayer St. (421-3315), attracts a big Brown crowd and shows first-run intellectual films and classics.

Sights

Providence's most notable historic sights cluster on **College Hill,** a 350-year-old neighborhood. **Brown University,** established in 1764, claims several 18th-century structures, proves the best source of information about the area. The Office of Admissions, itself housed in the historic Carliss-Brackett House at 45 Prospect St. (863-2378), distributes a free walking tour of the campus and gives tours daily at 10am and 2pm. (Open Mon.-Fri. 8am-4pm.) Check out **University, Sayles,** and **Wilson Halls,** and stroll down lamp-lined **Benefit Street.** At one of the oldest libraries in the nation, the **Providence Athaeneum,** 251 Benefit St. (421-6970), Edgar Allen Poe courted Sarah Helen Whitman, supposedly his inspiration for Annabel Lee—not surprising given the romantic air of this Greek Revival structure. Ask one of the librarians to show you the bust of Benjamin Franklin, the portrait of Poe, its "treasure" books, and the folio edition of Audubon's *Birds of America.* (Open June-Sept. Mon.-Fri. 8:30am-4:30pm; off-season Mon.-Fri. 8:30am-5:30pm, Sat. 9:30am-5:30pm. Free.) In addition to founding Rhode Island, Roger Williams created the Baptist Church; the **First Baptist Church of America,** built in 1775, stands at 75 N. Main St. Looking down from the hill, you'll see the **Rhode Island State Capitol** (277-2357), its enormous unsupported marble dome second in size only to St. Peter's in Rome. (Free guided tours Mon.-Fri. hourly 10am-2pm. Building open Mon.-Fri. 8:30am-4:30pm.)

At the nearby **RISD Museum of Art,** 224 Benefit St. (331-3511), you can view a first-rate collection of Greek, Roman, Asian, and impressionist art plus the gigantic, 10th-century Japanese Buddha and an ancient mummy. (Open Wed.-Sat. noon-5pm; winter Tues.-Wed. and Fri.-Sat. 10:30am-5pm, Thurs. noon-8pm, Sun. 2-5pm. Admission $2, seniors $1, ages 5-18 50¢.) Student art hits the walls during term time at the **Waterman Gallery,** in the same building. The **Woods-Gerry Gallery,** 62 Prospect St. (331-3511), shows both student and faculty creations. (Open Mon.-Wed. and Fri.-Sat. 11am-4pm, Thurs. 11am-7pm, Sun. 2-5pm.) In a handsome mansion at 110 Benevolent St., the **Museum of Rhode Island History** (331-8575) has four rooms of interesting exhibits. (Open Mon.-Thurs. 10am-4pm. Admission $1.50, seniors and students $1, ages 7-17 50¢.) The impressive **John Brown House,** 52 Power St. (331-8575), went up in 1786, funded by the wealthy China trade merchant. (Open Tues.-Sat. 11am-4pm, Sun. 1-4pm; Jan.-Feb. weekends by appointment. Admission $3.50, seniors and students $2.50, children $1.)

Thayer Street is a popular student hangout and shopping spot. Built in 1828 and the nation's oldest shopping mall, the **Arcade,** 65 Weybosset St. (456-5403), thrives on downtown's busiest commercial street. While the mall itself displays the Greek Revival style, current proprietors tend to the trendy Fro-Yo school.

For a quiet walk or jog, head to: the spacious grounds of **Roger Williams Park,** with its carousel and zoo, on the Cranston-Providence line; the lovely **Butler Hospital** (456-3700) estate; **Colt State Park,** in Bristol, where many local and national bands perform in summer; or the rolling green of **Swan Point Cemetery,** on Blackstone Blvd., where you can see the less-than-grotesque grave of horror writer H.P. Lovecraft.

Providence's revival as an agrarian and astrological powerhouse gives city inhabitants cause for celebration. On New Year's Eve, people wander the streets watching puppet shows, jazz bands, and Guatemalan dancers in a **First Night** celebration of the city's diversity. In early June, the **Festival of Historic Houses** lets tourists travel to the past and see ancient city homes by candlelight. In early September the **Providence Waterfront Festival** involves boat races, harbor cruises, and a landlubbers' arts and crafts fair. Call the visitors bureau for more information (274-1636).

Newport

Come on, share the wealth!
—Andrew Kaplan, Newport Fan

Despite all physical and astrological evidence to the contrary, Newport is not a city but an avatar of capitalism. This ancient capital seems quite capable of remembering the two not exactly innocent ages of its past, both involving ridiculous wealth. The way Dr. Kaplan taunts visitors in the promotional material should clearly indicate that this is no haven for budget travelers. The city, in reality, wants visitors to share *their* wealth with *it.*

Before the American Revolution, Newport was both one of the five largest towns in the northern half of the Americas and a thriving seaport enjoying the spoils of the triangle trade of rum, slaves, and molasses. Occupation by the British thwarted development until affluent vacationers targeted it as the ideal mid-19th-century retreat. In the "Gilded Age," Newport emerged unrivaled as the most popular resort in the U.S., with "summer cottages" built for the elite by the country's best architects—without regard for cost—in imitation of Neoclassical and baroque models. Crammed to the rafters with *objets d'art,* these "white elephants," as Henry James called them, testified to the determination of the *arrivistes* to purchase as much culture as possible.

Today, instead of fishing boats, Newport has 12-meter racing and sailing yachts and you'll only find fish wrapped in sauce with a soupçon of something. To avoid capitalism, visit in the off-season. In chillier days, the restaurants downtown offer fireplaces, hot cider and grog, and a softer sell. If you can't wait until the off-season, or if conspicuous consumption turns your stomach and not your head, consider retreating to one of the neighboring towns, whose demeanor better suits coastal towns than seats of trade.

Practical Information

Emergency: 911.

Visitor Information: Newport County Convention and Visitors Bureau, 23 America's Cup Ave. (849-8048 or 800-458-4843). Free maps. Open daily 8am-8pm; off-season 9am-5pm. **Newport Harbor Center,** 365 Thames St. More pamphlets and public restrooms. For more information on Newport call 800-242-1510 or 800-242-1520.

Bonanza Buses: Newport Gateway Center, 23 America's Cup Ave. (846-1820), next to the visitors bureau. To Boston (8 per day, 1½ hr., $10).

Rhode Island Public Transit Authority (RIPTA): 1547 W. Main Rd. (847-0209 or 800-662-5088). Very frequent service to Providence (1 hr., $2) and points between on Rte. 114. Buses leave from the Newport Gateway Center. Free Newport Loop bus (Memorial Day-Labor Day daily 10am-7pm) to main sights, shopping areas, and chamber of commerce. Office open Mon.-Fri 4:30am-8pm, Sat. 6am-7pm.

Car Rental: Newport Ford, 310 W. Main Rd. (846-1411). Compact $30 per day. 100 free mi., 15¢ each additional mi. Open Mon.-Fri. 8am-5pm. Must be 21 with a $200 credit card deposit.

Bike Rental: Ten Speed Spokes, 18 Elm St. (847-5609). Bikes of all speeds. 10-speeds $15 per day. Tandems $5 per day. Open Mon.-Sat. 9:30am-5:30pm, Sun. noon-5pm. Must have credit card and photo ID.

Post Office: 320 Thames St., opposite Perry Hill Market. Window service open Mon.-Fri. 7:30am-5:30pm, Sat. 9am-noon; lobby Mon.-Fri. 6am-7pm, Sat. 6am-5pm, Sun. 10am-5pm. **ZIP code:** 02840.

Area Code: 401.

Newport commands a boot-shaped peninsula on the southwest corner of Aquidneck Island in Narragansett Bay. The long span of the Newport Bridge (Rte. 138) connects the town to the smaller Conanicut Island to the west, which the Jamestown Bridge in turn connects to the mainland. The summer sanctuary, Block Island, lies 10 mi. southeast of Newport in the Block Island Sound. From Providence, take I-195 east to Rte. 114 south via Mt. Hope Bridge (45 min.). From Boston, take Rte. 128 south to Rte. 24 south to Rte. 114 south (called the West Main Rd. near Newport) or Rte. 138 south (the East Main Rd.). On summer weekends, beat the traffic by taking the back door into town: on Rte. 138 south, turn left onto Valley Rd. and continue past Newport Beach onto Memorial Blvd. (1½ hr.).

West Main Road becomes Broadway in town. **Thames Street,** the main drag on the waterfront, is pronounced as it looks, not like the river through London. Just about everything of interest in Newport is within walking distance. And walking is preferable to fighting the hellish traffic. The convenient RIPTA loop bus accesses most out-of-the-way spots.

Accommodations

Newport has no campgrounds, though a few fine ones cling in the area (see Near Newport below), and few cheap hotels. When staying in town, head for the visitors bureau for guest house brochures and free phones from which to call them. Guest houses offer bed and continental breakfast with colonial-style intimacy and orgasm. Those not fussy about sharing a bathroom or forgoing a sea view might find a double for $50. Singles are practically nonexistent. Avoid summer weekends, when many hotels and guest houses are booked solid two months in advance and rates rise by $10-$20. Also, be warned that many of Newport's cheaper accommodations close for the winter. **Bed and Breakfasts of Rhode Island, Inc.** (849-1298) can make a reservation for you in Newport at an average rate of $65 per night.

If you arrive in town after the visitors bureau closes, you'll have to try some guest houses on your own. At the beautiful 1890 **Queen Anne Inn,** 16 Clarke St. (846-5676), near Washington Sq., attractive rooms boast handsome wallpaper, bedspreads, and antique furniture. (Singles $40. Doubles $50-75. Open May-Oct.) Just outside Newport, in Middletown, is **Lindsey's Guest House,** 6 James St. (846-9386). Expect Eddie Haskell and the Beave to walk through the door at any minute. No substantial historic significance, but a solid breakfast and good rates compensate. (Rooms $50-60 weekends, $40-50 mid-week.)

Food

Seafood is the recurring theme here, high prices the recurrent nightmare. Takeout is always cheaper than sit-down. Life is what you make it. The young crowd favors the **Corner Store and Deli,** 372 Thames St., a restaurant-deli-grocery store with sandwiches ($2.75-4.75), salads, and Italian specialties to go. (Open daily 7am-10pm.) Eating downtown, you'll help restaurant owners meet their high rents. Along the waterfront and wharves, sandwiches, salads, and pasta dishes make good deals. Walk a few blocks away from downtown and time warp to the succession of true 1950s diners and New England seafood shacks. Sit at a booth and try Linda's Chili or Tish's Pea Soup at the **Franklin Spa,** 229 Franklin St. (Open Mon.-Sat. 6:30am-5pm, Sun. 6:30am-1pm.) Established in 1928, **The Newport Creamery,** at 49 Long Wharf Mall, has become a local institution. Just stop when you see the Golden Cow. Indulge in the enormous ice cream menu ($1.05-4.25). (Open daily 7am-11pm).

Dry Dock Seafood Restaurant, 448 Thames St., a few blocks south of the wharves. Small, cheap, homey seafood joint frequented by locals. Big, crispy fish and chips $5.25, lobster special $8.50. Burgers and fish sandwiches $1.50-6.25. Open Sun.-Thurs. 11am-10pm, Fri.-Sat. 11am-11pm.

The Island Omelette Shoppe, 1 Farewell St. Family-run diner feeding lots of local workers. Best breakfast in town; fast and cheap ($1-5). Open daily 6am-2pm.

Salas, 343 Thames St. Italian and Asian pasta with 8 sauces, in 3 serving sizes (½ lb. spaghetti with red clam sauce $4.50). Seafood $7-10; raw bar cheaper than most. Open daily 4-10pm.

Sights

The jewel in Newport's crown of historic districts, **The Point,** along Washington St. harborside, contains the famous Hunter House (1748) and six other homes of sea-captains and colonists of yore. Walking tours are included in the free *Best-Read Guide Newport,* available at the **Newport Historical Society,** 82 Town St. (846-0813). The society publishes its own, more detailed maps ($1), and leads two-hour walking tours through the downtown area. (Tours mid-June to late Sept. Fri.-Sat. at 10am. Tour $3, children free.) The society's **museum** of Newport history is free.

The most recent of the city's relics, the **Newport Mansions,** draws herds of tourists every summer. Seven of them are owned and run by the Preservation Society of Newport at 118 Mill St., which distributes walking maps of **Bellevue Avenue,** where most of these colossal beasts reside. **Cliff Walk** (take a right off the east end of Memorial Blvd.) offers a better view of the mansions, also affording a beautiful, rose-framed panorama of the ocean. Unless you want to go on a serious gilt trip, tours of the interiors are unnecessary. If you must venture inside, start at Cornelius Vanderbilt's **Breakers,** on Ochre Point Ave., the most famous and lavish of all. (Open July-Aug. Mon.-Wed. 10am-5pm, Thurs.-Sun. 9:30am-6pm; April-July and Sept.-Oct. daily 9am-5pm. Admission $6, ages 6-11 $3.50.) The **Marble House** and **Rosecliff,** both on Bellevue Ave., furnished settings for the movie *The Great Gatsby.* (Both mansions open May-Oct. daily 10am-5pm; April limited hours. Admission $5, ages 6-11 $3.) Several private palaces also open their doors to the public.

Cycle the 10-mi. loop along **Ocean Drive** for breathtaking scenery. On the way you'll pass sprawling and gaudy **Hammersmith Farm** (846-0420), the childhood home of Jackie Bouvier Kennedy Onassis and the "summer White House" in the early 60s. (Open June-Aug. daily 10am-7pm; April-May and Sept.-Oct. 10am-5pm; Nov. and March Sat.-Sun. only. Admission $5, children $2.)

The colonial buildings downtown are more unassuming than the mansions, but provide wonderful windows on that epoch. The 1765 **Wanton-Lyman Hazard House,** 17 Broadway (846-3622), the oldest standing house in Newport, has been restored in different period styles. (Open mid-June to Aug. daily 10am-5pm. Admission $2, children free.) The **White Horse Tavern,** on Marlborough St. (849-3600), the oldest drinking establishment in the country, dates to 1673, but the father of William Mayes, a notorious Red Sea pirate, first opened it as a tavern in 1687.

Since colonists fleeing Puritan Massachusetts founded Rhode Island for religious freedom, it comes as no surprise that the most interesting colonial buildings in town are houses of worship. The **Quaker Meeting House,** built in 1700, on the corner of Marlborough and Farewell St. (847-2481), displays Quaker plain inside and out. Zealots tore down the original steeple, criticized as too "papist," in 1807. (Open mid-June to Aug. Tues.-Sat. 10am-5pm. Admission $2, children free.) The **Touro Synagogue,** 83 Touro St. (847-4794), a beautifully restored Georgian building and the oldest synagogue in the U.S., dates back to 1763. It was to the Newport congregation that George Washington wrote the famous letter that describes the U.S. as giving "to bigotry no sanction, to persecution no assistance." (Free tours every ½ hr. in summer. Open late June-Sept. Sun.-Fri. 10am-5pm; spring and fall Sun.-Fri. 1-3pm; winter Sun. 1-3pm and by appointment.) Towering **Trinity Church,** facing Thames St. in Queen Anne Sq. (846-0660), boasts a pew reserved for George Washington back in the days when Newport was a revolutionary army stronghold. (Open Mon.-Sat. 10am-4pm, Sun. 11:30am-4pm. Free.) The beautiful, Gothic **St. Mary's Church,** at Spring St. and Memorial Blvd., is the oldest Catholic parish in the state. Jacqueline Bouvier and John F. Kennedy were married here. (Open Mon.-Fri. 7-11am. Free.)

The Redwood Library and Athenaeum, on 50 Bellevue Ave. (847-0292), built in 1748-1750, is the oldest library (and portrait gallery) in continuous use in the country. (Open daily 9:30am-5pm; winter 9am-5:30pm.) The nearby **Newport Art Museum,** 76 Bellevue Ave. (847-0179), has a fine collection of U.S. impressionist works collected in the 1864 Griswold House. Throughout the summer the museum holds musical picnics on its lawn. (Picnics free. Museum open Tues.-Sat. 10am-5pm, Sun. 1-5pm. Admission $2, seniors $1, children free.)

No racqueteer should miss the **Tennis Hall of Fame,** 194 Bellevue Ave. (849-3990), built in 1880, in the Newport Casino. The first U.S. national championships were held here one year later. The world-famous men's **Volvo Tennis Tournament** takes place here the second week of July, the galaxy-renowned women's **Virginia Slims Tournament** a week later. The Casino has one of the few facilities in the world for the ancient and arcane game of court tennis. (Open daily 10am-5pm; Oct.-April 11am-4pm. Admission $4, under 16 $2.)

Even those who don't sail should take some time to walk the plank onto vessels available for visits. Open to the public, the Bannister's Wharf Marina has housed the 12m yachts *Clipper, Independence, Courageous,* and *Gleam.* Check out the free *Newport This Week's Yachting & Recreation Guide* for a description of regattas and a calendar of events. Enter through Gate 1 of the U.S. Navy's training center on Coasters Harbor Island to view a different sort of sea power. Appearances to the contrary, tourism is not Newport's largest industry. The U.S. Navy is the town's largest employer, second in Rhode Island only to state government. On special occasions, you can tour the successors to the wooden and iron ships from the time of John Paul Jones. Visit the **Naval War College Museum** (863-8300) with interesting exhibits on naval history. (Open June-Sept. Mon.-Fri. 10am-4pm, Sat.-Sun. noon-4pm; Oct.-May Mon.-Fri. 10am-4pm. Free.)

After a few hours of touring Newport, you might think of escaping to the shore; unfortunately, the beaches crowd as frequently as the streets. The most popular of the shores is **First Beach,** or Easton's Beach, on Memorial Blvd., with its wonderful old beach houses and carousel. (Open Memorial Day-Labor Day Mon.-Fri. 9am-9pm, Sat.-Sun. 8am-9pm. Parking $5, weekends $8.) Those who prefer hiking over dunes to building sandcastles should try **Fort Adams State Park** south of town on Ocean Dr. (847-2400), with showers, picnic areas, and two fishing piers. (Entrance booth open daily 7:30am-4pm. Park closes 11pm-6am.) Other good beaches line Little Compton, Narragansett, and the shore between Watch Hill and Point Judith. For more details, consult the free *Ocean State Beach Guide,* available at the visitors center.

Entertainment

Summer drives Newport to hedonism. In July and August, lovers of classical, folk, and jazz each have a festival to call their own. The **Newport Music Festival** (849-0700) in July attracts pianists, violinists, and other classical musicians from around the world, presenting them in the ballrooms and lawns of the mansions. Tickets ($17-25) and information are available at the visitors bureau (849-8098) and through Ticketron (800-382-8080). In August, you might chorus with folksingers Joan Baez and the Indigo Girls at the **Newport Folk Festival** (212-496-9000), which runs two days, noon to dusk, rain or shine. Tickets ($20-22.50) are available through Ticketmaster. Later in the month, the **Newport Jazz Festival** (847-3700) comes to town. The setting for both festivals is a grassy field at Fort Adams State Park, overlooking the ocean. Purchase tickets ($15-50) in advance through the Tennis Hall of Fame on Bellevue Ave.

Newport's nightlife does an active and predictably trendy funky chicken. Local and out-of-state musicians play not just jazz at the snazzy pink and purple **Blue Pelican Jazz Club,** 40 W. Broadway (847-5675). This famous hotspot blows a diverse roster of performers. (Open daily 6pm-1am. Cover $6.) Down by the water at **Pelham East,** at the corner of Thames and Pelham (849-9460), they tend to play straight, hard-hitting rock 'n' roll. College kids flock here to hear the nightly live music. (Open daily noon-1am. Weekend cover $5.) Those longing still for the age of disco should visit **Maximillian's,** 108 William St. 2nd floor (849-4747), across the street from the Tennis Hall of Fame, one of the city's most popular audio-visually enhanced dance clubs. (Open Tues.-Sun 9pm-1am. Cover Sun. and Tues.-Thurs. $3, Fri.-Sat. $5.) Better yet, when you first sail into town, saunter down Bannister's Wharf and stop by the elegant, reserved, and atmospheric **Black Pearl Pub** (and café in good weather). (Open daily 11:30am-1am.)

Those seeking still more refined recreation should see a production of one of Newport's fine theatrical companies. The **Rhode Island Shakespeare Theater** (849-7892), on Broadway above the post office, in fact stages more U.S. than Elizabethan drama each season. (Tickets $13.) The **Newport Playhouse** (849-4618), on Connell Hwy., puts on light comedies and musicals. (Performances usually Thurs.-Sun. Tickets $15. Take Harrison Ave. bus from the YMCA.) Newport also has a resident modern dance group, the **Island Moving Company** (847-4470), which hosts a short summer season.

Balls whiz by at 188 mph, athletes a good deal more slowly, at the **Jai Alai Fronton,** 150 Admiral Kalbfus Rd. (849-5000 or 800-451-2500; 800-556-6900 outside RI), at the base of the Newport Bridge off Rte. 138. The place, one of the few in the country where the sport—and gambling on it—is legal, has impressive facilities. (Games May 5-Oct. 9 Mon.-Sat. at 7:30pm, matinees Mon. and Sat. at noon. Seats $2-3.50, standing room $1.) Read the weekly *Newport This Week* for more entertainment information.

Newport does not hibernate in the off-season. The large, active Celtic community has declared March **Irish Heritage Month** (849-8048), and sponsors a number of ethnic celebrations culminating in the St. Patrick's Day Parade in downtown Newport.

Near Newport: Conanicut and the Block Islands

On the western side of the Newport Bridge lies **Conanicut Island**, a sleepy, unassuming place with **Jamestown** at its heart. This mercifully undeveloped town consists of two streets dotted with fishing supply stores and craft shops. In the center of the island, the marvelous 1787 **Jamestown Windmill**, on North Rd., sits on a hill that affords a good view of the neighboring wildlife preserve where you may spot snowy egrets and blue herons. (Windmill open mid-June to Sept. Tues.-Sun. 1-4pm. Free.) Picnic or scuba dive at **Fort Wetherhill**, on Fort Wetherhill Rd. on the island's southeast shore (open 6am-11pm) or camp on the beach in **Fort Getty** (423-1363) on Fort Getty Rd. on the southwest portion of the island; stroll a few hundred yd. to Conanicut's second wildlife sanctuary. (Open May 25-Oct. 9. Sites $15.) Cozy and comfortable **Oyster Bar**, 22 Narragansett Ave., serves a mean chowder and local seafood at great prices ($3-10). The **East Ferry Market**, 47 Conanicut Ave., has the best coffee in the state, as well as sandwiches and pastries. (Open summer daily 6:30am-7pm; off-season Mon.-Fri. 6:30am-5pm, Sat. 6:30am-3pm, Sun. 8am-3pm.) In August, the Jamestown Yacht Club hosts the **Fool's Rules Regatta** (423-7492) in Potters Cove. Contestants must construct a sailboat from nonstandard material the day of the race, and coax it along the 500-yard course. Consult the free *This Week in South County* for information on other festivities.

Ten mi. southeast of Newport in the Atlantic, lovely **Block Island** has become an increasingly popular daytrip as Nantucket and Martha's Vineyard saturate with tourists. Weathered shingles, quaint buildings, and serenity endow the island with old New England charm. Bring a picnic, head due south from Old Harbor where the ferry lets you off, and hike to the Mohegan Bluffs. Those adventurous, careful, and strong enough can wind their way down to the Atlantic waters 70 yd. below. The **Southeast Lighthouse**, high in the cliffs, has warned sailors since 1875; its beacon shines the brightest of any on the Atlantic coast.

The **Block Island Chamber of Commerce** (466-2982; booth 466-2436), advises at the ferry dock in Old Harbor Drawer D, Block Island 02807. (Open Mon.-Fri. 9am-4pm, Sat. 9am-1pm; mid-Oct. to mid-May Mon.-Fri. approximately 10am-2pm.) You can obtain the free *Block Island Chamber of Commerce Directory* at the Newport Chamber of Commerce.

Cycling is the ideal way to explore the tiny (7 mi. × 3 mi.) island. Try the **Old Harbor Bike Shop** (466-2029), to the left when you exit the ferry. (10-speeds $2 per hr., $12.50 per day; single mopeds $12, $40; double mopeds $20, $60. Car rentals $55 per day, 20¢ per mi. Open daily 8:30am-7pm. Must be 21 with a credit card.)

Interstate Navigation Co., Galilee State Pier, Point Judith 02882 (401-783-4613; on Block Island 401-466-2261) runs one ferry per day (July 1-Sept. 10) between Providence and Block Island. (Departs at 8:30am, 3½ hr. Fare $7, $10.25 round-trip; bicycle $2.75. Stops at Ft. Adams at 10:30am, 2 hr. Fare $7, $8.75 round-trip; bicycle $1.75.) Year-round service to Block Island leaves only from Point Judith, near the town of Galilee, across Rhode Island Sound west of Newport. An interstate ferry leaves from Point Judith. (8-10 per day in summer down to 1 per day in winter; 1 hr.; fare $6.75, same-day round-trip $10, bicycle $1.75 each way, car $40.50 round-trip.)

The **police** can be reached at 466-2622, the **Coast Guard** at 466-2086. Block Island's post office sorts on Ocean Ave; the **ZIP code** is 02807. Since all phones are on the 466 exchange, only dial the last four digits while on the island.

Vermont

An old story has a Texas rancher going to Vermont to study the dairy farming industry. After spending the day touring pastures, barns, and farmhouses with his Vermont-born host, the Texan remarks, "You know, down in Texas, I can hop in my car and drive all day and still not reach the other side of my ranch."

"Ay-uh," says the Vermonter, "Had a car like that once myself."

Once known for their dry wit and laconic provincialism, Vermonters have more recently earned a reputation for their progressive, liberal politics, leading the way with anti-litter legislation several years ago, and more recently, passing a nuclear-freeze referendum. In addition, Burlington's Bernie Sanders became the first social-ist mayor of a major city in the U.S.

In the late 60s and early 70s, many dissatisfied young urbanites headed for a sim-pler, more peaceful existence in Vermont, setting up communes in Putney, the Northeast Kingdom, and elsewhere; hippies and long-time residents ended up dis-cussing organic farming techniques or the latest in wood stoves, all certain that Ver-mont offered the best possible quality of life. Since the 80s, professional Vermonters have BMWed here part-time to partake of country living in the summer and to ski in the winter, making Vermont a hot vacation spot. Information booths here are plentiful, helpful kiosks dot the highways, and nearly every town's chamber of com-merce has maps of stores and restaurants. But Vermonters are smart enough not to let big business ruin the pristine landscape, their biggest draw; billboards are out-lawed here. Vermont's park system fills only on September and October week-ends—a testament to the state's rural tranquility.

Practical Information

Capital: Montpelier.

Tourist Information: For lodging, events, attractions, dining, and camping, try either the **Ver-mont Travel Division,** 134 State St., Montpelier 05602 (828-3236; open Mon.-Fri. 7:45am-4:30pm; longer hours during fall foliage), or the **Chamber of Commerce,** P.O. Box 37, Mont-pelier 05602, on Granger Rd., I-89 exit 7 in Berlin (223-3443; open Mon.-Fri. 8:30am-5pm). For the scoop on exploring the great outdoors, try the **Department of Forests, Parks, and Recreation,** 103 S. Main St., Waterbury (244-8711; open Mon.-Fri. 7:45am-4:30pm); **U.S. Forest Supervisor,** Green Mountains National Forest, 151 West St., P.O. Box 519, Rutland 05702 (773-0300; open Mon.-Fri. 8am-4:30pm); and **District Ranger,** Green Mountains Na-tional Forest RFD#4, Middlebury 05753 (388-4362), or at RD#1, P.O. Box 108, Rochester 05767 (767-4261).

Public Transport: Vermont Transit Lines, 135 Saint Paul St., Burlington 05401 (864-6811 for information).

Time Zone: Eastern. **Postal Abbreviation:** VT.

Skiing

Twenty-four downhill resorts and 47 cross-country trails crisscross Vermont. For a free winter attractions packet, call the Vermont Travel Division (see Practical Information above), or write **Ski Vermont,** 134 State St., Montpelier 05602.

Vermont's famous downhill ski resorts offer a range of terrains, from easy "bunny" slopes to steep and mogul-covered runs, as well as a great variety of accom-modations, including cheap dorms. The best known resorts are: **Killington** (773-1500 or 773-1300; 107 trails, 18 lifts, 6 mountains); **Sugarbush** (583-2381; lodging 800-537-8427; 80 trails, 16 lifts, 2 mountains); **Stowe** (253-8521; lodging 800-247-8693; 44 trails, 10 lifts; see Stowe for more details); and **Jay Peak** (800-451-4449; 35 trails, 6 lifts). Vermont's abundance of cross-country resorts means you don't have to backtrack. Try: the **Trapp Family Lodge,** Stowe (253-8511; lodging 800-247-8693; 60 mi. of trails); **Mountain Meadows,** Killington (757-7077; 25 mi.); **Wood-stock** (457-2114; 47 mi.); and **Sugarbush-Rossignol** (583-2301 or 800-451-4320; 30 mi.).

Bennington

A minor industrial center and the state's third largest city (pop. 16,000), Benning-ton trumpets its status as the first chartered town in Vermont; historical sites abound. Pick up a map and a brochure describing **Historic Bennington Walking**

Tours at the **chamber of commerce,** Veteran's Memorial Dr. (447-3311) behind the deer park. From the bus terminal, turn right and walk up the street less than a mile. (Open daily 9am-5pm.) The town and state will celebrate their bicentennial in 1991, so expect a slew of festivals and celebrations; a reenactment of the Battle of Bennington is already scheduled for the summer.

The town is mostly built around the intersection of Rte. 9 (E. and W. Main St.) and Rte. 7 (streets running north and south). Walking through, you will pass many old buildings, although the only one you can glance into is the **Old First Church** (First Congregational Church). Established in 1702, the church was not only the home of the oldest Protestant religious organization in Vermont, but was also the first place in the U.S. to separate church and state. The building is still used for Sunday services (11am). (Open to the public late June-Oct. daily 10am-noon and 1-4pm.) Down the street is the **Bennington Museum,** W. Main St. (447-1571), with the world's largest collection of Grandma Moses's folk paintings and the oldest Stars and Stripes in existence. (Open March-late Dec. daily and some other winter weekends 9am-5pm. Admission $4.50, seniors and students $3.50, under 12 free.) Up the hill, the **Bennington Battle Monument,** a 306-ft. obelisk at the end of Monument Ave., commemorates General John Stark's victory over the British (gift shop 447-0550; open daily April 1-Oct. 31 9am-5pm; admission $1, under 12 50¢, under 5 free).

To escape the steady stream of traffic through the center of town try **Back-Road Country Tours** (442-3878). For $12.50 per person you get a one-hour jeep ride through the back roads of Bennington County with commentary on the local farms, covered bridges, wildlife, and folklore. (Open daily; trips leave from the chamber of commerce.)

There are a number of affordable restaurants in Bennington. **Geannelis' Restaurant,** 520 Main St., is very popular. The revolving menu hanging from the ceiling lists tasty sandwiches ($2-3), dinner ($4-7), and fine ice cream ($1.25). (Open Mon.-Sat. 6am-8pm, Sun. 7am-8pm.) **Occasionally Yogurt,** 604 Main St., has big salads ($2-5), natural vegetarian foods, and frozen yogurt occasionally topped with carob chips. (Open daily 11am-9pm.)

Affordable accommodations are much more occasional here. In town try the **Mid-town Motel,** 107 W. Main St. (447-0189), where rooms are dark but functional (singles $30, doubles $34). Further east is the **Homestead Motor Inn,** 924 E. Main St. (442-3143), with bright, clean rooms (singles $31, doubles $34). Camping, as usual, is far cheaper. **Greenwood Lodge and Tentsites,** P.O. Box 246, Bennington (442-2547), is an 8-mi. trip east on Rte. 9 in Woodford Valley. The Long Trail is just 3 mi. away. (Open July 1-Sept. 7, fall weekends, and some winter months. Dorms $10 with AYH card. Sites $10. Private family rooms from $25, slightly higher rates for fall foliage season. Linen, towels, and soap $2. Hot showers in lodge. Canoeing free.) You can also stay at **Woodford State Park** (447-7169), 10 mi. east on Rte. 9. (Open May 27-Oct. 14. Sites $9, reserved sites $12.) **Pine Hollow Camping Area** (823-5569), Old Military Rd., off Barber's Pond Rd. off U.S. 7, is 6 mi. south of Bennington, and offers swimming and tranquility. (Open May 15-Oct. 15. Sites $9.)

Bennington pins down the southwestern corner of Vermont, 39 mi. across the Green Mountains from Brattleboro, and 60 mi. south of Rutland on U.S. 7/7A. **Vermont Transit,** 126 Washington Ave. (442-4808), takes you to Middlebury, Rutland, Burlington, Montréal, and Albany, NY. (Open daily 9am-noon, 1:30-4:30pm.) Bennington's **ZIP code** is 05201; the **area code** is 802.

Bennington's neighboring towns offer interesting attractions of their own. Up Rte. 67A in North Bennington is the **Park-McCullough House** (442-5441), a beautifully restored Victorian mansion complete with carriage house and carefully groomed gardens. (Open early May-late Oct. daily 10am-4pm. Admission $3, ages 12-17 $1.50, under 12 free. Tours on the hour.) The family that owned the house gave generously to nearby **Bennington College** (442-5401), now renowned for its creative writing and arts departments. Pick up campus maps at the **Admissions Of-**

fice. (Open May-Aug. Mon.-Fri. 9am-3pm; Sept.-April Mon.-Fri. 9am-3pm, Sat. 9am-noon. Tours can be arranged.)

Fourteen mi. north on bucolic Rte. 7A is **Arlington,** one-time home of illustrator Norman Rockwell. An old church on Rte. 7A houses the **Norman Rockwell Exhibition,** a kitschy collection of old magazine covers by the artist (375-6423; open April-Oct. daily 9am-5pm; Nov.-March daily 10am-4pm). **Lake Shraftsbury State Park,** a few miles south of Arlington on Rte. 7A, has a fine picnic area, swimming at your own risk (no lifeguards), and boat rental. (Admission $1.50, ages 4-13 $1, under 4 free. Rowboats $3 per hr., canoes $4 per hr., pedal boats $5 per hr.)

Brattleboro

Southeastern Vermont is often charged with living too much in its past. This is certainly true of one of the largest towns in the area, Brattleboro (pop. 12,000). But the town lives in a more recent past than you might expect; Brattleboro is more a captive of the Age of Aquarius than colonial times. Indian prints are ubiquitous, the smell of patchouli wafts through the air, craft and food cooperatives abound, and bumpers are plastered with anti-nuclear slogans. The locals appreciate nature just as much as the tourists who rush in every fall to ogle the Connecticut River Valley's foliage.

Brattleboro is right on the Connecticut River, which you can explore by canoe. Rentals are available at **Connecticut River Safari,** (257-5008 or 603-363-4724) on Putney Rd. (Open Wed.-Sun. $12 per ½-day, $18 per day; longer packages available.) They also run a touring and guiding service on the Connecticut and other New England rivers. The **Brattleboro Outing Club** (603-399-4963), P.O. Box 335, Brattleboro, 05301, rents canoes and runs skiing programs. **Specialized Sports** (257-1017), on Putney Rd., specializes in used bikes ($14 the first day, $9 subsequent days).

The **Brattleboro Museum and Art Center** (257-0124), in the Old Railroad Station on Vernon St., overlooks the river. The museum has fine exhibitions of local artists' handicrafts, alongside a permanent collection of 19th-century Estey Organs, manufactured in Brattleboro. (Open May 13-Nov. 4 Tues.-Sun. noon-6pm. Admission $2, seniors $1, under 15 free.)

Inexpensive places to eat are easy to come by. The **Common Ground Community Restaurant,** 25 Eliot St., a workers' cooperative and favorite local hangout, serves a wide range of affordable vegetarian dishes in a relaxed, informal atmosphere. You can get soup, salad, bread, and beverage for $4. (Open June-Nov. Wed.-Sun. 11:30am-9pm; Dec.-May Sun.-Thurs. 11:30am-9pm, Fri.-Sat. 11:30am-8:30pm.) The **Backside Café,** 24 High St., serves delicious food in an artsy loft with rooftop dining. The Backside Chicken with mozzarella ($4) and a bottle of Bass or Sam Adams beer ($2.25) should please your insides. (Open Mon.-Thurs. 7:30am-4pm and 5-8:30, Fri. 7:30am-4pm and 5-9pm, Sat. 8am-3pm, Sun. 10am-3pm). For locally grown fruits, vegetables, and cider, go to the **farmers' markets** on the Town Common, Main St. (June 14-Sept. 13 Wed. 10am-2pm) or on Mink Farm, Rte. 9 west of town (May 13-Oct. 14 Sat. 9am-2pm).

The renovated **Latchis Hotel,** 2 Flat St. (254-6300), downtown, has nice rooms at decent prices, but they don't rent to anyone under 21. (Singles $38-52. Doubles $46-62.) Be careful as the neighborhood around Flat and Eliot St. can be rough at night. The **West Village,** 480 Western Ave. (254-5610), is about 3 mi. out of town on Rte. 9 in West Brattleboro. (Singles $30. Doubles $35.) Closer to town is the **Red Coach Motel** (254-4583) on Putney Rd. The rooms are clean, but in states of slight disrepair. (Singles $29. Doubles $55.) **Fort Dummer State Park,** Old Guildford Rd. (254-2610), just a few miles south on U.S. 5, has campsites with fireplaces, picnic tables, and bathroom facilities. (51 tentsites, $7.50 each. 10 lean-tos, $11 each. Firewood $1 per armload. Hot showers 25¢. Open May 27-Sept. 2.) **Molly Stark State Park** (464-5460) is 17 mi. west of town on Rte. 9. (24 tentsites, $7.50 each. 10 lean-tos, $11 each. Hot showers 25¢. Open May 25-Oct. 10.)

The nightlife of Brattleboro has two faces: one for jazz and reggae fans, the other for locals driving pick-ups. **Mole's Eye Café** (257-0771), at the corner of High and Main St., has jazz, reggae, and rock bands on Wednesday, Friday, and Saturday nights. (Open daily 11:30am to 1 or 2am. Light meals about $5. Cover $3. Wed. free.) **Colors,** 20 Elliot St. (254-8646), is a fun, relaxing place popular with both a gay and a straight clientele. Try a glass of Freixenet champagne ($2.50)—it will help you better appreciate the huge felt irises on the wall. (Open Sun.-Fri. 8pm-2am. Cover Thurs.-Sat. $2.) The **Arts Council of Windham County,** (357-1881) at 69 Main St. has local art openings the first Friday of every month, and plans to have poetry readings in 1991. The council can give you a free calendar of upcoming events, or you can call their 24-hr. events recording (257-1234).

The **chamber of commerce,** 180 Main St. (254-4565), is open Mon.-Fri. 8am-5pm. In summer, information booths are open on the Town Common off Putney Rd., and on Western Ave. just beyond the historic **Creamery Bridge** built in 1879. All can give you helpful, free guidebooks to Brattleboro.

Amtrak's "Montrealer" train from New York City and Springfield stops in Brattleboro behind the museum. Trains once daily to Montréal and south to Washington DC. Arrange tickets and reservations at **Lyon Travel,** 10 Elliot St. (254-6033; open Mon.-Fri. 9am-5pm, Sat. 10am-2pm). **Greyhound** and **Vermont Transit** stop in the parking lot behind the Texaco station at I-91 exit 3. Brattleboro is on Vermont Transit's Burlington-New York City route (3 per day, $33). Other destinations include Springfield, MA (3 per day, $11) and White River Junction (3 per day, $11), with connections to Montpelier, Waterbury, Burlington, and Montréal.

Brattleboro's **ZIP** code is 05301; The **area code** is 802.

White River Junction and West

Central Vermont is graced with quiet winding back roads and the sight of grazing cows in quiet green pastures. If you enjoy rural rubbernecking, plan an east-west trip along U.S. 4, or a north-south trip on Rte. 100. The roads are best reached from U.S. 5 or I-89, where they intersect with the Connecticut River at White River Junction. This unremarkable town serves as the major bus center for central and eastern Vermont. **Vermont Transit** (295-3011), on Rte. 5 just beyond the Wm. Tally House, has connections across New Hampshire, Burlington, and up and down the Connecticut River. (Office open Sun.-Fri. 7am-9pm, Sat. 7am-5pm.) **Amtrak** (295-7160), on Railroad Rd. off N. Main St., serves as a stop for the "Montrealer" train both south to New York City and Washington DC, and north to Essex Junction (near Burlington) and Montréal.

An **information booth** across Sykes St. from the bus station can fill your pockets with brochures on Vermont. (Open May 27-Oct. 15 daily 10am-5pm.) Also in the Junction you'll find the **Catamount Brewery,** 58 S. Main St. (296-2248), where you can sample delicious, unpasteurized amber ale produced in strict accordance with British brewing methods. (Store open Mon.-Sat. 9am-5pm, Sun. 1-5pm. Tours Tues. at 11am, Fri. at 1pm, Sat. at 11am and 1pm.)

For a quick bite to eat, stop at the **Polkadot Restaurant,** 1 N. Main St., a classic diner resting next to a retired Boston & Maine steam engine. Two pork chops with applesauce $5.50. (Open Mon.-Thurs. 5am-9pm, Fri.-Sat. 24 hr., Sun. 5am-9pm.) There are a few motels around, but the best bet for lodging is the old-style **Hotel Coolidge,** 17 S. Main St. (295-3118 or 800-622-1124), in the middle of town. The rooms are impeccably kept, but some of the cheaper rooms only have half-baths. (June-Oct. singles $22-50, doubles $27-55. Rates slightly lower in winter.) The **Vermonter Hotel,** 1 Gates St. (295-9755), has 20 cheesy but liveable singles without baths. ($25 per day, $65 per week).

Six miles west of White River Junction on U.S. 4 is **Woodstock,** a town which is part Vermont country village and part wealthy vacation resort. The pace for locals and tourists alike is slow, and even the traffic crawls. This is definitely not the place to look for nightlife. The Woodstock **chamber of commerce** at 18 Central St. will tell you what the town does offer and provide maps of trails for nearby mountains Peg and Tom; a half-hour walk up Mt. Tom will afford a good view of the town. (Open Mon.-Fri. 9am-5pm.) The chamber also sponsors an **information booth** (457-1042) in the middle of the village green. (Open late June to mid-Oct. Mon.-Fri. 9am-5pm, Sat.-Sun. 10am-3pm; mid-Oct. to late June, Sat.-Sun. 10am-2pm.) In addition there is the **Woodstock Town Crier,** a chalkboard with local listings on the corner of Elm and Church St.

The **Woodstock Historical Society,** 26 Elm St. (457-1822), is in the 19th-century **Dana House Museum,** which contains a rich collection of antique furniture and artifacts. (Open May-Oct. Mon.-Sat. 10am-5pm, Sun. 2-5pm. Admission $3.50, seniors $2.50, children $1.) The **Vermont Raptor Center,** part of the **Vermont Institute of Natural Sciences** (457-2779), on Church Hill Rd. about 2 mi. west of town, is a "living museum" introducing visitors to the owls and hawks of northern New England. (Open May-Oct. Wed.-Mon. 10am-4pm; Nov.-April Mon. and Wed.-Sat. 10am-4pm. Admission $3.50, ages 5-15 $1.) **Billings Farm and Museum** (457-2355) off River Rd., provides a great look into modern and 19th-century Vermont farm life with a working farm, a museum, and a restored 1890 farmhouse. (Open early May-late Oct. daily 10am-5pm.)

Eat beneath the gaze of a stone lion at **Bentley's Greenhouse,** 7 Elm St., a combination soda fountain, florist and sandwich shop. (Open Mon.-Wed. 8:30am-5:30pm, Thurs.-Sat. 8:30am-8pm, Sun. 8:30am-5pm.) The **Mountain Creamery,** 33 Central St., serves the best ice cream in town. Notable flavors include Myers rum raisin and Vermont maple walnut; a cone with one remarkably generous scoop costs $2.65. (Open daily 7am-6pm.) **The Deli at Woodstock,** just east of town on Rte. 4, has café-style dining and natural sodas (sandwiches $2.25-5.50).

A good place to spend the night is the beautifully remodeled **1826 House,** 57 River St. (457-1335; singles $45, doubles $50), with Bavarian antiques and a quiet back porch. The **Silver Lake Campground** (234-9974) is 9 mi. north of town on Rte. 12 near Barnard, with no public transportation available. (Open May 27-Oct. 14. Sites $13.50 per family, $2 each additional adult.)

To rent a quality bike and explore the scenery around Woodstock on wheels, go to **The Cyclery Plus,** at 36 Rte. 4 (457-3377), in West Woodstock. ($12 per half-day, $18 per day, $60 for 5 days. Open Mon.-Fri. 9am-6pm, Sat. 9am-5pm.) **Wilderness Trails** (295-7620) at the Quechee Inn, Clubhouse Rd., in Quechee will rent you a bike or canoe for the day. (1 person $14, 2 people $25, half-days and additional days $9.) **Quechee State Park** off Rte. 4 has hiking trails around **Quechee Gorge,** a spectacular 163-ft. drop from cliffs to the Ottauquechee River below. A bridge connecting the trails to the park's picnic grounds offers a view that makes you feel small and quite mortal; on the eastern side of the bridge an information booth can answer questions. The **Vermont Transit** agency in Woodstock (457-1325), at the Whippletree Shop, Central St., provides schedules and timetables of Vermont transit tours. To White River Junction (2 per day, $2.85) and Rutland (2 per day, $5.10.)

Genuine Vermont sharp cheddar cheese is made only in certain counties. One authentic producer is the **Plymouth Cheese Factory** (672-3650), on Rte. 100A 6 mi. south of U.S. 4 in **Plymouth.** (Open daily 8am-5:30pm; off-season daily 8am-5pm; closed Sun. Christmas-April.) Another big cheese from Plymouth, **Calvin Coolidge,** was born in this tiny village. Next door to his birthplace is the old homestead where in 1923 his father swore him in as president after learning of the sudden death of President Harding. (Open May 22-Oct. 18 daily 9:30am-5:30pm. Admission $1, children free.) Five mi. south on Rte. 100 lies glistening **Echo Lake,** a great place for a picnic and a swim. (Canoe or paddle boat rental $2 per hr. Admission $1.)

Middlebury

If you think soap-opera towns like Peyton Place and Pine Valley exist only in fantasy, you've never been to Middlebury. Villagers bike up and down **Main Street,** the town's backbone; children ramble through wide lanes carrying ice cream cones at dusk. The town has a friendly, bustling air, and the student population at nearby **Middlebury College** (388-3711, ext. 5338; open Mon.-Thurs. 9am-11pm, Fri. 9am-8:30pm, Sat. 11am-6pm, Sun. 11am-11pm), insures that things are never dull. In the summer, during the college's intensive language immersion programs, students speak only the language they are learning, even in cafés and fine restaurants. On campus there are free readings, dances, and concerts in a multitude of languages: here it helps to be at least bi-lingual since the college asks that English not be spoken on the premises all summer. If you begin to long for the sound of English, head out to Middlebury's famous **Breadloaf** campus (388-7945), off Rte. 125 just past Ripton, where you can hear it recited in dulcet tones at the literature summer school (late June to mid-Aug.), and the writer's conference at the end of August. Though some lectures are publicized during the summer, it is best to wander around, sit in on a few readings, and perhaps search for literary luminaries like John Updike, who have summered here in years past.

For more rugged pursuits head west to **University of Vermont's Morgan Horse Farm** (388-2077), which breeds sturdy, beautiful horses. Take Rte. 125 then Rte. 23 for 2½ mi. (Open May-Oct. daily 9am-4pm. Admission $2.50, teenagers $1, under 12 free. Tours available.)

Visit the studios of the **Vermont State Craft Center** (388-3177) at Frog Hollow, which sponsors exhibits by visiting artists and peddles an array of glass, pottery, carvings, and textiles created by Vermonters. (Open Mon.-Sat. 9:30am-5pm, and Sun. 11am-4pm; Jan.-May Mon.-Sat. 9:30am-5pm.) Downstairs in the house is the **Vermont Folklife Center** (388-4964), dedicated to preserving the state's oral and folk traditions by displaying the modern folk craft of local artists. (Open Mon.-Fri. 9am-5:30pm. Free.) The nearby **Sheldon Museum,** 1 Park St. (388-2117), one of the oldest community museums in the U.S., has a disturbing collection of antiques including a stuffed cat preserved over 100 years and a set of teeth extracted in the 19th century. (Open June-Oct. daily 10am-5pm; Nov.-April daily 1-4pm. Admission $2.50, seniors and students $2, under 12 50¢.) From there, walk down to Otter Creek and stroll across the **Marble Cutter Memorial Bridge,** which pays tribute to workers in Vermont's traditional industry while affording a fine view of the waterway.

Biking is a good way to see Middlebury, and is not too strenuous in the gentle hills that surround town. **Bicycle Holidays** (388-2453) rents like-new mountain bikes with saddle bags; they also plan tours. (First day $29, half-day $20, subsequent days $10.) You can rent simpler bikes and cross-country skis at the **Bike & Ski Touring Center,** 74 Main St. (388-6666; waxless cross-country skis $7.50 per day, waxable $5 per day; 3-speeds $1.50 per hr., $5 per day, $7.50 per weekend; open Mon.-Thurs. and Sat. 9:30am-5:30pm, Fri. 9:30am-8pm).

Cross-country skiing is all the rage here in winter; one look at the landscape will tell you why. Spend a day at **Lake Dunmore,** and from there hike up to **Silver Lake** with its canopy of birch trees and pines. On the way up, you'll pass by the beautiful **Falls of Lhana.** The north side of the lake makes for an invigorating, if chilly, dip unencumbered by a swimsuit. You might also want to stop by the **Robert Frost Interpretive Trail,** an easy ¾-mi. walk through wilderness 2 mi. east of Ripton on Rte. 25. Copies of Frost's poems adorn the Vermont landscape that inspired his work.

Middlebury's many fine restaurants cater primarily to those with large expense accounts, but the presence of year-round students assures the survival of cheaper places. **Calvi's,** 42 Main St., is an old-fashioned soda fountain with old-fashioned prices. Try their homemade ice cream in a cone ($1.25). (Open mid-June to early Sept. Mon.-Sat. 8am-10pm; mid-Sept. to early June Mon.-Sat. 8am-6pm.) Students also flock to **Mister Up's,** Bakery Lane, just off Main St. for its impressively eclectic ethnic menu, which includes beer-boiled shrimp ($4), Thai chicken satay ($4.25), and quesadilla ($5). (Open Mon.-Sat. 11:30am-midnight, Sun. 11am-midnight.) Another student roost is the **Vermont Country Kitchen,** 3 Park St., which sells a number of posh gourmet items, as well as reasonably priced sandwiches and a good selection of coffees. Try the California Dreamer, a savory cheese and veggie sandwich ($3.75). (Open Mon.-Fri. 7:30am-6pm, Sat.-Sun. 9am-6pm.)

Nightlife in Middlebury soars, again thanks to the college's proximity. Overlooking Otter Creek, the trendy **Woody's,** 5 Bakery Lane (388-4182), off Main St., has upscale dishes and drinks. Lunch prices are reasonable ($3.50-7) but items off the a la carte menu provide the best bet for a budget dinner. (Open Mon.-Sat. 11:30am-midnight, Sun. 10:30am-3pm and 5-9:30pm.) Across the street, **Amigos,** 4 Merchants Row (388-3624), serves up Mexican food ($2.50-12) and live local music Fridays and Saturdays from 10pm-1am. (Open Mon.-Sat. 1:30am-10pm, Sun. 4-10pm. Bar open nightly until midnight.)

Unfortunately, the area's cheapest accommodations are the farthest from town. **Homestead Bed and Breakfast** (545-2263), on Samson Rd. 2½ mi. from town, has two cheery rooms and two even cheerier hosts. (Singles $28. Doubles $35.) **Branbury State Park** (247-5925), 7 mi. south on U.S. 7, then 4 mi. south on Hwy. 53, will burn a smaller hole in your pocket. Situated on a lake, the park not only rents tentsites but boats for the day ($3-5). (Open May 27-Oct.14. Sites $11, lean-tos $14. Reservations recommended July 4-Aug. 15.) **Lake Dunmore Kampersville** (352-4501), 8 mi. south on U.S. 7, then 2 mi. east on 53, is a great place in spite of its kitschy name. (Open year-round. Sites $16.50 for 2 adults, children free, $5 per extra family on the same site. Reservations recommended, especially in July.)

Gather information on Middlebury and its environs at the friendly **Addison County Chamber of Commerce,** located in the historic Gamalid Painter House built in 1801, 2 Court St. (388-7951), just 50 yards from the bus stop. (Open daily 9am-5pm; off-season Mon.-Fri. 9am-5pm.)

Middlebury is on U.S. 7, at the base of the Green Mountains, 42 miles south of Burlington. The **Long Trail** passes by along the ridges in the **Green Mountain National Forest,** a few miles east. **Vermont Transit** buses stop at Keeler's Gulf, 16 Court St. (388-4373), west of Main St. Buses serve Albany, New York City, Boston, and Burlington.

Middlebury's **ZIP code** is 05753; the **area code** is 802.

Montpelier

Montpelier (pop. 8200) is a quiet, unassuming town, the capital of a state that is often understated but never unassuming. Montpelier lacks the glory of the neighboring mountains and the vigor of a student population; it does, however, have an 8-ft.-tall impassioned Ethan Allen. Crafted out of Vermont marble, Allen calls for the surrender of Fort Ticonderoga while heralding the presence of the proud, gold-domed **State House,** 115 State St. (open daily Mon.-Fri. 8am-4pm. Tours July to mid-Oct. Mon.-Fri. 10am-3:30pm, Sat. 11am-2:30pm) Located down the street is The Vermont Historical Society's **Vermont Museum and Library** at 109 State St. (828-2297), housed in the historic Pavilion building down the street from the state house, is yet another reminder that this is the capital; The library has approximately 45,000 tomes on the state's history (open Tues.-Fri. 9am-1:30pm), while the museum's exhibits encompass Vermont furniture, documents, and artifacts (open Mon.-Fri. 9am-4:30pm; admission $2, children 50¢). The **T.W. Woods Art Gallery,** at the corner of Ridge and College St. (828-8743), displays the work of a popular artist of the 19th century alongside work by contemporary Vermonters. (Open Tues.-Sun. 10am-4pm. Admission $2.)

Just to ensure that the capital is representative of most of Vermont, **Hubbard Park and Fitness Trails,** on Hubbard Park Dr., offer nature trails through 100 acres of preserved wilderness. (Open daily 9am-9pm.) Up Main St. onto Country Rd. is the **Morse Farm** (223-2740 or 800-242-2740), a working maple syrup farm that stays open year round. If you stop by in early spring though, you can see the maples being tapped. Guests are also free to wander the 300-acre farm, which gives a splendid panoramic view of the hills during foliage. The patriarch of the Morse family shows free films and gives tours of the sugarhouse.

Montpelier is also the happy home of the **New England Culinary Institute,** 250 Main St. (223-6324), and thus a fine place for a budget-blasting binge. The **Elm Street Cafe,** 38 Elm St., run by the institute's first-year students, serves nouvelle cuisine and delightful appetizers. (Lunch specials under $5.50. Dinners $5-15. Open Mon.-Fri. 7-10am, 11:30am-1:30pm and 5:30-9pm.) **Tubbs Restaurant,** 24 Elm St., is operated by second-year students and features French cuisine. (Lunch entrees $3-8; dinner entrees $13.50-18. Open Mon.-Fri. 11:30am-2pm and 6-9:30pm, Sat. 6-9:30pm.) The school's bakery, **La Brioche** (229-0443), occupies the same building and offers delicious pastries and cakes. Those who find the very notion of *coq au vin* repulsive should stop by the **Horn of the Moon Café,** 8 Langdon St., which uses Vermont cheese and organic produce to prepare vegetarian meals. (Open summer Mon.7am-3pm, Tues.-Sat. 7am-9pm, Sun. 10am-2pm; Mon. 7am-3pm, Tues.-Sat. 7am-9pm). Non-gourmands enjoy the **Wayside Restaurant,** east of town on Rte. 302 (223-6611), which trumpets its diner fare as "Yankee cooking at its best." (Hot sandwiches under $5. Open daily 9am-6pm.)

The **Vermont Travel Division,** 134 State St. (828-3236; open Mon.-Fri. 7:45am-4:30pm, Sat. 9am-3pm, Sun. 11am-3pm; longer hours in fall), can provide you with a list of restaurants and accommodations in the area, a helpful town map, and tourist information about the whole state. Try the beautifully maintained Victorian **Montpelier Bed and Breakfast,** 22 North St. (229-0878), about ½ mi. from the capitol. Very comfortable singles cost $25-38, doubles $42-60, all non-smoking. The cheaper rooms do not come with continental breakfast. The **Green Valley Campground** (223-6217), 6 mi. east of town on Rte. 2, though not very woodsy, does offer swimming and showers. (Open May-Oct.. Sites $10.50, pop-up $18.) **The Vermonter Hotel,** southeast of town on Rte. 302 (476-8541 or 479-9014), has sweet, immaculate rooms and a pleasant backyard. (Singles $31. Doubles $31-38.) In the heart of downtown. **Be Our Guest,** 35 School St., offers large, clean sunny rooms. (Doubles $25. Singles $20.) Make reservations because there are often weekly lodgers.

Montpelier rests just off I-89, 4 mi. northwest of Barre, 40 mi. southeast of Burlington, and 50 mi. northwest of White River Junction on the Winooski River. **Vermont Transit** is behind Chittenden Bank at 112 State St. (223-7112). Daily buses go to: Boston ($34), New York City ($65), White River Junction ($9), and Waterbury ($3). VT also offers service to Montréal and Portland, ME. (Open Mon.-Fri. 8:30am-6:30pm, Sat.-Sun. 8:30am-4:30pm.)

From Montpelier, you can explore the nearby **"Northeast Kingdom,"** three Vermont counties famous for their fall foliage. The town of **Craftsbury Commons,** in the Kingdom, is home to the **Craftsbury Center (AYH)** (586-7767), Hosmer Pond on Lost Nation Rd. ($10, nonmembers $40. Reservations required: write P.O. Box 31, Craftsbury Common 05827).

Montpelier's **ZIP code** is 05602; the **area code** is 802.

Stowe

Between Montpelier and Burlington lies **Stowe** (800-253-4754), one of the east's ski capitals. From November to April, people down the coast speed to the site of the highest peak in Vermont.

Quaint Stowe houses many ski resorts and four fine skiing areas. The hills are alive with the sound of some of the best cross-country skiing in the U.S., centered on Stowe's **Trapp Family Lodge,** Luce Hill Rd. (253-8511 or 800-826-7000). Alpine fans applaud **Mount Mansfield** (253-7311) and its close neighbor, **Spruce Peak,** and at higher points and prices, **Smuggler's Notch** (664-8851 or 800-451-8752). Skiing is an expensive undertaking—a one-day lift ticket will set you back about $35. A better bet might be the **Ski Vermont's Classics** program. A three-day $99 lift ticket (available at participating slopes) allows you to ski at any number of resorts in the area, including Mt. Mansfield and Smuggler's Notch. **Jim Shepard's Ski Shop** (253-4760) rents excellent downhill ($14) and cross-country skis ($10) for the day.

Stowe is still an attractive vacation option in the summer and is a good deal less expensive then. Rent mountain and road bikes at the **Mountain Bike Shop,** Mountain Rd. (253-7919; $6 per hr., $20 per day; open daily 9am-6pm). **Stowe Mountain Sports** on Mountain Rd. (253-4896) rents one- and 10-speeds ($10) and mountain bikes ($20) by the day. Pirate or rent canoes for the day at **Buccaneer Country Lodge**, 1390 Mountain Rd. (453-4772) for $25. Horseback riding is available at **Edson Hill Manor**, Edson Hill Rd. (253-8954 or 888-5137), for $18-23 per hour, and at **Topnotch at Stowe**, Rte. 108 (253-8585; guided tours $20, private lessons available).

Mt. Mansfield coordinates a variety of fun summer activities, all open daily in the summer from 9am to 5pm, weather permitting. The **Alpine Slide** on Spruce Peak, a concrete, gutter-shaped slide doused with streaming water, descends through beautiful woods and meadows. (Open mid-June to Sept. 2 daily 10am-5pm; weekends only May 27 to mid-June and Sept. 3-Oct. 14. Admission $6, children $4.) The **Gondola** runs up 4393 ft. above sea level to just below the summit of Mt. Mansfield (open mid-June to Oct. 14 daily 10am-5pm; weekends only May 27 to mid-June; fare $8.50, children $5). Or, for $9, you can burn out your brakes driving 20 minutes to the peak on the **Auto Toll Road** (open May 27-Oct. 14.) For a good daytrip, hike the **Long Trail** ascending Mt. Mansfield. Though there are a number of entrances to the trail on Mountain Rd., drive the particularly scenic route to the highest elevation point at Smuggler's Notch (not to be confused with the ski area), where the cliffs rise 1000 ft. above the pass; once, people smuggled cows into New England through this gap in the mountain. Today, an **information booth** here can point you to interesting sights on the trail, like Bingham Falls.

The socially conscious and fun-loving **Ben and Jerry's Ice Cream Factory** lies south on Rte. 100 (244-5641), a couple miles off I-89 in Waterbury. Starting in 1978 in a converted gas station, Ben and Jerry have since developed some of the best ice cream in the world. You can sample celebrated flavors such as Heath Bar Crunch, Rainforest Crunch, and White Russian. ($1 tours daily every ¼ hr 9am-4pm.) You can indulge at their store daily from 9am to 6pm.

For a more filling meal try the **Sunset Grille and Tap Room**, on Cottage Club Rd. off Mountain Rd., a friendly, down-home barbecue place with a vast selection of domestic beers and generous meals ($5-15). (Open daily 4:30pm-midnight.) All-American **Angelo's Pizza** on Mountain Rd. offers pizza ($1 per slice) and pasta ($4.75-7.50). (Open Mon.-Thurs. 11:30am-10pm, Fri.-Sat. 11:30am-midnight, Sun. 11:30am-10pm.) Right next door is the **Canton Chinese Restaurant** (253-4390), with a smiling Buddha and lunch specials starting at $2.75. (Open daily noon-11pm.)

For one of the few lodging bargains in town, the **Vermont State Ski Dorm** (253-4010) doubles as an AYH hostel from June 15 to October 15 ($8-10 per night). During the ski season they serve two meals a day and charge $35. Wipe your boots and help keep the place immaculate. The friendly and eccentric host of the **Golden Kitz**, Mountain Rd. (253-4217), offers travelers a relaxed and informal atmosphere, as well as theme bedrooms. (Singles with shared bath $26-40 in peak ski season; $18-28 in summer. Doubles $40-56 in the peak ski season, $36-40 in early and late ski season, and $28-50 in summer. Breakfast included.) Situated on a real brook, the **Gold Brook Campground** (253-7683), babbles 2 mi. south of the town center on Rte. 100. (Sites $10.50.) **Smuggler's Notch State Park** (253-4014) offers lean-tos ($11) and tent sites ($7.50). (Open May 19-Oct. 14; reservations suggested.)

Contact the **Stowe Area Association** on Main St. (253-7321 or 800-247-8693), right in the center of the village, for free booking service and summer information on the area's lodging, restaurants, and activities, including skiing. (Open summer Mon.-Fri. 9am-6pm, Sat. 10am-4pm, Sun. 11am-5pm; winter Mon.-Fri. 9am-8pm, Sat.-Sun. 9am-6pm.)

Stowe is centered around the intersection of Rte. 100 (Main St. in town) and Rte. 108 (Mountain Rd.). The ski areas all lie northwest of town on Rte. 108. Stowe is 12 mi. north of I-89's exit 10, which is 27 mi. southwest of Burlington. **Vermont Transit** runs one bus per day from Stowe to Newport and one to Burlington; both stop at the Commodore Inn, south of town on Rte. 100.

Stowe's **ZIP code** is 05672; the **area code** is 802.

Burlington

On the banks of gorgeous Lake Champlain, Burlington might at first seem to be just another waterside suburb. But this is Vermont, folks, and Burlington is the state's major city with a metropolitan population of roughly 130,000. Burlington's energy contradicts suburban lethargy, with the University of Vermont, Champlain College, and three other schools endowing the city with an engaging and youthful atmosphere.

Practical Information

Emergency: 911.

Tourist Information: Lake Champlain Regional Chamber of Commerce, 209 Battery St. (863-3489), right next to the ferry pier. Provides maps of the Burlington Bike Path and parks. Open Mon.-Fri. 8:30am-5pm, Sat.-Sun. 10am-2pm; late Sept.-late June Mon.-Fri. 8:30am-5pm.

Amtrak: 29 Railroad Ave., Essex Jct. (800-879-7298), 5 mi. from the center of Burlington. A stop for both the "Montrealer" and the "Yankee Clipper." Trains head north in the morning, south in the evening. To New York (2 per day, 9 hr., $66). Open daily 5:45am-noon, 1-6pm, and 7-11pm. Bus to downtown every ½ hr., 75¢.

Buses: Vermont Transit, 135 Saint Paul St. (864-6811), at Main St. Connections to Boston ($37), Montreal ($15), White River Junction ($13), Middlebury ($6.50), Bennington ($16.75), and Montpelier ($6.75). Open Mon.-Thurs. and Sat. 7am-8:30pm, Fri. and Sun. 7am-11:45pm.

Public Transport: Chittenden County Transit Authority (CCTA), 864-0211. Frequent, reliable service. Downtown hub at Cherry and Church St. Connections with Shelburne and other outlying areas. Buses operate Mon.-Sat. 5:45am-10:30pm, depending on routes. Fare 75¢, seniors and disabled 35¢, under 18 50¢.

Taxi: Yellow Cab, 864-7411. $1.20 per mile.

Bike Rental: Ski Rack, 81-85 Main St. (658-3313). Bikes $15-25 per day, tandems $35 per day. Open Mon.-Thurs. 9am-7pm, Fri. 9am-9pm, Sat. 9am-6pm, Sun. noon-5pm.

Help Lines: Women's Rape Crisis Center, 863-1236. Crises Services of Chittenden County, 656-3587.

Post Office: 11 Elmwood Ave. (863-6033), at Pearl St. Open Mon.-Fri. 8am-5pm, Sat. 9am-noon. ZIP code: 05401.

Area Code: 802.

Burlington is on the eastern shore of long, narrow Lake Champlain, 225 mi. northwest of Boston, 100 mi. south of Montreal. The center of Burlington is quite compact. An active pedestrian mall downtown swarms with craft vendors in the summertime. The city's hills and the expansion of its outskirts may make it necessary to take public transportation to reach the suburbs.

Accommodations, Camping, and Food

A local artist now owns Howden Cottage, 32 N. Champlain (864-7198), a charming bed and breakfast built in the 1820s. The YWCA, 278 Main St. (862-7520), lets dorm rooms and singles to women only. ($5 YWCA membership required. Singles $13. Doubles $15. Triples $16. Key deposit $5. Weekly: singles $47, doubles $50, triples $55, $20 with room deposit.) Three mi. from downtown, cozy Mrs. Farrell's Home Hostel (AYH), 27 Arlington Court (865-3730), has six beds for $9 per night for members, $11 for nonmembers. Reservations are required. North Beach Campsites, Institute Rd. (862-0942), is only 1½ mi. north of town on Rte. 127, along Lake Champlain. (Open May 15-Oct. 1. Sites $10-15. Showers 25¢, beach free. Vehicle charge $3.) Take the CCTA North Ave. bus leaving from the main city terminal on Saint Paul St. **Shelburne Campground,** Shelburne Rd. (985-2540), 1 mi. north of the center of Shelburne and 4 mi. south of Burlington, offers a pool, laundry facilities, and free showers. Buses stop right next to the campground. (Open April-early Oct. Sites $14 for 2 people, $1 each additional person.)

Henry's Diner, 155 Bank St., has been the place to meet the locals and eat good, inexpensive food since 1925. (Sandwiches $2-4, full meals $5-10. Open Mon. 7:30am-2pm, Tues.-Thurs. 6:30am-4pm, Fri.-Sat. 6:30am-8pm, Sun. 8am-2pm.) Henry's may have history, but its competition, **Oasis Diner,** 189 Bank St., is frozen in time. Men wearing white hats and aprons serve similar cuisine at similar prices in an aluminum setting. (Open Mon.-Sat. 5:30am-4:30pm.) A must-eat is **Noonies Deli,** 131 Main St., home of huge, delicious sandwiches on homemade bread ($3-4). (Open Mon.-Wed. 7am-10pm, Thurs.-Sat. 7am-1am, Sun. 8am-10pm.) Adrian from Amherst suggests you spend the extra cash at **Carbur's,** 115 Saint Paul St., close by Main St. The famous quint-decker Queen City special sandwiches ($10) make for good diversion while perusing the world's zaniest menu. (Open Sun.-Thurs. 11am-midnight, Fri.-Sat. 11am-1am.) Try the **Vt. Pasta Company,** 156 Church St., at the end of the pedestrian area, for a variety of pasta dishes ($5-8) and sandwiches ($2-4.50). (Open Mon.-Thurs. 10am-11pm, Fri.-Sat. 11:30am-11pm, Sun. 11am-10pm.) Finish off any meal with a trip to **Ben and Jerry's Ice Cream,** 169 Cherry St. (862-9620; open Mon.-Thurs. 10:30am-midnight, Fri.-Sat. 10:30am-1am, Sun. 11am-midnight) where you can watch them make ice cream in the front parlor. Good luck polishing off their 4½ pound "Vermonster," which includes 20 scoops of ice cream, 10 scoops of chopped walnuts, 7 scoops of strawberries, and 5 scoops of whipped cream. Taste a sample here and then head to B&J's factory tour in Waterbury (see Stowe).

For nightlife in Burlington there are a number of bars on Main St., notably the honky-tonk **Nectar's,** 188 Main St. (658-4771), where Boston-based and local bands play nightly. Mondays feature only bluegrass, Sundays jazz. Down Harps, Amstel Light ($3.25 ea.), or one of many domestics. (Open Sun.-Fri. 6am-2am, Sat. 6am-1am.) Say goodnight sweetheart, it's time to go to **Sha-na-na's,** 101 Main St. (865-2596), whose nightly DJs play mostly 50s and 60s music. Jitterbug lessons given Tuesday nights. (Open Mon.-Fri. 4pm-2am, Sat. 7pm-1am, Sun. 7pm-2am. Cover $3. Free buffet Mon.-Thurs. 4-9pm, Fri. 4-8pm.)

Sights and Entertainment

With its sprawling, low-lying suburbs, Burlington might not look like a cultural mecca, but it still manages to take full advantage of its scenic location, youthful exuberance, artistic community, and alluring history. **Church Street Transit Loop and Marketplace** downtown embodies this virtues; this historic district serves as a shopping center for modern northern Vermont; also displaying and selling the works of local artists. The historically inclined should also stroll through Victorian **South Willard Street,** which now houses Champlain College, and the campus of the **University of Vermont** (656-3480), founded in 1797. **City Hall Park,** in the heart of downtown, and **Battery Street Park,** right on Lake Champlain, are beautiful places to relax and bask in the scenery.

Plenty of food and drink for thought can be found at the **Vermont Pub and Brewery** (800-865-0500), 144 College St. at Saint Paul's, which offers affordable sandwiches and delicious homemade beers. If you can't quite figure out how Keller Original Vermont Lager is made, take a tour of the brewery downstairs. (Open Mon.-Thurs. 11:30am-12:30am, Fri.-Sat. 11:30am-1:30am, Sun. 2pm-midnight. Free tours Wed. at 4pm and Sat. at 8pm. Live entertainment nightly Thurs.-Sun.) Guides at **New England Dairy Foods,** 398-400 Pine St. (863-3968), will lead you around the largest quiche and cheesecake factory in New England and provide free samples. (Tours on the hour Mon.-Fri. 9am-1pm. Store open Mon.-Thurs. 9am-5:30pm, Fri. 9am-6:30pm, Sat. 9:30am-5pm.) For dessert head to the nearby **Champlain Choco-**

late Company, 431 Pine St. (864-1807), where you can see their rich, dark chocolate made on the premises. (Open Mon.-Fri. 9:30am-5:30pm, Sat. 9:30am-5pm.)

Summer culture vultures won't want to miss the many festivities Burlington offers: the **Champlain Shakespeare Festival** in mid-July, the **Vermont Mozart Festival** (862-7352) in July and early August, the **Festival of Fine Art** (869-9037) in early June, and the **Discover Jazz Festival** (863-7992) in early to mid-June.The Flynn Theatre Box Office, 153 Main St. (863-5966), handles sales for the Mozart and jazz performances. (Open Mon.-Fri. 10am-4:30pm, Sat. 10am-1pm.) The **Flynn Theatre** is a show unto itself. This movie house, built in 1930, has spectacular art deco decor and sponsors free folk concerts in Battery Park running from early June to late August. Contact the chamber of commerce for more information.

Near Burlington

Seven mi. south of Burlington in **Shelburne** is the **Shelburne Museum** (985-3344), which houses one of the best collections of Americana in the country. Beside 35 buildings transported from all over New England, 45-acre Shelburne has a covered bridge from Cambridge, a paddleboat and a lighthouse from Lake Champlain, and a bit of a local railroad. Catch also the fine collection of Degas, Cassatt, and Monet paintings. Tickets are valid for two days; you'll need both to cover the mile-long exhibit. (Open mid-May to mid-Oct. daily 9am-5pm. Admission $12.50, children $4.50.) Five mi. farther south on Rte. 7, the **Vermont Wildflower Farm** (425-3500), has a seed shop and 6½ acres of wildflower gardens to wander through. (Open May to mid-Oct. daily 10am-5pm. Admission May-June free; July-Oct. $2, seniors $1.50, under 12 free.)

Northeast of Burlington on Rte. 127 is the **Ethan Allen Homestead** (865-4556). In the 1780s, Allen, who forced the surrender of Fort Ticonderoga and helped establish the state of Vermont, built his cabin in what is now the Winooski Valley Park. A multi-media show and tour give insight into the hero and his state. (Open late April-late Oct. Summer Mon.-Sat. 10am-5pm, Sun. 1-5pm; spring and fall Tues.-Sun. 1-5pm.)

Both Burlington and Shelburne lie on **Lake Champlain,** the 100-mi.-long lake that separates Vermont from New York and Canada. Ferries crisscross the lake between Vermont's Green Mountains and New York's Adirondacks. The **Lake Champlain Ferry** (864-9804), at the bottom of King St., will ship you across the lake and back from Burlington's King St. Dock to Port Kent, NY. (June 21-Sept. 3 daily 7:30am-7:30pm, 14 per day; May 17-June 20 8am-5:30pm, 8 per day; Sept. 4-Oct. 21 8am-5:30pm, 8-11 per day. Fare $3, ages 6-12 $1, with car $11.50.) You can also take a ferry from Grand Isle to Plattsburg, NY, or go 14 mi. south of Burlington and take one from Charlotte, VT, to Essex, NY (either fare $1.50, ages 6-12 50¢, with car $6.50). A little less adventurous but just as rewarding is the **Spirit of Ethan Allen** scenic cruise (862-9685), departing from Burlington's Perkins Pier at the bottom of Maple St. The boat cruises along the Vermont coast, giving passengers a close-up view of the famous Thrust Fault, invisible from land. (Open May 26-Oct. 14. Cruises mid-May to early Sept. at 10am, noon, 2pm, and 4pm; early Sept. to mid-Oct. at noon and 2pm. Admission $7.25, ages 3-12 $3.50. Call about the more costly Captain's Dinner and Sunset Cruises.) The peak of nearby **Mt. Philo State Park.** (425-2390) affords great views of the environs. (Open daily 10am-sunset. Campsites $7. Admission $1.50, children $1.) Take the **Vermont Transit** bus from Burlington heading south along Rte. 7 to Vergennes. Twisting U.S. 2 cuts through the center of the lake by hopping from the mainland to Grand Isle to North Hero Island and then to Québec, Canada.

Several state campgrounds speckle the islands, and much of the surrounding land is wilderness. The marsh to the north is protected in the **Missiquoi National Wildlife Refuge.** Camp at **Burton Island State Park** (524-6353), accessible only by ferry (8:30am-6:30pm) from Kamp Kill Kare State Park, 50 mi. north of Burlington and 3½ mi. southwest of St. Albans off U.S. 7. The camp has 20 lean-to and tent sites ($15 and $11 respectively). **Grand Isle** has its own state park with camping (372-4300), just off U.S. 2 north of Keeler Bay. (Sites $9-11, lean-tos $12.50-14.)

THE MID-ATLANTIC

The diverse and densely populated states along the Eastern Seaboard tell the story of a nation's creation and development. With the first Puritan landing in Jameston, VA, and the bringing of African slaves here 13 years later, early colonists began the traditions of freedom, oppression, and capitalism. Philadelphia, the nation's first capital, celebrates constitutional democracy and free speech. The right to religious freedom is cherished by Mennonites and Amish. But perhaps the most cohesive elements of the Mid-Atlantic region lie in the the cold and convincing facts of economic success, political power, and urban growth. Or perhaps in the steel mill heritage of Pittsburgh and New Jersey; the pent-up history of Richmond and Williamsburg; the split-personality "Northern hospitality" and "Southern efficiency" of Washington, DC; or maybe just the lever-pulling neuroses of Atlantic City. Or perhaps not.

Travel

Fierce competition rules **airlines** for the traffic moving up and down the northeast corridor. Look for bargains in the big-city newspapers. **New York Air** offers low fares, and **Pan Am** has a cheap shuttle between Washington, DC and New York.

Train travel has taken hold in the Mid-Atlantic longer than in most regions of the U.S. **Amtrak** runs frequent "Northeast Corridor" trains that run north-south and connect Washington, Baltimore, Philadelphia, and New York. The east-west routes in Pennsylvania and West Virginia provide better service to remote areas than the bus companies. In larger cities such as Philadelphia and Washington, DC, Amtrak connects directly with city commuter-rail lines and bus lines.

Greyhound/Trailways covers the Mid-Atlantic states, including the Chesapeake Bay area. Large cities' local transit systems tend to be excellent. The efficient **New Jersey Transit System** links New York City and Philadelphia with Atlantic City and most New Jersey towns.

Look for ride boards at local colleges and universities instead of thumbing roadside. In all but the most rural areas, the frontier spirit of neighborliness vanished generations ago.

Finding reasonably priced **accommodations** in the cities becomes more difficult each year. The unfortunate flip side of gentrification means a marked increase in downtown hotel prices as older hotels give way to luxury conventioneers' inns. Regional Ys are closing residential facilities in many places. Budget hotel chains often skirt the edge of town. **Bed and breakfasts** are sometimes cheaper for longer stays: Philadelphia has the most B&B budget options. In beach areas, look for cottages available on a weekly basis. When in the mood to pamper yourself, consider going to a popular area in the off-season, when rates sometimes drop to one-half to one-third the seasonal cost. In Washington, DC, where "off-season" means every weekend, tickets to area attractions often come with room rental. **Youth hostels** shine bright in an otherwise dismal regional accommodations scene. AYH maintains an excellent chain of hostels in the big cities and a fair smattering on the coastlines.

Outdoors

The Mid-Atlantic states scream outdoor fun. The celebrated **Appalachian Trail** crosses the area. For information, contact the Appalachian Trail Conference, P.O. Box 807, Harpers Ferry, WV 25425 (304-535-6331). In Virginia, the **Blue Ridge Parkway** traverses the Shenandoah and Great Smoky Mountains. Other major outdoor areas include the national seashores along the coast, and the national forests in the Appalachians. Raft or backpack in the wilds of Pennsylvania and West Virginia's Allegheny Mountains. Wildlife refuges scattered along the Atlantic Ocean and its bays protect strange birds and wild ponies alike.

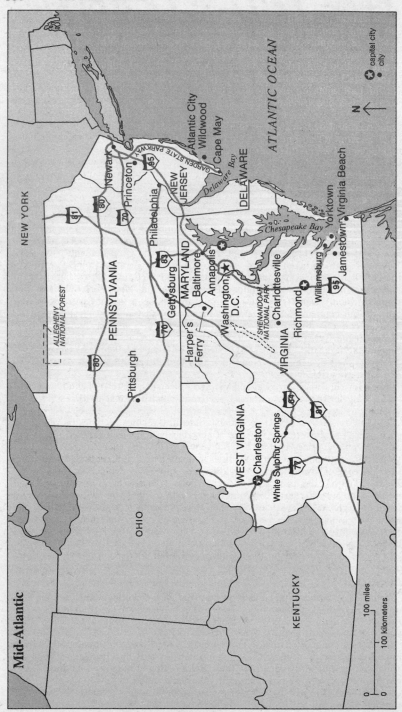

Bikers can choose between roads along flat beaches, through sloping valleys and gentle, rolling hills, or up arduous mountains. Biking is best during April, May, and from mid-September to mid-October. For information, contact one of the bicycle clubs that offer a variety of group tours, such as Bike VA, P.O. Box 203, Williamsburg, VA 23187 (804-253-2985), or Blue Ridge Biking, Inc., P.O. Box 504, Montezuma, NC 28653 (704-733-5566).

Near Maryland: Delaware

Delawareans strive to make up for their state's small size with a fierce pride in its rich historical past. They started by adopting "First State" as a slightly misleading nickname—now tourists the world over recognize that Delaware was the first to ratify the *U.S. Constitution* in 1787. To further solidify their standing as coolest state, ebullient residents will reveal the fact that Delaware has the lowest highest elevation of any state.

Most of Delaware's population sleeps in the northern industrial region, on the strip between Wilmington and Newark. Tourists usually associate the state with chemical industry and big corporations. Here, in 1938, nylon first saw the light of day. And it shimmered. But Delaware truly shines in the less synthetic regions of the seacoast; Lewes and Rehoboth Beach typify the soporific natural charm of the southern resort towns, while the Delaware Dunes stretch across more than 2000 acres of accessible seashore.

Practical Information

Capital: Dover.

Tourist Information: State Visitors Service, P.O. Box 1401, 99 King's Hwy., Dover 19903 (800-282-8667; 800-441-8846 outside DE). Open Mon.-Fri. 8am-4:30pm. Division of Fish and Wildlife, William Penn St., Dover 19901 (739-4431).

Time Zone: Eastern. Postal Abbreviation: DE.

Area Code: 302.

Lewes and Rehoboth Beach

The reserved atmosphere of these seaside retreats spells relief from the usual boardwalk fare. The beaches remain clean, the air stays salty, and the people, particularly in Lewes (pronounced "LOO-iss"), keep to themselves. Founded in 1613 by the Zwaanendael colony from Hoorn, Holland, Lewes rightly touts itself as Delaware's first town. To learn about Lewes, simply walk around town. To read more about it, try the **Lewes Chamber of Commerce** (645-8073), in the Fisher Martin House on King's Hwy. (Open Mon.-Sat. 10am-3pm.) The **Lighthouse Restaurant,** on Fisherman's Wharf just over the drawbridge in Lewes, flashes with occasionally brilliant food. (Open daily 7am-10pm.) Due east from Lewes, on the Atlantic Ocean, lurks the secluded **Cape Henlopen State Park** (645-8983), home to a seabird nesting colony, sparkling white "walking dunes," and campsites (645-2103) available on a first come, first serve basis (sites $12; open April-Oct.).

With a minimum of advance planning, you can join the committees of vacationing bureaucrats from Washington, DC who convene at the sand reefs of Rehoboth Beach on hot summer weekends—to mix and mingle with anyone who may donate to a future campaign. A popular spot for high school graduation celebrations, the beach also has a burgeoning gay community. The **chamber of commerce,** in the restored train station at 501 Rehoboth Ave. (800-441-1329 or 227-2233), provides brochures, but can't help much with budget accommodations. (Open Mon.-Fri. 9am-4:30pm, Sat. 10am-2pm.)

At the **Country Squire,** 17 Rehoboth Ave. (227-3985), you can talk with locals over one of the complete dinner specials (about $7). On Tuesdays (3-11pm), join the "Brown Collar" Gaming Club—a rag-tag collection of tourists and townies who gulp down beers ($3.75 per bucket) over a game of poker, darts, backgammon, bumper pool, or Trivial Pursuit. The breakfast special ($3), served at all times, is a lagniappe of sorts. (Open daily 7am-1am.) **Thrasher's** has served fries, and only fries, in enormous paper tubs ($5.75) for over 60 years. Bite too hastily into one of the tangy peanut-oil-soaked potato treats and understand how the place got its name. Locations on either side of the main drag, at 7 and 10 Rehoboth Ave., make avoiding it doubly difficult. (Open daily 11am-11pm.) Escape to **Nicola's Pizza,**at 1st St. and Rehoboth Ave., for some of the best 'za on the East Coast. (Open daily 11am-3pm.)

For inexpensive lodging, walk 1 block from the boardwalk to **The Lord Baltimore,** 16 Baltimore Ave. (227-2855), which has clean, antiquated, practically beachfront rooms. Ask for a porch room facing the ocean. (Singles and doubles from $35-65.) Or walk a little farther from the beach to the cluster of guest houses on the side lanes off 1st St., just north of Rehoboth Ave. **The Abbey Inn,** 31 Maryland Ave. (227-7023), is a warm, fuzzy place set back just far enough from the action. Call for reservations at least one week in advance, especially in summer. (2-day min. stay. Doubles from $33.) The **Big Oaks Family Campground,** P.O. Box 53 (645-6838), sprawls at the intersection of Rte. 1 and 270. (Sites $16.50.)

Greyhound/Trailways serves Lewes (flag stop at the parking lot for Tom Best's on Rte. 1; no phone) and Rehoboth Beach (227-7223; small station at 251 Rehoboth Ave.). Buses run to: Washington (3½ hr., $27); Baltimore (3¼ hr., $24); and Philadelphia (4 hr., $25). Lewes makes up on one end of the 70-minute **Cape May, NJ/Lewes, DE Ferry** route (Lewes terminal 645-6313; for schedule and fare information, see Cape May above). Grab a cab ($15) from the pier to reach Rehoboth. To get around within Rehoboth, use the free shuttle transportation run by the **Ruddertowne Complex** (227-3888; May 27-Sept. 2 daily 3pm-midnight every hr.), which serves points between Rehoboth and Dewey Beaches, including a stop at Rehoboth Ave.

The **post office** in Rehoboth reads your postcards at 179 Rehoboth Ave. (227-8406; open Mon.-Fri. 9am-5pm, Sat. 9am-noon). The **ZIP code** for Lewes and Rehoboth Beach is 19971; the **area code** is 302.

Maryland

Life in Maryland has centered on the Chesapeake Bay since the 17th century. Today, countless oysters and crabs jump out of the bay while its shipping lanes serve many mid-Atlantic cities. Yachts, Navy vessels, tankers, and trawlers alike anchor at the gleaming cities of Baltimore and Annapolis. Maryland also serves as "Weekend Warrior" home turf, with workers in the public and private sectors commuting into DC from the suburbs of the "Old Line State."

Practical Information

Capital: Annapolis.

Tourist Information: Office of Tourist Development, 217 E. Redwood St., Baltimore 21202 (333-6611 or 800-543-1036). **Forest and Parks Service,** Dept. of Natural Resources, Tawes State Office Bldg., Annapolis 21401 (974-3771).

Time Zone: Eastern. **Postal Abbreviation:** MD. **Area Code:** 301.

Baltimore

Once a center of East Coast shipping and industry, Baltimore declined structurally and economically from the late 1950s to the mid-70s, when then-mayor William Donald Schaefer began to clean up pollution, restore old buildings, and convert the Inner Harbor into a tourist playground. Today the Harborplace provides the inspiration for dozens of lookalike waterfront malls all along the eastern seaboard. Modern Baltimore still serves as Maryland's urban core. Near the downtown skyscrapers, old ethnic neighborhoods like Little Italy front Baltimore's signature row houses, whose unique façades stand for the city itself: polished marble steps representing the shiny Inner Harbor, straightforward brick for the proud and gritty urban environs. After the superb National Aquarium, try a stroll uphill to "Mt. Vernon" or through Fells Point during the day. North of downtown, prestigious Johns Hopkins University generates pre-meds, philosophers, and some of the nation's best lacrosse teams.

Practical Information

Emergency: 911.

Visitor Information: Office of Promotion and Tourism, 34 Marketplace, The Brokerage Bldg. #310 (837-4636), off Pratt St., 2 blocks north of the World Trade Center. Take bus #7, 10, or 27, or hop on the Inner Harbor trolley from any point along the water. Ask for *Baltimore Scene,* a monthly publication with excellent maps, lodging and eating hints, and schedules of events. Open Mon.-Fri. 9am-5pm. Information also at 600 Water St., in the Brokerage Bldg. (open Mon.-Fri. 10am-6pm); and in a booth at Harborplace on the downtown waterfront (open daily 10am-6pm). Satellite booth at Penn Station. Usually open late Fri. evenings, weekday mornings, and all day Sun.

Travelers Aid: 685-3569 (Mon.-Fri. 8:30am-5pm), 685-5874 (24-hr. hotline). Desks at Penn Station (open Mon.-Thurs. 9am-noon, Fri. 9am-1pm, Sat. 9am-1pm, Sun. 10am-5pm) and the Baltimore-Washington Airport (open Mon.-Fri. 9am-9pm, Sat.-Sun. 9am-5pm).

Baltimore-Washington International Airport (BWI): 859-7111. On Rte. 46 off the Baltimore-Washington Expressway, about 8 mi. south of the city center. Use BWI as your gateway to Baltimore or Washington, DC. Take Amtrak ($6) or MTA bus #16 downtown. **Airport limousines** (859-0800) run daily every ½ hr. 5am-midnight ($6). Hilton Hotel shuttle buses run every hr. ($14).

Amtrak: Penn Station, 1515 N. Charles St. (800-872-7245). Easily accessible by bus #3, 11, or 18 to Charles Station, downtown. Or take the Charles St. trolley to the Inner Harbor. Trains run about every hr. to: New York ($54), Washington, DC ($13), and Philadelphia ($25.50). Open daily 6am-10pm. Also serves Baltimore ($6) and Washington, DC ($10.50) from the Baltimore-Washington International Airport.

Greyhound/Trailways, 931-4000. 2 locations in Baltimore: one downtown at 210 W. Fayette St. (near Howard), the other 3 mi. east of downtown at 5625 O'Donnell St., near I-95. Frequent connections to: New York ($30), Washington, DC ($9), and Philadelphia ($13). Open 24 hr.

Public Transport: Mass Transit Administration (MTA), 109 E. Redwood St. (333-2700 or 760-4554 toll-free from Annapolis; both answered Mon.-Fri. 6am-11pm; 539-5000 24-hr. recording). Bus and rapid-rail system. Reliable service to most major sights within the city; service to outlying areas more complicated. Bus #16 serves the airport. Free *MTA Ride Guide,* available at any visitor information center. Some buses operate 24 hr. Fare $1, transfers 10¢. One-day **tourist pass** for unlimited travel anywhere in the city on any form of public transportation $2.25. Available at most visitor information centers and hotels. **Baltimore Trolley Works:** 501 Key Hwy. (396-4259). Operates two trolley routes downtown. The "Charles St." trolley runs north on Charles St. from the Inner Harbor to Penn Station and south along Maryland Ave. and Cathedral St. Mon.-Sat. 11am-7pm. The "Inner Harbor" trolley runs the length of the harbor from Pratt and Green St. to Fells Point. Mon.-Sat. 11am-10pm, Sun. 11am-7pm. Fare 25¢; no transfers.

Taxi: Yellow Cab, 685-1212.

Car Rental: Thrifty Rent-A-Car, 768-4900 or 800-367-2277. Offices at BWI Airport and 2030 N. Howard St. Economy cars from $31 per weekday, $18 per weekend day. Unlimited mi.

Under 25 $3 extra per day. Airport open 24 hr. Must be 21 with credit card or cash deposit.
Rent-A-Wreck, 9006 Liberty Rd., Randallstown (325-1185) and on Pulaski Hwy. near the
Baltimore Beltway (325-2757). From $24 per day. 60 free mi., 25¢ each additional mi. Open
Mon.-Fri. 8am-6pm, Sat. 8am-3pm. Must be 25.

Help Lines: Sexual Assault, 366-7273. Open 24 hr. **Gay Hotline and Information**, 837-8888.
Gay bars, meetings, and special events. Open daily 7:30-10pm, recording at all other times.

Post Office: On the 900 block of Fayette St. (347-4425). **ZIP code:** 21233.

Area Code: 301.

Baltimore lies in central Maryland, 100 mi. south of Philadelphia and about 150
mi. up the Chesapeake Bay from where it joins the Atlantic Ocean. The **Jones Falls
Expressway (I-83)** halves the city, and ends at the Inner Harbor. **I-95** and the
Baltimore-Washington Expressway (I-295) brush the southwest corner of the city
and lead directly to Washington. Drivers should expect delays when passing Baltimore on any route. Many of the tourist sites lie within 1 mi. west of I-83. The Baltimore Beltway, I-695, makes a loop around the city. Baltimore is a conglomeration
of several centuries of decentralized growth, with Old Baltimore roughly at the hub.
Since the streets are not numbered logically, except outside of downtown, a good
bus and road map (available at most bookstores and hotels) is essential. Remember
that *most* streets downtown are one-way. Less than an hour from DC on the expressway, and even closer (45 min.) to Annapolis, Baltimore makes an ideal daytrip.

Accommodations and Camping

Downtown cultivates few reasonable lodging options. **Amanda's Bed and Breakfast Reservation Service,** 1428 Park Ave. (225-0001), offers an alternative to budget
hotels and will also reserve for Annapolis B&Bs. (Singles and doubles from $50;
reservations recommended.)

Baltimore International Youth Hostel (AYH), 17 W. Mulberry St. (576-8880), near the
downtown bus and Amtrak terminals. Take the "Charles St." trolley or MTA bus #3, 11,
or 18. Elegant 3-story townhouse with 40 beds, kitchen, lounge, and baby grand piano. Members max. stay 6 nights, nonmembers 3 nights. Lockout 9:30am-5pm. Curfew 11pm. Chores
required. $10, nonmembers $13. Reservations recommended.

Abbey-Schaefer Hotel, 723 Saint Paul St. at Madison (332-0405), downtown. Take bus #3
or 9. High ceilings, big rooms, and an old, attractive lobby. Musty though tolerable rooms.
Huge chunks of paint may sprinkle you as you slumber. Singles $36. Doubles with private
bath $45. Deposit $10.

Rosedale Motel, 7940 Pulaski Hwy. (574-3662), inside the Baltimore Beltway, far east of
downtown. Don't let the ill-maintained office fool you—redecorated, spotless rooms in red
and blue, with private baths and curious hexagonal mirrors. Probably the best deal on the
Pulaski Hwy. motel strip since the places advertising lower prices don't include tax in billboard quotes. Singles $32. Doubles $35.

Capitol KOA, 768 Cecil Ave., Millersville (923-2771 or 987-7477), 10 mi. from the Baltimore
Beltway, 16 mi. from DC, 11 mi. from Annapolis. Full facilities, including pool. Take MD's
commuter train (Marc) to Odenton, MD (leaves from DC's Union Station, $7.60 round-trip)
and catch the campground's free shuttle bus from the Odenton station (leaves campground
at 7:15am, returns from Odenton at 6:30pm). Sites $17. Open April-Nov.

Food

Hard-shelled crabs, Baltimore's specialty, are served in many restaurants,
steamed, with a wooden mallet to break them open. Soft-shell varieties prove easier
to get at if more difficult to swallow.

Harborplace, at Pratt and Lombard St., has a beautiful view of the harbor and
food both fast and fancy. For enough money, some interesting Baltimore specialties
can be obtained from the chain stores in Harborplace: **Phillips'** crab cakes are
among the finest in Maryland, **Thrasher's** fries with vinegar are an Eastern Shore
tradition, **Gourmet Chips** dips potato chips into chocolate, and there's no better
Polish sausage than **Ostrowski's Polish Kielbasa.** (Harborplace open Mon.-Sat.

10am-9:30pm, Sun. noon-8pm.) Baltimore also has several enclosed markets. The largest and most famous, **Lexington Market,** on Lexington at Eutaw St., northwest of the harbor, provides an endless variety of produce, fresh meat, and seafood, plus most of the same food as Harborplace, often at cheaper prices. (Open Mon.-Sat. 8:30am-6pm. Take bus #7.)

No Da Gi, 2126 Maryland Ave., at 22nd St. Take bus #3, 9, or 11. Excellent Korean cuisine and a few Chinese and Japanese dishes. Goldfish stare at diners from central tank. Maki Sushi ($3-5), with plenty of Korean side dishes, a meal in itself. Exotic, authentic dishes. Lunch specials $6-7; dinners $8-15. Open Thurs.-Tues. 11am-11pm.

Ikaros, 4805 Eastern Ave., 2 mi. east of downtown. Take bus #10. A romantic hideaway in the heart of East Baltimore's Greek community. Try *avgolemono* soup, with egg, lemon, and rice ($1.25), or a big Greek salad ($2), the ideal opener for spinach and feta pies ($2.25). Open Sun.-Mon. and Wed.-Thurs. 11am-10pm, Fri.-Sat. 11am-11pm.

Haussner's, 3242 Eastern Ave. at Clinton. Take bus #10. An East Baltimore institution. Huge dining room full of impressive artwork and German cuisine. Pricey lunch and dinner entrees, but sandwiches from $5. Fluffy and fresh desserts $2-4. No shorts after 3pm; lines for dinner on weekends. Open Tues.-Sat. 11am-10pm.

Bertha's Dining Room, 734 S. Broadway at Lancaster (327-5795), in Fells Point. Plate of mussels $6.25; beer $1.75. Also has *paella* and fresh fish dishes. Jazz Tues. and Fri.-Sat. Dixieland Wed. 9pm-3am. Kitchen open Sun.-Thurs. 11:30am-11pm, Fri.-Sat. 11:30am-midnight. Bar until 3am.

Buddies, 313 N. Charles St. (332-4200). Good salad bar ($3.15 per lb.) Mon.-Fri. 11am-2:30pm. Beer $1.50. Live jazz Wed.-Sat. from 9:30pm. No cover. Open Mon.-Fri. 11am-1am, Sat. 2pm-1am.

Thompson's Sea Girt House, 5919 York Rd. (435-1800). Eat crab cakes here ($6.50 until 4pm) or have them shipped anywhere in the U.S. Open Mon.-Thurs. 11:30am-11pm, Fri. 11:30am-midnight, Sat. noon-midnight, Sun. 12:30-10pm.

Bo Brooks, 5415 Belair Rd. (488-2722). Complete seafood menu includes "Baltimore's Best Steamed Crabs." Family atmosphere. Dinner from $5. Take-out or eat in the popular tacky white dining room. Crab cake dinner from $5; instead share a platter of hard-shelled crabs (over $10). Carryout Mon.-Thurs. 5-9pm, Fri.-Sat. 5-11pm, Sun. 3:30-9pm; dining room Mon.-Thurs. 11:30am-3pm and 5-9:30pm, Fri. 11:30am-3pm and 5-11pm, Sat. 5-11pm, Sun. 3:30-9:15pm.

Sights

Baltimore's growth has not hindered its rich heritage. Shakespeare, Thames, and Fleet Street maintain their mid-18th century names and **Federal Hill,** overlooking Baltimore's harbor, celebrates Maryland's ratification of the *U.S. Constitution* in 1788. At the same time, Baltimore dresses up all over, with the **Inner Harbor** as the boutonière of the transformation. Most museums and attractions are within walking distance from this enormous port. Buses #7, 8, 10, 11, and most others will take you to or near the harbor.

Don't miss the **National Aquarium** on Pratt St. (576-3800), on the Harbor. The distinctive angular building sports exterior tiles copying nautical flag codes while the futuristic interior houses seven levels of aquatic life, including simulated habitats, a three-story walk-through coral reef, a shark tank, and a full-scale Amazon tropical forest. Also features a kids' Touch Tank, colorful marine photography, and subtle eco-propaganda on the walls. Arrive before 9am to avoid long lines; on weekends buy a ticket from the booth outside and return at the time (usually ½ hr. later) printed on the ticket. Excellent disabled access (except to the rain forest exhibit) includes separate entrance with no line—ask outside. (Open Mon.-Thurs. 9am-5pm, Fri.-Sun. 9am-8pm; Sept.-May Sat.-Thurs. 9am-5pm, Fri. 9am-8pm. Admission $9.25, seniors, students, and military $7.25, under 12 $5.50. Admission $2 Sept.-May Fri. after 5pm.)

Dominating the west side of the harbor, the frigate *Constellation,* the first commissioned ship of the U.S. Navy, sailed from 1797 until 1945, serving in the War of 1812, the Civil War, and as flagship of the Pacific Fleet during World War II.

(Open daily 10am-8pm; off-season 10am-4pm. Admission $2.75, seniors $1.50, children $1, active military free.) Also moored in the harbor are the U.S.S. *Torsk* submarine and the lightship *Chesapeake*. These two vessels make up the **Baltimore Maritime Museum** at Pier III (396-9304; open daily 9:30am-4:30pm; admission $3, seniors $2.50, children $1.50, active military free).

Continue down the harbor to Harborplace, Baltimore's trendy wharfside mall (open Mon.-Sat. 10am-9:30pm, Sun. noon-8pm). Also at this edge of the harbor, the **Maryland Science Center**, 601 Light St. (685-2370), offers science films, a planetarium, and an exhibit on computer technology. Don't miss the IMAX Theater's five-story screen and dazzling sound system. (Open Mon.-Thurs. 10am-6pm, Fri.-Sun. 10am-8pm; Sept.-May Mon.-Thurs. 10am-5pm, Fri.-Sun. 10am-6pm. Admission $7.50. Separate evening IMAX shows $5.)

The **Top of the World** observation deck on the pentagonal **World Trade Center** (837-4515) offers a fine, five-sided view of the city, plus small exhibits on famous Mobtown residents Thurgood Marshall, Ogden Nash, H.L. Mencken, and Poe. (Open Mon-Fri. 10am-5pm, Sat. 10am-7pm, Sun. 11am-6pm. Admission $2, ages 5-15 $1.)

To get a feel for Baltimore's historic districts, take bus #10 from Pratt St. to Broadway, and walk 2 blocks to **Fells Point,** passing through Little Italy on the way. This is authentic old Baltimore, with cobblestone streets, quaint shops, and historic pubs set against a backdrop of tug boats in the harbor. Stop in at the **Society for the Preservation of Federal Hill and Fells Point,** 812 S. Ann St. (675-6750), for an informative discussion of the area. (Open Mon.-Fri. 9am-4:30pm.)

Farther from the heart of town, the **Baltimore Museum of Art,** Charles St. at 32nd (396-7101), next to the Johns Hopkins University campus, houses the Isabel and Etta Cone collection of impressionist paintings. The Wurtzberger Sculpture Garden features works by Rodin, Manzu, Giacometti, and Epstein. (Open Tues.-Wed. 9am-4pm, Thurs. 10am-7pm, Fri. 9am-4pm, Sat.-Sun. 11am-6pm. Closed Aug. 18-31. Admission $2, under 18 free. Thurs. free. Take bus #3 or 11.)

The **Maryland Historical Society,** 201 W. Monument St. (685-3750), has Francis Scott Key's original manuscript for the "Star Spangled Banner," as well as 19th-century period rooms, U.S. portraiture, and silver. (Open Tues.-Fri. 10am-5pm, Sat. 9am-5pm; Oct.-April Sun. 1-5pm. Admission $2.50, seniors $1.50, ages 3-12 $1.) The **Peale Museum,** 800 E. Lombard St. (396-1149), lies 7 blocks north of Inner Harbor, just off I-83. Built in 1814, the building served as Baltimore's first City Hall; now it has a garden, sculptures, paintings, and an exhibit on Baltimore's rowhouses. (Open Tues.-Sat. 10am-5pm, Sun. noon-5pm. Free.) The **Walters Art Gallery,** 600 N. Charles St. at Centre (547-9000), keeps a large and diverse private collection (with loads of armor) in its imposing modern building. (Open Tues.-Sun. 11am-5pm. Tours Wed. at 12:30pm, Sun. at 2pm. Admissions $3, seniors $2, under 18 and students with ID free. Free Wed.)

Druid Hill Park (396-6106) contains the **Baltimore Zoo** (366-5466), a spectacular conservatory, and a lake surrounded by lush greenery. The zoo features elephants in a simulated savannah, Siberian tigers, and a waterfall. (Open daily 10am-5:20pm; Nov.-April 10am-4:20pm. Admission $5, seniors and children $3. Conservatory open daily 10am-4pm. Free. Take bus #4, 7, or 22 from Fayette St.) **Fort McHenry National Monument** (962-4290), located at the foot of E. Fort Ave., off Rte. 2 and Lawrence Ave., marks the spot where captive Francis Scott Key wrote the "Star Spangled Banner," for Roseanne Barr. Admission ($1 seniors and under 17 free) includes museum, fort, and an overlong film. (Open daily 9am-8pm; Sept.-late May 9am-5pm.)

Baltimore also holds a few interesting historic houses and birthplaces: **Edgar Allen Poe's House,** 203 N. Amity St. (396-4866; open April-Nov. Wed.-Sat. noon-4pm) and the **Babe Ruth Birthplace and Baltimore Orioles Museum,** 216 Emery St. (727-1539; open daily 10am-4pm).

Entertainment and Nightlife

Outdoor entertainment animates the Inner Harbor during the summer. The **Showcase of Nations,** a weekly series of outdoor fairs, celebrates a different culture each week. Though somewhat generic, the fairs are always fun, vending international fare and the ever-present crab cakes and beer.

Pier 6, at the Inner Harbor, has popular, jazz, and classical concerts (625-1400; 800-638-2444 outside MD). If you sit out on Pier 5, you can hear the music without paying the occasionally hefty admission. (Tickets $10-22.) Free concerts of all types take place every Sunday (7-8:30pm) April through Labor Day at the Harborplace Amphitheatre. The **Left Bank Jazz Society** (945-2266) has information on jazz performances. The Baltimore Arts Union's **BAU House,** 1713 N. Charles St. (659-5443) hosts frequent jazz concerts ($4-5), poetry readings, local art shows, chamber music, and rock 'n' roll. Bars and rock clubs cluster in Fells Point; well-known local and national alternative acts often play at **Max's on Broadway,** 735 S. Broadway (675-6297). Check the free weekly Baltimore *City Paper* for complete club listings.

Chesapeake Bay

The Chesapeake Bay, a long scraggly arm of the Atlantic Ocean that reaches from the coast of Virginia up through Maryland, nearly cleaves the state in two. For thousands of years, Native Americans worshipped the bay as the "Great Salt River." Originally, the water's shallowness and varying salinity made it one of the world's best oyster and blue crab breeding grounds. The centuries of development, however, have taken their toll on these waters. Despite recent conservation measures, fish, oysters, and crabs are slowly disappearing, sedimentation already filling and shortening many of the bay's tributaries. Within 10,000 years, the Chesapeake Bay may be a flat piece of oceanfront land.

The three states and one district that share its waters split the bay tourism. For pamphlets, write or call the Virginia Division of Tourism, the Maryland Office of Tourist Development, the Delaware State Visitors Center, or the Washington, DC Convention and Visitors Association. (All addresses and phone numbers in respective state or district introductions.)

The region's public transport system is ironically underdeveloped. Greyhound/Trailways bus #122, originating in New York City, goes to Salisbury, Princess Anne, Westover Junction, and Pocomoke City. Make connections with Washington, DC, Baltimore, or Philadelphia via Greyhound bus #127. Greyhound/Trailways also covers the eastern shores of the Chesapeake and Annapolis. The bay is bounded on the west by I-95; on the south by I-64; on the east by U.S. 9, 13, and 50; and on the north by U.S. 40.

Annapolis

Maryland's capital, an artistically renovated colonial port, boasts narrow streets, 16 miles of waterfront, and one of the country's highest concentrations of 18th-century Georgian architecture. Settled in 1649, Annapolis functioned as a temporary national capital and the meeting place of the Continental Congress from November 1783 to August 1784. The Annapolis Convention met here in 1786 to consider inter-state commercial disputes such as navigation rights of the Potomac. This convention preceded the Philadelphia Constitutional Convention, which was instrumental in ratifying the *U.S. Constitution.* In 1845 the U.S. Naval Academy was founded here, and its beautiful campus remains a major point of interest. Today the city makes a popular, charming stopover for tourists, glitzy yachts, and "romantic weekend getaways."

The interesting quarter of Annapolis extends south and east of its two central circles: **Church Circle,** containing St. Anne's Episcopal Church, and **State Circle,** site of the **Maryland State House** (974-3400), where the Continental Congress met to ratify the Treaty of Paris in 1784, ending the American Revolution. Inside, get

Maryland maps and brochures from the information desk, check out the few history exhibits, and watch the state legislature bicker in session. (Tours at 11am, 2pm, and 4pm. Open daily 9am-5pm. Free.) From State Circle, two arms stretch through the city: Main Street to the dock, and Maryland Avenue towards the naval academy. Follow Main St. for food and entertainment, Maryland Ave. for history. Annapolis is compact and easily walkable, provided you can find a parking space.

A walk down Maryland Ave. will take you near the **Paca House and Gardens,** 186 Prince George St. (263-5553). Governor William Paca, who designed the house himself, signed the Declaration of Independence. A visit to the beautifully restored estate finds a 1765 grandfather clock still ticking inside and trellises, water lilies, and gazebos outdoors. (Open Tues.-Sat. 10am-4pm, Sun. and holidays noon-4pm. Last tour at 3pm. Garden admission $2, house $3.50, both $5.) The big, elegant **Hammond-Harwood House,** 19 Maryland Ave. (269-1714), built in 1774, also retains period decor down to the candlesticks. (Open Tues.-Sat. 10am-5pm, Sun. 2-5pm; Nov.-March. Tues.-Sat. 10am-4pm, Sun. 1-4pm. Tours every ½ hr. Admission $3, under 19 $2.)

In an old church adjacent to Church Circle, the **Banneker-Douglass Museum,** 84 Franklin St. (269-2893), houses temporary exhibits and often photographs about African American life and history. (Open Tues.-Fri. 10am-3pm, Sat. noon-4pm. Free.)

Farther down Maryland Ave., (enter from King George St.) the prestigious **U.S. Naval Academy** commands harried, short-haired "plebes" (freshmen) in official sailor dress trying desperately to remember the words of the navy fight songs while the rest of the undergraduates, "middies" (for midshipmen), do their thing. **Bancroft Hall,** an imposing Georgian structure and the world's largest dormitory, houses the entire student body. In the yard outside Bancroft Hall, witness the noon lineup and formations of the disciplined students. **King Hall,** the academy's gargantuan dining hall, turns madhouse at lunchtime, serving the entire brigade in under four minutes. The hall even has its own brand of ketchup. For good luck, try to toss a penny into the quiver of the bronze statue of Tecumseh that stands out front. From a balcony past the high, stone lobby of Bancroft Hall you can survey the Naval Academy and an uninhabited model middie's dorm room.

Elsewhere on campus, the **Naval Museum** in Preble Hall (267-2109) has a simple collection of naval artifacts. (Open Mon.-Sat. 9am-4:45pm, Sun. 11am-4:45pm. Free.) Walking tours of the academy begin at the **Ricketts Hall** (267-6100) visitors center, directly inside the gates of the Academy at the end of Maryland Ave. (Tours March-May 10am-2pm on the hr.; June-Labor Day 9:30am-4pm every ½ hr.; Labor Day-Thanksgiving 10am-3pm on the hr. Tour $2, under 12 $1.)

The cheapest good eats in Annapolis swill at **Chick and Ruth's Velly,** 165 Main St. The all-day breakfast menu comes with unlimited free coffee. Grab a giant ice cream cone (99¢) or one of 22 kinds of doughnut. (Open 24 hr.) The more refined **Truffles,** 50 West St., allows you to cool down on a hot day with excellent salads, soups, and sandwiches and expansive, sugary desserts. (Open Mon.-Wed. 11am-4pm, Thurs. 11am-9pm, Fri.-Sat. 11am-10pm, Sun. 11am-3:30pm.) Back at the dock, visit the **Market House,** an indoor market with great seafood, chicken, candy, fruits, and vegetables. Try the oysters and clams ($3.50). (Open Mon.-Thurs. 9am-6pm, Fri.-Sat. 9am-7pm, Sun. 10am-7pm.)

Locals swear by **Marmaduke's Pub,** on Severn St. at 3rd (269-5420), across the bridge from the dock in Eastport. Sailors flock here Wednesday nights to watch videos of their races and partake of reasonably priced crabcakes. Wet your whistle with a "dark and stormy" (dark rum, ginger beer, and lime; $3), or draft beer. (Open daily 11:30am-2am. No cover downstairs. Weekend upstairs piano bar $5.) When driving to Marmaduke's, take the Eastport Bridge and ignore the "Eastport Bridge Detour" signs—the detour applies only to trucks. Spend a happy hour at **Uncle Harry's Outdoor Café,** 62 State Circle (263-4223), behind Harry Browne's. Beer ($2.25) and free steamed clams are sometimes seved with drinks, especially during winter Happy Hour (4-7pm). (Kitchen open daily 11am-3pm and 5-10pm. Bar until midnight. Occasional live music upstairs. No cover.) Later on, stroll down "Ego

Alley," the dock where the tan and fit parade and preen. Grab an ice cream cone and people-watch, or head into one of the many bars clustered in this section of town.

If you have a car, try **Haidi Zech**, 118 Claiburne Rd. (956-6038), a two-room B&B 6 mi. outside Annapolis. The friendly, accommodating proprietor will take you crabbing with her own equipment for free. (One guest $45, 2 guests $55; rates drop for stays over 2 nights. Take Rte. 2 south to Southbound Shores Dr., turn right, then left onto Locust St.) The small, immaculate **Scotlaur Inn**, 165 Main St. (268-5665), over Chick and Ruth's, has 10 lacy rooms with private baths. You'll have to climb stairs to get there, though. Rooms cost $60-75 on summer weekends, $50-55 during the week or off-season; if you call ahead and sound polite, rates may drop $5 when they're not busy. (Breakfast included.) A reasonable in-town B&B, **The Ark and Dove,** 149 Prince George St. (268-6277), sails two $63 rooms with shared bath, charming wooden furniture, and a player piano downstairs. (Reserve a month ahead.) For cheaper accommodations, wend your way to the **Capital KOA**, Millersville, MD, 11 mi. from Annapolis near Odenton. (For information and directions, see Baltimore or DC accommodations.)

Annapolis sits on Rte. 2, off U.S. 50/301, 50 mi. east of Washington, DC, and 30 mi. southeast of Baltimore. From DC, take U.S. 50 east to exit 70 (Rowe Blvd.) and follow signs to the historic district. From Baltimore, follow Rte. 2 south to U.S. 50 west, cross Severn River Bridge, then take exit 70. Baltimore's excellent **Mass Transit Authority** (760-4554) makes hourly runs from downtown Baltimore to Annapolis. (Express bus #210 Mon.-Fri. 6am-8pm, 1 hr., $2.05. Local bus #14 Mon.-Fri. 5am-midnight, Sat.-Sun. 6am-9pm, 90 min., $1.85.) **Greyhound/Trailways** connects Annapolis with Washington, DC (4 per day, 40 min., $11) and with towns on the far side of the Chesapeake Bay. Call the Baltimore or Washington Greyhound/Trailways stations for schedules. **Annapolis Transit,** 160 Duke of Gloucester St. (263-7964), operates a web of city buses connecting the historic district with the rest of town (Mon.-Sat. 6am-10pm, Sun. 8am-8pm). The free, efficient **Annapolis Trolley Shuttle** provides a park-and-ride service from the Navy/Marine Stadium parking lot, off Rte. 70, to the historic district (Mon.-Sat. every 20 min.).

Annapolis swims with offices, tours, and booths to help visitors. Try the **City of Annapolis Office of Public Information and Tourism,** 160 Duke of Gloucester St. (263-7940), or the **chamber of commerce,** 6 Dock St. (280-0445). (Both open Mon.-Fri. 9am-5pm.) On weekends the **information desk** at the Statehouse (974-3000) or the **visitors booth** near the dock (268-8687) can save stranded souls. Organized walking tours now start at the **Maritime Museum,** 77 Main St. next to the dock (267-8149 or 268-5576; 301-269-1910 from Baltimore; 202-858-5778 from DC). Two-hour tours leave daily at 1:30pm; October to January Saturday and Sunday at 1:30pm. ($6, seniors $5.50, under 18 $3.50.) The colonially costumed guides of **Three Centuries Tours,** 48 Maryland Ave. (263-5401), lead daily two-hour walking tours ($5) at 9:30am from the Annapolis Hilton, and at 1:30pm from the city dock.

Annapolis's **ZIP code** is 21401; the **area code** is 301.

Assateague and Chincoteague Islands

Sometime in the 1820s, the Spanish galleon *San Lorenzo* foundered off Maryland's short stretch of Atlantic coast. All human passengers were lost, but a few horses struggled ashore. More than a century and a half later, the Chincoteague ponies, descendants of those original survivors, still roam the unspoiled beaches of Assateague Island.

Assateague Island is divided into three parts. The **Assateague State Park** (301-641-2120), off U.S. 113 in southeastern Maryland, is a 2-mi. stretch with picnic areas, beaches, hot-water bathhouses, and campsites ($15). The **Assateague Island National Seashore** (301-641-1441), claims most of the long sandbar both north and south of the state park, and has its own campground (sites with cold water $9), beaches, and ranger station (301-641-3030). Free backcountry camping permits are available at the ranger station. Fire rings illuminate some relatively challenging (4-13 mi.) hikes; otherwise it's just you and nature.

The third part of the Assateague Island, the **Chincoteague National Wildlife Refuge** (804-336-6122), stretches along the south of the island on the Virginia side of the Maryland/Virginia border. The refuge functions as a temporary home for the threatened migratory peregrine falcon, a half million Canada and snow geese, and the beautiful Chincoteague ponies. At low tide, on the last Thursday in July, the wild ponies are herded together and made to swim from Assateague, MD, to Chincoteague, VA, where local fire department employees auction off the foals. The adults swim back to Assateague and reproduce again and provide next year's crop for the highest bidder. Bring plenty of insect repellent whenever you visit; six-legged nuisances also fill the island.

To get to Assateague Island, take **Greyhound/Trailways** to **Ocean City,** with daily express and local routes from Baltimore ($22), Washington, DC ($30), Norfolk, VA ($33), and Philadelphia ($33). The station in Ocean City idles at Philadelphia and 2nd St. (301-289-9307; open daily 10am-5pm). The **Ocean City Chamber of Commerce** (289-8559), on Rte. 50 at the southern edge of town, has information on accommodations. (Open Mon.-Sat. 9am-4:30pm, Sun. 10am-4pm.) To get to Assateague Island from Ocean City, take a taxi (289-8164; about $12). You can also reach Assateague from the town of Chincoteague, which lies on Chincoteague Island, 10 mi. east of U.S. 13. Greyhound/Trailways buses from Salisbury, MD, and Norfolk, VA, make a stop on U.S. 13 at T's Corner (804-824-5935), 11 mi. from town. For more information on the area, call or write to **Chincoteague Chamber of Commerce,** P.O. Box 258, Chincoteague, VA 23336 (804-336-6161; on Maddox Blvd.; open daily 9am-5pm).

New Jersey

> You from Joisey? I'm from Joisey. What exit?
> —Joe Piscopo

In his popular song "Born to Run," Bruce Springsteen of Asbury Park oddly echoed William Carlos Williams' epic poem *Paterson*. Describing the desire and need to flee from dying factory towns, the poet-king summed up the feelings of many residents of the so-called Garden State; visitors should take the words of the Boss as a warning. With only one youth hostel, Jersey has a superb interstate highway system for a reason. Know where your business is, take care of it quickly, and get the hell out. Done in this way and tolerating the expense, a few spots can be enjoyable. Green suburbs of "the City" up north like Oakland and Princeton spell relief from the smokestacks, while Atlantic City has a certain roulettish charm. Those gambling more for a tan should stick to Cape May at the state's southern tip. From the tips of the syringes washed up on the Jersey shore to the bottom chip in a stack of blackjack winnings, this state is a tourist Shangri-La, a paradise of the Eastern seaboard.

Practical Information

Capital: Trenton.

Tourist Information: State Division of Tourism, CN 826, Trenton 08625 (609-292-2470).

Gambling: Legal age 21.

Time Zone: Eastern. **Postal Abbreviation:** NJ.

Newark

The fourth-largest metropolitan region in the U.S., Newark has its own Broad Street lined with tall, new office complexes and an active port area. But New Yorkers and tourists with better places to go will eternally associate New Jersey's largest city with its airport. With daily overseas flights, this airport has a better reputation for on-time flights than either La Guardia or Kennedy Airport in New York.

New Jersey Transit (201-378-6300) runs express coaches to all airport terminals from Port Authority (42nd St. and Eighth Ave.) in midtown Manhattan, 24 hr. (Fare $5.) **Olympia Trails Coach** (212-964-6233) runs to the World Trade Center and Grand Central from Newark's north terminal and terminals A,B, and C (every 20 min. 6am-1am. Fare $5.) **PATH Trains** (212-732-8920) shuttle weary commuters to Newark's **train station** from New York's World Trade Center every 30 minutes. (Fare $1.) See New York Practical Information above for airport details.

If forced to stay in Newark overnight, try the **Airway Motor Inn,** 853 Rte. 1 and 9N, Elizabeth (201-354-3840), which has small, dark, but clean rooms. Ask for a room away from the highway and the parking lot. (Singles $32, weekends $40. Doubles $36, weekends $44. No reservations accepted. Take the Sheraton courtesy van—the Airway Motor Inn lies right around the corner.)

Newark Airport has no lockers; to store luggage during a layover, use **Unique Delivery,** Bldg. 51 (961-2250), next to North Terminal. Look for the unmarked gray door. They will pick up your luggage at the airport ($3) and store it for $1 per bag per day (backpacks $1.50). (Open daily 7:30am-midnight.)

Princeton

The town of Princeton slumbers peacefully off Rte. 1, 50 miles southwest of New York City and 11 miles north of Trenton. This quietly charming town's main attraction is Ivy-League **Princeton University** which has turned out presidents (James Madison and Woodrow Wilson), tycoons (J.P. Morgan), writers (F. Scott Fitzgerald), and movie stars (Jimmy Stewart and Brooke Shields). But no avatars.

Practical Information

Emergency: 911.

Visitor Information: Princeton University Communication/Publication Office, Stanhope Hall (258-3600). Campus maps and current information, including the *Princeton Weekly Bulletin,* with a calendar of events. Open Mon.-Fri. 8:30am-4:30pm. **Orange Key Guide Service,** 73 Nassau St. (258-3603), in the back entrance of MacLean House. Free campus tours, pamphlets, and maps. One-hr. tours Mon.-Sat. at 10am, 11am, 1:30pm, and 3:30pm, Sun. at 1:30 and 3:30pm. Office open Mon.-Sat. 9am-5pm, Sun. 1-5pm. **Princeton University Telephone Information,** 258-3000. Open daily 8am-11pm.

Airport: see Newark above.

Trains: Amtrak, 800-872-7245. Connects Princeton Junction, 3 mi. south of Princeton on Rte. 571, to New York City (7 per day, 1 hr., $21) and Philadelphia (7 per day, 1 hr., $17). Stops at Princeton only in the early morning and evening. Station open Mon.-Fri. 6am-8:30pm, Sat.-Sun. 7:15am-8:30pm. **New Jersey Transit** (201-460-8444, 800-772-2222 in NJ) runs 6am-midnight serving Princeton Junction. To New York City (1 hr., $9.25). Prices include a 5-min. ride on the "dinky," a small train connecting the town and campus to the outlying station. Dinky stops at University Place across from the McCarter Theater.

Buses: New Jersey Transit, 800-772-2222. Runs 6am-midnight. Buses stop at Princeton University and Palmer Sq. Take bus #606 to Trenton (every ½ hr., $1.90 exact change). **Suburban Transit** has 3 Princeton locations: Nassau Pharmacy, 80 Nassau St. (921-7400); Cox's Store, 182 Nassau St.; and Amoco Station, in Princeton Shopping Center. To New York (every ½ hr., $7, $13 round-trip).

Taxi: Associated Taxi Stand, 924-1222. Open daily 6am-midnight.

Post Office: 921-9563, in Palmer Sq. behind Tiger Park. Open Mon.-Fri. 8am-4:30pm, Sat. 8:30am-noon. ZIP code: 08542.

Area Code: 609.

Located in the green heart of the "Garden State," Princeton is within commuting distance of both New York City and Philadelphia. Driving from New York City, take the Holland Tunnel to the New Jersey Turnpike and exit at Hightstown. From Philadelphia, take I-95 north to Rte. 206, which leads to **Nassau Street,** Princeton's main strip, with shops clustered on one side and the university set back on the other. **Palmer Square,** the center of Princeton's business district, lies right off of Nassau between Witherspoon and Chambers St.

Accommodations, Food, and Entertainment

There are no budget accommodations in the town of Princeton. Budget motels clutter Rte. 1 and the environs of giant Quaker Bridge Mall, 4 mi. south of Princeton, served by local bus (see Practical Information above). The **Sleep-E-Hollow Motel,** 3000 U.S. 1, Lawrenceville (609-896-0900), rides 5 mi. south of Princeton, offering beds in small, well-worn rooms. Look out for the headless horseman. (Singles $28.50. Doubles $32.50.) For more than one person, the nearby **McIntosh Inn,** U.S. 1 and Quaker Bridge Mall (609-896-3700), is reasonable. Rooms come clean, large, and user-friendly. (Singles $42. Doubles $49. Extra cot $3.)

Most of Princeton's reasonably priced restaurants line Nassau and Witherspoon St., which intersects Nassau just across from the main gates of the university. Loud and crowded **P.J.'s Pancake House,** 154 Nassau St., has old wooden tables etched with student graffiti. The clamor gives way to a quieter breakfast crowd. Good food, but most meals cost $5-7. (Open Mon.-Thurs. 7:30am-10pm, Fri. 7:30am-midnight, Sat. 8am-midnight, Sun. 8am-10pm.) A popular student hangout and bar, **The Annex,** 128½ Nassau St., seems darker and often less noisy than P.J.'s, serving Italian entrees ($5-7), as well as omelettes and sandwiches ($2-3.50). (Open Mon.-Sat. 11am-1am.) The Mexican food at **Marita's Cantina,** 134 Nassau St., is only average, but the $6 all-you-can-eat lunch buffet (Mon.-Fri. 11:30am-2pm) will fuel you for days. A la carte items go for $2-5. Live bands play Thursdays. (Open daily 11:30am-11pm. Bar open until about 1:15am.) **Thomas Sweet's Ice Cream,** at Palmer Sq. across from the Nassau Inn, provides the perfect end to any meal. Have them blend a topping into their homemade ice cream ($2-3) or try the free sprinkles and one free topping on yogurt ($1.50-2.25). (Open Sun.-Thurs. 11am-11pm, Fri.-Sat. 11am-midnight.)

On May 17, 1955, Princeton students held one of the first pro-rock 'n' roll demonstrations in the U.S., blaring Bill Haley and the Comets's "Rock Around the Clock" until 1am when the Dean woke up and told them to turn it off. For some of that distilled male Ivy League tradition, down a drink in **The Tap Room,** in the basement of the Nassau Inn in Palmer Sq. (921-7500). A Princeton tradition since 1937, the pub has aging but freshly polished wood booths. Lovey Williams plays guitar Tuesday and Thursday nights until 10:30pm. (Open Mon.-Thurs. 11:30am-midnight, Fri.-Sat. 11:30am-1am.) Check Princeton's *Weekly Bulletin* for the scoop on films, concerts, and special events. Students and professional actors perform at **McCarter Theater** (452-5200), on campus in the Kresge Auditorium. (Box office open Mon.-Sat. noon-5pm.)

Sights

The 2500-acre landscaped campus of Gothic Princeton University seems to stretch on forever, virtually uninterrupted by streets of any kind. The **Orange Key** (see Practical Information above) provides free tours geared toward prospective students intent on hearing the myths and legends of the nation's fourth oldest school (founded in 1746). Those who become part of the school's graduating class can place a commemorative plaque and a patch of ivy on the outer wall of **Nassau Hall.** Completed in 1756, it stood as the colonies' largest stone edifice and Princeton's original university building; it also served as the capitol building of the original U.S. colonies for several months in the summer of 1783. The two magnificent bronze tigers represent the school's mascot. **Whig and Clio Hall,** named and modeled after a Greek temple, are home to the oldest college literary and debating club in the U.S. **Prospect Gardens,** a huge bed of flowers in the shape of Princeton's shield, grow particularly beautiful in the summertime.

The sculptures scattered throughout campus come from the $11 million **Putnam Collection.** The profile of one modern piece behind Nassau Hall bears a striking and comical resemblance to former President Richard M. Nixon. Picasso's *Head of a Woman* stands in front of the **University Art Museum** (452-3762). Tours of the outdoor sculptures (works by Alexander Calder, Henry Moore, Pablo Picasso, and David Smith) or of the museum's permanent indoor collection can be arranged through the university. (Open Tues.-Sat. 10am-4pm, Sun. 1-5pm. Free.)

Atlantic City

The riches-to-rags-to-riches tale of Atlantic City began over 50 years ago when it reigned as the monarch of resort towns. Vanderbilts and Girards graced the legendary boardwalk of the town whose opulence inspired the Depression-era board game for would-be-high-rollers, *Monopoly.* Fans of the game will be thrilled to see the real-life Boardwalk and Park Place that they've squabbled over for years. With the rise of competition from Florida resorts, the community chest began to close. Atlantic City landed on the luxury tax of the game board, suffering decades of decline, unemployment, and virtual abandonment.

But in 1976, state voters gave Atlantic City a reprieve by legalizing gambling, making the game a reality. Casinos sprang up by the Boardwalk, while the owners ignored the boarded-up streets below. The excessive, superficial wealth of the casinos makes it easy to forget the dirt and dank outside, especially since the owners make sure you never have to leave. Each velvet-soaked temple of tackiness has a dozen restaurants, entertainment, and even skyways connecting to other casinos. The chance to win big bucks draws everyone to Atlantic City, from high-rolling millionaires to senior citizens clutching their one last chance. One-quarter of the U.S. population lives within 300 miles of Atlantic City, and fortune-seeking pilgrims flock to its shore to toss the dice.

Practical Information

Emergency: 911.

Visitor Information: Public Relations Visitors Bureau, 2308 Pacific Ave. (348-7044), conveniently located near Mississippi Ave. Open Mon.-Fri. 9am-4:30pm. Next door is the **Atlantic City Convention and Visitors Bureau,** 2310 Pacific Ave. (348-7100 or 800-262-7395). Open Mon.-Fri. 9am-5pm.

Bader Field Airport: 345-6402. Serves New York/La Guardia, Philadelphia, Washington, DC, Newark, and other destinations. Buses run between Bader Field and the Boardwalk.

Amtrak, (800-872-7245), at Kirkman Blvd. off Michigan Ave. Follow Kirkman to its end, bear right, and follow the signs. To: New York City (1 per day, 2½ hr., $28); Philadelphia (5 per day, 1½ hr., $14); Washington, DC (1 per day, 3½ hr., $38). More connections to DC and NYC through Philly. Open Sun.-Thurs. 6am-10pm, Fri.-Sat. 6am-12:20am.

Buses: Greyhound/Trailways, 345-5403 or 344-4449. Buses every hr. to New York (2½ hr., $19) and Philadelphia (1¼ hr., $9). **New Jersey Transit,** 800-582-5946. Runs 6am-10pm. Hourly service to New York City ($21.50) and Philadelphia ($10), with connections to Ocean City ($1.50), Cape May ($3.50), and Hammonton ($3.25). Also runs along Atlantic Ave. (base fare $1). Both lines operate from **Atlantic City Municipal Bus Terminal,** Arkansas and Arctic Ave. Station and ticket offices open 24 hr.

Help Lines: Rape and Abuse Hotline, 646-6767.

Post Office: Martin Luther King and Pacific Ave. (345-4212). Open Mon.-Fri. 8:30am-5pm, Sat. 10am-noon. ZIP code: 08401.

Area Code: 609.

Atlantic City lies just past midway down New Jersey's coast, accessible by the Garden State Parkway. Hitching is not recommended.

Gamblers' specials make bus travel a cheap, efficient way to get to Atlantic City. Many casinos will give the bearer of a bus ticket receipt $10 in cash and sometimes a free meal. Look for deals in the yellow pages under "Bus Charters" in New Jersey, New York, Pennsylvania, Delaware, and Washington, DC. Greyhound/Trailways has same-day round-trip specials to Atlantic City.

Getting around Atlantic City is easy on foot. The casinos pack tightly together on the Boardwalk along the beach. When your winnings become too heavy to carry, you can hail a Rolling Chair, quite common along the Boardwalk. Though a bit of an investment ($1 per block for 2 people, 5-block min.), Atlantic City locals chat with you while they push. On the streets, catch a jitney ($1), running 24 hr. up and down Pacific Ave., or a NJ Transit Bus ($1) covering Atlantic Ave.

Accommodations and Camping

Large, red-carpeted, beachfront hotels have replaced four green houses, bumping smaller operators out of the game. A hundred bucks for a single is standard. Smaller hotels along Pacific Avenue, a block away from the Boardwalk, have rooms for less than $60, and rooms in Ocean City's guest houses are reasonably priced. Be sure to reserve ahead, especially on weekends. Many hotels lower their rates during the middle of the week. Winter is also slow in Atlantic City, as water temperature, gambling fervor, and hotel rates all drop significantly. Campsites closest to the action cost the most; the majority close September through April. Reserve a room or a site if you plan to visit in July or August.

Irish Pub and Inn, 164 St. James Pl. (344-9063), near the Boardwalk. Clean, cheap Celtic rooms with shared bath right next to the action. Nicely furnished Gaelic lobby and terrace with real Irish charm. Singles $25. Doubles $45. Key deposit $5. Open Feb.-Nov. The pub downstairs serves good Irish food 24 hr.

Hotel Cassino, 28 S. Georgia Ave. (344-0747), just off Pacific Ave. Small run-down rooms off a narrow hallway. Singles $35-40. Doubles $45. Key deposit $10. Open May-Oct.

Birch Grove Park Campground, Mill Rd. in Northfield (641-3778). 300 acres. Attractive and secluded but still near the casinos. Sites $15 for 2 people, with hookup $17.

Pleasantville Campground, 408 N. Mill Rd. 70 sites. Sites $24 for 4 people with full hookup.

Food

Each of the casinos has a wide selection of eateries intended to lure you and your wallet in. Some offer all-you-can-eat lunch or dinner buffets for $10-$12; sometimes you can catch a special for around $5. The town provides higher quality meals in a less noxious atmosphere. Since 1946, the White House Sub Shop, Mississippi and Arctic Ave., has served world-famous subs and sandwiches. Celebrity supporters include Bill Cosby, Johnny Mathis, and Frank Sinatra, rumored to have subs flown to him while he's on tour ($5-7.50, half-subs $2.50-4). (Open Mon.-Sat. 10am-midnight, Sun. 11am-midnight.) For renowned Italian food including the best pizza in town, hit Tony's Baltimore Grille, 2800 Atlantic Ave., at Iowa Ave. Open daily 11am-3am. Bar open 24 hr.) Though you may be turned off by the crowds, you can get great slices of pizza from one of the many Three Brothers from Italy joints on the Boardwalk.

Entertainment

Casinos

You have to see the casinos to believe them. Inside, thousands of square feet of flashing lights and plush carpet surround the milling crowds; few notice the one-way ceiling mirrors concealing the big-brother gambling monitors. Figures in formal wear embody Atlantic City's more glamorous past, but T-shirt-and-jeans gamblers now outnumber their flashy cohorts. The seductive rattle of chips and clicking of slot machines never stops. All casinos line Boardwalk, within a dice toss of each other. The biggest and newest of the casinos, Donald **Trump's Taj Mahal** (449-1000), commodifies a complex so expensive that missed payments threw Trump's billion-dollar empire into turmoil. Trump has two other casinos, each displaying his name in huge lights—the **Trump Castle** (441-2000) and **Trump Plaza** (441-6000). Other biggies are Bally's Park Place (340-2000), and Resorts International (344-6000). Caesar's Boardwalk Regency (348-4411), Harrah's Marina Hotel, (441-5000), and the Atlantis (344-4000), are hot clubs. Rounding out the list are the Claridge (340-3400) and Showboat (343-4000). The **Sands** (441-4000) and **Trop-World Casino** (340-4000) have extensive facilities that include golf and tennis. You may be amused by the two "moving sidewalks" that carry customers from the Boardwalk to the only two casinos without a Boardwalk entrance. Not surprisingly, these sidewalks move in only one direction.

Open nearly all the time (Mon.-Fri. 10am-4am, Sat.-Sun. 10am-6am), casinos douse you with alcohol as long as you are gambling (you must be 21 to get in) and many feign windows and clocks, preventing you from noticing the hours slip away. To curb your almost inevitable losses, stick to the cheaper games: blackjack, slot machines, and the low bets in roulette and craps. A book like John Scarne's *New Complete Guide to Gambling* will help you plan an intelligent strategy, but keep your eyes on your watch or you'll have spent five hours and five digits before you know what hit you.

Beaches and Boardwalk

You can bet the ocean is just a few spaces away. Atlantic City squats on the northern end of long, narrow **Absecon Island,** which has 7 mi. of beaches—some pure white, some lumpy gray. The **Atlantic City Beach** is free, and often crowded. Adjacent **Ventnor City's** sands are nicer. The legendary **Boardwalk** of Atlantic City has been given over to the purveyors of the quick fix, packed with junk-food stands, arcades, souvenir shops, and carnival amusements. Take a walk, jog, or bike in Ventnor City, where the Boardwalk's development tapers off.

Cape May

Good beach along the Atlantic blesses all the towns on the Jersey shore; for developers, the trick was deciding what to do with the village next door. While Atlantic City chose gambling and cheap pizza joints, Cape May expanded in a slightly different direction. The 5000 permanent residents (including the highest concentration of Mayflower descendents in the country) cultivate Cape May's image as a Victorian anachronism, a whalebone corset for tourists weary in body and mind. Century-old cottages turned inns stretch from the shore to the town's pedestrian mall. The tree-lined boulevards with wonderful flowerbeds and verandas make for a nice afternoon stroll, while the beach never lies more than two or three blocks away.

Tremendous pollution plagued the entire shore of New Jersey during the summer of 1988, after which the state launched a vigorous campaign to clean up the beaches. Since then the sand at Cape May actually glistens, still dotted with some of the famous Cape May diamonds (actually quartz pebbles that glow when cut and polished). When you unroll your beach towel on a city-protected beach (off Beach Ave.), make sure you have the **beach tag** which beachgoers over 12 must wear June to September from 10am to 5pm. Pick up a tag (daily $2, weekly $6, seasonal $10) from city hall (see below) or from the beach tag vendors roaming the shore.

The **Mid-Atlantic Center for the Arts,** 1048 Washington St. (884-5404), offers a multitude of tours and activities. Pick up *This Week in Cape May* in any of the public buildings or stores for a detailed listing. (Guided walking and trolley tours $4. 2-hr. guided cruises $7.) **Cape May Light House** and **Cape May Point State Park** (884-2159), just west of town, guide tourists, not ships. Built in 1859, the lighthouse offers a magnificent ragout of the New Jersey and Delaware coasts after a 199-step climb ($3).

When you're on a budget, prepare to be contented with burgers and sandwiches in Cape May since even the bars charge $13 and up for entrees. **The Ugly Mug,** 426 Washington St., a bar/restaurant in the mall, serves 12 ugly clams for half as many dollars. (Open Mon.-Sat. 11am-2am, Sun. noon-2am. Food served until 11pm.) **Carney's,** 401 Beach Ave. (884-4424), is the self-proclaimed "best bar in town" with live bands nightly. A mug of beer costs $2, sandwiches $4. (Snack menu served 3:30-10pm, bar open until 2am.) The **Ocean View Restaurant,** at Beach and Grant Ave., offers fine fresh seafood, to the tuna of $10-15. (Open daily 7am-10pm.) Free summer concerts enliven the town's bandstand.

Many of the well-preserved seaside mansions now take in nightly guests, although most cater to the well-heeled *New York Times* B&B set. Still several inns with reasonable rates fly in the thick of the action. The **Hotel Clinton,** 202 Perry St. (844-3993), at Lafayette St., has decent-sized singles ($25) and doubles ($35) with shared bath. Add $5 for weekend rates. (Open mid-June to early Sept. Call 516-799-8889 for off-season reservations.) Built in 1879, **Congress Hall,** 251 Beach Dr. (884-8421), between Perry and Congress St., presents itself as a gargantuan establishment weathered by a century of use. Though the cheapest rooms do the time-warp to the early 50s, they do it in a big way, complete with private baths and a pool. (Singles $25. Doubles $35. Weekends add $5, July-Sept. $15. Open May-Sept. Call 858-0670 for off-season reservations.) **Paris Inn,** 204 Perry St. (884-8015), near Lafayette St., has old but decent rooms with private baths. (Singles $30. Doubles $45. Weekends add $10.)

Campgrounds line Rte. 9 from Atlantic City to the Cape. The two closest to town are **Cold Springs Campground,** 541 New England Rd. (884-8717; sites $13, with hookup $15), and **Cape Island Campground,** 709 Rte. 9 (884-5777; sites $21, with hookup $24).

Despite its small size and geographic isolation, Cape May is easily accessible. By car from the north it's literally the end of the road—follow the Garden State Parkway south as far as it goes and you'll end up on Lafayette St. if you follow signs to Center City. From the south by car, bike, or foot, take a 70-minute ferry from Lewes, DE (terminal 302-645-6346) to Cape May (886-9699; for recorded schedule information 886-2718). Summer months 14 to 15 ferries cross per day, off-season 4 to 6. (Toll $16 for vehicle and driver, passengers $4, pedestrians $4, motorcyclists $13.50, bicyclists $7.) From Cape May, take bus #552 (14 per day, $1.40) from the depot to north Cape May and walk 1 mi. to the ferry.

The **Welcome Center,** 405 Lafayette St. (884-9562), provides a wagonload of friendly information about Cape May and free hotlines to inns and B&Bs. (Open Mon.-Sat. 9am-4pm.) As its name indicates, the **Chamber of Commerce and Bus Depot,** 609 Lafayette St. (884-5508), near Ocean St. across from the Acme, provides tourist information and a local stop for **New Jersey Transit** (800-582-5946; northern NJ 800-772-2222). Buses service Atlantic City ($3.50), Philadelphia ($13.75), and New York City ($24.50). (Terminal open July-Sept. daily 9am-8pm; off-season Mon.-Fri. 9am-8pm, Sat. 10am-8pm.) Like most legislatures, **City Hall,** 643 Washington St. (884-9525), sells beach tags required for beachgoers over 12 from June to September 10am to 5pm. Try your hand at polo at the **Village Bike Shop,** Washington and Ocean St. (884-8500), right off the mall. Also ask about the four-person tandem bike. (Open daily 6:30am-7pm. Bikes $3.50 per hr., $9 per day.)

Wildwood

Visiting Wildwood is like having a *really* greasy burger—though fun and strangely satisfying, you don't want to do it too often. The 2½-mi.-long Boardwalk vies with Atlantic City in tackiness, substituting legions of lusty adolescents for gamblers and mammoth roller-coasters for casinos. Wildwood is a beach-side amusement park, showcasing more rides than Disney World, and certainly as many balloon tosses, pizza joints, and soft-serve ice cream stands. Each of the rides cost one to seven tickets (35¢ each, 18 for $6, 36 for $11). Or you can buy an unlimited pass Monday-Friday ($10.50-12.50) from one of six booths near the rides. Two blocks inland from the Boardwalk, **Pacific Avenue** proffers restaurants, nightclubs, and theaters. For a map of the area, stop by the **Wildwood Tourist and Information Center,** on the Boardwalk (522-1407), at Schellinger Ave. (Open Mon.-Thurs. 8:30am-10pm, Fri.-Sun. 8:30am-11pm.)

The budget traveler should avoid the seafood restaurants which charge from $15 for dinner; the delis and sandwich shops lining Pacific Ave. provide a good alternative. Try **Luigi's Famous Cheesesteaks,** Pacific Ave. at Davis, the self-proclaimed King of Steaks, serving cheesesteaks and hoagies ($3.50). (Open Mon.-Sat. 11am-8pm.) You can get a decent slice of pizza on the Boardwalk for about $2, but for a good Italian meal in a quieter, cleaner setting check out **Rosauri's,** 3104 Pacific Ave., near Maple. Try the 12-in. pizza ($5). (Open daily 10am-7am.) The **Ocean Terrace,** 3616 Boardwalk, near the Boardwalk and Lincoln Ave., serves all-you-can-eat breakfasts from 8am ($4.50) and dinners from 4:30pm ($6). **Pompeo's Restaurant,** 17th Ave. and Boardwalk in N. Wildwood, has dinner specials with soup, salad, vegetables, entree, and dessert (4:30-6pm $8; after 6pm $9) and deep-fried Chesapeake oysters ($12).

Most of the motels next to the Boardwalk fill with vacationers, but many cheaper accommodations take in students working in Wildwood for the summer. The **Rosemont Hotel,** 230 E. Glenwood Ave. (522-6204), two blocks from the beach, offers singles ($22) and doubles ($35) with shared bath. **Sea Tag Lodge,** 226 E. Glenwood Ave. (522-6484), has rooms with rates based on double occupancy ($36 with private bath). Various independently run establishments rent "apartments and rooms" which generally resemble local motels. **Trio's Apartments and Rooms,** at 221 E. Glenwood (522-6996), has tiny rooms with shared bath for $35. (See Cape May above for the camping sites closest to Wildwood.)

Wildwood is a 40-minute drive south from Atlantic City and three hours from New York City via the Garden State Parkway. From the south, take I-95 to the Delaware Memorial Bridge; follow Rte. 49, and finally Rte. 47. **New Jersey Transit** (800-582-5946), has daily connections to Atlantic City ($3), Cape May ($1.75), and Philadelphia ($12.50), stopping at the Wildwood Municipal Bus Terminal, New Jersey and Oak Ave. (open daily 6:30am-10pm). **Local buses** cost $1.25 (884-5230).

The **post office** pushes paper at 3311 Atlantic Ave. (522-5421), at Oak. (Open Mon.-Fri. 9am-5pm.) Wildwood's **ZIP code** is 08260; the **area code** is 609.

Pennsylvania

While many associate the state with historic Philadelphia or industrial Pittsburgh, Pennsylvania rests on religious freedom. Driven by British persecution of his fellow Quakers, William Penn, Jr. petitioned the British Crown for a tract of land in North America in 1680. He arrived in 1682, named the colony after his father, and embarked on an experiment in religious tolerance that immediately attracted a diverse population. At the time of the American Revolution, Pennsylvania seemed destined to become the most prominent state in the new nation. The emerging colonies signed the Declaration of Independence in Philadelphia, the country's original capital and site of the First Continental Congress. However, other cities soon overshadowed it—New York City rapidly grew into the nation's most important commercial center, while Washington, DC usurped the role of nation's capital.

When the Industrial Revolution hit the U.S., Pennsylvania again made a strong start. Pittsburgh became the center of the nation's steel production, yet the largest U.S. industry, automobile manufacturing, eventually made its home in Detroit. The oil wells of Titusville caused the state to flourish once more until richer deposits in Texas and Oklahoma outstripped Pennsylvanian industry. Now the local steel industry stagnates and oil barely trickles from a few remaining wells. More recently, Three Mile Island helped Pennsylvania to claim the worst nuclear power plant accident in the U.S.

But Pennsylvania, a state accustomed to revolution, has recently rallied in the face of adversity. In 1976, Philadelphia groomed its historic shrines for its bicentennial celebration, and the tourist trade continues to boom. Even Pittsburgh, a city once dirty enough to fool streetlamps into burning in daytime, has initiated a cultural renaissance. But neither of Pennsylvania's two major cities overshadows the countryside between them. Pennsylvania's landscape, from the farms of Lancaster County to the deep river gorges of the Allegheny Plateau, retains the magnetism that drew Penn here 300 years ago. This state suits budget travelers well. Fifteen well-kept youth hostels are spaced no more than a day's bike ride apart, from Pittsburgh to Philadelphia.

Practical Information

Capital: Harrisburg.

Tourist Information: Bureau of Travel Development, 453 Forum Bldg., Harrisburg 17120 (717-787-5453 or 800-237-4363). Information on hotels, restaurants, and sights. Bureau of State Parks, P.O. Box 1467, Harrisburg 17120 (800-631-7105). The detailed, *Recreational Guide* is available at no charge at all visitor information centers.

Time Zone: Eastern. Postal Abbreviation: PA.

Philadelphia

Pennsylvanians like to boast via their license plates that "America starts here." Not that license plate mottos *ever* make sense, but Penn was neither the first state in the Union nor the site of the first U.S. settlement. Still, Philadelphia—the state's largest and most dynamic city—almost makes the claim viable. Here the *Declaration of Independence* first outlined a self-governed U.S. republic, and the *Constitution* planned the states in the nation's first capital. William Penn, perhaps the first famous U.S. colonist with a genuine belief in religious tolerance, founded the city. Benjamin Franklin, womanizer, brilliant diplomat, and leading intellectual behind the American Revolution, shaped the city's growth. Later, African Americans migrated north after the Civil War to influence and test the promises made by "the city of brotherly love." Today, the city that elected one of the first black mayors in the nation strikes a tenuous balance between its famous cheesesteaks and its cinematic side-of-beef abuser Rocky Balboa. Philly has provincial charm, cosmopolitan flavor, and street pretzel vendors who deliver both. With history, presence, and six college campuses the sights here are for once even worth seeing. Stop by Independence Hall, the Liberty Bell, the Franklin Institute, and maybe even have a Rocky-style run up the steps of the Fairmount Park Art Museum. In the process, ponder a few of the founding city's most challenging questions—what is liberty? who determines freedom? onions on that cheesesteak?

Practical Information

Emergency: 911.

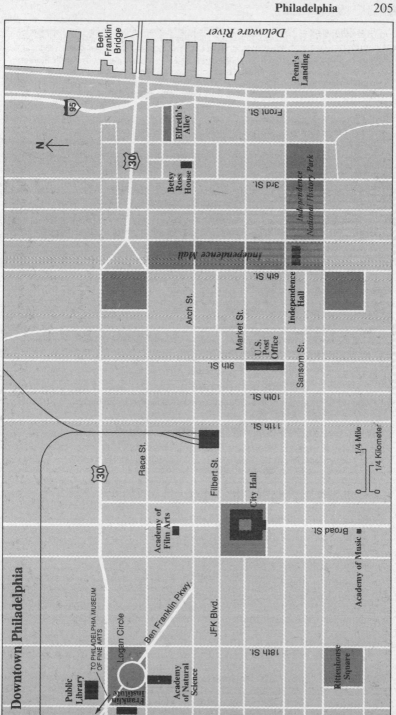

Downtown Philadelphia

Visitor Information: Visitors Center, 1525 John F. Kennedy Blvd. at 16th St. (636-1666). Pick up a free *Philadelphia Visitor's Guide* and the *Philadelphia Quarterly Calendar of Events.* Open daily 9am-6pm; off-season early 9am-5pm. **Directory Events Hotline,** 574-1200, ext. 2540. **Cultural Hotline,** 925-9000. **National Park Service Visitor Center,** 3rd and Chestnut (597-8974; 627-1776 for recording). Information on Independence Park, including maps, schedules, and the film *Independence.* Also distributes the *Visitor's Guide* and the *Quarterly Calendar of Events.* Open Sept.-June daily 9am-5pm; July-Aug. 9am-6pm. Film shown 9:30am-4:15pm. Tour assistance for non-English-speaking and the disabled.

Philadelphia International Airport: (information line 492-3181 from 6am-11pm), 8 mi. south-west of Center City on I-76. The 27-min. SEPTA Airport Rail Line runs from Center City to the airport. Trains leave daily 5:30am-11:25pm from 30th St. Station, Suburban Station, and Market East ($4.75). Last train from airport 12:10am. Cab fare downtown $21, but **Air-port Limelight Limousine** (342-5557) will deliver you to a hotel ($6) or a specific address downtown.

Amtrak: 30th St. Station, at 30th and Market St. (895-7123 or 800-872-7245), in University City. To New York City (every ½-hr., 2 hr., $28), Washington, DC (every ½-hr., 2 hr., $33), and points in western PA. Ticket office open daily 5am-10:30pm. Station open 24 hr. Trains run cheaply between Philadelphia and New York City; take the SEPTA commuter train to Trenton, NJ ($4.75), then hop on a New Jersey Transit train to NYC through Newark ($7.75).

Buses: Greyhound/Trailways, 10th and Filbert St. (931-4000), 1 block north of Market near the 10th and Market St. subway/commuter rail stop in the heart of Philadelphia. To: New York City ($14 per day, 2½ hr., Mon.-Thurs. $17, Fri.-Sun. $19); Washington, DC ($8 per day, 3½ hr., Mon.-Thurs. $22, Fri.-Sun. $26); Atlantic City (17 per day, 1½ hr., $10). **New Jersey Transit,** 800-582-5946. To Atlantic City ($10), Ocean City ($10.75), and other points on the New Jersey Shore.

Public Transport: Southeastern Pennsylvania Transportation Authority (SEPTA), 574-7800. Most buses operate 6:30am-1am, some all night. Extensive bus and rail service to suburbs. Two major subway routes: the Market St. line running east-west (including 30th St. Station and the historic area) and the Broad St. line running north-south (including the stadium com-plex in south Philadelphia). Subway unsafe after dark, but buses usually okay. Buses serve the 5-county area. Subway connects with commuter rails—the Main Line Local runs through the western suburb of Paoli ($3.50), and SEPTA runs north as far as Trenton, NJ ($4.75). Pick up a SEPTA **system map** ($1.50), and a good street map at any subway stop. Fare $1.50, 2 tokens for $2.10, transfers 40¢.

Taxi: Yellow Cab, 922-8400. **United Cab,** 625-9170.

Car Rental: Ugly Duckling Rent-a-Car, 4 Walnut St. (296-7177), Berwyn. Take SEPTA train west from Philadelphia to Daylesford, then a 5-min. walk to Walnut St. $17 per day, 13¢ per mi. Insurance $6 per day. Open Mon.-Sat. 8am-5pm. Must be 21. **Thrifty Rent-a-Car,** 365-3900 at the airport. Sub-compacts $31 per day, weekends $18 per day. Unlimited mi. but must not go farther south than DC or farther north than Massachusetts. Optional insur-ance $10 per day. Must be 25 with major credit card.

Help Lines: Gay Switchboard, 546-7100. Open daily 6-11pm.

Post Office: 30th and Market St. (596-5316), across from the Amtrak station. Open 24 hr. **ZIP code:** 19104.

Area Code: 215.

Philadelphia is 100 mi. from New York City, 133 mi. from Washington, DC, and 296 mi. from Boston. Founder William Penn, Jr., as a survivor of London's great fire in the 1660s, planned his city as a logical and easily accessible grid pattern of wide streets. The north-south streets ascend numerically from the **Delaware River,** flowing near Penn's Landing and Independence Hall on the east side, to the **Schuylkill River** (pronounced SCHOOL-kill) on the west. The first street is **Front,** the others follow consecutively from 2 to 69. **Center City** runs from 8th Street to the Schuylkill River. From north to south, the primary streets are Race, Arch, JFK, Market, Sansom, and South. The intersection of Broad (14th St.) and Market, loca-tion of City Hall, marks the focal point of Center City. The **Historic District** stretches from Front to 8th Street and from Vine to South Street. The sprawling, historic **University of Pennsylvania** rests on the far side of the Schuylkill River, about 1 mi. west of Center City. **University City** includes the Penn/Drexel area west of the Schuylkill River.

Accommodations and Camping

Downtown Philadelphia is saturated wtih luxury hotels, so anything inexpensive is popular. But if you make arrangements even a few days in advance, you should find comfortable lodging close to Center City for under $40. **Bed and Breakfast, Center City,** 1804 Pine St., Philadelphia 19103 (735-1137) can reserve you a room in a private home. (Singles $40-65. Doubles $45-75. Best to call 9am-9pm.) The **Philadelphia Naturalist and Work Camp Center,** P.O. Box 4755, Philadelphia 19134 (452-5240), rents beds to foreign students ($5 with light breakfast) and will arrange free room and board on a nearby farm in exchange for daily chores. Camping is available to the north and west of the city, but you must travel at least 15 mi.

Chamounix Mansion International Youth Hostel (AYH), West Fairmount Park (878-3676). Take bus #38 from JFK Blvd. to Ford and Cranston Rd., walk in the direction of the bus until Chamounix St., then turn left and follow until the road ends at hostel (about a 20-min. walk). In daylight take bus #38 to Fairmount Terr. apartments and follow the AYH sign 10 min. through a wooded path. Former country estate built in 1802. Clean and beautifully furnished, with 50 beds, showers, kitchen, and coin-operated laundry. Some basic groceries for sale. Extraordinarily friendly and helpful staff. Lockout 9:30am-4:30pm. Curfew 11pm. $9.50, nonmembers $12.50. Linen $2.

Old First Reformed Church, 4th and Race St. (922-4566), in Center City 1 block from the Independence Mall and 4 blocks from Penn's Landing. Historic church that converts its social hall to a youth hostel for 20. Mattresses on the floor, showers. 3-night max. stay. Check-in 5-10pm. Curfew 11pm. $10. Breakfast included. Open early July-late Aug.

The Divine Tracy Hotel, 20 S. 36th St. (382-4310), near Market St. in University City. Impeccably clean, quiet, and well-maintained rooms, though no bright Dick Tracy colors. Women must wear skirts and stockings at all times in the public areas of the hotel; men, long pants and socks with their shirts tucked in. Strictly single-sex floors. No smoking, vulgarity, obscenity, or blasphemy. Check-in 7am-11pm. Singles $20, with private bath $23-26. Shared doubles $17-20 per person. Fans and TVs for rent. The management does not permit alcohol or food (except small snacks) in the rooms, but the **Keyflower Dining Room** (386-2207) offers incredibly cheap and healthful, if bland, food. Entrees $1.75-2. Open to the public Mon.-Fri. 11:30am-2pm and 5-8pm.

International House, 3701 Chestnut St. (387-5125). Bus #21 stops right out front. Clean dorms in a modern complex built to house Philly's international students—must have student ID or affiliation with university or exchange program. May accept college graduates or professionals. Mostly singles in 10-room suites ($42). Reserve ahead if you want a suite with kitchen. Doubles, $50 **Eden** restaurant (see Food below) in the same building. Open year-round, but rooms scarce during school year.

The closest camping is across the Delaware River in New Jersey. Check out **Timberline Campground,** 117 Timber Lane, Clarksboro, NJ 08020 (609-423-6677), 15 mi. from Center City. Take 285 S. to exit 18A, Clarksboro, turn left and then right at the first stop sign, Cohawkin Rd. Go ½-mi. and turn right on Friendship Rd. Timber Lane is 1 block on the right. (Sites $11, with full hookup $13.50.) In Pennsylvania, **Tohickon Family Campground,** RD #3, Covered Bridge Rd. (933-5865) is on Rte. 29 about 25 mi. west of Philly. (Sites $20, with water $22.)

Food

More than 500 new restaurants have opened their doors in Philadelphia in the past decade, making the city one of the most exciting dining spots in the U.S. Inexpensive food abounds on Sansom St. between 17th and 18th; on South St. between 2nd and 7th; and on 2nd St. between Chestnut and Market. Numerous new places are opening up on **Penn's Landing,** on the Delaware River between Locust and Market St. Philadelphia's **Chinatown** lies right in the center of downtown action, bounded by 8th, 11th, Vine, and Race St. In **University City,** the University of Pennsylvania (UPenn) and Drexel University collide on the west side of Schuylkill

River making good cheap student eateries easy to find. Try the famous hoagie or cheesesteak, two local specialties. You may grow attached to the renowned Philly soft pretzel: have one for about 30¢ (with mustard) at a street-side vendor.

To stock up on staples, visit the **Italian Market** at 9th and Christian St. (Open daily dawn-dusk.) The **Reading Terminal Market**, at 12th and Arch St. (922-2317), is the place to go for picnic-packing, grocery-shopping, or a quick lunch. Since 1893, food stands have clustered together in this huge indoor market—selling fresh meats, produce, and delicious alternatives to modern fast-food courts. (Open Mon.-Sat. 8am-6pm.)

Historic District

Jim's Steaks, 4th and South. Take the 4th St. trolley or bus #10 down Locust St. A Philadelphia institution since 1939, serving some of the best steak sandwiches in town ($3.50-4). John Denver says he'd be a vegetarian if it weren't for Jim's cheesesteak. Eat to beat Jim's current record holder—11 steaks in 90 minutes. Open Mon.-Thurs. 10am-1am, Fri.-Sat. 10am-3am, Sun. noon-10pm.

Lee's Hoagies, 220 South St., near 2nd St. Authentic hoagies ($3-4.50) since 1953. The 3-ft. hoagie challenges even gluttonous tourists. Open Tues.-Thurs. 10am-11pm, Fri.-Sat. 10am-2am, Sun. 10am-10pm.

Fu Wing House, 639 South St., between 6th and 7th. Great hot-and-sour soup ($1.50). Entrees $6.75-9.25. Open Mon. and Wed.-Thurs. 5-11pm, Fri. 5pm-midnight, Sat. 4pm-midnight, Sun. 4-11pm.

Dickens Inn, Head House Sq., on 2nd St. between Pine and Lombard. Restaurant upstairs way upscale but tastes excellent. British country cooking served at the bakery—try a cornish pastie or shepherd's pie (both $3.75). Open Mon.-Tues. 8am-9pm, Wed.-Thurs. 8am-10pm, Fri. 8am-11pm, Sat. 8am-midnight, Sun. 10am-6pm. Pay slightly more at the bar, open daily 11:30am-1:30am.

Center City

Charlie's Famous Waterwheel Restaurant, downstairs at 1526 Samson St., between 15th and 16th St. First hoagie steak shop in Center City—their subs will sink you for days. Sandwiches and steaks with fresh fruit and vegetables ($5.25). Munch on free meatballs, pickles, and fried mushrooms at the counter while you wait. Open daily 11am-4pm.

Saladalley, 1720 Samson St. between 17th and 18th. Huge salad bar featuring truly innovative combinations of fresh fruits, vegetables, and homemade muffins. Try the pasta bows in walnut zucchini sauce ($8). Lunch $5.25, dinner $5.95. Open Mon.-Thurs. 11:30am-9pm, Fri.-Sat. 11:30am-10pm. 4 other locations.

University City

Audrey's Pit Barbecue, 113 S. 40th St., between Chestnut and Walnut. Considered the best barbecue joint in town. Funny guys Jack Nicholson and Redd Foxx eat here. Try the half-chicken or the barbecued beef sandwich ($3 each). Customers rave about the potato pie (90¢). Few seats, mostly take-out. Open Tues. 11:30am-7pm, Wed.-Thurs. 11:30am-10pm, Fri.-Sat. 11:30am-1am, Sun. 2-10pm.

Sweet Basil, 4000 Chestnut St., at 40th St. Cool and sophisticated. Eclectic menu with Indonesian, Cajun, and vegetarian entrees. Dinners $7-13. Open Mon.-Thurs. 5-10pm, Fri.-Sat. 5-10:30pm.

Barley and Hops, 3925 Walnut St., between 39th and 40th. Students swarm here for a respite from dining hall grub. Good burgers and sandwiches ($4-5). Open daily 11am-2am. Kitchen closes at 1am.

Eden, 3721 Chestnut St., at 38th St. Wholesome and satisfying grilled fish and chicken specialties served on a leafy terrace. No original sin here. Don't be put off by cafeteria-style dining. Great chicken stir-fry $6. Crab-cake sandwich with potatos $4.75. Students with I.D. 10% discount. Open Mon.-Sat. 11:30am-11pm. Bar open later.

Sights

"I went to Philadelphia," W.C. Fields quipped, "and it was closed." Though the city still sleeps fairly early, its fine collection of museums and an unmatched historical significance give Philly all the ingredients of a great town to visit, at least when it's open. A convenient way to see the sights rolls by on **Fairmount Park Trolley Tours** (879-4044 for recorded information). Sponsored by the city's park commission, the tours pass by all the major sights, and you may board or get off at your leisure. Tours (April-Nov. Wed.-Sun. 10am-4pm) leave every ½-hr. from the tourist center, 16th and JFK, and the Independence Park Visitors Center. (Admission $3; includes discounts at attractions.)

Independence Hall and the Historic District

The buildings of the **Independence National Historic Park** (open daily 9am-5pm; in summer 9am-8pm) witnessed events that have since passed into U.S. folklore. The park visitor center (see Practical Information above) makes a good starting point. Site of the signing of the *Declaration of Independence* in 1776, and the *Constitution* drafting and signing in 1787, **Independence Hall** lies between 5th and 6th St. on Chestnut. Engraved with a half-sun, George Washington's chair at the head of the assembly room prompted Ben Franklin to remark after the ratification of the Constitution that "Now at length I have the happiness to know that it is a rising and not a setting sun." (Free guided tours daily every 15-20 min.) The U.S. Congress first assembled in nearby **Congress Hall** (free self-guided tour), while its predecessor, the First Continental Congress, convened in **Carpenters' Hall,** 2 blocks away at 4th and Chestnut St. (Open Tues.-Sun. 10am-4pm.) North of Independence Hall lies the **Liberty Bell Pavilion.** The cracked Liberty Bell itself, one of the most famous U.S. symbols, refuses to toll even when vigorously prodded.

The remainder of the park contains preserved residential and commercial buildings of the Revolutionary era. Ben Franklin's home lies in **Franklin Court** to the north, on Market between 3rd and 4th St., and includes an underground museum and an architectural archeological exhibit. (Open daily 9am-5pm.) Nearby **Washington Square** has an eternal flame commemorating the **Tomb of the Unknown Soldier.** Across from Independence Hall is Philadelphia's branch of the **U.S. Mint,** 5th and Arch St. (597-7350) A self-paced guided tour explains the mechanized coin-making procedure. Open May-Sept. daily 9am-4:30pm, fall and winter Mon.-Sat. 9am-4:30pm. Free.

Tucked away near 2nd and Arch St. the quiet, residential **Elfreth's Alley,** allegedly "the oldest street in America," along which a penniless Ben Franklin walked when he arrived in town in 1723. On Arch near 3rd St. sits the tiny **Betsy Ross House,** where its namesake supposedly sewed the first flag of the original 13 states. **Christ Church,** on 2nd near Market, hosted the fashionable Quakers of colonial Philadelphia. Ben Franklin lies buried in the nearby Christ Church cemetery at 5th and Arch St. **Mikveh Israel,** the first Jewish congregation of Philadelphia, has a burial ground on Spruce near 8th St. Also see the Quaker meeting houses: the original **Free Quaker Meeting House** at 5th and Arch St., and a new and larger one at 4th and Arch St.

The **Afro-American Historical and Cultural Museum,** 7th and Arch St. (574-0380), stands as the first U.S. museum devoted solely to the history of African Americans. (Open Tues.-Sat. 10am-5pm, Sun. noon-6pm. Admission $3.50, seniors and children $1.75.)

Society Hill proper begins where the park ends, on Walnut St. between Front and 7th St. Now Philadelphia's most distinguished residential neighborhood, housing both old-timers and a new yuppie crowd, the area was originally a tract of land owned by the Free Society of Traders, a company formed to help William Penn, Jr. consolidate Pennsylvania. Federal-style townhouses dating back 300 years line picturesque cobblestone walks, illuminated by old-fashioned streetlamps. **Head House Square,** 2nd and Pine St., held a marketplace in 1745 and now houses restaurants, boutiques, and craft shops. An outdoor flea market occurs here summer weekends.

Located on the Delaware River, **Penn's Landing** (923-8181) is the largest freshwater port in the world. Among other vessels it holds the *Gazela,* a three-masted, 178-foot Portuguese square rigger built in 1883; the U.S.S. *Olympia,* Commodore

Dewey's flagship during the Spanish-American War (922-1898; tours daily 10am-4:30pm; admission $3, children $1.50); and the U.S.S. *Becuna,* a WWII submarine (tours in conjunction with the *Olympia*). The **Port of History,** Delaware Ave. and Walnut St. (925-3804) has quick changing exhibits. (Open Wed.-Sun. 10am-4:30pm. Admission $2, ages 5-12 $1.) The Delaware Landing is a great spot to soak up sun on a nice day. For $1.50 you can jump on **Penn's Landing Trolley** (627-0807), on Delaware Ave., between Catharine and Race St., which rolls along the waterfront giving guided tours.

Slightly out of the way lurks the **Edgar Allan Poe House,** 532 N. 7th St. (597-8780). Here the literary giant wrote some of his most macabre poems and stories, including *The Raven* and *The Tell-Tale Heart.* Please don't damage the floorboards. (Open daily 9am-5pm. Free.)

Center City

Center City, the area bounded by 12th, 23rd, Vine, and Pine St., whirls with activity. **City Hall,** Broad and Market St. (686-1776), an ornate structure of granite and marble with 20-ft.-thick foundation walls, is the nation's largest public municipal building. Until 1908, it also held the record for highest building in the U.S., helped by the 37-ft. statue of William Penn, Jr. on top. A municipal statute prohibited building higher than the top of Penn's hat until entrepreneurs in the mid-80's overturned it, finally launching Philadelphia into the skyscraper era. (Open Mon.-Fri. 7am-6pm. Free guided tours Mon.-Fri. at 12:30pm; meet in room 201.) The **Pennsylvania Academy of Fine Arts,** Broad and Cherry St. (972-7600), the country's first art school and one of its first museums, has an extensive collection of U.S. and British art including notable works by Charles Wilson Peale, Thomas Eakins, Winslow Homer, and a few contemporary artists. (Open Tues.-Sat. 10am-5pm, Sun. 11am-5pm. Tours Tues.-Fri. at 11am and 2pm, Sat.-Sun. at 2pm. Admission $5, seniors $3, students $2, under 12 free. Free Sat. 10am-1pm.)

Just south of **Rittenhouse Square,** 2010 Delancey St., the **Rosenbach Museum and Library** (732-1600), houses rare manuscripts and paintings, including the earliest-known copy of Cervantes' *Don Quixote.* (Open Sept.-July Tues.-Sun. 11am-4pm. Guided tours $2.50. Exhibitions only $1.50.) The nearby **Mütter Museum** (567-3737) of Philadelphia's College of Physicians displays gory medical paraphernalia including a death cast of Siamese twins and a tumor removed from President Cleveland's jaw. (Open Tues.-Fri. 10am-4pm. Free.) Ben Franklin founded the **Library Company of Philadelphia,** 1314 Locust St. near 13th St., over 250 years ago, as a club whose members' dues purchased books from England. A weather-worn statue of Franklin stands outside its present headquarters. The **Norman Rockwell Museum,** 6th and Sansom St. (922-4345) houses all of the artist's *Saturday Evening Post* cover works. (Open daily 10am-4pm. Admission $1.50, ages under 12 free.)

Benjamin Franklin Parkway

Nicknamed "America's Champs-Elysées," the Benjamin Franklin Parkway is a wide, diagonal deviation from William Penn's original grid pattern of city streets. Built in the 1920s, this tree- and flag-lined street connects Center City with Fairmount Park and the Schuylkill River. Admire the elegant architecture of the twin buildings at Logan Square, 19th and Parkway, that house the **Free Library of Philadelphia** and the **Municipal Court.**

At 20th and Parkway, the **Franklin Institute** (448-1200), whose **Science Center** amazes visitors with four floors of gadgets and games depicting the intricacies of space, time, motion, and the human body. A 20-ft. **Benjamin Franklin National Memorial** statue guards the entrance. In 1990, to commemorate the 200th anniversary of Franklin's death, the Institute unveiled the **Futures Center**—glimpses of life in the 21st century include simulated zero gravity and a timely, impressive set of exhibits on the changing global environment. (Futures Center open daily 9am-9:30pm. Science Center open daily 9am-5pm. Admission to both $7.50, seniors and children $6. After 5pm: $6, seniors and children $5.) The also brand new **Omniverse Theater** provides 180 deg. and 4½ stories of unparalleled visual experience. (Omniverse shows daily on the hour 9am-8pm. Admission $6, seniors and children $5.) **Fels Planetarium** boasts an advanced computer-driven projection system that simulates life billions of years beyond. (Shows Mon.-Thurs. at 12:15 and 2:15pm, Fri.-Sat. at 12:15, 2:15, 7:15, 8:15pm, Sun. at 12:15, 2:15, 4:15pm. Admission $5, seniors and children $4.) During the day, see all the sights for $11.50 (seniors and children $9.50) or check out any two for $9.50 (seniors and children $7.50). After 5pm, two attractions cost $8, seniors and children $7.

A ubiquitous casting of the *Gates of Hell* stands outside the **Rodin Museum,** at 22nd St. and the Parkway (787-5476), which houses the most complete collection of the artist's works outside Paris, including *The Thinker.* (Open Tues.-Sun. 10am-5pm. Free.) Try your hand at the sensual **Please Touch Museum,** 210 N. 21st St. (963-0666), designed specifically for children under eight. (Open daily 10am-4:30pm. Admission $4.50.)

The exhibit of precious gems and the 65-million-year-old dinosaur skeleton at the **Academy of Natural Sciences,** 19th and Parkway (299-1020), excite even the basest of human desires. (Open Mon.-Fri. 10am-4:30pm, Sat.-Sun. 10am-5pm. Admission $5.50, seniors $5, children $4.50.) Farther down 26th St., the **Philadelphia Museum of Art** (763-8100) protects one of the world's major art collections. In the nation's third largest museum you'll find Rubens' *Prometheus Bound,* Picasso's *Three Musicians,* and Duchamp's *Nude Descending a Staircase,* as well as extensive Asian, Egyptian, and decorative arts collections. (Open Tues.-Sun. 10am-5pm. Admission $5, seniors and students under 18 with ID $2. Free Sun. 10am-1pm.)

Fairmount Park sprawls behind the Philadelphia Museum of Art on both sides of the Schuylkill River. Bike trails and picnic areas abound, and the famous **Philadelphia Zoo** (243-1100), the oldest in the U.S., houses 1500 species in one corner of the park. (Open daily 9:30am-5pm. Admission $5.75, seniors and children $4.75.) Boathouse Row, which houses the shells of local crew teams, is especially beautiful when lit at night. During the day, hikers and non-hikers alike may wish to venture out to the northernmost arm of Fairmount Park, where trails leave the Schuylkill River and wind along secluded Wissahickon Creek for 5 mi. The **Horticultural Center,** off Belmont Ave. (879-4062; open Wed.-Sun. 9am-3pm) has greenhouses, Japanese gardening and periodic flower shows for free viewing.

West Philadelphia (University City)

West Philly is home to both the **University of Pennsylvania** and **Drexel University,** located across the Schuylkill from Center City, within easy walking distance of the 30th St. Station. Benjamin Franklin founded Penn in 1740. Fifteen years later the country's first medical school came to life, and students have been pulling all-nighters since then. The Penn campus provides a retreat of green lawns and red-brick quadrangles. Ritzy shops line Chestnut St. and boisterous fraternities line Spruce; warm weather brings out a varied collection of street vendors along the Drexel and Penn borders.

Penn's **University Museum of Archeology and Anthropology,** 33rd and Spruce St. (898-4000), houses one of the finest archeological collections in the world. (Open Sept.-June Tues.-Sat. 10am-4:30pm, Sun. 1-5pm. Admission $3, seniors and students $1.50.) In 1965, Andy Warhol had his first one-man show at the **Institute of Contemporary Art,** 34th and Walnut St. Today the gallery remains on the cutting edge of the art scene. (Open Thurs.-Tues. 10am-5pm, Wed. 10am-7pm. Admission $2, seniors and artists with a compelling work $1, students free. Free Wed.)

Entertainment

Check Friday's weekend magazine section in the Philadelphia *Inquirer* for entertainment listings. *City Paper,* distributed on Fridays for free, has weekly listings of city events. *Au Courant,* a gay and lesbian weekly newspaper, lists and advertises events throughout the Delaware Valley region. The bar scene enlivens University City with a younger crowd. Along South Street, there is a wide variety of live music on weekends. Stop by **Dobbs,** 304 South St. (928-1943), between 3rd and 4th, a mixed menu restaurant (entrees $6-8.50) with live rock nightly. (Open daily 6pm-2am.) Nearby **Penn's Landing** (923-4992) has free concerts in summer. Formerly under the direction of the late Eugene Ormandy, and now under Ricardo Muti, the **Philadelphia Academy of Music,** Broad and Locust St. (893-1930), houses the Philadelphia Orchestra, rated by many as the best in the U.S. The academy was modeled artistically after Milan's *La Scala* and acoustically after a perfect vacuum. The season runs from September through May. General admission tickets ($2) for seats in the amphitheater go on sale at the Locust St. entrance 45 minutes before Friday and Saturday concerts. Check with the box office for availability. The **Mann Music Center,** George's Hill (567-0707), near 52nd St. and Parkside Ave. in Fairmount Park, has 5000 seats under cover, 10,000 on outdoor benches and lawns and hosts summer Philadelphia Orchestra, ballet, jazz, and rock events. Pick up free lawn tickets June through August on the day of performance from the visitors center at 16th St. and JFK Blvd. (See Practical Information above). For the big-name shows (Billy Joel and Crosby, Stills, and Nash last year) sit just outside the theater for free. The **Robin Hood Dell East,** Strawberry Mansion Dr. (686-1776 or 477-8810 in summer), in Fairmount Park, brings in top names in pop, jazz, gospel, and ethnic dance in July and August. The Philadelphia Orchestra holds several free performances here in summer, and as many as 30,000 people gather on the lawn. Inquire at the visitors center (636-1666) for upcoming events. **Shubert Theater,** 250 S. Broad St., Center City (732-5446), has various dance, musical, and comedy performances year-round.

Philly has four professional sports franchises. The Phillies (baseball) and Eagles (football) play at **Veterans Stadium** (ticket office 463-5500), while the **Spectrum** (336-3600) houses the 76ers (basketball) and the Flyers (hockey).

Near Philadelphia: Valley Forge

Neither battles nor artillery bombardments took place here, but during the winter of 1777-78, 11,000 men quartered at Valley Forge under George Washington's leadership spent agonizing months fighting starvation and disease. Only 8000 survived. Nonetheless, inspired by the enthusiasm of General Washington and the news of a U.S. alliance with France, and drilled into efficiency by Inspector General Baron Von Steuben, the troops left Valley Forge stronger and better trained. They went on to victories in New Jersey and eventually reoccupied Philadelphia.

The park today encompasses over 2000 acres. (Open daily 6am-10pm.) Self-guided tours begin at the **visitors center** (783-7700), which also has a free museum and a 15-minute audio-visual program played daily twice per hour from 9am to 5:30pm. (Open daily 8:30am-5pm.) The tour features Washington's headquarters, reconstructed soldier huts and fortifications, and the Grand Parade Ground where the army drilled. And that's a fact, Jack. Admission to Washington's headquarters costs one Washington ($1), but most other exhibits and buildings in the park are free. Auto tapes rent for $6.40. The park has three picnic areas; although there is no camping within the park, campgrounds thrive nearby. A 5-mi. bike trail winds up and down the hills of the park. Rent bikes ($4 per hr., $11 per day) at the **Interpretive Association Bookstore** (783-1076; open daily 9am to 4:30pm).

To get to Valley Forge, take the Schuylkill Expressway westbound from Philadelphia for about 12 mi. Get off at the Valley Forge exit, then take Rte. 202 S. for 1 mi. and Rte. 422 W. for 3 mi. to another Valley Forge exit. SEPTA runs buses to the visitors center Monday through Friday only. Catch #125 at 16th and JFK. (Fare $3.10.)

Lancaster County

When flocks of German Anabaptists fled persecution in Europe for William Penn's bastion of religious freedom, locals quickly and wrongly labeled them the Pennsylvania Dutch. The name, a misunderstanding of the word *Deutschland* for

"Germany," stuck. Since the late 1700s, three distinct families of Anabaptists have lived in Lancaster County: **Brethren, Mennonites,** and **Amish.** The latter, and the Old Order Amish in particular, are famed for their lifestyle. Emphatically rejecting modern technology and fashion, they worship and educate their children at home, discouraging association with outsiders. Quite ironically, the modest Lancaster Amish community of 15,000 draws at least that many visitors each year, eager for a glimpse of the secluded country lifestyle of horse-drawn carriages, modest hats, and old-fashioned dress. In contrast to the Amish, some of the Mennonites embrace modern conveniences like cars and electricity. Many sell their farm goods at roadside stands or operate bed and breakfasts and craft shops. Lancaster County today has evolved into a strange mix of unbridled consumerism and plain living.

Lancaster County, even the concentrated spot of interest to tourists, covers a huge area. Cars are the vehicle of choice for most visitors. With wheels of any sort, you can pay a guide to hop in and show you around. **Alverta Moore** (626-2421) charges about $5 per hour. At the **Mennonite Information Center,** 2209 Millstream Rd. (299-0954; open Mon.-Sat. 8am-5pm), just off Rte. 30, you can hire a guide for $7.50 per hour (2-hr. minimum; available Mon.-Sat. 9:30am-9:30pm; Nov.-March 9:30am-4:30pm). Cars, though convenient, close you off from the countryside and can alienate even the well-intentioned while zooming by an Amish family's horse-drawn buggy. Note the triangular, fluorescent slow-moving signs mandated by law (and often protested by the Amish). **New Horizons,** 3495 Horizon Dr. (285-7607), will meet you at the train or bus station with a bike and pick it up there later, if you call ahead. (Bikes $12 per day. Free maps.) The Amish shun cars and for many, especially the young, bikes are the primary means of transport.

To see this country best, pick up maps at Lancaster City or Pennsylvania Dutch visitors bureaus (see below), veer off U.S. 30, and explore the winding roads. A good place to start, though, is the **People's Place,** on Main St./Rte. 340 (768-7171), in Intercourse 11 mi. east of Lancaster City. The acclaimed film *Who Are the Amish* shows every half hour from 9:30am to 5pm and **Amish World,** has charming hands-on exhibits on Amish and Mennonite life, from barn-raising to styles of hats. (Admission to one $2.50, children $1.50. To both $4.25, children $2.25.) The People's Place spans an entire block filled with bookstores, craft shops, and an art gallery. (Open Mon.-Sat. 9:30am-9:30pm; Nov.-March 9:30am-4:30pm.) If you have specific questions, seek out friendly locals at the Mennonite Information Center (see above) which also shows a free film *A Morning Song* every half hour.

A quiet metropolis in the heart of Dutch country, **Lancaster City,** the county seat, reflects the area's character well—clean, red-brick row houses gather around the historic Penn Square in the city center. At the **Lancaster Association of Commerce and Industry,** 100 Queen St. (397-3531), you can pick up guided walking tours of Lancaster City (April-Oct. Sun.-Fri. at 10am and 1:30pm, Sat. at 10am, 11am, 1:30pm; $3, seniors $2.50, students $1.50) or buy a worthwhile self-guided booklet ($1.50). To reserve a tour off-season call Pat (653-8225) or Harriet (394-2339). The center has its own rather avoidable film about Lancaster and a full line of brochures. (Open April-Oct. Mon.-Fri. 8:30am-5pm, Sat. 9am-4pm, Sun. 10am-3pm.; open 1 hr. later off-season.) Pick up a free **Map of Amish Farmlands** at any tourist spot in Lancaster County, or write to 340-23 Club, P.O. Box 239, Intercourse 17534.

The Amish don't take in visitors for meals, but if you ask around you may well find a Mennonite family that will share a meal and conversation. Ask the managers of your hotel or hostel if they know of some. A donation of $8 and a day's notice are usually required.

Just about everyone passing through Lancaster County expects a taste of real Dutch cuisine—and a flock of high priced "family-style" restaurants have sprouted up to please them. If you have the cash (all-you-can-eat meals $12-16) try any of the huge restaurants such as **The Amish Barn** spread thick on U.S. 30 and 340. Better still, drive farther from the city for smaller and more affordable *snitz, knepp,* and shoo fly pie. **Terre Hill Family Restaurant,** 213 E. Main St. (445-9233) in Terre Hill off Rte. 897 about 20 mi. south of Lancaster City, serves scrapple with vegetables and salad bar for $5.50. More varied fare can be found in Lancaster City. Don't miss the **Central Market,** in the northwest corner of Penn Sq., a huge food bazaar since 1899 with inexpensive meats, cheeses, vegetables, and sandwiches. (Open Tues. and Fri.-Sat. 5:30am-1:30pm.) Next door, **Habibi's,** 9 W. King St. (397-0152) fries a mean felafel for $3—ask for the special spices. (Open Mon. and Wed.-Thurs. 9:30am-5pm, Tues. and Fri.-Sat. 8am-5pm.

Hundreds of hotels, B&Bs, and campgrounds cluster in this area. Don't search for accommodations without stopping by the **Pennsylvania Dutch Visitors Bureau Information Center,** 501 Greenfield Rd. (299-8901), on the east side of Lancaster City just off Rte. 30. The bureau has walls of brochures and free phone lines to most area inns and campsites. Save $2 and avoid their film. (Open mid-May to early Sept. Sun.-Thurs. 8am-6pm, Fri.-Sat. 8am-7pm.) Three youth hostels on the county's eastern edge have cheap beds (check-out 9:30am; curfew 11pm; $7, nonmembers $10). Try the **Bowmansville Youth Hostel (AYH),** P.O. Box 157, Bowmansville 17507, on Rte. 625 at Maple Grove Rd. (215-445-4831). Close to though not easily accessible from I-76, this hostel is the most convenient of the three. The owners are extraordinarily friendly and helpful and the facilities are excellent, complete with kitchen and lounge. Take bus #12 to New Holland (last bus at 5:20pm) and walk or hitch the remaining 6 mi. The owners will also pick you up at Youer's Market (a #12 bus stop) if you call ahead. By car take Rte. 23 to Rte. 625 north. The **Marsh Creek Youth Hostel (AYH),** P.O. Box 376, E. Reeds Rd., Lyndel 19354 (215-458-5881), in Marsh Creek State Park, proves a challenge to find, but the well-kept house lies on a gorgeous lake. Amtrak stops in Downington 5 mi. away on its Philadelphia-Lancaster route. Call ahead and the owners will pick you up for $5. **Downington Cab** (269-3000) charges about $12. Fifteen mi. east, the **Geigertown Youth Hostel (AYH),** P.O. Box 49, Geigertown 19523 (215-286-9537; open March 2-Nov. 30), lies near French Creek State Park off Rte. 82. Though the area is beautiful, the hostel's remote location and ho-hum facilities may not merit the trip—the bunkrooms are musty and less-than-immaculate. Transportation from Reading, 15 mi. away, might be arranged if you call ahead.

There seem to be as many campgrounds as cows in this lush countryside. The closest year-round facility is **Old Millstream Camping Manor,** 2249 U.S. 30 E. (299-2314), 4 mi. east of Lancaster City. (Office open daily 8am-9pm. Sites $14, with hookup $17.) **Roamers Retreat,** 5005 Lincoln Hwy. (442-4287 or 800-525-5605), off U.S. 30 7½ mi. east of Rte. 896, opens only from April to October. (For reservations, call or write RD #1, P.O. Box 41B, Kinzers 17535. Sites $14.50, with hookup $16.) **Shady Grove,** P.O. Box 28, Adamstown 19501 (215-484-4225), on Rte. 272 at Rte. 897, has 80 sites with electricity ($15).

Greyhound/Trailways, 22 W. Clay St. (397-4861; open daily 7am-5:15pm) runs four buses per day between Lancaster City and Philadelphia (2 hr., $9). **Amtrak,** 53 McGovern Ave. (800-872-7245; reservations 24 hr.) makes the same trip (7 per day, 1 hr., $10.50). Lancaster City has its own bus system, **Red Rose Transit,** 47 N. Queen St. (397-4246), serving the city and the immediate countryside. Pick up route maps at the office. (Base fare 75¢, seniors free off-peak and Sat.-Sun.) The **ZIP code** for Lancaster City is 17604; the **area code** is 717.

Near Lancaster County

Milton S. Hershey, a Mennonite resident of eastern Pennsylvania's farms, failed in his first several jaunts into the business world. Then he found chocolate. Today the company that bears his name wonkas the world's largest chocolate factory in **Hershey** just across the northeastern border of Lancaster. Here street lights are shaped like candy kisses, streets named Chocolate and Cocoa. East of town at **Hershey Park** (800-437-7439), the **Chocolate World Visitors Center** (534-4900) presents a free, automated tour through a simulated chocolate factory. After viewing the processing of the cacao bean from tropical forests through the Oompas to final packaging, visitors emerge into a pavilion full of chocolate cookies, chocolate candy, chocolate milk, and Hershey sportswear—all for sale, of course. (Open daily 9am-6:45pm; early Sept. to mid-June 9am-4:45pm.)

Though Hershey Park amusement center has fairly unimpressive rides, meeting a walking talking Reese's cup just may be worth the hefty admission. (Open late May-early Sept. daily 10:30am-10pm. Admission $20, seniors $12.50, ages 4-8 $7. After 5pm $14. Parking $2.) Camp 8 mi. from Hershey and 15 mi. from Lancaster City at **Ridge Run Campground,** 867 Schwanger Rd., Elizabethtown 17022 (367-3454). Schwanger Rd. connects Rte. 230 and Rte. 283. (Sites $14.) **Greyhound/Trailways** (397-4861) goes to Hershey from Lancaster City (1 per day, 3 hr., $18), stopping at 337 W. Chocolate St..

Gettysburg

In November 1863, four months after 7000 men died in the Civil War's bloodiest battle, President Abraham Lincoln arrived in Gettysburg to dedicate a national cemetery—in a two-minute speech, rumored to have been written on the back of an envelope, Lincoln urged preservation of the union in one of the greatest orations in U.S. history. Lincoln's *Gettysburg Address* and the sheer enormity of the battle which prompted him to write it have established Gettysburg as the most famous battlefield in U.S. history. Each year, thousands of visitors heed Honest Abe's call to "resolve that these dead shall not have died in vain" and visit these Pennsylvania fields. The three-day battle (July 1-3, 1863) involved 170,000 soldiers who managed to shoot at each other across quite a large area; fields such as Valley of Death, Devil's Den, Bloody Run, and Cemetery Hill sprout a forest of monuments to those who fought.

Before attacking Gettysburg's swarms of Civil War memorabilia (including chess sets), get your bearings at the **National Park Visitors Information Center,** 1 mi. south of town on Washington St. (Bus #15; 334-1124; open daily 8am-6pm, Labor Day-Memorial Day 8am-5pm). Let the free map guide your tour by car or bike, or pay a park guide to show you the sights ($17 for a 2-hr. tour). On foot, forget about seeing the battlefield and concentrate on the worthwhile attractions around the park. A narrated **Electrical Map** presentation (every 45 min.) clearly shows the troop movements and action during the battle on a scale model of the fields (show $2, seniors $1.50, children free).

The exact spot of Lincoln's speech remains something of a mystery (he spoke somewhere in the national cemetery across from the visitors center) but the document itself is on display in the **Cyclorama Center** next to the visitors center. (Open daily 9am-5pm.) For an excellent perspective of the area, walk over to the **National Tower** (334-6754), whose high-speed elevators whisk you up 300 ft. for a spectacular view. (Open daily 9am-7:30pm. Admission $3.75, seniors $3.25, children $1.75.)

The **Eisenhower Farm,** where the 34th U.S. President spent his retirement years, adjoins the park's west side. Donated by the Eisenhower family, the farm is now a national historic site. Buy tickets and pick up the shuttle next door to the visitors center. The tour lasts about an hour. (Buses run every 15 min. Memorial Day-Labor Day daily 9am-4:15pm; Oct.-Dec. and Feb.-May Wed.-Sun. 9am-4:15pm. Tour $2.25, children 75¢.)

Contemporary Gettysburg may be an avatar of tackiness in many ways, but its eateries remain classy and affordable. The **Dutch Cupboard,** 523 Baltimore, serves up Pennsylvania Dutch specialties like *schnitz un knepp* (dried apples cooked with dumplings, $6.25) and the famous shoo fly pie (brown sugar, flour, special spices, and 2 kinds of molasses; $1.25). (Open daily 11am-9pm.) The candle-lit **Springhouse Tavern,** 89 Steinwehr Ave. (334-2100), lies in the basement of the Dobben House, Gettysburg's first building (1776), and an Underground Railroad shelter for runaway African slaves in the Civil War. Try a salamagundi (greens, ham, turkey, eggs, and cheeses, $5.25) or the "ordinary" (soup, salad, homemade bread and wine, $5.25).

The best place to sleep in Gettysburg remains the roomy and cheerful **Gettysburg Youth Hostel,** 27 Chambersburg St. (334-1020), on U.S. 30 just west of Lincoln Sq. in the center of town. (Kitchen, stereo, living room. Open 5-11pm. Check-out 9:30am. $7, nonmembers $10. Sleepsacks required.) The remarkably friendly hostel usually has space, but when you're lusting for a motel, the **Gettysburg Travel Council,** 35 Carlisle St., Lincoln Sq. (334-6274), has a full line of brochures—as well as maps and information on local attractions. The **Holland Tourist Court,** 2700 York Rd. (334-4380), 5 mi. east of town on U.S. 30, has six spacious singles and doubles from $28. There are several **campgrounds** in the area. Just 1 mi. south on Rte. 134 is **Artillery Ridge,** 610 Tarrytown Rd. (334-1288), which also runs a riding stable. (Sites $12.50 for 2 people, with hookup $15. Each additional person $2.) **Moyers Mountain Retreat,** in the delta of U.S. 15 and 30, has a heated outdoor pool and paths that connect to the **Appalachian Trail** (800-955-0208; sites $12 for 2 people, metered charge for electricity, extra person $2). Take 15 north to 94 north; the retreat is on the right.

Gettysburg orates in south-central Pennsylvania, off U.S. 15 about 30 mi. south of Harrisburg. Unfortunately, when the Union and Confederacy decided to go at each other here, they didn't have the traveler's convenience in mind. **Greyhound** has no station in town—they run one bus daily from Harrisburg (232-4251) that stops in front of the visitors center ($18).

The **post office** is at 155 Buford Ave. (337-3781; open Mon.-Fri. 8am-4:30pm, Sat. 8:30am-12:30pm). Gettysburg's **ZIP code** is 17325; the **area code** is 717.

Ohiopyle State Park

Hidden away in the forgotten landscapes of southwestern Pennsylvania lie some of the loveliest forests in the East, lifted by steep hills and cut by cascading rivers. Native Americans dubbed this part of the state "Ohiopehhle" ("white frothy water"), because of the grand Youghiogheny River Gorge (pronounced yock-a-gay-nee; "The Yock" to locals); the river provides the focal point of Pennsylvania's Ohiopyle State Park. The park's 18,000 acres supply hiking, fishing, hunting, and a complete range of winter activities, but the most popular activity is whitewater rafting along the river.

Lined up in a row on Rte. 381 in "downtown" Ohiopyle are four outfitters: **White Water Adventurers** (329-8531 or 800-992-7238); **Wilderness Voyageurs** (329-5517 or 800-272-4141); **Laurel Highlands River Tours** (329-8531 or 800-472-3846); and **Mountain Streams and Trails** (329-8810 or 800-245-4090). Guided trips on the Yock vary dramatically in price ($20-70 per person per day), depending on season, day of week, and difficulty. If you're an experienced river rat (or if you just happen to *enjoy* flipping boats) any of the above companies will rent you equipment. (Rafts about $9 per person, canoes $15, "duckies"—inflatable kayaks—about $15.) **Youghiogheny Outfitters** (329-4549) may be a bit cheaper since they do rental business only.

In order to do just about anything in the river you'll need a launch permit. They're free but get snatched up quickly. The **Park Information Center,** just off Rte. 381 on Dinnerbell Rd. (P.O. Box 105; 329-8591) recommends calling at least 30 days in advance. The 200 **campsites** ($7) that the office handles also require advanced booking—especially for summer weekends. (Open daily 8am-4pm; Nov.-April Mon.-Fri. 8am-4pm.) Fishing licenses ($20), required for ages 16 and over, are available at the Falls Market (see below).

Motels around Ohiopyle are sparse but the excellent **Ohiopyle Youth Hostel,** P.O. Box 99 (329-4476) sits right in the center of town off Rte. 381. Sue Moore has 24 bunks, a kitchen, a great yard, 6 cats, and 2 dogs—all for $6 per night, nonmembers $9. (Check-in 6-9pm.) **Falls Market and Overnight Rooms** (329-4973), on Rte. 381 in the center of town, rents singles ($22) and doubles ($30) with shared baths. The downstairs store has a decent selection of groceries and a snack-bar/restaurant. (Burgers $1.25, pancakes and bacon $2.25. Open daily 7am-7pm.)

Ohiopyle is on Rte. 381, 64 mi. southeast of Pittsburgh via Rte. 51 and U.S. 41. The closest public transport is to Uniontown, a large town about 20 mi. to the west on U.S. 40. **Greyhound/Trailways** serves **Uniontown** from Pittsburgh (3 per day, 1½ hr., $9). The **post office** (329-8650) is open Monday through Friday 7:30am to 4:30pm and Saturday 7:30am to 11:30am. The **ZIP code** is 15470. The **area code** for Ohiopyle and the surrounding area is 412.

Allegheny National Forest

Containing half a million acres of woodland stretching 40 mi. south of the New York state border, The Allegheny National Forest offers year-round recreational opportunities such as hunting, fishing, and trail biking. The forest makes an excellent detour on a cross-state jaunt on I-80, as its southern border is only 20 mi. from the interstate. A good first step is the **Kinzua Point Information Center** (726-1291), on Rte. 59. Friendly park employees have information on camping and recreation throughout the park. (Open May 27-Sept. 2 Sun.-Thurs. 9:30am-5:30pm, Fri.-Sat. 9:30am-8pm.) The forest divides into four quadrants, each with its own ranger station that provides maps and information about activities and facilities within its region. (Southwest: Marienville Ranger District (927-6628; open Mon.-Sat. 7am-5pm). Northwest: Sheffield Ranger District (968-3232; open Mon.-Fri. 8am-4pm). Northeast: Bradford Ranger District (362-4613; open daily 8am-4:30pm). Southeast: Ridgway Ranger District (776-6172; open Mon.-Fri. 7:30am-4pm). Swimming and beach passes for the park are available at the ranger stations ($2 per car). There is no charge for picnic sites or boat launches.

Camping facilities in the park are abundant and generally open from March to October. A "host" is available at most sights to assist campers and answer questions. (Sites $5-12, depending on the location and the time of year.) **Tracy Ridge** in the Bradford district and **Heart's Content** in the Sheffield district are particularly pretty. You can call 800-283-2267 to reserve sites, but the park keeps 50% as first come, first serve. You also don't even need a site to camp in the Allegheny; stay 1500 ft. from a major road or body of water and you can pitch a tent anywhere. **Kinzua Boat Rentals and Marina** on Rte. 59 (726-1650) rents canoes ($15 per hr., $18 per day), rowboats ($8.50 per hr., $20 per day), and motorboats ($12 per hr., $50 per day). Ask the rangers about sites accessible only by water.

From whatever direction you approach the Allegheny Forest, you'll encounter a small, rustic community near the park that offers groceries and accommodations. **Ridgway**, 25 mi. from I-80 (exit 16) at the southeastern corner, is especially scenic. **The Original,** 161 Main St., complete with jukebox, has great "baked" subs for $2.50-3 and burgers with fries for $2. (Open Mon.-Thurs. 11am-11pm, Fri.-Sat. 11am-midnight.) You can eat in the old train depot, now **Crispy's Fried Chicken,** at the intersection of Main St. and Montmorenci Rd. Two eggs with homefries and toast cost $1.50. (Open daily 7am-9pm.) The town of **Warren,** at the northeastern fringe of the forest where Rtes. 6 and 62 meet, has comparable services.

Greyhound Trailways serves Warren and Ridgway from Pittsburgh (about $28) as well as also from Philadelphia and Buffalo, NY. **Hitchhikers** should try to catch a ride to the forest at the bus station. Fortunately, U.S. 219 is a busy country road abuzz with truck traffic. When driving inside the forest yourself, be very careful during wet weather: about half the region is served only by dirt roads. The **area code** for this region is 814.

Pittsburgh

Though Charles Dickens called the city "Hell with the lid off" a century ago and the Steelers football team no longer wins the Superbowl, Pittsburgh today has much more to offer than steel mills belching smoke. The factories have been replaced by serene skyscrapers and colorful city parks; climb **Duquesne Incline** to the top of

Mt. Washington for a perfect view of this surprisingly beautiful city. Bridges cast geometric patterns on Pittsburgh's three famous rivers (the Monongahela, Allegheny, and Ohio), and the skyline stretches from the awe-inspiring **Cathedral of Learning** to the **PPG Place,** a startling glass tower with spires oddly imitating the cathedral's Gothic architecture.

Practical Information

Emergency: 911.

Visitor Information: Pittsburgh Convention and Visitors Bureau, 4 Gateway Ctr. (281-7711), downtown in a little glass building on Liberty Ave., across from the Hilton. Offers a 24-hr., up-to-date recording of events (391-6840), and aid for international visitors who don't speak English (624-7800). They city maps won't get you past downtown. AAA (for members only) and Travelers Aid have better maps (see below for both). Open May-Oct. Mon.-Fri. 9:30am-5pm, Sat.-Sun. 9:30am-3pm; Nov.-March Mon.-Fri. 9:30am-5pm, Sat. 9:30am-3pm.

Travelers Aid: Two locations; Greyhound Bus Terminal, 11th St. and Liberty Ave. (281-5474), and the airport (264-7110). Maps, tourist advice, and help for stranded travelers. Open Mon.-Fri. 9am-9pm, Sat.-Sun. 9am-5pm.

American Express, 2 PPG Place on Market Square (391-3202; for lost or stolen checks 800-221-7282). Open Mon.-Fri. 9am-5pm.

Greater Pittsburgh International Airport: 778-2525, 15 mi. west of downtown by I-279 and Rte. 60 in Moon Township. Serves most major airlines. **Airline Transportation Company,** 471-2250. Serves most downtown hotels (daily 5am-10pm, $9), Oakland (daily 7am-8pm, $9.50) and Monroeville (daily 6am-7pm, $13).

Amtrak: Liberty and Grant Ave. (800-872-7245 for reservations; 471-6170 for station information), on the northern edge of downtown next to Greyhound and the post office. Safe and very clean inside, but be cautious about walking from here to the city center at night. Open 24 hr. Ticket office open daily 8:30am-4pm, 5-5:15pm, 10:30pm-7:15am. To: Philadelphia (2 per day, 7½ hr., $60); New York (2 per day, 9 hr., $83); Chicago (2 per day, 9 hr., $75).

Greyhound/Trailways: 11th St. and Liberty Ave. (391-2300), on the northern outskirts of downtown. Large and fairly clean with police on duty. Station and ticket office open 24 hr. To: Philadelphia (7 hr., Mon.-Thurs. $42, Fri.-Sun. $46); New York (9 per day, 9-11 hr., Mon.-Thurs. $72, Fri.-Sun. $75); Chicago (4 per day, 9-11 hr., Mon.-Thurs. $49, Fri.-Sun. $59).

Public Transport: Port Authority of Allegheny County (PAT): 231-7000; bus information 231-5707. 165 bus routes. Fare $1.10, daily pass $4.50, weekend family pass $3.25. Tiny, 4-stop **subway** downtown is free. Schedules and maps at most department stores and in the Community Interest Showcase section of the yellow pages.

Taxi: Yellow Cab Company, 665-8100. **People's Cab Company,** 681-3131. **Diamond Cab,** 824-0984.

Car Rental: Rent-A-Wreck, 1200 Liberty Ave. (488-3440). $23 per day, 50 free mi., 15¢ each additional mi. Insurance $8. Open Mon.-Sat. 8am-5pm. Must be 21 with major credit card or a $150 cash deposit. **Alamo,** 930 Broadway Rd. (800-327-9633) airport area. Reserve 24 hr. in advance for $24 per day rate with unlimited mi. Optional insurance $11. Must be 21 with credit card. Under 25 surcharge $6.

American Automobile Assn. (AAA), at Wood St. and Oliver Ave. (338-4300). Open Mon.-Fri. 8:30am-3pm.

Help Lines: General Help Line, 255-1155. Open 24 hr. **Rape Action Hotline,** 765-2731. Open 24 hr. **Center for Victims of Violent Crime,** 1520 Penn Ave. (392-8582). Open 24 hr. **Persad Center, Inc.,** 441-0857, emergencies 392-2472. A counseling service for the gay community.

Post Office: 7th and Grant St. (642-4472; general delivery 642-4478). Open Mon.-Fri. 7am-6pm, Sat. 7am-2:30pm. **ZIP code:** 15230.

Area Code: 412.

Pittsburgh lies in southwestern Pennsylvania on I-79, 386 mi. from New York City, 308 mi. from Philadelphia, and 247 mi. from Washington, DC. The downtown area is a triangle formed by two rivers—the Allegheny on the north and the Monongahela to the south—coming together to form a third, the Ohio. Parallel to the Monongahela, streets in the downtown triangle number 1 through 7.

Accommodations and Camping

Reasonable accommodations are easy to find in Pittsburgh. Downtown is fairly safe, even at night; Pittsburgh has the lowest crime rate for a city of its size in the country.

Point Park College Youth Hostel (AYH), 201 Wood St. (392-3824), 8 blocks from the Greyhound Station. Catch a bus on Liberty Ave. or walk 5 blocks downtown on Grant St., take a right and walk 3 blocks on Forbes Ave. until Wood St., then turn left and walk 2 blocks. Closer to a hotel than a hostel—clean rooms with 2 beds and private bath. Office hours 8am-4pm. Check-in until 11pm (tell the guards you're a hosteler). Members only, $7.50. No kitchen but all-you-can-eat breakfast ($2.30) served in the 3rd-floor cafeteria 7-9:30am. Open early May-late Aug.

Carnegie-Mellon University, 1060 Morewood St. (268-2939), at Forbes in Oakland 2 blocks east of Craig St. Old-style dorm rooms, some with private baths. Excellent location in the heart of college town. Office hours Mon.-Fri. 8am-5pm. Check-in anytime with reservations. Singles $15. Doubles $20. Non-students: singles $18, doubles $25. Take $5 off per night for a week's stay. Open summer months only.

St. Regis Residence for Women, 50 Congress St. (281-9888), in the red brick church directly opposite the Civic Arena on Wylie St. past the Chatham Center. A 10-min. walk from the bus terminal, but take a cab at night. A Catholic-run home for women working and studying in the Pittsburgh area. Singles $10. Give them a day's notice.

Red Roof Inn, 6404 Stubenville Pike on Rte. 60 (787-7870), east of the Rte. 22-Rte. 30 junction near the airport. From the Greyhound station, take bus #26F. Singles $34. Doubles $41. Reservations necessary summer weekends.

The nearest campsite is the **Pittsburgh North Campground**, 6610 Mars Rd., Evans City 16033 (776-1150), 20 mi. from downtown. Take I-79 to the Mars exit. Facilities include tents and swimming. (Sites $15 for 2 people, extra adults $3, extra children $2. Hookup $2.50.) **Bethany Christian Campground**, R.D. #1, P.O. Box 217, Washington 15301 (483-6235), lies 20 mi. south of Pittsburgh on I-79.

Food

Elegant and expensive restaurants trisect Pittsburgh's inner triangle. Those in the South Side's **Station Square** are chic, while those in **Allegheny Square** to the north provide the overpriced fast food typical of new urban malls. On the East Side, the golf club "does" lunch on Walnut Street in Shadyside. Aside from the pizza joint/bars downtown, **Oakland** is your best bet for a good inexpensive meal. Forbes Ave., around the University of Pittsburgh, is packed with collegiate watering holes and cafés. Many of Pittsburgh's ethnic groups have stayed in the pockets where they originally settled, giving each neighborhood its own distinctive cuisine.

Original Hot Dog Shops, Inc., 3901 Forbes Ave., at Bouquet St. in Oakland. A rowdy, greasy Pittsburgh institution with the best dogs in town. Call it "the O" and they'll think you're a local. Dishes out 30,000 pounds of fries a week with dogs (from $1), pizza (slices $1), and burgers ($1.50). 50 kinds of beer including local brew Iron City. Open Sun.-Thurs. 9am-4:30pm, Fri.-Sat. 9am-6am.

Alexander's Pasta Express, 5104 S. Liberty Ave., in Bloomfield. Take bus #86A ("East Hills") to Liberty and S. Aiken Ave. An unpretentious and cozy Italian-American restaurant and bar. Great spinach and cheese ravioli with a meatball $5.50, New York strip steak $7. Open Mon.-Sat. 11am-12:30am, Sun. 11am-10:30pm.

Hot Licks, 5520 Walnut St., in the Theater Mall. Take bus #71B or D down 5th Ave., get off at Aiken, and walk north 2 blocks to Walnut. Calzones, subs, salads, and pizzas with a baseball theme. "Fowl Ball" chicken pizza $7. Nightly specials include 2-for-1 pizza on "Tequila Tuesday" and Wed. "Vodka and Wing" night. Barbecue chicken on a mesquite grill $5.25-8. A good stop before heading upstairs for jazz at the Balcony (see Nightlife below). Another, larger location at 1500 Washington Rd., in South Hills Mt. Lebanon. Take bus 41C.

Both open Mon.-Thurs. 11:30am-midnight, Fri.-Sat. 11:30am-2am, Sun. noon-midnight.
Kitchen closes 1 hr. earlier.

Suzie's Greek Specialties, 130 6th St. downtown. Specializes in homemade Greek dishes,
bread, and pastries ($6-8). Open Mon.-Fri. 11am-9pm, Sat. 4-11pm.

George Aiken's, 300 Forbes Ave., in Oakland. A local favorite for fried chicken and burgers
($1.75). Breakfast specials $1.50. Two dogs for $1. Open Mon.-Sat. 6am-9pm, Sun. 7am-7pm.

Bangkok Express, 410 1st. Ave., near Smithfield St. downtown. Tasty, spicy, Thai cuisine
served amid sparse decor. Lunches $5 with entree, soup, egg roll, and rice. Open Mon.-Fri.
11am-3pm.

Sights

   The **Golden Triangle,** formed by the Allegheny and Monongahela River, is home
to **Point State Park** and its famous 200-ft. fountain. The **Fort Pitt Blockhouse and
Museum** (281-9285) in the park dates back to the French and Indian War. (Open
Wed.-Sat. 9am-5pm, Sun. noon-5pm. Admission $1.50, seniors $1, children 50¢.)
PPG Place, on Stanwix St., is a high-rise complex with glass towers pointed like
church spires. (Open Mon.-Fri. 10am-6pm, Sat. 10am-5pm.) The square in front
features a musical fountain. Check the outdoor message board for times of free performances, ranging from Scottish brass bands to jazz. About 3 mi. east along the
Blvd. of the Allies in **Schenley Park,** the **Phipps Conservatory** (622-6914) conserves
2½ acres of happiness for the flower fanatic, bounded by Edwardian homes and
borders. (Open daily 9am-5pm. Admission $1.50, seniors and children 50¢, $1 more
for shows. Reserve tours at 622-6958). Founded in 1787, the **University of Pittsburgh** (624-4141; for tours call 624-7488) now stands in the shadow of the 42-story
Cathedral of Learning (624-6000) at Bigelow Blvd. between Forbes and 5th Ave.
The "cathedral," an academic building dedicated in 1934, features 22 "nationality
classrooms" designed and decorated by artisans from each of Pittsburgh's ethnic
traditions. **Carnegie-Mellon University** (268-2000) hyphenates right down the
street.
   Other city sights lie across the three rivers from the Golden Triangle. Northward,
across the Allegheny, steal a look at **Three Rivers Stadium,** where the Steelers and
Pirates play ball. The **Buhl Science Center** (237-3333), in **Allegheny Square,** has
special hands-on exhibits and sky shows that entertain both children and adults.
(Open Sun.-Thurs. 1-5pm, Fri. 1-9:30pm, Sat. 10am-5pm. Admission $4, ages under
18 $2.) To the west of Allegheny Sq. flies the tropical **Pittsburgh Aviary** (323-7234;
open daily 9am-4:30pm; admission $2, seniors and ages under 12 50¢; take bus
#16D or the Ft. Duquesne bridge).
   The **Pittsburgh Zoo** in Highland Park (441-6262; take "Negley" bus #71A or
"Highland" 71B) has a children's zoo, a reptile building, an aquarium, an Asian
forest, and an African savanna. (Open summer Mon.-Fri. 9am-5pm, Sat. 10am-
5pm, Sun. 10am-6pm; off-season Mon.-Fri. 9am-5pm, Sat. 10am-5pm. Admission
$3, seniors and children $1. Parking $2.)
   To get to the **South Side,** take the Smithfield Street Bridge across the Monongahela River. The star attraction here is **Station Square,** a cleverly renovated railway
terminal featuring shops and restaurants. The **Gateway Clipper Fleet** (355-7979;
tickets 355-7980) shares the riverbank and offers narrated sight-seeing cruises on
the three rivers. (Fare from $5.25.) **Mount Washington;** towers behind Station Sq.;
the trolleys **Duquesne** and **Monongahela Inclines** ascend the slope to an observation
platform. Even athletic types should climb the hill on the trolley to Grandview Ave.
along the edge of the mountain. (Open Mon.-Sat. 5:30am-12:45am, Sun. and holidays 8:45am-midnight. Fare $1.)
   Two of America's greatest financial legends, Andrew Carnegie and Henry Clay
Frick, made their fortunes in Pittsburgh. Their bequests to the city have greatly
enriched its cultural scene. The most spectacular of Carnegie's gifts are the art and
natural history museums, together called **The Carnegie,** at 4400 Forbes Ave. (622-
3131,) across the street from the Cathedral of Learning. The natural history section
is famous for its 500 dinosaur specimens, including an 84-ft. mammoth named for

the philanthropist himself—**Oiplodocus Carnegii.** The art museum's modern wing houses a collection strong in impressionist, post-impressionist, and 20th-century works. Every three years, The Carnegie hosts "The International," one of the country's oldest recurring contemporary art exhibits, next scheduled for 1993. (Open Tues.-Sat. 10am-5pm, Sun. 1-5pm. Take any bus to Oakland and get off at the Cathedral of Learning.)

While most know Henry Clay Frick for his art collection in New York, the **Frick Art Museum** 7227 Reynolds St., Point Breeze (371-0600), displays some of his early, less famous acquisitions. The permanent collection contains Italian, Flemish, and French works from the 13th through 18th centuries. **Clayton,** the Frick family mansion, opened to the public in the fall of 1989. Stroll through the two-acre gardens and the recently restored greenhouse and playhouse. (Open Wed.-Sat. 10am-5:30pm, Sun. noon-6pm. Free. Mansion tours $4.50. Take bus #67A, F, E, C, or 71C.)

Entertainment and Nightlife

Pittsburgh's metamorphosis from industrial to corporate town has happily resulted in the revitalization of its artistic seam. Pick up *In Pittsburgh* for free up-to-date entertainment listings and racy personals. The internationally acclaimed **Pittsburgh Symphony Orchestra** performs October through May at **Heinz Hall,** 600 Penn Ave. downtown; it gives free summer evening concerts outdoors at Point State Park (392-4000 for tickets and information). The **Pittsburgh Public Theater** (323-8200) is widely renowned but tickets cost a pretty penny: visitors with thin wallets should check out the **Three Rivers Shakespeare Festival** (624-4101), at University of Pittsburgh's Steven Foster Memorial Theater, near Forbes Ave. and Bigelow Blvd. downtown. The corps, consisting of students and professionals, performs late May to mid-August. Seniors and students can line up a half hour before showtime for 1/2-price tickets. Box office (624-7529) open 10am to showtime and Monday 10am to 4pm. (Tickets Tues.-Thurs. $15, Fri.-Sat. $18.) All-student casts perform with the **Young Company** at City Theater (tickets $9). The **Three Rivers Arts Festival** (261-7040 or 481-7040) takes place during three weeks in June, in Gateway Center, Point State Park, Allegheny Courthouse, and Station Square. The festival gives free exhibitions and demonstrations of painting, sculpture, and crafts, live performances of plays and music.

You can wet your whistle or flex your dance muscles at one of Pittsburgh's many nightspots. **Peter's Pub,** 116 Oakland Ave. (681-7465), is a raucous hangout frequented by U. Pitt's athletic teams. (Beer 75¢. Open Mon.-Sat. 11am-2am.) Also near the university is **C.J. Barney's Wooden Key,** 3907 Forbes Ave., absolutely jammed on Thursday, when $3 buys all-you-can-drink from 9pm to midnight. (Open Mon.-Sat. 11am-2am.) The jazz scene thrives in Pittsburgh: hear it nightly at Shadyside's **Balcony,** Theater Mall, 5520 Walnut St. (687-0110). (Live jazz Mon.-Thurs. 8:30pm-12:30am, Fri.-Sun. 9pm-1am. No cover. Take bus #71B or D down 5th Ave. to Aiken and walk north to Walnut St.) Or, if you don't mind the distance, head to the **James Street Tavern,** 422 Foreland Ave., North Side (323-2222). The restaurant upstairs is steep, but after 9pm on Thursday and Friday the jazz downstairs will amaze you. (No cover.)

Near Pittsburgh

The U.S. is loaded with celebrations of General and President George Washington, the founding father with the best rep and the worst teeth. **Fort Necessity,** on U.S. 40 near Rte. 381 (329-5512), necessitates a rare opportunity to remember when good ol' George got his cherry tree butt kicked. The site of Washington's surrender to the French in a battle that precipitated the French and Indian War, Fort Necessity has been rebuilt and features a half-hour talk (8 per day) by historians dressed up as English and French soldiers, in addition to a musket-firing demonstration. Chop down the door of the **Visitor Information Center** (open daily 9am-5:30pm;

Labor Day-Memorial Day 10:30am-5pm; admission $1, families $3). After his defeat, a promoted Washington regrouped forces to defeat the French in 1958 at **Fort Ligonier,** at the junction of Rte. 30 and 711, 60 mi. north of Necessity. (Open April-Oct. daily 9:30am-5pm. Admission $4, seniors $3, children $2.) Various groups reenact battles and camp life on some summer weekends.

Virginia

Virginia's disproportionate role in U.S. history began when the first successful British colonists landed at Jamestown in 1607. Thirteen years later, the first African slaves in North America arrived at Jamestown, initiating years of White "Tidewater" aristocracy and over three centuries of African American oppression. Thomas Jefferson, James Madison, and their peers crafted the Bill of Rights, proposing that "all men are created equal" while continuing to own African slaves. Yet, along with Massachusetts, Virginia led the colonists' revolt against England; here, at Yorktown, the British finally surrendered. Virginia is also the birthplace of eight U.S. presidents, including the first, George Washington. During most of the Civil War, however, Virginia worked against the Union, providing the Confederate capital of Richmond, as well as more industry, soldiers, and money than any other Southern state.

Today Virginia advertises its long, often polarized history in a host of Confederate street names, Robert E. Lee parks, fixed-up plantations, museums, and battlefields. Such nostalgia climaxes in Colonial Williamsburg, where guides in colonial costume show sweating tourists around the restored 18th-century capital. Meanwhile, near the nation's modern capital, proliferating suburbs and corporate headquarters coax northern Virginia—Fairfax County, Arlington, and Alexandria—into the Information Age. Much of the rest of the state remains farmland, with tobacco a major crop. Richmond provides nostalgia, the Blue Ridge Mountains purvey nature. In Charlottesville, gentility smothers intellect just as the naval base overwhelms Norfolk. This self-consciously Southern state may not have left behind the worst of its history, although in 1989, Virginia elected L. Douglas Wilder by a tiny margin as the nation's first African American governor.

Practical Information

Capital: Richmond.

Tourist Information: Virginia Division of Tourism, Bell Tower, Capitol Sq., 101 N. 9th St., Richmond 23219 (800-847-4882 or 786-4484). **Division of State Parks,** 1201 State Office Bldg., Richmond 23219 (226-1981). For the free **Virginia Accommodations Directory,** write to Virginia Travel Council, 7415 Brook Rd., P.O. Box 15067, Richmond 23227.

Time Zone: Eastern. **Postal Abbreviation:** VA.

Shenandoah National Park

Before 1926, when Congress authorized the establishment of Shenandoah National Park, the area held a series of rocky, threadbare farms along the Blue Ridge Mountains. Thirteen years later, the farmers and their families had been booted off their lands and the area returned to its "natural" state. Forests replaced fields, wild deer and bears devoured cows and pigs, and a two-lane highway, Skyline Drive, paved over dirt roads, complete with intermittent scenic overlooks where Sunday drivers could stop and gawk.

Today, such gawking comes naturally in Shenandoah; on clear days drivers and hikers can look out over miles of unspoiled ridges and treetops. In summer, the cool mountain air offers a respite from Virginia's typical heat and humidity. Go early in June to see mountain laurel blooming in the highlands. In fall Skyline Drive and its lodges instead grow choked with tourists enjoying the magnificent fall foliage.

Practical Information

Emergency (in park): 703-999-2227, or contact the nearest ranger. Collect calls accepted. You must dial the area code.

Park Information: 999-2226 daily 9am-5pm; 999-2227 for 24-hr. recorded message. Mailing address: Superintendent, Shenandoah National Park, Rte. 4, P.O. Box 348, Luray 22835.

Visitor Information: Dickey Ridge Visitors Center, mile 4.6 (635-3566), closest to the north entrance. Daily interpretative programs. Open April-Oct. daily 9am-5pm. Byrd Visitors Center, mile 50 (999-2243, ext. 281), in the center of the park. Movie and ʼ ʼuseum explain the history of the Blue Ridge Range and its mountain culture. Open March-Dec. daily 9am-5pm; Jan.-Feb. weekends only. Both stations offer changing exhibits on the park, free pamphlets detailing short hikes, daily posted weather updates, and ranger-led nature hikes.

Area Code: 703.

From its northern entrance at Front Royal to Rockfish Gap, 105 mi. farther south, Skyline Drive hugs the spine of the Blue Ridge and winds through Shenandoah National Park. The posted speed limit, 35 mph, gets tedious. The drive closes immediately after periods of bad weather. Most facilities hibernate from November through March. (Entrance $5 per vehicle, $2 per hiker, biker, or bus passenger; pass good for 7 days; seniors and disabled free.)

Miles along Skyline Dr. are measured north to south, beginning at Front Royal. There is no public transportation inside Shenandoah. Within the park, hitching opportunities are rare; outside the park, hitching is illegal. Greyhound sends buses to Waynesboro, near the park's southern entrance, twice per day from DC ($32, $60 round-trip), but no bus or train serves Front Royal. Rockfish Gap is only 25 mi. from Charlottesville on Rte. 64. You can also drive to Shenandoah from DC; take Rte. 66 west to 340 south. The 70-minute trip proves scenic in its own right in either direction.

When planning to stay more than a day, purchase the *Park Guide* ($1), a booklet containing all the park regulations, trail lists, and a description of the area's geological history. The *Guide to Skyline Drive* ($4.50) also provides information on accommodations and activities. The free *Shenandoah Overlook* newspaper reports seasonal and weekly events as well as practical information changes within the park. All three publications are available at both visitors centers.

Accommodations and Camping

The park maintains two "lodges"—fancy motels with cabins surrounding them—at Skyland (mile 42) and Big Meadows (mile 51). The more popular Skyland (999-2211 or 800-999-4714) proffers brown-and-green wood-furnished cabins ($38-70 with private bath) that differ little from the motel rooms (from $70 for 2 people). Rates rise in October (for the foliage) and fall $10 in November and December. Skyland closes December 15 through the end of March. Big Meadows (999-2221 or 800-999-4714) offers similar cabins and motel rooms in a smaller but no less crowded complex. (Cabins from $44 for 2 people. Rooms from $66. Extra $6 in Oct. Closed Nov.-April.) Both Skyland and Big Meadows contain restaurants (lunch from $4, dinner from $6). When the cheaper lodgings at Skyland are taken, the well-maintained array of cabins at Lewis Mountain (743-5108 or 800-999-4714), each with front porch and private bath, make the best deal. (One room $47. Two rooms $73. Each additional person $5. Extra $6 in Oct.) All three locations charge $2 more on Friday and Saturday nights. Reservations are usually necessary for all these accommodations, up to six months in advance for the fall season. Call the lodges or write ARA Virginia Sky-Line, P.O. Box 727, Luray 22835.

For cheaper accommodations, stay in Front Royal, at the gateway to the park. The **Skyline Resort Motel**, 622 S. Royal Ave. (635-5354), the closest and cheapest, resorts to huge, clean, lime-green rooms in separate pink stucco blocks. (Singles $23. Doubles $31. Extra $7 weekends.) The **Center City Motel**, 416 S. Royal Ave. (635-4050), has standard singles ($37) and doubles ($43). Reserve rooms for all Front Royal motels a few weeks in advance.

The park service maintains four major campgrounds: **Matthews Arm** (mile 22); **Big Meadows** (mile 51); **Lewis Mountain** (mile 58); and **Loft Mountain** (mile 80). All have stores, laundry facilities, and showers (no hookups). Big Meadows (992-2221), one of the larger sites, offers a wide range of activities like films and hikes; especially popular, reservations are required. (Visit your local Ticketron outlet or write Ticketron, Dept. R., 401 Hackensack Ave., Hackensack, NJ 07601.) The others are allotted on a first come, first served basis. Heavily wooded and uncluttered by mobile homes, Lewis Mountain makes for the happiest tenters. All sites cost $8 except Big Meadows ($10); call either visitors center to check on availability.

Back-country camping is free, but you must obtain a permit at a park entrance, a visitors center, one of the ranger stations, or the park headquarters halfway between Thornton Gap and Luray on U.S. 211. Back-country campers must set up 25 yd. from a water supply and out of sight of any trail, road, overlook, cabin, or other campsite. Since open fires are prohibited, bring cold food or a stove; boil water or drink bottled because some creeks are infected. Illegal camping carries a $50 fine. Hikers on the Appalachian Trail can make use of primitive open shelters, the three-sided structures with stone fireplaces strewn along the trail at approximately 7-mi. intervals. At full shelters, campers will often move over to make room for a new arrival. These shelters are reserved for through hikers with three or more nights in different locations stamped on their camping permits; casual hikers are now banned from them. The **Potomac Appalachian Trail Club** maintains six cabins in backcountry areas of the park. You must reserve in advance by writing to the club at 1718 N St. NW, Washington, DC 20036 (202-638-5306). The cabins contain bunk beds, water, and stoves; you must bring lanterns and food. Weeknight stays cost $3 per person, weekends $14 per group; one party member must be at least 21.

Sights and Activities

Trails criss-cross Shenandoah, the **Appalachian Trail** running the park's length. When your feet will take you no farther, saddle up a horse at the **stables** about a mile south of Skyland (mile 42.6; reservations at Skyland Lodge, 999-2211; open daily 8:30am-2:30pm; $14 per hr.). A yellow blaze marks horse trails, white or blue hikers-only. Bicyclists are prohibited on trails. Get trail maps at visitors centers.

One of the most strenuous hiking trails goes up **Old Rag Mountain**, 5 mi. from mile 45. The 7.2-mi. loop takes you through a tunnel and narrow splits in the rock where you must remove your pack to squirm through. (It's wise to bring a friend along. A thin one, though.) The stupendous view from the rocky summit makes every step of the hike worthwhile. This area, called **Whiteoak Canyon**, contains six spectacular waterfalls. The 5-mi. trail connecting these falls leads to **Limberlost**, a hemlock forest. For an easier hike try the **Dark Hollow Trail**, at mile 51, a ¾-mi. hike to a gorgeous set of falls—the closest falls to Skyline Dr. in the entire park.

Trout fishing is excellent in the rushing waters of **Whiteoak Canyon.** Try to visit in the spring when the water is at its fullest and there are still relatively few campers. Buy a five-day fishing license ($6) at visitors centers and area stores.

Drivers should enjoy **Mary's Rock Tunnel** (mile 32), where the road goes straight through almost 700 ft. of solid rock. One mi. farther north is **Thornton Gap** and its magnificent panorama. From the Matthews Arm campground (mile 22), you can hike up Hogback Mountain or stick to the road and view the twisting Shenandoah River from the **Hogback Overlook** (mile 21).

Take a break from hiking or driving at one of Shenandoah's seven **picnic areas** located at Dickey Ridge (mile 5), Elkwallow (mile 24), Pinnacles (mile 37), Big Meadows (mile 51), Lewis Mountain (mile 58), South River (mile 63), and Loft

Mountain (mile 80). All have tables, fireplaces, water fountains, and comfort stations. When you forget to pack a picnic basket, swing by the **Panorama Restaurant** (mile 31.5) for a meal and a view. (Sandwiches $4. Dinners $6-12. Open April-Nov. daily 9am-7pm.).

Blue Ridge Parkway

If you don't believe that the best things in life are free, this ride could change your mind. The 469 mi. of the Blue Ridge Parkway, continuous with Skyline Drive, run through Virginia and North Carolina connecting the **Shenandoah** and **Great Smoky Mountains National Parks** (see Tennessee). Administered by the National Park Service, the parkway adjoins hiking trails, campsites, and picnic grounds. Every bit as scenic as Skyline Drive, the Parkway remains much wilder and less crowded. From Shenandoah National Park, the road winds south through Virginia's **George Washington National Forest** from Waynesboro southwest to Roanoke. The forest offers spacious campgrounds, canoes for rent, and swimming in cold, clear mountain water at **Shenandoah Lake** (mile 16).

Self-guided nature trails range from the **Mountain Farm Trail** (mile 5.9), a 20-minute hike to a pleasant reconstructed homestead, to the **Hardwood Cove Natural Trail** (mile 167), a three-hour excursion. Of course, real devotees tackle the **Appalachian Trail**, which runs the length of the parkway. The Park Service hosts a variety of ranger-led interpretive activities.

Some of the more spectacular sights on and near the parkway include a 215-ft.-high, 90-ft.-long limestone arch called **Natural Bridge**, which now supports an unnatural highway and hosts unnatural nightly audio-visual shows (800-533-1410, 800-336-5727 outside VA; open daily 8am-dusk; admission $7, seniors $6, children $3.50). Thomas Jefferson bought the site from King George III for 20 shillings; George Washington also initialed it. Look for the "GW loves Martha" blazon still visible today. At **Mabry Mill** (mile 176.1), and **Humpback Rocks** (mile 5.8), you can simulate pioneer life, and at **Crabtree Meadows** (mile 339), you can purchase local crafts.

The **Blue Ridge Country AYH Hostel**, Rte. 2, P.O. Box 449, Galax 24333 (703-236-4962), rests only 100 ft. from the parkway at mile 214.5. (3-night max. stay. $8.25, nonmembers $11.25. For North Carolina hostels, see Asheville and Boone, in North Carolina.) There are nine **campgrounds** along the parkway, each with water and restrooms, located at miles 61, 86, 120, 167, 238, 297, 316, 339, and 409. The fee is $8; reservations are not accepted. Contact the parkway for information on backcountry and winter camping. Camping in the backcountry of the George Washington National Forest is free.

The cities and villages along the parkway offer a range of accommodations. For a complete listing, pick up a *Blue Ridge Parkway Directory* at one of the visitors centers, or the *Virginia Accommodations Directory*. The communities listed have easy access to the parkway and many, such as Asheville and Boone, NC, and Charlottesville, VA, have historic and cultural attractions of their own (see below).

Greyhound/Trailways provides access to the major towns around the Blue Ridge. Buses run to and from Richmond, Roanoke, Waynesboro, and Lexington; a bus serves Buchanan and Natural Bridge between Roanoke and Lexington once per day. For information, contact the station in Charlottesville (see Charlottesville Practical Information) or Greyhound/Trailways, 26 Salem Ave. SW (703-342-6761; open 24 hr.), in Roanoke.

For general information on the parkway, call **visitor information** in North Carolina (704-259-0779 or 704-259-0701). For additional details call the park service in Roanoke, VA (703-982-6458), or in Montebello, VA (703-377-2377). Write for information to **Blue Ridge Parkway Headquarters**, 200 BB&T Bldg., Asheville, NC 28801. Ten **visitors centers** lie along the parkway, plus seven stands where you can pick up brochures. Located at entry points where major highways intersect the Blue Ridge, the centers offer various exhibits, programs, and information facilities. Pick up a free copy of the helpful *Milepost* guide.

In an **emergency** call 800-727-5928 anywhere in VA or NC. Be sure to give your location to the nearest mile.

Charlottesville

This college town in the Blue Ridge foothills proudly bears the stamp of its patron Thomas Jefferson. Monticello, the cleverly constructed classical mansion he designed and then retired to, absorbs floods of tourists. The college "Mr. Jefferson" founded, the University of Virginia (pronounced you-vee-AY), dominates the town economically, geographically, and culturally, supporting both the town's pubs and writers/artists like Pulitzer Prize-winning Rita Dove. Even C-ville itself, low-lying, friendly, hip and compact, seems to reflect the third President's dream of well-informed, culturally aware citizens who choose to live close to the land. The Corner neighborhood near UVA has bookstores to browse and countless cheap eateries, but most commercial action and nightlife takes place in downtown proper, around E. Main St.

Practical Information

Emergency: 911. **Campus Police:** 4-7166 on UVA campus.

Visitor Information: Chamber of Commerce, 415 E. Market St. (295-3141), within walking distance of Amtrak, Greyhound/Trailways, and historic downtown. Open Mon.-Fri. 9am-5pm. **Thomas Jefferson Visitors Bureau,** Rte. 20 near I-64 (293-6789 or 977-1783). Take bus #8 ("Piedmont Community College") from 5th and Market St. Same information as chamber of commerce, plus state-wide brochures. Staff makes lodging inquiries and reservations. Free museum on Monticello and the Jefferson family. Open daily 9am-5:30pm. **University of Virginia,** at the rotunda in the center of campus (924-1019). Brochures and campus tour information. Open daily 9am-4:45pm. Brochures and student helpers also in **Newcomb Hall** on campus (no phone). Open daily 9am-10pm. Larger **university visitors center** off U.S. 250 west—follow the signs (924-7166). Answers as Campus Police. Wide selection of campus maps, transport schedules, entertainment guides, and hints on budget accommodations. Open 24 hr.

Amtrak: 810 W. Main St. (800-872-7245 or 296-4559), 7 blocks from downtown. To Washington, DC ($21) and New York ($76). Open daily 5:30am-9pm.

Greyhound/Trailways: 310 W. Main St. (295-5131), within 3 blocks of historic downtown. To: Richmond ($9.75), Washington, DC ($21), Norfolk ($24.75), and Lynchburg ($12). Open daily 6am-midnight.

Public Transport: Charlottesville Transit Service, 296-7433. Bus service within city limits, including most hotels and UVA campus locations. Buses operate Mon.-Sat. 6:20am-7pm. Maps available at both information centers, City Hall, and the UVA student center in Newcomb Hall. Fare 60¢, seniors and disabled 30¢, under 6 free. The more frequent blue **University of Virginia** buses require UVA ID or expensive long-term pass to board.

Yellow Cab: 295-4131. To Monticello $10.

Post Office: 1155 Seminole Trail (Rte. 29). Open Mon.-Fri. 8am-5:30pm, Sat. 8am-2pm. **ZIP code:** 22906.

Help Lines: Rape Crisis Line, 977-7273. Open daily 7pm-7am. **Lesbian & Gay Hotline,** 971-4942. Both UVA-affiliated.

Area Code: 804.

Charlottesville rests in the delta formed by Rte. 29, Rte. 250, and I-64. Streets number east to west, using compass directions; 5th St. NW is 10 blocks from (and parallel to) 5th St NE. Streets running east-west across the numbered streets are neither parallel nor logically named. C-ville has two downtowns: one on the west side near the university called **The Corner,** and **Historic Downtown** about a mile east. The two are connected by **University Avenue,** running east-west, which becomes **Main Street.**

Accommodations, Camping, and Food

Reasonably priced accommodations study near the university and at the junction of Rte. 29 north and the Rte. 250 bypass, also known as the Barracks Rd. area. **Guest House Bed and Breakfast** (979-7264; open noon-5pm) arranges rooms from $45 for a double. Because of the proximity of the Blue Ridge Mountains, camping facilities are readily available. For clean, standard motel rooms with TV, take bus #2 or 7 from the bus station or downtown to the **University Lodge,** 140 Emmet St. (295-5141; singles $38, doubles $44; each additional person $5). For slightly more upscale accommodations and a swimming pool, try the **Econolodge,** 400 Emmet St. (296-2104; singles $42, doubles $50). Above Chancellor's Drug Store near the campus, **Chancellor Apartments,** 1413½ University Ave. (295-5457), offers big rooms with faded but comfortable 19th-century furniture. (Curfew 11pm. No alcohol. Shared baths; sink in each room. Singles $14. Doubles $17. Each additional person $2. Call ahead.) Next door, **Anderson Apartments,** 1417½ University Ave. (295-2461), will reopen in 1991 after renovations and charge $20-30 a night for singles and doubles. The closest campground, **Cambrie Launch Charlottesville KOA,** Rte. 1, P.O. Box 144, 22901 (296-9881), provides sites for $16, with hookup $18.

You'll find good Southern chow in Charlottesville's unpretentious diners and family restaurants. **City Market,** 4th St. SW at Carver Recreation Center (971-3260), sells local produce, other foods, and homemade crafts. (Open mid-April to May and Aug.-Oct., Sat. 7am-noon; June-July Tues. 7-11am, Sat. 7am-noon.) For a homemade meal in a fun 50s atmosphere, complete with aqua-tiled walls and a rocking jukebox, pop into the **Blue Moon Diner,** 512 W. Main St., 2 blocks from the bus station. The great staff, large portions, and low prices (most dishes $1-4) will keep you smiling. (Open Mon.-Fri. 7am-10pm, Sat. 8am-10pm, Sun. 8am-4pm.) For a light, heathful meal, try the **Garden Gourmet,** 811 W. Main St. (295-9991), an all-natural eatery with international gourmet and vegetarian fare. You can't go wrong with the fresh salads (homemade dressing) or live folk, jazz, and rock music at dinner. (Open Mon.-Thurs. 11:30am-2:30pm and 5:30-9pm, Fri. 11:30am-2:30pm and 5:30-10pm, Sat. noon-3pm and 5:30-10pm.) Closer to the university, The Corner maintains a cluster of good cafés and delis. The **College Inn,** 1507 University Ave. is a popular, modest deli. (Lunch from $3, dinner from $4. Open daily 7am-11pm.)

Sights and Entertainment

Monticello, on Rte. 53 (295-8181 or 295-2657), is the house that took Mr. Jefferson 40 years to design and build. From the famous dome to the manicured lawns and gardens, the place exudes beauty and functional structure with automatic doors and dumbwaiter. (Open March-Oct. daily 8am-5pm; Nov.-Feb. 9am-4:30pm. Admission $7, Seniors $6, ages 6-11 $2.) Less than a mile away on Rte. 53, historic **Michie Tavern** (977-1234) still offers hospitality to travelers after 200 years. As one of Virginia's oldest remaining homesteads, the tavern offers a glimpse of 18th-century social life, a general store, and an operating grist mill. Experience disturbing colonial cuisine in "The Ordinary," a converted slave house. (Lunch buffet $9, ages 6-11 $2.75. Open daily 11:15am-3:30pm. Tavern-museum open daily 9am-5pm. Admission $5, ages 6-11 $1. Admission $3 if you lunch at The Ordinary.)

Mr. Jefferson's "academical village" has become the gorgeous **University of Virginia,** full of broad terraces, shaded hills, and brick buildings with incongruous Greek columns and lintels. The Roman Pantheon inspired the **Rotunda** (924-7969; open daily 9am-4:45pm), from which free historical tours leave daily at 10am, 11am, 2pm, 3pm, and 4pm. Stop by the **Fayerweather Gallery,** on Rugby Rd. to take in student art. Just down Rugby Rd., the university's **Bayly Art Museum,** includes a permanent display of small masterpieces from the Renaissance and most recent centuries, plus a good collection of colonial art and constantly changing exhibitions. (Open Tues.-Sun. 1-5pm. Free.) For more UVA information call 924-0311.

Today the university catches most of the limelight, but in colonial times the downtown area roller-boogied and breakdanced to the action. Now known as Historic Downtown, the area includes **Court Square,** the original commercial center, and **Swan Tavern** (now the Red Land Club; 296-6442), where early legislators gathered. Stop by the **Albermarle County Historical Society Museum** and pick up the *Guide to Historic Downtown Charlottesville,* a self-guided walking tour of the city. (All city buses go to historic downtown.) A few blocks from Court Sq. begins the Main St. **pedestrian mall,** home to jazz clubs and commercial art galleries including African and Native American art. Close by, browse **Daedalus Used Books** on 4th St. at Market (293-7595), the best in town. (Open Mon.-Fri. 10am-6pm, Sat. 10am-5pm, Sun. noon-4pm.)

C-ville loves jazz, doesn't mind rock & roll, and in general supports quite a few pubs. Bars open their doors around 8pm, and all close at 2am. **TRAX,** at 122 11th St. NW (295-8729), features alternative rock and international acts. (Cover varies.) **Miller's,** 109 W. Main St. (971-8511) has nightly jazz from Monday (no cover) to weekends (cover $2). Omnipresent posters and the free *C-Ville Review* magazine can tell you who plays where when. The **Court Square Tavern,** 500 Court Sq. (296-6111), lets you drink your way around the world, with over 100 imported beers.

Ash Lawn, on Rte. 6 (293-9539; open March.-Oct. daily 9am-6pm; Nov.-Feb. 10am-5pm), the 19th-century plantation home of President James Monroe, hosts a **Summer Music Festival** (box office 293-8000, open daily noon-6:30pm), featuring comic opera from mid-June to mid-August. (Tickets $10, seniors $9, students $7.) Also check the offerings of the **Heritage Theatre** (924-3376) for their summer play festival. Tickets ($12.50, seniors $11, students $8.50) are available at the box office at Culberth Theatre on the university campus. (Performances June-Aug. Mon.-Sat. at 8pm.)

Richmond

The former capital of the Confederate States of America, Richmond keeps one face turned toward its Civil War past, with numerous museums and restored houses displaying everything from troop movements to Confederate President Jefferson Davis' tablecloths. But in districts like the sprawling, beautiful Fan and formerly industrial Shockoe Bottom, another Richmond rears its coiffed and powdered head with relaxed, cultural savvy and excellent, inexpensive food. Richmond has also begun to recognize both faces' connection to an African American past, celebrated by the soon-to-open Black History Museum. Both Richmonds unite behind building gracious and welcome alternatives to life in pernennial northern rival Washington, DC.

Practical Information

Emergency: 911.

Visitor Information: Richmond Visitors Center, 1700 Robin Hood Rd. (358-5511), exit 14 off I-95/64, in a converted train depot. Helpful 6-min. video introduces the city's various attractions. Reserves accommodations, sometimes at heavy ($10-20) discounts. Arranges walking tours and provides quality maps. (Open May 27-Sept. 2 daily 9am-7pm; off-season 9am-5pm.) Brochure-only branch office at 301 E. Main St. downtown mainly plans conventions. State of Virginia visitors center in the **Bell Tower,** 101 N. 9th St. (786-4484), near the state capitol. Open Mon.-Fri. 8:15am-5pm, Sat.-Sun. 9:30am-4:30pm.

Amtrak: 7519 Staple Mills Rd. (264-9194 or 800-872-7245), out of town. Taxi fare to downtown $12. Open 24 hr.

Greyhound/Trailways: 2910 N. Boulevard (353-8903). Walk 2 blocks to the visitors center or take GRTC bus #24 north. To: Washington, DC ($16), Charlottesville ($9), Williamsburg ($9), Norfolk, VA ($18).

Public Transport: Greater Richmond Transit Co: 101 S. Davis St. (358-4782). Maps available in the basement of city hall, 900 E. Broad St., and in the Yellow Pages. Fare 75¢ (exact change), transfers 10¢. Buses serve most of Richmond infrequently, downtown frequently; most leave from Broad St. downtown. Bus #24 goes south to Broad St. and downtown. Unreliable trolleys serve downtown and Shockoe Slip. Fare 25¢.

Help Lines: Travelers Aid, 648-1767. **Rape Crisis Hotline,** 643-0888. Open 24 hr. **Psychiatric Crisis Intervention,** 780-8003 or 648-9225. Open 24 hr. **Gay Hotline,** 353-3626.

Post Office: 1801 Brook Rd. (775-6133). Take bus #22 or 37. Open Mon.-Fri. 7am-6pm. **ZIP code:** 23232.

Area Code: 804.

Locals describe Richmond's urban area as shaped like a closed ladies' fan placed east to west: the center is the **state capitol,** the short handle to the east is **Court End** and **Shockoe Button,** and the long western blade begins downtown and becomes the **Fan** neighborhood. Streets form a grid pattern but are not named logically except for 1st (west) through 14th (east) St. downtown. Both **I-95,** leading north to Washington, DC, and **195,** parallel to the James River, encircle the worthwhile urban area. **Route 64** heads northwest to Charlottesville and southeast to Williamsburg.

Accommodations and Camping

Budget motels around Richmond cluster along Williamsburg Rd., on the edge of town, and along Midlothian Turnpike south of the James River; public transport to these areas is infrequent at best. As usual, the farther away from downtown you stay, the less you have to pay. The visitors center distributes an extensive accommodations guide, but many of the prices are outdated. The obligatory spare-but-clean-roomed **Motel 6,** 5704 Williamsburg Rd., Sandston (222-7600), sleeps about 6 mi. east on Rte. 60, across from the airport. (Singles $27. Doubles $33. Take the "Seven Pines" bus.) Nearer town, the **Massad House Hotel,** 11 N. 4th St. (648-2893), 4 blocks from the capitol, has charming and comfortable rooms with shower and TV, recently upholstered in bright primary colors. Since these are the only inexpensive rooms downtown, they're often booked; in summer call a week ahead. (Singles $33. Doubles $40.) Three mi. from the center of town, the **Executive Inn,** 5215 W. Broad St. (288-4011), offers grand (by motel standards) but slightly faded rooms and a pool. Bus #6 runs frequently into town. (Singles $41. Doubles $44. Off-season: $35 and $37 respectively.) Most of Richmond's **B&Bs** reside in converted mansions along Monument Ave. (rooms $45-70). Call Lyn M. Benson at **Bensonhouse of Richmond** (648-7560 or 780-1522; Mon.-Fri. 10am-6pm), or **Abbey Hill Bed and Breakfast** (353-4656 or 355-5855) for more information.

The closest campground, **Pocahontas State Park,** 10300 Beach Rd. (796-4255), about 10 mi. south on Rte. 10 and Rte. 655, offers showers, biking, boating, lakes, and a huge pool. (Sites $8.50. No hookups. Pool $1.75, ages 3-12 $1.25.) Reserve a site by phone through Ticketron (490-3939; Virginia Beach office open April-Nov.).

Food and Nightlife

Richmond's great variety of good budget restaurants hides among the old trees and restored front porches in the spread-out, gentrified Fan district (bordered by Monument Ave., Main, Laurel St., and Boulevard). The **Commercial Café,** 111 N. Robinson St., serves the best barbecue in this barbecue-rich town. Sandwiches start at $5, but the genuine experience requires ribs—the "Taster" ($7) is quite filling, and the plates ($9-$14) can be shared. The ever-popular **Joe's Inn,** 205 N. Shields Ave., serves huge portions of spaghetti in a casual setting. (Lunches $3, dinners $7-8. Open daily 9am-2am.) The **Texas-Wisconsin Border Café,** 1501 W. Main St., features chili, potato pancakes, and *chalupas.* Signs above the bar read "Dixie Inn," "Secede," and "Eat Cheese Or Die." At night the café secedes as a popular bar. (Lunches $3-5. Dinners $5-9. Open daily 11am-2am.)

Downtown reels with cheap regular-guy lunch spots. **Gus' Corner Restaurant,** 100 N. 8th St., is a sandwich shop popular with Virginia politicians. The Lebanese marinated beef ($3.75) comes in a pita with onions and 12 seasonings. (Open Mon.-Fri. 6am-6pm.) **The Skull & Bones,** N. 12th St. at E. Marshall, 2 blocks from the Confederate White House, serves full, cafeteria-style meals (about $4) to local med students. (Open Mon.-Fri. 6am-9pm, Sat. 6:30am-3pm.) Anglophiles and homesick Brits should head for **Penny Lane,** 207 N. 7th St. (780-1682) a delightfully exaggerated pub with flags on the walls and soccer on the telly. (Open Sun.-Wed. 11am-4pm and 5-11pm, Thurs.-Sat. 11am-4pm and 5pm-1:30am. Live music Thurs.-Sat. 9pm-1:30am.) **Bill's Barbecue** sprinkles glorified fast food throughout town.

The Shockoe Slip district, from Main, Canal, and Cary St. between 10th and 14th St., features fancy shops in restored and repainted warehouses but few bargains. The **farmers market,** at N. 17th and E. Main St. nearby, has a fresh, excellent selection. **Peking Pavilion,** 1302 E. Cary St., offers excellent service, elegant decor, and gourmet Chinese food. Try the *kung pao* chicken. (Open Sun.-Thurs. 11:30am-2:15pm and 5-9:45pm, Fri. 11:30am-2:15pm and 5-10:45pm, Sat. 5-10:45pm only.)

Most other reputable bars and clubs are arrayed along Grace St. or elsewhere in the Fan. The **Metro,** at Broad and Laurel St., features local progressive bands most nights; the **Flood Zone,** 115 8th St. (644-0935), south of Shockoe Slip, offers bigger-name but still offbeat acts. (Ticket office open Tues.-Fri. 10am-6pm.)

Sights

Ever since Patrick Henry declared "Give me liberty or give me death" in Richmond's **St. John's Church,** 2401 E. Broad St. (648-5015), the river city has been quoting, memorializing, and bronzing its historical heroes. Sundays at 2pm an actor recreates the famous 1775 speech, given when the church served as the site of a Revolutionary Convention. (Open Mon.-Sat. 10am-3:30pm, Sun. 1-3:30pm.) Larger-than-life statues of George Washington and Thomas Jefferson grace the **State Capitol** grounds (786-4344). Jefferson designed the masterpiece of neoclassical architecture. Attendants arrange free tours. (Open daily 9am-5pm.) For more sculpture, follow Franklin Ave. from the capitol until it becomes **Monument Avenue,** lined with trees, gracious old houses, and towering statues of Confederate heroes. Note how Robert E. Lee, who survived the War, faces his beloved South, and Stonewall Jackson, who didn't, glares North.

North of the Capitol along Marshall St., the **Court End** district guards the most interesting historical sights. The **Confederate Museum,** 1202 E. Clay St. (649-1861), guards the world's largest Civil War artifact collection and gives tours of the **White House of the Confederacy** next door. Statues of Tragedy and Comedy grace the front door: decide for yourself which best describes the Confederacy. (Open Mon.-Sat. 10am-5pm, Sun. 1-5pm. Tours Mon., Wed., and Fri.-Sat. 10:30am-4:30pm, Tues. and Thurs. 11:30am-4:30pm, Sun. 1:15-4:30pm. Admission to museum or tour $4, seniors and college students with ID $3.50, under 13 $2.25; museum with tour $7, seniors and student $5, under 13 $3.50.)

The **Valentine Museum,** 1015 E. Clay St. (649-0711), fascinates with exhibits on local and Southern social and cultural history, such as tobacco and advertising. In 1991 Valentine offers a free restored historic home tour. (Open Mon.-Sat. 10am-5pm, Sun. noon-5pm. Admission $3.50, seniors $3, students $2.75, ages 7-12 $1.50.) Built in 1790, the **John Marshall House,** 818 E. Marshall St. (648-7998), home of the deeply influential chief justice, has been restored with authentic period and Marshall family furnishings. To see the house you must wait for a tour, which will begin every hour on the half-hour. (Open Tues.-Sat. 10am-5pm, Sun. 1-5pm. Admission $3.) Combination "Court End" tickets to the Confederate Museum and White House of the Confederacy, John Marshall House, and Valentine Museum (all within easy walking distance of each other) cost $9, seniors and students $8.50, under 13 $4.

East of the capitol, follow your tell-tale heart to the **Edgar Allan Poe Museum,** 1914-16 E. Main St. (648-5523). Poe memorabilia stuffs the oldest stone building in Richmond. (Open Tues.-Sat. 10am-4pm, Sun.-Mon. 1:30-4pm. Admission $4, seniors $3, students $2.)

Richmond is surprisingly rich in African American historic sights, many in the **Jackson Ward** neighborhood downtown. The **Maggie L. Walker National Historic Site,** 110 ½ E. Leigh St. (780-1380 or 226-1981), commemorates the life of an ex-slave's gifted daughter. Physically disabled, Maggie Walker advocated black women's rights and succeeded as founder and president of a bank. (Park rangers conduct house tours Wed.-Sun. 9am-5pm. Free.) The **Black History Museum and Cultural Center of Virginia,** 00 Clay St. (780-9093), should open in spring of 1991.

The Southeast's largest art museum, the **Virginia Museum of Fine Arts,** 2800 Grove Ave. at N. Boulevard downtown (367-0844), has an outstanding art nouveau gallery, a gorgeous collection (the largest outside the USSR) of Fabergé jewelry and Easter eggs made for the Russian czars, and a fine showing of U.S. contemporary and postmodern art. (Open Tues.-Wed. and Fri.-Sat. 11am-5pm, Thurs. 11am-10pm, Sun. 1-5pm.)

Richmond's early 20th-century rebuilders used the grand art deco style; some examples survive. The **Jefferson Hotel,** at Franklin and Adams St., (788-8000), is a breathtaking avatar of opulence whose grand piano is open for free to the public (serious players only, no "Chopsticks") nightly from 8pm-12:30am. At the **Byrd Theatre,** 2908 W. Cary St. (353-9911), you can view Hollywood's latest in extraordinary style: marble balconies, enormous stained-glass windows, and a Wurlitzer Organ that rises from the floor to entertain before each show.

Civil War buffs should pay a visit to the outskirts of Richmond to the **Richmond National Battlefield Park,** 3215 E. Broad St. (225-1981). The visitors center has extensive exhibits on the Civil War, as well as maps detailing the battlefields and fortifications surrounding the city. (Open daily 9am-5pm. Free.)

Free concerts abound here in summer; check **Style Weekly,** a free magazine available at the visitors center and around town, for information. Free entertainment often finds a home in **Dogwood Dell,** an outdoor theater below the **Carillon World War I Memorial,** on the 100-acre Maymont grounds. (Grounds open daily 10am-7pm; Nov.-March 10am-5pm.)

Williamsburg

At the end of the 17th century, when English aristocrats wore brocades and wigs, Williamsburg powdered its face as the capital of Virginia. During the Revolutionary War, the capital moved to Richmond, taking with it much of Williamsburg's grandeur. Then, in 1926, John D. Rockefeller, Jr.'s immense bank account came to the aid of the distressed city, restoring part of the town as a colonial village. His foundation still runs the restored section, a five- by seven-block town-within-a-town called Colonial Williamsburg, where fife and drum corps parade while cobblers, bookbinders, blacksmiths, and clockmakers go about their tasks using 200-year-old methods. Filled with events, the town might witness a Punch and Judy show, an evening of 18th-century theater, or a militia review on any given day. Though the fascinating and beautiful ex-capital claims to be a faithfully restored version of its 18th century self, don't look for dirt roads, open sewers, or African slaves. Williamsburg also prides itself on **William and Mary,** the second-oldest college in the United States. Outside Williamsburg, Virginia's other big tourist sights lie in wait; history buffs should see Yorktown, Jamestown, or one of the restored plantations, while amusement park aficionados should head to Busch Gardens.

Practical Information

Emergency: 911.

Visitor Information: Williamsburg Area Tourism and Conference Bureau, 201 Penniman Rd. (229-6511), about ½ mi. northwest of the transportation center. Free *Visitors Guide to Virginia's Historic Triangle.* Open Mon.-Fri. 8:30am-5pm. **Tourist Visitor Center,** Rte. 132-132y

(800-447-8679), 1 mi. northeast of the train station. Tickets and transportation to Colonial Williamsburg. Operated by the Colonial Williamsburg Foundation. Maps and guides to the historic district, including a guide for the disabled, available upstairs. Information including prices and discounts on Virginia sights downstairs.

Transportation Center: at the end of N. Boundary St., across from the fire station. **Amtrak,** 229-8750 or 800-872-7245. Direct service to: New York ($79), Washington, DC ($27), Philadelphia ($56), Baltimore ($32). Open Mon.-Tues. and Fri. 7:30am-9pm, Wed.-Thurs. and Sat. 7:30am-3pm, Sun. 1:30-9pm. **Greyhound/Trailways,** 229-1460. Ticket office open Mon.-Fri. 8am-6pm, Sat.-Sun. 8am-4pm. To: Richmond ($9), Norfolk ($9), Washington, DC ($20). **James City County Transit (JCCT),** 220-1621. Service along Rte. 60, from Merchants Sq. in the Historic District, west to Williamsburg Pottery, or east past Busch Gardens. No service to Yorktown or Jamestown. Operates Mon.-Sat. 6:15am-8:30pm. Fare $1, 25¢ per zone change; exact change required.

Williamsburg Limousine Service: 877-0279. Both the local taxi and cheapest guided tours. To Busch Gardens or Carter's Grove $6 round-trip. Guided tours to Jamestown ($19.50), Yorktown ($17.50), or both ($35), with admission fees included. Will take you to and from your Williamsburg lodgings. Make reservations for tours at least 24 hr. in advance; call between 9am-1am.

Post Office, 425 N. Boundary St. (229-4668). Open Mon.-Fri. 8am-5pm, Sat. 10am-noon. **ZIP codes:** 23185 (Williamsburg), 23490 (Yorktown), and 23081 (Jamestown).

Area Code: 804.

Williamsburg lies some 50 mi. southeast of Richmond between Jamestown (10 mi. away) and Yorktown (14 mi. away). The **Colonial Parkway,** which connects Williamsburg, Jamestown, and Yorktown, does not support commercial enterprise, helping to preserve an unspoiled atmosphere. Travelers should visit in late fall or early spring to avoid the crowds, high temperature, and humidity of summer. Also be aware that all the signs pointing to Colonial Williamsburg do not actually get there, but to the visitor center instead. To drive to the restored area proper, take the Lafayette St. exit off the Colonial Pkwy. Parking is surprisingly easy to find.

Accommodations and Camping

The few bargains in the Williamsburg area lie along Rte. 60 west or Rte. 31 south toward Jamestown. From Memorial Day to Labor Day, rooms are scarce and prices higher, so try to call at least two weeks in advance. Centrally located, family-run guest houses are clean, comfortable, cheap, and friendly alternatives to hotels. For a complete listing of accommodations, pick up a free copy of *Visitors Guide to Virginia's Historic Triangle* at the conference bureau, *not* at the visitor center (see Practical Information).

The closest hostel, **Sangraal-by-the-Sea Youth Hostel (AYH),** Rte. 626 (776-6500), near Urbanna, leaps 30 mi. away. They do provide rides to bus or train stations during business hours, but don't expect a daily ride to Williamsburg. ($9, nonmembers $11. Call ahead.) Closer to Williamsburg, **guest houses** are your best bet: some don't require reservations, but all expect you to call ahead, and most expect customers to avoid rowdiness and behave like houseguests. Five minutes from the historic district is **Mrs. H. J. Carter,** 903 Lafayette St. (229-1117). Dust mice would not dare hide under the four-poster beds in these large, airy singles and doubles. Prices range from $25 (1 person) to $35 (4 in 2 beds), but Mrs. Carter will not let unmarried men and women sleep in the same bed. **The Elms,** 708 Richmond Rd. (229-1551), offers elegant, colorful, antique-furnished rooms to one or two visitors for $21. Both houses sleep eight. **Holland's Sleepy Lodge,** 211 Harrison Ave. (229-6321), rents singles for $26.

Hotels close to the historic district, especially chain- or foundation-owned hotels, do not come cheap. The **Lafayette Motel,** 1220 Richmond Rd. (220-4900), a 10-minute walk from William & Mary, has clean, ordinary rooms with colonial-looking facades and a pool. (Singles $31-38. Doubles $55.) **Motel 6,** Rte. 60 W. (565-3433), 2½ mi. from Colonial Williamsburg, offers standard motel fare and a pool. (Singles $30. Doubles $36.)

Several campsites blanket the area. **Anvil Campgrounds,** 5243 Moretown Rd. (565-2300), 3 mi. west of Colonial Williamsburg Information Center on Rte. 60, offers a swimming pool, bathhouse, recreational hall, and store. (Sites $13-15, with hookup $20.) **Indian Village Campground,** 1811 Jamestown Rd. (229-8211), 2¼ mi. south on Rte. 31 from Rte. 199, has similar facilities and also rents cabins. (Sites $8-18. Call 5-9pm or leave message.) Nearby **Brass Lantern Campsites,** 1782 Jamestown Rd. (229-4320 or 229-9089), charges $10, with full hookup $14.

Food and Nightlife

Though Colonial Williamsburg proper contains several authentic-looking "taverns," few are cheap and most require reservations and forbid tank-tops. When you must eat in the historic district, stand in line for **Chowning's Tavern,** on Duke of Gloucester St., offering stews, sandwiches, and the misleadingly misspelled "Welsh Rabbit" (bread and cheese in beer sauce with ham) from $6. (Open daily 11:30am-3:30pm and 4pm-1am.) From 9pm on at Chowning's the **gambols** take place: costumed waiters serve mixed drinks, sing 18th-century ballads, and teach patrons how to play outdated dice and card games. **The Old Chickahominy House,** 1211 Jamestown Rd. (229-4689), rests over a mile from the historic district but make the trip. Share the antique and dried-flowers decor with pewter-haired locals whose ancestors survived "Starvation Winter" in Jamestown. Miss Melinda's "complete luncheon" is Virginia ham served on hot biscuits, fruit salad, a slice of buttermilk pie, and iced tea or coffee ($4.75). Expect a 20-min. wait for lunch. (Open daily 8:30-10:15am and 11:30am-2:15pm.)

During the summer, few William & Mary students stick around, but their hangouts, inexpensive and comfortable alternatives to fast-food and CWF fare, remain. In 50s wood and vinyl, **Paul's Deli Restaurant and Pizza,** 761 Scotland St., sells crisp *stromboli* for 2 ($6-7) and filling subs ($3-5). The "hot Italian" sub makes locals salivate. (Open daily 11am-2am.) Next door, the more upscale **Greenleafe Cafe** (220-3405) serves sandwiches, salads, and the like ($5-10), throbbing after 9pm on Wednesday (cover $2) with live folk music. (Open daily 11:30am-2am.) Both establishments are just a few blocks up Richmond Rd. from "Confusion Corner" where Colonial Williamsburg ends and W&M begins. For less pomp and more rustic circumstance, pack a picnic from one of the supermarkets clustered around the **Williamsburg Shopping Center,** at the intersection of Richmond Rd. and Lafayette St., or try the fast-food strip along Rte. 60. The rudimentary **farmers market** at Lafayette and North Henry St. sells cheap seafood or vegetables, depending on the farm.

Sights

Unless you plan to apply to W&M, you've probably come to see the restored gardens and buildings, crafts, tours, and costumed actors in the historic district also known as **Colonial Williamsburg.** The complex claims to re-create 18th-century Virginia, but it may introduce you to the ways of 19th-century robber barons. The Colonial Williamsburg Foundation (CWF) owns everything from the Governor's Palace to the lemonade stands and even most of the houses marked "private home"; most attractions require their exorbitant tickets. You even need a general admission ticket to enter the historic district, though this technicality is not enforced. All tickets entitle you to ride the CWF buses which circle the historic district every few minutes. A **Patriot's Pass** gains admission to all the town's attractions (except the former Rockefeller home, Bassett Hall) for one year, entrance to Carter's Grove, and a guided tour ($26, under 13 $17); a **Royal Governor's Pass** lasts 4 days and covers all the attractions in the town itself ($22.50, under 13 $15); and a **Basic Ticket** lets you into any 12 attractions except the Governor's Palace and the Decorative Arts Museum ($19, under 13 $12.50). Buy them at the CWF Visitor Center or from booths in town.

"Doing" the historic district without a ticket definitely saves money; for no charge, you can walk the streets, ogle the buildings, browse in the shops, march behind the fife and drum corps, lock yourself in the stockade, and even use the restrooms. Some shops that actually sell goods—notably the Apothecary by the Palace Green—are open to the public. Pretend you're Schwarzenegger in *Total Recall* and catch up to a guided **walking tour** moving about Colonial Williamsburg during the day. The poorly named "Other Half" tour relates the experience of Africans and African Americans. Outdoor events, including a mid-day cannon-firing, receive listings in the weekly *Visitor's Companion,* which is given away to ticketholders—many of whom conveniently leave it where non-ticket-holders can pick it up. A separate pamphlet detailing disabled access in Williamsburg is also available at the Tourist Information Center. Picnickers may find the best spots just outside the historic district on the elegant grounds of the **Abbey Aldrich Rockefeller Museum.** The adjacent unfenced swimming pool is officially open only to guests of CWF's hotels.

Those willing to pay shouldn't miss the **Governor's Palace,** on the Palace Green. This mansion housed the appointed governors of the Virginia colony until the last one fled in 1775. Reconstructed colonial sidearms and ceremonial sabers line the reconstructed walls, and the garden includes a hedge maze. (Separate admission $13.) The **Wallace Decorative Arts Museum** holds excellent collections of English furniture and ceramics. (Open Thurs.-Tues. 9am-5pm, Wed. 9am-5:30pm. Separate admission $7.50.)

Spreading west from the corner of Richmond and Jamestown Rd. ("Confusion Corner"), the other focal point of Williamsburg, **William and Mary,** is the second oldest college in the U.S. Chartered in 1693, the college has educated Presidents Jefferson, Monroe, and Tyler. The **Sir Christopher Wren Building,** also restored with Rockefeller money, is the oldest classroom building in the country. Nearby, in the historic district, sprawl the shops at **Merchant Square.** Park here and walk straight into Colonial Williamsburg.

Near Williamsburg

Jamestown and **Yorktown** are both important parts of the U.S. colonial story. The National Park System provides free, well-administered visitor's guides to both areas. Combination tickets to Yorktown Victory Center and to Jamestown Festival Park are available at either site for $9.50. At the **Jamestown National Historic Site** you'll see remains of the first permanent English settlement of 1607 and exhibits explaining colonial life. At the visitors center, skip the hokey film and catch a "living history" walking tour on which a guide portraying one of the colonists describes the Jamestown way of life. Call ahead (229-1733) for information since "living history" guides sometimes take the day off. (Site open daily 8:30am-6pm; off-season 9am-5:30pm. Entrance fee $5 per car, $2 per hiker or bicyclist.) Also see the nearby **Jamestown Festival Park** (229-1607), a museum commemorating the Jamestown settlement, with changing exhibits, a reconstruction of James Fort, a Native American village, and full-scale replicas of the 3 ships which brought the original settlers to Jamestown in 1607. A "living history" sailor even talks about the voyage. (Open daily 9am-5pm. Admission $6.50, under 13 $3.)

The American Revolution's last significant battle took place at Yorktown. British General Charles Lord Cornwallis and his men seized the town for use as a port in 1781. The colonies and the French soon surrounded and stormed the hold, forcing the British to surrender. Stop in at the national park's **visitors center** for a short movie explaining the event. Guided tours of the inner British defense line (a series of mounds and moats) are available throughout the day. With a car, take a 7-mi. self-guided tour of the battlefield, or rent a tape cassette and recorder for $2 in the visitors center. (Open daily 8:30am-6pm; last tape rented at 5pm.) The **Yorktown Victory Center** (887-1776), 1 block from Rte. 17 on Rte. 238, offers a museum filled with items from the Revolutionary War, as well as a film and an intriguing "living history" exhibit: in an encampment in front of the center, a troop of soldiers from the Continental Army of 1772 take a well-deserved break from active combat. Feel free to ask them about tomorrow's march or last week's massacre. (Open daily 9am-5pm. Admission $5, under 13 $2.50.)

Without a car, you won't find a cheap way to get to Jamestown or Yorktown; since the "towns" are tourist sights, guided tours provide the only transportation. With **Williamsburg Limousine,** a group of at least four people can see both Jamestown attractions in the morning ($19.50 per person), both Yorktown sights in the afternoon ($17.50 per person), or take the whole day and see both ($35).

The **James River plantations** buttressed the slave-holding Virginia aristocracy, built near the water to facilitate the planters' commercial and social life. **Carter's Grove Plantation,** 6 mi. east of Williamsburg on Rte. 60, is a masterpiece of Georgian architecture. Williamsburg Limousine (see above) offers two daily round-trip tours from Colonial Williamsburg ($5). Admission includes a self-guided tour of the still-active **Wolstenholme Town** archeology site (in front of the house), an early British settlement even more short-lived than nearby Jamestown. The plantation also includes a tour of restored African slave quarters. (Plantation and town open March-Nov. and Christmas week daily 9am-5pm. Admission $8, free with CWF Patriot's Pass.)

Berkeley Plantation, (829-6018), halfway between Richmond and Williamsburg on Rte. 5, witnessed the first Thanksgiving in 1619, and later the birth of U.S. Presidents Benjamin and William Henry Harrison. Pause and enjoy the terraced boxwood gardens. (Open daily 8am-5pm. Admission $8.) **Shirley Plantation** (821-5121 or 800-232-1613), west on Rte. 5, is a beautiful Queen Anne mansion which survived colonial wars, and, incredibly, the Civil War's destructive Peninsular Campaign. The Carter family still owns the land it began developing in 1613. (Open daily 9am-5pm; last tour at 4:30pm. Admission $6.) The largest frame house in the U.S., **Sherwood Forest Plantation** (829-5377), about 10 mi. from the Berkeley Plantation on Rte. 5, was the home of U.S. Presidents William Henry Harrison and John Tyler. (Grounds open daily 9am-5pm. Admission $2, children 50¢. Mansion open for tours by appointment. Tours $30 per group.)

When you tire of history, head to **Busch Gardens,** 3 mi. east of Williamsburg on Rte. 60 (253-3350). Rides, shows, and shops come together under a refreshingly European theme, "The Old Country." Join in on the raucous year-round Octoberfest in the German pavilion or take a free self-guided tour of the Anheuser-Busch Brewery. Williamsburg Limousine, the local buses, and Greyhound all serve Busch Gardens (see Practical Information above). (Open daily mid-May to early Sept; hours vary. Admission $20.) You can also cool off at **Water Country USA** on Rte. 199 E. (229-9300), ¼ mi. east of I-64. The new water theme park features a wave tank and water rides as well as variety shows. (Open mid-June to mid-Aug. daily 10am-8pm; late Aug.-early Sept. and late May to mid-June 10am-7pm. Admission $15.)jmd 8-15-90 wp jmd 8-28-90 am jmd 8-30 ff

Washington, DC

DC stands as the East Coast's only major city planned from scratch. Congress chose this riverbank forest as site of the nation's capital. When the Capitol's builders dammed creeks and cut down trees, standing water bred mosquitos that spread a virulent strain of malaria, giving rise to the enduring, provocative legend that DC was "built on a swamp." In the 1790s, French Pierre L'Enfant and African American Benjamin Banneker planned downtown and its most distinctive features—the grid pattern, the green Mall, and the Greek Revival buildings—successfully eliminating the fetid stench of disease, though not quite that of corruption.

Today, the government enclave downtown spreads flu-like out from the domed U.S. Capitol in block after block of marble-columned or smooth-walled façades, including the deservedly famous Smithsonian museums around the Mall. The city embraces satellite neighborhoods like Dupont Circle and Georgetown, as well as

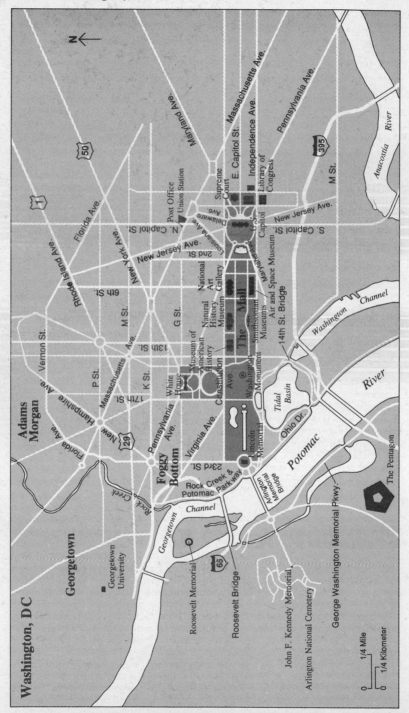

old townhouses, middle-class homes, the mansions of Foxhall Road, and the run-down buildings of Anacostia. Rock Creek Park, a long remnant of forest with the creek at its center, cuts the city in half.

As the nation's capital, the city grows along with the federal government. DC bloomed in the 1930s, when President Franklin D. Roosevelt's New Deal brought dozens of new acronyms and thousands of hopeful professionals to the Potomac. DC has always included a large and active African American community. The city's proximity to the South originally made it easy for freed African slaves to reach; later A. Philip Randolph's plan for a "March on Washington" in 1941 spurred the government to employ African Americans. Today people of African descent make up about 70% of the city's population. Yet this city is neither romantic nor trouble-free. The city divides both economically and geographically along race lines, still smarting from the riots of the 1960s. Whenever you emerge from the hi-tech "metro" subway, the homeless pose an unavoidable and striking contrast. Further, the largest private employer, the daily *Washington Post* newspaper, also feeds scandal-hungry DC residents, who hang on to every word. Not surprisingly, Washington, DC has more lawyers per capita than anywhere else in the U.S., and to help counteract it, more psychiatrists.

Practical Information

Emergency: 911.

Visitor Information: Visitor Information Center, 1455 Pennsylvania Ave. NW (789-7000), within the "Willard collection" of shops. A very helpful first stop. Ask for *Washington Visitors Map,* showing metro stops near points of interest, and *Washington's Attractions.* Language bank service in over 20 tongues. Open Mon.-Sat. 9am-5pm. **Washington Convention and Visitors Association (WCVA),** 1212 New York Ave. NW (789-7000). Open Mon.-Fri. 9am-5pm. Does not expect walk-ins. Write or call for copies of *Washington, DC: A Capital City* (for museum hours and exhibits to car rentals and accommodations) and *Washington, DC, Dining/Shopping Guide.* Brochures available in German, Japanese, French, and Spanish. **Events Hotline,** 737-8866. Recorded message.

International Visitors Information Service (IVIS): 733 15th St. NW #300 (783-6540). 24-hr. language bank in over 50 languages (after 11pm, emergency calls only). Office open Mon.-Fri. 9am-5pm.

Travelers Aid: Main office at 1015 12th St. NW (347-0101). Helpful for orientation to the city and in emergencies. Open Mon.-Fri. 9am-5pm. Desks at Union Station (347-0101; TDD 371-1937; open daily 9:30am-5:30pm); National Airport (684-3472; TDD 684-7886; open Sun.-Fri. 9am-9pm, Sat. 9am-6pm); and Dulles Airport (661-8636; TDD 471-9776; open Sun.-Fri. 10am-9pm, Sat. 10am-6pm).

Embassies: Australia, 1601 Massachusetts Ave. NW (797-3000). **U.K.,** 3100 Massachusetts Ave. NW (462-1340). **Canada,** 501 Pennsylvania Ave. NW (682-1740). **France,** 4101 Reservoir Rd. NW (944-6000). **Germany,** 4645 Reservoir Rd. NW (298-4000). **Ireland,** 2234 Massachusetts Ave. NW (462-3939). **Italy,** 1601 Fuller St. NW (328-5500). **Japan,** 2520 Massachusetts Ave. NW (234-2266). **New Zealand,** 37 Observatory Circle NW (328-4800). **Spain,** 2700 15th St. NW (265-0190).

Airports: See Getting There below.

Trains: See Getting There below.

Public Transport: See Orientation below.

Taxis: See Orientation below.

Car Rental: Cheapest in Arlington, VA, across the Potomac from downtown and easily accessible by Metrobus. **Arlington Rent-a-Car,** 3826 Lee Hwy., Arlington (524-3825). $16.50 per day, 15¢ per mi. Weekend (3-day) rental $48; 50 free mi., 10¢ each additional mi. Open Mon.-Fri. 10am-6pm, Sat. 11am-4pm. Must be 21; $200 deposit with major credit card, $250 without. **Bargain Buggies Rent-a-Car,** 912 N. Lincoln St., Arlington (841-0000). $16 per day, 16¢ per mi., $109 per week; 100 free mi., 16¢ each additional mi. Open Mon.-Fri. 8am-7pm, Sat.-Sun. 9am-3pm. Must be 21 with $400 deposit. **Thrifty Rent-a-Car,** 1001 12th St. NW (in DC, at 12th and K St.) and 4714 Miller Ave., Bethesda, MD (single phone number 986-0922). $32 per weekday, $27 per weekend day. 125 free mi. per day, 25¢ each additional mi.

Open Mon.-Fri. 7:30am-7:30pm, Sat. 7:30am-6pm, Sun. 9am-6pm. Must be 25 with major credit card.

Bike Rental: Metropolis Bikes, 709 8th St. SE (543-8900), at G St. SE near Capitol Hill. Unsafe south or southeast of Metropolis Bikes. $12 for 2 hr., $17 per day. Open Fri.-Wed. 11am-7pm, Thurs. 11am-9pm. Must have major credit card or $100-300 deposit.

Foreign Newspapers: American International News, 1825 Eye St. NW (223-2526). **Editorial El Mundo,** 1796 Columbia Rd. NW (387-2831), in Adams-Morgan (Spanish-language papers only). **Key Bridge Newsstand,** 3326 M St. NW (338-2626). **Newsroom Farragut Square,** 1001 Connecticut Ave. NW (872-0190), at 17th and K St.

Help Lines: DC Hotline, 223-2255. Open 24 hr. **DC Rape Crisis Center,** 333-7273. Open 24 hr. **Gay and Lesbian Switchboard,** 429-4971. Open daily 7:30-10:30pm.

Post Office: N. Capitol St. and Massachusetts Ave. NE (636-2200), across from Union Station. Open Mon.-Fri. 7am-midnight, Sat.-Sun. 7am-8pm. General Delivery at 900 Brentwood Rd. NE (636-1532), in a distant warehouse district. Open Mon.-Fri. 8am-3:30pm. **ZIP code:** 20002.

Area Code: 202.

Getting There

Unless you sail into Washington on the Potomac, you're sure to hit gridlock as you approach the city. You can miss the major traffic snarls by arriving out of commuter rush hours (Mon.-Fri. 7-10am and 3:30-6:30pm).

Highly confusing road signs mark all the interstates. The two main roads from Baltimore and the North are the **Baltimore-Washington (B-W) Parkway** and **I-95.** To go downtown, take the Parkway and follow signs for New York Ave. To get to the upper northwest quadrant, take I-95 to the Silver Spring exit onto the Capitol Beltway (I-495), then exit 20 ("Chevy Chase") onto Connecticut Ave. and take a left. From the south, take I-95 (which becomes I-395) directly to the 14th St. Bridge or the Memorial Bridge. Both lead downtown. From the west, take I-66 East over the Roosevelt Bridge and follow signs for Constitution Ave. I-66 is a simpler, faster way to get to the heart of Washington than I-495. Beware: to encourage car-pooling and fuel conservation, vehicles on I-66 East (Mon.-Fri. 7-9am) and I-66 West (Mon.-Fri. 4-6pm) must carry at least three people. Even out-of-towners have to pay the $50 fine if they break this law.

Three airports serve Washington. **National** (685-8000), 15 minutes from downtown, perches closest to DC, handling domestic flights only. Washington's Metrorail subway system (see Orientation below) whisks you from National to several downtown stops, or you can take a bus to the Capitol Hilton at 16th and K St. (Buses $7. Vans every ½ hr., $5.) Cab fare downtown costs about $8. **Dulles** (661-8020), 35 minutes from downtown, handles mostly international, transcontinental, and bargain flights. Buses, every half-hour, cost $12; taxi fare downtown $35-40. **Baltimore-Washington International** (261-1000) lies about 45 minutes from downtown. Buses, every half hour, will set you back $12; taxi fare downtown $40-45. Call the **Washington Flyer** (685-1400) for complete information on airport bus service to and from all three airports. Pan Am Airlines (845-8000) offers frequent shuttle service from National to LaGuardia Airport in New York City for $73 (under 21 and students with ID $49; seniors 10% discount).

Because planes often experience delays, Amtrak's **Metroliner** service (484-7540 or 800-872-7245) may be the fastest, although not necessarily the cheapest ($59, $83 round-trip), way to travel between New York and Washington. The trip between Penn Station and Union Station takes just over 3 hours. Metrorail's Red Line will take you from Union Station to other parts of the city.

Greyhound/Trailways, 1005 1st St. NE (565-2662), at L St., idles in a slightly unsafe area, but provides disabled facilities and frequent daily direct service to: Atlantic City (every 1½ hr., $22); Philadelphia (every 2-3 hr., $27); New York City (every ½-1 hr., $38); and Baltimore (every ½-1 hr., $9). Open 24 hr.

Orientation

The Capitol sits at the center of DC's street layout. The city's four **quadrants**—Northwest (NW), Northeast (NE), Southwest (SW), and Southeast (SE)—are bordered by three streets radiating in their eponymous directions from the Capitol: North Capitol, East Capitol, and South Capitol St. **The Mall,** not a shopping center but a grassy rectangle surrounded by the Smithsonian museums, extends west of the Capitol and divides NW from SW. Most of the city's sights, restaurants, and lodgings dwell in NW; most crime takes place in SE, out of sight from Capitol Hill.

Though out-of-town newspapers bill DC as "the murder capital of the nation," with more homicides per capita than any other U.S. city, most of the killings are drug-related disputes in areas tourists are unlikely to frequent. If you're not out alone, any place with pedestrians and restaurants should be reasonably safe at night, including Dupont Circle, Georgetown, and the well-lit parts of Adams-Morgan.

In theory, the city stretches out along "L'Enfant Plan," a grid pattern interrupted by avenues named for states; in practice, the grid often breaks down, especially in residential areas far from downtown. It's still useful for pedestrians and drivers. Numbered north-south streets run perpendicular to the east-west lettered streets. On either side of E. Capitol St. and the Mall, parallel streets run alphabetically from A-W. (Note: I St. is often written Eye St.) Once the letters of the alphabet are exhausted, two-syllable street names follow in alphabetical order (Ordway, Porter, Quebec), then three-syllable names (Brandywine, Chesapeake, Davenport), and, in farthest-north NW, trees and flowers (Jonquil, Kalmia). Avenues named for states are often major thoroughfares; those named for Eastern seaboard states (New York, Maryland, etc.) lead to the Capitol or the White House. **K Street** and **M Street** connect downtown to Georgetown. Take **Connecticut Avenue** from the White House through Dupont Circle, past the edge of Adams-Morgan and to the Maryland line. **Wisconsin Avenue** runs north from Georgetown to Friendship Heights and Montgomery County, MD. **16th Street** goes due north from downtown past Adams-Morgan and Rock Creek Park. **Massachusetts Avenue** links Dupont Circle, Union Station, and points east. Before setting out for your destination, check the quadrant indicator (NW, NE, SW, SE) of the address. Blocks on sequentially numbered and alphabetically ordered streets are numbered in increments of 100, making street addresses easy to locate. For example, 1350 Q St. is between 13th and 14th St. Addresses on state avenues (Wisconsin, for example) don't always follow this rule.

Washington's neighborhoods vary widely. **The Mall** is the park at the heart of the city, dotted with various memorials, the Capitol, the Smithsonian museums, and numerous government buildings. East of the Capitol, the **Capitol Hill** neighborhood extends around 11th St. NE and SE, a racially well-integrated community with its own local bars and restaurants. North of the Mall lies tiny **Chinatown.** **Adams-Morgan,** spanning from Connecticut Ave. and Calvert St. NW east along Columbia Rd. to 16th St. NW, remains the colorful, multi-ethnic center of DC's Hispanic community, though gentrification is currently underway. Hot bars, cool bookstores, and bargain ethnic food conglomerate here and in **Dupont Circle.** The circle itself joins Connecticut, Massachusetts, and New Hampshire Ave. with P and 19th St. NW; the neighborhood east, west, and north caters largely to gay residents. South of Dupont Circle is the downtown business district, where lawyers, federal employees, and couriers scurry between the postmodern buildings. Because DC bans buildings higher than the 13-story Washington Monument, there are no skyscrapers. **Georgetown,** centered around Wisconsin Ave. and M St. NW, studies across the river from Rosslyn, VA, where skyscrapers are legal. The student population of Georgetown University gives Georgetown the fun feel and rocking nightlife that tourists scuttle to each weekend. Self-descriptive **Embassy Row** lines Massachusetts Ave. between Dupont and Observatory Circles. The area bounded by Pennsylvania and Constitution Ave. and 18th and 26th St. NW, once a swamp, now answers to the name of **Foggy Bottom,** flaunting George Washington University, the

Kennedy Center, and the State Department. The grid pattern described above applies to all these neighborhoods except for Adams-Morgan, in which even longtime Washingtonians get lost. **Rock Creek Park,** a giant, undeveloped forest swath, reaches from near the Kennedy Center to DC's northern tip. Commuters drive home through it, and according to city legend, Charles de Gaulle once claimed the 8-sq.-mi. park was the French Embassy's backyard.

The grid and the state avenues make night driving easy in DC, but during business hours, Washington offers a nightmare of one-way streets and tangled traffic, despite its elegant design. Downtown and near the Mall, finding a parking space can prove a Herculean feat. Parking garages are exorbitant and metered spaces simply unavailable during much of the day. North of K St. outside rush hour (4-6:30pm) the determined driver can usually find a 2-hour-maximum metered space. Metered parking is free Monday to Saturday after about 7pm and all day on weekends. Traffic police are strict about parking violations, and fines steep. If, as on most of Constitution Ave., the signs read "No Parking 4-6:30pm, Mon.-Fri." do not saunter happily to your vehicle at 4:15pm; it probably won't be there. Some streets have "reversible lanes" whose proper direction depends on time of day; a few whole streets become one-way in rush hour. Watch for street signs indicating this.

Metrorail (637-7000), the Washington subway system, is a sight in its own right. (Main office at 600 5th St. NW. Open daily 6am-11:30pm.) The Dupont Circle Station has the longest escalator in the Western Hemisphere (204 ft.); throughout the system the architecture is futuristic, though sterile; the trains clean, quiet, crimefree, and air-conditioned. Pick up an easy-to-understand Metro map. Trains run every 10 or 15 minutes Monday to Friday 6am to midnight, Saturday 8am to midnight, and Sunday 10am to midnight. Rush-hour fares vary from $1.10 to $2.40, according to the distance you travel. At all other times, fares vary from 85¢ to $1.50. Computerized fare cards must be bought from machines in the station before you enter the subway and carried until you reach your destination. If you plan to connect with a bus after your ride, get a transfer pass from machines on the platform before boarding the train. To use the subway several times, buy a $5 or $10 fare card. The $5 weekend family tour pass allows a group of four unlimited travel on the Metrorail. (Available at the Metro Center Stop and from some hotel concierges.)

The extensive **Metrobus** (same phone, address, and hours as Metrorail) system reliably serves Georgetown, downtown, and the suburbs. Downtown, the bus stops every few blocks. Regular fare is 85¢, but again, rush-hour fares vary. Senior citizens and disabled people are eligible for reduced fares at all times with a valid WMATA ID card; children under 5 ride free when accompanied by a paying passenger. Send $1.50 to Metrobus and Metrorail for the new comprehensive map of bus and subway routes. Specify DC/MD or DC/VA. (ZIP code: 20001.)

Though most subway stops are listed below, Georgetown and most of Adams-Morgan are hard to reach by Metro. To reach Georgetown, get off at Foggy Bottom-GWU and walk west of Pennsylvania Ave. about 10 blocks to M St. NW; from Dupont Circle, take a D-2, D-4, D-6, or D-8 bus from 20th and P St. NW west to Wisconsin Ave. and Q St. Central Adams-Morgan is a long walk east along Calvert St. from its unofficial boundary at Connecticut and Calvert St. NW; take the Metro to the Woodley Park-Zoo stop.

DC has more **taxicabs** per capita than any other U.S. city, even though federal law keeps fares low enough for Congresspeople to taxi home—consequently no cab ride within DC should ever cost over $7 (unless you're going to Anacostia). Within DC, fares are determined by the number of often arbitrary zones you cross; zone maps are posted in cabs. Cabs to or from Maryland or Virginia are metered and exorbitant. Hail any cab downtown, but farther out, call **Yellow Cab** (544-1212). Be ready to give some directions or to send the first few cabs away.

Accommodations and Camping

Though notoriously expensive, Washington hotels offer a few bargains. Look for package deals and call the 800 numbers of the major national chains. Spetember,

May, and June are peak tourist months; the humidity drives businesspeople away during July and August, forcing hotels to lower their rates, especially on weekends. The **Holiday Inn Capitol Mall** (479-4000 or 800-465-4329) usually offers "bargains" from $59. For July and August weekends try the **Hotel Anthony**, 1823 L St. NW (223-4320 or 800-424-2970); normally a luxury business hotel, the Anthony drops rates as low as $50 for a single in July and August. Call to be sure. Summer housing at **American University** (885-2599) is available to anyone with valid college student ID, including foreign student tourists, for $75 per week. (2-week min. stay. Metro: Tenleytown. Kitchen facilities, cafeteria. Shuttle bus runs from Metro stop to dorms Mon.-Fri. 7:30am-midnight. Linens $5 per night. Rooms available June-Aug. Write to: American University Office of Summer Housing, McDowell Hall, Rm. 1, 4400 Massachusetts Ave. NW, WDC 20016.) Georgetown U. and Catholic U. housing is allowed only for "educational purposes," which can mean government interns or members of a summer program, but excludes tourists. **Georgetown University**, the most convenient, has singles ($16) or shared doubles ($13-15); write to G.U. Summer Housing, P.O. Box 2214, WDC 20057 or call 687-3999. (3-week min. stay. Bring your own linens. Requires mail application and 20% deposit. Rooms available June to mid-Aug.) **Catholic University** summer housing (319-5277) runs from $14 for a shared double to $18 for an air-conditioned single, with a three-day minimum stay. (Requires mail application and 20% deposit. Write to: Office of Resident Life, 108 St. Bonaventure Hall, Catholic University, WDC 20064. Rooms available mid-May to Aug. Metro: Brookland-CVA.) Write or call well in advance, preferably before May, for all three universities, in order to receive complicated contracts and information.

Area B&Bs are not cheap, though many provide deluxe rooms for a moderate price. Remember to check locations when using a B&B reservation service; some of the cheapest parade far out in the suburbs. **Bed and Breakfast, Ltd.** (328-3510) will reserve you a room at participating establishments for a $10 charge. (Summer: singles from $35, doubles from $45. Off-season extra $10. Call Mon.-Fri. 10am-5pm, Sat. 10am-1pm.) Also try the **Bed and Breakfast League, Ltd.** (363-7767; singles $35-55, doubles $45-65).

Campers have few options, none nearby. For information on parks in Maryland and northern Virginia, call the **National Park Service**, 1100 Ohio Dr. SW (485-9666; open Mon.-Fri. 8am-4pm), or **Dial-a-Park** (619-7275).

Washington International Youth Hostel (AYH), 1009 11th St. NW (737-2333), at K St. Metro: Metro Ctr., exit at G and 11th St. Clean and attractive bunks, bath, and kitchen in a recently renovated building. Friendly management. Separate facilities for men and women. 320-bed capacity. Secure storage area, lounges, laundry facilities. Disabled access. 6-day max. stay, longer if uncrowded. Lockout 11am-2:30pm. Check-in 7-10:30am and 2:30pm-midnight. Curfew midnight. Members only, $13. Linen $2. Memberships sold.

Swiss Inn, 1204 Massachusetts Ave. NW (371-1816). Metro: Metro Ctr. Friendly Swiss proprietor maintains 6 large, carpeted, well-maintained rooms. Coffee tables, private kitchen, private bath, and TV. Single $48. Double $58. Each additional person $10. Weekly: singles $288; doubles $348. Call to reserve a room at least 2 weeks ahead.

Adams Inn, 1744 Lanier Place NW (745-3600), 2 blocks from the center of Adams-Morgan. Metro: Woodley Park-Zoo (but a long walk). Elaborate, elegant Victorian townhouses with Persian rugs everywhere. Singles $45, with bath $60. Doubles $55, with bath $70. Each additional person $10. Breakfast included. Write or call for reservations weeks ahead Mon.-Sat. 9:30am-9pm, Sun. 1-9pm.

Allen Lee Hotel, 2224 F St. NW (331-1224), near George Washington University and Kennedy Center, within walking distance of the Mall and Georgetown. Metro: Foggy Bottom. Great price and location, but cleanliness sacrificed for convenience. Big, comfy beds, but dingy shared bathrooms. Singles $33, with private bath $40. Double $40, with private bath $56. Cot $6 extra. Cash and traveler's checks only. Reservations required in summer.

Kalorama Guest House at **Kalorama Park**, 1854 Mintwood Pl. NW (667-6369), and at **Woodley Park**, 2700 Cathedral Ave. NW (328-0860). Metro: Woodley Park-National Zoo. Friendly staff manages several Victorian townhouses in nice neighborhoods. Enjoy Continental breakfast and afternoon sherry in the oriental-carpeted living room. Smaller Mintwood

Pl. in the heart of Adams-Morgan houses mostly international travelers; Cathedral Ave. has fewer businesspeople. Laundry facilities. Rooms from $55 for 1 person, from $65 for 2. Private bath extra $20. Each additional guest $10. Rates drop $5-10 Nov.-Jan. Reservations with full prepayment or credit card required; cancel for full refund up to 2 weeks ahead.

University Inn, 2134 G St. NW (342-8020 or 800-842-1012). Metro: Foggy Bottom. In the heart of the GWU campus. Aging but clean rooms; slightly noisy but convenient neighborhood. Color TV. Laundry facilities. No private baths. Singles $59. Doubles $65. Weekend discounts available. Students with ID: singles $48, doubles $54; weekly $282 and $321 respectively.

Greenbelt Park, 6565 Greenbelt Rd., Greenbelt, MD 20770 (344-3948), 8-10 mi. and 3 traffic jams from town off the Baltimore-Washington Pkwy. Metro: from Metro Ctr. take Orange Line to New Carrollton, then bus T-16 to Crescent and Ridge Rd. (bus leaves hourly); $1.65 total fare. By car take Greenbelt exit off B-W Pkwy., keep right, pass light, and turn left after 1 mi. A green gem, run by the Feds. Quiet, spacious camping. Hiking trails. No hookup. Sites $6. First come, first served, but fills only for holidays and Grateful Dead concerts.

Capital KOA, 768 Cecil Ave., Millersville, MD 21108 (923-2771). Closer to Baltimore; 23 mi. from DC, 17 from Metro. By car take Rte. 50E to Rte. 3N, 11 mi. to Rte. 178. Pool and recreation room. Free games and movies. Hookups available. Sites $17. Cabins $24. Open April-Oct.

Food

Washington's ethnic eateries please the palates of foreign nationals from all over the globe, with Thai food slowly emerging as a DC specialty. When you get hungry in the Capitol Hill area, take the free Senator Subway from the Capitol to the cafeteria under the Dirksen side of the Senate Office Building. (Open Mon.-Fri. noon-2:30pm.) Sometimes the political stars deign to eat with mere mortals. The food is plain, but the government cafeterias offer some of the cheapest fare in DC. A flashing red light and siren in the dining room warn of an imminent House or Senate floor vote. Most of the Smithsonian buildings also have reasonably priced cafeterias. **Union Station,** Massachusetts and Delaware Ave. NE, has recently been remodeled to its former 1907 Beaux Arts glory and has a number of shops and eclectic eateries. The best bargain restaurants, however, center in **Dupont Circle** and **Adams-Morgan.** Choices range from Southern U.S. to Cuban and Ethiopian.

At the open-air market at the wharves on Maine Ave. and 9th St. SW, you can buy low-priced seafood straight from the Chesapeake Bay; go if only for the sights and smells. The food stands at **Eastern Market,** Independence Ave. and 9th St. SE on Capitol Hill, sell fresh produce, baked goods, meat, and seafood. (Metro: Eastern Market.) Parks and potential picnic sites are plentiful, especially near the White House.

Capitol Hill

Tune Inn, 331½ Pennsylvania Ave. SE. A real dive with 20-yr. veteran staff. Jukebox stocked with country & western oldies. Omelettes, sandwiches, roast beef and chicken; nothing over $4. Beer $1.75. Open Sun.-Thurs. 8am-2am, Fri.-Sat. 8am-3am. Min. order $3.

Hunan Dynasty, 215 Pennsylvania Ave. SE. Excellent tofu, *kung pao,* and other lunch specialties ($6). Ultra-modern surroundings include goldfish and white-collar Hill staff on "power lunches." Open Sun.-Thurs. 11am-10pm, Fri. Sat. 11am-11pm.

Kelly's Irish Times, 14 F St. NW (543-5433). Irish pub, Irish staff, Irish music some nights. Look for Yeats on the menu and the *Irish Times* on sale at the bar. Sandwiches and entrees $5-7. Beer from $2.25, Irish whiskey from $3.25. Open Sun.-Thurs. 10am-2am, Fri.-Sat. 11am-2am.

Hawk 'n' Dove, 329 Pennsylvania Ave. SE. Popular student pub and café. Wild game gazes out from the wall. Dinners $6-13, hearty sandwiches $5-8, midnight breakfast $5.50. Sun.-Thurs. 11am-2am, Fri.-Sat. 11am-3am.

Dupont Circle

The seriously bargain-minded or hurried can get cheap sandwiches ($3) and gyros from the many undistinguished neighborhood delis here, such as the **International Market** store, 2010 P St. NW (open daily 10am-5pm).

Sholl's Colonial Cafeteria, 1990 K St. NW, in the Esplanade Mall about 10 blocks from Dupont Circle. Good cooking at extraordinarily low prices: spaghetti ($1.75), chopped steak ($2), and roast beef ($2.75). Fresh food and generous portions, plus daily specials. Try the homemade pies. Open Mon.-Sat. 7am-2:30pm and 4-8pm.

Food for Thought, 1738 Connecticut Ave. NW (797-1095), 2 blocks from Dupont Circle. Veggie-hippie-folkie mecca with good, healthful food in a 60s atmosphere. Ten different vegetable and fruit salads, plus sandwiches and daily hot specials. Local musicians strum in the evenings. Bulletin boards announce everything from rallies to beach parties to rides to L.A. Lunch $6-8, dinner $6-11. Open Mon. 11:30am-3pm and 5pm-midnight, Tues.-Thurs. 11:30am-midnight, Fri. 11:30am-1am, Sat. noon-1am, Sun. 5pm-midnight.

Café-Petitto, 1724 Connecticut Ave. NW. Excellent Italian regional cooking in an understated atmosphere. Try the aesthetic antipasto buffet ($6) and fried Calabrian pizza. Dinner $6-10. Open daily 11:30am-midnight.

Kramer Books and Afterwards Café, 1517 Connecticut Ave. NW (387-3825). Bookshop dining tending to *nouvelle;* Washington's best pies, cakes, and mousses ($3.25-5). Hip crowds include theatergoers and DC's svelte literary scene. Live music Fri.-Sun after 10pm. Open Sun.-Thurs. 7:30am-11:45pm, Fri.-Sat. 24 hr.

Pan-Asian Noodles and Grill, 2020 P St. NW. Soups and unusual noodle-related dishes in 2 red-and-gray art-deco rooms. Vegetarian on request. Lunch from $6, dinner from $7. Open Mon.-Thurs. 11:30am-2:30pm and 5:30-10:30pm, Fri. 11:30am-2:30pm and 5:30-11pm, Sat. noon-2:30pm and 5:30-11pm, Sun. 5:30-10pm.

Volare Pizza, 2011 S St. NW, 3 blocks north of the Circle. Nothing fancy, just solid, cheap food in large portions. Full-meal daily specials, subs and enormous gyros ($4-5), whole pizzas ($4-6), and greasy breakfasts ($2-3). Open Mon.-Sat. 7am-11pm, Sun. 8am-10pm.

Georgetown

Washingtonians often eat dinner in Adams-Morgan, then come here for drinks, dessert, or a late-night snack; **Thomas Sweet,** Wisconsin Ave. and P St. NW, serves DC's best homemade ice cream and ices from $2 (open Sun.-Thurs. 9:30am-midnight, Fri.-Sat. 9:30am-1am).

Vietnam-Georgetown Restaurant, 2934 M St. NW. Excellent restaurant next to similarly great **Viet Huong,** 2928 M St. NW. Both serve fine crispy roll appetizers, gold-coin pork, and chicken with lemon grass entrees. Lunch at Vietnam-Georgetown $6, dinner $7-11. Open Mon.-Thurs. 11am-11pm, Fri.-Sat. noon-midnight, Sun. noon-11pm. Lunch at Viet Huong $5-6, dinner $6-11. Open Mon.-Fri. 11:30am-3pm and 5-10pm, Sat.-Sun. noon-11pm.

Georgetown Café, 1623 Wisconsin Ave. NW. Solid and deliciously greasy food with Middle Eastern dishes on the side (hummus and felafel $3). Breakfast anytime $1.50-3, lunch $3-4, dinner $3-7, with $2 beers. Open 24 hr.

Au Pied de Cochon/Aux Fruits de Mer, 1335 Wisconsin Ave. NW. The French entrees no bargain; come here for light fare, coffee, or excellent desserts ($2-4). Free, fresh rolls, and late-night crowds. Open 24 hr.

Madurai, 3318 M St. NW, above Zed's Ethiopian restaurant. Good Indian vegetarian dinners ($6-8); all-you-can-eat on Sun. night. Superb appetizers $1.50-3. Open daily noon-2:30pm and 5-10pm.

Gepetto's, 2917 M St. NW (333-2912). High-class crispy pizzas (from $10), with impossible stacks of meat on top—1 pie could feed 3 people. DC's best pizza say some. Open Mon.-Thurs. noon-11:30pm, Fri.-Sat. noon-1:30am, Sun. 4-11:30pm. They deliver.

Hamburger Hamlet, 3125 M St. NW. Some of the best burgers in DC, topped with everything from guacamole to caviar ($6). Sandwiches, salads, chili, and seafood $6-12. Big beers. Alas, poor Yorick. Open Sun.-Thurs. 11am-midnight, Fri.-Sat. 11am-1am.

Thai Taste of Georgetown, downstairs at 3287½ M St. NW. As good as its Connecticut Ave. cousin and usually less crowded. Delicious Thai food including whole fish, good satay, vegetarian entrees, and the ubiquitous *pad thai* (noodles, shrimp, pork, veggies, and spice grains). Dinner from $6. Open daily noon-2am.

Adams-Morgan

The Red Sea, 2463 18th St. NW (483-5000), and **Meskerem,** 2434 18th St. NW (462-4100). Consistent favorites among DC's burgeoning crop of Ethiopian restaurants. Use the traditional pancake bread, *injera,* to eat spicy lamb, beef, chicken, and vegetable *wats* (stews). Red Sea slightly cheaper (dinners $5-9) with live music Fri.-Sat., but Meskerem (dinners $6.50-9) offers archeological decor beneath a skylight and dining loft. Red Sea open Sun.-Thurs. 11:30am-11:30pm, Fri.-Sat. 11:30am-midnight. Meskerem open Mon.-Thurs. 5pm-midnight, Fri.-Sat. noon-12:30am, Sun. noon-midnight.

Thai Taste, 2606 Connecticut Ave. NW. Metro: Woodley Park-National Zoo. DC's black-and-neon magnet for Thai food lovers. Try the fried beef with chili paste and coconut milk, then Thai iced coffee ($1.50). Entrees $5-10, but $6 min. per person. Open Mon.-Thurs. 11:30am-10:30pm, Fri.-Sat. 11:30am-11pm, Sun. 5-10:30pm.

Mixtec, 1792 Columbia Rd. NW. Fantastic Mexican cuisine in a café setting. Rightly renowned for their *tacos al carbón* ($3 appetizer, $6 entree). Open Sun.-Thurs. 11am-10pm, Fri.-Sat. 9:30am-11:30pm.

Dante's, 1522 14th St. NW at Q St. Just as close to Dupont Circle—drive south on 16th St. NW from Adams-Morgan. Brand-new aqua-colored hangout for DC's tragically hip. Big, creative sandwiches like the "Hot Veg-o-Matic" ($5-7.50); skip the desserts. Open Mon. 5pm-3am, Tues.-Thurs. 11:30am-3am, Fri. 11:30am-4am, Sat. 5pm-4am, Sun. 11am-3pm (brunch) and 5pm-3am.

Fish Wings & Tings, 2418 18th St. NW. Carry-out lunch and dinner $4-10. Tiny, gaudy, and quasi-fast-food, but cultivating a reputation as DC's best Caribbean cuisine. Open Mon.-Thurs. noon-10pm, Fri.-Sat. noon-11pm.

Chinatown

This four-square-block neighborhood between 8th and 6th and Eye and G St. NW (Metro: Gallery Place) includes Chinese groceries, Chinese-language movie rentals, and the city's best Chinese restaurants. Do not come here alone at night.

Szechuan, 615 Eye St. NW (393-0130). Plush upstairs rooms offering DC's best Chinese food, especially the Szechuan/Hunan dishes. Excellent service. Lunch $6.50-8, dinner $7-15. Open Mon.-Thurs. 11am-11pm, Fri.-Sat. 11am-midnight, Sun. 11am-10pm. Free delivery downtown and in Adams-Morgan, including the youth hostel.

Szechuan Gallery, 617 H St. NW. Ignore the name, read the reviews on the door, and insist on the English-language "Taiwanese menu"—truly unusual Asian seafood at moderate prices. Try "fragrant crab." Dinner $5-10. Open Sun.-Thurs. 11am-3am, Fri.-Sat. 11am-4pm.

Chinatown Express, 744-746 6th St. NW (638-0424). Good, mainstream Chinese for the seriously budget-minded. Lunch specials ($3.25) Mon.-Fri. 10am-5pm. Dinner from $4.25. Open daily 10am-11pm.

Elsewhere

Florida Avenue Grill, 1100 Florida Ave. NW at 11th St. 2½ mi. north of the Mall. Metrobus: 11th St. or 16th St. to Florida Ave. Small diner overflowing with locals. Framed faces of boxers and entertainers beam down from the back wall. Awesome Southern-style food: breakfast with salmon cakes or spicy half-smoked sausage, eggs, grits, hotcakes, or southern biscuits ($3-4.50); lunch and dinner $4.25-7. Open Mon.-Sat. 6am-9pm.

Booeymonger, 5252 Wisconsin Ave. NW. Metro: Friendship Hts. Offbeat deli near the MD-DC line. Immense subs and sandwiches ($4-6), including vegetarian fare. Open daily 8am-1am; summer often until 2am.

Thai Flavor, 3709 McComb St. NW (966-0200), at Wisconsin Ave. NW. Take bus #30, 32, or 38 from Wisconsin and Q. Authentic and cheap Thai food with Thai customers. Try the *pad thai* or chicken with red basil. Delivery available for orders over $12. Lunch from $4. Dinner $6-12. Open Mon.-Sat. 11am-3pm and 5-10:45pm, Sun. 5-10:45pm.

Sights

Politics may be the business of Washington, but the city has cultural aspirations as well. DC's docket sports a wide array of museums, monuments, historic sites, parks, and libraries. An after-dark tour of the monuments provides a romantic escape from daytime heat and crowds. Don't make the common mistake of confining yourself to the Mall and its environs; some of DC's best sights hover far from it, including the Phillips Collection, the National Zoo, and Frederick Douglass' home. Some neighborhoods are even sights in themselves.

Tourmobile, 1000 Ohio Dr. SW, (554-7950 or 554-7020), a concession of the National Park Service, operates organized bus tours of Washington which stop at 18 major points of interest downtown. Ride all day in DC and/or to Arlington Cemetery ($8); you can also ride from 4 to 6pm one day and all day the next ($10). (Buses daily every 20 min. 9:30am-6:30pm.) Ride just to Arlington Cemetery ($2.75) or the Frederick Douglass House ($5). Tickets are half-price for children under 12. Buy tickets at one of the booths near eight major toursites or from the driver, and board at any stop on the Mall. You can reboard free anywhere. For the same prices, a fully equipped van for the disabled is available (554-7020; make reservations at least 24 hr. in advance). Gray Line, 50 Massachusetts Ave. NE (289-1995), offers pricey morning tours and affordable evening tours leaving at 8pm, from late October to late May at 7:30pm. (Evening tours $18, seniors with AARP card 10% discount, children $9.)

For a comprehensive two-hour narrated tour of the city aboard a trackless trolley, try Old Town Trolley Tours, 3150 V St. NE (269-3020). Buy tickets at the Old Post Office Pavilion, 1100 Pennsylvania Ave. NW, or from a hotel concierge, and catch a trolley at most major hotels. (Operates daily 9am-6pm; Labor Day-Memorial Day 9am-4pm. Tours $14, children $5. Reboard free.) Connoisseurs of the offbeat should try Scandal Tours (387-2259), which explore the more sensational side of Washington. See, among other things, the Pentagon, Watergate, and Gary Hart's townhouse. Tour guides imitate modern politicos. (Tours leave from the Washington Hilton, 1830 Connecticut Ave. NW Sat.-Sun. at 1 and 3pm. Tickets $27 plus $1-3 service charge; buy at the Hilton or through Ticketron, 800-543-3041.)

Capitol Hill

The beautiful, Renaissance-style Capitol Building (Metro: Capitol S. or Union Station) is a must-see. Walk by at night; if a lantern is lit high in the central dome, then congress is in session. (225-6827 or 224-3121; open daily 9am-4:30pm; free tours Mon.-Sat. every 15 min. 9am-3:45 pm; for disabled tour information 224-4048, TDD 224-4049.) To enter the visitors' galleries on your own, write your Representative or Senator for a pass. Those interested in seeing an actual congressional committee hearing should consult the Washington Post's daily "Today in Congress" column, usually placed in the front section.

Behind the Capitol at 1st St. and Maryland Ave. NE, the Supreme Court Building (479-3000) hands down various basement exhibits on the Court and Constitution. Check the "Court Calendar" of the Washington Post to see if the Court is in session. The court hears oral arguments from October to April from 10am to 3pm; queue at 9am to watch the whole argument or see five minutes of it as you walk through in the tourist line. Decisions are handed down in May and June at 10am. Metro: Capitol South. (Building open Mon.-Fri. 9am-4:30pm. Lecture tours every hr. Mon.-Fri. 9:30am-3:30pm when court not in session.)

Next to the Supreme Court looms the world's most comprehensive library, the Library of Congress, 1st St. and Independence Ave. SE (287-5000 for general info; tours 707-5458). The square modern marble Madison Building and the old ornate Jefferson Building comprise the vast complex. The architecture inside is breathtaking, and most library services are available to the public. Check out (not literally) the circular reading room from the second-floor visitors' gallery, the Gutenberg Bible, and the copies of Shakespeare's First Folio. (Open Mon.-Fri. 8:30am-9:30pm,

Sat.-Sun. and holidays 8:30am-6pm. Call for exhibits. Free 45-min. tours Mon.-Fri. every hr. 9am-4pm.)

Shakespeare buffs should also enjoy the **Folger Shakespeare Library and Theater,** 201 E. Capitol St. SE (544-7077 for public programs, 544-4000 for general information; library open Mon.-Sat. 10am-4pm). The small performance space resembles the Elizabethan Inns of Court theaters, in which Shakespeare's Blackfriars company performed. Today, an excellent company performs plays, not always Shakespearean. Reserve, if you can, months in advance; students should call the box office for rush-ticket availability. Metro: Capitol South. (Evening performances at 8pm, Sat. matinees at noon and 2pm. Tickets $21-35, seniors 20% off, students with ID 1 hr. before showtime ½-price. Box office 546-4000, open Mon. 10am-6pm, Tues.-Sat. noon-8pm, Sun. noon-7:30pm.)

The **Capital Children's Museum,** 800 3rd St. NE at H St. NE (543-8600, recorded message at 638-5437), offers "hands on" exhibits. Make tortillas, step inside a Native American burial ground, wander through a maze, or build a log cabin; there are enough activities here to occupy for several hours an army of children, all of whom must be accompanied by an adult. Metro: Union Station. (Admission $4, seniors and under 2 $1. Open daily 10am-5pm.)

Museums on the Mall

The **Smithsonian Institution** (357-2700 from 9am-5pm; 24-hr. recorded message 357-2020) is a glorious conglomeration of 14 galleries and museums, most of which recline on or near the Mall. Nearly 140 years ago, money from the bequest of English James Smithson founded the Smithsonian as the National Museum of the U.S. All attractions are free, wheelchair accessible, and offer written guides in French, German, Spanish, and Japanese with some Chinese, Arabic, and Portuguese. All open daily, generally from 10am to 5:30pm; in summer some extend their hours, and in winter some close on weekends. Exceptions are indicated below. In general, the science, history, and technology museums (Air and Space, American History, Natural History) draw large crowds, especially on summer weekends; the art museums only during touring exhibits. Allot at least two and a half days to see the Mall museums properly, four if you're a serious art buff. A 15-minute orientation film, a general information desk, and administrative offices showboat in **The Castle,** 1000 Jefferson Dr. SW, on the center of the Mall (357-2700, recording 357-2020, TDD 357-1729; open daily 9am-5pm). The Castle also stocks *Smithsonian: A Guide for Disabled Visitors,* but call a day in advance to request it. Get the free guides by writing to: Office of Public Affairs, Smithsonian Institution, WDC 20560. Cassette (free) and braille ($2) editions available. The outstanding **Smithsonian Folklife Festival** (287-3424), usually held in late June and early July, celebrates the arts and crafts of a different culture each year.

The **National Air and Space Museum,** 6th St. and Independence Ave. (357-2700), near the Capitol on the south side of the Mall, is the world's most-visited museum. Touch moon rocks and gawk at airplanes—the Wright brothers' *Kitty Hawk,* Lindbergh's *Spirit of St. Louis*—and spacecraft, including the command module from the first Apollo XI moon landing. Try to catch one of the astonishing 70mm movies shown on their five-story screen. Metro: L'Enfant Plaza. (Museum open daily 10am-5:30pm. Movie $2.25, seniors, students with ID, and children $1.25; weekend double features at 5:35 and 6:50pm $4 and $2.50. Shows and showtimes change frequently. Tours of museum highlights daily at 10:15am and 1pm. Recorded tours available in English, French, Spanish, German, Japanese, Portuguese, and Italian for $3, seniors and students $2.50.)

The spectacular interior space of the **East Wing** of the **National Gallery of Art,** 6th St. and Constitution Ave. NW (737-4215), close to the Capitol, is architect I.M. Pei's celebration of light and triangles. Look for the immense Calder mobile. The knife-edge corner of the building is one of the sharpest corners in modern architecture; according to legend, if you touch it, or even better, kiss it, you'll have good luck. The East Wing houses the more modern part of the gallery's painting collection. Built in the 1940s, the **West Wing** holds one of the world's greatest collections of European paintings in a serene pseudo-19th-century setting. Look for the Italian Renaissance pictures, then for Salvador Dali's famous *Last Supper,* hung in a different stairwell or small room each year. An underground moving walkway connects the East Wing, the West Wing, and the West Wing's cafeteria (lunch buffet $4). Check out the streamlined balconies and Greek columns on the brand-new Canadian Embassy next door. Metro: Archives or Judiciary Square. (Museums open Mon.-Sat. 10am-5pm, Sun. noon-5pm. Free East Wing tours Mon.-Fri. at 11:30am, Sat. at 11am, Sun at noon. West Wing introductory tours Mon.-Sat. at 3pm, Sun. at 1pm; guided tours in French, Spanish, German, and Italian given intermittently—call 842-6247 for details.)

The **Museum of African Art,** 950 Independence Ave. SW (357-4600; 357-2700 on weekends), dwells in the relaxing Quadrangle beside the Castle. Housed in an innovative, three-level, underground building, the museum displays a varied and authoritative collection of ceremonial masks and figures, textiles, sculpture, and functional objects. (Open daily 10am-5:30pm. 1-hr. tours leave from the information desk Mon.-Fri. at 10:30am, Sat.-Sun. at 10:30am, 1:30pm, and 3:30pm.)

The Smithsonian's newest museum, the **Arthur M. Sackler Gallery,** 1050 Independence Ave. SW (357-2700), shares the unique granite and glass building with the Museum of African Art. The Sackler's array of Asian and Near Eastern art includes jade, gold, silver, and bronze artifacts, ancient ritual objects, manuscripts, and 20th-century scrolls. A serene ornamental garden surrounds the museum. (Open daily 10am-5:30pm. Tours leave from the information desk daily at 11:30am.)

Next door, the **Hirshhorn Museum and Sculpture Garden,** at 7th St. and Independence Ave. SW (357-2700; 357-1300 for tour info), contains the most comprehensive collection of 19th- and 20th-century European and U.S. sculpture in the world, including small works by Rodin and Giacometti, with touring and permanent exhibits of modern painting and mixed-media from Picasso and Braque to the current avant-garde. The cylindrical Hirshhorn building has outraged traditionalists for decades. The gift shop sells art books and incomparable jazz and folklore records issued solely by the Smithsonian. The Sculpture Garden, on the Mall across from the main building, is a quiet oasis in the bustle of downtown DC, with works by Smith, Calder, and Aristide Maillol. (Open daily 10am-5:30pm. Tours Mon.-Fri. at 10:30am, noon, and 1:30pm, Sat. at 10:30am, noon, 1:30, and 2:30pm, Sun. 12:30-3:30pm hourly.)

Diagonally across the Mall from the Castle, the **National Museum of American History,** 14th St. and Constitution Ave. (357-1300), sits like a cluttered attic of rather cumbersome U.S. past. Among its always percolating exhibits are the original star-spangled banner and Horatio Greenough's infamous "topless" sculpture of George Washington. Next year's new goodies will include several rooms devoted to women in American reform movements 1890-1925. Visit the 1910-style ice cream parlor on the first floor for a grandiose banana split. (Open daily 10am-5:30pm. Tours Mon.-Fri. at 10am and 1pm, Sat. at 10am, 11am, and 1pm, Sun. at 11am and 1pm.)

You'll recognize the **National Museum of Natural History,** 10th St. and Constitution Ave. (357-2700), directly opposite the Castle, by the triceratops—popular with the playground set—standing outside. High points are the Hope Diamond, the Blue Whale, dinosaur skeletons, and an insect zoo. Anthropological exhibits include several galleries on Native American and Inuit life and customs. Kids love the Discovery Room and Naturalist Center. (Open daily 10am-5:30pm. Tours daily from the Rotunda at 10:30am and 1:30pm.)

The **Arts and Industries Museum,** 900 Jefferson Dr. SW (357-2700), motors next to the Castle on the south side of the Mall. Recreating the 1876 Centennial exhibition in Philadelphia, this museum looks like a huge, multi-national flea market. You can't ring the Liberty Bells made from sugar, tobacco, and cotton. (Open daily 10am-5:30pm. Free tours by appointment.)

Near the Mall

Among the fascinating permanent exhibits at the **National Archives,** at 7th St. and Constitution Ave. NW (501-5205), just north of the Mall, you'll find the Bill of Rights, the Declaration of Independence, the Constitution, and a 13th-century copy of the Magna Carta. You'll have to stand in a short line at the Constitution Ave. entrance to see them, though. Temporary photography and document exhibits cover local and U.S. history. From the 7th St. bus shelter beside the Archives, a shuttle leaves at 8am, 9:30am, 11:30am, 1:45pm, and 3:15pm for 845 S. Picket St., Alexandria, where you can hear the infamous Watergate tapes; call the Archives at 756-6498 for information. (Open daily 10am-9pm; Sept.-March 10am-5:30pm. Free.)

Also behind the line of museums on the North Mall, the **Federal Bureau of Investigation (FBI),** between 9th and 10th St. and Pennsylvania Ave. NW (324-3447), gives the most entertaining tour in Washington. Today's FBI seems not to have changed since the 60s TV show *Today's FBI;* stoic-faced agents/flight attendants explain how the Feds fight drugs, organized crime, and, egads, communist spies. Thrill to mementos of notorious criminals captured by the FBI, a laboratory of agents examining forensic specimens used to identify criminals, and the notorious live firearms demonstration. Not even prime-time TV offers such excitement. Arrive early in the morning or at least go on a weekday; lines for the hugely popular tour are often enormous. Metro: Federal Triangle or Metro Center. (Open Mon.-Fri. 8:45am-4:15pm. Free 1-hr. tours every 15 min.)

The **Bureau of Engraving and Printing,** 14th and C St. SW (447-9709), just south of the Washington Monument, offers continuous tours of the presses that annually print over $20 billion-worth of money and stamps. Look for the bins of shredded bills. Perhaps intoxicated with false consciousness, tourists have made this the area's longest line: skip breakfast or expect a 2-hr. wait. (Open Mon.-Fri. 9am-2pm. Self-guided tours. Free.)

The Smithsonian's **National Portrait Gallery,** 8th and F St. NW (357-2700), displays portraits of U.S. residents from all walks of life. See Gilbert Stuart's famous unfinished portraits of George and Martha Washington, the Hall of the Presidents, and the *Time* magazine cover collection. Metro: Gallery Place. (Open daily 10am-5:30pm. Tours Mon.-Fri. 10am-3pm, Sat.-Sun. and holidays 11am-2pm.) Often deserted, despite its excellent sampling of U.S. art from the classical to the modern abstract, the **National Museum of American Art,** 8th and G St. NW (357-2700), shares the building with the National Portrait Gallery. Temporary shows often explore representation and racial stereotypes. (Open daily 10am-5:30pm. Tours Mon.-Fri. at noon, Sat.-Sun. at 2pm.)

The **National Building Museum,** F St. NW (272-2448), between 4th and 5th St., honors great achievements in U.S. building arts and architecture. The museum building itself is stunning; look 150 ft. up at the 244 busts tucked in niches around the Old Pension Building's Great Hall. Metro: Judiciary Sq., F St. exit. (Open Mon.-Sat. 10am-4pm, Sun. and holidays noon-4pm. Tours Mon.-Fri. at 12:30pm, Sat.-Sun. at 12:30 and 1:30pm.)

Ford's Theater, 511 10th St. NW (426-6924), contains the Presidential Box, frozen in time on April 15, 1865, the night Lincoln was shot. The Lincoln Museum is downstairs. Across the street from Ford's Theater is the morbid **House Where Lincoln Died,** 526 10th St. NW (426-6830), worth a stop, if only for the furnishings and carefully restored rooms. Metro: Metro Center. (Open daily 9am-5pm. Ford's Theater sometimes closed Sat.-Sun. from 1pm. Free.)

The White House Area

For a summer visit to the **White House,** 1600 Pennsylvania Ave. NW (456-2200 or 456-7041), try to have the office of your Senator or Representative arrange a tour. Otherwise, you'll have to suffer through a one- or two-hour wait for the regular, abbreviated tour, which only takes you through five public rooms used for receptions. Disabled people can bypass the lines and ticket booths and enter through the northeast (exit) gate on Pennsylvania Ave. NW. Metro: McPherson Sq. or Farragut W. (Open Tues.-Sat. 10am-noon. Free tour tickets available at booth on the Ellipse, 755-7798; open daily 8am-noon.) In a stately 19th-century building at 17th St. between E St. and New York Ave. NW, the **Corcoran Gallery of Art** (638-3211), DC's largest and oldest private gallery, has a permanent U.S. and European collection. Devotees of the contemporary art scene come for the changing if no longer innovative shows in "Gallery One;" the gallery gained national exposure when it cancelled its 1989 Mapplethorpe photography exhibits. Metro: Farragut W. (Open Tues.-Wed. and Fri.-Sun. 10am-4:30pm, Thurs. 10am-9pm. Free tours daily at 12:30pm. Disabled access.) The **Renwick Gallery,** at 17th St. and Pennsylvania Ave. NW (357-1718 or 357-2700), bills itself as a "museum of American craft" and decorative arts, but most of the gallery isn't just for macrame buffs—1990's "New American Furniture" included a disorienting "cubist chest of drawers" and a table called "Mystery Robots Rip Off the Rain Forest." The **National Museum for Women in the Arts,** 1250 New York Ave. NW (783-5000), celebrates women's artistic contributions in its permanent collection and traveling exhibits. The beautifully renovated Renaissance revival building houses works in a multitude of media—fresco to photography, ceramics to silver, nylon to neon. Collection includes pieces by Georgia O'Keeffe, Mary Cassatt, Helen Frankenthaler. (Open Mon.-Sat. 10am-5pm, Sun. noon-5pm. Tours by appointment. Free.)

The **Organization of American States,** 17th St. at C St. NW (458-3000), contains an air-conditioned Mexican garden and small displays of Latin American arts and crafts. (Open Mon.-Fri. 9am-5pm.) It's traditional to get your picture taken sitting in the lap of the giant Albert Einstein statue outside the **National Academy of Sciences,** 2101 Constitution Ave. NW (393-8100; recording 334-2436). Exhibits indoors cover various scientific fields. **Lafayette Park,** across Pennsylvania Ave. from the White House, features statues of Revolutionary War generals and a representative sample of DC's sizable homeless population. Notice the Peace Park anti-nuclear vigils with gaudy, urgent signs and tattered tents.

Memorials

After you stand in a long line to take the elevator 555 ft. to the top of the tallest building in town, the **Washington Monument,** on the National Mall (426-6839), at 15th St. NW, will reward you with a perfect view down Constitution Ave. to the Capitol and across the Potomac River. Originally, the design included a large baroque base, but money ran out, resulting in its present phallic obelisk simplicity. (Stairs closed.) Spectacular **Fourth of July** festivities are held here, and during the rest of the summer the Washington Monument alternates with the Capitol building as the site of **free outdoor concerts** by the U.S. Military bands (June-Aug. at 8pm). Call the National Park Service recording **Dial-A-Park** (619-7275) for concert times, Mall events, and monument closings. Metro: Smithsonian. (Open April-Aug. daily 8am-midnight, last elevator 11:45pm; Sept.-March 9am-5pm.)

A visit to the **Lincoln Memorial,** West Potomac Park at 23rd St. NW (426-6895), is most memorable at twilight, when the image of the Washington Monument ripples in the long reflecting pool. The text of the Gettysburg Address embellishes the wall. Here, Martin Luther King, Jr. delivered his "I Have a Dream" speech, and African American operatic singer Marion Anderson sang from the steps when the Daughters of the American Revolution barred her entrance to Constitution Hall in 1939. Ask a Park Ranger for a guided tour request form between 8am-midnight. (Open 24 hr.) Walk around to the south side of the Tidal Basin, past the cherry trees, to the **Jefferson Memorial** (426-6821). Jefferson's imposing figure stands prominently in an open building adorned with excerpts of his famous writings. (Open daily 8am-midnight.) Cruise around the Tidal Basin in front of the memorial in a two-person paddleboat (484-0206; daily 10am-7:30pm, weather permitting; $7 per hr.)

The names of 58,175 U.S. citizens killed in the Vietnam War are carved into the haunting, black granite **Vietnam Veterans War Memorial** (426-6700), sunken into the ground on the north side of the reflecting pool at Constitution Ave. and 21st

St. NW. Designer Maya Ying Lin's eloquent design like "a rift in the earth" provokes violent and powerful emotions. Its eye-level simplicity and spare presentation confront the confusion and complexity of the war, and the nighttime reflections of the Capitol, the Washington Monument, and the Lincoln Memorial contrast ironically with the stark lists of the dead. After a bitter controversy over the aptness of such an abstract construction, Frederick Hart created a remarkably realistic statue of three veterans close to Lin's masterpiece.

The unforgettable World War II photograph of weary Marines triumphantly hoisting a U.S. flag on Mt. Suribachi has been immortalized in the largest bronze statue ever cast. The 78-ft. **Iwo Jima Statue Marine Corps Memorial** commemorates all U.S. Marines killed since 1775. Metro: Arlington Cemetery. (On Rte. 50, near Arlington Cemetery. Open 24 hr.)

Dupont Circle/Business District

Home to a plurality of DC's embassies, lobbyists, and good bookstores, the Dupont Circle neighborhood—roughly bounded by 16th, 23rd, S, and O St. NW—is the hub of Washington's ethnic, intellectual, and gay communities. Connecticut, Massachusetts, and New Hampshire Ave. intersect in Dupont Circle about 10 blocks north of the White House. Chess players, lunching office workers, and drug dealers populate the Circle's grassy island. Massachusetts Ave.'s Embassy Row runs west from the Circle. Walk north from Dupont Circle for the art museums, private galleries, and very snazzy townhouses; head a few blocks south to the glass-walled business district. Colorful and increasingly popular Adams-Morgan lies off upper Connecticut Ave., along Columbia Rd. In **Farragut Square,** 3 blocks south of Connecticut Ave., on 17th St. between Eye and K St. NW, picnic to the summer sounds of flute duets and jazz sax players.

The **Phillips Collection,** 1600-1612 21st St. at Q St. NW (387-2151), was the first museum of modern art in the U.S. and the best non-Smithsonian art museum in town. In addition to Renoir's masterpiece, *Luncheon of the Boating Party,* this intimate museum houses a connoisseur's choice of 19th- and 20th-century French painting and U.S. modernists such as Georgia O'Keeffe and Arthur Dove. Free chamber music and classical piano concerts take place from September to May Sundays at 5pm; check the *Washington Post's* "Weekend" for information. Metro: Dupont Circle, Q St. exit. (Open Tues.-Sat. 10am-5pm, Sun. 2-7pm. Free tours Wed. and Sat. at 2pm. Donation suggested. Disabled access.) The **Woodrow Wilson House,** 2340 S St. NW (673-4034), remains DC's only public past Presidential home, filled with artifacts from WW I, Wilson's administration, and the 1920s. (Open Tues.-Sat. 10am-4pm, Sun. noon-4pm. 1-hr. tours on request given by friendly, knowledgeable guides. Make reservations for tours for the blind and the hearing-impaired. Admission $3.50, seniors and students $2. Metro: Dupont Circle, Q St. exit.)

Andersen House, 2118 Massachusetts Ave. NW (785-2040), next to the Ritz-Carlton Hotel, remains as robber-baron and U.S. Ambassador Lars Andersen kept it in the 1880s and 90s. The stone columns hide a 2-story ballroom with indoor balconies and braided marble columns. The Society of the Cinncinnati (descendents of 1770s Continental Army officers) makes this decadent mansion its HQ. (Tours Tues.-Sat. 1-4pm; call ahead for wheelchair information. Free.)

For serious browsing, stop at **Second Story Books,** 2000 P St. NW (659-8884), with thousands of uncatalogued, previously-read paperbacks and hardcovers. (Open daily 10am-10pm. Metro: Dupont Circle.) **Lambda Rising,** 1625 Connecticut Ave. NW (462-6967), stocks work by and for gay people (open daily 10am-midnight); smaller **Lammas,** 1426 21st St. NW (775-8218) focuses on feminist literature and their resource directories provide data on gay and lesbian life in DC (open Mon.-Fri. 11am-9pm, Sat. 10am-9pm, Sun. noon-7pm).

The **Washington Post,** 1150 15th St., at L St. NW (334-7969), is the ubiquitous opiate in this town of news junkies; watch the next day's edition come to life on a guided tour, which includes the hectic newsroom, enormous presses and, inexplicably, the mailroom. Metro: Farragut North or Farragut West. (1-hour tours Mon.

and Thurs. at 10am, 11am, 1pm, 2pm, and 3pm. One-day reservation required. Free, no children under 11.)

Also in the business district, near the Post, are three small museums. The **National Geographic Explorer's Hall,** 17th and M St. NW (857-7588 or 857-7589; N.G. Society 857-7000), displays the world's largest free-standing globe and exhibits on early humanity and Colorado cliff dwellers. Metro: Farragut North. (Open Mon.-Sat. and holidays 9am-5pm, Sun. 10am-5pm. Disabled access.) The **B'nai B'rith Klutznick Museum,** 1640 Rhode Island Ave. NW (857-6583), contains Jewish cultural and ritual objects of importance, including George Washington's famous letter to the Newport, RI synagogue addressing religious freedom. Metro: Farragut North. (Open Sun.-Fri. 10am-5pm except Jewish holidays. Donation.) The genuinely disarming **National Rifle Association Museum,** 1600 Rhode Island Ave. NW (828-6255), maintains over 1000 firearms, including Teddy Roosevelt's pistol and Ronald Reagan's flintlock. (Open Mon.-Fri. 10am-4pm. Free.) Rather ironically, up 17th St. at Q St. NW is the **Trio Restaurant,** where African American civil rights organizers met to plan the 1963 March on Washington.

Georgetown

The settling of Georgetown preceded the construction of the District of Columbia, and some streets retain their original names. Today, Georgetown buzzes with constant activity. **M Street** and **Wisconsin Avenue,** the main streets running through Georgetown, overflow with unusual stores, fashionable clubs, expensive restaurants, and homeless people. A diverse crowd joins the weekend parade. When you're looking for the slightly offbeat, Georgetown probably has it, at a price. Some of DC's most beautiful townhouses line the winding streets off the main drags. Georgetown at night is fairly safe though, as usual, solo travelers should stay out of dark alleys. On weekend nights, gridlock reigns.

Georgetown is, not surprisingly, the home of **Georgetown University,** 3800 Reservoir Rd. NW (687-3600; general information 687-3634; student activities 687-3704), a Jesuit school known for fine academics and a stellar basketball team. The shady campus displays a wide variety of architectural styles including good examples of collegiate Gothic. The admissions office gives daily tours.

Dumbarton Oaks Museum and Garden, 1703 32nd St. NW (342-3233), a country estate just blocks from commercial Wisconsin Ave., features a rare collection of Pre-Columbian and Byzantine art in the mansion. But the garden provides the best reason to visit: the terraced, elaborate, blooming wonderland is never crowded on weekdays, making it DC's best cheap date. Metro: Dupont Circle, transfer to #30, 32, 34, 36, or 38 bus at 20th and P NW and get off after 32nd St. (Open Tues.-Sat. 2-5pm. Gardens open 2-6pm. Admission $2, seniors and children $1. Seniors free Wed. Free Nov.-March. Disabled access.)

When you (or your wallet) aren't in a bar-hopping mood, try the **Biograph Theater,** 2819 M St. NW (333-2696), showing obscure and often excellent art films from all over the globe. Bring your own popcorn.

Elsewhere

The **National Zoological Park,** on the 3000 block of Connecticut Ave. NW (673-4800 or 673-4717), is one of the largest and best-run zoos in the country. Highlights include two giant pandas, bald eagles, kangaroos, and a pair of full-grown tigers on their own grassy island. Follow the painted birdfeet to the high, enclosed walk-in "cage" of exotic birds. Metro: Woodley Park-National Zoo. (Grounds open daily 8am-8pm, buildings 9am-6pm; Sept. 16-April 30 8am-6pm, buildings 9am-4:30pm. Tours by special arrangement; call 673-4955.)

The Smithsonian's **Anacostia Museum** 1901 Fort Place SE (357-2700; 287-3369; TDD 357-1696), off Martin Luther King, Jr. Ave. SE, holds changing exhibits and occasional lectures and concerts focused on African American history and culture. Call during February (Black History Month) for special programs. Driving, take MLK Ave. to Morris Rd.; call Metro for the complex bus routes there. (Open daily 10am-5pm. Tours Mon.-Fri. at 10am, 11am, and 1pm. Free. Wheelchair accessible.)

Also in Anacostia, the **Frederick Douglass Home,** 1411 W St. SE (426-5961), chronicles the life of the great African American abolitionist. The house's objects still remain from when Douglass lived in it. Required 30-minute tours start hourly from the visitors center next door. (Open daily 9am-5pm. Free.)

Take in the spectacular view of Washington and the surrounding area from the Pilgrim Observation Gallery at **Washington National Cathedral,** Massachusetts and Wisconsin Ave. NW (537-6200). The sixth largest in the world and the second largest in the U.S., this impressive Gothic cathedral features intricate stained glass windows, stone carvings, and Woodrow Wilson's tomb. At night, stroll safely around the grounds and find the gazebos in the Bishop's Garden. Metro: Tenleytown, then bus #36 "Hillcrest." (Open Mon.-Fri. 10am-7:30pm, Sat.-Sun. 10am-4:30pm; Sept. 8-May 3 daily 10am-4:30pm. Grounds open 24 hr. Free. Continuous tours Mon.-Sat. 12:30-3:15pm, Sun. 12:30pm and 2:45pm.)

The **U.S. National Arboretum,** 3501 New York Ave. NE (475-4815), spreads across 444 acres of magnificently landscaped grounds with a special bonsai collection to make you feel tall. Metro: Stadium Armory, walk to 24th and R St. NE. (Open Mon.-Fri. 8am-5pm, Sat.-Sun. 10am-5pm. Bonsai collection open daily 10am-2:30pm. Call about facilities for the disabled.)

George Washington was counted among the engineers and architects of the **Chesapeake and Ohio Canal,** one of the country's first "think-big" schemes. The plan foresaw the Potomac River as the chief trade route between Europe and the Midwest. The Georgetown portion of the canal, now a charming national historic park (653-5844), hosts free jazz concerts on Sunday afternoons. The park runs parallel to the Potomac River all the way to Cumberland, MD, with 185 mi. of biking and hiking trails. You can rent boats, canoes, or bikes for the towpath at **Fletcher's Boat House,** 4940 Canal Rd. NW. (244-0461; bikes $6 per hr., $7 per day; must remain on C&O canal paths; rowboats and canoes $6 per hr., $14 per day; open Mon.-Fri. 9am-7:30pm, Sat.-Sun. 7:30am-7:30pm).

Outside the District

Great Falls Park (759-2925), 10 mi. outside the district on MacArthur Blvd., offers an excellent view of the falls and great picnic spots. Take advantage of hiking and riding trails, rock climbing, nature walks, and guided tours, and, for the more adventurous, excellent class-three rapids for kayaking, canoeing, or rafting.

The **Arlington National Cemetery,** located across Memorial Bridge in Arlington, VA (703-692-0931), holds 175,000 graves including those of Robert Kennedy, Joe Louis, and Oliver Wendell Holmes. The inscription on the **Tomb of the Unknown Soldier** reads, "Here rests in honored glory an American soldier known but to God." Watch for the changing of the Honor Guard every hour. An "eternal flame" burns next to the grave of John F. Kennedy. Metro: Blue to Arlington Cemetery, or take the $2.75 Tourmobile. (Open April-Sept. daily 8am-7pm; Oct.-March 8am-5pm.)

For a parking space, try the **Pentagon** (695-1776), across Memorial Bridge, the world's largest office building (23,000 employees). The Pentagon's mammoth parking lot blots out a good chunk of Arlington, VA. Hour-long tours of the Defense Department and Armed Forces' Headquarters include the Time-Life Collection of WWII art, Hall of Heroes, Flag Corridors, and more. (Tours every ½ hr. after security check at Tourbooth in Pentagon Metro stop. Open Mon.-Fri. 9:30am-3:30pm. Free.) Bring a photo ID for the preliminary security check. Non-U.S. citizens should bring their passports.

At **Alexandria's Old Town,** in Virginia, over 1000 18th-century buildings have undergone complete restoration. Major sights include the Torpedo Factory Art Center (where nearly 200 artists have their studios), Christ Church, George Washington's Masonic Memorial, and the Gadsby's Tavern Museum. A series of fine boutiques and restaurants adds to the excitement. To get to Alexandria, cross the 14th St. Bridge and go south on the George Washington Pkwy.; by Metro, take the yellow line to King St. Station and catch DASH bus #2 or 5 (60¢). For more information, call the Alexandria Visitors Center (703-549-0205).

Eight mi. south of Alexandria at the end of the parkway, **Mount Vernon** (703-780-2000) offers a history lesson. George Washington chose the loveliest spot on the whole length of the Potomac River for his house. A tour of the gardens and the African slave quarters surrounding the entry drive will give you a good idea of how a Southern tobacco plantation actually operated. The 30-acre grounds also hold Washington's tomb. (Open daily 9am-5pm; Nov.-Feb. 9am-4pm. Admission $5, seniors $4, children $2. Most buildings and grounds wheelchair-accessible.) Take the Yellow or Blue Metroline to National Airport, then bus #11H ("Fort Belvoire"). Gray Line and Tourmobile run tour buses to Mount Vernon (see Sights above). **Washington Boat Lines** (554-8000) runs crowded trips Tuesday to Sunday. (March-Nov. at 9am and 2pm, 4¾ hr. Fare $16.50, ages 6-11 $9.25. Cruise leaves from Pier 4, 6th and Water St. SW, in DC.)

Entertainment

Track the whirl of events and club listings with the free weekly *City Paper*, the "Weekend" section of every Friday's *Washington Post*, the monthly *Washingtonian* magazine ($2), or the free city magazines *Go* (monthly), *Where* (monthly), and *This Week in the Nation's Capital* (weekly).

Theater

DC hosts diverse drama spaces and companies. Broadway-style shows at the National Theater may perform beyond the scope of your wallet, but plenty of adventurous smaller theaters offer fascinating experimental, original, and repertory plays, often with political overtones.

The **National Theater**, 1321 Pennsylvania Ave. NW (800-233-3123 or 628-6161), one of the country's oldest, presents Broadway shows. Metro: Metro Center. Tickets run from $25-40. Same-day, half-price tickets and advance tickets are available for this and other theaters at **TICKETplace**, 12th and F St. NW (842-5387), at Metro Center, 12th St. exit. The **Arena Stage**, 6th St. and Maine Ave. SW (488-3300), has one of the best repertory companies in the nation. Metro: L'Enfant Plaza. Lower-budget, more experimental, and free local theaters are the **Source Theater**, 1835 14 St. NW (232-8012) and **Woolly Mammoth Theater**, 1401 Church St. NW (393-3939), both east of Dupont Circle, and the **Potomac Theater Project**, whose free 1990 season ran at the Georgetown Hall of Nations Theater, 1221 36th St. NW (863-9385).

The **John F. Kennedy Center for the Performing Arts**, 2700 F St. NW (467-4600), is a dazzling multi-theater complex that hosts performances by the Washington Opera, international ballet troupes, Broadway shows, and screenings for the American Film Institute. Take in the free view of the Potomac from the roof terrace. At Christmas, a free *Messiah* sing-along is held in the Opera House; call about when to line up for free tickets, they're given out several days before Christmas. Metro: Foggy Bottom. Seniors, students, military, and disabled people are eligible for half-price tickets to most KenCen shows before opening night, or for same-day performances after 6pm, after noon for matinee—positive ID a must. (Open daily 10am-9pm, later on performance nights. Free tours daily 10am-1pm.)

The **Wolf Trap Farm Park**, 1624 Trap Rd., Vienna, VA (255-1860), offers summer performances by famous ballet and dance companies, top-name musicians, symphonies, and occasionally ice skaters. Audiences sit indoors or lounge on the lawn outside the open-walled Filene Center.

Seasonal Events

Besides the events listed below, DC is home every year to countless marches, demonstrations, and protests, following quite literally in the steps of the 1963 Civil Rights March on Washington. Many are small, organized by media hounds or fringe political groups, but occasionally a big protest takes the town. In 1979, hordes of farmers demanding higher crop subsidies parked their tractors on and around the Mall, staying for weeks. The bigger marches are usually covered by the *Washington Post Metro* section a day or two in advance.

Martin Luther King, Jr.'s Birthday, 3rd Monday in Jan. (724-8062). A parade up Martin Luther King, Jr. Ave. SE, with speakers and local bands.

Black History Month, Feb. Special events and exhibits on African American history and culture, especially at Smithsonian museums (357-2700), DC Convention Center, and Martin Luther King, Jr. Public Library (727-0321)

Chinese New Year Parade, Feb. 18 (724-4091 or 638-1041). Lion and dragon dancers, drums, firecrackers, and street vendors line the streets of DC's Chinatown.

George Washington's Birthday Parade, Feb. 18, in Old Town Alexandria, VA. (703-838-4200). Drums, bands, and floats in "the USA's largest GW celebration." Mount Vernon also hosts special events for kids and adults (703-780-2000). On Feb. 16, 2 days before the parade, Fort Ward Park in Alexandria (4301 W. Braddock Rd.) offers a Revolutionary War encampment with simulated battle action from 10am-4pm.

Smithsonian Kite Festival, late March (357-3030). Go fly a kite or watch designers of all ages at the Washington Monument compete for prizes and trophies.

The National Cherry Blossom Festival, late March or early April (789-7000). Cherry Blossom Parade on Constitution Ave. from 7th to 17th St. Celebration of spring, the cherry blossoms, and Japanese-American friendship (the trees were given to the U.S. by Japan in 1912). Expensive tickets (728-1135) necessary for the April 6 Parade down Constitution Ave. Other events (some free) include fireworks, a fashion show, music, the Japanese Lantern Lighting ceremony, and a marathon.

White House Easter Egg Roll, April 1 (456-2200), on the White House South Lawn. Kids under 9 only; must be accompanied by an adult. Eggs and entertainment provided. 10am-2pm; free.

Shakespeare's Birthday Celebration, April 20 (544-7077). Exhibits, plays, Elizabethan music, food and children's events at the Folger Shakespeare Library, 201 E. Capital St. SE. Don't be misled: the Bard's actual birthday is April 23.

Asian Pacific American Heritage Festival, May 4 (354-5036). Food, crafts, and music from Thai to Hawaiian along the "Freedom Plaza" block of Pennsylvania Ave. downtown.

Greek Spring Festival, May 17-19 (829-2910). At and around St. Constantine and Helen Greek Orthodox Church, 4115 16th St. NW. Greek food, music, dancing, games, arts and crafts.

Malcolm X Day, May 19 (234-8755). Food, music and speeches in Anacostia Park honor the Malcolm X legacy.

National Symphony Orchestra Memorial Day Weekend Concert, May 26 (416-8100 or 619-7222), on the West Lawn of the capitol at 8pm. Free.

Dupont-Kalorama Museum Walk Day, June 1 (387-2151). Eight Dupont Circle-area museums and historic houses collaborate to offer free food, demonstrations, and tours.

Gay Pride Day, mid-June (667-0780 or 387-8401; evenings 833-3234). Rally and march for gay and lesbian pride and rights. No exact 1991 date yet.

Dance Africa DC, June 14-16 and 21-23 (269-1600), in and around Dance Place, 3225 8th St. NE. African food, crafts, clothing, music, and especially dance. Some performances require tickets; some free.

Bloomsday Ulysses Reading, June 15-17 (543-5433), at the Irish Times pub, 14 F St. NW. A lineup of readers from the DC literary and Irish communities take turns as a packed house hears all of Joyce's great novel read aloud. A 36-48-hr. endeavor.

Festival of American Folklife, June 26-30 and July 3-7 (357-2700), on the Mall. Huge Smithsonian-run fair demonstrating the crafts, customs, food, and music of a few selected states, territories and/or foreign countries to over a million visitors, with musicians, performers, and craftspeople imported from the featured regions.

Fourth of July, 619-7222. Festivities begin with a parade along the Mall (12:30pm) and the DC Free Jazz Festival (783-0360), with free concerts at Western Plaza. The National Symphony Orchestra performs on the Capitol steps (8pm), while crowds rock 'n' roll at the Washington Monument. Fireworks at 9:15pm. Washington's biggest blow-out of the year; expect massive and sometimes rowdy crowds. Take the subway and *not* a car.

Bastille Day Race, July 14 (452-1132 or 452-1126). Dominique's Restaurant sponsors the 12-block race, in which waiters carry champagne glasses on trays and demonstrate their juggling ability for the prize: a free trip to Paris. Race starts at 20th St. and Pennsylvania Ave. NW at noon.

Latin-American Festival, July 27-28. (833-9380) on the Mall. Free food, music, dance and theater from 40 Latin American nations.

African Cultural Festival, August 24-25 (347-0155 or 347-0171) on the Mall. Food, crafts, and music.

National Frisbee Festival, Aug. 31 (301-645-5043), on the Mall near the Air and Space Museum. The nation's largest non-competitive frisbee festival, with world-class champions and disc-catching dogs.

DC Blues Festival, Sept. 7 (483-0871). Free blues in Anacostia Park.

Adams Morgan Day, 2nd Sun. in Sept. (332-3292). A Latino *fiesta,* complete with food, arts, crafts, and music in DC's Hispanic Adams-Morgan area near 18th St. and Columbia Rd.

People's Christmas Tree Lighting, Dec. 11 (224-3069), Capitol West Lawn; **National Christmas Tree Lighting,** Dec. 12 (619-7222), on the Ellipse, outside the White House. In the latter the President himself flips the switch to light up a huge Christmas tree and a tall Hannukah Menorah at 5:30pm. Together these ignitions inaugurate the Pageant of Peace, on the Ellipse until Jan. 1, featuring nightly free choral performances with these and other brightly lit, constitutionally questionable religious displays in the background. Consult the *Washington Post* for information.

Smithsonian "Trees of Christmas" Display, Dec. 13-Jan. 5 (357-2700), outside the Museum of American History. Lots of trees, big and small, decked out in a splendid, multicultural array of ornaments.

Hannukah Festival, Dec. 25 (857-6583), at the B'nai B'rith Klutznick Museum, 1640 Rhode Island Ave. NW. Traditional Jewish music, food, and dance.

White House Candlelight Tours, tentatively Dec. 27-28 (456-2200). See the White House and its Christmas decorations by candles set in 6-ft.-high teak candlesticks. Tours start at 6pm, but line up at least an hour in advance. Call ahead.

New Year's Eve, 1100 Pennsylvania Ave. NW (289-4224), at the Old Post Office Pavilion. Throngs bid farewell to days of Auld Lang Syne amidst food, drink, live entertainment, and merriment at the city's largest party. Watch as the postage stamp drops from the Post Office Tower at midnight.

Nightlife

During the summer, Washington comes alive with music. The crowded amphitheater at the **Meriweather Post Pavilion** (982-1800) attracts big-name rock bands. (Take Rte. 270 to Columbia, MD, and follow the signs.) A series of summer concerts happens within the city as well. Every evening at 8pm, catch one of the **U.S. Military Bands** (475-1281) at either the West Terrace of the Capitol, or Sylvan Theatre on the Washington Monument grounds. (Information: Navy Band 433-6090; Army Band 696-3647; Marine Band 694-3502; Air Force Band 767-4310.) Museums often host free concerts as well (check the National Gallery of Art and the Air and Space Museum). If jazz and R&B move you more, try the **Carter Barron Amphitheater,** at 16th St. and Colorado Ave. NW (829-3200), offering concerts every weekend. (Tickets $5-15.)

DC's punk-rock scene is one of the nation's liveliest and most cohesive; in the 1980s, bands like Minor Threat and Fugazi fused crunchy guitar sounds, direct lyrics, and occasional reggae influence with a no-drugs, be-responsible attitude sometimes called "straight-edge." Besides listings below, good punk shows frequently take place in schools, churches, and other rented spaces; check the listings in *City Paper.* Most shows are all-ages, somewhat crowded, and quite safe for travelers. (Cover $2-5.) Call the D.C. Dept. of Parks and Recreation (673-7660) for dates and times of free summer outdoor punk shows at **Fort Reno Park,** at Nebraska Ave. and Davenport St. NW across from Wilson High School. (Metro: Tenleytown.)

DC's African American community originated the propulsive dance music called "go-go"—flagship bands include Chuck Brown and the Soul Searchers, Rare Essence, and E.U. of "Da Butt" fame. Unfortunately, most of the regular venues are hard to reach and probably unsafe for travelers. Look for posters and in *City Paper* for flyers advertising free concerts in parks.

One of the liveliest sections of the city, **Georgetown** is a great place to experience Washington nightlife. On Friday and Saturday evenings, streets fill with musicians, flower sellers, Hare Krishna devotees, rowdy students, and stylish socialites. Drinkers should beware of inflated prices; try the **Tombs,** 1226 36th St. NW (337-6668), near the Georgetown campus (open Mon.-Thurs. 11am-2am, Fri.-Sat. 11am-3am, Sun. 10am-2am), or the **American Café,** 1211 Wisconsin Ave. NW (944-9464), a good inexpensive restaurant (open Mon.-Thurs. 11am-3am, Fri.-Sat. 11am-4am, Sun. 10:30am-3am). Besides the general interest *City Paper* (see above), gay and lesbian travelers should pick up the free *Washington Blade,* available in stores and eateries around Dupont Circle. The best-distributed of the city's several African American interest papers is the *Washington Afro-American.*

Jazz

Blues Alley, 1073 Rear Wisconsin Ave. NW (337-4141). World-class jazz artists and Creole cuisine star at this Georgetown jazz supper club—located in an actual alley behind Wisconsin Ave.—for over 20 years. Dinner ($12-16) served from 6pm. Very good jazz every night, but the best-known artists come with world-class covers ($10-50) with frequent $5 per set (1½ hr.) food-or-drink min. Call for showtimes, prices, and reservations.

One Step Down, 2517 Pennsylvania Ave. NW (331-8863), near George Washington University. Metro: Foggy Bottom-GWU. Smaller and more casual than Blues Alley, also less expensive. Great local and out-of-town groups, usually from New York. All-jazz jukebox; free jam sessions Sat.-Sun. 3:30-7:30pm. Live jazz 5 nights per week, usually Sun.-Mon. and Thurs.-Sat. Cover for bands Mon.-Fri. $5, Sat.-Sun. $8.50-17. Often a food-or-2-drink min. order, but cheap sandwiches and burgers ($3.50-5). Open Sun.-Thurs. 10am-2am, Fri.-Sat. 10am-3am. Happy Hour 3-7pm. Ages under 21 welcome.

More Live Music

930 Club, 930 F St. NW (393-0930 or 638-2008). Metro: Metro Ctr. A star among DC nightclubs. Hot new alternative and progressive rock bands. Box office open Tues.-Fri. from 1pm. $3 to see 3 local bands; $7-14 for nationally known acts, which often sell out in advance. Under-21s admitted. Free Happy Hour video cabaret Fri. from 4pm.

d.c. space, 433 7th St. NW (347-4960 or 347-1445), at E St. Metro: Gallery Place. Space is the place for cabaret dinner theater, films, poetry readings, performance art, comedy, photography shows, and obscure, excellent rock and punk. Cover usually under $5. Monthly open-mike night—pay $2 or perform. Look for xeroxed monthly event-calendars in any record store. Showtimes Mon.-Thurs. at 8-10pm, Fri.-Sat. at 10-11pm.

Kilamanjaro, 1724 California St. NW (328-3838). Center of DC's Caribbean expatriate culture. Venue for reggae, worldbeat, and ethnic music from all over. Cover $5 after 9pm. Fri.-Sat. bigger names, often from Africa or the Caribbean; cover around $8 after 8pm. No shorts or tennis shoes. Happy Hour Fri.-Sun. 5-8pm with free snacks; cover $5, women free. Goat curry and other specialties $6.50-9.50. Open Fri.-Sat. 6pm-4am, Sun.-Thurs. 5pm-2am.

The Bayou, 3135 K St. NW (333-2897). Nightly rock 'n' roll. Lesser-known bands often attract a rough crowd; some all-ages shows, especially big-name college rock. Call for prices. Open Mon.-Thurs. and Sun. 8pm-2am, Fri.-Sat. 8pm-3am. Tickets $3-18.

Dance Clubs

Fifth Column, 915 F St. NW (393-3632). Tri-level dance floor in converted downtown bank. Fishtanks, sculptures, photography, and paintings by local artists abound. Open Tues.-Sat. at 10pm. Cover Tues. $3, Wed. $5, Thurs. $6, Fri. before 11pm $6 and after 11pm $8, Sat. $8. No sneakers or athletic wear. Must be 21. When too packed, try **The Vault,** next door at 911 F St. NW (347-8079), also a converted bank, but less popular and less artsy; younger crowd. Wed.-Thurs. $4, Fri.-Sat. $7. No dress code. Must be 21.

Opera, 1777 Columbia Rd. NW (265-6600), about 10 blocks from Woodley Park Zoo. Filled with young urban hipsters. Sleek place with a roomy, lighted dance floor, mezzanine for people-watching, and 2 bars. Top-40 and progessive music. Dancing Wed.-Thurs. 6pm-2am, Fri.-Sat. 6pm-3am, Sun. 6pm-2am. **Montana Café** in back has new cuisine dinners ($6-10). Café open Tues.-Thurs. 6-11pm, Sun. 6pm-midnight. Cover Wed. $3, Fri. $5, Sat. $7, Sun. $4. Thursday nights free, with "progressive music." Thurs. and Sat. are straight, Wed., Fri., and Sun. are gay. Must be 21.

Cities, 2424 18th St. NW (328-7194). Hotspot for eclectic dining and dancing crowd. Stays "in" by completely changing menu and decor every 4 months to highlight a new city. Dinner $12-16. Nightclub upstairs features contemporary disco, long bar, and lounge. Beers from $2.50 weeknights, from $3.25 Fri.-Sat. Impressive light-fare menu from $5. Restaurant open Sun.-Thurs. 6-11:30pm, Fri.-Sat. 6pm-midnight. Dancing Thurs.-Sat. from 10pm; variable cover $5-8. Bar open Mon.-Sat. 5pm-2am. Must be 21.

Tracks, 1111 1st St. SE at K St. (488-3320). Fri. night "college night" on Tracks' giant neon-lit dance floor, with min. age 18 and a mixed (gay and straight, African American and white) crowd. Sat.-Thurs. nights, gay African American men make up the dance floor's large population. Closes 5-6am weekends. Cheap beer ($2 per glass, $3 per pitcher weeknights) and many special events—pick up the Tracks newsletter in Dupont Circle stores for the week's calendar. Popular and safe club, but dangerous surrounding neighborhood; don't go without a car. Free Mon.-Tues., and nightly before 9pm; cover Wed.-Thurs. and Sun. $3, Fri.-Sat. $5.

Even More Clubs and Bars

Badlands, 1415 22nd at P St. NW (296-0505). Popular gay bar. Mixed ages, small dance floor, video room. Open Tues.-Thurs. 9pm-2am, Fri.-Sat. 9pm-3am, Sun. 9pm-2am. Cover: Tues. $2, Wed. $3, and Thurs.-Sat. $5.

Brickskeller, 1523 22nd St. NW (293-1885). Metro: Dupont Circle. Steaks and buffalo burgers ($4-14), but the real attraction is enormous selection of beer—over 500 brands. Mon.-Thurs. 11:30am-2am, Fri. 11:30am-2:30am, Sat. 6pm-2:30am, Sun. 6pm-1:30am. No cover. Ask about monthly beer-tastings ($20). On weekends, arrive early to avoid the crowds.

Comedy Cafe, 1520 K St. NW (638-5653). Metro: Farragut North. The best comedy club in town. Cover varies—on weekends $10, with dinner $16. Open-mike Thurs. Cover $2.50. Shows Fri. at 8:30 and 10:30pm, Sat. at 7:30, 9:30, and 11:30pm. Call for reservations.jmd 7-11-90 wp, man 8-13-90, jmd 8-17-90 jmd 8-29 am jmd 8-30

West Virginia

The Civil War era drew the boundary line between the Virginias, when most of Virginia seceded from the Union. The westernmost counties, choosing to keep their ties with the north, became a separate state in 1863, formalizing the longstanding rift between the mountainous and coastal regions.

West Virginia at last appears to be economically rising from the dust of its coal-mining history. Although cities such as Charleston still have colossal manufacturing plants, many towns have redirected their energies toward tourism. An example is the recent attempt to attract visitors to the majestic Allegheny Mountains. While years of neglect still show in the poor roads and occasional barren areas (from earlier strip-mining), an excellent state park system now enables visitors to hike, raft, and explore caverns throughout the rugged peaks.

Practical Information

Capital: Charleston.

Tourist Information: Travel Development Division, 1900 Washington St., State Capitol Complex, Bldg. 6, #B654, Charleston 25305 (348-2286 or 800-225-5982). **Division of Parks and Recreation,** 1900 Washington St., State Capitol Complex, Bldg. 6, #451, Charleston 25305. **U.S. Forest Service Supervisor's Office,** 200 Sycamore St., Elkins 26241 (636-1800).

Time Zone: Eastern. **Postal Abbreviation:** WV.

Area Code: 304.

Harpers Ferry

Lying at the confluence of the Shenandoah and Potomac Rivers and ringed by the Blue Ridge Mountains, tiny Harpers Ferry's interest is mainly historical. In October of 1859, the radical abolitionist John Brown led his 22-man "army of liberation" into the town to seize the U.S. arsenal here. Brown hoped his actions would incite a large-scale slave insurrection, but in two days, troops under the command of Robert E. Lee regained control of the town, and Brown was eventually hanged. Though the raid failed, it indicated the increasing emotional heat surrounding the slavery issue. Less than two years later, the debate escalated into civil war.

At the town's heart, restored 1850s buildings form the misnamed **Harpers Ferry National Park,** including a general store, tavern, blacksmith's shop, and the building where John Brown made his final stand. Costumed members of the National Park Service talk about daily life in the 19th century, the story of John Brown's raid, and the town's deconstruction during the Civil War. The best place to begin a tour of the town is at the **visitors information center** (535-6371), on Shenandoah St. in the park, where you will find orientation films, exhibits, and a host of activities explaining the area's historical significance. (Office and park open daily 8am-6pm; off-season 8am-5pm.) Don't miss the hourly movie about Brown's raid, featuring historical information and a debate over the morality of Brown's attack. History buffs should head to the **Park Service Book Store,** on High St., for its excellent collection of Civil War literature.

Those still curious about the raid should pay a visit to the **John Brown Wax Museum,** High St. at Potomac (536-6321). Here the life of John Brown and the story of his raid replay in a series of vignettes about as hot as wax can get. (Open March-Dec. daily 9am-5pm. Admission $2.)

But Harpers Ferry offers more than a look at the past. Nearby **Jefferson's Rock** provides a view that the statesman once declared "worth a trip across the Atlantic," including two rivers and three states. The old campus of **Storer University,** one of the first black colleges in the U.S., also rests nearby. Besides several steep local trails, Harpers Ferry offers easy access to the **Appalachian Trail** and the **Chesapeake and Ohio Towpath.** Appalachian Trail Conference Headquarters can be contacted at P.O. Box 807 (535-6331). The office itself perches 1 mi. from the restored town, at Jackson and Washington St. (Open Mon.-Fri. 9am-5pm, Sat.-Sun. 9am-4pm.) **Blue Ridge Outfitters** (725-3444), a few miles west of Harpers Ferry on Rte. 340 N., arranges several excursions, from two-hour canoe trips on the Shenandoah to three-day whitewater raft rides on Virginia's toughest waterways. Prices range accordingly, starting at $38. (Open daily 8am-7pm.) Several other excursion companies offer whitewater rafting at competitive rates; **River Riders,** P.O. Box 267, Knoxville, MD 21758 (301-834-8051 or 304-535-2663) runs trips from $28 per person, inner-tube trips from $20.

Look for most Harpers Ferry food around the restored town in undistinguished cafés; the best is probably the **Garden of Food** on High St. (Open Sun.-Fri. 11am-7:30pm, Sat. 11am-until.) The **Back Street Café,** on Potomac St., sells cheaper sandwiches ($2-3) and offers Saturday night "Ghost Tours" of the town ($2). (Open daily 10am-5pm.)

For accommodations try the **Harpers Ferry Hostel,** Rte. 2, P.O. Box 248E (301-834-7652), located across the C&O canal in Knoxville, MD. ($7; in winter $8.) Call about a ride from the Harpers Ferry train station. For a less hostel time, the **Hillside Motel,** 19105 Keep Tryst Rd. (301-834-8144), just across the bridge in Knoxville, MD, has rooms with TV and A/C. (Singles $26. Doubles $37.) The **Comfort Inn** at Rte. 340 and Union St. (535-6391; reservations 800-228-5150), a 10-minute walk from town, serves comforting coffee and doughnuts each morning—it also has wheelchair-accessible rooms. (Singles $44. Doubles $49. Weekends $47 and $52, respectively.)

You can **camp** along the C&O Canal, where sites rest 5 mi. apart, or in one of the five Maryland state park campgrounds lying within 30 mi. of Harpers Ferry.

The nearest are **Washington Monument State Park** (301-432-8065), 15 mi. north on Rte. 67 near Boonsboro (sites $4), and **Greenbrier State Park** (301-791-4767), a few miles north of Boonsboro on Rte. 66 between exits 35 and 42 on I-70 ($10). Far closer is the commercial **Camp Resort,** Rte. 3, P.O. Box 1300 (535-6895). Sites start at $18 for two people (with hookup $23, each additional adult $4).

Make Harpers Ferry a stop on the C&O Canal, or a daytrip (1 ½ hr. by car) out of Washington, DC. **Amtrak** (800-872-7245) serves Harpers Ferry directly from DC but trains go to DC only in the morning, from DC only in the afternoon ($13; call for reservations). The closest **Greyhound** bus stations are half-hour drives away in Winchester, VA, and Frederick, MD. To drive to Harpers Ferry from DC, take I-270 north to 340 west.

The **ZIP code** is 25425; the **area code** is 304.

Monongahela National Forest

Mammoth **Monongahela National Forest,** popular with canoers, succors deer, bear, wild turkeys, and spelunkers prowling around below ground in magnificent limestone caverns. But camping is the main attraction here, with 600 mi. of prize hiking trails and over 500 campsites to lure the adventurer. Camp in an established site ($10 or less), or sleep in the backcountry for free. Twenty-five mi. north on Rte. 92, the forest's **Lake Sherwood Area** (536-3660) offers fishing, hunting, swimming, hiking, and boating, as well as several campgrounds that rob from the rich to give to the poor. The campground fills only on major holidays. (2-week max. stay. Sites $8-9.) A three-hour drive north will bring you to **Blackwater Falls State Park** (800-225-5982), ¼ mi. southwest of Rte. 32. The park's dazzling centerpiece is the most popular waterfall in West Virginia. (Sites $8-9. Open April-Oct.) For advice and information on exploring Monongahela, visit the White Sulphur Springs **Forest Service Office,** in the Federal Bldg. (536-2144), at the corner of E. Main and Mountain Ave. (Open Mon.-Fri. 8am-4:45pm.) For information on the whole forest, which encompasses much of West Virginia's most scenic mountain country, contact the Supervisor's Office, Monongahela National Forest, 200 Sycamore St., Elkins 26241 (636-1800; Mon.-Fri. 8am-4:45pm).

SOUTHEAST

To the uninitiated, the Southeast looks like a glorious, endless beach. The Atlantic seaboard and Gulf Coast have some of the country's most beautiful and most popular oceanfront playgrounds. A long string of sun-soaked cities stretch along the shore, from North Carolina's Nag's Head to South Carolina's Myrtle Beach to Florida's Daytona and Miami Beach. To these add a dash of Disney World, the galaxy's most popular attraction, and you arrive at a vacationer's nirvana.

The region's reputation as a beach paradise can be very misleading, however. Apart from the vacation communities and the thriving Atlanta and Research Triangle areas, the agriculture-dependent Southeast has a pace and culture of its own. In many areas, you'll still be able to see the Confederate flag—a red background criss-crossed by blue-starred lines—flying above car dealerships and on the hoods of pickup trucks. Though it may show that the "Old South," and consequently some of the old segregationist values, are still around, whatever your ethnic or racial background there is little old-style violence—as the Southeast steps into the late twentieth century, mellowness rather than intolerance pervades.

Travel

In the winter months, waves of northern tourists flood the Southeastern beaches. Florida's Spring Break phenomenon, corresponding with college calendars, begins in February, peaks in mid-March, and tapers off in mid-April. Although the December-to-April crowds may make finding rooms difficult, this tourist activity can also be a blessing for the budget traveler. Look for advertisements of special deals on accommodations and transportation in northern newspapers and college publications. Summer brings crowds to Orlando, Myrtle Beach, the Outer Banks, and other amusement hot spots.

Atlanta's Hartsfield Airport, the world's second busiest, is the region's major air terminal. **Delta, Eastern,** and **Southern Airlines** are major carriers throughout the South. **U.S. Air** can fly you conveniently and inexpensively through Pittsburgh to most major Southern cities.

Amtrak trains begin in Boston and travel down the southeastern coast in two branches. One connects the midsection of North Carolina, western South Carolina, and Atlanta, then goes west to Alabama and eventually to New Orleans. The other travels down eastern North Carolina, South Carolina, and Georgia, and finishes up in Florida where, thanks to Henry Flagler (railroad magnate and co-founder of Standard Oil), railroad service is excellent. Unfortunately, no routes connect the two branches, though Amtrak does have service linking Florida with New Orleans.

Bus travelers should have few problems getting to most of the region's cities and towns. Atlanta is a central terminus for **Greyhound/Trailways,** and even the Great Smokies are brought within range by an infrequent schedule out of Asheville, NC. Though Greyhound recently encountered financial difficulty, it is still running most of its routes with reduced frequency. Since many of the routes run late, plan extra travel time for delays in making connections. The most poorly served areas are North Carolina's Outer Banks and Georgia's low country.

Car rental rates in Florida are consistently lower than anywhere else in the U.S. National companies drop their rates to $99 per week, and **Alamo** (800-327-9633) frequently offers $70 per week specials with low ($30) or non-existent drop-off fees. Find more good deals at **General** (800-327-7607), a regional company; **Value** (800-327-2501); **Holiday Pay-Less** (800-237-2804); and **Thrifty** (800-367-2277). **National** (800-227-7368) sometimes has special discounts and regulations for students and foreigners. Be sure to call around before you make reservations.

Youth hostels spread throughout the Appalachians and Florida, but aside from camping, there are few other bargain accommodations. Look for budget hotel

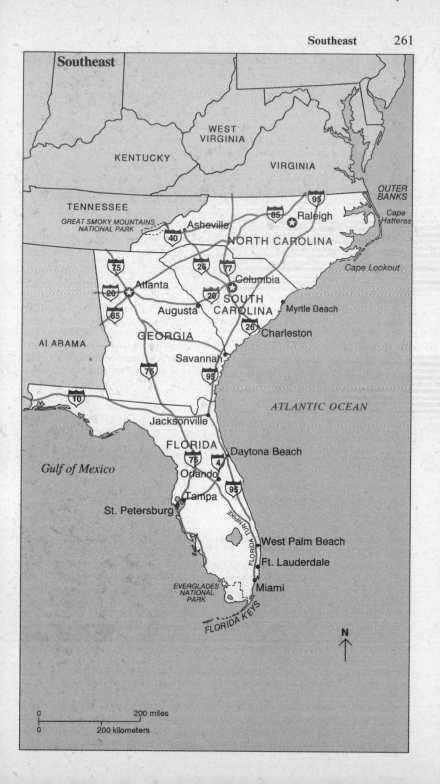

chains, such as **Motel 6** (505-891-6161) and **Econolodge** (800-446-6900) on the outskirts of cities. Winter is the high season here; the sweltering sun and high humidity
of June, July, and August often result in summertime bargains. **State parks** with
campsites are plentiful throughout the Southeast, and many **national forests** offer
free primitive camping.

Florida

In 1513 Ponce de León landed on the Florida coast near what would soon be
St. Augustine, in search of the elusive Fountain of Youth. The Sunshine State's
promise continues to seduce multitudes: senior citizens seek a retirement haven,
immigrants come in hope of greater opportunity, students pursue the prospect of
a deep tan and a cold beer, and adults and children alike race like mice through
the maze-like fantasy of Disney World.

However, an unpleasant side emerges in the land of the winter sun—Florida's
population boom continues to strain the state's resources, while commercial strips
and tremendous development in some areas has made once-pristine beaches into
eyesores. A steady flow of often unemployed illegal aliens continually floods into
southern Florida, exacerbating already volatile and fear-inspired race relations.
Most of the illegal drugs that reach northern cities enter through Florida, presenting
an overwhelming, often controversial drug enforcement problem. All of these factors mingle in the crucible of Miami, an immensely rich and frightening city.

Illusions and disillusionment aside, Florida caters to visitors worldwide. With
the profusion of ready-made entertainment centers, night clubs, amusement parks,
white sand, and topaz water, Florida's a beach.

Practical Information

Capital: Tallahassee.

Tourist Information: Florida Division of Tourism, 126 Van Buren St., Tallahassee 32301
(487-1462). Department of Natural Resources—Division of Recreation and Parks, 3900
Commonwealth Blvd. #613, Tallahassee 32303 (488-7326). U.S. Forest Service, 227 N.
Bruro St., P.O. Box 1050, Tallahassee 32302 (681-7265).

Time Zones: Eastern and Central (westernmost part of panhandle is 1 hr. behind Eastern).
Postal Abbreviation: FL.

Jacksonville and the North Coast

The gateway to Florida's frantic Atlantic Coast, Jacksonville (pop. 700,000) encompasses 840 square miles of laid-back landmass. Despite its vastness, the city has
yet to develop into the metropolis some locals envision. Major development along
the St. John's River and attempts to land a pro-football franchise still await their
fruition. In any case, Jacksonville remains a good place to start your travels in the
Southeast—its airport, Greyhound, and Amtrak terminals have many daily connections to most U.S. cities. Nearby Fort Clinch State Park and Little Talbot Island
State Park also preserve the best uncrowded and undeveloped beaches between
South Carolina and Key West.

Practical Information

Emergency: 911.

Visitors Center: Jacksonville Convention and Visitors Bureau, 6 E. Bay St. #200 (353-9736),
1½ blocks from the Jacksonville Landing. The free map of Duval County is a must in this
sprawling city. Pick up coupons for local hotels. Open Mon.-Fri. 7:30am-5pm.

Jacksonville International Airport, Airport Rd. (741-4902), 20 mi. north of downtown off I-95. The **Greyhound Airport Express** leaves the airport daily at 10am, 3:55pm, and 7:55pm; leaves downtown daily at 5:45 and 9:40pm. Fare $4, $4.70 if you buy your ticket at the airport.

Amtrak: 3570 Clifford Lane (locally 766-5110 or 800-872-7245), 6 mi. northwest of downtown off U.S. 1. To: Miami ($68), Washington, DC ($127), and Savannah ($33). Open 24 hr.

Greyhound/Trailways: 10 Pearl St. (356-1841), downtown. Plenty of blue plastic seats. A/C. To: Miami ($53), St. Augustine ($8), New Orleans ($84), and Washington, DC ($107). Open 24 hr.

Public Transport: Jacksonville Transportation Authority, 100 N. Myrtle St. (630-3100), downtown. Information kiosk at the intersection of W. Forsyth and N. Hogan St. Open Mon.-Fri. 6am-6pm. **BH-1** and **BH-2** buses go to the beach. Catch them near the corner of Pearl and Bay St., or in **Hemming Plaza,** a block away. BH-1 goes to Atlantic Blvd.; BH-2 to Beach Blvd. Fare $1.10. **Ferry** across St. John's River (251-3331) operates daily every ½ hr. 6:20am-10:15pm: takes you to Rte. A1A, a few mi. south of Little Talbot State Park on Little Talbot Island. Cars $1.50, pedestrians 10¢.

Taxi: Yellow Cab, 354-5511. Base fare $1.25, $1.25 per mi.

Car Rental: Alamo, 1735 Airport Rd. (800-327-9633), 5 min. from the terminal by free Alamo Shuttle. Sub-compacts $24 per day, $68 per week. Free drop-off in FL cities. Open 24 hr. Must be 21, extra $5 charge if under 25. Must have credit card or $100 deposit through a travel agent, $50 deposit if you pay 14 days in advance.

Post Office: 1100 King's Rd. (359-2840), downtown. Open Mon.-Fri. 8:30am-5pm, Sat. 9am-1pm. **ZIP code:** 32202.

Area Code: 904.

Jacksonville has three distinct areas, each a half-hour to an hour drive from the other. The first area, known as Jacksonville's Beaches, includes **Atlantic Beach, Neptune Beach,** and **Jacksonville Beach** from north to south. North of the St. John's River, on **Rte. A1A,** two more long stretches of beach make up part of **Fort Clinch State Park** and **Little Talbot State Park.** The third and last area, downtown Jacksonville, is of little interest beyond its shops and museums and can be *very* dangerous after dark. Major thoroughfares **Atlantic Boulevard** and **Beach Boulevard** run through the dead zone between Jacksonville and its beaches. Once in the beach region, **3rd Street** is the main drag, running parallel to the shore. Downtown is bisected by **Main Street,** which runs north from the north bank of the St. John's River. **Bay Street,** along the shore of St. John's River, and **Union Street** run east-west in the downtown area.

Accommodations and Camping

The biggest problem with Jacksonville accommodations is getting to them. The long distances can be frustrating, and unless you have a car or a fat bankroll for taxicabs, some of the places are darn near impossible to reach. Try to catch the Greyhound Shuttle from the airport: the last one leaves at 7:55pm. If you miss it, stay at a cheap airport hotel such as **Motel 6,** 10885 Hark Rd., Dunn Ave./Busch Dr. exit off I-95 (757-8600; singles $22), or the **Econolodge,** 1351 Airport Rd. (741-4844; singles $27). The **Salt Air Motel,** 425 Atlantic Blvd. (246-6465), offers bright, clean rooms. (Singles from $25. Doubles from $33. Call ahead in summer.) The **Ocean View Motel,** 60 Ocean View Dr. (246-9514), mostly rents rooms by the week. (All rooms $33 with kitchenette.)

The only campground accessible by public transportation is **Kathryn Abbey Hanna Park,** on Wonderwood Rd., Mayport (249-4700), south of Mayport Naval Base and north of Atlantic Beach. (Sites $10, campers $13.50. Park admission 50¢.) If you have a car, clinch a place at **Fort Clinch,** Rte. A1A (261-4212), on the St. John's River. (Sites $19, with electricity $21.) Even less of a cinch to get to, **Little Talbot Island State Park** (251-3231) lies 15 mi. south of Fort Clinch. (Sites $18, with electricity $20.)

Food

Rapid urban development and summer tourist crowds in Jacksonville have encouraged the growth of expensive "surf-and-turf" seafood restaurants. To avoid these, try local favorite **Patti's**, 7300 Beach Blvd., which has zesty spaghetti and other excellent Italian dishes, or check out **Bono's Barbeque**, on Beach Blvd. 2-3 mi. east of downtown. **Ritespot Restaurants** have two spots in Jacksonville: 665 Atlantic Blvd. (249-8666; open Mon.-Sat. 7am-10pm) and 4683 Ocean St., Mayport (246-2484; open Tues.-Thurs. and Sun. 11am-9pm, Fri.-Sat. 11am-10pm). These homey joints serve catch o' the day for $9, all-you-can-eat shrimp for $8.

If you eat downtown, look for cheap cuisine upstairs at the Jacksonville Landing, which has counters serving large portions of everything from pizza to egg foo-young. If nothing or no one there grabs you, try **Jack's Restaurant**, 229 W. Forsyth, where lunch specials or a fish dinner cost $4. (Open Mon.-Fri. 6am-3pm.)

Sights and Entertainment

There are virtually no sights of historic interest in Jacksonville because the entire city burned to the ground early in the century. To compensate, the city built a flashy new mall called the **Jacksonville Landing** on the downtown waterfront, and created the **Riverwalk** on the opposite bank. Kill an afternoon in town at the **Cummer Gallery**, 829 Riverside Ave. (336-6857), 1 block from the river, which has an excellent art collection and gorgeous Italian-style gardens. (Open Tues.-Fri. 10am-4pm, Sat. 1-5pm, Sun. 2-5pm. Donation.) The **Jacksonville Art Museum**, 4160 Boulevard Center Dr. (398-8336), has Chinese porcelain and pre-Columbian and modern art, as well as works by contemporary regional artists. (Open Tues.-Fri. 10am-4pm, Thurs. 10am-10pm, Sat.-Sun. 1-5pm.) Microscope out the **Museum of Science and History**, 1025 Gulf Life Dr. on the Southbank Riverwalk (396-7061), for its planetarium, endangered species aviary, and hands-on exhibits. (Open Mon.-Thurs. 10am-5pm, Fri.-Sat. 10am-6pm, Sunday 1-6pm. Admission $5, seniors, students, military, and children $3.) If you have a car and a hankering to head for the mountains, take a 7-mi. drive from downtown to the **Anheuser-Busch Brewery**, 111 Busch Dr. (751-0700), for the self-guided tour, a film of the beer-making process, and free samples. (Open Oct.-May Mon.-Sat. 10am-5pm. Free.)

Yet the beach, not the beer, is Jacksonville's main attraction. Golden and white sands extend most of the way south along the coast from Ponte Vedra to Fernandina. Neptune and Atlantic, two of the Jacksonville Beaches, attract the largest crowds, but the contrasting crystal blue sea and white sand make them well worth the trip.

After a day at the beach, try a night at **Fat Tuesday's**, Jacksonville Landing (353-0444), for ready-mixed ice drinks, music, finger food, and sandwiches from $5. Or try your luck at **Jacksonville Kennel Club** (646-0001), on McDuff Ave. 1½ mi. north of I-10, for dog racing. (Races Mon.-Sat. at 7:45pm. Admission to grandstand 50¢, clubhouse $2.)

Saint Augustine

Spanish adventurer Juan Ponce de León founded St. Augustine in 1565, making it the first European colony in North America and the oldest city in the U.S. Though he never found the legendary Fountain of Youth, de León did live to age 61, twice the expected life span at that time. Similarly, much of St. Augustine's original Spanish flavor has survived without the legend, thanks to the town's various preservation efforts. Today, in its dotage, the town is fairly quiet: its brick, palm-lined streets see few cars, and during the summer months the heat slows everything and everyone down. Yet historic sites, good food, and friendly people make St. Augustine well worth a few youthful days.

Practical Information

Emergency: 911.

Visitors Information: Visitors Center, 10 Castillo at San Marco Ave. (824-3334). From the Greyhound station, walk north on Ribeira, then right on Orange. Pick up hotel coupons and the free *Chamber of Commerce Map,* a comprehensive city guide. The ½-hr. movie, *St. Augustine Adventure,* cleverly introduces the city (every ½ hr., $2). Open daily 8:30am-5:30pm.

Greyhound/Trailways: 100 Malaga St. at King St. (829-6401). To Jacksonville (5 per day, 50 min., $11) and Daytona Beach (7 per day, 1 hr., $8). Open Mon.-Fri. 8am-5:30pm, Sat. 8am-4pm.

Taxi: Ancient City Taxi, 824-8161. From the bus station to motels on San Marco about $2.

Bike Rental: Buddy Larson's Bike Rental, 130 King St. (824-2402). $3 per hr. Open Mon.-Sat. 9am-5:30pm.

Help Lines: Rape Crisis, 355-7273 or 350-6808.

Post Office: King St. at Martin Luther King Ave. (829-8716). Open Mon.-Fri. 8:30am-5pm, Sat. 10am-1pm. **ZIP code:** 32084.

Area Code: 904.

St. Augustine guards the northeast coast of Florida, about 40 mi. south of Jacksonville and 47 mi. north of Daytona Beach. Unfortunately, the city has no public transportation, though most points of interest, like the bus station, tourist office, budget motels, and tourist district, are all within walking distance of one another. Historic St. Augustine, concentrated in the area between the **San Sebastian River** and the **Matanzas Bay** to the east, is easily covered on foot. **King Street,** running along the river, is the major east-west axis and crosses the bay to the beaches. **St. George Street,** also east-west, is closed to vehicular traffic and contains most of the shops and many sights in St. Augustine. **San Marco Avenue** and **Cordova Street** travel north-south. Winter brings a surge of activity to nearby **Vilano, Anastasia,** and **St. Augustine Beaches.**

Accommodations and Camping

Beyond the new, often full, youth hostel, you'll find several clusters of cheap motels in St. Augustine: one a short walk north of town on San Marco Ave.; another directly to the east of the historic district, over the Bridge of Lions along Anastasia Blvd.; and a third near Vilano Beach. Several inns in the historic district offer nice rooms, but rates start at $49 per night. Those traveling by automobile should consider the excellent seaside camping facilities at **Anastasia State Park.**

St. Augustine Hostel (AYH), 32 Treasury St. (829-6163), at Charlotte, 6 blocks from the Greyhound station. Large, dormitory-style rooms with shower and fans or A/C. Kitchen available. $10. Nonmembers $13. Guest bike rental $5 per day. Open for reservations 7:30am-9:30am and 5-10pm; information 9am-5pm.

American Motel, 42 San Marco Ave. (829-2292), near the visitors center. Owner won't take your money until you've inspected your room. He also provides transportation to and from the bus station when a car is available. Big, clean singles or doubles $26, weekends $35-43. Check visitors center for coupons.

The Palms Motor Inn, 137 San Marco Ave. (824-6181), ½ mi. from the visitors center. Pool. Old but clean rooms $26. Ask about discounts for *Let's Go* users.

Seabreeze Motel, 208 Anastasia Blvd. (829-8122), just over the Bridge of Lions east of the historic district. Clean rooms with A/C, TV. Pool. Good restaurants nearby. Singles $24. Doubles $28. Each additional person $4. Kitchenette $5 extra. Pick up coupon in visitors center for $66 3-night special.

The St. Francis Inn, 279 Saint George St. (824-6068), at Saint Francis St., 2 doors down from the Oldest House. Charming 10-room inn with a jungle of flowers and a tucked-away pool. Much of its original 18th-century interior preserved. Iced tea and juice served all day. Free bike use. Room with double bed $49, with twin beds $54. Cottage on premises with full kitchen and living room $104 for 4 people, $8 for each additional person. Continental breakfast included.

Anastasia State Recreation Area, on Rte. A1A (471-3033), 4 mi. south of the historic district. From town, cross the Bridge of Lions, and bear left just beyond the Alligator Farm. Open daily 8am-sundown. Sites $20, with electricity $22; $18 after the first night. Make reservations for weekends.

Food

The flood of daytime tourists and the abundance of budget eateries make lunch in St. Augustine's historic district a delight. Stroll Saint George St. to check the daily specials scrawled on blackboards outside each restaurant; locals prefer those clustered at the southern end of Saint George near King St. Finding a budget dinner in St. Augustine is trickier, since downtown is deserted after 5pm. However, an expedition along Anastasia Blvd. should unearth good meals for under $6. The seafood-wise will seek out the surf 'n' turf dinners ($6) at **Captain Jack's,** 410 Anastasia Blvd. (829-6846). Those with wheels interested in mass quantities of food should try the all-you-can-eat buffet at the **Quincey Family Steakhouse,** 2 mi. south of town on Rte. A1A at Ponce de León Mall. (Open Sun.-Thurs. 11am-10pm, Fri.-Sat. 11am-11pm.)

St. George Pharmacy and Restaurant, 121 Saint George St. Museum, luncheonette, and bookstore. Cheap sandwiches from $1.20; dinners from $2.50. Try the grilled cheese with a thick chocolate malt ($4). Breakfast special (egg, bacon, grits, toast or biscuit, and jelly) $2. Open Mon.-Fri. 7am-5pm, Sat.-Sun. 7:30am-5pm.

Café Camacho, 11-C Aviles St., at Charlotte St., 1 block from Saint George St. in the historic district. Part vintage clothes shop, part café. Serves delicious fruit shakes, soups, sandwiches, breakfast specials, vegetarian dishes, and an all-you-can-eat lunch bar from 11am-3pm ($5). Open Wed.-Mon. 7:30am-5pm.

O'Steen's, 205 Anastasia Blvd., 1½ mi. from downtown and 4 blocks from the Bridge of Lions. A lively local hangout with great prices. Arrive before 5pm to beat the dinner crowd. Daily special includes entree, salad or soup, and choice of 2 vegetables ($3.50, seafood $4.50). Open Mon.-Sat. 11am-8:30pm.

El Toro Con Sombrero, 10 Anastasia Blvd., on the left just over the Bridge of Lions from downtown. Look carefully because the sign is hidden by a sign for the adjoining sports bar. If you like Mexican food and 50s music, this is the place. Tacos $1.15. Open daily 7am-1am.

A New Dawn, 110 Anastasia Blvd. A health-conscious grocery store with a sandwich and juice counter. Delicious vegetarian sandwiches; try the Tofu Salad Surprise ($2.55). Fruit shakes and sodas $1-2. Open daily 8am-6pm.

Sights and Entertainment

Saint George St. is the center of the historic district, which begins at the Gates of the City near the visitors center and runs south past Cadiz St. and the Oldest Store. Visit **San Agustín Antiguo,** Gallegos House, Saint George St. (824-3355), St. Augustine's authentically restored 18th-century neighborhood, where artisans and villagers in period costumes describe the customs, crafts, and highlights of the Spaniards' New World existence. (Open daily 9am-5pm. Admission $2.50, seniors $2.25, students and ages 6-18 $1.35.) The oldest masonry fortress in the country, **Castillo de San Marcos,** 1 Castillo Dr. (829-6506), off San Marco Ave., has 14-ft. thick walls built of coquina, the local shellrock. The fort itself resembles a four-pointed star complete with a drawbridge and a murky moat. Inside you'll find a museum, a large courtyard surrounded by guardrooms, livery quarters for the garrison, a jail, a chapel, and the original cannons brought overseas by the Spanish. A cannon-firing ceremony happens once per day. (Open daily 9am-6pm; Nov.-April 9am-5:15pm. Admission $1, over 62 and under 12 free.)

St. Augustine has several old stores and museums. The self-descriptive **Oldest House,** 14 Saint Francis St. (824-2872), has been occupied continuously since its construction in the 1600s. (Open daily 9am-5pm. Admission $3, seniors $2.75, students $1.50.) The **Oldest Store Museum,** 4 Artillery Lane (829-9729), has over 100,000 odds and ends from the 18th and 19th centuries. (Open Mon.-Sat. 9am-5pm, Sun. noon-5pm. Admission $2.50.) Also in the old part of the city is the co-quina **Cathedral of St. Augustine,** begun in 1793. Although several fires destroyed parts of the cathedral, the walls and façade are original.

Six blocks north of the information center is the **Mission of Nombre de Dios,** Ocean St. (824-2809), a moss- and vine-covered mission which held the first Catho-lic service in the U.S. on September 8, 1565. Looming over the structure is a 208-ft. steel cross commemorating the city's founding. (Open Mon.-Fri. 8am-8pm, Sat.-Sun. 9am-8pm. Mass Mon.-Fri. at 8:30am, Sat. at 6pm, Sun. at 8am. Donation.) No trip to St. Augustine would be complete without a trek to the **Fountain of Youth,** 155 Magnolia Ave. (829-3168). Go right on Williams St. from San Marco Ave. and continue a few blocks past Nombre de Dios. (Open daily 9am-5pm. Admission $3.50, seniors $2.50, ages 6-12 $1.50.) In addition to drinking from the spring that Ponce de León mistakenly thought would give him eternal youth, you can see a statue of the explorer that does not age.

Though oil and water don't usually mix, Henry Flagler, co-founder of Standard Oil and a good friend of the Rockefellers, retired to St. Augustine. He built two hotels in the downtown area that the rich and famous once frequented, making St. Augustine the "Newport of the South." The former Ponce de León Hotel, at King and Cordova St., is now **Flagler College.** In summer the college is deserted, but during the school year students liven the town. In 1947, Chicago publisher and lover of large objects Otto Lightner converted the Alcazar Hotel into the **Lightner Mu-seum,** with an impressive collection of cut, blown, and burnished glass. (Open daily 9am-5pm. Admission $3, ages 12-18 $1.)

Visitors can tour St. Augustine by land or by sea. **St. Augustine Sight-Seeing Trains,** 170 San Marcos Ave. (829-6545), offers a variety of city tours lasting from one to eight hours. (Open daily 8am-5pm.) The one-hour tour ($9, ages 6-12 $4), a good introduction to the city, starts at the front of the visitors center. **Coleé Sight-Seeing Carriage Tours** (829-2818) begin near the entrance to the fort, take about an hour, and cover the historic area of St. Augustine. ($5 per hr. Open daily 8:30am-5pm.) The **Victory II Scenic Cruise Ships** (824-1806) navigate the emerald Matan-zas River. Catch the boat at the City Yacht Pier, 1 block south of the Bridge of Lions (leaves at 1, 2:45, 4:30, 6:45, and 8:30pm; cruises $6, under 12 $2).

On Anastasia Island, at **Anatasia State Park,** you can see Paul Green's *Cross and Sword,* Florida's official state play, telling the story of St. Augustine with the help of a large cast, booming cannons, and swordfights. (Admission $8, ages 6-12 $4; discounts for AAA members and large groups.)

With such a penchant for loudness and liquid, St. Augustine has an impressive array of bars. **Scarlett O'Hara's,** 70 Hypolita St. (824-6535), at Cordova St., is pop-ular with locals. The barbecue chicken sandwiches ($4) are filling and juicy, the drinks hefty and cool. Live entertainment begins at 9pm every night. (Open daily 11:30am-1am.) Try the **Milltop,** 19½ Saint George St. (829-2329), a tiny bar situ-ated above an old mill in the restored area. Local string musicians play on the tiny stage (daily 1pm-midnight). On St. Augustine Beach, **Panama Hattie's** (471-2255) caters to the post-college crowd. Pick up a copy of the *Today Tonight* newspaper, available at most grocery and convenience stores, for a complete listing of current concerts, events, and dinner specials.

Daytona Beach

Built for tourists, Daytona Beach changes with the seasons and the state of its shirt collars. In fall and winter it houses wide-lapelled senior citizens looking for sunshine. Spring Break brings thousands of tank-topped college students to its beaches for sun and fun, drinking and debauchery. In the summertime, it's quite literally a hot family vacation spot, with unbuttoned people from all over the coun-try coming to sunbathe or to watch one of the eight major road races at the nearby

Daytona Speedway. During any season, hundreds of cars roll along the beach within feet of sunbathers, or cruise the Atlantic Avenue strip. Hotels and fast food restaurants line the streets; if you're looking for scenery in Daytona Beach, forget it. Keep your eyes on the ocean for its spectacular sunsets.

Practical Information

Emergency: 911.

Visitor Information: Destination Daytona!, at the chamber of commerce, 126 E. Orange Ave., on City Island (255-0415 or 800-845-1234). Teleguide coupons! Open Mon.-Fri. 9am-5pm.

Travelers Aid: 771 Briarwood Dr. (252-4752, 24 hr.). Open Mon.-Fri. 8:30am-4:30pm.

Daytona Beach Regional Airport: 189 Midway Ave. (255-8441). The **Daytona-Orlando Transit Service (DOTS)** shuttle (257-5411) runs between Orlando's airport and Daytona (every 1½ hr. 4:30am-9pm, $20). Call ahead for reservations.

Amtrak: 2491 Old New York Ave., Deland (800-872-7245), 24 mi. west on Rte. 92. To: Orlando (2 per day, 1 hr., $7); Tampa (2 per day, 3 hr., $23); Ft. Lauderdale (1 per day, 6 hr., $49); Miami (1 per day, 7 hr., $53).

Greyhound: 138 S. Ridgewood Ave. (253-6576), 4 mi. west of the beach. Catch any of the several different routes to the beach at the Volusia County Terminal. To: Orlando (9 per day, 1 hr., $12.50); St. Augustine (5 per day, 1 hr., $11.50); Tampa (7 per day, 4 hr., $28); Ft. Lauderdale (8 per day, 6 hr., $32); Miami (11 per day, 8½ hr., $42). Open Mon.-Sat. 5am-1:30am, Sun. 5-8am and 10:30am-1:30am.

Public Transport: Votran Transit Company, at the corner of Palmetto and Bay (761-7700), on the mainland. Buses operate Mon.-Sat. 5:30am-6:30pm. Fare 60¢, transfers free. Free system maps available at hotels.

Taxi: AAA Cab Co., 253-2522. $1.25 per mi.

Car Rental: Alamo, at the airport (255-1511 or 800-327-9633). Sub-compact $21 per day, $71 per week with unlimited mileage. Free drop-off in Jacksonville or Ft. Lauderdale. Must be 21 with credit card or a $50 deposit through travel agent.

Help Lines: Rape Crisis and Sexual Abuse, 258-7273.

Post Office: 55 Granada Blvd., Ormond Beach (677-0333). Open Mon.-Fri. 8:30am-5pm, Sat. 9am-1pm. **ZIP code:** 32074.

Area Code: 904.

Daytona is 53 mi. northeast of Orlando and 90 mi. south of Jacksonville on Florida's northeast coast. The city of Daytona Beach is surrounded by water, with the Halifax River (Intracoastal Waterway) slicing through its middle and the Atlantic Ocean to the east. Central artery **Route A1A,** also known as **Atlantic Avenue,** is lined with cheesy hotels, tanning oil shops, and bars. **Broadway (U.S. 92)** divides Atlantic Ave. north-south. The beach, 23 mi. of hard-packed sand, encompasses four towns: hushed **Ormond Beach** to the north, rowdy **Daytona Beach** to the south, family-friendly **Daytona Beach Shores** farther south, and quiet **Ponce Inlet** at the very southern tip. Pay attention when hunting down street addresses, as the north-south streets often change numbering systems while passing through the various small towns along the ocean.

Accommodations and Camping

Almost all of Daytona's accommodations are on Atlantic Ave. (Rte. A1A), either on the beach or across the street; those off the beach offer the best deals. During Spring Break and big race weekends even the worst beach-back hotels become ridiculously overpriced; many cheaper and quieter hotels line the mainland along Ridgewood Ave. In summer and fall, prices plunge and most hotels offer special deals during the month of June when rooms can be had from $17. Cars are generally allowed on the beach from sunrise to sunset, with evening parking permitted in a few areas, but don't plan to sleep on these well-patrolled shores.

Daytona Beach International Youth Hostel (AYH), 140 S. Atlantic Ave. (258-6937), 1 block north of Broadway (U.S. 92). A big hostel near the beach with clean kitchen facilities and recreation room. Usually full of fun-loving international students. All rooms have A/C or fans, most have TVs. Owner takes hostelers on waterskiing trips to a freshwater lake ($5). Lockers available. $12, nonmembers $15. Weekly: members $70. Key deposit $5.

Camelia Hotel, 1055 N. Atlantic Ave. (252-9963). Neither luxurious nor on the beach, but clean and friendly. All rooms have cable TV. *Let's Go* users warmly welcomed. Pink bed-spreads, brown carpet. May-Feb. singles $18, doubles $22; Spring Break singles $60, doubles $70. Each additional person $4. Kitchen use $4.

Mil-Mark Motel, 1717 N. Atlantic Ave. (258-6238). Clean rooms with fluorescent orange lamps and late 70s decor, cable TV and A/C. Singles $18. Each additional person $5. Spring Break rooms $80-120.

Nova Family Campground, 1190 Herbert St. (767-0095), in Port Orange south of Daytona Beach, 10 min. from the shore. Take bus #7 or 15 from downtown or the beach. Shady sites, pool, grocery store. Open daily 9am-8pm. Sites $13. Open sites posted after hours; just register next day.

Tomoka State Park, 2099 N. Beach St. (677-3931), 6 mi. north of Daytona. Take bus #3 ("North Ridgewood") to Domicilio and walk 1 mi. north. Nature trails, a museum, and lots of shade. Also **Flagler Beach State Park,** Flagler Beach (439-3931), off A1A, 14 mi. farther north. Recreation area and beach. Sites for both $10, with hookup $12. Reserve 2 months in advance during peak seasons.

Food

Triple S Supermarket, 167 S. Atlantic Ave. (252-8431), across from the youth hostel, features deli sandwiches and subs ($1-3.50). For the freshest seafood, go down to Ponce Inlet; in the late afternoon you and the pelicans can watch the local fishing boats haul in your dinner. Local resorts often serve buffets in their bars, and you can usually eat as much as you want for the price of one drink. Try the **Holiday Inn,** 400 N. Atlantic Ave., which serves free, mediocre food every night from 5 to 8pm in its roof-top bar. Hostel managers can direct you to to the right resort each day of the week.

Manor Buffet, 101 Seabreeze Blvd. A fantastic place to stuff your face without draining your wallet. Dinners come with soup and salad bar. Mostly frequented by seniors—so don't show up in a wet swimsuit or Daisy Duke cutoffs. Menu low-sodium and low-fat. Lunch $3.25, dinner $4.25, drinks included. Open Mon.-Sat. 11am-3pm and 4-8pm, Sun. 11am-8pm.

Oyster Pub, 555 Seabreeze Blvd. A huge square bar where locals drink, eat hearty meat sand-wiches ($2-4), or slurp up the raw oysters (20¢) which are served all day. Open daily 11:30am-3am.

B & B Fisheries, 715 Broadway (252-6542). Family-owned business almost lives up to its motto, "If it swims . . . we have it." Take-out broiled flounder or sea trout lunches under $4. Lobster and catch-of-the-day specials for under $10. Open Mon.-Sat. 11am-9:30pm. Take-out service Mon.-Sat. 11:30am-8:30pm.

Gringo's Mexican Restaurant, 701 N. Atlantic Ave. Cozy place with good tacos and enchila-das. Plastic hornblower greets diners. Excellent enchilada combination platter $4.75. Open daily 5-10:30pm.

Sights and Events

Daytona's beach is its reason for being. During Spring Break, students from prac-tically every college in the country come here to get a head and body start on sum-mer. The beach itself resembles a traffic jam; dozens of cars, motorcycles, and rental dune buggies crawl along the hot sand. To avoid the inevitable bumper-to-bumper, you'll have to arrive early (6 or 7am) and leave early (3pm or so). You'll pay $3 to drive onto the beach, and police strictly enforce the 10 mph limit. Those in search of more beach and quiet should head north of Ormond to the undeveloped, uncrowded stretch between Ormond and Flagler Beach. **New Smyrna Beach,** 15 mi. south of Daytona Beach, is also less saturated with tourists. (Parking Mon.-Fri. $1, Sat.-Sun. $2.)

During Spring Break, concerts, hotel-sponsored parties, and other events cater to students questing for fun. Word of mouth provides the best information about these constantly changing events and inevitable beach parties, but also check the **Ocean Center,** a huge white building on Atlantic Ave. Buy tickets at the box office (254-4545 or 800-858-6444) around back on Wild Olive Ave. or at outlets in various malls and record stores throughout Daytona and Ormond. (Open Mon.-Fri. 9:30am-5pm.)

If you grow tired of racing around Daytona's beaches, its many racing events will do it for you. The **Daytona International Speedway,** 1801 Speedway Blvd. (254-6767), just off I-95 on U.S. 92, has racing from July through March, with most events taking place in February and July. (General admission to most races $20-25.) Events during Speed Week (Feb. 11-19) include the **Daytona 500** (Feb. 19), the **Goody's 300** (Feb. 18), and the **ARCA 200 World Championship Race** (Feb. 12). Tickets for these events run $20-45. The **Pepsi Firecracker 400 NASCAR Race** kicks into gear on the first Saturday in July. For information, contact the Ticket Office, Drawer S, Daytona Beach 32015 (254-6767). During the first weekend in March, **Motorcycle Week** culminates with the **Daytona 200 Motorcycle Classic;** call 254-6767 for tickets ($10) and information.

At the end of June at New Smyrna Beach, wax up your board for the **Aloe UP Surf Festival** (800-537-ALOE or 800-537-2563), where you can take a surfing workshop, go to the **Beach Bash Barbecue,** and listen to free reggae concerts.

Entertainment

A myriad of nightspots try unsuccessfully to imitate **Penrod's on the Beach,** 600 N. Atlantic Ave. (255-4471). Undoubtedly the hottest club during Spring Break, Penrod's hosts poolside parties, taco buffets, and daiquiri days. Cover ($9) includes admission to **Plantation,** its neighboring bar. **T.C.'s Top Dog** is a hot-dog eatery at 425 N. Atlantic Ave. (257-7766), 1 block off Seabreeze Blvd. Photos of past revelry line the inside walls of this little funhouse. For another fun club and bar check out **Razzle's,** 611 Seabreeze Blvd. (257-6236) or **Ocean Deck,** 127 S. Ocean Ave. (253-5224), on the beach behind the Mayan Hotel. As its name implies, Ocean Deck provides an open view of the ocean, a beach volleyball court, an extensive menu (most items under $7), and live reggae.

Orlando and Disney World

Though Orlando likes to tout itself as "the world's vacation center" and one of the country's fastest-growing cities, millions annually descend on this central Florida city for just one reason: Disney World, the world's most popular tourist attraction. Walt Disney selected the area south of Orlando as the place for his expanded version of California's Disneyland. Disney has since complemented the Magic Kingdom with the Epcot Center and the brand-new Disney-MGM Studios theme parks.

A number of parasitic attractions have sprouted nearby to cash in on Disney tourism. These usually take the form of expensive water or theme parks. Be warned: of the many ways to blow your dough in this land of illusions, you are best off spending your time and money at Disney first. Two exceptions to this rule are **Sea World** and the spanking new **Universal Studios Florida.** With fun and exciting exhibits and rides, both are well worth their admission price.

Downtown Orlando has little to offer other than pretty lakes and parks. For a change of pace, visit nearby **Winter Park,** home of posh Rollins College and an appealing college town that remains miraculously unaffected by the frenzied "entertainment" biz of its neighbor.

Practical Information

Emergency: 911.

Visitor Information: Orlando-Orange County Visitors and Convention Bureau, 8445 International Dr. (351-0412), several miles southwest of downtown at the Mercado (Spanish-style mall). Take bus #8, 21, 27, 28, or 29 from downtown. Maps and information on nearly all of the amusement park attractions in the area. Pick up a free bus system map. Open daily 8am-8pm.

Amtrak: 1400 Sligh Blvd. (843-7611 or 800-872-7245). 3 blocks east of I-4. Take S. Orange Ave., turn west on Columbia, then right on Sligh. To: Tampa (2 per day, 2 hr., $17); Jacksonville (2 per day, 3½ hr., $28); Miami (1 per day, 5½ hr., $47). Open daily 7am-9pm.

Greyhound/Trailways, 300 W. Amelia St. at Hughy Ave. (843-7720 for 24-hr. fare and ticket information), downtown near Sunshine Park 1 block east of I-4. To: Tampa (9 per day, 2½ hr., $18); Jacksonville (13 per day, 3 hr., $27); Miami (7 per day, 7 hr., $40). Open 24 hr.

Public Transport: Tri-County Transit, 438 Woods Ave. (841-8240 for information Mon.-Fri. 6:30am-6:30pm, Sat. 7:30am-5pm, Sun. 8am-4pm). Downtown terminal between Central and Pine St., 1 block west of Orange Ave. and 1 block east of I-4. Schedules available at most shopping malls, banks, and at the downtown terminal. Serves the airport, Sea World, Wet'n Wild, and a deliciously dense chocolate *torta.* Buses operate daily 6am-9pm. Fare 75¢, transfers 10¢.

Mears Motor Shuttle: 324 W. Gore St. (423-5566). Has a booth at the airport for transportation to most hotels, including the Airport Hostel. Cheapest transportation besides city bus #11 (which can be caught just outside the "B" terminal luggage claim 75¢), if you're alone and can't split taxi fare. Also runs from most hotels to Disney ($13 round-trip). Open 24 hr. Call one day in advance to reserve seat to Disney.

Taxi: Yellowcab; 422-4455. $2.25 first mi., $1.30 each additional mi.

Car Rental: Alamo, 8200 McCoy Rd. (857-8200 or 800-327-9633), near the airport. $25 per day, $78 per week. Under 25 $6 extra per day. Mandatory $12 refueling charge (don't fill the tank up before you turn it in). $40 drop-off fee to Jacksonville or Miami. Open 24 hr. Must have major credit card or a $50 deposit through travel agent.

Help Lines: Rape Hotline, 847-8811.

Post Office: 46 E. Robinson St. (843-5673), at Magnolia downtown. Open Mon. 7am-5pm, Tues.-Fri. 8am-5pm, Sat. 9am-noon. **ZIP code:** 32802.

Area Code: 407.

Orlando proper lies at the center of hundreds of small lakes and amusement parks. **Lake Eola** reclines at the center of the city, east of I-4 and south of Colonial Dr. Streets divide north-south by **Route 17-92 (Mills Avenue)** and east-west by **Colonial Drive.** I-4, supposedly an east-west expressway, actually runs north-south through the center of town. To get to either downtown youth hostel by car, take the Robinson St. exit.

Unlike other Florida vacation spots, the Orlando area is landlocked. Daytona swims 55 mi. to the northeast, St. Petersburg 100 mi. southwest, and Miami 230 mi. southeast. **Disney World** and **Sea World** are 15 to 20 mi. south of downtown on I-4; **Cypress Gardens** is 30 mi. south of Disney off U.S. 27 near Winter Haven. Transportation out to the parks is simple—most hotels offer a shuttle service to Disney, but you can take a city bus or call Mears Motor Shuttle. For Plantation Manor guests, the friendly managers take you to the theme park of your choice for $10 round-trip at most.

Accommodations and Camping

Orlando does not cater to the budget traveler. Prices for hotel rooms rise exponentially as you approach Disney World; plan to stay in a hostel or in downtown Orlando. Reservations are a good idea in December, January, March, and April, and on holidays. Former home of a Houston Astros farm club, giving rise to the name, **Kissimmee,** a few miles east of Disney World along U.S. 192 has some of the cheapest places to camp. There are no federal or state parks around the area, but one city park and six Orange County parks have campsites ($8, with hookup $11). Contact **Orange County Parks & Recreation Department,** 118 W. Kaley St. (420-4290), and **Orlando Parks Department,** 1206 W. Columbia (849-2283), for more information. (Both open Mon.-Fri. 9am-4:30pm.)

Orlando International Youth Hostel at Plantation Manor (AYH), 227 N. Eola Dr. (843-8888), at E. Robinson, downtown on the east shore of Lake Eola. Porch, TV room, kitchen facilities. Rooms sleep 4-6. A/C in some rooms. To Disney $10 round-trip; they also buy and sell tickets to Disney for $22, and may have a 4-day pass for $30. Hostel beds $11. Private rooms $27.

Airport Hostel, 3500 McCoy Rd. (859-3165 or 851-1612), off Daetwiler Rd. behind the La Quinta Motel. Take "Airport" bus #11 from the airport or downtown. Kitchen facilities, airplane fans in every room, and tropical fruit trees out back. $9. Breakfast included.

Young Women's Community Club (AYH), 107 E. Hillcrest St. (425-1076), at Magnolia, 4 blocks from Plantation Manor right behind the Orlando Sentinel. Take bus #10 or 12; staff recommends a taxi. Women aged 16-44 only. Clean, safe, and friendly. Pool. Flexible 3-night max. stay. $10. Weekly: $53. Good breakfast $2, dinner $4. No reservations accepted.

Travelodge, 409 Magnolia (423-1671), downtown. *Fancy* motel that takes in hostelers. Color TV, A/C. Adjoining 24-hr. restaurant. Doughnuts and orange juice each morning. Members only. Hard bed in double $15.

Sun Motel, 5020 W. Irlo Bronson Memorial Hwy., (396-6666) in Kissimmee. Very reasonable considering proximity to Disney World (4 mi.). Color TV, phone, pool. Singles $50. Doubles $55. Off-season $25 and $28, respectively.

KOA, U.S. 192 (396-2400 or 800-247-2728; 800-331-1453 outside FL), down the road from Twin Lakes. Kamping Kabins $33.50. Pool, tennis, store (open 7am-11pm). Even in season you're bound to get a site, but arrive early. Free buses twice per day to Disney. Office open 24 hr. Tent sites $20, with hookup $24. Each additional person $2.

Stage Stop Campground, 700 W. Rte. 50 (656-8000), 8 mi. north of Disney in Winter Garden. Take exit 80 off the Florida Turnpike N., then left on Rte. 50. Office open daily 8am-8:30pm. Sites with full hookup $14. Weekly: $84.

Food

Orlando has many cheap eateries, all accessible from downtown by foot or bus. To save money, avoid supping on Church St. or in the tourist-heavy International Drive area southwest of town. The Church Street area does offer occasional good deals on meals and beer (one of the pubs has a 5¢-beer night), posted weekly on billboards in the Church Street Mall.

Lilia's Grilled Delight, 3150 S. Orange Ave., 2 blocks south of Michigan St., 5 min. from the downtown business district. Small, modestly decorated Philippine restaurant but one of the best-kept secrets in town. Don't pass up *lumpia,* a tantalizing combination of sauteed meat, shrimp, vegetables, and peanut butter in a fried dough, or the *adobo,* the Philippine national dish. Lunch $3-5, dinner $4-7. Open Mon.-Sat. 11am-7pm; summer Mon.-Sat. 11am-2:30pm.

Numero Uno, 2499 S. Orange Ave. A "number one" local favorite serving tasty Cuban specialties in a casual setting. Roast pork dinner with rice, plantains, and salad about $8. Open Mon.-Thurs. 11am-9:30pm, Fri. 11am-10pm, Sat. 1-10pm.

Deeter's Restaurant and Pub, 17 W. Pine St., just up from Orange St. near the Church Street Mall. German American cuisine in an after-work-let's-have-a-beer atmosphere. Owner seen on German TV show, *Sprockets.* Try the amazing chicken in Reisling sauce ($8). Live entertainment Fri.-Sat. nights. Open Mon.-Sat. 11am-10:30pm.

Nature's Table, 331 N. Orange Ave., downtown. Vegetarian and healthful specialties. Delicious fruit and protein powder shakes ($1-2), yogurt, juice. Excellent, thick sandwiches under $4. Open Mon.-Fri. 9am-5pm.

Ronnie's Restaurant, 2702 Colonial Plaza, at Bumby St. just past the Colonial Plaza mall. Deco booths and counters from the 50s. Mix of Jewish, Cuban, and U.S. cuisine. The famous breakfast special (eggs, rolls, juice, coffee, and more) may fill you up for a few days ($4.65). Swell pancakes. Open Sun.-Thurs. 7am-11pm, Fri.-Sat. 7am-1am.

Forino New York Pizza-Deli, 47 E. Robinson. Gargantuan pizzas: a small ($8) feeds 2 easily. Also calzones and salad bar. Open Mon.-Sat. 10am-8pm.

Entertainment

The **Church Street Station**, 129 W. Church St. (422-2434), downtown between South and Garland St., is a slick, overpriced, block-long entertainment complex with five huge bar-restaurants, all variations on the theme of Orlando's early days. From 5pm, a $5 cover admits you to all of the bars. For more interesting, less expensive nightlife, explore **Orange Avenue** downtown. Several good bars and clubs have live music and dancing at very reasonable prices. The **Beach Club**, 70 N. Orange Ave. at Washington St. (841-7246), hosts DJ dancing or live reggae nightly.

Disney World

Admit it: you came to see Disney, the monarch of amusement parks, with a sprawling three-park labyrinth of kiddie rides, movie sets, and futuristic world displays. Sit back, relax, and forget reality for a while. Pretend that you're five years old again. Maybe six.

If bigger is better, Disney World certainly wins the prize for best park in the U.S. This World (824-4321 for information daily 8am-10pm) now divides into three continents: the **Magic Kingdom**, with its seven theme parks; the **Epcot Center**, part science fair, part World's Fair; and the newly completed **Disney-MGM Studios**, a real movie and TV studio combined with Magic Kingdom-style rides. All locate a few miles from each other in the town of Lake Buena Vista, 20 mi. west of Orlando via I-4.

A one-day entrance fee of $31 (ages 3-9 $25) admits you to *one* of the three parks; it also allows you to leave and return to the same park later in the day. A four-day **passport** ($100, ages 3-9 $80) admits you to all three and includes unlimited transportation on the Disney monorail, boats, buses, and trains. You can also opt for a five-day pass ($114, ages 3-9 $92). The multi-day passes need not be used on consecutive days, and they are valid forever. A few Disney attractions charge separate admissions: **River Country** ($11.75, ages 3-9 $9.25) and **Discovery Island** ($7.50, ages 3-9 $4)—for both $15, ages 3-9 $11; **Typhoon Lagoon** ($18.25, ages 3-9 $14.50); and **Pleasure Island**. ($10, over 18 only unless with adult). For descriptions, see Other Disney Attractions below.

Gray Line Tours (422-0744) and **Mears Motor Shuttle** offer transportation from most hotels to Disney World (depart hotel at 9am, departs Disney at 7pm; $11-13 round-trip). Major hotels and some campgrounds provide their own shuttles for guests. **Bikers** are stopped at the main gate and driven by security guards to the inner entrance where they can stash their bikes free of charge.

Disney World opens its gates 365 days per year, but hours fluctuate according to season. It's busy during the summer when school is out, but Christmas, Thanksgiving, Spring Break, and the month around Easter are "peak" times during which the park is packed. More people visit between Christmas and New Year's than at any other time of year. Since the crowd hits the main gates beginning at 10am, arrive as close to 9am as possible and seek out your favorite rides or exhibits before noon. You may wait from 15 minutes to an hour, sometimes even longer, at big attractions.

Magic Kingdom

Seven "lands" make up the Magic Kingdom. You enter on **Main Street, USA,** meant to capture the essence of turn-of-the-century hometown U.S. Architects have employed "forced perspective" here, building the ground floor of the shops 9/10 normal size, while the second and third stories get progressively smaller. Walt describes his vision in the "Walt Disney Movie" at the Hospitality House, to the right as you emerge from under the railroad station. The Main Street Cinema shows some great old silents. Late afternoons on Main Street turn gruesome, when the "All America Parade" marches through at 3pm: Take this chance to ride some of the more crowded attractions. Near the entrance, you'll find a steam train that tours the seven different lands.

The **Tomorrowland** area has rides and exhibits dealing with space travel and possible future lifestyles. The indoor roller coaster **Space Mountain** proves the high point of this section, if not the high point of the park, and is well worth the extensive wait.

The golden-spired Cinderella Castle marks the gateway to **Fantasyland,** where you'll find Dumbo the Elephant and a twirling teacup ride. Most who come off of the teacup ride most walk in a crooked line, as if the Salada is spiked. 20,000 Leagues Under the Sea gives a highpoint to the fantasy, as well as the beloved but beleaguered It's A Small World. You may never get the evil tune out of your head. Catch *Magic Journeys,* a plotless 3-D movie with excellent effects.

Liberty Square and **Frontierland** devote their resources to U.S. history and a celebration of Mark Twain. History buffs will enjoy the Hall of Presidents, and adventurers should catch the rickety, runaway Big Thunder Mountain Railroad rollercoaster. Haunted Mansion seems both scary and hilarious. A steamboat ride or a canoe trip which you help paddle both rest your feet from the seemingly endless trek. Also be sure to stop and see the Country Bear Jamboree.

Adventureland contains tropical islands. The Jungle Cruise takes a tongue-in-cheek tour through tropical waterways populated by not-so-authentic-looking wildlife. Pirates of the Caribbean explores caves where animated buccaneers battle, drink, and sing. The Swiss Family Robinson tree house, a replica of the shipwrecked family's home, provides logrolls of fun.

Epcot Center

In 1966, Walt Disney dreamed up an "Experimental Prototype Community Of Tomorrow" (EPCOT) that would evolve constantly, never be completed, and incorporate new ideas and industries from U.S. technology, functioning as a self-sufficient, futuristic utopia. Instead, today no humans live there and you may be put off by the not-so-subtle advertising that leaks into its corporate-sponsored attractions. Nevertheless, since Walt's vision stretches over twice the size of the Magic Kingdom, Epcot rarely seems crowded, and can be terrific fun.

Epcot splits into Future World and World Showcase. For smaller crowds, visit the former in the evening and the latter in the morning. The large trademark geosphere forms the entrance to **Future World and Spaceship Earth,** where visitors board a "time machine" for an interesting tour through the evolution of communication. A highlight of Future World is the **Journey Into Imagination,** which features the ever-popular 3-D *Captain Eo,* starring the moon-walking, sequin-gloved rock star Michael Jackson.

The rest of Epcot is the **World Showcase**—a series of international pavilions surrounding an artificial lake. Epcot opened Norway in the summer of 1988, and has undergone negotiation with Israel and Africa for new pavilions. A clichéed architectural style or monument, as well as typical food represents each country. People in costumes from past and present perform dances, theatrical skits, and other "cultural" entertainment at each pavilion. Before setting out around the lake, pick up a schedule of daily events at Epcot Center Information in Earth Station. Two of the best attractions are the 360° film made in China and 180° film made in France. Both include spectacular landscapes, some national history, and an inside look at the people of the respective countries. Another highpoint is Norway's thrilling **Maelstrom** ride. To get away from the incessant souvenir vending, try the Italian pavilion; La Gemma Elegant has beautiful Venetian glass bead necklaces and other items for very reasonable prices.

Every summer night at 10pm (off-season Sat. only), Epcot has a magnificent show called **Illuminations,** which features music from the represented nations accompanied by dancing, lights, and fireworks. The best vantage points are the porch of the **Cantina de San Angel** in the Mexican pavilion and the veranda near the United Kingdom's pavilion. Also be sure to check the daily event listing for the Courtyard

Trio times at the German Biergarten, and for theater and dancing shows at the America Garden Theater.

Orlando residents often buy season passes to Disney World just to eat at the pavilions in the World Showcase; many pay solely to eat at the **Restaurant Marrakesh** in the Moroccan Pavilion. Head chef Lahsen Abrache cooks delicious *brewat* (spicy minced beef fried in pastry) and *bastilla* (sweet and slightly spicy pie). A belly dancer performs in the restaurant every evening. (Lunch $8-12. Dinner $10-14. Make reservations in the mornings at Earth Station World Key Terminals.) The Mexican, French, and Italian pavillions also serve up excellent food at similar prices.

Disney-MGM Studios

Disney-MGM Studios have successfully created a "living movie set." Many of the familiar Disney characters dressed in Hollywood theme costumes stroll through the park, as do a host of characters dressed as directors, starlets, gossip columnists, and fans. A different real-live movie star leads a parade across Hollywood Boulevard every day. Events such as stunt shows and mini-theatricals take place continually throughout the park.

Like most things here the park has two parts: the first, the theme park, centers around Epcot-style rides and attractions, exploring the history of film and various elements of TV and film-making; the second and more interesting part of the studios is the two-hour **Backstage Studio Tour** through Disney's working studio. As expected the animation section is a high point, shown on a separate tour (10am-7pm), covering all stages of cartoon production.

Inside the Chinese Theater, take **The Great Movie Ride** in which you can see your favorite horror monster, Alien. Watch out for her second set of jaws—they really pop out quite a ways. Don't miss Catastrophe Canyon, where you can see, smell, and almost touch manmade floods, earthquakes, and fireballs. Star Tours highlights some of the movie *Star Wars'* special effects including space canyons, laser beams, and tie-fighters.

The **Muppets** have also been incorporated at Disney—be sure to catch their stage show "Here Come the Muppets," and watch for special guest appearances on Hollywood Boulevard by Kermit, Miss Piggy, Fozzie Bear, and others. Other puppet-like stars come here dialy—you may be able to catch a glimpse, shake the hand of, or get an autograph from Lauren Bacall, Bob Hope, or Vanna White.

Other Disney Attractions

For those who did not get enough amusement at the three main parks, Disney also offers several other attractions with different themes and separate admissions (see Disney World above). The newest is **Typhoon Lagoon,** a 50-acre water park centered around the world's largest wave-making pool. Surf the 7-ft. waves that appear out of nowhere every 90 seconds or snorkel in a salt water coral reef stocked with tropical fish and harmless sharks. Besides six water slides, the lagoon has a wonderful creek on which you can take a relaxing ride, an anomaly at Disney.

The other new addition is **Pleasure Island,** a sensual dining and entertainment complex with shops, restaurants, food carts, and entertainment. Built to resemble a swimming hole, **River Country** offers water slides, rope swings, and plenty of room to swim. Across Bay Lake from River Country is **Discovery Island,** a zoological park. Fairly uncrowded during the daytime and easily reached by car, all of the parks are in the Disney complex.

Near Orlando: Sea World, Cypress Gardens, and Universal Studios Florida

One of the country's largest marine parks, you need about six hours to see all of **Sea World,** 19 mi. southwest of Orlando off I-4 at Rte. 528 (407-351-3600 for operator; 407-351-0021 for recording). Shows feature marine mammals such as whales, dolphins, sea lions, seals and otters. Though the Seal and Otter Show and the USO waterski show are enjoyable, the killer whales **Baby Shamu** and **Baby Namu** are the big stars. Not only do they share the stage (or pool) with two beautiful white whales and two Orcas, but the trainers actually mix it up with the huge creatures and take rides on their snouts. People in the park gravitate towards Shamu Stadium before the show; arrive early to get a seat. After your brow gets sweaty, visit the air-conditioned **Fantasy Theater,** an educational show with live characters in costume. The smallest crowds cling in February and from September to October. Most hotel brochure counters and hostels have coupons for $2-3 off regular admission prices. (Open daily 8:30am-10pm; off-season daily 9am-7pm. Admission $25.50, ages 3-11 $21.20. Sky Tower ride $2.50 extra. Guided tours $5.50, children $4.50. Take bus #8.)

Cypress Gardens (813-324-2111; 407-351-6606 in Orlando), in Winter Haven, is a botanical garden with over 8000 varieties of plants and flowers. Take I-4 southwest to Rte. 27 south, then Rte. 540 west. The "Gardens of the World" feature plants, flowers, and sculptured mini-gardens depicting the horticultural styles of many countries and periods. Winding walkways and electric boat rides take you through the foliage. The main attraction is a water-ski show performed daily at 10am, noon, 2pm, and 4pm. Greyhound stops here once per day on its Tampa-West Palm Beach schedule ($20 from Tampa to Cypress Gardens; open daily 8am-9:30pm; in winter daily 9am-7pm. Admission $17, ages 6-11 $11.50.) Look for coupons at motels and visitors centers.

Newly opened in 1990, **Universal Studios Florida** (363-8000) is a two-in-one park containing a number of amazing theme rides: **Kongfrontation,** where King Kong will roughouse your cable car, an **E.T.** bike ride, and **Jaws,** a boat trip where you can see the shark used in the movie. Planned for the near future of 1991 is a **Back to the Future** ride, with seven-story high OMNIMAX surround screens and spectacular special effects.

Since the park also serves as a working studio making films, stars abound. Recently, Steve Martin played a dad in *Parenthood* here; Nickelodeon television programs are in continuous production. Universal also has a number of set blocks that you may have seen before in the movies, displaying Hollywood, Central Park, and Beverly Hills as well as the infamous Bates Motel from the *Psycho* films. The park will expand over the next few years, and admission prices will vary as the park swings into full-scale action. Call the studios for more information on current ticket prices.

Cocoa Beach/Cape Canaveral

Known primarily for its rocket launches, space shuttle blast-offs, and enormous NASA space center complex, the "Space Coast" also has uncrowded golden sand beaches and vast wildlife preserves. Even during spring break the place remains comfortable because most vacationers and sunbathers are neighborly Florida or Space Coast residents incognito.

The **Kennedy Space Center** (800-432-2153 for recorded information, in FL only), 8 mi. north of Cocoa Beach, is the site for all of NASA's flights. The Kennedy Center's **Spaceport USA** (452-2121 for reservations) provides a huge welcoming center for visitors. Try the two-hour bus tours of the complex and the IMAX film about the space shuttle, *The Dream is Alive,* projected on a five-and-a-half-story screen. (Tours depart from Spaceport USA daily 9:20am-6pm; $4 ages under 12 $1.75. Movie tickets $2.75, under 12 $1.75.) Buy tickets to both immediately upon arrival at the complex to avoid a long line. The center itself is free, as are the five movies in the Galaxy Theater and half-hour walking tours of the exhibits, among them the **NASA Art Gallery** with over 250 paintings and sculptures. The NASA Parkway, site of the visitors center, is accessible only by car via State Rd. 405. From Cocoa Beach, take Rte. A1A north until it turns west into Rte. 528, then follow Rte. 3 north to the Spaceport. With NASA's new ambitious twelve-a-year launch schedule, you may have a chance to watch the space shuttles Columbia, Atlantis, or Discovery thunder off into the blue skies above the cape. Don't count on it. Call (800-872-1969) for viewing dates.

Surrounding the NASA complex the marshy **Merritt Island Wildlife Refuge** (867-8667) fills with deer, sea turtles, alligators, and eagles. (Open daily 8am-sunset.) Just north of Merritt Island is **Canaveral National Seashore** (867-2805; open daily 6:30am-sunset), 67,000 acres of undeveloped beach and dunes, and home to more than 300 species of birds and mammals. (Take Rte. 406 east off U.S. 1 in Titusville.) Should you feel like shucking off your clothes and airing those places that don't usually see sun, a nude beach accessible to the public lies at the northern-most point of the seashore, near Turtle Mound.

For a bite to eat, try **Herbie K's Diner**, 2080 N. Atlantic Ave., south of Motel 6. A shiny chrome reproduction of a 50s diner, Herbie K's serves macaroni and cheese, chicken pot pie, happy haw (apple sauce), and hamburgers ($2). (Open 24 hr.) At the beach, **Motel 6**, 3701 N. Atlantic Ave. (783-3103), has a pool and large, clean rooms with TV and A/C. (Singles $30. Each additional person $8. Reservations required.) When Motel 6 is full, try the Gateway to the Stars Motel, 8701 Astronaut Blvd. (Rte. A1A) (783-0361), in Cape Canaveral. Big, old rooms sleep up to four people. (Rooms $30; Jan.-April $40.) If you get stuck in Cocoa or need a place to spend the night between bus connections, walk right behind the Grey-hound station to the **Dixie Motel**, 301 Forrest Ave. (632-1600), one block east of U.S. 1. for big clean rooms, a swimming pool, A/C, and friendly service. (Rooms $30 off-season.) Or pitch your tent at scenic **Jetty Park Campgrounds**, 400 East Jetty Rd. (783-7222), Cape Canaveral. (Sites $10, with hookup $16. Reservations necessary Jan.-May.)

The Cocoa Beach area, 50 mi. east of Orlando, consists of mainland towns Cocoa and Rockledge, oceanfront towns Cocoa Beach and Cape Canaveral, and Merritt Island in between. **Route A1A** runs through Cocoa Beach and Cape Canaveral, and **North Atlantic Avenue** runs parallel to the beach. Inaccessible by bus, Cocoa Beach also has no local public transportation. Cocoa, 8 mi. inland, is serviced by **Grey-hound**, 302 Main St. (636-3917), from Orlando ($13). From the bus station, taxi fare to Cocoa Beach is about $10 (call 783-8294). A **shuttle** service (784-3831) con-nects Cocoa Beach with Orlando International Airport, Disney World ($25), and the Kennedy Space Center ($12). Make reservations one day in advance and ask about special rates for groups of five or more.

The **Cocoa Beach Chamber of Commerce**, 1300 N. Atlantic Ave. (783-3650), in the Holiday Inn, has information on special events and can provide suggestions on cheap, temporary housing. (Open Mon.-Fri. 9am-5pm). The main office is at 400 Fortenberry Rd., Merritt Island (459-2200; open Mon.-Fri. 8:30am-5pm). For a comprehensive list of restaurants and all kinds of information about the area, ask at the **Broward County Tourist Development Council** (453-0823 or 800-872-1969), at the Kennedy Space Center.

Cocoa Beach's **ZIP code** is 32922; the **area code** is 407.

Fort Lauderdale

Every year, thousands of college students test their wings in Fort Lauderdale, the official U.S. Spring Break party capital. Every year, pale, lust-crazed flocks de-scend on the city and trade their No-Doze for Budweiser. Lately, however, the Spring Break crowds have begun to thin out in response to: an open-container law prohibiting partiers from drinking east of the Intercoastal Waterway; a 36-inch-high wall between the sand and A1A, compelling drunken revelers to cross at streetlights; and crack-downs on drunk driving, fake IDs, and indecent exposure. Yet the crowds that do remain still manage to enjoy the "adult entertainment."

In off-season, tourists less preoccupied with carnal fulfillment and more apprecia-tive of the land and ocean's beauty stroll the wide beach. Broad-sailed boats and luxury yachts cruise up and down the coast or anchor at the city's canals and ports.

When the Spring Break parties finally end, Fort Lauderdale breathes a huge sigh of relief.

Practical Information

Emergency: 911.

Visitor Information: Chamber of Commerce, 512 NE 3rd Ave. (462-6000), 3 blocks off of Federal Hwy. at 5th St. Pick up the helpful *Visitor's Guide* ($2). Open Mon.-Fri. 9am-5pm.

Fort Lauderdale/Hollywood International Airport: 3½ mi. south of downtown on U.S. 1 (Federal Hwy.), at exits 26 and 27 on I-95. Scheduled for expansions through 1991.

Amtrak: 200 SW 21st Terrace (463-8251 or 800-872-7245), just west of I-95, ¼ mi. south of Broward Blvd. Take bus #9, 10, or 81 from downtown. Daily service on "The Floridian" to: Miami (2 per day, 1½ hr., $6); Orlando (1 per day, 4 hr., $40); and Jacksonville (1 per day, 6 hr., $60). Open daily 7:30am-6:45pm.

Greyhound/Trailways: 513 NE 3rd St. (764-6551), 3 blocks north of Broward Blvd. at Federal Hwy., downtown. Unsavory location, especially at night. To: Orlando (2 per day, 3 hr., $37); Daytona Beach (2 per day, 3 hr., $38); and Tampa (2 per day, 2½ hr., $43). Open 24 hr.

Public Transport: Broward County Transit (BCT), 357-8400 (call Mon.-Fri. 7am-7pm, Sat. 8am-5pm, Sun. 8am-4pm). Extensive regional coverage. Most routes go to the terminal at the corner of 1st St. NW and 1st Ave. NW, downtown. Operates daily 6am-9pm every ½ hr. on most routes. Fare 75¢, seniors 35¢, students with I.D. 35¢, transfers 10¢. 7-day passes $8, available at beachfront hotels. Pick up a handy system map at the **Broward County Office Plaza,** 115 S. Andrews Ave., 1 block south of Broward Blvd. Students can reach Miami Beach for 35¢ from the downtown terminal.

Car Rental: Alamo, 2601 S. Federal Hwy. (525-4715 or 800-327-9633). Cheapest cars $25 per day, $70 per week. Unlimited mi., free drop-off in Daytona and Miami. Free shuttle to airport. Must be 21 with credit card, or $50 deposit through travel agent.

Bike Rentals: International Bicycle Shop, 1900 E. Sunrise Blvd. at N. Federal Hwy. (764-8800). Take bus #10 from downtown or bus #36 from A1A north of Sunrise. $10 per day, $35 per week. $100 deposit. Open Mon.-Fri. 10am-9pm, Sat. 9am-9pm, Sun. 11am-5pm. No minimum age. Avoid the expensive joints on the beach.

Taxi: Yellow Cab, 565-5400. **Public Service Taxi,** 587-9090.

Help Line: Crisis Hotline, 467-6333. Open 24 hr.

Post Office: 1900 W. Oakland Park Blvd. (527-2028). Open Mon.-Fri. 7:30am-5pm, Sat. 8:30am-2pm. **ZIP code:** 33319.

Area Code: 305.

Ft. Lauderdale drinks 27 mi. north of Miami and 43 mi. south of West Palm Beach on Florida's Atlantic Coast. Because I-95, which runs north-south and connects the three cities, is undergoing construction through 1992, it is often congested. **Alligator Alley** (Rte. 84/I-75) slithers 100 mi. west from Ft. Lauderdale across the Everglades to Naples and other small cities on the Gulf Coast of southern Florida.

Ft. Lauderdale is bigger than it looks. The city extends westward from its 23 mi. of beach to encompass nearly 450 sq. mi. of land area. Most of the maps show distances deceptively; when travelling from the beach to downtown, take a bus. Roads are divided into two types: streets and boulevards (east-west) and avenues (north-south). All are labeled NW, NE, SW, or SE according to the quadrant. **Broward Boulevard** divides the city east-west, **Andrews Avenue** north-south. The unpleasant downtown centers around the intersection of **Federal Highway** (U.S. 1) and **Las Olas Boulevard,** about 2 mi. west of the oceanfront. Between downtown and the waterfront, yachts fill the ritzy inlets of the **Intracoastal Waterway.** The strip (variously called Rte. A1A, N. Atlantic Blvd., 17th St. Causeway, Ocean Blvd., and Seabreeze Blvd.) runs along the beach for 4 mi. between **Oakland Park Boulevard** to the north and Las Olas Blvd. to the south. Las Olas Blvd. is the pricey shopping street; **Sunrise Boulevard** has most shopping malls. Both degenerate into ugly commercial strips west of downtown.

Accommodations and Camping

Hotel prices vary from slightly unreasonable to absolutely ridiculous, increasing exponentially as you approach prime beachfront. High season runs from mid-February to early April. Investigate package deals at the slightly worse-for-wear hotels along the strip in Ft. Lauderdale.

Small motels crowd each other like canned lemmings one or two blocks off the beach area; many offer efficiencies. Look along Birch Rd., one block back from Rte. A1A. **The Broward County Hotel and Motel Association** (462-0409) provides a free directory of area hotels. (Open Mon.-Fri. 9am-4:30pm.) Scan the *Ft. Lauderdale News* and the Broward Section of the *Miami Herald* for occasional listings of local residents who rent rooms to tourists in spring. Call 357-8100 for general information on camping in Broward County. Sleeping on the well-patrolled beaches is impossible between 9pm and sunrise.

Sol Y Mar Youth Hostel (AYH), 2839 Vistamar St. (566-1023), 2 blocks west of Rte. A1A, 1 block south of Sunrise Blvd. From downtown, take bus #40 to the intersection of Birch and Vista Mar. Pick-up at the bus station for $3.50. Clean and new two-room apartments with 6-8 beds and shower. Recreation room, barbecue, and nice pool. 5-min. walk to beach. Office open 9-11am and 5-7pm. $11, nonmembers $14.

International Youth Hostel, 905 NE 17th Terrace (467-0452). From downtown, take bus #30 to NE 15th Ave. and Sunrise Blvd. Walk east on Sunrise to NE 17th Terrace. Pick-up at bus station available. Shuttle service throughout FL. Ask about possible breakfast discount. Friendly manager, nice rooms with 7 beds and shower. A/C. Fills quickly during season; call ahead. Members $7, nonmembers $8.

Estoril Apartments, 2648 NE 32nd St. 33306 (563-3840; 800-548-9398 reservations only), 2 blocks west of the Intracoastal Waterway and 1 block north of Oakland Park Blvd. From downtown, take bus #20 to Coral Ridge Shopping Center and walk 2 blocks east on Oakland. Students can probably persuade the proprietors to pick them up from the bus station or airport. A 10-min. walk to the beach, but quiet and nice. Very clean rooms with A/C, TV, and a small kitchenette. Pool and barbecue. Students with *Let's Go* receive 10% discount. Office closes about 11pm. May-Dec.: singles $23; doubles $28. Jan.-April: singles $40-45. Reserve Feb.-March with 25% deposit.

Motel 6, 1801 State Rd. 84 (760-7999), 3 blocks east of I-95 and 3 mi. southwest of downtown. Take bus #14 to Rte. 84 and SW 15th Ave. and walk 3 blocks west. Far from the action. Clean, no-frills rooms. Singles $36. Doubles $42.50. Reserve far in advance for Sept.-May.

Ocean Lodge, 200-300 S. Ocean Blvd., Pompano Beach (442-2030), near the Ft. Lauderdale border on A1A. From downtown, take bus #11 north up A1A. Clean, attractive rooms. Singles $27, with kitchenette $30. Open May-Oct.

Easterlin County Park, 1000 NW 38th St., Oakland Park (776-4466), northwest of the intersection of Oakland Park and I-95, less than 4 mi. west of the strip and 3 mi. north of downtown. Take bus #14 from downtown to NW 38th St. or #72 along Oakland Park to Powerline Rd. By car take Sample exit from I-95. 2-week max. stay. Registration open 24 hr. Sites with electricity, barbecue pits, and picnic table $15.

Quiet Waters County Park, 6601 N. Powerline Rd. (NW 9th Ave.), Pompano Beach (360-1315), 10 mi. north of Oakland Park Blvd. I-95 exit 37. From downtown, take bus #14. Cramped, commercialized, but friendly. Bizarre 8-person "boatless water skiing" and other water sports. No electricity. Check-in 2-7pm. Fully equipped campsites (tent, mattresses, cooler, grill, canoe) for up to 6 people, Sun.-Thurs. $12, Fri.-Sat. $25 plus $20 refundable deposit.

Food

The clubs along the strip offer massive quantities of free grub during Happy Hour: surfboard-sized platters of wieners, chips, and hors d'oeuvres, or all-you-can-eat pizza and buffets. However, these bars have hefty cover charges (from $5) and expect you to buy a drink once you're there (from $2). In addition, these bars are nightclubs, not restaurants, and the quality of their cuisine proves it. The restaurants below serve "real" food.

Old Florida Bar-B-Q, 1388 E. Oakland Park Blvd. Take bus #10 or 20. Friendly service by owner Bill Claus. Great ribs, beans, and slaw ($13). Open Tues.-Sat. 11:30am-9:30pm.

The Laughing Yak, 3024 E. Commercial Blvd., across from Raindancer. Take bus #30 from downtown. For lunch try the vegetable in a pita and an iced tea with brown sugar ($4). For dinner you can cook your own Mongolian-style barbecue with the raw vegetable and meats of your choice (from $5). Open Mon.-Thurs. 11:30am-2pm and 5:30-10:30pm, Fri.-Sat. 11:30am-2pm and 5:30-11pm, Sun. 5:30-10pm.

Southport Raw Bar, 1536 Cordova Rd., by the 17th St. Causeway behind the Southport Mall on the Intracoastal Waterway. Take bus #40 from the strip or #30 from downtown. Aggressively marine decor. Spicy conch chowder $2, fried shrimp $4.75. Open Mon.-Sat. 11am-2am, Sun. noon-midnight.

Tina's Spaghetti House, 2110 S. Federal Hwy., just north of 17th St. Take bus #10 from downtown. Authentic red checkered tablecloths and hefty oak furniture. Popular with locals since 1952. Lunch specials $4-5. Spaghetti dinner $6-7. Open Mon.-Thurs. 11:30am-10pm, Fri. 11:30am-11pm, Sat. 4-11pm, Sun. 4-9pm.

Citizen Kane's, 2925 Commercial Blvd., between the Intracoastal Waterway and U.S. 1. Take bus #30 from downtown. Sandwiches $4-6. Great selection of bottled and imported beers. Maybe they'll tell you what "rosebud" means. Open Mon.-Sat. 11am-1am.

Grandma's Ice Cream, 3354 N. Ocean Blvd., just north of Oakland Park Blvd. Take bus #11 from downtown. Easily recognizable by the bright red 1901 Oldsmobile truck outside. Renowned for its incredible cinnammon ice cream. Open daily noon-11pm.

Sin

Ft. Lauderdale offers all kinds of licit and illicit entertainment by night. Mostly illicit. Planes flying over the beach hawk hedonistic Happy Hours at local watering spots. Students frequent the night spots on the A1A strip along the beach, with an emphasis on the word "strip." When going out, bring a driver's license or a passport as proof of age; most bars and nightclubs don't accept college IDs. Be warned that this is not the place for capuccino and conversation, but for topless doughnut shops and lubricated competitions.

For those who prefer garbed service, Bob and other friendly bartenders serve drinks and swell food all day long at **Banana Joe's on the Beach,** 837 N. Atlantic Blvd. (565-4446), at Sunrise and A1A. Come here to nurse an early-hour hangover, get started early with the day's revelry, or just watch the sunrise on the ocean. (Open Mon.-Fri. 7am-2am, Sat. 7am-3am, Sun. noon-2am. Kitchen open at 10:30am.)

Sights and Activities

Besides sun and sin, Fr. Lauderdale is pretty low on activities. To see why Ft. Lauderdale is called the "Venice of America," take a tour of its waterways aboard the **Jungle Queen,** located at the **Bahia Mar Yacht Center** on Rte. A1A, 3 blocks south of Las Olas Blvd. (3-hr. tours daily at 10am and 2pm. Fare $7, children $5.) For those desiring more intimate acquaintance with the ocean, **Bill's Sunrise Boat Rental,** 2025 E. Sunrise Blvd. (462-8962), offers equipment for a variety of water sports. On the beach, at 301 Seabreeze Blvd. (467-1316), Bill's charges $5 more for jet-skis and boats but also offers snorkeling trips (1½ hr., $25), windsurfer rentals ($30 for 3 hr., $50 per day; $300 deposit), and waterskiing boats and drivers ($75 per hr., up to 6 people).

Atlantis the Water Kingdom, 2700 Stirling Rd. (926-1000), is the third largest water theme park in the U.S. Admission includes unlimited use of the Slidewinder water slides and the Raging Rampage. If rain interrupts your day at Atlantis for 45 consecutive minutes or more, you receive a free raincheck to return another day. (Open summer daily 10am-10pm; off-season call for hours. Admission $13, seniors $7, ages 3-11 $10, under 3 free. Head south on I-95, exit at Stirling Rd., and turn left under the overpass.)

Miami

Barely a century ago, Ohio's wealthy Julia Tuttle bought herself some Biscayne Bay swampland and decided to start a city. Only after convincing ubiquitous Standard Oil magnate and Florida avatar Henry Flagler to build a railroad to the place did she manage to instigate the development of a major urban and cultural center. Today Miami stands as a complicated, international city. Though the rather rundown swampland aesthetic still permeates near the beach, and the entire city is often ruthlessly hot, downtown provides a slick "Miami Vice" charm and the ocean is mere moments away. Many smaller cultures make up this city: Little Havana, a well-established Cuban community; Coconut Grove, with its village-in-the-swampland bohemianism; placid, well-to-do Coral Gables, one of the country's earliest planned cities; and the African American communities of Liberty City and Overtown.

Practical Information

Emergency: 911.

Visitor Information: Greater Miami Convention and Visitors Bureau, 4770 Biscayne Blvd. (539-3000; 800-641-1111 outside Miami), a few blocks north of Rte. 195, on the 14th floor of County Bank Bldg. Pick up a *Map Manual,* essential for negotiating the different forms of public transit. Open Mon.-Fri. 8:30am-6pm, Sat. 9am-noon. **Coconut Grove Chamber of Commerce,** 2820 McFarlane Rd. (444-7270). Mountains of maps and advice. Open Mon.-Fri. 9am-5pm. The **Miami Beach Resort Hotel Association,** 407 Lincoln Rd. #10G (531-3553), can help you find a place on the beach. Open Mon.-Fri. 9am-5pm.

Miami International Airport: 7 mi. northwest of downtown (871-7515). Bus #20 is the most direct public transportation into downtown (bus #3 is also usable); from there, take bus C or K to south Miami Beach.

Amtrak: 8303 NW 37th Ave. (835-1221 or 800-872-7245), not far from the Northside station of Metrorail. Bus L goes directly to Lincoln Rd. Mall in south Miami Beach. Open daily 7am-7:45pm. To: Orlando (1 per day, 5½ hr., $47); Jacksonville (2 per day, 8 hr., $69); Washington, DC (2 per day, 22 hr., $144).

Greyhound/Trailways: 99 NE 4th St. (374-7222 for fare and schedule information). To: Orlando (8-10 per day, 6½ hr., $41); Jacksonville (8-10 per day, 11 hr., $53); Atlanta (6 per day, 15½ hr., $94). Ticket window open daily 5am-midnight.

Public Transport: Metro Dade Transportation, 638-6700; 6am-11pm for information. Complex system and buses tend to be quite tardy. The extensive **Metrobus** network converges downtown; most long bus trips transfer in this area. Lettered bus routes A through X serve Miami Beach. After dark, some stops are patrolled (indicated with a sign). Service daily 6am-8pm; major routes until 11pm or midnight. Fare 75¢. Pick up a *Map Manual* at the visitors bureau or at information stands at the corner of W. Flagler and NW 1st Ave. and on the Lincoln Rd. Mall in Miami Beach. Both open Mon.-Fri. 8am-5pm. Futuristic **Metrorail** service downtown. Fare $1, rail-bus transfers 25¢. The **Metromover** loop downtown, which runs 6:30am-7pm, is linked to the Metrorail stations.

Taxis: Yellow Cab, 444-4444. **Metro Taxi,** 888-8888. **Central Taxi,** 532-5555.

Car Rental: Value Rent-a-Car, 1620 Collins Ave., Miami Beach (532-8257). $19-20 per day, $99 per week. Open daily 8am-4pm. Must be 21 with credit card or $225 deposit. **Way-Lo,** 1701 Collins Ave. (871-4561), in the Ritz Plaza. $25 per day, $119 per week plus insurance. Open daily 8am-6pm. Must be 25 with credit card.

Auto Transport Company: Dependable Car Travel, 162 Sunny Isles Blvd. (945-4104). $21 per day, $89 per week. Open Mon.-Fri. 9am-5pm, Sat. 9am-noon. Must be 21 with a credit card or passport and foreign license.

Bike Rental: Miami Beach Cycle Center, 923 W. 39th St., Miami Beach (531-4161). $3 per hr., $12 per day, $32 per week, 2-hr. minimum. Open Mon.-Fri. 9:30am-6pm, Sat. 9:30am-5pm. Must be 18 with credit card or $40 deposit. **Dade Cycle Shop,** 3216 Grand Ave., Coconut Grove (443-6075). $3-6 per hr., $15-22 per day. Open daily 9am-6pm. Must have $10 deposit and driver's license or credit card.

Help Lines: Crisis Hotline, 358-4357. Rape Treatment Center and Hotline, 1611 NW 12th Ave. (549-7273). Gay Community Hotline, 759-3661. Center for Survival and Independent Living (C-SAIL), 1310 NW 16th St. (547-5444). Offers information on services for the disabled. Lines open Mon.-Fri. 8am-5pm.

Post Office: 500 NW 2nd Ave. (371-2911). Open Mon.-Fri. 8:30am-5pm, Sat. 8:30am-12:30pm. ZIP code: 33101.

Area Code: 305.

Miami squats on the east coast of Florida across the Strait of Florida from the Bahamas. The state's second largest east coast city, Miami, bench-presses 350 mi. from Jacksonville, 660 mi. southeast of Atlanta, and 860 mi. east of New Orleans.

Three highways criss-cross the Miami area. Just south of downtown, I-95, the most direct route north-south, runs into U.S. 1, known as the Dixie Highway. U.S. 1 goes as far as the Everglades entrance at Florida City and then all the way out to Key West. Route 836, a major east-west artery through town, connnects I-95 with the Florida Turnpike, passing the airport in between. Take Rte. 836 and the Turnpike to Florida City to avoid the traffic on Rte. 1.

When looking for street addresses, pay careful attention to the systematic street layout; it's *very* easy to confuse North Miami Beach, West Miami, Miami Beach, and Miami adresses. Streets in Miami run east-west, avenues north-south, and numbers into the hundreds refer to both. Miami divides into NE, NW, SE, and SW sections: the dividing lines (downtown) are Flagler Street (east-west) and Miami Avenue (north-south). Some numbered streets and avenues also have names—i.e., Le Jeune Rd. is SW 42nd Ave., and SW 40th St. is called Bird Rd.

Several four-lane causeways connect Miami to Miami Beach. The most useful is MacArthur Causeway, which feeds onto 5th St. in Miami Beach. Numbered streets run across the island, with numbers increasing as you go north; the main north-south drag is Collins Avenue. In South Miami Beach, Washington Avenue, 1 block to the west, is the main commercial strip, while Ocean Avenue, actually on the waterfront, lies 1 block east. The Rickenbacker Causeway is the only connection to Key Biscayne.

Spanish-speakers will have an advantage getting around Miami. The city has a large Spanish-speaking community; the *Miami Herald* now even puts out a Spanish edition of their paper. You may even run into problems on buses without it since many drivers only speak Spanish or limited English.

Accommodations and Camping

Finding cheap rooms in Miami should never pose a problem. Several hundred fleabag art deco hotels in South Miami Beach stand at your service. For safety, convenience, and security, stay north of 5th St. A "pullmanette" (40s lingo) is a room with a refrigerator, stove, and sink; getting one and some groceries allows you to save money on food. In South Florida, since any hotel room short of the Fontainebleau Hilton is likely to have 2-3 in. cockroaches ("palmetto bugs"), try not to take them as indicators of quality: they are actually shy, reticent, even beautiful creatures. In general, the peak season for Miami Beach runs late December to mid-March.

Camping is not allowed in Miami and the nearest campgrounds are north or west of the city. Those who can't bear to put their tents aside for a night or two should head on to one of the nearby national parks.

The Clay Hotel (AYH), 406 Española Way, Miami Beach (534-2988), on Washington Ave. between 14th and 15th St. Take bus C or K from downtown. Cheerful chaos reigns in the 7 buildings. Kitchen, laundry facilities, and ride boards. Very international crowd. Most rooms have 4 beds; 2 rooms share a bathroom. No curfew. $9, nonmembers $11. A/C $1. Hotel singles $17-20. Doubles $25-28. Key deposit $5.

Waves Hotel, 1060 Ocean Ave., Miami Beach (531-5835), on the beach at 11th St. Renovated, with friendly atmosphere. A/C, HBO, washer and dryer in basement. Singles and doubles April 1-Dec. 15 $40; 10% student discount in summer, and you can probably bargain down to $30. Pullmanette rates start $5 higher. Ocean views $10 higher. Key deposit $10, for pull-manettes $20.

San Juan Hotel, 1680 Collins Ave. (538-7531). Small, clean, old pullmanettes with dark car-pets, somewhat lumpy beds, and color TV. Good access to city buses. Singles and doubles $26.

Palmer House Hotel, 1119 Collins Ave., Miami Beach (538-7725), 3 blocks west of the beach. A, clean, venerable, art deco establishment with air-conditioned pullmanettes. Singles $30, off-season $27. Each additional person (up to 3) $4. $125 per week, off-season $100.

Miami Airways Motel, 5001 36th St. (883-4700). Will pick you up at nearby airport. Clean rooms, A/C, pool, HBO. Singles $32. Doubles $37.

Larry & Penny Thompson Memorial Campground, 12451 SW 184th St. (232-1049), a long way from anywhere. By car, drive 20-30 min. south along Dixie Hwy. Pretty grounds in a grove of mango trees. Laundry, store, and all facilities, plus artificial lake with swimming beach, beautiful park, and even water slides. Office open daily 8am-5pm, but takes late arriv-als. Lake open daily 10am-5pm. Sites $11, with hookup $17. Weekly: sites $67, with hookup $100.

Food

If you eat nothing else in Miami, be sure to try Cuban food. Specialties include *media noche* sandwiches (a sort of Cuban club sandwich on a soft roll, heated and compressed); *mamey,* a bright red ice cream concoction; rich *frijoles negros* (black beans); and *picadillo* (shredded beef and peas in tomato sauce, served with white rice). For Cuban sweets, seek out a *dulcería,* and punctuate your rambles around town with thimble-sized swallows of strong, sweet *café cubano* (25¢).

In Miami Beach, cheap restaurants are not common, but an array of fresh bak-eries and fruit stands can sustain you with melons, mangos, tomatoes, and carrots for under $3 per day.

La Rumba, 2008 Collins Ave., Miami Beach, between 20st and 21th St. Good, cheap Cuban food and noisy fun. Try their *arroz con pollo* (chicken with yellow rice; $6). Open daily 7:30am-midnight.

Flamingo Restaurant, 1454 Washington Ave., right down the street from the hostel. Friendly service, all in Spanish. Try the *pollo* (chicken) with pinto beans and rice $4. Open Mon.-Sat. 9am-7:30pm.

Wolfie's, 2038 Collins Ave., Miami Beach, at 21st St. Giant, extremely popular New York-style deli, famous for its cheesecake. Turkey on rye $6. Lunch $3-7, dinner $5-10. Open 24 hr. A 2nd Wolfie's is at **Rascal House,** 17190 Collins Ave., near Hallandale. Open daily 7am-1:45am.

Canton Too, 2614 Ponce de Leon Blvd., in Coral Gables. Indisputably the best Chinese food in Miami. Out-of-this-world honey chicken ($5). Open Mon.-Thurs. 11am-11pm, Fri.-Sat. 11am-midnight, Sun. 2-11pm.

Our Place Natural Foods Eatery, 830 Washington Ave., Miami Beach (674-1322). New Age books along with juices, salads, pita, tofutti, etc. Lunch $3-6, dinner $5-10. Live folk music on weekends. Open Mon.-Thurs. 11am-7pm, Fri.-Sat. 11am-11pm.

King's Ice Cream, 1831 SW 8th St., on Calle Ocho. Tropical fruit *helado* (ice cream) flavors include coconut (served in its own shell), *mamey,* and banana. Also try *churros* (thin Spanish donuts) or *café cubano* (10¢). Open daily 10am-11pm.

Sights

The best sight in Miami is the beach. When you get too burned or dazed, try the **Seaquarium,** 4400 Rickenbacker Causeway, Virginia Key (361-5703), just min-utes from downtown. While not on a par with Sea World in Orlando, it has a truly impressive array of shows, including obligatory dolphins, hungry sharks, and killer whales. The aquarium also displays tropical fish. (Open daily 9:30am-6:30pm; ticket office closes 5pm. Admission $14, children $10.) **Planet Ocean,** 3979 Rickenbacker Causeway (361-9455), across the street, offers a more educational atmosphere for uncovering the secrets of the deep. (Open daily 10am-6pm; ticket office closes 4:30pm. Admission $7.50, ages 4-12 $4.)

South Miami Beach, the swath of town between 6th and 23rd St., overwhelms with hundreds of hotels and apartments whose sun-faded pastel façades recall what sun-thirsty northerners of the 20s thought a tropical paradise should look like. The art deco palaces comprise the country's largest national historic district, and the only one to preserve 20th-century buildings. A fascinating mixture of people populates the area, including large retired and Latin immigrant communities; knowing Spanish is a big advantage here. A group called the **South Florida Art Center** (674-8278) has tried, with some success, to revive the fading Lincoln Rd. Mall as the center of a new art district. Their **cooperative gallery,** 942 Lincoln Rd. Mall, between Meridian and Lenox, exhibits the work of unknown artists; they have also helped others open their own galleries on the mall. (Gallery open Tues.-Thurs. and Sat. noon-6pm, Fri. noon-6pm and 7-11pm.)

On the waterfront downtown is Miami's newest attraction, the **Bayside** shopping complex, with fancy shops, exotic food booths, and live reggae or *salsa* on Friday and Saturday nights. For those interested in cinema's nautical leftovers, Bayside also refrigerates MGM's *Bounty,* used in the filming of *Mutiny on the Bounty.* Tours are given by guides in "authentic" (ripped) nautical clothing ($3.50, under 12 $1.50; tickets sold Sun.-Thurs. noon-8pm, Fri. noon-10pm, Sat. 10am-10pm).

On the bayfront between the Grove and downtown stands **Vizcaya** (579-2708 and 579-2808; recorded information 579-4813), set in acres of elaborately landscaped grounds. Built in 1916 by International Harvester heir James Deering, the four façades of this 70-room Italianate mansion hide a hodgepodge of European antiques. (Open daily 9:30am-5pm; last admission 4:30pm. Admission $5. Take bus #1 to 3251 S. Miami Ave., or Metrorail to Vizcaya.) Across the street from Vizcaya, both the **Museum of Science** and its **Planetarium,** 3280 S. Miami Ave. (854-4247; show information 854-2222), offer laser shows and their ilk; both congest with children. (Open daily 10am-6pm. Admission $5, ages 3-12 $3.50. Planetarium shows extra.)

Little Havana lies between SW 12th and SW 27th Ave. (take bus #3, 11, 14, 15, 17, 25, or 37). The street scenes of **Calle Ocho** (SW 8th St.) lie at the heart of this district; the corresponding section of W. Flager St. is a center of Cuban business. The **Little Havana Development Authority,** 970 SW 1st St. #407 (324-8127), arranges free walking tours that start from Domino Park, given one day's notice. You'll visit a cigar factory and some of the city's best shops and food stands. The works at the **Cuban Museum of Arts and Culture,** 1300 SW 12th Ave. (858-8006), reflect the bright colors and rhythms of Cuban art. Take bus #27. (Open Mon.-Fri. 10am-4:30pm, Sat.-Sun. 1-5pm. Donation.)

An entirely different atmosphere prevails on the bay south of downtown in self-consciously rustic **Coconut Grove** (take bus #1 or Metrorail from downtown). The grove centers around the intersection of Grand Ave. and Main Hwy. Drop into a watering hole like **Señor Frog's,** 3008 Grand Ave. (448-0999), home of bang-up tables and phenomenal salsa. (Open Sun.-Thurs. 10:30am-1am, Fri.-Sat. 10:30am-2am.)

Near Miami, the **Everglades National Park** teems with exotic life. Visit the park in winter or spring, when heat, humidity, storms, and bugs are at a minimum, and when wildlife congregates around the water. The park is accessible on the north via the Tamiami Trail (U.S. 41) or by the main park road (Rte. 9336) out of Florida City. The best way to tour the largely inaccessible park is to take Rte. 997 40 mi. through the flat grasslands to Flamingo, on Florida Bay, stopping at the various nature trails and pullouts along the way. Stop at the **visitors center,** P.O. Box 279, Homestead 33030 (247-6211), by the park headquarters just outside the entrance, to see a film on the Everglades and to pick up maps and information. (Open daily 8am-5pm.) The visitors center also sponsors a variety of hikes, canoe trips, and amphitheater programs. To get face-to-snout with an alligator, try the **Anhinga Trail,** 2 mi. beyond the entrance.

Entertainment

The climate of Miami nights won't force you indoors, but if you choose to take cover, the beach provides an array of good alternatives like pop-musicked **Club Nu,** Collins Ave. at 21st St. (cover around $11; dress code). For blues, try the **Peacock Cafe,** 2977 McFarlane Rd., Coconut Grove (445-0550; open Mon. 8pm-midnight, Tues.-Thurs. and Sun. 9pm-1am, Fri.-Sat. 10pm-2am). After the money's gone, head for **Friday Night Live,** at **South Point Park,** the very southern tip of Miami Beach, which features free city-sponsored concerts. (Call 579-6040 for information.) Down Washington Ave. at of Española Way, the **Cameo Theater** (532-6212) hosts live punk and other rock bands about once per week. For gay nightlife, check out **Uncle Charlie's,** 3673 Bird Ave. (442-8687), just off Dixie Hwy. (cover $1).

Performing Arts and Community Education (PACE) (856-1966) offers more than a thousand concerts each year (jazz, rock, soul, dixieland, reggae, salsa, bluegrass), most of which are free. For more information on what's happening in Miami, check *Miami-South Florida Magazine,* or the "Living Today," "Lively Arts," and Friday "Weekend" sections of the *Miami Herald.*

The Florida Keys

The coral rock islands, mangrove trees, and relaxed attitude of the people make the Florida Keys pleasant places to visit and live; with a character quite different from anywhere else in the U.S., these islands off the coast could even be a country in themselves. The Keys enjoy settings more Caribbean than Floridian with cool onshore breezes at night, wild tropical rainstorms, and of course sun hot enough to cook thick steaks, or skin. When the sun does set, clouds, heat lightning, and surrounding ocean provide an incredible accompaniment. Approximately 6 mi. off-shore, 100-yd. wide barrier reefs lie parallel to the Keys from Key Largo south to Key West. Adored by divers, these reefs harbour some of the ocean's most diverse and colorful marine life as well as hundred of wrecked ships and legendary lost treasure. There are also *very* few sharks.

The Keys run southwest into the ocean from the southern tip of Florida, accessible by the **Overseas Highway (U.S. 1). Mile markers,** which divide the highway into sections, replace street addresses to indicate the location of homes and businesses. They begin with mile 126 in Florida City and end with zero on the corner of Whitehead and Fleming St. in Key West.

Greyhound runs two buses per day to Key West from Miami, stopping in Coral Gables, Perrine, Homestead, Key Largo (451-3664), Marathon (743-3488), Big Pine Key, and Key West (296-9072). If there's a particular mile marker at which you need to get off, most drivers can be convinced to stop at the side of the road. Biking along U.S. 1 across the swamps between Florida City and Key Largo is impossible because the road lacks shoulders: Bring your bike on the bus.

The **area code** on the Keys is 305.

Key Largo

After crossing the thick swamps and crocodile marshland of Upper Florida Bay, Key Largo wheels out the first welcome of the Keys. Though a gateway of sorts—much like the wardrobe to magical Narnia—Largo is one of the longer Keys. Without a car it can be difficult to get around, although everything of importance lies within a 6 mi. range. Largo's **John Pennecamp State Park,** mile 102.5 (451-1202),.60 mi. from Miami, provides the visitor with a rare though somewhat murky view of the living reef off the Keys from glass-bottomed boats ($11-12). Mostly off-shore, the beautiful state park has the largest uninterrrupted stretch of the barrier reef in the Keys, the only underwater park in the country, and the only underwater Christ statue in the world. (Admission $2.50 for vehicle operator, each additional person $1.50. Camp sites $26, with hookup $28. Each additional night $2 discount.) The **Coral Reef Company** (451-1621 or 800-432-2871) sails visitors 6 mi. past mangrove swamps to the reef. (Snorkeling tours daily at 9am, noon, and 3pm. 1½ hr. of water time and a quickie lesson including gear for $18 at 9am, otherwise $20 per person.)

The Italian Fisherman, mile 104 (451-4471), has it all: fine food and a spectacular view of Florida Bay. Formerly an illegal gambling casino, this restaurant was the locale of some scenes from Bogart and Bacall's movie *Key Largo*. Try the thick-noodled spaghetti with delicious tomato sauce ($4) for lunch. (Dinners $6-14. Open daily 11am-11pm.) The seafood and selction of 99 beers of the **Crack'd Conch,** mile 105 (451-0732), is superb. Try the "Sorry Charlie" tuna fish sandwich ($4.50) or an entire key lime pie ($8.50). (Open Thurs.-Tues. noon-10pm.) With four locations, **Perry's,** serves fresh local seafood and charbroiled steaks, at mile 102; Ismorada, mile 82.5; Marathon, mile 52; and the most famous location at Key West, 3800 N. Roosevelt Blvd. (Lunch $4-9, dinner $6-16. Open daily 11am-11pm.) They also offer a "you hook 'em, we cook 'em" service for $2.50. **Mrs. Mac's Kitchen** mile 99.5, has out-of-this-world home-style cooking, pita bread sandwiches ($5) and a relaxed "Key-easy" atmosphere. (Open Mon.-Sat. 11am-10pm.) Other scenes from *Key Largo* were filmed at the **Carribean Club,** mile 104, a friendly local bar. The in-house band *Nasty Habits* dishes out hard rock to the locals and snapshots of Bogart and Bacall grace the walls. (Open daily 7am-4am.) When you're starring in your own late-night show, call **Sailboat John's Taxi** (852-6074) for a ride home.

After the state park's campsites fill up, try crowded but well-run **Kings Kamp Marina,** mile 103.5 (451-0010; sites by the ocean $18). Look for the concealed entrance on the northwest (gulf) side of U.S. 1. The **Hungry Pelican** mile 99.5 (451-3576), has beautiful bougainvillea vines in the trees and friendly owners Tom and Jerry Ray. Stuff your beak full in a clean, cozy trailer with a double bed for $30-35. Some other rooms are $40. The only other budget option, the **Sea Trails Motel** (852-8001), mile 98.5 on the bayside, has large but plain rooms with A/C, 1 double bed and 1 twin bed ($35). You won't see *Key Largo* here.

The **Florida Upper Keys Chamber of Commerce,** mile 105.5 (451-1414), at Rte. 905, has maps and brochures on local attractions, including scenes from the film *Key Largo*. (Open Mon.-Fri. 9am-5pm.) The **visitors center,** mile 103.4 (451-1414 or 800-822-1088) in the pink shopping center, has a cinematic selection of maps and brochures. (Open Mon.-Fri. 9am-5pm.) The dramatic mailroom scene from *Key Largo* was filmed at the **post office,** mile 100 (451-3155; open Oct.-June Mon.-Fri. 8am-4:30pm, Sat. 8am-noon). Key Largo's ZIP code is 33037; the area code is 305.

Key West

This is the end of the road. When searching for a tropical paradise, you can do no better than Key West. The island's pastel clapboard houses, hibiscus and bougainvillea vines, year-round tropical climate, and gin-clear waters make it a beautiful spot to visit in summer or winter.

Key West inhabitants have made their living salvaging wrecked ships, rolling cigars, gathering sponges, fishing for turtle and shrimp, and overcharging tourists for souvenirs. A railroad provided the original access to the island in 1912, built by, you guessed it, railroad guy Henry Flagler. A hurricane not only blew the stuffing out of the railroad, but tossed the dirt that Flagler used to fill some of the smaller channels into the ocean. Flagler's legacy to Key West remains with **Indian Key Fill,** the old railroad bridge running parallel to the highway in some spots, and in his cameo scene from the film *Key Largo*.

Like most of this region, the city of Key West has a relaxed atmosphere, hot sunshine, and spectacular sunsets, attracting travelers and famous authors like Tennessee Williams, Ernest Hemingway, Elizabeth Bishop, and Robert Frost over the years. Today, an easygoing diversity still attracts those outside the mainstream—a new generation of writers and artists, gay people (who own or manage more than half of Key West's businesses), recluses, adventurers, and eccentrics.

Practical Information

Emergency: 911.

Visitor Information: Key West Chamber of Commerce, 402 Wall St. (294-2587), in old Mallory Sq. Useful Humm's *Guide to the Florida Keys and Key West* available here. Accommodations list notes guest houses popular with gay people. Open daily 9am-5pm. **Key West Visitors Bureau,** P.O. Box 1147, Key West 33041 (296-3811 or 800-352-5397), produces a detailed guide to accommodations. Open Mon.-Fri. 9am-5pm. **Key West Welcome Center,** 3840 N. Roosevelt Blvd. (296-4444 or 800-284-4482), just north of the intersection of U.S. 1 and Roosevelt Blvd. Arranges accommodations, theater tickets, weddings, and reef trips if you call in advance. Open daily 9am-5pm.

Key West International Airport: on the southeast corner of the island. Serviced by Eastern and Piedmont airlines. No public bus service.

Greyhound/Trailways: 615½ Duval St. (296-9072). Obscure location in an alley behind Antonio's restaurant. To Miami stopping along all the Keys (2 per day, 5 hr., $33). Open Mon.-Sat. 7am-12:45pm and 2:30-5:30pm.

Public Transport: Key West Port and Transit Authority, City Hall (292-8159 or 292-8164). One bus (Old Town) runs clockwise around the island and Stock Island; the other (Mallory St.) runs counterclockwise. Pick up a clear and helpful free map from the chamber of commerce or any bus driver. Service Mon.-Sat. 6am-10pm, Sun. 6:40am-6:40pm. Fare 75¢, seniors and students 35¢. **Handicapped Transportation,** 294-8468.

Taxi: Key West Independent, 294-7277.

Car Rental: Alamo, Key Wester Inn, 975 S. Roosevelt Blvd. (294-6675 or 800-327-9633), near the airport. $33 per day, $132 per week. Under 25 $5 per day extra. Must be 21 with major credit card or $50 deposit through a travel agent. Drop-off in Miami a prohibitive $60.

Bike Rental: Key West Hostel, 718 South St. (296-5719). $6 per day, $30 per week. Hostel residents only. Open daily 8am-noon and 5-8pm. $20 deposit. **Bubba's Bike Rental,** 705 Duval St. (294-2618). $5 per day, $25 per week. Open daily 10am-5pm. Must have credit card or $50 deposit.

Help Line: 296-4357.

Post Office: 400 Whitehead St. (294-2257), 1 block west of Duval at Eaton. Open Mon.-Fri. 8:30am-5pm. **ZIP code:** 33040.

Area Code: 305.

Just 5 mi. long and 3 mi. wide and the southernmost point on the continental U.S., Key West lies at the end of Rte. 1, 160 mi. southwest of Miami. Only 90 mi. north of Havana, Cuba, Key West dips farther south than many islands in the Bahamas.

Divided into two sectors, the eastern part of the island, called "Des Moines" or "America" by some, harbors the tract houses, chain motels, shopping malls, and the airport. **Old Town,** the west side of town below White St., is cluttered with beautiful old conch houses. **Duval Street** is the main north-south thoroughfare in Old Town, **Truman Avenue** the major east-west route. Key West is cooler than mainland Florida in summer, and much warmer in winter.

On the way to and in the city of Key West, driving is slow; most of the highway is a two-lane road with only an occasional passing lane. Bikers beware: police enforce traffic laws. Use hand signals, stop at signs, and watch for one-way streets.

Accommodations and Camping

Beautiful weather resides year-round in Key West alongside tourists. As a result, good rooms at the nicer hotels go for up to $400 per day, especially during the winter holidays. There is no "off-season." Key West remains packed virtually year-round, with a lull of sorts from mid-September to mid-December; even then, don't expect to find a room for less than $40.

Try to bed down in Old Key West; the beautiful, 19th-century clapboard houses capture the flavor of the Keys: some of the guest houses in the Old Town offer complimentary breakfasts and some are for gay men exclusively. During the busy spring months, police tend to look the other way when people park overnight at the pull-outs by the Keys' bridges.

Key West Hostel, 718 South St. (296-5719), at Sea Shell Motel in Old Key West, 6 blocks west of Duval St. Take any bus to the corner of South and Reynolds St. Even has its own postcards. Rooms with 4 beds, shared bath. A/C at night. Dinners $1. Kitchen open until 9:30pm. No curfew. Office open daily 8am-noon and 5-8pm. $12, nonmembers $14. Key deposit $5. Motel rooms in summer $36, in winter $55. Call ahead to check availability; also call for late arrival.

Caribbean House, 226 Petronia St. (296-1600; 800-736-0179; 800-543-4518), at Thomas St. in Bahama Village. Brand new, Caribbean-style rooms with cool tile floors, A/C, TV, and ceiling fans. Comfy double beds. Norman, the friendly owner, may be able to place you in the completely furnished Caribbean Cottage (sleeps 5) or an unfurnished low-rent apartment for comfortable summer living. In-season: rooms $55, cottage $75. Summer: rooms $35, cottage $50. Apartments $600 per month.

Island House, 1129 Fleming St. (294-6284), at White St. Take any bus to the corner of White and Fleming. For gay men only. Rooms with A/C, fans, and radio; slick, ritzy atmosphere and decor. Sauna, pool, jacuzzi, and weight room. Singles in summer with shared bath $55; in winter $88.

Tilton Hilton, 511 Angela St. (294-8697), next to the Greyhound station near downtown. Plain rhyming rooms, as cheap as you'll find. Color TV, A/C. Singles in summer $30-34.

Jabour's Trailer Court, 223 Elizabeth St. (294-5723), 3 blocks from North Duval St. between Greene and Caroline St. Cramped trailer lots, but the only game in Old Town. Tents seldom turned away. Tents and vans $25 for 2 people, with hookup $30. Each additional person $3. Rates vary by season.

Boyd's Campground, 6401 Maloney Ave. (294-1465), on Stock Island. Take bus to Maloney Ave. from Stock Island. 12 acres on the ocean. Full facilities, including showers. Primitive sites $18. Water and electric $2 extra, A/C or heat $2 extra. Waterfront sites $3 extra.

Food

Expensive restaurants line festive Duval Street. Side streets offer lower prices and fewer crowds. Stock up on supplies at **Fausto's Food Palace,** 522 Fleming St. (296-5663), the best darn grocery store in Old Town. (Open Mon.-Sat. 8am-8pm, Sun. 8am-6pm.) Don't leave Key West without having a piece of (even a whole) **key lime pie,** although the genuine article with a tangy yellow filling is hard to find; key limes are not green. Pick up a copy of *The Masked Gourmet* ($1) at the Key West Welcome Center for reviews of pies and restaurants.

La Cubanita Restaurant, 601 Duval St. #3, at Southard. Noisy and fun. The best-priced Cuban food around. Try the Cuban sandwich ($3) or a palomilla steak dinner ($7.50). Open Mon.-Sat. 7am-9pm, Sun. 7am-3pm.

La Bodega, 829 Simonton St., 1 block east of Duval at Olivia. A cluttered old conch house favored by locals for cheap, thick sandwiches ($3-4) and fresh soups ($2.25). Open Mon.-Sat. 8am-11pm, Sun. 10am-11pm.

Half-Shell Fish Market, Land's End Village (294-5028), at the foot of Margaret St. on the waterfront 5 blocks east of Duval. Rowdy and popular with tourists. Great variety of seafood dinners $8-10. Famed for its spring conch chowder ($2.50). Open daily 11am-11pm.

El Cacique, 125 Duval St. Cuban food at reasonable prices. Homey and colorful. Filling lunch and dinner specials, with pork or local fish, black beans, and rice under $6. Try fried plantains, conch chowder, or bread pudding as side dishes, and flan ($1.25) for dessert. Open daily 8am-9pm.

Hercules Bar-B-Q, 3332 N. Roosevelt Blvd. (296-3846), just behind the Searstown Laundry, 1½ mi. west of Old Town. Take any bus to the Searstown Mall. A local secret, this tiny shack serves juicy, thick barbecue pork and beef sandwiches ($3). Take-out only. Open Mon.-Sat. 10:30am-9pm, Sun. 10:30am-7pm.

Blue Heaven Fruit Market, 729 Thomas St., 1 block from the Caribbean House. Hemingway used to drink beer and referee boxing matches at the Blue Heaven when it was a pool hall. Fresh fruits and lunch specials ($3). Try the wonderful fresh mango shakes ($1). Open Mon.-Sat. 10am-6pm.

Sights

Biking is a good way to see Key West, but first you might want to take the **Conch Tour Train** (294-5161), a narrated ride through Old Town, leaving from Mallory Sq. The touristy one-and-a-half-hour trip costs $11 (children $4) but guides provide a fascinating history of the area. (Operates daily 9am-4:30pm.) **Old Town Trolley** runs a similar tour, but you can get on and off throughout the day.

The glass-bottomed boat *Fireball* takes two-hour cruises to the reefs and back (296-6293; 3-4 per day; tickets $12, ages 3-12 $6). One of a few cruise specialists, the **Coral Princess Fleet,** 700 Front St. (296-3287), offers snorkeling trips with free instruction for beginners (2 per day, $24; open daily 8:30am-7:15pm). In summer, prices for snorkeling trips drop $5.

For many years a beacon for artists and writers, **Hemingway House,** 907 Whitehead St. (294-1575), on Olivia St., is where Papa wrote *For Whom the Bell Tolls* and *A Farewell to Arms.* Tour guides at the houses are notoriously awful; grin and bear it or traipse through the house on your own. About 50 cats (supposedly descendants of Hemingway's cats) make their home on the grounds. (Open daily 9am-5pm. Admission $5, children $1.) The **Audubon House,** 205 Whitehead St. (294-2116), built in the early 1800s, houses some fine antiques and a private collection of the works of ornithologist John James Audubon. (Open daily 9:30am-5pm. Admission $5, ages 6-12 $1.)

Down Whitehead St., past Hemingway House, you'll come to the **Southernmost Point** in the continental U.S. and the adjacent Southernmost Beach. A small, cone-shaped monument and a few conchshell hawkers mark the spot. The **Monroe County Beach,** off Atlantic Ave., has an old pier allowing access past the weed line. The **Old U.S. Naval Air Station** offers deep water swimming on Truman Beach ($1). **Mel Fisher's Treasure Exhibit,** 200 Greene St. (296-9936), will dazzle you with glorious gold. Fisher discovered the sunken treasures from the shipwrecked Spanish vessel, the Atocha. The National Geographic film is included in the entrance fee. (Open daily 10am-6pm, doors close 5:15pm. Admission $5, children $7.)

The **San Carlos Institute,** 516 Duval St., built in 1871, is a freshly restored paragon of Cuban architecture that shines with majorca tiles from Spain and now houses a research center for Hispanic studies. The **Haitian Art Company,** 600 Frances St. (296-8932), 6 blocks east of Duval St., is crammed full of vivid Caribbean artworks. (Open Mon.-Sat. 9am-5pm.)

Watching a sunset from the **Mallory Square Dock** is always a treat. Magicians, street entertainers, and hawkers of tacky wares work the crowd; swimmers and speedboaters show off; and the crowd always cheers when the sun slips into the Gulf with a blazing red farewell.

Every October, Key West holds a week-long celebration known as **Fantasy Fest,** which culminates in an extravagant parade. The entire population of the area turns out for the event in costumes that stretch the imagination. In April, the **Conch Republic** celebration is highlighted by a bed race, and the January-through-March **Old Island Days** features art exhibits, a conch shell-blowing contest, and the blessing of the shrimp fleet.

Entertainment

The daily *Key West Citizen* (sold in front of the post office) and monthly *Solares Hill* and *The Conch Republic* (available at the Key West Chamber of Commerce, lobbies, and waiting rooms) all cover events on the island. Nightlife in Key West revs up at 11pm, and runs until very late. Many establishments situate on or off Duval Street. Gay travelers can expect a little heckling from out-of-town cruisers at night, but violence is rare and hassles can be avoided by staying away from the straight bars at the far north end of Duval.

The Bull Bar, 224 Duval St. Not a place to nurse wine coolers; don't enter unless you're prepared to poison your esophagus with $1 schnapps shots. Live music nightly. Open Mon.-Sat. 10am-2am, Sun. noon-2am. The **Whistle Bar** upstairs opens at 5pm and closes at the same time as the Bull. Balcony overlooking Duval St. allows patrons to whistle at unsuspecting tourists—hence the name. Drinks 2-for-1 5-9pm.

Sloppy Joe's, 201 Duval St., at Greene (294-5717). Reputedly one of Papa Hemingway's preferred watering holes; the decor and rowdy tourists would probably now send him packing. Originally in Havana but moved to "Cayo Hueso" (i.e. Key West) when Castro rose to power. The bar's usual frenzy heightens during the Hemingway Days Festival in mid-July. Reasonable draft prices. Open daily 9am-until the sloppiness ends.

Captain Tony's Saloon, 428 Greene St. (294-1838). The oldest bar in Key West. Open daily noon-very, very late. Tony Tarracino, the owner, usually shows up at 9pm.

La Terraza de Martí (also called La Te Da), 1125 Duval (294-8435). Some of the best (albeit expensive) food in town. José Martí, the Cuban rebel, made incendiary speeches from the front balcony to raise money for the Cuban revolution in the 1890s. Open daily 10am-2am.

Tampa and St. Petersburg

The Gulf Coast communities of Tampa and St. Petersburg have a less raucous style than most Atlantic Coast vacation meccas. Not as sumerged in tourists, the two cities offer quiet beaches, beautiful harbors, and perfect weather year-round. One of the nation's fastest-growing cities and largest ports, Tampa contains thriving financial, industrial, and artistic communities. Across the bay, St. Petersburg caters to a relaxed, attractive retirement community, with oodles of health food shops and pharmacies. Meanwhile, the town's not-so-martyred beaches beckon with 28 miles of soft white sand, emerald water, and beautiful sunsets; perhaps as a result, the high season on the Gulf Coast runs from October to April.

Practical Information

Emergency: 911.

Visitor Information: Tampa/Hillsborough Convention and Visitors Association, 100 S. Ashley Dr. #850 (223-1111 or 800-826-8358). Teleguide coupons and some brochures. Open Mon.-Fri. 8am-4:45pm. West Tampa Chamber of Commerce, 3005 W. Columbus Dr. (879-2866). Open Mon.-Fri. 9am-5pm. Ybor City Chamber of Commerce, 1513 8th Ave. (248-3712). Open Mon.-Fri. 11am-3pm. St. Petersburg Chamber of Commerce, 401 3rd Ave. S. (821-4069). Open Mon.-Fri. 8:30am-5pm.

Travelers Aid: In Tampa, 253-5936. Open Mon.-Fri. 8:30am-4:30pm. In St. Pete, 823-4891.

Tampa International Airport: (276-3400) 5 mi. west of downtown. HARTline bus #30 runs between the airport and downtown Tampa. St. Petersburg Clearwater International Airport sits right across the bay. The Limo (822-3333) offers 24-hr. service from both airports to both cities and the beaches from Ft. Desoto to Clearwater ($10.50). Make reservations 12 hr. in advance.

Amtrak: In Tampa, 601 Nebraska Ave. (229-2473 or 800-872-7245), at Twiggs St., 1 block north of Kennedy. Two trains per day to: Orlando (2 hr., $18); Jacksonville (5 hr., $42); Savannah (8 hr., $71). Open dialy 7:30am-8pm. No trains go south of Tampa—no service to St. Pete. In St. Pete, 3601 31st St. N. (522-9475). Amtrak will transport you to Tampa by bus ($5).

Greyhound/Trailways: In Tampa, 610 E. Polk St. (229-1501 or 229-2112), next to Burger King downtown. To Miami (3 per day, 10 hr., $42) and Orlando (6 per day, 1½ hr., $18). In St. Pete, 180 9th St. N., downtown.

Public Transport: In Tampa, Hillsborough Area Regional Transit (HARTline), 254-4278. Fare 75¢, transfers 25¢. To get to St. Pete, take bus #100 express service from downtown to the Gateway Mall ($1). In St. Pete, St. Petersburg Municipal Transit System, 530-9911. Most routes depart form Williams Park at 1st Ave. N. and 3rd St. N. Ask for directions at the information booth there. Fare 75¢, transfers 10¢.

Help Lines: Rape Crisis, 530-7233. Gay/Lesbian Crisis Line, 586-4297.

ZIP codes: Tampa 33602, St. Pete 33713.

Area Code: 813.

Tampa sits at the corner of a bay in the middle of Florida's west coast, 85 mi. west of Orlando. The city divided into quarters by **Florida Avenue,** running east-west, and **Kennedy Boulevard,** which becomes **Frank Adams Drive** (Rte. 60), running north-south. Numbered avenues run east-west and numbered streets run north-south. You can reach Tampa on I-75 from the north, or I-4 from the east. St. Petersburg receives the stigmata 22 mi. southwest of Tampa, on the tip of the peninsula between the Gulf of Mexico and Tampa Bay. **Central Avenue** divides St. Pete east-west. **34th Street** (U.S. Hwy. 19) cuts north-south through the city and links up with the new **Sunshine-Skyway bridge** which connects St. Pete with the Bradenton-Sarasota area to the south. Avenues run east-west, streets north-south. The St. Pete beachfront is a chain of barrier islands accessible by bridge extending from Clearwater Beach in the north to Pass-a-Grille Beach in the south. Many towns on the islands offer quiet beaches and reasonably priced hotels and restaurants. From north to south, these towns include: **Clearwater Beach, Indian Rocks Beach, Madiera Beach, Treasure Island,** and **St. Petersburg Beach.** The stretch of beach past the Don CeSar Hotel (a pink montrosity recently declared an historical landmark) in St. Petersburg Beach and Pass-a-Grille Beach has the best sand, a devoted following, and the least pedestrian and motor traffic. Three causeways connect Tampa and St. Pete.

Accommodations and Camping

Inexpensive, convenient lodgings happen rarely in Tampa, but St. Petersburg has a youth hostel and many cheap motels along 4th St. N. and U.S. 19. Some establishments advertise singles for as little as $16, but these tend to be ancient and dirty. To avoid the worst neighborhoods, stay on the north end of 4th St. and the south end of U.S. 19. Fortunately, several inexpensive motels also line the St. Pete beach. In Tampa, you can try to contact the Overseas Information Center at the **University of South Florida** (974-3104) for help in finding accommodations. **Florida Suncoast Bed and Breakfast,** P.O. Box 12, Palm Harbor 33563 (784-5118), can arrange private lodgings in the area, as well as in Clearwater, Saratoga, and Bradenton (from $28). Write for an application for winter reservations, and apply at least one month in advance.

Tampa

Motel 6, 333 E. Fowler Ave. (932-4948), near Busch Gardens. From I-275, take the Fowler Ave. exit. On the northern outskirts of Tampa, 30 mi. from the beach. Well-used, small rooms. Singles $27. Each additional person $6.

Econolodge, 9202 N. 30th St. (935-7855 or 800-446-6900), near Busch Gardens. Swimming pool. Bright, clean rooms with A/C. Pick up the coupon in the orange *Welcome to Florida's Suncoast* map for a 1-4 person $33 per night special.

St. Petersburg

St. Petersburg International Hostel (AAIH), 215 Central Ave. (822-4095), at the Detroit Hotel downtown. Big, clean rooms with 2-4 beds, A/C; some with private bath. Kitchen and laundry facilities. Bike rental $10 per week. Call for pick-up at Greyhound or Amtrak stations. In the same building, **Club Detroit** offers live music 5 nights per week. Also, **Janus Landing** offers big name concerts like Depeche Mode. $11. Weekly: $50. Private rooms $18. Key deposit $5.

Kentucky Motel, 4246 4th St. N. (526-7373). Large, clean rooms with friendly owners, color TV, and free postcards. Singles $20. Doubles $22-25. Rooms $10 more Dec.-April.

AAA Motel, 6345 4th St. N. (525-5900). Small, clean rooms with A/C and satellite TV. Ask for a room in back to escape highway noise. Singles $18. Each additional person $2.

Grant Motel, 9046 4th St. N. (576-1369), 4 mi. north of town on U.S. 92. Pool. Clean rooms with A/C; most have fridge. Ask about the single for $21. Otherwise singles $26, doubles $28. Jan. 1-April 15 singles $37, doubles $39.

Buccaneer, 10800 and 10836 Gulf Blvd. (367-1908 or 800-826-2120), on Treasure Island. Quiet hotel with great beachfront rooms. Lends grills for cookouts. Doubles $29-38, with fridge $38-41. High season $45-62 and $65, respectively. Each additional person $6. Breakfast included. Key deposit $5.

Windjammer, 10450 Gulf Blvd., St. Pete Beach (360-4940). Large, clean rooms. Doubles $40-42, with kitchen $42-46. High season $50 and $52, respectively. Each additional person $5.

Fort DeSoto State Park (866-2662), composed of five islands at the southern end of a long chain of keys and islands, has the best camping. A wildlife sanctuary, the park makes a good daytrip or oceanside picnic spot. (2-day min. stay. Curfew 10pm. No alcohol. Sites $13.) Disregard the "no vacancy" sign at the toll booth (75¢) at the Pinellas Bayway exit. However, from January to April, you may want to make a reservation in person at the St. Petersburg County Building, 150 5th St. N. #63, or at least call ahead. In Tampa, try the **Busch Travel Park,** 10001 Malcolm McKinley Dr. (971-0008), ¼ mi. north of Busch Gardens, with a pool, store, recreation room, and train service to Busch Gardens and Adventure Island. (Tent sites $9. RV sites $15.)

Food

Prices for food leap high in Tampa, but cheap Cuban and Spanish establishments stretch all over the city. Black bean soup, gazpacho, and Cuban bread usually yield the best bargains. For Cuban food, Ybor City definitely has superior prices and atmosphere.

St. Petersburg's restaurants cater to its retired population—cheap, good, and low on sodium, they generally close by 8 or 9pm. Those hungry later should try St. Pete Beach or 4th St. The beach has several forgettable surf 'n' turf spots, but a few places serve excellent, cheap seafood.

Tampa

JD's, 2029 E. 7th Ave., in Ybor City. Take bus #12. Soups, sandwiches, and Cuban food in a roomy, low-key restaurant. Breakfast $2.50. Lunch $3-5. Open Mon.-Sat. 9am-3pm.

The Columbia, 2117 E. 7th Ave., in Ybor City. Elegant block-long Spanish restaurant. Oldest in the Sunshine State. Excellent meals accompanied by violinists and Flamenco dancers. Lunch $5-7. Dinners $9-25 plus $5 per person for entertainment. Open daily 11am-11pm.

The Loading Dock, 100 Madison St., downtown. Sandwiches $3-5. Try the "Flatbed" or the "Forklift" for a filling diesel-fueled meal. Open Mon.-Fri. 8am-8pm, Sat. 10:30am-2:30pm.

St. Pete

Goody Goody, 1119 Florida Ave. N., in Tarpon Springs. The best best burgers burgers ($2-2.30) in town. Decor straight out of *Lost in Space.* Open Mon.-Sat. 7:30am-7:30pm.

Crabby Bills, 402 Gulf Blvd., Indian Rocks Beach. Cheap, extensive menu. Ultra-casual atmosphere. Six blue crabs $5.50. Open Mon.-Thurs. 11am-10pm, Fri.-Sat. 11am-11pm. Arrive before 5pm to avoid substantial wait.

The Scandia, 19829 Gulf Blvd., Indian Shores. Danish theme invades. Small dining rooms, pleasant atmosphere. Dinners $6-11. Open Tues.-Sat. 11:30am-9pm, Sun. noon-8pm.

Ollie O's, 101 1st Ave. NE, St. Pete, in the Old Soreno Hotel 2 blocks from the youth hostel. Huge steaks with fries ($6) or soup and sandwich ($4). Open Mon.-Thurs. and Sat. 7am-5:30pm, Fri. 7am-6pm.

Sights and Activities

Tampa

Bounded roughly by 22nd Street, Nebraska Avenue, 5th Avenue, and Columbus Drive, **Ybor City** is Tampa's Latin Quarter. The area expanded rapidly after Vincent Martínez Ybor moved his cigar factories here from Key West in 1886. Although cigar manufacturing has been mechanized, some people still roll cigars by hand and sell them for $1 in **Ybor Square,** a 19th-century cigar factory converted into an upscale retail complex. (Open Mon.-Sat. 10am-9pm, Sun. noon-6pm. Free.) **Ybor City State Museum,** 1818 9th Ave. at 21st St. (247-6323), traces the development of Ybor City, Tampa, the cigar industry, and Cuban migration. (Open Tues.-Sat. 9am-noon and 1-5pm. Admission 50¢.) At **Three Birds Bookstore and Coffee Room,** 1518 7th Ave. (247-7041), you can sip a lemonade, get a sandwich, or enjoy a slice of cheesecake while you read the latest *Paris Review* or daily paper. Three Birds also offers extensive poetry and New Age book sections. (Open Mon.-Wed. 10am-7pm, Thurs.-Fri. 10am-10pm, Sat. 11am-10pm.) Aside from the square, the Ybor City area has remained relatively unspoiled by the rapid urban growth that typifies the rest of Tampa; **East 7th Avenue** still resembles an old neighborhood. Keep an ear out for jazz and a nose out for Spanish cuisine. Be careful not to stray more than two blocks north or south of 7th Ave. since the area becomes extremely dangerous, even during the daytime. Bus #5, 12, and 18 run to Ybor City from downtown.

Now part of the University of Tampa, the Moorish **Tampa Bay Hotel,** 401 W. Kennedy Blvd., once defined the most fashionable Florida coast resort hotel in 1889. Teddy Roosevelt trained his Rough Riders in the backyard before the Spanish-American War. The small **Henry B. Plant Museum** (253-3333), in a wing of the University of Tampa building, is an orgy of rococo craftsmanship and architecture. The exhibits themselves, which include Victorian furniture and Wedgewood pottery, pale in comparison to the architecture. (Guided tours at 1:30pm. Open Tues.-Sat. 10am-4pm. Donation.)

Downtown, the **Tampa Museum of Art,** 601 Doyle Carlton Dr. (223-8128), houses the Joseph Veach Nobre collection of classical and modern works. (Open Tues.-Sat. 10am-5pm, Wed. 10am-9pm, Sun. 1-5pm. Free.) Across from the University of South Florida, north of downtown, the **Museum of Science and Industry,** 4801 E. Fowler Ave. (985-5531), features a simulated hurricane. (Open daily 10am-4:30pm. Admission $2, ages 5-15 $1.)

The **waterfront** provides much of Tampa's atmosphere. Banana boats from South and Central America unload and tally their cargo every day at the docks on 139 Twiggs St., near 13th St. and Kennedy Blvd. Every year in February the *Jose Gasparilla,* a fully rigged pirate ship, loaded with hundreds of exuberant "pirates," "invades" Tampa and kicks off a month of parades and festivals, such as the **Gasparilla Sidewalk Art Festival.**

Enjoy everything from bumper cars to corkscrew rollercoasters at Tampa's questionably named **Busch Gardens—The Dark Continent,** 3000 Busch Blvd. at NE 40th (971-8282). Take I-275 to Busch Blvd., or take bus #5 from downtown. Not only are people confined to trains, boats, and walkways while giraffes, zebras, ostriches, and antelope roam freely across the park's 60-acre plain, but Busch Gardens has two of only 50 white Bengal tigers in existence. (Open daily 9am-8pm; off-season dialy 9:30am-6pm. Admission $21, infants free, 5-8pm $16. Parking $2.) A morning visit to the **Anheuser-Busch Hospitality House** inside the park provides a surefire way to make your afternoon more enjoyable. You must stand in line for each beer, with a three-drink limit.

St. Petersburg

St. Petersburg's main attraction is its coastline. **Pass-a-Grille Beach** may be the nicest, but the **municipal beach** at Treasure Island, accessible from Rte. 699 via Treasure Island Causeway, is free. When you're too sunburned to spend another day on the sand, head for **Sunken Gardens,** 1825 4th St. N. (896-3187), home of over 7000 varieties of exotic flowers and plants. (Open daily 9am-5:30pm. Admission $6, ages 3-11 $3.)

Opened in March 1982, the **Salvador Dalí Museum,** 1000 3rd St. S. (823-3767), in Poynter Park on the Bayboro Harbor waterfront, contains the world's largest collection of Dalí works and memorabilia—93 oil paintings, 1300 graphics, and even works from a 14-year-old Dalí. As Dalí himself said "Never a dully moment avec Dalí." (Tours available. Open Tues.-Sat. 10am-5pm, Sun. noon-5pm. Admission $3.50, seniors and students $2.50, ages under 8 free.) **Great Explorations,** 1120 4th St. S. (821-8885) is a museum with six hands-on exhibit areas not a Dickens adventure. Test your strength at the **Body Shop** where you can compare your muscles against scores taken from around the country. (Open Mon.-Sat. 10am-5pm, Sun. 1-5pm.) **The Pier,** at the end of 2nd Ave. NE (821-6164), extends out into Tampa Bay from St. Pete, ending in a five-story inverted pyramid complex that contains a shopping center, aquarium, and restaurant. (Open Mon.-Sat. at 10am, Sun. at 11am.)

Georgia

Georgians have begun to feel the peach of prosperity. Atlanta holds the rather unofficial title of "Capital of the New South," while Savannah's stately antebellum homes are undergoing restoration. The state is still largely agrarian, keeping Georgians up to their ears in their favorite fruit, the peach. With the Appalachians to the north and major rivers like the Chattahoochee originating around Atlanta, Georgia's resources for outdoor adventure are plentiful. As is the case in most of the South, the hospitality is peachy, making Georgia the perfect place for an extended visit.

Practical Information

Capital: Atlanta.

Tourist Information: **Department of Industry and Trade, Tourist Division,** 230 Peachtree St., Atlanta 30301 (656-3590), across from Atlanta Convention and Visitors Bureau. Write for or pick up a comprehensive *Georgia Travel Guide* open Mon.-Fri. 8 am-5pm. **Department of Natural Resources,** 270 Washington St. SW, Atlanta 30334 (800-542-7275; 800-342-7275 in GA). **U.S. Forest Service,** 1720 Peachtree Rd. NW, Atlanta 30367 (347-2385). Information on the Chattahoochee and Oconee National Forests. Open Mon.-Fri. 8am-4pm.

Time Zone: Eastern. **Postal Abbreviation: GA.**

Atlanta

Atlanta's seal, a Phoenix and the motto *Resurgens,* sums up the city's fabulous recovery since 1864, when Union General Sherman burned it to the ground. Today, Atlanta soars as the largest metropolitan area in the Southeast and a national economic powerhouse. The city contains the world's second busiest, but still beautiful, airport, the headquarters of Coca-Cola, and offices of over 400 of the Fortune 500 corporations. Nineteen institutions of higher learning, including Georgia Tech, Emory University, and Morehouse and Spellman colleges, call "The Big Peach" home.

Not surprisingly, fame and prosperity have diffused Atlanta's Old South flavor. An influx of transplanted Northerners and Californians, the third-largest gay population in the U.S., and a host of ethnic groups have lent the city a cosmopolitan air. Atlanta's progressivism in race relations only enhances these facts, with the city playing a vital role in the struggle for civil rights. The birthplace of Martin Luther King, Jr. witnessed unrest and activism during the 60s; by 1974, the city elected one of the nation's first African American mayors, Maynard Jackson, succeeded by King's colleague Andrew Young. Sleek and upbeat, Georgia's capital continues to aspire to its mythical reputation.

Practical Information

Emergency: 911.

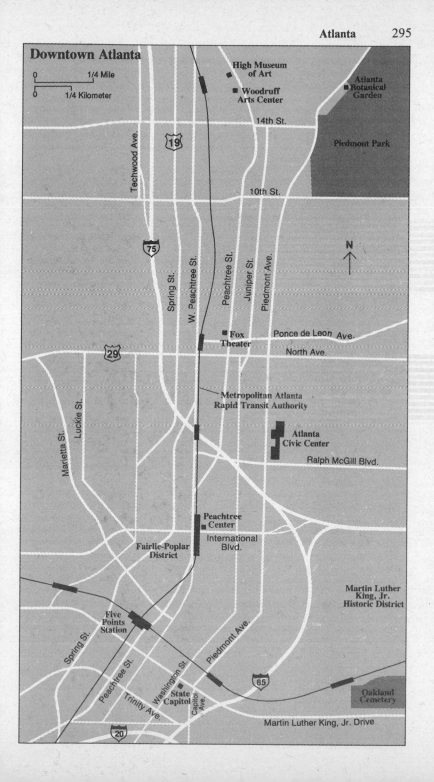

Downtown Atlanta

0   1/4 Mile
0   1/4 Kilometer

High Museum of Art

Woodruff Arts Center

Atlanta Botanical Garden

14th St.

Piedmont Park

10th St.

19

75

N

Techwood Ave.

Spring St.

W. Peachtree St.

Peachtree St.

Juniper St.

Piedmont Ave.

Fox Theater

Ponce de Leon Ave.

North Ave.

29

Metropolitan Atlanta Rapid Transit Authority

Luckie St.

Atlanta Civic Center

Ralph McGill Blvd.

Marietta St.

Peachtree Center

International Blvd.

Fairlie-Poplar District

Martin Luther King, Jr. Historic District

Five Points Station

Spring St.

Peachtree St.

Washington St.

Piedmont Ave.

Capitol Ave.

State Capitol

Trinity Ave.

85

Oakland Cemetery

Martin Luther King, Jr. Drive

20

Visitor Information: Atlanta Convention and Visitors Bureau, 233 Peachtree St. #200 (659-4270), Peachtree Center, Harris Tower, downtown. More aimed at conventions, but stop by to pick up a free copy of *Atlanta and Georgia Visitors' Guide* ($3 on newsstands). Open Mon.-Fri. 9am-5pm. Satellite information centers are at **Peachtree Center Mall** (521-6633), 233 Peachtree St. NE, and **Lenox Square Shopping Center** (266-1398), 3393 Peachtree Rd. NE, in Buckhead. Both open Mon.-Fri. 10am-5pm. Also at **Underground Atlanta,** Peachtree St. and Martin Luther King, Jr. Dr. (577-2148). Open daily 10am-5pm.

Travelers Aid: 81 International Blvd. (527-7400), in the downtown Greyhound terminal. Limited information on accommodations. Open Mon.-Fri. 8am-8pm, Sat. 10am-6pm. After hours, call 522-7370 for assistance.

Hartsfield International Airport: South of the city, bounded by I-75, I-85, and I-285. General information 530-6600; international services and flight information 530-2081. Headquarters of **Delta Airlines** (756-5000 or 800-523-7777). International travelers can get phone assistance in 6 languages at the **Calling Assistance Center,** a computerized telephone system in the international terminal. Subway is the easiest way to get downtown. The **Atlanta Airport Shuttle** (525-2177) runs vans from the airport to downtown, Emory, and Lenox Sq. (around $11). **Northside Airport Express** (455-1600) serves Stone Mountain, Marietta, and Dunwoody. Buses run daily 5am-midnight ($15-25).

Amtrak: 1688 Peachtree St. NW (872-9815), 3 mi. north of downtown at I-85. Take bus #23 to and from the "Arts Center" MARTA station. To: New Orleans (2 per day, 11 hr., $93); Washington, DC (2 per day, 14 hr., $111); Charlotte (1 per day, 5 hr., $48). Open daily 6:30am-9:30pm.

Greyhound/Trailways: 81 International Blvd. (522-6300), 1 block from Peachtree Center. MARTA: Peachtree Center. To: New Orleans (7 per day, 9 hr., $69); Washington, DC (8 per day, 16 hr., $94); Chattanooga (8 per day, 2½ hr., $22). Open 24 hr.

Public Transport: Metropolitan Atlanta Rapid Transit Authority (MARTA), 848-4711; schedule information Mon.-Fri. 6am-10pm, Sat.-Sun. 8am-4pm. Combined rail and bus system serves virtually all area attractions and hotels. Operates Mon.-Sat. 5am-1:30am, Sun. 6am-12:30am in most areas. Fare $1 exact change, transfers free. Unlimited weekly pass $9. Pick up a system map at the **MARTA Ride Store,** Five Points Station downtown, or at one of the satellite visitor bureaus. If you get confused, just find the nearest MARTA courtesy phone in each rail station.

Taxi: Checker, 351-1111. **London,** 688-5658. Base fare $1.50, $1.20 per mi.

Car Rental: Atlanta Rent-a-Car, 3185 Camp Creek Pkwy. (763-1160), just inside I-285, 3 mi. east of the airport. Nine other locations in the area including one at Cheshire Bridge Rd. and I-85, 1 mi. west of the Liddberg Center Railstop. Rates from $20 per day. 100 free mi., 15¢ each additional mi. Must be 21 with major credit card.

Help Lines: Rape Crisis Counseling, 659-7273. Open 24 hr. **Gay/Lesbian Center Help Line,** 892-0661. Open daily 6-11pm. Center located at 63 12th St. (876-5372).

Post Office: 3900 Crown Rd. (768-4126). Open Mon.-Fri. 7:30am-5pm. **ZIP code:** 30321.

Area Code: 404.

Atlanta rises from its own ashes in the northwest quadrant of the state, 150 mi. east of Birmingham, AL, and 113 mi. south of Chattanooga, TN. The city lies on north-south I-75 and I-85 and on east-west I-20. It is circumscribed by I-285 ("the perimeter").

Getting around is confusing at first because everything seems to be named Peachtree. However, of the 26 roads bearing that name, only one, **Peachtree Street,** is a major north-south thoroughfare, as are **Spring Street** and **Piedmont Avenue. Ponce De Leon Avenue** and **North Avenue** are major east-west routes. In the heart of downtown, the area to the west of I-75/85, south of International Blvd. and north of the capitol, where angled streets and shopping plazas run amok, there is no easily navigable plan.

Accommodations and Camping

When planning to stay in Atlanta for more than a few days, check with the **International Youth Travel Program (IYTP).** The convention and visitors bureau (see Practical Information above), will try to locate a single for $18. Unfortunately, since there are no hostels in Atlanta, the IYTP is your cheapest bet besides the YMCA. Unfortunately, these options do not apply for women from the U.S. **Bed and Breakfast Atlanta,** 1801 Piedmont Ave. NE (875-0525; call Mon.-Fri. 9am-noon or 2-5pm), offers singles from $35, doubles from $40.

Motel 6, 6 locations in the Atlanta area, all just outside the perimeter. Marietta, 2360 Delk Rd., exit 11 from I-75 (952-8161). Big, usually busy, hotel complex with large earth-toned rooms furnished with comfortable chairs. Pool. Singles $22. Each additional person $6. Another on I-285 at Chamblee-Turcker, exit 27 (455-8000), closer to the city. Two-story motel with pleasant clean rooms. Complete table and chair set and green curtains. Pool. Singles $24. each. Each additional person $6.

Travelodge, 1641 Peachtree St. NE (873-5731), in sight of the Amtrak station. Freshly painted, large hotel with attractive rooms and cushioned chairs. Complimentary coffee. Singles $39. Doubles $44.

Best Way Inn, 144 14th St. NW (873-4171), very, very near the highway. Tidy rooms with ugly paintings. Friendly management. Mexican restaurant. Pool. Singles $31. Doubles $36. Key deposit $5.

YMCA, 22 Butler St. (659-8085), between Edgewood and Auburn, 3 blocks from downtown. Men only, and usually full of semi-permanent residents. Community shower. Singles $16.50. Key deposit $5. Open Mon.-Fri. 9am-5pm. Hard to find space here, and they don't take reservations.

Arrowhead Campsites, I-20 W. and Six Flags Rd. (948-7302), 10 mi. west of downtown. Subway to Hightower, then bus to Six Flags in Austell, GA. Excellent facilities, including pool and laundry. Tent sites $11.75. RV sites $14.75.

Stone Mountain Family Campground, on U.S. 78 (498-5710), 16 mi. east of town. Exit 30-B off I-285 or subway to Avondale then "Stone Mountain" bus. Part of state park system. Tent sites $9. RV sites $9.50. Entrance fee $5 per car. Make reservations 2 weeks ahead.

Food

You really have to scrounge for inexpensive home-style Southern cooking when in Atlanta. Some favorite dishes to sample include fried chicken, black-eyed peas, okra, sweet potato pie, and mustard greens. Dip a hunk of cornbread into "pot likker," water used to cook greens, and enjoy. Atlanta's food offerings defy easy categorization, however. **Little Five Points,** is home to French African, Ethiopian, and vegetarian restaurants in many permutations; the rest of Atlanta is full of variety, too.

Do-it-yourselfers can procure produce at one of the South's largest outdoor markets, the **Atlanta State Farmers Market,** 16 Forest Pkwy. (366-6910), exit 78 off I-75 south. (No MARTA service.) The grocery in building K is open daily from 8am to 5pm. Fresh fruits, vegetables, eggs, and smoked meats are on sale in 80 acres of open-air, drive-through stalls. (Open Mon.-Fri. 10am-10pm, Sat.-Sun. 9am-9pm.) Travelers without a car may find the world-wide specialties of **Dekalb County Farmers Market,** 3000 E. Ponce De Leon Ave. (377-6400), near Stone Mountain more accessible. Take the subway to Avondale and then the "Stone Mountain" bus. (Open Tues.-Sun. 10am-9pm.)

Mary Mac's Tea Room, 224 Ponce De Leon Ave. NE. Take the "Georgia Tech" bus north. Famous for its amazing homemade cornbread and array of real Southern vegetables. Order by writing your own ticket. Waiters tend to rush you. Lunches $3-5, dinners $4-10. With student ID receive 10% discount at dinner. Open Mon.-Fri. 11am-4pm and 5-8pm.

The Varsity, 61 North Ave. NW at I-85. Take the subway to North Ave. station. Order at the world's largest drive-in or brave the masses to eat inside. Best known for chili dogs and the greasiest onion rings in the South. Employees have a language all their own. Eat in one of the giant TV rooms—1 room for each channel and vice-versa. Open Sun.-Thurs. 7am-12:30am, Fri.-Sat. 7am-2am.

Tortilla's, 774 Ponce De Leon Ave. Incredibly busy, neon-lit Mexican eatery. Cheap and luscious tacos $1.75, enormous gigantic super burrito $3. Open Mon.-Fri. 11am-10pm, Sat. noon-10pm.

Eat Your Vegetables Café, 438 Moreland Ave. NE, in the Little Five Points area. Mostly vegetarian foods (hummus, soyburgers, and salads) in a largely friendly atmosphere. Dinners $5-9. Open Mon.-Fri. 11:30am-2pm and 6-10:30pm, Sat. 5:30-10:30pm, Sun. 11am-3pm.

Touch of India, 962 Peachtree St. Three-course lunch specials $3-3.50. Popular with locals. Atmosphere and service worthy of a much more expensive restaurant. Dinners $5-10. Open daily 11:30am-2:30pm and 5:30-10:30pm.

Cha Gio Vietnamese Restaurant, 966 Peachtree St. NE at 10th St. (885-9387), next door to Touch of India. Three locations, all offering inexpensive, filling dinners ($4-6) in a welcoming, table-clothed environment. Open Mon.-Fri. 11am-3pm and 4-10pm, Sat. 11am-10pm, Sun. 11am-9pm.

Sights

Atlanta's sights scatter, but the effort it takes to find them usually pays off. The **Atlanta Preservation Center,** 401 the Flatiron Building, 84 Peachtree St. NW (522-4345), offers six walking tours of popular areas—Historic Downtown, West End and Wren's Nest, Oakland Cemetery, the capitol and Underground Atlanta, Inman Park, and Sweet Auburn—from April through November. A tour of the Fox Theater and environs is given year-round. All tours last about two hours. (Tours $3, seniors and students $2. Call for exact times and starting points.)

Visiting these areas on your own of course is the other economical option. Redeveloped **Underground Atlanta** is actually 6 blocks with over 120 shops, restaurants, and nightspots, all beneath the street. The entrance to Underground Atlanta is beside the "Five Points" subway stop. In the summer live musicians often play in and around Underground. (Shops open Mon.-Sat. 10am-9:30pm, Sun. noon-6pm. Bars and restaurants open later.) The recently opened **Atlanta Heritage Row,** 55 Upper Alabama St. (584-7879), documents the city's past and looks into the future with exhibits and films. (Open Tues.-Sat. 9:30am-7pm, Sun. 10am-5pm. Admission $4, children $3.) Newly opened adjacent to the shopping complex is the **World of Coca-Cola Pavilion,** 55 Martin Luther King, Jr. Dr. (676-5151), clearly identified by a Times Square-style neon Coca-Cola sign stretching 26ft. across. The $15 million facility highlights "the real thing's" humble beginnings in Atlanta with over 1000 artifacts and interactive displays. (Open Mon.-Sat. 10am-9:30pm, Sun. noon-6pm. Admission $2.50, seniors $2, children $1.50.)

Another big business in Atlanta, **Turner Broadcasting** and its Cable News Network (CNN), also promos a museum for curious visitors. The **CNN Studio tour,** at Techwood Dr. and Marietta St. (827-2300), demonstrates the day-to-day workings of a 24-hr. cable news station; witness the anchorpeople broadcasting the news live on the air beside the writers who produce the scripts. MARTA: Omni Station. (Open Mon.-Fri. 10am-5pm, Sat.-Sun. 10am-4pm. Tours on the hr. Admission $4, seniors and under 18 $2, under 5 free.)

Occasionally the CNN cameras turn a few blocks to the south on the **Georgia State Capitol,** Capitol Hill at Washington St. (656-2844). The gold that covers the dome was mined nearby in Dahlonega, GA. MARTA: George State. (Open Mon.-Fri. 9am-5pm, Sat. 11am-3pm, Sun. 1-3pm. Tours Mon.-Fri. on the hr. 10am-3pm except noon. Free.) Georgia moved into the nation's spotlight when home boy and past governor Jimmy Carter became U.S. President. Today the **Carter Presidential Center,** 1 Copenhill (331-3942), north of Little Five Points documents the Carter Administration (1977-1980) through exhibits and films; of course, the center also houses a Japanese garden and café. Take bus #16 to Cleburne Ave. from Five Points Station. (Open Mon.-Sat. 9am-4:45pm, Sun. noon-4:45pm. Admission $2.50, seniors $1.50, under 16 free.)

The birth and burial places, church, and a museum of the youngest man ever to be awarded a Nobel Peace Prize can all be explored in the **Martin Luther King Jr. National Historic Site.** Stop by its visitors center for an incredibly informative and helpful map of the **Sweet Auburn District,** also containing a short biography of King. **Ebenezer Baptist Church,** 407-13 Auburn Ave. (688-7263), where King pastored from 1960 to 1968, is now open to the public, as are Sunday worship services. (Open Mon.-Fri. 9:30am-noon and 1:30-4:30pm. Call for weekend hours. Donations accepted.) The 23½-acre area also includes the restored house where King was born, 501 Auburn Ave. (331-3919; open daily 10am-5pm, off-season 10am-3:30pm; free). King is buried at the **Martin Luther King Center for Nonviolent Social Change,** 449 Auburn Ave. (524-1956), which also holds a collection of King's personal effects and a film about his life. Take bus #3 from Peachtree/Alabama. (Open Mon.-Fri. 9am-5:30pm, Sat.-Sun. 10am-5:30pm. Admission $1.)

Just south of the King Memorial, **Oakland Cemetary,** 248 Oakland Ave. SE (577-8163), contains the graves of golfer Bobby Jones and **Gone With the Wind** author Margaret Mitchell. MARTA: King Memorial, 2 blocks south. (Open daily sunrise-sunset. Information center open Mon.-Fri. 9am-5:30pm. Free.) True *Gone with the Wind* fans can visit the Margaret Mitchell Room in the **Atlanta Public Library,** 126 Carnegie Way at Forsythe St. downtown. Here you'll find memorobilia such as autographed copies of her famous book. (Open Mon. and Fri. 9am-6pm, Tues.-Thurs. 9am-8pm, Sat. 10am-6pm, Sun. 2-6pm.)

Farther south of Oakland Cemetary in **Grant Park,** between Cherokee Ave. and Boulevard, the 40-acre **Zoo Atlanta** is undergoing a $25 million renovation with a new emphasis on natural habitats for the animals. Several entertaining animal shows stress conservation and the environment. Among the new exhibits is the Masai Mara, a re-creation of an African savannah, with an endangered black rhinoceros. Say "hi" to Willie B., Atlanta's favorite gorilla, in the African rain forest. (Open July-Aug. Mon.-Fri. 10am-5pm, Sat.-Sun. 10am-6pm.; Sept.-June daily 10am-5pm. Ticket office closes at 4:30pm. Admission $6.75, ages 3-11 $4.) Next door to Zoo Atlanta is **Cyclorama** (658-7625), the world's largest painting in the round. Completed in 1885, the 50-ft.-high, 900-ft. work depicts the 1864 Civil War Battle of Atlanta, complete with 3-D features and lighting and sound effects. Take bus #31 "Grant Park."(Open May-Aug. daily 9:30am-5:30pm; Sept.-April 9:30am-4:30pm. Admission $3.50, seniors $3, children $2.)

North of the city, on the other side of downtown, is **Piedmont Park,** where you can see the 60-acre **Atlanta Botanical Garden,** Piedmont Ave. at the Prado (876-5858) Stroll through five acres of landscaped gardens, a 15-acre hardwood forest with walking trails, and an exhibition hall. The Dorothy Chapman Fugua Conservatory holds hundreds of species of rare tropical plants. Take bus #36 "North Decatur" from the Arts Center subway stop. (Open Tues.-Sat. 9am-6pm, Sun. noon-6pm. Admission $4.50, seniors and children $2.25. Free Thurs. 1:30-6pm.) Just to the west of the park, the **Woodruff Arts Center,** 1280 Peachtree St. (892-3600; take the subway to Arts Center), houses the **High Museum** (892-4444) in Richard Meier's award-winning building of glass, steel, and white porcelain. The museum includes European decorative arts, European and U.S. paintings, photography, and a variety of (con)temporary art exhibits. (Open Tues. and Thurs.-Sat. 10am-5pm, Wed. 10am-9pm, Sun. noon-5pm. Admission $4, seniors and students with ID $2, children $1.) The museum branch at Georgia-Pacific Center (577-6939), 1 block south of Peachtree Center Station, is free (open Mon.-Fri. 11am-5pm).**The West End** is Atlanta's oldest neighborhood, dating back to 1835. Here hovers the **Wren's Nest,** 1050 Gordon St. (753-8535), home to Joel Chandler Harris, who popularized the African folk-tale trickster Br'er Rabbit through a somewhat stereotypical slave character, Uncle Remus. Take "Cascade" bus from West End Station. (Open Tues.-Sat. 10am-4pm, Sun. 2-4pm. Admission $3, seniors and teens $2, children $1.)

Buckhead, another famous neighborhood worth visiting, shows off one of the most beautiful residences in the Southeast. The Greek Revival **Governor's Mansion,** 391 West Paces Ferry Rd. (261-1776), bus #40 "West Paces Ferry" from Lenox Station, has elaborate gardens and furniture from the Federal period. (Tours Tues.-Thurs. 10-11:30am. Free.) In the same neighborhood, discover the **Atlanta Historical Society,** 3101 Andrew Dr. NW (261-1837). On the grounds are the **Swan House,** a lavish Anglo-Palladian Revival home, and the **Tullie Smith House,** an antebellum farmhouse. Don't miss the intriguing *Atlanta Resurgens* exhibit, in which famous and not-so-famous Atlantans praise the city. (Tours every ½ hr. Open Mon.-Sat. 9am-5:30pm, Sun. noon-5pm. Admission $6, seniors and students $4, children $3.)

For a different atmosphere, with African clothes, used books, and general hanging out, wander through the eclectic **Little Five Points Business District,** at the intersection of Moreland and Euclid Ave. NE, the center of Atlanta's bohemian community. The fortunate or psychotic may catch a glimpse of the psychedelic "Magic Bus" driven by the band YUR ("Your Universal Reality"), whose headquarters are in the neighborhood. Stroll through the second-hand clothing and record stores. Airborne disc afficionados should stop at **Identified Flying Objects,** 1164 Euclid Ave. NE, a Frisbee department store. (Open Mon.-Fri. noon-7pm, Sat.-Sun. noon-6pm.) Also visit the **Berman Gallery,** 1131 Euclid Ave. NE (525-2529), for its extensive Southern folk art collection.

A respite from the city is available at **Stone Mountain Park** (498-5600), 16 mi. east on U.S. 78, where a fabulous bas-relief monument to the Confederacy is carved into the world's largest mass of granite. The "Mount Rushmore of the South" features Jefferson Davis, Robert E. Lee, and Stonewall Jackson and measures 90 by 190 ft. Surrounded by a 3200-acre recreational area the mountain dwarfs the enormous statue. Check out the dazzling laser show on the side of the mountain each summer night at 9:30pm. Take bus #120 "Stone Mountain" from the Avondale subway stop. Buses leave only Mon.-Fri. at 4:30 and 7:50pm. (Park open daily 6am-midnight. Admission $5 per car.)

Six Flags, 7561 Six Flags Rd. SW (948-9290), at I-20 W., is one of the largest (331 acres) theme amusement parks in the nation, and includes several rollercosters, a free-fall machine, live shows, and whitewater rides. On summer weekends, the park is packed to the gills. Take bus #201 ("Six Flags") from Hightower Station; $1.25 one way. (Open summer daily roughly 10am-10pm. One-day admission $20, 2 days $22, seniors and children under 48 in. $10.)

Entertainment

For nearly surefire fun in Atlanta, buy a MARTA pass (see Practical Information above), and pick up one of the city's free publications on music and events. *Creative Loafing, Music Atlanta, the Hudspeth Report,* and "Weekend" in the Friday edition of the *Atlanta Journal* will all help you eat that peach. *Southern Voice* also has complete listings on gay and lesbian news and nightclubs throughout Atlanta. Look for free summer concerts in Atlanta's parks.

The outstanding **Woodruff Arts Center,** 1280 Peachtree St. NE (892-2414), houses the Atlanta Symphony and the Alliance Theater Company. For plays and movies also check the Moorish and Egyptian revival movie palace, the **Fox,** 660 Peachtree St. (881-1977), or the **Atlanta Civic Center,** 395 Piedmont St. (523-6275).

Atlanta's nightlife ripens to a frenetic, varied, and inexpensive softness. Night spots concentrate in Buckhead, Underground Atlanta, Little Five Points, and **Virginia Highlands,** a neighborhood east of downtown with trendy shops and a friendly, hip atmosphere. For blues, go to **Blind Willie's,** 828 N. Highland Ave. (873-2583), a dim, usually packed club with Cajun food and occasional big name acts. (Live music starts at 10pm. Open daily at 6pm. Cover Mon.-Fri. $3, Sat.-Sun. $5.) A college-age crowd usually fills Little Five Points in heading for **The Point,** 420 Moreland Ave. (577-6468), where you'll always get live music. (Open daily 4pm-until. Cover $3-6.) Only a few doors away the **Little Five Points Pub,** 1174 Euclid Ave. NE (577-7767), also opens with rock bands every night. Towards downtown, the newly opened **Masquerade,** 695 North Ave. (577-8178), is housed in an original turn-of-the-century mill. The bar has three different levels: heaven, with live hard-core music; purgatory, a more laid-back coffee house; and hell, progressive dance music. (Open Wed.-Thurs. 8pm-until, Fri. 8pm-4am, Sat. 9am-4. Cover $5-7. 18 and over.) **The Tower,** 735 Ralph McGill Blvd. (688-5463), is a popular lesbian bar and dance club. (Open Mon.-Thurs. 3:30pm-1am, Fri. 3:30pm-4am, Sat. 3:30pm-3am.) **Backstreet,** 845 Peachtree St. NE (873-1986), a hot gay dance spot stays open almost all night.

Underground Atlanta has the newest concept in suiting all tastes. A street called **Kenny's Alley** is composed solely of bars: a blues club, a dance emporium, a jazz bar, a country/western place, a New Orleans-style daquiri bar, and an oldies dancing spot. Fans of the Peachtree Three-Step must search elsewhere.

Savannah

General James Oglethorpe and 120 colonists founded Georgia, the thirteenth English colony, in February 1733 at Tamacraw Bluff on the Savannah River. Since then Savannah had a stint as the capital of Georgia, and both the first girl scout troop in the U.S. and Eli Whitney, inventor of the cotton gin, have made their homes here.

Ironically, when the price of cotton crashed at the turn of the century, many of the homes and warehouses along River Street fell into disrepair, and the townhouses and mansions that lined Savannah's boulevards became boarding houses or rubble. In the mid-1950s, a group of concerned citizens mobilized to restore the downtown area, preserving the numerous Federalist and English Regency houses as historic monuments. Today four historic forts, broad streets, and trees hung with Spanish moss only enhance the city's classic Southern aura.

Practical Information

Emergency: 911.

Visitor Information: Savannah Visitors Center, 301 Martin Luther King Blvd. (944-0456), at Liberty St. in a lavish former train station. Excellent free maps and guides. Open Mon.-Fri. 8:30am-5pm, Sat. Sun. 9am-5pm. The **Savannah Exposition,** in the same building, has photographs, exhibits, and 2 brief films depicting the city's history. Open daily 9am-4pm. Admission $2.25, seniors $2, teens $1.25, children 75¢.

Amtrak: 2611 Seaboard Coastline Dr. (234-2611 or 800-872-7245), 4 mi. outside the city. Taxi fare to city about $6. To Charleston, SC (2 per day, 1¾ hr., $23) and Washington, DC (3 per day, 11 hr., $110). Open 24 hr.

Greyhound: 610 E. Oglethorpe Ave. (232-2135), convenient to downtown. To: Jacksonville (11 per day, 3 hr., $22); Charleston, SC (3 per day, 2½ hr., $23); Washington, DC (8 per day, 17 hr., $87). Open 24 hr.

Public Transport: Chatham Area Transit (CAT), 233-5767. Buses operate daily 6am-11pm. Fare 75¢, transfers 5¢. **C&H Bus,** 530 Montgomery St. (232-7099). The only public transportation to Tybee Beach. Buses leave from the civic center in summer at 8:15am, 1:30pm, and 3:30pm, returning from the beach at 9:25am, 2:30pm, and 4:30pm. Fare $1.75.

Help Line: Rape Crisis Center, 233-7273.

Post Office: 2 N. Fahm St. (235-4646). Open Mon.-Fri. 8:30am-5pm. **ZIP code:** 31402.

Area Code: 912.

Savannah smiles on the coast of Georgia at the mouth of the **Savannah River,** which runs along the border with South Carolina. Charleston, SC, lies 100 mi. up the coast; Brunswick, GA lies 90 mi. to the south. The city stretches south from bluffs overlooking the river. The restored 2½-sq.-mi. **downtown historic district** is bordered by **East Broad** and **Martin Luther King Jr. Blvd.,** and on the north and south by the river and **Gaston Street.** This area is best explored on foot. **Tybee Island,** Savannah's beach, is 18 mi. east on Hwy. 80 and 26. Try to visit in just spring, the busiest and most beautiful season in Savannah.

Accommodations and Camping

Make your first stop in Savannah the **visitors center,** where a wide array of available coupons offer 15-20% discounts on area hotels. The downtown motels are clustered near the historic area, visitors center, and Greyhound station. The neighborhood is neither charming nor clean, but it's fairly safe. Do not stray south of Gaston St., however, where the historic district quickly deteriorates into a place you don't want to be alone in at night. For those with cars, Ogeechee Rd. (U.S. 17) has several independently owned budget options.

Thunderbird Inn, 611 W. Oglethorpe Ave. (232-2661), opposite the Greyhound station a few blocks from the historic district. Cinder-block walls and a charmless neighborhood, but the rooms are clean and cheap. Singles $28. Doubles $34. Off-season $23 and $25, respectively.

Quality Inn, 231 W. Boundary St. (232-3200), just west of the Greyhound station. Fairly luxurious rooms with cable TV and in-room movies. Ask about free transportation to the airport and bus station. Singles $40. Doubles $45. Rooms $32 (up to 4 people per room) with coupon from the visitors center.

Bed and Breakfast Inn, 117 Gordon St. (238-0518), on Chatham Sq. in the historic district. Pretty little rooms have TV, A/C, and shared bath. Singles $30. Doubles $38. Reservations required.

Budget Inn, 3702 Ogeechee Rd. (233-3633), a 15-min. drive from the historic district. Take bus #25B ("Towers and Ogeechee"). Comfortable rooms with TV and A/C. Pool. Singles and doubles $29, with coupon $24. Reservations recommended; call collect.

Sanddollar Motel, 11 16th St. (786-5362), at Tybee Island, 1½ mi. south on Butler Ave. A small, family-run motel practically on the beach. Most rooms rented weekly, but singles ($25, less in winter) may be available. Large parties often fill the place on summer weekends.

Skidaway Island State Park, Skidaway Rd. (356-2523), 6 mi. southeast of Savannah off Diamond Causeway. Inaccessible by public transportation. Follow Liberty St. east out of downtown; soon after it becomes Wheaton St., turn right on Waters Ave. and follow it to the Diamond Causeway. Heated showers. Open daily 7am-10pm.

Richmond Hill State Park, off Rte. 144 (727-2339), ½-hr. south of downtown; take exit 15 off I-95. Quieter than Skidaway and usually less crowded. Registration office open daily 8am-5pm. Sites $10.

Food

In Savannah cheap food is easy to come by. Try the waterfront area for budget meals in a pub-like atmosphere. The early-bird dinner specials at **Corky's,** 407 E. River St. (234-0113), range from $4-6. **Kevin Barry's Irish Pub,** 117 W. River St. (233-9626), has live Irish folk music Wednesday to Sunday after 9pm, as well as cheap drinks during Happy Hour.

Mrs. Wilkes Boarding House, 107 W. Jones St. (232-5997)—no sign. Home-style restaurant in the basement of a townhouse. A local favorite. Very budget—an all-you-can-eat lunch of meat, vegetables, breads, and iced tea $6.50. The 80-year-old Mrs. Wilkes still works the small dining room; Mr. Wilkes collects the money after you bring your dish to the sink. Go before 11:15am or after 2pm to avoid the wait, or go around back for a generous take-out picnic. Breakfast of grits, eggs, sausages, ham, corn, bread, muffins, juice and coffee ($3.75) served daily. Open Mon.-Fri. 8-9am and 11:30am-3pm.

Morrison's Family Dining, 15 Bull St., near Johnson Sq. downtown. Traditional U.S. and Southern cooking, multi-item menu. Full meals $3-5. Whole pies $2. The food is guaranteed—if you don't like it, you don't pay for it. Open Mon.-Fri. 6:30am-8pm, Sat.-Sun. 7:30am-8pm.

Hard Hearted Hannah's, 318 W. Saint Julian St., in the city market. Live jazz Mon.-Sat. night, and a soft-hearted omelette bar beginning at 10pm Fri.-Sat. Open Mon.-Sat. 4pm-until.

Bill Hilliard's, 3005 Victory Dr., Thunderbolt (354-5430), 4 mi. east of the historic district. Take the "Henry St." bus. Fresh seafood dinners with salad, hushpuppies, and fries from $7. Renowned buffets served Mon.-Sat. 11am-3pm ($5), Sun. 11am-9pm ($6). Open daily 11am-midnight.

Sights and Events

In addition to restored antebellum houses, the downtown area includes over 20 small parks and gardens. The **Historic Savannah Foundation,** 41 W. Broad St. (233-7703; 233-3597 for 24-hr. reservations), offers a variety of guided one- and two-hour tours ($6-10). You can also catch any number of bus and van tours ($6-9), leaving about every 10-15 minutes from outside the visitors center. Ask inside for details.

The best-known historic houses in Savannah are the **Owens-Thomas House,** 124 Abercorn St. (233-9743), on Oglethorpe Sq., and the **Davenport House,** 324 E. State St. (236-8097), a block away on Columbia Sq. The Owens-Thomas House is one of the best examples of English Regency architecture in the U.S. (Open Oct.-Aug. Sun.-Mon. 2-5pm., Tues.-Sat. 10am-5pm. Last tour at 4:30pm. Admission $3, students $2, children $1.) The Davenport House typifies the Federalist style and contains an excellent collection of Davenport china. By the 30s, the house had become a tenement and the owners planned to raze it for a parking lot. Its salvation in 1955 marked the birth of the Historical Savannah Foundation and the effort to restore the city. There are guided tours of the first floor every 15 minutes; explore the second and third floors at your leisure. (Open Mon.-Sat. 10am-4pm, Sun. 1:30-4pm. Last tour at 3:30pm. Admission $2.50, children $1.25.)

Lovers of Thin Mints, Scot-teas, and, of course, Savannahs should make a pilgrimage to the **Juliette Gordon Low Girl Scout National Center,** 142 Bull St. (233-4501), near Wright Square. The association's founder was born here on Halloween of 1860, possibly explaining the Girl Scouts' door-to-door treat-selling technique. The center's "cookie shrine," in one of the most beautiful houses in Savannah, contains an interesting collection of Girl Scout memorabilia. (Open Feb.-Nov. Mon.-Sat. 10am-4pm, Sun. 12:30-4:30pm; Dec.-Jan. Mon.-Tues. and Thurs.-Sat. 10am-4pm. Admission $3, ages under 18 $2.25.) One block down in **Johnson Square,** at the intersection of Bull and E. Saint Julian St., is the burial obelisk of Revolutionary War hero Nathaniel Green; a plaque containts an epitaph by the Marquis de Lafayette.

For a less conventional view of Savannah's history, arrange to tour the **Negro Heritage Trail,** visiting African American historic sites from early slave times to the present. Three different tours are available on request from the Savannah branch of the Association for the Study of Afro-American Life and History, King-Tisdell Cottage, Negro Heritage Trail, 514 E. Huntington St., Savannah 31405 (234-8000; open Mon.-Fri. noon-9pm). One day's notice is necessary; admission depends upon the particular tour.

In the past, Savannah's four forts have protected the city's inhabitants and shipping from the Spanish, the British, and other invaders. The most interesting of these is **Fort Pulaski National Monument** (786-5787), 15 mi. east of Savannah on Hwy. 80 and 26. (Open daily 8:30am-6:45pm. Summer admission $1 per person, max. $3 per carload; off-season free.) Fort Pulaski marks the battle site where walls were first introduced to rifled cannonry in the Civil War, making Pulaski and all forts obsolete. Built in the early 1800s **Fort Jackson** (232-3945), also along Hwy. 80 and 26, contains exhibits on the Revolution, the War of 1812, and the Civil War. Together with Fort Pulaski, it makes for a quick detour on a daytrip to Tybee Beach. (Open Tues.-Sun. 9am-5pm; off-season Sat.-Sun. 9am-5pm. Admission $1.75, seniors and students $1.25.)

Special events in Savannah include the **Hidden Garden of the Nogs Tour** (238-0248), on April 20-21, when private walled gardens are opened to the public, and the **Tybee Island Beach Bum's Parade** (786-5444), with a beach music festival and other island activities from June 18-20.

Brunswick and Environs

Beyond its hostel and the nearby beaches, laid-back Brunswick is of little interest to the traveler except as a relaxing layover between destinations. The **Hostel in the Forest (AYH)** is located 9 mi. west of Brunswick on U.S. 82 (though your maps and the AYH guide may say U.S. 84), just past a small convenience store. Take I-95 to exit 6 and travel west on U.S. 82 (a.k.a. 84) about 1½ mi. from the interchange until you see the white-lettered wooden sign set back in the trees along the eastbound lane. Make a U-turn ½ mi. farther along at Myer Hill Rd. The hostel itself is of low-impact construction ½ mi. back from the highway; every effort is made to keep the area surrounding the complex of geodesic domes and treehouses as natural as possible. There is no lock-out, no curfew, and few rules, and the low-key managers will shuttle you to the Brunswick Greyhound station for $2. (Call 264-9738, 265-0220, or 638-2623 usually after 5pm.) The manager can usually be convinced to use the pickup to make daytrips to Savannah, the Okefenokee Swamp, and the coastal islands. If possible, arrange to stay in one of the two treehouses at the hostel, each complete with a 25-square-foot picture window and a spacious double bed. Bring insect repellent if you plan to stay in the summertime since mosquitos and yellow biting flies abound. In addition to a peahen named Cleopatra and numerous chickens, the hostel also has an extensive patch of blueberry bushes; you can pick and eat as many berries as you wish from late May to mid-June. AYH members $6. Linens $1.

Twin Oaks Pit Barbecue, 2618 Norwick St. (265-3131), eight blocks from downtown Brunswick across from the Southern Bell building, features barbecued beef and chicken in sandwich ($2.50) or plate ($5) form. The breaded french fries are deep fried and delicious.

The nearby **Golden Isles,** which include **St. Simon's Island, Jekyll Island,** and **Sea Island,** have miles of white sand beaches. Transportation options are limited to hitchhiking, or getting a ride from a fellow hosteler. Near the isles, **Cumberland Island National Seashore** (882-4335) is 16 mi. of salt marsh, live-oak forest, and sand dune laced with a network of trails and interrupted only by a few decaying mansions. Reservations are necessary for overnight visits, but the effort is often rewarded; you can walk all day on the beaches and not see another person. Reservations by phone only: call daily 10:30am-4pm, no more than 8 weeks in advance. Sites are available on a standby basis 15 minutes before the twice-daily ferry departures to Cumberland Island. The **ferry** (45 min., $8) leaves from St. Mary's on the mainland at the terminus of Rte. 40, at the Florida border. Daily departures are at 9 and 11:45am, returning at 10:15am and 4:45pm, with an extra trip Fri.-Sun. at 3:40pm; off-season Thurs.-Mon. only.

The **Greyhound** station, at 1101 Glouster St. (265-2800; open Mon.-Sat. 8am-1pm and 4-11pm. Sun. 9am-noon and 4-11pm), offers service to Jacksonville (5 per day) and Savannah (4 per day).

The **area code** for the region is 912.

North Carolina

England's first attempt to colonize North America took place on the shores of North Carolina. This ill-fated episode ended when Sir Walter Raleigh's 1587 Roanoke Island settlement vanished inexplicably. Since then, a succession of pirates, patriots, and secessionists have brought adventure to the North Carolina coast. Today, the historic Outer Banks area is best known as an oceanfront playground, most of which is administered by the Cape Hatteras National Seashore.

The coast's wild streak contrasts sharply with both the mellow sophistication of the Raleigh, Durham, and Chapel Hill Research Triangle in the center of the state, and with the west's down-to-earth mountain culture. The natural beauty of the Blue Ridge Parkway and the Great Smoky Mountains rounds out the western border of this quietly grand and ever-gracious state.

Practical Information

Capital: Raleigh.

Tourist Information: Travel and Tourism Division, 430 N. Salisbury St., Raleigh 27611 (919-733-4171 or 800-847-4862). **Department of Natural Resources and Community Development,** Division of Parks and Recreation, P.O. Box 27287, Raleigh 27611.

Time Zone: Eastern. **Postal Abbreviation:** NC.

Outer Banks

Over the years, the Outer Banks have proven a treacherous place to live. An entire English colony settled on Roanoke Island in the late 16th century only to disappear in less than three years. Blackbeard called Ocracoke home in the early 18th century until a savvy serviceman struck down the buccaneer at Pamlico Sound. Most seafarers didn't fare well here; over 600 ships have foundered on the shoals of the Banks' southern shores. Fearing for their life, the Wright Brothers tried to fly the coop at the turn of the 20th century, but soared only a few hundred feet. All have left but a single cryptic clue to their fate: tourism.

The Outer Banks descends from unpleasant beach towns to idyllic wilderness. Narrow **Bodie Island,** on the Outer Banks' northern end, where the towns of Nags Head, Kitty Hawk, and Kill Devil Hills lie in wait, suffers high-density development and terrible traffic. To escape damnation, travel south on Rte. 12 through the magnificent wildlife preserves, past clusters of attractive if generic beach homes. Be afraid. Be very afraid. Head across Hatteras Inlet, to the remote town of **Ocracoke** on the island of the same name—here, at long last, you will find the Outer Banks' most delightfully desolate beaches.

Practical Information

Visitor Information: Aycock Brown Visitors Center, off Rte. 158, after the Wright Memorial Bridge, Bodie Island. Information on accommodations and picnic areas plus National Park Service schedules. Record sailfish welcomes visitors in the parking lot. Open Mon.-Thurs. 8:30am-6:30pm, Fri.-Sun. 8:30am-7:30pm; in winter Mon.-Fri. 9am-5pm.

Cape Hatteras National Seashore Information Centers: Bodie Island, Rte. 12 at Bodie Island Lighthouse (441-5711; information and special programs; open daily 9am-6pm; off-season 9am-5pm); **Hatteras Island,** Rte. 12 at Cape Hatteras (995-4474; camping information, demonstrations, and special programs; open daily 9am-6pm; off-season 9am-5pm); and **Ocracoke Island,** next to the ferry terminal at the south end of the island (928-4531; information on ferries, camping, lighthouses, and wild ponies; open daily 9am-5pm; mid-June to Aug. 9am-6pm).

Ferries: Toll ferries operate to Ocracoke from **Cedar Island,** east of New Bern on U.S. 70 (4-8 per day, 2¼ hr.) and **Swan Quarter,** on the northern side of Pamlico Sound off U.S. 264/Rte. 45 (2½ hr.), both on the mainland. $10 per car (reserve in advance), $1 per pedestrian, $2 per biker. (Cedar Island 225-3551, Swan Quarter 926-1111, Ocracoke 928-3841. All open daily 5:30am-8:30pm.) Free ferry across Hatteras Inlet between Hatteras and Ocracoke (operates daily 5am-11pm, 40 min.)

Taxi: Beach Cab, 441-2500. Serves Bodie Island and Manteo.

Car Rental: National, Mile 5½, Beach Rd. (800-328-4567 or 441-5488), Kill Devil Hills. $40 per day. 50 free mi., 22¢ each additional mi. Open daily 9am-5pm. Must be 21 with major credit card.

Bike Rental: Pony Island Motel (928-4411) and the **Slushy Stand** on Rte. 12, both on Ocracoke Island. $1 per hr. Open daily 8am-dusk.

Emergency: 911, north of the Oregon Inlet. **Ocracoke,** 928-4831.

ZIP Codes: Manteo 27954, Nags Head 27959, Ocracoke 27960.

Area Code: 919.

Four long, narrow islands strung north-to-south along half the length of the North Carolina coast comprise the Outer Banks. **Bodie Island** includes the towns of **Kitty Hawk, Kill Devil Hills,** and **Nags Head,** connecting to Elizabeth, NC, and Norfolk, VA, by U.S. 158. **Roanoke Island** swims between Bodie and the mainland on U.S. 64, and includes the town of **Manteo. Hatteras Island,** connected to Bodie by a bridge, stretches like a great sandy elbow. **Ocracoke Island,** the southernmost, is linked by free ferry to Hatteras Island, and by toll ferry to towns on the mainland. **Cape Hatteras National Seashore** encompasses Hatteras, Ocracoke, and the southern end of Bodie Island. On Bodie Island U.S. 158 and Rte. 12 run parallel to each other until the beginning of the preserve. After that Rte. 12 (also called Beach Rd.) continues south, stringing Bodie, Hatteras, and Ocracoke together with free bridges and ferries. Addresses on Bodie Island are determined by their distance in miles from the Wright Memorial Bridge.

Nags Head and Ocracoke lie 76 mi. apart and public transportation proves virtually nonexistent; cars are the transportation mode of choice. Though relatively safe and fairly common, hitching may require lengthy waits. The flat terrain makes hiking and biking pleasant, but the Outer Banks' ferocious traffic calls for extra caution; stick to Hatteras and Ocracoke for quieter routes.

Accommodations and Camping

Most motels cling to Rte. 12, mostly in the town of Nags Head; most will cost you plenty. For budget accommodations, try the town of Ocracoke. On all three islands the "in season" usually lasts from mid-June to Labor Day; rates are much higher and reservations are necessary. Reserve seven to 10 days ahead for weekday stays and up to a month for weekends. Rangers advise campers to bring extra-long tent spikes because of the loose dirt, and tents with extra-fine screens to keep out the flea-sized, biting "no-see-ums." Strong insect repellent is also helpful. Crashing on the beach is illegal.

Nags Head/Kill Devil Hills

Olde London Inn, Mile 12, Beach Rd. (441-7115), Nags Head oceanfront. No British graces but an oceanfront location, golf privileges, and recreational facilities. Huge picture windows offset drab decor in clean, spacious rooms. Cable TV, A/C, refrigerator. Singles or doubles $45-53; off-season $26-32.

The Ebbtide, Mile 10½, Beach Rd. (441-4913), Kill Devil Hills. A family type of place with spruce, wholesome rooms. Cable TV, A/C, and use of sedate pool and hot tub. Offers the "inside track" on local activities. Restaurant gives guests 10% discount, even on the 99¢ breakfast special. Singles or doubles $49-57; off-season $29-35. Oceanside triplex sleeps up to 8 $95; off-season $70.

Nettlewood Motel, Mile 7, Beach Rd. (441-5039), Kill Devil Hills, on both sides of the highway. Imagine that. Private beach access. Don't let the uninviting exterior, weed-infested driveway, and small rooms prevent you from enjoying this clean, comfortable motel. TV, A/C, refrigerator. 4-day min. stay on weekends. Singles or doubles $38, with efficiencies $54; off-season: rooms $25-30, with efficiencies $30-38. Free day for week-long stays.

Tanya's Ocean House, Mile 9½, Beach Rd. (441-2900), Kill Devil Hills. Slightly pricey, but oh-so-unique. Each room decorated along a different theme: literary types thrill to "the Library" and "the Gatsby." J.B. prefers "the Parlor" (with waterbed). Aquatic pleasures in pool or ocean. Singles or doubles $55-79; off-season $35-49.

Ocracoke

Sand Dollar Motel, off Rte. 12 (928-5571), Head south on Rte. 12, turn right at the Pony Island Inn, right at the Back Porch Restaurant, and left at the Edwards Motel. Accommodating owners make you feel at home in this breezy, quiet, immaculate motel. Singles $36. Doubles $45. Off-season: singles $30; doubles $35.

Beach House, just off Rte. 12 (928-4271), behind the Slushy Stand. B&B in 4 charming, clean, antique-filled rooms. Rooms $40; spring and fall $35; winter $30.

Edwards Motel, off Rte. 12 (928-4801), by the Back Porch Restaurant. Fish-cleaning facilities on premises. Bright assortment of accommodations, all with A/C and TV. Rooms with 2 double beds $42, with 2 double beds and 1 single bed $47; efficiencies $55; cottages $75-85. Off-season $35, $40, $50, and $65-70, respectively.

Oscar's House, on the ocean side of Rte. 12 (928-1311), 1 block from Silver Lake harbor. Quaint B&B with 4 rooms, shared baths. Memorial Day-June singles $45, doubles $55; July-Labor Day singles $50, doubles $60; off-season singles $40, doubles $50. Full vegetarian breakfast included.

There are five oceanside **campgrounds** on Cape Hatteras National Seashore, all open mid-April to mid-October. **Oregon Inlet** squats on the southern tip of Bodie

Island, **Salvo, Cape Point** (in Buxton), and **Frisco** near the elbow of Hatteras Island, and **Ocracoke** in the middle of Ocracoke Island. All have restrooms, cold running water, and grills. All sites (except Ocracoke's) cost $10, and rent on a first come, first serve basis. Reserve Ocracoke sites ($12) through **Ticketron Reservation Office**, P.O. Box 2715, San Francisco, CA 94126 (900-370-5566), or stop by the Ocracoke Ticketron terminal. For information, contact Cape Hatteras National Seashore, Rte. 1, P.O. Box 675, Manteo, NC 27954 (473-2111).

Food

The two best budget eateries in northern Outer Banks have a surprisingly south-of-the-border flavor; one seems the bizarre, drug-enhanced vision of the other. **Papagayo,** Mile 7½, Beach Rd. in Kill Devil Hills, serves spicy Mexican dinners ($7-9) and Fiesta Dip ($4) in an elegant, wood-paneled room overlooking the Atlantic. (Open Mon.-Thurs. 5:30-10pm, Fri.-Sun. 5:30-10:30pm.) Virtually across the street at Mile 8½ and Baum St., **Mex-Econo** (441-8226) assaults the senses alluringly. Vacuum cleaners dangle from the ceiling, punk bands like Buttsteak thrash almost nightly, and inexpensive innovative Mexican fare arrives on paper plates with tiny plastic cups of salsa and onions. Vegetarians thrill to the spinach enchiladas ($4) while seafood enthusiasts devour shark tacos ($4.50). Don't leave without an excursion to the bathroom. (Open daily noon-midnight.) For a more patriotic U.S. dining experience, say hi to **Sam and Omie's,** Mile 16, Beach Rd., near Whalebone junction, where stars and stripes complement "Sam"wiches ($2-5) and "Omie"lettes ($2-4). (Open Mon.-Sat. 7am-10pm, Sun. 7am-9pm.)

For a little life in your night, try popular **Kelly's Outer Banks Restaurant and Tavern,** Mile 10½, near the Wright Brothers National Memorial (open daily 4:30pm-1:30am). RV's (441-4963), on the Nags Head Causeway, offers sandwiches ($5-6), dinners ($9-14), live music, and an incredible view of the sunset over the sound. (Open daily 11am-10pm.)

In Ocracoke, you can't help but smile at the **Jolly Roger** (928-3703), a most mellow bar/grill/yogurt shop overlooking Silver Lake Harbor. Relax with a soft-shell crab sandwich ($3.25) and a pitcher of Michelob ($5) while watching the setting sun light up the Atlantic. For a quicker meal, **Trolley Stop One** has salads, subs ($2.50-4.50), and the cheapest burgers on the island. The fresh fish sandwich is a good catch for $3.25; reel in a complete dinner for $5.50. (Open Mon.-Sat. 11am-8pm, sun. 11am-3pm.) Amble by **Maria's Restaurant and Tavern** just to see this charming old dance hall. The 40-item salad bar, seafood, and Italian dinners will fill you up for $9-16. (Open daily noon-10pm.)

Sights and Activities

Many sights throughout the Outer Banks recount the region's colorful history, providing respite from the flurry of discos, fast-food joints, and water parks which draw pop-culture pilgrims each summer.

In Kill Devil Hills, visit the **Wright Brothers National Memorial,** Mile 8, U.S. 158 (441-7430), where Orville and Wilbur Wright made the world's first sustained, controlled power flight in 1903. You can see models of their planes, hear a detailed account of the day of the first flight, chat with the flight attendants, and view the dramatic monument which the U.S. government dedicated to the brothers in 1932. (Open daily 9am-7pm; winter 9am-5pm. Presentations every hr. 10am-5pm. Admission $1, $3 per car, free with seniors.) In nearby **Jockey's Ridge State Park,** home of the East Coast's largest sand dunes, hang-gliders float in the wind that Orville and Wilbur broke.

On **Roanoke Island,** the **Fort Raleigh National Historic Site,** off Rte. 64, offers three separately run attractions in one park. In the **Elizabeth Gardens** (473-3234), antique statues and fountains punctuate a beautiful display of flowers, herbs, and trees. (Open daily 9am-8pm; off-season 9am-5pm. Admission $2.50, under 12 free.) Behind door number two lies the theater where *The Lost Colony,* the oldest outdoor drama in the U.S., has been performing since 1937. The play celebrated its 50th year of production in 1990, having taken a four-year hiatus during World War II; theater lights might have drawn fire from German subs lurking offshore. The building itself is in its third incarnation: one burned down, one drowned in a hurricane, and the third cowers in the woods (473-3414; performed Mon.-Sat. mid-June to late Aug. at 8:30pm; tickets $10, seniors and disabled $9, under 12 $4; bring insect repellent). **Fort Raleigh** (473-5772) is a reconstructed 1585 battery—basically an unimpressive pile of dirt. The nearby visitors center contains a tiny museum and plays Elizabethan music as part of a losing battle to recall the earliest days of English activity in North America. (Open Mon.-Sat. 9am-8pm, Sun. 9am-5pm.) Lay your hands on a horseshoe crab and make faces at marine monsters in the Shark, Skate, and Ray Gallery at the **North Carolina Aquarium** (473-3493), 1 mi. west of Rte. 64. A full slate of educational programs keep things lively. (Open Mon.-Sat. 9am-5pm, Sun. 1-5pm. Donation.)

On Ocracoke Island, historical sights give way to the incessant, soothing surf. With the exception of the town of Ocracoke on the southern tip, the island remains a completely undeveloped national seashore. Speedy walkers or meandering cyclists can cover the same route as **Trolley Tours** (928-1111; $4, children $2) in less than an hour. Pick up a walking tour pamphlet at the visitor center. Better yet, stroll along and swim in the waters that smooch the pristine, unbothered shore. Park rangers offer a more informed angle on this most righteous endeavor, with nature walks, demonstrations, and interpretative talks. At the **Soundside Snorkel,** they teach visitors to snorkel. Bring tennis shoes and a swimsuit. (Wed. and Fri. at 2:30pm. Equipment rental $1. Make reservations at the Ocracoke Visitors Center from 9am the day before to 2:30pm the day of program.)

Raleigh, Durham, and Chapel Hill

Only the education of their residents surpasses the friendliness of Raleigh, Durham, and Chapel Hill, containing more PhDs per capita that any other part of the nation. What most connects the points of the Research Triangle is a detectable hospitality; people are usually willing to give directions or help alleviate that traveler's nightmare, walking, with a ride. Raleigh, the state capital, is an easygoing, historic town. Durham, the former tobacco mecca of the world, is now, ironically, a city devoted to medicine. Perhaps as a result of the city's many hospitals and research centers, one out of every two hundred people you meet in Durham is enrolled in one of the city's diet programs; known as the "Diet Capital of the World," 45 tons of excess weight are shed here annually. None of that dead weight can be found at Duke University, however, one of the greenest and most prestigious universities in the nation. Chapel Hill, just twenty miles down the road, holds its own both in education and scenery as the home of the nation's first state university and a law against cutting down all trees until they have been examined by a special tree inspector.

Practical Information

Emergency: 911.

Visitor Information: Raleigh Capitol Area Visitor Center, 301 N. Blount St. (733-3456). Focuses on buildings in the capitol area. Open Mon.-Fri. 8am-5pm, Sat. 9am-5pm, Sun. 1-5pm. **Durham Chamber of Commerce,** People's Security Building, 14th floor, 300 W. Morgan St. (682-2133). Not geared to the budget traveler. Complimentary maps and a great view of Durham. Open Mon.-Fri. 8:30am-5pm. **Chapel Hill Chamber of Commerce,** 104 S. Estes Dr. (967-7075). Open Mon.-Fri. 8:30am-5pm.

Raleigh-Durham Airport: 15 mi. northwest of Raleigh on U.S. 70 (840-2123). Many hotels and rental car agencies provide free airport limousine service (596-2361), if you make a reservation with them. Pick up helpful complimentary maps of Raleigh and Durham at the **information counter** on the airport's lower level.

Amtrak: 320 W. Cabarrus, Raleigh (833-7594 or 800-872-7245). To Miami (1 per day, 16 hr., $137) and Washington, DC (2 per day, 6 hr., $43). Open Mon.-Fri. 8am-9pm, Sat.-Sun. 8:30-11:30am and 6:30-9pm.

Greyhound/Trailways: Raleigh: 314 W. Jones St. (828-2567). To: Durham (6 per day, 40 min., $7) and Chapel Hill (5 per day, 80 min., $8). Good north-south coverage of NC. Also to: Greensboro (3 per day, 3 hr., $13); Richmond (7 per day, 3½ hr., $27); Charleston (1 per day, 8 hr., $37). Open 24 hr. **Durham:** 820 Morgan St. (687-4800), 1 block off Chapel Hill St. downtown, 2½ mi. northeast of Duke University. To: Chapel Hill (8 per day, 30 min.); Charlotte (3 per day, 4 hr.); Winston-Salem (4 per day, 3 hr.). Open daily 6:30am-11pm. **Chapel Hill:** 311 W. Franklin St. (942-3356), 4 blocks from the UNC campus. Open Mon.-Fri. 9am-4pm, Sat.-Sun. 8am-3:30pm.

Public Transport: Capital Area Transit, Raleigh (833-5701). Operates Mon.-Fri.; fewer buses on Sat. Fare 50¢. **Duke Power Company Transit Service,** Durham (688-4587). Most routes leave from the 1st Federal Building at Main St. on the loop, downtown. Buses operate daily 6am-6pm, some routes until 10pm. Fare 50¢, transfers 10¢.

Taxi: Safety Taxi, 832-8800. $1.20 per mile. **Shared Ride Taxi Service,** (822-5522). Transports seniors and the disabled ($1-2).

Help Lines: Rape Crisis, 755-6661.

Post Office: Raleigh: 310 New Bern Ave. (831-3661). Open Mon.-Fri. 8:30am-4:30pm, Sat. 8:30am-noon. **ZIP code:** 27611. **Durham:** 323 E. Chapel Hill St. (541-5466). Open Mon.-Fri. 8:30am-5pm. **ZIP code:** 27701. **Chapel Hill:** Franklin St., at the center of town. Open Mon.-Fri. 8:30am-5:30pm. **ZIP code:** 27514.

Area Code: 919.

Raleigh and Durham are 20 mi. apart, connected by U.S. 70; Durham and Chapel Hill are 10 mi. apart, connected by U.S. 15-501; Chapel Hill and Raleigh are 25 mi. apart, connected by I-40. They are between I-85 and I-95 in north-central North Carolina, just north of Everett Jordan Lake. Raleigh is the most urban of the three, while Chapel Hill's 729-acre UNC campus and Durham's 7,700-acre Duke University forest and Sarah P. Duke Gardens make the other two cities more suited to outdoor recreation and picnics.

Accommodations and Camping

Hotels in downtown Raleigh are expensive, but only of average quality. Try the YMCA and YWCA for the cheapest lodgings. Rooms in Durham are more moderately priced, but if you're on foot, many are difficult to reach from the center of town.

YMCA, 1601 Hillsborough St., Raleigh (832-6601), 5 blocks from Greyhound station. Small bright rooms and clean towels. Hall bath. Free use of recreation facilities. Singles $15.50. Call ahead since rooms are limited.

YWCA, 1012 Oberlin Rd., Raleigh (828-3205), ½ mile east of Cameron Village Shopping Center. Women only. Large, luxurious, and mostly residential facility. Hall bath. Free recreational facilities. Singles $15. Must have an informal interview with the director.

Carolina-Duke Motor Inn, I-85 at Guess Rd., Durham (286-0771). Clean rooms, with duck pictures on the walls and blue doors. Free Movie Channel. Swimming pool. Free shuttle bus to Duke University medical center on the main campus. 10% discount for *Let's Go* users, seniors, and AAA cardholders. Singles $29. Doubles $36. $3 for each additional person. The **Wabash Express** next door serves cheap breakfasts Tues.-Sat. and lunches Mon.-Sat.

Friendship Inn, 309 Hillsborough St., Raleigh (833-5771), 3 blocks west of the capitol, 2½ blocks from Greyhound. Clean, brown-curtained hotel rooms. Free local telephone calls, HBO, and Euro-bath soap in wall dispensers. Singles $31. Doubles $33.

Umstead State Park, U.S. 70 (787-3033), 5 mi. northwest of Raleigh. Tent and trailer sites. Large lake for fishing and hiking. Open June-Aug. 8am-9pm; Sept.-May shorter hours. Sites $5.

Food

The restaurants near the universities are best suited for the budget traveler in the triangle area. In Raleigh, **Hillsborough Street,** across from North Carolina State University, has a wide array of inexpensive restaurants and bakeries staffed, for the most part, by friendly students. The same can be said of **9th Street** in Durham and **Franklin Street** in Chapel Hill.

Ramshead Rath-Skellar, 157-A E. Franklin St., Chapel Hill (942-5158), right across from the campus. A student hang-out with a vast menu featuring pizza, sandwiches, and hot apple pie Louise. Ships' maidenheads, German beer steins, and old Italian wine bottles decorate eight different dining rooms with names like the "Rat Trap Lounge." "Flukey" Hayes, here since 1963, may cook your steak. Full meals $4-6. Open Mon.-Thurs. 11am-2:30pm and 5-9:30pm, Fri.-Sat. 11am-2:30pm and 5-10:30pm, Sun. 11am-2:30pm and 5-9pm.

The Ninth Street Bakery Shop, 754 9th St., Durham (286-0303). More than a bakery; sandwiches from $2.50. Try the dense bran or blueberry muffins. Live music nightly. Open Mon.-Thurs. 7am-7pm, Fri.-Sat. 8am-11pm, Sun. 8am-5pm.

Skylight Exchange, 405½ W. Rosemary St., Chapel Hill (933-5550). A sandwich restaurant with a huge brass espresso machine. Doubles as a used book and record store. Sandwiches $2-3. Live music on weekends. Open Mon.-Thurs. 10am-11pm, Fri.-Sat. 10am-1am, Sun. 1-9pm.

Side Street, 225 N. Bloodworth St., Raleigh (828-4927), at E. Lane St. 3 blocks from the capitol. Don't let the run-down exterior fool you—this is a classy place with antique furniture, flowers on the table from the florist's next door, and huge, filling sandwiches with exotic names. Salads too. All selections under $4.50. Open Mon.-Sat. 11am-3pm and 5-9pm.

Mariakakis Restaurant and Bakery, 15-501 Bypass, Chapel Hill (942-1453). A heck of a trek from campus, but it's worth the trip for comfortable chairs, an amazing selection of the world's beers, and free bread with most meals. Spaghetti $3. Large cheese pizza $6. Open Mon.-Sat. 11am-9pm.

Two Guys, 2504 Hillsborough St., Raleigh (832-2324), near campus. The outside of the restaurant is emblazoned with the old joke: "Two guys enter, one man leaves." The punch line is spicy pizza ($6.25) and large spaghetti portions ($3). Open Mon.-Wed. 11am-10pm, Thurs.-Sat. 11am-11pm, Sun. noon-10pm.

Bruegger's Bagel Bakery, 3 locations: 2302 Hillsborough St., Raleigh, (832-6118); 626 9th St., Durham (286-7897); 104 W. Franklin St., Chapel Hill (967-5248). Bagels 39¢. For the best bargain, buy a half-dozen "day-old" bagels for 99¢ and a tub of cream cheese ($1.55). Brand new stores. Open daily 6:30am-5pm.

Clyde Cooper's Barbeque, 109 E. Davie, Raleigh (832-7614), 1 block east of the Fayetteville Street Mall downtown. Try the deep-fried chicken or barbecued ribs while eyeing the picture of two kissing pigs near the counter. Dinners $4. Open Mon.-Sat. 10am-6pm.

Well Spring Grocery, 1002 9th St., Durham (286-2290). A health food grocery with a wide variety of inexpensive fruits, vegetables, and whole grains. Open Mon.-Sat. 9am-8pm.

Sights and Entertainment

While the triangle's main attractions are its universities, the city of Raleigh has its share of historical sights. The **capitol building,** in Union Square at Edenton and Salisbury, was built in 1840. (Open Mon.-Fri. 8am-5pm, Sat. 9am-5pm, Sun. 1-5pm. Tours available for large groups.) Across the street and around the corner at Bicentennial Square is the **Museum of Natural Sciences** (733-7450), which has fossils, gems, and animal exhibits including a live 17-ft. Burmese python named George. (Open Mon.-Sat. 9am-5pm Sun. 1-5pm. Free.) Just down the way at 109 E. Jones St., the **North Carolina Museum of History** (733-3894). Exhibits memorabilia from the state's Roanoke days to the present. (Open Tues.-Sat. 9am-4:30pm, Sun. 1-6pm. Free.) Pick up a brochure at the visitors center for a self-guided tour of the renovated 19th-century homes of **Historic Oakwood,** where eight North Carolina governors are buried. The **North Carolina Museum of Art,** 2110 Blue Ridge Blvd. (833-1935), off I-40 (Wade Ave. exit), has eight galleries with ancient Egyptian works and others by Raphael, Botticelli, Rubens, Monet, Wyeth, and O'Keeffe. (Open

Tues.-Sat. 9am-5pm, Fri. 9am-9pm, Sun. noon-5pm. Tours Tues.-Sat. at 1:30pm. Free.) A tour of **North Carolina State University** on Hillsborough St. (737-2437), includes the **Pulstar Nuclear Reactor** but no Homer Simpson. (Free tours during the semester Mon.-Fri. at noon, leaving from the Bell Tower on Hillsborough St.) Unless a nuclear accident occurs, none of these sights are all that glowing.

For more interesting, less urban sights, visit Chapel Hill where the **University of North Carolina** (962-0045), the oldest state university in the country, sprawls over 729 acres. Astronauts trained in celestial navigation until 1975 at the university's **Morehead Planetarium**, which houses one of 12 $2.2 million Zeiss Star projectors in existence. The planetarium puts up six different shows a year that involve a combination of films and Zeiss projections. Though aimed toward younger audiences these shows are well worth seeing and are conceived and produced while you watch. The best part of the planetarium is the staff of friendly UNC students, some of whom are trained operators of the Zeiss projector. The friendliest people you'll ever meet, most are willing to talk or give advice to stranded travelers. (Open Sun.-Fri. 12:30-5pm and 6:30-9:30pm. Admission $3, seniors, students, and children $2.50.) Over the next year special events will inundate the campus as UNC celebrates its bicentennial. Call the university number (962-0045) for information on sporting events and concerts at the Smith Center (a.k.a. the Dean Dome).

In Durham, **Duke University** is the major attraction. The **admissions office,** at 2138 Campus Dr. (684-3214), serves as a visitors center (open 8am-5pm). The **Duke Chapel** (tours and information 684-2572) is at the center of the university and has more than a million pieces of glass in 77 stained-glass windows which depict between 800 and 900 figures. The Duke Memorial Organ inside has 5000 pipes and hearing its music may bring tingles to the back of your neck. (Open daily during the school year 8am-5pm.)

To the left of the chapel is the walkway to the **Bryan Center,** Duke's maze-like student center, with a gift shop, a café, and a small art gallery; the information desk has brochures on activities, concerts, local buses, and free campus maps. Near West Campus on Anderson St. are the **Sarah Duke Gardens** (684-3698), with over 15 acres of landscaped gardens and tiered flower beds. Giant goldfish swim in a small pond near a vined gazebo where you can picnic in the shade. (Open daily 8am-dusk.) Take the free Duke campus shuttle bus to East Campus, which houses the **Duke Museum of Art** (684-5135), with a small but impressive collection. The six galleries are quiet and uncongested; you can relax and enjoy the works. (Open Mon.-Fri. 9am-5pm, Sat. 10am-1pm, Sun. 2-5pm. Free.) In the summer try to avoid stepping on math nerds and future editors at Duke's **Talent Identification Program** (TIP), a three-week training ground for youngsters to keep those PhDs coming. Also be sure to take the time to enjoy Duke's 7700-acre forest with more than 30 mi. of trails and drivable roads.

On the other side of Durham, up Guess Rd., is the **Duke Homestead,** 2828 Duke Homestead Rd. (477-5498). Washington Duke first started in the tobacco business here, and the beautiful estate is still a small working farm. (Open April-Oct. Mon.-Sat. 9am-5pm, Sun. 1-5pm; Nov.-March Tues.-Sat. 10am-4pm, Sun. 1-4pm.)

At night, students frequent bars along **Franklin Street** in Chapel Hill, and **9th Street** in Durham. Before doing the same, you can catch a **Durham Bulls** (688-8211) baseball game. The Bulls, a class A farm team for the Atlanta Braves, became far more famous after the movie "Bull Durham" was filmed in the ball park. (Reserved tickets $5, general admission $3.)

With three major universities in the Research Triangle area, there is always something to do, whether concert, guest lecture, exhibit, or athletic event. For a complete listing of activities in the triangle, pick up free copies of both the *Spectator* and *Independent* weekly magazines, available at most restaurants, bookstores, and hotels.

The Carolina Mountains

The sharp ridges and rolling slopes of the southern Appalachian mountain ranges create some of the East's most magnificent scenery. At one time, North Carolina's Edenic highlands belonged largely for the country's rich and famous. The Vanderbilts, for example, owned a large portion of the nearly 500,000-acre Pisgah National Forest, which they subsequently willed to the U.S. government. Today the Blue Ridge, Great Smoky, Black, Craggy, Pisgah, and Balsam Mountains that comprise the western half of North Carolina beckon budget travelers not billionaires. Campsites blanket the region, coexisting with elusive but inexpensive youth hostels and ski lodges. Enjoy the area's rugged wilderness while backpacking, canoeing, whitewater rafting, or cross-country skiing. Motorists and cyclists can follow the Blue Ridge Parkway to some unforgettable views (see Blue Ridge Parkway, VA).

The **Blue Ridge Mountains** divide into two areas. The first, northern area is the **High Country,** which includes the territory between the town of Boone and the town of Asheville, 100 mi. to the southwest. The second area comprises the **Great Smoky Mountain National Park** (see Great Smoky Mountain National Park, TN) and **Nanatahala National Forest.**

Boone

Named for famous frontiersman Daniel Boone, who built a cabin here in the 1760s on his journey into the western wilderness, this mountain town has a variety of year-round outdoor activities from hiking and rock climbing to whitewater rafting and skiing. Even in downtown Boone, along King Street, shops such as the Mast Gen'l Store and the Candy Barrel seem reminiscent of the not-so-distant pioneer past. Just around the corner, **Appalachian State University** brings a youthful spirit to the town along with many popular activities and cultural events.

Practical Information

Emergency: 911. **National Park Service/Blue Ridge Parkway Emergency,** 259-0701 or 800-727-5929.

Visitor Information: Boone Area Chamber of Commerce, 350 Blowing Rock Rd. (264-2225), just east of the intersection of Rte. 321 and 105 in the center of Boone, nearly 7 mi. north of the Blue Ridge Pkwy. Information on accommodations and sights. Open daily 9am-5pm. **North Carolina High Country Host,** 701 Blowing Rock Rd. (264-1299; 800-438-7500; 800-222-7515 in NC). Pick up copies of the *North Carolina High Country Host Area Travel Guide,* an informative and detailed map of the area, and the *Blue Ridge Parkway Directory,* a mile-by-mile description of all services and attractions located on or near the Parkway. Open daily 9am-5pm.

Greyhound/Trailways: At the AppalCart station on Winkler's Creek Rd. (262-0501), off Rte. 321 at Wendy's. Flag stop in Blowing Rock. One per day to Hickory and most points east, south, and west. To Hickory ($9) and Charlotte (2½ hr., $19). Open Mon.-Fri. 8am-5pm, Sat.- Sun. 1-5pm.

Public Transport: Boone AppalCart, on Winkler's Creek Rd. (264-2278). Local bus and van service; 3 routes. The Red Route links downtown Boone with ASU and the motels and restaurants on Blowing Rock Rd. The Green Route serves Rte. 421. Crosstown route between the campus and the new marketplace. The Red Route operates Mon.-Fri. every hr. 7am-7pm; Green Mon.-Fri. every hr. 7am-6pm; crosstown Mon.-Fri. 7am-11pm, Sat. 8am-6pm. Fare 50¢ in town, charged by zones in the rest of the county.

Post Office: 637 Blowing Rock Rd. (264-3813), and 103 W. King St. (262-1171). Open Mon.-Fri. 9am-5pm, Sat. 9am-noon. **ZIP code:** 28607.

Area Code: 704.

Boone lies in the northwest corner of the state, by the Pisgah National Forest, about 22 mi. from Tennessee and 99 mi. from Asheville (see below) along Blue Ridge Pkwy. Most of Boone's motels and businesses are on Rte. 321 (Blowing Rock

Rd.) and on the perpendicular Rte. 321-421 (King St.) Appalachian State University stands at their junction.

Coming from other points on the East Coast, use Charlotte as your gateway city to the mountains. **US Air** (800-428-4322) has established a hub at Charlotte's **Douglas Airport.**

Accommodations and Camping

Because of the wealthy visitors who escape to Boone's comfortably cool mountains in the summer and come to ski in the winter, the area has more than its share of expensive motels and B&Bs. However, good deals on motels, in addition to the hostels and camp sites in the area, make Boone a warm holiday for the budget traveler.

Blowing Rock Assembly Grounds (AYH), P.O. Box 974, Blowing Rock (295-7813), near the Blue Ridge Parkway, has small, primitive, but clean rooms. The grounds have communal bathrooms, sports facilities, and a cheap cafeteria, all in a gorgeous setting with access to hiking trails. Ask the bus driver to let you off at Blowing Rock Town Hall or at the Rte. 321 bypass and Sunset Dr., depending on the direction you're traveling—it's about 2 mi. from both points. Call the hostel for a pick-up, or turn left onto Sunset Dr., and where Sunset ends turn left 300 yd. and follow signs to B.R.A.G., and the hostel will be on your right. Primarily a retreat for religious groups; be prepared for a friendly but conservative atmosphere. $8, nonmembers $16. Package rates also available.

Most inexpensive hotels are concentrated along Blowing Rock Rd. (Hwy 321), or Hwy 105. The red-brick **Red Carpet Inn** may have simple rooms but they come with remote TV, a playground, and a savey pool. (Singles $32 Doubles $38.) The **High Country Inn,** Hwy 105 (264-1000) also has a pool and even a watermill by the entrance. Large, comfortable rooms. (Singles $39. Doubles $42.)

Choose between developed **campsites** and free primitive camping in the Boone area and the Pisgah National Forest. Along the Blue Ridge Pwy, spectacular sites without hookups are available for $7 at the **Julian Price Campground,** mile 297 (963-5911); **Linville Falls,** mile 316 (963-5911); and **Crabtree Meadows,** mile 340 (675-4444); (open May-Oct. only). Cabins in **Roan Mountain State Park** (800-421-6683) comfortably sleep six and are furnished with linens and cooking utensils. (Sun.-Thurs. $45.50, Fri.-Sat. $58. Weekly: $290.) The state park offers pool and tennis facilities and tends to attract smaller crowds than the campgrounds on the parkway. For more information call the Roan Mtn. Visitors Center at 615-772-3314.

Food

The North Carolina mountains are full of delicious family-style restaurants, mostly in B&Bs, at about $10 for all-you-can-eat feasts. The **Sunshine Inn** (295-3487) on Sunset Dr. in Blowing Rock, is a charming establishment. Picnicking, too, offers a fun and economical option in the mountains.

Woodland's, Hwy. 321 bypass, Blowing Rock (295-3651). Offers live entertainment nightly and an opportunity to "Eat in the Rough." Try authentic Carolina mountain barbecued pork and beef ($4-5). Open Mon.-Fri. 11am-midnight; kitchen closes at 10pm.

Red Onion, Hwy. 321 N. in Boone across from ASU. Heavenly pasta dishes (primavera $5), gourmet burgers, spicy Mexican specialties, and big sandwiches ($4-5). Open Sun.-Thurs. 11am-10pm, Fri.-Sat. 11am-10:30pm.

Dan'l Boone Inn, 105 Hardin St., at the junction of Rte. 321 and 421. Family style meals with ham biscuits 'n' plates heaped high with vegetables 'n' meat. All-you-can-eat $9. Open Mon.-Fri. 11am-9pm, Sat.-Sun. 8am-9pm.

Shadrack's Bar-B-Q and Seafood Barn, 729 Blowing Rock Rd., in an old roller-skating rink behind the Peddlar Steak House. Seats up to 600 people. All-you-can-eat barbecue pork, chicken, and ribs or fried catfish, accompanied by live bluegrass and exciting clogging ($9). Buffet Wed. 5:30-9pm, Fri. 5:30-10pm, Sat. 5:30-11pm; music begins at 7pm. Sun. lunch 11:30am-2pm ($7); music begins at 12:30pm.

Sights and Activities

An **Appalachian Summer** (262-6084) is a three-month, high-caliber festival of music, art, theater, and dance sponsored by Appalachian State University. In an open air amphitheater, **Horn in the West** (264-2120), located near Boone off Rte. 105, presents an outdoor drama of the American Revolution as fought in the southern Appalachians. (Shows Tues.-Sun. at 8:30pm. Admission $8-12. Reservations recommended.) Adjacent to the theater the **Daniel Boone Native Gardens** celebrate mountain foliage, while the **Hickory Ridge Homestead** documents 18th-century mountain life.

Use Boone as a base from which to explore the mountain towns to the west and south. The community of **Blowing Rock,** 7 mi. south at the entrance to the Blue Ridge Pkwy., is a folk artists' colony. Its namesake overhangs Johns River Gorge; chuck a piece of paper over the edge and the wind will blow it back into your face. AppalCart goes to the Blowing Rock Town Hall from Boone twice daily. Stop by **Parkway Craft Center,** mile 294 (295-7938), 2 mi. south of Blowing Rock Village, where members of the Southern Highland Handicraft Guild demonstrate their skills and sell their crafts. The craft center is located in the **Moses H. Cone Memorial Park,** 3500 acres of shaded walking trails and magnificent views. (Open May-Oct. daily 9am-5:30pm.)

Hikers should arm themselves with the invaluable large-scale map *100 Favorite Trails* ($2). Those interested in rock climbing should check out **Appalachian Mountain Sports** (264-3170), on Hwy. 105 S., in Boone. They offer professional (and expensive) instruction, mostly for small groups (1-3 people). The guides will meet you on the trail for a half-day of instruction, or a two- to three-day trip. (Open Mon.-Thurs. 10am-6pm, Fri. 10am-7pm, Sat. 9am-6pm, Sun. 10am-5pm. From $75 per person. Canoe rentals start at $12.50.) Consider joining one of the guided expeditions led by the staff of **Edge of the World,** P.O. Box 1137, Banner Elk (898-9550), on Rte. 184 downtown. A complete outdoor equipment and clothing store, the Edge leads many day-long backpacking, whitewater canoeing, rafting, spelunking and rock climbing trips all over the High Country for about $50. One of their most popular packages is a two-day summer backpacking trip across the Roan Mountain Balds which costs $75, including transportation, all equipment, 4 meals, instruction, and guide. Edge of the World also rents equipment. (Four-person tents $7 the 1st night, $6 the 2nd, $4 each additional night; 2-person tents $1 less each night. Also sleeping bags, sleeping pads, cook stoves, and backpacks.)

Downhill skiers can enjoy the Southeast's largest concentration of alpine resorts. Four concentrate in the Boone/Blowing Rock/Banner Elk area: **Appalachian Ski Mountain,** P.O. Box 106, Blowing Rock (800-322-2373; lift tickets weekends $26, weekdays $18, with full rental $27; **Ski Beech,** P.O. Box 1118, Beech Mountain (387-2011; lift tickets weekends $26, weekdays $21, with rentals $38 and $28, respectively); **Ski Hawknest,** Town of Seven Devils, 1605 Skyland Dr., Banner Elk (963-6561; lift tickets weekends $20, weekdays $10, with rentals $30 and $16, respectively); **Sugar Mountain,** P.O. Box 369, Banner Elk (898-4521 or 800-438-4555; lift tickets weekends $35, weekdays $25, with rentals $47 and $35, respectively). AppalCart (262-0501) runs a daily shuttle in winter to Sugar Mountain and four times per week to Ski Beech. Call the High Country Host (264-1299) for ski reports.

In a car, the 5-mi. access road to **Grandfather Mountain** (800-468-7325) reveals unparalleled views of the entire High Country area if you go on a clear day. At the top you'll find a private park featuring a mile-high suspension bridge and a small zoo ($6). To hike or camp on Grandfather Mt. you must get a permit ($3 per day), available at the Grandfather Mountain County Store on Rte. 221, Appalachian Mountain Sports, Edge of the World, or the Scotchman store at the Shanty Spring Trail at the junction of Rte. 105 and 184. (Contact the Backcountry Manager, Grandfather Mt., Linville, NC 28646 for more information. Mountain open April-Nov. daily 8am-8pm; Dec.-March 9am-4pm, weather permitting.) North Carolina Rte. 194, 226, 261, and 80 meander by the towns of Banner Elk, Beech, Elk Park, Bakersville, and Bandana, through verdant mountainsides and narrow valleys; by day, they're a sportscar driver's dream, but by night the absence of guardrails makes for a hair-raising experience.

Asheville

Asheville's hazy blue mountains, deep valleys, spectacular waterfalls, and plunging gorges embody classic Appalachian beauty. Driving the Blue Ridge Pwy., a part of the National Park Service, best reveals the scenic vistas that surround the city. The Appalachian Mountains prove fertile ground for the local arts and crafts community that fills festivals and galleries throughout the year. Asheville may be as famous for the reams of visitors who have enjoyed the natural beauty, small-town charm, and arts of the city as for the sights themselves. The **Biltmore Estate**, "Versailles of the South," home to George Vanderbilt and his designer-jean family, attracts herds of gawking tourists.

Practical Information

Emergency: 911.

Visitors Information: **Chamber of Commerce**, 151 Haywood St. (258-3858; 800-548-1300 in NC), off I-240 on the northwest end of downtown. Ask at the desk for the detailed city street map, city transit route map, and comprehensive sight-seeing guide. Open Mon.-Fri. 8:30am-5:30pm, Sat.-Sun. 9am-5pm.

Greyhound/Trailways: 2 Tunnel Rd. (253-5353), 2 mi. east of downtown, near the Beaucatcher Tunnel. Bus #13 ("Oteen/Beverly Hills") or 14 ("Haw Creek/Tunnel Rd.") runs to and from downtown every ½ hr. Last bus at 5:50pm. To: Charlotte (3 per day, 3 hr., $22); Knoxville (7 per day, 3 hr., $23); Atlanta ($39). Open daily 6:30am-10pm.

Public Transport: **Asheville Transit**, 360 W. Haywood (253-5691). Service within city limits. All routes converge on Pritchard Park downtown. Buses operate Mon.-Sat. 5:30am-7:30pm, most at ½-hr. intervals. Fare 60¢, transfers 30¢.

Post Office: 33 Coxe Ave. (257-4113), at Patton Ave. Open Mon.-Fri. 8:30am-5pm, Sat. 9am-noon. **ZIP code:** 28802.

Area Code: 704.

Asheville hugs the hills of the Blue Ridge Mountains in western North Carolina. Knoxville, TN, is 100 mi. to the northwest across Great Smoky Mountains National Park, and Winston-Salem lies 144 mi. east on I-40. Downtown Asheville is bordered by I-240 on the north and I-40 on the south. The Blue Ridge Pkwy. is accessible by I-40 east; the town of Boone (see above) sits 99 mi. farther along it to the northwest.

Accommodations and Camping

Asheville's independently owned motels outdo the budget chains. Many lean on **Merrimon Avenue,** north of the city (take bus #2 "Merrimon Avenue"), and on **Tunnel Road.** Make reservations early for periods around folk and craft festivals and holidays. For truly memorable, though expensive, accommodations in Asheville, stay at one of the B&Bs in the area. The **Bois d'Arc** (253-4345) and **Flint Street Inn** (253-6723) are two of the many guest houses; find more information on these country inns by calling or writing the chamber of commerce.

The **American Court Motel**, 85 Merrimon Ave. (253-4427), has tasteful, bright rooms with cable, A/C, pool, and laundromat. (Singles $34. Doubles $46.)Slightly farther from town, **Four Seasons Motor Inn**, 820 Merrimon Ave. (254-5324), breezes in with cheerful rooms and classic walk-in closets. (Singles $25. Double $28.) The incongruously named **Downtown Motel**, 65 Merrimon Ave. (253-9841), on Merrimon St. just north of the I-240 expressway, is a 10-minute walk from downtown (or take bus #2). This pleasant little blue building with somewhat dark rooms, and mismatched decor, keeps good-sized bathrooms and a pool. (Singles $28. Doubles $38.)

With the Blue Ridge Pkwy., Pisgah National Forest, and the Great Smokies easily accessible by car you can find a campsite to suit any taste. Close to town is **Bear Creek RV Park and Campground,** 81 S. Bear Creek Rd. (253-0798). Take I-40 exit 47, and look for the sign at the top of the hill. (Pool, laundry, groceries, and game room. Tent sites $12. RV sites with hookup $16.50.) In Pisgah National Forest, the nearest campground is **Powhatan,** off Rte. 191, 12 mi. southwest of Asheville. (Open May-Sept.)

Food

You'll find links in most major fast-food chains on **Tunnel Road** and **Biltmore Avenue,** though Asheville does offer some alternatives to the hamburger and frozen custard monarchs. The **Western North Carolina Farmers Market** (253-1691), at the intersection of I-240 and Rte. 191, near I-26, has plenty of fresh produce, as well as crafts. Take bus #16 to I-40, then walk ½ mi. (Open Mon.-Sat. 8am-6pm, Sun. 1-6pm.)

> **Bill Stanley's Barbeque and Bluegrass,** 20 South Spruce St., in the rear corner of a building adjacent to the police station. Hickory-cooked barbecue and fried chicken. Bluegrass and cloggers on the side begin at 8pm. All-you-can-eat buffet dinner $9, or just the music and dancing for $3. Open Tues.-Thurs. 11am-2pm and 6-11pm, Fri. 11am-2pm and 6pm-midnight, Sat. 6pm-midnight.

> **Boston Pizza,** 501 Merriman Ave. College hang-out serving amazing pizza (medium $7.75) with fresh vegetable toppings, and sub sandwiches. Open Tues.-Sat. 11am-11:30pm, Sun. noon-10pm.

> **The Hop,** 507 Merriman, next to Boston Pizza. You can rock it, you can roll it, at the Hop. After some pizza jump next door for homemade ice cream in this 50s-style joint that always packs a crowd. Open Mon.-Sat. 11:30am-11pm, Sun. 1-10pm.

> **Stone Soup,** at Broadway and Walnut St. Also on Wall St., downtown. A cooperative with freshly baked bread and nitrate-free sausage. Soup and sandwiches from $1.50. Packed from noon-2pm and for Sun. brunch. Open Mon.-Sat. 7am-4pm, Sun. 9:30am-1:30pm.

> **Malaprops Bookstore/Café,** 61 Haywood St. (254-6734), downtown in the basement of the bookstore. Gourmand coffees, bagels, tofu. Sandwiches $3-4. Occipital readings, great book curriculum, and walking staff. Open Mon.-Sat. 9am-8pm, Sun. noon-5pm.

> **Johnny O's Sandwich Shop,** 36 Battery Park Ave. Stand-up lunch counter. Cheeseburger 70¢. Open daily 6:30am-2:30pm.

Sights and Festivals

Elvis' Southern mansion, Graceland, is nothing compared to the Vanderbilt's **Biltmore Estate,** 1 North Pack Sq. (255-1700 or 800-543-2961). Take exit 50 off I-40, and go 3 blocks north. A tour of this true French Renaissance-style castle built in the 1890s can take all day depending on the crowds; try to arrive early in the morning. The self-guided tour winds through a portion of the 250-room chateau, viewing an indoor pool, a bowling alley, rooms full of Sargent paintings and Dürer prints, and enormous libraries of rare books. The surrounding gardens, designed by Central Park planner Frederick Law Olmsted, and a tour of the Biltmore winery, with sour wine tasting for those over 21, are included in the hefty admission price. (Open daily 9am-6pm; ticket office closes at 5pm. Winery open Mon.-Sat. at 11am, Sun. at 1pm. Admission $19, ages 12-17 $14, under 11 free.) George Vanderbilt had **Biltmore Village** built right outside the gates. This cozy shopping district contains craft galleries, antique stores, and a music shop.

Even the most famous of past visitors to Asheville did not have the privilege of staying at the Vanderbilt's chateau. You're not alone. Henry Ford, Thomas Edison, and F. Scott Fitzgerald all stayed in the towering **Grove Park Inn** when they passed through the peaceful mountain town. Made of stone from the surrounding mountains, the still-operating hotel has many pieces of original early-20th-century furniture and fireplaces you can literally walk into. To see sites really graced with famous people, visit the **Riverside Cemetery,** Birch St. off Montford Ave., north of I-240, where writers Thomas Wolfe and O. Henry are buried. The **Thomas Wolfe Memo-**

rial, 48 Spruce St. (253-8304), between Woodfin and Walnut St., was a boarding house run by Wolfe's mother and the novelist's boyhood home. Wolfe depicted the "Old Kentucky Home" as "Dixieland" in his first novel, *Look Homeward, Angel.* (Open Mon.-Sat. 9am-5pm, Sun. 1-5pm; hours vary in winter. Admission $1, students 50¢.)

Asheville's artistic tradition remains as strong as its literary one; visit the **Folk Art Center** (704-298-7928), east of Asheville at mile 382 on the Blue Ridge Pkwy., north of U.S. 70, to see outstanding work of the **Southern Highland Handicraft Guild.** (Open daily 9am-5pm. Free.) Each year around mid-July the Folk Art Center sponsors a **Guild Fair** (298-7928), at the Asheville Civic Center, off I-240 on Haywood St. Both the Folk Art Center and the chamber of commerce have more information on this weekend of craft demonstrations, dancing, and music.

A rare summer day goes by in Asheville when a festival is not taking place. At the end of July, the downtown **Belle Chere Festival** (253-1009) celebrates "beautiful living" with food and music. An **Appalachian Heritage Fair** (258-6111) occurs at the beginning of August. Also in August, the **Mountain Dance and Folk Festival** (257-1300) at the civic center, now in its 63rd season, has a 3-day competition in clog and square dancing, mountain traditional and bluegrass music, and individual musicianship. (Tickets $6-8.) The **Swannanoa Chamber Festival** (298-7613) in July has weekly chamber music concerts. ($10 per performance, $45 for a series ticket.)

South Carolina

From the Grand Strand to Charleston by the sea, and inland to Columbia, South Carolina is a state of pastureland and friendly folk. Many areas have yet to recover from the 1989 destruction of Hurricane Hugo, which bludgeoned the state with high winds, resulting in millions of dollars of damage to both coastal and inland cities. The storm threw six-ton yachts up on shore, and snapped trees at their midpoints like toothpicks.

Myrtle Beach is a tourist hotspot during the summer, and as such comes complete with flashing lights, all-night T-shirt shops, and expensive restaurants and hotels. Columbia, the capital, is slow-paced with not much to ogle, but it provides a nice change from hectic Myrtle Beach. Charleston is a beautiful city—most of the downtown area, a registered historic district, has been repainted, reshingled, and revamped following the storm. You'll need three or more days stay in Charleston to take in the city's flavor and favors.

Practical Information

Capital: Columbia.

Tourist Information: Department of Parks, Recreation, and Tourism, Edgar A. Brown Bldg., 1205 Pendleton St. #110, Columbia 29201 (734-0122). **U.S. Forest Service,** P.O. Box 970, Columbia 29202 (765-5222).

Time Zone: Eastern. **Postal Abbreviation:** SC.

Columbia

The capital is a quiet, unassuming city whose pervasive college-town flavor overshadows state politics. The University of South Carolina provides most of the city's excitement and nightlife. The city sprung up in 1786 when bureaucrats in nearby Charleston decided that their territory needed a proper capital city. Surveyors found some land near the Congaree River, cleared it, and within two decades, over 1000 people poured into one of America's first planned cities. President Woodrow Wilson called Columbia home during his boyhood and now thousands of USC students do the same. Stop by for a pleasant change from the high-powered sight-seeing of Charleston and the honky-tonk of Myrtle Beach.

Columbia's 18th-century aristocratic elegance has been preserved by the Historic Columbia Foundation in the **Robert Mills House,** 1616 Blanding St., 3 blocks east of Sumter St. (252-7742; tours Tues.-Sat. 10:45am-3:15pm, Sun. 1-5pm $3, students $1.50). Mills, one of America's first federal architects, designed the Washington Monument and 30 of South Carolina's public buildings. Across the street, at 1615 Blanding, is the **Hampton-Preston Mansion,** once used by Union forces as a Civil War headquarters. (Open Tues.-Sat. 10am-4pm, Sun. 1-5pm. Tours $3, students $1.50, under 6 free.) Stroll through USC's **Horseshoe,** at the junction of College and Sumter St., which holds the university's oldest buildings, dating from the beginning of the 19th century. The **McKissick Museum** (777-7251), at the top of the Horseshoe, offers scientific, folk and pottery exhibits, as well as selections from the university's extensive collection of Twentieth Century-Fox Movietonenews Newsreels. (Open Mon.-Fri. 9am-4pm, Sat. 10am-5pm, Sun. 1-5pm. Free.) Columbia's award-winning **Riverbanks Zoo,** on I-26 at Greystone Blvd., northwest of downtown, is called home by more than 2000 animals. See frogs, sharks, cobras, and tigers before stopping off at the concessions stand for a snow cone. (Open Mon.-Fri. 9am-4pm, Sat.-Sun. 9am-5pm. Admission $3.50, seniors $2, students $2.75, ages 3-12 $1.50.)

The new **South Carolina State Museum,** 301 Gervais St. (737-4595), beside the Gervais St. Bridge is located inside the historic Columbia Mills building. Exhibits include replicas of two denizens of the deep—a Great White Shark and the first submarine to sink an enemy ship. (Open Mon.-Sat. 10am-5pm, Sun, 1-5pm. Admission $3, seniors and college students with I.D. $2, ages 6-17 $1.25, under 6 free.)

The **Five Points** business district, at the junction of Harden, Devine, and Blossom St. (from downtown, take the "Veterans Hospital" bus), caters to Columbia's large student population. **Groucho's,** 611 Harden St. (799-5708), in the heart of Five Points, is a Columbia institution and anomaly—a New York-style Jewish deli serving large sandwiches at rock-bottom prices ($3-5). (Open Mon.-Fri. 10am-6pm, Thurs.-Fri. 7-11pm, Sat. 11am-4pm.) **Yesterday's Restaurant and Tavern,** 2030 Devine St. (799-0196), serves today's specialties on the newspapers under the lacquered tabletops. Enjoy complete dinner specials ($4-6) or vegetarian pies. (Open Sun.-Tues. 11:30am-1am, Wed.-Sat. 11:30am-2am.) **Kinch's Restaurant,** 1115 Assembly St. (256-3843), across the street from the State House, has an early bird breakfast special for $2. (Open daily 7am-4pm.) **The Columbia State Farmers Market,** Bluff Rd. (737-3016), across from the USC Football Stadium, is a good place to stock up on fresh produce shipped in from all corners of South Carolina. The university provides most of the city's excitement and nightlife. Try **Club 638,** 638 Harden St. (779-1953), at Five Points for dancing and revelry. Five Points abounds in bars; just walk through and pick your point.

The **USC Off-Campus Housing Office** (777-4174), in the "I" building on Devine St. is probably your best budget bet for beauty rest. They can link you up with owners of private homes in the university community who rent rooms. Otherwise, the only budget option downtown is the **Heart of Columbia,** 1011 Assembly St. (799-1140) with a shabby-looking exterior, but clean chambers in a heart-attack-free neighborhood. (Singles $29. Doubles $33.) Just west of downtown across the Congaree River, a number of inexpensive motels line Knox Abbot Dr. **Econo-lodge,** 827 Bush River Rd., off exit 108 at I-20 and I-26, has bright rooms, a swimming pool, A/C, and a movie channel. (Singles Sun.-Thurs. $24, Fri.-Sat. $35.) The **Sesquicentennial State Park** (788-2706) has sites with electricity and water ($8). Take "State Park" bus from downtown. By car, take I-20 to Two Notch Rd. (Rte. 1) exit, and head northeast 4 mi.

The **Greater Columbia Convention and Visitors Bureau,** 301 Gervais St. (254-0479). is not budget-oriented, but provides a free street map of the area with all the historical sights marked on it and a free coupon book for discounts at area hotels and restaurants. (Open Mon.-Fri. 8:30am-5pm, Sat. 10am-5pm.) The **University of South Carolina Information Desk,** Russell House Student Center, 2nd floor (777-

3196), on Green at Sumter St., across from the Horseshoe, provides campus maps, shuttle schedules, advice on nearby budget accommodations and the low-down on campus life and events. If you get stranded in the area and/or need transportation in a hurry, contact **Travelers Aid,** 1800 Main St. (733-5450; open Mon.-Fri. 9am-5pm).

Columbia is in the heart of South Carolina, at the junction of I-20, 26, and 77. It is 112 mi. from Charleston, 143 mi. from Myrtle Beach, 92 mi. from Charlotte, NC, and 215 mi. from Atlanta. Most buses running along the East Coast stop here. The **Congaree River** marks the western edge of the city. **Assembly Street** and **Sumter Street** are downtown's major north-south arteries; **Gervais Street** and **Calhoun Street** cut east-west. **Columbia Metropolitan Airport,** 300 Aviation Way (822-5000) is serviced by Delta, American, USAir, and others. **Amtrak,** 903 Gervais St. (252-8246 or 800-872-7245), has trains once per day to Washington, DC (9½ hr., $81); Miami (12 hr., $114); and Savannah (2 hr., $29). The northbound train leaves daily at 5:31am, the southbound train at 10:43pm. The station is open Mon.-Sat. 8:30am-4:30pm and 10:30pm-6:30am, Sun. 10:30pm-6:30am. **Greyhound/Trailways,** 2015 Gervais St. (779-0650), is near the intersection of Harden and Gervais St., about 1 mi. east of the capitol. Buses to: Charlotte, NC (5 per day, 2 hr., $20); Charleston, SC (5 per day, 2½ hr., $19); Atlanta (6 per day, 4½ hr., $38). Open 24 hr. **South Carolina Electric and Gas** (748-3019) operates local buses. Most routes start from the transfer depot at the corner of Assembly and Gervais St. Fare 50¢. Local **help lines** are **Helpline of the Midlands,** (771-4357), **Rape Crisis,** (252-8393), and **AIDS Information Line,** (779-7257). The **Richland Memorial Hospital,** 5 Richland Medical Park (265-7561), has emergency services and a walk-in clinic. Get up, a get, get down; emergency is 911 in this town.The**Post Office,** 1601 Assembly St. (733-4647), is open Mon. and Fri. 7:30am-6pm, Tues.-Thurs. 7:30am-5pm. Columbia's **ZIP code** is 29202; the **area code** is 803.

Myrtle Beach

Located mid-way along the 50-mile beach known as the **Grand Strand,** Myrtle Beach is more than a beach, it's a phenomenon—a living smorgasbord of American pop culture. Its white sand beaches, clean ocean water, 68 golf courses, and over 1000 restaurants and nightclubs, make Myrtle Beach the third most popular destination on the East Coast after Disney World and Atlantic City. With more than 40,000 rentable rooms and over 9000 individual campsites in the area, it sounds easy to find a cheap place to spend the night here, but during the summer, it is difficult, if not impossible, to find a hotel room for under $30. The streets of Myrtle Beach are lined with fireworks warehouses, all-you-can-eat restaurants, fast-food franchises, and gift shops. No less than 15 miniature golf courses enchant the area, including **Grand Prix Golf,** at the southern end of the strip (open daily 9am-midnight; $5), along with several waterparks, such as **Myrtle Waves,** (448-1026), on the U.S. 17 bypass at 10th Ave. N.

If the street activities aren't garish enough, use the flashing lights as a beacon and head toward the tacky museums at the beach center, Ocean Blvd. between 5th and 12th St. At the **Ripley's Believe It or Not Museum,** 901 N. Ocean Blvd. (448-2331), a film shows a man pulling a loaded wagon with his eyelids. (Admission $5.25, seniors, students, and military $4.25.) Launch into shopping ecstasy at the **Waccamaw Pottery and Outlet Park,** west of the beach on U.S. 501 between Myrtle Beach and Conway, a 500-acre complex of over 100 factory outlet stores. (Open in summer daily 9am-10pm.) For nightlife try **2001,** at Hwy. 17 N. and Lake Arrowhead Rd. (449-9434), or the **Afterdeck,** 9801 N. King's Hwy. (449-1550), where you can boogie, or do South Carolina's state dance, the *Shag* Monday to Saturday nights. Both clubs are located near **Restaurant Row,** the intersection of King's Hwy. and the Hwy. 17 bypass.

The restaurants in Myrtle Beach are largely predictable, overpriced steak-and-seafood places. You won't find any interesting budget fare here—look instead for local hangouts that serve burgers, sandwiches, and beer. **River City Café,** 21st Ave. N., serves huge juicy hamburgers, homemade fries, beer, wine, and free peanuts in a fun, collegiate atmosphere. (Open Mon.-Sat. 11am-10pm, Sun. 11:30am-9pm.) **K and W Cafeteria** (448-1669) has locations at both ends of town, on Business 17. At dinner expect a 40-minute wait. **Olympic Flame Restaurant and Pancake House,** 14th Ave. N. at Ocean Blvd., 1 block from the beach, starts the day right with fluffy pancakes ($2.25) and omelettes ($2.75). (Open daily 6:30am-10pm.) Or try **Mammy's Kitchen,** 11th Ave. N. at King's Hwy., for a breakfast special of hash-browns, toast, eggs, and bacon ($2). (Open daily 7am-noon and 4-9pm.)

For students, the most convenient places to stay are within 10 blocks north or south of the **Pavilion Amusement Park** area (8th and 9th Ave. N. at Ocean Blvd). From there, beaches, clubs and all-you-can-eat restaurants are within easy walking distance. The most inexpensive places are just west of the beach property in the 3rd St. area or on U.S. 17. You can often bargain for a lower hotel rate. Remember that in the off-season (Oct.-Feb.) prices plunge at most hotels. At the best budget oceanfront hotel, **La Roca Motel,** 1708 N. Ocean Blvd. (448-3341), owners Chong and Barry O'Leary offer the *Let's Go* user a 10% discount, a swimming pool, bright clean rooms, and helpful orientation tips. They also have a free barbecue each week. (Singles $20-30.) **Ocean West Motel,** 204 N. King's Hwy., has old but clean rooms with cable TV (Singles $35). The **King's Road Motor Lodge,** 1205 N. King's Hwy. (448-1625), two blocks from the Greyhound station, boasts bright rooms, a swimming pool, and a game room. (Singles $35; off-season $24. 10% discount for *Let's Go* users.) If you strike out at these places, try the **Beach Hotel and Motel Reservation Service** (local 626-7477, elsewhere 800-626-7477), which calls various member hotels free of charge to find the cheapest accommodations. For the best rates ask for "second row," the string of hotels across the street from the oceanfront properties. (Open Mon.-Fri. 9am-5pm.)

To distance yourself from the frenzied beach and enjoy the outdoors in a less infested incarnation, camp at **Myrtle Beach State Park** (238-5325). Just south of town off U.S. 17 and across from the air force base, the park encloses a stretch of non-commercial and relatively uncrowded shoreline. (Gates open daily 6am-midnight; off-season daily 6am-dark. Sites $14.) Some of the several private camp-grounds have rules against single campers, so call ahead if you're alone. **KOA Kam-pground,** on King's Hwy. at 5th Ave. S. (448-3421), is less than 1 mi. outside of town. (Sites with water and electricity $17.50, with full hookup $19.50. Call for reservations.) **Apache Family Campground,** 9700 King's Hwy. N. (449-7323), is slightly farther away. Some sites are on the beach, some in pine groves. (Families only. Sites $20-23.) Sleeping on the heavily patrolled beach is illegal, as are parties.

Stop at the **chamber of commerce,** 13th Ave. N. at King's Hwy. (626-7444), for free copies of *Beachcomber* and *Hot Times* as well as information on current activities. Also, pick up *Strand* magazine, a map of the area, bus schedules, and the yellow *Continuing Events* sheet which gives lisitings of current goings on. (Open Mon.-Fri. 8:30am-5pm, Sat. 9am-noon, Sun. noon-5pm.)

In Myrtle Beach, **U.S. 17,** also called **King's Highway,** runs north-south along the coastline and provides access to most points of interest. **Route 501** west in the direction of Conway leads to popular factory outlet stores. Myrtle Beach's **Greyhound** terminal, on 9th Ave. N. at U.S. 17 (448-2471), has connections to: Charleston (3 per day, 2 hr., $19); Florence (2 per day, 45 min., $15); and Wilmington (3 per day, 2 hr., $14). (Open Mon.-Fri. 8am-2:30pm and 7-8:45pm, Sat. 8am-2:30pm, Sun. 8-9am, noon-2:30pm, and 7-8:45pm.) To get around Myrtle Beach and Conway, use **Coastal Rapid Public Transit (CRPTA)** (626-9138 in Myrtle Beach; 248-7277 in Conway). Local fare 75¢; Conway to Myrtle Beach $1.25. Or rent a bike at **The Bike Shoppe,** 711 Broadway (448-5103; $5 per hr. for sturdy 1-speeds; license or credit card required for deposit).

The number for the local **police** is 448-3111. Myrtle Beach's **post office** is at 505 N. King's Hwy. (626-9533; open Mon.-Fri. 8:30am-5pm, Sat. 9am-noon). The **ZIP code** is 29577; the **area code** is 803.

Charleston

Razed by five different fires, and blown or shaken apart by more than 10 different hurricanes and earthquakes over the years, Charleston is currently recovering from the 135 mi. per hour winds, heavy rains, and destruction of September 1989's Hurricane Hugo. Though signs of destruction can still be seen here and there, the reconstruction is almost complete; fresh paint, new storefronts, and tree stumps mix with beautifully refurbished antebellum homes, old churches, and hidden gardens. Dukes, barons, and earls once presided over Charleston's great coastal plantations, leaving an historic downtown area which a traveler could spend weeks touring. The Charleston area also offers visitors the resources of the nearby Atlantic coastal islands. Most noticeably, the people of Charleston, in spite of the destruction they have endured, are some of the friendliest people you will meet on your journeys south. They survive the way they flourish—with a smile.

Practical Information

Emergency: 911.

Visitor Information Center: 85 Calhoun St. (722-8338), in front of the Municipal Auditorium. Walking tour map (50¢) has much historical information and good directions. The ½-hr. slide show, *The Charleston Adventure,* should not be confused with the remarkable *Dear Charleston,* but is a respectable overview of Charleston's past and present. Tickets $3, children $1.50. Open Mon.-Fri. 8:30am-5:30pm, Sat.-Sun. 8:30am-5pm.

Amtrak: 4565 Gaynor Ave. (744-8264), 8 mi. west of downtown. The "Durant Ave." bus will take you from the station to the historic district. Trains to: Richmond (2 per day, 7 hr., $75); Savannah (2 per day, 2 hr., $23); and Washington, DC (2 per day, 14 hr., $97). Open daily 6am-10pm.

Greyhound: 3610 Dorchester Rd. (744-4247), near I-26. Because the downtown bus station is closed this is the only one available, but try to avoid the area at night; it can be dangerous. To: Myrtle Beach (2 per day, 2 hr., $19); Savannah (2 per day, 3 hr., $23); Washington, DC (2 per day, 11 hr., $75). To get into town, take the **South Carolina Electric and Gas** bus marked "Broad St." or "South Battery" that stops right in front of the station and get off at the intersection of Meeting and Calhoun St. Pick up the bus marked "Navy Yard 5 mile Dorchester Rd.," at the same intersection to get back to the station from town. There are two "Navy Yard" buses so be sure to take the "5 mile Dorchester Rd." bus outbound; it's the only one that stops in front of the station. Open daily 6am-10pm.

Public Transport: South Carolina Electric and Gas Company (SCE&G) City Bus Service, 2469 Leeds Ave. (747-0922). Operates Mon.-Sat. 5:10am-1am. Fare 50¢. Also operates **Downtown Area Shuttle (DASH)** Mon.-Fri. 8am-5pm. Fare 50¢, transfers to other SCE&G buses free.

Car Rental: Thrifty Car Rental (552-7531 or 800-367-2277). $30 per day with 200 free mi., 20¢ each additional mi. Must be 25 with major credit card.

Bike Rental: The Bicycle Shoppe, 283 Meeting St. (722-8168). $3 per hr., $12 per day. Open daily 10am-5:30pm.

Taxi: North Area Taxi, 554-7575. Base fare $1.

Help Lines: Hotline, 744-4357. Open 24 hr. General counseling and comprehensive information on transient accommodations. **People Against Rape,** 722-7273. Open 24 hr.

Post Office: 11 Broad St. Open Mon.-Fri. 8am-5pm, Sat. 8am-noon. **ZIP code:** 29401.

Area Code: 803.

Charleston sits about 100 mi. north of Savannah and the same distance south of Myrtle Beach. The city dominates a peninsula situated midway along the South Carolina coastline. **Old Charleston** is confined to the southernmost point of the mile-wide peninsula below **Calhoun Street. Meeting, King,** and **East Bay Streets** are major north-south routes through the city.

Accommodations and Camping

Motel rooms in historic downtown Charleston are expensive. All the cheap motels are a good distance from downtown and not a practical option for those without cars. Investigate the accommodations just across the Ashley River on U.S. 17 South: several tiny establishments offer $12-15 rooms. For students the cheapest and best option in town is the **Rutledge Museum Guest House,** 114 Rutledge Ave. (722-7551), a beautiful historic home with shared rooms and free coffee, tea, hot chocolate, and cinnamon rolls each morning. ($15 per person; rates lower for extended stays.) The laid-back, friendly manager will not let you set foot in Charleston until she's given you a full orientation. If she can't house you, try **Charleston East Bed and Breakfast,** 1031 Tall Pine Rd. (884-8208), in Mt. Pleasant east of Charleston off U.S. 701. They will try to place you in one of their 16 private homes. (Rooms $30-50, $5-10 less for singles. Open for reservations Mon.-Sat. 10am-6pm.) **Motel 6,** 2058 Savannah Hwy. (556-5144), 4 mi. out at 7th Ave. is clean and pleasant, but far from downtown and frequently filled. (Singles $29, each additional person $6.)

There are several inexpensive campgrounds in the Charleston area, but not a one is near downtown. Eight mi. south on U.S. 17, try **Oak Plantation Campground** (766-5936; sites $9.50). Also look for **Pelican's Cove,** 97 Center St., at Folly Beach (588-2072; sites with full hookup $17).

Food and Nightlife

Most restaurants in the revamped downtown area are also expensive. If you choose to eat out, eat lunch, since most restaurants serve dinner selections at discounted prices.

Marina Variety Store/City Marina, Lockwood Blvd. Pleasant view of the Ashley River from an otherwise unremarkable dining room. Good shellfish and great nightly specials under $7. Open Mon.-Sat. 6:30am-3pm and 5-10pm, Sun. 6:30am-3pm.

Henry's, 54 N. Market St. (723-4363), at Anson. A local favorite. Not cheap, but the food is good, especially the grilled shrimp ($7.95). On weekends, live jazz upstairs starts at 9pm followed by a late-night breakfast. Open Mon.-Wed. 11:30am-10:30pm, Thurs.-Sun. 11:30am-1am.

Poogan's Porch, 72 Queen St., between King and Meeting St. Cajun cooking served in a tastefully restored city mansion. Sip iced tea on the veranda and pretend you're an authentic Charlestonian or Paul Newman, who has eaten here. Lunch is the only affordable meal ($6-8). Open daily 11:30am-2pm.

Alice's Restaurant, 973½ King St., at Cleveland, about 4 mi. north of downtown near Hampton Park and the Citadel. Southern cooking and reasonable burgers. Open Mon.-Thurs. 7:30am-10pm, Fri. 7:30am-12:30am, Sat. 11am-12:30am, Sun. 11am-7pm.

Before going out in Charleston, pick up a free copy of *Poor Richard's Omnibus,* available at grocery stores and street corners all over town; the PRO lists concerts and other events. Locals rarely dance the *Charleston* anymore, but night spots are anything but stodgy—even the ban on Sunday drinking has been lifted. Most bars and clubs are in the **Market Street** area. **Cafe 99,** 99 S. Meeting St. (577-4499), has nightly live entertainment, strong drinks ($2-4), and reasonably priced dinners ($4-7). (Open daily 11:30am-2am. No cover.) For the best bands go to **Myskyns Tavern,** 5 Faber St. (577-5595), near Market St., and have a drink ($1-3) at the enormous mahogany bar. For all-ages revelry try **Jukebox,** 4 Vendue Range (723-3431), which has an illuminated jukebox along one wall and a checkered dance floor. Or hang out with the locals on Friday and Saturday nights in front of **San Miguel's Mexican Restaurant** off Market St. (723-9745).

Sights and Events

Saturated with ancient homes, historical monuments, churches, galleries, and gardens, Charleston is a tourist's delight. A multitude of organized tours allow you to see the city by foot, car, bus, boat, trolley, or carriage. Several outfits have information and ticket centers near the visitors information center on Calhoun St.; others begin on Market St. near the historic district or along the waterfront. **Gray Line Water Tours** (722-1112) gives you your money's worth. Their two-hour boat rides leave daily at 10am, 12:30pm, and 3pm. (Fare $8. Reservations recommended.) For an appropriately old-fashioned view of the city, **Charleston Carriage**, 96 N. Market St. (577-0042), provides 50-minute horse-drawn tours of the city, starting from Buggy Whip Gift Shop (Fare $9, children $4.50; tours daily 9am-sunset). There is a free shuttle service from the visitors information center and downtown hotels. Before you start touring, though, see *Dear Charleston,* an internationally acclaimed documentary on the city's history recounted through the musings of long-time residents. The fast-paced, offbeat film is shown daily on the hour from 10am to 4pm (except 1pm) at the **Preservation Society Visitor Center,** 147 King St. (723-4381), and at **Dear Charleston Theater & Gifts,** 52 N. Market St. (577-4743; admission at both places $3.25, children $1.75). Matt gives it a thumbs up; Kevin gives it two snaps in a circle. The **Gibbes Gallery,** 135 Meeting St. (722-2706), has a fine collection of portraits by prominent American artists. (Open Sun.-Mon. 1-5pm, Tues.-Sat. 10am-5pm. Admission $2, seniors and students $1, children 50¢.)

The **Nathanial Russell House,** 51 Meeting St. (723-3646), features a magnificent staircase that spirals without support from floor to floor, giving an idea of how Charleston's wealthy merchant class lived in the early 19th century. The **Edmonston-Allston House,** 21 E. Battery St. (722-3405), looks out over Charleston Harbor. (Both open Mon.-Sat. 10am-5pm, Sun. 2-5pm. Admission to 1 house $4, to both $6. Get tickets to both homes at 52 Meeting St.) Founded in 1773, the **Charleston Museum,** 360 Meeting St. (722-2996), has a collection that ranges from natural history specimens to old sheet music, most connected in some way with the city. It also offers combination tickets for the museum itself and the three historic homes within easy walking distance: the **Aiken-Rhett Mansion** built in 1817; the 18th-century **Heyward-Washington House,** 87 Church St. (722-0354); and the **Joseph Manigault House,** 350 Meeting St. (722-2996). The Washington House includes the only 18th-century kitchen open to the public in Charleston. (Museum open Mon.-Sat. 9am-5pm, Sun. 1-5pm. Aiken-Rhett open daily 10am-5pm. Washington and Manigault both open Mon.-Sat. 10am-5pm, Sun. 1-5 pm. Admission to all 4 facilities $9, any 3 $7.)

A visit to Charleston just wouldn't be complete without a boat tour to **Fort Sumter** (722-1691), in the harbor. South Carolina, the first state to secede from the Union, started the Civil War by attacking this Union fortress on April 12, 1861. Over seven million pounds of metal were fired against the fort before those inside fled in February 1865. Tours ($7.50, ages 6-12 $3.75) leave several times daily from the Municipal Marina, at the foot of Calhoun St. and Lockwood Blvd. **Fort Sumter Tours,**the company that operates the tour boats to the fort, also offers tours to **Patriots' Point,** the world's largest naval and maritime museum. Here you can walk the decks of the retired U.S. aircraft carrier *Yorktown,* or pet the destroyer *Laffey's* huge fore and aft cannons.

If you are feeling a tad gun-shy, visit the **City Market,** downtown at Meeting St., which has an open air market daily from 9:30am to sunset. Vendors sell everything from porcelain sea animals to handwoven sweetgrass baskets.

Magnolia Gardens, (571-1266), 10 mi. out of town on Hwy. 61 off Rte. 17, is the 300-year-old ancestral home of the Drayton family, and treats visitors to 50 acres of gorgeous gardens with 900 varieties of camelia and 250 varieties of azalea. Get lost in the hedge maze. You'll probably want to skip the manor house, but do consider renting bicycles ($3 per hr.) to explore the neighboring swamp and bird sanctuary. (Open Sun.-Wed. 8am-6:30pm, Thurs.-Sat. 8am-8pm. Admission $7, seniors $6, teens $5, children $3.)

From mid-March to mid-April, the **Festival of Houses** (723-1623) celebrates Charleston's architecture and tradition, as many private homes open their doors to the public. Music, theater, dance, and opera converge on the city during **Spoleto Festival USA** (722-2764) in late May and early June. During **Christmas in Charleston** (723-7641), tours of many private homes and buildings are given, and many motels offer special reduced rates.

SOUTH CENTRAL

The land of Dixie got its name in the 1830s when Northern sailors traveling up the Mississippi River came back home with pockets full of foreign currency from Louisiana. The word "DIX" marked these ten dollar bank notes, reflecting southern Louisiana's French-speaking heritage; eventually the whole southern region along the river became known as "Dixie." A now-famous song of the same name was written in 1859, just before the Civil War, becoming a Southern battle hymn throughout the "War Between the States."

While the South no longer keeps separate currency, neither French nor Confederate, the region's separate culture persists. Well-known for their distinctive tastes, from grits to barbecue to Cajun crawfish, the states of Alabama, Arkansas, Kentucky, Louisiana, Mississippi, and Tennessee have also produced many of the nation's most original sounds—notably country, bluegrass, jazz, the blues, and the first riffs of rock 'n' roll. Hospitality also remains a trademark of the south central states; storekeepers usually send off customers with one "y'all"ism or another. A corresponding lack of hustle and bustle pervades even urban centers like Memphis and New Orleans. Overwhelmingly rural and agricultural, the region's wide-open spaces and lush, near-tropical forests make it one of the most beautiful parts of the country.

Travel

Seasonal fluctuations in travel in the South mean you can plan your trip either to join or avoid the crowds. Besides extraordinary Mardi Gras, many festivals and special events energize the area from March through September.

Greyhound/Trailways serves the region fairly comprehensively. However, many of the more remote locations, in Mississippi and Alabama especially, are served only once daily.

Amtrak is less reliable; many of the less populated areas are not served at all and several of the routes between larger towns and cities run only three times per week. Once-daily schedules cut through central Alabama to Atlanta, GA, north through central Mississippi to Memphis, TN, and Chicago, IL, and west along the Gulf Coast of Louisiana to Houston, TX. Arkansas is served on a St. Louis, MO, to Dallas, TX, run, Northern Kentucky has service, as well. Central and southern Georgia remain unserved.

Spend the extra money to rent a car, even for only a few days, in order to see the countryside. Take every opportunity to drive through rural areas on the (often poorly maintained) state and country roads. Farms are gradually being consolidated by large corporate owners, often making the landscape appear curiously devoid of residents. However, this slow erosion of the traditional way of life may be hard for the outside observer to spot. To those accustomed to a more developed United States, it often looks as if the lush rural hamlets haven't changed in decades. When behind your own steering wheel, don't try to make time near small towns since speed traps are not uncommon.

Apart from camping, there are few bargains on accommodations. The only hostels worthy of note are near the Blue Ridge Mountains, the Smokies, and in New Orleans. Look for budget hotel chains such as Motel 6, Days Inn (800-325-2525), and Econolodge (800-446-6900) on the outskirts of cities. **State parks** with camp-sites are fairly plentiful throughout the South; **national forests** dot the region, offering remote campgrounds and free primitive camping in unspectacular surroundings. Make room or campsite reservations when planning to visit betweeen March and September; local festivals held then often draw huge crowds.

South Central

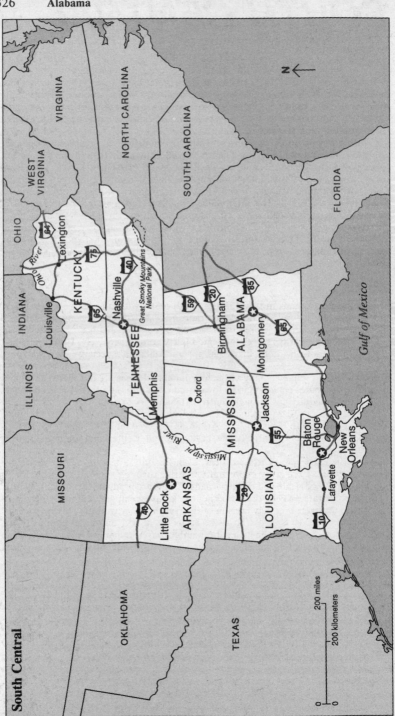

Alabama

Red clay earth and kudzu, a leafy vine that can grow one foot in length per day, extend throughout Alabama down to the Gulf of Mexico, though the state's name comes from the Native American word **Alibamo** meaning "thicket clearers." Yet this does little to clarify a surprisingly varied state; the northern part of Alabama alone contains wild Appalachian forests and Huntsville, a small city which has the NASA Space and Rocket Center and Space Camp. Alabama has also proved a focal point of the ongoing African American struggle for civil rights, from Rosa Parks refusing to relinquish her seat at the front of a Montgomery bus to Rev. Martin Luther King Jr.'s march from Selma. Today, while progressing even further economically and socially, this state in the "Heart of Dixie" maintains its untamed wilderness and hospitable charm.

Practical Information

Capital: Montgomery.

Tourist Information: Alabama Bureau of Tourism and Travel, 532 S. Perry St. (261-4169; 800-252-2262 outside AL). Open Mon.-Fri. 8am-5pm. **Travel Council, 600 Adams Ave. #254,** Montgomery 36104 (263-3407). **Division of Parks,** 64 N. Union St., Montgomery 36130 (800-252-7275).

Time Zone: Central (1 hr. behind Eastern). **Postal Abbreviation:** AL.

Birmingham

Literally and figuratively, the steel industry built Birmingham, drawing on the coal, iron ore, and limestone which exist naturally in the area's soil. Founded in 1871, the "Magic City" grew rapidly, its population more than tripling between 1900 and 1920. Today, Birmingham's supernatural growth has shot off in different directions. No longer an industrial town, the city's largest employer is the University of Alabama in Birmingham, which includes one of the best hospitals in the U.S., known for pioneering work in heart surgery.

No small-town Southern city, nearly a million people occupy Birmingham's metropolitan area. The city has risen a long way from the days of former police commissioner Eugene "Bull" Connor and his highly publicized racist attacks on nonviolent black protesters in 1963; Birmingham's first African-American mayor, Richard Arrington, has held office for over ten years.

Practical Information

Emergency: 911.

Visitor Information: Birmingham Visitor's Center, 1200 University Blvd. (254-1654). Maps, calendars, and coupons for accommodations. Open Mon.-Sat. 8:30am-5pm, Sun 1-5pm. Another location at the lower level of **Birmingham Municipal Airport** (254-1640), located east of downtown off Airport Hwy. Open daily 8:30am-8pm. **Greater Birmingham Convention and Visitors Bureau** in the **Chamber of Commerce,** 2027 1st Ave N., 3rd floor (252-9825), downtown. Open Mon.-Fri. 8:30am-5pm. For updated information on city events call **Funline,** 939-3866.

Amtrak: 1819 Morris Ave. (324-3033 or 800-872-7245), downtown. To: Montgomery ($11), Mobile ($53), and Atlanta ($30). Open daily 8:30am-4:30pm.

Greyhound/Trailways: 624 19th Ave. N. (252-7171). To: Montgomery ($14), Mobile ($38), and Atlanta ($19). Open 24 hr.

Public Transport: Metropolitan Area Express (MAX), 252-0101. Runs Mon.-Sat. 7am-6pm. Fare 80¢. **Downtown Area Runabout Transit (DART)** (252-0101), downtown area only if you can't tell. Runs Mon.-Fri. 10am-4pm. Fare 25¢.

Taxi: Yellow Cab of Birmingham, 252-1131. Base fare $1, $1.10 each additional mi.

Help Lines: Crisis Center, 323-7777. Rape Response, 323-7273.

Post Office: 351 24th St. N. (521-0209). Open Mon.-Fri. 7:30am-7pm. ZIP code: 35203.

Area Code: 205.

Birmingham reaches the rest of the country via three major highways: I-20 runs east to Atlanta; I-65 extends north to Nashville; and I-59 reaches northeast to Chattanooga, TN and southwest to Tuscaloosa. The downtown area grid system has avenues running east-west and streets running north-south. Major cultural and government buildings surround Linn Park, located between 19th and 21st St. N. on 7th Ave. N. The University of Alabama in Birmingham (UAB) extends along University Blvd. and 8th Ave. S. from 11th to 20th St.

Accommodations and Camping

Passport Inn, 820 20th St. S. (252-8041), 2 blocks from UAB. Large, clean rooms, tasteful decor in a convenient location. Singles $28. Doubles $33.

Ranch House, 2127 7th Ave. S. (322-0691). Near busy bars and restaurants; certainly not what it's name would suggest. Pleasant rooms with satellite TV. Pool. Singles $28. Doubles $35.50.

Economy Inn, 2224 5th Ave. N. (324-6688). Near some run-down buildings in the middle of downtown; not a great area at night. Sufficient rooms in a large hotel with an Indian restaurant downstairs. Singles $24. Doubles $29.

Oak Mountain State Park (663-3061), 15 mi. south of Birmingham off I-65 in Pelham. Heavily forested area with 85-acre recreational lake. Sites $8.25 for 1-4 people, with electricity $11.

Birmingham South KOA, 1235 Hwy. 33, (664-8832), 8 mi. south of I-459 on I-65 S. in Pelham. Pool, playground, and store. Sites $14, with full hookup $16.

Food

Just as coal and iron ore enrich Birmingham's soil, the city's restaurants are rich with food to satisfy any budget traveler. Right. In any case, barbecue remains the local specialty, although more ethnic variations have sprung up downtown. Explore Birmingham's inexpensive cosmopolitan options Five Points South, located at the intersection of Highland Ave. and 20th St. S. From pesto pizza with sun-dried tomatoes ($2 per slice) at Cosmo's Pizza, 2012 Magnolia Ave. (930-9971), to health-conscious vegetarian lunches, natural footware, and groceries at The Golden Temple 1901 11th Ave. S. (933-6333), between Birmingham's Five Points sandwiches the city's culinary diversity.

Café Bottega, 2240 Highland Ave. S. High red walls inside a sophisticated café. Fresh bread to dip in olive oil and Italian specialties brimming with fresh vegetables and herbs. Marinated pasta with sweet peas and mint $5.25. Open Mon.-Fri. 11am-11pm, Sat. 5-11pm.

Bogue's, 3028 Clairmont Ave. Short-order diner. *The* place for a true Southern brunch (cheese omelette with grits and biscuit, $3). Always busy weekend mornings. Open Mon.-Fri. 6am-2pm, Sat.-Sun. 6am-11:30am.

Hickory Pit, Cahaba Heights and White Oak Dr., Cahab Heights exit off Hwy. 280 S. Specializes in smoky barbecue chicken with your choice of red or white sauce $4. Owner's picture adorns one wall. Open Mon.-Thurs. 7am-8pm, Fri.-Sat. 7am-9pm.

Pita Stop, 1106 11th St. S., near UAB and Five Points. Delicious Middle Eastern and vegetarian specialties, felafel sandwiches ($4.25), and dinner plates ($6-8). Open Mon.-Thurs. 11am-9:30pm, Fri.-Sat. 11am-2pm and 5-10:30pm, Sun 11:30am-7:30pm.

Ollie's, 515 University Blvd., near Green Springs Hwy. True Bible Belt dining in an enormous 50s-style building. Pamphlets query "Is there really a Hell?" while you lustfully consume your beef. Sandwich $1.75, homemade pie $1.50. Open Mon.-Sat. 9:30am-8pm.

Sights

The remnants of Birmingham's steel industry are not easy to overlook, best exemplified by the gigantic **Sloss Furnaces National Historic Landmark** (324-1911), adjacent to the 1st Ave. N. viaduct off 32nd St. downtown. Though the blast furnaces closed 20 years ago, they now stand as the only preserved example of 20th-century iron-making in the world. Concerts, both rock and classical, are often molten here at night. (Open Tues.-Sat. 10am-4pm, Sun. noon-4pm. Free guided tours Sat.-Sun. at 1, 2, and 3pm.) Not Mr. Spock, but the Roman god of metal working, **Vulcan,** Valley Ave. at Hwy. 31 (328-6198), overwhelms Birmingham's skyline as the largest cast-iron statue in the world. Second only among statues to Lady Liberty in height, visitors can ride up this tribute to the city's steel industry and survey the city from its observation deck. The glowing torch that Vulcan carries has nothing directly to do with pig iron; instead it flies red when a car fatality has occured that day, remaining green when none occur. (Open daily 8am-10:30pm. Admission $1, under 6 free.)

Perhaps Birmingham's most famous landmark of the Civil Rights movement is the **Sixteenth Street Baptist Church,** 1530 6th Ave. N. (251-9402) at 16th St. N. In September 1963, months after a protest push which culminated in Martin Luther King's famous "Letter from a Birmingham Jail," white segregationists bombed the church, killing four black girls. Just the latest of bombings in so-called "Bombingham," the deaths spurred many protests at the church and in nearby **Kelly-Ingram Park,** at the corner of 5th Ave. and 16th St. N. Today a bronze statue of Martin Luther King, Jr. peacefully stands in the park; a **Civil Rights Museum** is scheduled to open next door to the park in late 1991.

Facing equally refreshing and urban **Linn Park,** the **Birmingham Museum of Art,** 2000 8th Ave. N. (254-2565), is currently undergoing an adventurous multi-million dollar renovation. The museum has U.S. paintings and English Wedgwood ceramics, as well as a superb collection of African textiles and sculpture, making it one of the most comprehensive exhibits in the Southeast.

Antebellum **Arlington,** 331 Cotton Ave. (780-5656), southwest of downtown, houses a fine array of Southern decorative arts from the 19th century. Go west on 1st Ave. N., which becomes Cotton Ave. to reach the stately white Greek Revival building which also hosts craft fairs throughout the year. (Open Tues.-Sat. 10am-4pm, Sun. 1-4pm. Admission $3, children $2.)

To learn more about the geology of the area, visit the **Red Mountain Museum and Cut,** 1421 22nd St. S. (933-4104). You can wander a walkway above the highway to see the different layers of rock formations inside Red Mountain, and maybe even excavate a fossil or two. The museum indoors has various exhibits on the prehistoric inhabitants of Alabama. (Open Tues.-Sat. 10am-4:30pm, Sun. 1-4:30pm. Admission $1.)

More lively creatures inhabit the **Birmingham Zoo,** 2630 Cahaba Rd. (879-0408), which features special exhibits on different predators and the behavior of social animals. Take zoo exit from U.S. 280 E. (Open daily 9:30am-5pm. Admission $3, children $1.50.) The zoo neighbors the **Birmingham Botanical Gardens,** 2612 Lane Park Rd. (879-1576). Look for the enormous greenhouse and elegant Japanese gardens, and the giant carp which fill its streams. (Open daily dawn-dusk. Free.)

Entertainment and Nightlife

Football fans make up Birmingham, or at least fill it on weekends when the University of Alabama plays at **Legion Field** (251-0537). If football isn't your game, you can catch the **Birmingham Barons** playing baseball at the Hoover Metropolitan Stadium, off I-459 beyond the Galleria Shopping Center, from spring to fall. (Admission $4.50.)

The historic **Alabama Theater,** 1817 3rd Ave. N. (251-0418), shows old movies on occasional weekends throughout the year. Their organ, the "Mighty Wurlitzer," usually entertains the audience before each showing. (Shows Fri.-Sat. at 7pm, Sun.

at 2pm. Admission $4, seniors $3, under 12 $2.) Pick up a free copy of *Fun and Stuff* or see the "Kudzu" in the Friday edition of *The Birmingham Post Herald* for listings of all movies, plays, and clubs in the area.

The **Five Points South** (or **Southside**) area has a high concentration of nightclubs. On cool summer nights many people grab outdoor tables in front of their favorite bars or just hang out by the fountain. Use caution here, and avoid parking or walking in dark alleys near the square; recent crimes in the area have even kept many longtime patrons away from the Southside.

Though not yet homonymous, Birmingham is becoming synonymous with live music. Those lucky enough to visit Birmingham in the middle of June for **City Stages** (251-1272) will hear everything from country to gospel to big name rock groups, with headliners such as Chuck Berry and Bo Diddley. The three-day festival also includes food, crafts, and children's activities. (Weekend pass $5.) For the hippest licks year-round check out **The Nick,** 2514 10th Ave. S. (252-3831). The poster-covered exterior asserts "the Nick . . . rocks." (Open Mon.-Sat. Live music nightly. Cover $2-5.) For jazz, blues, and even occasional Cajun music, the laid-back **Grundy's Music Room,** 1924 4th Ave. N. (323-3109), actually a basement club, has frequent guest artists. (Open Tues.-Sat. 3pm-until. Call for performance times and cover.) When Grundy's doesn't offer live tunes, you're better off with **The Burly Earl,** 2109 7th Ave. S. (322-5848), specializing in fried finger foods and local acoustic, blues, and sometimes rock sounds. (Restaurant open Mon.-Thurs. 10am-midnight, Fri.-Sat. 10am-2am. Live music Wed.-Thurs. 8:30pm-midnight, Fri.-Sat. 9:30pm-2am.)

Montgomery

Not only Alabama's geographic center, Montgomery is and always has been the state's political one, as well. Once the capital of the Confederacy in 1861, this former slave-holding town became the focus of the nationwide civil rights effort a century later, culminating in Martin Luther King's triumphant 1965 march from Selma to the steps of the state capitol. The close proximity of the Dexter Baptist Curch where Reverend King was pastor, the capitol building, and the newly unveiled Civil Rights Memorial testify to the struggles of African Americans here. Also the home of the Wright brothers' first flight school, which is now the Maxwell Air Force Base, Montgomery is a town of many diverse elements deeply rooted in its political heritage.

Practical Information

Emergency: 911.

Visitor Information: Visitor Information Center, 220 N. Hull St. (262-0013). Open Mon.-Fri. 8:30am-5pm, Sat.-Sun. 9am-4pm. **Chamber of Commerce,** 41 Commerce St. (834-5200). Open Mon.-Fri. 8am-5pm.

Travelers Aid: 265-0568. Operated by Salvation Army 24 hr.

Greyhound/Trailways: 210 S. Court St. (264-4518). To: Birmingham (8 per day, 3 hr., $14); Mobile (9 per day, 4 hr., $25); Tuskegee (2 per day, 1 hr., $6.50). Open 24 hr.

Public Transport: Montgomery Area Transit System (MATS), 701 N. McDonough St. (262-7321). Operates throughout the metropolitan area Mon.-Sat. 6am-5pm. Fare 80¢, transfers 10¢.

Taxi: Yellow Cab, 262-5225. $2.05 first mi., $1 each additional mi.

Help Lines: Council Against Rape, 264-7273. **Help-A-Crisis,** 279-7837. **Emergency Road Assistance,** 242-4128.

Post Office: 135 Catoma St. (244-7576). Open Mon.-Fri. 8am-5pm, Sat. 8am-noon. **ZIP code:** 36104.

Area Code: 205.

Montgomery is located at the intersection of I-65 and I-85, in south central Alabama, 91 mi. south of Birmingham, 192 mi. north of Mobile and the Gulf Coast. The downtown follows a grid pattern: **Madison Avenue** and **Dexter Avenue** are the major east-west routes; **Perry Street** and **Lawrence Street** run north-south.

Accommodations and Food

Accommodations are easy to procure for those with a car; I-65 at the Southern Blvd. exit overflows with cheap beds. Two well-maintained budget motels centrally located downtown are the **Capitol Inn,** 205 N. Goldthwaite St. (265-0541), at Heron St. near the bus station on a hill overlooking the city (singles $25, doubles $30) and the venerable, somewhat comfortable **Town Plaza,** 743 Madison Ave. (269-1561), at N. Ripley St. (singles $19, doubles $24). The Plaza, actually closer to the capitol, allows only adults. **The Inn South,** 4243 Inn South Ave. (288-7999), has nice new rooms, but is a 10-minute drive from downtown. (Rooms $27.) **KOA Campground,** ¼ mi. south of Hope Hull exit (288-0728), is 4 mi. from town and has a pool. (Tent sites $10, with water and electricity $14.)

There is rarely an empty seat for the Southern cooking at **The Farmer's Market Cafeteria,** 315 N. McDonough St. Free iced tea and ice cream comes with every inexpensive meal ($3-4). (Open Mon.-Fri. 5am-2pm.) **Chris's Hot Dogs,** 138 Dexter Ave., with over 70 years under its belt, is an even more extablished Montgomery institution. This small diner serves gourmet hot dogs ($1.20-2) and thick Brunswick stew ($1.50). (Open Mon.-Thurs. 8:30am-8pm, Fri. 8:30am-9pm, Sat. 10am-8pm.) For good Chinese food in Montgomery, try **The China Bowl,** 701 Madison Ave (832-4004), two blocks from the Town Plaza Motel. Fast food cooks in two giant woks 5 ft. from your nose. The inexpensive, large portions include a daily special of one entree, rice, egg roll, and a wonton ($3.75); take-out available. (Open Mon.-Thurs. 11am-9pm, Fri. 11am-9:30pm.)

Sights and Entertainment

Montgomery's newest, most powerful, and longest overdue sight, is the **Civil Rights Memorial,** 400 Washington Ave. at Hull St. Maya Lin, the Vietnam Memorial architect, also designed this dramatic, though minimal tribute to 40 men, women, and children who died fighting for civil rights. The outdoor monument bears names and dates of significant events on a circular black marble table over which water and flowers of remembrance continuously flow; a wall frames the table with Martin Luther King's words, " . . . Until Justice rolls down like waters and righteousness like a mighty stream." (Open daily.) The legacy and life of African American activism and faith can also be seen one block away at the **Dexter Avenue King Memorial Baptist Church,** 454 Dexter Ave. (263-3970), where King preached. At this 112-year-old church, Reverend King and other civil rights leaders organized the 1955 Montgomery bus boycott; 10 years later King would lead a nationwide civil rights march past this church to the Montgomery capitol. The basement mural chronicles the evolution of King and the nation's struggle during the 1960s. (Open Mon.-Fri. 8:30am-4pm. Free. Tours available.)

Three blocks north is **Old Alabama Town,** 310 N. Hull St. at Madison (263-4355), an artfully maintained historic district of 19th-century buildings. The complex includes a pioneer homestead, an 1892 grocery, a schoolhouse, an early African American church, and a freed slave's house. (Open Mon.-Sat. 9:30am-3:30pm, Sun. 1:30-3:30pm. Admission $5, ages 5-18 $1.50.)

While the **State Capitol** is closed to the public until late 1992 for restoration, visit the nearby **Alabama State History Museum and State Archives,** 624 Washington Ave. (261-4361). On exhibit are many Native American artifacts along with early military swords and medals. Stop by "Grandma's Attic" where you can try on antique furs and play with Tinker Toys. (Open Mon.-Fri. 8am-5pm, Sat.-Sun. 9am-5pm. Free.) Next door to the Archives is the elegant **First White House of** the **Confederacy,** 644 Washington Ave. (261-4624), which contains many original furnishings from Jefferson Davis's Confederate presidency. (Open Mon.-Fri. 8am-4:30pm, Sat.-Sun. 9am-4:30pm. Free.) Another restored home of interest is the **F. Scott and Zelda Fitzgerald Museum,** 919 Felder Ave. (262-1911), off Carter Hill Rd. Zelda, originally from Montgomery, lived here with Scott from October 1931 to April 1932. The museum contains a few of her paintings and some of his original manuscripts, as well as their strangely monogrammed bath towels. (Open Wed.-Sat. 10am-2pm.)

Fifteen minutes southeast of the downtown area is the **Montgomery Museum of Fine Arts,** 1 Museum Dr. (244-5700), off Woodmere Blvd. This attractive museum houses a substantial collection of 19th- and 20th-century paintings and graphics, as well as a unique interactive children's exhibit called "Artworks." (Open Tues.-Wed. and Fri.-Sat. 10am-5pm, Thurs. 10am-9pm, Sun. noon-5pm. Free.) Next door, also in **Wynton M. Blount Cultural Park,** is the **Alabama Shakespeare Festival,** 1 Festival Dr. (277-2273), one of the most remarkable sights in the South. This $22 million professional complex attracts some of the best Shakespearean actors and scholars in the world. The Festival, set in an English country park, stages a variety of plays including Broadway shows.

Entertainment in Montgomery does not end with the Bard, however. Get hammered at **The Rusty Nail,** 4115 Norman Bridge Rd. (288-6654), about a 10-minute drive directly south of downtown, where live rock bands play on weekends. (Open Mon.-Sat. 4pm-until.) For jazz or blues try **1048,** 1048 E. Fairview Ave. (834-1048), near Woodley Ave. (Open Mon.-Fri. 4pm-until and Sat. 6pm-until.) For further information on events in the city, call the chamber of commerce's 24-hr. **FunPhone** (265-2783).

Tuskegee

Late in the 19th century, after the Reconstruction, southern states segregated and disenfranchised "emancipated" African Americans. Booker T. Washington, himself a former slave, believed that African Americans could best combat repression through self-education and learning a trade. As a result, the curriculum at Washington's college, now **Tuskegee University,** revolved around practical endeavors such as agriculture and carpentry, with students constructing almost all of the campus buildings. Artist, teacher, and scientist George Washington Carver became head of the Agricultural Department at Tuskegee discovering he could prepare a full, varied meal using only the peanut.

Today more academically oriented Tuskegee covers over 160 acres and more subjects than ever; the buildings of Washington's original institute also comprise a national historical site. A walking tour of the campus begins at the **Carver Museum,** with the **Visitor Orientation Center** (727-6390) inside. (Both open daily 9am-4:30pm. Free.) **The Oaks,** Old Montgomery Rd., down the street from the museum, is a restored version of Washington's home. Free tours from the museum begin on the hour. (Free.)

Visitors can stay on campus in **Dorothy Hall,** 1212 Old Montgomery Rd. (727-8753; singles $24; doubles $28; rooms with shared bath and no A/C $11.) Reservations are advisable, since often there are no vacancies. During the academic year, the **Dorothy Hall Cafeteria** serves breakfast Mon.-Fri. 7:30-9am and lunch Mon.-Fri. 11:30am-1pm. For good cafeteria-style home cooking, try **Pierce's,** near the intersection of Fonville and E. Martin L. King Dr. a few blocks from campus. The vegetable plate ($2.50) or baked chicken with dressing ($2) are good bets. (Open Mon.-Fri. 7am-5pm, Sat. 7am-noon.)

To get to Tuskegee, take I-85 toward Atlanta and exit at Rte. 81 south. Turn right at the intersection of Rte. 81 and Old Montgomery Rd. (Rte. 126). **Greyhound** also has frequent service from Montgomery (1 hr., $6.50).

Tuskegee's **ZIP code** is 36083; the **area code** is 205.

Mobile

Mobile (pronounced mo-BEEL) is the South's best-kept secret; the splendor of its antebellum mansions, the serenity of its azalea-lined streets, and the warmth of both its climate and its people are enticing. The oldest of the major cities in Alabama, Mobile has an eclectic past, realized in its buildings. Named for the Maubilla tribe, but a French colony until 1718, Mobile's many influences can also be seen (for free) in the distinct Spanish and English architecture and in the forts around the city.

Mobile's location on the Gulf of Mexico has led to international invasion and international heritage. In many ways Mobile resembles the Mississippi Coast and New Orleans more than it does the rest of Alabama. Beautiful beaches are less than an hour away, and in fact, the first U.S. Mardi Gras took place in Mobile; the celebration still goes on here every year, but on a much smaller scale than in New Orleans.

Practical Information

Emergency: 911.

Visitor Information: Fort Condé Information Center, 150 S. Royal St. (434-7304), in a reconstructed French fort near Government St. Open daily 8am-5pm. **Mobile Convention and Visitors Bureau,** 1 St. Louis Center #2002 (433-5100; 800-662-6282 outside AL). Open Mon.-Fri. 8am-5pm.

Travelers Aid: 438-1625. Operated by the Salvation Army; ask for Travelers Services. Lines open Mon.-Fri. 9am-4:30pm.

Greyhound/Trailways: 201 Government Blvd. (432-1861), at S. Conception downtown. To: New Orleans (3 hr., $24); Montgomery (4 hr., $25); Birmingham (6 hr., $34). Open 24 hr.

Public Transport: Mobile Transit Authority (MTA), 344-5656. Major depots are at Bienville Sq., St. Joseph, and Dauphin St. Operates Mon.-Sat. 6am-7pm. Fare 50¢.

Taxi: Yellow Cab, 432-7711.

Help Lines: Rape Crisis, 473-7273. **Crisis Counseling,** 666-7900. Open 24 hr.

Post Office: 250 Saint Joseph St. (694-5917). Open Mon.-Fri. 8am-4:30pm, Sat. 8am-noon. **ZIP code:** 36601.

Area Code: 205.

Mobile Bay, on the Gulf of Mexico, is about 135 mi. east of New Orleans. The downtown district fronts the Mobile River. **Dauphin Street** and **Government Boulevard** are the major east-west routes. **Royal Street** and **St. Joseph Street** are the north-south byways. Some of Mobile's major attractions lie outside downtown. The *U.S.S. Alabama* is off the causeway leading out of the city; Dauphin Island is 30 mi. south.

Accommodations and Camping

Accommodations are both reasonable and accessible, but stop at the Fort Condé Information Center first; they'll make reservations for you at a 10 to 15% discount. The MTA runs a "Government St." bus regularly which reaches the Government St. motels listed below, but they are all within a 15-minute walk from downtown. For information on the area's many B&Bs, contact **Bed and Breakfast Mobile,** P.O. Box 66261, Mobile 36606 (205-473-2939).

Towne House Inn, 1061 Government St. (438-4653). Sterile but tidy rooms. Singles from $17. Doubles from $27, depending on number of people.

Economy Inn, 1119 Government St. (433-8800). Big beds, clean sheets, and dark-panelled walls. Try to get a ground floor room. Singles $18. Doubles $26.

Heart of Mobile Inn, 559 Government St. (433-0590). Dingy, cheap-looking, but sufficient rooms. Not quite in the heart of the city, but close—near the kidneys maybe. Singles $20. Doubles $25.

I-10 Kampground, 400 Theodore Dawes Rd. E. (653-9816), 7½ mi. west on I-10 (exit 13). No public transportation. Pool and laundry facilities. Sites $12.

Food

Because Mobile is on the gulf both seafood and southern cookin' are regional specialties. As well-known for its atmosphere as for its oysters ($5 for a dozen on the half shell), **Wintzels,** 605 Dauphin St., 6 blocks west of downtown, is covered inside with old anecdotes and sayings. A sign ouside boldly states, "We are famous for absolutely nothing although business is good." Elsewhere on Dauphin St., business also thrives at the newly opened **Mayer's,** 278 Dauphin St., two blocks west of Bienville Sq. Friendly service and southern fried chicken at good prices are this diner's specialties. Two pieces of chicken with fries and french bread are $3; also look for daily specials. (Open Mon.-Sat. 10am-10pm.) Closer to the water, **Argiro's,** 1320 Battleship Pkwy. (626-1060), next to the *U.S.S. Alabama,* provides cheap sandwiches ($2-3), southern specialties such as red beans and rice, and local color. Both businessmen and sailors frequent this small restaurant and country store. (Open daily 6am-10pm.)

Sights and Entertainment

Mobile encompasses four historic districts: **Church Street, DeToni Square, Old Dauphin Way,** and **Oakleigh Garden.** Each offers a unique array of architectural styles. The information center can give you maps for walking or driving tours of these former residences of cotton brokers and river pilots as well as the "shotgun" cottages of their servants.

Church St. divides into east and west subdistricts. The **Church Street East District,** closest to downtown, is the second-oldest of the districts. The homes showcase popular U.S. architectural styles of the mid- to late 19th century, including Federal, Greek Revival, Queen Anne, and Victorian. While on Church St., be sure and pass through the **Spanish Plaza,,** Hamilton and Government St., which honors Mobile's sibling city, Malaga, Spain while recalling Spain's early presence in Mobile. Also of interest in this area is the **Christ Episcopal Church,** 115 S. Conception St. (433-1842), opposite the tourist office at Fort Condé. Dedicated in 1842, the church contains beautiful German, Italian, and Tiffany stained glass windows.

In the **DeToni Historical District,** north of downtown, tour the tastefully restored **Richards-DAR House,** 256 North Joachim St. (434-7320), an award-winning example of antebellum Italianate architectural style. On slow days the staff may invite you in for tea and cookies. (Open Tues.-Sat. 10am-4pm, Sun. 1-4pm. Tours $2, children 50¢.) Brick townhouses with wrought-iron balconies fill the rest of the district.

Once a busy residential area, many houses near the historic district of **Old Dauphin Way** are now vacant. Attempts at revitalization, with new restaurants and clubs opening in the Victorian buildings, may bring new life to the area.

One of the most elegant buildings in Mobile is **Oakleigh,** 350 Oakleigh Place (432-1281) off Government St., with a cantilevered staircase and enormous windows that open onto all the balconies upstairs. Going away from downtown take a left on Roper St. Inside, a museum contains furnishings of the early Victorian, Empire, and Regency periods. (Open Mon.-Sat. 10am-4pm, Sun. 2-4pm. Tours every ½ hr.; last tour leaves at 3:30pm. Admission $4, seniors $3, college students with ID $2, children $1; tickets sold next door at the simple **Cox-Deasy House.**) For more information on Oakleigh's heyday and on other periods in Mobile's history visit the **Museum of the City of Mobile,** 355 Government St. (438-7569), which includes an exhibit of Mardi Gras queen costumes from the early 20th century.

The battleship *U.S.S. Alabama,* permanently moored at **Battleship Park** (433-2703), took part in every major World War II battle in the Pacific. The park is at the entrance of the Bankhead Tunnel, 2½ mi. east of town on I-10. Berthed along the port side of this intriguing ship is one of the most famous submarines of the war, the *U.S.S. Drum.* (Open daily 8am-sunset. Admission $5, ages 6-11 $2.50. Parking $1.)

Gray Line of Mobile (432-2229) leads interesting one-hour sight-seeing tours of the downtown historic areas from the **Fort Condé Information Center.** (Tours Mon.-Sat. at 10:30am and 2pm, Sun. at 2pm. Fare $7, children $3.)

For nighttime entertainment, stop in at **Trinity's Downtown,** 465 Auditorium Dr. (432-0000), where bands play rock and reggae Wednesday through Saturday nights. (Open Mon.-Thurs. 11am-midnight, Fri.-Sat. 11am-2am.) More live rock and reggae plays at **G.T. Henry's,** 462 Dauphin St. (432-0300), on a multi-layered stage. (Open Thurs.-Sat. from about 10pm. Small cover.) Two doors down is **Ivanhoe's,** 450-2 Dauphin St. (432-0400), where you can find the blues swimming alongside pool sharks. (Open Tues-Thurs. 3:30pm-1am, Mon. and Fri.-Sat. 7:30pm-2am. Small cover on weekends when bands play.)

For information on events and specific dates, call the 24-hr. recording **Tel-Events,** 342-0133.

Arkansas

Even as the smallest continental state in area west of the Mississippi, Arkansas stubbornly resists categorization. Though named for a mistranslated Native American word for "down river people," only the southeastern portion of the state resembles the flat, agricultural land of the Deep South. The rest of Arkansas has a little bit of everything: culturally autonomous Little Rock, a friendly community without all the grit, grime, or excitement of most big cities; Hot Springs, a resort town right out of the 1950s; the aptly named Eureka Springs, a pleasant surprise in the summer heat; and the rivers and hills of the breathtaking Ozark Mountains. For outdoorsfolk, this state offers some of the country's least crowded and most scenic national and state parks.

Practical Information

Capital: Little Rock.

Tourist Information: Arkansas Dept. of Parks and Tourism, 1 Capitol Mall, Little Rock 72201 (501-682-7777 or 800-643-8383).

Time Zone: Central (1 hr. behind Eastern). **Postal Abbreviation:** AR.

Little Rock

Abutting the Arkansas River, Little Rock serves as the political and geographical center of the state. In 1957, it served as the center of nationwide controversy, when Governor Orval Faubus led an often violent segregationist movement; using troops to prevent African American students from enrolling in Central High. The black "Little Rock Nine" enrolled only under national guard protection. Today an immaculate and integrated city surrounded by gently sloping hills, Little Rock rolls with a wealth of performing arts; unfortunately, as in other towns catering primarily to a yuppie crowd, entertainment for the budget traveler is limited. Take advice from the state license plate, which extols Arkansas as "The Natural State"—make like a stone and explore the nearby hills and waterways. After uncovering the history of the capital city's sights and homes, follow the paths to Hot Springs to the west and the Ozark Mountains to the northwest.

Practical Information

Emergency: 911.

Visitor Information: Arkansas Dept. of Parks and Tourism, 1 Capitol Mall (800-643-8383 or 800-482-8989 in-state), in a complex directly behind the capitol building. **Little Rock Bureau for Conventions and Visitors,** at Markham and Main St. (376-4781 or 800-844-7625), near the Greyhound station. Open Mon.-Fri. 9am-3:30pm; closed for lunch about 11:30am-12:30pm. **Telefun,** 372-3399. Activities listings for Little Rock.

Amtrak: Markham and Victory St. (372-6841 or 800-872-7245), near downtown. One train per day to St. Louis (7 hr., $65) and Dallas (7 hr., $72).

Greyhound/Trailways: 118 E. Washington St. (372-1861), across the river in North Little Rock. Use the walkway over the bridge to get downtown. Cab fare should run less than $4. To: St. Louis ($56 weekday); New Orleans ($61 weekday); and Memphis ($24 weekday). More expensive weekends.

Public Transport: Central Arkansas Transit (CAT), 614 Center St. (375-1163). Regular buses Mon.-Sat. every ½ hr. 6am-6:30pm. Very reliable service. Fare 80¢, transfers 10¢.

Taxi: Black and White Cab, (374-0333). Base fare 90¢, 90¢ each additional mi.

Help Lines: Rape Crisis, 375-5181. Open 24 hr. **First Call for Help,** 376-4567.

Post Office: 600 W. Capitol at 5th St. (377-6470). Open Mon.-Fri. 7am-5:15pm. **ZIP code:** 72201.

Area Code: 501.

Little Rock skips in the middle of Arkansas on I-40 just 140 mi. west of Memphis, and 335 mi. east of Oklahoma City. **I-30** also passes through Little Rock, 320 mi. northeast of Dallas. Most of Little Rock's streets were "planned" with no apparent pattern in mind. **Broadway** and **Main** are the major north-south arteries. **Markham** and all streets numbered one to 36 run east-west.

Accommodations and Camping

The Quapaw Inn Bed and Breakfast, 1868 S. Gaines St. (376-6873), 2 blocks west of 17th and Broadway. In a quaint Victorian house. Expensive for 1 person, but *the* place to stay for 2. Extremely friendly proprietor. Huge and delicious breakfast. (Rooms $35-45, each additional person $10.) Call in advance and ask for the *Let's Go* discount ($10).

Little Rock Inn, 6th and Center St. (376-8301), downtown. Large hotel with pool and saloon. Attractive rooms, often full. Singles $33. Doubles $38.

Econolodge, 322 E. Capitol (376-3661), downtown. Not a great neighborhood for women traveling alone. Spacious, spotless, and sunny rooms. Pool to beat the heat. Singles $27.50. Doubles $37.50.

Deluxe Inn, 308 E. Capitol (375-6411), next to Econolodge downtown. A step down in cleanliness, but spacious rooms with desk. Pool to boot. Singles $22. Doubles $28.

KOA Campground, Crystal Hill Rd. (758-4598), in North Little Rock 7 mi. from downtown between exit 12 on I-430 and exit 148 on I-48. Yet another pool. Sites from $16, with hookups $18.

Food

Though little distinguishes Little Rock's cuisine, the rice, chicken, and catfish that Arkansas produces beefs up its menus. Decent bargains smatter the city along with busy bars and live music.

Juanita's, 1300 S. Main St. The city's best Mexican food in a fun, loud, cantina atmosphere. Reasonable prices (entrees $6-10), nightly entertainment, and a hoppin' bar. Try Margarita night on Mon. ($1.75), or Sat. champagne brunch ($1.25 per glass). Hell, try 'em both. Open Mon.-Thurs. 11am-10pm, Fri. 11am-10:30pm, Sat. noon-10:30pm, Sun. 5:30-9pm.

The Los Angeles areas newest hostel....

The Santa Monica International AYH-Hostel

SANTA MONICA
INTERNATIONAL
AYH-HOSTEL

$ 12 per night for AYH/IYHF members

- 200 beds
- Recreation room
- T.V. lounge
- Library
- Self-serve kitchen
  & dining room
- Laundry room
- Open-air courtyard
- Traveler Information Center
- AYH Travel Store

- Located near many theaters &
  restaurants
- 7 miles from Los Angeles
  International Airport
- 3 blocks from Santa Monica
  Greyhound Bus Station
- Located near the Santa Monica
  beach & pier
- 1 mile from Venice Beach
- 8 miles from Malibu
- 15 miles from Hollywood

For more information or reservations, call or write :

Santa Monica International AYH-Hostel
1436 Second Street
Santa Monica, CA 90401
(213) 393-9913

American Youth Hostels

International Youth Hostel Federation Member

Solar Cafe, 1706 W. 3rd, across from Capitol. Former gas station and future energy source now specializing in healthy soups, sandwiches, and salads ($2.50-4). Open daily 7:30am-10pm.

Hungry's Cafe, 1001 W. 7th St. Raucous joint that revels in solid breakfasts as well as down-home lunch specials with 2 vegetables and bread for under $4. Good cap collection on the wall. Open Mon.-Fri. 6am-2pm.

The Oyster Bar, 3003 W. Markham St. Reasonably priced seafood and "Po'Boy" sandwiches ($4-5). Big screen TV, pool tables, cheap draft beer, and a decidedly laid-back atmosphere where paper towel rolls take the place of napkins. Open Mon.-Thurs. 11am-10pm, Fri.-Sat. 11am-10:30pm. Happy Hour Mon.-Fri. 3-6:30pm.

White Water Tavern, 2500 7th St. Popular gathering place and watering hole serving Southern cooking (full meal under $5). Try a foot-long hot dog ($2.50). Live music at night. Open Mon.-Sat. 11am-2am.

Center Street Cafe, 612 Center St. (372-9485). Blue-suited business luncheon spot. Home-cooked specialties like chicken-fried steak ($4.50), as well as sandwiches and salads. Entrees include 2 veggies and warm biscuits and run under $5. Open Mon.-Fri. 11am-2pm.

Sights

Little Rock's historic downtown district is known as the **Quapaw Quarter.** Pick up free walking tour guides at the **Quapaw Quarter District Office,** 1315 Scott St. (371-0075; open Mon.-Fri. 9am-5pm), or at the visitors bureau. These helpful guides have both labeled maps and brief histories of the historic buildings. Just one block away from the visitors bureau mopes the saucy **Old State House,** 300 W. Markham St. (371-1749), which served as the capitol from 1836 until the ceiling collapsed in 1899 while the legislature was in session. The restored building now provides a good starting point for a tour of downtown, with several engaging displays on the history of Arkansas. (Open Mon.-Sat. 9am-5pm, Sun. 1-5pm. Free.) The functioning **state capitol** (682-5080) at the west end of Capitol St. may look very familiar—it's actually a replica of the U.S. capitol in Washington, DC. Take a free self-guided tour or one of the 45-minute group tours given on the hour. (Open Mon.-Fri. 9am-4pm, Sat. 10am-5pm, Sun. 1-5pm. Call in advance on weekends.) For a look at the history of the townspeople of 19th-century Little Rock, visit the **Arkansas Territorial Restoration,** 214 E. Third St. (371-2348). Tours of four restored buildings include an old grog shop, and an exhibit of a typical old-fashoined print shop. (Open Mon.-Sat. 9am-5pm, Sun. 1-5pm. 50-min. tours every hr. on the hr. Admission $2, children $1. Free first Sun. of month.)

Along the banks of the Arkansas River, you'll find **Riverfront Park,** a pleasant place for a walk, and home to the legendary "Little Rock" itself. For the best access, go through the back of the Excelsior Hotel at Markham and Center St. It is easy to overlook the rock that juts out from the bank, and hard to believe that it once functioned as an important landmark for travelers going up the river. Take a ride on the paddle wheeler **Spirit** (376-4150; 1-hr. cruises $5, children $2.75; departing from the North Little Rock side of the Arkansas River Tues.-Sat. at 2pm). The town celebrates the waterway every year at **Riverfest,** on Memorial Day weekend.

A mile south of downtown is **MacArthur Park,** elegant home to several interesting museums and title of a great Donna Summer song. Particularly suited to children, the **Museum of Science and History,** housed in the old arsenal building where General Douglas MacArthur was born, has exhibits on Arkansas history. (Open Mon.-Sat. 9am-4:30pm, Sun. 1-4:30pm. Admission $1. Free Mon.) While in the park don't miss the **Arkansas Arts Center,** 9th and Commerce St. (372-400), and the **Decorative Arts Museum,** 7th and Rock St., the newest addition to the center and home to a collection of contemporary crafts. (Open Mon.-Sat. 10am-5pm, Sun. noon-5pm. Free.) The **War Memorial Park,** northwest of the state capitol off I-630 at Fair Park Blvd., houses the 40-acre **Little Rock Zoo** (666-2406), which simulates the animals' natural habitats. Most of the creatures can't tell the difference. But the elephant remembers. (Open daily 9:30am-4:30pm. Admission $1, children 50¢.)

The opening scene of *Gone With the Wind* features the **Old Mill Park,** Lakeshore Dr. at Fairway Ave. (682-7777) in North Little Rock, one of the city's most treasured attractions. The WPA constructed this water-powered grist mill during the Depression. (Open daily. Free.)

Archeologists are uncovering part of Arkansas' past that goes back much farther than the historic homes and parks, all the way to 700 AD. The **Toltec Mounds State Park** (961-9442), 15 mi. east of North Little Rock on Rte. 386, provided the political and religious center of the Plum Bayou people more than 1000 years ago. (Open Tues.-Sat. 8am-5pm, Sun. noon-5pm. Guided tours at 9:30am, 11am, 12:30pm, and 3:30pm. Admission $2, ages 6-15 $1.) Thirteen mi. west of Little Rock on Rte. 10 and then 2 mi. north on Rte. 300 is **Pinnacle Mountain State Park,** a fairly tame "wilderness park." After the moderately steep 1000-ft. climb to the top, you can take in a superb summit view. Look for fossils, and bring water on the hike. For more information, contact the Superintendent at Pinnacle Mountain State Park, R 1, Roland Rd., P.O. Box 34, Roland 72135 (868-5806). The park definitely merits a daytrip, but has no camping facilities.

Entertainment and Nightlife

Little Rock has an active cultural life, including a symphony, an opera, and community theaters. Conducted by Robert Henderson, the **Arkansas Symphony,** 2500 N. Tyler (666-1761), performs in Robinson Auditorium from September to May. (Tickets $9-20, students $3.)

The **Arkansas Opera Theatre** makes its new home at the **Wildwood Park for Performing Arts,** 20919 Denny Rd. (821-7275). Besides an opera festival in June, the park hosts children's theater and jazz concerts throughout the year. The professional **Arkansas Repertory Theatre,** at 6th and Main St. (378-0405), performs both conventional crowd-pleasers and avant-garde works. The **Community Theatre of Little Rock,** 1501 Maryland (376-4582), gives a series of family-oriented plays. For a change of pace, go see the **Rackensack Folklore Society** sing authentic Arkansas folk music at the Arkansas Arts Center. (First Mon. of each month at 7:30pm. Free.)

Live music plays almost nightly at a few spots around the city. Consult the free, bi-weekly *Spectrum,* or the *Nightflying* and *Today* monthlies to find out what's happening. Many good eateries also have good music. **Juanita's,** for example, has rock, reggae, and acoustic music Monday through Saturday, with a blues jam every Tuesday. The **Oyster Bar** gives good jazz every Monday ($3), and the **White Water Tavern** has down-home rock or country every night (See Food above for all three.)

Hot Springs

Get out of Little Rock and get to Hot Springs, an old-fashioned spa town in a national park established to preserve the natural springs. Bubbling up from the oak- and hickory-covered Hot Springs Mountain, the 143°F water totally purifies by the time it reaches the surface—NASA used the liquid to protect the Apollo mission moon rocks from bacteria. Hernando de Soto "discovered" the springs in 1541; Native Americans used Hot Springs many years previous as a neutral ground where many tribes met in peace. Since then, visitors from Franklin D. Roosevelt to Al Capone have come here to enjoy some peace of mind.

Hot Springs had its heyday in the 1920s, when the medicinal properties and healing powers of the springs made it one of the country's most popular resorts. The town has declined since the 40s, however; much like *Ghost,* the Patrick Swayze sleeper hit of the 1990 summer, today Hot Springs seems like a city that began to become a ghost town but changed its mind halfway through. There are some signs of revitalizing ectoplasm, however, with the national park, springs, and old-fashioned town definitely spiffy. The springs also provide one of the least expensive spa resorts in the nation.

The **Fordyce Bathhouse Visitor Center,** 300 Central Ave. (623-1433), offers information and fascinating tours on the surrounding wilderness areas and on the bathhouse itself, both of which are part of the Hot Springs National Park. The **Buckstaff** (623-2308) is the only bathhouse still functioning along the row. Baths are $9.50, massages $10. (Open Mon.-Fri. 7-11:45am and 1:30-3pm, Sat. 7-11:45am.) Down the street is the **Hot Springs Health Spa,** N. 500 Reserve (321-9664; bath $9, massage $12; open daily 9am-10pm).

When you're not bathing in the springs or hiking in the park, try cruising Lake Hamilton on the **Belle of Hot Springs** (525-4438), with one-hour narrated tours alongside the Ouachita Mountains and Lake Hamilton mansions. (Fare $7, children $3.25.) In town, the **Mountain Valley Spring Water Company,** 150 Central Ave. (623-6671), offers free samples and tours of its national headquarters. The **Magic Springs** amusement park, at 2001 Hwy. 70 E. (624-5411; 800-643-1212 outside AR), has a few musical shows and many children's rides. (Open summer Sun.-Fri. 10am-6pm, Sat. 10am-11pm. Admission $11, ages 3-11 $10.)

Nighttime family entertainment percolates throughout Hot Springs. The **Bathhouse Show,** 701 Central Ave. (623-1415), is a must-see two-hour comedy-musical-variety show tracing the history of Hot Springs musically, from the "boogie-woogie" years to the rock 'n' roll era. (Performances Tues.-Sun. at 8pm. Admission $7.50, seniors $7, children $3.75. Reservations required.) If you're just a little bit country, right in town the **Rocky Top Jubilee,** 1312 Central Ave. (623-7504), throws in some gospel and lots of comedy with the C&W. (Shows at 8pm. Admission $7.50, children $3.75. Reservations required.) A short drive out of town is the **Music Mountain Jamboree,** 3300 Albert Pike (767-3841) off Hwy. 270 W. Family-style country music shows take place nightly during the summer, and at various times throughout the year. (Shows at 8pm. Admission $8, children $4. Reservations required.)

Most of the town shuts down by dusk, but for late evening entertainment try the newly opened **Shucker's,** 801 Central Ave. (623-6200), in Spencer's Corner, which specializes in buckets and 40-oz. bottles of beer ($3.50).

Hot Springs has a number of small, inexpensive restaurants right in town. Snack on *beignets* (doughnuts without the hole; 75¢) and *café au lait* (75¢) at **Café New Orleans,** 210 Central Ave. (Open daily until 11:30pm. Live entertainment Fri. and Sat.) **Rod's Pizza Cellar,** at Spring and Broadway, serves delicious Italian specialties beneath bright neon for under $7. (Open Tues.-Thurs. 11am-10pm, Fri.-Sat. 11am-midnight, Sun. 11:30am-10pm.) For good 'ol country food, **Granny's Kitchen,** 332 Central Ave., has good deals on cheeseburgers with fries ($3) and granny's home-made pie. (Open daily from 7:30am.)

For the budget traveler who has a little stashed away in the ol' moneybelt, the **Arlington Hotel,** at Fountain and Central St. (623-7771), is a world-class resort—of yesteryear—at very reasonable rates. (Singles from $38. Doubles $48. Family rates with 2 double beds from $56.) Walk into a fairy tale at the **Best Motel,** 630 Ouachita (624-5736), which has gingerbread-like cabins, a storybook pool, and chairs for relaxing on the porch. (Singles $20. Doubles $30.) The **Perry Plaza Motel,** 1007 Park Ave. on Hwy. 7 (623-9814), offers air-conditioned suites with a bedroom, bathroom, and kitchen. (Sept.-Dec. and May $20; Feb.-April $40; off-season $22. Each additional person $5.) The motels clustered along Hwy. 7 and 88 have similar prices, although rates rise during the tourist season (Feb.-April); camping is far cheaper (see State Parks below).

Before touring Hot Springs, you should stop by the **visitors center,** downtown at the corner of Central and Reserve St. (624-3383), and pick up their valuable packet of coupons for many attractions and restaurants. Hot Springs becomes especially crowded during the horse racing season at nearby **Oaklawn** racetrack (Feb.-April): Don't get trampled in the stampede.

Hot Springs's **ZIP code** is 71901; the **area code** is 501.

State Parks Nearby

The 48,000-acre **Lake Ouachita Park** lies on the largest of three clear, beautiful, artificial lakes near Hot Springs. Travel 3 mi. west of Hot Springs on U.S. 270, then 12 mi. north on Rte. 227. Numerous islands lie just offshore where you can escape from civilization to enjoy the quiet coves and rocky beaches. Fishing is plentiful, and camping available from $5.50 per day (767-9366); fishing boats rent for $6 per day.

By car from Hot Springs you can readily reach **Lake Catherine Park,** which covers over 2000 acres of Ouachita Mountain, stretching along the shores of beautiful Lake Catherine. Campsites start at $5.50 per day (844-4176). Take exit 97 off I-30 at Malvern and go 12 mi. north on Rte. 171. (Canoe rentals $3.25 per hr., power boats $16 per ½ day, $24 per day.)

Ozarks

Beaten and worn by ages of weathering, one of the world's oldest mountain ranges now barely surpasses hill status in height. The terrain, however, is far more than just hilly with twisting switchback roads, steep scenic bluffs, and lush woods which make for a challenging vacationland. Ozark folk culture today is marked by reclusiveness and a fierce concern for preserving a way of life that includes musical and religious elements, such as fiddling and the Baptist Church.

While settling the land in northern Arkansas and southern Missouri required self-reliance and stubbornness, today's traveler should find things a bit tamer than they were a century ago. The Ozarks have become a major resort area for Missouri, Arkansas, and neighboring states; tacky gift shops have sprung up like weeds. The scenery, however, remains outstandingly rugged, and provides a beautiful background for long hikes. Arkansas folk love to canoe, fish, and float down the Ozarks' rivers, especially the Buffalo; likeminded travelers should arrive before midsummer, when the rivers begin to run too low for sport.

Few buses venture into the area, but hitching is good, and generally safe. Drivers should follow Rte. 7, 71, or 23 for best access and views. Eureka Springs to Huntsville on Rte. 23 south is a scenic one-hour drive. Also head east or west on Rte. 62 from Eureka Springs for attractive stretches. The **Arkansas Department of Parks and Tourism** (800-643-8383; see Arkansas Practical Information) can help with your trip. If you want to paddle a portion of the **Buffalo National River,** call the ranger station for camping and canoe rental info (449-4311; canoe rental $20 per day, cabin $40 per day), or contact Buffalo Point Concessions, HCR, P.O. Box 388, Yellville 72687 (449-6206). The **Arkansas Bikeways Commission,** 1200 Worthen Bank Bldg., Little Rock 72201, dispenses a bike trail map for the Ozark region. Also, the **Eureka Springs Chamber of Commerce,** (800-643-3546 outside Arkansas; 253-8737 in-state) has excellent vacation-planning material.

Ozark culture is alive and well southeast of Eureka Springs on Rte. 62 and then on Rte. 14 at the **Ozark Folk Center** (501-269-3851), near **Mountain View.** The center is a living museum of the cabin crafts, music, and lore of the Ozarks. Among the craftspeople practicing their trades in the **Crafts Forum** are a blacksmith, a basket maker, a potter, a gunsmith, and a furniture maker. Trams transport guests to the Crafts Forum from the visitors center. (Open Apr.-Oct. daily 10am-5pm. Admission $4.75, children $2.75.) Musicians give traditional concerts in the auditorium nightly at 7:30pm. The audience is invited to participate in the jigs. (Admission $5.25, children $3.25.) Seasonal events include the **Arkansas Folk Festival** and the **Mountain and Hammered Dulcimer Championships** (late April), the **Banjo Weekend** (mid-May), and the **Arkansas Old-Time Fiddlers Association State Championship** (late Sept.). The Fiddlers Championship is quite a sight as hundreds of old pros and young apprentices play authentic music of the Ozarks. Many of the people in this area are of Scottish or Irish descent, and the music shows clear signs of its Celtic roots.

Eureka Springs

In the early 19th century, the Osage spread reports of a wonderful spring with magical healing powers. White settlers flocked to the site and quickly established a small town from which they sold bottles of the miraculous water. Built on piousness and good marketing, Eureka Springs has since replaced its healing services with scenic and historical tourist attractions. Some faith does survive in **The Great Passion Play** (253-9200), which has brought recent fame to Eureka Springs. Modeled after Germany's Oberammergau Passion Play, which depicts Christ's last days, it is staged in a huge amphitheater atop a hill, drawing up to 4000 visitors each night. (Performances April-Oct. Tues.-Wed., Fri.-Sun. Tickets $8-11, ages 4-11 half-price. For reservations ask at your accommodations, or write P.O. Box 471, Eureka Springs 72632.) The amphitheater is off Rte. 62, just outside of town. **Gray Line Bus Tours** (253-9540) provides transportation to and from the play ($3 per person round-trip). They pick you up and drop you off at your hotel, motel, or campground. The theater is wheelchair-accessible.

For outdoor amusement, try the **Alpine Hiking Club** (253-9868), which sponsors Sunday hikes around town to places inaccessible by car. Hikers meet at the **New Orleans Hotel,** 63 Spring St. (spring-fall at 7:15am; winter at 1:15pm). There are about 80 different hikes and all levels of ability are welcome.

The town is filled with tourist-oriented restaurants. The **Gazebo,** in the Best Western Eureka Inn at the junction of Rte. 62 and 23 north, is a popular tourist dining spot with 1890s decor. The menu features Southern food and Arkansas catfish, but the best deal is your basic soup, cheese, fruit, and salad bar for $4.50. (Open daily 6:30am-9pm.) Get away from the usual tourist glitz at the **Wagon Wheel,** 84 S. Main St. (253-9934), a country-western bar decorated with antiques. (Open Mon.-Fri. 8am-2am, Sun. 10am-midnight.)

Accommodations in Eureka Springs are not difficult to find, but prices are impossible to foresee. They vary daily according to the crowds, from as low as $18 for singles in August to $45 during April; rates also drop on Mondays and Thursdays when Passion Players take a break. The **King's Hi-Way Inn,** 96 King's Hwy. (253-7311), is friendly and generally reasonable. (Singles $38. Doubles $42. $6 extra on weekends. Off-season singles and doubles $22.) The best package deal in town is **Keller's Country Dorm,** Rte. 62 (253-8418), 5 mi. east of town. For $24, you get a dorm bed, breakfast, dinner, and a reserved ticket to the Passion Play (additional nights $9). Call Richard Keller ahead of time to get this rate, generally reserved for church groups of 12 or more, but open to individuals. (Open April-Oct.)

There are several campgrounds near Eureka Springs, ranging in price from $5-10. **Pinehaven Campsites,** on Hwy. 62 (253-9052), 2 mi. east of town, charges $9 per tent and $14 for a full RV hookup. Farther out, but more picturesque **Lake Leatherwood,** 2 mi. west on Rte. 62 (253-8624), mostly sees tourists. Rates begin at $7 per tent. The **KOA Campground** (253-8036) is 3 mi. farther west on Rte. 62, then ¾ mi. south on Rte. 187. Sites $8-10. (Open April-Oct.)

For extra help in planning your time here, call the **Chamber of Commerce** (800-643-3546 or 253-8737), located on Rte. 62 just north of Rte. 23. (Open May-Oct. daily 9am-5pm; Nov.-April Mon.-Fri. 9am-5pm.) **Gray Line Bus Company** (253-9540) runs two-hour city tours at 9am, 11:30am, and 2:30pm from May 4 to early November. (Fare $8.25, ages under 17 free with paying adult, otherwise $6.) The buses will pick you up and return you to any motel or campground in Eureka Springs. (Pick-up times approximately 15 min. before tour departure time. Out-of-town pickup approximately 30 min. before departure time.) The town is also accessible by trolley. Check schedules at the chamber of commerce.

Eureka Springs's **ZIP code** is 72632; the **area code** is 501.

Kentucky

Stretching from the broad farms of its western quarter, past urban Louisville to the coal towns and poverty of Appalachian Ashland, Kentucky defines itself by hills, horses, and hospitality. Kentucky's title as the "Bluegrass State" is an apt one, describing not only its high grass and beautiful scenery, but also the fast hard-to-play country-folk music developed in rural parts of the state and rural Kentucky culture in general. Before the Civil War, Kentucky held slaves, slaveholders and abolitionists; Confederate President Jefferson Davis went to school in Lexington, while Kentucky-born President Abraham Lincoln sent Union troops to the state in 1862, preventing it from seceding. Even today, Kentuckians are intensely loyal—when "My Old Kentucky Home" is played at sports events, they stand up with hands over hearts. Today Kentucky's cities blend a vaunted Southern friendliness with more tolerance than you'll find in its southern neighbors, resulting in a state where visitors can't help feeling comfortable.

Practical Information

Capital: Frankfort.

Tourist Information: **Kentucky Department of Travel Development,** Capital Plaza Tower, 22nd floor, Frankfort 40601 (502-564-4930 or 800-225-8747). **Department of Parks,** Capital Plaza Tower, Frankfort 40601 (800-255-7275).

Time Zones: Central (1 hr. behind Eastern) and Eastern. **Postal Abbreviation:** KY.

Louisville

Perched on the Ohio River, just between the North and the South, Louisville (pronounced LOU-uh-vul) has its own way of doing things. An immigrants' town imbued with Southern grace and architecture, Louisville's beautiful Victorian neighborhoods surround smokestacks and the enormous meat-packing district of Butchertown.

People once visited Louisville only out of necessity; traders coming down the river from Pittsburgh had to stop here to avoid rapids. Today the spread-out, laid-back city has riverfront parks as well as the excellent orchestra, theater, and visual arts fostered by the University of Louisville. But despite dozens of citywide festivals, the year's main event is undoubtedly the Kentucky Derby. The nation's most prestigious horse race ends a week-long extravaganza, luring over half a million visitors who pay through the teeth for the less than pure necessity of this combination carnival, fashion display, and horse show. The $13 million wagered on Derby Day alone proves that Kentuckians are deadly serious about their racing—the prize is incredible prestige and $800,000 to the winning owner.

Practical Information

Emergency: 911.

Visitor Information: **Louisville Convention and Visitor Bureau,** 400 S. 1st St. (582-3732; 800-633-3384 outside Louisville; 800-626-5646 outside KY), at Liberty downtown. The standard goodies, including some bus schedules. Open Mon.-Fri. 8:30am-5pm, Sat. 8:30am-4pm, Sun. 10am-4pm. Visitor centers also in Standiford Field airport and in the Galeria Mall at 4th and Liberty St. downtown. **Concert Line,** 540-3210. Information on rock, jazz, and country performances.

Travelers Aid: 584-8186.

Airport: **Standiford Field** (367-4636), 15 min. south of downtown on I-65. Take bus #2 into the city.

Greyhound/Trailways: 720 W. Muhammad Ali Blvd. (585-3331), at 7th St. To: Indianapolis (6 per day, 2 hr., $19); Cincinnati (7 per day, 2 hr., $14.50); Chicago (7 per day, 6 hr., $53.50, $29 special); Nashville (10 per day, 3 hr., $22); Lexington (2 per day, 2 hr., $15). Storage lockers $1 first day, $3 each additional day. Open 24 hr.

Public Transport: Transit Authority River City (TARC), 585-1234. Major routes on the main intersecting streets off Broadway, running east-west, and off 4th St., running north-south. Operates daily 6am-midnight, but varies with bus route. Fare 60¢ during peak hours, 35¢ other times. Disabled access. Also runs a trolley on 4th Ave. from River Rd. to Broadway (free). Call for directions.

Taxi: Yellow Cab, 636-5511. Base fare $1.20, $1.40 per mi.

Car Rental: Dollar Rent-a-Car, in Standiford Field airport (366-6944). Weekends from $17 per day, weekdays $42. Open daily 6am-midnight. Must be 21 with credit card. Additional $6 per day for under 25. **Budget Rent-a-Car,** 4330 Crittenden Dr. (363-4300). From $40 per day. Open daily 6:30am-9pm. Must be 21 with major credit card or 25 without.

Help Lines: Rape Hot Line, 581-7273. **Crisis Center,** 589-4313. Both open 24 hr. **Gay and Lesbian Hotline,** 454-6699. Open daily 6pm-1am.

Medical Assistance: We Speak Your Language, 589-4450. Help in 41 languages.

Time Zone: Eastern.

Post Office: 1420 Gardner Lane (454-1632). Take the Louisville Zoo exit off Rte. 264 and follow Gardner Lane 1 mi. Open Mon.-Fri. 7:30am-7:30pm, Sat. 7:30am-1pm. **ZIP code:** 40232.

Area Code: 502.

Louisville sits 72 mi. west of Lexington, 101 mi. southwest of Cincinnati, OH, and 260 mi. east of St. Louis, MO. Major highways through the city include I-65 (north-south expressway), I-71, and I-64. The Henry Watterson Expressway, also called I-264, rings the city. The central downtown area is defined north-south by Main Street and Broadway, and east-west by Preston and 19th Street.

Aside from theater and riverfront attractions, much activity in Louisville takes place outside the central city, but the fairly extensive bus system goes to all major areas. Call TARC for help since written schedules are incomplete and sometimes confusing.

Accommodations

Though easy to find, accommodations in Louisville are not particularly cheap. If you want a bed during Derby Week, make a reservation at least six months to a year in advance; be prepared to pay high prices. The visitors center (see Practical Info above) will help after March 13. During Derby Weekend, the **University of Louisville** might allow camping (tents only) on their Belknap Campus soccer fields, about 1 mi. from the track ($5 per tent). At other times, if you don't choose one of the few affordable downtown options, try one of the many cheap motels that line the roads just outside town. **Kentucky Homes Bed and Breakfast** (635-7341) offers stays in private homes from $45. Call at least a few days ahead. Newburg (6 mi. away) and Bardstown (39 mi. away) are likely spots for budget accommodations.

Motel 6, 3304 Bardstown Rd. (456-2861), about 6 mi. southeast of downtown. Take Jefferson St. east from downtown, turn right on Baxter Ave., then bear left on Bardstown Rd., 3 mi. down. Or take bus #17 from Liberty and 7th St. Pool. Singles $25. Each additional person $6.

San Antonio Inn, 927 S. Second St. (582-3741). The cheapest lodging downtown and looks it. Rents rooms by the hr. Rough and shabby; women should steer clear. Singles $24, with phone $29.50. Doubles $35. Must be 21 with a photo ID.

Thrifty Dutchman Budget Motel, 3357 Fern Valley Rd. (968-8124), just off I-65. A hike from downtown. Take bus #18, but still expect a long walk. Clean, large rooms. Pool. Singles $31. Doubles $44.

Collier's Motor Court, 4810 Bardstown Rd. (499-1238), south of I-264. 30 min. from downtown by car, or take bus #17. Inconvenient, but well-maintained and cheap. Singles $28.50. Doubles $33.

Travelodge, 2nd and Liberty St. (583-2841), downtown behind the visitors center. Big, clean, and oh-so-convenient. Neighborhood Chinese restaurant provides room service. Singles $43. Doubles $45.

KOA, 900 Marriot Dr., Clarksville, IN (812-282-4474), across the bridge from downtown beside I-65; take the Stansifer Ave. exit. Grocery and playground; mini-golf and a fishing lake at the Sheraton across the street. Sites $15 for 2 people. Each additional person $3, under 18 $2. Kamping Kabins (for 2) $24. RV sites $17.50.

Food

Louisville's chefs whip up a wide variety of cuisines, but prices can be steep. Butchertown and the Churchill Downs area have several cheap delis and pizza places. Bardstown Rd. near Eastern Pkwy. offers budget pizzas and more expensive French cuisine.

The Rudyard Kipling, 422 W. Oak St. (636-1311). Take bus #4 from downtown. If you eat one dinner in Louisville, eat it here. Eclectic menu includes French, Mexican, and vegetarian entrees, Kentucky Burgoo (a regional stew), and other creative fare ($5-14). Half-jungle, half-colonial tavern rooms. Weekend nights feature piano music or rock 'n' roll; weeknights range from Celtic to bluegrass to folk music. Free Louisville Songwriters Cooperative acoustic music show each Mon. at 9pm. Open Mon.-Thurs. 11:30am-2pm and 5:30pm-until, Fri. 11:30am-until, Sat. 5:40pm-until. Call for events calendar. Wheelchair accessible.

Miller's Cafeteria, 429 S. 2nd St., downtown. Serve yourself a full breakfast or lunch (entree, pie, 2 vegetables, and drink) for $3-4. Big, comfortable dining room built in 1826 barely older than most of the customers. Open Mon.-Fri. 7am-2:30pm, Sun. 10am-2:30pm.

The Old Spaghetti Factory, 235 W. Market St., at 3rd St. downtown. Part of a national chain. Big helpings of spaghetti in a gorgeous remodeled turn-of-the-century department store. Trolley car in the floor. Full dinners with salad, bread, and ice cream $4-6. Popular with families—prepare to wait. Open Mon.-Thurs. 11:30am-2pm and 5-10pm, Fri. 11:30am-2pm and 5-11pm, Sat. 5-11pm, Sun. 4-10pm.

Another Place Sandwich Shop, 1514 Bardstown Rd. (458-8141). Take bus #17, 23, or 40 from downtown. Sandwiches, salads, and chili ($1.50-4) in a hip, two-story Victorian house. Loud rock 'n' roll and a well-equipped bar. Carry-out available. Open Mon.-Thurs. 8am-midnight, Fri.-Sat. 8am-1am, Sun. 8am-11pm.

Masterson's, 1830 S. 3rd St., near the University of Louisville. Take the #4 bus to "U of L" and walk. Popular with students and professors. Lunch buffet includes roast beef and fried chicken, with excellent desserts. The Taverna serves lunch and dinner for $5-8. Open Sun.-Thurs. 8am-11pm, Fri.-Sat. 8am-1am. All-you-can-eat Mon.-Fri. 11am-2pm ($4.25).

Mom's East End Cafe, 1605 Story Ave., near Hadley Pottery; take bus #15 or 31 from downtown. True Louisville eatery with TV, charming service, and visible kitchen. Limited, ordinary menu. Lunch or dinner under $4. Open Sun.-Thurs. 6am-9pm, Fri.-Sat. 6am-10pm.

Horses and Such

Even if you miss the Kentucky Derby, try to catch **Churchill Downs,** 700 Central Ave. (636-3541), 3 mi. south of downtown. Take bus #4 (4th St.) to Central Ave. Bet, watch a race, or just admire the twin spires, colonial columns, gardens, and sheer scale of the track. (Races April-June Tues.-Fri. 3:30-7:30pm, Sat.-Sun. 1-6pm; Oct-Nov. Tues.-Sun. 1-6pm. Grandstand seats $1.50, clubhouse $3, reserved clubhouse $5. Parking $2-3. Grounds open in racing season daily 10am-4pm.)

The **Kentucky Derby Festival** commences the week before the Derby and climaxes with the prestigious Run for the Roses the first Saturday in May. Balloon and steamboat races, music, and all manner of hullabaloo adorn the week. Seats for the Derby have a five-year waiting list. You can stand and watch from the grandstand or infield for $20, but get in line at the Downs early on Derby morning as these tickets aren't available any other way. 120,000 spectators flood the Downs each Derby day.

The **Kentucky Derby Museum** (637-1111), at Churchill Downs, provides the historical context essential for a true appreciation of the race's significance. The museum offers a slide presentation on a 360° screen, tours of the stadium, profiles of famous stables and trainers, a simulated horse-race for betting practice, and tips on what makes a horse a "sure thing." The huge Derby history exhibit reveals that African American trainers and jockeys dominated the race until the turn of the century. (Open daily 9am-5pm. Admission $3, seniors $2.50, ages 5-12 $1.50.)

The **Louisville Downs,** 4520 Poplar Level Rd. (964-6415), south of I-264, hosts harness racing during most of the year. There are three meets: July-Sept. Mon.-Sat.; Sept.-Oct. and Dec.-April Tues.-Sat. Post time is 7:30pm and 10-12 races leave the gates per night. (General admission $2, clubhouse $3. Minimum bet $2. Parking $2. Take bus #43 from downtown.)

If you're tired of being a spectator, go on a trail ride at **Iroquois Riding Stable,** 5216 New Cut Rd. (363-9159; $10 per hr.). Take 3d St. south to Southern Parkway or ride bus #4 or 6 to Iroquois Park.

Sights and Entertainment

Interesting antique, secondhand, and bookshops line **Bardstown Road** north and south of Eastern Pkwy. Just south of downtown and Oak St. (especially on 2nd through 4th St.) beautifully maintained Victorian homes comprise part of **Old Louisville.** Farther south, in University of Louisville territory, the **J.B. Speed Art Museum,** 2035 S. 3rd St. (636-2893), has an impressive collection of Dutch paintings and tapestries, Renaissance and contemporary art, and a sculpture court. The museum also has a touch-and-see gallery for visually impaired visitors. (Open Tues.-Sat. 10am-4pm, Sun. 1-5pm. Admission $2, seniors $1, students and children free. Free Sat.-Sun. Take bus #4.)

The **Riverfront Plaza** (625-3333), a landscape park overlooking the Ohio River, serves as the avatar of downtown Louisville. Call any time of year to find what festival or citywide event is taking place, as Louisville hosts many. The **Belle of Louisville** (625-2355), an authentic stern-wheeler, cruises the Ohio, leaving from Riverfront Plaza at the foot of 4th St. (Departs May 27-Sept. 2 Tues.-Sun. at 2pm. Sunset cruises Tues. and Thurs. 7-9pm; nighttime dance cruise Sat. 8:30-11:30pm. Fare $7, seniors $6, under 13 $3. Dance cruise $12, no discounts. Boarding begins 1 hr. before the ship leaves; arrive early especially during July.)

The **Museum of History and Science,** 727 W. Main St. (561-6100), downtown, emphasizes hands-on exhibits. Press your face against the window of an Apollo space capsule, then settle back and enjoy the four-story screen at the new IMAX theater. (Open Mon.-Thurs. 9am-5pm, Fri.-Sat. 9am-9pm, Sun. noon-5pm. Admission $4, children $3; $6 and $5 with IMAX tickets.) At the **Louisville Zoo,** 1100 Trevilian Way (459-2181), between Newbury and Poplar Level Rd. across I-264 from Louisville Downs, the animals are exhibited in neo-natural settings. Ride on an elephant's back or on the tiny train that circles the zoo. (Open Fri.-Tues. 10am-5pm, Wed.-Thurs. 10am-8pm; Sept.-April Tues.-Sun. 10am-4pm. Gate closes 1 hr. before zoo. Admission $4, seniors $1.75, children $2.)

Hillerich and Bradsby Co., 1525 Charleston-New Albany Rd., Jeffersonville, IN (585-5226), 6 mi. north of Louisville, manufactures the famous "Louisville Slugger" bat. (Tours Mon. and Fri. at 11am and 2pm except late June and first two weeks in July. Free. Go north on I-65 to exit for Rte. 131, then turn east.) **Hadley Pottery,** 1570 Story Ave. (584-2171), near Ohio St. just east of downtown, has been producing Mary Alice Hadley's gorgeous, unconventional pottery since 1940. (Free 30-min. tours Mon.-Fri. at 2pm. Shop open Mon.-Fri. 8:30am-4:30pm, Sat. 9am-12:30pm. Take bus #15 or 31.)

Louisville's thriving nightlife offers everything from bluegrass and Beethoven to Brecht and Beckett. Louisville's newest entertainment complex, the **Kentucky Center for the Arts,** 5 Riverfront Plaza (information and tickets 584-7777 or 800-283-7777), off Main St., hosts major performing arts groups, including the **Louisville Orchestra,** known for its repertoire of 20th-century music. The **Lonesome Pines** series showcases indigenous Kentucky music, including bluegrass. Ticket prices vary as wildly as the music, though student discounts are sometimes offered. The **Actors Theater,** 316 W. Main St. (584-1205), between 3rd and 4th St., a Tony award-winning repertory company, gives performances at 8pm and some matinees. Call for details. Tickets start at $15, with $7 student rush tickets available 15 minutes before each show. Bring a picnic dinner to **Shakespeare in the Park,** Central Park (634-8237), weekends between June 19 and August 9. (Performances at 8:30pm.) **The Kentucky,** 651 S. 4th (584-0960), shows unusual, obscure, and classic films and other arts events. Call the **Louisville Visual Arts Association,** 3005 Upper River Rd. (896-2146) for information on local artists' shows and events.

The **Phoenix Hill Tavern,** 644 Baxter Ave. (589-4957; take bus #17), resurrects live music in Louisville. Two bands play every Friday and Saturday night, with energetic country-rock on the first floor and cozy easy-listening on the second. Retreat to the roof-top bar or fresh-air patio. Local rock 'n' roll jams Tuesday to Thursday; weekends attract bigger names. (Open Tues.-Fri. 4pm-4am, Sat.-Sun. 6pm-4am. Dinner buffet Fri. only 5:30-7:30pm. Cover Tues.-Thurs. and Sun. $2, Fri.-Sat. after 8pm $3.) Escort service takes you to your car or to the bus stop after hours. The **Butchertown Pub,** at Story and Webster St. (583-2242), also has live bands and a dance floor; take "Market St." bus #15. Regional bands play college rock on weekends, with Monday and Tuesday nights sounding a bit more unusual. (Open Mon.-Thurs. 4pm-1am, Wed.-Fri.4pm-2am, Sat. 6pm-2am. Cover $2-3.) Bands play in University of Louisville's **Red Barn** (588-7332 or 588-6691) on Friday and Saturday nights. Some shows are all-ages.

A huge new complex at 120 S. Floyd St. serves the small but growing gay community with **Connections,** a flashy dance club. (Open Wed.-Sun. 9pm-4am. Cover $2-5 depending on night; Wed. no cover. Under-21s can dance but not drink.) The complex also contains a café, a video bar (open daily till 4am), and a theater which holds the Miss Gay USA pageant. Weeknights, many gay men prefer the **Discovery,** 116 E. Main St. (585-1116; open 9pm-4am), and lesbians the nearby **Carriage House,** on Main St.(587-0889).

Near Louisville

90% of the nation's bourbon hails from Kentucky, and 60% of that distills in Nelson and Bullitt Counties, close to Louisville. At **Jim Beam's American Outpost** (543-9877) in Clermont, 15 mi. west of Bardstown, Booker Noe, Jim Beam's grandson and current "master distiller," helps narrate a film about bourbon. Don't miss the free lemonade. From Louisville, take I-65 south to exit 112, then Rte. 245 south for 2½ mi. From Bardstown, take Rte. 245 north. (Open Mon.-Sat. 9am-4:30pm, Sun. 1-4pm. Free.) You can't actually tour Beam's huge distillery, but you can tour the **Maker's Mark Distillery** (865-2881), in Loretto, 19 mi. southeast of Bardstown. Take Rte. 49 to Rte. 52. This historic landmark shows how the nineteenth century made alcohol. (Tours Mon.-Sat. every hr. on the ½ hr. 10:30am-3:30pm. Free.) Neither site has a license to sell its liquors.

Bardstown proper hosts **The Stephen Foster Story** (626-1563), a showy, heavily promoted outdoor musical about America's first major songwriter, the author of "My Old Kentucky Home." (Performances mid-June to Labor Day Tues.-Sun. at 8:30pm, plus Sat. at 3pm. $9). **Kentuckyshow** (348-6501), an excellent and entertaining introduction to the state's history and culture, has moved from Louisville to the Old Bardstown Village and Civil War Museum on Old Bloomfield Rd. (Shows April-Oct. on the hr. Tues.-Sun. 11am-5pm. Admission $3.50 to museum and show, $3 for show only, seniors $2.50, children $2.) Greyhound leaves Louisville at 5pm nightly for Bardstown. By car, take I-65 south, then Rte. 245.

Now a national historic site, **Abraham Lincoln's birthplace** (358-3874) bulges 45 mi. south of Louisville near Hodgenville on U.S. 31 E. From Louisville, take I-65 down to Rte. 61; public transportation does not serve the area. Fifty-six steps representing the 56 years of Lincoln's life lead up to a stone monument sheltering the small log cabin. Much like the toys, only a few of the Lincoln logs that you see are believed to be original. A slow-moving film describes Lincoln's ties to Kentucky. (Open June-Aug. daily 8am-6:45pm; Sept.-Oct. and May 8am-5:45pm; Nov.-April 8am-4:45pm. Free.)

Hundreds of enormous caves and narrow passageways wind through **Mammoth Cave National Park** (758-2320), 80 mi. south of Louisville off I-65, west on Rte. 70. Mammoth Cave comprises the world's longest network of cavern corridors—over 325 mi. in length. Devoted spelunkers (ages 16 and over) will want to try the six-hour "Wild Cave Tour" in summer ($25); also available are two-hour, 2-mi. historical walking tours ($3.50, seniors and children $1.75) and 90-minute tours for the disabled ($4). Since the caves stay at 54°F year-round, bring a sweater. (Visitors center open daily 7:30am-7:30pm; off-season 7:30am-5:30pm.) Greyhound serves **Cave City,** just east of I-65 on Rte. 70 but the national park still lies miles away. **Gray Line** (637-6511; ask for the Gray Line) gives tours and bus rides to the caves. Call a few days ahead.

The **area code** for the Mammoth Caves area is 502.

Lexington

In 1775, an exploring party camping in Kentucky, hearing news of the Battle of Lexington in far-off Massachusetts, named the spot after the skirmish. No longer merely derived from the North, Lexington has grown to become Kentucky's second-largest city and the world's largest burley tobacco center in its own right. With a recently rehabilitated and expanded downtown area, Lexington has managed urban renewal with remarkable style, even retaining its charming original neighborhoods. The University of Kentucky's huge campus extends east from South Limestone St., providing a clientele for several distinctive eateries and shops.

Much like their namesake, inhabitants of this gracious city are still concerned with victory, gaining fame for their dedication to horse breeding and training. Instead of suburbs Lexington has thousand-acre farms of blue grass and white fences. With over 150 horse farms gracing the Lexington area, the stables have nurtured such greats as Citation, Lucky Debonair, and Majestic Prince.

Practical Information

Emergency: 911.

Visitor Information: Greater Lexington Convention and Visitors Bureau, 430 W. Vine St. #363 (233-1221), in the convention center. Brochures, maps, and bus schedules. Open Mon.-Fri. 8:30am-5pm, Sat. 10am-5pm. Information centers also grace I-75 north and south of Lexington.

Airport: Bluegrass Field, 4000 Versailles Rd. (254-9336). Serves regional airlines and regional flights; often easier to fly to Louisville's Standiford Field.

Greyhound: 477 New Circle Rd. (255-4261). Lets passengers off north of Main St. Take Lex-Tran bus #6 downtown. Open daily 6:45am-11:30pm. To: Louisville (4 per day, 1½ hr., $15); Cincinnati, OH (7 per day, 1½ hr., $15); Knoxville, TN (9 per day, 3 hr., $38.50).

Public Transport: Lex-Tran, 109 W. London Ave. (252-4936). Good system serving the university and city outskirts. Most buses leave from Vine or Main St. Fare 60¢, transfers 10¢. 10¢ trolley serves downtown area. Operates daily 7am-5:30pm.

Taxi: Lexington Yellow Cab, 231-8294. Base fare $1.90, $1.35 per mi.

Help Line: Rape Crisis, 253-2511. Open 24 hr.

Time Zone: Eastern.

Post Office: 1088 Nandino Blvd. (231-6700). Open Mon.-Fri. 8:30am-5pm, Sat. 9am-1pm. **ZIP code:** 40511.

Area Code: 606.

Lexington rises out of the rolling pasturelands of central Kentucky, 72 mi. east of Louisville, 80 mi. south of Cincinnati on I-75. **New Circle Road** highway, which is intersected by many roads that connect the downtown district to the surrounding towns, also surrounds the city. **High, Vine,** and **Main Streets** are the major east-west routes downtown; **Limestone Street** and **Broadway** the north-south thorough-fares.

Accommodations and Camping

The concentration of horse-related wealth in the Lexington area tends to ride accommodation prices up. The cheapest places gallop out of the city on roads beyond New Circle Rd. If you're having trouble on your own, **Dial-A-Accommodations,** 430. W. Vine St. #363 (233-7299), will locate and reserve a room free of charge in a requested area of town and within a specific price range. (Open Mon.-Fri. 9:30am-5pm.)

University of Kentucky, Apartment Housing (257-3721). Full kitchen and private bathroom. Fold-out sleeper. Rooms also available during the school year space permitting. 14-day max. stay. $21. Call ahead on a weekday. Available June-Aug. You may have to explain that you only want a short stay; longer-term rentals to UK affiliates only.

Kimball House Motel, 267 S. Limestone St. (252-9565), downtown. An avatar of charm. Clean, antique-filled rooms transport you to a turn-of-the-century boarding house. Friendly, helpful management. Some singles (1st floor, no A/C, shared bath) just $20. Ask for them specifically; they often fill by late afternoon. Otherwise, cheapest singles $24. Doubles $28. Key deposit $5.

YMCA, 239 E. High St. (254-9622), downtown. Men only. Dormitory-style rooms with bed and dresser. If full, the Y will offer you space in the Salvation Army's homeless shelter on W. Main St. Singles $20, with private bath $30. Weekly: $85. Key deposit $5. Call at least a few days ahead.

Bryan Station Inn, 273 New Circle Rd. (299-4162). Take Limestone St. north from downtown and turn right onto Rte. 4. Clean, pleasant rooms in the middle of a motel/fast-food strip. Singles $26. Doubles $28. Rates decrease the longer you stay.

Good, cheap campgrounds abound around Lexington; unfortunately, you need a car to reach them. The **Kentucky Horse Park Campground,** 4089 Ironworks Pike (233-4303), 10 mi. north off I-75, offers a free shuttle to the KY Horse Park and Museum. (2-week max. stay. Sites $9, with hookup $12.)

Food

Lexington specializes in good, down-home bluegrass food. The few distinctive restaurants are near the university. Downtown, avoid the chic new retail area and explore the surrounding streets for hidden delis and sandwich shops.

Alfalfa Restaurant, 557 S. Limestone St. (253-0014), across from Memorial Hall at the university. Take bus #2A. Fantastic home-cooked international and vegetarian meals. Complete dinners with salad, bread, and entree under $10. Excellent, filling soups and exotic salads from $2. Live music nightly. Open Tues.-Thurs. 5:30-9pm (in summer until 9:30pm), Fri. 5:30-10pm, Sat. 10am-2pm and 5:30-10pm, Sun. 10am-2pm.

Hall's on the River, on Boonesboro Rd., 30 min. southwest of downtown. Follow Richmond Rd., which turns into Athens Boonesboro Rd. Pass the I-75 interchange—Hall's lies exactly 8 mi. away. Sample the "hot brown" (the Kentuckian version of an open-faced turkey sandwich with ham and a special sauce) and other local dishes. Entrees with 2 side dishes $8-12. Open Mon.-Thurs. 11:30am-10pm, Fri.-Sat. 11:30am-11pm.

Joe Bologna's, 103 W. Maxwell St., at S. Limestone 5 blocks south of Main. College hangout popular for its pizza ($4-10). J-O-E has a way with B-O-L-O-G-N-A. Extra napkins necessary for the juicy gourmet cheesesteak. Open Mon.-Thurs. 11am-midnight, Fri.-Sat. 11am-1am, Sun. noon-11pm.

High on Rose Cantina, 301 E. High St. (252-9498). Hearty Mexican dishes (all entrees with beans, chips, and salsa) $4-7. Get high on the cheap beer and rowdy rock and country music. Open Mon.-Sat. 11am-1am, Sun. 11am-11pm.

Central Christian Church Cafeteria, 219 E. Short St., 1 block north of Main St. Decent country food—greens and cornbread, fried fish, homemade pies—for under $3. Open Mon.-Fri. 6:30am-2pm.

Sights and Nightlife

To escape the stifling swamp conditions farther south, antebellum plantation owners built beautiful summer retreats in milder Lexington. The most attractive of these stately houses preen only a few blocks northeast of the town center, in the Gratz Park area near the public library. In addition to their past, the wrap-around porches, wooden minarets, stone foundations, and rose-covered trellises distinguish these from the neighborhood's newer homes.

The **Hunt Morgan House,** 201 N. Mill St. (253-0362), hunkers down at the end of the park across from the library. Built in 1814 by John Wesley Hunt, the first millionaire west of the Alleghenies, the house later witnessed the birth of Thomas Hunt Morgan, who won a Nobel Prize in 1933 for proving the existence of the gene. Yet the house's most colorful inhabitant was Confederate General John Hunt Morgan. Chased by Union troops, the general once rode his horse up the front steps and into the house, leaned down to kiss his mother, and rode out the back door. What a guy. Visit the house to see its Federal-period design and weird color schemes. (Tours Tues.-Sat. 10am-4pm, Sun. 2-5pm. Admission $4, ages 6-12 $1.50.)

Kentucky's loyalties divided sharply in the Civil War. Mary Todd grew up five blocks from the Hunt-Morgan House; later she married Abraham Lincoln. The **Mary Todd Lincoln House** oscillates at 578 W. Main St. (233-6666; open April 1-Dec. 15 Tues.-Sat. 10am-4pm; admission $3).

Transylvania University, west of Broadway and north of 3rd St. (233-8242), became the first U.S. college west of the Alleghenies. Its Greek Revival buildings aren't quite as impressive as its alumni list—two vice-presidents, 50 senators, 100 representatives, 36 governors, and 34 ambassadors. Legend has it, however, that it long labored under a curse that caused various freak accidents including the decapitation of a sleepy bloodhound named Zan. Only the burial of the man supposedly responsible, an eccentric professor named Rafinesque, broke the curse. (Guided tours upon request Mon.-Fri. 9am-4pm. Call 233-8120.) On Richmond Rd. at E. Main St., you can admire **Ashland** (266-8581), the 20-acre homestead of statesman Henry Clay. The mansion's carved ash interior came from trees that grew on the property. (Open May-Oct. Mon.-Sat. 9:30am-4:30pm, Sun. 1-4:30pm; Nov.-April Mon.-Sat. 10am-4pm. Admission $4, children $1.50. Take bus #4A on Main St.)

The sprawling **University of Kentucky** (257-7173) gives free campus tours in "Old Blue," an English double-decker bus, at 10am and 2pm weekdays (call 257-3595). On campus, UK's new **Art Museum** (257-5716) holds Native American relics and modern U.S. art (open Tues.-Sun. noon-5pm); its **Museum of Anthropology** (257-7112) also opened recently (open Mon.-Fri. 8am-5pm). Call 257-7173 and ask what's happening on UK's constantly changing arts calendar.

Lexington's sparse nightlife includes some fun clubs and bars. You can do the humpty-hump at **Breeding's,** 509 W. Main St. (255-2822) or go upstairs to **The Brewery,** a friendly and authentic country-western bar (both open daily 8am-1am). **Comedy on Broadway,** 142 N. Broadway (254-5653), features stand-up comics most nights. **The Bar,** 224 E. Main St. (255-1551), a disco popular with gay men and women, stays open until 3:30am on Saturday. (Open daily until 1:30am. Cover $3 Fri.-Sat.). **The Wrocklage,** 361 W. Shore St. (231-7655), serves up alternative and punkish rock, and **Lynagh's,** in University Plaza at Woodland and Euclid St. (259-9944), serves as a good neighborhood pub.

Horses and Seasonal Events

Horse farms, for the most part, no longer permit tourists to come and gawk. One exception is **Spendthrift Farm,** 884 Ironworks Pike (299-5271), 8 mi. northeast of downtown. (Free tours Feb.-July Mon.-Sat. 10am-noon; Aug.-Jan. Mon.-Sat. 10am-2pm. Take Broadway until it becomes Paris Pike, turn left onto Ironworks.)

The pretty (pretty touristy, that is) **Kentucky Horse Park,** 4089 Ironworks Pike, exit 120 (233-4303), 10 mi. north on I-75, is a state park with full facilities for equestrians, a museum, two films, and the Man O' War Monument. (Open mid-March to Oct. daily 9am-5pm; times vary the rest of the year. Admission $8, ages 7-12 $4. Horse-drawn vehicle tours included.)

If horse racing is more your style, visit the **Keeneland Race Track,** 4201 Versailles Rd. (254-3412), west on U.S. 60. (Races Oct. and April; post time 1pm. Admission $2.) The public can observe morning workouts. (April-Oct. daily 6-10am.) The final prep race for the Kentucky Derby occurs here in April. The **Red Mile Harness Track,** 847 S. Broadway (255-0752; take bus #3 on S. Broadway), has racing from April to June and also in September. (Post time 7:30pm. Last week in Sept. post time 1:30pm.) The crowds run the gamut from wholesome families to seasoned gamblers. (Admission $1.50, reserved seating $3, programs $2, parking free. Seniors free Thurs.) Morning workouts (7:30am-noon) open to the public during racing season.

In June, the **Festival of the Bluegrass** (846-4995), at Masterson Station Park, attracts thousands for a Kentucky-style hootenanny. Camping at the festival grounds is free. The **Lexington Junior League Horse Show** (mid-July), the largest outdoor show in the nation, unfolds its pageantry at the Red Mile (see above).

Near Lexington

Outside Lexington, in **Richmond,** exit 95 off I-70, is **White Hall** (623-9178), home of the abolitionist (not the boxer) Cassius M. Clay, Henry's cousin. The elegant mansion really consists of two houses, one Georgian and one Italianate. The one-hour tour covers seven different living levels. (Open April-Aug. Mon.-Sun. 9am-4:30pm; Sept.-Oct. Wed.-Sun. 9am-4:30pm. Guided tours only. Admission $3, under 13 $2.) **Fort Boonesborough** (527-3328), a re-creation of one of Daniel Boone's forts, also graces Richmond. The park has films about the pioneers, samples of 18th-century crafts, and a small museum. (Open April-Aug. daily 9am-5:30pm; Sept.-Oct. Wed.-Sun. 9am-5:30pm. Admission $3, ages 6-12 $1.75. Combination White Hall/Boonesborough ticket $4.)

Ten mi. south of Richmond and 30 mi. south of Lexington, where the bluegrass meets the mountains, lies **Berea,** home of **Berea College** (986-9341), a tuition-free school founded in 1855. Many of the 1500 students, most from Appalachia, pay for their expenses by operating the school's crafts center. Campus tours leave from the corner of **Boone Tavern.** (Tours Mon.-Fri. at 9am, 10am, 1pm, and 3pm, Sat. at 1 and 2pm.) The **Appalachian Museum** (986-9341, ext. 6078), Jackson St. on campus, charts regional history through arts and crafts. (Open Mon.-Sat. 9am-6pm, Sun. 1-6pm. Closed Jan.)

Because of the emphasis on craft skills at Berea College, the town has a concentration of galleries, gift shops, and workshops. Of particular interest is **Churchill Weavers,** Lorraine Court (986-3127), north of town off I-75 and U.S. 25, the largest hand-weaving firm in the country. (Free tours Mon.-Fri. 9am-noon and 1-4pm. Gift shop open Mon.-Sat. 9am-6pm, Sun. noon-6pm.) The student-run crafts center has two locations: the **Boone Tavern Gift Shop,** in the hotel (986-9341, ext. 5233; open Mon.-Sat. 8am-8pm, Sun. noon-8pm), and the **Log House Sales Room,** on Estill St. (986-9341, ext. 5225; open Mon.-Sat. 8am-5pm, Sun. 1-5pm). During May and early fall, the town floods with tourists for the good folk music and food at the **Kentucky Guild of Artists' and Craftsmen's Fair,** in Indian Fort Theater. In mid-August, the local **McClain Family Band** rolls out their annual bluegrass festival (986-8111) on their Big Hill Farm. To reach Berea, take Greyhound bus #360 (3 per day), on the Lexington-Knoxville route, which will leave you at the B&B Grocery the college and Boone Tavern.

A celibate sect akin to the Amish ("Pennsylvania Dutch"), the Shakers, practiced the simple life between Harrodsburg and Lexington, about 25 mi. southwest on U.S. 68, at the **Shaker Village** (734-5411). The 5000-acre farm features 27 restored Shaker buildings. A tour includes demonstrations of everything from apple-butter-making to coopering (barrel-making). (Open daily 9am-6pm. Admission $6.50, ages

12-17 $3, ages 6-11 50¢.) Though the last Shaker to live here died in 1923, you can still eat and sleep in original Shaker buildings. (Dinner $12-14. Singles $30-55. Doubles $45-65. Reservations required.) Greyhound bus #350 runs to Harrodsburg, 7 mi. from the village.

The **Red River Valley,** in the northern section of the Daniel Boone National Forest, approximately 50 mi. southeast of Lexington, draws visitors from around the country. A day outing from Lexington will show why song and square dance have immortalized this spacious land of sandstone cliffs and stone arches. **Natural Bridge State Park** (663-2214) 12 mi. south of Slade, highlights the major attraction of the upper valley. The Red River Gorge highlights the lower valley. Greyhound bus #296 will get you to Stanton (10 mi. west of Slade) and a **U.S. Forest Service Office** (663-2853). If you're driving, take the Mountain Parkway (south off I-64) straight to Slade, and explore the region bounded by the scenic loop road, Rte. 715. Camp at **Natural Bridge State Resort Park** (800-325-1710). The campground, complete with pool, facilities for the disabled, boat rental, and organized square dances, hosts the **National Mountain Style Square Dance and Clogging Festival,** a celebration of Appalachian folkdances. (Admission $1-2. Tent sites $8.50, with hookup $10.)

Cumberland Gap

Almost completely uncommercialized **Cumberland Gap National Historical Park** is home to Daniel Boone's **Wilderness Trail,** a natural passage through an 800-ft. break in the Appalachian Mountains. The park surrounds the route that Boone and 30 axe-wielding pioneers blazed along a Shawnee and Cherokee Buffalo trail, in 1775.

Today the park provides 50 mi. of trails of varying length. Atop Brush Mountain lies the **Hensley Settlement,** a collection of 12 farms worked for 50 years until abandoned in the 1940s. The settlers lived in an isolated encampment of rough-hewn chestnut log houses. Since 1965, the park service has restored five farmsteads, the schoolhouse, and cemetery. You can reach the settlement by a 35½-mi. hike each way or in a four-wheel-drive vehicle. Worthwhile three-hour tours depart several times per day ($4, children $2). Make reservations at the **National Park Visitors Center** (606-248-2817), located about 200yd. from Middlesboro, KY, off U.S. 25 E., where rangers offer a series of free walking tours, educational and historical programs, and exhibits in the summer. (Open daily mid-June to Aug. 8am-6pm; Sept. to mid-June daily 8am-5pm.)

You can canoe, kayak, and whitewater raft on rapids year-round. The Cumberland River can be reached from the **Cumberland Falls State Resort Park** (800-325-0063), southwest of Corbin on KY Rte. 90 off U.S. 25 W., about 65 mi. from the Cumberland Gap Historical Park. Along the way, stop in **Corbin,** KY, for lunch at **The Original Kentucky Fried Chicken Restaurant,** junction of U.S. 25 E. and U.S. 25 W., to share the dream of the late Colonel Sanders, pioneer of fast food and avatar of the goatee. (Open daily 7am-11pm.) Raft from Rte. 90, 5 mi. east of the enormous falls. By a full moon the falls show the only known moonbow in the Western Hemisphere. On a clear winter evening the moonbow looks colorful, but at other times it appears as a translucent arch of light. (Public pool. Tent sites at the park $8.50. Buffet lunch at the lodge $5, dinner $8.) **Sheltowee Trace Outfitters** (679-5026) offers rafting trips on the river, as does **Cumberland Outdoor Adventures,** on KY Rte. 90, 5 mi. east of Cumberland Falls.

There is a **campground** on Rte. 58 in Virginia (Sites $8, free firewood, quiet rule in effect 10pm-6am). Free permits, available at the visitor's center, are required for backcountry camping. Make reservations to stay at one of the group sites or shelters. ($1 per person.) For non-campers, there is a string of uninspiring but cheap motels along U.S. 25 E. in Middlesboro. The **Parkview Motel** (606-248-4516), very convenient to the park, has wood-paneled rooms with original paintings, spotless bathrooms, and satellite TV. (Singles $24. Doubles $30.)

Louisiana

Thomas Jefferson struck quite a bargain when he purchased the Louisiana Territory from Napoleon for $15 million in 1803. Not only did he gain a region of tremendous natural wealth, he considerably increased the social diversity of a young United States. Only the richness of the alluvial soil matches Louisiana's cultural heritage, each successive wave of settlers leaving its own layer of ethnic sediment. Native Americans prospered in the swampy wetlands, with traces of their civilizations still evident in a few parks and museums throughout the state. The arrival of the Acadians, French settlers expelled from Nova Scotia by the British in 1755, augmented the original French population of the early 18th century. These Cajuns (a corruption of "Acadians") retreated to the swampy Louisiana hinterland, creating distinctive dialects, music, folklore, and trendy cuisine. Their influence combined with that of other elements to create a flavorful gumbo of settlers.

Today visitors to Louisiana will experience the state's unusual spice. French terms tend to creep into the local dialect, not just from the Cajuns, but from Creoles, whose French, Spanish, and African descent created a distinct tongue and cuisine. Equally spicy is zydeco, the hot dance music with lyrics in patois, or regional French. While Louisiana has suffered severely from the regional oil depression, it has regrouped behind the tourist industry and offers plenty of inexpensive activities suitable to any palate.

Practical Information

Capital: Baton Rouge.

Tourist Information: State Travel Office, P.O. Box 94291, Capitol Station, Baton Rouge 70804 (342-7317 or 800-334-8626). Open daily 8am-4pm. Office of State Parks, P.O. Box 1111, Baton Rouge 70821. Open Mon.-Fri. 9am-5pm.

Time Zone: Central (1 hr. behind Eastern). Postal Abbreviation: LA.

New Orleans

Founded around 1718 by the French, ceded to the Spanish in 1762, and then reacquired by the French, New Orleans had already existed quite happily for almost a century before it became a U.S. territory in 1803. However, it is more New Orleans' African American heritage than its European one that gives it unique musical and culinary flavors. African American jazz engendered New Orleans by combining traditional African rhythms and percussion with brass instruments popular in the U.S. Spicy New Orleans-style dishes such as gumbo also originated with vital ingredients from Africa including the slippery vegetable avatar, okra. In addition to jazz, the vibrant sounds of New Orleans range from Cajun and zydeco tones to down-home blues.

New Orleans ("N'awlins" to locals) seems Mediterranean or Caribbean in contrast to the more straight-laced Anglo-Saxon cities on the Atlantic Coast. In the 19th century, the red-light district known as "Storyville" simmered with revelry. Today, it's still a city that loves to party. From Tennessee Williams' *Streetcar Named Desire* to Anne Rice's vampire chronicles, the seductiveness of New Orleans is striking.

The climax for the "city that care forgot" is the Mardi Gras celebration held the week before Ash Wednesday, usually in late February. Anxious to have as much fun as their religion and bodies will allow before Lent, the townspeople and countless tourists parade, dance, sing, and drink until midnight of Mardi Gras ("Fat Tuesday") itself.

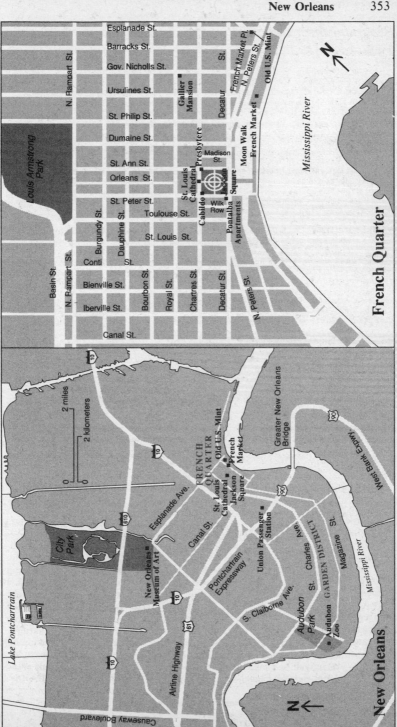

French Quarter

Esplanade St.
Barracks St.
Gov. Nicholls St.
Ursulines St.
St. Philip St.
Dumaine St.
St. Ann St.
Orleans St.
St. Peter St.
Toulouse St.
St. Louis St.
Conti St.
Bienville St.
Iberville St.
Canal St.

N. Rampart St.
Basin St.
N. Rampart St.
Burgundy St.
Dauphine St.
Bourbon St.
Royal St.
Chartres St.
Decatur St.
N. Peters St.

Louis Armstrong Park

Gallier Mansion
Decatur St.
French Market Pl.
N. Peters St.
Old U.S. Mint

St. Louis Cathedral
Presbytere
Madison St.
Moon Walk
French Market

Cabildo
Wilk Row
Jackson Square
Pontalba Apartments

Mississippi River

New Orleans

Lake Pontchartrain
Causeway Boulevard

City Park

New Orleans Museum of Art

Esplanade Ave.

FRENCH QUARTER
St. Louis Cathedral
Jackson Square
Old U.S. Mint
French Market

Greater New Orleans Bridge

Canal St.

Union Passenger Station

Pontchartrain Expressway

Airline Highway

S. Claiborne Ave.

Audubon Park
St. Charles Ave.
Magazine St.
GARDEN DISTRICT
Audubon Zoo

West Bank Expwy.

Mississippi River

2 miles
2 kilometers

Practical Information

Emergency: 911.

Visitor Information: To plan your vacation before you leave home, write or call the **Greater New Orleans Tourist and Convention Commission** (566-5011), 1520 Sugar Bowl Dr., New Orleans, LA 70112. Once in town, go to the main floor of the Superdome. Open Mon.-Fri. 8:30am-5pm. More convenient and very helpful is the **New Orleans/Louisiana Tourist Center,** 529 St. Ann, Jackson Square (566-5031), in the French Quarter. Free city and walking tour maps. Open daily 10am-6pm. **Tourist Information Service,** 525-5000.

Travelers Aid: 936 St. Charles Ave. (525-8726), at the YMCA. Assists stranded people by providing temporary shelter, food, and counseling. Open Mon.-Fri. 8am-4pm.

Moisant International Airport: (464-0831) 15 mi. west of the city. Served by the major domestic airlines as well as by larger Latin American carriers. **Louisiana Transit Authority** (737-9611) runs between the airport and downtown at Elk and Tulane every 30-45 min. for $1.10 in exact coins. Pick-up in front of Hertz. Airport limousine shuttles to downtown hotels cost $8, cabs $18.

Buses and Trains: Union Passenger Terminal, 1001 Loyola Ave., a 10-min. walk to Canal St. via Elk. Terminus for statewide interstate bus and train systems. Open 24 hr. for tickets and information. **Amtrak,** 528-1610 or 800-872-7245. To Memphis (1 per day, 8 hr., $69) and Houston (3 per week, 8 hr., $67). **Greyhound/Trailways,** 525-9371. To: Baton Rouge (29 per day, 2 hr., $13; $9 college rate); Memphis (5 per day, 11 hr., $56); Houston (9 per day, 9 hr., $40).

Public Transport: Regional Transit Authority (RTA), Plaza Tower, 101 Dauphin St., 4th floor (569-2700), at Canal. Bus schedules and transit information. Office open Mon.-Fri. 8:30am-5pm. Phone line provides 24-hr. route information. All buses pass by Canal St., at the edge of the French Quarter. Major buses and streetcars run 24 hr. Fare 60¢, transfers 5¢. One- and three-day passes are also available.

Taxi: United Cabs, 522-9771. **Checker Yellow Cabs,** 943-2411. **Liberty Bell Cabs,** 822-5974. Base fare $1.10, each additional mi. $1.10.

Car Rental: Budget Car Rental, 1317 Canal (467-2277), plus 6 more locations. $40 per day, $25 on weekends. 100 free mi. Add $5 per day if under 25. Open daily 7am-midnight. Must be 21 with credit card or 25 with a cash deposit.

Bike Rental: Bicycle Michael's, 618 Frenchman (945-9505), a few blocks west of the Quarter. $3.50 per hr., $12.50 per day. Weekly rates available. Open Mon.-Sat. 10am-7pm.

Help Lines: Gay Counseling Line, 522-5815. Usually operates nightly 5-11pm. **Crisis Line,** 523-2673.

Post Office: 701 Loyola Ave. (589-2201), near the Union Passenger Terminal, a 10-min. walk from Canal St. Open Mon.-Fri. 8:30am-4:30pm, Sat. 8:30am-noon. **ZIP code:** 70140.

Area Code: 504.

Although part of the Mississippi Delta, New Orleans is not actually on the Gulf of Mexico. The city is tucked between a bend in the **Mississippi River** and the southern shore of **Lake Pontchartrain.** Jackson, MS is 210 mi. north; Atlanta 480 mi. to the northeast; Houston 350 mi. west along the gulf. Keep in mind that the main streets of the city follow the curve in the river; it's easy to get lost even though New Orleans is fairly small. There are many one-way streets, drivers must sometimes make U-turns to cross intersections. The major tourist area is the small **French Quarter (Vieux Carré),** bounded by the Mississippi River, **Canal Street, Esplanade Avenue,** and **Rampart Street.** Streets in the French Quarter follow a grid pattern, and traveling on foot is not difficult. The **Garden District** is west of downtown. Buses to all parts of the city pass by Canal St. at the edge of the Quarter.

Even by day, much of New Orleans is unsafe, in particular the tenement areas directly to the north of the French Quarter and those directly northwest of Lee Circle. Even the quaint-looking side streets of the Quarter are dangerous at night—stick to busy, well-lit thoroughfares. Take a cab back to your lodgings when returning late at night from the Quarter.

Accommodations

Finding inexpensive yet decent accommodations in the French Quarter is as difficult as finding a sober citizen on Fat Tuesday. Try one of the few inexpensive **bed and breakfasts** around the Garden District, the best of which are listed below. Dormitory rooms with semi-private baths are available at **Loyola University** (865-3735), from June to August ($20 per person).

During Mardi Gras there is not a vacant room in the city and prices invariably rise. **Jazzfest** in late April also makes budget rooms scarce; reserve accommodations as far ahead as possible.

Marquette House (AYH), 2253 Carondelet St. (523-3014), in an antebellum house near the Garden District only minutes by streetcar to the Quarter. Usually teeming with travelers. Lounge, dining room, and kitchen. Lockers available. Check-in &:30am-1pm and 3-11pm. $10.50, nonmembers $13.50. Private doubles $22, nonmembers $25. Linen $1. Key deposit $5. Reservation for Mardi Gras must be paid in full in advance; include self-addressed, stamped envelope.

St. Charles Guest House, 1748 Prytania St. (523-6556) in a quiet, lovely neighborhood near the Garden District and St. Charles streetcar. Beautiful house with a plant-covered patio and a pool. Singles $25, with private bath $35-38. Doubles from $40. Continental breakfast included. Ask about $12.50 per person student rate.

Prytania Inn, 1415 Prytania St. (566-1515). Near the Garden District, 1 block from the St. Charles streetcar, which runs to the French Quarter in about 10 min. Light, airy rooms surround a shaded patio. Free laundry facilities. Singles from $29. Doubles from $33. Sumptuous 2-course breakfast included.

Old World Inn, 1330 Prytania St. (566-1330), 1 block from the St. Charles streetcar. Multicolored carpeting and walls covered with paintings create a slightly tacky but homey atmosphere. Singles from $27.50. Doubles from $35. One quint for $75. Complimentary juice and coffee in the morning.

YMCA, 936 St. Charles Ave. (586-9622), on Lee Circle. Drab though sufficient rooms in a large building complex at the heart of downtown. For men and women. Singles $26. Doubles $31.

LaSalle Hotel, 1113 Canal St. (523-5831 or 800-521-9450), 4 blocks east of Bourbon St. downtown. Unsafe area at night alone. Elegant lobby with coffee around the clock on an antique sideboard. Rooms dark and less inspiring than the entrance. Free movies. Singles $27, with bath $39. Doubles $30, with bath $45. Reservations recommended.

Camping

The several campgrounds near New Orleans are tough to reach via public transportation which is unavailable or infrequent to some sites. Try, nonetheless, if only to get away from the crowds in the French Quarter, and enjoy Louisiana's beautiful forests, lakes, and bayous. Bring insect repellent; the mosquitos are vicious.

Bayou Segnette State Park, 7777 Westbank Expressway (436-1107). RTA bus transport available. Enchanting park. Cabins on the bayou $50 for up to 8 people. Primitive campsites $10.

KOA West, 219 S. Starrett, River Ridge 70123 (467-1792), off highway I-10. RTA bus transport available. Pool, laundry facilities. Sites $21 for 2 people.

St. Bernard State Park, P.O. Box 534, Violet 70092 (682-2101), 18 mi. southeast of New Orleans. Take I-10 to Rte. 47 south and go left on Rte. 39 through Violet and Poydras. Nearest public transport to New Orleans ½ mi. away. Pool. Registration until 10pm. Sites $12, seniors $7.

Parc d'Orleans II, 10910 Chef Menteur Hwy. (242-6176; 800-535-2598 outside LA), 3 mi. east of the junction of I-10 and U.S. 90 (Chef Menteur Hwy.). Near public transport into the city. Pool, laundry facilities. Sites from $13.

Fontainebleau State Park, P.O. Box 152, Mandeville 70448 (626-8052), southeast of Mandeville on U.S. 190, on the shores of Lake Ponchartrain. Farthest from New Orleans of all the campgrounds. Sites $9.

Food

In an ancient Francophone cant, New Orleans means "good food." Today, there are more restaurants per capita in New Orleans than in any city except Paris. Acadian refugees, Spaniards, Italians, and African and Native Americans have all influenced New Orleans's distinctive culinary style. Hot, spicy, and delicious Cajun cooking combines of French, Spanish, and African styles: hot peppers, meats, and seafood abound. Jambalaya (rice with meat, vegetables, sometimes fish or shrimp, and a piquant red pepper sauce) is an example of this hearty fare that packs a punch. Creole food comes from a similar heritage as Cajun, but is traditionally more delicate; try some shrimp *etouffé* as an example. A Southern breakfast of grits, eggs, bacon, and corn bread will satisfy even the biggest of eaters. For lunch, try a seafood po'boy (a long french-bread sandwich filled with fried oysters or shrimp) or red beans and rice. Also sample the tiny crawfish, the southern freshwater cousin of the Maine lobster. Besides local specialties, New Orleans houses some of the most famous and innovative restaurants in the world. Oysters Rockefeller originated at **Antoine's,** 725 St. Louis St. (581-4422; open Mon.-Sat. noon-2pm and 5:30-9:30pm), but just getting a table can prove as difficult as paying the bill (expect more than $20 per person). **Le Ruth's,** 636 Franklin St. (362-4929), farther from the French Quarter, serves elegant French cuisine. You need not bust your budget at these expensive restaurants to get a taste of New Orleans, though; excellent food can be found almost anywhere.

Cool off in the summer months with a "snow ball" (sno-cone) from **Hansen's Snow-Blitz Sweet Shop,** 4801 Tchoupitoulas St. (891-9788). Expect a line. (Open Tues.-Fri. and Sun. 3-9pm.) Indulge yourself with some Creole pralines; some of the best and cheapest bake at **Laura's Candies,** 600 Conti and 155 Royal St. (525-3880; open daily 9am-10pm). The **French Market,** between Decatur and N. Peters St. on the east side of the French Quarter, sells fresh vegetables. The grocery stores on Decatur St. have the rest of the fixings you'll need for a picnic.

French Quarter

Acme Oyster House, 724 Iberville. Slurp fresh oysters shucked before your eyes (6 for $3.50, 12 for $6) or sit at the red checkered tables for a good ol' po'boy. Open Mon.-Sat. 11am-10pm, Sun. noon-7pm.

Quarter Scene Restaurant, 900 Dumaine. This cornerside café serves delicious salads and seafood and pasta entrees ($4-7). A tasty surprise is the *Dumaine* ($4), a peanut butter and banana sandwich topped with nuts and honey. Open 24 hr., except Tues. closes at 11:30 pm.

Croissant d'Or, 617 Ursuline St. In a historic building that was the first ice cream parlor in New Orleans. Delicious, reasonably-priced French pastries that won't chip your teeth. Open daily 7am-5pm.

Mama Rosa's, 616 N. Rampart, on the edge of the French Quarter. The best pizza in New Orleans (10-in. cheese $7.25). Also serves heaping salads and gumbo ($3). Open Tues.-Thurs. 10:30am-10:30pm, Fri.-Sun. 10:30am-11:30pm.

Café du Monde, French Market at the intersection of Decatur and Saint Ann St. A people-watching paradise since the 1860s. Drink *café au lait* and down perfectly prepared hot *beignets* with powdered sugar (3 for 75¢). Open 24 hr.

Outside the Quarter

Franky and Johnny's, 321 Arabella, off Tchoupitoulas southwest of downtown towards Tulane. Good seafood and po'boys served in a fun and lively atmosphere. Try the turtle soup ($2.50). Open Mon.-Thurs. 11am-11pm, Fri.-Sat. 11am-midnight, Sun. 11am-10pm.

Camellia Grill, 626 S. Carrollton Ave. Take the St. Charles streetcar away from the Quarter to the Tulane area. One of the finest diners in America, complete with friendly napkins and cloth servers, or vice-versa. Try the chef's special omelette ($5.50) or partake in the amazing pecan pie. Expect a wait on weekend mornings. Open Sun.-Wed. 8am-1am, Thurs.-Sat. 8am-2am.

Domilise's, 5240 Annunciation. Also uptown. This neighborhood restaurant serves the best po'boys in New Orleans, huge and cheap (around $3.50). Open Mon.-Fri. 9am-7pm, Sat. 10am-7pm.

Bluebird Café, 3625 Prytania St. Delicious healthy sandwiches (around $3) and hearty Southern breakfasts. Open Mon.-Fri. 7am-3pm, Sat.-Sun. 8am-3pm.

Mais Oui, 5908 Magazine Ave. Home cooking at its best. But yes! Delicious corn bread and gumbo. Entrees run from $5-8 and the menu changes daily. Bring your own wine. Open Mon.-Fri. 11:30am-2:45pm and 5:30-8:45pm, Sat. 5:30-8:45pm.

Mother's Restaurant, 401 Poydras, 4 blocks north of Bourbon St. Yo mama has been serving up unparalleled crawfish *etouffé* ($5.25) and seafood po'boys to locals for almost half a century. Entrees from $4.25. Open Mon.-Sat. 5am-10pm, Sun 7am-10pm.

Joey K's, 3001 Magazine St. This comfortable neighborhood restaurant serves good seafood, Italian food ($5-7), and po'boys ($3.25-4.50). Open Mon.- Fri. 11am-10pm, Sat. 8am-10pm.

All Natural, 5517 Magazine St. (891-2651). Mostly a take-out health food store, but tables await outside. Great sandwiches. Probably the only place in the world serving vegetarian Jambalaya ($5 with salad). Open Mon.-Fri. 10am-7pm, Sat. 9am-7pm, Sun. 10am-5pm.

Sights

French Quarter

Allow yourself at least a full day to take in the Quarter at leisure. The oldest section of the city, it is justly famous for its ornate wrought-iron balconies, French architecture, and joyous atmosphere. Known as the **Vieux Carré,** meaning Old Square, the historic district of New Orleans offers interesting used book and record stores, museums and shops that pawn off ceramic masks and cheap T-shirts to innocent tourists. There's a large gay community here; check out local newsletters *Impact* and *Ambush* for more information on gay events and nightlife. Walk through the residential section down **Dumaine Street** toward **Rampart Street** to escape the more crowded area near the river. Stop in at a neighborhood bar; tourists are taken in stride here and you should feel welcome.

Jackson Square is the heart of the Quarter. Centered around a bronze equestrian statue of General Andrew Jackson, the victor of the Battle of New Orleans, the square boogies with artists, mimes, musicians, and magicians. Across the street, the **Moonwalk** offers a scenic view of the river and shipping wharves. The **Louisiana State Museum** encompasses four different buildings, three of which (the **Cabildo, Presbytère,** and **1850 House**) are in Jackson Square. They contain artifacts, papers, and other changing exhibits on the history of Louisiana and New Orleans. The fourth, the **Old U.S. Mint,** 400 Esplanade (568-6968), lies outside the Quarter, housing interesting collections on the history of African Americans, jazz, and Mardi Gras. All buildings except for the Cabildo are open for touring. (All open Wed.-Sun. 10am-5pm. Admission $3, seniors and students $2, under 12 free.)

The rich cultural history of the French Quarter has made it a National Historical Park, and free tours are given by the **Jean Lafitte National Historical Park,** 916-918 North Peters (589-2636), located in the back section of the French Market at Decatur and Saint Phillip St. The National Park Service also conducts a "City of the Dead" tour of local cemeteries (reservations required). These unique burial grounds, which the travelers in the film *Easy Rider* found psychedelic, are accessible to anyone. Just wander into **St. Louis Cemetery #1** on the corner of Basin and Conti St. to the north of the French Quarter. The elaborate above-ground tombs which crowd the yard date back to 1789. Be careful here, however; ghosts won't bother you, but other dangerous characters might.

Back in the Quarter, several historical homes open their doors to the public. One of the most interesting is the **Hermann-Grima House,** 820 Saint Louis St. (525-5661; tours every ½ hr.; open Mon.-Sat. 10am-3:30pm; admission $3.50, seniors $2.50, students $1.50). Creole cooking demonstrations are offered from October through May on Thursdays. The **Gallier House,** 1132 Royal St. (523-6722; see Museums below) is considered one of the best small museums in the country. And no wonder: visitors are given free refreshments after the tours.

Outside the Quarter

The French Quarter is certainly not the only interesting aspect of New Orleans. In the southernmost corner of the Quarter at the "foot of Canal St." where the riverboats dock, is the **World Trade Center,** the **Old Customs House,** and **Riverwalk,** a multi-million dollar conglomeration of overpriced shops overlooking the port. You can take the **Canal St. Ferry** to Algiers Point until about 9pm for a 25-minute view of the Mississippi River (free). For a bird's-eye view of the city take the elevator up to the 31st floor observation deck of the **World Trade Center,** #2 Canal St., or better yet, buy an expensive drink at the **Top of the Mart,** (522-9795) a revolving bar on the 33rd floor that is particularly enchanting at sunset. (Open Mon.-Fri. 10am-1am, Sat. 11am-2am, Sun. 4pm-midnight.)

Scheduled to open in the fall of 1990, the **Aquarium of the Americas** (861-2537) lies across from the World Trade Center, directly on the river. The Aquarium will hold over a million gallons of water to let visitors can see the environments of underwater creatures from North, Central, and South America. (Admission $7.50, seniors $6, children $4. Open daily 9:30am-9pm until Dec. 1990, then open Mon.-Wed. and Sat.-Sun. 9:30am-6pm and Thurs. 9:30am-8pm.)

Also relatively new in the downtown area, the **Warehouse Arts District,** on Julia St. between Commerce and Baronne, contains historic architecture and contemporary art galleries housed in revitalized warehouse buildings. Exhibits range from Southern folk art to experimental sculpture. Maps of the area are available in each gallery. Scheduled to open in fall 1990 is the **Contemporary Arts Center,** 900 Camp St. (523-1216) in an extraordinary modern building.

Many diverse elements of New Orleans lie outside downtown. Though the streetcar named "Desire" was derailed long ago, you can take the **St. Charles Street Car** to the west of the French Quarter to view some of the city's finest buildings, including the elegant, mint-condition 19th-century homes along **Saint Charles Avenue.** This old-fashioned train takes you through some of New Orleans's most beautiful neighborhoods at a leisurely pace for a mere 60¢. Be sure to disembark at the **Garden District,** an opulent neighborhood between Jackson and Louisiana Ave. The legacies of French, Italian, Spanish, and American architecture create an extraordinary combination of magnificent structures, rich colors, lacy ironworks, and of course, exquisite gardens. Many have no basements and are raised several feet above the ground, affording protection from the swamp on which New Orleans was built. The wet foundation of the city even troubles the dead—all the city's cemeteries must be elevated to let the deceased rest in peace above water. The Jean Lafitte National Historical Park Service (see French Quarter Sights above) also leads a daily walking tour of this district. You can also pick up a copy of a self-guided tour at their office.

The St. Charles Street Car runs all the way to **Audubon Park,** across from Tulane University. Designed by the same architects who planned Central Park in New York City, Audubon contains lagoons, statues, stables, and the delightful **Audubon Zoo** (861-2537): a re-created Louisiana swamp, which hosts numerous alligators, is just one of the many excellent exhibits. A free museum shuttle whisks you from the Audubon Park entrance (streetcar stop #36) to the zoo. (Zoo open Mon.-Fri. 9:30am-5pm, Sat.-Sun. 9:30am-6pm. Admission $6, seniors and children $3.) You can return to the old quarter from Audubon Park by steamboat; the *Cotton Blossom* (586-8777) sails the Mississippi daily from Canal St. to the zoo and back. Though it costs more than the streetcar ($5.50, children $4.50), the antique vessel allows good views of the port. (Hour-long trips from Canal St. at 9:30am, 12:15pm, and 3pm, from the zoo at 11am, 1:45pm, and 4:30pm.) You can find quite a bit of nature a 10-minute drive north of the Quarter, in **City Park,** at the corner of City Park Ave and Marconie Dr. (482-4888), accessible by the Esplanade or City Park bus. This 1500-acre park is one of the five largest city parks in the U.S.—even bigger than New York City's Central Park. Besides the **Museum of Art** (see Museums below), it contains a botanical garden, golf courses, tennis courts, 800-year-old oak trees, lagoons, and a miniature train, unlike New York City's Central Park.

One of the most unique sights near New Orleans, the coastal wetlands that line Lake Salvador, make up another segment of the Jean Lafitte National Historical Park called the **Barataria Unit** (689-2002). Unfortunately, the park can only be reached with a car, but the free park service swamp tours almost warrant renting one. The park is off the West Bank Expressway across the Mississippi River down Barataria Blvd. (Hwy. 45).

A trip to Louisiana is not complete without seeing its mysterious bayous and "sleeping waters." **Riverboat cruises** offer swamp tours and other water journeys. Those with spare time and money may want to jump aboard the **Cajun Queen** or **Creole Queen** (524-0814), which offer various cruises (1½-5 hr., $10-14) giving an anecdote-filled, if not royal, history of New Orleans, Cajun, and Creole life. Also available are tours of bayou country and the Beauregard Plantation aboard **The Voyageur** (523-5555). Tours leave the ferry landing at the foot of Canal St. daily at 10am and return around 3pm. (Tickets $9.50, children $4.75.)

Museums

Gallier House Museum, 1118-1132 Royal St., French Quarter (523-6722). This elegant restored residence brings alive the taste and lifestyle of mid-19th century New Orleans. Tours every ½ hr., last tour at 4pm. Open Mon.-Sat. 10am-4:30pm. Admission $4, seniors and students $3, children $2.25.

New Orleans Historic Voodoo Museum, 724 Dumaine (523-7685). Small French Quarter museum full of occult displays and artifacts centering around New Orleans voodoo queen Marie Laveau. Not for the faint-hearted. Buy *gris-gris,* a specially blessed good luck pouch, in the gift shop. Open daily 10am-dusk. Admission $3, seniors and students $2, children $1.

Musée Conti Wax Museum, 917 Conti St. (525-2605). One of the world's finest houses of wax. The voodoo display and haunted dungeon are perennial favorites. Open daily 10am-5pm except during Mardi Gras. Admission $5, ages 13-18 $3, under 13 $2.

New Orleans Museum of Art, City Park (488-2631). Take the Esplanade bus from Canal and Rampart. Small collection of local decorative arts, opulent works by the jeweler Fabergé, and a strong collection of French paintings including works by Degas. Open Tues.-Sun. 10am-5pm. Admission $4, seniors and children $2.

Confederate Museum, 929 Camp St. (523-4522). An extensive collection of Civil War records and artifacts. Located just west of Lee Circle, in an ivy-covered stone building. Open Mon.-Sat. 10am-4pm. Admission $3, seniors $2, children 50¢.

Louisiana Nature and Science Center, 11000 Lake Forest Blvd. (246-5672), in Joe Brown Memorial Park. Hard to reach without a car, but a wonderful escape from the frivolity of the French Quarter. Trail walks, exhibits, planetarium shows, laser shows, and 86 acres of natural wildlife preserve. Open Mon.-Fri. 9am-5pm, Sat.-Sun. noon-5pm. Admission $3, seniors $2, children $1, families $7.

Entertainment and Nightlife

You've come to the right place. On any night of the week, at any time of year, multitudes of people join the constant festival of the French Quarter. And that's only the beginning. After exploring the more traditional jazz, blues, and brass sound of the Quarter, assay the rest of the city for less tourist-oriented bands playing to a more local clientele. Check *OffBeat* for maps of the clubs; try *Gambit,* the free weekly entertainment newspaper, or the Friday edition of the Times-Picayune's entertainment guide "Lagniappe" to find out who's playing where.

Traditional New Orleans jazz, born here at the turn of the century in Armstrong Park, can still be enjoyed at tiny, dimly lit, historic **Preservation Hall,** 726 Saint Peter St. (523-8939). If you don't arrive before the doors open, be prepared for a lengthy wait in line and poor visibility and sweaty standing-room only inside. (Admission $3; no drinks are sold, although you can bring your own soft drinks. Doors open at 8pm; music begins at 8:30pm and goes on until midnight.)

Keep your ears open for **Cajun** and **zydeco** bands, a local specialty. Using accordions, washboards, triangles and drums, they perform hot dance tunes (to which locals expertly two-step) and exuberantly sappy waltzes. Their traditional fare is the *fais do-do,* a lengthy, wonderfully sweaty dance. Anyone who thinks couple-dancing went out in the 50s should try one of these; just grab a partner and throw yourself into the rhythm. The locally based **Radiators** do it up real spicy.

The annual **New Orleans Jazz Festival** (522-4786), held at the fairgrounds in late April, features music played simultaneously on six stages. The festival also includes a Cajun food and crafts festival. Though loads of fun and musically exhilarating, the restival grows more zoo-like each year. Book your room early.

French Quarter

New Orleans bars stay open late, and few bars adhere to a strict schedule or entrance policy. In general, they open around 11am and close around 3am. Most bars in this area are very expensive, charging $3-5 for drinks. Yet on most blocks you can find cheap draft beer and "Hurricanes," sweet drinks made of juice and rum; visitors can totter around the streets and listen to great music without going broke.

The Napoleon House, 500 Chartres St. (524-9752). One of the world's great watering holes; popular with locals. Located on the ground floor of the Old Girod House, built as an exile home for Napoleon in a plan to spirit him away from St. Helena. The "Avatar Ambrosia" is delicious, especially when chased with Dixie beer. Food served. Open Mon.-Fri. until 1am, Sat.-Sun. until 2am.

The Absinthe Bar, 400 Bourbon St. (525-8108). Reasonable drinks for the French Quarter, with a blues band sometimes led by Bryan Lee. Has seen the likes of Mark Twain, Franklin D. Roosevelt, the Rolling Stones, and Humphrey Bogart. Open Sun.-Thurs. 5:30pm-2am, Fri.-Sat. 5:30pm-3am.

Pat O'Brien's, 718 Saint Peter St. (525-4823). The busiest bar in the French Quarter, full of happy tourists. You can listen to the pianos in one room, mix with local students in another, or lounge beneath huge fans near a fountain in the courtyard. Home of the original Hurricane; purchase your first in a souvenir glass ($6). Open Sun.-Thurs. 10am-4am, Fri.-Sat. 10am-5am.

Bourbon Pub/Parade, 801 Bourbon St. (529-2107). This gay dance bar sponsors a "Tea dance" on Sun. with all the beer you can drink for $5. Open 24 hr. Dancing nightly 9pm-until.

Old Absinthe House, 240 Bourbon St. (523-3181). The marble absinthe fountain inside has been dry since absinthe was outlawed. The Absinthe Frappe is a reinvention of the infamous drink with anisette or Pernod liqueur ($3.75). Food served. Reputed to be the oldest bar in the U.S.

Blue Crystal, 1135 Decatur St. (586-0339), on the other side of Jackson Park from the Bourbon Street bars. Progressive dance music for a younger crowd. The walls glow blue and green.

Storyville Jazz Hall, 1104 Decatur St. (525-8199). This large music hall opens onto the street and hosts a variety of bands from Southern metal to cool jazz. Generally a concert hall; call for times and ticket information.

Outside the Quarter

Many great bars frolic outside the French Quarter—those below are grouped according to nearby landmarks.

Cafe Brasil, 2100 Chartres St. (947-9386), off Frenchman St. just outside of the French Quarter. Neon lights and comfortable armchairs fill this art gallery/theater space/bar. Live jazz and reggae bands. Open daily 10:30pm-until.

Snug Harbor, 626 Frenchman St. (949-0696), just east of the Quarter near Decatur. Blues vocalists Charmaine Neville and Amasa Miller sing here regularly, giving 2 shows per night. The cover is no bargain, but Mon. evening with Ms. Neville is worth $8. You can also hear, but not see, the soulful music from the bar in the front room. Food served. Open daily 4pm-4am.

Benny's Bar, 938 Valence St. (895-4905), uptown. Hole-in-the-wall look-alike home of some of the city's best blues. Open daily, music starts around 11pm. No cover.

Tipitina's, 501 Napoleon Ave. (897-3943). This locally renowned establishment attracts the best local bands and even some big names. Favorite bar of late jazz pianist Professor Longhair; a bust of him now graces the front hall. Though the prof's pedagogy is no longer, the club books a wide variety of music. Best to call ahead for times and prices. Cover $3-10.

Michaul's, 701 Magazine St. (522-5517), at Girnod. Cover usually $3, free if you eat dinner there (entrees $7-13). A huge floor for Cajun dancing; they will even teach you how. Open with music Mon.-Fri. 7:30pm-11:30pm, Sat. 8pm-midnight.

Maple Leaf Bar, 8316 Oak St. (866-5323), near Tulane University. The best local dance bar, offering zydeco and Cajun music where everyone does the two-step. Also has poetry readings Sun. at 3pm. The party begins Sun.-Thurs. at 10pm, Fri.-Sat. at 10:30pm. Cover $3-5.

Muddy Water's, 8301 Oak St. (966-7174), near Tulane. Live music every night, mostly blues. Serves food and extracts a small cover. Open Sun.-Thurs. 11am-4am, Fri.-Sat. 11am-7am.

Jimmy's, 8200 Willow St. (866-9549), off Carrollton Ave. near Tulane. Popular bar featuring mostly good 'ol rock 'n' roll. Open with live music Wed.-Sun. 10pm-until.

The F&M Patio Bar, 4841 Tchoupitoulas (895-6784). Where all the yuppie uptowners go for late-night fun. Pool tables, juke boxes, and a patio bar add to the entertainment. This place really starts rocking around 1am and keeps on rolling until morning.

Igor's, 2133 St. Charles Ave. (522-7913). Take the St. Charles streetcar. This laundromat, pool room, bar and restaurant is the hot spot for lodgers at the Marquette House. Cheap food (10-in. pizza $3.75). The ol' wash and dry will never be the same again. Always a spin cycle. Open 24 hr.

St. Charles Tavern, 1433 St. Charles Ave. (523-9823). Have a blast at this neighborhood gathering spot, frequented by friendly cops and cabbies. Cheap salad bar ($3.45) and pizza ($3). Open 24 hr.

Plantations

River Road, a winding street that follows the Mississippi River, holds several preserved plantations from the 19th century. Pick up a copy of *Great River Road Plantation Parade: A River of Riches* at the New Orleans or Baton Rouge visitors centers for a good map and descriptions of the houses. Also free and frequent ferries cross the Mississippi at Plaquemine, White Castle, and between Lutcher and Vacherie. A tour of all the plantations would be quite expensive, though; all have steep admission charges. Skip most of the plantations since they all emphasize the same ostentatiousness of the Old South before the Civil War. The tours also fail to mention the hundreds of African slaves that lived in the cramped quarters behind the houses. Those below are listed in order from New Orleans to Baton Rouge.

San Francisco Plantation House, Rte. 44 (535-2341), 2 mi. north of Reserve, 23 mi. from New Orleans on the north bank of the Mississippi. Beautifully restored plantation built in 1856. Galleried in the old Creole style with the main living room on the 2nd floor. Exterior painted 3 different colors with many colorfully decorated ceilings. (Open daily 10am-4pm. Admission $5.50, children $2.50.)

Houmas House, River Rd., Burnside (473-7841), just over halfway to Baton Rouge on the northern bank of the Mississippi. Setting for the movie **Hush, Hush, Sweet Charlotte,** starring Bette Davis and Olivia DeHavilland. Built in 2 sections: the rear constructed in the last quarter of the 18th century; the Greek Revival mansion in front in 1840. Beautiful gardens and furnishings. Open Feb.-Oct. daily 10am-5pm; Nov.-Jan. 10am-4pm. Admission $5, students $3, children $2.

Nottoway, Rte. 405 (545-2730), between Bayou Goula and White Castle, 20 mi. south of Baton Rouge on the southern bank of the Mississippi. Largest plantation home in the South often called the "White Castle of Louisiana." An incredible 64-room mansion with 22 columns, a large ballroom, and a 3-story stairway. The first choice of David O. Selznick for filming *Gone with the Wind* but the owners didn't give a damn and simply wouldn't allow it. Open daily 9am-5pm. Admission and 1-hr. guided tour $8, children $3.

Baton Rouge

In the heart of Louisiana's plantation country, Baton Rouge provides a quiet retreat from the revelry of New Orleans. Today, the city seems curiously uncrowded and devoid of traffic. The controversial but always colorful Huey Long held court in this capital city until he was felled by an assassin's bullet in 1935. Nicknamed the "Kingfisher" after his successful political overthrow of the Louisiana aristocracy, Governor Long's corrupt populist political machine gained him fame and did not injure his reputation; a huge statue of the governor stands guard in front of the tallest capitol in the U.S. Besides politicians, the action in Baton Rouge centers around students. Visit **Louisiana State University** and **Southern University,** the nation's largest predominantly black university, to see the city's youthful side.

Practical Information

Emergency: 911.

Visitor Information: **Baton Rouge Convention and Visitors Bureau,** 838 North Blvd. (383-1825). Pick up the visitors guide but don't expect too much from the staff. Open daily 8am-5pm.

Greyhound/Trailways: 1253 Florida Blvd. (343-4891), at 13th St. A 15-min. walk from downtown. Unsafe area at night. To New Orleans (11 per day, 2 hr., $13) and Lafayette (6 per day, 1 hr., $8). Open 24 hr.

Public Transport: **Capital City Transportation:** 336-0821. Main terminal at 22nd and Florida Blvd. Buses run Mon.-Sat. approximately 6:30am-6:30pm. Service to LSU decent, otherwise unreliable and/or infrequent. Fare 75¢, transfers 10¢.

Help Lines: **Crisis Intervention/Suicide Prevention Center,** 924-3900. **Rape Crisis,** 383-7273. Both open 24 hr.

Post Office: 750 Florida Blvd. (381-0713), off River Rd. Open Mon.-Fri. 8:30am-4:30pm, Sat. 9-11am. **ZIP code:** 70821.

Area Code: 504.

Baton Rouge relaxes 80 mi. northwest of New Orleans up I-10 and the meandering Mississippi. I-10 connects Baton Rouge with Lafayette (52 mi. away) and Acadiana on the west. The state capitol sits on the east bank of the river; the city spreads eastward. The heart of downtown, directly south of the capitol, runs until **Government Street. Highland Road** leads south from downtown directly into LSU.

Accommodations, Camping, Food, Nightlife, et al.

Most budget accommodations lie outside of town along east-west Florida Blvd., (U.S. 190), or north-south Airline Hwy. (U.S. 61). **Louisiana State University** provides cheap accommodations at their on-campus hotel run out of Pleasant Hall (387-0297). Take bus #7 ("University") from North Blvd. behind the Old State Capitol. The flat rate of $38 covers as many friends as you can fit, comfortably about four people. **The Budgetel Inn,** 10555 Reiger Rd. (291-6600 or 800-428-3438), has very welcoming, neat rooms. (Singles $29. Doubles $36.) The **Alamo Plaza Hotel Courts,** 4243 Florida Blvd. (924-7231), has spacious rooms with cable TV and an occasional bug. Take bus #6 ("Sherwood Forest") east on Florida Blvd. from the Greyhound station. (Singles $22. Doubles $26.) The **KOA Campground** 7628 Vincent Rd. (664-7281), KOs 12 mi. east of Baton Rouge (Denham Springs exit off I-12). Well-maintained sites include clean facilities and pool. (Sites $12.50 for 2 people, with hookup $14.)

The best places to eat in Baton Rouge are near Louisiana State University (LSU) on **Highland Road.** Try **The Chimes,** 3357 Highland (383-1754), across the street from LSU, for burgers, po'boys, seafood, fried alligator ($5.50), live entertainment, and a selection of 70 different beers. Also refreshing are the veggie sandwich ($3.50) and the daily $1 beer specials. (Open Mon.-Fri. 11:30am-2am, Sat. 4pm-midnight,

Sun. noon-midnight.) Nearby **Louie's Café,** 209 W. State, is a 24-hr. grill famous for its stir-fried vegetable omelettes served anytime (around $4). Right behind Louie's is local favorite **The Bayou,** 124 W. Chimes (346-1765), the site of the bar scene and the concealing plant in *sex, lies, and videotape*. You can play free pool from 5 to 8pm and drink select longnecks for 99¢. Downtown, you can't miss the **Frostop Drive-In,** 402 Government, with a giant rootbeer mug spinning on a post outside and a Wurlitzer jukebox spinning platters inside. Try the delicious root beer floats ($1.50) and sandwiches ($2). (Open Mon.-Fri. 9:30am-8:30pm, Sat. 10:30am-8:30pm, Sun. 11am-8pm.) The hippest edition of Baton Rouge nightlife is the **One-gieme Art Bar,** 1109 Highland (393-9335), with art openings and original music ranging from flamenco guitar to experimental rock. (Open Mon.-Sat. 8pm-2am.)

Sights

The most prominent building in Baton Rouge is also the first one you should visit. Huey Long ordered the unique **Louisiana State Capitol** (342-7317), a magnificent modern skyscraper, built in a mere 14 months between 1931 and 1932. The front lobby alone merits a visit, but visitors should also go to the free 27th-floor observation deck. (Open daily 8am-4:30pm.) One of the most interesting in the U.S., the building attests to the power of Long's personality. Look for the plaque in a back corridor indicating the spot of his assassination; look in front under the statue to see his burial place. The **Old State Capitol,** at River Rd. and North Blvd., an eccentric Gothic Revival castle, offers free tours. (Open Tues.-Sat. 9am-4:30pm.) Just south of downtown, the **Beauregard District** boasts typically ornate antebellum homes. Walk down North Blvd. from the Old State Capitol to the visitors center to take in the beauty of this neighborhood.

Just a block away from the Old State Capitol on River Rd. floats the **Riverside Museum** of the Louisiana Arts and Science Center (344-9463). Climb on the old steam engine and train cars parked next door. The museum also has a good collection of sculpture, photographs, and paintings by contemporary Louisiana artists. (Open Tues.-Fri. 10am-3pm, Sat. 10am-4pm, Sun. 1-4pm. Admission $1.50; seniors, students, and children 75¢.) The museum runs the **Old Governor's Mansion,** the chief executive's residence from 1930-1963, at North Blvd. and St. Charles St. (Open Sat. 10am-4pm, Sun. 1-4pm. Admission $2.)

Those who don't have a car to visit outlying plantations (see Plantations under New Orleans) can visit the well-restored **Magnolia Mound Plantation,** 2161 Nicholson Dr. (343-4955), the only plantation on the regular bus line. (Open Tues.-Sat. 10am-4pm, Sun. 1-4pm; last tour at 3:30pm. Admission $3.50, seniors $2.50, students $1.50.) While most of the plantations have little mention of the African slaves and servants who worked on the plantations, the **LSU Rural Life Museum,** 6200 Burden Lane (765-2437) off Perkins Rd., re-creates everyday rural life in pre-industrial Louisiana. The authentically furnished shops, cabins, and storage houses adjoin meticulous azalea-filled gardens. (Open Mon.-Fri. 8:30am-4pm. Admission $3, children $2.)

Tour the harbor in the *Samuel Clemens* steamboat (381-9606), which departs from Florida Blvd. at the river for one-hour cruises. (Tours March-Sept. daily at 10am, noon, and 2pm; Oct.-March Wed.-Sun. at 10am, noon, and 2pm. Admission $5, children $3.) Open for inspection, the *U.S.S. Kidd* (342-1942), a World War II destroyer, throws tantrums on the river just outside the Louisiana Naval War Memorial Museum. (Open daily 9am-5pm. Ship and museum admission $3.50, children $2. Ship only $1, children 50¢.)

Acadiana

In 1755, the English goverment expelled French settlers from their homes in Nova Scotia. Moving down the Atlantic coastline and into the Caribbean, the so-called Acadians still received a hostile reception; Massachusetts, Georgia, and

South Carolina made them indentured servants. The Acadians soon realized that their only hope for freedom lay in reaching the French territory of Louisiana and settling on the Gulf Slope. Many of the present-day inhabitants of St. Martin, Lafayette, Iberia, and St. Mary parishes descended from these settlers.

Since the 18th century, many factors have threatened Acadian culture with extinction. Louisiana passed laws in the 1920s forcing Acadian schoolchildren to speak English. The oil boom of the past few decades has also endangered Acadian cultural survival. Oil executives and developers envisioned Lafayette, a center of Acadian life, as the Houston of Louisiana, threatening this small town and its neighbors with mass culture. However, the proud people of southern Louisiana have resisted homogenization, making the state officially bilingual and establishing a state agency to preserve Acadian French in schools and in the media.

Today "Cajun Country" spans the southern portion of the state, from Houma in the east to the Texas border. Mostly bayou and swampland, the unique natural environment here has intertwined with Cajun culture. The music and the cuisine, especially, symbolize the ruggedness of this traditional, family-centered society. Try some crawfish or dance the two-step to a fiddle and an accordion to sample Cajun life.

Lafayette

Lafayette makes a fine base for exploring Acadiana, filled with historical villages and museums of traditional Cajun life; besides the Acadian sites, however, the city has little to offer the tourist. The town centered oil businesses in southern Louisiana in the 70s and 80s, but the drop in crude prices stalled growth.

Opened in April 1990, **Vermilionville**, 1600 Surrey St. (233-4077), is an historic bayou attraction. Full of music, crafts, and food, this re-creation of an Acadian settlement educates as it entertains. (Open Sun.-Thurs. 10am-6pm, Fri.-Sat. 9am-9pm. Admission $8, seniors $6.50, ages 6-18 $5.) A folk life museum of restored 19th-century homes, **Acadian Village**, 200 Greenleaf Rd. (981-2364), 10 mi. from the tourist center, offers another view of Cajun life. Take U.S. 167 north, turn right on Ridge Rd., left on Mouton, and then follow the signs. (Open daily 10am-5pm. Admission $4, seniors $3, students $1.50.) The **Lafayette Museum**, 1122 Lafayette St. (234-2208), contains heirlooms, antiques, and Mardi Gras costumes. (Open Tues.-Sat. 9am-5pm, Sun. 3-5pm. Admission $3, seniors $2, students and children $1.)

Built on the edge of the Atchafalaya Swamp, Lafeyette links up with Baton Rouge via a triumph of modern engineering, the Atchafalaya Freeway, a 32-mi. bridge over the bayous. Get closer to the elements by embarking upon one of the **Atchafalaya Basin Swamp Tours** (228-8567), in the nearby town of Henderson. The captain explains the harvesting of crawfish and the building of the interstate highway on unstable swamp mud. (Tours leave at 10am, 1pm, 3pm, and 5pm. Fare $7, children $4.)

Cajun restaurants with live music and dancing have popped up all over Lafayette, but they tend to be expensive. **Mulates**, 325 Mills Ave., Beaux Bridge, calls itself the most famous Cajun restaurant in the world, and the autographs on the door support its claim. Cajun seafood dinners cost $10-15. (Open Mon.-Sat. 7am-10:30pm, Sun. 11am-11pm. Music noon-2pm and 7:30-10pm.) In downtown Lafayette, visit **Le Café des Artistes,** 537 Jefferson St., a chic gathering place. Menu includes fruit crepes and sandwiches ($3.75-4.25) on French bread with sprouts served on a bed of modern art. (Open Tues.-Fri. 11am-2pm and 5-10pm, Sat. 9am-2pm and 5-11:30pm.) Down the road is **Chris' Poboys,** 631 Jefferson St. (234-1696), which not surprisingly offers po'boys ($4-5) and seafood platters. (Open Mon.-Fri. 11am-9pm.)

Several motels are a $3 cabfare from the bus station. The close **Travelodge Oil Center,** 1101 Pinhook Rd. (234-7402) has large, attractive rooms, cable TV, pastel, and a pool. (Singles $23. Doubles $26.) The **Super 8,** 2224 N. Evangeline Thruway (232-8826), just off I-10, has ample, plain-looking rooms, a pool, and a stunning view of the highway. (Singles $30. Doubles $32.) Other inexpensive chain motels line Evangeline Thruway, including **La Quinta** (233-5610) and **Motel 6,** (233-2055). Avoid motels on Cameron St.; this area is unsafe. If you have extra cash, treat yourself to bed and breakfast at **Til Frere's House,** 1905 Verot School Rd. (984-9347), which has antique-filled rooms, private baths, Turkish towel robes, large breakfasts, complimentary drinks (mint juleps always on hand) and snacks. (Singles $55. Doubles $65. Mention *Let's Go* and you may get a 10% discount.) The closest campground is lakeside **KOA Lafayette** (235-2739), 5 mi. west of town on I-10 (exit 97), with a complete store and a pool. (Sites $14, a few small cabins $22-25.)

Pick up a copy of *The Times* (available at restaurants and gas stations all over town) to find out about what's going down this week. Considering its size and location, Lafayette has a surprising amount of after-hours entertainment, including the **Cajun Dance,** a world-class concert hall that regularly brings in acts and concerts of national prominence. For a lagniappe of sorts, Lafayette kicks off spring and fall weekends with **Downtown Alive!,** a series of free concerts featuring everything from new wave to Cajun and zydeco. (All concerts Fri. at 5:30pm. Call 268-5566 for information.) The **Festival International de Louisiane** (232-8086) in late April blends the music, visual arts, and cooking of this region into a francophone festival that pays tribute to the influence of the French upon southwestern Louisiana.

Lafayette stands at Louisiana's major crossroad. I-10 leads east to New Orleans (130 mi.) and west to Lake Charles (76 mi.); U.S. 90 heads south to New Iberia (20 mi.) and the bayou country; U.S. 167 runs north into central Louisiana. Lafayette also provides a railroad stop for Amtrak's *Sunset Limited,* linking the city with New Orleans (1 per day, 3 hr., $26), Houston (3 per wk., 5 hr., $47), and Los Angeles. The unstaffed station is at 133 E. Grant St., near the bus station; tickets must be purchased in advance through a travel agent. **Greyhound,** 315 Lee Ave. (235-1541), connects Lafayette to New Orleans (7 per day, 2½ hr., $19) and Baton Rouge (7 per day, 1 hr., $8), as well as to small towns such as New Iberia (2 per day, ½ hr., $3). The **Lafayette Bus System,** 400 Dorset (261-8570), runs infrequently, and not on Sundays (fare 45¢). But you'll need a car to really explore Acadiana and the Gulf Coast bayou country. **Thrifty Rent-a-Car,** 401 E. Pinhook (237-1282), usually has the best deals, though even these aren't so great. ($32.75 per day, 150 free mi. Must be 21 with major credit card.)

The **post office** is at 1105 Moss (232-4800). Lafayette's **ZIP code** is 70501; the **area code** is 318.

New Iberia and Southcentral Louisiana

While other plantations made their fortunes off cotton, most plantations in southern Louisiana grew sugarcane. Today most of these stay in private hands, but **Shadows on the Teche,** 317 E. Main St. (369-6446), is open to the public. Built in 1831, a Southern aristocrat saved the crumbling mansion from neglect after the Civil War. (Open daily 9am-4:30pm. Admission $4, children $2.)

Seven mi. away is **Avery Island,** on Rte. 329 off Rte. 90, actually a salt dome that resembles an island. Avery houses the world-famous **Tabasco Pepper Sauce** factory, where the McIlhenny family has produced the famous condiment for nearly a century. Guided tours include a sample taste. You may join the cult of Tabasco Sauce lovers. Kev did. (Open Mon.-Fri. 9-11:45am and 1-3:45pm, Sat. 9-11:45am. Free. 50¢ toll to enter the island.) Nearby lie the **Jungle Gardens** (369-6243), 250 acres developed in the 19th century by E. A. McIlhenny that include waterways, a lovely wisteria arch, camelia gardens, Chinese bamboo, alligators, and an 800-year-old statue of the Buddha. The jungle's sanctuary for herons and egrets helped save the snowy egret from extinction. This elegant bird, once hunted for the long plumes it grows during mating season, now nests in the gardens from February to mid-summer. (Open daily 9am-6pm. Admission $4.50, children $3.50.)

For a unique look at swamp and bayou wildlife, take an **Airboat Tour** (229-4457) of Lake Fausse Point and the surrounding area. (Tickets $40 for 4 people.)

New Iberia crouches 21 mi. southeast of Lafayette on U.S. 90. **Amtrak** (800-872-7245) serves New Iberia between New Orleans and Lafayette. **Greyhound** (364-

8571) pulls into town at 101 Perry St. Buses head to Morgan City ($6), New Orleans ($17), and Lafayette ($3) three times per day.

The **Tourist Information Center** propagandizes at 2690 Center St. (365-1540), at the intersection of Hwy. 14. (Open daily 9am-5pm.) The **post office** is at 817 E. Dale St. (364-4568). The **ZIP code** is 70560; the **area code** is 318.

Acadian Wildlife

Much of Acadiana is lush wilderness. The subtropical environment supports many species through a mixture of marsh, bottomland hardwoods, and stagnant backwater areas called bayous. Explore this bayou country about 40 mi. southeast of New Iberia near Bayou Vista to fish, see wildlife, or enjoy the jungle-like terrain. **Atchafalaya Delta Wildlife Area,** rich in birdlife, lies at the mouth of the Atchafalaya River in St. Mary Parish. The preserve encompasses bayous, potholes, low and high marsh, and dry ground. Rails, snipes, coot, and gallinules thrive here. Access it by boat launch from Morgan City near the Bayou Boeuf locks. Primitive campsites are available in the area.

The center of **Attakapas Wildlife Area,** in southern St. Martin and Iberia Parishes, lies 20 mi. northwest of Morgan City and 10 mi. northeast of Franklin. Flat swampland composes most of this hauntingly beautiful area, which includes a large amount of raised land used as a refuge by animals during flooding. In Attakapas cypress-tupelo, oak, maple, and hackberry grow on the high ground, and a cornucopia of swamp plants flourish in the wetlands. Hunting for squirrels, deer, and rabbits is popular here. You may also encounter local residents such as beavers, otters, muskrats, raccoons, bobcats, hawks, and gators. Once again, the area can be reached by boat; public launches leave from Morgan City on Rte. 70. Watch for signposts. Say "No" to drugs. No camping is allowed.

Mississippi

Perhaps one of the most sung about places in the U.S., Mississippi is poor economically, but rich historically. Mississippi's African American heritage has long stood at the core of the state's past. Not only did the blues originate from African slave songs in the Delta, the flat agricultural land around the Mississippi River, but Mississippians Robert Johnson and B.B. King popularized this great art form. Largely because of its firmly entrenched segregation, Mississippi provided one of the more public arenas for the Civil Rights Movement; from James Meredith's integration of "Ole Miss," to Freedom Summer and the Mississippi Freedom Democratic Party, African American activism paved the way for a more equitable New South.

When traveling today, try getting off the interstate to explore the lush forests, swamps, and countryside. A major passageway for hundreds of years, the Natchez Trace winds gracefully through the shade from Natchez, Mississippi to Nashville, Tennessee, passing through a beautiful national park and many historic landmarks. The park service helps you travel at a leisurely pace by strictly enforcing the Trace's 50-mph speed limit.

Practical Information

Capital: Jackson.

Tourist Information: Division of Tourism, 1301 Walter Siller Bldg., 550 High St. (359-3414 or 800-647-2290). Open Mon.-Fri. 8am-5pm. **Bureau of Parks and Recreation,** P.O. Box 10600, Jackson 39209.

Time Zone: Central (1 hr. behind Eastern). **Postal Abbreviation:** MS.

Jackson

Not a state capital, Jackson is the only major urban area in Mississippi. A hybrid of a briskly growing sunbelt city and sleepy Deep South town, Jackson reels with 20th-century activity, but without the teeming throngs of most major cities. Sights and stores here keep the hours of a smaller town—the historic and business districts barely come to life during working hours, and never create the tense atmosphere of a big metropolis. But most of Jackson's uniqueness lies outside the downtown area altogether. Located directly on the breathtaking **Natchez Trace Parkway,** Jackson has shaded campsites, cool reservoirs, national forests, and Native American mounds only minutes away.

Practical Information

Emergency: 911.

Visitor Information: Tourist Information Center, 1100 Lakeland Dr. (960-1800), off I-55 Lakeland exit. Open Mon.-Sat. 8am-4:30pm, Sun. 1-4:30pm. **Convention and Visitors Bureau,** 921 N. President St. (960-1891), downtown. Open Mon.-Fri. 8:30am-5pm.

Travelers Aid: 352-4481.

Allen C. Thompson Municipal Airport: East of downtown, off I-20. Cab fare to downtown approximately $13.

Amtrak: 300 W. Capitol St. (355-6350). To Memphis (1 per day, 4 hr., $42) and New Orleans (1 per day, 4 hr., $39). Open daily 7:30-10:30am and 5-7:30pm.

Greyhound/Trailways: 201 S. Jefferson St. (353-6342). Unsafe area at night. To: Dallas (4 per day, 10 hr., $68); Montgomery (7 per day, 7 hr.; $43); Memphis (1 per day, 4½ hr., $35). Open 24 hr.

Public Transport: Jackson Transit System (JATRAN) (948-3840), in the Federal Bldg. downtown. Limited service. Bus schedules and maps posted at most bus stops. Buses operate Mon.-Fri. 6am-5:30pm, Sat. 7am-6pm. Fare 60¢, transfers 10¢.

Help Lines: First Call for Help, 352-4357. Information referral service. **Rape Hotline,** 982-7273. **Mississippi Gay Alliance,** 961-4140.

Taxi: Veterans Cab, 355-8319. Base fare $1.10, $1 per mi.

Post Office: 401 E. South St. (968-0572). Open Mon.-Fri. 7am-7pm, Sat. 8am-noon. **ZIP code:** 39201.

Area Code: 601.

Jackson lies at the intersection of I-55 (north to Memphis, south to New Orleans) and I-20. Highways 49, 51, and 80, as well as the scenic Natchez Trace (which stretches 550 mi. from Natchez to Nashville, TN) can get you there. **State Street** runs north-south through downtown, **High Street** east-west.

Accommodations

There are few motels dowtown; however, with a car you can easily find inexpensive rooms along I-20 and I-55.

Sun 'n' Sand Motel, 401 N. Lamar St. (354-2501), downtown. Large, sunny rooms surround a tree-covered courtyard with a funny V-shaped pool. Very 50s oranges and aquas—even a Polynesian oom. Cable TV. Singles $30. Doubles $35.

Admiral Benbow Inn, 905 N. State St. (948-4161), downtown. Comfortable, clean rooms and a nice pool. Lovely, spacious rooms with remote control TV and tasteful bedspreads around a shaded courtyard. Singles $35. Doubles $40.

Red Roof Inn, 700 Larson St. (969-5006), by the fairgrounds downtown, but not as convenient as Admirals and Sun. Right next to highway, though fresh greenery surrounds building. Pleasant abodes with 2 comfortable chairs and color-coordinated linens. Singles $29. Doubles $37.

Motel 6, 970 I-20 Frontage Rd. (948-3692). Next door to noisy truck stop. Tidy and small white-walled rooms boats spotless bathrooms. Pool. Singles $21. $6 each additional person.

Food

Jackson eateries specialize in catfish and plate lunch specials, catering to both the young, professional crowd and older regulars. Most establishments are inexpensive and lively.

Primo's, 1016 N. State St. A Jackson tradition. Excellent, cheap Southern food; breakfasts with creamy grits and huge omelettes under $3. Vegetable plates, too, by gosh! Open Mon.-Fri. 7am-9:30pm, Sat.-Sun. 8am-9:30pm.

The Elite Cafe, 141 E. Capitol. Unpretentious lunch spot with great homemade cornbread, rolls, and veal cutlets. Plate lunch specials with 2 vegetables and bread under $4.50. Be prepared to wait in line during lunch rush. Open Mon.-Fri. 7am-9:30pm, Sat. 5-9:30pm.

The Iron Horse Grill, 320 W. Pearl St., at Gallatin. A huge converted smokehouse with a small cataract falling from the second floor. Primarily Tex-Mex ($5-8); steak and seafood entrees more expensive. A pianist accompanies lunch and dinner. Open Mon.-Sat. 11am-10pm.

Kiefer's, 705 Poplar Blvd., off Fortification St. Young crowds frequent this Greek restaurant, where you can bring your own wine. Gyro platters under $5. Open daily 11am-11pm.

Sights and Entertainment

Next door to the visitors center and the baseball stadium grows The Mississippi Agriculture and Forestry/National Agricultural Aviation Museum, 1150 Lakeland Dr. (354-6113), an avatar of Mississippi's strong ties to the fertile soil and air. The center includes real planes and original tools as well as a working farm. (Open Tues.-Sat. 9am-5pm, Sun. 1-5pm. Admission $3, seniors $2.75, children $1.) The old and the new compete everywhere in Jackson to the point that the city has two capitol buildings. Built in 1840, the Old State Capitol (354-6222), at the intersection of Capitol and State St., now houses an excellent museum of Mississippi's often dramatic history, including artifacts from original Native American settlements and documentaries on the Civil Rights Movement. (Open Mon.-Fri. 8am-5pm, Sat. 9:30am-4:30pm, Sun. 12:30-4:30pm. Free.) The state legislature's current home is the beautiful New State Capitol (359-3114), at Mississippi and Congress St., completed in 1903. A huge restoration project in 1979 has preserved the beaux arts grandeur of the building, complete with a gold-leaf covered eagle perched on the capitol dome. (Guided 45-min. tours Mon.-Fri. at 9am, 10am, 11am, 1:30pm, 2:30pm, and 3:30pm. Open Mon.-Fri. 8am-5pm, Sat. 10am-4pm, Sun. 1-4pm. Free.)

The downtown area maintains several other museums worth a visit. The Mississippi Museum of Art, at Pascagoula and Lamar St. (960-1515), has a fabulous collection of Americana and a fun participatory Impression Gallery for kids. (Open Tues.-Sat. 10am-5pm, Sun. noon-4pm. Admission $2, children $1; students free Tues.-Thurs.) Next door is the Russell C. Davis Planetarium (960-1550), considered one of the best in the world. (Galactic and musical shows Tues.-Fri. at 8pm; Sat. at 2, 4, and 8pm; Sun. at 2 and 4pm. Admission $4, seniors and children $2.50.) Look for a terrific presentation of nature and wildlife for the whole family at the Mississippi Museum of Natural Science on Jefferson St. (354-7303), across from the fairground. (Open Mon.-Fri. 8am-5pm, Sat. 9:30am-4:30pm.) And don't miss the Greek Revival Governor's Mansion (359-3175), a national historic landmark. The tours on the half hour are an enlightening introduction to Mississippian politics. (Open Tues.-Fri. 9:30-11am.) For a more in-depth look at some fine architecture, visit the Manship House, 420 E. Fortification (961-4724), a short walk north from the New Capitol. Charles Henry Manship, the Civil War mayor of Jackson, built this Gothic Revival "cottage villa," now restored to its 19th-century condition. (Open Tues.-Fri. 9am-4pm, Sat.-Sun. 1-4pm.) Sherman occupied Jackson's oldest house, The Oaks, 823 N. Jefferson St. (353-9339), built in 1746, during the siege of the city in 1863. (Open Mon.-Fri. 10am-4pm, Sat.-Sun. 1:30-4pm. Admission $2, students $1.)

The **Smith-Robertson Museum and Cultural Center,** 528 Bloom St. (960-1457), directly behind the Sun 'n' Sand Motel, presents and preserves Mississippi's African American history. This large and getting larger museum once housedf the state's first black public school, which *Native Son* author Richard Wright attended until the eighth grade. Now it includes folk art, photographs, and excellent exhibits of the Civil Rights Movement, particularly the role of African American women in Mississippi history. (Open Tues.-Sat. 9am-5pm, Sun. 2-5pm. Admission $1, children 50¢.)

After soaking in the history of life and politics in Jackson, soak up some music and fun at **Hal & Mal's Restaurant and Oyster Bar,** 200 Commerce St. (948-0888), which entertains in a converted warehouse. Reggae to innovative rock bands play Thursday through Saturday nights. (Restaurant open Mon.-Sat. 11am-10pm; bar open until 1am. Cover varies.)

Oxford

A visit to Oxford's town square reveals a simple beauty and charm which can't help but perpetuate the mythical image of life in a small Southern community. The quaint and almost too-perfect set-up centers around a monument to Confederate soldiers and the white sandstone **Lafayette County Courthouse.** It's no wonder that Oxford's own William Faulkner based his fictional Yoknapatawpha County on his picturesque hometown.

Beyond its literary aura, Oxford's status as a full-fledged college town dispells any Southern myths. At the **University of Mississippi** (known affectionately as "Ole Miss"), academic buildings surround the shaded yard called The Grove, while student social life revolves around football games and the Greek system. Though its physical environment has remained idyllic, the 1960s marked years of turmoil for the university. African American students, James Meredith first among them, struggled to enroll here; the nation watched as John F. Kennedy ordered troops to Oxford to protect registering students.

While in the town square, be sure to stop by the **Tourist Information Center** (232-2149), though hours sometimes vary from a shortage of volunteers. (Open Mon.-Sat. 8am-noon and 1-5pm. Sometimes closed Sat.) After the information center closes, turn the corner to **Square Books,** 200 Lamar St. (236-2262), where friendly advice combines with Faulkner postcards and an impressive collection of Southern writing. (Open Mon.-Sat. 9am-9pm, Sun. noon-5pm.)

A walk down South Lamar and along Old Taylor Rd., or better yet, on a path through Bailey's Woods from behind the Skipworth Museum on Museum Ave., leads to **Rowan Oak** (234-3284 or 232-7318). This former home of William Faulkner is tucked in a bend in Old Taylor Rd. Don't miss Faulkner's office in the back of the house where an outline to his novel *A Fable* adheres to the walls. (Open Tues.-Sat. 10am-noon and 2-4pm, Sun. 2-4pm.)

Faulkner studies continue at the university's **Center for the Study of Southern Culture** at the Barnard Observatory (232-5993), where scholars from all over the world gather for a conference on Bill each August. The center also houses year-round exhibits on Southern culture. (Open Mon.-Fri. 8:15am-4:45pm. Free.) Other resources include the **Blues Archive** across the street, 340 Farley Hall (232-7753), which houses B.B. King's personal collection of over 10,000 records. (Open Mon.-Fri. 8:30am-5pm.)

For grits and biscuits and other Southern fare in the heart of the square, **Smitty's,** 208 S. Lamar, has a full breakfast for under $4. (Open Mon.-Sat. 6am-9pm, Sun. 8am-9pm.) You'll also find restaurants which cater to the fun-loving and budget-conscious students of Ole Miss within walking distance of the square. **The Gin,** 201 Harrison St. (234-0024), 1 block southeast of Oxford Sq., is a converted cotton warehouse where lively crowds gather, especially for the live weekend bands. Sandwiches and burgers run under $6. (Open Mon.-Wed. and Sat. 11am-midnight, Thurs.-Fri. 11am-1am.) **The Hoka Café**, right next door at 304 S. 14th St., recieves kudos for its ceiling tapestries, blues posters, and cheesecake, but also serves sandwiches and catfish ($3-6). (Open daily 11am-"whenever, but usually by 2am.") **Square Books** (see above), in the square, serves square sandwiches ($2-4) and killer sweets (brandy bread pecan and pudding squares) in a café upstairs from the bookstore. **Café Olé**, 1612 University Ave., ¼ mi. east of the town square, serves incredible Mexican food including vegetarian specialties like spinach enchiladas ($2.50) and vegetable fajitas ($6.75). (Open Mon.-Fri. 11am-2pm and 5-10pm, Sat. 5-10pm.)

Nightlife usually centers around rockin' bands at the Gin and "artsy" movies virtually every night at the Hoka (see above). **Syd and Harry's**, 118 Van Buren Ave. (236-3193), in the square, has the best music in town. Dance five nights a week to a mixture of blues, rock, and progressive music, or just cuddle up with your favorite beer. (Open Mon. and Wed. 4pm-midnight, Thurs.-Fri 4pm-1am, Sat. 5pm-midnight.)

Plan ahead for lodgings: rooms are scarce in Oxford during football games (many weekends Sept.-Nov.), graduation (2nd week in May), and the Faulkner Festival (in late July). Behind the pink doors with white hearts of **The Ole Miss Motel**, 1517 E. University Ave. (234-2424), lurk comfortable rooms with cable TV and some refrigerators. (Singles $28. Doubles $34.) **The University Inn**, 2201 Jackson Ave. (234-7013), about 1 mi. from the university, is more luxurious, offering steamrooms, whirlpools, and a pool. (Singles $34. Doubles $40. Pool $2.) **Johnson's Motor Inn**, 2305 Jackson Ave. (234-3611), right next door, has spacious, clean, but lived-in rooms. (Singles $26. Doubles $30.)

Oxford fictionalizes 23 mi. east of I-55 and 130 mi. southeast of Memphis, TN on Rte. 6. For the most part, the town is small enough to cover easily on foot. University Avenue is the major east-west thoroughfare, intersecting with Lamar a few blocks south of the town square. Van Buren Avenue and Jackson Avenue cross the square parallel to University Ave.

Before touring Oxford, you should stop by the **Oxford Tourism Council**, 229 W. Jackson Ave. near Ole Miss (234-4651; open Mon.-Thurs. 9am-5pm, Fri. 9am-4pm). At the **Greyhound** station, 925 Van Buren Ave. (234-1424), make connections to Memphis (1 per day, 2 hr., $15) and Birmingham (1 per day, 4 hr., $31). Mississippi is notorious for its infrequent and inconvenient Greyhound routes.

Oxford's **post office** dislocates at 911 Jackson Ave. (234-5615). The city's **ZIP code** is 38655; the **area code** is 601.

Vicksburg

Started as a mission by Rev. Newit Vick in 1814, Vicksburg holds notoriety for its role in the Civil War. Its verdant hills and prime location on the Mississippi River proved extremely strategic for the Confederate forces, though not strategic enough: after a 47-day siege, the Union forces gained control over the "Gibraltar of the South," on July 4, 1863, the same day that Gettysburg fell. The loss of this critical river city meant the death of the Confederacy.

Today the war-torn countryside has been restored to its natural state, though markers of combat sites and prominent memorials pepper the grass-covered 1700-acre **Vicksburg National Military Park**, (636-0583 or 636-9421; 800-221-3536 outside MS) that surrounds the city. It's best to drive to the battlefield, museums, and cemetery east of town on Clay St. at exit 4B off I-20. (Admission $3 per car, $1 per person on bus, seniors and children free.) The visitors center at the entrance provides maps. Take a guide with you on a two-hour driving tour ($15) of the military park or drive the 16-mi. trail yourself. (Open summer daily 8am-8pm; off-season daily 8am-5pm.)

Within the park, visit the **National Cemetery** and the **U.S.S. Cairo Museum** (636-2199). The museum's centerpiece is the restored iron-clad gunboat *Cairo* (KAY-ro), the first vessel ever sunk by a remotely detonated mine. The museum displays a fascinating array of artifacts preserved for over a century after the ship sunk in the waters of the Yazoo River. (Open daily 8am-7:30pm; off-season 8am-5pm. Free.) To learn more of the events of the battle at Vicksburg, be sure to catch **"Vanishing Glory,"** 717 Clay St. (634-1863), a multi-media theatrical panorama. (Shows daily on the hour 10am-5pm; admission $3.50, ages 6-18 $2.)

The **Old Court House Museum,** 1008 Cherry St. (636-0741), presides over Vicksburg's town center, 3 mi. from the park's entrance. Once used as a prison for captured Union soldiers during the Siege of Vicksburg, today many consider it one of the South's finest Civil War museums, with everything from newspapers printed on the back of wallpaper to Jefferson Davis's tie. (Open Mon.-Sat. 8:30am-4:30pm, Sun. 1:30-4:30pm. Admission $1.75, seniors $1.25, ages under 18 $1.)

Next door, continuing the martial theme, is **Toys and Soldiers, A Museum,** 1100 Cherry St. (638-1986), where 27,000 toy soldiers from all over the world await you. (Open Mon.-Sat. 9am-4:30pm, Sun. 1:30-4:30pm. Tours $2, ages under 18 $1.50, families $5.) Two blocks away lie the **Museum of Coca-Cola History and Memorabilia** and the **Biedenharn Candy Company,** 1107 Washington St. (638-6514), which first bottled Coca-Cola. The museum displays Coke memorabilia from as far back as 1894, and sells Coke floats and over 100 different Coca-Cola items. (Open Mon.-Sat. 9am-5pm, Sun. 1:30-4:30pm. Admission $1.75, children $1.25. Disabled access.)

After taking time to wander around some of Washington Street's old-fashioned brick-paved roads, you'll end up not far from several fine antebellum homes. **Balfour House,** 1002 Crawford St. (638-3690), served as local headquarters for the Union Army after they took Vicksburg. Look down the three-story vertigo-inducing spiral staircase. (Open daily 9am-5pm. Admission $5, children $2.) The **Martha Vick House,** 1300 Grove St. (638-7036), was the home of Martha Vick, an unmarried daughter of Reverend Vick. But of course. The restored building contains many elegant French paintings. (Open daily 9am-5pm. Admission $5, ages 12-18 $2.) The latter, like many of the restored Vicksburg estates, doubles as a B&B (ask at the visitor's center).

While downtown, chow down at **Burger Village,** 1220 Washington St., home of inexpensive ground beef on buns. (Open Mon.-Thurs. 9am-6pm, Fri.-Sat. 9am-7pm.) The **New Orleans Café,** 1100 Washington St., provides sandwiches for under $6 and Cajun specialties and seafood for more. (Open Sun.-Fri. 11am-10pm, Sat. 11am-midnight.) Don't look far for a bar; inside the restaurant is the lively **Other Side Lounge.** (Open Mon.-Sat. 11am-2am, Sun. 11am-midnight.) Across the street is **Miller's Still Lounge,** a real Southern watering hole with live entertainment and popcorn smells nightly. (Open Sun.-Thurs. 11am-midnight, Fri.-Sat. 11am-2am.) A mile south of downtown, **Ruben's,** 3421 Washington St., offers Miss-Mex lunch specials starting at $4. (Open Mon.-Thurs. 11am-9pm, Fri.-Sat. 11am-10pm.) From there take a short drive south on Washington St. to the **Louisiana Circle,** a secluded overview serving truly breathtaking vistas of the great Mississippi River.

You can easily find cheap accommodations in Vicksburg, except around July 4th weekend when the military park's reenactment brings thousands of tourists and inflated hotel rates. Since most hotels are located by the park, don't expect to stay in town. The **Hillcrest Motel,** 4503 Hwy. 80 E. (638-1491), has spacious, ground-floor singles for $20 and doubles for $23. The **Scottish Inn,** I-20 at Hwy 80 E. (638-5511), provides dank and worn singles for $23, doubles for $26. The **Vicksburg Battlefield Kampground,** 4407 I-20 Frontage Rd. (636-9946), has a pool and laundromat. (Sites $10-12 for 2 people.)

For more information about Vicksburg, visit the **Tourist Information Center** (636-9421), directly across the street from the park. (Open daily 8am-5pm.) Unfortunately, you'll need a car to see most of Vicksburg: the bus station, the information center, the downtown area, and the far end of the sprawling military park are at the small city's four extremes.

Vicksburg lies 30 mi. west of Jackson on I-20, and 200 mi. north of New Orleans. The **Greyhound/Trailways** (636-1230) station is inconveniently located at 3324 Hall's Ferry Rd., off Frontage Rd.; buses run to Jackson (8 per day, 1 hr., $8). The

Rape and Sexual Assault Service (636-6120) answers calls 24 hr. Vicksburg's ZIP code is 39180; the area code is 601.

Biloxi and the Mississippi Coast

Billed as the South's Riviera, **Biloxi** and its neighbors Gulfport and Pascagoula have tossed aside their tranquil origins to become hyped-up resorts. Biloxi, ironically a Native American word meaning "first people," once served as the centerpiece of the Old Spanish Trail from Florida to the California missions. Today, known as Highway 90 or Beach Boulevard, the "trail" is lined with fast-food operations, hotels, and new condominiums. Less tacky than the coastline in Florida's Panhandle, Mississippi's gulf shores achieve partial redemption thanks to their subtropical scenery. The so-called Spanish Moss hanging from the oak trees along the roads is neither Spanish nor moss, but actually a plant related to the pineapple, living off the moisture in the air. Biloxi also sits on the world's longest (26 mi.) man-made beach, the **Gulf Islands National Seashore**.

Between Biloxi and Gulfport you'll find the mansions, pavilions, and grounds of **Beauvoir**, 2244 Beach Blvd. at Beauvoir Rd. (388-1313), the last home and current shrine of Confederate President Jefferson Davis. (Open daily 9am-5pm. Admission $4, children $2.) Also along the shoreline is the **Biloxi Lighthouse,** which, according to legend, was painted black after President Lincoln's assassination. Actually, it needed a paint job because it had rusted. Today it's snowy white, and open seasonally for viewing the gulf and the town. (Open March-Oct. daily 9am-sunset. Admission 50¢.) For a jaunt around the city take the **Ole Biloxi Train Tour,** a 1½-hr. ride that begins at the lighthouse; the first tour leaves at 9:30am. (Tour $5, children $2.50.)

Swimming goes on until well past Labor Day in the warm water of Biloxi's beaches, but the shore often a bit unsightly. Hurricane Camille devastated this area 20 years ago and the coast has never fully recovered. Nearby **Ship Island,** in the national seashore, which served as the Union's command center for the pivotal Battle of New Orleans, has consistently crystal blue waters: *USA Today* called it one of the nation's 10 best beaches. Hiking is also fabulous, but beware of alligators and wear plenty of sunscreen. **Boats** to the island depart from Biloxi's Buena Vista Motel, Central Beach Blvd. (432-2197; 6-hr. trips mid-May to Sept. daily at 9am and noon; April to mid-May Sat.-Sun. at 9am and noon; fare $11, children $5). You can camp overnight on **Horn Island** or **East Ship Island;** just remember to pack insect repellent.

Accommodations on the coast can be very costly; the cheapest places are located beyond the reach of public transportation. Several motels offer singles and doubles for about $25 to $35 mid-week in summer, with even higher rates on weekends. Half a dozen mediocre motels with good prices surround the **Biloxi Hilton,** some with rates as low as $15 for a single off-season. One of the nicest of these, the **Motel 6** at 2476 Beach Blvd. (388-5130), sits in a modern building with spruce new rooms and a pool. (Singles $27. Doubles $36.) Rates here do not rise on weekends. Camping is also a cheap alternative; rates vary from $10-15 depending on the season. The most convenient site is the **Biloxi Beach Campground,** 3162 W. Beach Blvd. (432-2755). Farther from town are **Martin's Lake and Campground,** 14601 Parker Rd. (875-9157), 1 mi. north of I-10 at exit 50 in Ocean Springs, and the campground at **Gulf Islands National Seashore, Davis Bayou** (875-3962) on Hanley Rd. off U.S. 90 also in Ocean Springs.

The **Biloxi Chamber of Commerce,** 1048 Beach Blvd. (374-2717), across from the lighthouse, eagerly offers aid to tourists. (Open Mon.-Fri. 8:30am-5pm.) The **Biloxi Tourist Information Center,** 710 E. Beach Blvd. (374-3105), down the street from the bus station, has many helpful brochures. (Open Mon.-Fri. 8am-6pm, Sat. 9am-6pm, Sun. noon-5pm.) For more information contact the **Mississippi Gulf Coast Convention and Visitor's Bureau,** 135 Courthouse Rd. (896-6699 of 800-237-9493).

Biloxi lies 90 mi. east of New Orleans and 70 mi. west of Mobile. Jackson is 170 mi. inland. Getting into and out of Biloxi is rarely problematic because intercity buses serve the town well. **Greyhound/Trailways,** 322 Main St. (436-4336), offers frequent service to New Orleans (15 per day, 2½ hr., $16) and Jackson (2 per day, 4 hr., $24). **Coast Area Transit** (896-8080) operates buses (marked "Beach") along the beach on U.S. 90 from Biloxi to Gulfport. (Buses supposedly operate Mon.-Sat. every 70 min. Board at any intersection. Fare 75¢.)

The **post office** is at 135 Main St. (432-0311), near the bus station. (Open Mon.-Fri. 8:30am-5pm, Sat. 9am-noon.) Biloxi's **ZIP code** is 39530; its **area code** is 601.

Tennessee

Tennessee encompasses three distinct regions corresponding roughly to the great loops in the Tennessee River. Eastern Tennessee is hillbilly country, home to the beautiful Great Smoky Mountains while the rolling farmlands of central Tennessee surround the rhinestone glitter of Nashville. The western portion of the state looks to Memphis and the Mississippi River for the maintenance of a more "Southern" way of life. Tennessee's geographic distinctions crystallized culturally during the Civil War, when a ferocious rift developed between the pro-Union eastern section and the Confederate west. This divided state contributed legendary local sons Davy Crockett and Andrew Jackson to U.S. history, but it also earned a measure of notoriety for its backwoods mentality. The Scopes "Monkey Trial" took place in Dayton in 1925, forbidding the teaching of evolution here until 1967. Aided by FDR's Tennessee Valley Authority (TVA) dams and a host of other New Deal initials, however, Tennessee today appears to be coming out of the woods. The sounds of country and bluegrass along with a wealth of crafts, which began with the first pioneers in the untrammeled Tennessee wilderness, unite the state's regional triumvirate. Nashville and Memphis attract millions of visitors each year to their respective musical shrines, while serving double duty as major commercial centers for the mid-South.

Practical Information

Capital: Nashville.

Tourist Information: Tennessee Dept. of Tourist Development, P.O. Box 23170, Nashville 37202 (741-2158). Open Mon.-Fri. 8am-4:30pm. **Tennessee State Parks Information,** 701 Broadway, Nashville 37203 (742-6667).

Time Zone: Central (Memphis and Nashville; 1 hr. behind Eastern) and Eastern (Chattanooga, Knoxville). **Postal Abbreviation:** TN.

Memphis

Follow your ears in the southwestern corner of Tennessee to Memphis, the birthplace of rock 'n' roll and home of the blues. W.C. Handy, who played on legendary Beale Street, published the first blues piece here in 1912, appropriately titled "Memphis Blues." Later, Elvis Presley popularized the fusion of southern country music with African American blues and gospel, becoming the "King of Rock 'n' Roll."

Memphis also lies at the spiritual if not geographical center of the mid-south commercial region, which includes western Tennessee, Arkansas, Missouri, Alabama, and Mississippi. The nation's 15th-largest city, Memphis headquarters several large corporations. From anywhere in the country, each and every package sent through Federal Express winds up at Memphis for sorting; this also means you can get the city's famous barbecue ribs sent from local restaurants to anywhere in the country absolutely, positively overnight.

Practical Information

Emergency: 911.

Visitors Information Center: 207 Beale St. (526-4880), 2 blocks south on 2nd St. and 2 blocks east on Beale from the Greyhound station. Quite helpful, with everything from bus maps to restaurant guides. Open daily 9am-6pm.

Memphis International Airport: just south of the southern loop of I-240. Taxi fare to the city $12-13—negotiate in advance. Public transport to and from the airport only $1.25, but a long and difficult trip for a traveler unfamiliar with the area.

Amtrak: 545 S. Main St. (526-0052 or 800-872-7245), at Calhoun on the southern edge of downtown. Unsafe area during the day, very dangerous at night. To New Orleans (1 per day, 7½ hr., $69, round-trip from $76) and Houston (1 per day, 14 hr., $137). Open Mon.-Sat. 8am-12:30pm, 1:30-5pm, 9pm-6am, Sun. 9pm-6am.

Greyhound/Trailways: 203 Union Ave. (523-7676), at 4th St. downtown. Unsafe area at night. To Nashville ($37) and New Orleans ($61). Open 24 hr.

Public Transport: Memphis Area Transit Authority (MATA), 61 S. Main St. (274-6282). Extensive bus routes cover most suburbs but buses take their time and do not run frequently. The 2 major downtown stops are at Front and Jefferson St. and at 2nd St. and Madison Ave. Operates Mon.-Fri. 5am-5pm, major lines until 11pm; less frequent service Sat.-Sun. Fare 85¢.

Taxi: Yellow Cab, 526-2121. $2.35 first mi., $1.10 each additional mi.

Crisis Line: 247-7477. Open 24 hr. Also refers to other numbers.

Time Zone: Central (1 hr. behind Eastern).

Post Office: 555 S. 3rd St. (521-2140), at Calhoun St. Take bus #13. Open Mon.-Fri. 8:30am-5:30pm, Sat. 10am-2pm. **ZIP code:** 38101.

Area Code: 901.

Memphis spreads out from the east bank of the **Mississippi River** in the southwest corner of Tennessee, 200 mi. southwest of Nashville and 300 mi. south of St. Louis, MO. **I-240** circles Memphis. Downtown, named avenues run east-west and numbered ones north-south. **Madison Avenue** bifurcates north and south addresses. Two main thoroughfares, Poplar and Union Avenues, lead to the heart of the city from the east; 2nd and 3rd Streets arrive from the south.

Accommodations

The accommodations outlook in Memphis is fair to good for those with a car; otherwise you will have to take an unreliable bus to reach reasonably priced lodgings. Downtown establishments are expensive, but cab fare to the hinterlands may make them seem more reasonable. Less expensive but less comfortable motels grace Elvis Presley Blvd. near Graceland. Book ahead if you are coming between August 12-16, when Elvis fans from around the universe gather to pay tribute on the anniversary of his death. The visitors information center has a thorough listing of lodgings. Contact **Bed and Breakfast in Memphis,** P.O. Box 41621, Memphis 38174 (726-5920), for guest rooms in Memphis homes. French- and Spanish-speaking hosts are available. (Singles $27-55. Doubles $32-55.)

Lowenstein-Long House/Castle Hostelry (AYH), 1084 Poplar and 217 N. Waldran (527-7174). Convenient location—a long but possible walk from downtown, or accessible by bus #50 from 3rd St. Beautiful accommodations in an elegant Victorian mansion. Laundry facilities. $10, nonmembers $13.

River Place Inn, 100 North Front St. (526-0583), overlooking the water. Upscale hotel with great rooms from $48. The visitors information center has a $35 coupon for 1-4 people.

Regal 8 Inn, 1360 Springbrook Rd. (396-3620), just east of intersection of Elvis and Brooks Rd. near Graceland. Not regal nor fit for the King but pleasant rooms with white painted brick walls and spotless bathrooms. Enjoy free coffee and doughnuts after a morning swim. Free shuttle to and from airport. Singles $27. Doubles $36.

Motel 6, I-55 at Brooks Rd. (346-0992), near Graceland. Small but tidy. Pool. Singles $27. Doubles $33.

Food

When a smoky, spicy smell follows you almost everywhere, you are either extremely paranoid, malodorous, or in Memphis, where barbecue reigns. The city hosts the World Championship Barbecue Cooking Contest in May. But don't fret if gnawing on ribs isn't your thing: Memphis has plenty of other Southern style-restaurants with down-home favorites like fried chicken, catfish, chitlins, and fresh vegetables.

The Rendezvous, Downtown Alley, in the alley across from the Peabody Hotel off Union St., between the Ramada and Days Inns. A Memphis legend, serving large portions of ribs ($6.50-9), and cheaper sandwiches ($3). Open Tues.-Thurs. 4:30pm-midnight, Fri.-Sat. noon-midnight.

Mike's Barbeque Pit, 73 Monroe, near the river downtown. Traditional diner serves barbecue, grill food, and tamales. Full meals under $5. Open Mon.-Fri. 6am-3pm, Sat. 7am-2pm.

P and H Café, 1532 Madison Ave. (274-9794). The initials aptly stand for Poor and Hungry. This local favorite serves huge burgers, plate lunches, and grill food ($3-5). Say hi to *Mona Lisa.* Local bands occasionally play Sat. night. Open Mon.-Sat. 11am-3am.

The North End, 346 N. Main St. (526-0319), downtown. Dark but cozy. Extensive menu includes tamales, wild rice, and creole dishes ($3-8). Delicious vegetarian meals for under $5. Great Hot Fudge Pie ($2.50). Happy Hour 4-7pm. Live music Wed.-Sun. with a small cover (around $3). Open daily 11am-3am. Next door **356 North Main** offers a similar menu, but with stir-fry specialties. No music but no cover.

Leonard's Barbecue Pit, 1140 Bellevue Blvd. S. An old Elvis haunt near Graceland serving good barbecue ($3-5). Cute ceramic pigs in the window modeled after the King during his later reign. Open Mon.-Sat. 10am-5pm.

Spaghetti Warehouse, 40 W. Huling St., off S. Front St. Great friendly family restaurant. Get a filling plate of pasta, salad, and bread for under $5 in a restored trolley car or on a carousel. Open Mon.-Thurs. 11am-10pm, Fri. 11am-11pm, Sat. noon-11pm, Sun. noon-10pm.

Front St. Delicatessen, 77 S. Front St. Lunchtime streetside deli with almost no room to sit inside. Popular with local yuppies. Patio dining in sunny weather. Hot lunch specials $4. Open Mon.-Fri. 8am-4pm, Sat. 11am-3pm.

Sights

Elvis Presley has become somewhat of a deity in people's minds since his death in 1977, and his home, heaven. Don't come to **Graceland** (pronounced GRACE-lin), 10 mi. south of downtown at 3794 Elvis Presley Blvd. (332-3322; 800-238-2000 outside TN), looking for a glimpse into the reality of the King's world. The built-up complex resembles an amusement park, with visitors shuffling from one room to another until the ride is over. The varying surfaces of the rooms, from the mirrored halls and ceilings to the carpeted walls of the Jungle Room, provide excitement and insight into Elvis' eclectic, multi-tiered style. Elvis bought the mansion when he was only 22, and lived/grew there until his death. The King and his family are buried next door in the Meditation Gardens, completing the religious experience that is Graceland.

Across the street, you can visit several Elvis museums, including the **Elvis Presley Car Museum.** This huge hall has 20 of Presley's cars and an indoor drive-in movie theater which shows clips from 31 of the movies Elvis made. Also open for tourists is Elvis' personal plane, named for his daughter, the *Lisa Marie*—look for his bed with a safety belt. In one of the gift shops, say hello to Elvis' Uncle Vestor who dispenses witticisms for free while he works. Like most of the people you meet here, Vestor makes Graceland a unique experience. Tickets are sold across the street from Graceland and reservations are recommended. Admission to the mansion costs $8, children $4.75; the entire package (including car museum, plane, a 20-min. film, and customized bus) costs $16, children $11. Take Lauderdale/Elvis Presley bus #13 from 3rd and Union. (Open mid-June to mid-Aug. daily 8am-8pm; early June and late Aug. 8am-7pm; Sept.-April 9am-6pm; May 8am-6pm.)

A musical tour of Memphis goes beyond Graceland, into other locations downtown. Most famous is **Beale Street.** Historical signs and the statue of W.C. Handy explain the birthplace of the blues. After a long period of neglect, this neighborhood once again has music pouring from almost every door; live music seeps into the park. Moved to Beale St., the **W.C. Handy Home and Museum,** 352 Beale (527-2583), exhibits music and photographs. (Open daily 9am-6pm; call for an appointment.) A five-and-dime store run by the same family since 1876, **A. Schwab,** 163 Beale St. (523-9782), still offers old-fashioned bargains. A "museum" of relics-never-sold gathers dust on the mezzanine floor, including an array of voodoo potions and powders. Elvis used to buy some of his flashier ensembles here. (Open Mon.-Sat. 9am-5pm. Free guided tours.) Avid music fans like U2 might want to visit tiny **Sun Studio,** 706 Union Ave. (521-0664), where Elvis, Jerry Lee Lewis, Johnny Cash, and Carl Perkins first ventilated their vocal chords for producer Sam Phillips. (Thirty-min. tours every hr. on the ½ hr. Open daily 10:30am-5:30pm. Admission $4, children $2.)

Scheduled to open in June of 1991, **The Great American Pyramid** (800-627-9726) is not the latest game show but the latest extravaganza in Memphis. You won't be able to miss the 32-story-high, six-acre-wide shining pyramid that will hold the American Music Hall of Fame, the Memphis Music Experience, the College Football Hall of Fame, and a 20,000 seat arena. The whole experience will include daily music shows indoors and in outdoor parks; admission will be $25, children $17.50.

Until June of 1991, visitors must settle for **Mud Island,** 125 N. Front St. (576-7241), which will lycanthropically turn into **Festival Island** when the Pyramid opens. Now Mud Island holds a fascinating museum on the Mississippi River which includes comprehensive music history exhibits and a 5-block replica of the river. Bring a bathing suit for the Gulf of Mexico, a huge swimming pool. Catch a "Sunset Party" Wednesday evenings from early May to Labor Day. (Open daily April-late Nov., hours change seasonally. Pick up a calendar of events at the visitors information center. Admission $6, seniors and children $4. Beach and park only $3.) Your budget may not accommodate the expensive restaurants along the river, but a stroll along the Mississippi costs not a cent. The river runs clear where it passes Memphis, making the sunsets especially memorable.

In the heart of downtown lies the luxurious **Peabody Hotel,** 149 Union St., the social center of Memphis society in the first half of this century. Folklore once said that the Mississippi Delta began in its lobby. Now the hotel keeps ducks in its indoor fountain; every day at 11am and 5pm the management rolls out the red carpet and the ducks waddle to and from the elevator with piano accompaniment. Get there early because sometimes ducks are impatient.

On April 4, 1968, a sniper assassinated Rev. Martin Luther King, Jr. at the **Lorraine Motel,** 406 Mulberry St. The second-floor motel room near the site of the shooting is being converted into a museum and civil rights center (to be completed in 1991).

Found at 3rd and Beale St. and other spots around the city, the "Showboat" bus runs 7am-11pm taking you to all the sights of midtown. Buy an all-day ticket for $2. A major sight is the **Victorian Village,** which consists of 18 mansions in various stages of restoration and preservation. The **Mallory-Neeley House,** 652 Adams St. (523-1484), one of the village's two mansions open to the public, went up in the mid-19th century and has yet to come down. Most of its original furniture remains intact. (Open Tues.-Sat. 10am-4pm, Sun. 1-4pm. Admission $4, seniors and students $3.) For a look at a different lifestyle during the same era, the **Magerney House,** 198 Adams St. (526-4464), held the middle-class home of Eugene Magerney, who helped establish Memphis's first public schools. (Open Tues.-Sat. 10am-4pm. Free.)

Set in attractive Overton Park, the **Memphis Brooks Museum of Art** (722-3500) houses a mid-sized collection of impressionist painting and 19th-century U.S. art.

(Open Tues.-Sat. 10am-5pm, Sun. 1-5pm. Admission $2, seniors, students, and children $1. Free Fri.) The **Memphis Zoo and Aquarium** (726-4775) swings next door. (Open daily 9am-4:30pm. Admission $3.25, seniors and children $1.50. Free Mon. after 3:30pm.) Another beautiful art and nature complex is the **Dixon Gallery and Gardens,** 4339 Park Ave. (761-5250; open Tues.-Sat. 10am-5pm, Sun. 1pm-5pm; admission $2, children $1; free Tues.).

For a less tranquil day, visit **Libertyland,** 940 Early Maxwell Blvd. (274-1776), an amusement park near MSU. (Open mid-June to late Aug. Tues.-Sat. 10am-9pm, Sun. noon-9pm; mid-April to early June and late Aug.-early Sept. Sat. 10am-9pm, Sun. noon-9pm. Admission $6, seniors $3. "Thrill ride" ticket $6 extra.)

Entertainment and Nightlife

Blues blows nightly all over Beale St., usually with a small cover charge ($3-5), but many evenings free blues fills the air from street performers in the park. Get down with tourists at the **Rum Boogie Cafe,** 182 Beale St. (528-0150), or ride the red carpet to **Club Royale,** 349 Beale St. (527-5404) for live music with an older, better-dressed Memphis crowd.

Key magazine, distributed by the visitors information center, the free *Memphis Flyer,* or the "Playbook" section of the Friday morning *Memphis Commercial Appeal* will give you an idea of what's going down around town. The **Antenna Club,** 1588 Madison Ave. (725-9812), receives the city's hip progressive rock and hard core music. For harder-core music downtown, go to **GDI's on the River,** 287 S. Front St. (526-1086).

The majestic **Orpheum Theater,** 89 Beale St. (525-7800), is a classic movie palace, complete with 15-ft.-high Czechoslovakian chandeliers and an organ. The theater shows classic movies on weekends along with an organ prelude, a cartoon, and a Buck Rogers episode (sorry, no Gil Gerard). The **Memphis Chicks,** 800 Home Run Lane (272-1687), near Libertyland, are a big hit with fans of Southern League baseball. (Reserved seats $4, general admission $2.75.)

Nashville

The capital of Tennessee since 1843, Nashville is probably better known for its country music than for its big-city politics. Though banjo picking and boot stomping have entrenched themselves in Tennessee's central city, this town has something to satisfy everyone's musical tastes. Whether a terrific symphony, local folk music, or the newest rock, the area's major recording studios perpetuate some of the best, though perhaps not the latest, sounds. Behind this musical harmony breakdances "the Wall Street of the South," a slick, choreographed financial hub. The same city that headquarters the Southern Baptists and higher morality also provides a center of the fine arts and higher learning, with Vanderbilt and Fisk University. Nashville is a large, eclectic, unapologetically glitzy place that marches to its own mirthful drummer.

Practical Information

Emergency: 911.

Visitor Information: Nashville Area Chamber of Commerce, 161 4th Ave. N. (259-4755), between Commerce and Union St. downtown. Ask for the *Hotel/Motel Guide,* the *Nashville Dining & Entertainment Guide,* and a *Calendar of Events.* Information booth in main lobby open Mon.-Fri. 8am-5pm. **Nashville Tourist Information Center,** I-65 at James Robertson Pkwy. exit 85 (259-4747), about ½ mi. east of the state capitol, just over the bridge. Take bus #3 ("Meridian") east on Broadway. Complete maps marked with all the attractions. Open daily until sunset. *Spotlight on the Arts* ($3.50) is available at the **Metro Arts Commission,** 111 4th Ave. S. (259-6374).

Travelers Aid: 256-3168. Open Mon.-Fri. 8:30am-4pm.

Metropolitan Airport: 8 mi. south of downtown. Limos $8 one way, taxis $12-14, MTA buses 75¢.

Greyhound: 200 8th Ave. S. (256-6141), at Demonbreun St., 2 blocks south of Broadway downtown. Borders on a rough neighborhood. To: Memphis (9 per day, 4 hr., $37); Washington, DC (7 per day, 16 hr., $89); Atlanta (7 per day, 7½ hr., $29); Louisville (14 per day, 4 hr., $22). Open 24 hr.

Public Transport: Metropolitan Transit Authority (MTA), 242-4433. Buses operate Mon.-Fri. 5am-midnight, less frequent service Sat.-Sun. Fare 75¢, zone crossing or transfers 10¢. The **Nashville Trolley** (242-4433) runs daily in the downtown area every 10 min. for only 25¢.

Taxi: Nashville Cab, 242-7070. 90¢ first mi., $1.30 each additional mi.

Help Lines: Crisis Line, 244-7444. **Rape Hotline,** 327-1110. **Handicapped Information,** 259-6676. **Gay and Lesbian Switchboard,** 297-0008.

Time Zone: Central (1 hr. behind Eastern).

Post Office: 901 Broadway (255-9447), across from the Sheraton and next to Union Station downtown. Open Mon.-Fri. 8am-6pm, Sat. 8am-noon. **ZIP code:** 37202.

Area Code: 615.

Nashville is located on the **Cumberland River** smack in the middle of Tennessee, 178 mi. west of Knoxville, and 209 mi. northeast of Memphis. Take I-40 or I-24 from the east or west and I-65 from the north or south.

The names of Nashville's streets seem undeniably fickle. **Broadway,** the main east-west thoroughfare, becomes **West End Avenue** just outside downtown at I-40, and later becomes **Harding Road.** Downtown, numbered avenues run north-south, parallel to the Cumberland River. The curve of **James Robertson Parkway** encloses the north end, becoming **Main Street** on the other side of the river (later Gallatin Pike), and **McGavock Street** at the south end. The area between 2nd and 7th Ave., south of Broadway, is unsafe at night.

Accommodations and Camping

Finding a room in Nashville is not difficult, just expensive. Most places cling within 20 mi. of downtown. Make reservations well in advance, especially for weekend stays. A dense concentration of budget motels line W. Trinity Lane and Brick Church Pike at I-65, north of downtown. Even cheaper hotels inhabit the area around Dickerson Rd. and Murfreesboro, but the neighborhood is seedy at best and not recommended for women. When traveling in a small group, an efficiency suite is an economical option: **Lexington Hotel Suites,** 2425 Atrium Way (883-5201), off Briley Pkwy. behind the Holiday Inn, east of downtown, offers a queen-size bed and a hide-a-bed for $75. Or contact **Bed and Breakfast of Middle Tennessee** (297-0883; singles $25-40, doubles $50-75). **Hallmark Inns,** part of a local chain, are cheaper than the national chains.

Motel 111, 800 James Robertson Pkwy. (244-2630), near tourist information center downtown. Nice building with elevator and 50s-style wallpaper. Comfortable, likable rooms. Singles $24. Doubles $29.

The Cumberland Inn, I-65 N. and Trinity Lane (226-1600). Neat brick exterior. Cheerful rooms with big beds, table, and chairs. Singles $26.50. Doubles $33.50.

Motel 6, 311 W. Trinity Lane (227-9696), at exit 87B off I-24/I-65; 323 Cartwright St., Goodlettsville (859-9674), take the Long Hollow Pike west, off I-65, then turn right onto Cartwright; and 95 Wallace Rd. (333-9933), take exit 56 from I-24, go west on Harding Pl. 1 block, left at Traveler's Inn Lane, and left on Largo. Tidy, efficient white rooms with dark curtains. Singles $28. Each additional person $6.

Tudor Inn-Downtown, 750 James Robertson Pkwy. (244-8970), at 8th Ave. N. Take bus #8 on 8th Ave. from the Greyhound station. Next door to Motel 111. Dark but clean rooms. Singles $30, weekends $32. Doubles $33.

Three campgrounds within walking distance of Opryland USA can also be reached by public transport from 5th St. For the **Fiddler's Inn North Campground** (885-1440), the **Nashville Travel Park** (889-4225), and the **Two Rivers Campground** (883-8559), take the Briley Pkwy. north to McGavock Pike, and exit west onto Music Valley Dr. (Sites $15-17 for 2 people.) Ten minutes north of Opryland is the **Nashville KOA**, 708 N. Dickerson Rd. (859-0075), I-65 in Goodlettsville, exit 98. Tell 'em Dave sent you. (Sites $12-17.)

Food

The influence of the Nashville sound even extends into the local delicacies. Pick up a Goo-Goo cluster (peanuts, chocolate, caramel, and marshmallow) at any store and you'll bite into the initials of the Grand Ole Opry. Pecan Pie is another favorite dessert, perfect after spicy barbecue or fried chicken. Restaurants for collegiate tastes and budgets cram the 2000 block of Elliston Place, near Vanderbilt. The **farmers market,** north of the capitol between 3rd and 7th Ave., sells fresh fruits and vegetables until sunset.

> **Loveless Motel Restaurant,** Hwy. 100 (646-9700), at Rte. 5, 15 mi. southwest of town. Accessible by car only. True country-style cooking at its best and most unrequited. Famous for its preserves, fried chicken, and hickory-smoked ham. To experience a truly heavy Southern meal try the homemade biscuits with red-eye gravy, a special blend of ham drippings and coffee ($3-8). Open Tues.-Sat. 8am-2pm and 5-9pm, Sun. 8am-9pm. Reservations recommended weekends.

> **Slice of Life,** 1811 Division, next to music studios. Fresh bread and vegetarian Tex-Mex with wholesome ingredients, one of many healthy alternatives to high-cholesterol Southern cuisine. Quesadillas under $5. Open Mon.-Sat. 7am-9pm, Sun. 8am-9pm.

> **International Market,** 2010-B Belmont Blvd. Asian grocery with a large Thai buffet ($4-6). Crowded for lunch. Open daily 10:30am-9pm.

> **Rotiers,** 2413 Elliston Place (327-9892). Traditional "greasy spoon" without the grease. Good sandwiches and specials ($3-5). No croissants here. Open daily 9am-11:35pm.

> **Brown's Diner,** 2102 Blair Blvd. (269-5509), near Vanderbilt. Dilapidated diner with expanded dining room. Great for fun college atmosphere, but food less than exciting. Burgers $4-5. Open Mon.-Sat. 11am-10:30pm. Bar serves until midnight.

Sights

Music Row, the home of Nashville's most famous industry, whistles along Division and Demonbreun St. from 16th to 19th Ave. S., bounded on the south by Grand Ave. (Take bus #3 to 17th Ave. and walk south.) After surviving the mobs outside the **Country Music Hall of Fame,** 4 Music Sq. E. (256-1639) at Division St., you can gawk at Elvis' "solid gold" Cadillac and other country music memorabilia. Included in the admission is a tour of RCA's historic **Studio B,** where you can see how stars like Dolly Parton and U.S. Respresentative from Massachusetts Chet Atkins recorded their first hits by experimenting with the instruments and equipment yourself. (Open June-Aug. daily 8am-8pm; Sept.-May 9am-5pm. Admission $6.50, ages 6-11 $1.75, under 6 free.) When you want to record your own hit, the **Recording Studio of America,** 1510 Division St. (254-1282), underneath the Barbara Mandrell Country Museum, lets you do your own vocals on pre-recorded, high-quality 24-track backgrounds to popular country and pop tunes. Choose a set and make a video, too. (Audio recording $13, video $20. Open June-Aug. daily 8am-8pm; Sept.-May daily 9am-5pm.)

A 15-minute walk west from Music Row along West End Ave. to **Centennial Park** will soon explain why Nashville calls itself the "Athens of the South." In the park stands an exact-size replica of the **Parthenon** (259-6358). Originally built as a temporary exhibit for the Tennessee Centennial in 1897, the Parthenon made such a splash that the model was rebuilt in more durable form. In the summer of 1990, the museum installed a 42-ft. replica of **Athena,** the goddess of wisdom, completing a perfect reproduction of the original monument with the largest indoor sculpture in the Western Hemisphere. Unlike the oringinal, this building houses the Cowan Collection of American Paintings in the basement galleries during April, August, and December. Watch Greek theater performed on the steps in mid-July and August. (Open Tues.-Sat. 9am-4:30pm, Sun. 1-5pm. Admission $2.50, children $1.25.)

A walk through the downtown area reveals more of Nashville's eclectic architecture. **Union Station Hotel,** 1001 Broadway, is a towering restored turn-of-the-century train station and one of the best known landmarks in Nashville. The **Ryman Auditorium,** 116 5th Ave. N. (254-1445), off Broadway at 5th, housed a tabernacle and the Grand Ole Opry in previous incarnations. (Guided tours daily 8:30am-4:30pm. Admission $2, ages 6-12 $1.) Turn up 2nd Ave. from Broadway to study the cast-iron and masonry façades of the handsome commercial buildings from the 1870s and 1880s, many of which have been converted into restaurants and nightspots. The **Tennessee State Capitol,** Charlotte Ave. (741-0830), a handsome Greek Revival structure atop the hill next to downtown, offers free guided tours. (Open Mon.-Fri. 9am-4pm, Sat. 10am-5pm, Sun. 1-5pm.) Across the street is the **Tennessee State Museum,** 505 Deaderick (741-2692). (Open Mon.-Sat. 10am-5pm, Sun. 1-5pm. Free.)

When you tire of the downtown area, rest at the **Cheekwood Botanical Gardens and Fine Arts Center,** Forest Park Dr. (356-8000), 7 mi. southwest of town. The well-kept, leisurely, English-style gardens are a welcome change from Nashville's glitz. Take bus #3 ("West End/Belle Meade") from downtown to Belle Meade Blvd. and Page Rd. (Open Tues.-Sat. 9am-5pm, Sun. 1-5pm. Admission $3.50, seniors and students $2, ages 7-17 50¢). The nearby **Belle Meade Mansion,** 110 Leake Ave. (356-0501), at Harding Rd., displays Southern antebellum opulence at the site of the nation's first thoroughbred breeding farm. (Two tours per hr., last tour at 4pm. Open Mon.-Sat. 9am-5pm, Sun. 1-5pm. Admission $4, ages 13-18 $3.50, 6-12 $2.)

Thirteen mi. east of town is the **Hermitage,** 4580 Rachel's Lane (889-2941); take exit 221 off I-40. Andrew Jackson's beautiful manor house sits on 625 acres making an ideal spot for a picnic. Beware the crowded summer months. (Open daily 9am-5pm. Admission $7, seniors $6.50, ages 6-13 $3.50.)

Fisk University's **Van Vechten Gallery,** 17th Ave. N. (329-8543), exhibits a distinguished collection of U.S. art. The gallery owns a portion of the Alfred Steiglitz Collection, donated to Fisk by Georgia O'Keeffe, Steiglitz's widow. Other exhibits feature her work in addition to a range of photography and African art. (Open Tues.-Fri. 10am-5pm, Sat.-Sun. 1-5pm. Admission $2.50, elementary and high school students free.)

Entertainment

Nashville offers a wide and dazzling array of inexpensive nightspots. Many feature the country tunes for which the town is known while others cater to jazz, rock, bluegrass, or folk music fans. The *Tennessean* has entertainment listings Fridays and Sundays; the *Nashville Banner* Thursday afternoon. The Nashville *Key,* available at the chamber of commerce, also informs. Comprehensive listings for all live music and events in the area also abound in free copies of *Nashville Scene* or *Metro* around town. Muse over these publications plus many more at **Moskós,** 2204-B Elliston Place (327-3562), while stalling at their tasty muncheonette. (Open daily 8am-midnight.)

A cross between Las Vegas glitz and Disneyland purity, with the best in country music thrown in, **Opryland USA** (889-6700) remains Nashville's largest draw. The amusement park part contains all the requisite family attractions from roller coasters to cotton candy, but also gives over 10 live music shows, each performed several times in different areas throughout the day, from 9am-sunset. At other times, country music pipes throughout the entire park. (Open late March-late April and early Oct.-early Nov. Sat.-Sun.; early May-late May and early Sept.-late Sept. Fri.-Sun.; late May-early Sept. daily; Admission $20, 2 days $25.) The **Grand Ole Opry** moved here from the town center in 1976. *The* place to hear country music, the Opry stomps every Friday and Saturday night. Matinees are added during peak tourist season (March-Sept.). Tickets cost $12-14 Friday and Saturday nights, $9.75-12 for matinees; reserve them from Grand Ole Opry, 2808 Opryland Dr., Nashville 37214. Enclose a check or money order, or call 615-889-3060. General admission tickets can be purchased at the box office only, starting at 9am on Tuesday for weekend shows. Check the Friday morning *Tennessean* for a list of performers.

Many stars got their start at the somewhat sleazy **Tootsie's Orchid Lounge,** 422 Broadway (251-9725), which still has good C&W music and affordable drinks. For years the owner Tootsie Bess, lent money to struggling musicians until they could get on the Ole Opry. Not recommended for women traveling alone. (Open Mon.-Sat. 10am-3am, Sun. noon-3am.) The more genteel **Blue Bird Cafe,** 4104 Hillsboro Rd. (383-1461), in Green Hills, plays blues, folk, soft rock, and a smidgen of jazz. Women traveling solo will feel comfortable in this mellow, clean-cut establishment. Dinner, served until 8:30pm, consists of salads and sandwiches ($4-6.50). Music begins at 9:30pm. Go west on Broadway, then south on 21st, which turns into Hillsboro Rd. (Open Mon.-Sat. 5:30pm-1am. Cover $4-5.) The **Station Inn,** 402 12th Ave. S. (255-3307), offers serious bluegrass. (Open Tues.-Sat. 7pm-until. Music starts at 9pm. Cover $4. Free Sun. night jam session.) West of downtown, the **Bluegrass Inn,** 1914 Broadway (329-1112), has beer, chips, and bluegrass music with a cinderblock-and-cement motif. A good-natured sort of place, the cover (around $4) depends on who's picking. (Open Wed.-Thurs. 9pm-midnight, Fri.-Sat. 9pm-1am.)

There's more to entertainment in Nashville than country music; just visit during the first weekend in June for the outdoor **Summer Lights** (259-6374) downtown, when top rock,, jazz, reggae, classical, and, of course, country performers all jam simultaneously. For information on **Nashville Symphony** tickets and performances, call Ticketmaster at 741-2787. Rock bands play to a college audience at the **Exit/In,** 2208 Elliston Place (321-4400), near the Vanderbilt campus. (Bands start around 10:30pm. Cover about $4.) In a huge renovated warehouse downtown **Ace of Clubs,** 114 2nd S. (254-2237), packs 'em in for grand ol'e rock 'n' roll. (Open daily. Music around 9pm. Cover $4-7.) **The World's End,** 1713 Church St. (329-3480), is a popular gay restaurant and dance club with a huge video screen. It would be silly to miss the wealth of live music in the city, but villagers don't put just spring water on their pool tables at **Springwater,** 115 27th Ave N. (320-0345), near the Parthenon. And near Vanderbilt try **The Villager,** 1719 21st Ave. S. (298-3020).

Great Smoky Mountain National Park

The largest wilderness area in the eastern U.S., Great Smoky Mountain National Park encompasses a half-million acres of gray-green Appalachian peaks, bounded on either side by misty North Carolina and Tennessee valleys. Bears, wild hogs, white-tailed deer, groundhogs, wild turkeys, and more than 1500 species of flowering plants make their homes here. Whispering conifer forests line the mountain ridges at elevations of over 6000 ft., rhododendrons burst into their full glory in June and July, and by mid-October, the sloping mountain flanks have become a giant crazy-quilt of color, reminiscent of the area's well-preserved crafts tradition.

Start any exploration of the area with a visit to one of the park's three visitors centers. **Sugarlands,** on Newfound Gap Rd., 2 mi. south of Gatlinburg, is the park's headquarters. (Open in summer daily 8am-7pm; spring and fall 8am-5pm; winter 8am-4:30pm.) **Cades Cove** (436-1275) is in the park's western valley, 22 mi. southwest of Sugarlands on Little River Rd., 15 mi. southwest of Townsend, TN. (Open in summer daily 9:30am-7pm; fall 8:30am-5:30pm; spring 9:30am-5:30pm.) The **Oconaluftee Visitors Center,** 4 mi. north of Cherokee, NC (497-9147), serves travelers entering the park from the Blue Ridge Parkway and all points south and east (open same hours as Sugarlands). The park **information line** (615-436-1200; open daily 8:30am-4:30pm) telelinks all three visitors centers. The rangers can answer travel questions, field emergency message calls, and trace lost and found equipment.

At each visitors center you'll find displays amplifying the park's natural and cultural resources, bulletin boards displaying emergency messages or public information, brochures and films, and comfort stations. Be sure to ask for *The Smokies Guide,* a newspaper offering a comprehensive explanation of the park's changing natural graces. The helpful journal also includes practical information on tours and other activities, such as rafting or horseback riding. The standard park service brochure, *Great Smoky Mountains,* provides the best driving map in the region. Hikers should ask the visitors center staff for assistance in locating an appropriately detailed backcountry map. You can also tune your car radio to 1610 AM at various marked points for information.

Gatlinburg connects to Cherokee, NC on Newfound Gap Road (U.S. 441). Even if one's destination is the serene hills and trails of the mountains, it is difficult to resist the Vegas-like charm of this little resort town. Mobs of tourists occupy its bizarre corners ranging from a quick-fix wedding chapel to a wax museum holding a candle to President Bush. The **Space Needle's** electric elevator ride transports its customers to a moving view the Smokies, or perhaps to breathe mountain air not tainted with the hot scent of bargain shopping. Gatlinburg reveals itself to be a Bizarro world of tourist delights full of shops, churches, restaurants, and attractions. Also unique to Gatlinburg is the way the town twists and squeezes into every square inch of space along a heavily trafficked strip, appearing in the same abrupt way it ends. For more down-to-earth guidance and a copy of the helpful *In the Smokies* stop in at the **Tourist Information Center,** 520 Pkwy. (615-436-4178), conveniently located on the strip. (Open May-Oct. Mon.-Sat. 8am-8pm, Sun. 9am-5pm; Nov.-April Mon.-Sat. 8am-6pm, Sun. 9am-5pm.)

Back to life, back to reality, back to the park, nine hundred mi. of hiking trails and 170 mi. of road criss-cross the park. The **Appalachian Trail** is the park's central north-south boulevard (hikers only). A road goes all the way up to **Clingman's Dome,** the highest point. **Little River Road** works its way through the southwest quadrant of the park, out to the 11-mi. Cades Cove loop. A self-guided auto-tour leads to many small parking areas from which you can walk (¼ to ½ mi.) to the sites of old hand-built buildings, the last vestiges of a vital mountain community that occupied the area in the 1850s. Along the short and pretty walkways it is not uncommon to encounter wildlife, even bears. The park service advises visitors to practice caution and treat the bears, as all wildlife, with all due respect. For information, contact the **Appalachian Trail Conference,** P.O. Box 807, Harper's Ferry, WV 25425.

Accommodations and Camping

A free permit is required for backcountry camping at the park's many primitive sites. Just follow the simple self-registration procedures posted at outlying ranger stations and at the three visitors centers. To stay at one of the "rationed" primitive campgrounds, you'll have to obtain in-person or telephone authorization from the park headquarters. (Sites with pcinic table and fireplace $5-7. Toilet and sink facilities. No showers.) Sites at three (**Smokemont, Elkmont,** and **Cades Cove**) of the Smokies' 10 developed campgrounds accept reservations; the remainder are first come, first serve. (Sites $10.) For those hauling a trailer or staying at one of the park's campgrounds near the main roads during the summer, reservations are a must. Obtain them at least eight weeks in advance by writing to Ticketron, P.O. Box 62429, Virginia Beach, VA 23462 (900-370-5566).

Three youth hostels locate in the area around the park. The closest is **Bell's Wa-Floy Mountain Village (AYH),** Rte. 3, P.O. Box 611 (615-436-7700), 10 mi. east of Gatlinburg on Rte. 321. From the center of Gatlinburg catch the east-bound trolley (25¢) to the end of the line. From there, it's a 5-mi. walk to Wa-Floy. Trolley service also runs past Wa-Floy from Gatlinburg three times per day—ask in town or call for times. Located centrally in the Wa-Floy Retreat (which doubles as the

Steiner Bell Center for Physical and Spiritual Rejuvenation), the hostel is no more than a rustic cabin divided into a few single-sex apartments with kitchenettes. The interior is shabby but clean, though the showers are dark, moldy, and unpleasant. Yet peacocks and ducks, unaware of the shower conditions, roam the lovely grounds complete with a pool, tennis courts, meditation area, chapel, and requisite murmuring stream. The proprietor, Mrs. Floy Steiner Bell, may welcome you warmly with her poetry. ($10, nonmembers $12. Call for reservations at least one day ahead.) On the other side of the park, about 35 mi. away on a slow, winding road in North Carolina, you can vegetate after a hike or river ride in the spacious communal living room of Louise Phillip's **Smokeseege Lodge (AYH)**, P.O. Box 179, Dillsboro (704-586-8658), on Rte. 441, 11 mi. south of Cherokee. Walk from the nearest Greyhound/Trailways stop, nearly 3 mi. away in Sylva, NC. If you're driving from the Smokies, watch carefully on the right-hand side of Rte. 441 for a small, triangular AYH logo—the hostel is at the end of a gravel road. Kitchen facilities are available; no smoking or drinking permitted. (Lockout 9am-5pm. Curfew 11pm. $7, nonmembers $17. Call ahead for availability. Open April-Oct.) Further south, near Wesser, the bustling **Nantahala Outdoor Center (NOC)**, U.S. 19 W., P.O. Box 41, Bryson City (704-488-2175), 80 mi. from Gatlinburg and 13 mi. from downtown Bryson City, welcomes both seasoned hikers and inexperienced adventurers. Located in the **Nantahala National Forest,** the NOC is not an official hostel, but does offer cheap beds. Staying at the NOC is a good idea when planning a whitewater rafting trip or taking advantage of the other programs offered there; keep in mind the center is not a convenient trip from the GSM park or Gatlinburg. Bunks occupy simple wooden cabins at "base camp" on the far side of the river and fairly large-sized motel rooms with kitchenettes. Showers, kitchen, linen, and laundry facilities included. ($7. Call ahead for reservations.) Next to the NOC's general store and equipment sales department, their riverfront restaurant serves hearty, affordable country-style food ($3-5).

The NOC's rates for 2½-hr. whitewater rafting expeditions are pricey, but you can rent your own raft for a self-designed trip down the Nantahala River (Sun.-Fri. $12, Sat. $15. One-person inflatable "duckies" $22 per day.) The NOC also rents canoes and kayaks and offers instruction for the novice. Most trips have minimum age or weight limits; daycare service is available at the center. Trip prices include transportation to the put-in site and all equipment. Don't let *Deliverance* steer you clear.

Hike on the Appalachian Trail to explore some of the old forest service roads. The NOC staff will gladly assist if you need help charting an appropriate daytrip.

The NOC also maintains seasonal "outposts" on the **Ocoee, Nolichucky, Chattoga,** and **French Broad Rivers,** all within 100 mi. of its Bryson City headquarters. Although these do not have overnight facilities, a rafting expedition on any of these rivers makes a satisfying daytrip if you have a car. Be sure to look into NOC's 20% discounts during March and April.

GREAT LAKES

The Great Lakes change mood with considerable speed. One day they're as smooth as a backyard kiddie pool, the next as choppy and dark as the North Atlantic, sending 20-foot swells over seawalls and sucking down 50,000-ton freighters. The largest and deepest, Lake Superior, also has the least populated and most scenic coasts. Lake Michigan is a sports-lover's paradise, with deep-water fishing, swimming, sailing, and dunes for hang gliding. Though Erie has suffered the most from industry, vigilant citizens and strict regulations have helped the shallowest of the lakes regain its former beauty.

In contrast to the lakes, the dark forests and rural farmlands sheathed in fields of wheat and corn seem tame. The only motion for miles may be a red-tailed hawk winging overhead. In the 19th and early 20th centuries, European immigrants came by the millions—some farmers in search of rich soil, others hoping to tap the land's iron and copper deposits. Cities like Milwaukee and Cincinnati sprang up as commercial hubs for transporting the region's raw materials.

The era of the "New Frontier," which brought the meteoric growth of the railroads and auto industries pivotal to the nation's development, has long since disappeared. Though hard hit by inflation and economic changes in the mid-70s, the large cities around the Great Lakes have battled back while still maintaining their traditional blend of urban energy and heartland charm. Minneapolis and St. Paul make a sophisticated center for the arts; Indianapolis proves a pit stop for U.S. sports activity; and Cleveland and Detroit, most devastated by the industrial slump, have revamped their cityscapes with innovation. Chicago sits at the heart of the region. Its world-class music, architecture, and restaurants join hands with a gritty brand of politics and an unpretentious sensibility.

Travel

Small regional airlines serve major Great Lake cities best. Operating out of Chicago's Midway Airport, **Midway Airlines** (800-621-5700) offers cheap flights and many specials to East Coast and Midwest cities. (New York to Chicago $312 on Sat.-Sun., $270 otherwise; Chicago to Detroit $26.) **Northwest Airlines** (800-225-2525) flies mainly to northern cities and the West Coast, using Minneapolis and Detroit as hubs (Detroit to Los Angeles $343). Book one month in advance for discount fares. **United** (800-241-6522) is not always as cheap but is certainly convenient, with a Chicago hub serving most Midwestern cities nonstop (Chicago to Minneapolis $285).

Amtrak's national hub is Chicago, with routes radiating throughout the southern Great Lakes region. Only one route serves Wisconsin and Minnesota, with a branch to the Twin Cities; northern Michigan lacks train service altogether. But you'll have no trouble getting around by bus in the more populous areas of the Great Lakes states. **Greyhound** provides the most extensive coverage, particularly in Wisconsin and Minnesota. Greyhound buses and connecting lines completely encircle Lake Michigan along shoreside highways, but serve the Upper Peninsula only in the middle of the night. Regional bus companies include **Indian Trails** in Michigan, **Badger Bus** in Wisconsin, and **Indiana Motor Bus.**

The Great Lakes region stands out as the only area in the central U.S. well served by **youth hostels.** Conveniently, these hostels tend to lie near established bike trails and access points to canoe routes. Approximately 20 hostels stretch across Michigan from Detroit northwest to the central Lake Michigan shore. Ohio has a well-spaced smattering of hostels, while Minnesota has a cluster around the Twin Cities. Southern Wisconsin has several more. Indiana and Illinois, except for Chicago, are hostel wastelands. Look for a room or an extra bed at one of the many college campuses. State universities often have huge numbers of dorm rooms for sharing or renting,

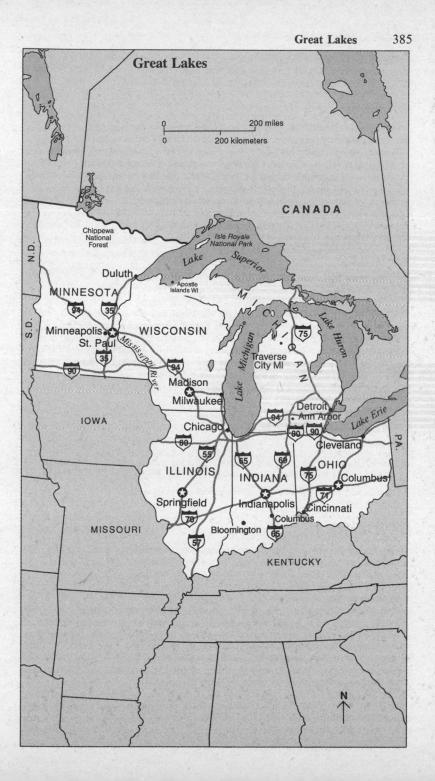

Great Lakes

especially during the sumer, when motels in popular tourist areas double and even triple their prices. Illinois, Indiana, and Wisconsin have an ample supply of **Motel 6's** and slightly more expensive **Red Roof Inns** (800-843-7663).

Outdoors

Surprisingly, the most scenic car and bike routes in the southern Great Lake states trace not the lake coasts, but the southern parts of Indiana and Ohio. Rugged cliffs, deep valleys, and lush forests stand in contrast to the flatlands of the north; especially dazzling are Hoosier and Wayne National Forests in Indiana and Ohio, respectively. Minnesota's Boundary Waters and the forests and craggy coasts of Michigan's U. P. challenge the intrepid nature lover with untamed wilderness. For general information on the National Park Service properties, contact the Midwest Regional Office, 1709 Jackson St., Omaha, NE 68102 (402-221-3471). Contact the National Forest Service's Regional Office at 310 W. Wisconsin Ave., Milwaukee, WI 53203.

Illinois

Illinois divides into two distinct parts: Chicago and the rest of Illinois, called "downstate" by Illini. No longer "Second City," Chicago is now the third largest metropolis in the U.S., teeming with diverse communities and a thriving, diverse economy. Downstate is blessed with stability and fertility—quiet farm country with the kind of open space that inspired the science fiction novels of Ray Bradbury, born in Wankegan. Illinois' two halves share an economy based on agriculture as well as the self-confidence that comes from knowing that they are the heart of both the Grain Belt and the U.S.

Practical Information

Capital: Springfield.

Tourist Information: **Office of Tourism**, 620 E. Adams St., Springfield 62701 (217-782-7500). **Travel Center**, 310 S. Michigan Ave., Chicago 60604 (312-793-4732).

Time Zone: Central (1 hr. behind Eastern). Postal Abbreviation: IL.

Chicago

The Pottawattamie people who first came upon this patch of prairie at the edge of Lake Michigan dubbed it *Chikagu,* or "City of the Wild Onion;" some say it really meant "City of the Big Smell." Modern Chi-town has displaced the Pottawattamie and their vegetables, but the name and both its meanings have stuck along with countless other epithets for the Midwest's largest city. Locals and out-of-towners know Chicago as "the Windy City," a catchy pair of trochees referring not to the stiff breezes which whip through the downtown streets but to the hot air from the mouths of certain turn-of-the-century revivalist preachers. Supercilious New Yorkers may write Chicago off as merely the nation's "Second City," and census-hungry Angelenos may relegate it to third place, but die-hard Chicagoans will always insist that Carl Sandburg's "City of the Big Shoulders" knocks out any civic competitor with the guts to climb into the ring.

The Chicago *Tribune* once speculated what the city would be like without Lake Michigan. Forgoing the obvious conclusion (that it simply wouldn't exist), the author described a horrible scenario of endless sprawl in all directions, severe water shortages, and a sickly population menaced by the mosquitoes swarming out of nearby swamps. As it is, Chicago's healthy lakefront resulted from a historical

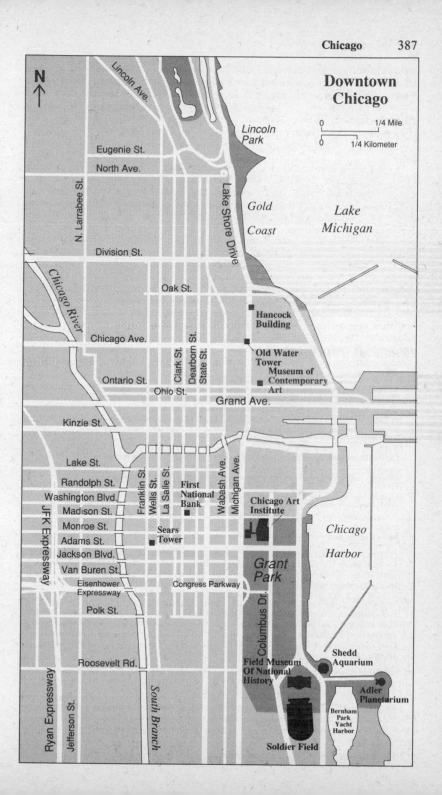

N

**Downtown
Chicago**

0   1/4 Mile

0   1/4 Kilometer

Lincoln Ave.

Lincoln
Park

Lake
Michigan

Eugenie St.

North Ave.

N. Larrabee St.

Lake Shore Drive

Gold

Coast

Division St.

Chicago River

Oak St.

Hancock
Building

Chicago Ave.

Old Water
Tower

Clark St.

Dearborn St.

State St.

Museum of
Contemporary
Art

Ontario St.

Ohio St.

Grand Ave.

Kinzie St.

Lake St.

Randolph St.

Franklin St.

Wells St.

La Salle St.

Wabash Ave.

Michigan Ave.

Washington Blvd.

First
National
Bank

Chicago Art
Institute

Madison St.

Monroe St.

JFK Expressway

Sears
Tower

Adams St.

Chicago

Harbor

Jackson Blvd.

Van Buren St.

Grant
Park

Eisenhower
Expressway

Congress Parkway

Polk St.

Roosevelt Rd.

Ryan Expressway

Jefferson St.

South Branch

Columbus Dr.

Shedd
Aquarium

Field Museum
Of National
History

Adler
Planetarium

Bernham
Park
Yacht
Harbor

Soldier Field

rather than a geographical accident—the Great Fire of 1871. Allegedly started when Mrs. O'Leary's cow kicked over a lantern in a hay-filled shed, this immense bonfire destroyed most of the city. Two decades later, Daniel Burnham instituted a formal riot-proof rebuilding plan which had the fortunate side-effect of reserving all of Chicago's 27 miles of lakefront property for public beaches, parks, and harbors. A product of visionary modern architects like Frank Lloyd Wright and Louis Sullivan, the postcard-perfect skyline sprouts up three of the world's tallest buildings.

Beyond the lakefront and elegant downtown areas, Chicago preserves much of the no-nonsense grittiness it had when Upton Sinclair grimly termed it *The Jungle*. The stockyards and freight depots which made the Armours and the Pullmans rich have remained closed for decades, but local trains still rattle by every ten minutes on the city's signature elevated tracks. Chicago's extreme racial polarization—the North Side is predominantly white, the South Side predominantly African American—often obscures the tremendous diversity of the city's checkerboard ethnic neighborhoods, which erupt in an endless chain of festivals every summer. Some old West Side neighborhoods still conduct daily business entirely in Polish, a reminder that Chicago has more Poles than any city besides Warsaw.

Such cultural variety has inspired a score of major museums, an impressive collection of public sculpture, one of the world's finest symphonies, excellent small theaters, and the University of Chicago, which in turn has produced more Nobel laureates than any university in the world.

Practical Information

Emergency: 911.

Visitor Information: Chicago Tourism Council Visitors Information Center, 163 E. Pearson (280-5740), in the Water Tower Pumping Station. Pick up a copy of the *Chicago Visitors Guide.* Open daily 9:30am-5pm. **Chicago Chamber of Commerce,** 200 N. LaSalle (580-6900), at Lake St. Open Mon.-Fri. 8:30am-4:45pm. **Tourist Information Center,** 310 S. Michigan Ave. (793-2094), across from the Art Institute. Open Mon.-Fri. 9am-5pm.

Travelers and Immigrants Aid: 327 S. LaSalle St. (435-4500; after hours 222-0265). Open daily 8:30am-5pm. Other locations at O'Hare Airport (686-7562; open daily 8am-9pm), Greyhound (435-4537); and Union Station (435-4500; open daily 8:30am-5pm). The main office provides language assistance, legal aid, and information for the disabled.

Consulates: Australia, 321 N. Clark St. (221-1515); **Canada,** 310 S. Michigan Ave. (427-1031); **France,**737 N. Michigan Ave. (787-5359); **West Germany,** 104 S. Michigan Ave. (263-0850); **Ireland,** 400 N. Michigan Ave. (337-1868); **Israel,** 111 E. Wacker Dr. (565-3300); **Italy,** 500 N. Michigan Ave. (467-1550); **Mexico,** 300 N. Michigan Ave. (726-3942); **U.K.,** 33 N. Dearborn St. (346-1810). Most open Mon.-Fri. 9am-5pm.

O'Hare International Airport: Off I-90. Inventor of the layover and holding pattern. Depending on traffic, a trip between downtown and O'Hare can take up to 2 hr. The **Rapid Train** runs between the Airport El station and downtown. Plan 40 min.-1 hr. for the ride. **Continental Air Transport** (454-7800) connects the airport to selected downtown and suburban locations. Runs every 30 min. 6am-11:30pm. Fare $12. **Midway Airport,** on the western edge of the South Side often offers less expensive flights. To get downtown, take CTA bus #54B to Archer, then ride bus #49, 62, or 162 to State St. For an extra 20¢, the 99M express runs from Midway downtown 6:30-8:15am and from downtown to Midway during the afternoon rush hour. Continental Air Transport costs $9. For limousine service to either airport, call **C.W. Limousine Service** (493-2700). Rides from the South Side, as well as between the two airports (both $9.75). Airport baggage lockers $1 per day.

Amtrak: Union Station (558-1075 or 800-872-7245), Canal and Adams St. downtown. Take the El to State and Adams, then walk up Adams 7 blocks. Amtrak's main hub. Station open 24 hr.; tickets sold daily 7:30am-10pm. Baggage check $1 per day.

Greyhound: 630 W. Harrison St. (781-2900), on corner of Jefferson and Desplaines. Take the El to Linton. The hub in central U.S. Also serves as home base for several smaller companies covering the Midwest. To: Milwaukee ($13), Detroit ($21-25), and St. Louis ($24-29). Open 24 hr.

Public Transport: See Transportation below.

Taxi: Yellow Cab, 829-4222.

Car Rental: Fender Benders Rent-a-Car, 1545 N. Wells St. (280-8554), 1½ blocks from the Sedgwick El stop. $27 per day, $145 per week. 50 free mi., 15¢ each additional mi. Open Mon.-Fri. 8:30am-6:30pm. Must be 25 with major credit card.

Auto Transport Company: National U-Drive, 2116 N. Cicero Ave. (889-7737).

Help Lines: Metro Help, 929-5150. 24-hr. crisis line. Rape Crisis Line, 708-872-7799. Open 24 hr. Gay Horizon Hotline, 929-4357.

Medical Emergency: Cook County Hospital, 633-6000. Take the Congress A train to the Medical Center Stop.

Medical Walk-in Clinic: MedFirst, 310 N. Michigan Ave. (726-0577). Non-emergency medical care. Open Sun.-Fri. 8am-6pm, Sat. 8am-5pm.

Post Office: 433 W. Van Buren St. (765-3210), 2 blocks from Union Station. Open 24 hr. except Sun. ZIP code: 60607.

Area Code: 312 (for numbers in Chicago), 708 (for numbers outside Chicago's municipal boundaries). All numbers listed here without area code are in the 312 area.

Orientation

Chicago runs north-south along 29 mi. of southwest Lake Michigan lakefront, with a slight western tilt. The city and its suburbs sprawl across the entire northeastern corner of Illinois. Most cross-country road, rail, and airplane trips in the northern U.S. pass through Chicago.

Despite its vast size, Chicago is neatly organized. The grid-like pattern of streets centers at **State Street,** the east-west axis, and **Madison Street,** the north-south axis. State and Madison also mark a busy commercial area called the **State Street Mall.** If you need to determine the location of a given address, find out what "hundred" N., S., E., or W. the street is numbered. Each block increases by 100 in number (with a few exceptions) as the distance from State and Madison increases. East numbers are few because the lake gets in the way. South streets are usually numbered (not named), with the exception of 1200 S., known as Roosevelt. Once you leave Chicago municipal boundaries, this may break down, as each suburb maintains its own numbering system.

Chicago's other neighborhoods are diverse and frequently polarized. If you arrive by bus or train, you'll be in Chicago's **Loop,** the skyscraper-studded downtown area surrounded by elevated train tracks. This neighborhood remains safe during the business day, but not after dark. Just south of the Loop and southwest of the natural history museum lies **Pilsen,** a center of Chicago's Latino community. **Chinatown** is just south of Pilsen. Avoid the **Near South Side,** in the south 30s, and the wastelands of the **Near West Side,** west of I-90/94—two of the more dangerous urban slums in the U.S. In general, don't go south of Cermak or east of Halstead St. Ritzy business and residential districts extend north of the Loop along Michigan Ave. into the affluent north lakeshore, culminating in the wealthy suburbs on the northern edge of Cook County. Working and middle-class neighborhoods extend outward from the core city area. The western and northern districts have mixed ethnic neighborhoods including Greeks, Italians, Indians, Native Americans, and Southeast Asians. Poles are concentrated near Oak Park. **Uptown** is home to Vietnamese and other Southeast Asians (in Argyle), and clusters of Haitians and Native Americans. Irish neighborhoods dot the western portion of the city. The South Side is overwhelmingly African American, while the northern suburb of **Skokie** contains a well-known Jewish community. Just southeast of Chicago, blue-collar workers labor in **Gary, IN,** a languishing steel giant and home of the Jackson Five.

Transportation

The **Chicago Transit Authority,** part of the **Regional Transit Authority** (836-7000 in the city, 800-972-7000 in the suburbs), runs rapid transit trains, subways, and buses. The CTA runs 24 hr., but late-night service is infrequent and unsafe in some areas, especially the South Side. Some stations do not operate at all at night. Maps are available at many stations, the Water Tower Information Center, and the RTA Office. The **elevated rapid transit train** system, called the **El,** bounds the major downtown section of the city, the Loop. Trains marked "A," "B," or "all stops" may run on the same tracks, stopping at stations designated "A," "B," or "all stations," respectively. Also, different routes may run along the same tracks in places. Because of Chicago's grid-like layout, many bus lines run for several mi. along one straight road. Train fare is $1.25, bus fare from 6-9am and 3-6pm $1.25. Ten tokens good for one train or bus ride each any time of day cost $9. Remember to get a transfer (25¢) from the driver when you board the bus or enter the El stop, which will get you two more rides in the following two hours. A $60 month pass is available in many supermarkets, including the Jewel and Dominick's chains.

On Sundays and holidays from Memorial Day weekend to the end of September, you can tour Chicago's cultural attractions on CTA's **Culture Buses** (every 30 min. 10:30am-4:55pm; fare $2.50, seniors and children $1.25). A transfer from a previous ride reduces the price to $1, seniors and children 40¢. Three routes serve the North, South, and West Sides. Many sights and museums described below are on a Culture Bus route, and some offer a discount upon presentation of a Culture Bus Supertransfer. You can use the Culture Bus Supertransfer all day.

Several major highways crisscross the city and urban area. The **Eisenhower (I-290)** cuts west from the Loop. **I-90** pivots around the Eisenhower; to the northwest it's called the **Kennedy,** to the south, the **Dan Ryan.** The **Edens (I-94)** splits off from the Kennedy and heads north to the suburbs. **I-294** rings the city. Some of the highways require tolls (about 40¢).

Accommodations

With budget lodgings in Chicago, you get what you pay for, sometimes even less. Women especially might want to play it safe and stay in less thrifty hotels. Besides still-expensive weekend specials ($60-80) that are often unavailable because of conventions, try **Chicago Bed and Breakfast,** 1704 Crilly Court, Chicago 60014 (951-0085), a referral service that offers over 60 rooms of varying prices throughout the city and outlying areas. (From $40 per person. Cooking facilities often available.) **Exel Inns** (800-356-8013; singles $43), and **Motel 6** (708-818-8088; singles $25, doubles $36), are national motel chains with locations in the suburbs accessible to travelers with cars.

Chicago International Hostel (AYH and IYH), 6318 N. Winthrop (262-1011). Take Howard St. northbound train to Loyola Station. Walk south and east on Sheridan Rd. to Winthrop, then ½ block south. Clean rooms in a safe and convenient neighborhood. Good place to meet traveling students. Kitchen. Laundry room available. Check-in 4-9:30 pm. Lockout midnight. $10, nonmembers $13. Linen included.

International House (AYH), 1414 E. 59th St., Hyde Park (753-2270), off Lake Shore Dr. Take the Illinois Central Railroad to 59th St. and walk ½ block west. Part of the University of Chicago. 200 comfortable dorm-style rooms. Shared bath. Cheap cafeteria. $14, nonmembers $23. Open mid-June to Aug. Reservations required.

Baker Hall, National College of Education, 2808 Sheridan Rd. (708-256-5150), between the Baha'i Temple and Evanston Hospital. Take the northbound train from Howard to Central St. Delightful dormitory with shared bath, cafeteria. Singles $20. Doubles $30. Open June-Aug. Usually booked; try reserving several months in advance.

Hotel Cass, 640 N. Wabash (787-4030), just north of the Loop. Take subway to Grand St. Convenient location, clean rooms. Singles $35. Doubles $40. A/C $5. Key deposit $5.

Hotel Wacker, 111 W. Huron (787-1386), Near North Side. Small, slightly shabby rooms. Singles $35. Doubles $45. Weekly: $80-85. Key and linen deposit $5.

YMCA and YWCA, 30 W. Chicago Ave. (944-6211). Good security, bare rooms, some unpleasant clientele. Singles $24-30. Doubles $35. Key deposit $5. Students: $75 per week; $228 per month; bring a letter from your registrar.

YMCA, 3333 N. Marshfield Ave. (248-3333), near North Side and Lincoln Ave. district. El to Paulina. Men only, min. age 19. All singles. Much less attractive than the hostels for the short-term visitor, but low weekly rates ($65-70). $14 per day. Key deposit $5.

Leaning Tower YMCA, 6300 W. Touhy (647-1122), in Niles. From Howard El stop, take bus #290. Look for ¼-scale replica of the Leaning Tower of Pisa. Private baths. Singles $27. Doubles $30. Off-season $4-5 less. Key deposit $5. Call ahead for reservations.

Pioneer Motel, 8835 Ogden Ave., Brookfield (708-485-9686), on U.S. 34, 3 mi. east of I-294 in the western suburbs. Accessible only by car. Clean, comfortable rooms, tile floors. Singles $27. Each additional person $2. $5 key deposit.

Brookfield Motel, 8804 Ogden Ave., Brookfield (708-485-0948) next to Pioneer Motel. Pleasant, clean, carpeted rooms. Singles $27. Doubles $32.

Food

The "Windy City" is also a city that eats—very well. Like many urban dwellers, Chicagoans flee downtown come dusk; most of the best food finds lie far away from the Loop, in busy nightlife districts or tiny neighborhoods. One of Chi-town's favorite fillers is its renowned pizza, which features a thick crust covered with melted cheese, fresh sausage, sauteed onions and peppers, and a spicy sauce made from fresh whole tomatoes. Besides pizza, you can sample especially good Southeast Asian, Mexican, and Greek food. Dig into anything from Thai noodles to sizzling ribs, another Chicago specialty, at the city's **Taste of Chicago Festival,** where 80 vendors tickle your tastebuds in late June and early July. Expect to spend $10-15 as you sample various foods. The Festival grills and thrills along Michigan Ave. near the Art Institute. Spectacular fireworks accompany the food of July 4. *Chicago* magazine ($2) offers a comprehensive restaurant guide with honest and thorough listings cross-indexed by price, cuisine, and location.

Pizza

Pizzeria Uno, 29 E. Ohio, and **Due,** 619 N. Wabash. Uno is where it all began. In 1943, owner Ike Sewall introduced Chicago-style deep dish pizza, and though the graffiti-stained walls have been painted over and the restaurant is franchised across the nation, the pizza remains damn good. Due sits right up the street, has a terrace and more room than Uno's, but the legend is lacking. Pizzas $5-15. Uno open daily 11:30am-7pm; Due open Mon.-Thurs. 11:30am-1:30am, Fri. 11:30am-2:30am, Sat. noon-2:30am, Sun. noon-11:30pm.

Edwardo's has 10 locations including: 1212 N. Dearborn (337-4490), Near North Side; 521 S. Dearborn (939-3366), downtown; and 1321 E. 57th St. (241-7960), in Hyde Park. Vegetable-fanciers will love the spinach or broccoli soufflé pizza ($11). Hours vary by location. N. Dearborn location open Mon.-Thurs. 11am-12:30am, Fri.-Sat. 11am-1:30am, Sun. 11am-11:30pm.

Gino's East, 160 E. Superior. Wait 30-40 min. while they make your "pizza de résistance." Graffiti-covered wall. Small pan pizza ($6) serves 2 people with ease. Open Mon.-Thurs. 11am-11pm; Fri.-Sat.11am-midnight, Sun. noon-10pm.

Loop

For a cheaper alternative to most Loop dining, try the surprisingly good fast-food pizza, fish, potato, and burger joints in the basement of the State of Illinois Building at Randolph and Clarke St. Entrees run $2.50-$4.

The Berghoff, 17 W. Adams. Moderately priced German and American fare, including terrific strudel and home-brewed beer. German pot roast $7. Open Mon.-Thurs. 11am-9:30pm, Fri.-Sat. 11am-10pm.

Milty's Super Deli, 65 E. Wacker Pl. Old deli favorites corned beef ($4.25) and beef brisket ($4.25). Open Mon.-Fri. 6:30am-5pm, Sat. 8am-2:30pm.

Near North

John Barleycorn Memorial Pub, 658 W. Belden Ave. (348-8899), at Lincoln Ave. English-style pub attracts an artsy, intellectual crowd by playing classical music and showing art slides on 3 large screens. Model ship collection rides the walls. Reasonably priced menu includes burgers ($5). Open daily 10am-2am. Kitchen open until 1am.

Billy Goat's Tavern, 430 N. Michigan Ave., hidden on lower Michigan Ave., an underground street. Go down through what looks like a subway entrance in front of the Tribune building. Inspiration for Saturday Night Live's legendary "Cheezborger, cheezborger—no Pepsi, Coke" greasy spoon. Ask for a nifty goat hat. Cheezborgers $1.80. Open Sun.-Fri. 7am-2am, Sat. 7am-3am.

Ed Debevic's, 640 N. Wells, and 660 Lake Cook, Deerfield (945-3242). The 1990s avatar of the typical diner. Burgers, chicken pot pie, and other all-American dishes. Full dinners $5. Packed on weekend nights. N. Wells location open Mon.-Thurs. 11am-midnight, Fri. 11am-1am, Sat. 10am-1am, Sun. 10am-11pm. Deerfield location closes a bit earlier.

North Side

Cafe Phoenicia, 2814 N. Halsted St. (549-7088). El to Diversey then 2 blocks on Diversey to Halstead. A tribute to the Phoenician alphabet and nautical tableaux spice up the walls of this little Lebanese outfit. Outstanding hummus $3, lamb kebab $8. Open Mon.-Sat. 11:30am-2pm and 5-10:30pm, Sun. 4-9:30pm. Reservations required on weekends.

Mekong, 4953 N. Broadway, at Argyle St. Busy, spotless Vietnamese restaurant. Tasty soups $3.50-4, fried noodles $5-10. Open Sun.-Tues. and Thurs. 10am-10pm, Wed. 4-10pm, Fri.-Sat. 10am-11pm.

Heartland Cafe, 7000 N. Glenwood (465-8005), at Lunt Ave. Cheap, delicious food, complete with live folk and jazz Fri. and Sat. evenings, outdoor café, and a hip bookstore. Dinner entrees $7.25-9.50. Open Mon.-Thurs. 9am-1am, Fri.-Sat. 9am-3am, Sun. 9am-2am. Kitchen open until 11pm; until midnight Sat. Cover varies.

Marco's Paradise, 3358 N. Sheffield (281-4848), down the street from Wrigley Field. Private and claustrophobic downstairs, open and airy first floor. Try the large *enchiladas mexicanas* ($5.75) or *carne asada* (skirt steak, $9). Open Sun.-Thurs. 11am-midnight, Fri.-Sat. 11am-2am. Reservations suggested on weekends.

Tokyo Marina, 5058 N. Clark St. Cleaved into two rooms—one a sushi bar and one with less trendy Japanese food. Entrees $6.50-7.50. Open daily 11:30am-11pm.

Launa Thai, 5951-5 N. Broadway, between Thorndale and Elmdale Ave. Winsome family-run restaurant. Curry dishes $3.75-4.50. Open Mon.-Fri. noon-2pm and 5-10pm, Sat.-Sun. noon-10pm.

North Shore

Slice of Life, 4120 Dempster, Skokie. El to Howard, then bus #215 to Crawford and Dempster. Fresh, delicious, kosher deep-dish pizza (small $5.50). Fresh fish specials also a treat. Open Sun.-Thurs. 11:30am-9pm, Fri. 11:30am-2am, Sat. sunset-2am.

Blind Faith Cafe, 525 Dempster, Evanston. Take the Evanston train to Dempster. The antithesis of the greasy spoon. Wholesome, natural vegetarian food. Order one of their exotic entrees like Udon Noti Yaki ($8) on blind faith or ask your waiter to explain the ingredients. And you will find your way home.

La Choza, 7630 N. Paulina, Evanston, 1 block west of Howard El stop. Seedy, broken neon storefront conceals a vine-covered canopied terrace in the back. Chow down on the "Mexico City" (enchilada, tostada, beans, and rice; $5.35). Open Tues.-Thurs. 4-11pm, Fri. 2-11:30pm, Sat. 2-midnight, Sun. 2-10:30pm.

Walker Bros. Original Pancake House, 153 Green Bay Rd., at Wilmette between Central and Lake. Take Northwest Metro train to Wilmette Station, then walk down Green Bay Rd. Stunning collection of stained glass and Tiffany lamps cowers in fear of rampant children. Heavenly apple pancakes ($6). Huge lines for Sunday brunch. Open Sun.-Thurs. 7am-10:30pm, Fri.-Sat. 7am-midnight.

South Side

Medici on 57th, 1327 E. 57th St., Hyde Park. University of Chicago students flock here for custom-made burgers ($4-5). "Garbage" pizza (everything on it) just $5.75. Open Sun.-Thurs. 7am-12:30am, Fri.-Sat. 9am-1am.

Three Happiness, 2130 S. Wentworth Ave., or across the street at 209 W. Cermak Rd. in Chinatown. Visible from the Cermak/Chinatown El stop. Choose between the upstairs restaurant and the little storefront across the way. Expect long lines Sun. for Chicago's best *dim sum* (items $1.75), served around noon. Reinforce your wallet if you plan to stay for dinner ($10-12). Open Mon.-Thurs. 10am-midnight, Fri.-Sat. 10am-1am, Sun. 10am-10pm.

Near West Side and Oak Park

Al's Italian Beef, 1079 W. Taylor St., at Aberdeen, near Little Italy. Take a number. Standing and eating at the counter is customary as there are no tables or chairs. Great Italian beef sandwiches ($2.75) and fries. Wash your meal down at the lemonade stand across the street. Open Mon.-Sat. 9am-1am.

The Parthenon, 314 S. Halsted St. in Greektown. Enjoy anything from gyros ($6) to *saganaki* (cheese flamed in brandy, $3.25). Dinners $4.25-13.50. Open Sun.-Thurs. 11am-1am.

Sights

While public transportation and your feet will serve you well around town, guided tours provide a less demanding alternative. Tours start near major hotels; you must make reservations. **American Sight-seeing Tours-Chicago,** 520 S. Michigan Ave. (427-3100), has two- to eight-hour tours with boat tours in the summer ($12-37). **Gray Line of Chicago,** 33 E. Monroe St. (346-9506), has three to seven-hour tours and three-hour cruises ($18-24). **Mercury Sight-seeing Boats** (332-1353) and **Shoreline Marine Sight-seeing Boat** (708-673-3399) offer charter cruises for $5-8.

Museums

Admission to each of Chicago's major museums is free at least one day per week. The "Big Five" allow exploration of everything from the ocean to landscape painting to the stars; a handful of smaller collections represent diverse ethnic groups and professional interests. For more information, call the **Chicago Council on Fine Arts Hotline** at 346-3278 (24 hrs.), or get the informative pamphlet *Chicago Museums* at a the tourist information office.

Museum of Science and Industry, 5700 S. Lake Shore Dr. (684-1414). Hands-on exhibits ensure a crowd of children, overgrown and otherwise. Highlights include the Apollo 8 command module, a German submarine, a life-sized replica of a coal mine, a 16-ft. human heart, and a new exhibit on learning disabilities. Open Mon.-Fri. 9:30am-4pm, Sat.-Sun. 9:30-5:30pm; May 27-Sept. 2 daily 9:30am-5:30pm. Free.

The Oriental Institute, 1155 E. 58th St. (702-9520), on the University of Chicago campus, offers an extraordinary collection of ancient Near Eastern art and archeological treasures despite its politically incorrect name. You can't miss the massive statue of Tutankaman. Open Tues.-Sat. 10am-4pm, Sun. noon-4pm. Free.

Field Museum of Natural History, Roosevelt Rd. at Lake Shore Dr. (922-9410), across from the aquarium. Geological, anthropological, botanical, and zoological exhibits. Don't miss the Egyptian mummies, the Native American Halls, the Hall of Gems, and the dinosaur display. Open daily 9am-5pm. Admission $3, seniors and students $2, families $10. Free Thurs.

The Adler Planetarium, 1300 S. Lake Shore Dr. (322-0300). Astronomy exhibits and a sophisticated skyshow. Don't overlook the Astro-Center, a $4-million subterranean addition. Skyshow 5 times per day in the summer, less frequently in the winter. Planetarium open mid-June to Aug. daily 9:30am-5pm Mon.-Thurs. 9:30am-4:30pm, Fri. 9:30am-9pm, Sat.-Sun. 9:30am-5pm. Exhibits free. Admission to the shows $3, seniors free, ages 6-17 $1.50.

The Art Institute of Chicago, Michigan Ave. at Adams St. (443-3500). The city's premier art museum. Finest collection of French impressionist paintings west of Paris. Also works by El Greco, Chagall, Van Gogh, Picasso, and Rembrandt. Call to find out about temporary exhibits. Open Mon. and Wed.-Fri. 10:30am-4:30pm, Tues. 10:30am-8pm, Sat. 10am-5pm, Sun. and holidays noon-5pm. Donation $5, seniors and students $2.50. Free Tues.

Shedd Aquarium, 1200 S. Lake Shore Dr. (939-2438). The world's largest indoor aquarium with over 6600 species of fresh and saltwater fish in 206 exhibition tanks including a Caribbean reef. The Oceanarium, scheduled for completion in 1990, will feature small whales, dolphins, seals, and other marine mammals. Open March-Oct. daily 9am-5pm; Nov.-Feb. 10am-5pm.

DuSable Museum of African-American History, 740 E. 56th Pl. and Cottage Grove (947-0600), Washington Park. Illuminating exhibit on everything from ancient African sculpture to the 60s black arts movement. Open Mon.-Fri. 9am-5pm, Sat.-Sun. noon-5pm. Admission $2, seniors and students $1, under 13 50¢. Free Thurs.

The Museum of Contemporary Art, 237 E. Ontario (280-2660), within walking distance of the Water Tower. Exhibits change often. One gallery devoted to local artists. Open Tues.-Sat. 10am-5pm, Sun. noon-5pm. Admission $4, seniors and students $2. Free Tues.

Peace Museum, 430 W. Erie (440-1860). Daring, multimedia exhibits that may turn even the most bellicose visitor from hawk to dove. Open Tues.-Sun. noon-5pm, Thurs. noon-8pm. Admission $3.50, seniors and students $2.

Outdoors

A string of lovely lakefront parks fringes the area between Chicago proper and Lake Michigan. On a sunny afternoon, a cavalcade of sunbathers, dog walkers, roller skaters, and skateboard artists ply the shore, yet everyone still has room to stake out a private little piece of the paradise. Lincoln, Grant, Burnham, and Jackson Parks are operated by the Recreation Department (294-2200).

Lake Michigan lures swimmers to the **Lincoln Park Beach** and the **Oak Street Beach,** on the North Side. Both crowded, popular swimming spots soak in the sun. The smaller and rockier beaches between 49th and 57th St. on the South Side are also clean, accessible, and equipped with changing houses. (Open mid-June to early Sept. daily 9am-dusk.) The beaches are unsafe after dark. Call the Chicago Parks District for further information (294-2333).

Lincoln Park, 2021 N. Stockton Dr. (871-3999; bus #151 or 156), rents paddleboats by the hour ($7, with $2 deposit) and the half-hour ($4, with $1 deposit). The Park District maintains jurisdiction over eight harbors from May 15 to October 15 for powerboats and sailboats. Great apes, farm animals, and snow leopards are just a few of the inhabitants of **Lincoln Park Zoo,** 2045 N. Lincoln Park W. (294-4660). You can also walk among the cactus in the **Lincoln Park Conservatory** (294-4770). (Both open daily 9am-5pm. Free.) Be warned that muggers haunt the park after dark.

Spend a relaxing summer day at **Grant Park,** on the waterfront between Roosevelt Rd. and Monroe St., east of Michigan Ave. An hour-long, computer-operated light display takes place at **Buckingham Fountain** each night at 9pm. Jets of water spray 90 ft. into the air, illuminated by colored lights hidden in the fountain base. You can also rent ice skates in the winter ($2.50) or bring your own roller skates to the **Richard J. Daley Bicentennial Plaza** (294-4792), in Grant Park. The **Garfield Park Conservatory,** 300 N. Central Park (533-1281), El to Pulaski then walk east, has palms, cacti, ferns, and tropical plants enclosed in its 4½ acres. (Open daily 9am-5pm. Free.) The **Chicago Botanic Garden,** Lake Cook Rd., Glencoe (708-835-5440), ½ mi. east of Edens Expressway, El to Howard then bus #214 (533-1281), is a lush 300-acre tract featuring a wide variety of carefully nurtured plants. Especially beautiful are the Japanese Garden, set on three islands, and the Rose Garden. (Open daily 8am-sunset. Parking $3, includes admission.)

The Loop

After the Great Fire of 1871 left the city a pile of ashes Chicago became a workshop for leading architects such as Daniel Burnham, Louis Sullivan, and later Mies Van der Rohe, whose Chicago School transformed urban design throughout the world by creating, among other things, the modern skyscraper. The Loop is a mecca for architecture buffs. A walking tour (1½ hr.) takes you past pioneer skyscrapers; dazzling masterworks of art deco, international style, and postmodern architecture; impressive modern sculpture; and the world's tallest building.

The best place to start is the **ArchiCenter,** 330 S. Dearborn (782-1776). Volunteers lead excellent walking tours (from $5, often less for seniors and students; call for exact prices), and the center offers lectures, photography exhibits, and a bookstore. The center is appropriately located, since the **Monadnock Building** was the last of important wall-bearing construction before Chicago's architects developed the skyscraper's revolutionary steel-frame.

From the ArchiCenter, go west on Jackson Blvd. to LaSalle St. Here at the **Board of Trade Building,** 141 W. Jackson (435-3490), designed by Holabird and Root just before the 1929 stock market crash, you'll see the real forces that drive Chicago. Cosmopolitan art deco ornament goes head-to-head with a huge monument to Ceres, the Greek goddess of grain, standing 609 ft. above street level. At the fifth-floor visitors gallery (open Mon.-Fri. 9am-2pm), you can watch the frantic trading of Midwestern farm goods at the world's oldest and largest commodity futures exchange.

Continue west on Jackson to Franklin St., and the unmissable looming 110-story 1707-ft. **Sears Tower,** 233 W. Wacker (875-9696). On a clear day, from the skydeck of the world's tallest building you can see four states. (Open daily 9am-midnight. Admission $3.75, under 15 $2.25.)

The First National Bank Building and Plaza (732-6037) stands about 2 blocks northeast, at the corner of Clark and Monroe St. The world's largest bank building sweeps the eye to the sky with its diagonal slope. Marc Chagall's vivid mosaic, *The Four Seasons,* lines the block and sets off a public space often used for concerts and lunchtime entertainment.

One street over is State and Madison, the most famous block of "State Street that great street" and the focal point of the Chicago street grid. Louis Sullivan's Carson Pirie Scott store building is marked by exquisite ironwork and the famous extra-large Chicago window though the grid-like modular construction has been altered by additions. Try to also visit Sullivan's other masterpiece, the **Auditorium Building,** several blocks south, at the corner of Congress and Michigan. Beautiful design and flawless acoustics highlight this Chicago landmark.

No one knows exactly what the Picasso sculpture at the foot of **Daley Center Plaza** is supposed to represent, although it has marked this public space at the corner of Dearborn and Washington since 1967. Across the street rests Joan Miró's *Chicago,* the sculptor's gift to the city.

One block north takes you to Randolph and Clark and the controversial, visually stunning **State of Illinois Building,** designed by Helmut Jalm in 1985. A hypermodern version of a town square, the structure features a sloping atrium, circular floors that allow full view of hundreds of employees and elevators and escalators with their guts exposed. One of the Loop's many fine and incomprehensible modern sculptures, *Monument`a la bęte debout,* by Jean Dubuffet, stands in the plaza.

As you wander around the Loop, notice the murals decorating the temporary walls that surround construction sites, usually witty homages to the city of Chicago painted by local schoolchildren.

Near North

The city's ritziest district lies above the Loop along the lake, just past the Michigan Ave. Bridge which affords a good view of the Near North. Overlooking the stretch is the **Tribune Tower,** 435 N. Michigan Ave., a Gothic skyscraper resulting from a hotly-contested international design competition in the 20s. The building houses one of Chicago's major newspapers; quotations celebrating freedom of the press emblazon the inside lobby.

Chicago's **Magnificent Mile,** along Michigan Ave. north of the Chicago River, is a conglomeration of chic shops and galleries. En route you'll pass the **Chicago Water Tower and Pumping Station,** (467-7114) at the corner of Michigan and Pearson Ave. Only these two public structures, built in 1867, survived the Great Chicago Fire. The pumping station, which still supplies water to nearly 400,000 people on the North Side, now houses the multimedia production *Here's Chicago.* For $4.75 (seniors and students $3.50, under 12 $2.50), you can briefly tour the pumping station, watch a 45-minute slide portrayal of Chicago, and see a slick 10-minute aerial view of the city. (Open Sun.-Thurs. 10am-5pm, Fri.-Sat. 10am-5:30pm.) Across the street is **Water Tower Place,** a ritzy new vertical shopping mall, worth a browse. A short walk north on Michigan Ave. leads to the **John Hancock Center,** 875 N. Michigan (751-3681), a towering office building with observation decks.

Beautiful old mansions and apartment buildings fill the streets between the Water Tower and Lincoln Park. Known as the **Gold Coast**, the area has long been the elite residential enclave of the city. The early industrialists and city founders made their homes here and, lately, many families have decided to move back in from the suburbs. Lake Michigan and the Oak St. Beach shimmer a few more blocks east. Urban renewal has made **Lincoln Park** the popular choice for upscale residents. Bounded by Armitage to the south and Diversey Ave. to the north, lakeside Lincoln Park is also a center for recreation and nightlife, with beautiful harbors and parks, and some of the city's liveliest clubs and restaurants along North Halsted and Lincoln Ave.

If you hear the bells of St. Michael's Church, you're in **Old Town,** a neighborhood where eclectic galleries, shops, and nightspots crowd gentrified streets. Absorb some of the architectural atmosphere while strolling the W. Menomonee and W. Eugenie St. area. In early June, the Old Town Art Fair attracts artists and craftspeople from across the country. Many residents open their restored homes to the public. (Take bus #151 to Lincoln Park and walk south down Clark or Wells St.)

North Side and North Shore

Extending from Diversey Ave. to Howard St., the North Side offers a mix of ethnically diverse residential neighborhoods. **Graceland Cemetery** runs through the heart of the area along Clark St. Elaborate tombs and monuments designed by the likes of Louis Sullivan and Lorado Taft make the burial ground one of Chicago's most interesting sights and a posthumous status symbol. The ArchiCenter (922-3432; see The Loop above) offers tours several times daily, and the cemetery office at the northeast corner of Clark St. and Irving Park Rd. has guidebooks for sightseers.

Though they finally lost their battle against night baseball in 1988, **Wrigleyville** residents remain, like much of the North Side, fiercely loyal to the Chicago Cubs. Just east of Graceland Cemetery, at the corner of Clark St. and Addison, tiny, ivy-covered **Wrigley Field** is the North Side's most famous institution, well worth a pilgrimage for the serious baseball fan. After a game, walk along Clark St. in one of the city's busiest nightlife districts, where restaurants, sportsbars, and music clubs abound.

The North Shore encompasses many separate municipalities, including Evanston, Skokie, Wilmette, and Glencoe. Skokie is well-known for its large Jewish community, and Wilmette contains the **Baha'i House of Worship,** Shendan Rd. and Linden Ave. (708-256-4400), an 11-sided dome in an ornate Near-Eastern style, modeled on the House of Worship in Haifa, Israel. (Open mid-May to mid-Oct. daily 10am-10pm; mid-Oct. to mid-May. 10am-5pm.) El to Howard Station, then commuter rail to Wilmette, Fourth St. and Linden Ave., then walk two blocks east on Linden.

South Side

A hodgepodge of neighborhoods with distinct boundaries, the South Side is not uniformly safe for the blithe out-of-towner; however, exercise caution and a visit here can prove truly rewarding. The South Side features some of Chicago's most vital ethnic communities, beautiful buildings, and points of historical interest.

Seven mi. south of the Loop along the lake, the **University of Chicago's** beautiful, Neo-Gothic campus dominates the **Hyde Park** neighborhood. A former retreat for the city's artists and musicians, the park became the first U.S. community to undergo urban renewal in the 50s, and now is a calm island of intellectualism in a sea of dangerous neighborhoods. The University of Chicago police force is Illinois' second largest. When visiting the campus, don't stray out of Hyde Park's boundaries.

The artists return in June for the **57th Street Art Fair.** The neighborhood also features Frank Lloyd Wright's famous **Robie House,** at the corner of Woodlawn Ave. and 58th St. Tours ($2, $3 on Sun.) depart daily at noon. Representative of the Prairie school, this large house blends into the surrounding trees and its low horizontal lines now house university offices. Unfortunately, the original furniture was removed to the nearby **Smart Gallery**, at 5550 S. Greenwood Ave. (702-0200). From the Loop, take bus #6 ("Jefferson Express") or the Illinois Central Railroad from the Randolph St. Station south to 57th St. Be careful after dark. (Open Tues.-Fri. 10-4, Sat. 10-6, Sun. 2-6. Free.)

Neighboring **Kenwood** is the home of Jesse Jackson's Operation PUSH headquarters at 50th and Drexel, as well as the Middle Eastern "Castle" of Elijah Muhammad, one-time mentor of activist Malcolm X and boxer Muhammad Ali. Although this eclectic area is far safer than its neighbor to the north, the untutored traveler should beware. Chinatown is a small but unbreakable piece of China, near the Cermak El stop.

Once considered the nation's most perfect community, **Pullman Historic District** on the southeast side began in 1885, when George Pullman, the inventor of the sleeping car, hired British architect Solon S. Beman to design a model working town so that his Palace Car Company employees would be "healthier, happier, and more productive." Unfortunately, worker resentment over Pullman's power bothered the earliest of suburbs. For local flavor and a chat with some serious history buffs, try the **Hotel Florence**, 11111 Forrestville Ave. (785-8900), the center of the 19th-century community, which now houses a restaurant and the **Historic Pullman Foundation** (785-8181). By car, take I-94 to W. 111th St; by train, take the Illinois Central Gulf Railroad to 111th St./Pullman. (Tours leave from the hotel the first Sun. of each month May-Oct. Admission $3.50, seniors $3, students $2.)

Home of the Democratic machine, **Bridgeport** symbolizes (for many) the Old Chicago. The Irish neighborhood at 37th and Halsted has given Chicago four of its mayors, including Richard Daley.

Near West Side

The Near West Side, bounded by Wacker St. to the east and Ogden Ave. to the west, is a fascinating group of tiny ethnic enclaves. Farther out, however, looms the West Side, one of the most dismal slums in the U.S. Dangerous neighborhoods lie side-by-side with the safe ones, so be careful and aware of where you are. **Greektown** might not be as Greek now, but several blocks of authentic restaurants (north of the Eisenhower on Halsted) do remain, continuing to draw people from all over the city.

A few blocks down Halsted (take the #8 Halsted bus) the historic **Hull House** stands as a reminder of Chicago's role in turn-of-the-century reform movements. Here, Jane Addams devoted her life to her settlement house and earned her reputation as a champion of social justice and welfare. Hull House has been relocated to 800 S. Halsted, but painstaking restoration, a slide show, and thoughtful exhibits about Near West Side history make the **Hull House Museum** (413-5353), at the same location, a fascinating part of a visit to Chicago. (Open Mon.-Fri. 10am-4pm; summer Mon.-Fri. 10am-4pm, Sun. noon-5pm. Free.)

Little Italy, along Taylor St., remains a tighter residential area than its Greek neighbor. Charming storefront restaurants, delis, and bakeries serve this relatively self-contained community. Nearby, the **University of Illinois at Chicago** rises above area neighborhoods, a striking monument to austere modern architecture.

Oak Park

Ten mi. west of downtown on the Eisenhower (I-290) sprouts **Oak Park.** Ernest Hemingway lived here, as did Frank Lloyd Wright, who endowed the community with 25 of his spectacular homes and buildings. The **visitors center,** 158 Forest Ave. (708-848-1500), has maps and guidebooks. (Open daily 10am-5pm.) Don't miss the **Frank Lloyd Wright House and Studio** 951 Chicago Ave. (708-848-1500), with his beautiful 1898 workplace and original furniture. (Admission $5, recorded tours $2 extra. Tours Mon.-Fri. at 11am, 1pm, and 3pm, frequently Sat.-Sun. 11am-4pm. By car, exit north from the Eisenhower on Harlem Ave. and follow markers. By train, take the Lake St./Dan Ryan El to Harlem/Marion stop.)

Entertainment

To stay on top of Chicago events, grab a copy of the free weekly *Chicago Reader,* on many streetcorners, or tune in to **WXRT** 93.1 FM. *Chicago* magazine has exhaustive club listings. The **Bears** play football at Soldier's Field, the **White Sox** swing in the South Side at Comiskey Park, and the **Cubs** play ball at gorgeous Wrigley Field. Michael Jordan and the **Bulls** dunk at Chicago Stadium. For current sports events, call **Sports Information** (976-1313).

Theater

Chicago is one of the foremost theater centers of North America. Though most tickets are expensive you can buy half-price tickets on the day of performance at **Hot Tix Booths,** 24 S. State St., downtown. (Open Mon. noon-6pm, Tues.-Fri. 10am-6pm, Sat. 10am-5pm. Tickets for Sun. shows on sale Sat.) There are also booths in Oak Park Mall and Evanston (1616 Sherman). Phone **Curtain Call** (977-1755) for information on ticket availability, schedules, and Hot Tix booths. **Ticket Master** (800-233-3123) offers tickets to many theaters. Also check with theaters to see if they sell half-price student rush tickets 30 minutes before showtime.

Over the last decade, Chicago has fostered a number of smaller theaters similar to the off-off-Broadway houses in New York City. Mostly located on the North Side and known as "Off-Loop" theaters, these houses specialize in original drama. David Mamet got his start at **Steppenwolf Theater,** 2540 N. Lincoln Ave. (472-4141; tickets $8). Major theaters for Broadway-bound productions are located in the downtown area. The **Shubert Theater,** 22 W. Monroe St. (977-1700), and the **Blackstone Theater,** 60 E. Balbo St. (341-8455), near State St., both stage Broadway productions. The better-known Shubert costs more ($15-38). The Blackstone's shows start at $10, and students get a 10% discount. Several suburban playhouses also offer the works of major playwrights. Check the free *Chicago Theater Guide,* available at Hot Tix booths, for complete listings.

Body Politic Theater and **Victory Gardens Theater,** both at 2261 N. Lincoln Ave. (871-3007). Various genres; often host touring companies. Downstairs, the Victory Gardens presents drama by Chicago playwrights. Tickets for both $15-23.

Organic Theater Co., 3319 N. Clark St. (327-5588). Original works and avant-garde adaptations. Showtimes Tues.-Fri. at 8pm, Sat. at 6:30 and 9:30pm, Sun. at 3 and 8pm. Tickets $15-23.

Wisdom Bridge Theater, 1559 W. Howard St. (743-6442). 1 ½ blocks east of the Howard El stop. Mostly new material or creative postmodern productions, such as a Kabuki *Macbeth.* Showtimes vary. Tickets $20-24. Call for student discount.

Kuumba Professional Theater, 343 S. Dearborn (461-9000). The most established of the city's many black theater groups. Showtime usually 8pm. Tickets $12-15.

Apollo Theatre, 2540 N. Lincoln (935-6100). Launched *A Soldier's Play.* Tickets $8-16, students ½ price.

Comedy

Chicago boasts a multitude of comedy clubs, the most famous being the **Second City Comedy Revue,** 1616 N. Wells St. (337-3992). Busting guts for nearly 30 years with its satirical spoofs of Chicago life and politics, Second City graduated John Candy, Bill Murray, and the late John Belushi and Gilda Radner among others. (Shows Sun.-Thurs. at 9pm, Fri.-Sat. at 8:30 and 11pm. Tickets $5 Mon., $9.50 Sun.-Thurs., $10.50 Fri.-Sat. Reservations recommended, but during the week you can often get in if you show up 1 hr. early.) A free improvisation session follows the show. **Second City etc.** offers up yet more comedy next door (same phone number, times and prices). A branch of Second City, accessible only by car, jokes in Rolling Meadows (708-806-1555).

Dance, Classical Music, and Opera

Many top-notch international dance companies, including ballet, ethnic, and modern troupes, perform in the **Auditorium Theater**, 50 E. Congress Parkway (922-2110). Call **FINEART** (346-3278), a cultural events hotline sponsored by the Chicago Office of Fine Arts, for details. The **Ballet Chicago** (993-7575) performs in season at various locations. They produce Neo-Classical ballet, particularly the work of George Balanchine. (Tickets $15-30. Call for student discounts.) **MoMing**, 1034 W. Barry (472-9894), celebrates avant-garde dance in a warehouse building on the North Side. On two weekends in mid-July, you can watch for just $2. (Performances usually $8-12.) The **Chicago City Ballet** performs at the auditorium under the direction of Maria Tallchief. (Tickets $25-48.)

The **Chicago Symphony Orchestra (CSO)**, conducted by Sir George Solti, performs in **Orchestra Hall**, 220 S. Michigan Ave. (435-8111). Renowned guest artists highlight the season (Sept. 28-June 9). Tickets ($12-44) are hard to come by, but regularly scheduled non-subscription and university nights do pop up. If you're lucky, someone will have cancelled a ticket recently. Ask for a student discount. The CSO has a summer season at **Ravinia Festival** in suburban Highland Park (see Seasonal Events below). In summer every Wednesday at noon, the **Chicago Public Library Cultural Center**, 78 E. Washington St. (346-3278), hosts free outdoor concerts. Other free cultural events are scheduled too; call their information line.

The **Lyric Opera of Chicago,** Civic Opera House, 20 N. Wacker Dr. (332-2240 or 332-2244), still puts on some of the most popular shows in town. The season runs from September to January. Tickets ($16-78) are often sold out.

Seasonal Events

Like Chicago's architecture, the city's summer celebrations are executed on a grand scale. City dwellers head for the lakefront beaches and parks, or jam the outdoor cafés and beer gardens. The regionally famous **Ravinia Festival** (312-728-4642), in the northern suburb of Highland Park, runs from late June to late September. The Chicago Symphony Orchestra, ballet troupes, folk and jazz musicians, and comedians perform throughout the festival's 14-week season. (Shows start between 7:30 and 8:30pm. Admission $10-20. $6-7 buys you a patch of ground for a blanket and picnic.) To reach Ravinia Park, take the Chicago and Northwestern Commuter Railway to the main gate ($3.75), or the Ravinia bus service from the Loop ($8 round-trip).

Chi-town also offers several free summer festivals on the lakeshore. The **Fourth of July Celebration** (744-3315), in Grant Park, draws huge crowds for its fireworks display and performance of Tchaikovsky's *1812 Overture.* Prime your buds for the **Taste of Chicago** festival in the week before July 4th. Chicago's best chefs set out booths with endless samples; you can stuff yourself with everything from sushi to barbecue for $16. In mid-July, Lake Shore Park, Lake Shore Dr., and Chicago Ave. are the scene of the **Air and Water Show,** featuring several days of boat races, parades, hang gliding events, and stunt flying, as well as a performance by the Blue Angels precision fliers.

Chicago's **Blues Festival** (744-3315), in early June, presents homegrown music to the thousands who turn out at the **Petrillo Music Shell** in Grant Park. Even more of a spectacle are the **Chicago Gospel Festival**, in July, and the **Chicago Jazz Festival,** at the end of August. On a smaller scale, Chicago also has over 75 ethnic and neighborhood festivals. Call the 24-hr. Special Events Hotline (744-3315) for information.

Nightlife

Chicago's frenetic nightlife is a grab bag of music, clubs, bars, and more music. "Sweet home Chicago" takes pride in the innumerable blues perfomers who have played there (a strip of 43rd St. was recently renamed Muddy Waters Drive). For other tastes, jazz, folk, reggae, and punk clubs jam people all over the North Side. Aspiring pick-up artists swing over to **Rush and Division,** an intersection that has replaced the stockyards as one of the great meat markets of the world. To get away from the crowds, head to a little neighborhood spot for a lot of atmosphere. Call the **Jazz Hotline** (666-1881). Ask at your favorite bar about pub crawls, where a bus will ferry you between bars for a total $5 cover.

Blues

B.L.U.E.S. etcetera, 1124 W. Belmont (549-9436), El to Belmont then 3 blocks west on Belmont Ave. In general, with the aid of a dance floor, a more energetic blues bar than its sibling location **B.L.U.E.S.,** 2519 N. Halsted St. (528-1012), El to Fullerton, then westbound Fullerton bus. Cramped, but the music is unbeatable. Music starts Mon.-Thurs. at 9pm, Fri.-Sun. at 8:30. Open Sun.-Fri. 8pm-2am, Sat. 8pm-3am. Cover Sun.-Thurs. $5, Fri.-Sat. $7.

Kingston Mines, 2548 N. Halsted St. (477-4646), just north of B.L.U.E.S. Shows 6 nights per week. Watch for the "Blue Monday" jam session. Music starts at 9:30pm. Open Sun.-Fri. until 4am, Sat. until 5am. Cover Mon. $5, Tues.-Thurs. and Sun. $7, Fri.-Sat. $8.

New Checkerboard Lounge, 423 Muddy Waters Dr. (624-3240). Chicago's oldest blues club and the last authentic remnant of the old days. In a shady, unsafe South Side neighborhood, but a worthwhile pilgrimage for the serious fan. Music starts Mon.-Fri. at 9:30pm, Sat. at 10pm, Sun. at 8pm. Closing time varies. Cover $3-5.

Wise Fools Pub, 2270 N. Lincoln St. (929-1510), El to Fullerton, then go south on Lincoln. Intimate Lincoln Park setting for top blues artists. Mon. night's Big Band Jazz series also great fun. Music 9:30pm-1:30am. Bar open daily 4pm-2am. Cover $4-8.

Other

Butch McGuires, 20 W. Division St. (337-9080), at Rush St. Originator of the singles bar. Owner estimates that "over 2400 couples have met here and gotten married" since 1961—he's a little fuzzier on divorce statistics. Once on Rush St., check out the other area hang-outs. Drinks $1.75-4.25. Open Mon.-Thurs. 10:30am-2am, Fri. 10:30am-4am, Sat. 9:30am-5am, Sun. 9:30am-midnight.

Cabaret Metro, 3730 N. Clark (549-3604). Cutting-edge concerts from $6 and Wed. night "Rock Against Depression" extravaganzas ($4 for men, women free) entertain a hip, young crowd. Open Sun.-Fri. 9:30pm-4am, Sat. 9:30pm-5am.

Christopher Street, 3458 N. Halsted (975-9244). Lots of guppies (gay urban professionals) swim in this attractive, upscale fishbowl with 3 bars, a huge dance floor, and aquarium wallpaper. Drinks $2-4. Open Sun.-Fri. 4pm-4am, Sat. 4pm-5am. Cover Fri.-Sat. $3 ($1 goes to AIDS research).

Danny's, 1951 W. Dickens Ave. (489-6457), Bucktown. Zebratone walls, Elvis memorabilia, and a jukebox with everything from the Ramones to Tammy Wynette. Favorite with artsy locals. Not in the safest neighborhood, but great fun once you arrive. Open daily 5pm-2am, Sat. 5pm-3am.

Jazz Showcase, 636 S. Michigan (427-4300), in the Blackstone Hotel downtown. Number-one choice for serious jazz fans. During the jazz festival, big names heat up the elegant surroundings with impromptu jam sessions. No smoking allowed. Music Tues.-Sun. at 8pm and 10pm, Fri.-Sat. at 9 and 11pm. Closing time and cover vary.

No Exit, 6970 N. Glenwood (743-3355), in Rogers Park. This North Side coffeehouse has live nightly jazz, but no Avatar or Inez. While the musicians warm up, you can too by reading Sartre or playing chess. Sandwiches $3.25. Open daily 4pm-until. Cover free-$5.

Wild Hare & Singing Armadillo Frog Sanctuary, 3350 N. Clark (327-0800), El to Addison. Near Wrigley Field. Live rastafarian bands play nightly to a packed house. Open daily until 2-3am. Cover $3-5.

Sluggers World Class Sports Bar, Inc., 3540 N. Clark (248-0055), near Wrigley Field. El to Addison. If TV monitors tuned to every sporting event imaginable don't turn you on, maybe the gameroom with ski ball, trampoline hoop, and the city's only indoor batting cage will. Drink prices rise 50¢ during Cubs games, but on Wed. nights beer is only 75¢. Open Sun.-Fri. 11am-2am, Sat. 11am-3am.

Tania's, 2659 N. Milwaukee Ave. (235-7120). Exotic dinner and dancing adventure with hot *salsa cumbia* and *merengue* bands. No jeans. Live music Wed.-Mon. Open daily 11am-4am. No cover, but a 2-drink minimum.

Baja Beach Club, 401 E. Illinois St. (222-1992), on the North Pier. Newly popular, especially with an older crowd. Video games but no beach. Open Sun.-Tues. 11am-2am, Wed.-Thurs. 11am-3am, Fri. 11am-4am, Sat. 11am-5am.

Springfield

Springfield poet Vachel Lindsay wrote, "In our little town a mourning figure walks, and will not rest." This ghoulish shade of Abraham Lincoln, who settled in Springfield in 1837 to practice law, still stalks Springfield incessantly; the city is completely mobilized to help tourists see Old Abe memorabilia. The state capital's efforts, much like the place and its people, are always tasteful but very insistent.

Practical Information

Emergency: 911.

Visitor Information: Springfield Convention and Visitors Bureau, 109 N. 7th St. (789-2360 or 800-545-7300). Open Mon.-Fri. 8am-5pm. **Central Illinois Tourism Council,** 631 E. Washington St. (525-7980). **Lincoln Home Visitors Center,** 426 S. 7th (789-2357). Open daily 8:30am-5pm. All locations have very useful brochures on restaurants, hotels, camping, events, recreation, and services for seniors and the disabled.

Amtrak: 3rd and Washington St. (800-872-7245), near downtown. To Chicago (2-4 per day, 4 hr., $31) and St. Louis (2-4 per day, 2½ hr., $19). Those passing through on Amtrak can stop over in Springfield free. Lockers 50¢ first day, $1 subsequent days. Open daily 6am-9:30pm.

Greyhound: 2351 S. Dinkser (544-8466), on the eastern edge of town. Take a cab downtown ($5). To Chicago ($25) and St. Louis ($12). Open 7:30am-10:30pm. Those passing through town by bus can stop off at no extra charge.

Public Transport: Springfield Mass Transit District, 928 S. 9th St. (522-5531). Pick up maps at headquarters or at the tourist office on Adams. All 12 lines serve the downtown area along 5th, 6th, or Monroe St., near the Old State Capitol Plaza. Fare 50¢, transfers free. Buses operate Mon.-Sat. 6am-6pm. **Access Illinois Transit Service (AITS)** (522-8594). Buses seniors and the disabled. Call 24 hr. in advance to arrange trip.

Taxi: Lincoln Yellow Cab, 523-4545 or 522-7766.

Post Office: 2105 E. Cook St. (788-7200), at Weir St. Open Mon.-Fri. 7:45am-5:30pm, Sat. 8am-noon. **ZIP code:** 62703.

Area Code: 217.

I-55 connects Springfield with Chicago, 200 mi. northeast, and St. Louis, 90 mi. southwest. I-72 passes through from the east, and U.S. 36 from the west. Numbered streets in Springfield run north-south, but only on the east side of the city. All other streets have names, with **Washington Street** dividing north-south addresses.

Accommodations and Camping

Most inexpensive places congregate in the eastern and southern parts of the city, off I-55 and U.S. 36; bus service from downtown to these outlying areas is limited. Downtown rooms cost $10-30 more. Make reservations on holiday weekends and during the State Fair in mid-August. Downtown hotels may be booked solid on weekdays when the legislature is in session. Check with the visitors bureau about finding reasonable weekend packages offered by slightly more upscale hotels. All accommodations listed below have color TV and A/C.

Best Inns of America, 500 N. 1st St. (522-1100). Clean, bright, comfortable rooms. Pool. Singles $34. Doubles $36-42. Continental breakfast included. Key deposit $1.

Best Rest Inn, 700 N. Dirksen Pkwy. (522-1100 or 800-237-8466). Take the "Bergen Park-Grandview" bus to the 700 block of Milton, then go 3 blocks east. The second-best in Springfield. Singles $24. Doubles $28.

Motel 6, 3125 Wide Track Dr. (789-1063), near Dirksen Pkwy. at the intersection of I-90 and State Rte. 29. Standard motel room fare and a pool. Singles $23. Doubles $29.

Lincoln Motel, 2929 S. 6th St. (525-6670). Clean rooms with the hotel's name written on the bedspreads in marker. Ghost of the President occasionally caught loitering in the hall. Singles $20. Doubles $28.

Travel Inn, 500 S. 9th St. (528-4341), near downtown. Unkempt exterior with clean, somewhat shabby but fairly large rooms. Singles $25. Doubles $28. Weekly: $100.

For camping, try **Mister Lincoln's Campground**, 3045 Stanton Ave. (529-8206), next to the car dealership 4 mi. southeast of downtown. Large area for RVs dominates the campground, with a field for tents on the side and showers. Take bus #10 ("Laketown"). Tent sites $6, with electricity $14, $6 each additional person. Open March-Dec.

Food

Horseshoe sandwiches gallop to the forefront of Springfield cuisine. Looking more like what ends up *on* horseshoes than horseshoes, these tasty concoctions consist of ham on prairie toast covered by a tangy cheese sauce and french fries. In and around the **Vinegar Hill Mall**, at 1st and Cook St., a number of moderately priced restaurants serve horseshoes, barbecued ribs, Mexican and Italian food, and seafood. Plan accordingly because Springfield tends to start shutting down between 3 and 5pm.

Joe Gallina's Pizza, 432 E. Monroe. Joe himself calls out the orders in Italian; Italian songs occupy part of the jukebox. Quite big small cheese pizza $4. Open Mon.-Thurs. 11am-11pm, Fri.-Sat. 11am-midnight.

Feedstore, 528 E. Adams St., across from the Old State Capitol. Nothing fancy inside, just good food. Sandwiches $2.75-3.75. No-choice special $4.25. Open Mon.-Sat. 11am-3pm.

Saputo's, 801 E. Munroe at 8th St., 2 blocks from Lincoln's home. Family-owned and - operated for 40 years. Red lighting, red table cloths, red chairs, and—of course—red tomato sauce. Tasty southern Italian cuisine. Large baked lasagna $4.25. Open Mon.-Fri. 10:30am-midnight, Sat. 5pm-midnight, Sun. 5-10pm.

Norb-Andy's, 518 E. Capitol, 2½ blocks east of the New State Capitol. Emphatically nautical theme: oars, ships, and a backward-running clock all decorate this politico-hangout. A jazz guitar player often strums in the corner. Horseshoes $4.75-6. All-American dinner entrees $7-19. Open Mon.-Fri. 11am-10pm, Sat. 11am-11pm. Bar open Mon.-Sat. 11am-11pm.

Sights

Springfield presents its tourist attractions zealously. Just pick up one of the many pamphlets at most museums and, of course, tourist offices for all the necessary info. Pleasing to most budgets, all Lincoln sights are free. The **Lincoln Home Visitors Center**, 426 S. 8th St. at Jackson (523-0222), shows an 18-minute film on "Mr. Lincoln's Springfield." The **Lincoln Home** (492-4150), the only one Abe ever owned, also sits at 8th and Jackson, in a restored 19th-century neighborhood. (Open daily 8:30am-5pm; bad weather may reduce winter hours. 10-min. tours every 5-10 min. from the front of the home. Arrive early to avoid the crowds. Free, but you must pick up passes at the Visitors Center.) A few blocks northwest, at 6th and Adams right before the Old State Capitol, you'll find the **Lincoln-Herndon Law Offices** (782-4836), where Honest Abe practiced before ascending the political ranks. (Under renovation indefinitely. Open for tours only daily 9am-5pm; last tour at 4:15. Free.) Around the corner to the left across from the Downtown Mall lies the **Old State Capitol** (782-7691), a weathered limestone edifice with a majesty that rivals its Greek models. In 1858, Lincoln delivered his stirring and prophetic "House Divided" speech here, warning that the nation's contradictory pro-slavery and abolitionist government could prove a volatile source of dissolution. A manuscript copy of Lincoln's Gettysburg Address is on display. (Open daily 9am-5pm. Tours daily. Free.) The **New State Capitol**, four blocks away at 2nd and Capitol (782-2099), is also worth seeing, for its art and politics. (Tours Mon.-Fri. 8am-4pm, Sat.-Sun. 9am-3:30pm. Open to public longer.)

Springfield is not just Lincolnville, U.S.A. Don't miss the **Dana-Thomas House,** 301 E. Lawrence Ave. (782-6776), 6 blocks south of the Old State Capitol. This stunning and well-preserved 1902 home resulted from one of Frank Lloyd Wright's early experiments in design, providing a wonderful example of the Prairie School style. The furniture and fixtures are Wright orginals as well. (Open Thurs.-Mon. 9am-5pm. 1-hr. tours every ½ hr. Free.) The **Illinois State Museum,** Spring and Edwards St. (782-7386), complements displays on the area's original Native American inhabitants with presentations of contemporary Illinois art. (Open Mon.-Sat. 8:30am-5pm, Sun. noon-5pm.)

Indiana

The difference between two popular explanations for Indiana's nickname of "Hoosier" typifies the competition between the state's rural and industrial traditions. One explanation holds the name to be a corruption of the pioneer's call to visitors at the door, "who's there?"; the other claims that its use spread from Louisville where the labor contractor Samuel Hoosier employed Indiana workers who later became known as Hoosiers. Today, more than half a century later, visitors still find two Indianas: the heavily industrialized northern cities and the slower-paced agricultural southern counties.

In this outsider's view of the rural and the urban Indiana, the latter wins out unfairly. Too many people associate Indiana only with Gary's smokestacks and the Indianapolis 500; perhaps the best way to see the state is to recognize the connection between the farms and the factories. Visit the athletic, urban mecca of Indianapolis, but don't miss the rolling green hills and rural beauty downstate. The state that produced wholesome TV celebrities David Letterman and Jane Pauley also features beautiful scenery, especially during the fall when the foliage around Columbus puts on a spectacular show.

Practical Information

Capital: Indianapolis.

Tourist Information: **Indiana Division of Tourism,** 1 N. Capitol #700, Indianapolis 46204 (232-8860; 800-289-6646 in IN). **Division of State Parks,** 616 State Office Bldg., Indianapolis 46204 (232-4124).

Time Zones: Eastern and Central (1 hr. behind Eastern). During the summer, eastern Indiana does not observe Daylight Savings Time and corresponds to the other half of the state.

Postal Abbreviation: IN.

Indianapolis

Unlike gasahol, the short-lived corn-based petroleum alternative of the late 70s, Indianapolis has successfully managed to combine cars and corn. The two have mixed to fuel Indiana's premiere city into a cultural center which today would never run former weathercaster David Letterman out of town for warning of hail "the size of canned hams," as it once did. Indianapolis is a city driven by a passion for cars and sports, seen in its wide California-style streets and the international Pan Am games, held here in 1987. Each Memorial Day weekend the Indy 500 combines exhaust and exhaustion in the largest single-day sporting event in the world.

Practical Information

Emergency: 911 or 632-7575.

Visitor Information: Indianapolis City Center, 201 S. Capital St. (237-5200), in the Pan Am Plaza across from the Hoosierdome. Open Mon.-Fri. 10am-5:30pm, Sat. 10am-4pm. Fun Fone, 237-5210. Recording of the week's events, sporting, theatrical, and otherwise.

Indianapolis International Airport: 7 mi. southwest of downtown near I-465. To get to the city center, take bus #9 ("West Washington").

Amtrak: 350 S. Illinois (263-0550 or 800-872-7245), behind Union Station. Somewhat deserted but relatively safe area. To Chicago ($38) only. Open Sun. 9-10:30pm, Mon. and Wed. 5:30am-4pm and 9-10:30pm, Tues. and Thurs. 8am-4pm and 9-11:45pm, Fri. 8am-4pm and 9-10:30pm, Sat. 9-11:45pm.)

Greyhound: 127 N. Capital Ave. (635-4501), downtown at E. Ohio St. 1 block from Monument Circle. Fairly safe area. To: Chicago ($25.25), Columbus ($24), and Louisville ($25.25). Open 24 hr. Indiana Trails operates out of the same station and serves cities within the state.

Public Transport: Metro Bus, 14 E. Washington St. (632-1900 or 635-3344), 1 block from Monument Circle. Open Mon.-Fri. 7:30am-5:30pm. Fare 75¢, rush hour $1. Transfers 25¢. Special disabled service P.O. Box 2383, Indianapolis 46206 (632-3000).

Taxi: Yellow Cab, 637-5421.

Car Rental: Louie's Rent-a-Bent, 2233 E. Washington St. (632-4429), 2½ mi. east of downtown. From $11 per day plus 10¢ per mi.; weekly $99 with unlimited mi. Car must not leave the state. Check carefully to make sure car's in good shape. Open Mon.-Fri. 9am-6pm, Sat. 9am-5pm. Required $150 deposit may be paid with credit card.

Help Lines: Crisis and Suicide Hotline, 632-7575. Mayor's Handicapped Hotline, 236-3620.

Time Zone: Eastern.

Post Office: 125 W. South St. (464-6000), across from Amtrak. Open Mon.-Wed. and Fri. 7am-5:30pm, Thurs. 7am-6pm. ZIP code: 46206.

Area Code: 317.

Indianapolis lies 183 mi. south of Chicago, and 113 mi. north of Louisville. I-465 rings the city and provides access to all points downtown. The center of Indianapolis is located just south of **Monument Circle** at the intersection of **Washington Street** (U.S. 40) and **Meridian Street.** Washington divides the city north-south; Meridian east-west.

Accommodations and Camping

Indianapolis offers plenty of budget motels; however, most lie about 5 mi. from downtown off I-465, with bus service to these areas very limited. For the Indy 500 in May, motels jack up their rates, especially on weekends; make reservations one year in advance.

Medical Tower Inn, 1633 N. Capitol Ave. (925-9831), in the tall building across from the Methodist Hospital. Hospital clean and well-maintained. Singles $38. Doubles $48. With student ID $8 discount.

Dollar Inn, 4630 Lafayette Ave. (293-9060), immediately south of I-65. Convenient to the Speedway and Eagle Creek Park. Small, clean rooms. Singles $22. Doubles $27. Key deposit $2.

Indy East Motel, 5855 E. Washington St. (357-8323). Take #8 bus. Clean if stale rooms. Singles $22. Doubles $30. Key deposit $2.

Atlas Hotel, 433½ E. Washington St. (630-4109). Take #8 bus from downtown. Small, dirty rooms with no bath. Singles $10. Weekly: $50.

Kamper Korner, 1951 W. Edgewood Ave. (788-1488), 1 mi. south of I-465 on Rte. 37. No bus service. Open area with no shade. Laundry, grocery, showers, free fishing and swimming. Enforced quiet hours 11pm-7am. Tent sites $14, with water and hookup $15. Limited services Nov. to mid-March.

Food and Nightlife

Indianapolis greets visitors with a variety of restaurants that range from holes-in-the-wall to trendy locales decked out in vintage kitsch.

Tourists and residents alike head for **Union Station**, 39 Jackson Pl. (266-8740), near the Hoosier Dome 4 blocks south of Monument Circle. This 13-acre maze of restaurants, shops, dance clubs, bars, and hotels sells every edible substance imaginable in a beautiful, authentically refurbished rail depot. The second-level oval rings with moderately priced ethnic eateries. (Entrees average $2.50-5. Open Mon.-Thurs. 10am-9pm, Fri.-Sat. 10am-10pm, Sun. 11am-6pm.)

Acapulco Joe's, 365 N. Illinois Ave., downtown. The hot 'n' spicy food will sear your taste-buds. For the average Joe, they offer peanut butter and jelly sandwiches. 3 tacos $6.50. Open Mon.-Thurs. 7am-9pm, Fri.-Sat. 7am-10pm.

Iaria's, 317 S. College Ave., about 10 blocks from downtown. A 50s throwback, with shiny vinyl furniture and chrome chairs. Spaghetti and meatball dinner $6. Open Mon.-Thurs. 11am-9:30pm, Fri. 11am-11pm, Sat. noon-11pm.

The City Market, 222 E. Market St., 2 blocks east of Monument Circle. Renovated 19th-century building with produce stands and 15 ethnic markets. Prices reasonable but not rock-bottom. Open Mon.-Sat. 6am-6pm.

Nightlife makes waves 6 mi. north of the downtown area in **Broad Ripple**, at College Ave. and 62nd St., typically swamped with students and yuppies. The area has charming ethnic restaurants and art studios in original frame houses, as well as some artsy bars. **The Patio Lounge**, 6308 Guilford Ave. (253-0799), sponsors underground bands for $1-3 cover. (Open Mon.-Fri. 5pm-3am, Sat. 8pm-3am. Take "College-Broad Ripple" bus #17 north from central downtown.)

Sights

Often obscured by the hubbub surrounding the Indy 500, Indianapolis cultural attractions promise a pleasant afternoon. The slogan "Where children grow up and adults don't have to" describes the city's museums; "Please touch" is the motto of the **Children's Museum** at 3000 N. Meridian St. (294-5437). Kids help run hands-on exhibits, which include a turn-of-the-century carousel, a huge train collection, heavy petting zoos, and high-tech electronic wizardry. (Open Tues.-Sat. 10am-5pm, Sun. noon-5pm. Free.) The **Indianapolis Museum of Art**, 1200 W. 38th (923-1331), houses a large collection of Turner paintings and watercolors as well as Robert Indiana's LOVE sculpture. The museum sits among 154 acres of park, beautifully landscaped with gardens and nature trails. (Open Tues.-Sun. 11am-5pm. Free, except for special exhibits.) The **Eiteljorg Museum**, 334 N. Senate Ave. (636-9378), west of downtown, features Native American and Western art. (Open Tues.-Sat. 10am-5pm, Sun. noon-5pm. Admission $2, seniors $1.50, under 12 $1.) Stunning African and Egyptian decor graces the **Walker Theatre**, 617 Indiana Ave. (635-6915). Erected in 1927, the theater symbolizes Indianapolis' African American community, hosting such jazz greats as Louis Armstrong and Dinah Washington. The complex also sponsors plays, dance performances, and a week-long black film festival in late October. Even those who don't make one of the shows should go just to see the splendid interior. Upstairs in the ballroom, the **Jazz on the Avenue** series offers live music every Friday night.

The Indianapolis 500

When in Indianapolis, do as the locals do and visit the **Indianapolis Motor Speedway**, 4790 W. 16th St. (241-2500). Take the Speedway exit off I-465 or bus #25 ("West 16th"). A shrine dedicated to the automobile, this 1909 behemoth encloses an entire 18-hole golf course. Except in May, you can take a bus ride around the 2½-mi. track for $1. The adjacent **Speedway Museum** (Indy Hall of Fame) houses a collection of Indy race cars and antique autos, as well as racing memorabilia and videotapes highlighting historic Indy moments. (Open daily 9am-5pm. Admission $1, under 16 free.)

The country's passion for the automobile reaches a frenzy during the **500 Festival** when 33 aerodynamic, turbocharged, 2½-mi.-to-the-gallon race cars circle the asphalt track at speeds over 225 mph. Beginning with the time trials (the two weekends in mid-May preceding the race), the party culminates with a big blowout on the Sunday of Memorial Day weekend (weather permitting). Book hotel reservations early and buy tickets in advance. For ticket information, call 248-6700 (open daily 9am-5pm). The 500 isn't the only race in town; call for information on other auto events at the **Indianapolis Raceway Park,** 9901 Crawfordsville Rd. (293-7223), near the intersection of I-74 and I-465.

Bloomington

Bloomington is most famous for "Hoosier Hysteria," a condition characterized by reverence for its basketball team. **Indiana University,** the proud home of this deeply loved team, also contains the town's only other attractions. Although vast, the IU campus is best explored on foot. Brochures describing walking tours are available at the tourist information office; expect a blister or two. The university has a superb rare book collection at the **Lilly Library,** E. 7th St. (855-2452; open Mon.-Thurs. 8am-8pm, Fri. 8am-5pm, Sat. 9am-5pm, Sun. 1-5pm. Free). Across the street, the **University Art Museum** (855-4826), yet another triangular structure designed by I.M. Pei, houses exhibits of ancient Mediterranean, Asian, and African art. (Open Tues.-Sat. 9am-5pm, Sun. 1-5pm. Free.) The university also has a superb music department; visit the **Musical Arts Center** (885-9053), on Jordan Ave., where terrific opera performances, symphony concerts, musicals, and free popular concerts take place Wednesdays during term-time. (Tickets $8-12, students $3-6.) Those craving food or information should visit the huge **Indiana Memorial Union** (856-6381), on 7th St., which has a deli (open daily 9:30am-4pm) on the mezzanine floor and a campus information booth on the first floor.

Tickets to a Hoosier basketball game are not surprisingly hard to come by unless you know a friendly student. Other sporting events include the **Little 500** bike race held in the university stadium on the third Saturday in April: the movie *Breaking Away* portrayed this event as a town-gown showdown; in reality it's just an opportunity for students and alumni to party.

As in many large university towns, the campus blends in with the town streets. The shops and restaurants in Bloomington concentrate in the block bordered by 4th and 7th Street running east-west, and College and Walnut Street traveling south and north, respectively. Student hangouts line Kirkwood Ave. For delicious Greek fare (gyro $3), a safe bet is the **Trojan Horse,** 100 E. Kirkwood. (Open Mon.-Thurs. 11am-11pm, Fri.-Sat. 11am-midnight, Sun. 3-9pm.) **Nick's English Hut,** 423 E. Kirkwood, serving burgers ($2.50-3.35) and beer (pound jars $1.10, pitchers $4.25), combines the atmosphere of a traditional tavern with the energy of a college hotspot. (Open Mon.-Sat. 11am-2am, Sun. noon-midnight.) Slightly removed from the college scene, **The Snow Lion,** 113 S. Grant St., serves Tibetan food in quiet and elegant surroundings. (Seafood entrees $7-10. Open daily 5-10pm.)

In staying overnight, try to avoid home game weekends, "Little 500" day in April, and graduation week, when rates are higher and hotels booked solid. In a seedy neighborhood, the **Downtown Motel,** 509 N. College Ave. (336-6881), right around the corner from the Greyhound station and an easy walk to the university, has clean if musty rooms. (Singles $25. Doubles $30. Key deposit $1.) Farther north, the **Stony Crest Motel,** 1300 N. Walnut St. (332-9491), at 17th St., has clean rooms and a swimming pool. (Singles $26. Doubles $29.) Campers should try the **Riddle Point Campground** (332-5220) on Lake Lemon. Take Rte. 45 north of town, then Tunnel Road north to the end. A beautiful lake surrounds this rustic site. (Showers available. Primitive site $7, with hookup $10.) **Harding Ridge Federal Campground** (837-9453), 7 mi. south on Rte. 446, presides on the shore of Lake Monroe. (Primitive sites $7, with hookup $9.) Also on the lake is the **Paynetown-Monroe Reservoir** (837-9490), 4 mi. south on Rte. 446. (Primitive sites $3, with hookup $8.) The **Bloomington/Monroe County Visitors Bureau,** 2855 N. Walnut St. (334-8900 or 800-678-9828), north of town off Rte. 37, has information on sights, restaurants, and lodging in and around Bloomington and Monroe County. The **Greyhound** station, 535 N. Walnut St. at 10th (332-1522), receives buses about 8 blocks from campus, and serves Indianapolis ($9.50). (Open Mon.-Fri. 4:30am-5:30pm, Sat. 4:30am-4pm, Sun. bus times only.)

Bloomington's **ZIP code** is 47401; the **area code** is 812.

Columbus

After World War II, when the Cummins Engine Company decided that Columbus' educational facilities lagged behind the times, the company set up a fund to pay architectural fees for school buildings, stipulating that the architect must be of world stature. Since then, churches, fire stations, and everything in between have sprung up under this innovative program. Columbus is now home to 50 public and private buildings that make up the most concentrated collection of contemporary architecture in the world.

Before starting on your tour, stop at the helpful **visitors center,** 506 5th St. (372-1954), at Franklin. The extension of the Indianapolis Museum of Art beautifies the second floor. (Visitors center open March-Nov. Mon.-Sat. 9am-5pm, Sun. 10am-2pm; Nov.-March Mon.-Sat. 9am-5pm. Museum open Mon.-Wed. and Fri.-Sun. 10am-2pm, Thurs. 10am-5pm.) Bus tours ($7) also leave from the visitors center (Mon.-Fri. at 10am, Sat. at 10am and 2pm).

A walking tour of downtown takes about 90 minutes. A block away from the visitors center, downtown's well-preserved Victorian homes set off I.M. Pei's **Cleo Rogers Library,** complete with Henry Moore sculpture, and the **First Christian Church,** a cube accompanied by a rectangular tower, by Eero Saarinen (designer of the St. Louis Gateway Arch). To the south stands **St. Peter's Lutheran Church** by Gunnar Birkerts with its spike-like steeple. Of the other specially commissioned buildings, must-sees include: Eero Saarinen's stunning **North Christian Church,** whose futuristic exterior has been copied all over the world; Harry Weese's **Otter Creek Clubhouse,** which sits atop what some consider the nation's finest golf course; and the ultramodern **Commons,** a shopping mall housing a performance center, art gallery, and an indoor playground all designed by Cesar Pelli.

The Commons contains a couple of casual eateries, but head instead across the street to **Zaharako's** (known locally as "The Greeks"), 329 Washington St. Established in 1900, the restaurant features onyx soda fountains, a 50-ft. mahogany bar, Tiffany lamps, and marble counters. Come for ice cream, candy, or hearty sandwiches ($1.25-2.25). (Open Mon.-Sat. 10am-5pm.) The **Imperial 400 Motor Inn,** 101 W. 3rd St. (372-2835), offers comfortable rooms with artwork on the walls and leather chairs, a heated pool, and a convenient location. (Singles $30-36. Doubles $30-40.) Though its rooms are rather dark, the **Dollar Inn,** west of town at Hwy. 46 and I-65 is a good buy for the buck. (Single $22. $5 each additional person. Key deposit $2.) **KOA** (342-6229) sets up camp 6 mi. south on I-65 at Ogleville. (Primitive sites $12, with hookup and water $15. $3 each additional person.) **Greyhound** idles at 204 E. 8th St. (376-3821) and sends four buses daily to Indianapolis ($10.25). (Open Mon.-Fri. 9am-5:45pm, Sat. 8:45am-12:45pm.)

The **ZIP code** for Columbus is 47401; the **area code** is 812.

Michigan

Gerald Ford, Malcolm X, and Madonna do not make the most likely trio. But all three grew up in Michigan, the state that offers more variety than any other in the Midwest. University towns like Ann Arbor serve as strongholds for liberals and young scholars; industrial powerhouses like Detroit still supply the nation with three-quarters of its cars, despite the auto industry's slump less than a decade ago. Michigan also chimes in with natural beauty, from the rugged, solitary forests of the Upper Peninsula to the shimmering waters of the magnificent fresh-water shoreline. The excitement of the city and the tranquility of nature combine to make Michigan an attractive place to study, work, or kick back and relax.

Practical Information

Capital: Lansing.

Tourist Information: Michigan Travel Bureau, 333 S. Capitol Ave., Lansing 48933 (800-543-2937). Department of Natural Resources, Information Services Center, Steven T. Mason Bldg., P.O. Box 30028, Lansing 48909 (373-1220). Detailed information on state parks, forests, campsites, and other public facilities.

Time Zones: Eastern. The westernmost fifth of the Upper Peninsula is Central (1 hr. behind Eastern).Postal Abbreviation: MI.

Detroit

Detroit has suffered a great deal in the past few decades. In the 60s, as the country danced to the African American Motown sound, the world watched Detroit's black and white communities clash during some of the worst riots of the Civil Rights Movement. Following the riots, many white residents headed to the suburbs, leaving thousands of deserted houses and buildings behind. The auto industry declined, unemployment skyrocketed, and the frustrated people of Detroit brought more violence to the half-abandoned city.

Recently things have taken a turn for the better. Whether to lure in big corporations (and big money) or out of genuine compassion for the city and people of Detroit, businesspeople and citizens have spent billions on a successful renovation of the downtown area. The silver towers of the Renaissance Center line the emerald Detroit River, as do numerous new hotels, shopping centers, and office buildings. Residential areas such as Indian Village east of downtown have undergone massive renovation as well, and the mostly African American city is slowly becoming more racially mixed. Ethnic festivals held downtown every summer weekend reveal the residents' newly found pride and excitement.

Practical Information

Emergency: 911.

Visitor Information: Detroit Convention and Visitors Bureau, on Hart Plaza at 2 E. Jefferson St. (567-1170). From the Greyhound terminal, turn right at Randolph St., then right onto Jefferson. Pick up the free Detroit Visitors Guide. Open daily 9am-5pm. Also at 100 Renaissance Center #1950 (259-4333). Open Mon.-Fri. 9am-5pm. Call What's Line, 567-1170, for a recorded listing of entertainment events. Ticketmaster, 645-6666.

Travelers Aid: 211 W. Congress, 3rd floor (962-6740).

Detroit Metropolitan Airport: (942-3550), 21 mi. west of downtown off I-94. Commuter Transportation Company and Kirby Tours (963-8585 or 800-521-0711) have shuttles to downtown ($10 to hotels, $15 anywhere else). Taxi fare downtown is a steep $25.

Amtrak: 2601 Rose St. (964-5335 or 800-872-7245), on 17th St., 1½ blocks south of Michigan Ave. To Chicago ($31) and Cleveland ($33). Open daily 6:30am-1am.

Greyhound: 130 E. Congress at Randolph St. (963-9840), downtown. For connections to city buses, walk ½ block west on Congress St. to Woodward Ave., then north to Cadillac Sq. To: Chicago ($14), Toronto ($25), and New York ($98). Open 24 hr.; ticket office open daily 5:45am-1:30am.

Public Transport: Detroit Department of Transportation (DOT), 1301 E. Warren (833-7692). Carefully policed public transport system. Serves the downtown area, with limited service to the suburbs. Most buses operate until 1am. Fare $1, transfers 10¢. **People Mover,** Detroit Transportation Corporation, 150 Michigan Ave. (224-2160). Ultramodern tramway facility circles the Central Business District with 13 stops. Fare 50¢. **Southeastern Michigan Area Regional Transit (SMART),** 962-5515. Bus service to the suburbs. Fare $1-2.50, transfers 10¢.

Taxi: Unity Cab, 834-3300.

Car Rental: Call-a-Car, 877 E. Eight Mile Rd. (541-2700), in Hazel Park at I-75. From $20 per day; 100 free mi., 15¢ each additional mi. Must be 21 with credit card and insurance. Car must not leave MI.

Help Lines: Crisis Hotline, 224-7000. **Gay and Lesbian Crisis Line,** 398-4297.

Time Zone: Eastern.

Post Office: 1401 W. Fort (226-8301), at 8th St. Open Mon.-Fri. 8am-5:30pm, Sat. 8:30am-noon. **ZIP Code:** 48200.

Area Code: 313.

Detroit faces Windsor, Ontario across the Detroit River, lying 275 mi. east of Chicago, above Lake Erie on the banks of the river. The sprawling suburban area does not lend itself to personification. Years of mass exodus from downtown have created a ring of affluent suburbs and ethnic neighborhoods.

One-way streets and punctual parking meter personnel carefully monitor the Motor City's well-maintained and surprisingly uncrowded road system. Detroit's streets form a grid, with the major east-west arteries, known as the "Mile Roads," marked out in 1-mi. segments north of downtown. **Eight Mile Road** is the northern boundary of the city. I-94 heads east from the airport as the **Detroit Industrial Parkway** to downtown, where it becomes the **Ford Freeway.** South of downtown, I-75 is known as the **Fisher Freeway;** north of downtown, it turns into the **Chrysler Freeway.** I-96 is called **Jeffries Freeway,** and Rte. 10 is the **Lodge Highway.**

If you plan to stay for more than a few days, get a copy of *Monthly Detroit* ($1.50) at a local newsstand. It gives detailed listings of events, nightspots, restaurants, tours, sports, theater, and dance.

Accommodations and Camping

Although weekend specials are available at many downtown hotels, few other options are both cheap *and* safe. If you opt for cheap, be sure to arrive in daylight and be willing to forgo nightlife. The area around the Amtrak station is unsafe. The Greyhound station, near the gentrified riverfront, attracts a varied crowd—don't leave the station alone on foot after dark. It's best to take a bus, cab, or car to reach other parts of the city.

Teahouse of the Golden Dragon Home Hostel, 8585 Harding Ave. (756-2676), in Centerline, north of 10 Mile Rd. off Kyle. Take SMART bus #510 or 515. Rooms double as personal space for housemother. Chorus of clocks chime through the night. $5.

Country Grandma's Home Hostel (AYH), 22330 Bell Rd. (753-4901), in New Boston, midway between Detroit and Ann Arbor. Close to Metro Parks. $7, nonmembers $10 (includes temporary membership); additional nights $7.

Red Roof Inn, 2350 Rochester Rd. (689-4391), in Troy, ½ hr. from downtown. Take exit 67 off I-75. Singles $34. Doubles $36.

Roadway Inn, 8230 Merriman Rd. (729-7600), just outside the Detroit Metro airport. Accessible only by car; take I-94 to Merriman Rd. Free shuttle service to and from airport. Singles $32. Doubles $38.

Mercy College of Detroit, 8200 W. Outer Dr. (592-6170), 11 mi. from downtown off the Lodge Freeway (Rte. 10). Campus secure, but surrounding area shaky. Sinks in rooms, shared bath. Kitchen and laundry facilities. Singles $12. Doubles $18.

University of Windsor, Vanier Hall, Wyandotte St. W. and Huron Church Rd. (519-973-7074), in Windsor, Canada, near the USA Bridge. Take the Tunnel Bus, then bus #1C. Less convenient, but much safer and more pleasant than comparable accommodations on the U.S. side. Clean, spacious rooms with A/C. Singles CDN$24. Doubles CDN$40. Student rate CDN$14.50. Price reduced 12% for American money. Open May-Aug.

You'll have to trek some distance if you want to camp. A dozen state parks with campgrounds lie about 40 mi. out, off I-75, 96, and 94. **Sterling State Park** (289-2715) lies 37 mi. south of Detroit, ½ mi. off of I-75 just north of the city of Monroe. (Open 24 hr. Sites $9, including electricity.) The **Detroit-Greenfield KOA,** 6680 Bunton Rd. (482-7722), is about 30 mi. from downtown Detroit and 3 mi. east of Ypsilanti. From I-94 (exit 187), go 1 mi. south onto Rawsonville Rd., turn right onto Textile Rd., then go 1 mi. and turn left onto Bunton—the campground is ½ mi. farther. (216 sites. $17 for 2 people, with water and hookup $20. Each additional person $3, ages 4-17 $2. Open March 30-Nov. 18.) The **Windsor South Resort Kampground** (519-726-5200) 6480 Texas Rd., offers comparable rates (CDN$15.50) and facilities, with 10% discount for U.S. dollars. Take the tunnel or bridge to Hwy. 3, then go south on Howard Ave. to Texas Rd.

Food and Nightlife

Ethnic food is the best budget option in Detroit. From late April to mid-September, Hart Plaza, in the Civic Center along the river downtown, is the scene of a series of African American, Arabic, German, Irish, Mexican, Ukrainian, and other weekend festivals. The *Do it in Detroit* brochure, available at the visitors bureau, lists ethnic festivals held at Hart Plaza (224-1184). To savor the essence of **Greektown,** munch on *baklava* as you stroll down Monroe Ave., about 4 blocks northeast of the Ren Cen. **Trappers Alley,** 508 Monroe Ave. (963-5445), houses 90 food and retail shops. (Open Mon.-Thurs. 10am-9pm, Fri.-Sat. 10am-midnight, Sun. noon-7pm.) **Eastern Market** (833-1560), at Gratiot and Russell Ave. just north of Fisher Freeway, has hawked meat and produce outdoors since 1892. (Open Mon.-Fri. 5am-noon, Sat. 5am-5pm.) Another popular area for eating, drinking, and listening to music is the **Rivertown** area in the renovated **Warehouse District,** 1 mi. east of the Ren Cen off E. Jefferson Ave. **Mexican Town,** a lively neighborhood south of Tiger Stadium, has a number of terrific restaurants.

Pizza Papalis Taverna, 553 Monroe Ave., in Greektown, doesn't serve Greek food but is a comfortable restaurant and bar with delicious pizza. Try the 6-in. Chicago-style junior pizza ($3.45). Open daily 11am-1am.

Xochimilco Restaurant, 3409 Bagley, in Mexican Town. People come from all over Michigan to enjoy the *botanes* (chips smothered with refried beans), Mexican sausages, and other goodies ($4.75-6.75). Huge servings and hugely popular, so plan to wait 20-30 min. Open daily 11am-4am.

Woodbridge Tavern, 289 St. Aubin St. (259-0578), at Woodbridge in Rivertown. Comfortable old-style bar, restored to its original 20s character, complete with a honky-tonk piano and an outdoor terrace known as Marcia's Vineyard. Sandwiches and burgers $3.50-5. Open Mon.-Sat. 6:30am-2am, Sun. noon-11pm. Live classic rock 'n' roll Thurs.-Sun. No cover.

Niki's Taverna, 735 Beaubien St. (961-4303), just south of Monroe St., close to the Ren Cen in Greektown. White-collar lunch crowd. Gyros with fries $5.50. Open Mon.-Thurs. 11:30am-3:30am, Fri.-Sun. 11:30am-5am.

Alvin's Finer Delicatessen and Detroit Bar, 5756 Cass (832-2355), across the street from Wayne State University. Deli sandwiches $2.50-3.75. Open daily 11am-6pm. Bar open until 2am Thurs.-Tues. Live music in the back room ranges from acoustic to dance to jazz Thurs.-Mon. Cover $2-5.

Jacoby's, 624 Brush St., near the Greyhound station, 2 blocks north of the Ren Cen. Continues its 85-year German tradition of beer and *sauerbraten* after being rebuilt following a fire in 1989. Great drinks, fantastic fresh perch, and small but delicious sandwiches all under $5. Open Mon.-Wed. 11am-10pm, Thurs.-Fri. 11am-11pm.

Soup Kitchen Saloon, 1585 Franklin (259-2643), at Orleans in Rivertown. Try a taste of Nantucket for dinner (cornmeal-fried oysters $9). Open Mon.-Thurs. 11am-midnight, Fri.-Sat. noon-2am, Sun. 3pm-midnight. Top blues and jazz performers Wed.-Sun. at 9pm. Cover varies, but usually $2-6.

St. Andrew's Hall, 431 E. Congress (961-6358), 2 blocks north of the Ren Cen. Remodeled church offers no avatars, only live performances by local and big-name bands. The DJs at **The Shelter,** in the basement, provide all types of alternative music Tues.-Sun. nights.

Sights

The sparkling waterfront district is quite small and takes no more than a day to explore. The **Civic Center** and **Renaissance Center (Ren Cen)** between E. Jefferson St. and the waterfront, display striking modern architecture. Tours of the Ren Cen are given regularly. (For general Ren Cen information call 568-5600; tour information 341-6810; lines open daily 9am-5pm.)

The Civic Center includes the **Philip A. Hart Plaza** (224-1185), a 10-acre "people place" that holds free concerts in summer, ethnic festivals on summer weekends (afternoons and evenings), and ice skating in the winter. Look for the spiraling **Pylon** and the computerized **Dodge Fountain,** known as the "flying donut," designed by Noguchi. Across the street is the striking and controversial **Joe Louis Monument,** a huge black arm and fist suspended on cables and designed by Robert Graham. The Civic Center also includes **Cobo Hall** (224-1010), one of the nation's largest convention centers. The **Joe Louis Arena** (567-6000) next door, home of the Detroit Red Wings hockey team, also hosts a variety of concerts and other events, as does **Cobo Arena** (567-6000), on the other side of Cobo Hall.

Just north of downtown, the magnificent **Fox Theatre,** 2211 Woodward Ave. (567-6000), has been painstakingly renovated. Now, as in 1928, the Fox is a gilt picture palace of impressive dimensions and gaudy decorations. Diana Ross, Aretha Franklin, and Stevie Wonder auditioned here for Motown Records in the 60s; today it hosts a variety of drama, comedy, and musical productions. **The Detroit Institute of Arts (DIA),** 5200 Woodward Ave. (833-7900), 2½ mi. north of downtown, has one of the nation's most comprehensive fine arts collections. Diego Rivera's spectacular 1932 *Detroit Industry* frescoes alone merit a visit. (Open Tues.-Sun. 9:30am-5:30pm. Donation.) The institute is part of Detroit's **Cultural Center,** a 40-block cluster of public and private cultural institutions bordered by Wayne State University (take bus #53). A quick walk from the DIA takes you into the "Streets of Old Detroit" at the **Detroit Historical Museum,** 5401 Woodward Ave. (833-1805; open Wed.-Sun. 9:30am-5pm; donation). Right next door, you can conduct experiments at the **Detroit Science Center,** 5020 John R. St. (577-8400; open Tues.-Fri. 9am-4pm, Sat. 10am-6pm, Sun. noon-6pm; admission $5, seniors and ages 6-12 $4, ages 4-5 $2). Explore technical and social aspects of the Underground Railroad at the **Museum of African American History,** 301 Frederick Douglass (833-9800; open Wed.-Sat. 9:30-5pm, Sun. 1-5pm; donation). Though Barry Gordy's Motown Record Company has moved to Los Angeles, the **Motown Records Museum,** 2648 W. Grand Blvd. (867-0991), preserves its memories. Downstairs, shop around the primitive studio in which the Jackson Five, Marvin Gaye, Smokey Robinson, and Diana Ross recorded the tunes that made them famous. (Open Mon.-Sat. 10am-5pm, Sun. 2-5pm. Admission $3, ages under 12 $2.) The museum lies east of Rosa Parks Blvd., about 1 mi. west of the John C. Lodge Freeway. Take the "Dexter Avenue" bus right to the museum from downtown.)

The colossal **Henry Ford Museum,** and **Greenfield Village,** 20900 Oakwood Blvd., off I-94 in Dearborn (271-1620 or 271-1976; 24 hr.), definitely warrant a foray into the suburbs. The 12-acre museum has more than the expected parade of antique cars: other sensational items include the chair Lincoln sat in and the car Kennedy rode in when they each were assassinated. Greenfield Village is a collection of 80 transplanted historic buildings, including a turn-of-the-century amusement park, the Wright brothers' bicycle shop, the courtroom where Lincoln practiced law, Puritan homes, and various shops, houses, and taverns, all set in a beautiful 240-acre park. (Open daily 9am-5pm. Admission to museum and village $10.50 each, seniors $9.50, ages 5-12 $5.25. 2-day combination tickets $18, children $9. Take SMART bus #200 or 250.)

If you're looking for a safe, quiet refuge from the city bustle, head to **Belle Isle Park** (267-7115), a 985-acre island in the Detroit River (open 24 hr.). Take a car or pick up DOT bus #25 (eastbound) at the corner of Jefferson and Randolf (in front of the Ren Cen) to MacArthur Bridge, then transfer to Belle Isle bus #4. Designed by Frederick Law Olmsted, Belle Isle has a variety of recreational facilities and fishing spots, as well as a conservatory, several fantastic playgrounds, an aquarium, and a small zoo. Most buildings are open daily from 10am to 5pm. Ask the driver for a brochure about walking and bus tours of the island.

Events

* America's Motor City turns into the Monte Carlo of the Midwest for one great week each year. The **Detroit Grand Prix** (259-5400), the only Formula One World Championship race in the U.S., takes place the third week in June. The time trials are held the Friday and Saturday before the race from 8:30am to 7:15pm on Friday and 8:30am to 5:45pm on Saturday. The course follows the city streets by the Ren Cen. (Tickets about $3 for Fri., $10 for Sat., $25 for Sun. 3-day reserved grandstand seat $95-120.)

Jazz fans jet to Detroit during Labor Day weekend for the **Montreux-Detroit Jazz Festival** (259-5400), the U.S. half of the Swiss Montreux International Jazz Festival. Held in Hart Plaza, most concerts are free, except for headliners such as Dizzy Gillespie and Wynton Marsalis.

Ann Arbor

Dominated by the University of Michigan and its 20,000 undergraduates, Ann Arbor is one of the most progressive, cultured, and lively university towns in the U.S., combining a relaxed small-town atmosphere with world-class arts. Smoking marijuana brings only a $25 fine, an anomaly anywhere in the U.S., but especially in the conservative Midwest.

Ann Arbor is basically a laid-back college town, but when the students leave, locals indulge in a little celebrating. During **Art Fair Week** in late July, hundreds of thousands of people pack the city and clog the streets to see the **Ann Arbor Street Art Fair**, the **State Street Area Art Fair**, and the world-famous **Summer Art Fair**. Also drawing crowds from late June to mid-July, the **Ann Arbor Summer Festival** features numerous dance and theater productions, as well as performances by musicians famous in styles ranging from jazz to country-western to classical. On the last Saturdays of June, July, and August, the **German Festival** highlights the German heritage common to most of the upper Midwest, while the **Ethnic Fair** in early September celebrates food, culture, and crafts from around the world. Call the visitors bureau for details.

In the realm of inanimate culture, the university features some top-notch free museums. The **University of Michigan Art Museum (UMAM)**, at the corner of State and University (747-0519), houses a small but choice collection of works from around the world (open Tues.-Fri. 10am-4pm, Sat.-Sun. 1-5pm). Paths for biking, jogging, or just walking crisscross the town and lead through the **Nichols Arboretum**, a university-owned park off Geddes Ave., just northeast of downtown. The paths also run through the gorgeous **Gallup Park**, 3000 Fuller Rd. (662-9319), on the Huron River, also northeast of downtown. Here small, man-made islands connected by arched bridges form ponds for water sports and fishing. (Both parks open daily 6am-10pm.) In the summer, you can rent bikes and canoes at Gallup. (Bike rental $3 first hr., $1 each additional hr. Canoes $6 first hr., $1 each additional hr., Sat.-Sun. $1 extra. Rental Mon.-Fri. 11am-9pm, Sat.-Sun. 9am-9pm. Must have a $10 cash deposit and driver's license.) On warm afternoons, pastorally inclined students haunt the beautiful **Mathaei Botanical Gardens**, 1800 N. Dixboro Rd. (998-7060). Call the Park and Recreation Department (994-2780 or 769-9140) for additional information about Ann Arbor's parks.

During the academic year you can get cheap food (entrees $2-5) at the **U of M Cafeteria**, West Quad, 541 Thompson St., or at the **Michigan League**, 911 N. University Ave. (Both open Mon.-Sat. 7:15am-7:30pm; summer Mon.-Sat. 11:30am-7:30pm.) The **U of M Union**, 530 S. State St., also offers a melange of restaurants, specialty shops, and bookstores. If you don't mind shelling out more than $5, you'll find lots of nice places playing Simon and Garfunkel songs. Most student hangouts are on **State Street** close to Central Campus and in the **South University Street** "Village" uptown, complete with lively restaurants and bars.

Drink your beer from pint jars on the outdoor balcony at **Casa Dominick's**, 812 Monroe, across from the law quad. Tasty pasta, pizza, and Italian dishes $4-5; pints of beer $1.75. (Open Mon.-Thurs. and Sat. 10am-10pm, Fri. 10am-11pm, Sun. 4-8pm. Bar open Mon.-Thurs. 4-10pm, Fri. 4-11pm.) **Good Time Charley's**, 1140 S. University St., has very popular outdoor tables, but its indoor hanging plants make either setting equally enjoyable. Dinners $3.50-7. (Open Mon.-Sat. 11am-2am, Sun. 4pm-midnight.) Doubling as an amateur art gallery, **Park Avenue Delicatessen**, 211 S. State St. (665-9535), exhibits Bell of the Ball sandwiches (bell peppers, onions, salami, mustard on french bread) for $4.75. (Open Mon.-Sat. 11am-7pm, Sun. 11am-6pm.) Not to be outdone, the **Espresso Royale Café**, 324 S. State St., provides a nice, airy atmosphere, fruit drinks, and a large variety of coffees; it too displays art. Drinks 70¢-$2. (Open Mon.-Fri. 7am-midnight, Sat.-Sun. 9am-midnight.) Pack a picnic at the **farmers market** that springs up every Saturday and Wednesday (7am-3pm), outside the Kerrytown Mall on N. 5th Ave.

Ann Arbor has excellent nightspots that cater to its club-hopping college population. Look for blues, reggae, and rock 'n' roll at **Rick's American Café**, 611 Church St. (996-2747). Voted the best bar in Ann Arbor for the sixth straight year in 1990, Rick's has hosted well-known alternative bands like 10,000 Maniacs. (Open Mon.-Thurs. and Sat. 7:30pm-2am, Fri. 3pm-2am. Cover $2-5; more for big acts.) Great posters advertise **The Blind Pig**, 208 S. 1st St. (996-8555), and its live rock 'n' roll and blues. (Open daily 9am-2am, Fri. 6pm-2am. Cover $3-15.)**Del Rio**, 122 W. Washington (761-2530), at Ashley, isn't as much of a college student hangout, but it provides a pleasant restaurant/bar with free jazz Sunday nights. It is also managed cooperatively by its employees—a vestige of a fast-dying Ann Arbor tradition. (Open Mon.-Fri. 11:30am-1:45am, Sat. noon-1:45am, Sun. 5:30pm-1:45am.)

For information on current classical performances, contact the **University Musical Society** (764-2538; open Mon.-Fri. 10am-6pm) or the **Ann Arbor Symphony Orchestra**, 527 E. Liberty (994-4801). Live jazz can be heard every night in Ann Arbor; for information, call **Eclipse Jazz** (763-0046) or ask around. The **Ann Arbor Civic Theatre**, 1035 S. Main St., performs plays year-round. (Call the visitors bureau for schedule and prices; call 763-8587 to order tickets.)

Despite a predominance of expensive hotels and motels in Ann Arbor, it is possible to find reasonable accommodations rates. Book way ahead if you plan to stay during commencement (early May), during any home-game weekend (in the fall), or during the Summer Art Fair (late July). The **University of Michigan** has rooms available year-round. **Cambridge House**, West Quad, 541 Thompson St. (764-0185), is the most expensive of the dorms (singles $38), but it has carpeting, color TV with cable, and private bathrooms; it is also located in the heart of campus. **Mary Markley**, 1503 Washington Hts. (764-1126), near the hospital, and **Baits Dorm**, Hubbard Rd., North Campus (764-0130) have standard cinder-block walls and tile floors, but are comfortable and worth the money. (Singles $19. Doubles $27.) Markley's location is probably better; Baits, though peaceful, is across the river 2 mi. away. (Reservations for dorms can be made at 764-5325.) **Red Roof Inn**, 3621 Plymouth Rd. (996-5800), U.S. 23 (exit 41), has singles for $38, doubles for $46. The **Ann**

Arbor YMCA, 350 S. 5th Ave. at William St. (663-0536), in downtown Ann Arbor, allows women. Clean, dorm-style rooms have shared bath with laundry facilities available. (Singles $21. Weekly: $76.) **Embassy Hotel,** 200 E. Huron (662-7100), has a convenient location that compensates for small, often unavailable rooms. (Singles $28. Doubles $33.)

Ann Arbor lies 40 mi. west of Detroit on I-94, approximately 20 mi. from **Detroit Metro Airport. Commuter Transportation Company** and **Kirby Tours** (278-2224 or 800-527-0711 outside MI) run frequent shuttles between the airport and the U of M Union (around $12). Ann Arbor's layout is a well-planned grid. **Main Street** divides the town east-west while **Huron Street** divides it north-south. The central campus of the university lies 5-6 blocks east of Main St., south of E. Huron St. (about a 15-min. walk from the center of town).

The **Ann Arbor Convention and Visitors Bureau,** 211 E. Huron St. #6 (995-7281), has free guides about area attractions, cultural activities, accommodations, and the university. (Open Mon.-Fri. 8:30am-5pm.) **University of Michigan Information** is reached at 763-4636 (open Tues.-Sat. 7am-2pm, Sun.-Mon. 9am-1pm). **Amtrak,** 325 Depot St. (994-4906 or 800-872-7245), offers train service to Chicago ($31) and Detroit ($8). (Open daily 7:30am-11:30pm). **Greyhound,** 116 W. Huron St. (662-5212), at Ashley St. downtown, 1 block off Main St., offers frequent service to Detroit ($6.75) and Chicago ($21). (Open daily 7:30am-6:30pm). The **Ann Arbor Transportation Authority** (973-6500 or 996-0400) runs 25 routes serving Ann Arbor and a few nearby towns. Most buses operate daily 6:45am-10:15pm. (Fare 60¢, seniors and students 30¢. Office open Mon.-Fri. 8am-5pm.) **Emergency** here is 911 and the 24-hr. **Sexual Assault Crisis Line** is 936-3333.

Ann Arbor's **time zone** is Eastern. The **post office** is at 2075 W. Stadium Blvd. (665-1100; open Mon.-Fri. 7:30am-5pm). The **ZIP code** is 48106; the **area code** is 313.

Lake Michigan Shore

The 350-mi. eastern shore of Lake Michigan stretches south from the Mackinaw Bridge to the Indiana border. Tourists flock here to enjoy high dunes of sugary sand, superb fishing, abundant fruit harvests through October, and deep snow in winter. Many of the region's attractions center around forked **Grand Traverse Bay** and **Traverse City,** the "cherry capital of the world," at the southern tip of the bay. Fishing is best in the **Au Sable** and **Manistee Rivers.** The rich fudge sold in numerous specialty shops, however, seems to have the biggest pull on tourists, whom locals dub "fudgies." The **West Michigan Tourist Association,** 136 E. Fulton, Grand Rapids 49503 (616-456-8557), offers copious free literature on this area. (Open Mon.-Fri. 8:45am-5pm.) **Greyhound** (see Traverse City below) serves the coast.

Traverse City and Environs

In summer, vacationers head to Traverse City for its sandy beaches and annual **Cherry Festival,** held the first full week in July. Traverse City produces 50% of the world's sweet and tart cherries. The locals are friendly and the city full of intimate cafés and overpriced knick-knack shops. The surrounding landscape of sparkling blue water, cool forests, and magnificent sand dunes makes this region a Great Lakes paradise, though a crowded and expensive one. Grand Traverse Bay is the focal point for swimming, boating, and scuba diving. Free beaches and public access sites dot its shores. Look for the large flock of white swans.

According to local legend, the mammoth sand dunes 30 mi. northwest of Traverse City are a sleeping mother bear, waiting for her cubs—the **Manitou Islands**—to finish a swim across the lake. According to scientific theory, ice-age glaciers left behind the islands which now comprise the **Sleeping Bear Dunes National Lakeshore.** Nature constantly resculpts the dunes, and some rise a precipitous 400 ft. above the shore of Lake Michigan. The best place to see the dunes is on **Pierce**

Stocking Scenic Drive, off M-109 just north of the town of Empire. A ferry (256-9061 or 271-4217) runs out of Leland to South Manitou Island in summer. (Ferries leave daily at 10am, return at 5pm. Round-trip $14, $16 if you are camping; children under $12 receive a $4 discount.) The park and centers rent canoes, and remain open in winter for cross-country skiing.

The renowned **Interlochen Center for the Arts** (276-9221) rests between two lakes just south of Traverse City on Rte. 137. Here, the high-powered **National Music Camp** instructs over 2000 young artists and musicians each summer in the visual arts, theater, dance, music, and pretension. Performances are usually free or cost only $1-2 during the **International Arts Festival,** held from late June to mid-August. Recent guest performers included Peter, Paul, and Mary and John Denver. The **Interlochen Arts Academy** at the center offers performances almost every weekend in winter as well. The 1200-acre wooded grounds are open year-round, and free tours leave the information center Monday to Saturday at 10am and 2:30pm, Sunday at 3pm. Across the road, the huge **Interlochen State Park** (276-9511) has camping (primitive sites $5, with hookup $9, plus a $3 vehicle permit). The park store rents row boats ($12 per 12-hr., $15 per 24-hr., $20 deposit or driver's license required).

Traverse City has a multitude of fast-food restaurants along E. Front St., but smaller, cheaper, and more appetizing restaurants dot the town. **Stone Soup,** 115 E. Front St. (941-1190), downtown, serves splendid salads ($3-5.75) and "sandriginals," daily special sandwiches ($5.25). (Open Mon.-Sat. 7am-4pm, Sun. 9am-3pm.) The **Omelette Shop and Bakery,** 124 Cass St. (946-0912), makes great omelettes ($3.25-5.25), soups, muffins, and ratatouille *frittata.* (Open daily 7am-3pm.) **D.J. Kelly's,** 120 Park St. (941-4550), has enough bowties, green upholstery, and expensive sandwiches to remind you of the clubhouse after the 18th hole. (Fondues $5-5.50. Open Mon.-Thurs. 5-10pm, Fri.-Sat. 5-11pm.)

Sleep in the woods at the **Brookwood Home Hostel (AYH),** 538 Thomas Rd. (352-4296), in Frankfort near the Sleeping Bear Dunes, almost 50 mi. south of Traverse City on Hwy. 31. The large cottage has 12 beds. ($6. Open mid-June to Sept. 20.) Another option is the **Honey House Home Hostel,** 613 S. Bayshore (264-9768), in Elk Rapids, 18 mi. north of Traverse City, where you'll find 15 beds but no showers. ($5, nonmembers $6. Open May-Oct.) The **Victoriana Bed and Breakfast,** 622 Washington St. (929-1009), near downtown, has four comfortable, almost grand, rooms decorated with family heirlooms. (Singles $40. Doubles $45. Suite $65. Big breakfast and afternoon tea included.) The **Northwestern Michigan Community College,** East Hall, 1701 E. Front St. (922-1406), offers dorms with shared bath. (Singles $15. Doubles $25. Suite with private bath $50. Reservations recommended. Open summer only.) **D. Orr Haus Motor Lodge,** 894 Munson Ave. (263-7685), has clean, no-frills motel rooms right across the street from a nice state beach. (Singles and doubles $26.50. Weekends $5 more.)

There are hundreds of **campgrounds** around Traverse City—in state parks and forests, the Manistee and Huron National Forests, and various parks run by local townships and counties. The West Michigan Tourist Association's *Carefree Days* gives a comprehensive list of public and private sites. State parks usually charge $7-9. As usual, the national forests (723-2211 or 723-3161) are probably the best deal ($4-7). Sleeping Bear Dunes National Lakeshore (326-5134) has two campgrounds: **DH Day** (334-4634) in Glen Arbor, and **Platte River** (325-5881) in Honor. DH Day costs $6 per vehicle; Platte River costs a few dollars more because of recent renovation. Both campgrounds fill up on mid-summer weekends.

The **Greyhound** station at 3233 Cass Rd., near downtown, Detroit ($36). (Open Mon.-Fri. 8am-5pm.) **Bay Area Transportation Authority** (941-2324) buses run once per hour on scheduled routes ($1.50 per ride) and may provide personal transportation. (Open Mon.-Fri. 6am-6pm, Sat. 9am-5pm.)

For visitor information, contact the **Grand Traverse Chamber of Commerce,** 202 E. Grandview Pkwy. (947-5075; open Mon.-Fri. 9am-3pm, Sat. 10am-3pm), or the **Grand Traverse Convention and Visitors Bureau,** 415 Munson Ave. #200 (947-1120 or 800-872-8377; open Mon.-Fri. 9am-5pm). Ask for the *Traverse City Guide*

and *Carefree Days*. Call the **Michigan Department of Natural Resources** for information on state parks (947-7193) or state forest campgrounds (946-4920; open Mon.-Fri. 8am-5pm). For a listing of local events and entertainment, pick up the weekly *Traverse City Record-Eagle Summer Magazine*, free at the visitors bureau and in many stores.
   The area's **time zone** is Eastern. The **post office** is at 202 S. Union St. (946-9616); open Mon.-Fri. 8am-5pm). Traverse City's **ZIP code** is 49684; the **area code** is 616.

North of Traverse City: Charlevoix and Mackinaw City

   Hemingway set some of his Nick Adams stories on the stretch of coast near **Charlevoix** (pronounced SHAR-le-voy), north of Traverse City on U.S. 31. The town, which lies on a ½-mi.-wide ribbon of land between Lake Michigan and Lake Charlevoix, attracts more tourists than in Hemingway's time, as upscale downstaters triple Charlevoix's population in summer. An artsy and aesthetically stunning town, Charlevoix is worth the trip even if you're not a Hemingway fan.
   Fort Michilimackinac (436-5563) guards the straits between Lakes Michigan and Superior, just as it did in the 18th century, though **Mackinaw City,** the town that grew around the fort, is out to trap tourists, not invading troops. (Tours of the fort daily 10:15am-6pm. Admission $5.50, ages 6-12 $2.75.) **Mackinac Island** (which prohibits cars) has another fort, **Fort Mackinac** (906-847-3328), many Victorian homes, and the **Grand Hotel** (906-847-3331), an elegant, gracious summer resort with the world's longest porch. Horse-drawn carriages cart guests all over the island (906-847-3325; $6-10 per person; open daily 8:30am-5pm). Tourist-tempting fudge shops originated on the island. (Ferries leave June-Aug. every hr., May and Sept.-Nov. every other hr.; round-trip $9, ages 6-12 $5.75.) **Greyhound** has a flag stop at the Standard gas station in downtown Mackinaw City. (See Upper Peninsula below for ferry service to Mackinac Island and St. Ignace.)
   The small **Durance Home Hostel (AYH),** 541 N. Mercer (547-2937) in Charlevoix, is run by a delightful woman who feeds her guests plenty of stories and raspberries ($3.25). Or rough it at **Fisherman's Island State Park,** (547-6641) 3 mi. southwest of Charlevoix. The **Petoskey Regional Chamber of Commerce,** 401 E. Mitchell (347-4150) in Petoskey, 18 mi. north of Charlevoix, has information on the area's attractions. The Mackinaw **travel information center** (436-5566), off I-75, is loaded with brochures. Try to visit in fall, when the fiery foliage is reflected in clear, cold water.

Upper Peninsula

   A multimillion-acre forestland bordered by three of the world's largest lakes, Michigan's Upper Peninsula (U.P.) is one of the most scenic and unspoiled stretches of land in the Great Lakes region.
   Greyhound is the major carrier on the Peninsula. Lower Peninsula schedules connect at St. Ignace to Sault Ste. Marie and U.S. 2 across to Escanaba. In Escanaba and in Ironwood, routes from Wisconsin, Duluth, and Chicago link with service to Marquette and the Keweenaw Peninsula. If you are traveling by bus in the U.P., connections will require a wait of approximately one day and half of a night, since buses travel only at night. While this may help save on accommodations costs, it makes for a weary traveler. Try to get some sleep on the beautiful beaches; life is very tranquil in the U.P.

Eastern Upper Peninsula

   The low, eastern reaches of the U.P. contain vast quiet lakes and forests, deserted lakeshore dunes, and lonely, mosquito-infested marshes—sanctuary for hikers, cross-country skiers, anglers, canoeists, and compulsive scratchers. Contact the **Upper Peninsula Travel and Recreational Association,** P.O. Box 400, Iron Mountain 49801, for general information. The **U.S. Forestry Service,** Hiawatha National

Forest, 2727 N. Lincoln Rd., Escanaba 49829, has guides and maps to help you plan a trip into the wilderness. The towns of Manistique on the Lake Michigan shore and Grand Marais (see Superior North Shore above) on the Superior coast offer supplies, information, food, and accommodations. Contact the Grand Marais Chamber of Commerce, P.O. Box 118, Grand Marais 49839 (494-2766).

Les Cheneaux Islands, due south of the Soo Canal on Lake Huron, are a labyrinth of 35 forest-covered islets and pure, delicious water. Hill's Marina, in Hessel on MI Rte. 134 (484-2640), rents 14-ft. aluminum motor boats (7½ horsepower, $35 per day including a tank of gas). Hiawatha National Forest maintains Government Island as an uninhabited area. You can dock your boat and camp here.

U.S. 2 from the north end of the bridge in St. Ignace west to Naubinway follows some lovely, unspoiled, and practically deserted lakeshore. The white sand dunes of enormous Lake Michigan resemble ocean beaches. Numerous inexpensive motels line U.S. 2. Sleep in or near Manistique, where you can find a whole range of accommodations and outgoing locals. Most motels are priced from $32 to $36 in the summer. The Marina Guest House, 230 Arbutas (341-5147), is a clean, well-kept B&B. (Singles $30. Doubles and suites $45-50. Reservations recommended.) The Beachcomber Motel (341-2567) offers clean rooms. At night, guests are lulled to sleep by the waves of Lake Michigan and the semis on U.S. 2. (Singles $29. Doubles $36.) The big sandwiches ($3.50-4) at Sunny Shores Restaurant next door will brighten your day. (Open daily 6:30am-9pm.) For supplementary information, contact the Schoolcraft County Chamber of Commerce, on U.S. 2 just west of Manistique (341-5010; open Mon.-Fri. 8am-6pm, Sat.-Sun. 9am-4pm).

Excellent swimming opportunities splash around Manistique. An especially beautiful, sandy beach lies 2 mi. west of the city limits, just off Rte. 2. Handsome and clean Indian Lake State Park (341-2355) lies 5 mi. west. (300 sites; $9. Tents or tepees rent at $6 per night.) Camper's Market (341-5614) rents canoes. ($10 per day, $7 per half-day; $20 deposit required.) Downtown, you may unknowingly cross the Siphon Bridge, the nation's only "floating bridge," which may soon be landlocked. Twelve mi. west of Manistique, visit the amazing Big Spring, a 45-ft. deep, 45°F pond of crystal clear water and brown trout—early residents called it the "mirror of heaven."

Directly north of Manistique, the Pictured Rocks National Lakeshore (387-2607) stretches along the Superior coast. Here, the rain, wind, and ice of Lake Superior have carved the sandstone cliffs into multicolored arches and columns, with caves dotting the steep walls about the lake. The lakeshore offers beaches, primitive camping, and inland lakes for fishing and swimming. For a better perspective on the stone formations, Pictured Rocks Boat Cruises (494-2611) will take you along the shoreline, with frequent departures in summer and early fall. (Tickets $10, ages 6-12 $5, under 5 free.) A section of the scenic North Country Hiking Trail traverses the park, with free campsites en route. This trail crosses the entire U.P. and winds south through the Lower Peninsula into Ohio.

The area code for the U.P. is 906.

Isle Royale National Park

No cars are allowed in America's most unspoiled national park, a 45-by-9-mi. island in Lake Superior. Ponds, lakes, and forest wilderness cover the rock foundation of Isle Royale, creating a natural sanctuary where humans are only guests. More than 100 mi. of hiking trails lace the island, threading past beaches and lookout points, through thick hardwood forests and ancient Native American copper mining pits. The Greenstone Ridge Trail follows the backbone of the island from Rock Harbor Lodge. Ojibway Lookout, on Mt. Franklin, affords a good view of the Canadian shore 15 mi. away. Monument Rock, 70 ft. tall, challenges even experienced climbers. Lookout Louise, also on the trail, offers one of the most beautiful views in the park. For a superlative time, go to Ray's Island, the largest island in the largest lake on the largest island in the largest freshwater lake in the world.

The park is open for **camping** between mid-June and early September, but beware of fog and mosquitoes in June and early July. Nights are always cold (mid-40°F in June): Bring warm clothes. Plan also to bring your own tent rather than relying on shelters. There are 31 campsites along the shores and on inland lakes. Permits, free and available at any ranger station, are required for backcountry camping. There are three **ranger stations:** Windigo on the western tip of the island; Rock Harbor on the eastern tip of the island; and near Siskiwit Lake, on the south shore, midway between Windigo and Rock Harbor. Be sure to boil water for at least two minutes or use a 25-micron filter, as it is infested with a nasty tapeworm, and iodine tablets and charcoal purification are not sufficient. Campers can buy supplies and groceries at Rock Harbor and limited amounts at Windigo. Ferries run from **Houghton** (906-482-0984), on the Upper Peninsula, twice per week from mid-June to August ($37 one way); and from **Copper Harbor** (906-289-4437), also on the U.P., from mid-May through September, 2-7 days per week depending on the month ($30 one way). From **Grand Portage, MN** (715-392-2100), ferries run three days per week from mid-May to mid-June, daily from mid-June through August. (Windigo one way $25, Rock Harbor one way $30. Day cruise 9:30am-6pm $30. Reservations recommended.

Minnesota

Minnesota's nickname, "Land of 10,000 Lakes," expresses the state's modest character. Although the total number of lakes actually tallies closer to 15,000, Minnesotans prefer to round the figure down. Inclement weather and sparsely populated land have somehow inspired Minnesotans with an energetic, cooperative spirit. State residents are almost always ready to help a neighbor or a stranger, whether aid comes as a push out of a snowdrift or as social welfare policies championed by Minnesota's own Hubert Humphrey and Walter Mondale.

The Midwestern prairie meets the North Woods in this state. Neatly laid out family farms give way to wild tracts of lake-spangled forest toward the Canadian border. One of the most beautiful canoeing areas in the country, Minnesota's Boundary Waters weave through wilderness that has never felt the rubber tread of the dreaded Winnebago. This landscape felt like the old country to 19th-century immigrant farmers from Germany and Scandinavia, whose descendants still populate much of the state. Even in the cosmopolitan Twin Cities of Minneapolis and St. Paul, longtime residents pronounce "Minn-eh-soh-ta" with a Nordic sweetness, stretching their "oh"s out nice and long.

Practical Information

Capital: St. Paul.

Tourist Information: Minnesota Travel Information Center, 375 Jackson St., 250 Skyway Level, St. Paul 55101 (296-5029 or 800-657-3700). Open Mon.-Fri. 8am-5pm.

Time Zone: Central (1 hr. behind Eastern). **Postal Abbreviation:** MN.

Minneapolis and St. Paul

The Twin Cities are two of the most culturally exciting and aesthetically pleasing cities in the U.S., altering the stereotype of the city as a place to work and play but not to live. Inhabited not just by Scandinavian descendants, the Twin Cities are very cosmopolitan; people of many ethnic and cultural backgrounds lend diversity to the thriving arts community, local restaurants, and general atmosphere. An abundance of lakes, parks, and attractive houses plus good urban planning make the Twin Cities a beautiful place as well.

Yet despite their name, the Twin Cities are hardly twins. Minneapolis has an artsy image, with more museums, parks, and a stronger artistic community than St. Paul. The music scene in particular is unbeatable, spawning rugged bands like Hüsker Dü, the Replacements, and Babes in Toyland; here Prince and other members of his royal family crowned the "Minneapolis sound."

While Minneapolis grew from water power harnessed at the Mississippi, St. Paul grew from whiskey. Originally dubbed Pig's Eye, after one-eyed whiskey seller "Pig's Eye" Parrant, St. Paul still retains a grittier, less saintly style. St. Paul is no urban martyr, however. This state capital has Victorian homes, historic landmarks, and nationally recognized performing arts, even if overshadowed by its more charming twin.

Practical Information

Emergency: 911.

Visitor Information: Minneapolis Convention and Visitors Association, 1219 Marquette Ave. (348-4313 or 800-445-7412). Open Mon.-Fri. 8am-5pm. **St. Paul Convention and Visitors Bureau,** 600 NCL Tower, 445 Minnesota St. (297-6985 or 800-627-6101). Open Mon.-Fri. 8am-5pm. **Greater Minneapolis Chamber of Commerce,** 81 S. 9th St., Quinlan Bldg. #200 (370-9132). Open Mon.-Fri. 8am-5pm. **St. Paul Chamber of Commerce,** #600, North Central Life Tower, 445 Minnesota St. (222-5561). Open Mon.-Fri. 8am-5pm. **Cityline,** 645-6060. Information on local events, concerts, weather, news, sports, and much more.

Travelers Aid: 404 S. 8th St. (335-5000), Minneapolis. Open Mon.-Fri. 8:30am-4pm. Also at the airport (726-9435). Emergency shelter help. Open Mon.-Sat. 8am-8pm, Sun. noon-8pm.

Twin Cities International Airport: 7 mi. south of the cities, on I-494 in Bloomington. **Northwest Airlines** has its headquarters here. Limousines (726-6400) run to downtown and suburban hotels, leaving from the lower level near baggage claim (6am-midnight; fare $7.50). Take bus #35 to Minneapolis (fare 85¢; service available 6-8am and 3-4:45pm). Otherwise, take bus #7 to Washington Ave. in Minneapolis, or transfer at Fort Snelling for bus #9 to downtown St. Paul. Ask for a transfer. Taxis are about $18 to Minneapolis and $15 to St. Paul.

Amtrak: 730 Transfer Rd. (800-872-7245), on the east bank off University Ave. SE, between the Twin Cities. A nice station, but a fair distance from both downtowns. Trains to Chicago (8½ hr., $66).

Greyhound: In **Minneapolis,** 29 9th St. at 1st Ave. N. (371-3311), 1 block northwest of Hennepin Ave. Very convenient. 24-hr. security. To: Chicago ($55), New York ($129), and Seattle ($119). Open daily 5:45am-2:15am. In **St. Paul,** 7th St. at St. Peter (222-0509), 3 blocks east of the Civic Center, downtown. A little deserted, even in the daytime; don't hang around outside. Open daily 5:45am-8:10pm.

Public Transport: Metropolitan Transit Commission, 560 6th Ave. N. (827-7733). Call for information and directions Mon.-Fri. 6am-11pm, Sat.-Sun. 7am-11pm. Schedules and route maps available at: tourism information center, Coffman Student Union, 300 Washington Ave. SE, University of Minnesota; Comstock Hall Housing Office, 210 Delaware St. SE, University of Minnesota; and the MTC store, 719 Marquette, in downtown Minneapolis. Bus service for both cities. Some buses operate 4:30am-12:45am, others shut down earlier. Fare 75¢ peak, 50¢ off-peak, ages under 18 25¢ off-peak. **University of Minnesota Bus,** 625-9000. Buses run 7am-10pm. Free to campus locations and even into St. Paul, if you are a student. Off-campus routes 35-50¢, 75¢ peak.

Car Rental: Ugly Duckling Rent-A-Car, 6405 Cedar Ave. S. (861-7545), Minneapolis, near the airport. From $17 per day with 100 free mi., weekly from $100. Open Mon.-Fri. 9am-6pm, Sat. noon-3pm, or by appointment. Must technically be 25, but ages 21 and over usually allowed. Major credit card or a $200 deposit required.

Taxi: Yellow Taxi, 824-4444, in Minneapolis. **Yellow Cab,** 222-4433, in St. Paul. Base rate $1.25, $1.20 per mi.

Help Lines: Gay-Lesbian Helpline, 822-8661. **Rape Crisis Line,** 2431 Hennepin Ave. (825-4357). Open 24 hr.

Post Office: In **Minneapolis,** 1st St. and Marquette Ave. (349-4935), next to the Mississippi River. General Delivery open Mon.-Fri. 8:30am-5pm, Sat. 9am-noon. **ZIP code:** 55401. In **St. Paul,** 180 E. Kellogg Blvd. (293-3021). Open same hours. **ZIP code:** 55101.

Area Code: 612.

Minneapolis and St. Paul lie 405 mi. northwest of Chicago on I-94 and 252 mi. north of Des Moines, IA, on I-35. The two cities are on either side of the curving **Mississippi River;** Minneapolis is 8 mi. northwest of St. Paul on I-94. Minneapolis's layout is straightforward—streets run east-west and avenues run north-south. **Hennepin Avenue** crosses the Mississippi and goes through downtown, curving south toward uptown. Outside of downtown, most avenues are in alphabetical order as you travel west. St. Paul's streets are more confusing to navigate. **Grand Avenue** (east-west) and **Snelling Avenue** (north-south) are major thoroughfares. **University Avenue** connects the Twin Cities.

Accommodations and Camping

A good budget lodging is hard to find in the Twin Cities. While cheap airport hotels abound, their cleanliness and safety are often inadequate. The convention and visitors bureaus have useful lists of **bed and breakfasts.** The **University of Minnesota Housing Office** (624-2994), in Comstock Hall, has a list of rooms in different locations around the city that rent on a daily ($5-15) or weekly basis. The **Oakmere Home Hostel (AYH),** 8212 Oakmere Rd. (944-1210), in Bloomington, has singles for $10. The nice, wood-paneled rooms overlook a lake, but the hostel's fairly remote suburban location makes it virtually unreachable without a car.

College of St. Catherine, Caecilian Hall, 2004 Randolph Ave. (690-6604), St. Paul. Take St. Paul bus #7 or 14, or call for directions. 103 stark but quiet dorm rooms near the river in a nice neighborhood. Shared bath, kitchenette. Singles $12. Doubles $20. Open June to mid-Aug.

Kaz's Home Hostel (AYH), 5100 Dupont Ave. S. (822-8286), in South Minneapolis. Take bus #4 to Bryant and 50th, then walk 2 blocks west on 50th to Dupont. Only 6 blocks from Lake Harriet. Four beds in spacious rooms. Check-in 5-9pm. Curfew 11pm. Members only, $8. Reservations required.

Evelo's Bed and Breakfast, 2301 Bryant Ave. (374-9656), in South Minneapolis. A 15-min. walk from uptown or take bus #17 from downtown. Three comfortable rooms with elegant wallpapering and furnishings in a beautiful house filled with Victorian artifacts. Friendly owners. Singles $45. Doubles $55. Reservations required.

Town and Country Campground, 12630 Boone Ave. S. (445-1756), 15 mi. south of downtown Minneapolis. From I-35W, go west on Rte. 13 to Rte. 101 for ½ mi., then left onto Boone Ave. 60 sites—the closest to the Twin Cities. Plenty of shade and family-run, but you can hear the freeway. Sites $10 for 2, with electricity $13, full hookup $15. Each additional person $1.

Minneapolis Northwest I-94 KOA, (420-2255), on Rte. 101 west of I-94 exit 213, 15 mi. north of Minneapolis. Noisy kids and all the klassic KOA amenities: pool, sauna, and showers. Sites $13-17.50. Each additional person $2.

Food

The Twin Cities specialize in casual dining; a gourmet sandwich or salad and a steaming cup of coffee is the favored fare. During the past decade demographics and tastes have changed: many of the Scandinavian smorgasbords have given way to Vietnamese and natural food restaurants. The **uptown** Prince once sang about ("it's where I wanna be") is now popular with a young, artsy crowd, while the **Warehouse District** in Minneapolis and St. Paul's **Victoria Crossing** tend to draw more yuppies. Near the University of Minnesota, **Dinkytown** and the **West Bank** cater to student needs. For cheaper food and ethnic specialties, try **Northeast Minneapolis** or explore St. Paul.

Minneapolis

The New Riverside Cafe, 329 Cedar Ave. (333-4814), West Bank. Take bus #73. The self-proclaimed "Biomagnetic Center of the Universe." Full vegetarian meals served cafeteria-style amidst unframed works by local artists. Nightly live jazz and bluegrass. Sandwiches and Mexican dishes $2-4. Open Mon.-Thurs. 7am-11pm, Fri. 7am-midnight, Sat. 8am-midnight, Sun. 9am-1:30pm. Performances Tues.-Thurs. at 7pm, Fri.-Sat. at 9pm. No cover.

It's Greek to Me, 626 Lake St. at Lyndale Ave. Take bus #4 south. Great Greek food, complemented by traditional costumes hanging on the walls. Gyros $3.50. Dinners $6-10. Open daily 11am-11pm.

Matin, 416 1st Ave. N. downtown. Elegant Vietnamese food with French flair. All-you-can-eat lunch buffet $5.75, entrees $3.25-5.75. Try the *xao cu nang* (tofu or mushrooms sautéed in garlic sauce with rice; $4.75). Open Mon.-Fri. 11am-2:30pm, Mon.-Thurs. 5-10pm, Fri.-Sat. 5-11pm.

The Malt Shop, 50th St. at Bryant Ave. in South Minneapolis (take bus #4), or Snelling at I-94, St. Paul (take bus #1 or 94). An old-time soda fountain; try a phenomenal fresh fruit malt or shake ($2.60). Minneapolis shop open Mon.-Thurs. 11am-10:30pm, Fri. 11am-11pm, Sat. 8:30am-11pm, Sun. 8:30am-10:30pm. St. Paul shop open Sun.-Thurs. 7:30am-10:30pm, Fri.-Sat. 7:30am-11pm.

Two Pesos, 1320 W. Lake St. uptown. Take bus #21 or 94L from St. Paul. The fast-food aura is quickly forgotten on the outdoor patio, cool even in the most sweltering weather. Two soft tacos $3.50. Bottled Mexican beer $2, margaritas $1.50. Open Mon.-Sat. 10:30am-2am, Sun. 10:30am-midnight.

Annie's Parlor, 313 14th Ave. SE, in Dinkytown, and 406 Cedar Ave., West Bank. Malts that are a meal in themselves ($3) and great hamburgers ($3-4.25). Open Mon.-Thurs. 11am-11pm, Fri.-Sat. 11am-midnight, Sun. noon-11pm.

Vescio's, 406 14th Ave. SE, in Dinkytown. Take bus #6 to 4th St. Solid mom-and-pop Italian fare with friendly service. Pasta $5.50-8. Open Tues.-Thurs. 11am-11pm, Fri.-Sat. 11am-12:30am, Sun. 3-10pm.

St. Paul

Café Latté, 850 Grand Ave., across the street from Victoria Crossing. Cafeteria-style, but elegant, with bi-level seating and neon accents to match its accented name. Delicious soups, salads ($3-4.25), pastries, and espresso. Steamed milk drinks called Hot Moos $1.50; try the Swedish Hot Moo with cinnamon, cardamon, and maple syrup. Lines usually long. Open Mon.-Thurs. 10am-11pm, Fri. 10am-midnight, Sat. 9am-midnight, Sun. 9am-10pm.

Willow Gate, 767 Cleveland Ave. S., ½ mi. south of the College of St. Catherine. Take bus #7. This Chinese restaurant offers enormous and delicious dinners ($4-7), as well as (can you believe it?) complimentary tea. Subgum fried rice (with chicken, pork, and shrimp) $4.75. Open Mon.-Thurs. 11:30am-9pm, Fri.-Sat. 11:30am-10:30pm, Sun. 4-9:30pm.

Sawatdee, 289 E. 5th St., downtown next to the Farmers Market. Take bus #50. Delicious Thai food enhanced by great ambience—antique street lamps light the tables. Stir-fried shrimp with peppers $8, other entrees $6-18. Open Sun.-Thurs. 11am-10pm, Fri.-Sat. 11am-11pm.

Mickey's Dining Car, 36 W. 7th St., across from the Greyhound station. Small, cheap, and convenient; a great spot for wee-hour munchies runs. Steak and eggs from $4, lunch and dinner from $3. Open 24 hr.

St. Paul Farmers Market, 5th St. at Wall Market (227-6856), downtown. Fresh produce and baked goods. Get there before 10am on Sat. for the best quality and widest selection. Call to verify location and hours. Open Sat. 6am-1pm, Sun. 8am-1pm May-Oct.

Sights

Minneapolis

One look at the beautiful lakes right in the middle of the city explains Minneapolitans' civic pride. **Lake of Isles,** off Franklin Ave., about 1½ mi. from downtown, is ringed by stately mansions. It's hard to believe you're in the middle of the city when you walk through throngs of Canadian geese and breathe the countrified air. Bikers, skaters, and joggers constantly round **Lake Calhoun,** on the west end of Lake St. south of Lake of Isles, making it a hectic social and recreational hotspot. Rent skates and Kaplanesque roller blades at **Rolling Soles,** 1700 W. Lake St. (823-5711; skates $3 per hr., $7.50 per day; blades $5 per hr., $10 per day; open daily

10am-9pm). The **Minneapolis Park and Recreation Board** (348-5406) rents canoes ($4.50 per hr.) at the northeast corner of Lake Calhoun. Situated in a more residential neighborhood, **Lake Harriet** has a tiny paddleboat, a stage with occasional free concerts, and an endless stream of joggers. The city provides 28 mi. of trails along these lakes for cycling, roller skating, roller blading, jogging, or strolling on a sunny afternoon. The circumference of each lake is about 3 mi. and paths are well maintained; take bus #28 to all three (lakes, that is).

One of the top modern art museums in the country, the **Walker Art Center**, 725 Vineland Place (375-7600), a few blocks from downtown, draws thousands with daring exhibits and an impressive permanent collection, including works by Lichtenstein and Warhol. And don't miss the beautiful bronze sculpture by Isamu Noguchi titled *Avatar*. Inside is an excellent, not-too-expensive café (sandwiches $1.50-2.50; open Tues.-Sun. 11:30am-3pm), while adjacent is the Guthrie Theater (see Entertainment). (Art center open Tues.-Sat. 10am-8pm, Sun. 11am-5pm. Admission $3, seniors free, ages 12-18 $2.) Next to the Walker, the **Minneapolis Sculpture Garden** displays dozens of sculptures and a fountain in a "room" of exquisitely landscaped trees and flowers. The **Minneapolis Institute of Arts**, 2400 3rd Ave. S. (870-3131), contains Egyptian, Chinese, American, and European art. (Open Tues.-Sat. 10am-5pm, Thurs. 10am-9pm, Sun. noon-5pm. Free. Admission to special exhibits $2, students and ages 12-18 $1, seniors and under 12 free; free to all Thurs. 5-9pm. Take bus #9.)

St. Anthony Falls and Upper Locks, downtown at 1 Portland Ave. (333-5336), has a free observation deck that overlooks the Mississippi River. (Open April-Nov. daily 8am-10pm.) Several miles downstream, Minnehaha Park provides a breathtaking view of **Minnehaha Falls,** immortalized in Longfellow's longwinded *Song of Hiawatha*. (Take bus #7 from Hennepin Ave. downtown.)

St. Paul

The capital city remains fairly sedate and, frankly, sterile on weekends. Battle school field trips to see the golden horses atop the ornate **state capitol,** Cedar and Aurora St. (296-3962 or 296-2881; open Mon.-Fri. 9am-5pm, Sat. 10am-4pm, Sun. 1-4pm). The nearby **Minnesota Historical Society** (296-6126) is closed until the fall of 1992, when it will reopen in a new building between Kellogg Blvd. and Ireland Blvd. The museum has displays about St. Paul's early Scandinavian settlers and Native Americans, along with a wealth of information in its extensive libraries. The appropriately named **Landmark Center,** 75 W. 5th St. (292-3272), a grandly restored 1894 federal court building with towers and turrets, houses a collection of pianos, art exhibits, a concert hall, and four restored courtrooms. (Open Mon.-Wed. and Fri. 8am-5pm, Thurs. 8am-8pm, Sat. 10am-5pm, Sun. 1-5pm. Free. Tours given Thurs. at 11am and Sun. at 2pm.) **St. Paul's Cathedral,** 239 Selby Ave. (228-1766), is a scaled-down but beautiful version of St. Peter's in Rome. (Open daily 6am-6pm.)

Summit Avenue, west of downtown, displays the nation's longest stretch of Victorian homes, including the Governor's Mansion and the former homes of F. Scott Fitzgerald and railroad magnate James J. Hill. Railroad fortunes in the 19th century built most of these houses, known as the "Grand Old Ladies of Summit Avenue."

St. Paulites are justifiably proud of their space-age **Science Museum,** 30 E. 10th St. (221-9400 or 221-9451), near the intersection of Exchange and Wabasha St. A giant iguana sculpture stands guard outside, while inside the **McKnight-3M Omnitheater** presents a dizzying array of films. (Open Tues.-Sat. 9:30am-9pm, Sun. 11am-9pm. Tickets for exhibits $3.50, for theater $4.50, combination $5.50. Seniors and under 12 receive $1 discounts.)

When you tire of touring, go inside and have a brew at **Stroh Brewing Company,** 707 E. Minnehaha (778-3275), with free tours and samples. (Open Mon.-Fri. 1-4pm.)

Entertainment and Events

With more theaters per capita than any U.S. city outside of New York, the Twin Cities' vibrant drama scene has something for everyone. The shining star of the thriving theater community is the **Guthrie Theater,** 725 Vineland Place (377-2224), just off Hennepin Ave. in Minneapolis, adjacent to the Walker Art Center. The Guthrie repertory company performs here from June to March. (Box office open Mon.-Sat. 9am-8pm, Sun. 11am-7pm. Tickets $6-34, rush tickets 10 min. before the show $6.) **Loring Park,** near the Walker Art Center, is the focal point of Minneapolis's large and politically powerful gay community. On Monday evenings in the summer, the park hosts free local bands, followed by vintage films, on the hill toward the north edge. (Take bus #1, 4, 6, or 28 going south.)

The **Children's Theater Company,** 3rd Ave. at 24th S. (874-0400), adjacent to the Minneapolis Institute of Art, puts on classics and innovative productions for all ages from September to June. (Box office open Mon.-Sat. 9am-5pm, Sun. noon-4pm except during summer. Tickets $11-18, seniors, students, and children $8-14. Student rush tickets 15 min. before performance $6.)

In the summer from early July to early August, **Orchestra Hall,** 1111 Nicollet Mall (371-5600 or 371-5656), downtown Minneapolis, hosts the not-so surprisingly titled **Summerfest,** a month-long celebration of Viennese music performed by the **Minnesota Orchestra.** (Box office open Mon.-Sat. 10am-6pm. Tickets $6-40. Student rush tickets 15 min. before show $4.) Don't miss the free coffee concerts and nighttime dance lessons at nearby **Peavey Plaza,** in Nicollet Mall between 11th and 12th St., surrounding a spectacular fountain (no wading allowed).

St. Paul's glass-and-brick, accordion-fronted **Ordway Music Theater,** 345 Washington St. (224-4222), is one of the most beautiful public spaces for music in the country. The **St. Paul Chamber Orchestra,** the **Schubert Club,** and the **Minnesota Opera Company** perform here. (Box office open Mon.-Sat. 10am-5:30pm. Tickets $12-36.)

A passel of comedy and improvisational clubs make the Twin Cities a downright hilarious place to visit. Dudley Riggs' **Brave New Workshop,** 2605 Hennepin Ave. (332-6620), has consistently good musical comedy shows in an intimate club. (Box office open Tues.-Sat. 4-10pm. Performances Tues.-Sat. at 8pm. Tickets $10 weekdays, $12 weekends.) **Stevie Ray's,** W. 28th at Hennepin Ave. (872-0305), in South Minneapolis, features local stand-up comics, usually good ones. (Shows Wed.-Sun. at 8pm, additional show Fri.-Sat. at 10:30pm. Wed.-Thurs. $7, Fri.-Sat. $9, Sun. $4.50. Fri. improv soap operas $3.) For swinging singles fun, go to **St. Anthony's Wharf** (378-7058), in St. Anthony Main, a restored mattress warehouse next to Riverplace. (Glass of Budweiser $1.75. Open Mon.-Fri. 11:30am-10pm, Sat.-Sun. 11:30am-11:30pm.) The **400 Bar,** 4th St. at Cedar Ave. (332-2903), on the West Bank, is a great place to escape the mattress madness and just have a good time. This friendly, neighborhood bar features live music nightly on a miniscule stage. (Open daily noon-1am. Occasional $2 cover.) A sizzling downtown club (and Prince's old haunt) is **First Avenue and 7th St. Entry,** (338-8388), with reggae, rock 'n' roll, funk, house, thrash, and heavy metal. But no chamber music. Live bands play every night. Band members occasionally toss combs to patrons waiting on line. (Open Mon.-Sat. 8pm-1am, Sun. teen night 7pm-midnight. Cover $1-5, for concerts $6-12.)

There are several gay and lesbian bars in the Twin Cities, including **The Gay '90s,** Hennepin Ave. at 4th St. (333-7755; open daily 8am-1am.) Look for *Equal Time, Gaze,* or *GLC Voice,* free on newspaper stands, for more information on gay and lesbian activities, or call the gay and lesbian information line at 822-0127.

For general information on the local music scene and other events, pick up the free *City Pages* or *Twin Cities Reader,* available throughout the Cities. Free outdoor blues, jazz, and rock concerts are held along the riverfront near St. Anthony Falls. (Call 724-8437 for information.)

Some of Minneapolis's most popular forms of entertainment take place outdoors. In January, the 10-day **St. Paul Winter Carnival,** near the state capitol, cures cabin fever with ice sculptures, ice fishing, parades, and skating contests. Both cities get into the swing of things in July. St. Paul celebrates **Taste of Minnesota,** on the Capitol Mall during the Fourth, then **Riverfest** for a week in late July, with big name bands, food stands, and rides in Harriet Island Park. Also in July, the 9-day **Minneapolis Aquatennial** begins, with concerts, parades, art exhibits, and kids dripping sno-cones on their strollers. (Call 922-9000 for information on all these events.) During late August and early September, spend a day at the **Minnesota State Fair,** at Snelling and Como, one of the largest in the nation. If the human zoo has become too much, talk to the animals at the **Minnesota Zoo,** on Hwy. 32 (432-9000). Walk around, or ride the all-weather monorail. (Open Mon.-Sat. 10am-6pm, Sun. 10am-8pm; off-season daily 10am-4pm. Admission $4, seniors $2, ages 6-16 $1.50. Parking $1.)

The "Homerdome," also know as the **Hubert H. Humphrey Metrodome,** 501 Chicago Ave. S. (375-1366), in downtown Minneapolis, houses most of the Twin Cities' professional sports teams.

Northern Minnesota

Chippewa National Forest Area

The Norway pine forests, interspersed with lovely strands of birch, thicken as you move north into **Chippewa National Forest** (335-2226), source of the mighty Mississippi River. Camping and canoeing are popular activities thanks to hundreds of lakes in the area. Leech, Cass, and Winnibigoshish (win-nuh-buh-GAH-shish or simply "Winnie") are the largest, but also the most crowded with speedboats. The national forest shares territory with the **Leech Lake Indian Reservation,** home of 4560 members of the Minnesota Chippewa tribe, the fourth largest tribe in the U.S. The Chippewa moved into this area in the early 1700s from the Atlantic Ocean, through the Great Lakes, successfully pushing out the Sioux. In the mid-1800s, the government seized most of the Chippewa's land, setting up reservations like Leech Lake.

Use the town of Walker on Leech Lake as a gateway to the Chippewa National Forest. Travelers can find information on the tourist facilities at the **Leech Lake Area Chamber of Commerce** on Rte. 371 downtown (547-1313 or 800-833-1118; open daily 8am-5:30pm). Information on abundant, cheap outdoor activities is available just east of the chamber of commerce at the **forest office** (547-1044; open Mon.-Fri. 7:30am-5pm). **Greyhound** runs from Minneapolis to Walker (2 per day, 4 hr., $21), stopping at the Lake View Laundromat, Minnesota at Michigan Ave., just east of the chamber of commerce.

The less-than-mighty **Headwaters of the Mississippi** trickle out of **Lake Itasca,** 30 mi. west of Walker on Rte. 200, the only place where mere mortals can easily wade across the Mississippi. Campsites in the park are usually not crowded. (Sites $8, with electricity $10. 2-day vehicle permit $3.25.) The **Itasca State Park Office** (266-3654) through the north entrance, down County Rd. 38, has more information. (Open daily 8am-10pm.) You can also get there via Bemidji , which has a **Greyhound** stop (Duluth-Bemidji $16).

The **area code** is 218.

The Superior North Shore

The North Shore begins with the majestic Sawtooth Mountains just north of Duluth and extends 150 wild and wooded mi. to Canada. This stretch, defined by **Highway 61 (North Shore Drive),** encompasses virtually all of Minnesota's Superior lakeshore and supports multitudes of bears, moose, and the only remaining wolf population in the contiguous 48 states. In summer multitudes of humans flock to the towns dotting the coastline to fish, camp, hike, and canoe, attracted by the cool and breezy weather.

During the warmer months, many outdoor enthusiasts drive or bike their way up the coast along Hwy. 61, beginning in Duluth. Bring warm clothes, since even in summer temperatures can drop into the low 40s at night. And bring your money bags unless you plan to camp: over 200 years ago, locals trapped beaver, but now they prey on tourists.

A recently completed hiking trail runs from Duluth to Canada, along the Superior coast. For tenderfoot daytrippers, the trail provides easy access to accommodations, transportation, and food along the way. For more information write to the **Superior Trail Hiking Association,** P.O. Box 2175, Tofte 55615 (226-3539). Caramel-colored water splashes over the jagged rocks at **Gooseberry Falls,** a popular swimming hole 40 mi. up the coast from Duluth. Sleep within earshot of the falls at the **Gooseberry Falls Campground** (834-3787; sites $12, including state park sticker; make reservations for July and Aug.). Just north of the falls, **Split Rock Lighthouse** looks out over one of the most treacherous stretches of water around. The rocks below, endowed with strange magnetic qualities, made compasses useless and lured unwary sailors into their Scylla-and-Charybdis arms. The **History Center** (226-4372), next to the lighthouse atop a 120-ft. cliff, offers exhibits on famous shipwrecks and a film on the old days of Split Rock, though no cyclops or Greek gods. (Lighthouse and history center open daily May 15-Oct. 15 9am-5pm; off-season Fri.-Sun. noon-4pm. Admission consists of a $3.25 state park sticker.) Camp next door at **Split Rock Lighthouse State Park** (226-3065; sites $11.75, including state park sticker). Make reservations two weeks in advance.

Grand Marais makes a good base for excursions into nearby portions of the **Boundary Waters Canoe Area Wilderness.** This unique area covers over two million acres of forests, containing 1100 lakes. There are no roads, phones, electricity, or private dwellings here, and no motorized vehicles are allowed. Permits are required to enter the BWCAW from May to September. The 60-mi. **Gunflint Trail,** now widened into an auto road, begins in Grand Marais and continues northwest into the BWCAW. Reward yourself at the end of the trail with a stay in the well-kept cabins at **"Spirit of the Land" Island AYH Hostel** (388-2241), in Seagull Lake. ($10. $2 boat transport. Meals $3-5. Closed Nov.-Dec. and April.) The **Tip of the Arrowhead Tourist Information Center,** Broadway and 1st Ave. (387-2524), has a wealth of information about the area. The National Forest Ranger station at the base of the trail, ¼ mi. south of town, offers even more information, and issues BWCAW permits for individual ports of entry into the wilderness. (Open summer daily 6am-6pm.) **Wilderness Waters Outfitters** (387-2525), just south of Grand Marais on Rte. 61, rents canoes. ($13 per day, $12 per day for more than 3 day trips; $10 deposit required. Paddles, life jackets, and a car rack are included. Open May-Oct. daily 7am-7pm.)

Motels charge at least $25 for a single, but campground space is easy to find. The **Grand Marais Recreation Area** (387-1712), off Rte. 61 in town, offers a great view of Lake Superior. Pitch your tent by the small inlet and eat breakfast with the ducks. (Office open daily 6am-10pm. Sites $10, with water and electricity $12.50, with full hookup $14. Open May to mid-Oct.)

Grand Marais's **area code** is 218.

Duluth

Still the largest inland port on the Great Lakes, the once-booming railroad hub of Duluth relies on the thousands of tourists who come to see the city's historic mansions, beautiful parks, and spectacular views of Lake Superior. Minnesota's "refrigerated city," known for its abnormally cold weather, also offers a great place to gear up for a fishing, camping, or driving excursion into northwestern Minnesota.

The best thing about Duluth is its proximity to majestic Lake Superior. Take a tour of the harbor on **Duluth Superior Excursions,** 5th Ave. W. at Waterfront (722-6218), behind the Duluth Arena and Auditorium. (Boats depart mid-May to early June and early Sept. to mid-Oct. 10:30am-4:30pm every 2 hr.; early June-early Sept.

9:30am-7:30pm every 2 hr. Admission $7, ages 3-11 $3.25.) Reach new summer heights by climbing to the top of empty **Enger Tower,** 18th Ave. W. on Skyline Parkway. You can see all of Duluth-Superior Harbor, and up to 30 mi. farther on a clear day. **Hawk Ridge,** 4 mi. north of downtown off Skyline Blvd., creates a bird-watcher's paradise. A tremendous number and variety of hawks cruise by between late August and early November on their way south.

For indoor entertainment, visit **The Depot,** 506 W. Michigan St. (727-8025), in the old Amtrak station, where the **Lake Superior Museum of Transportation** captures Duluth's railroad and logging heritage. (Open daily 10am-5pm; Sept. 2-May 27 Mon.-Sat. 10am-5pm, Sun. 1-5pm. Admission $4, seniors $3, families $11, ages 6-17 $2.) Also known as the **St. Louis County Heritage and Arts Center,** the Depot houses the **Duluth Playhouse** (722-0349; box office open Mon.-Fri. 9am-4pm, until 8pm on nights of performances; tickets $5-6, seniors and students $4-5), the **Duluth Ballet** (722-2314), and the **Duluth-Superior Symphony Orchestra** (722-7429). Mansion-lovers should head to **Glensheen,** 3300 London Rd. (724-8863). This 39-room neo-Jacobean spectacle has beautiful Edwardian furnishings and landscaped grounds that overlook the lakes. (Open Feb.-Dec. Thurs.-Tues. 9am-4pm; Jan. Sat.-Sun. 1-3pm; more tours in summer and on weekends. Admission $5.50, seniors and ages 13-17 $4.25, under 12 $2.50; less in winter. Make reservations in summer.)

After a day of sight-seeing, head to one of the city parks. Free outdoor concerts are held at **Chester Bowl** and **Lake Superior Zoological Gardens** (624-1502) in Fairmont Park in West Duluth. **Bayfront Park** hosts the **International Folk Festival** (727-8025 or 722-7425) on the first Saturday in August. Call the Park and Recreation Department (723-3337) for more information.

Two downtown shopping centers—the restored **Fitger's** brewery, 600 E. Superior St. (722-5624), and the more modern **Holiday Center**—have a number of pleasant restaurants ranging from fast-food joints to elegant dining spots. **Grandma's Saloon and Deli,** 522 Lake Ave. S., packs people into a room that combines old-time atmosphere and lots of old advertising signs. Those under 21 can't enter unless accompanied by an adult. (Sandwiches $4.25-6.50, spaghetti $7. Open daily 11am-midnight.) Despite the name, **Sir Benedict's Tavern on the Lake,** 805 E. Superior St. (728-1192), is much more laid-back. Pick up a made-to-order sandwich ($3.40-4.20) and choose from the many imported beers ($2.30). Outside tables overlook the lake. (Live bluegrass Wed., Celtic music every 3rd Thurs. Open Mon.-Tues. and Thurs. 11am-11pm, Wed. 11am-midnight, Fri.-Sat. 11am-12:30am.) Afterwards, head to the **Portland Malte Shoppe,** 714 E. Superior, for a huge, delicious malt ($2.80; open daily 11am-11pm).

The **AYH youth hostel** at the **YWCA,** 202 W. 2nd St. (722-7425), is an exception to Duluth's inflated bedroom price rule. The dorms are small but carpeted, with a TV room, a kitchen, laundry facilities, and a weight room. ($9, nonmembers $22 per night or $55 per week.) The **College of St. Scholastica,** 1200 Kenwood Ave. (723-6483), often has spacious, pleasant rooms in summer at its secluded campus. (Doubles with shared bath $32. Make reservations.) **Jay Cooke State Park** (384-4610), southwest of Duluth on I-35, has 84 campsites. (Open daily 8am-10pm. Sites $8.50. Vehicle permit $3.25.) **Spirit Mountain,** 9500 Spirit Mountain Pl. (628-2891), near the ski resort of the same name, is 10 mi. south on I-35, on the top of the hill. (Sites with electricity $13, with electricity and water $15.)

Greyhound, 2212 W. Superior (722-5591), 2 mi. west of downtown, serves Michigan's Upper Peninsula, Hancock, and Calumet ($66). The **Duluth Transit Authority (DTA)** serves the downtown and outlying areas. Consult maps in bus shelters or call 722-7283. (Fare 75¢, seniors 35¢.)

The **Convention and Visitors Bureau,** at Endion Station, 100 Lake Place Dr. (722-4011; open Mon.-Fri. 9am-4:45pm), and the summer **visitors center** on the waterfront at Harbor Dr. (722-5501; open daily 9am-7:30pm), have an ample supply of brochures and Duluth maps. Duluth rocks 154 mi. northeast of the Twin Cities on I-35.

The Duluth **post office** is at 2800 W. Michigan (723-2590), near the bus station. (Open Mon.-Fri. 8am-5pm, Sat. 9am-noon.) Duluth's **ZIP code** is 55806; its **area code** is 218.

Ohio

This state just doesn't quit. Undaunted by the rustbelt depression of the late 1970s, the Ohio Seven—a constellation of cities representing nearly four-fifths of the nation's leading industries—pushes ahead with plans for the future. At opposite ends of the state, Cleveland and Cincinnati have revamped their downtowns, cleaned up pollution, and fostered a resurgence in the arts, all the while retaining their own distinct flavor. In the center of the state, Columbus gained recognition by a 1989 *Newsweek* article as one of the best places to live in the country. And for two centuries, farmers in central and northeastern Ohio have raised crops and tended dairylands.

On the eastern edge of the Midwest, Ohio lays claim to several major waterways and some of the nation's most fertile pastures. The geography that fosters industry and agriculture also features numerous outdoor attractions. With vacation spots like the Lake Erie Shore and the lush southern forests, it's no surprise that the state's name comes from an Iroquois word meaning "beautiful."

Practical Information

Capital: Columbus.

Tourist Information: State Office of Travel and Tourism, 77 S. High St., P.O. Box 1001, Columbus 43215 (614-466-8844). **Greater Columbus Convention and Visitors Bureau,** 1 Columbus Bldg., 10 W. Broad St. #1300, Columbus 43215 (614-221-6623 or 800-821-5784). Open Mon.-Fri. 8am-5pm.

Time Zone: Eastern. **Postal Abbreviation:** OH.

Cleveland

Despite the success of Gilded Age magnates like Rockefeller and Hanna, Cleveland has always been a tough, industrial city, witnessed by the abandoned railroad bridges, steel factories, and warehouses lining the Cuyahoga River. In the 1970s Cleveland became the first major city to default on its loans since the Great Depression and turned into a national joke after the filthy Cuyahoga River caught fire downtown. Now Cleveland is experiencing a major rebirth. Planners have spent billions on downtown construction, waterfront development, and historic renovation; the city's thriving arts community and I. M. Pei's much-anticipated Rock and Roll Hall of Fame have also put it in a different national spotlight. Cleveland is certainly no longer the "Mistake on the Lake."

Practical Information

Emergency: 911.

Visitor Information: Cleveland Convention and Visitors Bureau, 3100 Tower City Ctr. (621-7981 or 800-321-1001), in Terminal Tower at Public Square. Free maps and helpful staff. **Cleveland Fun Phone,** 621-8860, a 24-hr. entertainment hotline. **Language Bank** and **Nationalities Service Center,** 781-4560, are open 24 hr.

Cleveland Hopkins International Airport: (265-6030) in Brookpark, 10 mi. west of downtown, but accessible on the RTA airport rapid line, which goes to the Terminal Tower on train #66X ("Red Line") for $1.

Amtrak: 200 Cleveland Memorial Shoreway NE (696-5115 or 800-872-7245), east of City Hall. Open Mon.-Sat. 4am-1pm, 2-5:30pm, and midnight-3am; Sun. 4-8:45am and midnight-3am. To New York ($90) and Chicago ($70).

Greyhound: 1465 Chester Ave. (781-0520; schedules and fares 781-1400), at E. 14th St. near RTA bus lines and about 7 blocks east of Terminal Tower. Frequent and convenient service to Chicago and New York City; good coverage of Ohio. To Pittsburgh ($19), Cincinnati ($36), and Indianapolis ($48).

Regional Transit Authority (RTA): 2019 Ontario Ave. (566-5074), across the street from Terminal Tower. Schedules for city buses and rapid transit lines. Open Mon.-Fri. 7:30am-5:30pm. Information by phone Mon.-Sat. 6am-6pm (621-9500). Service daily 4:30am-12:30am. Bus lines, connecting with the Rapid stops, provide public transport to most of the metropolitan area. Fare $1 (free transfers to buses), buses 85¢.

Taxi: Yellow Cab, 623-1500. 24 hr.

Time/Weather Line: 931-1212. 24 hr.

Help Line: Rape Crisis Line, 391-3912. 24 hr.

Post Office: 2400 Orange St. (443-4199 or 443-4096). Open Mon.-Fri. 8am-7pm. **ZIP code:** 44101.

Area Code: 216

Cleveland spreads out south of Lake Erie and extends to crowded suburbs, including Cleveland Heights and Shaker Heights to the east, Garfield Heights to the southeast, and Parma to the southwest. **Terminal Tower** in **Public Square** divides the city into east and west. To reach Public Square from I-90 or I-71, follow the Ontario Ave./Broadway exit. From I-77, take the 9th St. exit to Euclid Ave., which runs into the Square. From the Amtrak station, follow Lakeside Ave. and turn onto Ontario, which leads to the tower. Almost all of the RTA trains and buses run downtown.

Accommodations and Camping

Cheap lodgings are simply not available in downtown Cleveland. Travelers are better off staying in the suburbs. Hotel taxes are a hefty 10%, not included in the prices listed below.

If you know your plans well in advance, try calling **Cleveland Private Lodgings** (321-3213), which places people in homes around the city for as low as $25. All arrangements are made through the office. Leave enough time for a letter of confirmation. (Open Mon.-Tues. and Thurs.-Fri. 9am-noon and 3-5pm.)

Stanford House Hostel (AYH), 6093 Stanford Rd. (467-8711), 22 mi. south of Cleveland in Peninsula. Exit 12 off I-80. Take bus #77F to Snowville Rd. Beautifully restored Greek Revival farmhouse is on National Register of Historic Places. Excellent facilities, friendly houseparent. All hostelers required to perform a task (vacuuming, emptying the trash, etc.). Check-in 5-9pm. Flexible curfew 11pm. $8, sleep sack $2. Reservations only.

Lakewood Manor Motel, 12019 Lake Ave. (226-4800), about 3 mi. west of downtown in Lakewood. Take bus #55CX . Neat, severe. TV, central A/C. Complimentary coffee daily and doughnuts on weekends. Singles $32. Doubles $40.

Gateway Motel, 29865 Euclid Ave. (943-6777), 10 mi. east of Public Sq. in Wickliffe. Take Euclid Ave. exit off I-90 or bus #28X. Spacious, clean rooms with A/C and color TV. Singles $25. Doubles $30.

Red Roof Inn, 29595 Clemens Rd. (892-7920), at I-90 and Crocker Rd., exit 156. Eleven mi. west of downtown in Westlake. Better than average for this chain. Spacious rooms with nice wallpaper. Singles $36. Doubles $47.

Forty minutes east of downtown, off I-480 in Streetsboro, are two campgrounds: **Woodside Lake Park,** 2256 Frost Rd. (626-4251; tent sites for 2 $15, with electricity $16; each additional guest $2, ages 3-17 75¢); and **Valley View Lake Resort,** 8326 Ferguson (626-2041; tent sites $17, water and hookup available).

Food

You'll find Cleveland's culinary treats in the tiny neighborhoods that surround the downtown area. To satiate that lust for hot corned beef, just step into one of the dozens of delis in the city center. The open-air, European-style **West Side Market, W. 25th and Lorain Ave.** (781-3663), is a great place to get a feel for the people of Cleveland while buying fresh produce, ethnic baked goods and meats, and goat heads. There are 185 vendors and a poultry house for the adventurous. (Open Mon. and Wed. 7am-4pm, Fri.-Sat. 7am-7pm.)

Tommy's, 1820 Coventry Rd., just up the hill from University Circle. Take bus #9x east to Mayfield and Coventry Rd. Delicious, healthy pita bread sandwiches ($2.50-5.25) and friendly service. Try the Brownie Monster for dessert. Open Mon.-Sat. 7:30am-10pm, Sun. 9am-5pm.

Mama Santa's, 12305 Mayfield Rd., in Little Italy just east of University Circle. Authentic Sicilian food served beneath subdued lighting. Medium pizza $3.25, spaghetti $4.25. Open Mon.-Thurs. 11am-midnight, Fri.-Sat. 11am-1am.

Downtown Coffee Shoppe, 1150 Huron Rd., 8 blocks from Public Sq. This Mom-and-Pop diner on a calm street behind Euclid Ave. has simple sandwiches and burgers $1.25-2.50. Open Mon.-Fri. 6am-5pm.

Sights and Entertainment

Cleveland has a wide variety of things to see and do. 1990 witnessed the opening of the long-awaited **Tower City Center** (771-0033), a three-story shopping complex in the Terminal Tower. Although essentially just a luxury mall with prices to match, it is notable as an emblem of the tremendous renovation and revitalization of downtown Cleveland.

One of the most beautiful things about Cleveland is Lake Erie, best seen at **Cleveland Lakefront State Park** (881-8141), 2 mi. west of downtown and accessible from Lake Ave. or Cleveland Memorial Shoreway. This mile-long beach is a great place to swim, play frisbee, picnic in the shaded, grassy areas, or simply sit and watch the waves roll in.

The east side of Cleveland plays host to most of the city's arts activities. **Playhouse Square Center,** 1501 Euclid Ave. (241-6000), just east of downtown, is the third-largest performing arts center in the nation. The **Cleveland Opera** (575-0900) and the famous **Cleveland Ballet** (621-2260) perform there, as do many other artists and organizations. Located 5 mi. east of the city, **University Circle** is a cluster of 75 cultural institutions. Check with the helpful visitors bureau for details on museums, live music, and drama. The world-class **Cleveland Museum of Art,** 11150 East Blvd. (421-7340), in University Circle, contains a fine collection of 19th-century French and American impressionist paintings, as well as a version of Rodin's "The Thinker." A beautiful plaza and pond on which to ponder face the museum. (Open Tues. and Thurs.-Fri. 10am-5:45pm, Wed. 10am-9:45pm, Sat. 10am-4:45pm, Sun. 1-5:45pm. Free.) Nearby is the **Cleveland Museum of Natural History,** Wade Oval (231-4600), where you can see the only extant skull of the fearsome Pygmy Tyrant *(Nanatyrannus).* (Open Mon.-Sat. 10am-5pm, Sun. 1-5:30pm. Admission $3.75, seniors, students, and children $1.75. Free Tues. and Thurs.) The renowned **Cleveland Orchestra,** one of the nation's best, has its home in University Circle at Severance Hall, 11001 Euclid Ave. (231-1111; $10-23, depending on the seating). During the summer, however, the orchestra performs at **Blossom Music Center,** 1145 W. Steels Corners Rd., Cuyahoga Falls (920-8040). University Circle itself is safe, but some of the neighborhoods immediately surrounding it are rough, especially at night, so use caution. East of University Circle, in a nice neighborhood, is the **Dobama Theatre,** 1846 Coventry Rd., Cleveland Hts. (932-6838). This little-known theater gives terrific, inexpensive ($5-8) performances in an intimate, living-room atmosphere.

A great deal of Cleveland's nightlife is focused in the **Flats,** the former industrial core of the city along both banks of the Cuyahoga River. Located just west of Public

Square, the northernmost section of the Flats contains several nightclubs and restaurants. On weekend nights, expect large crowds and larger traffic jams. On the east side of the river, from the deck at **Rumrunners**, 1124 Old River Rd. (696-6070), you can watch the sunset across the water through the steel frames of old railroad bridges. Live bands play often, and draft beer is $1.25. (Open daily 11am-2am. Occasional $2 cover.) **Peabody's Down Under**, 1059 Old River Rd. (241-0792 or 241-2451) draws crowds not for the view, but for the variety of local and nationally famous rock 'n' roll bands that play most nights. (Open daily 8pm-2:30am. Cover $4-18 depending on the band.) On the west side of the river are several other clubs, including **Shooters**, 1148 Main Ave. (861-6900), a beautiful bar/restaurant with a great view of the river and Lake Erie. Prices are fairly high (dinners $7-10), but you can capture the flavor of Cleveland nightlife inexpensively by taking your drink to the in-deck pool. (Open Mon.-Sat. 11:30am-1:30am, Sun. 11am-1:30am.) When you tire of fluorescent pink tank tops and wine coolers, stop by the **Euclid Tavern**, 11629 Euclid Ave. (229-7788), just east of University Circle, the place for good conversation and great music. Live bands play nightly; every Saturday the place is packed to hear the phenomenal Mr. Stress Blues Band. (Open 24 hr. Beer $1.50.)

In the shadow of Cleveland's metropolitan hustle and bustle lie the Amish communities of bucolic **Holmes County**. Originally Swiss Mennonites, the Amish broke with the main body to create their own sect. Following Jacob Amman, they came to America in 1728 to practice their more austere lifestyle undisturbed. In Ohio, they settled south of Cleveland in rural Holmes, Wayne, and Tuscarawas counties. Outsiders can visit the **Amish Farm** (893-2951), in Berlin, which offers a film presentation, demonstrations of non-electrical appliances, and a tour of the grounds. (Open April 1-Nov. 1 Mon.-Sat. 10am-6pm. Tour $2.25, children $1. Buggy ride $2.75.) Unserved by public transportation, Berlin lies 70 mi. south of Cleveland on Rte. 39, 17 pastoral mi. west of I-77.

Lake Erie Islands

"Ohio's Scenic Playground," the Lake Erie Island region can be either quaint or garish, depending on where you go. The area around the regional center on the mainland, **Sandusky**, tends toward the latter, with an abundance of neon signs and billboards; still, downtown Sandusky is not as commercial as the surrounding highways. Once the last stop in the U.S. for escaped African slaves fleeing to Canada via the Underground Railroad, Sandusky lies on Rte. 2, 55 mi. west of Cleveland and 45 mi. southeast of Toledo.

Near Sandusky, experience **Cedar Point**, the scenic playground's scenic amusement park (627-2350) off Rte. 6. Take the Ohio Turnpike (I-80) to exit 7 and follow signs north on U.S. 250 to the home of the Magnum XL200, the world's largest, fastest, longest, and steepest roller coaster. (Open mid-May to mid-Sept. daily, 9am-10pm. Admission $20, seniors $12.75, under 48 in. $11, under 3 years free. After 5pm, when the lines diminish, the admission drops to $11.) In Sandusky savor the **Erie County Vineyard Days**, each fall from mid-September to November. Sandusky and the Erie Islands lost their monopoly on U.S. wine production after Prohibition and the Great Depression, but today the area still ferments in an orgy of libations that would do Dionysius proud. For more information, contact the **Visitors and Convention Bureau**, 231 W. Washington Row (625-2984; open Mon.-Fri. 8am-6pm, Sat. 10am-4pm), or the **Tourist Information Center**, 5510 Milan Rd. (626-5721; open May 27-Sept. 2 daily 8am-6pm).

Greyhound, 6513 Milan Rd. (625-6907) offers bus service from Sandusky to Cleveland ($13.25), Detroit ($24.25), and Chicago ($49.50). The **Greyhound Shuttle** runs to downtown Sandusky ($4) and Cedar Point ($5).

Cheap accommodations are difficult to find in Ohio's vacationland, especially during summer weekends. Rates are extremely flexible and tend to soar during the peak tourist season, so try to schedule an off-season visit. In Sandusky, sample one of the motels east of downtown along Cleveland Rd. The **Tudor Inn Motel**, 2214

Cleveland Rd. (626-0775), has a cabin available during the summer for $27 and motel rooms year-round for $29. A hundred yards away, **Bayshore Estates RV Park and Campsite,** 2311 Cleveland Rd. (625-7906), has tent sites for $11, with hookup $13. Camping is also available at the **Crystal Rock Campground,** 710 Crystal Rock Rd. (684-7177), off Rte. 6 south of Rte. 2, with extensive facilities, including a pool (sites $16, with hookup $19.50).

Just northwest of Sandusky, accessible by Rte. 2, is **Marblehead Peninsula** and the adjoining **Catawba Island.** This area is less cluttered than Sandusky and brings you closer to the region's scenic aspects. On the northeast side of Marblehead, **Lakeside,** on North Shore Blvd., is one of the last of the Chautauqua villages. This 19th-century Methodist retreat has economy rooms in its **Hotel Lakeside** (798-4461). Take Rte. 2 to Rte. 163, heading toward the tip of Marblehead. (Singles $17. Doubles $20. Grounds admission fee $7, children $5. Overnight auto pass $1, includes free entertainment at the compound's Hoover Auditorium.) **Poor Richard's Inn,** 317 Maple St. (798-5405), is 2 blocks up the street from the Hotel Lakeside. (Singles $18. Doubles $23.) Camping is also available at Lakeside (tent sites $7, with hookup $11). A couple of miles from the Catawba Point ferry dock, try the **East Harbor State Park** (734-4424), on Rte. 269 off I-65. (Open 24 hr. Tent sites $8.)

Kelleys Island, the largest U.S. island in Lake Erie, is a laid-back, relaxing island with none of Sandusky's neon glitter and all of the region's famous beauty. In addition to the beaches, examine the water-filled, abandoned limestone quarries in the island's interior. Near the town on the island's southern shore you can see **Inscription Rock,** a slab of limestone covered with Erie American pictographs over four centuries old. On the north shore, 30,000 year-old glacial grooves gouged the limestone an impressive 15 ft. deep, 35 ft. wide, and 400 ft. long. The best way to tour the island is by bicycle; rent from **The Other House** (746-2236), near the ferry deck on the southwest shore ($9 per day, $10 deposit). Golf carts ($10 per hr., $25 per half-day) but not spinach can be rented from **Popeye's,** also near the ferry dock. The best (the only) place to camp is **Kelleys Island State Park** (746-2546), on the north shore near the glacial grooves (sites $6). **Neuman Boat Line,** 101 E. Shoreline Dr. (626-5557), in Sandusky, serves Kelleys Island by ferry. Ferries run more frequently between Kelleys Island and the Marblehead dock, on the eastern tip of the peninsula (April-Oct. every hr. dawn to dusk, half-hourly during weekends. Taking your vehicle across can add hours to your wait. One way $3.50, children 6-11 $2, car $6.50, bike $1.)

The **Bass Island chain** extends far into Lake Erie to the west of Kelleys Island; **South Bass Island,** shaped like an hourglass, is the largest and most populous of the three. If Kelleys is the relaxing island, then South Bass, or Put-In-Bay as it is commonly known, is the lively, exciting island with a party atmosphere. The town of **Put-In-Bay,** 2 mi. northeast of the ferry dock, is packed on summer weekends with people from all over attracted by the nightlife scene. The **Round House Bar,** 234 Lorain Ave. (285-4595, ext. 110), downtown, bulges with people listening to talented live bands that perform nightly. A glass of Budweiser is $1.75. (Open daily noon-1am.)

Stuck to the hourglass's waist at the town of Put-In-Bay is **Perry's Victory and International Peace Memorial,** the world's tallest doric column (352 ft.), erected to commemorate Commodore Oliver Hazard Perry's victory over the British in the War of 1812. (Open Mon.-Fri. 10am-6pm, Sat.-Sun. 10am-7pm. Elevator $1.) Also located in Put-In-Bay, the **Heineman Winery,** Catawba Ave. (285-2811), gives intimate tours of the grounds, including a look at **Crystal Cave,** one of the world's largest geodes. (Open late May to mid-Sept. daily 11am-5pm. Admission $3, children $1.)

On the island, you can camp and swim at **South Bass Island State Park** (285-2112; open daily 8am-5pm; tent sites $7). **Island Bike Rental,** Langrum Rd. (285-2016), across from the ferry dock, not surprisingly rents island bikes ($2 per hr., $6 per day). The **Miller Boat Line** (285-2421) serves Put-in-Bay from Catawba Point. Take the Put-in-Bay exit, Rte. 53, north from Rte. 2 until it ends. (Ferries late March to mid-Nov. every hr.; early June-early Sept. every ½ hr. One way $3.50, children $1, cars $6.50, bikes $1.50.)

Miller Boat Line also serves **Middle Bass Island,** where you can visit the fortress-like **Lonz Winery** (285-5411) and sample their vintage. (Open mid-May tolate Sept.) The **area code** for the islands is 419.

Columbus

In the heart of Ohio lies **Columbus,** the state's capital and most populous city (619,000). The downtown area sprawls around the architecturally stellar **state capitol** and **Capitol Square** at Broad and High St. (466-2125; open daily 9am-5pm), while also containing two excellent museums. The **Columbus Museum of Art,** 480 E. Broad St. (221-6801), has a fine collection of European masterpieces. (Open Tues. and Thurs.- Fri. 11am-5pm, Wed. 11am-9pm, Sat. 10am-5pm, Sun. 11am-5pm. Admission $3.50, seniors, students, and ages 6-17 $1. Fri. free.) Ohio's **Center of Science and Industry (COSI),** 280 E. Broad St. (228-2674), feautures hands-on mechanized exhibits. (Open Mon.-Sat. 10am-5pm, Sun. 1-5:30pm. Admission $5, seniors, students, and children $3, families $15.)

The rapidly growing **Columbus Zoo,** 9990 Riverside Dr. (645-3400) in Powell, contains the world's largest cheetah collection, the largest U.S. display of reptiles and amphibians, and the world's first captive-born gorilla. (Open May 27-Sept. 2 daily 9am-6pm; off-season daily 9am-5pm. Admission $4, ages 2-11 $2, under 2 free.)

Head to **Bernie's Bagels and Deli,** 1896 N. High St., for delicious warm sandwiches ($2-5). The low-ceilinged basement setting resembles a fall-out shelter, but the nightly live gigs make it cozy rather than claustrophobic. For an above-ground dining experience, choose from 1000 bottles of wine to accompany the moderately priced Mediterranean cuisine at **A La Carte,** 2333 N. High St. (294-6783). The outdoor tables are particularly popular. (Open Mon.-Thurs. 11am-9:30pm, Fri.-Sat. 11am-11pm, Sun. 11am-9pm.) Just south of Capitol Square is the **German Village,** first settled in 1843 and now the largest privately funded restored historical area in the U.S. Visitors can tour stately brick homes and patronize old-style beer halls and restaurants. At **Schmidt's Sausage House,** 240 E. Kossuth St. (444-6800), tap your feet to the live music nightly while eating brats and German potato salad. (Open Mon. 11am-10pm, Tues.-Thurs. 11am-11:30pm, Fri.-Sat. 11am-midnight, Sun. 11am-9pm.) For information, call or visit the helpful **German Village Society,** 634 S. 3rd St. (221-8888). (Open Mon.-Fri. 9am-4pm.)

Two mi. north of downtown Columbus looms gargantuan **Ohio State University;** its enrollment of over 58,000 students is the largest in the United States. **Visitor Information** is in Mershon Auditorium at 30 W. 15th Ave. (292-0428 or 292-0418), at N. High St. The students support a lively nightlife, with most of the activity on **North High Street. Papa Joe's,** 1573 N. High St. (421-7272), is a popular pick-up spot for rowdy seniors. On Wednesdays, buckets of beer are a mere drop in the bucket at $5. (Open daily 7pm-2:30am. Admission 50¢.) **Newport's,** 1722 N. High St. (291-8829), regularly features famous bands or plays dance music for a sweaty, energetic crowd. (Call for admission information and music schedule.)

The beautiful **Heart of Ohio Hostel (AYH),** 95 E. 12th Ave. (294-7157), 1 block from OSU, has outstanding facilities for $8. Check-in 5-9pm, curfew 11pm. Rooms in apartment houses near campus are cheap, abundant, and well advertised during the summer, when OSU students leave them vacant. Contact **De Santis Properties** (291-7368; 451-8715 evenings) for information. Downtown accommodations are much more expensive.

Visitors to the city can contact the **Greater Columbus Convention and Visitors Bureau,** 10 W. Broad St. #1300 (221-6623 or 800-234-2657). Open Mon.-Fri. 8am-5pm. **Greyhound,** 111 E. Town St. (221-5311), offers the most frequent and complete service from downtown Columbus to Cincinnati ($19), Cleveland ($19), and Chicago ($56.50). Public transportation in the city is run by the **Central Ohio Tran-**

sit **Authority (COTA),** 177 S. High St. (228-1776). (Open Mon.-Fri. 8:30am-5:30pm. Fare 75¢, express $1, transfers 10¢.) All travelers should beware of the extensive construction that will take place near Capitol Square until 1992.
The **area code** for Columbus is 614; the **ZIP code** is 43016.

Near Columbus

The pun about Ohio being round on both ends and high in the middle is hardly accurate. In the southeastern end of the state, Pleistocene glaciers plowed into the land creating narrow valleys, steep hills, and ragged rock formations which are currently swathed in dense green forests. **U.S. 50,** running east from Cincinnati to Parkersburg, roughly follows the southern route of the Buckeye Trail.

Along U.S. 50 lie the spectacular Native American burial grounds constructed by the Adena, Hopewell, and Fort Ancient "Moundbuilders." Among the most interesting is the **Mound City Group National Monument** (774-1125), on Rte. 104, 3 mi. north of Chillicothe. Within a 13-acre area hunch 24 still-mysterious Hopewell burial mounds. The adjoining museum elucidates theories about Hopewell society based on the mounds' configuration. (Monument open daily dawn-dusk. Museum open daily 8am-5pm. Admission $1, max. $3 per vehicle, seniors and ages under 17 free.) Check with park officials for information on other nearby mounds. **Chillicothe** itself merits a visit for the Greek Revival mansions of the northwest territory's first capital.

Ten mi. south of Chillicothe off U.S. 23, you can camp at **Scioto Trail State Park** (663-2125; office open Mon.-Fri. 8am-11pm; 24-hr. self-registration; primitive camping free; designated sites $4, with electricity $8). Four mi. from the bus station is the **Chillicothe Home Hostel (AYH),** 1940 Egypt Pike Rd. (775-3632 or 773-3989). A phenomenal beer can collection covers the walls of one available room. (Members only. $5. Reservations required.)

Greyhound, 302 E. Main St. (775-2013), serves Chillicothe from both Cincinnati($27.25) and Columbus ($11.25).

About 30 mi. east of Chillicothe, U.S. 50 passes near **Hocking Hills State Park,** accessible by Rte. 93 north or Rte. 56 west. Rugged terrain marked with waterfalls, gorges, cliffs, and caves make this area the most beautiful in the state. **Ash Cave,** east of South Bloomingville on Rte. 56, gouges 80 acres out of a horseshoe-shaped rock. A trickling stream falls over the edge of this cliff to a pool at the cave entrance. **Cantwell Cliffs,** southwest of Rockbridge on Rte. 374, is another horseshoe-shaped precipice. Also visit the deep gorge **Cedar Falls, Conkles Hollow,** and **Rock House,** a stone structure stuck precariously in a perpendicular cliff. All of these sights are preserved and run by the state park system. Camp at **Old Man's Cave,** off State Rte. 664 (385-6165; primitive camping $4; designated sites with pool $7, with electricity and pool $10).
The **area code** for these here parts is 614.

Cincinnati

Longfellow called it the "Queen City of the West." In the 1850s, less romantic folk nicknamed it "Porkopolis," a tribute to its position as the world's largest pork-packing center. As a legacy of this era, winged pigs guard the entrance of the city's **Sawyer Point Park** downtown. Though swine no longer snort through the streets and the West has since expanded to the Pacific, Cincinnati still combines cosmopolitan charm with pig-in-a-poke comfort.

Mark Twain purportedly claimed that if the world suddenly stopped dead, it would take Cincinnati 20 years to figure it out. Snuggled in a valley surrounded by seven rolling hills and the Ohio River, downtown Cincinnati is much more reminiscent of an old-fashioned town square than of an urban center, mostly because the streets are clean and the people friendly.

Practical Information

Emergency: 911.

Visitor Information: Cincinnati Convention and Visitors Bureau, 300 W. 6th St. (621-2142). Open Mon.-Fri. 8:45am-5pm. Pick up an *Official Visitors Guide.* **Information Booth** in Fountain Square. Open Mon.-Sat. 8:30am-5:30pm. **Info Line,** 421-4636. Lists plays, opera, cruises, and symphonies.

Airport: Greater Cincinnati International Airport, in Independence, KY, 13 mi. south of Cincinnati. The **Jetport Express** (283-3702) shuttles passengers to downtown (about $8).

Amtrak: 1901 River Rd. (921-4172 or 800-872-7245). To Indianapolis ($29) and Chicago ($57).

Greyhound: 1005 Gilbert Ave. (352-6000), just past the intersection of E. Court and Broadway. To: Indianapolis ($19); Louisville, KY ($19); Cleveland ($36). Open 24 hr.

Public Transport: Queen City Metro, 122 W. Fifth St. (621-4455). Office has bus schedules and information. Telephone information Mon.-Fri. 6:30am-7pm, Sat.-Sun. 8am-5pm. Most buses run out of Government Sq. at 5th and Main St., to outlying communities. Peak fare 65¢, other times 50¢, weekends 35¢.

Taxi: Yellow Cab, 241-2100. Base fare $1.50, $1.20 per mile, $3 minimum.

Weather Line: 241-1010.

Help Lines: Rape Crisis Center, 216 E. 9th St. (381-5610), downtown. **Gay/Lesbian Community Switchboard:** 221-7800.

Post Office: 122 W. 5th St. (684-5664), between Walnut and Vine St. Open Mon.-Fri. 8am-5pm, Sat. 8am-1pm. **ZIP code:** 45202.

Area Code: 513.

Cincinnati is in southwestern Ohio, 78 mi. due north of Lexington, KY, and 100 mi. southeast of Indianapolis. **Fountain Square,** E. 5th at Vine St., is the focal point of the downtown business community. Cross streets are numbered and designated East or West, with Vine Street as the divider. **Riverfront Stadium,** the **Serpentine Wall,** and the **Riverwalk** are down by the river. The University of Cincinnati spreads out from Clifton, north of the city. Overlooking downtown from the east, **Mt. Adams,** adjoining Eden Park, harbors some of Cincinnati's most active nightlife.

Accommodations and Camping

Cincinnati has many motels, but most of the cheap places are outside the heart of the city. Cars and reservations are recommended, especially on nights of Reds baseball games and on weekends. Campgrounds are also a long way out of town.

Cincinnati Home Hostel (AYH), 2200 Maplewood Ave. (651-2329), in a slightly run-down neighborhood 2 mi. north of downtown. A three-story house now being renovated. Large rooms, TV downstairs. Singles $6.

College of Mount St. Joseph, 5701 Delhi Pike (244-4327), about 8 mi. west of downtown off Rte. 50. Immaculate rooms in a quiet, though remote location. Excellent facilities. Singles $15. Doubles $20. Cafeteria lunch and dinner $3.50.

Evendale Motel, 10165 Reading Rd. (563-1570), ½ hr. from downtown. Small, dark, but clean rooms. Singles and doubles $23.

Red Roof Inn, 5300 Kennedy Ave. (531-6589), off I-71 at Ridge Rd. Run-of-the-roof basics from the national chain. Singles $39. Doubles $50.

Ohio Valley Bed and Breakfast, 6876 Taylor Mills Rd. (606-356-7865), in Independence, KY. Singles and doubles in a variety of area homes as low as $40. Call well in advance for reservations.

Camp Shore Campgrounds, Rte. 56 in Aurora, IN (812-438-2135), 30 mi. west of Cincinnati on the Ohio River. Tent sites with hookup $12.

Rose Gardens Resort—KOA Campgrounds, I-75 exit 166 (606-428-2000), 30 mi. south of Cincinnati. Award-winning landscaping. Tent sites $16. Cabins $25, including water and electricity. Make reservations.

Food

The city that gave us the first soap opera and the first baseball franchise (the Redlegs) presents as its great culinary contribution **Cincinnati chili.** To the usual meat and beans, locals add your choice of spaghetti, onions, and cheese, often with a hot dog to boot, all for about $2.50. With few exceptions, Cincinnatians swear by the abundant **Gold Star Chili, Skyline,** and **Empress** fast-food chains.

Camp Washington Chili, Hopple and Colerain Ave., 1 block west of I-75. A legendary greasy spoon. Open Mon.-Sat. 24 hr.

Izzy's, 819 Elm St., also 610 Main St. A Cincinnati institution founded in 1901. Izzy has passed away, but his tradition of good-natured insults endures. Overstuffed kosher sandwiches with potato pancake $3-4. Izzy's famous reuben $4.50. Open Mon.-Fri. 7am-5pm, Sat. 7am-4pm; Main St. restaurant open Mon.-Sat. 7am-9pm.

Montgomery Inn, 9440 Montgomery Rd., east off I-71, exit 12. Few customers would contest their claim to the world's best ribs. Friendly family atmosphere. Ribs $11-14. Open Mon.-Thurs. 11am-11pm, Fri. 11am-midnight, Sat. 4pm-midnight, Sun. 4-10pm.

Graeter's, 41 E. 4th St., downtown, and 11 other locations. Since 1870, Graeter's has dished out fresh ice cream with giant chocolate chips. Medium cone $1.80. Open Mon.-Sat. 11am-5:30pm.

Findlay Market, 18th at Elm St., 2 mi. north of downtown. Produce and picnic items $3-5. Open Wed. 7am-1:30pm, Fri.-Sat. 7am-6pm.

Sights and Events

Downtown Cincinnati revolves around the **Tyler Davidson Fountain,** the ideal spot to people-watch while you feign admiration for the gorgeous architecture. If you squint your eyes, you can almost see Les Nesman rushing to WKRP to deliver the daily hog report. Check out the expansive gardens and daring design at **Procter and Gamble Plaza,** just east of Fountain Square, or walk along **Fountain Square South,** a shopping and business complex connected by a series of second-floor skywalks. When the visual stimuli exhaust you, prick up your ears for a free concert in front of the fountain. The **Downtown Council,** 120 W. 5th St. (579-3191), has more information. (Open Mon.-Fri. 9am-5pm.)

Close to Fountain Square, the **Contemporary Arts Center,** 115 E. 5th St., 2nd floor (721-0390), by Walnut, has survived a nationally publicized attack by some Cincinnati citizens on its exhibition of sexually explicit photographs by Robert Mapplethorpe. With a newly enhanced reputation among the national arts community, it continues to change its exhibits frequently, offering evening films, music, and multi-media performances. (Open Mon.-Sat. 10am-6pm, Sun. 1-5pm. Admission $4, seniors and students $3. Mon. free.)

The **Cincinnati Zoo,** 3400 Vine St. (281-4700), at Forest Ave., can be reached by car (take Dana Ave. off I-75 or I-71), or by bus (#78 or 49 from Vine and 5th St.) *Newsweek* called it one of the world's "sexiest zoos"; the lush greenery and cageless habitats evidently encourage the zoo's gorillas and famous white Bengal tigers to reproduce enthusiastically. (Open in summer daily 9am-8pm, entrance closes at 6pm; off-season 9am-6pm, entrance closes at 5pm. Admission $5.75, seniors and ages under 12 $2.50.)

On a cliff overlooking downtown from the east, the Mt. Adams/Eden Park area gives Cincinnati a bit of bohemian charm. Shaded by the trees of Eden Park, the **Cincinnati Art Museum** (721-5204) features a permanent collection spanning 5000 years, as well as exceptional exhibits of musical instruments and Middle Eastern artifacts. (Open Tues., Thurs.-Sat. 10am-5pm, Wed. 10am-9pm, Sun. noon-5pm. Admission $3, seniors $1.50, students $2, under 18 free. Sat. free. Take bus #49 to Eden Park Dr. By car, follow Gilbert Ave. northeast from downtown.) Step into a tropical rain forest in the **Krohn Conservatory** (352-4086), one of the largest public greenhouses in the world. (Open daily 10am-5pm. Suggested donation $1.50, seniors and ages under 15 $1.) The **Taft Museum,** 316 Pike St. (241-0343), downtown, has a beautiful collection of painted enamels, as well as pieces by Rembrandt and Whistler. (Open Mon.-Sat. 10am-5pm, Sun. 2-5pm. Suggested donation $2, seniors and students $1.)

On the west side of town, the **Union Terminal,** 1031 Western Ave. (241-7257), near the Ezzard Charles Dr. exit off I-75 (take bus #1), is a fine example of art deco architecture that boasts the world's highest unsupported dome. Renovations have closed the terminal museum until 1991.

Procter and Gamble offers good, clean fun on its tours of its home plant, **Ivorydale,** 5201 Spring Grove Ave. (721-8230). Watch the world's largest soap manufacturer at work while you learn a little about the history of the U.S. hygeine industry. (Tours Tues.-Thurs. Reservations required.)

Cincinnati is fanatical about sports. The **Reds** major league baseball team (421-7337) and the **Bengals** NFL football team (621-3550) both play in **Riverfront Stadium.** The **Riverfront Coliseum** (241-1818), a Cincinnati landmark, hosts other sports events and major concerts year-round. During the second week of July **Summerfair** (800-582-5804), a large art festival, is held at **Coney Island,** 6201 Kellogg Ave. (232-8230).

The **Riverwalk** by the **Serpentine Wall** is a pleasant place to stroll along the Ohio River, with free summer concerts held at the **Pavilion.** The area was totally revamped for the state's 1988 bicentennial. At the **Bicentennial Commons,** exquisite recreational facilities and a timeline of Ohio history span about a mile. Even those who have graduated from jungle gym days should bounce on the rubber floor. On Labor Day, get seats early for **Riverfest,** one of the nation's largest fireworks displays.

Entertainment and Nightlife

The cliff-hanging communities that line the steep streets of Mt. Adams also support a vivacious arts and entertainment industry. Perched on its own wooded hill is the **Playhouse in the Park,** 962 Mt. Adams Circle (421-3888), a theater-in-the-round remarkably adaptable to many styles of drama. The regular season runs mid-September to July, with special summer programs as well. Accessible to the vision and hearing impaired. (Tickets $14-25.50, 15 min. before the show student rush tickets $8.50.)

For a drink and a voyage back to the 19th century, try **Arnold's,** 210 E. 8th St. (421-6234), Cincinnati's oldest tavern, between Main St. and Sycamore downtown. After 9pm, traditional jazz, ragtime, and swing are served alongside sandwiches ($4-5) and dinners ($6-10). (Open Mon.-Fri. 11am-10pm, Sat. 4-10pm.) Check out the antique toys inside or listen to jazz and blues in the courtyard at **Blind Lemon,** 936 Hatch St. (241-3885), at St. Gregory St. in Mt. Adams. Draft beer $2. (Open Mon.-Fri. 4pm-2:30am, Sat. 6:30pm-2:30am, Sun. 3pm-2:30am. Music at 9:30pm.) The **City View Tavern,** also in Mt. Adams at 403 Oregon St. (241-8439), off Monastery St., is hard to find, but worth the effort. This down-to-earth local favorite proudly displays an article heralding it as one of the best dives in Cincinnati. The deck in back offers a great view of the city's skyline and the Ohio River. Local draft beer 90¢. (Open Mon.-Fri. noon-1am, Sat. 1pm-1am, Sun. 2-11pm.)

The University of Cincinnati's **Conservatory of Music** (556-9430) often gives free classical and experimental concerts. Slightly more upscale, the **Music Hall,** 1243 Elm St. (721-8222), by Ezzard Charles Dr., has wonderful acoustics: the **Cincinnati Symphony Orchestra** (621-1919) performs here from September to May. (Tickets $7-32. Discounted rush tickets 10 min. before the performance.) Other companies performing at the Music Hall are the **Cincinnati Opera** (241-2742; limited summer productions; tickets $7-32) and the **Cincinnati Ballet Company** (621-5219; performances Sept.-May; tickets $6-42). For updates, call **Dial the Arts** (751-2787).

Near Cincinnati

If you can't get to California's Napa or Sonoma Valleys, the next best thing may be **Meiers Wine Cellars,** 6955 Plainfield Pike (891-2900). Take I-71 to exit 12 or I-75 to Galbraith Rd. Free tours of Ohio's oldest and largest winery allow you to observe the entire wine-making operation and taste its fruits. (Free tours May 27-Oct. 31 Mon.-Sat.; Nov.-May must have at least 12 people to tour.)

In Mason, 24 mi. north of Cincinnati off I-71 at exit #24, the **Kings Island** amusement park (241-5600) cages The Beast, the world's second-fastest roller coaster. Admission entitles you to unlimited rides and attractions, but emphatically not the food. Pack a picnic or a very thick wallet. Lines diminish after dark. (Open May 27-Sept. 2 Sun.-Fri. 10am-10pm, Sat. 10am-11pm. Admission $21.)

Wisconsin

The state that calls itself "America's Dairyland" is also one of the nation's most popular playlands, with forests, rivers, and lakes to suit the tenacious and the tenderfoot alike. Lake Superior to the north and Lake Michigan to the east give the Wisconsin coast the natural beauty that makes the Great Lake area famous. Wisconsin's appeal comes not just from nature; Wisconsin residents pick up where the wilderness leaves off. Here you can enjoy such diverse pleasures as Milwaukee's ethnic festivals, Madison's annual autumn march to legalize marijuana, or the Door County fishboil, a social event of culinary proportions.

Practical Information

Capital: Madison.

Tourist Information: Division of Tourism, 123 W. Washington St., Madison 53707 (266-2161, 266-6797, or 800-372-2737).

Time Zone: Central (1 hr. behind Eastern). **Postal Abbreviation:** WI.

Milwaukee

After Milwaukee opened for settlement in 1835, it quickly became the home of Irish, German, and East Coast emigrants. Together they gave the city its reputation for *gemutlichkeit*—hospitality. An international array of more recent immigrants, including Italians, Poles, and Hispanics, has combined with the Teutonic culture, as the city now welcomes more travelers than ever to its beautiful lakefront. For today's visitor, the best part of Milwaukee may be its vital ethnic communities—during the summer, one of them throws a city-wide party every weekend. The self-proclaimed "City of Fabulous Festivals" has top-notch museums, quality arts organizations, and plenty of beer, baklava, and bagpipes.

Practical Information

Emergency: 911

Visitor Information: Greater Milwaukee Convention and Visitors Bureau, 756 N. Milwaukee St. (273-3950), downtown. Open Mon.-Fri. 8am-6pm. Also at the airport (open Mon.-Fri. 7am-9:30pm, Sat. 10am-6pm, Sun. 1-9:30pm) and Grand Avenue Mall at 3rd St. (open Mon.-Fri. 10am-8pm, Sat. 10am-6pm, Sun. noon-5pm). Pick up a copy of *The Greater Milwaukee Dining and Visitors Guide.* **Fun Line** (799-1177) and **Rockline** (276-7625) give local entertainment information. Both open 24 hr.

Travelers Aid: At the airport (747-5245). Open daily 9am-9pm.

Amtrak: 433 W. St. Paul Ave. (800-872-7245), at 5th St. 3 blocks from the bus terminal. To Chicago ($14.50). Open Mon.-Fri. 6am-9pm, Sat.-Sun. 7:30am-9pm.

Buses: Greyhound, 606 N. 7th St. (272-8900), off W. Michigan St. downtown. Open daily 5am-11:30pm. To Chicago ($13) and Madison ($6). **Wisconsin Coach,** in the Greyhound terminal (542-8861). Service to outlying areas of Wisconsin. Open daily 6am-9pm. **Badger Bus,,** across the street (276-7490). To Madison (6 per day, $6.50).

Public Transport: Milwaukee County Transit System, 1942 N. 17th St. (344-6711). Efficient service in the metro area. Most lines run 5:30am to the wee hours. Fare $1, seniors 50¢ with Medicare card.

Car Rental: Suburban Car Rental, 4939 S. Howell (482-0300), across from Mitchell Airport. From $16 per day. Unlimited mi. within Wisconsin; outside Wisconsin, 150 free mi., 15¢ each additional mi. $10 collision insurance. Open Mon.-Fri. 7am-9pm, Sat. 9am-5pm, Sun. noon-9pm. Must be 21 with liability insurance and major credit card.

Taxi: City Veteran Taxi, 643-5522 or 653-1212. Base rate $1.25, $1.25 per mi.

Auto Transport Company: Auto Driveaway Co., 9039 W. National Ave. (962-0008 or 327-5252), in West Alice. Open Mon.-Fri. 8am-5pm, Sat. 8am-noon. Must be 21 with a good driving record.

Help Lines: Crisis Intervention Center, 257-7222. Open 24 hr. **Rape Crisis Line,** 547-4600 or 542-3828. **Gay People's Union Hotline,** 562-7010.

Post Office: 345 W. St. Paul Ave. (287-2530), south along 4th Ave. from downtown, next to the Amtrak station. Open Mon.-Fri. 7:30am-6pm. **ZIP code:** 53201.

Area Code: 414.

Wisconsin's largest city in both area and population (664,000) occupies about 15 mi. of the **Lake Michigan** shoreline in the southeastern corner of the state. Milwaukee lies 90 mi. north of Chicago, 80 mi. east of Madison on I-94, and 340 mi. east of Minneapolis on I-90/94. The downtown area is a few miles back from the lakeshore. The **Milwaukee River** flows north-south just east of downtown, dividing streets east-west and breaking the city's grid pattern.

Accommodations and Camping

Sleeping rarely comes cheap in downtown Milwaukee, but there are two attractive hostels nearby, as well as the convenient University of Wisconsin dorms.

Red Barn Youth Hostel (AYH), 6750 W. Loomis Rd. (529-3299), 13 mi. southwest of downtown via Rte. 894, exit Loomis. Take bus #10 or 30 westbound on Wisconsin Ave., get off at 35th St., and take the #35 southbound to the Loomis and Ramsey intersection; cross over to the Pick and Save store and walk ¾ mi. Rustic, slightly dark rooms in an enormous, red barn. Friendly houseparents. $5, nonmembers $8. Open May-Oct.

University of Wisconsin at Milwaukee (UWM): Sandburg Halls, 3400 N. Maryland Ave. (229-4065). Take bus #30 north to Hartford St. and look for the tall stone building. Private rooms part of suites. Laundry, cafeteria available. Singles with shared bath $19. Doubles $25-35. Open May 31-Aug. 15.

Halter Home Hostel (AYH), 2956 N. 77th St. (258-7692), 4 mi. west of downtown. Take bus #57 to 76th and Center St. In a quiet, residential neighborhood. Closer of the two hostels, but also smaller: 4 beds in 2 comfortable bedrooms. Members only, $8.

Hotel Wisconsin, 720 N. 3rd St. (271-4900), across from the Grand Avenue Mall. 250 old but clean rooms at a convenient downtown location. Singles $44. Doubles $49. Key deposit $3. Phone deposit $2.

Motel 6, 5037 S. Howell Ave. (482-4414), near the airport. Take bus #80 southbound at the corner of 6th and Wisconsin; get off at Edgerton and Howell. Outdoor pool. Singles $29,, Doubles $35. Fills quickly; consider making reservations.

State Fairgrounds (257-8844); take Madison exit off I-94 west, then 84th St. to the fairgrounds. No tents, only RVs. Often noisy. Sites $14. Very full for the State Fair in early Aug.

Country View Campgrounds, S. Craig Rd. (662-3654), 4 mi. west of Big Bend, a 40-min. drive southwest. Take Rte. 15, exit at Hwy. F, turn left to reach Big Bend. Tent sites for 2 $15, full hookup $17. Each additional adult $7.50, each additional child $1.

Food

Milwaukee does not cater to dainty eaters—prices here are small, portions are big. The bohemian **Brady Street** area to the north has many Italian restaurants, and the **South Side** is heavily Polish. Many students and young professionals have lunch on the **Grand Avenue Mall's** third floor, a huge *Speisegarten* ("meal garden") that cultivates reasonable ethnic and fast food places. **East Side** eateries are a little more cosmopolitan, often serving cappuccino in place of *kielbasa*. The UWM cafeteria, on the main floor of the student union, offers good, cheap chow.

Kalt's, 2856 N. Oakland, at Locust on the East Side. Delicious burgers and German food. German beer steins hang everywhere, surrounding a huge suspended moose head. Lunch $2.50-5.50, dinner $7.25-12.25. Live comedy Thurs.-Sun. at 7:30pm, additional show Fri.-Sat. at 10pm. Admission $5-7. Call Comedy Sportz (962-8888) for reservations. Free hors d'oeuvres Mon.-Wed. 4-6pm, Thurs.-Fri. 3-6pm. Open Mon.-Wed. 4pm-midnight, Thurs. 11am-1am, Fri.-Sat. 11am-2am, Sun. 2-11pm.

Webster's Bookstore and Cafe, 2551 Downer Ave., at Webster Place on the East Side. Not yet in the dictionary, but fast becoming a local institution. French-American café for would-be poets. Try the *croque monsieur* (ham 'n' cheese croissant; $4), or the soufflé pizza ($4). Outdoor seating, great bookstore, and friendly staff. Open Mon.-Sat. 7am-midnight, Sun. 7am-5pm.

Abu's Jerusalem of the Gold, 1978 N. Farwell, at Lafayette on the East Side. A wall-inscribed poem dedicated to Abu, exotic tapestries, and plenty of kitsch adorn this tiny corner restaurant. Try the rosewater lemonade. Plenty of veggie entrees, including felafel sandwich ($2.25) and kebab dinner ($6.50). Open Mon.-Thurs. 11:30am-9pm, Fri. 11:30am-2am, Sat. 11:30am-4am, Sun. 1:30-9pm.

Albanese's, 701 E. Keefe Ave., 3 mi. north of downtown, 3 blocks west of Humboldt. Generous portions of homemade Italian food (pasta dishes $5.25-6.25). Open Mon.-Thurs. 11:30am-1:30pm and 5:30-10:30pm, Fri. 11:30am-1:30pm and 5:30-11:30pm, Sat. 5:30-11:30pm, Sun. 5-9:30pm. Closed Sundays during July and August.

Sights

Historic Milwaukee, Inc., P.O. Box 2132 (277-7795), offers tours (usually one per day) focusing on ethnic heritage, original settlements, and architecture ($2-3). Ask about Milwaukee's many beautiful churches, including **St. Josaphat's Basilica**, 2336 S. 6th St. (645-5623), a turn-of-the-century landmark with a dome larger than the Taj Mahal's. Make phone arrangements to see the church, since it's is usually locked.

Riverwest is a racially mixed neighborhood where activists and workers rub shoulders. The **Woodland Pattern Book Center**, 720 E. Locust (263-5001), has a large selection of small press publications. The center also sponsors poetry readings, lectures, and gallery shows that attract local and national artists. (Open Tues.-Fri. noon-8pm, Sat.-Sun. noon-5pm.)

If the center doesn't satisfy your craving for art, turn to one of Milwaukee's excellent museums. The **Milwaukee Public Museum**, 800 W. Wells St. (278-2700), at N. 8th St., allows visitors to walk through incredibly realistic exhibits of the streets of Old Milwaukee and a European village, complete with cobblestones and two-story shops. Other terrific exhibits focus on Native American settlements and North American wildlife. (Open Mon. noon-8pm, Tues.-Sun. 9am-5pm. Admission $4, under 18 $2.) The lakefront **Milwaukee Art Museum**, in the War Memorial Building, 750 N. Lincoln Memorial Dr. (271-9508), houses a diverse collection of Haitian art, 19th-century German art, and U.S. sculpture and paintings, including two of Warhol's soup cans. (Open Tues.-Wed. and Fri.-Sat. 10am-5pm, Thurs. noon-9pm, Sun. noon-5pm. Admission $3, seniors, students, and disabled people $1.50.) Visit the **Villa Terrace**, 2220 N. Terrace Ave. (271-3656), an Italian-style villa on the East Side that's now a decorative arts museum. (Open Wed.-Sun. 1-5pm. Admission

$1.) Also try the large and picturesque **Bradley Sculpture Garden,** 2145 Brown Deer Rd. (271-9509; 276-6840 to schedule a tour; reservations only, two weeks in advance; admission with scheduled tour group $2.50, students $1.50, seniors and children $1). The **Charles Allis Art Museum,** 1801 N. Prospect Ave. (278-8295), at Royall Ave., is an English Tudor mansion with a fine collection of Chinese, Japanese, Korean, Persian, Greek, and Roman artifacts, as well as U.S. and European furniture. (Open Wed. 1-5pm and 7-9pm, Thurs.-Sun. 1-5pm. Free. Take bus #30.) The **Mitchell Park Conservatory,** 524 S. Layton Blvd. (649-9800), at 27th St., better known as "The Domes," recreates a desert, a rain forest, and seasonal displays in a series of three seven-story conical glass domes. (Open daily 9am-5pm. Admission $2.50, seniors $1.25, under 18 and disabled people $1. Take bus #27.) Four mi. west, you'll find the **Milwaukee County Zoo,** 10001 W. Bluemound Rd. (771-3040), where zebras and cheetahs roam next to each other in the only prey-predator exhibit in the U.S. Also look for the black rhinos and the trumpeter swans (*not* together in the same exhibit). (Open Mon.-Sat. 9am-5pm, Sun. 9am-6pm; shorter hours in winter. Admission $4.50, under 12 $2.50. Parking $3. Take bus #10.)

Across the river from the PAC (see Events below), the stone and ivy **Milwaukee County Historical Center,** 910 N. 3rd St. (273-8288), details the early years of the city with many artifacts, photographs, documents, and displays. (Open Mon.-Fri. 9:30am-5pm, Sat. 10am-5pm, Sun. 1-5pm. Free.)

Since beer made Milwaukee famous, touring a brewery proves quite a sobering experience. The **Miller Brewery,** 4251 W. State St. (931-2467), offers free one-hour tours with free samples. (3 tours per hr. Mon.-Sat. 10am-3:30pm. Must be 21.)

Events and Entertainment

During almost every summer weekend, the Milwaukee lakefront throws a city-wide party or ethnic festival. One of the best is the **Summerfest** (273-3378), held over 11 days in late June and early July, fronting a potpourri of musical performances, culinary specialties from 30 restaurants, and an arts and crafts marketplace. Tots should enjoy the circus watershow and children's theater. (Admission $6, $5 in advance.) The **Rainbow Summer** is a series of free lunchtime concerts throughout the summer, featuring jazz, bluegrass and country music. Concerts are held weekdays from noon to 1:15pm in the Peck Pavilion at the Performing Arts Center (see below). Milwaukeeans line the streets for **The Great Circus Parade** (273-7877) in mid-July, an authentic re-creation of turn-of-the-century processions, with trained animals, daredevils, costumed performers, and 75 original wagons. (Call their office for information on special weekend packages at local hotels and motels during the parade.) In early August the **Wisconsin State Fair** (257-8800) rolls into town, toting big-name entertainment, 12 stages, exhibits, contests, rides, fireworks, and, of course, a pie-baking contest. (Admission $4, under 11 free.) For updates on upcoming fairs and events, call 789-5000 and punch in 2116 when asked.

For entertainment on a strict budget, Milwaukee's colleges and universities satisfy with films, concerts, lectures, theater, and exhibits. Call the **Marquette University Information Center** (288-7250; open Mon.-Fri. 9am-1pm; closed during summer; 224-7115 24 hr.) or the **University of Wisconsin-Milwaukee Union** (229-4825; open Mon.-Thurs. 7:30am-10pm, Fri.-Sat. 7:30am-11pm, Sun. 8:30am-10pm). For quality arts performances, visit the modern white stone **Performing Art Center (PAC),** 929 N. Water St. (800-472-4458), across the river from Père Marquette Park. The PAC hosts the Milwaukee Symphony Orchestra, First Stage Milwaukee, Ballet Company, and the Florentine Opera Company. (Tickets $10-30.) The **Skylight Comic Opera,** 813 N. Jefferson (271-8815), at E. Wells St., is well known for its contemporary and classic opera performances. (Box office open Mon.-Fri. noon-6pm and one hr. before shows. Tickets $18-25, seniors $2 discount, students ½ price day of show.) .

Nightlife

If you've got the time, Milwaukee has the bars. By some estimates, there are over 6000 of them here—about one for every 100 Milwaukeans. Downtown bars are more accessible to tourists, but more expensive. For lower prices and less hype, head east to the campus area. (Downtown pitchers $4.50-5.25, mixed drinks $2-2.50; campus area pitchers $3.50-4.50, mixed drinks $1.50.)

Downtown, come in from the cold to **Safehouse,** 779 N. Front St. (271-2007). Step through a bookcase passage and enter a bizarre world of spy hideouts, James Bond music, and a phone booth with 90 sound effects. A brass plate labeled "International Exports, Ltd." marks the entrance. Draft beer costs $1.25, simple dinners $4-5. (Open Mon.-Sat. 11:30am-2am, Sun. 5pm-2am. Cover $1-2 on weekends.) For British-style drinking fun, dip into **John Hawk's Pub,** 607 N. Broadway (562-2137), on the National Register of Historic Places. A glass of beer costs $1.75. (Open daily 11am-2am, live jazz Fri.-Sat. at 9:30pm.) The college crowd dances downtown to a selection of top-40 or progressive tunes at **Bermudas,** 500 N. Water St. (765-0891), at Clybourn 1 block from Broadway. They also sponsor some under 21 college nights. (Open Tues.-Thurs. 8pm-2am, Fri.-Sat. 8pm-2:30am. Cover $2 Fri.-Sat., $4 Mon. and Wed.

On the East Side, North Ave. has a string of campus bars: **Von Trier's,** 2235 N. Farwell (272-1775), at North, is the nicest. Don't miss the ceiling mural of the town of Trier. No pitchers—strictly bottled imports in the lavish German interior or on the large outdoor patio. Bottles average $2.75. (Open Mon.-Fri. 4pm-2am, Sat.-Sun. 4pm-2:30am.) **Hooligan's,** a block or so south at 2017 North Ave. (273-5230), is smaller, louder, and rowdier. (Open daily 11am-2:30am. Pitchers $4.50. Live music on Mon. at 9:30pm. Cover $2-4.) A few blocks down at **RC's,** 1530 E. North Ave. (273-1100), next to McDonald's, you can have a close encounter of the preppy kind. (Pitchers $4.) **Judge's Irish Pub,** 1431 E. North Ave. (224-0605), across the street, has a more eclectic clientele and a tented beer garden (pitchers $3.75-6).

Madison

In the predominantly conservative Midwest, Madison has gained fame for its liberal attitudes and established itself as Wisconsin's intellectual and political center. Despite the city's fall from hippiedom, a mixture of punkers, frat boys, socialists, and Bible-thumping fundamentalists spices up life on the isthmus encompassing the downtown/university area. Four sparkling lakes, wide, bike-safe streets, a huge arboretum, and over 150 city parks take the edge off urban life in this capital city.

Practical Information

Emergency: 911.

Visitor Information: Greater Madison Convention and Visitors Bureau, 121 W. Doty Ave. (255-0701). Open Mon.-Fri. 8am-5pm. **State of Wisconsin Tourist Information Center,** 123 W. Washington St. (266-2161 or 800-372-2737), a few blocks from the visitors bureau and 1 block from the capitol. Open Mon.-Fri. 8am-4:30pm. **Campus assistance,** 420 N. Lake St. (263-2400), near State St. Open Mon.-Fri. 8am-8pm, Sat. 10am-2pm, with longer weekend hours during the school year. **Gay-Lesbian Center,** 255-4297. **Concert Line,** 271-7625. Open 24 hr.

Dane County Airport: 4000 International Lane (246-3380), in the northeast corner of town. About a 20-min. drive from campus. Badger Cab to campus costs $5-6. The "Burr Oaks" bus is only 75¢, but with suitcases it's a long walk to the Packer Ave. bus stop.

Greyhound: 931 E. Main St. (257-9511 or 257-3050), off E. Washington Ave. 10 blocks from the capitol. Open daily 7am-7:20pm, sporadically late at night, but always 15 min. before buses scheduled leave or arrive. To: Milwaukee ($6), Green Bay ($19, students with ID $14.50), and Minneapolis ($39, students with ID $23). **Badger Bus,** 2 S. Bedford (255-6771), at W. Washington Ave. Open daily 7am-10pm. Regular runs to Milwaukee only (6 per day, 1½ hr., $6.50). Usually faster than Greyhound. **Jen Calder Bus,** 217 S. Hamilton (255-0525).

Main office a few blocks southeast of the capitol, but call to find convenient on-campus ticket stops. Trips "directly to your airline" at Chicago's O'Hare Airport cost $14. Buses 12 times per day 3:30am-8:30pm.

Public Transport: Madison Metropolitan Bus Transit (MMTA), 266-4466. Excellent system with efficient service to all parts of the city. All buses eventually converge on Capitol Sq., at the top of State St. Buses operate daily 6am-11pm. Fare 75¢, campus 35¢. **Women's Transit Authority,** 263-1700. Offers free, safe rides for women, 7pm-2am. Service prompt in an emergency; otherwise, expect a 1- to 2-hr. wait.

Taxi: Badger Cab, 256-5566. Ride-share system with $2 base fare, additional 50¢ per zone. Greyhound station to the UW campus about $2. **Union Cab,** 256-4400. From Greyhound station to UW campus $3-4, airport to campus $8-9.

Car Rental: Thrifty Car Rental, 332 W. Johnson St. (255-4297). $16 per day, 16¢ per mi. $65 weekend rate includes 300 free mi. Must be 21 with driver's license and major credit card in your name.

Bike Rental: Budget Bicycle Center, 1202 Regent St. at Charter St. (251-8413). $6 per day, $11 per weekend, $21 per week. Free tour maps. Open Mon.-Fri. 10am-8pm, Sat. 10am-7pm, Sun. noon-5pm.

Help Lines: Rape Crisis, 251-7273. Open 24 hr. **Gay Crisis Line,** 255-4297. Open daily 9am-6pm.

Post Office: 3902 Milwaukee St. (246-1287). A 15-min. bus ride from downtown on the "Buckeye" bus. Open Mon. 8am-7pm, Tues.-Fri. 8am-6pm, Sat. 9:30am-1pm. 24-hr. pickup in the lobby. There is also a branch 2 blocks south of the capitol building, at 215 King Jr. Blvd. Open Mon.-Fri. 7:30am-5pm, Sat. 8:30am-noon. **ZIP code:** 53714.

Area Code: 608.

U.S. 12 surrounds Madison to the south and west; I-90/94 comes around on the north and east. U.S. 151 intersects both from southwest to northeast, running along Washington and Park St., which both go downtown. Madison overflows from a narrow isthmus between large Lake Mendota on the northwest and small Lake Monona on the southeast. Most sights are on the isthmus. **State Street** is a tree-lined pedestrian concourse that runs from the capitol toward the student union, the cultural center of the city. Madison is a cyclist-oriented city, complete with bike traffic lights and bike cops.

Accommodations and Camping

There are several reasonably priced accommodations in Madison, but rooms are often booked, even on weeknights; try to make advance reservations. Inexpensive motels congregate almost exclusively off U.S. 12 near its intersection with I-90/94.

University of Wisconsin dorms: Six hotel rooms in the **Memorial Union,** 800 Langdon (262-1583), overlooking Lake Mendota; 14 rooms at **Union South,** 227 N. Randall St. (263-2600), near the football stadium. Nice, comfortable, convenient. Singles $43. Doubles $47. **Short Course,** 1450 Linden Dr. (262-2270), has standard dorm rooms. Singles $15. Doubles $12 per person. Triples $10 per person. Dorms available mid-March to Sept. for those who have a legitimate reason to visit campus, such as visiting friends at UW. Reserve by phone.

University YMCA (AYH), 306 N. Brooks St. (257-2534), right beside the UW campus. From the Greyhound station, turn left on Main St. and walk 2 blocks to bus stop; all local buses here go to University Ave. Get off at N. Brooks St. and walk left. Room for 4 men and 4 women in run-down, dingy dorms. Questions about the hostel are only answered 10am-3pm and during check-in, 7pm-midnight. $8, nonmembers same price if there is room.

YWCA, 101 E. Mifflin (257-7722), at Capitol Sq. and Pinckney, 11 blocks from the Greyhound station; turn left onto Main St. and walk 2 blocks to the bus stop. Take any bus to Capitol Sq. Women only, though men can be registered with women in doubles. No visitors. Singles $16, with bath $19.

Lake Kegonsa State Park (873-9695), about 15 mi. southeast of Madison off U.S. 51. Attractive tent sites $12.75 for non-WI residents (park admission $6, camping fee $6.75); sites $7.50 for WI residents.

Babcock County Park (246-3896), 5-10 min. from Kegonsa in the town of MacFarland, by Lake Waubesa. Not as big or beautiful as Kegonsa, but showers, flush toilets, and a nearby laundromat are a bonus. $10, electricity included. Open May-Nov.

Mendota County Park, County Rd. M (246-3896), 2 mi. northwest of Madison off University Ave., overlooking beautiful Lake Mendota. Sites $10.

Madison KOA (846-4528), 11 mi. north off I-94 (exit 126). More of an RV park, with no shade and lots of gravel. Tent sites $14.50 for 2, trailer $17; each with full hookup. Each additional person $1.50. Open April 15-Nov. 1.

Food and Nightlife

At lunchtime, carts selling fresh cherries, ethnic specialties like felafel, and blended fruit smoothies fill the square at the end of State St. In summer, buy inexpensive fresh fruits, vegetables, breads, cakes, and cheeses at the open-air **Farmers Market,** Capitol Sq. concourse (Sat. 6:30am-2pm).

Sunprint Cafe, 638 State St. on the 2nd floor. A light, vegetarian alternative. Delicious salads and sandwiches $3.50-5. Great banana muffins 90¢. Doubles as a small gallery. Open Mon.-Thurs. 7am-10pm, Fri.-Sat. 7am-11pm, Sun. 9am-3pm.

El Charro, 600 Williamson St., in the Gateway. If you don't mind plastic plates and cutlery, come here for authentic, tasty, and inexpensive chow. Breakfast $2.75, 4 chicken tamales $3. Open Mon.-Fri. 11am-9pm, Sat. 8am-9pm.

Madison Bagel Company, 309 N. Henry St. Locals and visitors, especially from the east coast, flock here for huge, delicious bagels better than most in the Midwest. Eight kinds of bagels and as many flavors of cream cheese. Plain bagel 60¢, with cream cheese $1.25, bagel sandwiches $1.25-4.50. Open Mon.-Sat. 7am-midnight, Sun. 7am-5pm.

Ella's Kosher Deli and Ice Cream Parlor, 425 State St., halfway between the capitol and the University of Wisconsin; also Lake St. location at 2902 E. Washington Ave. Voted Madison's best deli 1985-89. Sandwiches $2.25-4.50. Hot-fudge fantasies $3. Open Mon.-Wed. 8am-11pm, Thurs.-Sat. 8am-midnight, Sun. 9am-9pm.

Steep and Brew, 544 State St. One of the best of Madison's many new tea houses, offering coffee in its various forms and flavors ($1.50), fruit drinks ($1.25-1.75), and tea (65¢). Outdoor seating available. Open Mon.-Thurs. 8am-10pm, Fri. 8am-11:30pm, Sat. 9am-11:30pm, Sun. 11am-8pm.

Madison's bars are smaller, less glittery, and less gimmicky than those in Milwaukee. However, while Milwaukee's brewing industry shrinks, Madison's only grows as the local Capital Garten Brau prospers. For jocks and cheap drink specials (mixed drinks $2, tap beer $1), patronize **Joe Hart's,** 704 University Ave., at Lake St. (Open Mon.-Thurs. 11:30am-12:45am, Fri. 11:30am-2am, Sat. 6pm-2am, Sun. 6pm-12:45am.) For more variety, walk from the capitol down King St. to Wilson, turn left, and 2 blocks down is the **Cardinal Bar,** 418 E. Wilson (251-0080). (Dance music plays Tues.-Sun. 9pm-2am. Bar opens at 5pm daily. Fri.-Sat. open until 2:30am. Cover $2 Fri.-Sat., $1 Wed.-Thurs.)

For a low-key, smoky atmosphere go to the **602 Club,** at 602 University Ave. (256-5204). (Mixed drinks $1.50. Draft pints $1. Open Mon.-Wed. 11:30am-1am, Thurs. 11:30am-2am, Fri.-Sat. 11:30am-2:30am.) For good live music, head to the **Club de Wash Tavern,** 636 W. Washington Ave. at Francis St. (256-3302), in the Hotel Washington Building. Artists belt out blues, rock, and reggae nightly. (Beer 75¢ per glass, $2.50 pitchers Tuesday nights. Open Sun.-Thurs. 10:30am-2am, Fri.-Sat. 10:30am-2:30am.) **Essenhaus,** 514 E. Wilson (255-4674), at Blair St., claims an authentic German bar experience, complete with live polka some nights. Servers in *lederhosen* and *dirndls* bring Boots o' Beer (about 2 liters each) for $8.50. (Open Tues.-Wed. and Sat.-Sun. 3pm-1am, Thurs. 11:30am-2am, Fri. 11:30am-1am.)

The nightspot that best combines all these different types is the **Memorial Union,** 800 Langdon St. (262-1583). Indoors is the **Rathskeller,** strewn with tables and pitchers of Miller beer ($3.75). (Open daily 11:30am-midnight.) Outside the Rathskeller you'll find the **Union Terrace,** with multicolored tables overlooking beautiful Lake Mendota. Diversions here range from chess to raucous live bands; check *Union Today,* posted daily in the Union, for events. Inside the Union, next to the Rathskeller, is an inexpensive cafeteria. (Open Mon.-Sat. 9am-9pm, Sun. 9am-8pm.) All events at the Union are free; the building is open daily 7am-midnight.

Sights and Activities

Madison is a city of lakes and parks where hiking, picnicking, biking, swimming, and sailing prove the order of the day. Many Madisonians turn out to feed the ducks at the free **Vilas Park Zoo,** at Drake and Grant St. (266-4732; open daily 9:30am-8pm; take the "Burr Oaks" bus). **Vilas Beach,** off Wingra Dr. on the south side of the zoo, accomodates windsurfers and blaring radios. **Wingra Park** (233-5332), off Monroe St., a 15-minute walk from the Vilas area on Knickerbocker Rd., has a more sedate, family atmosphere. Rent windsurfing equipment for $10 per hour, or canoes ($6 first 1½ hr., $2.50 each additional hr.). The zoo, the beach, and the park are all on Wingra Lake, 1 mi. southwest of Capitol Square.

The Memorial Union is a pleasant place in the daytime, where local musicians occasionally accompany those swimming off the dock. For people-watching, there are few better arenas on the planet. Leave yourself time for some **Babcock Hall Ice Cream** (262-5959), made by UW's dairy service students (90¢). Work it off with a run from Memorial Union out to **Picnic Point.** The Union boathouse (262-7351) rents canoes for $3 per hour, $10 per day; windsurfing equipment $10 per hour. (Open daily 11am-sunset.)

Take a free guided tour of the **state capitol** (266-0382) if you find yourself at a loss for excitement (tours every hr. Mon.-Sat. 9am-3pm, Sun. 1-3pm). The ascending triangles of the **Unitarian Church,** 900 University Bay Dr., south of downtown, are yet another example of Frank Lloyd Wright's work. (Take the "L line" or "G line" bus.)

Much like a refrigerator, the University of Wisconsin provides a magnet for cultural activities. Its **Elvehjem Museum of Art,** 800 University Ave. (263-2246), has furniture, graphic, and decorative arts from ancient and modern times. (Open Mon.-Sat. 9am-4:45pm, Sun. 11am-4:45pm. Free.) Over a dozen campus theater, music, and dance groups perform regularly. Check kiosks for campus events, as well as notices for Madison's professional theater groups and movie houses.

The **Madison Art Center,** 211 State St. (257-0158), features changing exhibits and workshops, and sometimes has performances in the lobby. Along with an outstanding modern art collection it occasionally displays 19th-century Japanese prints. (Open Tues.-Thurs. 11am-5pm, Fri. 11am-9pm, Sat. 10am-5pm, Sun. 1-5pm. Donation requested; one paid show per year $3, seniors and students $2.) In the same building, the **Civic Center** (266-9055) is the home of Madison's own repertory company and features dance, musical, and theatrical performances year-round. (Tickets $8-12. Box office open Mon.-Fri. 11am-5:30pm, Sat. 9am-1pm. Take the "Mendota" or "A West" bus.) At the **Coliseum,** 1881 Exposition Center Mall E. (257-5686), more renowned musical groups perform. (Tickets $15-18. Box office open Mon.-Fri. 9am-5pm.) During the school year, the **University Theater,** Vilas Hall, 821 University Ave. (262-1500), offers classical music events for about $4.

Door County

Door County, the beautiful, 40-mi. long peninsula stretching north into Lake Michigan, attracts more visitors every year, and for good reasons. The penisula (technically an island cut off from the rest of Wisconsin by the Sturgeon Bay Canal) hosts famous fishcooking parties (known as fishboils), and boasts five state parks, 250 mi. of shoreline, and eight inland lakes. Despite the recent tourist onslaught, the peninsula remains low-key and relaxed; streets often don't have addresses, and businesses often close "around sunset." For the time being, Door County, like its namesake, is wide open to visitors, providing stores, restaurants, and parks, while managing to shut out reckless developers.

Practical Information

Emergency: 911

Visitor Information: Door County Chamber of Commerce, 6443 Green Bay Rd. (743-4456), on Hwy. 42/57 entering Sturgeon Bay. Friendly staff with free brochures for every village on the peninsula and biking maps (25¢). Mailing address P.O. Box 346, Station A. Triphone, a free 24-hr. service located outside the chamber of commerce, which allows you to call any hotel on the peninsula, as well as restaurant, police, weather, and fishing hotlines. Open June-Oct. Mon.-Fri. 8am-5pm, Sat. 10am-4pm; off-season Mon.-Fri. 8am-5pm. Each village also has its own visitors center.

Car Rental: Phil Young Car Rental, 120 N. 14th Ave. (743-9228). $20 per day, 10¢ per mi. Call a week ahead in summer. Open Mon.-Fri. 7am-5pm, Sat. 8am-noon. Must be 21 with driver's license and a credit card or a $50 deposit plus estimated cost.

Other Rentals: Nor Door Sport and Cyclery, Fish Creek (868-2275), at the entrance to Peninsula State Park. Mountain bikes $7 per hr., $20 per day; 18- and 21-speeds $5 per hr., $15 per day, $30 for 3 days. Open mid-May to Oct. The Boat House, Fish Creek (868-3745). Mopeds $12.50 for the 1st hr., $7.50 each additional hr. Must have $50 deposit and driver's license. Rental includes $5 admission fee to nearby Peninsula State Park. Kurtz Corral, 3 mi. east of Carlsville on C.R. "I" (743-6742). Horseback riding on 300 acres. $17 per hr., children's rides $15; instruction included. Open May-Oct. daily 9am-3pm and 4-6pm.

Police: 123 S. 5th Ave. (743-4133), in Sturgeon Bay.

Post Office: 359 Louisiana (743-2681), at 4th St. in Sturgeon Bay. Open Mon.-Fri. 9am-5pm.

Area Code: 414.

The real Door County begins north of **Sturgeon Bay,** though the county line lies south. Highways 42 and 57 converge, flow through Sturgeon Bay, and then split again—57 running up the eastern coast of the peninsula, 42 up the western side. The peninsula is 200 mi. northwest of Madison (take Hwy. 151 and then 57 north) and 150 mi. north of Milwaukee (take Hwy. 43, then 42, north), and has no land access except Sturgeon Bay. Summer is high season in Door's 12 villages, the biggest of which are **Fish Creek** (rhymes with "fish stick"), **Sister Bay,** and **Ephraim.** There is no public transportation on the peninsula.

Accommodations and Camping

Motels here are uniformly expensive. There are few options outside the $50-70 range, but if you arrive on a slow night you might be able to bargain down to $40 or less. Otherwise, try camping, which brings you closer to the peninsula's beauty.

Those more interested in the peninsula's motels should shack up at **Liberty Park Lodge** (864-2025), in Sister Bay north of downtown on Rte. 42, where you still can sit on the huge porch and watch the sun set over the lake. (Lodge rooms $40-52.) Or try **Chal-A Motel,** 3910 Hwy. 42 57 (743-6788), 3 mi. north of the bridge in Sturgeon Bay. (July-Oct. singles $39, doubles $44; Nov.-June singles $24, doubles $34.) The outgoing manager will offer guests advice; she also runs a museum on the grounds with over 1000 dolls, antique cars, and Christmas window mechanicals.

Camping is the way to go in Door County, and four out of the five **state parks** surveyed (all except Rock Island; open daily 6am-11pm) have sites. Daily park admission costs $6; an annual admission sticker $28. Camping is an additional $6.7-10 (electricity $1.75 extra) at each park. **Peninsula State Park,** P.O. Box 218, Fish Creek 54212 (868-3258), by Fish Creek village, is the largest, with 472 sites. Reserved sites (with showers and flush toilets) are hard to get in high season, but 127 sites are kept open for walk-ins—still, try to come early in the morning. (Sites $10.) Peninsula has 20 mi. of shoreline, a spectacular view from Eagle Tower, and 17 mi. of hiking. **Potawatomi State Park,** 3740 Park Dr., Sturgeon Bay 54235 (743-8869), just outside Sturgeon Bay off Hwy. 42/57, has 125 campsites, half of which are open to walk-ins. Write for reservations. (Sites $8.50.) **Newport State Park,** at the tip of the peninsula, 6 or 7 mi. from Ellison Bay off Hwy. 42, has only 16 sites and does not allow motorized vehicles. (Sites $10.) To get to **Rock Island State Park,** take the ferry from Gill's Rock to Washington Island (see Sights and Activities) and another ferry (847-2425 or 847-2252; $5 round-trip, $3 children) to Rock Island. (40 sites. $6.75. Open May-Dec.)

The best private campground is **Path of Pines** (868-3332), in Fish Creek, which has scenic sites and a truly hospitable staff. It's 1 mi. east of the perennially packed Peninsula, on County "F" off Hwy. 42. (Sites $13, $15 with water and electricity. Each additional adult $2.25.)

Food and Drink

Many people come to Door County just for the **fishboils,** not a trout with blemishes, but a Scandinavian tradition dating back to 19th-century lumberjacks. As much a ceremony as it is a meal, the boil produces billowing heat that meets with the cool twilight air off Lake Michigan. The best fishboils (all $8-9) are at: **White Gull Inn,** in Fish Creek (868-3517; May-Oct. Wed. and Fri.-Sun.; Nov.-April Wed. and Sat. at 5:45, 7, and 8:15pm; reservations required); the **Edgewater Restaurant,** in Ephraim (854-4034; June to mid-Oct. Mon.-Sat. at 5:30 and 6:45 pm; reservations recommended); and **The Viking,** at Ellison Bay (854-2998; mid-May to Nov. 4:30-8pm). Cherries are another county tradition, and each fishboil ends with a big slice of cherry pie.

In Door County, you're better off stocking up at grocery stores and farm markets than sitting down at a restaurant. **Piggly Wiggly,** on Country Walk Rd. (854-2391), in Sister Bay, is probably the best place to get groceries. Another is located at Cherry Point Mall in Sturgeon Bay. (Open Mon.-Sat. 8am-8pm, Sun. 8am-5pm.) **Hy-Line Orchards,** (868-3067) on Hwy. 42 between Juddville and Egg Harbor, is a huge barn full of produce and a few old Model T's. Try the cherry cider. (Open daily 8am-8pm.) Door County wines and fresh produce are sold at **Ray's Cherry Hut,** ½ mi. south of Fish Creek on Hwy. 42. (Open mid-May to Nov. daily 7:30am-6:30pm.)

Al Johnson's Swedish Restaurant, in Sister Bay on Hwy. 42 down the hill and 2 blocks past the information center. Excellent, authentic Swedish food popular with locals and visitors alike. Goats keep the sod roof trimmed. Swedish pancakes and meatballs $5. Open daily 6am-9pm.

Bayside Tavern, Fish Creek on Hwy. 42. Serves serious burgers ($2-4) and a delicious Friday perch fry ($7). Also a hip bar. Beer 75¢. No one under 21 admitted. Open daily 11am-10pm.

The Fish Creek General Store, Fish Creek. The best deal on prepared food on the peninsula. Thick deli sandwiches with potato chips $2.25. Carry-out only. Open May-Nov. daily 8am-8pm.

Kirkegaard's Yum-Yum Tree, in Bailey's Harbor. Floats $1.75, sundaes $1.75-2.50, cones 85¢, beer brats $1.50, deli sandwiches $2-4, and plenty of Danish philosophy for dessert. Open mid-May to Nov. daily 10am-10pm.

Sights and Activities

Door County is best seen by bike; you miss much of Door's beauty by driving. **Cave Point County Park** offers the most stunning views of the peninsula. The park is on Cave Point Rd. off Hwy. 57, just south of Jacksonport. (Open daily 6am-10pm. Free.) Next door is **Whitefish Dunes State Park,** with 10 mi. of hiking through a well-kept wildlife preserve. (Open daily 8am-8pm. Admission $6.) There are small public beaches all along Door's 250-mi. shoreline; one of the nicest is Lakeside Park at **Jacksonport.** The beach is wide and sandy, backed by a shady park and playground. (Open daily 6am-10pm. Free.) You can go windsurfing off the public beach at Ephraim, in front of the Edgewater Restaurant and Motel. **Windsurf Door County** (854-4071), across from the public beach at South Shore Pier, rents boards ($10 per hr., $45 per day; $100 deposit or major credit card required). **Peninsula**

State Park, a few miles south of Ephraim in Fish Creek, has 3763 acres of forested land. Ride a moped or bicycle along the 20 mi. of shoreline road, or mix, mingle, and sunbathe at **Nicolet Beach** in the park. From the immense Eagle Tower 1 mi. east of the beach, 110 steps up, you can see clear across the lake to Michigan and Mike's house. (Open daily 6am-11pm. Admission $5 for cars, $1 for bikes, under 18 free.)

Kangaroo Lake, the largest of the eight inland lakes on this thin peninsula, offers warmer swimming and a less intimidating stretch of water. Kangaroo Lake Road, south of Bailey's Harbor off Hwy. 57, provides lake access; follow the county roads around the lake to find your own secluded swimming spot. The **Ridges Sanctuary,** north of Bailey's Harbor off Hwy. "Q," has an appealing nature trail that leads to an abandoned lighthouse. (Open daily 10am-6pm. Free.) **Newport State Park,** 6 mi. east of Ellison Bay on Newport Dr. off Hwy. 42, provides more satisfying hiking than Peninsula (vehicles not allowed). Newport has an expansive 3000-ft. swimming beach and 13 mi. of shoreline on Lake Michigan and on inland Europe Lake.

For more scenic seclusion, seek out **Washington Island,** off the tip of the Door Peninsula; ferries run by Washington Island Ferry Line (847-2546; one-way for cars $6.50, fare $2.75, ages 6-11 $1.50) and Island Clipper (854-2972; round-trip $5.50, $3 children) both leave Gills Rock and Northport Pier several times daily.

Apostle Islands

Over the past million or so years, glaciers have sculpted the Great Lakes along with the scenic archipelago known as the Apostle Islands. Today 20 of the 22 islands are protected as a national lakeshore. Summer tourists visit the wind- and wave-whipped caves by the thousands, camping on the unspoiled sandstone bluffs.

All Apostle Islands excursions begin in the sleepy mainland town of **Bayfield,** which has a number of crafts shops and restaurants. For live music and good cheer, head to **Bates Bar,** 14 S. Broad St. (779-5356), where grinning gargoyles are imprisoned in wood around the bar. (Open Mon.-Fri. 4pm-2am, Sat. 1pm-2am, Sun. 1-6pm. Live blues or rock 'n' roll Fri.-Sat. Cover $2.)

Madeline Island is the largest and most visited island of the lot, and a few good restaurants line Main Street in its only town, **La Pointe.** At **Beach Club,** enjoy the relaxed atmosphere and a view of the lake. (Svelte shrimp basket with fries $6. Open summer daily 11am-3:30pm and 5:30-9:30pm.) **Grandpa Tony's,** in downtown La Pointe, has inexpensive, quite edible chow (burgers $2-3) and delicious ice cream (small cone $1.50). (Open summer Mon.-Fri. 8am-9pm, Sat.-Sun. 8am-10pm.) Join the bronzed and beautiful aprés-windsurfing set at **The Pub** (747-6315) ½ mi. south of town in Grennke's Inn. Though pricy, the seafood or steak dinners ($12-16) are a treat. (Open April-Nov. daily 7:30am-10pm. Hours fluctuate each month.)

Legend has it that the islands were named in the 18th century when a band of pirates called the Twelve Apostles hid out on Oak Island. Today you don't have to hide to stay there, as long as you get a free camper's permit, available at the **National Lakeshore Headquarters Visitors Center,** 410 Washington Ave. in Bayfield (779-3397). The permit allows you to camp on 19 of the 22 islands. Madeline Island has two campgrounds. **Big Bay Town Park** is 6½ mi. from La Pointe, right next to the beautiful Big Bay Lagoon. (Primitive sites $13.25 for out-of-staters, including state park sticker.) Across the lagoon, **Big Bay State Park** has sites for $10.75, including state park sticker. Camping is also available on the mainland at **Apostle Islands View Campground,** Hwy. 13 (779-5524; in winter 742-3303), ½ mi. south of Bayfield. (Sites $9-14, depending on season.)

Aside from camping, the **Frostman Home,** 24 N. 3rd St. (779-3239), Bayfield, has three comfortable rooms for $25. Down the street and around the corner, **Greunke's Inn,** 17 Rittenhouse Ave. (779-5480), has pleasant, old-fashioned rooms from $28. Madeline Island has several motels. On Colonel Woods Blvd., you can be surrounded by walls of knotty pine at **La Pointe Lodgings Motel** (747-5205 or 779-5596; singles $55, off-season $35). Across the street, the **Madeline Island Motel**

(747-3000) has clean rooms. (Singles $37-41. Doubles $41-$45.) The "high season" summer months find accommodations scarce, so reserve in advance.

A few hundred years ago, the Chippewa came to Madeline Island from the Atlantic in search of the *megis shell,* a light in the sky that was supposed to bring prosperity and health. The **Madeline Island Historical Museum** (747-2415), right off the dock, offers lessons in Chippewa, trading, and logging history of the islands. (Open late May-early Oct. daily 9am-5pm. Admission $1.50, seniors $1.20, ages 5-17 50¢.) **Indian Burial Ground** 1 mi. south of La Pointe, has meandering dirt paths that lead to the graves of early settlers and christianized Chippewa, including Chief Great Buffalo. Towards the end of the day, head to **Sunset Bay** on the north side of the island. **Madeline Island Tours** (747-2051) offers two or three 1¼-hour tours of the island each day (admission $5, ages 5-11 $2.75).

The other islands have subtler charms of their own. The sandstone quarries of Basswood and Hermit Island, as well as the abandoned logging and fishing camps on some of the others, are mute reminders of a more vigorous and animated era. Some of the sea caves on Devils Island are large enough to maneuver a small boat inside. Museums in their own right, the restored lighthouses on Sand, Raspberry, Michigan, Outer, and Devils Island offer spectacular views of the surrounding country. A good way to visit all of these sights is on one of three narrated cruises provided by the **Apostle Islands Cruise Service** (779-3925; tickets $17, children $9).

The Apostle Islands lie off the northern tip of Wisconsin and are easily accessible from Bayfield, off Hwy. 13. They are 90 mi. from Duluth, 220 mi. from the Twin Cities, and 465 mi. from Chicago. Transportation to Raspberry and Stockton Islands, as well as cruises past all the islands, is provided by the **Apostle Islands Cruise Service** (779-3925; $47 round-trip). The rest of the islands can be reached by the **Water Taxi** (779-5153) for a considerably higher price. Ferry service to and from Bayfield and La Pointe is also provided by **Madeline Island Ferry Line** (747-2051); summer ferries daily every ½ hr. 6am-11pm; less frequently March-June and Sept.-Dec; tickets $2.25, ages 6-11 $1.50, cars $5.25). A nearby **Greyhound** station is in **Ashland, WI,** 101 2nd St. (682-4010), 22 mi. southeast of Bayfield. (Ashland-Duluth $7.) The **Bay Area Rural Transit (BART)** offers a shuttle. (Last one at 3:20pm to Bayfield. 4 per day. Fare $1.80, seniors $1.10, students $1.50.) Rent mopeds at **Motion to Go** in the La Pointe Lodgings Motel. ($7-10 per hr., $45 per day. Open summer daily 9am-9pm. Driver's license required as deposit.) Rent fat-tired bicycles at **Island Bike Rental** (747-5442), ½ block north of the town dock in La Pointe. ($2 per hr., $10 per day. Tandem or bike $5 per hr. Open May 27-early Oct. daily 10am-5:30pm.)

The **Bayfield Chamber of Commerce,** 42 S. Broad St. (779-3335) and the **Madeline Island Chamber of Commerce,** Main St. (747-2801), provide helpful information, especially concerning accommodations. (Both open summer daily 9am-5pm.) The **Apostle Islands National Lakeshore Headquarters Visitors Center,** 410 Washington Ave. in Bayfield (779-3397) can answer more questions. (Open daily 8am-6pm; off-season Mon.-Fri. 8am-4:30pm.)

The La Pointe **post office** (747-3712) lies just off the dock on Madeline Island. (Open Mon.-Fri. 9am-4:30pm, Sat. 9:30am-1pm.) The **ZIP code** is 54850.

The **area code** for the Apostle Islands is 715.

GREAT PLAINS

The Great Plains are to be explored as they are lived—slowly and to the fullest. Over 200 years ago, a newborn nation stretched westward onto this land. In U.S. culture, this area remains the territory of Laura Ingalls Wilder and Wild Bill Hickok, of the farmer and the pioneer. Before the Homestead Act of 1862, white Americans saw the plains simply as a huge, flat barrier to be traversed on the way to the fertile valleys of the West Coast. The new law, and the new transcontinental railroad, began an economic boom that essentially lasted until the Great Depression of the 30s, when the fertile "bread basket" became an impoverished Dust Bowl. Since then, thanks to modern farming techniques, the region has regained its status as the nation's largest grain and livestock producer. The land's original Native American inhabitants seem less well-remembered, although their names grace numerous towns, rivers, streets, and monuments. Yet there are more monuments to the "conquest" of the prairie than to the prairie's first dwellers. Native Americans retain ownership of only a small fraction of their homeland, while suffering from the socio-economic consequences of such displacement. Though many Native Americans have begun movements to regain their land, most remain relegated to reservations and natural history museums. And although the U.S. government made the Great Plains the artificial home of thousands, Native Americans in turn have strongly influenced this area, perhaps more than any other region in the country.

They may lack the glamor and excitement of the East and West Coasts, but the Great Plains deserve respect. More than a passing topic for a John Cougar Mellencamp song or subject material for a pickup truck commercial, the Great Plains are the nation's heartland, reflecting the rural, small-town, and agricultural U.S. While this rustic aspect brings frequent dismissal of the Plains as "empty" and "boring," they certainly have a charm, even a mystique, of their own.

Some of the friendliest and most honest people in the U.S., those who live in the Plains possess a great deal of respect for the land; many make their living off it, paying attention to its condition and fluctuations as though it were an extension of their own body. When you stop on a country road or stroll through a field, with nothing but green corn, golden wheat, or "amber waves of grain" stretching for miles, it is not difficult to see why.

Many of the small towns of the Great Plains, scattered in the oceans of crops and prairie at county crossroads throughout the region, have no more than a gas station or general store, a sprinkling of houses in a "plus"-shape around the intersection, and 500 people. Upon realizing how many such towns thrive here, you know that this is life in the Great Plains. With few major cities in the region, small-town and rural life best reflects the spirit of the Plains: insular yet friendly, calm yet hardworking, simple yet enchanting.

Travel

More than a few corn and wheat fields separate the towns of the Great Plains—the cross-country driver can expect to pass many hours watching fence posts go by. Those with the time and the inclination can enjoy the rural life and landscape by experiencing it at a leisurely pace. Yet from the interstates, the Great Plains can seem as boring as the endless stretch of black pavement before you. To truly enjoy the plains, get onto one of the flat, straight-as-an-arrow country roads that runs parallel to the freeway. Here you'll discover the fields and the small towns that make up the true center of the U.S.

Greyhound/Trailways follows the major interstates. In Iowa, Greyhound connects with other local lines that honor the Ameripass, including South Dakota's **Jack Rabbit** and Arkansas' **Iowa Lines. Jefferson Lines,** another Greyhound affili-

Great Plains

CANADA

NORTH DAKOTA

Lake Sakakawea

THEODORE ROOSEVELT NATIONAL PARK

S.D.

Bismarck

94

MINNESOTA

SOUTH DAKOTA

Pierre

29

Rapid City

N.D.

BLACK HILLS

BADLANDS NATIONAL PARK

90

Missouri River

IOWA

Cedar Rapids

NEBRASKA

80

Omaha

Des Moines

Lincoln

ILLINOIS

WISCONSIN

N
↑

COLO.

70

Topeka

Kansas City

St. Louis

KANSAS

135

Wichita

MISSOURI

35

Tulsa

Oklahoma City

ARKANSAS

OKLAHOMA

TEXAS

0   200 miles

0   200 kilometers

ate, breaks the east-west pattern by running a few lines from central Minnesota through Iowa, Kansas, and Missouri to Arkansas and Oklahoma. **Amtrak** crosses the plains states on three routes from Chicago. Since the trains usually run at night, Amtrak is a good option for getting across the region, but not for exploring it or even watching it tumble by.

Car travel is the best way to explore the Great Plains. Rentals are cheap, but beware of extreme heat in the summer and biting cold in the winter; air conditioning and heat are strongly recommended.

If you're **bicycling,** try to plan your route west to east. In the summer, a strong wind blows across the unbroken horizon out of the Rockies. Those traveling from east to west might consider taking their bikes onto a bus for portions of the trip.

The Great Plains have a notably low density of hostels—seven of 'em in seven states—but you'll encounter numerous cheap motels. Local motels, usually the least expensive, at times run as low as $15 per night. The best deals often line the interstates outside of towns. Campsites are plentiful, and car travelers can sleep all over the region in state park campsites.

Outdoors

The "amber waves of grain" originally sprouted out of the Great Plains, and still form a veritable ocean of corn and wheat. Early travelers actually experienced seasickness riding through the waves of wild grass. Three vacation areas bait tourists and break the undulating rhythm of the plains: the **Badlands** and **Black Hills** of South Dakota, and the picturesque **Ozarks** of Missouri. All have extensive state and/or national park services and recreational facilities.

Many visitors to the plains are on constant lookout for an Uncle Henry look-alike screaming, "It's a twister, it's a twister!" Tornadoes actually occur quite infrequently here, and most collapse back into the clouds from which they came without touching the ground.

Many animals make this harsh land their home. Several species of deer lope through the hills, while rabbits and prairie dogs burrow in the sod and geese and pheasant fly overhead. You can see wild bison in some isolated areas such as the Badlands. Most of the wild prairie has been put to the plow, but occasional patches are protected by state and national parks. For information on the national park properties in the Great Plains, contact the National Parks Midwest Regional Office, 1709 Jackson St., Omaha, NE 68102 (402-221-3471).

Iowa

Native Americans named this area Iowa, "the beautiful country," but luckily they didn't see the state from its freeways, which streak straight through the flattest parts of an already level state. To see Iowa's real beauty, you have to turn off the freeway and onto the old roads that wind and plunge through fairy-tale meadows, hills, and thickets. Here, far from the beaten concrete trail, you can cast your line into one of more than 19,000 miles of fishing streams, bike the 52-mile Cedar Valley Nature Trail from Cedar Rapids to Cedar Falls, or travel through time to one of the many traditional communities established in Iowa.

Practical Information

Capital: Des Moines.

Tourist Information: Iowa Department of Economic Development, 200 E. Grand Ave., Des Moines 50309 (515-281-3100). **Conservation Commission,** Wallace Bldg., Des Moines 50319 (515-281-5145).

Time Zone: Central (1 hr. behind Eastern). **Postal Abbreviation:** IA.

Des Moines

If you're expecting downtown Des Moines, the capital of Iowa, to be a friendly, safe, quiet place where the tallest building is the two-story chamber of commerce, forget it. Friendly and safe, yes. Quiet, no—at least not during business hours. Des Moines's workforce bustles in and out of downtown's cluster of mini-skyscrapers. Home to over 50 insurance companies and a world-class art museum and musical events, Des Moines exhibits a growing array of big-city pleasures. However, the capital never loses sight of the state it represents. Every year, Des Moines hosts the **Iowa State Fair**, bringing cows, pigs, and corn to this nine-to-five city.

Practical Information

Emergency: 911.

Visitor Information: Des Moines Convention and Visitors Bureau, in the Kaleidoscope Skywalk at 6th and Walnut St. (244-2444), at the Hub Tower. The office at Des Moines International Airport (287-4396) has information for airborne travelers. Open Mon.-Sat. 10am-10pm, Sun. 2-10pm. **Events Hotline,** 283-2220. The main office (no walk-ins) is at 309 Court Ave. #300 (286-4960 or 800-451-2625). Open Mon.-Sat. 10am-5:30pm.

Des Moines International Airport: Fleur Dr. at Army Post Rd. (285-5857), about 5 mi. southwest of downtown.

Greyhound: 1107 Keosauqua Way (243-5211), at 12th St. just northwest of downtown. To: Kansas City (4 per day, 4 hr., $31); St. Louis (6 per day, 9½ hr., $60); Chicago (9 per day, 8-9 hr., $60). Open 24 hr.

Public Transport: Metropolitan Transit Authority (MTA), 1100 MTA Lane (283-8100), just south of the 9th St. viaduct. Open Mon.-Fri. 6am-6pm, Sat. 7am-5pm. Pick up maps at the MTA office or any Dahl's market. Routes converge at 6th and Walnut St. Buses operate Mon.-Fri. 6:20am-6:15pm, Sat. 6:45am-5:50pm. Fare 60¢, transfers 5¢.

Taxi: Capitol Cab, 282-8111. **Yellow Cab,** 243-1111. $1.40 base rate, $1.20 each additional mi. Airport to downtown $7.

Car Rental: Budget (287-2612), at the airport. $36 per day, 100 free mi. per day. Open Mon.-Fri. and Sun. 8am-11:30pm, Sat. 8am-10pm. Must be 21 and have major credit card. Under 25 add an extra $7.50.

Help Lines: Crisis Intervention, 244-1000. **Gay/Lesbian Resource Center,** 277-1454. Open Mon.-Thurs. 4-10pm, Sun. 4-8pm.

Post Office: 1165 2nd Ave. (283-7500), just north of I-235, downtown. Open Mon.-Fri. 8:30am-5:30pm. **ZIP code:** 50314.

Area Code: 515.

Des Moines lies near the center of Iowa at the intersection of I-35 and I-80. Numbered streets run north-south, named streets east-west. Numbering begins at the **Des Moines River** and increases east or west, starting at **South Union** where the river twists east. **Grand Avenue** divides addresses north-south along the numbered streets. Other east-west thoroughfares are **Locust Street, Park Avenue, Douglas Avenue,** and **Hickman Road.**

Accommodations and Camping

Finding cheap accommodations in Des Moines is usually no problem, though you should make reservations for visits in March (high school sports tournament season) and in August, when the State Fair comes to town. Several cheap motels cluster around I-80 and Merle Hay Rd., 5 mi. northwest of downtown. Take bus #4 ("Urbandale") or #6 ("West 9th") from downtown.

Econo Lodge, 5626 Douglas Ave. (278-1601), across from Merle Hay Mall. Ugly but safe neighborhood. Bus stop in front. Large, newly furnished rooms with cable TV, complimentary coffee, doughnuts, and newspaper. Spa and sauna. Singles $30. Doubles $33.

Royal Motel, 3718 Douglas Ave. (274-0459), northwest of downtown 1 mi. from Merle Hay Mall. Take bus #6. Clean, comfortable, cottage-like rooms. Singles $27 weekdays, $30 weekends. Doubles $32 weekdays, $35 weekends.

YMCA, 101 Locust St. (288-2424), at 1st St. downtown on the west bank of the river. Small rooms, some of which are quite dirty. A convenient downtown location. Lounge, laundry, and swimming pool. Singles $19.50, key deposit $5.

YWCA, 717 Grand Ave. (244-8961), across from the Marriott Hotel downtown. In a safe area. Women only. Clean dorm-style rooms with access to lounge, kitchen, and laundry. Singles $59 per week, doubles $44 per week. No daily rental.

Iowa State Fairgrounds Campgrounds, E. 30th St. at Grand Ave. (262-3111, ext. 266). Take bus #1 or 2. 1600 campsites on a grassy, wooded hill. Very nice—but crowded at fair time. Water spigots at all sites, but no fires allowed. Office open Mon.-Fri. 8am-4:30pm, fee collected in the morning. $8 per vehicle.

Walnut Woods State Park, S.W. 52 Ave. (285-4502), 4 mi. south of the city on Rte. 5. Floods out about once per year; if the front gate is locked, it's for a good reason. Primitive sites $4, with electricity $6. Office open daily 4am-10:30pm.

Food

Cheap, clean fast-food places are located on the lower level of the **Locust Mall** downtown on 8th and Locust St. (246-6010). **Kaleidoscope Skywalk** (286-4988), just east of the Locust Hall, at 6th and Walnut St. in the Hub Tower, also has quick eats. Both restaurant-o-ramas close at 5:30pm; sup here early. **Court Avenue,** 2 blocks south of Locust around 3rd St., has a few reasonable Mexican and Italian restaurants in a renovated warehouse. A popular **farmers market** (286-4987) holds court at 4th and Court Ave. every Saturday from 7am to 1pm.

Spaghetti Works, 310 Court Ave. Old-fashioned interior with a fire truck for a salad bar. Watch out for the 50-ft. green-red-and-blue sea serpent twisting and churning on the wall. Large portions. Spaghetti dinners with salad and garlic bread $3.75-6, lunch versions $3-4. Open Mon.-Thurs. 11:30am-2pm and 5-10pm, Fri.-Sat. 11:30am-2pm and 5-11pm, Sun. 11:30am-2pm and 4-9:30pm.

Babe's, 417 6th St., across from the Locust Mall. In its 50-year history, this restaurant has attracted such luminaries as Diane Sawyer and Bob Barker, but neither of its namesakes, Ruth or the Big Ox. Dinners $8-12. Try the Offenburger (ground chuck, ham, swiss cheese, lettuce, and tomato) for $4.50.

Juke Box Saturday Night, 206 3rd St. (243-0707). Hot spot for fun and drink. Decorative '57 Chevy motif. Aid the digestion process by participating in the frequent hula-hoop, twist, and jitterbug contests. Drinks average $2.50. Happy Hour Mon.-Fri. 7-8pm. Open Mon.-Fri. 5pm-2am, Sat. 6pm-2am, Sun. 6pm-midnight.

Sights

From downtown you can see the green and gold domes of the **state capitol** (281-5591), on E. 9th St. across the river and up Grand Ave., where bureaucrats make the laws that shape Iowa's future. (Tours every hr. Mon.-Fri. 9:15am-3:15pm.) You can catch a glimpse of the glamor and excitement of Iowa politics during legislative observations (Jan.-May) any time the legislature decides to meet. You may even spot Senator Fred Grandy, Gopher of TV's "Love Boat," up on the Lido deck. Take bus #5 "E. 6th and 9th St.," 1 "Fairgrounds," 2, 4, or 7.) Three blocks away, the **Iowa State Historical Museum and Archives,** at Pennsylvania and Grand Ave. (242-5147), is a beautiful new building with three floors of exhibits on Iowa's natural, industrial, and social history, as well as a monolithic neon outdoor sculpture called the *Plains Aurora.* (Museum open Tues.-Sat. 9am-4:30pm, Sun. noon-4:30pm. Free. Take bus #7.)

Most cultural sights cluster west of downtown. The **Des Moines Art Center,** 4700 Grand Ave. (277-4405), is acclaimed for its wing of stark white porcelain tile designed by I.M. Pei. Modern art predominates, but the museum also has Native American, impressionist, and optics exhibits. (OpenTues.-Wed. and Fri.-Sat. 11am-5pm, Thurs. 11am-9pm, Sun. noon-5pm. Admission $2, seniors and students $1.

Free Thurs. all day and until 1pm Fri.-Wed. Take "West Des Moines" bus #1.) Down the street across Greenwood Park, the **Science Center of Iowa**, 4500 Grand Ave. (274-4138), is chock full of entertaining permanent exhibits and occasional traveling exhibits. (Open Mon.-Sat. 10am-5pm, Sun. noon-5pm. Admission $4, seniors $2.50, under 12 $2.) Flapper-era cosmetic manufacturer Carl Weeks realized his fantasy of owning a home just like the King of Britain's after he had salvaged enough ceilings, staircases, and artifacts from English Tudor mansions to complete **Salisbury House**, 4025 Tonawanda Dr. (279-9711; public tours Mon.-Thurs. at 2pm or by appointment; admission $2.) Two mi. away stands the grandiose Victorian mansion **Terrace Hill**, 2800 Grand Ave. (281-3604), built in 1869 and currently the governor's mansion. (Free tours March-Dec. Mon.-Thurs. 10am-1:30pm, Sun. 1-4:30pm every 30 min.)

The **Iowa State Fair,** one of the largest in the nation, captivates Des Moines for 10 days during the middle of August. Traditional events include agricultural displays, tractor pulls, chuckwagon races, and demolition derbies, but many open contests have been added to the fair over the years: tobacco-spitting, rolling-pin-throwing, and hog-calling, to name a few. For information contact the Administration Building, Iowa State Fair Grounds, Des Moines 50306 (262-3111). 24-hr. information line.

Iowa City

Once the seat of Iowa's territorial and state government, Iowa City lost its capital status in 1857 to the more centrally located Des Moines. Today, the University of Iowa dominates the city; its 30,000 students comprise half of the town's winter population. Not only is Iowa City remote, but it is also one of the state's few remotely hip towns.

After the legislature moved away, the **Old Capitol** (335-0548) became the first building owned by the University of Iowa. Recently renovated for the second time, the gold dome now serves as the centerpiece for both the university and the town. Stop by the **Old Capitol National Monument** for a free tour. (Call ahead for larger groups. Open Mon.-Sat. 10am-3pm, Sun. noon-4pm.) MacBride Hall, next door, houses the **Museum of Natural History** (335-0480), on Clinton St. at Jefferson. (Open Mon.-Sat. 9:30am-4:30pm, Sun. 12:30-4:30pm. Free.) Five blocks west of the Old Capitol, the eclectic **Museum of Art** (335-1727), on N. Riverside Dr., houses paintings, sculpture, antique silver, traveling exhibits, and U of I student and faculty work. (Open Tues.-Sat. 10am-5pm, Sun. noon-5pm. Free.) While on campus, you may want to stop by the **Iowa Memorial Union**, at Madison and Jefferson, a half-block from the Old Capitol. (Open Mon.-Sat. 8am-9pm, Sun. noon-4pm.) Both students and ducks frequent the outdoor patios and gardens. Inside, the **Union Station** serves food cafeteria-style. (Sandwiches $1.50-2.75. Open daily 10am-7pm.) Glasses of beer cost 75¢ at the river-level **Wheelroom**. (Open summer Mon.-Sat. 4-10pm.)

At **The Kitchen**, 9 S. Dubuque St. (337-5444), local "cooking artists" concoct dishes in a small open kitchen, spreading a smorgasbord of spicy aromas throughout that canvas they call a café. All pasta dishes are $5-7. (Open Mon.-Sat. 11am-2:30pm and 5-9:30pm.) **Vito's**, 118 E. College St. (339-1393), in the pedestrian concourse just east of the capitol, serves huge, delicious sandiches with fries ($4-5.25) and a variety of salads ($2) in a beautiful wood-paneled and brick interior. The corps of ceiling fans mesmerizes. (Open Mon.-Wed. 11am-12:30am, Thurs.-Sat. 11am-2am, Sun. 11am-10pm.) For dessert, no place beats the **Great Midwestern Icecream Co.**, 126 Washington (337-7243), at the head of the pedestrian concourse. Generous cones cost $1.25 and include a scoop of ice cream. (Open Mon.-Thurs. 7am-11pm, Fri. 7am-midnight, Sat. 8am-midnight, Sun. 10am-11pm.) On Wednesday night (5:30-7:30pm) and Saturday morning (7:30-11:30am), when the cows come home, a **farmers market** (356-5000) is held at Van Buren and Washington next to City Hall.

The **Wesley Youth Hostel (AYH)**, 120 N. Dubuque St. (338-1179), 6 blocks from the Greyhound station, has cots in clean rooms with access to showers and a kitchen. A free medical clinic operates downstairs. (Check-in 7-9pm. Curfew 10pm. Members and students $8, others $16.) The cheapest motel rooms around are in **Coralville**, 2 mi. west of Iowa City off I-80 exit 242. Take the "First Ave. Coralville" bus from the University of Iowa Pentacrest. The **Motel 6,** at 810 1st Ave. in Coralville (354-0030), has an outdoor pool and cable TV. (Singles $27. Doubles $33.) The nearby **Sunset Motel**, 28 1st Ave. (354-4009), has simple rooms with cable TV and free coffee. (Singles $22. Doubles $29.)

Iowa City is 110 mi. east of Des Moines, just south of I-80. The Greek Revival buildings of the Old Capitol area are known as the **Pentacrest.** To the east is a pedestrian concourse filled with trees, benches, and fountains, and lined with restaurants and shops. **Greyhound, Burlington Trailways,** and **Jefferson Bus Lines** share a station at 404 E. College Ave. (337-2127), at Gilbert St., making connections to Minneapolis, St. Louis, Des Moines, and Omaha. (Station open Mon.-Fri. 6:30am-9pm, Sat. 6:30am-8pm, Sun. 6:30am-8pm and 10pm-8am.) **Iowa City Transit** (356-5151) and **Coralville Transit** (351-7711) service the entire area for 50¢. **Cambus** serves the campus area for free. For visitor information, stop by the **Convention and Visitors Bureau,** 325 E. Washington St. (337-9637; open Mon.-Fri. 8am-5pm), or the **Campus Information Center** (335-3055), on the first floor of the Iowa Memorial Union (open Mon.-Sat. 8am-9pm, Sun. noon-4pm).

The **post office** for Iowa City is at 400 S. Clinton (354-1560; open Mon.-Fri. 8:30am-5pm, Sat. 9:30am-1pm); the **ZIP code** is 52240. Iowa City's **area code** is 319.

The Amana Colonies

In 1714, the religious movement known as the Community of True Inspiration began in Germany. Migrating to the U.S. and settling momentarily in Buffalo, New York in 1842, the followers headed to Iowa for a more rural existence in 1855, where they settled in the seven villages known as the Amana Colonies. Initially, the inhabitants led a totally communal lifestyle. The experiment fell through during the Great Depression, and today it is primarily the church that gives the colonies a sense of cultural and spiritual unity. Although affiliated with neither the Amish nor the Mennonites, the Amana colonists adhere to a similarly spartan existence.

In keeping with the old world village feel, there are no addresses in the colonies, only place names. Anything that isn't on the road leading into town is easily found by following the profusion of signs that point to attractions off the main thoroughfare.

Start your visit with a history lesson at the **Museum of Amana History** (622-3567) in Amana on the "central artery." The museum runs a sentimental, overly patriotic, but informative slide show every hour on the half-hour. (Open July-Aug. Mon.-Sat. 9:30am-5pm, Sun. noon-5pm; Sept.-June Mon.-Sat. 10am-5pm. Admission $2, children $1.) The **Woolen Mill Machine Shop Museum** (622-3432), in Amana, gives free tours of the mill. Buy your Amana blankets, sweaters, and clothes here. (Open Mon.-Sat. 8am-6pm, Sun. 11am-5pm. Tours Mon.-Sat. every hr. 9am-4pm.) Across the street, watch artisans plane, carve, and sand wooden creations in occasional open workshops at the **Amana Furniture and Clock Shop** (622-3291; open Mon.-Sat. 9am-5pm, Sun. noon-5pm). In Middle Amana, at the **Communal Kitchen Museum** (622-3567), you can tour the former site of all local food preparation. (Open May-Oct. daily 9am-5pm. Admission $1.) At **Hahn's Hearth Oven Bakery** (622-3439), next door, the scrumptious products of the colonies' only functional open-hearth oven are sold. Simple pleasures include a loaf of bread ($1.25) and cinnamon rolls (50¢). (Open April-Oct. Tues.-Sat. 7am to sell-out around 4:30pm; Nov.-Dec. Wed. and Sat. only.)

Amana is probably best known for its delicious, wholesome food. The **Amana Society Bread and Pastry Shop** (622-3600), across from the Amana Museum, sells fragrant, fresh breads and pastries. A 6-in. honey loaf costs only 60¢, while an opa (5-in. cinnamon pastry) is yours for 80¢. (Open mid-April to mid-Nov. Mon.-Sat. 8am-5pm, Sun. noon-4pm.) Once you've had your ration of bread, go on a free wine-tasting spree at one of the several wineries in town. Wines range from the standard grape to brews fermented from rhubarb and dandelions. When you're ready for heartier fare, try the **Colony Inn** (622-3471), which serves hefty portions of delicious German and American food, such as ham, fried chicken, bratwurst, and sauerkraut. Dinners ($10-12) and lunches ($7) are served with cottage cheese, bread, diced ham, sauerkraut, fruit salad, and mashed potatoes. Breakfast ($6) is an all-you-can-eat orgy of fruit salad, huge pancakes, fried eggs, thick sausage patties, bacon, and a bowl piled high with hashbrowns. (Open Mon.-Sat. 7:30am-10:30pm, Sun. 11am-8pm.)

Most lodging options consist of pricey but personal B&Bs such as **Lucille's Bett und Breakfast** (668-1185), **Dusk to Dawn Bed and Breakfast** (622-3029), and **Joy's Bed and Breakfast** (642-7787). The **Rettig House Bed and Breakfast** (622-3386), in Middle Amana, has been in the family for four generations and the family does not allow smoking, drinking, or, ironically, children under 12. (Singles and doubles $38.50.) The only camping is at the **Amana Community Park** in Middle Amana (622-3732). (Sites $2.50 per vehicle, $3.50 with electricity and water.)

The Amana Colonies lie 10 mi. north of I-80, clustered around the intersection of U.S. 6, Rte. 220, and Rte. 151. From Iowa City, take Rte. 6 west to Rte. 151; from Des Moines, take exit 220 off I-80 east to Rte. 6 and Rte. 151. Stop by the **Amana Colonies Visitor Center,** just west of Amana on Rte. 220 (622-6262; open Mon.-Wed. 9am-5pm, Thurs.-Sat. 9am-10pm, Sun. 10am-5pm).

Amana's **ZIP code** is 52203; the **area code** is 319.

Cedar Rapids

Although Cedar Rapids is the principal industrial city of eastern Iowa, the pace of life in this "City of Five Seasons" (the fifth being the time to relax and enjoy oneself) remains slow. Named after the surging rapids of the Cedar River running through its center, Cedar Rapids' residents meander rather than march, and are rarely too pressed for time to strike up a conversation.

The **Science Station,** 427 1st St. S.E. (366-0968), across the street from the Ground Transportation Center, features hands-on scientific fun. (Open Tues.-Sat. 9am-5pm, Sun. 1-4pm. Admission $2, seniors and children $1.50.) The spiffy **Cedar Rapids Museum of Art,** 324 3rd St. S.E. (366-7503), features the world's largest collection of the works of Marvin Cone, Grant Wood, and Mauricio Lasansky, plus a children's gallery. (Open Tues.-Wed. and Fri.-Sat. 10am-4pm, Thurs. 10am-7pm, Sun. noon-3pm. Free.) From 1870 to 1910, thousands of Czechoslovakian immigrants settled in Cedar Rapids. Take bus #7 to 16th Ave. and C St. to visit the **Czech Village,** on 16th Ave. between 1st St. and C St. S.W., where you can stroll along the historic streets and visit traditional Czech watering holes and bakeries. At the end of the block you'll find the **Czech Museum and Library,** 10 16th Ave. S.W. (362-8500), which houses the largest collection of traditional costumes outside Czechoslovakia. (Open Tues.-Sat. 9:30am-4pm; Dec.-Jan. Sat. 9:30am-4pm. Admission $2.50, ages 8-13 $1.)

Downtown Cedar Rapids is filled with moderately priced restaurants and delis. **Sub King Box Office Deli,** 218 3rd St. S.E., has good sandwiches ($1-4) and 3-in. subs ($1.75-2.75). (Open Mon.-Fri. 8am-5:30pm, Sat. 10am-3pm.) For free chips with your dinner, stop by **Gringo's Mexican Restaurant,** downtown at 207 1st Ave. S.E. Try the beef enchiladas with rice and beans ($3.75). (Open Mon.-Thurs. 11am-10:30pm, Fri.-Sat. 11am-11pm, Sun. 4:30-9pm.) In the Czech Village sample *houskas* (braided raisin bread) or *kolace* (fruit-filled sweet rolls) at family-owned **Sykora's Bakery,** 73 16th Ave. S.W. (open daily 6am-5pm). Try more substantial Czech meals at **Konecny's,** 72 16th Ave. S.W., a local favorite. Sandwiches cost

$1-2, goulash $1; fortunate travelers may catch the sausage and sauerkraut special for $3.75. (Open daily 6-10am and 11am-2pm.)

There are plenty of budget motels on 16th Ave. S.W. The **Shady Acres Motel,** 1791 16th Ave. (362-3111), is a row of cottage-like, spotlessly clean rooms atop acres of rolling hills and huge oaks. Rooms have A/C, showers, and TV, but no phone. (Singles $18. Doubles $22. Take bus #10 to the K-Mart 5 blocks away.) **The Village Inn Motel,** 100 F Ave. NW (366-5323), across the river from the Quaker Oats factory, is 4 blocks from downtown and 8 blocks from the Greyhound station. The large, quiet rooms include cable TV. (Singles $30. Doubles $38.) **Exel Inn,** 616 33rd Ave. S.W. (366-2475), 5 mi. from downtown, boasts clean rooms, comfortable beds, free coffee, and HBO. (Singles $27. Doubles $34.)

Cedar Rapids is 150 mi. east of Des Moines at the junction of I-380 and Rte. 30 and 151. The Amana Colonies are 19 mi. southwest. The **Greyhound/Trailways** station, 145 Transit Way S.E. (364-4167), sends buses to: Des Moines (4 per day, 3 hr., $13); Chicago (4 per day, 6½ hr., $35); and Kansas City (3 per day, 7-11 hr., $56.50). Get around town in **Easyride** buses. (Buses run daily 5:30am-5:30pm; fare 50¢, seniors 25¢, students 30¢, transfers 10¢, reduced fare with receipts from many local restaurants.) All routes stop at the **Ground Transportation Center,** 200 4th Ave. S.E. (398-5335), across from the Greyhound station. For taxis, try **Yellow Cab** (365-1444).

For information on sights, accommodations, and attractions, contact the **Cedar Rapids Area Convention and Visitors Bureau,** 119 1st Ave. SE (398-5009; open Mon.-Fri. 8am-5pm, Sat. 9am-4pm). Or call the **Visitor Info Line** (398-9660).

The **post office** is at 615 6th Ave. S.E. (399-2911; open Mon.-Fri. 8:30am-5pm, Sat. 9am-noon). Cedar Rapids' **ZIP code** is 52401; the **area code** is 319.

Kansas

At the Deep Rock Café in Colby, Kansas, a mid-afternoon gathering of older farmers in baseball caps talk about everything from Gorbachev to their golf games in spare, poker-like voices. World politics affect Kansas growers almost as much as the weather, acting in some ways to deprovincialize this landlocked state. Today, highway signs reading "every Kansas farmer feeds you and 75 others" indicate the Sunflower State's status as the chief wheat producer for the U.S. Kansas also supplies bread for much of the Soviet Union, ironically with the same winter wheat Russian immigrants brought here in the 1870s. This hardy "Turkey Red" crop became one of the few survivors of the drought and duststorms that plagued the Midwest in the 1930s.

Much like winter wheat, immigration has strengthened and shaped this state named for the Kansa tribes, far more than in the surrounding Great Plains. Liberal Massachusetts thinkers founded Topeka and Lawrence in the 1850s, to ensure personally that Kansas remain a "free," anti-slavery, state. After fending off attacks from pro-slavery "Bushwackers" from Missouri, Kansas held the all African American community of Nicodemus, established by "exodusters" seeking opportunity. Kansan activists later helped shape the women's rights movement with the first female mayor. Such politics seemed somehow natural here, in a state filled with influential anti-industrial populists, even including the Scarecrow in L. Frank Baum's *The Wizard of Oz.*

Of course, despite Kansas' relationships with the East Coast and world markets, quirky, small-town rituals persist. The state fair, held in Hutchinson during the second and third weeks of September, is more delightful than dizzying: sure, it has ferris wheels and roller-coaster rides, but the fair also features baked goods, quilting contests, and hog auctions. Unbeknownst to most, Kansas is also the home of the Garden of Eden (at the corner of 2nd and Kansas, in Lucas, just off I-70 on Hwy.

181 in the virtual center of the U.S.), a meticulous re-creation first planted in 1907. (Open summer daily 9am-6pm; winter 10am-4pm.)

Practical Information

Capital: Topeka.

Tourist Information: Department of Economic Development, 400 W. 8th, 5th floor, Topeka 66603 (296-2009). Kansas Park and Resources Authority, 503 Kansas Ave., 6th floor, Topeka 66603 (296-2281).

Time Zone: Central (1 hr. behind Eastern). Postal Abbreviation: KS.

Wichita

When Coronado, the first European to explore the Great Plains, came to the present-day site of Wichita, he was so disappointed that he had his guide strangled for misleading him. Though no one found the mythical Quivira or city of gold, by the 1870s settlers had taken a permanent shine to the place and stubbornly called their home town such endearing names as the "Peerless Princess of the Plains," and the "Wonderfully Worthy Wombat." Today one of the largest aircraft manufacturing centers in the U.S., Wichita lures tourists to its worthiness with a wellspring of festivals, attractions, and rumors of gold.

The **Old Cowtown Historic Village Museum,** 1871 Sim Park Dr. (264-6398), takes you back to boisterous cattle days through the 30 buildings that comprised the town during the 1870s. (Open daily 10am-5pm; Jan.-Feb. Mon.-Fri. 10am-5pm. Admission $2.50, ages 6-12 $1.50, under 6 free.) In the equally worthwhile **Wichita-Sedgwick County Historical Museum,** 204 S. Main (295-9314), posh antique furniture and heirlooms sit beside historical oddities, such as the hatchet used by crusading prohibitionist Carrie Nation when she demolished the bar of the Carey Hotel. (Open Tues.-Fri. 11am-4pm, Sat.-Sun. 1-5pm. Admission $1, ages 6-16 50¢.) Further from the center of town is the **Mid-American Indian Center and Museum,** 650 N. Seneca (262-5221), which showcases traditional and modern works by Native American artists. The late Blackbear Bosin's monolithic sculpture, *Keeper of the Plains,* stands guard over the grounds. (Open Mon.-Sat. 10am-5pm; off-season Tues.-Sat. 10am-5pm, Sun. 1-5pm. Admission $1.75, seniors $1, under 14 $1.25.)

The campus of **Wichita State University,** at N. Hillside and 17th St., contains an outdoor sculpture collection comprised of 53 works, including pieces by Rodin, Moore, Nevilson, and Hepworth. Free sculpture maps are available at the **Edwin A. Ulrich Museum of Art** (689-3664), also on campus. One whole side of this unmissable building contains a gigantic glass mosaic mural by Joan Miró. (Open mid-Aug. to mid-June Wed. 9:30am-8pm, Thurs.-Fri. 9:30am-5pm, Sat.-Sun. 1-5pm. Free.) Take "East 17th" or "East 13th" bus from Century II.

Meat spells meals in Wichita. And if you have only one meat in Wichita, go to **Doc's Steakhouse,** 1515 N. Broadway, where the most expensive entree is the 18-oz. T-bone at $7.75. (Open Mon.-Thurs. 11:30am-9:30pm, Fri. 11:30am-11pm, Sat. 4-11pm.) The **Old Mill Tasty Shop,** 604 E. Douglas, recalls a long-lost Wichita with its old-time soda fountain and spitoons. Sandwiches and ice cream treats cost 50¢-$2. (Open Mon.-Fri. 11am-3pm, Sat. 8am-5pm.) **Dyne Quik,** 1202 N. Broadway, is homey, although grotesquely misspelled and cramped, awfurring catfish with potatoes, bread, and coffee for $3.50 or a 21-piece shrimp dinner for $5. (Open Mon.-Fri. 5:15am-3pm, Sat. 5:15am-1:30pm.)

Wichita presents a Quivira of cheap hotels. Try South Broadway, though be wary of the neighborhood. The **Mark 8 Inn,** 1130 N. Broadway (265-4679), is hard to beat, with clean rooms, huge pillows, in-room movies, and refrigerators. (Singles $24. Doubles $27.) Closer to downtown and the bus station is the **Royal Lodge,** 320 E. Kellogg (263-8877), with a dated but clean interior and cable TV. (Singles $25, with king-size bed $30. Doubles $32.) Several other cheap but palatable motels line East Kellogg 5 to 8 mi. from downtown. The **Wichita KOA Kampground,** 15520 Maple Ave. (722-1154), 5 mi. west of I-235 on U.S. 54, has private showers, a laundromat, gameroom, pool, and convenience store. (Office open daily 8:30am-6pm. Tent sites $11.25 for 2 people, with hookup $16. Each additional person $1.50.) Wichita sits on I-35, 170 mi. north of Oklahoma City and about 200 mi. southwest of Kansas City. **Main Street** is the major north-south thoroughfare. **Douglas Avenue** lies between numbered east-west streets to the north and named east-west streets to the south. The **Convention and Visitors Bureau,** on 100 S. Main St. (265-2800), has a "Quarterly Calendar" of local events. (Open Mon.-Fri. 8am-5pm.) The **Wichita Fun Phone** (262-7474) lists current festivals, activities, sports, and entertainment.

The closest **Amtrak** station is in Newton, 25 mi. north of Wichita, at 5th and Main St. (283-7533; tickets sold Mon.-Fri. 9am-1pm and 1:30-5:30pm). One train chugs daily to Kansas City (4 hr., $49) and Dodge City (2½ hr., $39). **Greyhound/Trailways** provides bus service to the Newton Amtrak station for $6; schedules vary. The Greyhound/Trailways station is located at 312 S. Broadway (265-7711), 2 blocks east of Main St. and 2 blocks south of Douglas Ave. Buses serve: Kansas City (4 per day, 4 hr., $36); Denver (2 per day, 12 hr., $64); Dodge City (2 per day, 3 hr., $20.25); Dallas (4 per day, 9 hr., $64). (Open daily 3:30am-1:30am.) The **post office** posts at 7117 W. Harry (946-4511), at Airport Rd. (Open Mon.-Fri. 8am-4:30pm, Sat. 8am-noon.) Wichita's **ZIP code** is 67276; the **area code** is 316.

Dodge City

Legends haunt Dodge City, the avatar of cowtowns. At the turn of the century, wranglers, gunfighters, prostitutes, and other lawless types used the town as a stopover along the Santa Fe trail: chaos ensued. At one time **Front Street,** the main drag, had one saloon for every 50 citizens. Since most, according to legend, died "with their boots on" in drunken brawls and heated gunfights, their makeshift cemetery became known as Boot Hill. In actuality, fewer people were shot or stabbed in Dodge City in all of its heyday than are killed in acts of violence every three days in New York City. Seems the town had more newspapers (at one time five) than knock-down, drag-out violence, the storytelling competition doing much to magnify a few intoxicated incidents.

Yet for a taste of life during Dodge City's wild heyday, saunter on down to the **Boot Hill Village Museum,** a block-long complex replicating the Boot Hill cemetery and Front St. as they looked in the 1870s. Among the buildings is the **Boot Hill Museum,** which displays a 1903 Santa Fe locomotive and the restored and furnished **Hardesty House,** a rancher's Gothic Revival home. On summer evenings the **Long Branch Saloon** holds a variety show at 7:30pm, preceded by a campy gunfight. (Open daily 8am-7:30pm; Sept.-May Mon.-Sat. 9am-5pm, Sun. 1-5pm. Show $3.75. Admission to museum $4.50, seniors and children $4, families $13; off-season $3, $1, and $13, respectively.)

Catty corner from Boot Hill is the **Kansas Teachers' Hall of Fame** and **Wax Museum,** at 603 5th Ave. (225-7311; open Mon.-Sat. 10:30am-8:30pm, Sun. 1-5pm). Admission to the Hall of Fame is free; the wax museum costs $2. Unless you know an old teacher honored there, the Hall of Fame is a better place to begin a brief downtown walking tour than to browse. Walk up 5th Ave. to Spruce, and head east. At 4th Ave. and Spruce, on the lawn outside the chamber of commerce (227-3119), sits the town memorial sculpture garden, carved by the late dentist O.H. Simpson. Monuments include "Lest We Forget," an enormous, mournful-eyed cow bust honoring the seven million longhorns sent to market from Dodge City during the 1870s and 80s, early evidence that animal rights activism began in the West. Dr. Simpson also sculpted pairs of stone cowboy boots placed toes-up in mock burial form, but most were stolen.

On the corner of 2nd Ave. and Spruce sits the old, round, historic Carnegie Library, complete with stained-glass windows and a reading patio out back, now the **Carnegie Art Center** (open Tues.-Fri. noon-5pm, Sat. 11am-3pm). Walk down 2nd Ave. to Front St. to check out "El Capitan," yet another enormous longhorn cattle statue commemorating the 1870s cattle drives, this one sculpted in bronze by Jasper d'Ambrosi. The trail of quirky, bovine sympathy art continues at the **Hyplains Dressed Beef** packing plant (227-7135), south of Wyatt Earp Blvd., on Trail St. between 2nd and 3rd Ave. Kansas artist Stan Herd, more known for planting and plowing fields to look like Van Gogh's "Sunflowers," painted a wrap-around mural depicting Kansas history, from the first horse introduced by Spaniards in the 1500s to the last wild buffalo, around 1890.

Today, longhorn cattle parade through town only during **Dodge City Days** (227-2176) at the end of July, when the city recalls its past with a rodeo, a beauty pageant, a pancake-eating contest, turtle racing, and a huge festival.

If all of these cow pictures make you hungry (you heartless swine), head to yet another **Muddy Waters**, 2303 W. Wyatt Earp Blvd., for a ½-lb. burger ($2.50), or the less barbaric giant tostada ($4.75), in a very bar-like atmosphere ($1 draws). (Open Mon.-Wed. 11am-10pm, Thurs.-Sat. 11am-2am. Food served till 11pm.) To forgo beef altogther, try **Ozzie's** at North and "A" Ave., for fried most everything including chicken dinners ($5.25). Take Central north from downtown, and go west on the bypass. (Open Tues.-Fri. 4pm-2am, Sat.-Sun. noon-2am.) Inside the Boot Hill Museum you can get all the barbecued beef and fixings you can eat at the **Chuckwagon Barbecue** ($6, ages 6-12 $4; open June-Aug. daily 5:30-7:30pm).

A warning to the carless: except for the Western Inn Motel across from the bus station (rooms $30-40), most motels rustle 4 mi. west along Wyatt Earp Blvd., a quite busy highway that becomes U.S. 50 outside of town. The **Holiday Motel**, 2100 W. Wyatt Earp (227-2169), rounds up cheap, clean, big rooms with HBO, and a nice pool. (Singles $20. Doubles $27. 10% discount for seniors.) The **Econolodge**, 1610 W. Wyatt Earp (225-0231), has lots o' features at moderate rates: free HBO, indoor pool, jacuzzi, sauna, gameroom, bovine, dry cleaning service, laundry facilities, and shuttle service. (Singles $27. Doubles $36.) There are two adequate campgrounds close to town—the highly developed **Gunsmoke Campground**, W. Hwy. 50 (227-8247), 3 mi. west of Front St. (tent sites $9 for 2 people, RV sites with hookup $13; each additional person $1.50) and the **Water Sports Campground Recreation**, 500 Cherry St. (225-9003), on a small lake 10 blocks south from Front St. on 2nd Ave. (sites $9; swimming $1.50).

Dodge City barebacks 150 mi. west of Wichita on Rte. 54, north of the Oklahoma panhandle, and 310 mi. east of Colorado Springs on U.S. 50. The center of town and hub of all business activity is, and historically has been, the railway. **Amtrak** (800-872-7245) runs out of the **Santa Fe Station**, a century-old national historic landmark at Central and Wyatt Earp Blvd. Contact a travel agent, since no tickets are sold at the station. One train daily heads eastbound, and one westbound, to: Kansas City (7 hr., $79), La Junta, CO (2 hr., $54), and Lamy, NM (8 hr., $85). **Greyhound/Trailways**, 2425 E. Wyatt Earp Blvd. (225-1617), serves Dodge twice daily from Wichita ($20.25). (Open Mon.-Sat. 8am-5pm.) There is no public transportation in town. The **post office** meters at 700 Central (227-8616; open Mon.-Fri. 8:15am-4:30pm, Sat. 11am-1pm). Dodge City's **ZIP code** is 67801; the **area code** is 316.

Lawrence

With its wide tree-lined avenues and gracious Victorian houses, Lawrence's placidity hides a stormier side. In the mid-19th century it stood in the crossfire of antebellum disputes over slavery; pro-slavery Missourians repeatedly burned, sacked, and raided it before and during the Civil War. The abolitionist New England Emigrant Aid Company founded the town, and even considered naming it "New Boston." Instead they called themselves "Jayhawks" after a mythical bird that worries its prey before devouring it. Still enjoying the flavor of intimidation, Lawrence, home to the University of Kansas and plenty of former hippies, explodes the stereotype of a conservative Kansas town.

The small but stately **Elizabeth Watkins Community Museum**, 1047 Massachusetts St. (841-4109), displays the relics of Lawrence's tumultuous past, with emphasis on the Civil War era. The bottom floor is devoted to the Kansas **Sports Hall of Fame**, with bios, photos, and mementos. (Open Tues.-Sat. 10am-4pm, Sun. 1:30-4pm. Donation.) On the **University of Kansas** campus you can see Comanche, a dead stuffed horse, who, when alive, was the only survivor of Custer's Last Stand. He and other stuffed animals just sit and stare in the **Museum of Natural History**, in Dyche Hall at 14th and Jayhawk Blvd. (864-4540, 864-4450 on weekends; open Mon.-Sat. 8am-5pm, Sun. 1-5pm; donation). Aesthetes should stop by the **Helen Foresman Spencer Museum of Art**, 1301 Mississippi St. (864-4710), to appreciate a fine collection of Renaissance and baroque painting and sculpture, as well as a provocative cheese sauce. (Open Tues.-Sat. 8:30am-5pm, Sun. noon-5pm. Free.)

The large student population in Lawrence supports several tasty, reasonably priced restaurants most in the granola lover grain. Vegetarians rejoice. The **Paradise Café**, 728 Mass. St., will toss you a veggie-burger made of lentils, oats, and walnuts for $3. (Open Mon.-Tues. 8am-2:30pm, Wed.-Sat. 6:30am-2:30pm and 5-10pm, Sun. 8am-2:30pm.) For the Depression-minded, the café serves a "no more hard times special" with brown rice, pinto beans, and a huge piece of cornbread for just $3. The crowded **Tin Pan Alley**, 1105 Mass. St., has great Mexican and domestic food, plus breakfast anytime. Parents watch out—a sign above the door reads "All unattended children will be sold as slaves." (Open Mon.-Sat. 11am-10pm, Sun. 11am-9pm.) For coffee and New Age books, try **Pywackers**, ½ block north of Mass. St. on 9th St. Also known as the "Unknown Café," it has vegetarian sandwiches ($3.25), pastry, herbal tea, and sweet, enlightened management. (Open Mon.-Fri. 8am-6pm, Sat. 9am-5pm.) A **farmers market** sprouts up thrice weekly at 10th and Vermont. (Open Sat. 6:30-10:30am, Tuesday and Thursday 4-6:30pm.)

At 12th and Indiana, a block north of the student union, sits Lawrence's alternative triangle, with an upstairs coffeehouse, the **Glass Onion**, featuring an international daily grind for 75¢ (open Mon.-Thurs. 10am-9am, Fri.-Sat. 10am-11pm) and the ever popular **Yellow Sub** downstairs. The Beatles serve incredibly scrumptious and addictive subs and half-subs ($2.50-6) amid Elvis posters. (Open summer Mon.-Thurs. and Sun. 10am-10pm, Fri.-Sat. 10am-midnight; late Aug.-late May Mon.-Thurs. and Sun. 10am-midnight, Fri.-Sat. 10am-1am.) Next door, the **Crossing**, 618 W. 12th St., has an especially popular front deck doubling as an impromptu Friday afternoon club. Quality live local bands blare Saturday nights. (Open Mon.-Sat. 11am-midnight. Cover with bands $2.)

Lawrence has riots to offer the restless at night. For great live jazz, enter the **Jazzhaus**, 926½ Massachusetts St. (749-3320; open daily 4pm-2am). The **Bottleneck**, 737 New Hampshire, a block north of Mass. St. downtown, hosts progressive live rock, reggae acts, and alternative music nights. Cover varies with act, from free to $8. (Open Mon.-Sat. 3pm-2am.) The skatepunk crowd heads through the cornfields to the **Outhouse**, 4 mi. east of Mass. St. on 15th (841-8879), for live, all ages punk shows and serious slam dancing. Resident William S. Burroughs has been known to recite lyrics over local punk compositions here. Ask at **Rudi's Pizza**, 12th and Indiana behind the Crossing, about Outhouse times and performers. For culture fiends and the more sedate, A. Drians Taub, **Liberty Hall**, at 642 Mass. St. (749-1912), shows first-run art/indy films nightly. Call for prices and showtimes.

When you feel like spending the night after all this revelry, try the **College Motel**, 1703 W. 6th (843-0131), a short walk uphill from the bus station. Clean rooms come with A/C and a pool. (Singles $25-28. Doubles $32.) The small **Jayhawk Motel**, 1004 N. 3rd (843-4131), farther from the center of town, has fairly clean, sunless rooms. (Singles $20. Doubles $22.) Another option is the **G.S. Pearson Dormitory**, 500 W. 11th St. (864-4884), at the end of Louisiana St. Standard dorm rooms lack private baths and phones, but are spotlessly clean and ultra-secure. Mention that you are scouting the University of Kansas, or are participating in orientation. (Singles $15. Doubles $20.)

Lawrence is a very pretty 30-mi. drive west of Kansas City on Kansas Rte. 10, and 25 mi. east of Topeka on I-70. The main drag is **Massachusetts Street,** short Kansas blocks between 7th and 11th Ave. The **Amtrak** station is at 413 E. 7th St. (843-7172 or 800-872-7245), a few blocks east of downtown. Trains run once per day to: Kansas City (1 hr., $12.50); St. Louis (8 hr., $54); and Chicago (10 hr., $98). Since no tickets are sold at the station, try a travel agency, such as the one at 704 Mass. St. (842-4000; open Mon.-Fri. 9am-5pm, Thurs. 9am-8pm, Sat. 9am-12:30pm). **Greyhound/Trailways** and **Jefferson Lines** share a depot at 1401 W. 6th St. (843-5622), at Michigan, 7 blocks from Mass. St. (Open Mon.-Fri. 7am-5pm and 7-10:30pm; Sat. 7-10am, 2:30-4:30pm, 7-8:15pm, and 9:15-10:30pm; Sun. 7-9am, noon-4:30pm, and 7-10:30pm). Buses go to: Kansas City (8 per day, 1 hr., $10.50); Wichita (4 per day, 4 hr., $24); Des Moines (4 per day, 6½ hr., $43.50); Dodge City (1 per day, 9 hr., $40.50); Denver (3 per day, 12 hr., $69); and Topeka (7 per day, ½ hr., $5). The **Lawrence Bus Co.,** 841 Pennsylvania (842-0544 or 864-3506) runs full service September through May. In summer, the "Union" bus runs only between the campus and downtown, once every hour at 25 minutes past the hour. The "Trailridge" bus goes between 6th St. hotels, the bus station, and downtown. (Buses operate daily 7am-6pm. Fare 75¢.) For a cab, call **A-1 City Cab** (842-2432; bus station to K.U. $3.50).

The **chamber of commerce,** 823 Vermont (843-4411), has listings of historic buildings and a map of town. (Open Mon.-Fri. 8:30am-5pm.) For information on goings-on in town, call the **University of Kansas Information Hotline** (864-3506).

Lawrence's **ZIP code** is 66044; the **area code** is 913.

Topeka

Like Lawrence, its neighbor 25 miles to the east, Topeka was founded in 1854 by abolitionist settlers, who wanted to ensure with their bodies and votes, that Kansas remain a free state. When Kansas was admitted to the Union as a free state in 1861, Topeka became the capital, with only 200 residents.

Today the **state capitol building,** bounded by 10th and 8th Ave. and Jackson and Harrison St. (296-3966), has a beautiful dome and rather hokey murals of John Brown and the settling of the plains. Free tours let you ride in the old glass elevator to the dome. (Tours Mon. and Thurs.-Fri. from 9-11am and 1-3pm on the hr.) Try the cheap sandwiches downstairs. (Building open for meanderers Mon.-Sat. 7:30am-5:30pm, Sun. 8am-5pm.) Those who inevitably have time to kill, or think it's out to kill them, should head to the **Menninger Museum,** 5800 SW 6th Ave. (273-7500), next door to the world-famous psychiatric hospital also founded by Karl Menninger. Along with a fascinating history of psychiatry, the museum's galleries also have insane amounts of art. (Open Tues.-Fri. 10am-5pm, Sat. 11am-5pm. Donation.) Take the #3 "West 6th" bus from downtown.

One block east of the state capitol, **Poor Richard's Café,** 705 S. Kansas Ave., struggles as the only late-night place in town. Besides burgers and delicious shakes, Dick also serves breakfast all day in booths with personal jukeboxes. (Open Mon.-Sat. 11am-3am.) Every 10 minutes from 11am to 1:30pm, a 10¢ trolley runs along Kansas Ave. For a bit more boursin, **Annie's Place,** at the corner of Huntoon and Gage in the Gage Shopping Center, has broiled chicken sandwiches ($4.25), half-pound burgers ($4), and bathtub-sized chef salads ($5). (Open Mon.-Thurs. 11am-10pm, Fri.-Sat. 11am-11pm, Sun. 11am-9pm.) Take the #4 "Huntoon" bus.)

The **Amtrak** station is at 5th and holiday (357-5362 or 800-872-7245). One train goes west and one east daily to: Lawrence (½ hr., $8), Kansas City (1½ hr., $14), and St. Louis (6 hr., $55). **Greyhound/Trailways** is at 200 S.E. 3rd (233-2301) at Quincy, a few blocks northeast of the capitol. Buses motor to: Kansas City (6 per day, 1½ hr., $9.50); Lawrence (6 per day, 35 min., $5); Denver (3 per day, 11 hr., $69); Wichita (4 per day, 3 hr., $19); and Dodge City (1 per day, 8 hr., $38.50).

(Open Mon.-Fri. 7am-10pm; Sat. 7am-4pm and 8-10pm; Sun. 7-11:30am, 3-4pm and 8-10pm.) **Topeka Transit** provides local bus transportation (354-9571; Mon.-Fri. 6am-6:30pm, Sat. 8am-6:30pm; fare 70¢, seniors 35¢). Topeka's General Delivery **ZIP code** is 66601; the **area code** is 913.

Missouri

Missouri, the state whose 1850 "Compromise" between slavery and freedom led to the Civil War, often resembles the South more than the Great Plains. Defined by the nation's two greatest rivers, the state in actuality has very little to do with compromise—Mark Twain (Samuel Clemens) of Hannibal wrote *Huckleberry Finn* as a discussion of slavery, while other Missourians stormed Kansas to ensure it followed in Missouri's pro-slavery footsteps.

Today, the Missouri landscape stretches from the "Missourah" plains in the east and north into the "Missouree" low Ozark mountains in the south, along the way encompassing former jazz giant Kansas City, and St. Louis, gateway to the West. Today the birthplace of "English" poet T.S. Eliot and "Southern" playwright Tennessee Williams certainly lives up to its challenging "Show Me State" motto.

Practical Information

Capital: Jefferson City.

Tourist Information: Missouri Division of Tourism, Department MT-90, P.O. Box 1055, Jefferson City 65102 (751-4133; 869-7110 in St. Louis). **Missouri Department of Natural Resources,** 1915 Southridge, P.O. Box 176, Jefferson City 65102 (751-3443 or 800-334-6946).

Time Zone: Central (1 hr. behind Eastern). **Postal Abbreviation: MO.**

St. Louis

When Pierre Laclede founded this trading post over two centuries ago, he envisioned its future as a great city of the New World. Steamboat trade on the Mississippi and the birth of powerful brewing and distilling industries helped realize Laclede's ambition. Today, as a vibrant cultural center, St. Louis is a pleasure to tour, thanks in great part to renewed interest in preserving historic housing and in developing and beautifying neighborhoods. An important transportation center when it opened in 1894, **St. Louis Union Station** marks a National Historic Landmark, as well as a festive shopping center in the downtown district. Flowers and trees grace the **Soulard Historic District** in South St. Louis, only recently rescued from urban decay. Farther west lie the charming **Central West End** and the many attractions in **Forest Park,** the largest urban park in the country. At the **Riverfront** and **Laclede's Landing,** riverboats rest along the banks of the muddy and mighty Mississippi.

Practical Information

Emergency: 911.

Visitor Information: Convention and Visitors Bureau, 10 S. Broadway #300 (421-1023 or 800-247-9791), at Market St. Open daily 8:30am-5pm. **St. Louis Visitors Center,** 445 N. Memorial Dr. at Washington (241-1764), at Gentry Landing. Pick up the *St. Louis Visitors Guide,* maps, brochures, and friendly advice. Open daily 10:30am-4:30pm. Other visitor information locations at the airport and at Kiener Plaza; hours often irregular. Call **Fun Phone,** 421-2100, for info on special events.

Travelers Aid: 809 N. Broadway (241-5820). Open Mon.-Fri. 8:30am-5pm, Sat. 10am-2pm.

Lambert St. Louis International Airport: (426-8000), 12 mi. northwest of the city on I-70. Served by Bi-State "Natural Bridge" bus #104 (runs once per hr. 5:50am-5:45pm from 9th and Locust St.) and Greyhound.

Amtrak: 550 S. 16th St. (331-3300 or 800-872-7245), at Market St. downtown. To: Chicago, Dallas, New Orleans, Denver, and Kansas City, MO; prices vary. Open daily 6am-midnight. Additional passenger station in Kirkwood (966-6475), at Argonne Dr. and Kirkwood Rd.

Greyhound: 809 N. Broadway (231-7800), north of the business district. A major hub for the midwest. To: Kansas City, MO (4-5 per day, $36); Chicago ($35); Indianapolis ($29); Oklahoma City ($88); Memphis ($49). Airport service. Open 24 hr. Additional station in Kirkwood at 11001 Manchester (965-4444). Open Mon.-Fri. 8am-midnight.

Public Transport: Bi-State, (231-2345 in St. Louis; 800-223-3287 in E. St. Louis). Extensive service, but buses infrequent during off-peak hours. Buses daily, with reduced service on weekends and holidays. Maps and schedules available at the Bi-State Development Agency, 707 N. 1st St., on Laclede's Landing, or at the reference desk of the public library's main branch, 13th and Olive St. Fare 85¢, transfers 15¢; seniors and disabled 40¢, transfers free. Free in the downtown area (bordered by I-40, Broadway, Jefferson, and Cole). The **Levee Line,** the way to get around downtown, also offers free service to points of interest between Union Station and the Riverfront.

Taxi: Yellow Cab, 991-1200.

Car Rental: Cut-Rate Car Rental, 10232 Natural Bridge (426-2323). $28 per day. 150 free mi., 18¢ each additional mi. Open Mon.-Fri. 6am-10pm, Sat.-Sun. 9am-10pm. Must be 21 with major credit card.

Help Lines: Rape Crisis, 531-2003. Open 24 hr. **Gay and Lesbian Hotline,** 367-0084.

24-Hr. Pharmacy: 351-2100.

Post Office: 1720 Market St. (436-5255). Open Mon.-Fri. 7am-5pm. Open 24 hr. for stamp purchase and express mail pickup. **ZIP code:** 63166.

Area Code: 314 (in Missouri); 618 (in Illinois)

The **Mississippi River** divides St. Louis from its unsafe Illinois neighbor, East St. Louis. The city of St. Louis, a small crescent, hugs the river; the suburbs (the "county") fan out in all directions. University City, home of Washington University, lies west of downtown. I-44, I-55, I-64, and I-70 meet in St. Louis. **Route 40/64** is the main drag running east-west through the entire metropolitan area. Downtown, **Market Street** divides the city north-south. Numbered streets begin at and run parallel to the river, with **1st Street** closest to the river. Besides East St. Louis, the most dangerous areas are the Near South Side and some of the North Side.

Accommodations

The motels and universities that offer budget accommodations generally locate several miles from downtown. Buses do serve the major suburban arteries, but the trip back to the city may require an inordinate amount of time.

Huckleberry Finn Youth Hostel (AYH), 1904-1906 S. 12th St. (241-0076), 2 blocks north of Russel St. in S. St. Louis. From downtown, take bus #73 ("Carondelet"), but don't walk; it is just past an unsafe neighborhood. Shabby alleyway entrance but the small rooms are neat. Dorm-style accomodations, 4-8 beds per room. Open doors; guard your belongings. While you're here, ask about the area hikes and tours that AYH sponsers. Office open 6-10pm and 7-9:30am. $10, nonmembers $13.

Washington University: Shepley and Eliot Halls (889-5050 or 727-6337) at the corner of Big Bend Blvd. and Forsyth. Buses #91 and 93 take 40 min. from downtown. Clean dorm rooms offer bare essentials. A/C. Singles $14. Doubles $24. Reservations required. Open May 25-Aug. 20.

Motel 6, 4576 Woodson Rd. (427-1313), in N. St. Louis County. Take bus #104 ("Natural Bridge"). Two hr. from Washington University. Inconvenient, but dependable. Singles $30. Doubles $35.

Food

Although noted for its German and French heritage, St. Louis' best culinary creations emerge from Italian and U.S. traditions. The young and affluent gravitate to **Laclede's Landing** and the **Central West End.** Downtown on the riverfront, Laclede's Landing has experienced an amazing transformation from industrial wasteland to popular nightspot. Bars and dance clubs in this area occupy restored 19th-century buildings; most have no cover charge. Reach the landing by walking north along the river from the Gateway Arch or towards the river along Washington St. Call 241-5875 for information on the landing. The Central West End caters to a slightly older crowd. Just north of Lindell Blvd., for 5 blocks along Euclid Ave., a slew of restaurants has won the urban professional seal of approval. Take bus #93 ("Lindell") from Broadway and Locust downtown.

Farther west, **Clayton** offers a pleasant setting for window-shopping and dining. Historic **South St. Louis** (the "Italian Hill,") and the University City Loop (Delmar Blvd. west of Skinker) offer dozens of restaurants.

Blueberry Hill, 6504 Delmar (727-0880), near Washington University. Jukebox rumored to have a library of 30,000 records. Living entertainment in the Elvis Room every Fri.-Sat. Sandwiches and specialties $3.50-4.25. Open Mon.-Sat. 11am-2am, Sun. 11am-11pm.

Posh Nosh, 8115 Maryland, in Clayton. Containers of complimentary dill pickles under the yellow awning to placate your appetite while you wait for $3 deli sandwiches. Open Mon.-Fri. 10am-8pm, Sat. 10am-7pm.

Amighetti Bakery, 101 N. Broadway, downtown, and 5141 Wilson Ave., in S. St. Louis near I-44. Take bus #95 to Wilson Ave. Order one of Amighetti's locally renowned sandwiches ($4-5) from the express window or join the white-collar lunch crowd inside. Open Mon.-Fri. 10am-3pm, Sat. 10:30am-2pm; express window Mon.-Fri. 11am-6:30pm.

Rossino's, 204 N. Sarah, 1 block south of Lindell, just outside the eastern edge of the Central West End. Take bus #93 from Washington and Broadway. Downstairs, slightly upscale establishment serving Italian food. Pasta with meatballs $5.25. Open for lunch Mon.-Fri. 11am-2pm; dinner Mon. 6-11pm, Tues.-Thurs. 5-11pm, Fri.-Sat. 5pm-1am, Sun. 5-10pm.

Ted Drewe's Frozen Custard, 6726 Chippewa, and 4224 S. Grand (352-7376). The place for the summertime St. Louis experience. Stand in line to order chocolate-chip banana concrete ice cream. Toppings blended, as in a concrete mixer, but the ice cream stays hard enough to turn the cup over and not fall out. Open March-Dec. Sun.-Thurs. 11am-midnight, Fri.-Sat. 11am-1am.

Sights

Visible from 10mi. away, the **Gateway Arch** (425-4465) on Memorial Dr. by the Mississippi River, stands as the nation's tallest monument at 630ft. Designed by Finnish architect Eero Saarinen, the arch celebrates St. Louis' former role as a pioneer gateway. On a cloudless day you can see 30 mi. of city stretching lazily on one side as the "monstrous big" Mississippi flows by on the other. Just in case you wondered, the stainless steel arch is an inverted catenary curve, the shape assumed by a chain hanging freely between two points. A train rides up the monument daily in summer from 8am to 9:15pm; in winter 9am to 6pm. (Tickets $2.50, children 50¢.) Spend your one- to two-hour wait at the **Museum of Westward Expansion,** under the arch. Don't miss (you couldn't if you tried) the *Monument to the Dream,* a half-hour documentary chronicling the sculpture's construction shown in summer 17 times per day. (Film $1. Museum open same hours as arch.)

Sightseers can also take in St. Louis from the water on a cruise with **Gateway Riverboat Cruises** (621-4040), which leaves from docks on the river right in front of the arch. Departures in summer every 45 minutes begin at 10:15 daily; in spring and fall every 1½ hr., beginning at 11am. (Cruise $6.50, children $3.50.)

Facing the arch two blocks to the west stands the **Old Courthouse,** site of the Dred Scott decision, a landmark case in which the court determined that a slave passing through "free soil" where slavery was banned did not subsequently become free. The museum housed here provides a wonderful view of downtown St. Louis.

(Open daily 8am-4:30pm. Free.) From the courthouse, walk up Market St. for about 1 mi. or take the free, frequent Levee Line bus to the magnificent old **Union Station.** Currently an indoor shopping mall, the station nostalgically recalls the demise of the St. Louis railroad in the 1950s.

Walk south of downtown down Tucker Blvd. (preferably during daylight hours) or take bus #73 ("Carondelet") to **South St. Louis.** The city proclaimed this a historic district in the early 70s; it once housed German and East European immigrants, great numbers of whom worked in the breweries. Young couples and families are now revitalizing South St. Louis, but have not yet displaced an older generation of immigrants. Though dangerous after dark, the end of 12th St. in the historic district features the **Anheuser-Busch Brewery,** 1127 Pestalozzi St. (577-2626 or 577-2153), at 13th and Lynch. Take bus #40 ("Broadway") or 73 from downtown. Watch the beer-making process from barley to bottling and meet the famous Clydesdale horses. The 70-minute tour stops in the hospitality room, where guests can sample each beer Anheuser-Busch produces. Don't get too excited about the free beer, however—you get the boot out after only 15 minutes. (Tours in summer Mon.-Sat. 10am-5pm; off-season 9am-4pm. Free, but you must pick up a ticket at the office first.)

Also in South St. Louis, built on grounds left by botanist Henry Shaw, grow the internationally acclaimed **Missouri Botanical Gardens,** 4344 Shaw (577-5100), north of Tower Grove Park. From downtown, take bus #99 ("Lafayette") from 4th and Locust St. going west, or take I-44 by car. Get off at Shaw and Tower Grove. The gardens display plants and flowers from all over the globe; the Japanese garden truly soothes. (Open May 27-Sept. 2 daily 9am-8pm; off-season 9am-5pm. Admission $2, seniors $1, under 12 free. Free Sat. mornings.)

To the north and west of downtown, and worth as much of your time as the rest of St. Louis, **Forest Park,** hosted the 1904 World's Fair and St. Louis Exposition. Take bus #93 ("Lindell") from downtown. The park contains two museums, a zoo, a planetarium, a 12,000-seat amphitheater, a grand canal, and countless picnic areas, pathways, and flying golf balls. Don't miss the **Missouri Historical Society** (361-1424), at the corner of Lindell and DeBaliviere on the north side of the park, filled with U.S. memorabilia including an exhibit devoted to Charles Lindbergh's flight across the Atlantic in the "Spirit of St. Louis." (Open Tues.-Sun. 9:30am-4:45pm. Free.) High atop Art Hill, just to the southwest stands an equestrian statue of France's Louis IX the city's namesake, and the only Louis of France to achieve sainthood. The king beckons with his raised sword toward the **St. Louis Art Museum** (721-0067), which contains masterpieces of Asian, Renaissance, and impressionist art. (Open Tues. 1:30-8:30pm, Wed.-Sat. 10am-5pm, Sun. 11am-4pm. Free.) Near the southern edge of the park lies the **St. Louis Zoo** (781-0900). Marlin Perkins, rugged former host of the TV show *Wild Kingdom,* turned the zoo into a world-class institution. His sidekick, Jim, still probably did all the dirty stuff. At the Living World exhibit, view computer-generated images of future evolutionary stages of humans. (Open daily 9am-5pm. Free.) The **St. Louis Science Center-Forest Park** (289-4400) offers hands-on exhibits and a planetarium projector. (Admission to planetarium $3, children $2. Admission to Discovery Room 50¢.)

Near Forest Park, **Washington University** livens things up with interesting campus and students, as well as a noteworthy faculty. The **Cathedral of St. Louis,** 4431 Lindell Ave. (533-2824), just north of Forest Park at Newstead, successfully if strangely combines Romanesque, Byzantine, Gothic, and baroque styles. Gold-flecked mosaics depict episodes from 19th-century church history in Missouri. (Free tour Sun. at 1pm. Open daily 7am-6pm. Take "Lindell" bus #93 from downtown.) **The Crafts Alliance Gallery,** 6640 Delmar Blvd. (725-1151), north of Washington University, shows ceramic, enamel, glass, metal, and textile works by U.S. craftspeople. (Open Tues.-Fri. noon-5pm, Sat. 10am-5pm. Free. From downtown, take bus #91 on Washington St.)

The **Magic House,** 516 S. Kirkwood Rd. (822-8900), can be a hair-raising good time—place your hand on the van de Graff generator to find out how. (Open May 27-Sept. 2 Tues.-Thurs. and Sat. 10am-6pm, Fri. 10am-9pm, Sun. noon-6pm; off-season Tues.-Thurs. 3-6pm, Fri. 3-9pm, Sat. 10am-6pm, Sun. noon-6pm. Adults $2.50, under 12 $2.)

The second largest of its kind in the U.S., **Laumeier Sculpture Park,** 12580 Rott Rd. (821-1209), cultivates over 50 contemporary works on 96 acres. The park also hosts free outdoor jazz concerts on Sunday evenings during the summer. (Open daily 8am-½ hr. past sunset. Gallery open Wed.-Sat. 10am-5pm, Sun. noon-5pm. Free.)

See the world's only 1936 vintage bowling pin car at the **National Bowling Hall of Fame and Museum,** 111 Stadium Plaza (231-6340), across from Busch Stadium. Even if bowling doesn't strike you as fascinating, the museum provides an afternoon's entertainment; you can even bowl a few frames yourself. (Open May 27-Sept. 2) Mon.-Sat. 9am-7pm, Sun. noon-7pm; off-season Mon.-Sat. 9am-5pm, Sun. noon-5pm. Admission $3, seniors $2, children $1.50.)

Entertainment

St. Louis's heart belongs to ragtime and brassy Dixieland jazz. In the early 1900s, showboats carrying Dixieland and rag regularly traveled to and from Chicago and New Orleans. St. Louis, a natural stopover, fell head over heels in love with the music and, happily, has never recovered. For purists, the annual **National Ragtime Festival** takes place on a riverboat in mid-June. (Tickets $19.50.) Those with thin wallets can try sitting by the boat and listening to the music from the pavement. Float down the Mississippi while listening to jazz on the *President* (621-4040), a five-story paddleboat. (2½-hr. cruise Tues. at 10:30am, Wed.-Sun. at 10:30am and 7pm. Adults $9.50, children $4.75; rates higher at night. Open June-Oct.)

Laclede's Landing, just north of the arch, is St. Louis's evening hotspot. Bars and restaurants featuring jazz, blues, and reggae fill "the landing." Try **Muddy Waters,** 724 N. 1st St. (421-5335), for live music from a band called *Dichotomy* on weekends. (Open Mon.-Sat. 11am-3am, Sun. noon-3am.) The **Funnybone Comedy Club,** 940 W. Port Plaza (469-6692), offers national headliners for a modest price and a two-drink minimum. (Wed.-Thurs. and Sun. $6, Fri.-Sat. $8-9.)

Founded in 1880, the **St. Louis Symphony Orchestra** is one of the finest in the country. **Powell Hall,** 718 N. Grand (534-1700), which houses the 101-member orchestra, provides acoustic and visual magnificence. (Performances Sept.-May Thurs. at 8pm, Fri.-Sat. at 8:30pm, Sun. at 3 and 7:30pm. Box office open Mon.-Sat. 9am-5pm and before performances. Tickets $9-40. Take bus #97 to Grand Ave.)

St. Louis offers the theater-goer many choices. The **Municipal Opera** (361-1900), the "Muny," performs hit musicals in Forest Park during the summer. Tickets cost up to $28.50, but the rear 1200 seats, quite far from the stage, are free. Arrive around 6:15pm for 8:15pm shows and bring a picnic (no bottles). Hot dogs and beer are also sold at moderate prices. **The Opera Theatre of St. Louis,** 130 Edgar Rd., Webster Groves (961-0171), although usually booked, features new and classic operas in English. (Performances Tues.-Sun. Tickets $7.50-45.) Tour the **Fabulous Fox Theatre** (534-1678) for $2.50 (under 12 $1.50; Tues., Thurs., and Sat. at 10:30am; call for reservations), or pay a little more for Broadway shows, classic films, Las Vegas, country, and rock stars. Renovated and reopened in 1982, the Fox was originally a 1930s movie palace.

St. Louis Cardinals baseball games (421-3060; Tickets $5-8.50; April-Oct.) swing at Busch Stadium, downtown. **Blues** hockey games (781-5300) take place at the Arena. (Sept.-May; tickets $10-21.) The Cardinals football franchise headed for sunny Phoenix a few years back.

Kansas City

Set up as a trading post in 1821 by a French fur trader, Kansas City had already sprawled into a rollicking river city long before the time Kansas and Missouri drew state lines. Today, as a result, two Kansas Cities exist, at least in theory: one in Kansas, and one in Missouri. Though no one notices the boundary between the cities until tax time, Kansas City, KS, pocketed with ethnic neighborhoods like Strawberry Hill, is a bit more residential. More audible in Kansas City, MO is Missouri River culture, and its strains of New Orleans jazz off the Mississippi. A 1920s haven for gamblers, prostitutes, stray cowpokes, and musicians, now Kansas City's almost nostalgic love of the river can be felt not just as a passageway for Mississippi Delta culture, but as the thing that distinguishes the Missouri side of Kansas City from the surrounding treeless plains and from its sibling city to the west.

Practical Information

Emergency: 911.

Visitor Information: Visitors Center, 1100 Main St. #2550 (221-5242 or 800-767-7700), in the City Center Square bldg. downtown. Pick up *A Visitor's Guide to Kansas City.* Open Mon.-Fri. 8:30am-4:30pm. Also at 4010 Blue Ridge Cutoff (861-8800), just off I-70 next to the stadium. Daily Visitors Information (474-9600) is a recorded listing of theater activity in the downtown area. Jazz Hotline, 931-2888. Ticketmaster, 931-3330.

Kansas City International Airport: (243-5237) 18 mi. northwest of Kansas City off I-29. The KCI Express Bus (243-5950) departs from airport gate #63 at 6:30am, then every ½ hr. 8am-9pm, and at 11:30pm; bus goes to the Greyhound station, Crown Center, and the Country Club Plaza and takes 45 min.-1 hr. (fare $11). Bus #29 goes to the airport (fare 85¢) but takes much longer and leaves only in the early morning and late afternoon.

Amtrak: 2200 Main St. (421-3622 or 800-872-7245), directly across from Crown Center. Take bus #28, 31, 40, 51, 53, 54, 56, or 57. To St. Louis (2 per day, 5½ hr., $40-60) and Chicago (2 per day, 9 hr., $74). Open 24 hr.

Greyhound/Trailways: 1101 N. Troost (698-0080 or 221-2835). To: St. Louis (7 per day, 4-5 hr., $36); Chicago (6 per day, 11 hr., $49); Des Moines (4 per day, 5 hr., $39); Omaha (4 per day, 3-4 hr., $38); Lawrence (7 per day, 1 hr., $10). Open daily 4:30am-12:30am.

Kansas City Area Transportation Authority (Metro): 1350 E. 17th St. (221-0660; open Mon.-Fri. 6am-6pm), at Brooklyn. Excellent downtown coverage. Fare 75¢, plus 10¢ for crossing zones. Free transfers; free return receipt available downtown. Pick up maps and schedules at headquarters, airport gate #62, or on buses.

Taxi: Checker Cab, 474-8294. Yellow Cab, 471-5000. Fare about $25 from airport to downtown; determine fare before trip.

Car Rental: Thrifty Car Rental, 2001 Baltimore (842-8550 or 800-367-2277), 1 block west of 20th and Main St; also at the KCI airport (464-5670). Compact Mon.-Thurs. $32 per day, Fri.-Sun. $17 per day with 150 free mi., 25¢ each additional mi. Drivers under 25 must add $3. Must be 21 with major credit card. Two-day minimum rental.

Post Office: 315 W. Pershing Rd. (374-9275), near the train station. Open Mon.-Fri. 8am-6:30pm, Sat. 8am-12:30pm. General Delivery open Mon.-Fri. 8am-5:30pm. ZIP code: 64108.

Area Codes: 913 in Kansas, 816 in Missouri.

Quite ironically, almost every sight worth visiting in KC lies south of the Missouri River on the Missouri side of town; KCMO, as it is known, is organized like a grid with numbered streets running east-west and named streets running north-south. Main Street, the central artery, divides the city east-west and cuts north-south, close to the farmers market and the central business district of Crown Center, Westport, and the Country Club Plaza. Remember the KC metropolitan area sprawls two states, and travel may take a while, particularly without a car. All listings are for Kansas City, MO, unless otherwise noted.

Accommodations

Kansas City is a big convention center and can usually accommodate everyone looking for a room. The least expensive lodgings are near the interstate highways, especially those leading from Kansas City to Independence, MO. Downtown, most hotels are either expensive or uninhabitable, with a few exceptions; most on the Kansas side require a car.

Travelodge, two locations. **Downtown:** 921 Cherry St. (471-1266), at 9th St. Take bus #12. Secure rooms in an unsafe neighborhood. Desirable only if you want to be downtown. Singles $34. Doubles $37. **Midtown:** 3240 Broadway (531-9250), just north of Westport. Bright, secure rooms in a lively area, near several jazz spots. Security guard at night. Singles $30-35. Doubles $40.

White Haven Motor Lodge, 8039 Metcalf (649-8200 or 800-722-2892), 4 blocks west of state line, on the Kansas side. Amusing, 1950s-style family motor lodge where even prices don't seem to have caught up with the times. Wrought-iron-fenced-in pool, restaurant, HBO. Free coffee and 5¢ doughnuts in the morning. Singles $32. Doubles $39. Triples $41. Quads $43.

Traveler's Inn, 606 E. 31st (861-4100), off I-435 at I-70 and U.S. 40 at exit 7A. Take bus #28. Pleasant but brown rooms, indoor pool, spa, gameroom, laundry, free cable TV. Incongruous but inviting Indian retaurant. Free morning coffee. Singles $28-32. Doubles $37. Key deposit $2.

Days Inn, 5100 E. Linwood Blvd. (923-0070), off I-70 at Van Brunt exit. Take the "Linwood" bus from Main St. downtown. Newly renovated, bright blue carpeted rooms. Especially kind management. Hilariously small pool. Free coffee and breakfast. Singles $29. Doubles $34.

Food

Kansas City rustles up a herd of meaty, juicy barbecue restaurants that serve unusually tangy ribs. For fresh produce year-round, visit the **farmers market,** in the River Quay area, at 5th and Walnut St. Arrive in the morning, especially on Saturday.

Arthur Bryant's, 1727 Brooklyn St. at 17th, about 1 mi. east of downtown. Take bus #71 ("Prospect") or 8. A local legend. The meat and sauce are superb and the servings are more than generous. Barbecued beef sandwiches ($5.75) are thick enough to stuff any living human. Open Mon.-Thurs. 10am-9:30pm, Fri.-Sat. 10am-10pm, Sun. 11am-8pm.

Gates & Sons Bar-B-Q, Swope Pkwy. and the Pasco. Best ribs in town. Barbecue beef sandwiches ($4) with large enough short end rib portions to eat for 2 days. Kevin has. Even the steak fries are meaty. Open Mon.-Thurs. 11am-2am, Fri.-Sat. 11am-3am, Sun. 11am-midnight. Also at 12th and Brooklyn St. (483-3880).

The Golden Ox, 1600 Genesee. Take bus #12 to the stockyards. Best steak in Kansas City. Lunch $4-6, dinner $10-17. Open Mon.-Fri. 11:20am-10pm, Sat. 4:30-10:30pm, Sun. 4-9pm. The restaurant runs a more reasonably priced **cafeteria** next door—enter through the Stockyards Building. Dine with (and on) local livestock for about $3. Open daily 6am-1:30pm.

Strouds, 1015 E. 85th St., off Troost. Sign proclaims "We choke our own chickens." Don't choke on the incredible fried chicken with cinnamon rolls, biscuits, and honey. Enormous dinners ($7-12) in a weathered wooden hut. Open Mon.-Thurs. 4-10pm, Fri. 11am-11pm, Sat. 2-11pm, Sun. 11am-10pm.

Stephenson's Old Apple Farm Restaurant, 16401 E. U.S. 40, several mi. from downtown. The hickory-smoked specialties are worth the trip and the prices. The accompanying side dishes (fruit salad, apple fritters, and corn relish) are as noteworthy as the entrees themselves. Open Mon.-Fri. 11:30am-10pm, Sat. 11:30am-11pm, Sun. 10am-9pm.

TheProspect, 4109 Pennsylvania, off Westport Rd. in Westport. Elegant sky-lit, light wood decor. Herbivores can choose from innovative salads and pasta dishes. Dinner $6-10. Courtyard open in summer. Open Sun.-Thurs. 11am-10pm, Fri.-Sat. 11am-1am.

The Pumpernickel Deli, 319 E. 11th St., 4 blocks from downtown. Friendly, busy place with simple, no-frills decor. Often sells cheap, fresh veggies outside. Sandwiches $1-2.50, with the jumbo hoagie topping the menu ($2.60). Sunrise special of bagels, ham, egg, and cheese $1.50. Open Mon.-Fri. 7:30am-6:30pm, Sat. 9am-3pm.

Lamar's Do-Nuts, 240 E. Linwood. Amazingly fresh, sweet, scrumptious doughnuts (30¢). Open Mon.-Sat. 6am-6pm, Sun. 6:30am-4pm.

Sights

Built in 1922, the **Country Club Plaza** (known as "the Plaza") is the oldest and perhaps most picturesque U.S. shopping center, located 2½ mi. south of Crown Center. Modeled after buildings in Seville, Spain, the plaza sprouts fountains, sculptures, hand-painted tiles, and reliefs of grinning gargoyles on every corner.

A few blocks to the northeast, the **Nelson-Atkins Museum of Fine Art**, 45th Terrace at Rockhill (751-1278), is renowned for its East Asian collection. Children on tours hush as they pass the synthetic, blue-uniformed museum guard made by Duane Hanson. Whisper in the Buddhist temple, and the Henry Moore Sculpture Garden. (Open Tues.-Sat. 10am-5pm, Sun. 1-5pm. Admission $3, students $1. Free admission to permanent exhibits Sun. Take bus #40, 56, or 57 from Main St. or Crown Center.)

Two mi. north of the plaza is **Crown Center**, 2450 Grand Ave. (274-8444), at Pershing. The headquarters of Hallmark Cards, it houses a maze of restaurants and shops alongside a hotel with a five-story indoor waterfall. Inside, the **Hallmark Visitors Center** (274-5672) fetchingly and with great joy illustrates the process and history of greeting card production. (Visitors center open Mon.-Fri. 9am-5pm, Sat. 9:30am-4:30pm. Free.) Also in the Crown Center are the **Coterie Children's Theatre** (474-6552) and the **Ice Terrace** (274-8411), KC's only public ice skating rink; take bus #40, 56, or 57, or any trolley from downtown ($3). The Crown Center has free **Concerts in the Park** every Friday evening at 8pm during the summer. Last summer's performers included Yusef Islam, Amy Grant, the Guess Who, and the Grateful Dead. Run through a huge fountain designed for running through; you can't have more fun on a hot summer night with your clothes on. Just to the west stands the **Liberty Memorial**, 100 W. 26th St. (221-1918), a tribute to those who died in World War I. Ride the elevator to the top for a fantastic view, then visit the free museum. (Open Tues.-Sun. 9:30am-4:30pm. Elevators $2, students 50¢, ages under 11 25¢.)

Entertainment

Formerly the crossroads of the Santa Fe, Oregon, and California Trails, and an outfitting post for travelers to the west, now nightspots are the only things that pack the restored **Westport** area (931-3586), located near Broadway and Westport Rd. a ½-mi. north of the plaza. **Blayney's**, 415 Westport Rd. (561-3747), in a small basement, still manages to host live bands six nights per week, offering reggae, rock, and/or jazz. Monday is "Blues Night." (Open Mon.-Sat. 7pm-3am. Max cover $2.) The oldest bar in KC, **Kelly's Westport Inn**, 500 Westport Rd. (753-9193), gets rowdy around sundown. (Open Mon.-Sat. 6am-1am.) Next door, **Stanford & Sons** offers one of the only live comedy shows in town. (Showtimes Mon.-Thurs. 9pm, Fri.-Sat. at 8 and 11pm. Cover Mon.-Thurs. $5, Fri.-Sat. $7. Must be 21.)

There is no shortage of jazz in KC. In the 20s, the city was part of a famous triangle that included Chicago and New Orleans. Count Basie and his "Kansas City Sound" reigned at the River City bars, while Charlie "Yardbird" Parker, who gained his fame in New York, soared in the open environment. Stop by the **Grand Emporium Hotel and Saloon**, 3832 Main St. (531-1504), to hear jazz bands play on Friday and Saturday; weekdays feature rock, blues, and reggae bands. (Open Mon.-Sat. 9am-3am.) **Kiki's Bon-Ton Maison**, 1515 Westport Rd. (931-9417), features KC's best in-house soul band, the Bon-Ton Soul Accordian Band on Wednesdays 9-11pm and Saturdays at 10:30pm. Kiki's serves up cajun food with the zydeco and hosts the annual Crawfish Festival (complete with a "Crawfish Look-Alike Contest") the last weekend in May. (Open Mon.-Thurs. 11am-midnight, Fri.-Sat. 11am-1am. Food until 10pm.) You'll find earthly paradise at **Milton's Jazz**, 805 W. 39th St. (753-9476). The late Miltie once sponsored Basie, Parker, and other jazz greats. (Live music Fri.-Sat. 8pm-1am. Cover $2.) **City Lights**, 7425 Broadway (444-6969) may not be as nostalgic, but it is dependable and fun with live bands Tuesday to Saturday 9pm to 1am. (Open Mon.-Sat. 4pm-1:30am. Cover $4.)

Café Lulu, 1706 W. 39th St. on the Kansas side (931-5858) hosts a "Spoken Word" reading series and performance art on Monday nights from 9-11pm. Meals are served until midnight, with no cover. The **Human Observation Lab** (the "Lab"), 1012 McGee (842-1655), presents itself eponymously as a forum for in-house art bands, performers, and the just plain weird. Bring a writing utensil. The door is always open, but officially opens at 7:30pm. Cover varies. Get ahold of *KC Pitch* magazine (561-0601) for current listings of local music and club happenings.

Sports fans will be bowled over by the massive **Harry S. Truman Sports Complex** and even Howard Cosell could not muster enough inscrutable superlatives to describe **Arrowhead Stadium**, 1 Arrowhead Dr. (924-3333), home of the Chiefs football team (924-9400). Next door, the water-fountained, artificial turf-clad wonder of **Royals Stadium**, 1 Royal Way (921-8000), is home to the Royals baseball team. The stadium express bus runs from downtown on game days.

Nebraska

The Platte River is the source of Nebraska's name, which comes from an Omaha word meaning "river in the flatness." Many of Nebraska's place names, such as Tecumseh, Ogallala, and Otoe recall the people who populated this territory prior to European settlement. For almost two decades after the Homestead Act of 1862, settlers fought with Crazy Horse, Red Cloud, and Dull Knife, turning Nebraska into a battlefield. Today agriculture dominates the harsh landscape of Nebraska, which still manages to produce much of the food consumed by the other 49 states.

Practical Information

Capital: Lincoln.

Population: 1,605,900.

Tourist Information: **Nebraska Department of Economic Development**, P.O. Box 94666, Lincoln 68509 (471-3796). **Nebraska Game and Parks Commission**, 2200 N. 33rd St., Lincoln 68503 (464-0641). Permits for campgrounds and park areas ($10). Open Mon.-Fri. 8am-5pm.

Time Zone: Central (1 hr. behind Eastern) and Mountain (2 hr. behind Eastern). **Postal Abbreviation:** NE.

Omaha

Omaha, just across the Missouri River from Council Bluffs, Iowa, is an old packing house and railroad town. Flanked to the west by corn and cow country, to the south by apple orchards, and tangled with Union Pacific Railroad lines, Omaha is the crossroads for many of our nation's calories. History has seen immigrants from Bohemia, freed African slaves, and, more recently, Mexican migrant workers, all come to Omaha for jobs in the packing houses. Evidence of these ethnic communities appears most prominently on grocery shelves where corn tortillas with Spanish labels sit alongside bags of Vic's popcorn and Czechoslovakian liver dumplings. A nearby cemetery remembers the winter of 1846, when the Mormons passed through on their way to Utah. Ironically, it is the history of Native Americans in Omaha which is most elusive; mostly in the place names of the region can their influence be seen.

Practical Information

Emergency: 911.

Visitor Information: **Nebraska/Omaha Tourist Information Center**, 1212 Deer Park Blvd. (595-3990), at I-80 and 13th St. (Rte. 73/75). Take bus #6 from downtown. Open April-

Oct. daily 9am-5pm. **Douglas County Tourism and Convention Bureau,** 1819 Farnam St. #1200 (444-4660), in the Omaha-Douglas Civic Center. City bus schedules in the basement, behind the cafeteria area. Open daily 8:30am-4:30pm. **Mayor's Commission on the Handicapped,** 444-5021. Information on transportation, access, and services. Open Mon.-Fri. 8am-4:30pm. **Events Hotline,** 444-6800.

Amtrak: 1003 S. 9th St. (342-1501 or 800-872-7245). One train per day to: Chicago (9 hr., $93); Denver (9 hr., $98); Salt Lake City (24 hr., $164). Open Mon.-Fri. 6:30am-3:30pm and 10:30pm-7:30am, Sat.-Sun. 10:30pm-7:30am.

Greyhound: 1601 Jackson (341-1900). To: Kansas City (3 per day, 4½ hr., $38.50); Chicago (8 per day, 12 hr., $69); Denver (4 per day, 10½-12 hr., $69). Open 24 hr.

Public Transport: Metro Area Transit (MAT), 2615 Cuming St. (341-0800). Maps available at the Park Fair Mall, 16th and Douglas near the Greyhound station. Open Mon.-Sat. 6am-9pm, Sun. 7am-9pm. Buses have thorough service for downtown, Creighton University area, North Omaha, and 24th St., but don't reach as far as M street and 107th, where several budget hotels are located. Fare 75¢, transfers 5¢. Bus #28 ("Airport") from 10th St. serves the airport twice early in the morning and twice late in the afternoon, in case you suddenly have to flee by air.

Taxi: Happy Cab, 339-0110. $1.20 first mile, $1 each additional mile. Fare to airport $7.

Car Rental: Rent-a-Wreck, 501 N. 17th St. (344-2001), at Cass St. $18 per day with 50 free mi., 10¢ each additional mi. Open Mon.-Sat. 7:30am-6pm. Must be 21 with major credit card or $100 deposit.

Help Lines: Crisis Line, Inc., 341-9111 or 341-9112. **Rape Crisis,** 345-7273. **Gay/Lesbian Crisis Line** (in Lincoln), 475-5710.

Time Zone: Central (1 hr. behind Eastern).

Post Office: 1124 Pacific St. (348-2895). Open Mon.-Fri. 7:30am-5pm, Sat. 7:30am-noon. **ZIP code:** 68108.

Area Code: 402.

Omaha sits along the Missouri River, halfway up Nebraska's eastern border, about 125 mi. west of Des Moines on I-80. I-80 cuts east-west through southern greater Omaha, then dips down to the southwest for a 50-mi. leg to Lincoln. I-480 runs along the western edge of downtown to join I-80. I-29 runs north-south on the western side of the Missouri River. Numbered north-south streets begin at the river; named roads run east-west. **Dodge Street** divides the city north-south. When night falls, avoid 24th St., and stay close to Creighton University at 25th and California. However, the area from 10th to 19th St. between Dodge and Jackson is considered safe.

Accommodations and Camping

Many budget motels are off the L or 84th St. exits from I-80, 6½ mi. southwest of downtown. Buses #11, 21, and 55 service the area.

Budgetel Inn, 10760 M St. (592-5200) near 108th. Bus #55 will get you only as close as 108th and Q. Best value in town. Free continental breakfast delivered to room, which already has coffee and coffeemaker. Singles $28-34, with kingsize bed $29-36. Doubles $30-36.

Motel 6, 10708 M St. (331-3161), adjacent to the Budgetel Inn. Basic bed-and-Bible rooms, with HBO and phone. Singles $26. Doubles $32.

Super 8, 7111 Spring St. (390-0700), near 72nd and Grover St. Take bus #11 or 21. Non-smoking rooms, cable TV. Restaurants nearby, though you can stay in and enjoy the popcorn vending machine. Singles $31. Doubles $37. Also at 108th and L St. (339-2250; singles $30, doubles $37).

Econolodge, 2211 Douglas St. (345-9565 or 800-446-6900). Ideal for the carless. Secure downtown location compromised by slightly frayed neighborhood. Free coffee and doughnuts in the morning. Singles $32. Doubles $42.

Bellevue Campground, at Haworth Park (291-3379), on the Missouri River 10 mi. from downtown at Hwy. 370. Take the infrequent bus #50 ("Bellevue") from 17th and Dodge to Mission and Franklin, and walk down Mission. Showers, toilets, and shelters. Tent sites $4, with hookup $7. Free water. Open daily 6am-10pm, but stragglers can enter after hours if they're quiet.

Food and Nightlife

Once a warehouse district, the **Old Market**, on Howard St. between 10th and 13th, has been converted into a real estate developer's dream with quaint shops, restaurants, and bars. **Coyote's Bar and Grill**, 1217 Howard St. (345-2047) howls with fun Tex-Mex appetizers like "Holy Avocado" ($3.75), salads, chili, and staggeringly large burgers ($3.50-4) in hip wood and bevelled glass surroundings. (Open Mon.-Thurs. 11am-11pm, Fri.-Sat. 5pm-10pm.) **Trini's**, 1020 Howard St. (346-8400) marinates, sautées, and composes profoundly authentic Mexican and vegetarian food in an elegant, candlelit cavern. Menu translated into English; dinner $2.50-7. (Open Mon.-Thurs. 11:30am-10pm, Fri.-Sat. 11:30am-11pm, Sun. 1-8pm.) The **Bohemian Café**, 1406 S. 13th St. in South Omaha's old Slavic neighborhood, sells shirts to loyal locals that read "Czech us out." Highly carnivore-friendly fare, accompanied by onions and potatoes, all under $6. (Open daily 11am-10pm.) **Joe Tess' Place**, 5424 S. 24th St., at U St. in South Omaha (take bus #6 from Farnam and 16th) is renowned for its fresh, fried carp and catfish served with thin-sliced potatoes and rye bread. Entrees $3-7. (Open Mon.-Thurs. 10:30am-11pm, Fri.-Sat. 10:30am-midnight, Sun. 11am-11pm.) If you want *real* Nebraska fare, just walk into any movie theatre and ask for popcorn.

Punk, progressive rock, and Irish folk music have each somehow managed to find venues in Omaha. Check out the window of the **Antiquarium Bookstore**, 1215 Harney in the Old Market, for information on coming shows. For tickets, call Tix-Ticket Clearinghouse at 342-7107. **Sokol Hall**, at 13th and Martha (346-9802), headlines local and national punk and progressive rock bands. (Tickets around $5.) In the Old Market area, head to the **Howard St. Tavern**, 1112 Howard St. (341-0433). The local crowds and good music create a pleasant atmosphere. Live music downstairs; 60s and 70s music upstairs. (Open Mon.-Sat. 3pm-1am, Sun. 7pm-1am. Cover $2-3.50.) **Omaha's Magic Theater**, 1417 Farnam St. (346-1227; call Mon.-Fri. 9am-5:30pm), is devoted to the development of new American musicals. (Evening performances Fri.-Mon. Tickets $5, seniors and students $2.)

The best dance club in town, **The Max**, 1417 Jackson (346-4110), caters to gay men with five bars, a disco dance floor, DJ, patio, and fountains. (Open daily 4pm-1am. Cover $3.) Another gay bar, **The Run**, 1715 Leavenworth (449-8703) is popular for its "after hours" weekends from 1:35am-3:45am, when $4 gets you enough coffee, soda, and music to last the night. (Otherwise open daily 2pm-1am. No cover.) **Chesterfield**, 1950 St. Mary's Ave. (342-1244) is a lesbian bar, with occasional entertainment. (Open daily 3pm-1am.)

Sights

Omaha's **Joslyn Art Museum**, 2200 Dodge St. (342-3300), is a three-story art deco landmark with a fantastic courtyard and an excellent display of Native American blankets, baskets, and other artifacts. In the summer, they host "Jazz on the Green" each Thursday from 7-9pm. (Open Tues.-Wed, Fri.-Sat. 10am-5pm, Thurs. 10am-9pm, Sun. 1-5pm. Admission $2, seniors and ages under 12 $1. Free Sat. 10am-noon.)

The **Western Heritage Museum**, 801 S. 10th St. (444-5071), has an historic schoolroom and soda fountain among its exhibits, but its main attraction is its architecture. Built in the old Union Pacific Railroad Station in 1929, the museum glitters with kitsch. (Open May 27-Sept. 2 daily 8am-8pm; off-season Tues.-Sat. 10am-5pm, Sun. 1-5pm. Admission $2, ages under 12 $1.) Housed in the historic Nebraska Telephone Building, the **Great Plains Black Museum**, 2213 Lake St. (345-2212), presents the history of African American migration to the Great Plains in photographs, musical instruments, documents, dolls, and quilts. Especially compelling are the portraits and biographies of the first African American women to settle in Nebraska, as well as the exhibit commemorating the life of Malcolm X, born Malcolm Little in Omaha in 1925. (Open Mon.-Fri. 8am-4:30pm. Donation $2. Take bus #8 from 19th and Farnam, or #9 from Dodge.)

The **Omaha Children's Museum**, 551 S. 18th St. (342-6164), features hands-on science and art exhibits. (Open June-Aug. Tues.-Sat. 10am-5pm, Sun. 1-5pm; Sept.-May Tues.-Fri. 2:30-5pm, Sat. 10am-5pm, Sun. 1-5pm.) The **Henry Doorly Zoo**, 3701 S. 10th St. (733-8400), at Deer Park Blvd., is home to white Siberian tigers and the largest enclosed aviary in North America. (Open April-Oct. Mon.-Fri. 9:30am-5pm, Sat.-Sun. 9:30am-6pm; in winter daily 9:30am-4pm, Mutual Education Building and aquarium only. Admission $5, children $2.50.)

Lincoln

From nearly 20 miles away the Nebraska State Capitol is visible, soaring far above the city and farmlands below. The "Tower on the Plains," remarkable for its streamlined exterior and detailed interior, is an appropriate centerpiece for Lincoln, itself an oasis of learning, legislating, and culture on the prairie.

In 1867, Lancaster settlers renamed their outpost Lincoln, in honor of the recently deceased president; soon after the fledgling city became the state's capital. This hospitable pioneer town is now the seat of the nation's only one-house state legislature, and home of the "Big Red" Cornhuskers, the University of Nebraska's beloved football team.

Practical Information

Emergency: 911.

Visitor Information: Tourist Offices, 1221 N St. #606 (477-6300). Open Mon.-Fri. 8am-4:45pm. Also at 105 S. 9th St. (477-6300), at O St. downtown. Open late May-Sept. daily 9am-5pm. **League of Human Dignity,** 1423 O St. (471-7871). Advice and aid, including local transportation for disabled persons. Open Mon.-Fri. 8am-5pm. **24-hr. Visitor Information Line,** 477-6300.

Amtrak: 201 N. 7th St. (476-1295 or 800-872-7245). To Omaha (1 per day, 1 hr., $13) and Denver (1 per day, 7½ hr., $96). Open daily 11pm-7am, Mon.-Wed. 6am-3pm.

Greyhound: 940 P St. (474-1071), close to downtown and city campus. Buses run east-west to Omaha (7 per day weekdays, 6 per day weekends, 1 hr., $11.25) and Chicago (6 per day, 10-12 hr., $74). Open Mon.-Fri. 7am-6pm, Sat. 8am-6pm, Sun. 2-6pm.

Public Transport: Lincoln Transportation System, 710 J St. (476-1234). Open Mon.-Fri. 7am-4:30pm. All buses stop at 11th and O St. Mon.-Sat. 6am-7pm. Fare 65¢. "Star shuttle" buses (10¢) serve downtown Mon.-Fri. 9:30am-5pm.

Taxi: Yellow Cab, 477-4111. $2.50 first mi., $1 each additional mi.

Car Rental: Economy Rent-a-Car, 2912 N. 38th St. (466-3344), 1 block south of Adams. $10 per day with 50 free mi., 12¢ each additional mi. Cars cannot cross state line. Open Mon.-Fri. 7:30am-5:30pm, Sat. 8am-1pm. Must be 21 with major credit card or $250 cash deposit.

Help Lines: Rape Crisis, 471-7273. 24 hr. **Gay/Lesbian Support Line,** 475-4967 or 472-5644. **Committee Offering Lesbian and Gay Events (COLAGE),** 474-2454, at University of Nebraska. **Hotline for the Handicapped,** 471-3656 or 800-742-7594. **Lodging Hotline,** 476-2192.

Post Office: 700 R St. (473-1695). Open Mon.-Fri. 7:30am-5pm, Sat. 9am-noon. **ZIP code:** 68508.

Area Code: 402.

Lincoln is in southeastern Nebraska, 55 mi. southwest of Omaha on I-80, accessible by train or bus. **O Street** is the main east-west drag, splitting the town north-south. Alphabetized streets increase northwards. **First Street,** running north-south, sits along **Salt Creek,** west of downtown. The **University of Nebraska** (472-7211) is on the northern border of downtown. Check the **student union** on 14th at R St.

for ride boards (at main entrance) and cheap food. Most places of interest are within walking distance of downtown, except for the university's **East Campus**. Take the university shuttle from Lyman Hall, available only during the academic year, or bus #4 ("University Place").

Accommodations and Camping

The small, ministry-run **Cornerstone Hostel (AYH)**, 640 N. 16th St. (476-0355 or 476-0926), is located on the university's downtown campus. Two big carpeted rooms with couches, tables, and futons serve as single-sex dorm rooms. Bring a sleeping bag or blankets and pillow. No showers but full kitchen. (Curfew 11pm. $4, members only.) Nonmembers (and moneyed AYHers) can stay downtown at the gorgeous, family-run **Town House Mini-Suite Motel**, 18th and M St. (475-3000). Each one-bedroom apartment has a pull-out couch, great beds, a furnished kitchen with coffeemaker, cable TV, and access to a microwave. (Singles $34. Doubles $39.) The **Great Plains Motel**, 2732 O St. (476-3253), maintains nicer rooms than most hotels in this price range with pleasant wood-paneled furnishings, thick beige carpeting, and refrigerators. Free coffee and HBO. Take bus #1 ("East Havelock") from downtown. (Singles $29.50. Doubles $36.)

The best place to camp is at **Branched Oak Lake** (464-0641, ext. 245), 12 mi. north of town on Rte. 34, where facilities include showers and restrooms. (Sites $6, with electricity $8.) Campers need a Nebraska park entry permit ($10), available at area concessions, lake headquarters, or at the Nebraska Game and Parks Commission in Lincoln (see Nebraska Practical Information).

Food and Entertainment

Strawberries, pastry, tie-dye shirts, and a coffee stand are the excuses for a crafts-and fruit-filled **Farmers Market** held downtown every Saturday morning from June to October on 7th St. between P and Q St. Bohemia thrives at Lincoln's **Coffeehouse**, 1324 P St. (477-6611), where high ceilings, slow fans, excellent coffee served in huge glass mugs (50¢), and a bookstore converge. 'Tis a most inviting place to relax, chat, snack, and read. Alongside other birkenstocky fare, a vegetarian sandwich or salad ($3-4) is offered daily. A "poetry quilt" on the back wall invites new submissions in the tradition of poet and former patron Lawrence Ferlinghetti. You can sell your used philosophy, poetry, and regional American literature books here, lightening your load while you find out about upcoming concerts and readings. (Open Mon.-Thurs. 7am-midnight, Fri.-Sat. 7am-1am, Sun. noon-midnight.) Locals swear by the more prosaic fare at **Spaghetti Works**, 228 N. 12th St., where lunch is $4 and dinner just $5. (Open Mon.-Thurs. 11:30am-2pm and 5-10pm, Fri. 11:30am-2pm and 5-11pm, Sat. 11:30am-2:30pm and 5-11pm, Sun. 5-9pm.) **Noodles Comedy Club** is upstairs. (Shows Thurs. at 8:30pm, Fri.-Sat. at 7:30 and 9:45pm.) Students and locals alike flock to **Valentino's**, 3457 Holdrege, near the East Campus, for great pizza, pasta, antipasto, and buffets. Buffets happen Mon.-Sat. 11am-2pm ($4.75) and 4-9pm ($6); Sunday brunch serves itself at noon ($5.50). (Open Sun.-Thurs. 11am-11pm, Fri. 11am-12:30am, Sat. 11am-1am.) A second Valentino's is at 232 N. 13th St. (475-1501), near the city campus; there's yet another in Topeka, KS which Kevin enjoys.

A bar-goers bar, **P.O. Pears**, 322 S. 9th St. (476-8551) has an enormous mechanized windmill contraption in the back room. Draft beer is 69¢, burger and fries $3. (Open daily 11:30am-1am; open at 10am on football Saturdays.) Twenty-one-year-old animals can enjoy the **Zoo Bar**, 136 N. 14th St. (435-8754), where jazz avatar Charlie Parker got his nickname "Yardbird" sitting in with the Jay McShane band. The live blues, zydeco, and jazz make you forget you're in Nebraska. (Open Mon.-Fri. 3pm-1am, Sat. noon-1am, Sun. 6-11pm. Music starts at 9pm. Free-$10 cover, depending on act.) **Duffy's Tavern**, 1412 O St. (474-3543), attracts a sophisticated local crowd to one of Lincoln's only alternative music bars. Draft beers 65-75¢. (Open daily 1pm-1am. Cover $2-8.) **Julio's**, 132 S. 13th St. (477-5122), has

Tex-Mex, gourmet burgers, and a Happy Hour (Mon.-Fri. 3-7pm and 11pm-1am; draws 75¢, pitchers $2.25) enlivened by live jazz every Thursday night at 8:30pm. Look for the old black lead, red brick, and bevelled glass of the telephone building. (Open Sun.-Wed. 11am-11pm, Thurs.-Sat. 11am-midnight; bar open daily to 1am.) Do not pass Go, do not collect $200, and go directly to **Boardwalk,** 104 N. 20th St. (435-9412 or 474-5692), a gay bar and dance club. Admits both men and women. (Open daily 3pm-1am. Happy Hour 3-9pm.)

Sights

The **capitol building,** 14th at K St. (471-0448), maintains all the pomp and majesty of an art deco museum. Its floor, reminiscent of a Native American blanket in design, is an incredible mosaic of inlaid Belgian and Italian marble; each pattern contains the history of some aspect of the land and peoples of Nebraska. (Open daily 9am-5pm. Excellent tours on the hour. Free.)

The **Sheldon Memorial Art Gallery,** 12th and R St. (472-2461), on the university's city campus, is not to be missed. The cool, white building designed by Philip Johnson is as great a work of art as any painting or sculpture in its collection. Featured artists include Hopper, O'Keefe, Rothko, Brancusi, Calder, Moore, and Rodin. The **Sheldon Film Theatre** (472-5353) runs independent and art films. (Gallery open Tues.-Wed. 10am-5pm, Thurs.-Sat. 10am-5pm and 7-9pm, Sun. 2-9pm.)

An unusually large mammoth named "Archie," short for its genus name, *Archidiscodon,* poses with several other fossil buddies in the **University of Nebraska State Museum** (472-2642), in Morrill Hall at 14th and U St. (Open summer Mon.-Fri. 10:30am-noon and 1:30-4:30pm, Sat.-Sun. 2-4pm; academic year Tues.-Fri. 2:30-4:30pm, Sat.-Sun. 2-4pm. Donation requested.)

Shoot the duck at the **National Museum of Roller Skating,** 7700 A St. (489-8811), the self-proclaimed "definitive source for the history of roller skating" and final resting place of some great costumes. Take bus #5 ("Bryan Hospital") from downtown. (Open Mon.-Fri. 9am-5pm. Free.)

North Dakota

Though a state (the 39th) since 1889, North Dakota and most of its windswept terrain remains a mystery to travelers. Those who do visit often pass like wildfire through the eastern prairie to the more sensational "badlands," the infertile, pockmarked buttes dominating the western half of the state. Those in search of solitude, however, should savor the tranquil expanses of farmland before moving on to the tourist-filled western towns. Yet, no matter where you go in North Dakota, eager locals will make you feel at home. People here are about as sparse as snow in June (there are fewer than 10 per square mile), but they are twice as amiable. North Dakotans epitomize the Midwestern adage: cold hands, warm heart.

Practical Information

Capital: Bismarck.

Tourist Information: Tourism Promotion Division, Liberty Memorial Bldg., Capitol Grounds, Bismarck 58505 (224-2525 or 800-472-2100; 800-437-2077 outside ND). **Parks and Recreation Department,** 1424 W. Century Ave. #202, Bismarck 58502 (224-4887).

Time Zone: Central (1 hr. behind Eastern) and Mountain (2 hr. behind Eastern). **Postal Abbreviation:** ND.

Area Code: 701.

Bismarck

When the first rails crossed the slopes of the Rockies, this pleasant frontier town on the east bank of the Missouri River became the terminus for the Northern Pacific Railway. Leaders renamed it Bismarck in honor of the current Chancellor of Germany, hoping to attract German investment in the budding railroad company. Today, while Germany once again becomes an economic force to contend with, Bismarck remains North Dakota's modest capital. With 75,000 residents, it also stands tall as the state's second largest city, known in post-Cold War circles as "Little Berlin," but without the thrill of reunification and the tourism it sparks.

Bismarck takes every opportunity to tout its 20-story art deco **State Capitol,** 900 East Blvd. (224-2480). Built in the early 1930s when art deco raged, the building foreshadowed not only the end of the Cold War, but also the end of dramatic statements by architects in North Dakota. Walk across the wide green lawn in front of the capitol to reach the **North Dakota Heritage Center** (224-2666) with sophisticated exhibits inside on the Plains tribes, the buffalo, and the history of white settlement. (Open Mon.-Thurs. 8am-5pm, Fri. 8am-8pm, Sat. 9am-5pm, Sun. 11am-5pm. Free.) The less showy but equally informative **Camp Hancock Historic Site,** at the intersection of 1st Ave. and Main St. (224-2666), originally housed workers on the Northern Pacific Railroad. (Open Wed.-Sun. 1-5pm.)

Below **Mandan,** on the opposite bank of the Missouri, lies **Fort Lincoln,** a campsite built for the same purpose. General Custer's march towards his fatal meeting with Sitting Bull at Little Bighorn began here. The fort is part of the worthwhile **Fort Lincoln State Park** (663-9571), which also features a reconstructed Mandan village on its original site, renovated army blockhouses, and a small collection of artifacts and memorabilia from Native Americans and early settlers. (Park open daily 8am-sunset; Sept.-May Mon.-Fri. 9am-sunset. Museum open daily 9am-9pm; Sept.-May Mon.-Fri. 9am-5pm.)

At the end of July, join lifetime fans and lifers at the **Annual North Dakota Prison Rodeo,** held at the penitentiary east of Bismarck. In the first week of August, watch for the **Art Fair,** held on the Capitol Mall lawn. Call ahead (255-3285) for information on the **United Tribes Pow Wow,** held in early September, one of the largest gatherings of Native Americans in the nation; enjoy the dancing, singing, foods and crafts of many tribes. To find out more about local entertainment, drop by or call the new **Bismarck Civic Center,** at the terminus of Sweet Ave. E.(222-6491), for a schedule of events.

Bismarck has several local diners that serve tasty, inexpensive meals. The **Little Cottage Cafe,** 2513 E. Main St., brings in droves of workers at the lunch whistle and families at dinnertime. Fantastic muffins cost 90¢, an 8-oz. sirloin steak $5.25. (Open daily 6am-10pm.) The **Drumstick Cafe,** 307 N. 3rd St., serves breakfast all day. The home-baked desserts (fresh strawberry pie 95¢) and fresh-ground coffee are superb. Sandwiches are $2-3.50. (Open Mon.-Sat. 24 hr.) For an intimate family dinner complete with classical music, try **Caspar's East 40,** 1401 E. Interchange Ave. (258-7222). The service is fast and friendly, the food delicious. Get a Chicken teriyaki dinner for $5.25. Reservations preferred.

The **Highway Motel,** 6319 E. Main St. (223-0506), 2 mi. east on Rte. 10, rents rooms to local workers by the month, but they often have space for those staying only a night or two. (Singles $15. Doubles $23.) **Motel 6,** 2433 State St. (255-6878), right off I-94, offers clean, small rooms and a pool. (Singles $25. Doubles $31. Under 18 free.) Your best bet closer to town is the **Bismarck Motor Hotel,** 2301 E. Main Ave. (223-2474). (Singles $19. Doubles $30.)

The **Hillcrest Campground** (255-4334), 1½ mi. out of town on E. Main St., provides showers and scenery from April to September. (Sites $5.) The edenic **General Sibley Park** (222-1844), 4 mi. south of Bismarck on S. Washington St., merits a visit even if you don't stay the night. Those who do decide to stay should call ahead for reservations, and then set up camp in a glen of huge, shady trees on the banks of the Missouri River. The park has showers. (Sites $5, with full hookup $9.) **Fort Lincoln State Park** (663-9571), 5 mi. south of Mandan on Rte. 1806, has a quiet campground on the east bank of the Missouri. (Sites $8, with water and electricity $10. Daily pass to park and showers included.)

Most of **Bismarck** is contained within an oval formed by I-94 and its corollary Business 94, otherwise known as **Main Street.** Bismarck's small downtown shopping district coalesces where the Wall once stood in the southwest curve of this oval, bounded by Washington St. and 9th St. on the west and east, and Rosser Ave. and Business 94 on the north and south.

The **Bismarck-Mandan Convention and Visitors Bureau** provides propaganda at 523 N. 4th St. (222-4308). (Open Mon.-Fri. 8am-5pm.) The largely defense-oriented **Bismarck Municipal Airport,** 2½ mi. south of Bismarck, lies near the intersection of University Dr. (Rte. 1804) and Airport Rd. **Greyhound,** 1237 W. Divide (223-6576), 3 inconvenient mi. west of downtown off I-94 exit 35, provides service to Minneapolis (10 hr., $47) and Seattle (1½ days, $145). (Open Mon.-Fri. 3:30-5am, 8am-1pm, and 4-9pm, Sat.-Sun. 3:30-5am, 9am-12:30pm, and 6-9pm.) Bismarck's **time zone** is Central (1 hr. behind Eastern), except for Fort Lincoln, which is Mountain (2 hr. behind Eastern). The **post office** is at 220 E. Rosser Ave. (221-6517; open Mon.-Fri. 8am-5pm, Sat. 10-noon); the **ZIP code:** is 58501. Bismarck's **area code** is 701.

Theodore Roosevelt National Memorial Park and Medora

President Theodore Roosevelt appreciated the beauty of the Badlands' red and brown-hued lunar formations so much that he bought a ranch here. After Roosevelt's mother and wife (who were two different people) died on the same day, he came here in search of "physical and spiritual renewal;" today's visitor can find the same peace among the quiet canyons and dramatic rocky outcroppings which earned the park the name "rough-rider country."

The park divides into a south unit and a north unit. The entrance to the better-developed **south unit,** (time zone: Mountain) is just north of I-94 in the historic frontier town of **Medora.** Restored with the tourist in mind, Medora is a place to hold tightly to your purse strings. Limit your shopping to **Joe Ferris' General Store** (623-4447), spotless and still inexpensive. (Open daily 8am-8pm.) For more immediate nourishment, stop by the **Badlands Bake Shoppe,** four doors to the left of Ferris, for a mid-day snack. Large muffins cost 85¢, a loaf of Dakota bread—perfect hiking food—$2.25. (Open May-Sept. daily 8am-4pm.) In pleasant weather, indulge at the **Chuckwagon Bar-B-Q,** an outdoor buffet ($8, children $4) serving ribs and chicken in the summertime. (Open daily 4:30-7pm.) Budget motels are even harder to find than budget food, but the **Dietz Motel,** 401 Broadway (623-4455), offers clean spacious basement rooms at the lowest rates in town. Owned by North Dakota's own special gift to the world of comedy. (Singles from $10. Doubles from $25.)

Medora's only sight is the **Badlands Wax Museum,** on Main St. (623-4451), which tells you all there is to know about the town. (Open Tues.-Sat. 10am-9pm, Sun.-Mon. 10am-7pm. Admission $2, children $1.) **Greyhound** serves Medora from the Dietz Motel, with two buses daily to Bismarck ($20) and Billings, MT ($53).

Start your exploration of the park at the **visitors center** (623-4466) on the western edge of town. The center serves as a mini-museum, displaying a few of Teddy's guns, spurs, and old letters; it also shows a beautiful film of winter badlands scenes. Be sure to pick up a copy of *Frontier Fragments,* the park newspaper, which lists a variety of ranger-led talks, walks, and demonstrations. (Open daily 8am-8pm; Sept.-May 8am-4:30pm. Inquire at desk for film showtimes.) Here you pay the park entrance fee ($3 for vehicles, $1 for pedestrians). Then either follow the 36-mi. scenic loop through the park, or drive to one of the unpaved trails that start from the loop and foot it deep into the wilderness. Don't miss the world's third-largest **petrified** forest, 14 mi. into the park. **Painted Canyon Overlook,** 7 mi. east of Medora, also has a **visitors center** (575-4020; open daily 8am-8pm), picnic tables, and a breathtaking view of the badlands.

The **north unit** of the park is 75 mi. from the south unit on Rte. 85. (time zone: Central). Most of the land is wilderness; very few people visit, and fewer still stay overnight. As a result, backcountry hiking possibilities are endless. Check in at the ranger station (623-4466 or 842-2333) for information and a free overnight camping permit. (Open daily 8am-4:30pm.) As a compromise between the wilderness and Medora, the park maintains **Squaw Creek Campground,** 5 mi. west of the north unit entrance. (Sites $6.) For more information on the park, write to Theodore Roosevelt National Memorial Park, Medora 58645.

Oklahoma

Until 1907, when it finally achieved statehood, Oklahoma was known as "Indian Territory." In the late 1830s President Andrew Jackson ordered five tribes from the southeastern United States to relocate to this wilderness; the Cherokees still refer to this tragic march, on which over one-fourth of the tribe died from hunger and disease, as the "Trail of Tears." Another relocation in 1889 moved the so-called Five Civilized Tribes from the East and nearly a dozen displaced tribes from the North and West to tiny plots of land in Oklahoma in order to make room for white settlers. April 22, 1889, marked the first Oklahoma Land Run during which settlers, at an appointed time, rushed to stake their claims; those homesteaders who snuck across the border before the gun earned Oklahoma the name "Sooner State."

During the 20th century, Oklahoma's economic status plummeted from the dramatic oil boom of 1904 to the devastating Dust Bowl of the Great Depression. The latter resulted from massive erosion caused by prolonged drought and destructive farming techniques. The near total crop failure forced many settlers to wander west in search of new land or other employment, much like the Joad family in John Steinbeck's *The Grapes of Wrath.* While in recent years the state has suffered from its dependence on the seesawing oil business, the longstanding Native American culture and downhome friendliness that characterize Oklahoma make it a pleasant place to visit.

Practical Information

Capital: Oklahoma City.

Tourist Information: **Oklahoma Tourism and Recreation Department,** 500 Will Rogers Building, Oklahoma City 73105 (521-2409 or 800-652-6552 out of state), in the capitol complex.

Time Zone: Central (1 hr. behind Eastern). Postal Abbreviation: OK.

Tulsa

Tulsa lies in the heart of Green Country, a region known for its wooded hills, fertile farmlands, and immense lakes. Named by the Creek and founded by a group of white settlers who discovered black gold on the banks of the Arkansas River, Tulsa has earned the title "Oil Capital of the World" for containing more oil company headquarters than any other city. Though the moniker disappeared with the boom, the oil tycoons left behind an eclectic if somewhat eccentric architectural legacy of art deco skyscrapers, French villas, and Georgian mansions. Tulsa is also home to the second largest Native American population of any U.S. metropolitan region.

Orientation and Practical Information

Emergency: 911.

Visitor Information: Convention and Visitors Division, Metropolitan Tulsa Chamber of Commerce, 616 S. Boston (585-1201 or 800-558-3311). **Information Center,** in the kiosk on the east side of the Civic Center, at Denver and 5th St., 5 blocks west of the bus station. Open Mon.-Thurs. 7am-5pm, Fri. 7-11am.

Greyhound/Trailways: 317 S. Detroit (584-4427). To: Oklahoma City (8 per day, 2 hr., $12.50); St. Louis (9 per day, 7½-9½ hr., $58); Kansas City (4 per day, 6-8 hr., $49, students $46; $36.75 at 1am and 4am); Dallas (6 per day, 7 hr., $50; 2 weeks in advance $25). Lockers $1. Open 24 hr.

Public Transport: Metropolitan Tulsa Transit Authority, 510 S. Rockford (582-2100). Buses run daily 9am-3pm. Fare 60¢, transfers 5¢, seniors and disabled 30¢, ages 5-18 50¢, under 5 free with adult. Maps and schedules available at the main office (open Mon.-Sat. 9am-5:30pm), the chamber of commerce, and most libraries, but are not always reliable.

Taxi: Yellow Cab, 582-6161.

Bike Rental: River Trail Sports Center, 3949 Riverside Dr. (743-5898), at 41st St. Five-speeds $4 per hr., $12 per day. Open Mon.-Sat. 10am-7pm, Sun. 11am-6pm. Must have driver's license or cash deposit.

Help Lines: 583-4357, for information, referral, and crisis intervention. Open 24 hr. **Gay Information Line,** 743-4297. Open daily 8-10pm.

Post Office: 333 W. 4th St. (599-6800). Open Mon.-Fri. 8:30am-5pm. **ZIP code:** 74101.

Area Code: 918.

Tulsa sits on I-44, 100 mi. from Oklahoma City in the northeastern corner of the state. All "South" addresses are along the numbered east-west streets, which begin downtown. Named streets lie in alphabetical order, with the alphabet beginning at north-south avenues on both sides of **Main Street,** and at east-west streets 1 block north of **First Street.** Streets named after the western cities are on the west side of town, eastern on the east side. If possible, navigate Tulsa by car. Outside of downtown, sidewalks are scarce and bus routes limited.

Accommodations and Camping

Most cheap accommodations in Tulsa are outside the city center. An exception is the **YMCA,** 515 S. Denver (583-6201), open to men only. Ask for a room on the third floor. Guests have access to pool and gym; the office is open 24 hr. (Singles $10.) The cheapest downtown motel is the **Darby Lane Inn,** 416 W. 6th St. (584-4461). Clean, recently remodeled rooms have cable TV. (Singles $34. Doubles $40. Call for reservations.) Outside downtown, budget motels abound along I-244 and bordering streets. The **Gateway Motor Inn,** 5600 W. Skelly Dr. (446-6611), 8 mi. from downtown off I-44, is one of about a dozen area motels mostly serving truckers. Take bus #17 and get off at Reasor's Grocery. Rooms are clean with enormous beds, cable TV, and HBO. (Singles from $19. Doubles $27.) Across I-44 (but inaccessible by bus), **Days Inn,** 1016 N. Garnett Rd. (438-5050), about 7 mi. east of town off I-244, has clean rooms with HBO. (Singles $18. Doubles $23.) The **Roadway Motel,** 4724 S. Yale (496-9300), just south of I-44, is notable for its central location. From downtown take bus #15, get off at 49th and Yale, and walk 2 blocks north. (Singles $25. Doubles $30.)

The **KOA Kampground,** 193 East Ave. (266-4227), ½ mi. west of the Will Rogers Turnpike Gate off I-44, has a pool, laundry room, and game room. (Sites $14, with hookup $15.) **Keystone State Park** (865-4991) offers three campgrounds along the shores of Lake Keystone, 20 mi. west of Tulsa on the Cimarron Turnpike (U.S. 64). The wooded park offers hiking, swimming, boating, and excellent catfish and bass fishing. Four-person cabins with fireplaces and kitchenettes are also available for $40; call 800-522-8565 for reservations.

Food

The menu changes every day at **Nelson's Buffeteria**, 514 S. Boston (584-9969). Operating since 1929 and currently run by Nelson Jr., the cafeteria is now a Tulsa landmark. Most of the servers have been here since the oil boom. Generous breakfast specials ($2-3) are served from 8:30 to 10:30am. Try the famous chicken-fried steak ($4.50). (Open daily 6am-2:30pm.) The best barbecue in town, **Elmer's**, 4128 S. Peoria, sells sliced beef, bologna, and sparerib dinners ($4-7). (Open Mon.-Thurs. 11am-9:45pm, Fri.-Sat. 11am-11:45pm.) For a more genteel dining experience, turn the corner at 41st St. just east of Peoria to **Mary's Bread Basket**, 1405 E. 41st. The owner, Mary Gubser, has written several cookbooks and sells 15 kinds of bread. Try the vichyssoise ($2.50) or a sandwich and salad ($3-5). (Open Mon.-Fri. 7am-5:30pm, Sat. 7am-2:30pm). The giant pink **Casa Bonita**, 2120 S. Sheridan Rd., offers large Mexican dinners ($5-7) in a highly entertaining atmosphere. The dining areas range in decor from rustic, candle-lit caves to a somewhat authentic south-of-the-border village. (Open Sun.-Thurs. 11am-9:30pm, Fri.-Sat. 11am-10pm). The 50s-style **Metro Diner**, 3001 E. 11th St. at College, has a ton of funky memorabilia and an obligatory soda fountain. They specialize in sinfully rich fountain treats, burgers ($3.50-5), and homemade pies ($1.75). Seniors receive a 10% discount. (Open Mon.-Thurs. 6:30am-midnight, Fri.-Sat. 6:30am-1am, Sun. 6:30am-11pm.) Keep in mind that most downtown restaurants close at 3pm on weekdays and 1pm on Saturdays.

Sights and Entertainment

The **Thomas Gilcrease Museum**, 1400 Gilcrease Museum Rd. (582-3122), at Newton St. and 25th Ave., 2 mi. northwest of downtown, contains the world's largest collection of American art. Works on display include a large number of Remington sculptures and Russell paintings, along with Native American jewelry, masks, and weapons. Take bus #7 ("Gilcrease") from downtown. (Open Mon.-Sat. 9am-5pm, Sun. 1-5pm. Donation requested.) The **Philbrook Art Center**, 2727 S. Rockford Rd. (749-7941), in the former Renaissance villa of an oil baron, now houses a collection of Native American pottery and artifacts alongside Renaissance paintings and sculptures. Picnic by the lovely pond on the grounds. Take bus #16 ("S. Peoria") from downtown. (Open Tues.-Sat. 10am-5pm, Sun. 1-5pm. Admission $3, seniors and college students $1.50, other students and children free.) The **Fenster Museum of Jewish Art**, 1223 E. 17th Pl. (582-3732), housed in B'nai Emunah Synagogue, contains an impressive collection of Judaica exhibits spanning from 2000 BC to the present.

You won't find any student bars around **Oral Roberts University (ORU)**, 7777 S. Lewis (495-6161), since smoking, drinking, and dancing are prohibited on this Christian campus. Visit the university regardless of your religious affiliation or degree of interest, if only to stand in awe before the bizarre, gold-mirrored, angled architecture. Inside the **Prayer Tower** (495-6807) visitors can walk through an exhibition honoring the university's founder. Choirs sing in the background, spotlights illuminate mementos from Roberts's childhood, and doors open and close automatically as if by divine command. A Jesus some 900 ft. tall appeared to Oral Roberts and instructed him to build the **O.R. City of Faith Hospital**, which recently fell from financial grace. The new management does not dwarf the 60-story building, now a cancer research center. Nobody's quite sure what to do with the 80-ft.-high praying hands still looming at the entrance. The **ORU Healing Outreach** (496-7700) hosts a "Journey Through the Bible" tour, where Old Testament scenes are recreated in life-like, three-dimensional exhibits. (Open Mon.-Sat. 10:30am-4:30pm, Sun. 1-5pm. Tours every 15-20 min. Free.) The university is about 6 mi. south of downtown Tulsa between Lewis and Harvard Ave. Take bus #9 ("S. Lewis"). (Prayer Tower and visitors center open Mon.-Sat. 9am-4:30pm, Sunday 1-4:30pm.)

Fans of art deco architecture will want to visit the **Boston Avenue United Methodist Church**, 1301 S. Boston (583-5181). Built in 1929, the house of worship is vaguely suggestive of the witch's palace in *The Wizard of Oz*. Climb the 14-story tower for a skyline view of downtown Tulsa. Free tours are given after 11am services on Sunday (about 12:15pm) or for specially scheduled groups.

Rodgers and Hammerstein's *Oklahoma!* continues its run at the **Discoveryland Amphitheater** (245-0242), 10 mi. west of Tulsa on 41st St., accessible only by car. Though the musical gives a somewhat romanticized introduction to Oklahoma's history, a performance under the stars is a treat. Be sure to arrive early for the pre-show barbecue, starting at 5:30pm. (Shows June-Aug. Mon.-Sat. at 8pm. Admission $12, ages under 12 $7. For tickets call 245-6552 or 800-338-6552; write 2502 E. 71st St., Tulsa 74136. Barbecue $6.50, children $4.50.) The most moving commemoration of Native American heritage is the **Trail of Tears Drama,** performed in Tahlequah, 66 mi. east of Tulsa on Rte. 51. This show reenacting the Cherokees' tragic march from the Carolinas to Oklahoma provides a dramatic alternative to the romance of song and dance. (Performances June-Sept. 2 Mon.-Sat. at 8pm. For tickets, call 456-6007 or 800-544-4705, or write P.O. Box 515, Tahlequah, OK 74465; reservations are recommended. Admission $8, ages under 13 $4.)

At night, head out of downtown to the bars along 15th St. east of Peoria, or in the 30s along S. Peoria. Down at the **Sunset Grill,** 3410 S. Peoria (744-5550), no cover for every night's rowdy rock bands accompanies free popcorn and a free buffet at midnight. You must be 21 to enter. Drinks $2-3. (Open daily 8pm-2am.) To keep up-to-date on Tulsa's nightlife, pick up a free copy of *Uptown News* at a newsstand, bookstore, or the chamber of commerce.

The best times to visit Tulsa are during annual special events like the **International Mayfest** (582-6435) in mid-May. This outdoor food, arts, and performance festival takes place in downtown Tulsa over a five-day period. The mid-August **Pow-Wow** held at Mohawk Park just northwest of the airport attracts Native Americans from dozens of different tribes. The four-day festival includes a trade fair, arts and crafts exhibits, and nightly dancing contests which visitors may attend. Admission is $3 per carload.

Oklahoma City

Oklahoma City began on April 22, 1889 with a gunshot that sent settlers swarming by foot, horseback, covered wagon, and bike into the newly opened Oklahoma territory. A few eager souls literally jumped the gun to get a head start on staking their claims, earning the name "sooner."By the 1930s homesteaders hit the "oil from the sky" that sprayed out of Oklahoma City's wells, bringing the capital wealth and notoriety. Today, a working well still sits on the grounds of the capitol building, but only as a symbol of years past as most of the state's oil has long since disappeared. While Tulsa is more Ozark in character, Oklahoma City is cowboy country; cattle auctions still take place in OKC stockyards. For sightseeing, a car is the best mode of transportation since attractions like Remington Park and the National Cowboy Hall of Fame lie along the highway and buses are infrequent.

Orientation and Practical Information

Emergency: 911.

Visitor Information: Chamber of Commerce Tourist Information, 4 Santa Fe Plaza (278-8912), at the corner of Gaylord. Open Mon.-Fri. 8am-4:30pm.

Travelers Aid: 601 NW 5th (232-5507), at Main. Open Mon.-Fri. 8am-4:30pm.

Will Rogers Memorial Airport: (681-5311), southwest of downtown. **Airport Limousine, Inc.,** 3805 S. Meridian (685-2638), has van service to downtown ($9).

Greyhound/Trailways: 427 W. Sheridan Ave. (235-6425), at Walker. In a seedy part of town. Take city bus #5, 6, 11, or 12. To: Tulsa (6 per day, 2 hr., $11); Dallas (4 per day, 5 hr., $35); Kansas City (5 per day, 10 hr., $49). Open 24 hr.

Public Transport: Masstrans, 300 E. California Blvd. (235-7433). Bus service Mon.-Sat. 6am-5:40pm. All routes radiate from the station at Reno and Gaylord, where maps are available. Route numbers vary depending on the direction of travel. Fare 75¢.

Taxi: Yellow Cab, 232-6161. $2 first mi., $1 each additional mi. Airport to downtown fare $12.

Car Rental: Rent-a-Wreck, 2930 NW 39th Expressway (946-9288). Used cars $28 per day with 125 free mi., 20¢ each additional mi. Open Mon.-Fri. 9am-5pm, Sat. 8:30am-noon. Must be 21 with major credit card.

Bike Rental: Miller's Bicycle Distribution, 739 Asp Ave. (321-8296). Ten-speeds $2 per day. Open Mon.-Fri. 9am-6pm, Sat. 9am-3pm. Major credit card or $75 cash deposit required.

Help Lines: Crisis Hotline, 848-2273. **Rape Crisis,** 524-7273. Both open 24 hr.

Post Office: 320 SW 5th St. (278-6300). Open Mon.-Fri. 8:30am-5:30pm, Sat. 9am-noon. **ZIP code:** 73125.

Area Code: 405.

Oklahoma City (pop. 445,300) lies virtually at the center of the state. I-35 and I-40 intersect at right angles in the city. Dallas is about 200 mi. to the south. Streets are organized more or less on a grid. **Main Street** divides the town east-west.

Accommodations, Camping, and Food

The **YMCA,** 125 NW 5th St. (232-6101), has tolerable rooms for men only with shared bath. (Singles $10.75.) The **Myriad Motor Inn,** 1305 Classen (235-2384), at NW 13th and N. Shartel in a pleasant neighborhood near downtown, is one of the best deals in the city. Long list of attractive features includes outdoor pool, adjoining restaurant and nice rooms with color TV. Large country breakfast is included. (Singles $23. Doubles $28.) The **Brass Lantern Inn,** 700 NW 9th St. (232-0505), across from St. Anthony's Hospital, has clean, quiet, comfortable and amply lit rooms. (Singles $25. Doubles $30.) I-35 near Oklahoma City is lined with inexpensive hotels that offer singles for under $25.

Oklahoma City has two readily accessible campgrounds. **RCA,** 12115 Northeast Expressway (478-0278), next to Frontier City Amusement Park 10 mi. north of the city on I-35, has a pool, laundry room, and showers. (Tent sites for two $11, RV sites with hookup $14. Each additional person $1.) The nearest state-run campground lies on Lake Thunderbird about 30 mi. south of OKC at **Little River State Park** (360-3572 or 364-7634). Take I-40 East to the Choctaw Rd. exit, then south until the road ends. (Tent sites $4, $5 in area with gate attendant; showers included. Office open 8am-5pm.)

Since Oklahoma City has the largest feeder cattle market in the U.S., beef tops most menus. Downtown, the concourse under **Skirvin Plaza** is filled with inexpensive lunch spots. Enter from the Skirvin or Sheridan Century hotels. (Open daily 11am-3pm.) The **Cattlemen's Café,** 1309 S. Agnew (236-0416), near the stockyards, serves its namesakes well. Menu features prime rib dinner ($6.50), navy bean soup with cornbread ($1), and sandwiches. (Open 24 hr.) Try "Oklahoma crepes" (chicken, cream cheese, and jack cheese enchiladas topped with sour cream) for $6 while you relax in flowered neon at **Pump's Bar and Grill,** 5700 N. Western (840-4369). Burgers, sandwiches, and specialties $3.50-7. (Open Sun.-Thurs. 11am-11pm, Fri.-Sat. 11am-midnight.)

Sights and Entertainment

The **Oklahoma City Stockyards,** 2500 Exchange Ave. (235-8675), are the busiest in the world. Cattle auctions, held here Monday through Wednesday, begin at 7 or 8am and sometimes last into the night. Monday and Tuesday are the busiest days; Monday morning is the best time to visit. An auctioneer fires bids in a rapid-fire monotone as cowhands chase the cattle through a maze of gates and passages into the auction building. Visitors can enter this building free of charge via a catwalk over the pens, leading from the parking lot east of the auction house. To reach the stockyards, take bus #11 from Hudson downtown to S. Agnew Ave.

The plight of Native Americans along the "Trail of Tears" is commemorated by James Earle Fraser's *The End of the Trail.* Ironically, his sculpture of a man slumped over an exhausted pony is on display at the **National Cowboy Hall of Fame and Western Heritage Center,** 1700 N.E. 63rd St. (478-2250). Along with Frederic Remington sculptures and cowboy memorabilia, you'll find John Wayne's collection of Pueblo kachina dolls. Every summer, the museum showcases 150 works of the National Academy of Western Art. Take bus #22 from downtown. (Open May 27-Sept. 2 daily 8:30am-6pm; off-season daily 9am-5pm. Admission $5, seniors $4, ages 6-12 $3.) Just across I-44 from the Cowboy Hall of Fame, the enormous $97 million **Remington Park,** offers entertainment to horse-lovers and gamblers alike. Aside from racing tracks, the grounds include two lakes, a grassy park, and several restaurants. (Open Wed.-Sun. 11am-5pm, racing starts at 1pm. Admission $2, seniors $1, ages under 18 $1 and must be accompanied by an adult.)

Gas lamps and spacious mansions are the hallmarks of **Heritage Hill,** a grand ol' neighborhood of restored turn-of-the-century houses. The **Overholser Mansion,** 405 NW 15th St. (528-8485), built in 1903, is a good example of Victorian architecture filled with elaborate Limoges china services, Venetian crystal, and Meissen vases. This mansion was once the social center of Oklahoma City. (Open Tues.-Fri. 10am-4pm, Sat.-Sun. 2-4pm. Free tours every hr.) **Nichols Hills,** just north of Oklahoma City, is another community loaded with gorgeous homes. Take bus #5 (from Walker and Main) past 63rd, and wander west.

The **Kirkpatrick Center Museum Complex,** 2100 NE 52nd St. (427-5461), a sort of educational amusement park, looks like a mall but is actually a conglomeration of eight separate museums, each colorful and entertaining in its own right. Highlights are the **Air and Space Museum** and the **International Photography Hall of Fame.** Take bus #22. (Open May 27-Sept. 2 Mon.-Sat. 9am-6pm, Sun. noon-6pm; off-season Mon.-Fri. 9am-5pm, Sat. 9am-6pm, Sun. noon-6pm. Admission to all 8 museums $5, seniors and ages 5-12 $3.)

For a night of country dancing and music, try **Doc Severinson's,** 201 N. Meridian (946-2300). When Doc and his band are busy with *The Tonight Show,* other groups take Tommy's lead and fill in. (Open Wed.-Sat. from 4:30pm. Ticket office open Wed.-Sat. 10am-10pm. Prices vary with performers; no charge for the house band.) The **Oklahoma Opry,** 404 W. Commerce (632-8322), is home to a posse of country music stars. (Regular performances Sat. at 8pm.) The **Black Liberated Arts Center,** 1901 N. Ellison (528-4666), provides plays and musical events at the Classen Theater from October to May.

South Dakota

South Dakota is not just the flat, boring state that jaded coastal types often ignore. From the forested granite crags of the Black Hills to the glacial lakes of the northeast, the Coyote State has more to offer visitors than might be expected. First discovered by Europeans in 1792, South Dakota's Native American population actually predates white settlers by almost 1000 years. Clashes between the two cultures grew most violent when white men staked claims on sacred Sioux territory in the 1800s. Things are considerably more peaceful nowadays, as South Dakota welcomes visitors with open arms—and open cash registers. Visitors from both U.S. coasts making the most of local hospitality have also made tourism the state's second largest industry, after agriculture.

Practical Information

Capital: Pierre.

Tourist Information: **Division of Tourism,** 221 S. Central, in Capitol Lake Plaza, P.O. Box 1000, Pierre 57051 (773-3301 or 800-952-2217; 800-843-1930 outside SD). Open Mon.-Fri. 8am-5pm. **U.S. Forest Service,** Custer 57730 (673-2551). Camping stamps for the national forest, Golden Eagle passes for those over 62, and Black Hills National Forest maps ($1). Open Mon.-Fri. 8am-5pm. **Division of Parks and Recreation,** Capitol Bldg., Pierre 57501 (773-3391). Information on state parks and campgrounds. Open Mon.-Fri. 8am-5pm.

Time Zones: Central (1 hr. behind Eastern) and Mountain (2 hr. behind Eastern). **Postal Abbreviation:** SD.

Rapid City

Rapid City's location, approximately 40 mi. east of the Wyoming border, makes it an ideal base from which to explore both the Black Hills and the Badlands. Every summer the area welcomes about 2.2 million tourists, over 40 times the city's permanent population.

Practical Information

Emergency: 911.

Visitor Information: Rapid City Chamber of Commerce, Visitors Bureau, 444 Mt. Rushmore Rd. N. (343-1744), in the Civic Center. Visitors bureau open May 27-Sept. 2 daily 7am-6pm; chamber of commerce open year-round Mon.-Fri. 8am-5pm.

Buses: Milo Barber Transportation Center, 333 6th St. (348-3300), downtown. **Jack Rabbit Lines** runs east from Rapid City. To Pierre (1 per day, 3 hr., $36) and Sioux Falls (Mon.-Thurs. 2 per day, 8 hr., $64). **Powder River Lines** services Wyoming and Montana. To Cheyenne (2 per day, 8½ hr., $56.50) and Billings (2 per day, 9 hr., $69). **Arrow Stage Lines** runs to Nebraska and Iowa. To Omaha (3 per day, 13 hr., $62). All 3 honor the Greyhound Ameripass. Station open Mon.-Fri. 6am-11pm, Sat.-Sun. 6am-1pm, 4-5:30pm, and 9:30-11pm.

Public Transport: Milo Barber Transportation Center, 348-7433. City bus transportation available by reservation. Call 24 hr. in advance. One way trip $1, seniors 50¢. Office open Mon.-Fri. 6am-5:30pm.

Taxi: Rapid Taxi, 348-8080. Base fare $2, $1 per mi.

Car Rental: Black Hills Car Rental, 301 Campbell (342-6696). Budget cars $16 per day plus 16¢ per mi., subject to availability. Open Mon.-Fri. 8am-5pm, Sat. 9am-4pm. Must be 21 with a major credit card.

Time Zone: Mountain (2 hr. behind Eastern).

Post Office: 500 East Blvd. (394-8600), several blocks east of downtown. Open Mon.-Fri. 8am-5pm, Sat. 9:30am-12:30pm. **ZIP code:** 57701.

Area Code: 605.

Orienting yourself may be difficult at first, since Rapid City sprawls across 27 flat sq. mi., and few of the buildings in town stand taller than four stories. The center of the downtown area is bordered on the east and west by 6th and 9th Street, and on the north and south by Omaha and Kansas City Street.

Accommodations, Camping, and Food

The **AYH hostel,** downtown in the YMCA, 815 Kansas City St. (342-8538), consists of 12 cots, with no separation between men and women. Access to kitchen and YMCA facilities is available, but no bedding is provided. A cot for the night costs $4 for AYH members or any young foreigner.

Rapid City accommodations are considerably more expensive during the summer. Make reservations, since budget motels often fill up weeks in advance. The **Big Sky Motel,** 4080 Tower Rd. (348-3200), sits on a hill just south of town, affording a spectacular view of the city and the surrounding farmland. (Spotless but phoneless singles $28, doubles $43.) **Motel 6** is less conveniently located northeast of town, off I-90 exit 59, about a $4 cab trip from downtown. Some rooms have disabled access. Pool available. (Singles $30. Doubles $36.) **The Bel Air Inn,** 2101 Rushmore Rd. (343-5126), has a pool and cable TV. (Singles $30. Doubles $37.) **The Berry Patch Campground,** 1860 E. North St. (341-5588), 1 mi. east of I-90 off exit 60, has 14 grass campsites, gameroom, playground, showers, and swimming. (Tent sites $12.50 for 2, with hookup April 12-Oct. 1 $16. Each additional person $1.50.)

Aunt Jane's, 807 Columbus (341-4529), on the first floor of a Victorian house stuffed with antiques, will sate your appetite. Aunt Jane prepares her own recipes, such as the Rocky Mountain salad sandwich (ham, swiss cheese, and peaches; $3.25). (Open Mon.-Fri. 8am-4:30pm, Sat. 9am-2pm.) **Tally's,** 530 6th St. (342-7621), downtown under the orange awning, serves family-style country meals such as chicken-fried steak ($5.75). (Open daily 7am-8pm; Sept. 2-May 27 7am-7pm.) Don't miss the 5¢ cookies at **Ray's Retail Bakery,** 729 Main (343-4720; open Mon.-Sat. 5am-5pm). The **Flying T** (342-1905), 6 mi. south on U.S. 16, next to the Reptile Gardens, serves a chuck wagon meal on a tin plate for $10, under 11 $4, singing cowboys included. Dinner (7:30pm sharp) and a Western musical show (8:15pm) are offered every night.

Sights and Entertainment

Tourism rears its flashing neon head in Rapid City. If you brought your walking shoes, take the **Rapid City Walking Tour** of the historic and well-preserved downtown area; pick up a guide at the visitors center. The **Sioux Indian Museum** and the **Pioneer Museum** (both 348-0557), 515 West Blvd., between Main and St. Joseph St. in Halley Park, present interesting but limited exhibits. (Open Mon.-Sat. 9am-5pm, Sun. 1-5pm; Oct.-May Tues.-Sat. 10am-5pm, Sun. 1-5pm.) **The Museum of Geology,** 501 E. Saint Joseph St. (394-2467), in the administration building of the School of Mines and Technology, just east of Main St., exhibits the beautiful minerals and textbook fossils of the Badlands. (Open Mon.-Sat. 8am-6pm, Sun. noon-6pm; off-season Mon.-Fri. 8am-5pm, Sat. 9am-2pm, Sun. 1-4pm. Free.) The **Dahl Fine Arts Center,** 7th and Quincy St., houses rotating exhibits of local and Native American art, as well as the enormous "Cyclorama of American History," a circular 200-ft. mural. (Open Mon.-Thurs. 9am-8pm, Fri.-Sat. 9am-5pm, Sun. 1-5pm.) For more information, ask at the visitors center.

For nightlife, try Main St. between 9th and Mt. Rushmore St. **Filly's Food, Fun, and Firewater** (348-8300), in the Hilton, is a fantastic spot for a quiet drink or a comedy show. (Shows Fri.-Sat. at 9 and 11pm. Open Mon.-Sat. 11am-2am, Sun. noon-midnight. Cover $5-6.) For boot-stompin' country-western music and dancing, head to **Boot Hill,** 826 Main St. (343-1931), where live bands perform nightly. (Open Mon.-Sat. 3pm-2am, Sun. 5-11:30pm. Cover Tues.-Sat. $2.)

Black Hills

The Black Hills, so named for the dark sheen that distance lends to the green pines covering the hills, have long been considered sacred by the Sioux living to the north. The treaty of 1868 gave the Black Hills and the rest of South Dakota west of the Missouri River to the Sioux, but in a hardly unprecedented move the gold rush of 1877-79 broke the treaty. Since then, white residents have dominated the forested hills, white granite spires, and expansive underground caves with their logging, mining, and tourism. Recently, the Sioux took their claims to federal court and, in 1980, the Supreme Court awarded them a "just compensation" of $200 million. The Sioux, however, refused to accept the money, wanting only the return of their land. Legislative efforts to address this conflict have, to date, met with slow death by Congressional inertia.

I-90 skirts the northern border of the Black Hills through Spearfish in the west and Rapid City in the east. The interconnecting road system through the hills is difficult to navigate without a good map; pick up one for free at the Rapid City Chamber of Commerce.

Powder River Lines serves only Deadwood, Lead, and Hot Springs (see Rapid City Practical Information). Rent a car to explore the area thoroughly. Alternatively, take advantage of the excellent and informative **Gray Line** tours (342-4461). Tickets can be purchased at Rapid City motels, hotels, and campgrounds. Make reservations, or call one hour before departure; they will pick you up at your motel. Tour #1 is the most complete Black Hills tour, going to Mt. Rushmore, Black Hills National Forest, Custer State Park, Needles Highway, and the Crazy Horse Monument (mid-May to mid-Oct. daily, 8 hr., $24). Tour #2 goes north through the Black Hills to the historic western towns of Lead and Deadwood, Mt. Moriah Cemetery, and the Black Hills mining museum (June-Aug. daily, 8 hr., $26). Tour #4 heads to Spearfish for the Black Hills Passion Play (June-Aug. Sun., Tues., and Thurs., 5 hr., $18). Tour #5 provides nighttime transportation to Mt. Rushmore, which is illuminated for viewing (June 1-Sept. 2 daily, 4½ hr., $8).

Hiking in the hills is quite enjoyable—there is little underbrush beneath the conifer canopy, and there are many abandoned mines and strange rock outcroppings to explore. Since rainy, cool weather is common in May and June, dress accordingly.

Black Hills National Forest

The Black Hills, like other national forests, adheres to the principle of "multiple use"; mining, logging, ranching, and tourism all take place in close proximity. Visitors may feel inundated by the latter activity. Seemingly around every bend in the Black Hills' narrow, sinuous roads lurk "don't miss" attractions like reptile farms and Flintstone Campgrounds—or a billboard advertising them. Visit the forest outside of the peak July to mid-September tourist season, when cars and campers descend on the area in a rush for the modern-day gold of glow-in-the-dark souvenirs.

The most convenient information centers are the **Pactola Ranger District**, 803 Soo San Dr., Rapid City (343-1567; open Mon.-Fri. 8am-5pm), and the **Spearfish Ranger District**, 226 Colorado Blvd., Spearfish (642-4622; open Mon.-Fri. 8am-5pm). The main information office and visitors center at **Pactola Reservoir**, 17 mi. west of Rapid City on U.S. 385, has forestry exhibits in the summer in addition to the usual tourist literature. You can buy supplies before you head off to the hinterland at small grocery stores in Keystone and Custer, or at the KOA campground 5 mi. west of Mt. Rushmore on Rte. 244.

Camping in the national forest is virtually unrestricted. To save money the adventurous way, disappear down one of the many dirt roads (make sure it isn't someone's driveway) and set up camp. This option is safe, free, legal, and fun, but watch for poison ivy and afternoon thunder showers. The most popular established campgrounds include **Bear Gulch** and **Pactola** (343-4283), on the Pactola Reservoir just south of the junction of Rte. 44 and U.S. 385. (Sites $9-11.) Other favorites include the **Willow Creek Horse Camp**, in the North Cave Gap Area ($10 reservation fee, $15 charge for 1-10 people) and **Sheridan Lake Campground** (574-2873 or 800-283-2267), east of Hill City on U.S. 385 (sites $9-11), both of which provide picnic tables, pit toilets, and water hydrants. These campgrounds often fill up in the summer, but you can reserve a spot by calling or writing ahead. For more information, contact the Pactola or Spearfish Ranger District (see above). As a last resort, try the **Hill City-Mt. Rushmore KOA** (574-2525), 5 mi. west of Mt. Rushmore on Rte. 244. The KOA cabins come with facilities including showers, a stove, a heated pool, laundry facilities, and free shuttle service to Mt. Rushmore. (Office open daily 7am-11pm; Oct.-April 8am-10pm. Sites $15 for 2 people, $18 with water and electricity, $20 with full hookup.)

Mt. Rushmore National Monument

South Dakota historian Doane Robinson originally conceived this "shrine of democracy" in 1923 as a memorial for local Western heroes such as Kit Carson. By its completion in 1941, the monument portrayed the 60-ft.-tall faces of George Washington, Thomas Jefferson, Abraham Lincoln, and Theodore Roosevelt. Millions have stood in awe before the four granite patriarchs; some, however, find it odd and distasteful that only white Americans are enshrined in sacred Sioux hills. From Rapid City, take U.S. 16 to Keystone and Rte. 244 up to the mountain. The **visitors center** (574-2523) has the usual multi-media exhibitions as well as braille brochures and wheelchairs. Programs for the disabled are held daily at 9pm. (Visitors center open daily 8am-10pm; Sept. 18-May 14 8am-5pm.) Nearby **Borglum's Sculptor's Studio** holds the plaster model of the sculptor's mountain carving, as well as his tools and plans. (Ranger talks held in summer every hr. 9:30am-6pm; studio open daily 9am-8pm.) Between the visitors center and the studio sits the **Mt. Rushmore Memorial Ampitheater,** the locale of the evening sculpture-lighting programs. (May 14-Sept. 4 program 9pm, sculpture lit 9:30-10:30pm; Sept. 5-16 program 8pm, sculpture lit 8:30-9:30pm.)

Custer State Park

Peter Norbeck, governor of South Dakota during the 1970s, loved to hike among the thin, towering rock formations that haunt the area south of Sylvan Lake and Mt. Rushmore. Norbeck not only created Custer State Park to preserve the area's treasures, but spectacular **Needles Highway** as well, which follows his favorite hiking route. He purposely kept the highway narrow and winding so that newcomers could experience the pleasures of discovery. Watch for mountain goats and bighorn sheep among the rocky spires. For information, contact HCR 83, P.O. Box 70, Custer 57730 (255-4515; open Mon.-Fri. 7:30am-5pm). There is a daily entrance fee ($3, under 11 free, $6 per carload). At the entrance, ask for a copy of *Tatanka,* the informative Custer State Park newspaper. The **Peter Norbeck Welcome Center** (255-4464), on U.S. 16A, 1 mi. west of the State Game Lodge, is the park's central information center. (Open June-Aug. daily 8am-8pm.) All eight **state park campgrounds** charge $7-8 per night and have showers and restrooms. Restaurants and concessions are available at any of the four park lodges—State Game, Blue Bell, Sylvan Lake, and Legion Lake—but you can save money by shopping at the local general stores in Custer, Hermosa, or Keystone.

Sylvan Lake, Needles Hwy. (Rte. 87), proves as lovely as its name, with hiking trails, fishing, horse concessions, paddle boats, and canoes. Horse rides are available at Blue Bell Lodge ($12 per hr., under 12 $10; $20 for 2 hr., under 12 $17). Boat rentals are available at Legion Lake Lodge ($2.50 per person for ½ hr.). All lakes and streams permit fishing, with a $6 daily license available at the four area lodges. Five-day nonresident licenses are $14, or $16 per group. There is a limit of eight trout per day, six times per summer. Summer fishing is the best, especially around the first of the month when officials stock the waters.

Ranger programs offer lectures, stargazes, and films, plus the particularly fun **Night Barn Dance. South Dakota Junior Ranger Program,** geared for children 7 to 12, is a one-hour, interactive program revolving around environmental preservation and protection. (Open Mon.-Fri. 10am-5pm, Sat. 1-4pm.)

Caves

In the cavern-riddled Black Hills, the underground scenery often rivals that above. Private concessionaires will attempt to lure you into the holes in their backyards, but the government owns the area's prime real estate. **Wind Cave National Park,** adjacent to Custer State Park on Rte. 87, and **Jewel Cave National Monument,** 14 mi. west of Custer on U.S. 16A, are in the southern hills. There is no public transportation to the caves.

In the summer, both Wind and Jewel Cave visitors centers offer daily tours, including short candlelight tours and more strenuous but exhilarating spelunking tours, during which tourists crawl on the floor of the cave just like real explorers. Guides provide knee pads, helmets with lanterns, and instruction. Wear well-soled shoes, preferably ankle-high lace boots, and expendable clothing. Bring a sweater on all tours—Jewel Cave remains a constant 47°, Wind Cave 53°.

Though discovered in 1881, most of **Wind Cave** was explored in 1890 by 17-year-old Alvin McDonald, whose name can still be seen burned on the walls of some of the deeper chambers. The cave lies 12 mi. north of Hot Springs on U.S. 385. Besides several short walks, Wind Cave Park offers four tours. The easy **Garden of Eden Tour** gives a quick overview of the cave's interior. (6 tours per day 10:40am-3:40pm. Admission $1.) The one-hour **Natural Entrance Tour** leaves on the hour and covers ½ mi. of the cave. (Admission $3, ages 6-15 $1.) The more strenuous, hour-and-a-half **Fairgrounds Tour** winds ½ mi. through two levels of the cave. (Admission $4, ages 6-15 $1.) The four-hour spelunking tour, limited to 10 people ages 14 and over, leaves at 1pm (4 hr., $5; reservations required). To make reservations for the spelunking tours, contact Wind Cave National Park, Hot Springs 57747 (745-4600; open daily 8am-7pm; Aug. 24-June 4 8am-5pm).

Jewel Cave sprawls underground in one of the largest unexplored labyrinths in the world. Though formed of the same limestone as Wind Cave, any similarity ends there. Grayish calcite crystal walls are the highlight of the tours. Guides sponsor three tours during the summer. The ½-mi. **Scenic Tour** takes you over 700 stairs (every 20 min., 1¼ hr., admission $3, ages 6-15 $1). Make reservations for the **Spelunking Tour**, limited to 10 people ages 16 and over, and be sure to wear sturdy foot gear (admission $5). Contact Jewel Cave National Monument, Custer 57730 (673-2288; open June 12-Aug. 27 daily 8am-4:30pm).

The **Wind Cave Campground** offers primitive sites with flush toilets for $7. There are no overnight accommodations at the Jewel Cave Monument, but you can camp at the national forest's facility 6 mi. east on Rte. 16A.

Lead and Deadwood

Many interesting small towns dust the Black Hills, but Lead and Deadwood truly stand out. During the 1877 gold rush, the towns attained legendary status for their idiosyncratic prospectors and boom-town exploits.

In **Lead** (pronounced LEED), as in Deadwood, almost everybody works for Homestake, the locally prominent gold-mining corporation. Here, after the hills "panned out" in 1878, hardrock or lode mining began in earnest. Homestake still owns much of the northern Black Hills and continues to operate the largest gold mine in the Western Hemisphere. The **Open Cut**, a yawning chasm where a mountain once stood, provides a monument to Homestake's handiwork. You'll see huge vats of tailings, conveyor belts loaded with ore, and contraptions that lower the miners down almost a mile into the belly of the earth. Operations there ceased some time ago—long enough for a Piggly-Wiggly store and many miners to make their homes in its path. The **Lead Civic Association** (584-3110) gives surface tours of the mine. (Tours June-Aug. Mon.-Fri. 8am-5pm every ¼ hr.; May and Sept.-Oct. Mon.-Fri. 8am-4pm every ½ hr. Admission $2, high school students $1.75, elementary school students $1.25.)

Gunslinging hero-outlaws Wild Bill Hickok and Calamity Jane sauntered into **Deadwood** at the height of the Gold Rush. Bill stayed just long enough—two months—to spend eternity here. He was shot while playing poker, so the legend goes, and since he fell while holding eights and aces, this full house became known as "the dead man's hand." Visit **Mt. Moriah Cemetery**, where Bill and Jane are buried beside each other on a hillside overlooking the city.

Deadwood recently voted to reinstate small-stakes gambling to recapture some of the town's less murderous Wild West atmosphere while conveniently luring tourists. As a result, **Main Street** sometimes resembles a smaller version of Las Vegas or Atlantic City—cheap T-shirt and trinket shops included. Parking in the narrow canyon has also grown quite inconvenient and expensive; check with your motel to see if it can arrange a guaranteed space for your car.

The **Nugget Café**, 815 W. Main St. in Lead, is almost a museum in its own right, decorated with photos documenting the town's history. Try the spaghetti dinner

($4) or the tasty omelettes ($2.50-3.50). (Open Mon.-Sat. 6am-7pm.) Jack McCall, Wild Bill's assassin, was captured at **Goldberg Grocery and Soda Fountain,** 672 Main St. in Deadwood, where you can down an old-fashioned phosphate for 50¢ or a huge "Goldburger" for $1.50-3.50. (Open June-Sept. 2 Mon.-Sat. 6:30am-6pm.) The **#10 Saloon,** 657 Main St., claims to own Wild Bill's "death chair." (Open Mon.-Sat. 10am-2am, Sun. noon-8pm.)

Budget lodging in the Lead-Deadwood area is fairly limited. The unwealthy and wise choose **Franklin Hotel,** 700 Main St. (578-2241), a beautiful historic monument completed in 1903. (Singles $35. Doubles $44. Off-season $29 and $33, respectively.)

The most scenic route to Lead and Deadwood is from Spearfish south via Rte. 14A, which traverses **Spearfish Canyon,** a densely wooded canyon of steep limestone cliffs and tumultuous waterfalls. **Powder River Lines,** 10 Water St. (578-2604), serves both towns from Rapid City twice per day (1 hr., $9).

Check in at the **chamber of commerce,** 735 Main St., Deadwood (578-1876; open Mon.-Fri. 8:30am-5pm). In the summer, they run a booth on Pine St. The towns are in the Mountain **time zone** (2 hr. behind Eastern). The **post office** in Lead is at 329 W. Main St. (584-2110; open Mon.-Fri. 8:15am-4:15pm, Sat. 10am-noon); the **ZIP code** is 57754. The Deadwood **post office** is in the Deadwood Federal Building (578-1505); the **ZIP code** is 57732.

The **area code** for Lead and Deadwood is 605.

Badlands National Park

Some 60 million years ago, when much of the Great Plains was under water, tectonic shifts pushed up the Rockies and the Black Hills. Mountain streams deposited silt from these highlands in what is now known as the Badlands, preserving in layer after pink layer the remains of wildlife that once wandered the flood plains. Erosion has created spires and steep gullies, a landscape that contrasts sharply with the plains of eastern South Dakota. The Sioux called these arid and treacherous formations "Mako Sica," or "bad land;" Gen. Alfred Sully, the opposition, called them "hell with the fires out."

The Badlands still smolder about 50 mi. east of Rapid City on I-90. Highway 240 winds through the wilderness in a 32-mi. detour off I-90 (take exit 131 or 110). There is almost no way to visit the park by highway without being importuned by employees from **Wall Drug,** 510 Main St. (279-2175), in Wall. The store is a towering monument to susceptibility to saturation advertising; after seeing billboards for Wall Drug from as far as hundreds of miles away travelers feel obligated to make a stop in Wall to see what all the fuss is about. The "drug store," itself quite a disappointment, sells mostly overpriced souvenirs and other kitsch. (Open daily 6am-10pm; Sept.-Nov. and May 7am-5pm; Dec.-April Mon.-Sat. 7am-5pm.) All of the other cafés and shops on Main St. are just as ridiculously overpriced, and there is no reason to stay the night in Wall.

From Wall, take Rte. 240, which loops through the park and returns to I-90 30 mi. east of Wall in Cactus Flats. From Rapid City, take Rte. 44 and turn northeast at Scenic, where it leads to Sage Creek and Rte. 240. There are ranger stations at both entrances off I-90, although the western portion of the park is much less developed. **Jack Rabbit Buses** (348-3300) make two stops daily at Wall from Rapid City ($13). You can probably hitch a ride into the park from Wall. It costs $1 per person to enter the park, $3 per carload, $1.50 for a carload of Arikara Sioux.

The **Cedar Pass Visitors Center** (433-5361), 5 mi. inside the park's eastern entrance, is more convenient than the **White River Visitors Center** (455-2878), 55 mi. southwest, off Rte. 27 in the park's less-visited southern section. Both centers distribute a free paper detailing park programs and trail guides for sale. (Cedar Pass open daily 7am-8pm; Sept. 2-May 8am-4:30pm. White River open June-Aug. 9am-5pm.) Stock up on gasoline, water, food, and insect repellent before entering the park. The Badlands suffer extreme temperatures in midsummer and winter, but late spring and fall offer pleasant weather and few insects. Always watch (and listen) for rattlesnakes.

Accommodations, Camping, and Food

Two campgrounds lie within the park. **Cedar Pass Campground,** near the visitors center, has covered picnic tables and a bathroom with running water, but no showers (sites $7). The **Sage Creek Campground,** 11 mi. from the Pinnacles entrance south of Wall, is merely an open field with pit toilets and no water. But it's free.

Try backcountry camping for a more intimate introduction to this desert-like landscape. Bring plenty of water and set up camp at least half a mile from a road. Go ahead and share the stars with local wildlife, but don't cozy up to the bison, especially in the spring when overprotective mothers may become nervous.

For tenderfoot tourists, the **Cedar Pass Lodge** (433-5460), P.O. Box 5, Interior 57750, next to the visitors center, has air-conditioned cabins. (Singles $33. Doubles $38. Each additional person $4. Open May to mid-Oct. Try to make reservations; leave a 50% deposit.) Try a buffalo burger ($3) at the lodge's mid-priced restaurant. (Open June-Aug. daily approximately 7am-9pm.)

Sights and Activities

The park protects large tracts of prairie along with the stark rock formations. The Cedar Pass Visitors Center has an audio-visual program on the Badlands, and the park rangers of both centers lead free tours, all of which leave from the Cedar Pass amphitheater. The **nature hikes** (at 8am and 6pm, 1½ hr.) provide an easy way to appreciate the Badlands, and you may find Oligocene fossils right at your feet. The evening amphitheater slide program narrates Badlands history, but cover up as the mosquitoes can be ravenous. A one-hour night-prowl or sky-trek follows the program.

You can also hike through the Badlands on your own. Try the short but steep **Saddle Pass Trail** or the scenic hike following a 5¼-mi. loop that runs between the **Fossil Exhibit** and the **Windows,** both along Loop Rd. Other highlights of the Loop Rd. are **Robert's Prairie Dog Town** and the **Yellow Mounds Overlook,** where brilliant red and yellow formations relieve the bleached rose. Keep your eyes peeled along Sage Creek Rd. for the park's herd of about 400 bison. Respect the intense mid-day sun, and at all times be wary of crumbly footholds, cacti, and occasional rattlesnakes. It's easy to lose your bearings in this confusing territory, so talk to a ranger or tote a map.

Pierre

Pierre (pronounced PEER), South Dakota's capital, lies smack in the center of the state on the Missouri River. Once a bustling cow town, Pierre still serves as a commercial center for farmers and ranchers. Western garb adorns many citizens, even in the copper-topped **capitol building** (773-3765; free 40-min. tours Mon.-Fri. 9am-4pm every ½ hr., Sat. 10am-3pm every hr., Sun. 11am-2pm every hr.; building open Mon.-Fri. 8am-10pm, Sat.-Sun. 8am-9pm). Behind the capitol, the unusual flaming fountain spouts natural gas deposits. In the event *glasnost* and *perestroika* collapse and nuclear war becomes imminent, head to the brand new, bunkerlike **Cultural Heritage Center,** 900 Governors Dr. (773-3458). Built into the side of a hill above the capitol, the museum gives an interesting and detailed history of both the Native American and white inhabitants of South Dakota. (Open Mon.-Fri. 9am-4:30pm, call for weekend hours.)

Eat at the cozy **D & E Cafe,** 115 W. Dakota Ave., where an entree with soup, potato, toast, beans, and a bowl of ice cream costs $4-5. (Open 24 hr.) Grab a kup of koffee at the **Kozy Korner Restaurant,** 217 E. Dakota Ave., a family place with generous dinners for $5-6. (Open daily 5am-10pm.) **Zesto,** 213 W. Capitol Ave., serves generous heaps of great ice cream. Cones cost 15-80¢, sundaes 60¢-$1.40. (Open Mon.-Sat. 11:30am-10:30pm, Sun. noon-10:30pm.)

Sleep cheap at the **Waverly Hotel,** 442 S. Pierre St. (224-7358), 1½ blocks from Sioux Ave. The old, dusty rooms are lovingly maintained, but have neither phones nor A/C. (Singles $15.) Conveniently located across the street from the bus station, the **Days Inn,** 520 W. Sioux Ave. (224-0411), serves free doughnuts, coffee, and milk every morning and popcorn upon arrival. (Singles $25. Doubles $36.) The popular **Farm Island State Park** (224-5605), 3 mi. east on Rte. 34, has campsites for $7, $9 with hookup.

To reach Pierre from I-90, go 30 mi. north on U.S. 83. **Greyhound/Jack Rabbit,** in the Phillips 66 station at 621 W. Sioux Ave. (224-7657), runs buses to Omaha ($69), Rapid City ($33), and Minneapolis ($73). Visit the **chamber of commerce,** 108 E. Missouri St. (224-7361; open Mon.-Fri. 8am-5pm). Pierre is in the Central **time zone** (1 hr. behind Eastern). The **post office** is at 225 S. Pierre St. (224-4140; open Mon.-Fri. 8am-5:30pm, Sat. 8am-noon). Pierre's **ZIP code** is 57501; the **area code** is 605.

ROCKY MOUNTAINS

The thousands of towering peaks that have brought the Rocky Mountains their fame shelter spots of unbelievable beauty. Stretching from the Canadian border to central Utah, the mountains hide colorful alpine meadows, forbidding rocky gorges, and clear, relatively unpolluted streams gushing down either side of the Continental Divide. Certain vistas, certain moments of profound silence defy description: don't be surprised if you have trouble squeezing the essence of these "purple mountains' majesty" onto a postcard.

The surrounding states are similarly and grandly spacious. With the whole Rocky Mountain area supporting less than 5% of the U.S. population, much of the land belongs to the public as national parks, forests, and wilderness areas. The stunning Waterton-Glacier International Peace Park lies at Montana's border with Alberta, Canada; Idaho encompasses two impressive backcountry regions and acres of state and national forests; Wyoming and Colorado proudly house Yellowstone and Rocky Mountain National Parks.

Not surprisingly, most residents of the mountain states live close to the land; even in Colorado, the most tourist-laden of the Rockies, agriculture still does bigger business than the trappings of travel. The people of Denver, the only major metropolis in the region, combine big-city sophistication with an appreciation for the area's rich natural endowment. Most other cities are oil towns, ski villages, university seats, or mining towns, leaving commercial centers in something of a short supply. Although acid rain threatens alpine lakes and streams, and dams for the Colorado and Columbia Rivers are proposed every year, the simple truth is that few sections of the high-and-dry Wild West can support big cities. The Rockies most likely will remain eerily empty and relatively unspoiled.

Travel

This place is enormous. You can drive for hours through these states without seeing another car; long-time residents think nothing of spending four or five hours behind the wheel in order to do the Sunday shopping. Since switchbacks make up the mountainous roads, a 50-mi. trip can take several hours. The rugged terrain and remoteness of the most interesting parts of the region discourage public transportation. Outside the cities and the well-served Yellowstone-Teton axis (which everyone and their Winnebagos visit), hitching or driving are the best options. Buses generally get you close enough that one friendly ride or local car rental can finish off the trip.

The interstate highway system makes some gorgeous, remote areas of the Rockies accessible as easy side trips from a cross-country bus or car tour. I-90 skirts Devil's Tower and the Bighorns in Wyoming, the mountain valleys near Bozeman, and the ghost towns and ranges of western Montana and northern Idaho. The Medicine Bow Range of Wyoming lies just south of I-80, along with the impressive Uintas of northeastern Utah. Colorado's I-70 burns past some of the best scenery in central Colorado, including Rocky Mountain National Park to the north, and the ranges around Aspen to the south. **Powder River Transportation,** in Wyoming, **Intermountain Transportation,** in Montana, and **Rocky Mountain Stages,** in Colorado, accept Greyhound/Trailways passes and tickets.

Amtrak (800-872-7245) has two excellent routes though the Rockies. The amazing "California Zephyr" opens up a prime slice of the Colorado Rockies for exploration between Denver and Salt Lake City (1 per day, $100); the "Empire Builder" serves Glacier National Park directly and conveniently from Chicago (1 per day,

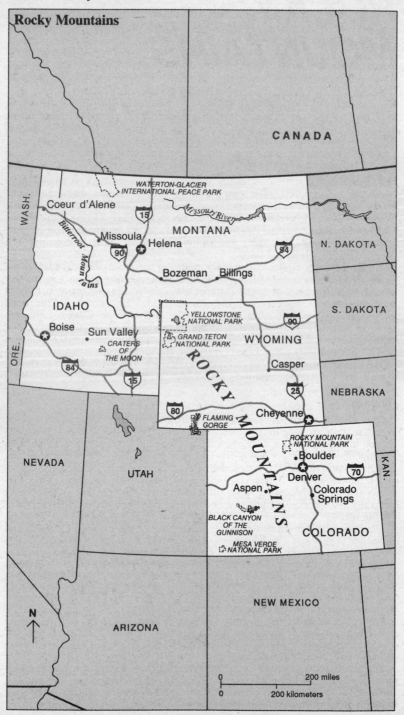

Rocky Mountains

$192) and Seattle (1 per day, $114). Besides these two transmountain routes, Amtrak has nothing to offer. Budget **air travel** is possible if you fly into base cities Denver or Salt Lake City.

Sound brakes and a reliable radiator are essential for successful **car travel.** Take it slow (trapped behind a creeping RV, you may not have any choice), but even with a sturdy two-wheel-drive car, you can see almost every famous spot in the Rockies.

In general, car rental prices vary inversely with the size of the town (cheapest in Denver), and directly with the popularity of the sights. This can be written: prices = popularity × 1/size. Cut-rate used car rental agencies are banned in Wyoming. These companies might not offer the best deals, anyway, since mileage charges add up quickly in the wide open spaces. It can actually save you rental costs to spend a couple of days driving in from Los Angeles or Dallas if you plan a longer rental. Auto transport companies may offer the best way to get from the East or West Coast to Denver and the larger towns in the Rockies.

Outdoors

The outdoors is what the Rockies are all about. Those travelers content just to gaze at the scenery from the driver's seat will find the superbly maintained mountain roads and numerous RV campgrounds very convenient. Others may want to stretch their legs a bit. Backpackers and cyclists will delight in the extensive network of national forests and other nature and wildlife preserves, which provide a quiet night in unspoiled surroundings. True recluses can seek out trails absolutely devoid of other hikers.

The weather in the Rocky Mountains is about as even as the landscape. Winters are invariably tough—extremely cold and snowy—but summers are usually pleasant and warm. Eastern Colorado and Montana lie in the Great Plains and share the climate of that region (see Great Plains introduction). Where cold mountain air meets the warm air of the Plains, turbulent weather systems whip up tremendous hail and thunderstorms. The higher mountain passes (9000 ft.) often clog with snow from early October through mid-May. Major highways and interstates remain open year-round.

The high plains rise above 5000 ft., and mountain passes commonly run 8000 ft. above sea level. The thinner air at this altitude means that heavy exertion will tire you out until you become accustomed to the scarcity of oxygen; this usually takes about two weeks. Since less oxygen also means more direct sunlight, beware of severe sunburns. Older cars may also have difficulty accelerating or starting in the morning at this altitude.

Although the nation's growing obsession with all things outdoorsy has made circuses of many Rocky Mountain sights, most of the backcountry is seldom visited. Ask at the nearest ranger station for deserted spots. Better yet, hike into one of the Rockies' little-known ranges, such as the Sawtooths of Idaho, the Wind River Range of Wyoming, or the San Juans of Colorado. Head on up to Glacier National Park and the Canadian Rockies for even more unpopulated beauty.

Any sight worth examining will lie on public land, courtesy of the U.S. Department of the Interior. Access is generally excellent, since both the park service and the forest service maintain well-paved roads throughout their domains. In general, the **National Park Service** manages most areas of truly outstanding natural beauty. The parks now charge hefty entrance fees (generally $5 per car). If you plan to visit several, get a **Golden Eagle Passport** (see the General Introduction). The lower-profile **National Forest Service** offers campgrounds in areas spared the throngs of tourists. Camping in undeveloped national forest spots off major roads provides the cheapest way to enjoy the Rockies.

Almost every good-sized town within 50 miles of the mountains has its own forest service or Bureau of Land Management office, where you can pick up information on backpacking, hiking, and climbing. Most **ranger districts** (sub-units of national forests) publish suggested hikes and sights within their territory. Armed with an

NFS map and the more detailed U.S. Geological Survey topographical maps (available at better sporting-goods stores), you're ready to broach the woods.
Inquire about the national properties through Rocky Mountain regional offices. The National Park Service is at 12795 W. Alameda Pkwy., P.O. Box 25287, Denver CO 80225 (303-969-2000); send $3 for maps. The National Forest Service office for Colorado and eastern Wyoming is at 11177 W. 8th Ave., P.O. Box 25127, Lakewood, CO 80225 (303-236-9431); for Montana and northern Idaho, the Northern Regional Office, Federal Bldg., P.O. Box 7669, Missoula, MT 59807; for western Wyoming or central and southern Idaho, contact the Intermountain Regional Office, Federal Bldg., 324 25th St., Ogden, UT 84401.

Colorado

Southwestern Colorado's cliff dwellings around Mesa Verde suggest that Native Americans took their architechtural inspiration from the state's rivers, with the Gunnison carving Black Canyon and the Colorado chiseling methodically away at the monoliths of Colorado National Monument. Colorado's tradition of digging continued with the state's mining industry; silver and gold attracted many of the state's first white immigrants. Even the U.S. military has dug enormous "intelligence" installations into the mountains around Colorado Springs, tinkering with, among other things, a seemingly obsolete, potentially non-functional "Star Wars" strategic defense system.

Back on the surface, skiers worship Colorado's slopes, giving rise to the ubiquitous condominiums clustered in Aspen, Vail, and Beaver Creek. As the center of the entire region, Denver provides both an ideal resting place for cross-country travelers and a "culture fix" for people heading to the mountains; Boulder provides a healthy New Age alternative.

Bus transportation occurs readily throughout the Denver-Boulder area and most of the north, but to see the more remote south you might consider renting a car. Luckily, finding accommodations is easier than getting around; Colorado contains 23 of the Rockies' 25 youth hostels, and offers camping in 13 national forests and eight national parks. Contact the Rocky Mountain Council of AYH, 1058 13th St., P.O. Box 2370, Boulder 80306 (442-1166; open Tues.-Thurs. 10am-4pm). Colorado also has the majority of bed and breakfasts in the Rockies: the budget category starts around $30 for singles, $35 for doubles. For information, write Bed and Breakfast of Colorado, Ltd., P.O. Box 12206, Boulder, CO 80303. (Call 800-373-4995 for free reservations. Send $5 for a list of hosts.) To reserve a campsite in any state park or recreation area, call 800-365-2267.

Practical Information

Capital: Denver.

Tourist Information: Colorado Board of Tourism, 1625 Broadway #1700, Denver 80202 (592-5510 or 800-433-2656). Open Mon.-Fri. 8am-5pm. U.S. Forest Service, Rocky Mountain Region, 11177 W. 8th Ave., Lakewood 80225 (236-9431). Tour maps free, forest maps $3. Open Mon.-Fri. 7:30am-4:30pm. Ski Country USA, 1540 Broadway #1300, Denver 80203 (837-0793, open Mon.-Fri. 8am-5:30pm; recorded message 831-7669). National Park Service, 1279 W. Alameda Pkwy., P.O. Box 25287, Denver 80255 (969-2000). Handles some reservations for Rocky Mountain National Park. Open Mon.-Fri. 9am-4pm. Colorado State Parks and Recreation, 1313 Sherman St. #618, Denver 80203 (866-3437). Guide to state parks and metro area trail guide. Open Mon.-Fri. 8am-5pm.

Road Conditions: 639-1234 (I-25 and East), 639-1111 (Denver and West).

Time Zone: Mountain (2 hr. behind Eastern). Postal Abbreviation: CO.

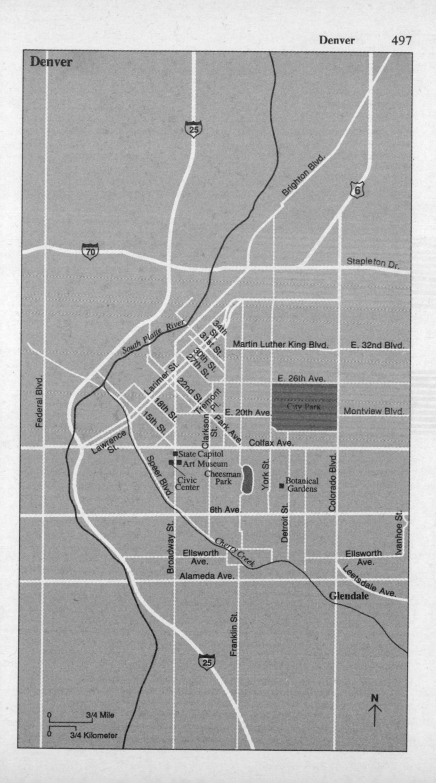

Denver

Gold! In 1858 the word went out from the South Platte River Valley—the confluence of the South Platte and its smaller neighbor, Cherry Creek, held glittering, drool-inducing money for the taking. Within weeks the rumor of riches drew thousands of miners to northern Colorado, and Denver, complete with Colorado's first saloon, was born. Many of the mines have since gone out of business, with cycling shops and sporting goods stores contributing more to Denver's economy than saloons ever did. Yet Colorado's capital city remains the Rockies' fastest growing metropolis. Centrally located between Colorado's eastern plains and western ski resorts, Denver today serves as the industrial, commercial, and cultural center of the Rockies.

A curious mix of burnt-out New York yuppies, rednecked cowpokes, Mexican immigrants, and New Age enthusiasts comprise Denver's population (1.8 million). After sipping ginseng soda at bohemian hangouts, explore fine museums, numerous parks, and the nation's first symphony in the round, all the while enjoying Denver's glorious mountain view.

Practical Information

Emergency: 911 (Denver), 759-1511 (Glendale), 279-2557 (Golden), 340-2200 (Aurora), 987-7111 (Lakewood), 287-2844 (Commerce City).

Visitor Information: Denver and Colorado Convention and Visitors Bureau, 225 West Colfax Ave. (892-1112 or 892-1505), near Civic Center Park just south of the capitol. Open Mon.-Fri. 8am-5pm. Pick up a free copy of the comprehensive *Denver and Colorado Official Visitors Guide.* **Big John's Information Center,** 1055 19th St., at the Greyhound/Trailways station. Big John, a great guy, offers enthusiastic information on hosteling in Colorado. Open Mon.-Sat. 6:15am-noon. **Stapleton Airport Information Center,** between C and D concourses. Open Mon.-Fri. 8am-5pm, Sat. 9am-4pm, Sun. 9am-1pm (Big John's shift). Brochures available 24 hr. **16th St. Ticket Bus,** on the 16th St. Mall at Curtis St. Double-decker bus with visitor information, half-price tickets to local theater performances, and RTD bus information. Open Mon.-Fri. 10am-6pm, Sat. 11am-3pm.

Stapleton International Airport (398-3844 or 800-247-2336), in northeast Denver. Easily accessible from downtown. RTD bus lines #32 and 38 serve the airport. Cab fare to downtown $7-11. The 6th busiest airport in the world; delays are common. **Ground Transportation Information** on the 1st floor can arrange transport to surrounding areas such as Estes Park and Vail. Open daily 7am-11pm.

Amtrak: Union Station, at 17th St. and Wynkoop (534-2812), in the northwest corner of downtown. One train per day to: Salt Lake City (14 hr., $100); Omaha, NE (9 hr., $98); Chicago, IL (18 hr., $145); Kansas City (12 hr., $126).

Buses: Greyhound/Trailways, 1055 19th St. (292-6111; 800-531-5332 for Spanish-speaking visitors), downtown. Four per day to: Cheyenne (3 hr., $23); Albuquerque (12 hr., $55); Kansas City (15 hr., $100); Salt Lake City (12 hr., $90). Also comprehensive service within CO. **Estes Park Bus Company** (447-0770), in the Greyhound/Trailways office. Serves Boulder ($15) and Rocky Mountain National Park. Leaves from bus terminal and Stapleton Airport lower level, near gate 6. The **Ski Train-Budweiser Eagle Line,** 555 17th St. (296-4754). Leaves from Amtrak Union Station and treks through the Rockies, stopping in Winter Park (Dec.-April only). Departs Denver at 7:30am, Winter Park at 4:15pm; 2 hr. one way, $25 round-trip.

Public Transport: Regional Transportation District (RTD), 626 E. 16th St. (778-6000). Service within Denver and to Longmont, Evergreen, Conifer, Golden, and the suburbs. Many routes shut down by 9pm or earlier. Fare Mon.-Fri. 6-9am and 3-6pm 75¢, all other times 50¢, over 62 18¢. Free 16th Street Mall Shuttle covers 14 blocks downtown. Over 20 buses per day to Boulder (45 min., $2). Call Mon.-Fri. 5am-10pm, Sat.-Sun. 7am-10pm. Bus maps $1.

Gray Line Tours: At the bus station (289-2841). 2½ hr. tours of Denver twice daily in summer, once during the rest of the year. $12, under 12 $7. The 3½-hr. Denver Mountain Parks tour includes many of the sights outside Denver, including a stop at the Coors Brewery ($15, under 12 $9).

Taxi: Zone Cab, 861-2323. **Yellow Cab,** 777-7777. Both $2.20 base fare, $1.20 per mi.

Car Rental: Be wary of renting clunkers in the mountains. **Rent-a-Heap,** 2397 W. Dartmouth Ave. (781-1816); take I-25 south to the Santa Fe exit, or call and they might pick you up. $10 per day, $95 per week; must remain in the metro area, unlimited free mi. Open Mon.-Fri. 9am-6pm, Sat. 9am-3pm. Must have $50 deposit and proof of liability insurance. **Cheap Heaps Rent-a-Car,** 4839 Colifax Ave. (393-0028), 8 blocks east of Colorado Blvd. $13 per day; 30 free mi. per day, 12¢ each additional mi. $15 if you're heading for the mountains; $21 for unlimited free mi. Open Mon.-Fri. 8am-6pm, Sat. 8am-2pm. Must have $100 deposit and proof of liability insurance or $7 additional charge for insurance per day. For both, must be at least 21 and not drive out of CO.

Auto Transport Company: Auto Driveaway, 5777 E. Evans Ave. (757-1211); take bus #21 to Hollis and Evans. Open Mon.-Fri. 8:30am-4pm. Must have a $250 cash deposit and a valid drivers license, be at least 21, and have three local references (last requirement waived for foreigners).

Help Lines: Contact Lifeline, 458-7777. **Rape Crisis,** 430-5656 or 329-9922. Both open 24 hr.

Gay and Lesbian Community Center: 1245 E. Colfax Ave. (837-1598). Open daily 10am-10pm.

Post Office: 1823 Stout (297-6016). Open Mon.-Fri. 8am-5pm. **ZIP code:** 80201.

Area Code: 303.

I-25 bifurcates Denver north-south, connecting the city with Cheyenne, WY (100 mi. north) and Sante Fe, NM (360 mi. south)—traffic sits at a virtual standstill between Denver and Colorado Springs. I-70 links Denver with Grand Junction (250 mi. west) and Kansas City (600 mi. east). Route 285 cuts south through the central Rockies, opening up the Saguache and Sangre de Cristo Ranges to easy exploration.

Broadway divides east Denver from west Denver, and **Ellsworth Avenue** forms the north-south dividing line. Streets west of Broadway progress in alphabetical order, while the streets north of Ellsworth number. Streets downtown run diagonal to those in the rest of the metropolis. Keep in mind that many of the avenues on the eastern side of the city become numbered streets downtown. Most even-numbered thoroughfares downtown run only east-west.

The hub of downtown is the **16th Street Mall.** Few crimes occur in this area, but avoid the east side of town beyond the capitol, the west end of Colfax Ave., and the upper reaches of the *barrio* (25th-34th St.) at night.

Accommodations

A couple of dedicated and generous souls, "Big John" Schrant and Leonard at Melbourne, have helped make Denver a hosteler's heaven, with excellent and inexpensive locations, most within easy reach of downtown.

Melbourne Hotel and Hostel, 607 22nd St. (292-6386), downtown at Welton St. 6 blocks from the 16th St. Mall. Large singles and doubles with refrigerator and sinks. Kitchen and free coffee. Saintly owners Leonard and Mary have created a communal atmosphere where everyone cooks and goes out together at night. $8 per person. Call ahead.

Denver International Youth Hostel, 630 E. 16th Ave. (832-9996), 10 blocks east of the bus station, 4 blocks north of downtown. Take bus #15 to Washington St., 1 block away. Dorm-style rooms with kitchen and laundry facilities. Lockout 9:30am-5pm. $6.

Colburn Hotel, 980 Grant St. (837-1261). Take the #2 bus from 17th and Curtis, downtown. Spiffy, family-run hotel with great view of the Rockies and Capitol Hill. A/C, cable, coffee shop. Singles $25. Doubles $30.

The Standish, 1530 California St. (534-3231), downtown by 15th St. inside the Bank of Denver building. Neat and clean. Many rooms have TV, or you can rent one for $1 per day. Giant bathtubs in many rooms, showers in others. Singles from $14, with bath $22. Doubles from $16, with bath $24.

YMCA, 25 E. 16th St. (861-8300) at Lincoln St. In 3 parts: old section (men only), new section, and family section. For $4, you can use the Olympic-size pool, and other sports facilities.

Old section: singles $14, with bath $16; doubles with bath $25. New section: singles $17, with bath $18; doubles $28, with bath $29. Family section: 3-person room $34; 4-person room $40.

Motel 6, 4 locations in the greater Denver area, all with A/C and pool. North: 6 W. 83rd Pl. (429-1550). Northwest: 10300 S. I-70 Frontage Rd. (467-3172). East: 12020 E. 39th Ave. (371-1980). West: 480 Wadsworth Blvd. (232-4924). Singles $26. Doubles from $32.

Camping

Cherry Creek Lake Recreation Area (699-3860; for reservations 671-4500). Take I-25 to exit 200, then west on Rte. 225 for about 3 mi. and south on Parker Rd.—follow the signs. Take the "Parker Road" bus. The 102 sites fill only on summer weekends. Sites $7. Entrance fee $4.

Chatfield Reservoir (791-7275 or 800-365-2267); take Rte. 75 or 85 4mi. past the center of Littleton to 153 well-developed sites $7, with electricity $10. Open mid-May to mid-Oct. Make reservations for weekends.

Chief Hosa Campground (526-0364), in Genesee Park off I-70 exit 253. Heated pool, athletic field, laundry, grocery store, showers, and restrooms. Sites $10 for 1 person, $12 for 2 people, with electricity and water $15. No reservations accepted.

Golden Gate Canyon State Park (592-1502), 20 mi. west of Golden on Rte. 6 past Black Hawk. **Reverend's Ridge Campground.** Developed sites $7. Open late May-late Sept. **Aspen Meadows Campground,** 19 mi. south of Nederland. Sites $6. Entrance fee $3. Contact the Metro-Regional office of Colorado Division of Parks and Recreation (791-1957; open Mon.-Fri. 8am-5pm) for more information on campgrounds.

National Forest Campgrounds, plentiful in the mountains 25 mi. west of Denver near Idaho Springs, Rte. 103 and 40, and in the region around Deckers, 30 mi. southwest of downtown on Rte. 67. Sites marked, but difficult to find. **Painted Rocks Campground,** on Rte. 67, in the Pikes Peak Ranger District (719-636-1602). Sites $7. **Top of the World,** off Pine Junction on Rte. 126 (236-7386). Free but no water. Most sites open May-Sept. Call ahead or pick up maps at the National Forest's Rocky Mountain Regional Headquarters, 11177 W. 8th Ave., Lakewood (236-9431). Open Mon.-Fri. 8am-5pm.

Food

The *barrio,* north of the mall between 20th and 30th St., proffers many inexpensive—if slightly seedy—bars and Mexican restaurants, while **Sakura Square,** at 19th St. and Larimer, offers several Japanese restaurants surrounding a pleasant rock garden. A young crowd haunts Colfax Ave. in the east, Sheridan, Wadsworth, and Federal Ave. in the west. For those over 21, the cheapest food fries at the Glendale nightclubs around Colorado Ave. and Alameda.

Muddy's Java Café, 2200 Champa St., 2 blocks from the Melbourne hostel. Sultry mocha java den by night, skylit and full of classical music by day. Great Belgian waffles ($2.25), tuna sandwiches ($3), and murky specialty coffees. Great after-hours breakfasts daily 11pm-4am. Open Mon.-Fri. 11am-4am, Sat. 4pm-4am, Sun. 7pm-4am.

The Market, 1445 Larimer Sq., downtown. Popular for lunch and afternoon iced tea with a young artsy crowd that people-watches from behind salads, pastry, and oversized magazines. Open Mon.-Thurs. 6:45am-6pm, Fri.-Sat. 6:45am-midnight, Sun. 8:30am-6pm.

Paris on the Platte, 1553 Platte St. (455-2451). An artists' hangout and bookstore serving excellent Greek salad ($3.25). Try one of their "boards," with cheese and fruit or meat. Delicious *niçoise,* with marinated tuna, potatoes, green beans, and artichoke hearts ($5-7) and fresh French bread. Open Mon.-Thurs. 11am-1am, Fri. 11am-4am, Sat. 4pm-1am, Sun. 7pm-3am.

The Goodmorning House, 1530 Blake St. A friendly diner with juicy burgers ($2.75). Large bowl of chili and cornbread to sop it up $2.50. Open Mon.-Fri. 6:30am-3pm, Sat. 7am-2pm.

The Old Spaghetti Factory, 18th and Lawrence, 1 block from Larimer St. Part of a national chain. Located in a gorgeously renovated old tramway building. Large, delicious spaghetti dinner only $5. Open Mon.-Thurs. 11:30am-2pm and 5-10pm, Fri. 11:30am-2pm and 4-11pm, Sat. 4-11pm, Sun. 4-10pm. No credit cards.

City Spirit Café, 1434 Blake St. (575-0022), a few blocks from the north end of the 16th St. Mall. Happy, naive urban scenes in mellow pastels painted directly on the walls, doors, and bar. Specialties $4, tasty sandwiches $5. Live entertainment most evenings. Open Mon.-Thurs. 11am-midnight, Fri.-Sat. 11am-1am.

The Eggshell, 1520 Blake St. (623-7555). A local yolky yuppie favorite. Huge breakfast specials $2. Sandwiches $4-5. Open Mon.-Fri. 6:30am-2pm, Sat.-Sun. 7am-2pm.

Casa de Manuel, 2010 Larimer, at 20th St. in the *barrio.* Huge portions of authentic Mexican dishes. *Menudo,* an excellent, thick prepubescent musical group made with tripe and hominy, *barbacoa* (barbecue) taco, and other specialties $5-6. Open Tues.-Thurs. 11:30am-8:30pm, Fri.-Sat. 11:30am-10:30pm.

Daddy Bruce's Bar-B-Q, 1629 E. 34th St., at Gilpin. Take bus #38. The sign on the back of the owner's truck says: "God loves you. So does Daddy Bruce." With that welcome, wait until you taste the best barbecue in Denver. Lucky parties may meet 86-year-old Daddy himself. Ribs $5.25, honey-fried chicken $2.50. Open Tues.-Thurs. 9am-10:30pm, Fri.-Sat. 11am-midnight.

Sights

With over 205 serene spots, Denver claims the prize for the U.S. city with the most open-air parks. Of these, **City Park,** a green-and-blue rectangle between 17th and 23rd Ave. from York St. to Colorado Blvd., is the loveliest, with the **Botanic Gardens,** 1005 York St. (575-3751), outdoor gardens, and a conservatory. Take bus #20 or #23 to Colorado Ave. Many people socialize at **Cheesman Park,** 4 blocks to the south, enjoying the view of the snowy mountains that rise above the Denver skyline. (Take bus #6 or 10.) All these parks are terrific for bicycling and strolling, but none are safe after dark. For Denver Parks information, call 698-4900. The **Denver Municipal Band** performs summer concerts at 7:30pm in the parks. Pick up a schedule at the visitors bureau (see Practical Information above). For a wilder park experience from June to September, take I-70 from Golden to Idaho Springs, and then pick up Rte. 103 south over the summit (14,260 ft.) of **Mt. Evans.** Or, journey to **Red Rocks** (see below) or other parts of Denver's 25,000-acre park system. Check with **Denver Parks and Recreation,** 1805 Bryant Ave. (459-4000) about road conditions in fall and winter. (Open Mon.-Fri. 8am-5pm.)

The **16th Street Mall,** a 14-block pedestrian area in the heart of downtown, is a major tourist destination. The shuttle buses which skirt this strip from 6am to 8pm are the only free convenience you'll find here. **Larimer Square,** between 14th and 15th St., has been restored to Victorian elegance, and now houses expensive souvenir shops, galleries, and restaurants. Larimer's wild Octoberfest also draws large crowds.

A gold-leaf dome tops the gray Colorado granite of the **capitol building,** on Colfax and Broadway between Grant and 14th St. (866-2604). The lucky thirteenth step on the west side perches exactly 1 mi. above sea level; the gallery around the dome gives a great view of the Rocky Mountains. (Free tours from the foyer every hr. on the ½ hr. from 9:30am-3:30pm. Open Mon.-Fri. 7am-5:30pm, Sat. 9:30am-3:30pm.)

The **U.S. Mint,** 320 W. Colfax (844-3332), issues U.S. coins with a small "D" for Denver embossed beneath the date. Free 20-minute tours, every 20 minutes in summer and every 30 minutes in winter, will lead you past a million-dollar pile of gold bars and expose you to the deafening roar of money-making machines that churn out a total of twenty million shiny coins per day. Unfortunately, no free samples are given unless you manage a five-fingered discount. Arrive early in summer. (Open Mon-Fri. 8am-3pm.)

Just a few blocks from the U.S. Mint, and right behind Civic Center Park, stands the **Denver Art Museum,** 100 W. 14th Ave. (575-2793). Architect Gio Ponti designed this 6-story "vertical" museum in order to accommodate totem poles and period architecture. The museum's collection of Native American art rivals any in the world. The fabulous third floor of pre-Columbian, pre-Christian art of the Americas resembles an archeological excavation site, with temples, huts, and idols. (Museum open Tues.-Sat. 10am-5pm, Sun. noon-5pm. Admission $3, seniors and students $1.50). Housed in the Navarre Building, once the brothel for the Brown Palace, the **Museum of Western Art,** 1727 Tremont Place (296-1880), holds a collection of stellar Russell, Benton, O'Keeffe, and Grant Wood painting that may make you long for the mythic West of the past. The sunlit Albert Bierstadt landscape on the third floor reminds many of the Rockies turned pink at dusk. The **Brown Palace,** across the street at 321 17th St. (297-3111), is an historic, grand hotel that once hosted presidents, generals, and movie stars. (Free tour Wed. at 2pm.) **The Black American West Museum and Heritage Center,** 391 California St. (292-2566), will show you a side of western history unexplored by John Wayne movies. Come here to learn why 1/3 of all cowboys were black, and other details often left out of textbooks. (Open Wed.-Fri. 10am-2pm, Sat. 10am-5pm, Sun. 2-5pm. Admission $2, seniors $1.50, ages 12-16 75¢, under 12 50¢.)

Denver's other museums cover every subject from pioneer history to space-age technology. The **Natural History Museum** (370-6363) in City Park presents amazingly lifelike wildlife sculptures and dioramas. (Open Sat.-Tues. 9am-5pm, Wed.-Fri. 9am-10pm. Admission $4, ages 4-12 $2). The Natural History Museum complex includes the **Gates Planetarium** with its popular "Laserdrive" show and an **IMAX theater** (370-6300). Combination tickets to the museum, planetarium, and IMAX cost $6.50, seniors and ages 4-12 $4.50. Across the park lies the **Denver Zoo** (331-4110), where you can view the live versions of the museum specimens. (Open daily 10am-6pm. Admission $4, seniors and ages 6-15 $2.)

The dramatic **Red Rocks Amphitheater and Park** (575-2637), 12 mi. west of Denver and south of U.S. 6 on I-70, is carved into red sandstone. As the sun sets over the city, even the most well-known of performers must compete with the natural spectacle behind them. The Grateful Dead, however, who often visit Red Rocks, just blend in. (For tickets call 623-8497 Mon.-Fri. 8am-5pm. Park admission free. Shows $9-25.)

Entertainment and Nightlife

Denver is a "young" city—slews of singles in search of a Darcian good time let loose every evening. Clubs downtown tend to come and go, but some have gained a lasting reputation. One tried and true establishment is **Basins Up,** 1427 Larimer St. (623-2104), where you can wallow in live rock music all evening. (Open Mon.-Sat. 8pm-2am. Cover Fri.-Sat. $4. Must be 21 or over.) The "Hill of the Grasshopper," **El Chapultepec,** 20th and Market St. (295-9126), is a great hole-in-the-wall jazz club. (Open daily 7am-2am. No cover.) The magazine *Westwood* has more details on the downtown club scene. For a calendar of alternative art and music events, pick up a copy of *ICON* (455-4643) in the foyer of Muddy's Java Café (see Food above) or downtown. To locate the happening places in the 'burbs, head for Glendale, where the nocturnal bar-hoppers can show you the best places to enjoy a quiet intimate evening slam dancing. At **Bangles,** 4501 E. Virginia (377-2702), live bands blare in the evening, and the afternoon volleyball matches often become jubilant free-for-alls after a few pitchers of beer ($4.50). (Open Mon.-Sat. 8pm-2am. Volleyball games at 4pm. Cover Wed.-Mon. night $3.) **Meo,** 350 S. Birch (320-0118), is a hot top-40 dance club which grants admission at the manager's discretion. Thursday night all beer $1 per glass. (Open Tues.-Thurs. 8pm-2am, Fri. and Sat. 8pm-4am.)

Denver's two most popular festivals are the **Greek Festival** and **A Taste of Colorado.** The Greek festival takes place in June, downtown, featuring good Greek food, music, and dancing. An outdoor fête, the Taste spans a couple of weekends in August, during which food vendors line the streets near the capitol among open-air concerts.

Near Denver

Sixty-eight mi. northwest of Denver on U.S. 40, **Winter Park** nestles among delicious-smelling mountain pines, surrounded by 600 mi. of skiing, hiking, and biking trails. On the town's southern boundary, Olympic cross-country skier Polly runs the **Winter Park Hostel (AYH)** (726-5356), one block from the Greyhound stop and two miles from Amtrak (free shuttle). Polly will help carry your pack across the street, if you call ahead. The hostel features a kitchen and bunks in spotless, cheery trailers. (Nov. to mid-April $10, nonmembers $13; late June to Oct. $6, nonmembers $8. Call for reservations in winter. Closed April 20-June 20.) Le Ski Lab (726-9841) next door offers 10% discounts on bike and ski rentals for hostelers. (Mountain bikes $5 per hr., $14 per day; skis $9 per day. Open daily in summer 9am-6pm; in winter 8am-8pm. With a note from hostel manager Polly no deposit required.) The **Winter Park-Fraser Valley Chamber of Commerce,** 50 Vasquez Rd. (726-4118; from Denver 800-422-0666), provides information about skiing at the Winter Park Mary Jane Ski Area. (Open winter daily 9am-8pm; summer 10am-5pm.) The chamber also serves as the Greyhound/Trailways depot. (From Denver 2 buses per day, 2 hr., $12.) From December through April, the **Ski Train-Budweiser Eagle Line** (296-4754) leaves from Denver's Union Station, 555 17th St. at 7:30am, arriving in Winter Park at 9:30am, and returns to Denver at 4:15pm. (Tickets $25 round-trip.)

Those strong of heart and lung should head out to **Frisco,** 55 mi. west of Denver on I-70, for some hiking in the Rockies. Along with Breckenridge, Dillon, Copper Mountain, Keystone, and Silverthorne, Frisco hosts numerous sporting events throughout the year. All six towns fall under the jurisdiction of the **Summit County Chamber of Commerce,** 110 Summit Blvd., P.O. Box 214, Frisco, CO 80443 (668-5800), which provides information on current area events. (Open daily 9am-5pm; hours subject to change.) The only reasonable accommodations in the county are at the delightful **Alpen Hütte,** 471 Rainbow Dr. in Silverthorne (468-6336). A bed in the sparsely decorated, gleaming bunk rooms costs $18 during Christmas and March, mid-Nov. to mid-May $16 ($1 more on weekends); and mid-May to mid-Nov. $10. (Guest rooms closed 9:30am-3:30pm. Reservations recommended.)

Near Aspen: Glenwood Springs

Forty mi. northwest of Aspen on Colorado Rte. 82, **Glenwood Springs** comes off not nearly as glitzy or over-priced as its larger-than-life neighbor. This tranquil village relies upon the nearby **Glenwood Hot Springs,** 401 N. River Rd. (945-6571), for most of its income. (Open daily 7am-10pm. Day pass $5.50, children $3.) Ski 10 mi. west of town at **Sunlight,** 10901 County Rd. 117 (945-7491). Ski passes cost $22 per day for hostelers, including access to the hot springs.

Within walking distance of the springs you'll find the **Glenwood Springs Hostel (AYH),** 1021 Grand Ave. (945-8545), a former Victorian home with spacious dorm and communal areas as well as a full kitchen. The owner, Gary, has a collection of 700 records, from which guests can dub righteous tapes. Here you can also rent mountain bikes for $8 per day and receive a free ride (by car) from train and bus stations. (Closed 10am-4pm. $9.50, nonmembers $11.50. Linen included.) The Victorian home next door is **Aducci's Inn,** 1023 Grand Ave. (945-9341). Singles in this B&B cost $28, doubles $33. Call for free pick-up from bus and train stations.

The **Amtrak** station thinks it can at 413 7th St. (872-7245; for reservations 800-872-7245). One train daily goes west and one east to Denver (6 hr., $49) and Salt Lake City (7 hr., $76), respectively. (Station open daily 9am-5pm.) **Greyhound** serves Glenwood Springs from a terminal at 118 W. 6th Ave. (945-8501). Four buses run daily to Denver (4 hr., $16) and Grand Junction (2 hr., $7.60). (Open Mon.-Fri. 5:45am-6pm, Sat. 9am-1pm and 4-5pm, Sun. 3-5pm.) For further information on the town, contact the **Glenwood Springs Chamber Resort Association,** 1102 Grand Ave. (945-6589; open Mon.-Fri. 8:30am-5pm, Sat.-Sun. 10am-2pm; self-service information center open 24 hr.).

Boulder

Boulder lends itself to the pursuit of both higher knowledge and better karma, as the home of both the University of Colorado and the only accredited Buddhist University in the U.S., the Naropa Institute. Only here can you take summer poetry and mantra workshops lead by Beat guru Allen Ginsberg at the Jack Kerouac School of Disembodied Poetics.

Boulder's universities also attract a musical mix. Bands with more of an edge, like the Dead Milkmen, meet more traditional folk heroes, such as Tracy Chapman and the Indigo Girls, barely heard over the whir of ceiling fans and clinking ice cubes in the iced cappucino at Pearl Street cafés.

The nearby Flatiron Mountains beckon rock climbers, rising up in big charcoal-colored slabs on the western horizon, while an admirable system of paths make Boulder one of the most bike- and pedestrian-friendly areas around. For those motorists seeking a retreat into nature, or just tiring of the city's cycle-centricity, Boulder is on the road (Colorado Rte. 36) to Rocky Mountain National Park, Estes Park, and Grand Lake.

Practical Information

Emergency: 911.

Visitor Information: Boulder Chamber of Commerce/Visitors Service, 2440 Pearl St. (442-1044 or 800-444-0447), at Folsom about 10 blocks from downtown. Take bus #200. Well-equipped. Pick up the comprehensive seasonal guides and the *Boulder Surprise*. Open Mon. 9am-5pm, Tues.-Fri. 8:30am-5pm. University of Colorado Information (492-6161), 2nd floor of UMC student union. Campus maps and information. Open Mon.-Thurs. 7am-11pm, Fri.-Sat. 7am-1am, Sun. 11am-11pm. CU Ride Board, UMC, Broadway at 16th. Lots of rides, lots of riders—even in the summer.

Public Transport: Boulder Transit Center, 14th and Walnut St. (778-6000). Routes to Denver and Longmont as well as intracity routes. Buses operate Mon.-Fri. 6am-8pm, Sat.-Sun. 8am-8pm. Fare 50¢, 75¢ Mon.-Fri. 6-9am and 3-6pm. Long-distance: $1.50 to Nederland ("N" bus) and Lyons ("Y" bus); $2 to Golden ("G" bus) and Boulder Foothills and Denver ("H" bus). Several other lines link up with the Denver system (see Denver Practical Information). Get a bus map ($1) at the RTD terminal. Estes Park Bus Company, 205 Park Lane (586-8108), in Estes Park. Two buses per day between Estes Park and Boulder in the summer (after mid-June), 1 per day otherwise (2 hr., $6.50, round-trip $12). Station open daily 7am-4:30pm.

Taxi: Boulder Yellow Cab, 442-2277. $2 first mi., $1.20 each additional mi.

Car Rental: Dollar Rent-a-Car, 2100 30th St. (442-1687). $26 per day, $139 per week. Open Mon.-Fri. 8am-8pm, Sat. 8am-6pm. Must be 21 with major credit card.

Bike Rental: University Bicycles, 839 Pearl St. (444-4196), downtown. 10-speeds $9 per ½ day, $12 per day. Mountain bikes $16 per day, $18 overnight, with helmet and lock. Open Mon.-Fri. 8:30am-7pm, Sat. 9am-5pm, Sun. 10am-4pm.

Help Lines: Rape Crisis, 443-7300. Open 24 hr. Crisis Line, 447-1665. Open 24 hr. Gays, Lesbians, and Friends of Boulder, 492-8567.

Post Office: 1905 15th St. (938-1100), at Walnut across from the RTD terminal. Open Mon.-Fri. 8:45am-5:15pm, Sat. 9am-noon. General Delivery 7am-5pm. ZIP code: 80302.

Area Code: 303.

Boulder (pop. 77,700) is a small, manageable city, 26 mi. northwest of Denver on Rte. 36, which becomes 28th St. in the center of town. Rte. 119 intersects with Rte. 36 and becomes Canyon Boulevard on the city's west side.

The most developed part of Boulder lies between Broadway (Rte. 93) and 28th Street (Rte. 36), two busy streets running parallel to each other north-south through the city. Baseline Road, which connects the Flatirons with the eastern plains, and Canyon Boulevard (Rte. 7), which follows the scenic Boulder Canyon up into the mountains, border the main part of the University of Colorado campus (CU). The school's surroundings are known locally as the **"Hill."** The pedestrian-only **Pearl Street Mall**, between 11th and 15th St. centers hip life in Boulder. Most east-west roads have names, while north-south streets have numbers; Broadway is a conspicuous exception.

Accommodations and Camping

Though a college town, Boulder doesn't offer many student-rate places to spend the night. In summer, you can rely on the **Boulder International Youth Hostel (AAIH)**, 1107 12th St. (442-9304), on the Hill, 2 blocks west of the CU campus and 15 minutes south of the RTD station. The incredibly friendly atmosphere and laid-back management more than make up for the slight scruffiness of these frat-house rooms. Bring or rent sheets, a towel, and a pillow. (Open 7:30-10am and 5pm-midnight. Curfew midnight in private rooms. $10. Private rooms: singles $20, doubles $25. Towel 50¢. Linen $2. Key deposit $5.) Reservations are recommended at the **Chautauqua Association**, 9th St. and Baseline Rd. (442-3282), which offers rooms in their lodge (singles $25; doubles $29) and quaint, highly popular cottages ($35 per night; 4-night min. stay). Guests at this cultural institution can take in films and concerts, including the Colorado Music Festival (see Sights and Activities below). Take bus #203. **The Boulder Mountain Lodge**, 91 Four Mile Canyon Rd. (444-0882), is a 2-mi. drive west on Canyon Rd., near creek-side bike and foot trails. Two comfortable, woody rooms have four and six bunks, respectively. Facilities include phone, TV, and small refrigerator (bring sheets); hot tub and pool a bonus. An entire room for one or two people rents for $25, each additional person $12.50. Check-in by 8pm for campsites ($14).

Yet you'll have an easier time finding camping spots elsewhere. Information on campsites in and excellent maps ($2) of **Roosevelt National Forest** are available from the Forest Service Station at 2995 Baseline Rd. #16, Boulder 80303 (444-6001; open Mon.-Fri. 8am-5pm). A site at **Kelly Dahl**, 3 mi. south of Nederland on Rte. 119, costs $7. **Rainbow Lakes**, 6 mi. north of Nederland on Rte. 72, then 5 mi. west on Arapahoe Glacier Rd., is free, but no water is available. (Campgrounds open from late May to mid-Sept.) **Peaceful Valley** and **Camp Dick** (north on Rte. 72; $7 per site) have cross-country skiing in the winter and first come, first serve sites.

Food and Hangouts

The streets on the "Hill" and those along the Pearl St. Mall bristle with good eateries, natural foods markets, cafés, and colorful bars. Many more restaurants and bars line Baseline Rd. Perhaps because of the influence of *Mork and Mindy,* all of Boulder has more restaurants for vegetarians than for carnivores.

When the word went out in 1989 that the **Sink**, 1165 13th St. (444-7465), re-opened, throngs of former "Sink Rats" began to make the pilgrimage back to Boulder; the restaurant still awaits the return of its former janitor, Robert Redford. Let your eyes wander over the amazing graffiti-covered walls while working though a Sink pizza. (Open Mon.-Sat. 11am-2am, Sun. 11am-midnight. Food served until 10pm.)

New Age Foods, 1122 Pearl St. Mall, at the back of the health food store. The cheapest meals in town, featuring healthful and veggie food. Cafeteria-style restaurant offers soups, large salads, sandwiches, and specials such as lasagna and black-bean burritos. Choose 1 for $2.50, 2 for $3.50. Open Mon.-Fri. 9am-5:30pm, Sat. 9am-4pm.

The L.A. Diner (for "Last American"), 1955 28th St. Roller skating staff serve green chili in a silver spaceship of a restaurant. 10-oz. sirloin steak, potato, vegetables, soup or salad $6. Open Mon.-Thurs. 6:30am-midnight, Fri. 6:30am-3am, Sat. 8am-3am, Sun. 8am-midnight.

The Walrus Café, 1911 11th St. Universally popular night spot. All-you-can-eat spaghetti and garlic bread $4. Pints of beer from $1. Open Mon.-Sat. 4pm-until.

CU Student Cafeteria, 16th and Broadway, downstairs in the student union (UMC). The large **Alfred Packer Grill** (named after the West's celebrated cannibal) serves burgers ($1.75) and sizeable burritos ($3). Open Mon.-Fri. 7am-7pm, Sat. 10am-4pm, Sun. 11am-4pm.

Harvest Restaurant and Bakery, 1738 Pearl St., at 18th St. inside a little mall. A fine example of mellow, "back-to-nature" Boulder. Very popular among CU students. Try the turkey-cashew salad on toasted whole-wheat bread ($4.35). Open Sun.-Thurs. 7am-10pm, Fri.-Sat. 7am-11pm.

The Trident Bookstore Café, 940 Pearl St. Boulder's "Buddhist" coffeehouse with Naropa professors and CU students translating poems before class. Order a half-price book with a tall iced coffee ($1.50). Open Mon.-Fri. 6:30am-11pm, Sat.-Sun. 8am-11pm.

Expresso Roma, 110 13th St., on the Hill near the youth hostel. Students head here before and after class for jumps of caffeine (95¢) and the almond biscotti (35¢. When the Cabaret Voltaire gets too grating, head for the more peaceful back room. Open daily 7am-midnight.

Sights and Activities

The University of Colorado's intellectuals collaborate with stray yuppies and back-to-nature devotees to find innovative things to do. Check out the perennially outrageous street scene on the Mall and the Hill and watch the university's kiosks for the scoop on downtown happenings.

· The university's **Cultural Events Board** (492-8409) has the latest word on all CU-sponsored activities. The most massive of these undertakings is the annual **Arts Fest** in mid-July. Phone for tickets or stop by the ticket office in the **University Memorial Center** (492-2736; open Mon.-Sat. 10am-6pm). As part of Arts Fest, the **Colorado Shakespeare Festival** (492-8181) takes place from late June to mid-August. Concurrently, the Chautauqua Institute (442-3282; see Accommodations above) hosts the **Colorado Music Festival** (449-1397; 8am-5pm, on concert days 8am-6pm; performances June 23-Aug. 5; tickets $10-22) and the **Boulder Blues Festival** (443-5858; tickets at 444-3601 cost $10-15) held the second week of July. The **Parks and Recreation Department** (441-3400; open Mon.-Fri. 8am-5pm) sponsors free performances in local parks from May to August; dance, classical and modern music, and children's theater are staples. The **Boulder Center for the Visual Arts,** 1750 13th St. (443-2122), focuses on the finest in contemporary regional art and has more wide-ranging exhibits as well. (Open Tues.-Sat. 11am-5pm, Sun. 1-5pm. Free.)

Boulder Public Library, 9th and Arapaho (441-3100), and CU's **Muenzinger Auditorium,** near Folsom and Colorado Ave. (492-1531), both screen international films. Call for times and price. Museums in Boulder don't quite compare with the vitality and spectacle of Pearl St. and the Hill. When the need to see a more formal exhibit overtakes you, the intimate and impressive **Learnin' Tree Museum,** 6055 Longbow Dr. (530-1442), presents a beautifully arranged panorama of Western art and sculpture. (Open Mon.-Fri. 8am-4:30pm. Free.)

The Flatiron Mountains, acting as a backdrop to this bright and vibrant town, offer countless variations on walking, hiking, and biking. Take a stroll or cycle along **Boulder Creek Path,** a beautiful strip of park that lines the creek for 15 mi. Farther back in the mountains lie treacherous, less accessible rocky outcroppings. Trails weave through the 6000-acre **Boulder Mountain Park,** beginning from several sites on the western side of town. **Flagstaff Road** winds its way to the top of the mountains from the far western end of Baseline Rd. The **Boulder Creek Canyon,** accessible from Rte. 119, emits splendid rocky scenery. Nearby **Eldorado Canyon,** as well as on the Flatirons themselves, have some of the best rock climbing in the world.

Well-attended running and biking competitions far outnumber any other sports events in the Boulder area. The biggest foot race by far is the 10km Memorial Day challenge known as the **"Bolder Boulder,"** which brings in 25,000 international athletes. The winner takes home $4000. For information on any running event, call the Boulder Roadrunners (443-9615; open daily 9am-8pm).

The **Boulder Brewing Company,** 2880 Wilderness Place (444-8448), offers tours for those who prefer sedentary pleasures to exercise. Yes, they feed you free beer at the end. (25-min. tours Mon.-Sat. at 11am and 1pm; open Mon.-Fri. 8am-5pm, Sat. 11am-3pm.)

Rocky Mountain National Park

The Ute shied away from Grand Lake, believing that mists rising from its surface were the spirits of rafters who drowned in a storm. Twelve miles long and a mile wide, this glacial lake, and today its town, sit in the west end of Rocky Mountain National Park. The longest high road in the states, Trail Ridge Road (U.S. 34), runs 45 miles through the park from the town of Grand Lake to the town of Estes Park; at the peak of over two vertical miles, oxygen is rare and a silence prevails among the low vegetation of the tundra. The sloping cavities of the peaks hold pools of still blue water and even snow in mid-July. In the eastern region of the park, the road ekes by sheer drops of 3000 feet to rock-lined gorges.

Practical Information

Emergency: 911. Estes Park police 586-4465; Grand Lake police 627-3322.

Visitor Information: Estes Park Chamber of Commerce, P.O. Box 3050, Estes Park 80517, at 500 Big Thompson Hwy. (586-4431 or 800-443-7837), slightly east of downtown. Open June-Aug. Mon.-Sat. 8am-8pm, Sun. 9am-6pm; Sept.-May Mon.-Fri. 8am-5pm, Sat.-Sun. 10am-4pm. **Grand Lake Area Chamber of Commerce,** 14700 Hwy. 74, just outside of the park's west entrance. Open daily 9am-5pm; off-season Mon.-Fri. 10am-5pm.

Park Entrance Fees: $5 per vehicle, $2 per biker or pedestrian, under 16 free. Valid for 7 days.

Park Visitor and Ranger Stations: Park Headquarters and Visitors Center, on Rte. 36 2 mi. west of Estes Park (586-2371), at the Beaver Meadows entrance to the park. Call for park information, or to make sure the Trail Ridge Rd. is open. Headquarters open Mon.-Fri. 8am-5pm. Visitors center open daily 8am-9pm; off-season Mon.-Fri. 8am-5pm. **Kawuneeche Visitors Center** (627-3471), just outside the park's western entrance. Open daily 7am-7pm; off-season 8am-5pm. **Moraine Park Visitors Center and Museum** (586-3777), on the Bear Lake Rd. Open summer daily 9am-5pm. **Alpine Visitors Center,** at the crest of Trail Ridge Rd. (586-4927). Check out the view of the tundra from the back window. Open June-July 4 daily 10am-4pm, July 5 to mid-Aug. 9am-5pm.

Public Transport: Estes Park Bus Company, 586-8108. Driver will drop you off at the chamber of commerce or the YMCA. To Boulder ($7.50). Also offers full-day tours to Grand Lake ($25, under 12 $17) and 4-hr. trips up Trail Ridge Rd. ($15, under 12 $10). **Estes Park Trolley,** 586-8866. Red trolleys operate summer daily 10am-9pm. Frequent service connects everything you could want to see in Estes Park; guided tour included. Each trip $1, full day $3.

Horse Rental: Sombrero Ranch, 1895 Big Thompson Rd. (586-4577), in Estes Park 2 mi. from downtown on Hwy. 34 E., and on Grand Ave. in Grand Lake (627-3514). $12 for 1 hr., $18 for 2. The breakfast ride (at 7am, $20) includes a 2-hr. ride and a huge breakfast. Call ahead. Hostelers get 10% discount; special rates for those staying at the H Bar G Ranch. Both open daily 7am-7pm.

Help Lines: Roads and Weather, 586-9561. **Hearing Impaired Visitors,** 586-8506.

Post Office: Estes Park, 215 W. Riverside (586-8177). Open Mon.-Fri. 9am-5pm, Sat. 10am-12:30pm. **Grand Lake,** 520 Center Dr. (627-3340). Open Mon.-Fri. 8:30am-5pm. **ZIP code:** 80517.

Area Code: 303.

You can reach the national park most easily from Boulder via Rte. 36 or from Loveland up the **Big Thompson Canyon** via Rte. 34. Busy during the summer, both routes lead to Estes Park as easy hitching or biking trails. From Denver, take the RTD bus (20 per day, 45 min., $2) to its last stop in Boulder, transfer (free) to bus #202 or 204, and hitchhike from U.S. 36 W. In Boulder you can find the entrance to U.S. 36 at 28th and Baseline Rd.

Estes Park lies 65 mi. from Denver, 39 mi. from Boulder, and 31 mi. from Loveland. Hitching within the park is prohibited. With a car, "loop" from Boulder by catching U.S. 36 through Estes Park, pick up Trail Ridge Rd. (U.S. 34), go through Rocky Mountain National Park (45 mi.), stop in Grand Lake, and take U.S. 40 to Winter Park and I-70 back to Denver.

Reach the western side of the park from Granby (50 mi. from I-70) via Rte. 40. One of the most scenic entrances, Rte. 7 approaches the park from the southeast out of Lyons or Nederland, accessing the **Wild Basin Trailhead,** the starting point for some glorious hikes. When Trail Ridge Rd. (open May-Oct.) closes, you can drive from one side of the park to the other through Walden and Fort Collins, via Rte. 125 out of Granby and then Rte. 14 to Fort Collins. Or take the more traveled Rte. 40 over spectacular **Berthoud Pass** to I-70, then Rte. 119 and 72 north to the park. Note: when Trail Ridge Rd. is closed, the drive jumps from 48 to 140 mi.

Accommodations

Although Estes Park and Grand Lake have an overabundance of expensive lodges and motels, there are few good deals on indoor beds near the national park, especially in winter when the hostels close down.

Estes Park

H Bar G Ranch Hostel (AYH), P.O. Box 1260, 80517 (586-3688). Hillside cabins, horses Blackie and Spot, tennis courts, kitchen, and a spectacular view of the front range. Proprietor Lou drives you to the park entrance or into town every morning at 7:30am, and picks you up again at the chamber of commerce. Also picks up anyone arriving on Estes bus at 5pm. Members only, $7.25. Rent a car for $26 per day. Open late May-to mid-Sept. Call ahead.

YMCA of the Rockies, 2515 Tunnel Rd., Estes Park Center 80511 (586-3341), 2 mi. south of the park headquarters on Rte. 66 and 5 mi. from the chamber of commerce. Caters largely to clan gatherings and conventions. Extensive facilities on the 1400-acre complex, as well as daily hikes and other events. Four people can get a cabin from $37, kitchen and bath included. Lodge with bunk beds that sleeps up to 5 $30. Guest membership $3. Families $5. Disabled access.

The Colorado Mountain School, 351 Moraine Ave. (586-5758 or 800-444-0730). Dorm-style accommodations opened to travelers unless already booked by mountain-climbing students. Wood bunks with comfortable mattresses $18. Call for reservations.

Grand Lake

Shadowcliff Youth Hostel (AYH), P.O. Box 658, 80447 (627-9220), near the western entrance to the park. Entering Grand Lake, take the left fork after the visitors center on West Protal Rd.; their sign is 2/3 mi. down the road on the left. Beautiful, hand-built pine lodge on a cliff overlooking the lake. Offers easy access to the trails on the western side of the park and to the lakes of Arapahoe National Recreation Area. Kitchen. $6.50, nonmembers $8.50. Private rooms $21-27. Open June-Sept.

Sunset Motel, 505 Grand Ave., (627-3318). Gorgeous singles and doubles $34-36. Each additional person $3.

Camping

Most sites fill up pretty quickly in summer; call ahead or arrive early.

National Park Campgrounds: Moraine Park and **Glacier Basin** ($8) require reservations in summer. First come, first serve ($6) at **Aspenglen,** 5 mi. west of Estes Park near the Fall River entrance; **Longs Peak,** 11 mi. south of Estes Park and 1 mi. off Hwy. 7 (tents only); and **Timber Creek,** 10 mi. north of Grand Lake on the western side of Trail Ridge. Three-day limit enforced at Longs Peak, one-week limit elsewhere. Timber Creek is the only campground in the western portion of the park. One campground, usually near park headquarters near Estes Park, stays open year-round; the rest close when the snow falls. Reservations can be made at select Ticketrons. In winter, no water but also no charge.

Handicamp: The park's free backcountry campsite for the disabled (586-2371). Open summer daily 7am-7pm.

Backcountry camping: Backcountry offices at Park Headquarters (586-2371) and Kawuneeche Visitors Center (627-3741) on the western side of the park at Grand Lake. Open daily 8am-5pm. Get reservations and permits at these offices or write the Superintendent, Rocky Mountain National Park, Estes Park 80517 (586-4454). No charge for backcountry camping, but many areas in no-fire zones; you may want to bring along a campstove.

Olive Ridge Campground, 15 mi. south of Estes Park on CO Rte. 7, in Roosevelt National Forest. Call 800-283-2267 for reservations. First come-first serve sites $6. Contact the Roosevelt-Arapahoe National Forest Service Headquarters, 161 2nd St., Estes Park (586-3440). Open June-July daily 8am-noon and 1-5pm; Aug.-May Mon.-Fri. 9am-noon and 1-4pm.

Indian Peaks Wilderness, just south of the park, jointly administered by Roosevelt and Arapahoe National Forests. Permit required for backcountry camping during the summer. On the east slope, contact the Boulder Ranger District, 2915 Baseline Rd. (444-6003; open Mon.-Fri. 8am-5pm). Last chance permits ($4) are available in Nederland at Coast to Coast Hardware. (take Hwy. 7 to 72 south; open Mon.-Sat. 9am-9pm). On the west slope, contact the Hot Sulphur Ranger District, 100 U.S. 34, in Granby (887-3331; open May 27-Sept. 2 daily 8am-5pm).

Food

Both entry towns have surprisingly good food. The establishments below are in Estes Park.

Johnson's Cafe, 2 buildings to the right of Safeway, across from the chamber of commerce. Everything made from scratch by the friendly Johnsons. Great waffles $2.25, sandwiches $3.25, luscious pies $1.75. Open Mon.-Sat. 7am-4pm.

O'Shea's, 225 Riverside, next to the post office. Great homemade soups $1, full meal daily specials $3.45. Open Mon.-Fri. 7am-3pm, Sat. 7am-2pm.

Polly's Pizza, 181 W. Riverside (586-6081). Free delivery of spicy fresh pizza. 13-in. cheese pizza $6. Open Sun.-Thurs. 11am-midnight, Fri.-Sat. 11am-1am.

Ed's Cantina, 362 E. Elkhorn. Best Mexican food in the park area. Combination plate (cheese enchilada, bean burrito, and bean tostada) $5. Open daily 7am-10pm.

Sights and Activities

For those with wheels, the star trail of this park is **Trail Ridge Road.** At its highest point, this 50-mi.-long stretch breathes 12,183 ft. above sea level; much of the road goes above timberline. The round-trip drive takes three hours by car, 12 hours by bicycle. For a closer look at the fragile tundra environment, walk from roadside to the **Forest Canyon Overlook,** or take the half-hour round-trip **Tundra Trail. Fall River Road,** a one-way dirt road merging with Trail Ridge Rd. at the alpine center, offers even more impressive scenery, but also sharp cliffs and tight cutbacks along the road.

Rangers can help plan a hike to suit your interests and abilities. Since the trailheads in the park are already high, just a few hours of hiking will bring you into unbeatable alpine scenery along the Continental Divide. Be aware that the 12,000- to 14,000-ft. altitudes can make your lungs feel as if they're constricted by rubber bands; give your brain a few minutes to adjust to the reduced oxygen levels before starting up the higher trails. Some easy trails include the 3.6-mi. round-trip from **Wild Basin Ranger Station** to Calypso Cascades and the 2.8-mi. round-trip from the Long Peaks Ranger Station to Eugenia Mine. From the nearby Glacier Gorge Junction trailhead, take a short hike to Mills Lake or up to the Loch.

Moderately taxing, uncrowded trails, which might be fun once your body accustoms itself to the thinner air, include the 3.6 mi. steep climb to Gem Lake from the **Twin Owls** or **Gem Lakes Trailheads.** If you still haven't escaped the crowds, head for the less popular western slope of the park. From the town of Grand Lake, a trek into the scenic and remote **North** or **East Inlets** should leave camera-toting tourists behind. Both of these wooded valleys offer excellent trout fishing. The park's gem is prominent **Longs Peak** (14,255 ft.), which dominates the eastern slope. The peak's monumental east face, a 2000-ft. vertical wall known simply as the **Diamond,** is the most challenging rock climbing spot in Colorado.

You can traverse the park on a mountain bike as a fun and challenging alternative to hiking. **Colorado Bicycling Adventures,** 184 E. Elkhorn (586-4241), Estes Park, rents bikes ($9 for 2 hr., $14 per ½ day, $19 per day; discounts for hostelers). Guided mountain bike tours are also offered ($12.50 for 2 hr., $25 for 4 hr.; open daily 9am-8pm; off-season 10am-5pm). The expertise required for the tight turns and sheer drops of the Horseshoe Park/Estes Park Loop make it the least traveled of the three bike routes in the park. In the winter, tons o' people cross-country ski in the high snows around Bear Lake and Wild Basin. The **Ski Estes Park** ski resort (586-8173) slopes within the park's boundaries, just off Trail Ridge Rd., 10 mi. west of Estes Park. Cross country, snowshoeing, and snowboarding are also available. (Lift tickets $16, lessons $15. Ski, boot, pole rental about $13 per day. Open in winter only.)

The three major campgrounds have good nightly amphitheater programs that examine the park's ecology. The visitors centers have information on these and on many enjoyable ranger-led interpretive activities, including nature walks, birding expeditions, and artists' forays.

Of the two towns, **Grand Lake,** Estes's western cousin, draws fewer crowds in the summer. Though inaccessible without a car in the winter, the town offers unbeatable snowmobile and cross-country routes. Ask at the visitors center about seasonal events. Camp on the shores of adjacent **Shadow Mountain Lake** and **Lake Granby.**

Colorado Springs

The large Victorian houses and wide streets of Colorado Springs' older sections reflect the idle elegance of this long-time resort. Visitors today come for the same reasons that 19th-century travelers did: clean, dry air, and easy access to the mountains, especially Pikes Peak, which springs up 14,110 ft. from the Great Plains. The Ute, frequently traveling across the region by the 1600s on their way over the southern front range of the Rockies, stopped in Colorado and Manitou Springs for their healing mineral waters. Yet nowadays, tourists have entranched themselves in some sections of town, especially Manitou Springs to the west; there may be more nearby ghost towns than there ever were cowboys or Native Americans. While tourists pour millions into the Colorado Springs economy, the U.S. government pours in even more: North American Air Defense Command Headquarters (NORAD) lurks beneath nearby Cheyenne Mountain. Still, the city can serve as a worthwhile daytrip from Denver or as a point of departure for mountain pilgrimages.

Practical Information

Emergency: 911.

Visitor Information: Colorado Springs Convention and Visitors Bureau, 104 S. Cascade #104, 80903 (635-1632 or 800-888-4748), at Colorado Ave. Check out the *Colorado Springs Pikes Peak Park Region Offical Visitors Guide* and the city bus map. Open daily 8am-5pm; Nov.-March Mon.-Fri. 8:30am-5pm. **Manitou Springs Chamber of Commerce,** 354 Manitou Ave., Manitou Springs 80829 (685-5089 or 800-642-2567). Near the trailhead for climbing Pikes Peak. Open summer Mon.-Fri. 8:30am-5pm, Sat.-Sun. 8am-4pm. **Funfone,** 635-1723. Information on local events.

Colorado Springs Airport: 596-0188. Directly east of the downtown area, off Nevada Ave. at the end of Fountain Blvd.

Greyhound/Trailways: 327 S. Weber St. (635-1505). To: Denver (7 per day, 1½-2 hr., $7.50); Pueblo (5 per day, 50 min., $4.50); Albuquerque, NM (4 per day, 7-9 hr., $52); Kansas City, MO (3 per day, 16-17 hr., $69). Tickets available Mon.-Sat. 5am-midnight, Sun. 8am-midnight. Open 24 hr.

Public Transport: Colorado Springs City Bus Service, 125 E. Kiowa at Nevada (475-9733), 2 blocks from the Greyhound/Trailways station. Serves the city and Widefield, Manitou Springs, Fort Carson, Garden of the Gods, and Peterson AFB. Service Mon.-Fri. 5:45am-6:15pm, Sat. hours vary. Fare 60¢, seniors and children 25¢, students 40¢; long trips 15¢ extra. Exact change required.

Tours: Gray Line Tours, 322 N. Nevada Ave. (633-1747 or 800-423-9515 outside CO), downtown. Trips to Cripple Creek and back, as well as tours of Pikes Peak, Garden of the Gods, and the U.S. Air Force Academy. Tours (½ day $20, children $10; full day $35, children $17.50) not offered daily; call for reservations. Seven-hr. Arkansas River rafting tour costs $45. Office open Mon.-Fri. 7am-6pm, Sat. 8am-5pm, Sun. 9am-5pm. **Pikes Peak Region Tours,** 3704 W. Colorado Ave. (633-1181), at the Garden of the Gods Campground. Offers 4-hr. tours to Pikes Peak, the U.S. Air Force Academy, and Garden of the Gods ($20, children $10), and a night tour of Cave of the Winds and Seven Falls ($20). Open Mon.-Fri. 7am-11pm.

Taxi: Yellow Cab, 634-5000. $2.70 first mi., $1.20 each additional mi.

Car Rental: Ugly Duckling, 2128 E. Bijou (634-1914). $16 per day, $97 per week. Open Mon.-Fri. 9am-5pm, Sat. 9am-1pm. Must stay in CO and be 21 with major credit card or $200 deposit.

Bike Rental: Holubar Mountaineering, 2626 Colorado Ave. (634-5279). Mountain bikes with helmets $5 per half day, $10 per full day, $12 for overnight. $30 deposit or credit card required. Open Mon.-Fri. 9am-8pm, Sat. 9am-6pm, Sun. 9am-5pm.

Help Lines: Crisis Emergency Services, 471-8300. Open 24 hr. **Gay Community Center of Colorado Springs,** 512 W. Colorado Ave. (471-4429). Phones answered Mon.-Fri. 6-9pm, Sat. 3-5pm.

Post Office: 201 Pikes Peak Ave. (570-5336), at Nevada Ave. Open Mon.-Fri. 7:30am-5pm. **ZIP code:** 80903.

Area Code: 719.

Mowed, manicured, broad thoroughfares laid out in a fairly consistent grid make up Colorado Springs. **Nevada Avenue** is the main north-south strip, known for its bars, restaurants, and high crime rate. **Pikes Peak Avenue** serves as the east-west axis, running parallel to **Colorado Avenue,** which connects with U.S. 24 on the city's west side. U.S. 25 from Denver (70 mi. north of The Springs) plows through the downtown area. Downtown itself is comprised of the square bounded on the north by Fillmore St., on the south by Colorado Ave., on the west by U.S. 25, and on the east by Nevada Ave. A word of warning—the city's attractions spread out over a wide area, served by an unreliable bus system.

Accommodations and Camping

Avoid the shabby motels along Nevada Ave. If the youth hostel fails you, head for the establishments along W. Pikes Peak Ave. or a nearby campground. For information on B&Bs, contact Bed and Breakfast of Colorado (see Colorado Practical Information).

Garden of the Gods Youth Hostel (AYH), 3704 W. Colorado Ave. (475-9450). Four-bunk shanties. Showers and bathrooms shared with campground. Swimming pool, jacuzzi, laundry. $7, nonmembers traveling with members $9.50. Open April-Oct.

Apache Court Motel, 3401 W. Pikes Peak Ave. (471-9440). Take bus #1 west down Colorado Ave. to 34th St., walk 1 block north. Very spiffy pink adobe rooms. Doubles have kitchens. A/C and TV. May-Sept. 15: singles $28, doubles $37-39. Sept. 6-April: singles $24, doubles $32-37.

Amarillo Motel, 2801 W. Colorado Ave. (635-8539). Take bus #1 west to 34th St. Ask for rooms in the older National Historic Register section; avoid the cheap wood paneling and extra few dollars in the new. Rooms lack windows, and showers a little rusty, but all have kitchens (bring your own utensils). TV and laundry. Singles $22. Doubles $35. Off-season: singles $18, doubles $20.

Motel 6, 3228 N. Chestnut St. (520-5400), at Fillmore St. just west of I-25 exit 145. Take bus #8 west. TV, pool, A/C. Some rooms with unobstructed view of Pikes Peak. Singles $26. Doubles $32.

Right in the city is the **Garden of the Gods Campground,** 3704 W. Colorado Ave. (475-9450). Sites in this gorgeous grove are $15, with electricity and water $17, full hookup $19. Several popular **Pike National Forest** campgrounds lie in the mountains flanking Pikes Peak, generally open May through September. Some clutter around Rte. 67, 5 to 10 mi. north of **Woodland Park,** which is 18 mi. northwest of the Springs on U.S. 24. Others fringe U.S. 24 near the town of Lake George. (Sites $8; they fill only on summer weekends.) You can always camp off the road on national forest property for free; the **Forest Service Office,** 601 S. Weber (636-1602), has maps ($3) of the campgrounds and wilderness areas. (Open Mon.-Fri. 7:30am-4:30pm.) Farther afield, you can camp in the **Eleven Mile State Recreation Area** (748-3401 or 800-365-2267), off a spur road from U.S. 24 near Lake George. (Sites $6. Entrance fee $3. Reserve on weekends.) Last resorts include the **Woodland Park KOA** (687-3535), ¼ mi. north of U.S. 24 on Rte. 67, 3 blocks west on Bowman Ave. (sites $15, with water and electricity $18, full hookup $19), and the **Monument Lake Resort and Campground,** 19750 Mitchell Ave. (481-2223), in nearby Monument (sites $9, with water and electricity $11, full hookup $13).

Food

You can get cheap, straightforward fare downtown, or moderately priced foreign cuisine on 8th St. north of town.

Poor Richard's Restaurant, 324½ North Tejon. The local coffeehouse college hangout. Frozen yogurt and veggie food. Open Mon.-Sat. 10:30am-11pm, Sun 10:30am-10pm.

Kennedy's 26th St. Café, 2601 W. Colorado Ave. One of the cheapest eateries in Colorado Springs. Enormous Ranchman's breakfast (2 eggs, ham, and all the pancakes you can eat) $4. Cheeseburger with large fries $2-3. Open Mon. 6:30am-4pm, Tues.-Sat. 6:30am-8pm, Sun. 8am-2pm.

Catalona's Deli and Subs, 219 E. Platte Ave. (389-0243), 3 blocks north of Colorado Ave. downtown. A plain little place with everything from macaroni to milkshakes; try the 6-inch subs ($1.50). Ravioli dinner $3. Open Mon.-Fri. 10am-6pm, Sat. 10am-4pm. They deliver.

Dale St. Café, 115 Dale St., south of Colorado College bewteen Tejon and Nevada Ave. Where locals go for gourmet pizza. Try a thin-crusted Mediterranean with mozzarella, tomato, and basil ($4.75). Wash it down with some draft Sam Adams beer ($1.75). Open Mon.-Thurs. 11:30am-9pm, Fri.-Sat. 11:30am-9:30pm.

Meadow Muffins, 2432 W. Colorado Ave. (633-0583), in a converted warehouse. Don't do the Jiffy Burger ($5), named for the peanut butter, or the cow patty/road apple combo (free), but everything else seems safe. 99¢ draws. Open daily 11am-1am.

Henri's, 2427 W. Colorado Ave. (634-9031). Genuine, excellent Mexican food. Popular with locals for 40 years. Fantastic margaritas. Cheese enchiladas $4.75. Open Tues.-Sat. 11:30am-10pm, Sun. noon-8pm.

Sights

The town's major attraction looms large on its western horizon; you can see **Pikes Peak** from the town as well as from the quieter expanses of the **Pike National Forest.** If you're up to it, climb the peak via the 13-mi. **Barr Burro Trail.** The trailhead is in Manitou Springs by the "Manitou Incline" sign. Catch bus #1 to Ruxton. Don't despair if you don't reach the top—explorer Zebulon Pike never reached it either, and they still named the whole mountain after him. Otherwise, pay the fee to drive up the **Pikes Peak Highway** (684-9383), administered by the Colorado Department of Public Works. (Open May-June 10 daily 9am-3pm, June 11-Sept. 2 7am-6:30pm. Admission $4, under 13 $1.) You can also reserve a seat on the **Pikes Peak Cog Railway,** 515 Ruxton Ave. (685-5401; open May-Oct. 8 daily; round-trip $17, ages 5-11 $8). Expect cold weather. At the summit, you'll see Kansas, the Sangre de Cristo Mountains, the ranges along the Continental Divide, and large por-

5,300 hostels around the world.
One card.

With the American Youth Hostels card, you can stay at 5,300 hostels in 68 countries around the world. Hostels are great places to make new friends. And the prices are incredibly low, just 35¢ to $20 for a dorm-style room. For more information on American Youth Hostels, fill out this card or call us at 202-783-6161.

Name _____

Address _____

City/State _____ Zip _____

Phone _____

Permanent Address (If Different From Above)

Address _____

City/State _____ Zip _____

Phone _____

YES, I am interested in American Youth Hostels. Please tell me more about:

☐ Membership

☐ Trips & Tours

☐ Eurailpass

☐ Travel Accessories

☐ Volunteer Opportunities

☐ Special Events In My Community

INTERNATIONAL YOUTH HOSTEL FEDERATION
American Youth Hostels

```
PLACE
STAMP
HERE
```

INTERNATIONAL YOUTH HOSTEL FEDERATION
American Youth Hostels
Dept. 801
P.O. Box 37613
Washington, DC 20013-7613

LET'S GO: USA

tions of Adrian's Locks. Note that even when the temperature is in the 80s in Colorado Springs, Pikes Peak only warms up to the mid-30s; roads often remain icy through the summer.

Pikes Peak is not Colorado Springs' only outdoor attraction. The **Garden of the Gods City Park,** 1401 Recreation Way (578-6939), composed of red rock monuments perhaps once part of a Native American holy land, now rings a pleasantly secluded picnic and hiking area. (Free. Visitors center open daily 9am-5pm; off-season 10am-4pm.) Don't miss the "kissing camels," just a few minutes walk from the park's south entrance. For more strenuous hiking, head for the **Cave of the Winds** (685-5444), 6 mi. west of exit 141 off I-25. Guided tours of the fantastically contorted caverns happen every 15 minutes daily from 9am to 9pm; off-season from 10am to·5pm. Just above Manitou Springs on Rte. 24 lies the **Manitou Cliff Dwellings Museum** (685-5242), U.S. 24 bypass, where you can wander through a pueblo of ancient Anasazi buildings. (Open daily June-Aug. 9am-6pm; May-Oct. 10am-5pm. Admission $2.75, under 11 $1.25.)

Buried in a hollowed-out cave 1800 ft. below Cheyenne Mountain, the **North American Air Defense Command Headquarters (NORAD)** (554-7321) lies in wait. This telecommunications complex makes up one of the key elements in U.S. nuclear strategy. Headquarters for the controversial "Star Wars" space defense system are being erected nearby. The **Peterson Air Force Base,** on the far east side of the city, offers a visitors center and the **Edward J. Peterson Space Command Museum** (554-4915; open Tues.-Fri. 9am-5pm, Sat. 10am-5pm; off-season Mon.-Sat. 9am-5pm; free). Take bus #2.

The **United States Air Force Academy,** a college for future officers, marches 12 mi. north of town on I-25; it's chapel has some of the most distinctive architecture in Colorado. On weekdays during the school year, uniformed cadets gather at 11:55am near the chapel for the cadet lunch formation—a big production just to chow down. The **visitors center** (472-2000) has self-guided tour maps, information on the many special events, and guided tours every 30 minutes during the summer. (Open daily 9am-5pm.)

The **Pioneers' Museum,** downtown at 215 S. Tejon St. (578-6650), covers the settling of Colorado Springs, including a display on the techniques and instruments of a pioneer doctor. (Open Mon.-Sat. 10am-5pm, Sun. 1-5pm.) Everything you ever wanted to know about mining awaits at the **Western Museum of Mining and Industry,** 1025 N. Gate Rd. (598-8850; open daily 9am-4pm; admission $3, ages 5-17 $1). Take exit 156-A off I-25. And all your questions about those famous Olympians will be answered at the **U.S. Olympic Complex,** 1750 E. Boulder St. (578-4618 or 578-4644), which offers informative 1½-hour tours that include a film. (Open Mon.-Sat. 9am-4pm, Sun. noon-4pm.) Take bus #1 east to Farragut.

For information about the arts in Colorado Springs, drop in at the **Colorado Springs Fine Arts Center,** 30 W. Dale (634-5583; open Tues.-Fri. 9am-5pm, Sat. 10am-5pm, Sun. 1-5pm), or call **Colorado College** (389-6606), which stocks the city with cultural events, including the **Summer Festival of the Arts.** Tickets and info available at Worner Campus Center, at Cascade and Cache La Poudre St. (Open Mon.-Fri. 8am-5pm.)

At night, Colorado College's literati find comfortable reading at **Poor Richard's Espresso Bar,** adjacent to the bookstore (see Food above). The bar occasionally hosts comedy, acoustic performances, and readings. (Open Mon.-Thurs. 7am-midnight, Fri.-Sat. 7am-2am, Sun. 7am-10pm.) The **Dublin House,** 1850 Dominion Way at Academy St. (528-1704), is a popular sports bar, with Sunday night blues downstairs. (Open Mon.-Thurs. 4pm-2am, Fri.-Sun. 11am-2am. Music starts at 9pm. Cover $3.)

Near Colorado Springs: Cripple Creek

Forgotten mining towns pepper the area about Colorado Springs, crumbling reminders of the state's glory days. Down on **Cripple Creek,** two hours from Colorado Springs via Rte. 67 off U.S. 24, resides the **Mollie Kathleen Gold Mine** (689-2465),

1 mi. north of town on Hwy. 67. Every 15-20 minutes during the day, miners lead tours down a 1000-ft.-deep shaft. (Open May-Oct. daily 9am-5pm. Tours $6, under 12 $5.) For information about other activities, try the **Cripple Creek Chamber of Commerce,** P.O. Box 650, Cripple Creek 80813 (689-2169 or 689-2307).

In a car (with good suspension), the most exciting way to reach Cripple Creek is via **Phantom Creek Road.** This route takes off from U.S. 50, 30 mi. southwest of Colorado Springs, and meanders up an ever-narrowing canyon, in which the vertical walls get closer and closer to the road. Finally, near the tourist-haunt mining town of Victor, the road reaches a 9000-ft. highland. Cripple Creek still lies 6 mi. ahead. On the return trip, take the most scenic route over the unpaved **Gold Camp Road** (open only in summer), once described by Teddy Roosevelt as the "trip that bankrupts the English language."

Aspen

A world-renowned hermitage of dedicated musicians and elite skiers, Aspen looms as every budget traveler's worst nightmare.

Like countless other Colorado resort areas, Aspen once held prosperous mining town. When the streams of silver began to dry up in the 1940s, the shanty settlement went into a 20-year decline. But the Aspen of the 90s exhibits no signs of its past hardship; condos with seven-digit retail values line the outskirts of the nation's best-known resort community. Some have even been audacious enough to suggest that this community has become too exclusive, but these objections have done little to reverse Aspen's popularity with the upper class or Hunter Thompson and his gonzo lifestyle. In this glitzy town, low-budget living will probably remain as much a thing of the past as the forsaken mining industry.

Practical Information

Emergency: 911.

Visitor Information: Visitors Center, at the Wheeler Opera House, 320 E. Hyman Ave. (925-1940). Pick up free *What to Do in Aspen and Snowmass.* Open daily 8am-7pm; winter 10am-5pm. **Aspen Chamber and Resort Association,** 303 E. Main St. (925-1940). Open Mon.-Fri. 8am-5pm. **Aspen District of the White River National Forest Ranger Station,** 806 W. Hallam at N. 7th St. (925-3445). Information for hikers and a map of the whole forest ($2). Open July 7-Sept. 2 Mon.-Sat. 8am-5pm; off-season Mon.-Fri. 8am-5pm. **24-Hr. Forest Information,** 920-1664 (recording).

Pitkin County Airport: (920-5380), 4 mi. west of town on Hwy. 82. **Continental** (925-4350) and **United** (925-3400) each offer 8 daily flights from Denver ($98). Roaring Fork buses shuttle visitors into town from the Airport Business Center (50¢).

Public Transport: Roaring Fork Transit Agency, 450 Durant Ave. (925-8484), 1 block from the mall. Service in summer daily 7am-midnight; in winter 7am-1am. Buses to Snowmass, Woody Creek, and other points down valley as far as El Jebel daily 6:15am-12:15am; in winter 6:15am-1am. One bus per day round-trip to Maroon Bells ($3 one way). Free shuttles around town. Out-of-town service 50¢-$2.50.

Taxi: High Mountain, 925-8294. Base fare $2.85, $1.80 per mi. To airport $10. In winter, call **Aspen Carriage Co.** (925-4289) for a horse-drawn sleigh ride.

Car Rental: National, (800-227-7368), at the airport. Economy cars $37 per day, $160 per week. 70 free mi., 33¢ each additional mi. Must be 25 with major credit card.

Bike Rental: The Hub, 315 E. Hyman St. (925-7970). Mountain bikes with helmets $6 per hr., $15 per half day, $20 per day. Open daily 9am-8pm. Must have credit card or $500 deposit.

Weather Line: 831-7669.

Help Lines: Crisis Line, 800-332-6804. Open 24 hr. **Gay Community of Aspen,** 925-9249.

Post Office: 235 Puppy Smith Rd. (925-7523). Open Mon.-Fri. 9am-5pm, Sat. 9am-noon. ZIP code: 81611.

Area Code: 303.

Aspen slaloms 195 mi. southwest of Denver. In the winter, however, you must take I-70 west to Glenwood Springs before you can pick up CO Rte. 82 south to Aspen, thus adding about 70 mi. to the trip.

Once in Aspen, you will have no trouble getting around. CO Rte. 82 forms **Main Street**, to the south of which lies the downtown shopping district, and to the north of which lie opulent villas.

Accommodations and Camping

Budget accommodations don't come easy in Aspen. Luckily, though, surrounding national forests offer inexpensive summer camping, and some reasonably priced skiers' dorms, double as guest houses in summer. The largest crowds and highest rates arrive in late December, February, and March. Consider lodging in Glenwood Springs, 70 mi. north of Aspen, where inexpensive accommodations are plentiful.

Little Red Ski Haus, 118 E. Cooper (925-3333), 2 blocks west of downtown. Clean, bright, wood-paneled rooms. Vivacious, helpful manager. In winter, singles and dorm bunks $26-30. Doubles from $48. Off-season: singles $20, doubles $40. Breakfast included. Wed. night spaghetti dinner $5. Call before coming, to make sure there's space.

Aspen International Hostel at the St. Moritz Lodge, 334 W. Hyman Ave. (925-3220). Dorms, shared baths. Pool, jacuzzi, sauna. Look at the room before you handing over any money. In winter bunks $29, off-season $20.

Alpine Lodge, 1240 Hwy. 82 E. (925-7351), ½ mi. east of town just beyond Independence Pass. B&B run by sweet polyglot family. Luxurious singles $33. Doubles $40. Huge sunny room downstairs with bunks, for small groups, $60.

Unless 6 ft. of snow covers the ground, try camping in the mountains nearby. Hike well into the forest and camp for free, or use one of the nine **national forest campgrounds** within 15 mi. of Aspen. Maroon Creek offers beautiful campgrounds: Maroon Lake, Silver Bar, Silver Bell, and Silver Queen are on Maroon Creek Rd. just west of Aspen. (3-day max. stay. No reservations; sites fill well before noon. Open July-early Sept.) Southeast of Aspen on Rte. 82 toward Independence Pass there are six campgrounds: Difficult, Lincoln Gulch, Dispersed Sites, Weller, Lost Man, and Portal. Ironically, Difficult is the only one with water (14-day max. stay; sites $6). The others are free and have a five-day maximum stay.

Food

The best eateries in Aspen make their meals on Main St. **The Main Street Bakery,** 201 E. Main St. (925-6446), offers sweets, stir fry ($5), gourmet soups ($3), and a reprieve from pretension. (Open Mon.-Sat. 6:30am-9:30pm, Sun. 7:30am-4pm.) Two doors east of the Explore bookstore (see Entertainment and Nightlife below) is the the **In and Out House,** 233 E. Main St. (925-6647), a miniscule hole-in-the-wall that doles out huge sandwiches on fresh-baked bread ($1.85-3.50) to long lines of music students at lunch. Arrive around 11:30am to beat the crowd. (Open Mon.-Fri. 9am-9pm, Sat.-Sun. 9am-4pm.) **The Red Onion,** 420 E. Cooper St. (925-9043), still on its original site after almost 100 years, has lots of antique woodwork to go with burgers and sandwiches ($4-5) and good *fajitas* ($7.75). Look for a coupon at the visitors center. (Open daily 11:30am-10pm.) The local coffeehouse, **Pour la France,** 411 E. Main St. (920-1151), serves a mean continental breakfast ($3.25) in the morning, pastries and coffees in the evening. A good place for pretentious conversation. (Open Sun.-Thurs. 7am-10pm, Fri.-Sat. 7am-11pm.) **The Popcorn Wagon,** on the corner of Mill and E. Hyman Ave., across from the Wheeler Opera House sells the only thing you can afford after lodging in Aspen. Great chocolate crepes as well ($1.50). (Open Mon.-Sat. 11am-2am, Sun. 11am-midnight.)

Entertainment and Nightlife

Aspen's active après-skiers support an equally active nightlife. Students frequent the **Cooper Street Pier,** 500 E. Cooper St. (925-7758), where a chili dog and fries ($3) and a glass of draft beer (75¢) are the combo of choice. (Restaurant open daily 11am-11pm. Bar open 11am-2pm.) At **The Tippler,** 535 E. Dean Ave. (925-4977), you'll find a more seasoned crowd, also downing 75¢ drafts. (Open Tues.-Sat. 9am-2am.) **Little Annie's,** 517 E. Hyman Ave. (925-1098), has been known to host the jet set, but usually flies a wider range of patrons. (Restaurant open daily 11:30am-11:30pm. Bar open 11am-2am.) The scene at **André's,** on the third floor at 312 S. Galeria (925-6200), changes every time you turn around; business talk, student antics, and gay socializing make this one of the liveliest places in town. Live music Monday to Saturday from 10:30pm to 1:30am. Intellectual discussions, esoteric jokes, and mouth-watering scents fill the air at the **Explore Booksellers and Coffee Shop,** 221 E. Main St. (925-5336). Read as many of the shop's books as you'd like for free, served upstairs over tea and a table. (Open Sun.-Thurs. 10am-10pm, Fri.-Sat. 10am-midnight.)

In addition to a passel of annual artistic rituals, Aspen hosts many seasonal and even nightly cultural events. For tickets and the scoop on local dance, theater, and film in the entire Aspen area, call the **Wheeler Opera House Box Office,** 320 E. Hyman Ave. (925-7250; open Mon.-Sat. 10am-5pm).

Activities and Sights

The hills surrounding town contain four ski areas; **Aspen Mountain, Buttermilk Mountain,** and **Snowmass Ski Area** (925-1221) sell interchangeable lift tickets. ($33-35, seniors with ID $20, under 12 $17. Daily hours: Aspen Mtn. 9am-3:30pm, Buttermilk Mtn. 9am-4pm, Snowmass 8:30am-3:30pm.) **Aspen Highlands** (925-5300) does not provide interchangeable tickets. ($33, seniors with ID and children $17. Open daily 9am-4pm.) Favorite slopes include **Sheer Rock Face** at Aspen, **Nipple** at Buttermilk, and **Catholic School** at Snowmass.

Needless to say, you can enjoy the mountains without shelling out money to ski. The ghost towns of **Ashcroft** and **Independence** open their doors to visitors in the summer, and hiking in the Maroon Bells and Elk Mountains is permitted when the snow isn't too deep. Maroon and Crater Lakes are popular destinations in this relatively unspoiled area. Shuttles run twice every hour and have been instituted to spare the Maroon Creek Valley from automobile emissions and noise. (Fare $2.50, seniors and children $1.) Free shuttle buses to Highlands leave from Aspen's Rubey Park 15 and 45 minutes after the hour. Biking up to **Maroon Lake** is popular and fairly strenuous. From the trailhead, hike the 1.6-mi. turnpike through aspen groves to **Crater Lake,** and continue through high passes to more distant destinations in the **Maroon Bells-Snowmass Wilderness.** Pick up a topographical map in Aspen before beginning your ascent. The **Ute Mountaineer,** 308 S. Mill St. (925-2849; open daily 9am-8pm), and **Carl's Pharmacy,** 306 E. Main St. (925-3273; open daily 8am-10pm), both sell maps for $2.50.

Undoubtedly Aspen's most famous event, the **Aspen Music Festival** (925-9042) holds sway over the town from late June to August. Free bus transportation goes from Rubey Park downtown to "the Tent," south of town, before and after all concerts. Picnic outside the tent and listen for free; afternoon rehearsals are also free. (Concerts June-late Aug. Tickets $8-25. Sun. rehearsals $2.) Aspen's only museum, the **Wheeler-Stallard House,** 620 W. Bleecker St. (925-3721), is also home to the symbiotic **Aspen Historical Society,** which offers tours of the house daily from 1 to 4pm during peak tourist season. The talk includes many fascinating details about the mining history of Aspen, including the notorious brownie floor. (Admission $3, children 50¢.)

Great Sand Dunes National Monument

After Colorado's splendid mountains begin to look the same, make a path for the unique mountains of sand at the northwest edge of the **San Luis Valley.** The 700-ft. dunes lap the base of the **Sangre de Christo Range,** commemorating thousands of years of wind-blown accumulation. The progress of the dunes at passes in the range is checked by the shallow but persistent **Medano Creek.** Visitors can wade across the creek from April to mid-July. For a short hike, head out on Mosca Trail, a ½-mi. jaunt into the desert sands. Try to avoid the intense afternoon heat.

Rangers preside over daily naturalist activities, hikes, and other programs. Full schedules are available at the **visitors center** (378-2312), ½ mi. past the entrance gate, where you can also view a 15-minute film on the dunes, shown every 15 minutes. (Open daily 8am-8pm; Sept. 2-May 27 8am-5pm. Entrance fee for vehicles $3, pedestrians and bikers $1.) For more information contact the Superintendent, Great Sand Dunes NM, Mosca 81146 (378-2312).

For those who crave more than just the first wave of dunes, the **Oasis** complex (378-2222) on the southern boundary also provides four-wheel-drive tours of the backcountry. The tour takes the rugged Medano Pass Primitive Road into the nether regions of the monument. (4 tours daily, 3 hr., $14, under 12 $8. Discounts for seniors.)

Pinyon Flats, the monument's campground, fills quickly in summer. Camping here among the prickly pear cacti is first come, first serve. Bring mosquito repellent in June. (Sites $6.) If the park's sites are full, you can camp at Oasis. (Sites $8 for 2 people, with hookup $11.50. Each additional person $2.50. Showers included.) **Backcountry camping** requires a free permit. For information on nearby National Forest Campgrounds, contact the Rio Grande National Forest Service Office, 1803 W. Hwy. 160, Monte Vista, CO 81144 (852-5941). All developed sites are $5-7.

Great Sand Dunes National Monument blows 32 mi. northeast of Alamosa and 112 mi. west of Pueblo, on Rte. 150 off U.S. 160. **Greyhound/Trailways** sends one bus per day out of Denver to Alamosa (5 hr., $35), whose depot is at 511 4th St. (589-4948; open Mon.-Fri. 9am-1pm and 4-6pm, Sat. 11am-12:30pm and 5-6pm). Hitching to the monument is simple, especially from Rte. 150. Avoid the poorly maintained country road from Mosca on Rte. 17. For emergencies within the park, call the **Colorado State Patrol** (589-5807).

Mesa Verde National Park

Six long centuries ago, Native American tribes settled and cultivated the desert mesas of southwestern Colorado. In 1200 AD, they constructed and settled in the cliff dwellings until 1376 when they mysteriously abandoned their shelters. The Navajo tribes that arrived in the area in 1450, named the previous inhabitants the Anasazi or the "ancient ones." Today only four of the 1000 archeological sites are open to constant touring, because the fragile sandstone wears quickly under human feet. Since such caution causes some congestion within the park, arrive early.

Entrance fees to the park are $5 per car, $2 per pedestrian or cyclist. The southern portion of the park divides into the **Chapin Mesa** and the **Wetherill Mesa.** A stop at the **Spruce Tree Museum and Visitors Center** (529-4543), near the cliffs at the southern end of the park, offers information and three-hour guided tours. (2 tours each morning. $8, under 12 $4. Open daily 8am-6:30pm; off-season Mon.-Fri. 8am-5pm.) On Wetherhill Mesa, tours run only from June to September and leave from Far View Lodge (6 hr.; $10, under 12 $4). You may take self-guided tours up ladders and through passageways of the Anasazi dwellings. Spruce Tree House is one of the better-preserved ruins. To get an overview of the Anasazi lifestyle, visit the **Spruce Tree Museum** (529-4475) at the Chapin Visitors Center. (Open daily 8am-6:30pm.)

The **Far View Visitors Center** (529-4523), close to the north rim on the way to the Morfield campground (see below), can also be of assistance. (Open in summer daily 8am-5pm.) The **Morfield Ranger Station** in the park's northwest corner (529-4548), offers a six-hour excursion departing from the Morfield campground. (Tours $10, under 12 $4. Station open summer daily 8am-5pm.)

Mesa Verde's only lodging, **Far View Motor Lodge** (529-4421), is extremely expensive, but a few nearby motels can put you up for under $30. Try the **Ute Mountain Motel**, 531 S. Broadway (565-8507) in Cortez, CO. (Singles from $24. Doubles from $34.) However, it's best to stay at the nearby **Durango Hostel** (see Durango). The only camping in Mesa Verde is at **Morfield Campground**, (529-4474; off-season 529-4421) 4 mi. inside the park, with some beautiful and secluded sites. (Sites $7, with full hookup $14.50. Showers 85¢ for 10 min.) Outside the park, ¼ mi. east on Hwy. 160, is the **Double A Campground and R.V. Park** (565-3517; sites $12, with hookup $15.50).

The park's main entrance is off U.S. 160, 36 mi. from Durango and 10 mi. from Cortez. Greyhound/Trailways will drop you off in either town on its daily Durango-Cortez run, but only in the wee hours of the morning. Stations are at Frontier Plaza (565-7379) in Cortez, and at 225 8th Ave. (247-1581) in Durango. From Cortez, you can ride the park employee shuttle (May 15-Oct. 15), which leaves from 317 E. Main St. daily at 6:45am, and returns from the park at 5:30pm ($3.60 one way). **Durango Transportation** (259-4818) will take you on a nine-hour tour of the park ($27, children $13.50); bring a lunch. Since sights lie up to 40 mi. apart, a car is very helpful. Van transportation is also available at the Far View Lodge for self-guided tours with 24-hr. notice.

Mesa Verde's **ZIP code** is 81330; nearby Mancos is 81328. The **area code** is 303.

San Juan Mountains

Ask Coloradans about their favorite mountain retreats and they'll most likely name a peak, lake, stream, or town in the San Juan Range of southwestern Colorado. Four national forests—the Uncompahgre (pronounced un-cum-PAH-gray), the Gunnison, the San Juan, and the Rio Grande—encompass this sprawling range.

Durango is an ideal base camp for forages into these mountains. In particular, the **Weminuche Wilderness**, northeast of Durango, tempts the hardy backpacker with a particularly large expanse of hilly terrain. You can hike for miles without seeing a tree, and wild sweeping vistas are the rule. Get maps and information on hiking in the San Juans from **Pine Needle Mountaineering**, Main Mall, Durango 81301 (247-8728; open Mon.-Sat. 9am-9pm, Sun. 11am-4pm; winter Mon.-Sat. 9am-6pm, Sun. 11am-4pm; maps $2.50).

The San Juan area is easily accessible on U.S. 50, traveled by hundreds of thousands of tourists each summer. **Greyhound/Trailways** and **Rocky Mountain Stages** service the area, but very poorly; **hitchhiking** is an only slightly better alternative. Car travel is the best option in this region.

On a happier note, the San Juans are loaded with AYH hostels and campgrounds, making them one of the most economical places to visit in Colorado.

Durango

As Will Rogers once put it, Durango is "out of the way, and glad of it." Despite its increasing popularity as a tourist destination, Durango retains an almost insidiously relaxed small-town atmosphere. Come to see nearby Mesa Verde and to raft down the Animas River, but don't be surprised if you end up staying longer than you expected. Winter is Durango's busiest season, when nearby **Purgatory Resort** (247-9000), 20 mi. north on U.S. 550, hosts skiers of all levels. (Lift tickets $30, children $14.)

Durango is best known for the **Narrow Gauge Railroad**, 479 Main St. (247-2733), which runs along the Animas River Valley to the gilded tourist town of Silverton.

Old-fashioned locomotives pull a string of sight-seeing cars through the mountains four times per day; you must make reservations in advance. The ride is even worth the $37 round-trip fare (children $18.75). To backpack into the scenic **Chicago** and **New York Basins,** buy a round-trip ticket to Needleton ($34). The train will drop you off here on its trip to Silverton. When you decide to leave the high country, return to Needleton and flag the train, but you must have exactly $17 to board if you don't have a return pass. For more information on the train and its services for backpackers, contact the Durango and Silverton Narrow Gauge Railroad, 479 Main St., Durango 81301. (Offices open May-Aug. daily 6am-9pm; Aug.-Oct. 7am-7pm; Oct.-May 8am-5pm.)

For river rafting, **Rivers West,** 520 Main St. (259-5077), has the best rates. ($10 per hr., $19 for 2 hr. plus lunch, $25 for an hr. plus a steak dinner. Children 20% discount. Open daily 8am-9pm.) **Durango Rivertrips,** 720 Main St. (259-0289), organize two-hour rides in two-person rafts. ($15; open daily 9am-9pm). When you feel like biking about town, pick up gear from **Hassle Free Sports,** 2615 Main St. (259-3874; bikes $8 per hr., $20 per day; open Mon.-Sat. 8:30am-6pm, Sun. 10am-4pm; must have driver's license and major credit card).

Food in Durango is overpriced on the whole. Buy provisions at **City Market,** on Hwy. 550, 1 block down 9th St., and at 3130 Main St. (Both open 24 hr.) Or breakfast with the locals at **Carver's Bakery,** 1022 Main Ave., which has good bread and breakfast specials ($2-4). (Open Mon.-Sat. 6:30am-10pm, Sun. 6:30am-2pm.) The **Durango Diner,** 957 Main St., serves ample cheeseburgers ($2.25) and boasts a singing cook. (Open Mon.-Sat. 6am-2pm, Sun. 7am-1pm.) **Clancy's Bar,** 128 E. 6th St. (247-2626), serves good sandwiches ($4.50), offers veggie dishes on request, and has live entertainment on weekends and some weekdays. (Open daily 11am-midnight. Bar open 4:30pm-1am.)

The simplest way to ensure a pleasant stay in Durango is to rest up at the **Durango Youth Hostel,** 543 E. 2nd Ave. (247-9905 or 247-5477), a quaint old building 1 block from downtown. David, the friendly host, will encumber you with sight-seeing tips, fresh vegetables from his garden, and stories about hippie guru Timothy Leary. (Check-in 5-10pm. Check-out 7-10am. $8, nonmembers $9. Make reservations in winter.) The **Central Hotel and Hostel,** 975 Main St. (247-0330), has a TV in each of the clean and pleasant rooms. (Singles $25. Doubles $28.) The **Cottonwood Camper Park,** on U.S. 160 (247-1977), 1/3 mi. west of town, has tent sites for $12, with electricity and water $15, full hookup $16.

Durango parks at the intersection of U.S. 160 (east to Alamosa, 150 mi.) and U.S. 550 (south to Farmington, NM, 45 mi.). Streets run perpendicular to avenues, but everyone calls Main Avenue "Main Street." **Greyhound/Trailways,** 275 E. 8th Ave. (259-2755), serves Grand Junction ($28), Denver ($47), and Albuquerque ($33). (Open Mon.-Fri. 7am-5:30pm, Sat. 7am-noon and 4:30-5:30pm, Sun. 7-10am and 4:30-5:30pm.)

Durango's **ZIP code** is 81301; the **area code** is 303.

Ouray

Once upon a time Ouray (pronounced yer-RAY) prospered as, you guessed it, a gold and silver mining town. Surrounding 5000-ft. peaks dwarf this grape-sized hamlet in the Uncompahgre (pronounced un-com-PAH-gray) National Forest. The town itself prepares well for hikers and climbers, with numerous sports shops to equip and keep track of you through their hiker registration service. After a hike or a ski tour, soak in the **Onvis Hot Springs** (626-5324), right off the "Million Dollar Highway" (U.S. 550) on the northern outskirts. (Open Mon.-Sat. 9am-10pm, Sun. 9am-7pm; off-season Wed.-Mon. noon-9pm. Admission $4, seniors and children $2.75, ages 13-17 $3.50.) Though rumors persist, the name "Million Dollar Highway" does not, in fact, indicate that the road is paved with silver and gold.

Experience the heritage of Ouray on a tour of the **Bachelor-Syracuse Mine,** County Rd. 14, P.O. Drawer 380 W. (325-4500), just off Hwy. 550. Sit in an ore cart and careen 3350 ft. along a real mine shaft right into the heart of the mountain.

Rides leave on the hour. (Open late May-late Sept. daily 9am-5pm. Admission $7, under 12 $4.) Once you resurface, head to the southwest end of town to see the **Box Canyon Falls,** a 285-ft. cataract. (Open mid-May to mid-Oct. daily 8am-8pm. Admission $1.25, seniors $1, ages 4-12 75¢, under 4 free.)

Rent a jeep in Ouray and four-wheel over the Imogene Pass to Telluride (see Telluride below). The prices are as steep as the trail but you'll not likely forget the stupendously beautiful trip past waterfalls, mountain peaks, alpine flowers, ice fields, yellow-bellied marmots, and old mining towns. Reserve a jeep as far in advance as possible. **San Juan Scenic Jeep Tours,** 480 Main St. (325-4444 or 325-4154), rents jeeps for $50 per ½ day, $75 per day. (Open daily 7am-6pm. $50 deposit required.) To pedal the mountains, rent a bike ($15 per ½ day, $20 per day; $1 for helmet) at **Downhill Biking,** 825 Main St. (325-4284; open daily 8am-6pm).

A national forest **campground** (325-4061) perches above Ouray, roughly 1 mi. south on U.S. 550. (Sites $5. Open May-Sept.) The **Ouray KOA** (325-4736) has some streamside sites, and comfortable grassy spots for primitive camping. (Sites $14.50, with electricity and water $16.50, full hookup $17.50.) For indoor accommodations, journey 10 mi. down valley to **Ridgway,** at the intersection of U.S. 550 and Rte. 62, where the **Adobe Hostel and Cantina,** Lidell Dr. (626-5939) serves up pleasant, affordable rooms in the back of a small, elegant restaurant. Some rooms have lofts; all have Mexican blankets, wonderful feather beds, free muffin and coffee in the morning. Bunks $13. Singles $32. Doubles $38.

Ouray's **ZIP** code is 81427; the **area code** is 303.

Telluride

Home to the first bank Butch Cassidy ever robbed (the San Miguel), Telluride has a history right out of a 1930s black-and-white film. Prize fighter Jack Dempsey used to wash dishes in the Senate, fittingly a popular saloon/brothel that frequently required Dempsey to serve as bouncer. Of course, now it serves delicious Greek food (see below). The Sheridan Hotel (see below) hosted actresses Sarah Bernhardt and Lillian Gish on cross-country theater tours, while Vice President William Jennings Bryan, who delivered his "Cross of Gold" speech in Telluride, stayed here. More recently, in his autobiography *Speak, Memory,* Vladimir Nabokov relates his pursuit through Telluride of a particularly rare type of butterfly. Not so rare (especially after its devaluation) was the silver that attracted all the less aesthetically inclined hoodlums to Telluride in the first place, beginning in 1875.

Today, music lovers, "high-concept" environmentalists, and downhill skiers and mountain bikers inhabit Telluride, lingering for a weekend or several years. These young nomads, with an insatiable appetite for bluegrass, foreign film and outdoor sports, lend Telluride the slightly "groovy" and daredevilish atmosphere of a college town. Self-proclaimed atheists can be spied crossing themselves before tipping their planks down "Spiral Stairs" and "the Plunge," two of the Rockies' most gutwrenching slopes. For more information, contact the **Telluride Company,** P.O. Box 307, 81435 (728-3856).

Yet neither rockslide nor snowmelt signal the end of the festivities in Telluride. The quality and number of summer arts festivals seems staggering when you consider that only 1500 people call the town home. While get-togethers occur just about every weekend in summer and fall, the most renowned include the **Bluegrass Festival** in late June—last year the likes of James Taylor and the Nitty Gritty Dirt Band attracted crowds of 13,000. Though music stores sell tickets ($25 per night, $75 for the weekend) from Grand Junction to Aspen, people have managed to sneak in. On the weekend of the festivals, you can easily find dishwashing or food serving jobs in exchange for tickets to the show. Telluride also hosts a **Talking Gourds** poetry fest (late June), a **Composer to Composer** festival (mid-July), which last year featured Laurie Anderson, and a **Jazz Festival** (early Aug.), among others. You can often hear the music festivals all over town, all day, and deep into the night as you try to sleep. Above all, the **Telluride International Film Festival** (Labor Day weekend), now in its 17th year, draws famous actors and directors from all over the globe. Guests in years past have included Academy Award-winning actor Daniel Day Lewis, and trendy director David Lynch. Contact the **Telluride Chamber Resort Association,** upstairs at Rose's (728-3041), at the entrance to town, for more information. (Open Mon.-Fri. 9am-7pm, Sat.-Sun. 10am-7pm.) For 24-hr. recorded information call the **Festival Hotline** (728-6079).

The **visitors center** lies next to the **Coonskin Chairlift,** which will haul you up 10,000 ft. for an excellent view of Pikes Peak and the La Sal Mountains. (Open Thurs.-Mon. 11am-3pm. Fare $5, seniors and children $3.) The biking, hiking and backpacking opportunities around Telluride are endless; ghost towns and lakes tucked behind stern mountain crags fill the wild terrain. For an enjoyable day hike, trek up the San Miguel River Canyon to **Bridal Veil Falls.** Drive to the end of Rte. 145 and hike the steep, misty dirt road to the spectacular waterfall. **Paragon Ski and Sport,** 213 W. Colorado Ave. (728-4525), is drew up the blueprints for camping supplies, bikes, and skis. (Open summer Mon.-Thurs. 9am-7pm, Fri.-Sun. 9am-8pm; winter daily 8am-9pm.) Stop at the local sportshop or **Between the Covers** bookstore, 224 W. Colorado Ave., for trail guides and maps.

The **Oak Street Inn (AYH),** 134 N. Oak St. (728-3383), has two-level loft dorms complete with saunas. ($14.50, in summer $12.50, nonmembers $22. Showers $3.) When they're out of beds, head for the **New Sheridan Hotel,** 231 W. Colorado (728-4351), where a 3-bunk room for 1-3 people goes for $26. Be warned that the Sheridan is considering a major "upscaling." You can **camp** in the east end of town in a town-operated facility with water, restrooms, and showers. (Two-week max. stay. Sites $5.) **Sunshine,** 4 mi. southwest on Rte. 145 toward Cortez, and **Matterhorn,** 10 mi. farther on Rte. 145, are well-developed national forest campgrounds; the latter can accommodate trailers with hookup. (Two-week max. stay. Sites $5.) Accessible by jeep roads, several free primitive campgrounds locate nearby. During festival times, you can crash just about anywhere in town, and hot showers are mercifully available at the high school ($1).

Baked in Telluride, 127 S. Fir St., has enough rich coffee and delicious pastry, pizza, and bagels (42¢) to get you through a festival weekend without sleeping. Invest in one of their mugs ($2), and refill it endlessly for 50¢, while conserving styrofoam trees. (Open daily 6am-10pm.) The **Athena Senate,** 123 S. Spruce, serves elegant Greek appetizers, omelettes, and late night/early morning food. (Open Mon.-Sat. 11am-3am, Sun. 11am-12:30am; during Bluegrass Fest until 5am.) Delicious Italian fare bakes at **Eddie's Café,** 300 W. Colorado (728-5335) including 8-in. pizzas ($4.25) and other dinner specials $7-11. At **Froggies's Popcorn Wagon,** on the corner of Fir and Colorado Ave., sit on the shaded outdoor deck admiring the mountains with a papoose-sized bag of warm buttery popcorn ($1) or a vegetarian crêpe ($2). (Open daily 11am-until.)

You can only get to Telluride by car, on Rte. 550 or Rte. 145. Telluride's **post office** stamps and sorts at 101 E. Colorado Ave. (728-3900; open Mon.-Fri. 9am-5pm, Sat. 10am-noon). The **ZIP code** is 81435; the **area code** is 303.

Black Canyon of the Gunnison National Monument

According to the geologist who first mapped this area, "no other canyon in North America combines the depth, narrowness, sheerness, and somber countenance of the Black Canyon." The geologist was right. Sculpted by the Gunnison River, this steely black canyon drops 2500 ft. into the earth's crust. Sunlight strikes the canyon floor only once per day, at high noon.

The **North Rim** of the canyon is more remote, accessible only via a 12-mi. dirt road which leaves CO Rte. 92 near the Crawford Reservoir. Seven overlooks position along the rim, and a self-guiding nature trail starts from the campground. The better developed, more populated **South Rim** is most easily reached from U.S. 50 via CO Rte. 347 just outside of Montrose. An 8-mi. scenic drive along this rim boasts spectacular **Chasm View,** where you can peer down a sheer vertical drop of 2000 ft. Inspired hikers can descend to the bottom of the canyon; the least difficult trail (more like a controlled slide) drops 1800 ft. over a distance of 1 mi. At certain points you must hoist yourself up on a chain in order to gain ground. Suffice it to say, this hike is not to be undertaken lightly. Registration and advice from a ranger are required before any descent. For more information, write the Superintendent, Gunnison National Monument, P.O. Box 1648, Montrose 81401, or call the **visitors center** at 249-1915. (Guided nature walks at 11am and 4pm. Campfire program daily at 9pm. Meet at the visitors center. Open May 27-Sept.2 daily 8am-8pm.) A short walk down from the visitors center affords a view startling enough in its steepness to require chest-high rails to protect the dizzy from falling.

Camp in either rim's beautiful desert **campground.** Each has pit toilets and charcoal grills; the southern one has an amphitheater with evening programs in summer. Water is available, but use it sparingly. (Sites $6.) You can collect wood with some difficulty, or let George Washington collect it at a store on the turn-off from U.S. 50. Backcountry camping and driftwood fires in the canyon bottom are permitted; beware of the abundant poison ivy.

The closest town to the monument is **Montrose,** with administrative offices for the monument located at 2233 E. Main St. (249-7036; open Mon.-Fri. 8am-4:30pm). Look to the **Mesa Hotel,** 10 N. Townsend Ave. (249-3773), at the junction of Rte. 550 and 50, for quaint, clean, cheap rooms. (Singles $13, with bath $20. Doubles $23.) Across the street moos the **Stockman's Café & Bar,** 320 E. Main St., serving hearty Western and Mexican meals. (Open Thurs.-Tues. 7am-midnight.) The town's **visitors center** assists at 2490 S. Townsend Ave. (249-1726; open May-Oct. daily 9am-5pm).

A few miles south of Montrose on Hwy. 550, the **Ute Indian Museum,** 17253 Chipeta Dr. (249-3098), is a brilliant find, exhibiting costumes from the Bear Dance, the bilingual letters of chief Ouray (leader of the Southern Ute tribe), and rare accounts of the Native American experience during the past two centuries. (Open May 27-Sept.2 Mon.-Sat. 10am-5pm, Sun. 1-5pm. Admission $2, seniors and children $1.)

Greyhound serves Montrose, 50 N. Townsend Ave. (249-6673), and Gunnison, 625 E. Main St. (249-2624). Gunnison lies about 55 mi. east of Montrose on U.S. 50. The bus will drop you off at the junction of Rte. 50 and 347, 6 mi. from the canyon. **Western Express Taxi** (249-8880) will drive you in from Montrose for about $14. Entrance to the monument costs $3 for vehicles, $1 for pedestrians and bikers.

Montrose's **ZIP code** is 81401. The **area code** for the region is 303.

Crested Butte

After leading a hunting expedition of several men to Crested Butte in 1873, Alfie Packer returned home alone a few days later, appearing strangely pudgier and wealthier. At a trial accusing Packer of murder, robbery, and cannibalism, the presiding judge declared, "This state had seven Democrats, and you ate five of them."

Bizarre politics and anthropophagy aside, Crested Butte is a ski town limited in size by encircling mountains and difficult roads. Two routes lead to town, both only accessible to car or mountain bike. Reach Crested Butte from the south by taking I-50 to Gunnison and picking up CO Rte. 135, which heads north 30 mi. to town. From June to October on Hwy. 70 to the north, take CO Rte. 82 15 mi. south from Glenwood Springs to Carbondale, picking up CO Rte. 133, which leads to Crested Butte through seasonal Kebbler Pass: Be warned that the pass is a 30-mi. dirt and gravel road, though the surrounding cedar trees and deer may be worth the ground tooth enamel.

The **Mount Crested Butte** ski area opens from late November to early April. For a winter brochure and lift reservations contact Crested Butte Vacations, P.O. Box A, Mt. Crested Butte 81225 (800-544-8448). Buses run in season 10 times per day bewteen the mount and Crested Butte, on the hour, starting at 7am, from the corner of 6th and Elk St.

In summer, Crested Butte has one of the best **4th of July parades** around, with the whole town, including the fire and police departments, making floats and dousing each other with assorted alcoholic beverages. As people recover, Crested Butte hosts an annual **wildflower festival,** (July 4-8), with hikes, art exhibits, and photography workshops. In early August, the town hosts a Festival of the Arts. All of these summer festivals, parades, and celebrations attempt to assuage the effects of withdrawal for ski addicts throughout the mild season. For more information, call the **chamber of commerce** (349-6438 or 800-545-4505), located at 2nd and Elk across the street from the Forest Queen. Get hiking and mountain bike trail maps here as well. **Three-River Outfitters,** 315 6th St. (349-5011), at the four-way stop at the end of Elk St., rents out "fat tire" mountain bikes (helmet and water bottle included) for $8 per half day, $15 per day. (Open daily 8am-6pm.)

At night, Crested Butte behaves like a college town, but without the lectures. The **Eldorado Cafe** ("the Eldo") at 215 Elk Ave. (349-6430), absolutely sweats with local youths dancing themselves into oblivion to live bands. Great food enhances the fun. (Open daily 11am-2am. Closed most of June. Cover around $2. ID required.) Do some pre-Eldo carbo-loading at **Donita's Cantina,** 4th and Elk, which serves incredibly yummy Mexican food (guacamole $3.25). (Open daily 5-9:30pm.) For coffee and sweets go to the **Bakery Café,** at 3rd and Elk (349-7280; open daily 7:30am-8:30pm). Next door, **The Cook, His Wife, the Thief, and Her Lover,** 400 Anthropophagy Dr., serves up the best human flesh in town, and it won't cost you an arm and a leg. Try the filling Packerburger ($6.50), or the mouth-watering avatart ($1.50). Nibble on a piece of Raoul for $1.75. (Open Mon. midnight-2:15am.)

In town, stay at the **Forest Queen Hotel** (349-5336), on the corner of 2nd and Elk St. Ask Thelma Cornman, a columnist for the local paper, about her recent travels to Iran, Oman, Pakistan, and Spain. (Early Jan.-late Dec.: bunks $12; doubles $25, with private bath $30. Late December-early January: bunks $14; doubles $30, with private bath $35. Great breakfast included.)

Grand Junction

Grand Junction gets its hyperbolic name from the confluence of the Colorado and Gunnison rivers as well as the Rio Grande and Denver Railroads. As western Colorado's trade and agricultural center, this quiet city serves as a fantastic base for explorations of the Gunnison Valley and the western San Juans.

Some excellent restaurants also meet in Grand Junction. **Dos Hombres Restaurant,** 421 Branch Dr., just south of Broadway (Rte. 340) on the southern bank of the Colorado River, serves great Mexican food in a casual, family-style setting. A second Dos Hombres está in the Coronado Plaza in Clifton. (Combination dinners $3.75-5.25. Open daily 11am-10pm.) During the day, the **B & J Coffee Shop,** 400 Main St., in the back of a downtown dime store, has some unintentionally charming touches, like coke in bottles, a soda fountain, and full meals for $4.75, along with fat, iced cinnamon rolls. (Open Mon.-Sat. 6:30am-4:30pm.) **The Bayou,** 159 Colorado Ave., 1½ blocks from the hostel, serves gumbo and other Cajun food. (Open daily 11:30am-10pm.)

Two of the most affordable lodgings lie within walking distance of the bus and train stations downtown. The old **Melrose Hotel (AYH),** 337 Colorado Ave. between 3rd and 4th St., is an immaculate, well-maintained old hotel with oodles of old-fashioned Old World charm. ($11, nonmembers $15, with bath $18. Doubles $18, with bath $20.) **La Court Motor Lodge,** 120 S. 1st St. (242-3310), offers A/C, huge tubs, beautiful wood furniture, and general luxury, including a gorgeous, Spanish-tiled pool. (Singles $25. Doubles $30.) And there's always **Motel 6,** 776 Horizon Dr. (243-2628), though in this case a bit far from downtown. (Singles $26. Doubles $32.) Camping in **Highline State Park** (858-7208), 22 mi. from town and 7 mi. north of exit 15 on I-70, or **Island Acres State Park** (464-0548), 15 mi. east on the banks of the Colorado River, costs $6 per site plus a $3 day pass. A **KOA,** 3238 F Rd. (434-6644), knocks them out in Clifton, just east of Grand Junction off I-70. (Sites $13.75, with electricity and water $15.75, full hookup $17.75.)

For literature on the area, visit the **Tourist Information Center**, 759 Horizon Dr., Suite F (243-1001; open Mon.-Sat. 9am-8pm, Sun. 9am-5pm; off-season Mon.-Sat. 9am-5pm, Sun. 9:30am-1pm), or the **Convention and Visitors Bureau**, at 3rd and Grand downtown (800-352-5286; open Mon.-Fri. 9am-5pm). Or contact the **Chamber of Commerce** at P.O. Box 1330, Grand Junction 81052 (242-3214).

Grand Junction lies at the juncture of U.S. 50 and 24 in northwestern Colorado. U.S. 6 connects these two highways in town. Denver skies 228 mi. to the east; Salt Lake City slouches 240 mi. to the west. The **bus station**, 230 S. 5th S. (242-6012) has service to: Denver (3 per day, 7 hr. $22); Salt Lake City (1 per day, 8 hr., $30); and Los Angeles (1 per day, $84). (Open Mon.-Sat. 3:30am-5:10pm and 9pm-12:30am, Sun. 3:30-7:45am, noon-5:10pm, and 9pm-12:30am.)

Grand Junction's **post office** is at 241 N. 4th St.; **ZIP code** 81502; **area code** 303.

Near Grand Junction

Fifty mi. east of Grand Junction lies **Grand Mesa** (Large Table), the world's largest flat-top mountain. Some 600 million years ago, a 300-ft.-thick flow of lava covered the area where the mesa now stands. Since then, erosion has worn down the surrounding land by over 5000 ft., but the lava cap has preserved Grand Mesa's original height. An ancient Native American story tells how an enormous eagle who lived on the rim of Grand Mesa snatched up a human child in its beak and flew off. The child's vengeful father found the eagle's nest and tossed out the eaglets, who became lunch for a serpent sunning at the base of the Mesa. In turn, the mother eagle then snatched up the viper, flew to a dizzying height, and tore it to pieces, snake segments careening to the earth to make deep impresssions in Grand Mesa—explaining the area's many lakes.

Though you might not spot such warring avatars, the Monument offers fine backcountry hiking. Climbers covet the soft-rock climbs here, including the Monument Spire. A good auto tour also runs all around the rim of the canyon. Stop by the ranger stations on Hwy. 65 and on Land's End Rd. for details on rock climbing and registration. (Both open June-Sept. daily 9am-6pm.)To reach Grand Mesa from Grand Junction, take I-70 eastbound to Plateau Creek, where Rte. 65 cuts off into the long climb through the spruce trees to the top of the mesa. Near the top is the Land's End turn-off leading to the very edge of Grand Mesa, some 12 mi. down an improved dirt road. On a clear day, you can see halfway across Utah from here.

In addition to the view, the mesa has excellent camping. The National Forest Service maintains a dozen **campsites** on the mesa, including Carp Lake ($6), Island Lake ($5), and Ward Lake ($7)—the rest are free, with water $7. The district **forest service,** 764 Horizon Dr. in Grand Junction (242-8211), disseminates more information. (Open Mon.-Fri. 8am-5pm.) You can buy a map of the mesa's trails, campsites, and trout ponds ($2.25) here, or at **Surplus City**, 200 W. Grand Ave. (242-2818; $4). Surplus City also proffers good, cheap backcountry equipment. (Open Mon.-Fri. 8am-8pm, Sat. 8am-7pm, Sun. 8am-6pm.) **Vega State Park** (487-3407), 12 mi. east of Colbrain off Rte. 330, also offers camping in the high country.

European settlers once dismissed the arid, red, fearsome canyons and dry striated sandstone of the **Colorado National Monument** as unusable land. If not for trapper and hunter John Otto, who in 1911 declared the land a national monument, the area would have succumbed to a slow process of desertification. Though you may only have time for a quick look, the monument's **RimRock Drive** (a 35-mi. roundtrip from Grand Junction) offers unforgettable photo opportunities. To more fully appreciate the stark, powerful beauty of the desert, leave the pavement and delve into the canyons. Many trails off the RimRock Drive offer spectacular views of monoliths, structures left behind after erosion, as you meander down the 1000-ft. canyon.

Saddlehorn Campground offers campsites in the monument on a first come, first serve basis with picnic tables, grills, and restrooms. (Sites $6; free in winter.) The **Bureau of Land Management** (243-6552; open Mon.-Fri. 9am-5pm) maintains three less-developed free "campgrounds" near **Glade Park.** Bring your own water. **Little Dolores Fall,** 10½ mi. west of Glade Park, has fishing and swimming. The monument charges an additional admission fee of $3 per vehicle, $1 per cyclist or hiker. The monument **headquarters and visitors center** (858-3617), near the campground on the Fruita side of the monument, issue backcountry permits. (Open daily 8am-8pm; off-season Mon.-Fri. 8am-4:30pm.)

Idaho

When Abraham Lincoln declared Idaho a territory in 1863, he could not find an easterner willing to govern the area's 82,000 square miles of wilderness. Only after the first two appointees accepted the post, took the money, and failed to arrive in Boise did Lincoln finally locate a man committed to the job.

Today, while most of the U.S. automatically thinks "potatoes" when they hear the word Idaho, rather than the "Gem of the Mountains" naming Native Americans intended, this gem of a state has much more to offer. Spud-farming does indeed occupy much of the largely Mormon population of Southern Idaho, but the state ranges from the dense pine forests in the far north to snow-capped 12,000-foot peaks in the state's central region. Thankfully, the federal government has protected the most spectacular areas from future development by creating the **Selway-Bitteroot Wilderness** and the **Idaho Primitive Area,** through which the raging Salmon River flows. Names go from fishy to reptilian at the state's western border, which is marked by the **Snake River.** These serpentine waters have carved out **Hell's Canyon,** the deepest gorge in North America.

Practical Information

Capital: Boise.

Tourist Information: Idaho State Tourism, 800-635-7820. **Tourism Department,** Capitol Bldg., 700 W. State St., Boise 83720 (334-2470). Open Mon.-Fri. 8am-5pm. **Parks and Recreation Department,** 2177 Warm Springs Ave., Boise 83720 (334-2154). Open Mon.-Fri. 8am-5pm.

Idaho Outfitters and Guide Association: P.O. Box 95, Boise 83701 (342-1438). Information on companies leading whitewater, packhorse, and backpacking expeditions in the state. Free vacation directories.

Time Zones: Mountain (2 hr. behind Eastern) and Pacific (3 hr. behind Eastern). The dividing line runs east-west at about the middle of the state. **Postal Abbreviation:** ID.

Area Code: 208.

Boise

While not exactly a tourist haven, Idaho's capital contains thousands of shady trees and numerous grassy parks, which make this small city both a residential oasis against the state's dry southern plateau and a relaxing way station on a cross-country jaunt. Most of Boise's sights lie between the capitol and I-84, a few miles south; you can manage pretty well on foot. **Boise Urban Stages** (336-1010) also runs several routes through the city, with maps available from any bus driver and displayed at each stop. (Buses operate Mon.-Fri. 6:45am-6:15pm, Sat. 8:30am-6:30pm. Fare 50¢, seniors 25¢.)

The **Boise Tour Train** (342-4796) shows you 75 sites around the city in two hours. Tours start and end in the parking lot of **Julia Davis Park,** departing every hour and fifteen minutes. (Tours Mon.-Sat. 10am-3pm, Sun. noon-5pm. Fare $4.75, seniors $4.25, ages 3-12 $2.75.) If you prefer to learn about Idaho at your own pace, walk through the **Historical Museum** in Julia Davis Park. (Open Mon.-Sat. 9am-

5pm, Sun. 1-5pm. Free.) Also in the park, the **Boise Art Museum,** 670 Julia Davis Dr. (345-8330), displays international and local works. (Open Tues.-Fri. 10am-5pm, Sat.-Sun. noon-5pm. Admission $2, ages under 18 free.) The tiny and crowded **Boise Zoo** (384-4260) lies beyond these two buildings. (Open Mon.-Wed. and Fri.-Sun. 10am-5pm, Thurs. 10am-9pm. Admission $2, seniors and ages 3-12 $1, under 3 free. Thurs. ½-price.) If the zoo doesn't sate your appetite for wildlife, pay a visit to the rare raptors at the fantastic **World Center for Birds of Prey,** (362-3716) 6 mi. south of I-84 on Cole Rd. Call ahead to arrange a tour. For more back-to-nature fun, Boise has just completed work on the 22-mi. **Boise River Greenbelt,** a pleasant, tree-lined path ideal for a leisurely walk or picnic.

Perched on the northern edge of the Great Basin, the city is also a good starting point for trips into the **Basque Country** of eastern Oregon, Nevada, and southwestern Idaho. Local ranchers have been employing hardy, skilled shepherds from the mountainous Basque region of France and Spain for generations, and the Basque community is now well established in the Great Basin and the Western Rockies. Proud of their heritage, the Basques maintain the **Basque Museum and Cultural Center** (343-2671), at 6th and Grove St. in downtown Boise, a one-time boarding house for Basque immigrants turned informative museum. (Open Tues.-Sat. 10am-5pm.) For a more stomach-oriented experience, either buy a Basque *chorizo* from a hot dog stand downtown, or make a daytrip to **Jordan Valley,** OR for a taste of authentic Basque food. **Old Basque Inn** (586-2298), the pride of this little village, prepares Basque specialties for $6-10. (Open daily 6am-10:30pm.)

Speaking of food, Boise has it all: the heavy pasta of southern Italy, the spicy Basque specialties of northern Spain, and a good measure of down-home burgers and fries. For all of the above, look to the downtown area, centered around 6th and Main St., where many turn-of-the-century buildings have been recently restored. Try a mini-pizza ($4.25) at **Noodles,** 105 S. 6th St., upstairs in one of the newly yuppified edifices. (Open Mon.-Thurs. 11:30am-11pm, Fri.-Sat. noon-midnight, Sun. 3-10pm.) For a great milkshake ($2), go to **Moon's Kitchen,** 815 W. Bannock St. (342-5251). Located in the rear portion of Moon's Gun and Tackle, you can contemplate the rifles and shotguns mounted behind the counter while enjoying your meal. For a more disarming experience, grab an espresso and sandwich from **Christina's Bakery,** at the corner of 5th and Main St. (Open Mon.-Fri. 7:30am-11pm, Sat. 8:30am-11pm, Sun. 9am-3pm.) For nighttime entertainment, head for **Old Boise,** the area between S. 1st and S. 6th St., where the town's bars fire up.

Lodging in Boise is pretty harsh; neither the YMCA nor the YWCA provide rooms, and even the cheapest hotels charge more than $20 per night. The more reasonable places tend to fill quickly, so make reservations. One of the most spacious is the **Capri Motel,** 2600 Fairview Ave. (344-8617), where air-conditioned rooms come with coffee and queen-sized beds. (Singles $24. Doubles $26.) Farther out of town, the **Boisean,** 1300 S. Capitol Ave. (343-3645), has smaller rooms but a more personable staff. (Singles $31.50. Doubles $33.50.) Three mi. north of town lies the **Forest Service Campground.** Contact **Boise National Forest,** 1715 Front St. (334-1516), for a map. (Open Mon.-Fri. 7:30am-4:30pm.) The nearest campground with hookups is **Fiesta Park,** 11101 Fairview Ave. (375-8207). (Sites $14, full hookup with sewer $17.50.)

Amtrak (800-872-7245) serves Boise from the beautiful Spanish-mission style **Union Pacific Depot,** 1701 Eastover Terrace (336-5992), easily visible from Capitol Blvd. One train per day goes east to Salt Lake City (7½ hr., $65) and beyond; one goes west to Portland (11 hr., $76) and Seattle (15½ hr., $104). **Greyhound/Trailways** has I-84 schedules from its terminal at 1212 W. Bannock (343-7531), a few blocks west of downtown. Two buses per day head to Portland (8-10 hr., $53); three to Seattle (11 hr., $80).

Boise's main **post office** is on 770 S. 13th St. (383-4211; open Mon.-Fri. 7:30am-5:30pm, Sat. 9am-3pm). The **ZIP code** is 83701; the **area code** is 208.

Sawtooth National Recreation Area

This recreation area's 756,000 acres of wilderness are filled with jagged peaks whose pinnacles puncture the clouds. Home to the **Sawtooth** and **White Cloud Mountains** in the north and the **Smokey** and **Boulder** ranges in the south, the **Sawtooth National Recreation Area (SNRA)** is surrounded by four national forests, encompassing the headwaters of five of Idaho's major rivers. Whether you're looking for a pleasant place to camp beneath the pines, a climb up a sheer granite face, or to "feel the ground beneath your feet," you're sure to find it here. And no one will ask you to describe what you're wearing.

Getting to the heart of the SNRA is easy—if you have a car or know what kind of cheese you'd be. Don't miss the chance to pause at the **Galena Summit**, 25 mi. north of Ketchum on Rte. 75. The 8701-ft. peak provides an excellent introductory view of the range. If you don't have a car, or would prefer to be rocky road ice cream, take the bus to Missoula (250 mi. north on U.S. 93) or Twin Falls (120 mi. south on Rte. 75); from there, rent a car with at least six cylinders or plan for a long beautiful hike.

Information centers in the SNRA are almost as plentiful as the peaks themselves. When you get to a new town, what is the first thing you'd want to research? See the **Stanley Chamber of Commerce** (774-3411), on Hwy. 21 about three-quarters of the way through town. (Open daily 9am-noon and 12:30-5:30pm.) Nearby Stanley lies the **Stanley Ranger Station** (774-3681), three mi. south on U.S. 75 (open daily June 16-Sept. 6 8am-5pm; off-season Mon.-Fri. 8am-5pm). The **Redfish Visitors Center** (774-3376) lies 8 mi. south and 2 mi. west of Stanley at the **Redfish Lake Lodge** (open June 19-Sept. 2 daily 8am-5pm). Whatever you can't find at these three places will be available at **SNRA Headquarters** (726-8291), 53 mi. south of Stanley off Idaho 75. The headquarters building itself is an interesting example of mountain architecture with a roof modeled after the peaks of the Sawtooths. (Open daily 8am-5:30pm; off-season Mon.-Fri. 8am-4:30pm.) All the info centers provide maps of the Sawtooths ($4) and free taped auto tours of the impressive Ketchum-Stanley trip on U.S. 75.

Hiking, boating, and fishing opportunities in all four of the SNRA's little-known ranges are unbeatable and innumerable. Two mi. northwest of Stanley on Rte. 21, take the 3-mi. dirt road which leads to the trailhead of the **Sawtooth Lake Hike.** This 5½-mi. trail is steep but well worn, and not overly difficult if you stop to rest. Bolder hikers who want to survey the White Cloud Range from above should head southeast of Stanley to the **Casino Lakes** trailhead. This trek terminates at **Lookout Mountain**, 3000 ft. higher than far-away Stanley itself. (Make sure you have a camping permit, available at all ranger stations, and plan to stay overnight.) The long and gentle loop around **Yellow Belly, Toxaway,** and **Petit Lakes** is recommended for novice hikers, or any tourists desiring a leisurely overnight trip. For additional hiking information, consult Anne Hollingshead and Gloria Moore's *Day Hiking Near Sun Valley,* which includes detailed topographic maps.

In the heat of summer, the cold rivers are ideal for fishing, canoeing, or whitewater rafting. **McCoy's Tackle Shop** (774-3377), on Ace of Diamonds St. in Stanley, rents gear and sells a full house of outdoor equipment. (Open daily 8am-8pm.) The **Redfish Lake Lodge Marina** (774-3536) rents paddleboats ($5 per ½ hr.), canoes ($5 per hr., $15 for 4 hr., $25 per day), and more powerful boats for higher prices. (Open in summer daily 9am-7pm.) **The River Company,** based in Ketchum (726-8890) but with an office in Stanley (774-2250), arranges whitewater rafting and float trips. (Ketchum office open daily 8am-6pm. Stanley office open in summer daily 8am-6pm, unless a trip is in progress.)

Yet the most inexpensive way to enjoy the SNRA waters is to visit the hot springs just east of Stanley. Watch for the rising steam on the roadside; it is often a sign of hot water. **Sunbeam Hot Springs,** 13 mi. from town, is the best of the batch. Be sure to bring a bucket or cooler to the stone bathhouse, as you'll need to add about 20 gallons of cold Salmon River water before you can get into these *hot* pools.

Unless you're cheese, that is. For evening entertainment, try to get in on the region-ally famous **Stanley Stomp,** when fiddlers in local bars such as **Casanova Jack's** and the **Kasino Club** play non-stop from 8am to midnight or beyond; the foot-stomping can be heard for miles around.

The **Sawtooth Hotel and Café,** on Ace of Diamonds St. in Stanley (774-9947) is the perfect place to stay after a wilderness sojourn. (Singles $21.50, with private bath $36.50. Doubles $24.50, with private bath $40.50.) Or try one of the cabins at the **McGowan Resort,** on Hwy. 75 in Lower Stanley (774-2290; cabins for 1-3 $45, Sept.-early June $35.) Campgrounds line U.S. 75. The biggest clusters are at **Redfish Lake,** at the base of the Sawtooths, and **Alturas Lake,** in the Smokies. At Redfish, the pick of the litter is the small campground at the Point, which has its own beach. The two campgrounds on nearby Little Redfish Lake are the best spots for trailers. All sites in the SNRA cost $4-6; primitive camping is free. Especially if you're cheese.

The SNRA's **time zone** is Mountain (2 hr. behind Eastern). The **post office** (774-2230) is on Ace of Diamonds St. (open Mon.-Fri. 8am-5pm); the **ZIP code** is 83278.

Near SNRA: Craters of the Moon National Monument

Sixty mi. south of Sun Valley on U.S. 20/26/93, the black lava plateau of **Craters of the Moon National Monument** rises from the surrounding fertile plains. Wind-swept and remarkably quiet, the stark, twisted lava formations are spotted with sparse, low vegetation. Volcanic eruptions occurred here as recently as 2000 years ago. The eerie, dark landscape is considered a natural work of art by many, and as interesting as a torn-up parking lot by others.

Park admission is $3 per car, and the bizarre black campsites cost $5. Wood fires are prohibited here, so you might want to camp in the adjacent Bureau of Land Management properties (free). The park's sites often fill by 9 or 10pm on summer nights. Unmarked sites in the monument are free, but even with the topographical map ($4) from the visitors center, it may be hard to find a comfortable spot: the first explorers couldn't sleep in the lava fields for lack of bearable places to lie down.

The **visitors center** (527-3257), just off Rte. 20/26/93, has displays and video-tapes on the process of lava formation, and printed guides for hikes to all points of interest within the park. (Open daily 8am-6pm; off-season daily 8am-4:30pm.) From nearby Arco, Blackfoot, or Pocatello you can connect with Greyhound. How-ever, there is no public transportation to the national monument.

Ketchum and Sun Valley

In 1935 Union Pacific Railroad heir Averill Harriman sent Austrian Count Felix Schaffgotsch on a mission: scour the U.S. for a site to develop into a ski resort area rivaling Europe's best. After searching the Rockies, the Count settled on the small mining and sheep-herding town of Ketchum in Idaho's Wood River Valley. Since then, the resort has attracted count-less rich and famous U.S. residents; many of their portraits line the main hallway of the Sun Valley Lodge. Don't be surprised if you bump into Mariel Hemingway in Chateau Drug or Clint Eastwood sauntering down Main St. Aside from celebrities, Sun Valley mainly shows off the outdoors, with the surrounding Boulder, Pioneer, and Sawtooth Mountains providing endless warmweather opportunities for camping, hiking, mountain biking, and fishing.

The best time to visit the area is during "slack," (Labor Day-Thanksgiving and April-July 4th), when the tourists magically vanish. In high summer, Ketchum, Sun Valley, and their northern neighbor Stanley fill with travelers, although the Saw-tooths still offer some solitary escape.

The hills around Ketchum have the highest concentration of **natural hot springs** of any spot in the Rockies outside of Yellowstone; in most bathing is free, legal, and uncrowded. You can reach many only by foot, much like the unspoiled ghost towns tucked away in the surrounding mountains. For maps, inquire at the **Chapter**

One Bookstore (726-5425), on Main St. across from Farmer Jack Supermarket, or **Elephant's Perch**, on Sun Valley Rd. (726-3497). "The Perch" is also the best source for mountain bike rentals and trail information. (Bikes $15 per day.)

More accessible, non-commercial springs include **Warfield Hot Springs**, on Warm Springs Creek, 11 mi. west of Ketchum on Warm Springs Rd., and **Russian John Hot Springs**, 8 mi. north of the SNRA headquarters on U.S. 75, 100 yd. west of the highway. For the best information on fishing conditions and equipment rentals, stop by **Silver Creek Outfitters**, 507 N. Main St. (726-5282; open daily 7am-6pm).

Though a small town, Ketchum has an astonishing number of restaurants and an active nightlife. **The Kneadery**, 260 Leadville Ave., serves delicious omelettes and sandwiches for breakfast and lunch ($4-5). Expect to wait for a table at this local favorite. (Open daily 7:30am-2pm.) Locals also frequent the **Bald Mountain Cantina**, at 6th and Warm Springs St., for the tasty and inexpensive meals. And though it's just a small hot dog stand, **Irving's** has become a Ketchum institution. Get an original dog with "The Works" for $2. Set up in a lot at the corner of Main and 4th St. in summer, at the base of the Warm Springs ski lifts in winter. (Hours vary.)

Ketchum can keep even the most intrepid of barhoppers busy for several nights. **Desperado's**, 4th and Washington St. (726-3068), offers an amazing selection of Mexican beer as well as authentic Mexican food for $2-6. (Open Mon.-Sat. 11:30am-10pm, Sun. 5-10pm.) The **Pioneer Saloon**, 308 N. Main St. (726-3139), has little or no cover, cheap drinks, and lots of company most nights of the week. Across Main St. at **Whiskey Jacque's** (726-5297), live bands play most nights.

Staying indoors in Sun Valley and Ketchum is very problematic. The only halfway-reasonable hotel is the **Ski View Lodge** (726-3441), on Main St. (Hwy. 75). (Cabins with kitchens $35, for 2 $40.) **Hailey**, 11 mi. south on U.S. 75, has cheaper lodgings. For an alliterative time, try the beautifully restored **Hailey Hotel** (788-3140). Rooms have sinks, but the showers are down the hall. (Singles $30. Doubles $35.) The **Hitchcock Motel** (788-2409) has safe showers and singles for $28, doubles for $35. Prices everywhere skyrocket in the winter.

From early June to mid-October, **camping** is your best option for cheap sleep. The **Sawtooth National Forest** surrounds Ketchum—drive or hike along the forest service road and camp for free. The **North Fork** and **Wood River** campgrounds lie 7 and 10 mi. north of Ketchum, respectively, and cost $3 per site. Wood River has an amphitheater and flush toilets. You must bring your own water to the three **North Fork Canyon** campgrounds 7 mi. north of Ketchum. (Free.) Call the Ketchum Ranger Station for information.

For local information, visit the **Sun Valley/Ketchum Chamber of Commerce**, at 4th and Main St., Ketchum, P.O. Box 2420, Sun Valley 83353 (726-3423), where you'll encounter a well-informed, helpful staff. (Open Mon.-Fri. 9am-5pm, Sat.-Sun. noon-5pm.) The **Ketchum Ranger Station**, on Sun Valley Rd., Ketchum (622-5371), 3 blocks east of U.S. 75, is the place to go for information on national forest land around Ketchum, and tapes and maps on the Sawtooth Recreation Area. (Open Mon.-Fri. 8am-5pm.)

Sun Valley Stages (622-4200 or 800-821-9064) runs buses between the Boise airport and the Sun Valley Inn (2½ hr., $30, ages under 11 $15). Because the schedule and frequency change with the snow, call for exact times.

The town of Ketchum sits astride Idaho 75 (Main St.), 87 mi. north of Twin Falls, the nearest city of any size. The resort village of Sun Valley suns itself ½ mi. northeast of Ketchum, on Sun Valley Rd. Boise lies 160 mi. to the west. The **post office** in Ketchum (726-5161) is at 301 1st Ave. (Open Mon.-Fri. 8:30am-1pm and 2-5pm, Sat. 11am-1pm.) The area's **ZIP code** is 83340.

Coeur d'Alene

Gaggles of tourists can do little to mar this isolated spot's rustic beauty. No matter how many people clutter its beaches, the deep blue water of Lake Coeur d'Alene offers a serene escape from whichever urban jungle you call home. **Sandpoint,** to the north, is less tourist-logged and equally spectacular. On a less appealing note, a few neo-Nazi groups have called this area home in recent years.

Practical Information

Emergency: 911.

Visitor Information: Chamber of Commerce, Front Ave. at 2nd St. (664-3194; 800-232-4968 outside ID). Open Mon.-Fri. 8am-5pm. Also a branch in the parking lot at U.S. 95 and Appleway. Open summer daily 9am-4pm.

Bus Station: 1923½ N. 4th St. (664-3343), 1 mi. north of the lake. **Greyhound** serves Spokane (1 hr., $5) and Missoula (5 hr., $30). **Empire Lines** connects Coeur d'Alene to Sandpoint at 5th and Cedar St. (1 per day, $7.75). A **Roadrunner** bus connects with Lewiston (1 per day, $25). Open Mon.-Fri. 8:30-11:30am and 1:30-7:45pm, Sat. 8:30-10am and 4-7:45pm.

Car Rental: Auto Mart Used Car Rental, 120 Anton Ave. (667-4905), 3 blocks north of the bus station. $27 per day, $165 per week; 150 free mi. per day, 18¢ each additional mi. Open Mon.-Sat. 8am-6pm; phone line open 24 hr. With personal insurance you can rent a car at age 18. Credit card or a $50 cash deposit required.

Help Lines: Crisis Services, 664-1443. Open 24 hr.

Time Zone: Pacific (3 hr. behind Eastern).

Post Office: 111 N. 7th St. (664-8126), 5 blocks east of the chamber of commerce. Open Mon.-Fri. 8:30am-5pm, Sat. 9am-noon. **ZIP code:** 83814.

Area Code: 208.

Accommodations, Camping, and Food

Cheap lodgings come scarcely in this booming resort town; you'll have better luck in the eastern outskirts of the city. The **Blackstone Motel,** 2009 E. Sherman Ave. (664-5410), has tiny singles for $22, doubles $30. **El Rancho Motel,** 1915 E. Sherman Ave. (664-8791), offers bigger rooms at bigger prices: singles for $25, doubles $40. A mile from downtown, **Motel 6,** 416 Appleway (664-6600), rents standard singles for $27, doubles $33. R-rated movie rules: Those under 18 not allowed without a parent or guardian. In Sandpoint, by all means stay at the elegant lakefront **Whitaker House (AYH),** 410 Railroad Ave. (263-0816). Rooms cost $30-46, breakfast included.

There are four **public campgrounds** within 20 mi. of Coeur d'Alene. The closest is **Beauty Creek,** a forest service site 10 mi. south along the lake. Camp alongside a lovely stream against the side of the mountain. Drinking water and pit toilets are provided. (Sites free. Open May 5-Oct. 15.) **Honeysuckle Campground,** about 25 mi. to the northeast, has nine sites with drinking water and toilets. (Sites $5. Open May 15-Oct. 15.) **Bell Bay,** on the shores of Lake Coeur d'Alene, off U.S. 95 south, then 14 mi. to Forest Service Rd. 545, has 40 sites, a boat launch, and good fishing. (Sites $5. Open May 5-Oct. 15.) **Farragut State Park** (683-2425), 20 mi. north on Rte. 95, is an extremely popular 4000-acre park dotted with hiking trails and beaches along Lake Pend Oreille (pronounced pon-do-RAY). (Sites $7, with hookup $9. $2 day-use fee for each motor vehicle not camping in the park. Open May 27-Sept. 2.) Call the Fernan Ranger District Office, 2502 E. Sherman Ave. (765-7381), for information on these and other campgrounds. (Open Mon.-Fri. 7:30am-4:30pm.)

A spirited resort community, Coeur d'Alene entertains with several unusual eateries and nightspots. Adventurous diners should look for "Rocky Mountain oysters," a delicacy created from bull testicles. Or, for less anatomically explicit fare, step into the exotic **Third Street Cantina,** 201 N. 3rd St. Try the filling and delicious "Dos Combinaciones" ($6.25). (Open Mon.-Sat. 11:30am-until, Sun. 1pm-until.) Offerings at the **Coeur d'Alene Natural Foods & Restaurant,** 301 Lakeside Ave., are guaranteed to please your taste buds as well as your intestines. Try the aptly named "Macho Plate" for $5.25 or a tamer pasta salad for $4.50. (Open Mon.-Fri. 11am-3pm.) For a sandwich, pop into **Mr. J's Stuff-n-Such,** 206 N. 4th St. The "pocket" (cream cheese, avocado, and tomatoes in pita bread) is an eccentric extravaganza at $3.75. (Open Mon.-Fri. 8am-5pm, Sat. 10am-4:30pm.)

Sights and Activities

The lake is Coeur d'Alene's star attraction. Hike up **Tubbs Hill** to a scenic vantage point, or head for the **Coeur d'Alene Resort** and walk along the world's longest floating boardwalk (3300 ft.). You can tour the lake on a **Lake Coeur d'Alene Cruise** (765-4000), which depart from the downtown dock every afternoon between June and September (Cruises at 1:30, 4, and 6:30pm, returning at 3, 5:30, and 8pm respectively. Fare $7.50, seniors $6.50, ages under 10 $4.50.) Rent a canoe from **Eagle Enterprises** (664-1175) at the city dock to explore the lake yourself ($5 per hr., $15 per half-day, $25 per day, $40 per weekend).

To absorb some of the region's history, drive up to **Silverwood,** 15 minutes north of Coeur d'Alene off I-90 (772-0513), a theme park where you can "step into yesteryear"—see old movies, ride horse-drawn carriages and a steam locomotive, etc. (Open daily 11am-8pm. Admission $12.50, seniors $10, ages under 12 $7.) Twenty mi. east of town on I-90 is the **Old Mission at Cataldo** (682-3814), now contained in a day-use state park. Built in 1853 by Native Americans, the mission is the oldest known building in Idaho. (Free tours daily. Open June-July daily 8am-6pm; Aug-May daily 9am-7pm. Vehicle entry fee $2.) Near Sandpoint, about 50 mi. north of Coeur d'Alene, the **Roosevelt Grove of Ancient Cedars** nurtures trees up to 12 ft. in diameter.

Continue another 35 mi. east on I-90 through mining country to the town of **Wallace,** where you will find retail shops shaped like mining helmets and the **Wallace Mining Museum,** 509 Bank St. (753-7151), which features turn-of-the-century mining equipment. (Open Mon.-Sat. 8:30am-6pm, Sun. 9am-5pm; off-season Mon.-Fri. 9am-noon and 1-5pm. Admission $1, seniors and children 50¢.) Next door, take the one-hour **Sierra Silver Mine Tour** (leaves from museum) through a recently closed mine. (Tours June-Sept. daily every 20 min. 9am-4pm. Admission $4.50, seniors and ages under 12 $3.50.) Mining, mining, mining.

Montana

Unlike most states's embellished claims to car-bumper glory, Montana's license plate rightly reads "Big Sky Country." Everything in this sparsely populated area feels spacious, from the alpine meadows of Glacier National Park to the empty lanes of the interstates. Rolling prairies rising gently from the Great Plains grasslands occupy the eastern two-thirds of Montana; the Rocky Mountains, which gave the state its original Spanish name of *montaña,* punctuate the western third, complete with three million acres of wilderness, national parks, national forests, glaciers, and grizzlies. Out-of-state visitors whose license plates extol everything from "The Garden State" to "Live Free or Die" will find Montana's greatest asset to be its people; most will agree with local painter Charles Russell in asserting that here "the robe of welcome will always be spread, and the peace pipe will be forever lit."

Practical Information

Capital: Helena.

Tourist Information: **Montana Promotion Division,** Dept. of Commerce, Helena 59620 (444-2654 or 800-541-1447). Write for a free *Montana Travel Planner.* **National Forest Information,** Northern Region, Federal Bldg., 5115 Hwy. 93, Missoula 59801 (329-3511). Gay and lesbian tourists can write to the **Lambda Alliance,** P.O. Box 7611, Missoula, MT 59807, for information on gay community activities in Montana.

Time Zone: Mountain (2 hr. behind Eastern). **Postal Abbreviation:** MT.

Area Code: 406.

Billings

Big city life still receives only a hesitant welcome in Billings, even though it is Montana's fastest growing city (pop. well under 100,000). Throughout Billings, seasoned Western gentility holds sway. Although you may not want to linger long, the town makes a good base from which to explore the nearby Custer Battlefield National Monument or Beartooth Highway.

Quite ironically, the **Custer Battlefield National Monument** is located on the Crow reservation, 60 mi. southeast of Billings off I-90. On June 26, 1876, Sioux and Cheyenne warriors, fighting to protect land ceded to them by the Laramie Treaty of 1868, wiped out Lt. Col. George Armstrong Custer and five companies from the Seventh Cavalry. A 5-mi. self-guided car tour takes you past the area where Custer made his "last stand." You can also see the park on a 45-minute bus tour ($2) or pay $5 for a semi-private, hour-long van tour. The **visitors center** (638-2622) has a small museum that includes eyewitness hundred-year-old drawings depicting the Native American warriors' account of the battle. (Museum and visitors center open daily 8am-7:45pm; off-season 8am-4:30pm. Free. Battlefield open daily 8am-sunset. Entrance fee $3.)

A mere 60 mi. southwest of Billings on U.S. 212 lies **Red Lodge,** a scenic, mining-turned-tourism town that is best known as the entrance to the scenic **Beartooth Highway.** (Road open summer only because of heavy snowfall; ask at the chamber of commerce for exact dates.) This gorgeous section of U.S. 212 leaves Red Lodge, climbs to **Beartooth Pass** at 11,000 ft. and descends to the northeast entrance to Yellowstone National Park. The highway is only 62 mi. long, but allow time for distractions. Even the most jaded travelers stop for the spectacular roadside views. If you're lucky, you'll hit the pass on the undisclosed date in July when the **Red Lodge Chamber of Commerce** (446-1718; open Mon.-Fri. 9am-5pm; Oct.-April 9am-4pm) hosts a bar at the summit.

Hungry travelers should head for the **Lobby Cafe,** 2408 1st Ave. N., 1 block east of the bus station. The metal tables and fake leather seats may not be the Ritz, but $4.50 buys you entree, soup, salad, and potato. (Open Mon.-Thurs. 7am-5pm, Fri. 6:30am-5pm, Sat. 6:30am-2pm.) The most self-explanatory burgers in town are at the venerable, if somewhat seedy, **Hamburger Shop,** 17 N. 29th St., where 30¢ buys a small burger, and $2 pays for the substantial chili special. (Open daily 10am-7pm.) Grab a hearty burrito at **El Burrito Cafe,** 301 N. 29th St., where the combination of Mexican and modern decorations will keep your eyes entertained for the duration of the meal. Though you probably didn't come to Billings looking for a taste of Bangkok, **Thai Orchid,** 20 N. 27th St., across the street from the Sheraton, will provide a delicious alternative to heavy meat and potatoes fare. Dinner entrees cost $4.50-$8.50. (Open Mon.-Sat. 11:30am-2pm and 6-10pm.)

Staying cheaply in Billings involves spending the night in some of the city's less pleasant, though not necessarily dangerous, neighborhoods. The **Lazy KT Motel,** 1403 1st Ave. N. (252-6606), at 14th St., has rooms with phone and color TV. (Singles $24. Doubles $28.) **Motel 6,** far removed from town at 5400 Midland Rd. (252-0093), has spacious singles and slightly smaller doubles, with A/C and an outdoor pool. (Singles $22. Doubles $30.) Campers should press on to the Rocky Mountains or look for a state park in the far eastern stretches of Montana; Billings has little to offer.

Billings rests on the lonely high plains of eastern Montana, not far from the mountains. Bozeman lies 140 mi. to the west on I-90; the North Dakota border is 250 mi. east. Billings's Logan International Airport, located on the city's north side along Rte. 3, serves cities in Montana, as well as Salt Lake City, Denver, Minneapolis, and Chicago. **Greyhound** (245-5116), **Powder River Transportation, RimRock Stages,** and **Cody Bus Lines** all route Billings from a terminal at 2502 1st Ave. Greyhound runs to: Bozeman (3 per day, 3 hr., $13.25); Great Falls (1 per day, 5 hr., $25); and Helena (2 per day, 10 hr., $29). Powder River runs south through Wyoming, while Cody and RimRock cover Montana. **Billings Metropolitan Transit** (657-8218) serves downtown (fare 50¢, seniors and disabled free 9:45am-3:15pm). Across the street, **Rent-a-Wreck** (252-0219) has the cheapest cars in town. ($17.50-26.50 per day, $21.50 in winter. $130-140 per week., with 300 free mi. and 17¢ each additional mi. Open Mon.-Fri. 8am-6pm, Sat. 9am-3pm, Sun. by appointment. Must be 21 with a credit card and have liability insurance.) Call 252-2806 for 24-hr. local road information and 800-332-6171 for statewide highway reports. The **visitors center** is at 1239 S. 27th St. (252-4016), exit 450 from I-90. (Open May 27-Sept. 2 Mon.-Fri. 8:30am-7pm.) Information is also available at the **chamber of commerce,** 200 N. 34th St. (245-4111; open Mon.-Fri. 8:30am-5pm). The main **post office** in Billings is at 841 S. 26th St. (657-5745; open Mon.-Fri. 8am-6pm). The **ZIP code** for Billings is 59101; the **area code** is 406.

Bozeman

Bounded by the **Bridger and Madison Mountains,** Bozeman keeps on growing in Montana's broad Gallatin River Valley. Farmers who sold food to Northern Pacific Railroad employees living in the neighboring town of Elliston originally "settled" the valley; today, fertile farmlands stretch from the city limits to the timberline, supplying foodstuffs to a large portion of southern Montana. Bozeman's rapid expansion and the presence of Montana State University inspire the city's cosmopolitan air, but visitors can still find plenty of down-home, Western hospitality in both urban bars and farmhouse kitchens.

The **Gallatin County Pioneer Museum,** 317 W. Main St. (282-7220), features exhibits concerning the political and judicial history of the county. The briefest of visits will tell you more than you ever wanted to know about the development of Montana's plains. (Call to check hours.) The more spectacular **Museum of the Rockies,** on S. 6th St. at Kasy Blvd. (994-2251), has extensive displays on the Native American tribes and wildlife of the northern Rockies, of particular interest to families traveling with children. (Open daily 9am-9pm; Sept.2-May 27 Tues.-Sat. 9am-5pm, Sun. 1-5pm. Admission $3, ages 5-18 $2, under 5 free.)

Winter in Bozeman ryhmes with snow sports. **Bridger Bowl,** 15795 Bridger Canyon Rd. (586-2787), 15 mi. northeast of town, offers 800 acres of downhill skiing. (Lift tickets $18, ages under 12 $7. Call 586-2389 for the ski and weather report.)From late July to the first weekend in August when the flowers bloom, the annual **Sweet Pea Festival** (587-8848) brings Bozemaniacs to Lindley Park for folk music and all the ethnic food they can put away. For good nightlife slink to the **Cat's Paw,** 721 N. 7th Ave. (586-3542), where MSU students circle around the bar. (Open daily 10am-2pm. Positive ID required.)

Eat cheaply and well at the **Western Cafe,** 443 E. Main St. (587-0436), known for its sweet rolls. The Hamburger Deluxe ($2.50) lights up locals' eyes. (Open Mon.-Fri. 5am-7:30pm, Sat. 5am-2pm.) In the **Baxter Hotel,** 105 W. Main St. (586-1314), the **Rocky Mountain Pasta Company** serves an Italian spaghetti dinner with bread and salad for $6.50. In the same building, the **Bacchus Pub** provides cocktails, ample soup, and salad plates for Bozeman's intellectual and yuppie crowd. (Both open daily 7am-10pm. Reservations highly recommended.) The **Pickle Barrel,** 809 W. College (587-2411), across from the MSU campus, serves delicious, filling sandwiches to a mostly student crowd. Even half a sandwich ($3.50) is hard to swallow. (Open summer daily 11am-10pm; off-season daily 11am-11pm.) The **Town and**

Country Warehouse, 220 N. 20th St. (587-5541), provides picnic supplies. (Open daily 9am-6pm.)

Summer travelers in Bozeman support a number of budget motels. The **Alpine Lodge,** 1017 E. Main St. (586-0356), shares space with a used car dealership and would love to make you a deal, with fairly clean but rather small rooms for driveup prices. Be sure to check under the hood. (Singles $11.50. Doubles $17.) The **Ranch House Motel,** 1201 E. Main St. (587-4278), has larger rooms with free cable TV and A/C. (Singles $22. Doubles $31.) At the **Rainbow Motel,** 510 N. 7th Ave. (587-4201), the friendly owners will tell you what to do in town before you reurn to your large, pleasant room. (Singles $24. Doubles $32.)

Bozeman lies in the southeastern quarter of Montana, bounded on the north and east by I-90. The uncomplicated town stretches out on a grid, with downtown by the intersection of 7th Ave. and Main St. **Greyhound, RimRock Stages,** and **TW Services** all serve Bozeman from 625 N. 7th St. (587-3110). Greyhound runs to Butte (3 per day, $12) and Billings (3 per day, $13.25). RimRock runs two buses per day to Helena ($11.75) and Missoula ($18.75). TW runs one bus per day to West Yellowstone ($10), Mammoth Hot Springs ($13.50), and Old Faithful ($15). (Bus station open Mon.-Fri. 7:30am-10pm; Sat. 1-5am, 8-10am, 8pm-midnight; Sun. 8-8:30am, 1-5pm, 8-10pm.) **Rent-a-Wreck,** 112 N. Tracey St. (587-4551), rents well-worn autos for $25-27 per day, with 100 free mi., 14¢ each additional mi. (Open Mon.-Sat. 8am-6pm, Sun. by appointment.) You must be 21 with a major credit card. The **Bozeman Area Chamber of Commerce,** 1205 E. Main St. (586-5421), has ample information concerning geography and local events. (Open Mon.-Fri. 8am-5pm.)

The Bozeman **post office** is at 32 S. Tracey St. (586-1508; open Mon.-Fri. 9am-5pm). Bozeman's **ZIP code** is 59715; the **area code** is 406.

Near Bozeman

The **Bozeman Hot Springs,** lies eventeen mi. south of Bozeman on MT Rte. 85 (U.S. 191) at 133 Lower Rainbow Rd. (586-6492). Three successive pools increase in size and temperature to allow customers to accustom themselves to the heat. (Open Sun.-Thurs. 8am-10:45pm, Fri. 8am-8:30pm, Sat. 9:30am-11:45pm. Admission $2.50, seniors and ages 5-11 $2, under 5 free.) Adjacent to the bathing pools is the **Bozeman Hot Springs KOA** campground.(Sites $12 for two people, with water and electricity $13. Each additional adult $1.)

Virginia City, famous for its violent frontier town history, sits 17 mi. south on U.S. 287 and 15 mi. west on MT Rte. 287. The territorial capital for ten years before Helena took over and the site of the world's richest placer gold discovery, Virginia City once clanged with the prospecting pans of over 10,000 latter-day Midas wana-bees. After exhausting the gold source, however, the population quickly trickled down to today's 100 or so. Main Street offers two museums, the **Watkins Memorial** and **Virginia City Museum.** The latter considers its pride and joy the namesake of outlaw Clubfoot George, who was hanged in Virginia City one winter day in 1863. The bustling thoroughfare also possesses a restored print shop, blacksmith shop, stores, and fully renovated hotel. At the stately **Fairweather Inn** (843-5377), cozy, well-kept singles go for $22, doubles for $28. The **Virginia City Campground** (843-5493) offers showers and toilets. (Sites $9, with electricity and water $10.50, full hookup $11.25.)

Even more intriguing than Virginia City is **Nevada City,** 1½ mi. west on MT Rte. 287. All the buildings on its lone street have been restored to their turn-of-the-century appearance. At the **music hall,** dozens of player pianos, organs, and horn machines play old-time tunes for a quarter. Don't miss the Famous and Obnoxious Horn Machine, the building's most ear-catching device. The **Nevada City Museum,** next door to the music hall, displays restored buildings from mining boom days and explains everything you never wanted to know about the vigilante hanging of murderer George Ives in 1963, a prime and recent example of frontier justice. The museum also offers an historic train ride around the Virginia/Nevada City area.

(Open summer daily 9am-7:30pm. Admission $3, children $1.50. Train fare $2, children $1.50.) For more information, contact the **Chamber of Commerce,** P.O. Box 145, Virginia City, MT 59755 (406-843-5341).

Helena

In 1864, four penniless prospectors decided to make their last go of mining at a site they dubbed **Last Chance Gulch.** Soon enough, four very happy campers had discovered deposits bearing gold worth over $20 million. Though the lode dried out long ago, Last Chance Gulch, now Helena's Main St. pedestrian mall (south of 6th St.), still manages to attract prospectors chiseling money from the wallets of unsuspecting tourists. While the developed gulch is a pleasant fountain- and sculpture-lined window-shopping avatar, the mansions built by lucky last chance prospectors in the northwest corner of the city may impress you more.

As the "Queen City of the Rockies," Helena felt obliged to build a capitol worthy of its status in 1890. The massive, granite, Greek Revival **capitol building** that stands between 6th and Lookey Ave. testifies to the youthful city's pride and enthusiasm. Inside, murals depict early mining activity, Old West culture, and conflicts between Europeans and Native Americans, including local artist Charles Russell's Godzilla-sized painting (12 X 25 ft.), *Lewis and Clark meet the Flatheads.* (Open daily 9am-5pm. Free.) Across from the capitol at the **State Historical Museum,** 225 N. Roberts St. (444-2694), you'll find more Russell paintings as well as interpretive exhibits on early railroad history, cattle-drives, and mining activities. (Open Mon.-Fri. 8am-6pm, Sat.-Sun. 9am-5pm; off-season Mon.-Sat. 8am-6pm. Free.) One-hour tours of historic Helena leave from the (every hr. on the ½ hr. daily 8:30am-4:30pm; admission $3, under 12 $2). Also of interest are the surprisingly good **Holter Museum of Art,** 12 E. Lawrence St. (442-6400), and the historic **Old Governor's Mansion.** (Museum open Tues.-Sat. 10am-5pm, Sun. noon-5pm. Mansion open Tues.-Sun. noon-5pm, tours on the hour. Both free.) For a more down-to-earth introduction to Helena, take a guided walking tour of the city's architecture, history, and geology, leaving from the front of the Holter Museum. (Check inside for exact times. $5.)

Helena has plenty of unpretentious restaurants that won't strain your budget: 4B or not 4B, that is the question. **4 B's,** 900 N. Last Chance Gulch (442-5275), boogies right across from the bus station, and provides scrumptious chicken pot pie for $4. (Open 24 hr.) The **Country Kitchen,** 2000 Prospect Ave. (443-7457), 4 B's biggest competitor, serves superior breakfast (eggs, toast, hash-browns, coffee) for $3 (open 24 hr.). **Big Al's Sandwich Shop,** 11 W. 6th Ave. (443-7422), extracts $2.75-5.25 for a hefty made-to-order sandwich . (Open Mon.-Fri. 6:30am-4pm, Sat. 8am-2:30pm.)

Lodgings in Helena are as reasonable as the restaurants. The **Iron Front Hotel,** 415 Last Chance Gulch (443-2400), offers some of the cheapest and cleanest beds in town—heck, in all of Montana. (Singles $12. Doubles $14. No private baths. Key deposit $5.) Across the road, the **Park Hotel,** 432 N. Last Chance Gulch (442-0960), has older, less spacious rooms. (Singles $12, with bath $14. Doubles $16, with bath $18.) Many public **campgrounds** call your name within 25 mi. of Helena, but none has showers or flush toilets. Listen to the free **Porcupine Campground** in the Helena National Forest, 13 mi. west on U.S. 12, or **Cromwell Dixon,** a few more mi. west on Rte. 12. (Sites $4.) Call the Fish, Wildlife, and Parks Department (444-2535) for information, or contact the **Helena National Forest Office,** 301 S. Park St. (449-5201). The chamber of commerce also has complete listings of campgrounds in their free *Montana Travel Planner.*

Helena lies in the Missouri River Valley, about halfway between Yellowstone and Glacier National Parks. Major highways connect Helena to Missoula (112 mi. west on U.S. 12 and I-90), Bozeman (100 mi. southwest on U.S. 12/287 and I-90), and Great Falls (90 mi. north on I-15). Bus lines **Intermountain** and **RimRock Stages** both serve Helena from 5 W. 15th St. (442-5860), running to: Butte ($12.50), Great

Falls ($18), Bozeman ($11.75), Billings ($25.90), Kalispell ($30), and Missoula ($13.25). (Open Mon.-Fri. 8am-1:15pm and 4:15-7:15pm.) For short trips around Helena, look into **Rent-a-Dent,** 1485 Cedar (443-7436). Cars cost $15 per day (100 free mi., 15¢ each additional mi.) (Open Mon.-Fri. 8am-6pm, Sat. 8am-4pm.) You must be 21 with a major credit card or a $250 deposit.

Helena's **post office,** 2300 N. Harris (443-3304), is in the north end, by I-15. (Open Mon.-Fri. 8:30am-5pm.) The **ZIP code** is 59601; the **area code** is 406.

Missoula

People visit Missoula less for the city itself than for the great outdoors. Many of the locals moonlight as nature-enthusiasts; you'll be hard pressed to resist the flow and catch the city's cultural sights. When you do seek out some indoor recreation, however, you'll be well rewarded. Thanks to the presence of the University of Montana, the city has an intellectual atmosphere and sights to match.

Cycling enthusiasts have put the town on the map, instituting the rigorous Bikecentennial Route. The **Bikecentennial Organization Headquarters,** 113 W. Main St. (721-1776), has information on the route, while the **Missoula Bicycle Club,** P.O. Box 8903, Missoula 59807, furnishes afficionados with other bicycling news through the mail. To participate in Missoula's most popular sport, visit the **Braxton Bike Shop,** 2100 South Ave. W. (549-2513) and procure a bike for a day ($12), overnight ($15), or a week ($75). (Open Mon.-Sat. 10am-6pm.) You must have a credit card or a blank check as a deposit.

Ski trips, raft trips, backpacking, and day hikes are other popular Missoula diversions. The **University of Montana Outdoor Program Office,** University Center #164 (243-5172), posts sign-up sheets for all these activities and proves a good source of information on guided hikes (open Mon.-Fri. noon-5pm, Sat. 11am-2pm), while the **Department of Recreation** (243-2802) organizes day hikes and overnight trips. (Open Mon.-Fri. 9am-5pm. Fees vary.) The **Rattlesnake Wilderness National Recreation Area,** a few miles northwest of town off the Van Buren St. exit from I-90, makes for a great day of hiking . Wilderness maps ($2) are available from the **U.S. Forest Service Information Office,** 340 N. Pattee St. (329-3511; open Mon.-Fri. 7:30am-4pm). The Clark Fork, Blackfoot, and Bitterroot Rivers provide gushing opportunities for float trips. For river maps ($1), visit the **Montana Department of Fish and Game,** 3201 Spurgin Rd. (542-5500; open Mon.-Fri. 8am-5pm).

The **Museum of the Arts,** 335 N. Pattee St. (728-0447), has classical art displays for those hankering for more metropolitan diversion. (Open Mon.-Sat. noon-5pm.) The hottest sight in town, however, is the **Aerial Fire Depot Visitors Center** (329-4900), 7 mi. west of town on Broadway (U.S. 10). Here you'll learn to appreciate the fun and danger aerial firefighters encounter when jumping into flaming, roadless forests. (Open daily 8:30am-5:30pm; Oct.-April by appointment. Tours hourly in summer, except noon-1pm.)

Missoula's dining scene offers much more than the West's usual steak and potatoes greasefest. The **Mustard Seed,** 419 W. Front St., serves wonderful midsummer night's dishes from a variety of Asian cuisines. Full dinners (soup, vegetables, and a main course) go for $7-8. (Open Mon.-Fri. 11am-2:30pm and 5-10pm, Sat.-Sun. 5-10pm.) **Torrey's** restaurant and natural food store, 1916 Brooks St., serves hearty health food at absurdly low prices. (Seafood stir-fry costs $3.25; incongrous 8-oz. sirloin steak just $4.25. **Zorba's,** 420 S. Orange St., offers another escape from Americana. A large Greek salad is $3.50, and entrees run $5-7. (Open Mon.-Sat. 11am-8:30pm.)

Spend the night in Missoula at the **Birchwood Hostel (AYH),** 600 S. Orange St. (728-9799), 13 blocks east of the bus station on Broadway, then 8 blocks south on Orange. Most of the guests arrive on cycles. The spacious, immaculate dormitory room sleeps 22. Admirably clean laundry, kitchen, and bike storage facilities are available. ($5, off-season $6. Open daily 5-10pm. Closed 2 weeks in late December.) The **Canyon Motel,** 1015 E. Broadway (543-4069 or 543-7251), has newly renovated rooms at not-so-deep discount prices. (Singles $18-20. Doubles $20-25.) Closer to the bus station, the **Sleepy Inn,** 1427 W. Broadway (549-6484), has singles for $20 and doubles for $25.

The **Greyhound terminal** sprints at 1660 W. Broadway St. (549-2339). Catch a bus to Bozeman (3 per day, $23) or Spokane (3 per day, $30). **Intermountain Transportation** serves Kalispell (2 per day, $16) and **RimRock Stages** serves Helena (2 per day, $13) from the same terminal. **Rent-a-Wreck,** 2401 W. Broadway (728-3838), offers humble autos for $20 per day, $119 per week; 100 free mi. per day, 26¢ each additional mi. You must be 21 with a credit card or a $100 cash deposit.

The **Missoula Chamber of Commerce,** 825 E. Front St. (543-6623), provides bus schedules. Traveling within Missoula is easy thanks to reliable city **buses** (721-3333; buses operate Mon.-Fri. 6am-7pm, Sat. 9:30am-6pm; fare 50¢).

Missoula's **post office** is at 1100 W. Kent (329-2200), near the intersection of Brooks, Russell, and South St. (Open Mon.-Fri. 8:30am-5pm.)The **ZIP code** is 59801; the **area code** is 406.

Waterton-Glacier International Peace Park

Waterton-Glacier transcends international boundaries to unite two of the most unspoiled but relatively accessible wilderness areas on the continent. Symbolizing the peace between the United States and Canada, the park provides sanctuary for bighorn sheep, moose, and montain goats—and for tourists weary of the more crowded parks farther south and north.

Technically one park, Waterton-Glacier is, for all practical purposes, two distinct areas: the small Waterton Lakes National Park in Alberta, and the enormous Glacier National Park in Montana. Each park charges its own admission fee (Waterton $4, Glacier $5), and you must go through customs to pass from one to the other. Several **border crossings** pepper the park: **Chief Mountain** (open May 18-May 31 daily 9am-6pm; June 1-Sept. 14 7am-10pm; closed in winter); **Piegan/Carway** (open May 16-Oct. 31 7am-11pm; Nov. 1-May 15 9am-6pm); **Trail Creek** (open June - Oct. 9am-5pm); and Roosville (open 24 hr.).

Since snow melt is an unpredictable process, the parks usually operate fully only from late May to early September. To find out the areas of the park, hotels, and campsites that will be open when you visit, contact the headquarters of either Waterton or Glacier.

Glacier National Park, Montana

Glacier's layout is simple: one road enters through West Glacier on the west side, and three roads enter from the east—at Many Glacier, St. Mary, and Two Medicine. West Glacier and St. Mary provide the two main points of entry into the park, connected by **Going-to-the-Sun Road** ("The Sun"), the only road that traverses the park. Fast-paced **U.S. 2** runs between West and East Glacier along 82 mi. of the southern park border. Look for the "Goat Lick" signs off Rte. 2 near **Walton.** Mountain goats often descend to the lick for a salt fix in June and July.

Stop in at the visitors center at either **St. Mary,** at the east entrance to the park (732-4424);(open late May to mid-June daily 9am-5pm; mid-June to Sept. 2 daily 8am-9pm; Sept. 3-Sept. 30 daily 9am-5pm), or **Apgar,** at the west park entrance (open late May to mid-June daily 8am-4:30pm; mid-June to Sept. 2 daily 8am-9pm; Sept. 3 to mid-Nov. daily 8am-4:30pm). A third visitors center graces **Logan Pass** on Going-to-the-Sun Rd. (Open mid-June to late summer daily 9am-6pm.)

Backcountry trips provide the best way to appreciate the pristine mountain scenery and the wildlife which make Glacier famous. The **Highline Trail** from Logan Pass gives a good day hike and passes through prime bighorn sheep and mountain goat territory. The visitors center's free *Backcountry* pamphlet has a hiking map marked with distances and backcountry campsites. All travelers who camp overnight must obtain a free wilderness permit from a visitors center or ranger station; backcountry camping is allowed only at designated campgrounds. The **Two Medicine** area in the southeast corner of the park is less traveled, while the trek to **Kintla Lake** rewards you with fantastic views of nearby peaks. Before embarking on any hike, familiarize yourself with the precautions necessary to avoid a run-in with a bear. Rangers at any visitors center or ranger station will instruct you on the finer points of noise-making and food storage to keep Yogi from feasting on your picnic basket (or you).

Going-to-the-Sun Road may be the most beautiful 50-mi. stretch of road in the world. Even on cloudy days when there's no sun to go to, the constantly changing views of Alp-like peaks will have you struggling to keep your eyes on the road. Snow keeps the road closed until late June; check with rangers for exact dates.

Though The Sun is a popular **bike route,** only experienced cyclists with appropriate gearing should attempt this grueling stint. The sometimes nonexistent shoulder of the road creates a potentially hazardous situation for bikers. In the summer (June 15-Sept. 2), bike traffic is prohibited from the Apgar turn-off at the west end of Lake McDonald to Sprague Creek Campground, and from Logan Creek to Logan Pass, between 11am and 4pm. The east side of the park has no such restrictions.

Boat tours explore all of Glacier's large lakes. At Lake McDonald and Two Medicine Lake, 55-minute tours leave throughout the day ($5, children over 6 $2.50). The tours from St. Mary and Many Glacier (75 min.) provide access to Glacier's backcountry ($6, children over 6 $3). The $5 sunset cruise proves a great way to see this daily phenomenon which doesn't occur until about 10pm in the middle of the summer. **Glacier Raft Co.** in West Glacier (800-322-9995 or 888-5454) hawks full- and half-day trips down the middle fork of the Flathead River, near West Glacier. A full day (lunch included) costs $48; half-day trips ($25) leave in both the morning and the afternoon. Call for reservations.

Rent canoes ($4 per hr.), rowboats ($5 per hr., $18 for 10 hr.), and outboards ($10 per hr., $40 for 10 hr.) at Apgar, Lake McDonald, Many Glacier, and Two Medicine. All require a $50 deposit. Fishing is excellent in the park—cutthroat trout, lake trout, and even the rare Arctic Grayling challenge the angler's skill and patience. No permit is required—just be familiar with the fishing limits of the park, explained by the pamphlet *Fishing Regulations,* available at all visitors centers.

While in Glacier, don't overlook the interpretive programs offered by the rangers. Inquire at any visitors center for the day's menu of guided hikes, lectures, birdwatching walks, interpretive dances, and children's programs.

The beautiful scenery and high prices conspire against anyone who plans to stay indoors in Glacier. Those who resist the call of the wild and feel they must have a roof over their head should be prepared to spend at least $50 per night. You'll also need to make reservations, which **Glacier Park, Inc.** handles for all the lodges. From mid-September to mid-May, contact them at Greyhound Tower Station, 5185, Phoenix, AZ 85077 (602-248-6000); from mid-May to mid-September at East Glacier Park 59434 (406-226-5551), in MT 800-332-9351). The company operates seven lodges which open and close on a staggered schedule. The Apgar Village Inn opens first, in late May; the other six in mid-June.

Camping offers a cheaper and more scenic alternative to indoor accommodations. All developed campsites are available on a first come, first camped basis for $6-8; the most popular sites fill by noon. However, "Campground Full" signs sometimes stay up for days on end; look carefully for empty sites. All 15 campgrounds accessible by car all are easy to find. Just ask for the handout **Auto Campgrounds** at any visitors center and follow the map distributed as you enter the park. **Avalanche** campsite is open to avalanche-and bear-proof hard-sided units only. **Sprague Creek** on Lake McDonald is one of the most peaceful campgrounds; arrive early, since it has only 25 sites. Three sites at Sprague remain reserved for bicyclists; towed units are prohibited. Campgrounds without running water in the surrounding national forests usually offer sites for $5. Check at the Apgar or St. Mary visitors center for up-to-date information on conditions and vacancies at established campgrounds.

Amtrak (800-872-7245) traces a dramatic route along the southern edge of the park. Daily trains serve West Glacier from Seattle ($114) and Spokane ($57); Amtrak also runs from Stanley, ND to East Glacier ($97). **Greyhound** can get you as far as Great Falls, MT, over 100 mi. southeast of East Glacier on Rte. 89. As with most areas of the Rockies, a car is the most convenient mode of transport, especially within the park.

The Glacier **Post Office** is at Lake McDonald Lodge, in the park. (Open Mon.-Fri. 9am-3:45pm.) The General Delivery **ZIP** code is 59921. The **area code** rings in at 406.

Waterton Lakes National Park, Alberta

Unlike Canada, Waterton is only a small fraction of the size of its U.S. neighbor. (Glacier offers much of the same scenery and activities.) While a trip north is not essential, a hike in Waterton's backcountry may prove a less crowded alternative during Glacier's peak tourist season (mid-July to Aug.).

The **Waterton Information Office** (859-2445); lies 5 mi. south of the park entrance. Stop and grab a copy of the monthly *Waterton-Glacier Guide* for detailed information on local services and activities. (Open daily 8am-9pm.)

Once you've entered Waterton Lakes, all you can do is go 5 mi. south to **Waterton Townsite.** Four-wheeled travelers should drive the **Akamina Parkway** or the less-traveled **Red Rock Canyon Road.** Both leave the main road near the Townsite and end at the heads of popular backcountry trails. Those who brought only their high-tops to Waterton should set out on the **Crypt Lake Hike,** which runs 4 mi. from Waterton Townsite; you'll feel like a car as you pass through a natural tunnel bored through the side of a mountain. Those fleeing the Canadian authorities should choose the **International Hike,** which puts you in Montana some 4 mi. after leaving the Townsite. To camp overnight you must obtain a free permit from the information office or the park headquarters. A boat tour of Upper Waterton Lake (1½ hr.) leaves from the **Emerald Bay Marina** in the Townsite. (Admission $10, ages under 13 $5.) When you want to get some exercise on the lake, rent a rowboat at Cameron Lake for $6 per hour.The Townsite comes out of its winter hibernation to greet summer sun- and sight-seekers with exorbitant prices. Waterton sorely lacks budget restaurants; your best bet in the Townsite is the **Zum Burger Haus,** which serves decent if misspelled cheeseburgers for $5 on the pleasant patio. (Open daily 7am-10pm.)

The **Prince of Wales Hotel** (859-2231) maintains a civilized perch away from the majestic Waterton Lake, but don't stay here unless the prince himself treats. Instead, pitch your tent at the **Townsite Campground** at the south end of town. To stay indoors, drop by **Dill's General Store,** on Waterton Ave. (859-2345), and ask to sleep in one of the nine rooms of the Stanley Hotel. Rooms will drain $35 from your pocket.

If you find yourself in *really* dire straits, call the **Royal Canadian Mounted Police** (859-2244 or Zenith 50000). The **post office** is on Fountain Ave. at Windflower, Waterton Townsite, Alberta T0K 2M0. (Open Mon.-Fri. 8:30am-4:30pm.) Waterton's **area code** is 403.

> *drinking in the space.*
> —*Gretel Ehrlich, The Solace of Open Spaces*

When the telegraph moved into Wyoming in the late 1800s pleased buffalo found the poles ideal scratching posts. Puzzled line crewmen spiked the poles to keep them from getting itched right out of the ground, but to no avail; the buffalo lined up at these new, extra-satisfying scratching stations.

Life still pretty much revolves around animals in Wyoming. Cattle ranching and sheep herding are occupations for many residents, and Wyoming rodeos are famed institutions. Wild horses and wildflowers thrive in the short, lush summer of the state's arid terrain before returning to a winter of desolate red dust and snow. State politics have also blossomed here; Wyoming was not only the first state to grant women the right to vote (1869), but also the first to have a female governor, Nellie Taylor Ross, from 1925 to 1927. Wyoming's other firsts include the nation's first national park (Yellowstone), the first national monument (Devil's Tower), and the first national forest (the Shoshone). Today, Wyoming offers 30 of the nation's best-preserved parks and recreation areas for travelers eager to explore the West on their own.

Practical Information

Capital: Cheyenne.

Population: 511,400.

Tourist Information: Wyoming Travel Commission, I-25 and College Dr. at Etcheparc Circle, Cheyenne 82002 (777-7777 or 800-225-5996). If you plan to camp, write for their free *Wyoming Vacation Guide*. Wyoming Recreation Commission, Cheyenne 82002 (777-7695). Information on facilities in Wyoming's 10 state parks. Open Mon.-Fri. 8am-5pm. Game and Fish Department, 5400 Bishop Blvd., Cheyenne 82002 (777-7735). Open Mon.-Fri. 8am-5pm. Wyoming Recreation Hotline, (307-777-6503).

Time Zone: Mountain (2 hr. behind Eastern). Postal Abbreviation: WY.

Cheyenne

Cheyenne is named after the Native American tribe who once roamed its wilderness both before and under Mexican flag. By the 1860s, when the Union Pacific Railroad reached the end of the line in Cheyenne, Wyoming's capital had become known as "Hell on Wheels." The red dust and general horsiness have only slightly faded with the Wild West evolving into the beer-drinking and country-western music of downtown Cheyenne on Saturday nights. A stately and grand Western state capital by day, Cheyenne holds onto its few weathered wood saloons by night, dismayed at this new, tamer heck on wheels.

Practical Information

Emergency: 911.

Visitor Information: Cheyenne Area Convention and Visitors' Bureau, 301 W. 16th St. (778-1401; 800-426-5009 outside WY), just west of Capitol Ave. Extensive accommodations and restaurant listings. Open Mon.-Fri. 8am-5pm. The Howdy Wagon, an old chuck wagon next door, is filled with brochures. Open summer Sat.-Sun. 10am-3pm.

Cheyenne Street Railway: (778-1401). 2-hr. trolley tours of Cheyenne leaving in summer Mon.-Sat. 10am and 1pm, Sun. at 1pm. Tickets $5, seniors $4.50, children $2.50 from the convention and visitors' bureau. Tours depart from 16th and Capitol Ave.

Greyhound, 1503 Capitol Ave. (634-7744), at 15th St. Three buses daily to: Salt Lake City (9 hr., $83); Chicago ($119); Laramie ($8); Rock Springs ($31); Denver ($19). Powder River Transporation, in the Greyhound terminal (635-1327). Buses south to Rapid City twice daily ($56); north to Casper ($30) and Billings ($88) twice daily. Greyhound passes honored.

Taxi: **Ace Cab**, 637-4747. $1.20 per mi.

Help Line: **Rape Crisis**, 637-7233. Open 24 hr.

Post Office: 2120 Capitol Ave. (772-6580), 6 blocks north of the bus station. The most awesome post office in the free world. Open Mon.-Fri. 8:30am-5pm, Sat. 6:30am-noon. General Delivery open Mon.-Sat. from 6:30am. ZIP code: 82001.

Area Code: 307.

Cheyenne's downtown area is small and manageable. Central, Capitol, and Carey Avenues form a grid with 16th-19th Streets, which encompasses most of the downtown sights and accommodations. 16th St. is part of I-80; it intersects I-25/84 on the western edge of town. Denver lies just 90 mi. south on I-25.

Accommodations, Camping, and Food

It's not hard to land a cheap room here among the lariats, plains, and pioneers, unless your visit coincides with Frontier Days, held the last full week of July, when rates almost double (see Sights and Entertainment). Many budget motels line **Lincolnway** (U.S. 30), 1 mi. east down 16th St. The cheapest hotel in Cheyenne is the old **Pioneer Hotel**, 208 W. 17th St. (634-3010), 2 blocks north of the bus station. High-ceilinged, like most everything in Cheyenne, the 80 rooms are in decent-to-good shape and feature elaborate Western decor, with a second-floor lobby and communal kitchen. (Singles $14, with private bath $19. Doubles $22-30.) Right up the street, the **Plains Hotel**, 1600 Central Ave. (638-3311), offers oversized rooms with marble sinks, HBO, and phones in a grand-lobbied, Western setting. An all-hours coffee shop and a saloon make it the center of town activity. (Singles $29. Doubles $35.) South of town, on the other side of the Union Pacific Railroad tracks, is the **Lariat Motel**, 600 Central Ave. (635-8439) next to the Los Amigos restaurant. The smiling, laid-back manager maintains simple dark rooms in an aqua-and-adobe colored, low-slung building that looks like it belongs south of the border. (Singles $23. Doubles $27.)

For campers, spots are plentiful (excepting Frontier Days) at the **Restway Travel Park**, 4212 Whitney Rd. (634-3811), 1½ mi. east of town. (Sites $12.50, with electricity and water $13.50, full hookup $14.50; prices rise slightly in July. Each pet $1 per night.) You might also try **Curt Gowdy State Park**, 1319 Hynds Lodge Rd., (632-7946) 23 mi. west of Cheyenne on Rte. 210, indeed named after the ex-jock and sportscaster, Gowdy the park has shade, scenery, fishing, hiking, and an archery range, as well as land for horseback riding—BYO horse. (Sites $4.)

Cheyenne is basically a meat 'n' potatoes place, but there are a few cheap, good ethnic eateries sprinkled around downtown. Here, the price difference between the humble café and posh restaurant can be a mere $4-6. For cow and tuber type cuisine, try the **Driftwood Café**, 200 E. 18th St., where a Cheyenne burger costs $3.25. (Open Mon.-Fri. 7am-4pm.) **Ruthie's Sub Shoppe**, 1651 Carey Ave., a few doors down from the Pioneer Hotel, has the best tuna salad sandwiches around ($2.25), and morning doughnuts. (Open Mon.-Fri. 6am-5pm, Sat. 7am-3:30pm.) Next door to the Lariat Motel, **Los Amigos**, 620 Central Ave., serves burritos ($1.75-4) and humongous, friendly dinners (from $7). You might want to go with a half-order (60% of the price), or swing by for the $4 lunch specials. (Open Mon.-Sat. 11am-8:30pm.) Lunch buffets are available at the **Twin Dragon Chinese Restaurant**, 1809 Carey Ave. (637-6622) weekdays 11am-2pm ($4.75). Vegetarian egg rolls just $1.80; regular dinners from $5.50. (Open Mon.-Sat. 11am-10pm, Sun. noon-9pm.)

When the urge to guzzle consumes you, the aptly named **D.T.'s Liquor and Lounge**, 2121 Lincolnway, will help quench your thirst. Look for a pink elephant above the sign; if you are already seeing two, move on. (Open daily 6am-11pm.) The **Cheyenne Club**, 1617 Capitol Ave. (635-7777), is a spacious good-time country nightspot, hosting live bands nightly at 8:30pm. You must be 19 to enter and 21 to drink. (Open Mon.-Thurs. and Sat. 8:30pm-2am, Fri. 5pm-2am. Cover $1.)

Sights and Entertainment

If you're within 500 mi. of Cheyenne between July 21 and 30, make every possible effort to attend the **Cheyenne Frontier Days,** nine days of non-stop Western hoopla. The town doubles in size as anyone worth a grain of Western salt comes to see the world's oldest and largest rodeo competition and partake of the free pancake breakfasts (every other day in the parking lot across from the chamber of commerce), parades, and square dances. Most remain inebriated for the better part of the week. Reserve accommodations in advance or camp nearby. For information, contact Cheyenne Frontier Days, P.O. Box 2666, Cheyenne 82003 (800-543-2339; 800-227-6336 outside WY; open Mon.-Fri. 8am-5pm).

If you miss Frontier Days, don't despair; Old West events are the major source of entertainment for Cheyenne's history-oriented public. Throughout June and July the Cheyenne Gunslingers perform a mock **Old Cheyenne Gunfight,** at W. 16th and Carey St., to prove that justice reigns in Wyoming territory. (Shows Mon.-Fri. at 6pm, Sat. at noon. Free.) The **Cheyenne Frontier Days Old West Museum** (778-7290), in **Frontier Park** at 8th and Carey St., is a half-hour walk north down Carey St. The museum chronicles the rodeo's history from 1897 to the present, housing an "Old West" saloon and an extensive collection of Oglala Sioux clothing and artifacts. (Open Mon.-Sat. 8am-7pm, Sun. 10am-6pm; off-season daily 11am-5pm. Admission $2, seniors $1, families $5, ages under 12 free.)

The **Wyoming State Museum,** 2301 Central Ave. (777-7024), has an especially digestible history of Wyoming's cowboys, sheepherders and women suffragists, along with exhibits on the Oglala, Cheyenne, and Shoshone who preceded them. (Open Mon.-Fri. 8:30am-5pm, Sat. 10am-4pm, Sun. noon-4pm; off-season closed Sun. Free.) The **Wyoming State Capitol Building,** at the base of Capitol Ave. on 24th St. (777-7220), shows off its stained glass windows and yellowed photographs to tour groups trekking through. (Open Mon.-Fri. 8:30am-4:30pm. Summer tours every 15 min.)

This oversized cowtown rolls up the streets at night; except for a few bars, the downtown goes to sleep at 5pm. One delightful exception is the **Old Fashioned Melodrama,** playing at the **Old Atlas Theater** (638-6543 mornings, 635-0199 aft. and eve.), an old vaudeville house at 211 W. 16th St., between Capitol and Carey Ave. (Shows July-late Aug. Wed.-Sat. 7pm. Tickets $4, under 12 $2.50.) To find out about beauty pageants and other theatrical events contact the **Cheyenne Civic Center,** 510 W. 20th St. (637-6363; box office open Mon.-Fri. 11am-5:30pm).

Casper and Environs

Built primarily as a stop for the Union Pacific Railroad, Casper's history differs little from hundreds of other railroad towns. Nevertheless, Casperites pride themselves on their city's one claim to fame—nine of the pioneer trails leading west, including the Oregon and Bozeman trails, met and intersected at a point not far from what now is the city's southern limit. Hence Casper's nicknames, "the Hub" and "the Heart of Big Wyoming"; disparage them within earshot of local residents at your own risk.

Casper's other pride and joy, **Fort Caspar** (235-8462), 4205 W. 13th St., is an old reconstructed army fort on the western side of town. Lt. Caspar Collins, who died while trying to warn Sgt. Amos Custard of an impending Native American attack, gave his name to the fort; the city also bears his name, albeit misspelled because of a postal clerk's error. An informative museum sits on the site. (Open Mon.-Fri. 9am-6pm, Sat. 9am-5pm, Sun. noon-5pm; off-season Mon.-Fri. 9am-5pm, Sun. 2-5pm. Free.) From here you can hike to Muddy Mountain or Lookout Point to survey the terrain that hosted some of the last bloody conflicts between Native Americans and white pioneers.

Forty-five mi. northwest of Casper on U.S. 20/26, you can see **Devil's Kitchen** (also called **Hell's Half Acre**), a 320-acre bowl serving up hundreds of colorfully crazy spires and caves. Fifty-five mi. out on WY Rte. 220, **Independence Rock** still freely welcomes travelers to the entrance of a hellish stretch of the voyage across Wyoming. In 1840, Father Peter DeSmet nicknamed it the "Great Registry of the Desert," honoring the renegades and Mormon pioneers who etched their names into the rock. Explore the abandoned prospecting town on **Casper Mountain** or follow the **Lee McCune Braille Trail** through Casper Mountain's **Skunk Hollow**. If you're here at the end of August, check out the week-long **Central Wyoming Fair and Rodeo,** 1700 Fairgrounds Rd. (266-4228), which keeps the town in an extended state of Western hoopla with parades, demolition derbies, livestock shows, and, of course, rodeos.

Casper Mountain, 11 mi. south of Casper, hosts the **Hogadon Ski Area** (266-1600), with 60 acres of trails and runs rising 8000 ft. above sea level. For ski rental, stop in at **Mountain Sports,** 543 S. Center St. (266-1136), where downhill and cross-country skis go for $15 per day, $70 per week. (Open winter Mon.-Sat. 9am-6pm, Sun. noon-5pm; summer Mon.-Sat. 9am-6pm. Credit card or cost of equipment in cash required.) For information on ski conditions, contact **Community Recreation, Inc.** (235-8383; open Mon.-Fri. 8am-5pm). Even if you don't ski, ride up Casper Mountain to enjoy the magnificent view of Casper and the plains north of the city.

Since the recent failure of the oil economy, prices are conveniently low in Casper. At the **Cheese Barrel,** 544 S. Center St., cheese gets incorporated into nearly every concoction except the beverages. Try the pita vegehead ($3.50), and be sure to have at least one order of cheese bread ($1 for 2 gooey slices). (Open Mon.-Sat. 7am-3pm.) **Anthony's,** 241 S. Center St., serves huge portions of Italian food (spaghetti $4.75) by candlelight. (Open Mon.-Sat. 11:30am-2pm and 5-10pm, Sun. 9am-2pm and 5-10pm.)

If you're looking to stay overnight in Casper, check out the **Travelier Motel,** 500 E. 1st St. (237-9343), which offers spotless rooms near the center of town. (Singles $16.50. Doubles $18.) The **Topper Motel,** 728 East A St. (237-8407), 6 blocks east of the bus depot, is a spacious and clean double decker. (Singles $18.50. Doubles $23-40.)

Campers can bunk down at the **Ft. Caspar Campground,** 4205 W. 13th St. (234-3260; tents $10; full hookup $13) or **Casper Mountain Park,** 12 mi. south of Casper on Rte. 251, near Ponderosa Park (sites $4). **Alcova Lake Campground,** 32 mi. southwest of Casper on County Rd. 407 off Hwy. 220, is a popular recreation area with beaches, boats, and private cabins. (Sites $4.) The **Hell's Half Acre Campground** (472-0018), 45 mi. west on U.S. 20-26, has showers and hookups (full hookup $10.40 for 2). The **Natona County Parks Office,** 182 Casper Mt. Park, provides information about camping in the greater Casper area. (Open Mon.-Fri. 9am-5pm.)

The informative **Casper Chamber of Commerce** commerces at 500 N. Center St. (234-5311; open Mon.-Fri. 8am-7pm, Sat.-Sun. 10am-7pm; off-season Mon.-Fri. 8am-5pm). The **Powder River Transportation Services,** 596 N. Poplar (266-1904), sends two buses per day to: Buffalo ($20), Sheridan ($25), Cheyenne ($29), Billings ($56), and Rapid City ($49). **Casper Affordable Used Car Rental,** 131 E. 5th St. (237-1733), rents cars for $22 per day, $150 per week; 100 free mi., 15¢ each additional mi. (Open Mon.-Fri. 8am-5:30pm. Must be 22 with a major credit card or $200 deposit.)

Casper's main **post office** stands guard on 150 East B St. (266-4000; open Mon.-Fri. 7:30am-5:30pm). The **ZIP** code is 82601; the **area code** is 307.

Bighorn Mountains

The Bighorns erupt from the hilly pastureland of northern Wyoming, a dramatic backdrop to the grazing cattle and sprawling ranch houses at their feet. Here in the 1860s, violent clashes occurred between the Sioux, defending their traditional hunting grounds, and incoming settlers. Cavalry posts such as **Fort Phil Kearny,** on U.S. 87 between Buffalo and Sheridan, could do little to protect the settlers. The war reached a climax at the **Fetterman Massacre,** in which several hundred Sioux warriors wiped out Lt. Col. Fetterman's patrol. As a result, settlers and soldiers left the Bighorns to the Sioux. However, though the Native Americans won the battle, they lost the war. Within 20 years, settlers made the Bighorns permanent cattle country.

For sheer solitude, you can't beat the Bighorns' **Cloud Peak Wilderness.** To get to **Cloud Peak,** the 13,175-ft. summit of the range, most hikers enter at **Painted Rock Creek,** accessible from the town of Tensleep, 70 mi. west of Buffalo on the western slope. The most convenient access to the wilderness area, though, is from the trailheads near U.S. 16, 25 mi. west of Buffalo. From the **Hunter Corrals** trailhead, move to beautiful **Mistymoon Lake,** an ideal base for strikes at the high peaks beyond. You can also enter the wilderness area from U.S. 14 out of Sheridan in the north.

Campgrounds fill the forest, and all sites cost $6 per night. Near the Buffalo entrance **Lost Cabin Middle Fork** and **Crazy Woman** boast magnificent scenery, as do **Cabin Creek** and **Porcupine** campgrounds near Sheridan. If you choose not to venture into the mountains, you can spend the night free just off Coffeen St. in Sheridan's grassy **Washington Park.**

Most travelers will want to use either Buffalo or Sheridan as a base town from which to explore the mountains. The **Mountain View Motel** is by far the most appealing of Buffalo's cheap lodgings. Pine cabins with TV, A/C, and/or heating complement the owners' assiduous service. (Singles $18-$20. Doubles $28-32. $2 less in the off-season.) Stock up on sandwiches at the **Breadboard,** 57 S. Main St. (684-2318), where a large "Freight Train" (roast beef and turkey with all the toppings) costs $3.20. (Open Mon.-Sat. 11am-8pm.)

If you get bored of the outdoors, a visit to the **Jim Gatchell Museum of the West,** 10 Fort St. (684-9331), or the museum and outdoor exhibits at the former site of Fort Phil Kearny (on U.S. 97 between Buffalo and Sheridan; open daily 8am-6pm; Oct. 16-May 14 Sat.-Sun. 1-5pm) may fend off malaise. Both testify to the tangled relations between local Native Americans and the encroaching pioneers.

The **Buffalo Chamber of Commerce** informs at 55 N. Main St. (684-5544), 8 blocks south of the bus station. (Open Mon.-Fri. 9am-5pm.) In the summer, you can also visit the Buffalo summer information center, 2 mi. east on Hwy. 16. (Open July-Aug. daily 10am-7pm; June and Sept. daily 11am-6pm.) The **U.S. Forest Service Offices,** at 300 Spruce St. (684-7981), will answer your questions about the Buffalo District in the Bighorns, and sell you a road and trail map of the area ($2). (Open Mon.-Fri. 8am-4:30pm.) At **Alabam's,** 421 Fort St. (684-7452), you can buy topographical maps ($2.50) as well as hunting, fishing, or camping supplies. (Open daily 6am-9:30pm; off-season daily 6am-8pm.)

The town of **Sheridan,** 30 mi. to the north of Buffalo, escaped most of the military activity of the 1860s. But Sheridan has its own claim to fame: Buffalo Bill Cody used to sit on the porch of the once luxurious **Sheridan Inn,** at 5th and Broadway, as he interviewed cowboy hopefuls for his *Wild West Show.* The inn has recently hit hard times, and may soon close. Motels, many with budget rates, line the town's two main drags, Coffeen Ave. and Main St. Try the **Parkway Motel,** which offers large, cheerfully decorated singles for $18 and doubles for $24.

Sheridan's **U.S. Forest Service Office,** 1969 S. Sheridan Ave. (672-0751), offers maps of the Bighorns ($2), along with numerous pamphlets on how to navigate them safely. The **Sheridan Chamber of Commerce,** 5th St. at I-90 (672-2485), can also provide information on the National Forest, as well as other useful tips for lodging and activities in Sheridan. (Open daily 8am-8pm.)

Nestled at the junction of I-90 (east to the Black Hills area and north to Billings, MT) and I-25 (south to Casper, Cheyenne, and Denver), **Buffalo** is easy to reach. **Powder River Transportation** serves Buffalo from a terminal at the **Frontier Inn,** 800 N. Main St. (684-7453), where twice daily you can catch a bus north to Sheridan ($8) and Billings ($33), or south to Cheyenne ($33). Buffalo, as the crossroads of north-central Wyoming, remains a good place for hitchhikers to catch rides to the southern cities of Casper and Cheyenne. Getting a lift on the freeway in Sheridan is more difficult. But never fear, true believer—**Powder River buses** run from the depot at the **Rancher Motel,** 1552 Coffeen Ave. (672-8147), to: Billings (2 per day, $27.25); Buffalo (2 per day, $8); and Cheyenne (2 per day, $44). (Station open Mon.-Fri. 8am-5am; Sat. 9am-noon, 4-5:30pm, 9:30-11pm, 2:30-5:30am; Sun. 10am-noon, 4-5:30pm, 9:30-11pm, 2:30-5:30am.)

The **time zone** for both Sheridan and Buffalo is Mountain (2 hr. behind Eastern.) The **ZIP code** for Buffalo is 82834, and for Sheridan 82801. The **area code** for the Bighorns is 307.

Eastern Wyoming: Medicine Bow Range, Laramie, and Saratoga

As you travel west from Cheyenne into the **Pole Mountain** division of Medicine Bow National Forest, the gentle prairie gives way to hilly forests and parks that have yet to lure tourists in any great numbers. **Happy Jack Road** (Rte. 210) parallels I-80 for a scenic 38 mi. from Cheyenne to Laramie, home of the University of Wyoming. **Curt Gowdy State Park,** mid-way between the two cities, is a prime hiking area with beautiful lakes and great fishing, and is frequented by university students (see Cheyenne Accommodations). The **Vedauwoo** ("earthbound spirits," pronounced vee-dah-voo) **National Park,** 20 mi. west of Cheyenne off I-80, offers some of the finest rock climbing in the world (entrance fee $2). Call the Forest Service (745-8971) for further info.

Greyhound can get you from Cheyenne to the **Laramie Terminal,** 1358 N. 2nd St. (742-0896; 2 per day, $8.50; terminal open Mon.-Fri. 8:30am-5:30pm, Sat. 9am-1pm). Named after a French fur trapper, Laramie makes a rather interesting rest stop if you arrive during June, when the University of Wyoming campus hosts a **Western Arts Music Festival,** or during the second full week of July when the town parties Western style with **Jubilee Days.** The **Laramie Chamber of Commerce,** 3rd and Park St. (745-7339), has information on all events. (Open daily 9am-6pm; off-season daily 8am-5pm.) The **UW Department of Theater and Dance,** P.O. Box 3951, University Station, Laramie 82071, can provide information on campus and cultural occasions. The box office, in the lobby of the Fine Arts building (766-3212), is open the week before a production daily from noon-4pm.

Stop in for a quick bite in Laramie at the **Downtown Café,** 215 Grand Ave., for a cheeseburger ($3), order of fries, soda, and dessert. (Open Mon.-Sat. 6am-2pm.) Stay at the **Thunderbird Motel,** 1369 N. 3rd St. (745-4871), 2 blocks south of the bus station. Cruise into clean, spacious rooms with A/C and cable TV. (Singles $19.50. Doubles $22.50.)

The **North Platte River Valley** and its central town, Saratoga, are even better-kept secrets than Medicine Bow. Route 130 from Laramie west to Saratoga is a stunning, summer-only passage directly up and over the 11,000-ft. **Snowy Range Pass** (742-8981; 800-442-8321 in southeastern WY). This route over the mountains will save you 40 mi. Just before the summit, you'll pass through **Centennial,** a tiny ski resort town legendary for its lost gold mine. Not far from Centennial, you'll come upon **Saratoga,** still unsullied by massive tourist invasions. A hundred mi. from Laramie and only 20 mi. south of I-80 (exit 235), Saratoga draws crowds with the delightful **Hobo Hot Springs,** a natural 110°F mineral water source that is directed into a large sand-bottomed pool. When you get too hot, simply climb over the low wall into the rejuvenating North Platte River.

Wyoming has designated the 70-mi. stretch of the **North Platte River** that connect Saratoga to Colorado's norther border a "blue ribbon" trout stream. Contact the **Game and Fish Department,** in Medicine Bow (379-2337), or inquire at the well-equipped **Saratoga-Platte Valley Chamber of Commerce,** 102 W. Bridge St. (326-8855). **Great Rocky Mountain Outfitters,** 216 E. Walnut St. (326-8750), offers fun-filled float trips (half-day $20, full day $40). The chamber of commerce has a more extensive list of tour companies operating similar expeditions on the North Platte, as well as a list of local accommodations. (Open June-Sept. Mon.-Fri. 9am-6pm; Oct.-May Mon.-Fri. 9am-5pm.)

Should your creel run dry, try **Wally's Pizza**, 110 E. Bridge St. (326-8472), the only budget alternative in town and a culinary rarity in this part of Wyoming. It serves a "vegetarian special" (cheeses, avocado, mushroom, cucumber, and sprouts) and huge sandwiches on fresh-baked bread ($4.50) in a cozy setting. (Open Mon.-Sat. 11am-10pm, Sun. noon-9pm.)

The best place to stay in Saratoga is the **Wolf Hotel**, 101 E. Bridge St. (326-5525), on WY Rte. 130 at the town's only main corner. This charming, renovated building is a registered national historic landmark. Rooms have most basic amenities except telephones. (Singles $12, with bath $17. Doubles $23.) The saloon and dining rooms downstairs evoke the 1890s. Reservations are recommended for busy summer weekends. The **Silver Moon Motel**, 412 E. Bridge St. (326-5974), is near the river. Clean rooms come with TV. (Singles $24. Doubles $30.)

Medicine Bow National Forest is a camper's paradise. Of the over 30 campgrounds, about half are free; all have toilets and drinking water. The closest ones to Saratoga are: **Jack Creek Campground**, 20 mi. west on Rte. 500, then 8 mi. south on a forest service road (open mid-June to Oct.; free); **Lincoln Park Campground**, 21 mi. southeast on Rte. 130, then 4 mi. north on a forest service road (open mid-May to Sept., $3); and **South Brush Creek**, 2 mi. beyond Lincoln Park (open mid-May to Sept., $4). Other sites cluster around Centennial and Laramie. Call the **ranger station** (326-5258) for more information.

The **Sierra Madre Range**, on the western slope of the North Platte Watershed, boasts some of the best camping and hiking in the national forest. The town of **Encampment**, just 40 mi. south of I-80 on Rte. 230, is a good base for forays into the mountains. A 16-mi.-long aerial tramway—the longest in the world—used to supply the hungry copper smelters of Encampment with a steady supply of ore. The town now claims an excellent **museum** (327-5310 or 327-5744) of mining days, with several complete buildings from the town's turn-of-the-century boom period. (Open May 27-Sept.2 daily 1-5pm; off-season Sat.-Sun. 1-5pm. Free guided tours by appointment.)

For maps and information on hiking, camping, cross-country skiing, and other kinds of recreation in this area, contact the Medicine Bow National Forest, 605 Skyline Dr., Laramie 82070 (745-8971; open Mon.-Fri. 7:30am-5pm, Sat.-Sun. 7:30am-4pm; off-season Mon.-Fri. 7:30am-5pm.) Also try the **chamber of commerce**, P.O. Box 456, Medicine Bow 82329 (379-2255; open Mon.-Wed. 8am-2pm), and the **ranger station** in Saratoga, 212 S. 1st St. (326-5258; open Mon.-Fri. 7:30am-5pm). The Laramie **post office** is at 105 W. Main St. (326-5611; open Mon. and Fri. 8:30am-5pm, Tues.-Thurs. 8am-5pm, Sat. 8:30-9:30am). The **ZIP code** is 82331; the **area code** is 307.

Yellowstone National Park

Had legendary mountain man John Colter studied the classics of world literature, he probably would have compared his 1807 trek into the Yellowstone area with a descent into Dante's Inferno. In any case, his graphic descriptions of boiling, sulfuric pits, spouting geysers, and smelly mudpots inspired a half-century of popular stories about "Colter's Hell." In 1870 the first official survey party, the Washburn Expedition, reached the area. As they came over a mountain ridge, the explorers were shocked by a fountain of boiling water and steam jetting 130 ft. into the air. Members of the expedition watched it erupt nine times and named it "Old Faithful" before leaving the Upper Geyser Basin. One year later, President Grant declared Yellowstone a national park, the world's first.

Visitors in Grant's time might have encountered 50 other tourists amid Yellowstone's 3472 square miles. Today's tourist will find the park cluttered with the cars and RVs of 50,000-odd people. The park's main attractions are huge, tranquil Yellowstone Lake, the 2100-ft.-deep Yellowstone River Canyon, and the world's largest collection of reeking, sputtering geysers, mudspots, hot springs, and fumaroles (steam-spewing holes in the ground). In the back country, you'll have the chance to observe the park's abundant bear, elk, moose, bison, and bighorn sheep, escaping the hordes of tourists in the bargain.

In 1988 Yellowstone was ravaged by a blaze that charred almost half the park. Crowds in Yellowstone doubled in 1989 in an extraordinary example of disaster tourism, with people pouring in to see "what really happened." While the effects of the fire are still visible throughout much of the park, crowd size should return to normal, which is still quite large, in 1991. The scarred forests do make for interesting, if somewhat macabre, viewing; rangers have erected exhibits throughout the park to better explain the fire's effects.

Practical Information

Emergency: 911.

Park Information and Headquarters: Superintendent, Mammoth Hot Springs, Yellowstone National Park 82190 (344-7381). The switchboard serves all visitors centers and park service phones. General information, campground availability, and emergencies. Headquarters open off-season Mon.-Fri. 8am-5pm. **Park Admission:** $10 for non-commercial vehicles, $4 for pedestrians and bikers. Good for one week.

Visitors Centers and Ranger Stations: Most regions in this vast park have their own center/station. The district rangers have a good deal of autonomy in making regulations for hiking and camping, so check in at each area. All visitors centers have guides for the disabled and give backcountry permits, or have a partner ranger station that does. Each visitors center's display focuses on a different theme. **Mammoth Hot Springs** (344-2357): natural and human history. Open June-Aug. daily 8am-7pm; Sept.-May daily 8:30am-5pm. **Grant Village** (344-6602): wilderness. Open summer only, daily 8am-6pm. **Old Faithful/Madison** (344-6001): geysers. Open April-Nov. daily 8am-6pm; Dec.-March daily 8am-4:30pm. **Fishing Bridge** (344-6150): wildlife and Yellowstone Lake. Open daily 8am-6pm; off-season daily 9am-5pm. **Canyon** (344-6205): natural history and history of canyon area. Open July-Aug. daily 8am-6pm; Sept.-June daily 9am-5pm. **Norris** (344-7733): park museum. Open daily 8am-6pm. **Tower/Roosevelt Ranger Station** (344-7746): special temporary exhibits. Open daily 8am-5pm. *Discover Yellowstone,* the park's activities guide, has a thorough listing of tours and programs at each center.

Radio Information: Tune to 1606AM for service information and radical interpretive metadiscourse within the park.

Foreign Visitors Aid: 800-225-3050. The park has a multilingual staff of rangers. Brochures available in French, German, Spanish, and Japanese.

West Yellowstone Chamber of Commerce: P.O. Box 458, West Yellowstone, MT 59758 (406-646-7701). Located at the intersection of Canyon and Yellowstone St., 2 blocks west of the park entrance. Open daily 9am-6pm; off-season Mon.-Fri. 9am-6pm.

Greyhound: 127 Yellowstone Ave., W. Yellowstone, MT (406-646-7666). Two buses per day northeast to Bozeman (2 hr., morning bus $16, evening bus $10), and 1 per day south to Salt Lake City (7½ hr., $59). Open summers only, daily 8am-8pm.

TW Services, Inc.: 344-7311. Monopolizes concessions within the park. Nine-hour bus tours of the lower portion of the park leave daily from all lodges ($22, ages under 12 $18). Similar tours of the northern region leave Gardiner, MT, and the lodges at Mammoth Lake and Fishing Bridge ($14-21, depending on where you start and end). Individual legs of this extensive network of tour loops can get you as far as the Grand Tetons or Jackson, but the system is inefficient, and costs much more money than it's worth. Fares add up quickly. (West Yellowstone to Old Faithful, 3 per day, $6.40, children $3.20; does not include park entrance fee.)

Gray Line Tours: 211 W. Yellowstone Ave, West Yellowstone, MT (406-646-9374). Offers full-day tours from West Yellowstone around the lower loop ($25.50, ages under 12 $9), upper loop ($23.50, ages under 12 $8), and Grand Tetons ($34, ages under 12 $12). Open daily 8am-5pm.

Car Rental: Payless Auto Rental, 225 W. Yellowstone Ave., West Yellowstone, MT. (406-646-9561), inside the Traveler's Lodge. $35 per day with 100 free mi., 25¢ each additional mi. Open daily 8am-7pm. Must be 21 with a credit card, $100 deposit, or passport.

Bike Rental: Yellowstone Bicycles, 132 Madison Ave., West Yellowstone, MT (406-646-7815). $15 per day. Open daily 8am-9pm.

Horse Rental: Mammoth Hot Springs Hotel, from late May- mid-Sept. **Roosevelt Lodge,** mid-June-Sept. 2. **Canyon Lodge,** June 4-Sept. 2. $10.30 per hr., $19.50 for 2 hr. Call TW Services (394-7901) for more information.

Medical Facilities: Lake Clinic, Pharmacy, and **Hospital** at Lake Hotel (242-7241). Clinic open May-Sept. daily 8:30am-5pm. Hospital Emergency Room open May-Sept. 24 hr. **Old Faithful Clinic,** at Old Faithful Inn (545-7325). Open May-Oct. daily 8:30am-5pm. **Mammoth Clinic,** at Mammoth Hot Springs (342-7965). Open Mon.-Fri. 8:30am-5pm.

Post Offices: Old Faithful Station, in the park behind the visitors center. Open Mon.-Fri. 8:30am-4pm. **ZIP code:** 82190. **West Yellowstone, MT,** 17 Madison Ave. Open Mon.-Fri. 8:30am-5pm. **ZIP code:** 59758.

Area Codes: 307 (in the park), 406 (in West Yellowstone and Gardiner). Unless otherwise indicated phone numbers have a 307 area code.

The bulk of Yellowstone National Park lies in the northwest corner of Wyoming with slivers spilling into Montana and Idaho. **West Yellowstone, MT,** at the park's western entrance, and **Gardiner, MT,** at the northern entrance, are the most built-up and expensive towns along the edge of the park. The southern entry to the park is through Grand Teton National Park.

Yellowstone's extensive system of roads circulates its millions of visitors. Side roads branch off to the park entrances and some of the lesser-known sights. It's unwise to bike or walk around the deserted roads at night since you may risk startling large wild animals. Approaching any wild beast at any time is illegal and extremely unsafe, and those who don't remain at least 100 ft. from bison, bear, or moose risk being mauled, gored to death, or made the victim of a *Far Side* cartoon.

The park's high season extends from about June 15 to September 15. If you visit during this period expect large crowds, clogged roads, and motels and campsites filled to capacity. A better option is to visit either in late spring or early fall, when the Winnebagos and the tame animals they transport are safely home.

Accommodations

Cabin-seekers will find options galore within the park. Standard hotel and motel rooms for the nature-weary also abound, but to keep your grip on the amenities of modern living cheaply, the towns at the park's entry-points may be your best bet.

In The Park

TW Services (344-7311) controls all of the accommodations within the park, and uses a special set of classifications for budget cabins. All cabins or rooms should be reserved well in advance of the June to September tourist season.

Old Faithful Inn and Lodge, near the west Yellowstone entrance. Offers pleasant Roughrider cabins without bath ($17) and Frontier cabins with bath ($30). Well-appointed hotel rooms from $32, with private bath $48.

Roosevelt Lodge, in the northwest corner. A favorite campsite of Teddy Roosevelt. Provides the cheapest and most scenic indoor accommodations around. Rustic shelters $16, each with a wood-burning stove (bring your own bedding and towel). Also Roughrider cabins ($17—bring your own towel) and more spacious "family" cabins with toilet ($33).

Mammoth Hot Springs, 18 mi. west of Roosevelt area, near the north entrance. Unremarkable budget cabins $21. Frontier cabins with private baths from $46.

Lake Yellowstone Hotel and Cabins, near the south entrance. Overpriced, but with a nice view of the lake. Frontier cabins identical to Old Faithful's ($39) and Western cabins with a little more space ($61).

Canyon Village. Less authentic and more expensive than Roosevelt Lodge's cabins, but slightly closer to the popular Old Faithful area. Frontier cabins $46, Western cabins $61.

West Yellowstone, MT

West Yellowstone International Hostel, at the Madison Hotel and Motel, 139 Yellowstone Ave. (406-646-7745). Friendly manager presides over old but clean, wood-adorned hotel. Singles $25, with bath $27. Doubles with bath $32. Rooms $2 cheaper in the spring. Hostelers stay in more crowded rooms for $12, nonmembers $15. Open May 27-mid-Oct.

Alpine Motel, 120 Madison (406-646-7544). Plastic but clean rooms with cable TV and A/C. Singles $26. Doubles $31.

Traveler's Lodge, 225 W. Yellowstone Ave. (406-646-9561). Comfortable, large rooms; ask for one away from the hot tub. Singles $40, off-season $26. Doubles $42, off-season $28. $5 discount if you rent a car from them (see Practical Information above).

Ho-Hum Motel, 126 Canyon Rd. (646-7746). Small, dark, but clean. With so-so effort, you can do better than Ho-Hum. Singles $32. Doubles $40.

Gardiner, MT.

Located about 90 min. northeast of West Yellowstone, Gardiner served as the original entrance to the park and is considerably smaller and less tacky than its neighbor.

The Town Motel (848-7322), across from the park's northern entrance. Pleasant, wood-paneled, carpeted rooms. Singles $25. Doubles $28.

Wilson's Yellowstone River Motel (406-848-7303), ½ block east of U.S. 89. Large, well-decorated rooms overseen by friendly manager. Singles $30. Doubles $34.

Hillcrest Cottages (848-7353), on U.S. 89 near where it crosses the Yellowstone River. Small but clean singles $21. Doubles $26. Seven nights for the price of 6.

Camping

All developed campsites are available on a first come-first serve basis exceptfor the **Bridge Bay Campground,** which reserves sites up to eight weeks in advance through Ticketron (900-370-7070). During summer months, most campgrounds fill by 2pm. All regular sites cost $5-9. Arrive very early, especially on weekends and holidays. If all sites are full, try the free campgrounds outside the park in the surrounding national forest land. Bring a stove or plan to hike a bit in search of firewood. Except for **Mammoth Campground,** all camping areas close for the winter.

Two of the most beautiful and restful areas are **Slough Creek Campground,** 10 mi. northeast of Tower Junction (open May-Oct.), and **Pebble Creek Campground,** 15 mi. farther down the same road (open June-Sept.). Both relatively uncrowded spots have good fishing. **Canyon Village** and **Fishing Bridge Campgrounds** are for non-tenting travelers only (RV hookup $17; open June-Sept.). The popular and scenic campgrounds at **Norris** (open May-Sept.) and **Madison** (open May-Oct.) fill early (by 1pm), while others, such as **Fishing Bridge, Canyon,** and **Pebble Creek,** sometimes have sites until 6pm. **Bridge Bay** (open May-Sept.), **Indian Creek** (open June-Sept.), and **Mammoth** (open year-round) campgrounds are treeless and non-scenic. You'd be better off camping in the **Gallatin National Forest** to the northwest. Good sites line Hwy. 20, 287, 191, and 89. Call the Park Headquarters (344-7381) for information on any of Yellowstone's campgrounds. Madison, Norris, Bridge Bay, Grant, and Lewis Lake campgrounds all have special hiker/biker areas, and charge only $1 for tent sites.

More than 95%, or two million acres, of the park is backcountry. To venture overnight into the wilds of Yellowstone, you must obtain a free **wilderness permit** from a ranger station or visitors center. Be sure you understand the most recent instructions regarding closing of campgrounds and trails due to bears and other wildlife. The more popular areas fill up in high season, but you can reserve a permit up to 48 hr. in advance.

The campgrounds at Grant, Village Lake, Fishing Bridge, and Canyon all have coin-operated laundries and pay showers ($1 plus 25¢ for towel or soap). The lodges at Mammoth and Old Faithful have no laundry facilities but will let you use their showers for $1.50.

To discourage bears, all campers should keep clean camps and store food in a locked car or suspended 10 ft. above ground and 4 ft. horizontally from a post or tree trunk.

Food

Be very choosy when buying food in the park, as the restaurants, snack bars, and cafeterias are quite expensive. If possible, stick to the **general stores** at each lodging location (open daily 7:30am-10pm) and try to stock up on price-regulated items.

Sights and Activities

TW Services, for unbelievable amounts of money, will sell you tours, horseback rides, and chuckwagon dinners until the cows come home. But given enough time, your eyes and feet will do an even better job than TW's tours, without placing you in danger of bankruptcy. Hiking to the main attractions is much easier if you make reservations at the cabins closest to the sights you most want to see.

The geysers that made Yellowstone famous are clustered on the western side of the park, near the West Yellowstone entrance. **Old Faithful,** while neither the largest, the highest, nor the most regular geyser, is certainly the most popular; it gushes in the **Upper Geyser Basin,** 16 mi. south of **Madison Junction** where the entry road splits north-south. Since its discovery in 1870, the grandaddy of geysers has consistently erupted with a whoosh of spray and steam (5000-8000 gallons worth) every 45 to 70 minutes. Avoiding crowds here in summer is nearly impossible unless you come for the blasts at dusk or in the wee hours of the morning. Enjoy elk and other geysers in the surrounding **Firehole Valley.** Swimming in any hot springs or geysers is prohibited, but you can swim in the **Firehole River,** ¾ of the way up Firehole Canyon Drive (turn south just after Madison Jct.), or in the **Boiling River,** 2½ mi. north of Mammoth, which is not really hot enough to cook pasta. Still, do not swim alone, and beware of strong currents.

From Old Faithful, take the easy 1½-mi. walk to **Morning Glory Pool,** a park favorite, or head 8 mi. north to the **Lower Geyser Basin,** where examples of all four types of geothermic activity (geysers, mudpots, hot springs, and fumaroles) steam, bubble, and spray together. The regular star here is **Echinus,** which erupts about every hour from a large basin of water. If you are lucky enough to witness it, the biggest show on earth is put on by **Steamboat,** the largest geyser in the world. Eruptions can last 20 minutes and top 400 ft. The last such enormous eruption occured on June 4, 1990, after about a year of dormancy; Ben was in the park researching that day and missed the whole thing. Don't hold your breath for another one soon, but if Ben's sad tale is any indication of increasing activity, you might get lucky.

Whether you're waiting for geysers to erupt or watching them shoot skyward, don't go too close as the crust of earth around a geyser is only 2 ft. deep, and falling into one of these boiling sulfuric pits could be detrimental to your health. Pets are not allowed in the basin unlike Benny-Boy Blue.

Mammoth Hot Springs has famous hot springs terraces, built of multicolored bifurcated limestone deposits which add 6 in. every year. Wildlife is quite abundant in the northern part of the park, both along the road from Mammoth to Roosevelt, perhaps on the road itself, and past Roosevelt in the Lamar Valley. Hitch from Mammoth to Roosevelt if you might want to try the scenic 4-mi. hike south to **Tower Falls.**

The pride of the western area of the park is the **Grand Canyon of the Yellowstone,** carved through glacial deposits and amber, volcanic bedrock. For the best views, hike or drive to the 308-ft. Lower Falls at Artist Point, on the southern rim, or head for Lookout Point on the northern rim. All along the canyon's 19- mi. rim, keep an eye out for the rare bighorn sheep, and at dawn or dusk the bear-viewing management area (at the intersection of the northern rim and Tower roads) should be loaded with opportunities to use your binoculars.

Yellowstone Lake, 16 mi. south of the Canyon's rim at the southeastern corner of the park, contains tons o' trout; after procuring a free Yellowstone fishing permit, catch a few, and have the chef fry them for you in the Yellowstone Hotel Dining Room. Most other lakes and streams allow catch-and-release fishing only. The aptly yellow **Lake Yellowstone Hotel**, originally built in 1891, and renovated in 1989, merits a visit though its room rates put it well out of the range of most budget travelers. The bright, airy lobby with large windows provides a magnificent view of the lake. Walks around the main body of the lake, as well as those that take you around one of the lake's three fingers, are scenic, and serene rather than strenuous. Nearby **Mud Volcano**, close to Yellowstone Lake, features boiling sulfuric earth and the **Dragon's Mouth**, a vociferous steaming hole that early explorers reportedly heard all the way from the lake. You'll smell it that far away for sure.

Although most of the spectacular sights in the park are accessible by car, a hiking trip through the backcountry will remove you from the masses. The multilayered petrified forest of **Specimen Ridge** and the geyser basins at **Shoshone** and **Heart Lakes** are only accessible by well-kept trails. **Cascade Corner**, in the southwest, is a lovely area accessible by trails from Belcher. Over 1000 mi. of trails crisscross the park, but many are poorly marked. If you plan to hike, pick up a topographical trail map ($2.50) at any visitors center and ask a ranger to describe all forks in the trail and the wording of trail markings. Even after annoying the ranger, allow yourself extra time (at least 1 hr. per day) in case you lose the trail.

Winter

Yellowstone can be as rewarding blanketed with snow during winter as blanketed with tourists during summer. Native animals can still be seen clustered around the sparse vegetation, while the traveling well-wrapped humans convert the park into snowboarding city. Cross-country skiing, ranger-sponsored snowshoe tours, and evening programs with hot chocolate and noisy snowmobile excursions are all available at off-season rates. Contact Park Headquarters (344-7381), **Snowmobile Touring** (545-7249), or the **visitors centers** at Mammoth Hot Springs, Old Faithful (mid-Dec.-mid-March), and West Yellowstone (mid-Dec.-mid-March). In winter, the Mammoth Hotel converts two rooms into a youth hostel, each of which holds six people ($6 per person).

Plowed roads make winter bus service available to West Yellowstone and Flagg Ranch on the west and south borders; the Mammoth-Tower-Cooke City park road is kept open and accessible from Bozeman via Gardiner. All other roads are used by snowmobilers and the snowcoach only. The **snowcoach**, a heated, enclosed tank-like vehicle, run by TW Services, provides transportation from the south gate at Flagg Ranch, the west gate at West Yellowstone, and the north gate at Mammoth to bring travelers to the Old Faithful Lodge. With a permit (free from any visitors center), you may use the undeveloped backcountry sites. But exercise caution: people do get snowed in. You can find heated restrooms at Madison and Mammoth campgrounds. Food is available at Old Faithful and the **Canyon Snack Shop**, snowmobile fuel at Old Faithful, Mammoth, and Canyon. The **Three Bears Hotel**, 217 W. Yellowstone Ave. (406-646-7353), rents snowmobiles ($68 per day, $75 for 2 people).

Grand Teton National Park

When French fur trappers first peered into Wyoming's wilderness from the eastern border of Idaho, they found themselves face to face with three craggy peaks, all topping 12,000 ft. In an attempt to make the imposing landscape seem more trapper-friendly, they dubbed the mutant mountains "Les Trois Tetons," French for "the three breasts." Though they eventually did discover that the mountains belonged to a much larger range, the Frenchmen still never realized that mountains are not breasts, and only changed the name to "Les Grands Tetons." The misnomer stuck and today the snowy heights of Grand Teton National Park delight modern hikers and cyclists with miles of strenuous trails. The less adventurous appreciate the rugged appearance of the Tetons; the craggy pinnacles and shining glaciers possess an extraordinary beauty. Most visitors will appreciate the park's relative lack of crowds in comparison with Yellowstone, its sometimes zoo-like neighbor to the north.

Practical Information

Emergency: 911.

Park Headquarters: Superintendent, Grand Teton National Park, P.O. Drawer 170, Moose 83012 (733-2820). Office at the Moose Visitors Center. Open Mon.-Fri. 8am-4:30pm.

Park Entrance Fees: $10 per car, $4 per pedestrian or bicycle, $5 per family (non-motorized), under 16 (non-motorized) free. Good for 7 days for both the Tetons and Yellowstone.

Visitors Center: Moose, Rockefeller Pkwy. at the southern tip of the park (733-2880). Open June-Aug. daily 8am-7pm; Sept.-May daily 8am-5pm. Jenny Lake, next to the Jenny Lake Campground. Open June-Aug. daily 8am-7pm; Sept.-May daily 8am-5pm. Colter Bay, on Jackson Lake in the northern part of the park (543-2467). Open early June-early Sept. daily 8am-7pm; May and late Sept. daily 8am-5pm. Signal Mountain, between Colter Bay and Moose (543-2516). Open May 13-June 30 daily 8am-5pm. Park information brochures available in braille, French, German, Japanese, and Spanish. Topographical maps ($3). Pick up the *Teewinot* newspaper (free) for a complete list of park activities, lodgings, and facilities.

Park Information and Road and Weather Conditions: 733-2220; 24-hr. recording.

Bike Rental: Colter Bay General Store. 1-speed bikes $2 per hr., $9 per day. Open daily 7:30am-10pm. $20 deposit and 2 IDs required. Call the Grand Teton Lodge Co. (733-2811 or 543-2855) for more information. Mountain Bike Outfitters, Inc. (733-3314), at Dorman's in Moose. Quality mountain bikes $5 per hr., $22 per day. Open summer daily 9am-6pm. Credit card or deposit required.

Medical Care: Grand Teton Medical Clinic, Jackson Lake Lodge (543-2514 or 733-8002 after hours), near the Chevron station. Open June to mid-Sept. daily 10am-6pm. In a dire emergency, contact St. Johns's Hospital (733-3636), in Jackson.

Post Office: In Colter Bay General Store. Open mid-May to mid-Sept. Mon.-Fri. 8am-noon and 1-5pm, Sat. 9am-1pm. ZIP codes: Colter Bay 83001, Moose 83021, Moran 83013, Kelly 83011.

Area Code: 307.

The national park occupies most of the space between Jackson to the south and Yellowstone National Park to the north. Rockefeller Parkway connects the two parks and is open year-round. The park is directly accessible from all directions except the west. Hitching from Jackson is easy; hitching from Yellowstone may be more time-consuming.

Accommodations

If you want to stay indoors, grit your teeth and open your wallet. The Grand Teton Lodge Co. controls nearly all the lodging within the park. Make reservations for any Grand Teton Lodge establishment by writing the Reservations Manager, Grand Teton Lodge Co., P.O. Box 240, Moran 83013 (543-2855 or 800-628-9988 outside Wyoming). Accommodations are available late May through early October, and are most expensive from late June to early August. Reservations are recommended to insure a place to hibernate. (See Jackson below for accommodations outside the park.)

Colter Bay Tent Cabins: Cheapest accommodations in the park, but not the place to stay in extremely cold weather. Canvas shelters with wood-burning stoves, table, and 4-person bunks. Sleeping bags, wood, cooking utensils, and ice chests available for rent. (Call Maintenance, 543-1081). Cabins $17 for 2, each additional person $2. Restrooms and showers ($1.50) nearby.

Colter Bay Log Cabins: Quaint, well-maintained log cabins near Jackson Lake. Room with semi-private bath $25, with private bath $45-65. Two-room cabins with bath $65-85.

Flagg Ranch Village: P.O. Box 187, Moran 83013 (543-2861 or 800-443-2311), on the Snake River near the park's northern entrance. Simple, clean cabins with semi-private bath $26. Slightly larger rustic cabins $36, with private bath $38.

Camping

Camping is the way to see the Tetons without emptying your savings account. The park service maintains six campgrounds, all on a first come-first serve basis (sites $7). In addition, there are two trailer parks and acres of backcountry open to visitors whenever the snow's not too deep. RVs are welcome in all but Jenny Lake, but hookups are unavailable. Information is available at any visitors center.

Park Campgrounds: All campgrounds have rest rooms, cold water, fire rings, grocery store, and picnic tables. **Jenny Lake:** 49 highly coveted sites; arrive early. No RVs. **Signal Mountain:** A few mi. south of Colter Bay. 86 spots, usually full by noon. **Colter Bay:** 310 sites, shower and laundromat. Usually full by 2pm. **Snake River** and **Lizard Creek:** Northern campgrounds, with 60 sites, convenient to Yellowstone. Fills in late afternoon. **Gros Ventre:** On the park's southern border. 360 sites. A good bet if you arrive late. Max. stay in Jenny Lake 7 days, all others 14 days. Reservations required for large groups.

Colter Bay RV Park: 112 sites, electrical hookups. Reserved through Grand Teton Lodge Co. (733-2811 or 543-2855). Grocery store and eateries. Sites June-Aug. $17, May and Sept. $15. Showers $1.50, towel rental $1.25.

Flagg Ranch Village Camping: Operated by Flagg Ranch Village (543-2861 or 800-443-2311). Grocery and eateries on the grounds. Sites $9.50 for 2, $13.50 with hookups. Make reservations.

For **backcountry camping,** reserve a spot in a camping zone in a mountain canyon or on the shores of a lake by submitting an itinerary to the permit office at **Moose Ranger Station** (733-2880) from January 1 to June 1. Pick up the permit on the morning of the first day of your hike. Two-thirds of all spots left open are available on a first come-first serve basis; you can get a permit up to 24 hr. before setting out at the Moose or Jenny Lake Ranger Stations. (Open daily 8am-7pm.) Camping is unrestricted in some off-trail backcountry areas (though you must have a permit). Wood fires are not permitted above 7000 ft. As the weather can be severe, even in the summer, backcountry campers should be somewhat experienced before venturing far from civilization.

Food

As in Yellowstone, the best way to eat in the Tetons is to bring your own food. If this isn't possible, stick to what non-perishables you can pick up at the **Flagg Ranch Grocery Store** (open daily 7am-10pm; reduced hours in winter), or **Dornan's Grocery** in Moose (open daily 8am-6pm; reduced hours in winter). In Jackson, you can stock up on goodies at **Albertson's** supermarket.

Sights and Activities

As the youngest mountain range in North America, the Tetons provide hikers, bikers, climbers, rafters, and sightseers with challenges and vistas not found in more eroded ranges. The Grand Teton itself rises 13,700 ft. from the valley floor virtually without foothills. While Yellowstone wows visitors with its geysers and mudpots, Grand Teton's geology boasts some of the most scenic mountains in the U.S., if not the world.

Cascade Canyon Trail, one of the least arduous (and therefore more popular) hikes, originates at Jenny Lake. To start, take a boat trip (operated by Grand Teton Lodge Co.) across Jenny Lake (fare $2.25, round-trip $3; children $1.25, round-trip

$1.50), or hike the 2-mi. trail around the lake. Trail guides (25¢) are available at the trailhead. A ½-mi. from the trail entrance lies the **Hidden Falls Waterfall;** the hardy can trek 6 mi. further to **Lake Solitude.** Another pleasant day hike, popular for its views of wildlife, is the 4-mi. walk from Colter Bay to **Hermitage Point.** The **Amphitheater Lake Trail,** which begins just south of Jenny Lake at the Lupine Meadows parking lot, will take you 9 breathtaking mi. up to one of the park's many glacial lakes. Those who were bighorn sheep in past lives can take the challenge of **Static Peak Divide,** a 15-mi. trail that climbs 4020 ft. and offers some of the best lookouts in the park. All information centers provide pamphlets about the day hikes and sell the *Teton Trails* guide ($1.85).

Those who prefer floating to walking should rent boats at the **Colter Bay Marina** for a leisurely afternoon on Jackson Lake. (Rowboats $5 per hr. Canoes $5.50 per hr. Motorboats $12 per hr., 2 hr. min.; $50 deposit required. Open daily 7am-6pm.) Call Grand Teton Lodge Co. (733-2811 or 543-2811) for more information. **Signal Mountain Marina** (543-2831) rents a greater variety of boats, but charges more. (Rowboats and canoes $5 per hr. Motorboats $12.50 per hr. Waterski boats and pontoons $25 per hr. Open daily 7am-6pm.) The **Grand Teton Lodge Company** (543-2855 or 733-2811) can take you on scenic Snake River float trips within the park. (10½-mi. half-day trip $21.50, ages under 17 $12.50. 20½-mi. luncheon or supper trips $29, ages under 17 $19.) **Fishing** in the park's lakes, rivers, and streams is excellent. Wyoming state fishing licenses ($5) are required and may be purchased at the visitors centers and ranger stations.

The **American Indian Art Museum** (543-2467), in the Colter Bay Visitors Center, offers an extensive private collection of Native American artwork, artifacts, movies, and workshops. (Open June-Sept. daily 8am-7pm; May and late Sept. daily 8am-5pm. Free.) During July and August you can see Cheyenne, Cherokee, Apache, and Sioux dances at Jackson Lake Lodge (Fri. at 8:30pm). At the Moose and Colter's Bay Visitors Centers, rangers lead a variety of activities aimed at educating visitors about such subjects as the ecology, geology, wildlife, and history of the Tetons. Check the *Teewinot* for exact times, as schedules change daily.

In the winter, all hiking trails and the unplowed sections of Teton Park Road are open to cross-country skiers. Pick up the trail map *Winter in the Tetons* at the Moose Visitors Center. From January through March, naturalists lead **snowshoe hikes** from Moose Visitors Center (733-2880; snowshoes distributed free). Call for reservations. **Snowmobiling** along the park's well-powdered trails and up into Yellowstone is a noisy but popular winter activity. Grab a map and guide at the Jackson Chamber of Commerce, 10 mi. south of Moose. For a steep fee you can rent snowmobiles at Signal Mt. Lodge, Flagg Ranch Village, or down in Jackson; an additional $5 registration fee is required for all snowmobile use in the park. All campgrounds close during the winter. The Colter Bay parking lot is available for RVs and cars, and backcountry snow camping (only for those who know what they're doing) is allowed with a free permit from Moose. Check with a ranger station for current weather conditions and avalanche danger. Many early trappers froze to death in the 10-ft. drifts.

Jackson

Like Denim, that avatar of the Wild West, Jackson has developed from an all-purpose workcloth into a pasteled, button-flied, stonewashed and acid-dipped-for-effect designer fabric. Today, Jackson overflows with camera-snapping tourists making comical efforts to look like "real Westerners" amongst Ralph Lauren stores. But cowboys roamed Jackson long before the Tetons became a recreational destination, and plenty of Marlboro women still call this uninhibited Western city home. These residents are the genuine articles: their hats are Stetsons, their ragged bandanas aren't just for show, and the stuff on their boots—don't ask, it's not shinola.

Practical Information

Emergency: 911.

Visitor Information: Jackson Hole Area Chamber of Commerce, 532 N. Cache St. (733-3316), in a modern wooden split-level with grass on the roof. A crucial information stop. Open mid-June to mid-Sept. daily 8am-8pm; off-season daily 8:30am-5pm. **Bridger-Teton National Forest Headquarters,** 340 N. Cache St. (733-2752), 2 blocks south of the chamber of commerce. Maps $2-8. Open daily 7:45am-5:30pm; off-season daily 7:45am-4:30pm.

Buses: Jackson-Rock Springs Stages, 72 S. Glenwood St. (733-3135). Daily bus to Pinedale ($10.50) and Rock Springs ($18). Greyhound passes not honored. Open Mon.-Fri. 10-11:30am, Sat.-Sun. 10:30-11:30am. Connections with **Greyhound** at the Rock Springs terminal, 1005 Dewar Ave. (362-2931). Open Mon.-Fri. 8am-5pm, Sat. 8am-noon. **Grand Teton Lodge Co.** (733-2811) runs a shuttle twice daily in summer to Jackson Lake Lodge ($5.25, $4 park entrance fee not included).

Bus Tours: Powder River Tours, 565 N. Cache St. (733-2136). Full-day tour of the Tetons with boat ride on Jenny Lake ($34). **Grayline Tours,** 330 N. Glenwood St. (733-4325), in front of Dirty Jack's Theatre. Full-day tours of Grand Teton National Park and Yellowstone National Park lower loop ($36). Call for reservations. **Wild West Jeep Tours** (733-9036), P.O. Box 7506, Jackson 83001. In summer only, half-day tours of the Tetons and other areas ($27, seniors $24.50, ages under 12 $14.) Call for reservations.

Car Rental: Rent-A-Wreck, 1650 W. Martin Ln. (733-5014). $21 per day, $116 per week; 125 free mi., 20¢ each additional mi. Open Mon.-Fri. 8am-5:30pm. Must be 21 with credit card or a $300 cash deposit. Must stay within 200 mi. of Jackson.

Ski and Bike Rental: Hoback Sports, 40 S. Millward (733-5335). 10-speeds $17 per day, mountain bikes $20 per day; lower rates for longer rentals. Skis $13 per day. Open daily 9am-7pm. Must have credit card or enough cash to cover the cost of the equipment. **Skinny Skis,** 65 W. Delovey St. (733-6094). Skis $9 per day, $17 for mountaineering. Open daily 9am-9pm. Major credit card or deposit for value of equipment.

Weather Line, 733-1731. 24-hr. recording.

Help Lines: Rape Crisis Line, 733-5162. **Road Information,** 733-9966, outside WY 800-442-7850.

Post Office: 220 W. Pearl St. (733-3650), 2 blocks east of Cache St. Open Mon.-Fri. 8:30am-5pm. **ZIP code:** 83001.

Area Code: 307.

Although most services in Jackson are terribly expensive, the town makes an ideal base for trips into the Tetons, 10 mi. north, or the Wind River Range, 70 mi. southeast. U.S. 191, the usual southern entry to town, ties Jackson to I-80 at Rock Springs (180 mi. south). This road continues north into Grand Teton Park and eventually reaches Yellowstone, 70 mi. to the north. The streets of Jackson are centered around **Town Square,** a small park on Broadway and Cache St.

Accommodations, Camping, and Food

Jackson's constant influx of tourists ensures that if you don't book ahead rooms will be small and expensive at best, and non-existent at worst. Fortunately you can sleep affordably in one of the two local hostels. **The Bunkhouse,** in the basement of the Anvil Motel, 215 N. Cache St. (733-3668), has a lounge, kitchenette, laundromat, ski storage, and, as the name implies, one large but quiet sleeping room with comfortable bunks. ($15; off-season $10. Linens $2.) **The Hostel (AYH),** P.O. Box 546, Teton Village 83025 (733-3415), near the ski slopes, 12 mi. northwest of Jackson, is a budgetary oasis among the condos and lodges of Teton Village, and a favorite of skiers because of its location. Game room, TV room, ski waxing room, and movies nightly. Accommodations range from dorm-style rooms ($14.50 per bunk, $16 for nonmembers) to private suites ($34 for 2 people, $42 for 3 or 4). All are clean and well maintained. If you prefer to stay in a Jackson motel, the **Lazy X Motel,** 325 N. Cache St. (733-3673), offers moderately priced attractive rooms during the summer. (Singles $34. Doubles $40.) You can always fall back on **Motel**

6, 1370 W. Broadway (733-1620), even though their rates rise steadily as the peak season approaches. (Singles from $35. Doubles from $42.)

Though it doesn't offer amazing scenery, Jackson's RV/tent campground, the **Wagon Wheel Village** (733-4588), doesn't charge an arm and a leg either. Call for reservations. (Sites from $16.50.) Cheaper sites and more pleasant surroundings are available in the **Bridger-Teton National Forest** surrounding Jackson. Hike up Cache Creek to the south of town, or drive toward Alpine Junction on U.S. 26/89 to find spots. Check the map at the chamber of commerce for a complete list of campgrounds. (Sites $4-10.)

The Bunnery, 130 N. Cache St., in the "Hole-in-the-Wall" mall, has the best breakfast in town—2 eggs, peaches, cottage cheese, toast $3.25. Sandwiches $3.50-4. (Open daily 7am-2pm.) For great burgers in a bright art deco setting, try the **Cadillac Grill,** Cache St. The huge bacon-cheeseburger ($5) will fill you up without emptying your wallet. On weekdays, a mixture of Western barbecue and Mexican delicacies is set out at **Pedro's,** 139 N. Cache St. for the $3 all-you-can-eat buffet. (Open summer daily 11am-8:30pm.) Just down the street, **Alexander's Lone Star Cafe,** 335 N. Cache St., specializes in great barbecue sandwiches ($3-3.75) and giant dinners ($6-8). (Open daily 7am-9:30pm.) For a cheap, light meal, away from the cache on Cache St., head to **Pearl St. Bagels,** 145 Pearl St., where a myriad of bagel-sandwiches are under $3. (Open Mon.-Fri. 6:30am-3pm, Sat.-Sun. 7:30am-3pm.)

Nightlife and Activities

Western saddles serve as bar stools at the **Million Dollar Cowboy Bar,** 25 N. Cache St. (733-2207), Town Square. This Jackson institution attracts a mixed group of cowpokes, high society types, and even some gay cowboys. (Open Mon.-Sat. 10am-2am, Sun. 11am-2am. Live music Mon.-Sat. 9pm-2am. Cover $3-6 after 8:30pm.)

Cultural activities in Jackson fall into two camps—the rambunctious foot-stomping Western celebrations and the more formal, sedate presentations of music and art. Every summer evening except Sunday, the Town Square hosts an episode of the **Longest-Running Shoot-Out in the World.** For $2.50 on Friday evenings at 8pm, you can join in at the **Teton Twirlers Square Dance,** in the fair building on the rodeo grounds (733-5269 or 543-2825). Each June, the town celebrates the opening of the **Jackson Hole Rodeo** (733-2805; open June-Aug. Wed. and Sat. 8pm; tickets $5-8). The prestigious **Grand Teton Music Festival** (733-1128) holds court in Teton Village from mid-July through August. (Performances nightly at 8:30pm; student tickets $3-5. Fri. and Sat. symphony at 8:30pm; student tickets $9. Reserve in advance.) And on Memorial Day, the town bulges at the seams as tourists, locals, and nearby Native American tribes pour in for the dances and parades of **Old West Days.** Throughout September, the **Jackson Hole Fall Arts Festival** attracts painters, dancers, actors, and musicians to Jackson's four main theaters.

Between May 15 and Labor Day over 100,000 city slickers and backwoods folk go white-water rafting out of Jackson. **Mad River Boat Trips,** 1060 S. Hwy. 89 (733-6203), offers the cheapest white-water and scenic raft trips (from $20), though the **Barker-Ewing Co.,** 45 W. Broadway (733-1000), is stiff competition (from $25). Cheaper thrills include a lift 10,452 ft. up Rendez-Vous Mountain on the **Jackson Hole Aerial Tram** (733-2292; fare $10, seniors $8, teens $6, ages 6-12 $2). In winter, the **Jackson Hole Ski Resort** (733-2292) at Teton Village offers some of the steepest, most challenging skiing in the country.

The Wildlife Museum (733-4909), in Grand Teton Plaza on Broadway, exhibits the trophies of local hunters in extremely realistic settings. (Open May-Oct. daily 9am-6pm. Admission $2, families $5, ages 6-12 $1, under 6 free.)

Wind River Range

Named by the Arapahoe for the turbulent rivers that tumble down to the sloping, windswept farmlands on the range's eastern border, the Winds are the most spectacular of Wyoming's mountains. Seven enormous glaciers, acres of forests, and miles of primitive wilderness bear this out. The difficulty of traveling far into the Wind River range, however, keeps the region unspoiled by tourist traffic.

There are no roads into the range: it lies smack in the middle of a tremendous oval formed by U.S. 191, which runs along the western side, and U.S. 26/28/287, which follows along the range's eastern edge. From the western side, the trails are accessible from **Pinedale;** if you're coming from the east, the closest you'll get is **Lander.** Since most of the range's finest scenery lies in the **Bridger Wilderness Area** on the western slope, Pinedale is the prime starting point for hiking expeditions. Stop at **Pinedale Ranger District Office,** 210 W. Pine St., P.O. Box 220 (367-4326), before you venture into the range. (Open Mon.-Sat. 7:45am-4:30pm; off-season Mon.-Fri. 7:45am-4:30pm.) Fishing permits and information are available at sporting goods stores and at the **Wyoming Game and Fish Department,** 117 S. Sublette (367-4352; open Mon.-Fri. 8am-5pm; permits $5 per day, $15 per week, $40 per month). U.S. Geological Survey topographic maps ($4) are essential for trips into the backcountry. Pick up the standard 7½-minute map sections at **Faler's Hardware,** 341 E. Pine (367-2324), a giant sporting goods and general store in Pinedale. (open Mon.-Sat. 7am-7pm, Sun. 8am-5pm.)

Note: Novice backpackers should not venture deep into the Winds without guidance. The rugged terrain and unpredictable weather can make conditions challenging at best, dangerous at worst. In some areas of the Winds you can go weeks without meeting other humans, so don't expect quick help if you run into trouble. Beginners are advised to stick to trails closest to the range's perimeter.

The two most popular trailheads are at the end of the 16-mi. access road that heads east out of Pinedale. The trails begin at **Elkhart Park** above giant Fremont Lake, where you will find yet another information center. (Open daily 8am-8pm.) From there, head 9 mi. up the trail to the beautiful **Seneca Lakes;** hardy mountaineers will want to continue 18 mi. through **Indian Pass** to the glaciers beyond. You can climb **Fremont Peak** (13,745 ft.) from here. The other trailhead at Elkhart will take you into the **Pine Creek** drainage, an angler's nirvana. Beyond the canyon, the trail continues up to **Crows Nest Lookout** and **Glimpse Lake,** which provide beautiful bird's eye views of the icy surroundings.

Other popular destinations from Pinedale include **Gannett Peak** (at 13,804 ft., the highest mountain in the state), 10 mi. east, and **Big Sandy,** 50 mi. southeast on U.S. 191. Rock climbers from all over the world converge at the Big Sandy trailhead for the 8-mi. jaunt into **Cirque of the Towers,** where sheer cliffs hem in hikers. At the northwestern end of the Wind Range sits its most famous peak, **Squaretop.** Begin at **Green River Lake,** northwest of Pinedale on Rte. 352 off U.S. 191, for a good two-day loop around this aptly named mountain. This area and the trail leading to the Cirque are the only crowded spots in the range.

Access to the Winds from the other side is more time-consuming because of the longer, gentler eastern slope. One of the showpieces of this area is the broad **Shoshone Lake,** which lies at the crest of the **Shoshone Trail.** A few miles beyond the lake, the Shoshone Trail joins the **Fork Trail,** which leads into the tangled heart of the **Popo Agie** (pronounced po-PO-zhuh) **Wilderness.** Approach this unspoiled area from Lander via the Sinks Canyon Rd. west through geologically impressive **Sinks Canyon State Park** on Rte. 131. There are two small campgrounds here (sites $4; arrive by 3pm).

The **Lander Ranger District Offices** (332-5460), on U.S. 287, can give you information on the Popo Agie Wilderness. (Open Mon.-Fri. 8am-noon and 1-5pm.) For information on hiking in **Fitzpatrick Wilderness** in the northwestern Winds, write to the forest service offices at P.O. Box 186, Dubois 82513. For information on the eastern side of the Winds, write the Shoshone National Forest, P.O. Box 961, Cody

82414. To find out about the **Wind River Indian Reservation,** contact the Joint Council of Shoshone and Arapahoe Tribes, P.O. Box 217, Fort Washakie 82514.

In Pinedale, you needn't don blue jeans to eat at **The Wrangler Cafe,** 310 E. Pine St., where burgers with all the fixin's go for $3.25 and fantastic homemade pie costs $1.85. (Open Mon.-Fri. 6am-10pm, Sat.-Sun. 6am-8pm.) South of town on U.S. 191, **King Cone** serves a much-vaunted burger ($2), and a variety of shakes and sweets. You might want to bring sunglasses, as the restaurant and even the rocks in the surrounding parking lot are painted garish shades of flourescent green, purple, and orange. For food in Lander, try **The Breadboard,** 125 E. Main St., where you can sink a hardy sub for $3. (Open Mon.-Fri. 11am-8pm., Sat. 11am-4pm.) A local favorite is **The Commons,** 170 E. Main St. Wrap yourself around the waffles and bacon breakfast ($2.80). (Open daily 6am-11pm.)

The **Pinedale Chamber of Commerce,** 32 E. Pine (367-2242), has a list of accommodations and area sights. Stop here before choosing a room or campsite. (Open June-Sept. daily 8:30am-5:30pm.) Clean, comfortable accommodations with A/C are available at both the **Pine Creek Motel,** 650 W. Pine St. (367-2191), and the **Teton Court Motel,** 123 E. Magnolia (367-4317). Singles at Pine Creek from $24, at Teton from $26. Doubles at both from $32. Nearby **Trail's End** has free camping; sites at **Fremont Lake** (367-4326) go for $6. Unobstructed views of the Winds will cost you only $4 at the **Elkhart Park** campground, at the end of the road past Fremont Lake.

If you decide to shack up in Lander, visit the **Lander Chamber of Commerce,** 160 N. 1st St. (332-3892), for information on lodgings and current activities. (Open Mon.-Fri. 9am-5pm.) For bikers and hikers, the cheapest rooms are at **Ma's Boarding House,** Mortimer Ln. (332-3123, ask for Pat Focht), at the southern end of Lander. (Overnight bunk with shower $5. Camping $1. Breakfast-and-a-hug $3.) Your next best bet is the **Downtown Motel,** where clean but phoneless singles cost $22.

Jackson-Rock Springs Stages serve Pinedale once per day from the terminal at 1005 Dewar Ave. (362-6161) in Rock Springs ($10.50), and from the stop at 72 S. Glenwood St. (733-3135) in Jackson ($10.50). The flag stop in Pinedale is at the northern Phillips 66 station (367-4311). Greyhound passes are not honored. **Powder River Transportation** can connect you with Lander from Jackson or Casper; Greyhound passes are honored.

Pinedale's **ZIP code** is 82941; Lander's 82520. The **area code** for the Winds is 307.

Near the Winds

The great plains stretch southwest from Lander as far as the eye can see and the lonely expanses of sagebrush are broken only by the glaring blacktop of U.S. 28. Thirty mi. from Lander down this empty highway lie the remains of **South Pass City** and **Atlantic City,** two erstwhile mining towns whose crumbling wooden buildings stand as monuments to both the stamina and avarice of Wyoming's first pioneers.

Recent restoration efforts have helped to refurbish both communities, and the interesting historical displays in the **South Pass Visitors Center** merit a drive down the 5-mi. dirt detour from the highway. (Open Mon.-Fri. 9am-5pm. Ask a local for directions.) This rough-and-ready frontier community also played an important role in the women's suffrage movement. William Bright, a representative from South Pass City, wrote and introduced the bill which, when passed in 1869, made Wyoming the first territory to allow women the right to vote and hold office. The National Forest Service maintains a splendid forested **campground** just out of town near Atlantic City. (Sites $4.)

Eighty-five mi. northeast of Lander on U.S. 20, the comic book-sounding city of Thermopolis maintains the world's largest single mineral hot springs at **Hot Springs State Park** (864-3771). In 1896, the U.S. purchased the springs from the Shoshone and Arapahoe tribes for $60,000 worth of cattle and food supplies, on stipulation that the "public" would always be allowed to bathe for free. To ensure this, the state maintains a clean but rotten-egg-smelling bathhouse on the grounds of the state park. (Open Mon.-Sat. 8am-6pm, Sun. noon-6pm. Towel and bathing suit rental 50¢.)

The **chamber of commerce,** 220 Park St. (864-2636), in the State Park Building, provides adequate assistance and a schedule of special events in Thermopolis. (Open Mon.-Fri. 8am-5pm.) If need be, you can stay at the simple **Plaza Hotel** (864-2251), on the park ground, where slightly run-down singles without shower start at $12, doubles at $35. **Pumpernicks,** 512 Broadway, serves delicious sandwiches ($2.50-5), salads, and steaks, and has Old West memorabilia strung up along the walls. (Open Mon.-Sat. 7am-9pm, Sat.-Sun. 9am-10pm.) **The Sideboard Cafe,** 109 S. 6th St., serves ample hamburgers for $2.75 and straightforward but good dinners for $4.75-7. (Open daily 6am-10pm.)

TEXAS

Texas remains both bilingual and bicultural. European American culture celebrates Texas's past as an independent republic and cultivates an image of rugged masculinity typified by the cattle rancher with the mile-long Cadillac and the avaricious oil-baron J.R. Ewing. This culture's creed, "the bigger, the better," pervades urban centers such as Houston and Dallas with their conglomerations of shiny new skyscrapers. Alongside this longhorn tradition, a vibrant Mexican American culture has developed and survived. To visitors, its most palpable and visible contributions to the "Lone Star State" are addictively spicy food and distinctive architecture. Yet, "Tex-Mex" means more than a trendy and tasty cuisine; it represents also a balance of cultures and conquests in the largest state in the continental U.S.

Practical Information

Capital: Austin.

Tourist Information: Texas Division of Tourism, P.O. Box 12728, Austin 78711 (512-463-8586). U.S. Forest Service, P.O. Box 130, Lufkin 75901 (409-831-2246). State Parks and Recreation Areas, Austin Headquarters Complex, 4200 Smith School Rd., Austin 78744 (512-463-4630).

Time Zones: Central (1 hr. behind Eastern) and Mountain (2 hr. behind Eastern). Postal Abbreviation: TX.

Travel

Car travelers have the run of most of this huge state, but public transport serves areas frequented by tourists. The constellation of major cities in eastern Texas forms a triangle with Dallas/Ft. Worth, San Antonio, and Houston/Galveston at the corners, and Austin part way along the San Antonio-Dallas leg. Each leg measures 200-300 mi. in length. Interstate highways, frequent bus schedules, and Amtrak routes connect the points. Kerrville Bus Lines, a Greyhound affiliate, covers the entire region, while Greyhound/Trailways zooms along the edges.

Outside this triangle, the two areas of greatest interest to visitors are western Texas and the Gulf Coast/Mexican Border area, accessible by interstates and bus routes. Greyhound has frequent service on I-10 and I-20 into western Texas and convenient service to Corpus Christi and the southern border towns. Greyhound's affiliate, TNM&O Coaches, provides thorough regional coverage in northwestern Texas and southern New Mexico. El Paso/Ciudad Juárez, a major urban area straddling the Mexican border, is a convenient base for exploring western Texas and southern New Mexico.

San Antonio, El Paso, Austin, and Houston each have a hostel, and the state's very own B&B organization arranges stays in private homes in many Texas cities and towns. The "budget" class charges $25-40 for singles, $30-50 for doubles.

Regional cuisine, like most of Texan culture, is enriched by the state's Mexican heritage. "Tex-Mex" is a variation of the dishes served across the border. Chefs throw jalapeño peppers into chili as casually as a Burger King crew chief might shake salt on french fries. Mexican pastries and genuine longhorn beef are a must. Have your steak "chicken-fried" and pour on cream sauce, or try a big Texas-style T-bone.

Outdoors

Some folks say Texas has only two seasons: summer and January. It's hot in summer. Really hot. The heat is more bearable in the west, where the air is dry, but the humidity in the coastal area is stifling. Winter varies across the state, from warm and mild in the south to potentially severe and blizzardy in the northern panhandle.

Texas

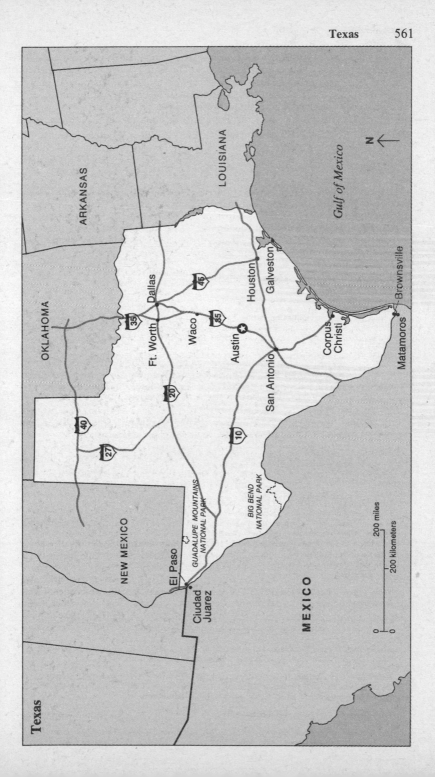

Take advantage of the state's wide open space by camping. Bring a tent and tons of repellent to deter the mosquito squadrons. The state park system has excellent camping at over 60 parks, recreation areas, and historic sites. Some parks charge an admission fee of $2 per car, 50¢ per pedestrian or bicyclist. Sites usually cost $4. In the open ranching countryside of western Texas or in the Hill Country, finding sites should present few problems. For a broader overview of the state and desert survival, see the Southwest Introduction.

Dallas

Local institutions such as Neiman-Marcus stores, the colorful nocturnal skyline, and the Cowboys football team and cheerleader dynasty typify Dallas's preoccupation with commerce and hype. As shown in the television series "Dallas," business is of primary interest in the "silicon prairie," where affluence is emphasized, not downplayed. Yet it is the Mexican culture, permeating everything from food to language, that tempers this soap opera glitz with a far greater richness.

Practical Information

Emergency: 911

Visitor Information: Dallas Convention and Visitors Bureau, 1201 Elm St. #200 (746-6677). Open Mon.-Fri. 8:30am-5pm. **Union Station Visitor Center,** 400 S. Houston Ave. (954-1111), in a booth in the lobby. Open daily 9am-5pm. **Special Events Info Line,** 746-6679.

Dallas-Ft. Worth International Airport: (212-574-8888), 17 mi. northwest of downtown. Big like everything in Texas. Sprawling, conversational computer-run shuttle system makes even the longest layover bearable. **Love Field** (670-7275; take bus #39) has mostly intra-Texas flights. To get downtown from either airport, take the **Super Shuttle,** 729 E. Dallas Rd. (817-329-2001; in terminal, dial 02 on phone at ground transport services). 24-hr. service. DFW airport to downtown $12, Love Field to downtown $8.

Amtrak: 400 S. Houston Ave. (653-1101 or 800-872-7245), in Union Station, next to Reunion Tower. One train per day to Houston (6 hr., $40) and St. Louis (15 hr., $122).

Greyhound/Trailways: 205 S. Lamar (655-7000), at Commerce 3 blocks east and 1 block north of Union Station. To: Houston (7 per day, 6 hr., $27); San Antonio (11 per day, 6 hr., $32); El Paso (6 per day, 12½ hr., $75); New Orleans (8 per day, 12½ hr., $82). Open 24 hr.

Public Transport: Dallas Area Rapid Transit (DART), 601 Pacific Ave. (979-1111 or 934-3278). Serves most suburbs; routes radiate from downtown. Service 5am-midnight, to suburbs 5am-8pm. Base fare 75¢, more with zone changes. Information desk open Mon.-Fri. 8:30am-4:45pm. Maps available at Main and Akard St. Mon.-Fri. 8am-5pm, or at Elm and Ervay St. Mon.-Fri. 7am-6pm. **Hop-a-Bus** (979-1111) is DART's downtown Dallas service, with a park-and-ride system. Four routes (blue, red, orange, and green) run about every 10 min. Fare 35¢, transfers free. Look for buses with a blue bunny, a red kangaroo, an orange cricket, or a green frog.

Taxi: Yellow Cab Co., 426-6262. $1.30 first mi., $1 each additional mi. DFW Airport to downtown $20.

Car Rental: All-State Rent-a-Car, 3206 Live Oak (741-3118). $25 per day with 100 free mi. Open Mon.-Sat. 7:30am-6pm. Must be 21 with major credit card.

Bike Rental: Bicycle Exchange, 11716 Ferguson Rd. (270-9269). Rates from $60 per week. Open Mon.-Fri. 9am-7pm, Sat. 9am-5pm. Must have a credit card.

Help Lines: Gay Hotline, 368-6283. Open daily 7:30pm-midnight. **Community Center,** 3920 Cedar Springs (528-4233). **Senior Citizen Call Action Center,** 1500 Marilla St. (744-3600). Information on reduced fares, recreational activites, and health care.

Time Zone: Central (1 hr. behind Eastern).

Post Office: 400 N. Ervay St. (953-3045), on Thanksgiving Sq. downtown. Open Mon.-Fri. 8am-4:30pm, Sat. 8am-noon. **ZIP code:** 75201; General Delivery, 75221; **Area Code:** 214.

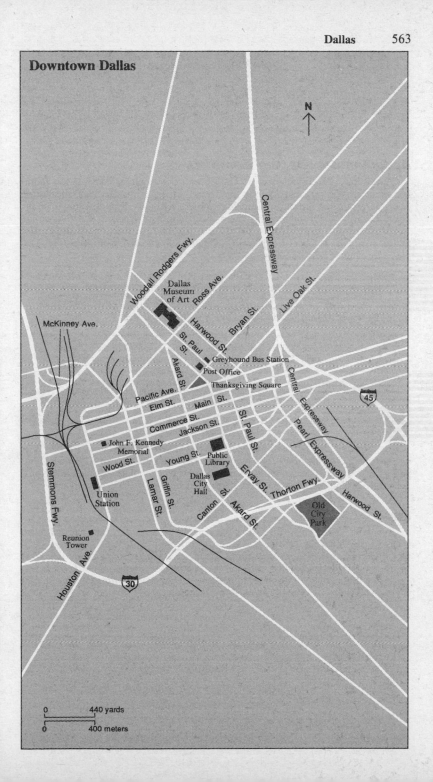

Downtown Dallas

N

Woodall Rodgers Fwy.

Central Expressway

Dallas Museum of Art

Ross Ave.

Live Oak St.

McKinney Ave.

Harwood St.

Bryan St.

St. Paul St.

Greyhound Bus Station

Post Office

Akard St.

Thanksgiving Square

Pacific Ave.

Elm St.

Main St.

Central Expressway

45

Commerce St.

Jackson St.

St. Paul St.

Pearl Expressway

John F. Kennedy Memorial

Young St.

Public Library

Stemmons Fwy.

Wood St.

Dallas City Hall

Ervay St.

Thorton Fwy.

Harwood St.

Union Station

Lamar St.

Griffin St.

Canton St.

Akard St.

Old City Park

Reunion Tower

Houston Ave.

30

0   440 yards
0   400 meters

Dallas (pop. 1,062,000) is in the northeast corner of Texas, near the border of Oklahoma and Arkansas. Houston is 240 mi. to the south, El Paso 620 mi. to the west. Downtown Dallas will confuse pedestrians and drivers alike. Streets are laid out along two separate grids that meet at a 45° angle. Pedestrians beware: jaywalking is illegal and subject to a $25 fine. Also please note that the Greyhound station is actually on the corner of Lamar and Commerce St., and not where the map indicates.

Accommodations and Camping

Conventions are big business in Dallas, and the resulting demand for rooms boosts rates, as do big events such as the Texas State Fair (mid-Oct.) and the Cotton Bowl (Jan. 1). Most restaurants and nightlife are well outside of downtown, so it's not necessarily worthwhile to stay there. The suburbs of Irving and Arlington are full of inexpensive motels. **Motel 6** (505-891-6161) has 11 locations in the greater Dallas area. Also consider **Exel Inns** (800-356-8013) and **Red Roof Inns** (800-843-7663) for singles from $34-40.

Dallas International Hostel, 10230 Harry Hines Blvd. (358-3211), at the Anchor Motel. From downtown, take bus #40 to the corner of Willowbrook and Harry Hines, and walk ½ block north on Harry Hines. Area known for its prostitution. Women should not walk alone here at night. Safe, simply-furnished motel-style rooms sleep 3 and are rarely full. Check in 7-9am and 5-11pm. $10, nonmembers $19. Mandatory linen $1.50.

Bed and Breakfast Texas Style, 4224 W. Red Bird Lane, Dallas 75237 (298-5433 or 298-8586). Hosts are friendly Dallas families who'll meet you at a hotel or the bus station by special request. Singles $25-29. Doubles $30-40. Reservations strongly recommended; make 'em at least 2 weeks in advance.

Dallas Budget Inn, 4001 Live Oak (826-7110). Take bus #1 or 20 from downtown. The neighborhood is seedy, but close to downtown. Passable rooms. Singles $25. Doubles $28.

Welcome Inn, 3243 Merrifield (826-3510), at the Dolphin St. exit off I-30 East. Cheery, comfortable rooms with mint green decor. Singles $30. Doubles $33.

If you have a car and camping gear, try the **Hi-Ho Campground,** 200 W. Bear Creek Rd. (223-8574), south of town. Take I-35 14½ mi. to exit 412, turn right, and go 2 more mi. (Tent sites $10 for 2, $14.50 with hookup. $1 each additional person.) Sleeping in Dallas parks is illegal and unsafe.

Food

Greenville Avenue in North Dallas has miles of restaurants. (Take bus #1 down Greenville.) **McKinney Avenue** also offers a variety of cheap eats. For more ideas, pick up a copy of the Friday weekend guide of the *Dallas Morning News.* The **West End Historic District,** popular with family vacationers, supplies ample food, beverage, and entertainment in the heart of downtown. For fast Tex-Mex food and a variety of small shops, explore the **West End Marketplace,** 603 Munger St. (954-4350). The **Farmers Produce Market,** 1010 S. Pearl Expressway (748-2082), between Pearl and Central Expressway near I-30, has good buys. (Open daily sunrise-sunset.)

Guadalajara, 4405 Ross. Piñata-packed interior, patioed exterior. Superb view of Dallas. Combination dinners $5, steak and seafood specialties $7-10. Open Mon.-Thurs. 11am-3am, Fri. 11am-4am, Sat. 9am-4am, Sun. 9am-3am.

Farmer's Grill, 807 Park Ave., at the corner of Cadiz and Canton. Excellent cobbler, prepared with market fruit each morning. Complete Texas country dinners $4-5. Open Mon.-Fri. 6am-3pm. Bar open until 9pm.

Herrera's Cafe, 4001 Maple Ave. (528-9644). Take bus #29. Informal decor doesn't daunt businesspeople in suits and dresses who partake of the excellent Tex-Mex dinners. Filling meals $4-6. Bring your own beer, and expect to wait on weekends. Open Mon. and Wed.-Thurs. 10am-9pm, Fri. 10am-10pm, Sat. 9am-10pm, Sun. 9am-9pm.

Old Spaghetti Warehouse, 1815 N. Market (651-8475), in the heart of the West End. Excellent Italian food in a colorful pasta emporium. Spaghetti plates $3-5, specialties $6-9. Crowded at lunchtime. Open Sun.-Thurs. 11am-10pm, Fri. 11am-midnight, Sat. noon-midnight.

White Rock Yacht Club, 7324 Gaston Ave., just west of Garland. A quirky, unpretentious place with pool tables and peanut shell-littered floors. Yacht club tacos $4.50. No entree over $6, but portions are small. Free peanuts. Open Mon.-Sat. 11am-2am, Sun. noon-2am.

Colter's, 11827 Abrams (680-1990). Over 10 locations in the Dallas area, though all are pretty far from downtown. Generous portions of hickory-smoked barbecue amid rustic country decor. Great onion rings. Bring a church bulletin on Sun. to get 15% off your bill. Sandwiches $3, dinners $5-7. Open Sun.-Thurs. 11am-9:30pm, Fri.-Sat. 11am-10pm.

Sights

Dallas has no easily discernible history. Originally an inland port in the mid-19th century, it eventually became a railroad town and then an oil city. Take in the what you can of Dallas's present from the top of **Reunion Tower** (741-3663; open Mon.-Fri. 10am-10pm, Sat.-Sun. 9am-midnight; admission $2, seniors and children $1). On your way out, explore the adjoining **Union Station,** 400 S. Houston Ave., one of the city's few grand old buildings.

Walking north along Houston you'll come upon the **Texas School Book Depository,** from where, on November 22, 1963, Lee Harvey Oswald shot President John F. Kennedy. The site is now **The Sixth Floor,** 411 Elm St. (653-6666), an unabashedly worshipful museum commemorating Kennedy's life and detailing his assassination. (Open Sun.-Fri. 10am-6pm, Sat. 10am-7pm. Last tickets sold one hr. before closing. Admission $4, seniors $3, students $2. Audio tours $2.) The **John F. Kennedy Memorial,** designed by Philip Johnson, stands at Market and Main St.

Continue north along Houston to reach the heart of the **West End Historic District** (747-7470), which perhaps should be renamed the West End Dining and Drinking District. The converted red brick warehouse neighborhood culminates in the **West End Marketplace,** 603 Munger Ave., a passel of fast-food eateries, bars, and shops. (Open Mon.-Thurs. 11am-10pm, Fri.-Sat. 11am-midnight, Sun. noon-8pm.)

Walking east along Ross Avenue from the historic district leads you to the new **Arts District,** the centerpiece of which is the **Dallas Museum of Art,** 1717 N. Harwood St. (922-1200). The museum offers an excellent collection of Indonesian, impressionist, modern, and U.S. decorative art. There is also an outdoor sculpture garden and an art room for children. (Museum open Tues.-Wed. and Fri.-Sat. 10am-5pm, Thurs. 10am-9pm, Sun. and holidays noon-5pm. Children's room open Wed.-Thurs. and Sat. noon-5pm. Admission to both free.)

Walking south from the museum on St. Paul, toward the downtown area, turn right on Bryan St. and walk 1 block to **Thanksgiving Square,** (969-1977), a tiny park beneath massive towers. Built below street-level, with gardens and quiet waterfalls, the square is both an example of successful urban design and a respite from the city's busy streets. (Open Mon.-Fri. 9am-5pm, Sat.-Sun. and holidays 1-5pm.) Continue south from Thanksgiving Square along Ervay St. to the imposing, $32-million **Dallas City Hall** (670-3957), designed by the omnipresent I.M. Pei.

About nine long blocks south of City Hall on Ervay St. is the **Old City Park,** at Gano St. (421-5141). The park, indeed the oldest, is also one of the most popular recreation areas and lunch spots in the city. Open spaces and picnic facilities are scattered among restored buildings, which include a railroad depot and a church. (Park open daily dawn to dusk. Exhibit buildings open Tues.-Fri. 10am-4pm, Sat.-Sun. 1:30-4:30pm. Tours $4, seniors and ages 6-12 $3.)

State Fair Park (670-8400), southeast of downtown on 2nd Ave. by the Cotton Bowl, is home to numerous museums, all within walking distance of each other. A standout is the **Museum of Natural History** (670-8457), which has a small permanent display on prehistoric life. (Open Mon.-Sat. 9am-5pm, Sun. noon-5pm. Admission free for permanent exhibits; prices vary for temporary exhibits.) Other buildings include the **Aquarium** (670-8441; open daily 9am-5pm); the **Age of Steam**

Museum (421-8754; open Thurs.-Fri. 9am-1pm, Sat.-Sun. 11am-5pm; admission $2, under 16 $1); the **Science Place** (428-5555; open Tues.-Sun. 9:30am-5:30pm; admission $5, seniors and ages 7-16 $2); and the **Dallas Garden Center,** at 2nd and Forest Ave. (428-7476; open Mon.-Sat. 10am-5pm, Sun. 12:30-5pm).

The **Dallas Arboretum and Botanical Garden** (327-3990), off Garland Rd. in northeast Dallas, comprises 66 acres of country just outside the city. (Open March-Oct. Tues.-Sun. 10am-6pm; Nov.-Feb. Tues.-Sun. 10am-5pm. Admission $3, seniors $2, ages under 12 $1.)

Entertainment

Dallas, like most other cities (and intros), offers a surprising mix of the serious and the frivolous. Check the *Dallas Observer* or weekend sections of local papers for complete entertainment listings. Enjoy free summer theater during July and August at the **Shakespeare in the Park** festival (599-2778), at Samuell-Grand Park just northeast of State Fair Park between Grand Ave. and Samuell Blvd. Two plays are performed annually; each runs about two weeks. The **Music Hall** (565-1116), in State Fair Park, houses the **Dallas Symphony Orchestra** (692-0203) from January to May and in September (tickets $7-18); the **Dallas Civic Opera** (827-3320) in November and December (tickets $6-45, 50% student discount in certain sections); the **Dallas Ballet,** which performs the *Nutcracker* in late December; and the **Dallas Summer Musicals** (787-2000) from June to August, with performances nightly (tickets $5-35, cash only). KVIL (369-8500) sells half-price tickets on performance days. (Tickets on sale noon-6pm, for matinees 9am-noon.)

Greenville Avenue is home to a variety of bars and nightclubs, including **Aw Shucks,** 3601 Greenville Ave. (821-9449), an outdoor seafood bar just south of Mockingbird Lane. Sit outside on a warm Texas evening, gosh darnit, and enjoy a cool beer ($1.25) with raw oysters ($3-7). (Open Mon.-Thurs. 11am-11pm, Fri.-Sat. 11am-11:45pm, Sun. 11:30am-10pm.) McKinney Avenue, parallel to and a few blocks west of Central Ave., is another center of nightlife, with the **Hard Rock Cafe,** 2601 McKinney (855-0007), at its hub. Enjoy loud music and nightly dancing. (Open daily 11am-2am. No cover.) The **Historic West End,** downtown on Market and Munger St., also writhes with nightlife. Pay one cover charge ($5-8) for all eight of the packed clubs on **Dallas Alley.** Look for the colorful neon arches at the tip of the West End. Nearby is the **Outback Pub,** 1701 N. Market St. (761-9355), a pseudo-Aussie lounge/restaurant with a large selection of beers to help you pretend you're eating a vegemite sandwich. The pub proffers live rock nightly. (Open daily 11am-2am. No cover.) One of the most popular clubs is **Dick's Last Resort,** 1701 N. Market St. (747-0001), which plays "loud and obnoxious Dixieland" and prides itself on its insolent employees. But aw shucks, with a motto like "No cover—no dress code," it's far from a last resort. (Open Mon.-Thurs. 11am-midnight, Fri.-Sat. 11am-2am.)

Even those Dallasites who like to think of themselves as a refined and reserved sometimes get caught up in the rowdy Texan spirit and head to country-western dance halls. **Belle Star,** 7724 N. Central Expressway at Southwestern (739-3435), takes its name from a tough 19th-century outlaw. Like Belle herself, some of the customers here get rambunctious. The large dance floor has made this place a popular hangout, but the real action doesn't begin until around 9:30pm. (Open Wed.-Sat. 7pm-2am, Sun. 4pm-midnight. Cover $3, free before 8:30pm. Free dance lessons Sun. 4-8pm.)

Six Flags Over Texas (817-640-8900), 15 mi. from downtown off I-30 in Arlington, is the original link in the nationwide amusement park chain. The name alludes to the six governments that have presided over the state through the years. This is a thrill-lover's paradise, complete and replete, we repeat, with rides, restaurants, shops, and entertainment theaters. The hefty admission charge ($20, over 55 years or under 4 ft. $14) includes unlimited access to all rides and attractions. (Open June-Aug. Sun.-Thurs. 10am-10pm, Fri.-Sat. 10am-midnight; March-May and Sept.-Oct. Sat.-Sun. 10am-8pm. Parking $3.)

Austin

Apart from the magnificent capitol building and the omnipresent longhorns of the state university, you'd never guess that Austin is in Texas. The city has a reputation as a sanctuary for panhandlers and a destination for intellectuals, music lovers, the young, and the restless. Unlike Houston and Dallas, downtown Austin has not sprouted towering glass boxes; the 50,000-plus student body of the University of Texas (UT) seems to generate unpredictability and a dose of radicalism. Amidst rapidly tapering urban growth, state politics and university students still dominate Austin. When you've had your fill of Lone Stars, explore the hill country of Texas, with Austin as your base.

Practical Information

Emergency: 911.

Visitor Information: Austin Tourist Center, 412 E. 6th St. (478-0098). Open Mon.-Fri. 8:30am-5pm, Sat.-Sun. 1-5pm. **Tourist Information Center** (463-8586), 11th and Congress, in the state capitol. Open daily 8am-5pm. **Texas Parks and Wildlife,** 389-4800 or 800-792-1112 in TX. Open Mon.-Fri. 8am-5pm. Call for information on camping outside Austin. Or write to or visit Texas Parks and Wildlife Dept., 4200 Smith School Rd., Austin 78744.

Amtrak: 250 N. Lamar Blvd. (476-5684 or 800-872-7245). To: Dallas (7 per week, 6 hr., $36); San Antonio (7 per week, 3 hr., $13); El Paso (3 per week, 10 hr., $117). No Houston service.

Greyhound/Trailways: 916 E. Koenig (458-5267), several miles north of downtown off I-35. Pick up buses to downtown at the Highland Mall across the street. To: San Antonio (11 per day, 2-3 hr., $11); Houston (11 per day, 3-4 hr., $16); Dallas (10 per day, 4 hr., $27); El Paso via San Antonio (5 per day, 14 hr., $75). Open 24 hr.

Public Transport: Capitol Metro, 504 Congress (474-1200; line open Mon.-Sat. 6am-midnight, Sun. 6am-7pm). Maps and schedules available here Mon.-Fri. 7am-6pm, Sat. 9am-1pm, or at the Austin Chamber of Commerce, across from the tourist center. Fare 50¢, seniors, children, and disabled 25¢. Downtown, the **Armadillo Express** connects major downtown points and runs every 10-15 min. in old-fashioned green trolley cars Mon.-Fri. 6:30am-10pm, Sat. 11am-7pm. Fare 25¢. The **University of Texas Shuttle Bus** serves the campus area. Map and schedule at the UT Information Center (471-3151) or any library, including the Main Library, 8th and Guadalupe St.

Taxi: Yellow Cab, 472-1111. Base fare $1.25, $1.25 per mi. Airport to downtown $7.50.

Car Rental: Rent-A-Wreck, 6820 Guadalupe (454-8621). $20-22 per day, 100 free mi., 19¢ each additional mi. Open Mon.-Fri. 8am-6:30pm, Sat.-Sun. 10am-3:30pm. Must be 21 with major credit card.

Bike Rental: University Schwinn, 2901 N. Lamar Blvd. (474-6696). Mountain bikes only $20 per day. $300 deposit required. Open Mon.-Fri. 10am-7pm, Sat. 10am-6pm.

Help Lines: Crisis Intervention Hotline, 472-4357. **Austin Rape Crisis Center,** 440-7273.

Time Zone: Central (1 hr. behind Eastern).

Post Office: 300 E. 9th St. (929-1250). Open Mon.-Fri. 7:30am-6pm, Sat. 8am-noon. **ZIP code:** 78767.

Area Code: 512.

Austin (pop. 750,000) lies 78 mi. northeast of San Antonio, 192 mi. south of Dallas on I-35, and 164 mi. west Houston on U.S. 290. Highway signs lead to the **capitol area** near Congress Ave. and 11th St., in the center of the city. **Congress Avenue** runs from the **Colorado River** in the south 12 blocks to the capitol and then seven more blocks to the **University of Texas (UT)** in the north. The university splits numbered streets into east and west and includes most tourist spots in this stretch. Austin is a cyclist's paradise, with roller-coaster hills and clearly marked bikeways.

Accommodations and Camping

Cheap accommodations abound in Austin. Three UT co-ops rent rooms to hostelers and include three meals per day at no extra cost. The aptly named **21st St. Co-op,** W. 21st St. (476-1857) charges $10 for large, comfortable rooms. Facilities include TV room, laundry, recreation room, and piano. The place ills rapidly in summer. To get from the bus station to the hostel, take bus #15 to 7th and Congress St., walk down 7th 1 block to Colorado, and take #3 to 21st and Nueces St.; those who get there too late should wander two blocks west to the end of 21st St. to the **Pearl Street Co-op,** on Pearl St. of all the places. This co-op offers the same deal as 21st, but with access to a beautiful courtyard pool. (Rooms $13.) Just a few blocks away, **Taos Hall,** 2612 Guadalupe (474-6905), provides three meals and a bed for just $10. You're most likely to get a private room here, and when you stay for dinner, the friendly residents will give you a welcoming round of applause. As if that's not enough sleeping around, a couple blocks away is the **Goodall Wooten Dorm,** 2112 Guadalupe (472-1343). The "Woo" has private rooms with a small refrigerator, plus access to a TV room and basketball courts. Call ahead. (Rooms $15.)

Farther from the center of town but still conveniently located is the newly opened **Austin International Youth Hostel (AYH),** 2200 S. Lakeshore Blvd. (444-2294). From the Greyhound station take bus #7 ("Duval") to Lakeshore Blvd. and walk about ½ mi. to the hostel. From I-35 east, exit at Riverside, head east, and turn left at Lakeshore Blvd. The Hostel has a kitchen, A/C, and nearby grocery stores ($8.)

I-35, running north and south of Austin, features a string of inexpensive hotels well outside downtown. **Motel 6** has two locations along I-35, both with clean rooms, a pool, and HBO-blessed color TV. **North,** 9420 N. I-35 at the Rundberg exit (339-6161), lies 12 mi. north of the capitol off N. Lamar and E. Rundberg Lane. Take a bus to Fawnridge and walk 4 blocks. (Singles $20. Doubles $26.) The opposite-minded **South,** 2707 I-35 (444-5882), near the Woodward exit, is 7 mi. south of the capitol near St. Edward's University. (Singles $22. Doubles $28.)

Camping is no problem after a 15- to 45-minute drive. The **Austin Capitol KOA** (444-6322), 6 mi. south of the city along I-35, offers a pool, game room, laundry, grocery, and playground. Some cabins are available. (Sites $14 for 2 people.) The **Emma Long Metropolitan Park,** 2000 Barton Spring (346-1831), a large preserve in the bend of the Colorado River, 6½ mi. off Rte. 2222, has hookups, tent sites, and a boat ramp. Contact the visitors center or the Highland Lakes Tourist Association for more information (see Practical Information above).

Food

Two main districts compete for Austin's restaurant trade. Along the west side of the UT campus, **Guadalupe Street** has scores of fast-food joints and convenience stores, including the **Party Barn,** with drive-through beer. Those who disdain the $3 all-you-can-eat pizza buffets and sub shops that line the drag can eat in the UT Union ($2-5). The second district clusters around **Sixth Street,** south of the capitol. Here the battle for Happy Hour business rages with special intensity to the delight of many; three-for-one drink specials and free hors d'oeuvres are common.

Sam's Bar-B-Que, 2000 E. 12th St. Take bus #12 or 6 eastbound. Some of the best and friendliest barbecue in the Southwest. Tiny, dive-like interior clogged with locals on weekends. Barbecue plates (with beans and potato salad) $4. Open Mon.-Thurs. 10am-3:30am, Fri.-Sat. 10am-5am, Sun. 10am-3am.

Trudy's Texas Star, 409 W. 30th St. Fine Tex-Mex dinner entrees $7-9, with a fantastic array of margaritas. Famous for their *migas,* a corn tortilla soufflé ($4). Open Mon.-Thurs. 7am-midnight, Fri.-Sat. 7am-4am, Sun. 8am-midnight.

Sholz Garden, 1607 San Jacinto (477-4171), near the capitol. An Austin landmark recognized by the legislature as "epitomizing the finest traditions of the German heritage of our state." German only in name, of course. Great chicken-fried steaks and Tex-Mex meals ($5-6). Live country-rock music and excellent jazz. Open Mon.-Thurs. 11am-midnight, Fri.-Sat. 11am-2am.

Texas Chili Parlor, 1409 Lavaca. Hot chili and Tex-Mex ($5-7) in a barroom atmosphere as spicy as its food. Happy Hour daily 3-7pm. Open daily 11am-1am.

Old Bakery and Emporium, 1006 N. Congress, near the capitol. Cheap sweets and light lunches in an old stone home. Sandwiches $1.75-2. Open Mon.-Fri. 9am-4pm.

Sights

Not to be outdone by Washington, in 1882 Texans built their **state capitol,** Congress Ave. (463-0063), 7 ft. higher than the national capitol. This colossal building with colorful inlaid marble floors has "Texas" inscribed on everything from door hinges to hallway benches. (Open during legislative session 24 hr.; off-season 6am-11pm. Free tours Mon.-Sat. 8:30am-4:30pm. Tourist information center open daily 8am-5pm.) Across the street from the capitol, at 11th and Colorado St., sleeps the **Governor's Mansion** (463-5516), built in 1856. The bottom level stores the furniture of the past 10 Texas governors. (Free tours Mon.-Fri. every 20 min. 10am-11:40am.)

The **University of Texas at Austin,** the wealthiest public university in the country, enrolls over 50,000 students. Its **visitors centers** (471-1420) reside in Sid Richardson Hall, adjacent to the LBJ Library, and at the corner of Martin Luther King and Red River Rd. The **Harry Ransom Center,** Guadalupe at 21st St. (471-8944), displays an obligatory Gutenburg Bible as well as medieval, 20th-century U.S., and Latin American art. (Open Mon.-Sat. 9am-5pm, Sun. 1-5pm. Free.)

The **Laguna Gloria Art Museum,** 3809 W. 35th St. (458-8191), 8 mi. from the capitol, in a Mediterranean villa-lookalike, displays the city's best exhibits on a rotating basis and features 20th-century artwork. With rolling, spacious grounds that overlook **Lake Austin,** the Laguna often hosts inexpensive evening concerts, plays, and seasonal festivals. Take bus #21. (Docent tours Sun. at 2pm. Open Tues.-Sat. 10am-5pm, Thurs. 10am-9pm, Sun. 1-5pm. Admission $2, seniors and students $1, ages under 16 free. Free Thurs.)

Near the capitol is **St. Mary's Cathedral,** E. 10th and Brazos St., an ornate sanctuary and the closest Austin comes to Gothic architecture. Many flock to riverside **Zilker Park,** 2201 Barton Springs Rd., just south of the Colorado River, on hot afternoons. **Barton Springs Pool,** in the park (476-9044), is a popular swimming hole banked by walnut and pecan trees. The unchlorinated, spring-fed pool is 1000 ft. long and 200 ft. wide. Beware: the pool's temperature rarely rises above 60°F. Get away from the crowd and avoid paying by walking upstream (take an inner tube) and swimming at any spot that looks nice. (Admission $1.75, Sat.-Sun. $2, ages 12-18 50¢, under 12 25¢. Swimming free and at your own risk Nov.-Jan.) Zilker Park also has a botanical garden (477-8672), rentable canoes (478-3852), playgrounds, playing fields, and picnic areas. Parking inside the grounds costs $2, but is free on the roads near the entrance.

Entertainment

Austin draws musicians from all over the country and has boosted many to fame. Pick up a free copy of the **Austin Chronicle,** available at book and record stores, for listings of who's in town. For honky-tonk and two-steppin' action visit the **Broken Spoke,** 3201 S. Lamar Blvd. (442-6189), Austin's liveliest dance hall. (Open Mon.-Tues. 9:30am-11:30pm, Wed. and Fri. 9:30am-1am, Thurs. 9:30am-12:30am, Sat. 11am-2am. Dancing Wed.-Sat. Cover Wed.-Sat. $4-5; no cover Mon.-Tues.) Students frequent the **Continental Club,** 1315 S. Congress (441-2444), for everything from punk-a-billy and new wave to folk music. (Cover $4.) Wander along 6th St., especially on weeknights when there are no crowds and no cover charges, to sample the bands from the sidewalk. For solid Texan music, try **Raven's Garage** (482-9272), on Red River just north of 6th St., where bands rev up in an old garage. Women should be careful as this street is not well lit. On campus, the **Cactus Cafe,** 24th and Guadalupe (471-8228), hosts different musicians almost every night.

(Hours vary, but usually open 8am-1am. Cover $2-12.) Next door, the **Texas Tavern** (471-5651) favors country music and serves fast food. (Hours vary, but usually open 11:30am-1:45am. Cover $2-5.) Those journeying out to Lake Travis should seek out the **Oasis Cantina De Lago**, 6550 Comanche Trail (266-2441), a restaurant and bar with a gorgeous sunset view. (Open Sun.-Thurs. 11am-9pm, Fri.-Sat. 11am-10pm. No cover.)

From early May through late August, the **Zilker Park Hillside Theater**, 2000 Barton Springs Rd. (499-2000), on Rte. 2244, produces free variety shows and concerts under the stars. Shows usually start between 7 and 9pm. The **Austin Symphony Orchestra** sponsors concerts of all kinds in the amphitheater at 1101 Red River Rd. (476-6064), downtown, while UT's **Performing Arts Center**, 23rd at E. Campus Dr. (471-1444), screens major touring theater companies, operas, and the like.

Film fans can try the **Varsity Repertory Theater**, 2402 Guadalupe (474-4351), which hosts new and unusual movies and foreign films. The historic **Paramount Theater**, 713 Congress (472-5470), has a daily double-feature oldies film festival (admission $4, seniors, students, and ages under 12 $2.50).

San Antonio

The Alamo stands as a ghostly historical reminder haunting the center of San Antonio, right next to the posh, lively Rivercenter shopping mall. Many of the famous battle's descendants still live and remember in the city; now, however, European and Mexican American culture coexist peacefully, shaping the politics and economy of San Antonio. Spanish architecture, south-of-the-border food, and an ethnically diverse population give the city its distinctive appeal.

Practical Information

Emergency: 911.

Visitor Information Center: 317 Alamo Plaza (299-8155), downtown across from the Alamo. Open daily 9am-5:30pm.

San Antonio International Airport (821-3411), north of town. Served by I-410 and Hwy. 281. Cabs to downtown $11.25. Super Van Shuttle departs for downtown every 15 min. 6am-6:45pm, every 45 min. 6:45pm-midnight. Fare $6, children $3.

Amtrak: 1174 E. Commerce St. (223-3226 or 800-872-7245), off the I-37 Montana St. exit. To: Dallas (7 per week, 8 hr., $43); Houston (3 per week, 4 hr., $42); El Paso (3 per week, 11½ hr., $106).

Greyhound: 500 N. Saint Mary's St. (270-5800; 270-5860 in Spanish), or 151 Crossroads Blvd. (732-7441), 1 mi. south of I-10. To: Houston (10 per day, 4 hr., $24); Dallas (13 per day, 6 hr., $32); El Paso (5 per day, 11 hr., $72). Open 24 hr.

Public Transport: VIA Metropolitan Transit, 112 Soledad (227-2020), between Commerce and Houston. Buses operate 5am-10:30pm, but many routes stop at 5pm. Inconvenient service to outlying areas. Fare 40¢ (more with zone changes), express 75¢. Cheap (10¢) and frequent streetcars operate downtown Mon.-Fri. 7am-8pm, Sat. 9am-8pm. Office open daily 6am-8pm.

Taxi: Yellow Cab, 226-4242. Checker Cab, 222-2151. Both $2.50 for first mi., $1 each additional mi.

Car Rental: Chuck's Rent-A-Clunker, 3249 SW Military Dr. (922-9464). $13-25 per day with 100 free mi. Must be 19 with a major credit card. Open Mon.-Fri. 8am-7pm, Sat. 9am-4pm, Sun. 10am-6pm.

Help Lines: Rape Crisis Center, 349-7273. Open 24 hr. Presa Community Service Center, 532-5295. Referrals and transport for elderly and disabled. Open Mon.-Fri. 8:30am-noon and 1-4pm.

Time Zone: Central (1 hr. behind Eastern).

Post Office: 615 E. Houston (227-3399), 1 block from the Alamo. Open Mon.-Fri. 8:30am-5:30pm. General Delivery: 10410 Perrin-Beitel Rd. (650-1630); really in the boondocks—about 15 mi. northeast of town. **ZIP code:** 78205.

Area Code: 512.

San Antonio (pop. 951,000) stands about 80 mi. south of Austin and about 150 mi. north of Nuevo Laredo on the Mexican border. I-35 and I-10 meet just south of town and I-37 shoots southeast to Corpus Christi. The **Riverwalk** and its canal form a rough circle in the center of town. **The Alamo** (northeast), **Hemisfair Plaza** (southeast) and **La Villita** (south) lie just outside the circle. **Commerce Street** connects downtown to **Market Square** and **El Mercado**, about 10 blocks west.

Accommodations and Camping

Since San Antonio is a popular city, downtown hotel managers have no reason to keep prices low. Further, San Antonio's dearth of rivers and lakes means that there are few good campsites. The best value in public camping is about 30 mi. north of town at Canyon Lake in **Guadalupe River State Park** (512-438-2656; sites $4). Inexpensive motels cluster along Broadway between downtown and Brackenridge Park. Drivers should follow I-35 north to find cheaper and often safer accomodations within 15 mi. of town.

Bullis House Inn San Antonio International Hostel (AYH), 621 Pierce St. (223-9426), 2 mi. northeast of the Alamo, across the street from Fort Sam Houston. From downtown take bus #11 to Grayson St. and get off at the stop after the Stop & Go store. Friendly hostel in a quiet neighborhood. Cramped but clean rooms. Pool, kitchen. Lockout 11am-5pm. Curfew 11pm, but night key available ($5 deposit). $10, nonmembers $12. Private singles from $17, nonmembers from $19. Doubles from $24, nonmembers from $26. Linen $2. Fills in summer.

Elmira Motor Inn, 1126 East Elmira (222-9463), about 3 blocks east of St. Mary's, a little over 1 mi. north of downtown. Large, clean rooms. More luxurious than most at this price. Singles $24. Doubles $26.

The Traveler's Hotel, 220 N. Broadway (226-4381), about 5 blocks northwest of the Alamo. Comfortable but rather gloomy rooms and eccentric residents. Large singles $16.50, with private bath $22.50. Doubles $21, with private bath $27.

Motel 6, 138 North W. White Rd. (333-1850), 4 mi. east of downtown near I-10. Take bus #24 from downtown. Clean, though sparsely furnished. TV and pool. Singles $24. Doubles $30. Reservations required.

El Tejas Motel, 2727 Roosevelt Ave. (533-7123), at E. Southcross, 3 mi. south of downtown near the missions. Take bus #42. Family-run with some waterbeds, color TV, and a pool. Somewhat musty rooms have playing-card walls. Singles $22. Doubles $28. Extra $2 on weekends.

San Antonio KOA, 602 Gembler Rd. (224-9296), 6 mi. from downtown. Take bus #24 ("Industrial Park") from the corner of Houston and Alamo downtown. Showers, laundry, A/C, pool, playground, movies, fishing pond. Sites $12.75 for 2, each additional person $2.

Yogi Bear's Jellystone Park, 2617 Roosevelt Ave. (532-8310), 3 mi. south of downtown. Smarter than the average park. Showers, laundry, pool, spa, playground. Next to golf course and restaurants. Open daily 8am-8pm. Tent sites $12 for 2. RV sites $16 for 2. Each additional person $2. Children free.

Food

Downtown San Antonio's Mexican food goes down disappointingly blandly. Explore the area east of S. Alamo and S. Saint Mary's St. for better Mexican food and barbecue. The Riverwalk abounds with waterfront cafés. **Pig Stand** diners offer decent, cheap food all over this part of Texas; the branch at 801 S. Presa, off S. Alamo, is open 24 hr. North of town, many East Asian restaurants line Broadway across from Breckenridge.

Casa Río, 430 E. Commerce (225-6718). Brightly decorated tables along the river, serenading mariachis, tasty Mexican cuisine, and a bargain to boot. Entrees $4-7. A la carte items $1.50-

3. Open Mon.-Thurs. 11:30am-9:30pm, Fri.-Sat. 11:30am-10pm, Sun. noon-9:30pm. Usually crowded—large parties should make reservations.

Big Bend, 511 Riverwalk, near the Hyatt. Best *fajitas* on the river. A bit expensive, but large portions and good atmosphere compensate. Margaritas $2, draft beer $1 during Happy Hour (Mon.-Fri. 2-7pm). Open Sun.-Thurs. 9am-1am, Fri.-Sat. 9am-2am.

Hung Fong Chinese and American Restaurant, 3624 Broadway, 2 mi. north of downtown. Take bus #14. The oldest Chinese restaurant in San Antonio. Consistently good and crowded. Big portions. Try the egg rolls and lemon chicken. Meals $3-8. Open Mon.-Thurs. 11am-11pm, Fri. 11am-midnight, Sat. 11:30am-midnight, Sun. 11:30am-11pm.

Josephine Street Cafe, 400 East Josephine (224-6169), just northeast of downtown in a poor neighborhood. The semi-anonymous local hangout immortalized as the sultry neon diner on tourist posters. Steaks, chicken, fish, and Cajun dishes $5-10. Open Mon.-Thurs. 11am-10pm, Fri. 11am-11pm.

Sights

The Missions

The four missions along the San Antonio River once formed the basis of San Antonio; the city still preserves their remains in the **San Antonio Missions National Historical Park.** To reach the missions by car or bike, follow the blue-and-white "Mission Trail" signs beginning on S. Saint Mary's St. downtown. **San Antonio City Tours** (680-8724), in front of the Alamo, provides a two-hour tour of all the missions and the Alamo for $10, while **Tours for Kids,** 15411 Aviole Way (496-6030), offers what you might guess (9am-3pm). Bus #42 stops right in front of Mission San José, within walking distance of Mission Concepción. All of the missions are open daily 9am to 6pm; September to May from 8am to 5pm. For general information on the missions, call 229-5701.

Mission Concepción, 807 Mission Rd. (533-7109), 4 mi. south of the Alamo off E. Mitchell St. The oldest unrestored church in North America (1731). Traces of the once-colorful frescoes still visible. Sun. mass 5:50pm.

Mission San José, 6529 San Jose Blvd. (922-0543). The "Queen of the Missions" (1720), with its own irrigation system, a church with a gorgeous sculpted rose window, and numerous restored buildings. The largest of San Antonio's missions, it provides the best sense of these self-contained Spanish institutions. Catholic services (including a noon "Mariachi Mass") are held 5 times on Sunday.

Espada Aqueduct, 10040 Espada Rd, about 4 mi. south of Mission San José. Features a tiny chapel and a functioning mile-long aqueduct, built between 1731 and 1745.

Mission San Juan Capistrano (534-3161) and **Mission San Francisco de la Espada** (627-2064), both a swallow's flight off Roosevelt Ave., 10 mi. south of downtown. Smaller and simpler than the other missions, but best at evoking the sense of isolation these imperial outposts once knew.

Downtown Tourist District

"Be silent, friend, here heroes died to blaze a trail for other men." Disobeying orders to retreat with their cannons, the defenders of the Alamo, outnumbered 20 to one, held off the Mexican army for 12 days. Then, on the morning of the thirteenth day, Mexican buglers blew the infamous *deguello*—"No Quarter, No Prisoners." Forty-six days later General Sam Houston's small army defeated the Mexicans at San Jacinto amidst cries of "Remember the Alamo!" Now only tourists attack the **Alamo** (225-1391), at the center of Alamo Plaza, by the junction of Houston and Alamo St., and sno-cone vendors are the only defenders. A single chapel and a barracks preserved by the state are all that remain of the former Spanish mission. Adobe. (Open Mon.-Sat. 9am-5:30pm, Sun. 10am-5:30pm. Free.) The **Long Barracks Museum and Library,** 315 Alamo Plaza (224-1836), houses Alamo memorabilia. (Open Mon.-Sat. 9am-5:30pm.)

Heading southwest from the Alamo, black signs indicate access points to the **Paseo del Río (Riverwalk),** with shaded stone pathways following a winding canal built in the 1930s by the WPA. Lined with picturesque gardens, shops, and cafés, and connecting most of the major downtown sights, the Riverwalk is well-patrolled, safe, and especially beautiful at night. Ride the entire length of the Riverwalk by taking a boat ($2, children $1) from the front of the Hilton Hotel. The **Alamo Imax Theater** (225-4629), in River Center, shows a docudrama Alamo film on its six-story screen. (7 ws 10am-7pm. Admission $5.75, seniors and military $4.75, children $3.75.) Nearby and newly transformed, **La Villita** (299-8610) houses crafts shops and art studios. (Open daily 10am-6pm.)

Hemisfair Plaza, on S. Alamo (229-8570), the site of the 1968 World's Fair, is another top tourist spot. The city often uses the plaza, surrounded by restaurants, museums, and historic houses, for special events. The **Tower of the Americas,** 200 S. Alamo (299-8615), rises 750 ft. above the dusty plains, dominating the meager skyline. Get a broad view of the city from the observation deck on top. (Open daily 8am-11pm. Admission $2, seniors $1.25, ages 4-11 $1.) Within the plaza stroll through the free museums, including the **Institute of Texan Cultures,** (226-7651; open Tues.-Sun. 9am-5pm; parking $1) and the **Mexican Cultural Institute** (227-0123), filled entirely with modern Mexican art (open Tues.-Fri. 10am-7pm, Sat.-Sun. noon-6pm). On a spot near Hemisfair on Commerce St., across from the San Antonio Convention Center, German Americans erected **St. Joseph's Church** in 1868. Since this beautiful old church stubbornly refused to move, a local department store chain built their establishment around it.

A few blocks west, between Commerce and Dolorosa St. at Laredo, is the Main Plaza and city hall. Directly behind the city hall lies the **Spanish Governor's Palace,** 105 Plaza de Armas (224-0601). Built in Colonial Spanish style in 1772, the house has carved doors and an enclosed, shaded patio and garden. (Open Mon.-Sat. 9am-5pm, Sun. 10am-5pm. Admission $1, children 50¢.)

Market Square, 514 W. Commerce (229-8600), is a center for the sale of both schlocky souvenirs and handmade local crafts. The walkway **El Mercado** continues the block-long retail stretch. At the nearby **Farmers Market,** you can buy produce, Mexican chilis, pastries, candy, and spices. Come late in the day, when prices are lower and vendors willing to haggle. (Open June-Aug. daily 10am-8pm; Sept.-May daily 10am-6pm.)

San Antonio North and South

Head to **Brackenridge Park,** main entrance 3900 N. Broadway (735-8641), 5 mi. north of the Alamo, for a day of unusual sight-seeing. The 343-acre showplace includes an aerial tramway (rides $1.75), a Japanese sunken garden, stone bridges, and a miniature railway. Also in the park, the **San Antonio Zoo,** 3903 N. Saint Mary's St. (734-7183), is one of the country's largest, housing over 3500 animals from 800 species in natural settings, as well as an extensive African mammal exhibit. (Open daily 9:30am-6:30pm; Nov.-March daily 9:30am-5pm. Admission $5, seniors $3.50, ages 3-11 $1.) At the **Witte Museum,** 3801 Broadway (226-5544), permanent exhibits focus on Texas wildlife while curators mount new shows. (Open Mon. and Wed.-Sat. 10am-6pm, Tues. 10am-9pm, Sun. noon-6pm; off-season closes at 5pm. Admission $3, seniors and students $1.50, ages 6-12 $1. Free Thurs. 3-9pm.) The 38-acre **Botanical Center,** 555 Funston Pl. (821-5115), 1 mi. east of Brackenridge Park, includes the largest conservatory in the Southwest. (Open Tues.-Sun. 9am-6pm. Admission $2.50.)

The **San Antonio Museum of Art,** 200 W. Jones Ave., just north of the city center, inhabits a restored Lone Star Brewery building. As in most breweries, towers, turrets, and spacious rooms decorated with ornate columns house Taxan furniture and pre-Columbian, Native American, Spanish Colonial, and Mexican folk art. (Open Mon. and Wed.-Sat. 10am-5pm, Tues. 10am-9pm, Sun. noon-6pm. Admission $3.50, seniors $2, students $1.50, ages 6-12 $1. Free Tues. 3-9pm.) The former estate of Marion Koogler McNay, the **McNay Art Institute,** 6000 N. New Braunfels (824-5368), displays a collection of mostly post-impressionist European art. It also has a charming inner courtyard with sculpture fountains and meticulous landscaping. (Open Tues.-Sat. 9am-5pm, Sun. 2-5pm. Free.)

The **Lone Star Brewing Company,** 600 Lone Star Blvd. (226-8301), is about 2 mi. south of the city. Trigger-happy Albert Friedrich had managed to accumulate a collection of 3500 animal heads, horns and antlers when he opened the Buckhorn in 1887. What better place to put them than in his bar? Now you have to look at them on tours which leave every 30 minutes, and provide beer samples. As in most breweries, you'll see lots of taxidermy but won't learn how the brewery works. (Open daily 9:30am-5pm. Admission $2.50, seniors $2, ages 6-11 $1.)

Entertainment

Celebrating its centennial in April 1991, the 10-day **Fiesta San Antonio** ushers in spring as it does each year. Concerts, parades, and plenty of Tex-Mex food commemorate the victory at San Jacinto and honor the heroes at the Alamo. The 100th anniversary celebration will feature sky divers and a dramatic reenactment of the first parade in 1891.

For fun after dark, stroll down the Riverwalk. For those who prefer just looking at pictures of fun after dark, peruse the Friday *Express* or the weekly *Current* as a guide to concerts and entertainment. **Floore's Country Store,** 14464 Old Bandera Rd. (695-8827), toward the northwestern outskirts, is an old hangout of country music star Willie Nelson. Dancing takes place outside on a large cement platform. (Cover varies.) **Mendiola's Ballroom,** 16490 I-35 south (622-9204), is the city's best Mexican dance hall. On Saturdays, the doors are thrown open and dancers of all ages crowd the gigantic floor. (Take I-35 south from downtown. Admission $5.) Some of the best jazz in the city plays at **Jim Cullen's Landing,** 123 Losoya (222-1234), in the Hyatt downtown. The music inside starts at 9pm and goes until around 2am. A jazz quartet performs on Sunday nights. The riverside café outside opens at 11:30am. (Cover $3.)

Corpus Christi

Located smack dab on the Gulf of Mexico shoreline, Corpus Christi (pop. 225,000) combines longhorn pride with the attractions of a coastal town. Local eagerness for tourism, fueled by a downturn of the petroleum industry, has added to the town's drawing power, particularly for the budget traveler. The part of Corpus Christi discovered by Spanish explorer Alonzo de Pineda in 1515 now serves as a base for the two major industries of petroleum and agriculture, while remaining the hub of city life. Corpus Christi looks toward the water with its restaurants reflecting a unique blend of Tex-Mex and seafood tastes. Because Corpus Christi is essentially an outdoor city, come prepared to swim, sail, waterski, golf, or otherwise enjoy the pier. Sunshine certainly compensates for what Corpus Christi lacks in high culture.

Practical Information

Emergency: 911

Visitor Information: Convention and Visitors Bureau, 1201 N. Shoreline (882-5603), where I-37 meets the water. Piles of pamphlets, bus schedules, and local maps. Open Mon.-Fri. 8:30am-5pm. Weekend information available at the **Corpus Christi Museum,** 1900 N. Chaparral (883-2862). Open Sat. 10am-5pm, Sun. 1-5pm. The **Information Line** (854-8540) provides information on events, restaurants, clubs, and shopping.

Corpus Christi International Airport, 1000 International Dr. (289-2675), west of downtown, bordered by Rte. 44 (Agnes St.) and Joe Mireur Rd. Call your airline for reservations and schedule information. Cabs to downtown about $7.

Greyhound: 702 N. Chaparral (882-2516), at Starr downtown. To: Dallas (5 per day, 8 hr., $51); Houston (14 per day, 5 hr., $28); Austin (6 per day, 5 hr., $29). Open 24 hr.

Public Transport: Regional Transit Authority (The "B"), 882-1722. Pick up route maps and schedules at the main station on the corner of Water and Schatzel St. or at the visitors bureau.

Central transfer point is City Hall, downtown. Service Mon.-Sat. except holidays until around 8pm. Fare 50¢, seniors, disabled, students, and children 25¢.

Taxi: Island Shuttle Cab Company, 949-8850. Fare $1 per mi. Major credit cards accepted.

Car Rental: Thrifty, 1928 N. Padre Island Dr. (289-0041), at Leopard St. $33 per day, 150 free mi. each day, 20¢ each additional mi. Weekends $19 per day, 100 free mi. each day. Open Mon.-Fri. 6am-9pm, Sat.-Sun. 8am-9pm. Must be 21 with a major credit card. Under 25 surcharge $3.

Help Lines: 24-Hour Crisis Hotline, 887-9816. **Crisis Services,** 887-9818. **Women's Shelter,** 881-8888. Open 24 hr.

Post Office: 809 Nueces Bay Blvd. (886-2200). Open Mon.-Fri. 8am-5pm, Sat. 7:30am-noon. **ZIP code:** 78469.

Area Code: 512.

Corpus Christi's tourist district follows **Shoreline Drive,** which borders the gulf coast. The downtown business district lies 1 mi. west. Unfortunately, the streets don't quite follow a grid pattern, and the largely one-way roads downtown may frustrate drivers, sending them in circles up and down the bluff. **Agnes Street** and **Leopard Street** are the easiest routes to follow when approaching downtown from the west. Agnes St. goes directly downtown from the airport; Leopard follows a parallel path from most of the cheaper motels. Both streets end within one block of Shoreline Dr.

Accommodations and Food

Sandwiched between the visitors bureau and the ultra-posh Wyndham Hotel is the **Sand and Sea Budget Inn,** 1013 N. Shoreline Dr. (882-6518), where I-37 meets the water. Rooms have a small foyer, plush carpet, and you can't beat the location. Since there are only four singles, try to make a reservation. (Singles $24. Doubles $30, with bay view $35. Key deposit $5.)

While the northwest section of Corpus Christi lacks the convenience and public transport of downtown lodging, it does have the best motel bargains. Find ecosleep at the **Ecomotel,** 6033 Leopard St. (289-1116). Exit I-37 north at Corn Products Rd. and turn left at light. By bus, take #27 from downtown right to the motel: Be sure to check a schedule, since the bus runs infrequently. Clean, ecocomfortable, dimly lit rooms—you may have to turn on the TV to read these words. (Singles $20. Doubles $28.) Nearby is the standard yet reliable **Motel 6,** 845 Lantana St. (289-9397). Take exit 3B from I-37 north, 4B from I-37 south. (Singles $20. Doubles $27.) Campers should head to **Padre Island National Seashore** or **Mustang State Park** (see Padre Island National Seashore below). Also, **Nueces River City Park** (241-1464), north on I-37 (exit 16 at Nueces River), has free tent sites and 3-day RV permits.

Corpus Christi's downtown area transubstantiates into many inexpensive and tasty eating establishments. **Bahia,** 224 Chaparral (884-6555), serves simple but rib-sticking Mexican breakfasts and lunches. The authentic food compensates for the tacky decor. Try *nopalitos* (cactus and egg on a tortilla; $1.25) or a taco and two enchiladas with rice beans, tea, and dessert ($3.75). Live entertainment rocks the house on Friday from 7 to 9pm. (Open Mon.-Thurs. 7am-3pm, Fri. 7am-3pm and 6-9pm, Sat. 8am-3pm.) Just down the street, the **Sea Gulf Villa Cafe,** 412 N. Chaparral, lets you build your own breakfast *tacquito* (any 4 items $1.25) or try three bean, cheese, and veggie *chalupas* for $3.25. Large portions and quick service. (Open Mon.-Sat. 7am-3pm.) Run aground the **Cajun Reef,** 1002 N. Chaparral, and its all-you-can-eat lunch buffet ($4.80). Run-down exterior but inviting interior. Dinner entrees run $8-10. (Open Mon.-Thurs. 11:30am-9pm, Fri.-Sat. 11:30am-10pm.)

Corpus Christi is the home of **Whataburger,** a chain of superior fast-food joints. With 23 locations in the city, there is ample chance to sample their made-to-order burgers ($2) or malts ($1.25). Most locations open 24 hr.

Few restaurants lie within walking distance of the Ecomotel and other northwest motels except for the **Little Venice Restaurant,** inside the Ecomotel, which offers an Italian all-you-can-eat buffet for $3.75. The filling breakfast of pancakes, eggs, and ham or sausage costs just $2. (Open Mon.-Sat. 6am-10pm, Sun. 6am-2pm.)

Sights

Corpus Christi's shoreline seems ready-made for tourists; wide sidewalks with distance markers (for joggers) and graduated steps leading up from the water (for more sedentary sea-gazers) border almost 2 mi. of Corpus Christi Bay. More tourism than industry fills the docks and piers, with restaurant showboats and sightseeing ferries netting a daily catch of the finless *photo visitaurus ridiculus.*

Sights are concentrated along the gulf shore. On the north end of Shoreline Dr., the Convention Center houses the **Art Museum of South Texas,** 1902 N. Shoreline (884-3844), whose small but impressive collection includes works by Monet, Matisse, Picasso, Rembrandt, Goya, and Ansel Adams. Disabled access. (Open Tues.-Fri. 10am-5pm, Sat. 10am-6pm, Sun. 1-6pm. Free.) **The Harbor Playhouse,** 1 Bayfront Park (882-3356), less than 100 yds. away, presents classic and contemporary plays as well as musicals; during the summer it usually offers a series of melodramas. A quirky children's theater gives weekend matinee performances at the same location. (Tickets $8-10 for professional shows. Performances Fri.-Sat. at 8pm, Sun. at 3pm.) Across the street is the quirky **Corpus Christi Museum,** 1900 N. Chaparral (883-2862), with quirky hands-on animal exhibits for quirky kids. (Open Tues.-Fri. 10am-5pm, Sat.-Sun. noon-5pm. Free.) Two blocks to the southwest sits **Heritage Park** (883-0639), a neighborhood with the old homes of nine of the city's patriarchs, all open to visitors. Tours are quick (about 15 min.) and fun. (Generally open Mon.-Fri. 10am-4pm, but hours vary in each house. Tours Sat. at 12:30 and 12:45pm. Call 883-0639 for group tours. Free.)

Corpus Christi works to attract shoppers in an effort to pump money into its weary economy. Take the **trolley** (289-2600) from the north shoreline to the **Sunrise** or **Padre Island Mall.** The trolley travels along the posh and scenic Ocean Dr. The pseudo-old-time trolleys run every hour from the motels on Shoreline Dr. to the malls. Trolley #72 serves the malls; #73 gives scenic tours. Catch both at Bayfront Plaza or beachfront hotels. (Fare Mon.-Fri. 50¢, Sat. 10¢.)

Padre Island National Seashore

One of only eight national seashores, Padre Island National Seashore (PINS) boasts unadulterated seascapes, clean sand dunes, perfectly preserved wildlife refuges, and an ideal environment for jet skiing and surf sailing. Condos and tacky souvenir shops have sprung up around the junction of the Padre Isles and the John F. Kennedy Causeway, the only access route; yet, after about 4 mi. they disappear back into the depths whence they came. The majority of the 80 mi. of seashore remains preserved.

Driving and hiking along the beach prove two of the most popular activities at PINS. Because of the loose sand, four-wheel drive vehicles are needed to traverse the length of the beach. Cars must stop 30 mi. shy of the end of the national seashore at the Mansfield Cut, since there is no bridge across the channel. Though the seashore has no hiking trails, the **Malaquite** (pronounced MAL-a-kee) **Ranger Station** (949-8173), 3½ mi. south of the park entrance, conducts hikes and programs throughout the year. (Call 949-8060 for information on group programs.) They also provide first aid and emergency assistance.

Entry into PINS costs $3. For just a daytrip to the beach, however, go to the beautiful and uncrowded **North Beach** (24 mi. from Corpus Christi), which lies just before the $3 checkpoint.

The headquarters for PINS lie, ironically, outside the island in nearby Corpus Christi. The **PINS Visitors Center,** 9405 S. Padre Island Dr. (512-937-2621), pro-

LET'S GO Travel
1991 CATALOGUE

LET'S PACK IT UP

Let's Go Pack/Suitcase:
Lightweight and versatile. Carry-on size
(24" x 14" x 10"). Hideaway suspension (internal
frame). Waterproof Cordura nylon. Lifetime
guarantee. Detachable day-pack.
Navy blue or grey.

10014 Suitcase   **$144.95**
Free shoulder strap and
Let's Go travel diary.

Passport/Money Case:
Zippered pouch of waterproof nylon.
71/2" x 41/2". Navy or grey.
10011 Passport Case   **$6.50**

Undercover Neck Pouch:
Ripstop nylon and soft Cambrelle. 61/2" x 5".
Two separate pockets. Black or tan.
10012 Neck Pouch   **$6.95**

Fanny Pack:
Pack cloth nylon. Three compartments.
Charcoal or Marine Blue.
10013 Fanny Pack   **$13.95**

Let's Go Travel Books:
Europe; USA; Britain/Ireland;
France; Italy; Spain/Portugal/Morocco; Greece;
Israel/Egypt; Mexico; California/Hawaii; Pacific
Northwest; London; New York City.
1016 Specify USA; Europe   **$13.9!**
1017 Specify Country   **$12.9!**
1018 Specify New York or London $9.9!
This is $1.00 off the cover price!

International Youth Hostel Guide for
Europe and the Mediterranean:
Lists over 3,000 hostels. A must.
10015 IYHG   **$10.9!**
FREE map of hostels worldwide.

Sleepsack: (Required at all hostels)
78" x 30" with 18" pillow pocket. Durable
poly/cotton, folds to pouch size. Washable.
Doubles as a sleeping bag liner.
10010 Sleepsack   **$13.9!**

LET'S GO® Travel
We wrote the book on budget travel

1991-1992 American Youth Hostel Card

(AYH): Recommended for every hosteler, this card is required by many hostels and brings discounts at others. Applicants must be US residents. Valid internationally.

10022	**Adult AYH (ages 18-55)**	**$25.00**
10035	**Youth AYH (under age 18)**	**$10.00**
10023	**Plastic Case**	**$0.75**

FREE directory of hostels in the USA.

LET'S SEE SOME I.D.

1991 International Student Identification Card

(ISIC): Provides discounts on accommodations, cultural events, air fares and, this year, increased accident/medical insurance. Valid from 9/1/90–12/31/91.

10020	**ISIC**	**$14.00**

FREE "International Student Travel Guide" and insurance information.

1991 International Teacher Identification Card

(ITIC): Similar benefits to the ISIC.

10024	**ITIC**	**$15.00**

FREE "International Student Travel Guide" and insurance information.

1991 Youth International Education Exchange Card

(YIEE): Similar benefits to the ISIC. Available for non-students under the age of 26. Valid by calendar year.

10021	**YIEE**	**$14.00**

FREE "Discounts for Youth Travel."

Eurail Pass: the best way to travel Europe.

First Class

10025	15 Day	**$390.**
10026	21 Day	**$498.**
10027	1 Month	**$616.**
10028	2 Months	**$840.**
10029	3 Months	**$1042.**

Flexipass

10030	5 Days within 15	**$230.**
10031	9 Days within 21	**$398.**
10032	14 Days in 1 month	**$498.**

Eurail Youth Pass (Under 26)

10033	1 Month	**$425.**
10034	2 Months	**$560.**
10036	15 days in 3 months	**$340.**
10037	30 days in 3 months	**$540.**

Child Passes (age 4-12) also available.

All Eurail Pass orders include FREE: Eurail Map, Pocket Timetable and Traveler's Guide.

LET'S GO® Travel

One source for all your travel needs

LET'S GET STARTED

PLEASE PRINT OR TYPE. Incomplete applications will be returned.

International Student/Teacher Identity Card (ISIC / ITIC) application enclose:
- ❶ Dated proof of current FULL-TIME status: letter from registrar or administration or copy of transcript or proof of payment.
- ❷ One picture (1½" x 2") signed on the reverse side. Applicants must be at least 12 years old.

Youth International Exchange Card (YIEE) application enclose:
- ❶ Proof of birthdate (copy of passport or birth certificate). Applicants must be age 12 – 25.
- ❷ One picture (1½" x 2") signed on the reverse side.
- ❸ Passport number _____ ❹ Sex: M   F

Last Name_____First Name_____

Street_____

Continental U.S. Addresses only. We do not ship to P.O. Boxes

City_____State_____Zip Code_____

Phone (   )_____—_____Citizenship_____

School/College_____Date Trip Begins_____/_____/_____

ITEM NUMBER	DESCRIPTION	QUAN-TITY	UNIT OR SET PRICE	TOTAL PRICE
		Total Price		
		Total Shipping and Handling		
		Optional Rush Handling (add $9.95)		
		Mass. Residents (5% sales tax on Gear, Books & Maps)		
			TOTAL:	

Shipping and Handling
If your order totals: Add
Up to 30.00 $2.00
30.01 to 100.00 $3.25
Over 100.00 $5.25

Please allow 2-3 weeks for delivery.
RUSH ORDERS DELIVERED WITHIN ONE WEEK OF OUR RECEIPT.
Enclose check or money order payable to Harvard Student Agencies, Inc.

LET'S GO Travel

Harvard Student Agencies, Inc. Thayer Hall–B Cambridge, MA 02138
(617) 495-9649   1-800-5LETSGO

vides information on weather conditions, safety precautions, and sight-seeing opportunities in nearby **Mustang State Park** and **Port Aransas**. (Open Mon.-Sat. 8:30am-4:30pm.) Within the national seashore, the **Malaquite Visitors Center** (512-949-8068), about 14 mi. south of the JFK Causeway turn-off, supplies similar information while also offering exhibits and wildlife guidebooks. (Open June-Aug. daily 9am-6pm; Sept-May daily 9am-4pm.)

The **PINS Campground** (949-8173) consists of an asphalt area for RVs, with restrooms and cold-rinse showers. (Sites $4.) Five mi. of beach are devoted to primitive camping, and free camping is permitted wherever vehicle driving is allowed. Near the national seashore is the **Balli County Park**, on Park Rd. 22 (949-8121), 3½ mi. from the JFK Causeway. Running water, electricity, and hot showers are available. (3-day max. stay. Sites $4, with hookup $8.50. Water key deposit $5.) Those who value creature comforts should head a few miles farther north to the **Mustang State Park Campground** (749-5246), on Park Rd. 53, 6 mi. from the JFK Causeway, for electricity, running water, dump stations, restrooms, hot showers, shelters, trailer sites, and picnic tables. Make reservations; there's often a waiting list, especially in winter when the "snowbirds" (northern tourists) arrive. (Entry fee $2. Camping fee $9.)

Motorists enter the PINS via the JFK Causeway, which runs through the Flour Bluff area of Corpus Christi. PINS is difficult to reach by public transportation. Corpus Christi bus #10 (which makes only 2 trips per day Mon.-Fri.) takes you to the tip of the Padre Isles (get off at Padre Isles Park-n-Ride). To reach the national seashore, call the **Island Shuttle Service** (949-8850; fare $1 per mi.). Note that round-trip distance from the bus stop to the Malaquite Visitors Center is over 30 mi. There is no post office on the PINS; mail should be sent general delivery to Flour Bluff sub-station, 10139 Security Dr. (937-3530), Corpus Christi. (Open Mon.-Fri. 8am-5pm, Sat. 10am-noon.) The **ZIP code** is 78418.

Houston

Houston began in the wake of Texas's battle for independence from Mexico when two New York speculators bought 2000 acres of land on Buffalo Bayou. In just nine years the settlement emerged as a major cotton shipping port, only to grow just as rapidly into an energy center after the discovery of an oil gusher in 1901. Not surprisingly, Houston's geographical expansion parallels its history of quick economic growth; in all, the city covers almost 500 sq. mi. The absence of zoning laws, combined with a recklessly swift building boom in the 70s and early 80s, has resulted in a peculiar architectural mix. A museum, an historic home, a 7-Eleven, and a mini-mall may share the same city block, while the downtown area showcases an oil-fed array of modern skyscrapers.

Practical Information

Emergency: 911.

Greater Houston Convention and Visitors Bureau: 3300 Main St. (523-5050), at Stuart, 10 blocks south of I-45 outside of the downtown area. Take any bus serving the southern portion of Main St. (#7, 8, 14, 25, 65, 70, or 78). Open Mon.-Fri. 8:30am-5pm.

Travelers Aid: 1600 Louisiana St. (223-8946), at the YMCA. Open daily 6am-midnight. **24-hr. help line:** 668-0911. Offices also at 2630 Westridge St., off Main St. near the Astrodome, and at the Greyhound station and the Houston Intercontinental Airport.

Houston Intercontinental Airport: (230-3000), 25 mi. north of downtown. Get to the city center via the **Airport Express** (523-8888). Buses depart every 30 min. between 7am and 12:30am (fare $8.50, children $4.25). **Hobby Airport** is 9 mi. south of downtown, just west of I-45. Take bus #73 to Texas Medical Center and then catch any bus to downtown. **Hobby Airport Limousine Service** leaves Hobby for downtown every 30 min. between 7:30am and 11:30pm (fare $4.35, ages under 13 free). **Southwest Airlines** (237-1221) has commuter flights to most major Texas cities. Flights from Hobby to San Antonio, Dallas, and Austin as low as $24 one way with 21-day advance purchase. Standard one way fare to San Antonio, Austin, or Dallas $69.

Amtrak: 902 Washington Ave. (224-1577 or 800-872-7245), in a rough neighborhood. During the day, catch a bus by walking west on Washington (away from downtown) to the intersection with Houston Ave. At night, call a cab. To: San Antonio (3 per week, 4 hr., $42); New Orleans (3 per week, 9 hr., $68); El Paso (3 per week, 16 hr., $132).

Greyhound/Trailways: 2121 S. Main St. (222-1161), on or near several local bus routes. Walk west toward downtown on Texas to the intersection of Main St. for local buses. Unsafe area. To: San Antonio (6 per day, 4 hr., $27); New Orleans (8 per day, 9 hr., $40); Dallas (5 per day, 5 hr., $24-32); El Paso (4 per day, 16 hr., $90); Corpus Christi (5 per day, 5 hr., $28); Galveston (5 per day, 1½ hr., $9). Open 24 hr.

Public Transport: Metro Bus System. For route and schedule information, call 635-4000 (Mon.-Fri. 6am-8pm, Sat.-Sun. 8am-5pm). An all-encompassing system that can take you from NASA (15 mi. southeast of town) to Katy (25 mi. west of town). Get system maps at the Customer Services Center, 912 Dallas St. (658-0854; open Mon.-Fri. 10am-6pm). Individual route maps can also be obtained at Metro headquarters, 500 Jefferson at Smith, 12th floor; the Houston Public Library, 500 McKinney at Bagby (236-1313); or at the Metro Ride store at Fannin and Capitol. Buses operate 6am-midnight. Fare 70¢, zone changes 10¢.

Taxi: Yellow Cab, 236-1111. Base rate $2.40 plus $1.15 per mi.

Car Rental: Rent-A-Heap Cheap, 5722 Southwest Freeway (977-7771). Cars from $25 a day with 100 free mi., 25¢ each additional mi. Open Mon.-Fri. 9am-7pm, Sat.-Sun. 9am-5pm. Must be 21 with major credit card.

Help Lines: Crisis Center Hotline, 228-1505. Open 24 hr. **Rape Crisis,** 528-7273. Open 24 hr. **Gay Switchboard of Houston,** 529-3211. Counseling, medical and legal referrals, and entertainment information. Open daily 3pm-midnight.

Time Zone: Central (1 hr. behind Eastern).

Post Office: 401 Franklin St. (227-1474). Open Mon.-Fri. 9am-5pm, Sat. 9am-1pm. **ZIP code:** 77052.

Area Code: 713.

Houston (pop. 3,232,000) lies 35 mi. inland from the Gulf of Mexico. New Orleans is 350 mi. east on the same coastline, which is paralleled by I-10; Dallas is a 240-mi. drive north on I-45; San Antonio is 200 mi. nearly due west on I-10. The flat Texas terrain supports several mini-downtowns. True "downtown" Houston, a squarish grid of interlocking one-way streets, borders the Buffalo Bayou at the intersection of I-10 and I-45. The city's notorious traffic jams will halt drivers during rush hour, but a car in Houston is almost a must—distances are vast and bus service is infrequent. Houstonians orient themselves by **"The Loop,"** I-610, which lassoes the city center at a radius of 6 mi. Anything inside The Loop is easily accessible by car or bus. Find rooms on the southern side of the city, near Montrose Ave., the museums, Hermann Park, Rice University, and Perry House for easy access to several bus lines and points of interest.

Accommodations and Camping

An important convention center, Houston offers hundreds of hotels; those downtown are the most expensive. The cheaper motels are concentrated southwest of downtown by the Astrodome and **South Main Street,** and along the **Katy Freeway** (I-10 west) on the other side of the city. Singles are as low as $18, doubles as low as $20. The rooms may be decent once you get inside, but this part of town is quite dangerous at night. (Buses #8 and 9 go down S. Main, and #19, 31, and 39 go out along the Katy Freeway.) Although safe rooms in the $25-35 range are rare, many of the best hotels in the city offer rooms for 1-4 people at under $50 on the weekends.

Perry House, Houston International Hostel (AYH), 5302 Crawford (523-1009), at Oakdale. From the Greyhound station, take bus #8 or 9 south to the Oakdale stop and then walk east 6 blocks on Oakdale to Crawford. Clean and friendly, in a quiet neighborhood near museums and restaurants. Owner of the house offers tours around the city. Lockout 10am-5pm. $10. Linen $1.50.

Houston Youth Hostel, 5530 Hillman #2 (926-3444). Take bus #36 to Lawndale at Dismuke. Only 6 beds, but rarely full. A less hectic atmosphere than most AYH-affiliates, but also less roomy. Coed dorm room. No curfew. $7. Linen $1.

YMCA, 1600 Louisiana Ave. (659-8501), between Pease and Leeland St. Separate women's floor. Good downtown location and a short ride from the Westheimer nightlife. Clean but minimalist rooms. No private baths. Rooms $15. Key deposit $2. Another branch at 7903 South Loop E. (643-4396) is farther from downtown but has cheaper rooms. Take bus #40 ("Telephone"). Men only. $13. Key deposit $10.

Grant Motor Inn, 8200 Main St. (668-8000), near the Astrodome. Clean and safe. Cable TV, swingset, and pool. Singles $28. Doubles $36. Make summer reservations in advance.

The Roadrunner, 8500 S. Main St. (666-4971), near the Astrodome. Mediocre Acme-style rooms despite Satanic phone number. Ask to see a few before you unpack. Avoid flattened coyotes in lobby. Singles $22. Doubles $26.

Motel 6, 3223 South Loop E. (664-6425), near the Astrodome. Simply furnished, but neat. Area can be dangerous at night. Singles $27. Doubles $30.

There are only two campgrounds in the Houston area. Both the **KOA Houston North,** 1620 Peachleaf (442-3700), off north Loop 610, and the **Houston Campground,** 710 State Hwy. 6 S. (493-2391), are out in the boondocks, inaccessible by Metro Bus. KOA charges $14.50 per site for two, $2 each additional adult, $1.50 each additional child. Houston Campground charges $11 per site for two, $3 each additional adult, $1.50 each additional child.

Food

As a port town, Houston has witnessed the arrival of many immigrants (today its Indochinese population is the second largest in the nation), and its range of restaurants reflects this. Houston cuisine includes Mexican and Vietnamese food, and the state specialty, barbecue. Look for reasonably priced restaurants among the shops and boutiques along **Westheimer Street,** especially near the intersection with Montrose. This area, referred to as "Montrose," is Houston's answer to Greenwich Village. This area is also popular with gay men. Bus #82 follows Westheimer from downtown to well past The Loop. For great Vietnamese cuisine, go to **Milam Street,** where it intersects Elgin St., just south of downtown.

Good Company Barbecue, 5109 Kirby Dr. A busy Texas tradition, complete with picnic tables and loud country music. Sliced pork and rib barbecue, as well as chicken and sandwiches ($3-7). Open Mon.-Sat. 11am-10pm, Sun. noon-10pm.

Hobbit Hole, 1715 S. Shepherd Dr., a few blocks off Westheimer. Take bus #35. For the hard-core Tolkien buff or the dedicated vegetarian. Try the "Gandalf," a meatless treat with mushrooms, avocado, and melted cheese ($5.25). Entrees $4-8. Open Mon.-Thurs. 11am-11pm, Fri.-Sat. 11am-midnight, Sun. 11:30am-10pm.

Pappasitos Cantina, 6445 Richmond. Great Mexican food (entrees $6-16), including award-winning *fajitas,* served to the vibrant strains of *mariachi* music. Open Sun.-Thurs. 11am-11pm, Fri.-Sat. 11am-midnight.

Luther's Bar-B-Q, 8777 S. Main St. One of eleven locations in the Houston area. Good Texas barbecue entrees ($3-6) and free refills on iced tea. Open Sun.-Thurs. 11am-10pm, Fri.-Sat. 11am-11pm.

Van Loc, 3010 Milam St. (528-6441). Vietnamese and Chinese food at reasonable prices (entrees $5-8). The great all-you-can-eat luncheon buffet ($3.65) includes iced tea but no funky cold medina. Open daily 10am-midnight.

Cadillac Bar, 1802 N. Shepherd Dr., at the Katy Freeway (I-10), northwest of downtown. Take bus #75, change to #26 at Shepherd Dr. and Allen Pkwy. Wild fun and authentic Mexican food. Try the "Mexican Flag," a flaming shot of liquor. Tacos and enchiladas $5-7; heartier entrees more expensive. Open Mon.-Thurs. 11am-10:30pm, Fri. 11am-midnight, Sat. noon-midnight., Sun. noon-10pm.

The Marble Slab, 3939 Montrose (523-3035). The latest ice cream hotspot—special flavors and mix-ins prepared on its namesake tabletop. Homemade ice cream in a cone with one mix-in $2. Open Mon.-Thurs. 11:30am-11pm, Fri.-Sat. 11:30am-midnight, Sun. noon-11pm.

Sights

Houston's gigantic urban sprawl has created several clusters of skycrapers; Galleria and the Medical Center by themselves would dwarf the skyline of some comparable cities. Start your journey in the true downtown, the focal point of virtually all of the city's bus routes.

In the southwest corner of the downtown area is **Sam Houston Park,** just west of Bagby St. between Lamar and McKinney St. **St. John's Lutheran Church,** built in 1891 by German farmers, contains the original pulpit and pews. Catch the one-hour tour to see four buildings in the park. (Tours on the hr. Mon.-Sat. 10am-3pm, Sun. 1-4pm. Tickets $4, students and seniors $2).

Central downtown is a shopper's subterranean paradise. Hundreds of shops and restaurants line the underground **Houston Tunnel System,** which connects all the major buildings in downtown Houston, extending from the Civic Center to the Tenneco Building and the Hyatt Regency. On hot days, everyone ducks into the air-conditioned passageways to escape the heat and humidity. To navigate the tunnels, pick up a map at the Houston Public Library, the Pennzoil Place, or the Texas Commerce Bank.

Head westward along Westheimer to the **Galleria,** an extravagant, Texas-sized shopping mall with an ice-skating rink surrounded by pricey stores. (Rink open Sun.-Fri. noon-5pm and 8-10pm, Sat. noon-10pm. Skate rental $7.) Next door is the **Transco Tower,** 2800 Post Oak Blvd. (439-2000), Houston's latest monument outside of downtown. The view from the top is impressive; just walk in and take an elevator to the 51st floor. Don't miss the **Wall of Water Fountain,** in front of the Transco—it's on the scale of a waterfall.

Back toward downtown, just east of Montrose, are two of the city's smaller but most highly acclaimed museums. The **Menil Collection,** 1515 Sul Ross (525-9400), displays both ancient and 20th-century art. (Open Wed.-Sun. 11am-7pm.) One block away, the **Rothko Chapel,** 1409 Sul Ross (524-9839), houses some of the artist's works. The paintings in this tranquil place seem to blend into the walls; it's easy to mistake them for background. (Open daily 10am-6pm.)

Antique-lovers will want to see **Bayou Bend,** in **Memorial Park,** the palatial mansion of millionaire Ima Hogg (*yes,* that's her real name), daughter of turn-of-the-century Texan governor Jim Hogg. Admire the collection of 17th- to 19th-century decorative art. The **Bayou Bend Museum,** 1 Westcott St. (529-8773), is 3 mi. from downtown just off Memorial Dr., and quite at home in posh River Oaks. Take bus #16, 17, or 84. (Tours Tues.-Sat. $4, seniors $3. Call ahead. Closed Aug. Disabled access.)

On Main Street, 3½ mi. south of downtown, lies the beautifully landscaped **Hermann Park,** near all of Houston's major museums. The **Houston Museum of Natural Science** (639-4600) offers a splendid display of gems and minerals, permanent exhibits on petroleum, a hands-on gallery geared toward children, and a planetarium and IMAX theater to boot. (Open Sun.-Mon. noon-5pm, Tues.-Sat. 9am-5pm. Admission $2.50, seniors and children $2.) The **Houston Zoological Gardens** (525-3300) feature small mammals, hippopotami, and alligators. (Open Tues.-Sun. 10am-6pm. Admission $2.50, seniors $2, ages 3-12 50¢.) The **Museum of Fine Arts,** 1001 Bissonet (639-7300) adjoins the north side of Hermann Park. Designed by Mies van der Rohe, the museum boasts a strong collection of impressionist and post-impressionist works, as well as a slew of Remingtons. (Open Tues.-Wed. and Fri.-Sat. 10am-5pm, Thurs. 10am-9pm, Sun. 12:15-6pm. Admission $2, seniors and college students $1, under 18 free. Free Thurs.) Across the street, the **Contemporary Arts Museum,** 5216 Montrose St. (526-3129), has multi-media exhibits. (Open Tues.-Sat. 10am-5pm, Sun. noon-6pm. Free.) Also located on the park grounds are sports facilities, a zoo, a kiddie train, and the Miller Outdoor Theater (see Entertainment below). The University of Houston, Texas Southern University, and Rice University congregate in this part of town.

The **Astrodome**, Loop 610 at Kirby Dr. (799-9555), a mammoth indoor arena, is the home of the **Oilers** football team and the **Astros** baseball team. (Tours daily 11am, 1pm, 3pm, and 5pm; off-season 11am, 1pm, and 3pm. Admission $2.75, ages under 7 free. Parking $3). At these prices, you're better off paying admission to a game. Football tickets are hard to get, but seats for the Astros are usually available and cost only $3, reflective of the perennial quality of the team. (Call 526-1709 for tickets.)

Wander down Space Age memory lane at NASA's **Lyndon B. Johnson Space Center** (483-4321), where models of Gemini, Apollo, Skylab, and the space shuttle are displayed in a free walk-through museum. This NASA is the home of Mission Control, which is still central headquarters for peopled space flights; when astronauts ask, "Do you read me, Houston?" the folks here answer. (Control center open daily 9am-4pm. Free.) By car, go 21 mi. south of downtown on I-45. The carless should take the Park and Ride Shuttle #246 from downtown.

Terminus of the gruesomely polluted Houston Ship Channel, the **Port of Houston** leads the nation in foreign trade. Free 90-minute guided harbor tours are offered on the inspection boat *Sam Houston.* (Tours Tues.-Wed. and Fri.-Sat. at 10am and 2:30pm, Thurs. and Sun. at 2:30pm.) Reservations for these deservedly popular tours usually must be requested four to six weeks in advance, but you can join one if the boat doesn't reach its 90-person capacity. Call to make last-minute reservations. To reach the port, drive 5 mi. east from downtown on Clinton Dr., or take bus #48 to the Port Authority gate. For more information or reservations, write or call Port of Houston Authority, P.O. Box 2562, Houston 77252 (225-4044; open Mon.-Fri. 8am-5pm).

Entertainment

Whether you're in the mood for a few cold beers in an urban-professional hangout or some serious country "kicker" dancing, Houston has the bar for you. The Westheimer strip offers the largest variety of places for no cover.

Rub elbows with venture capitalists and post-punks alike at **The Ale House,** 2425 W. Alabama at Kirby (521-2333). The bi-level bar and beer garden offer over 100 brands of beer served with a British accent. Upstairs you'll find mostly New Wave music and dancing. (Open daily noon-midnight.) A similar mix can be encountered at the more exclusive **Cody's Restaurant and Club,** penthouse of 3400 Montrose St. (522-9747), which offers a view of the skyline. Sit inside or out on the balcony, and listen to live jazz. (Open Tues.-Fri. 4pm-2am, Sat. 6pm-2am. Informal dress.) **Sam's Place,** 5710 Richmond Ave. (781-1605) is a real Texan hangout, especially on Sunday afternoons when a band plays outdoors (5-10pm) and various booths proffer different beers. An indoor band continues from 7pm-1am. (Happy Hour Mon.-Fri. 4-8pm and Mon.-Thurs. 11pm-closing. Open Mon.-Sat. 11am-2am, Sun. noon-2am. Clothes required.) **The Red Lion,** 7315 Main St. (795-5000), features cheap beer and nightly entertainment that ranges from bluegrass to heavy metal. (Open Mon.-Fri. 11am-2am, Sat. 4pm-2am, Sun. 4-10pm.)

Houston offers ballet, opera, and symphony at **Jones Hall,** 615 Louisiana Blvd. Tickets for the **Houston Symphony Orchestra** (224-4240) cost $5-23. The season runs from September to May. During July, the symphony gives free concerts on Tuesday, Thursday, and Saturday at noon in the Tenneco Building Plaza. The **Houston Grand Opera** (546-0200) produces seven operas per season, with performances from October through May. (Tickets $5-25, 50% student discount ½ hr. before performance.) Call 227-2787 for information on the ballet, opera, or symphony. If you're visiting Houston in the summer, take advantage of the **Miller Outdoor Theater** in Hermann Park (520-3290). The symphony, opera, and ballet companies stage free concerts here in the evenings from May to August, and the annual **Shakespeare Festival** arrives for the last week of July and first week in August. The downtown **Alley Theater** (228-8421) stages Broadway-caliber productions at moderate prices. (Tickets $14-28. Student rush seats 15 min. before curtain $5.) Comedy-lovers should visit the **Comedy Workshop,** 2105 San Felipe (524-7333; nightly shows $2-4). For last-minute, half-price tickets to many of Houston's sporting events, musical and theatrical productions, and nightclubs, take advantage of **Showtix** discount ticket center, located at 400 Rusk, at Smith in Tranquility Park (227-9292; open Tues.-Sat. 11am-5:30pm); and 11140 Westheimer St. at Wilcrest (open Mon.-Fri. 11am-5pm, Sat. 10am-noon).

Near Houston: Galveston Island

Fifty mi. southeast of Houston on I-45, the narrow, sandy island of **Galveston** (pop. 65,000) offers not only a beach resort's requisite T-shirt shops, ice cream stands, and video arcades, but also beautiful historic homes, shady, oak-lined streets, and even a few quiet, deserted beaches.

It's hard to fathom, but prior to the devastating hurricane of 1900, this was the largest and wealthiest city in Texas. With the city almost fully decimated, the survivors of that storm swore that Galveston would be rebuilt better and stronger than ever. Although the city never regained its prominence, the 10-mi. concrete seawall that gives the main thoroughfare its name is testament to Galveston's resolve. An unfortunate result is that your "beachside" motel may not be precisely that. The island's natural beaches are located at its extreme ends; below the seawall the shore-line is rocky and swimming is prohibited.

A warning to visitors: Galveston's streets are set up in a grid that appears elementary. Lettered streets (A to U½) run north-south, numbered streets run east-west, with **Seawall** following the southern coastline. But it's incredibly easy to get completely lost because most streets have two names. For example, Avenue J and Broadway are the same, as are 25th Street and Rosenberg.

You can surround yourself with families, partying teenagers, and high-spirited volleyball games at **Stewart Beach,** near 4th and Seawall. If you prefer an older, quieter, student crowd, try **Pirates Beach,** about 3 mi. west of 95th and Seawall. There are two **Beach Pocket Parks** on the west end of the island, just east of Pirates Beach, with bathrooms, showers, playgrounds, and a concession stand. (Parking $3.)

After a day at the beach, visit the **Strand,** on Strand St., between 20th and 24th St., a national historic landmark of nearly 50 restored Victorian buildings; today it consists of restaurants, gift shops, and clothing stores. Cool off with a delectable root-beer malt ($1.75) at **LaKing's Confectionery,** 2323 Strand (762-6100), a large, old-fashioned ice-cream parlor and candy factory. (Open Sun.-Thurs. 10am-9pm, Fri.-Sun. 10am-10pm.) One of the island's two **visitors centers,** located 2 blocks over at 2016 Strand (765-7834; open Mon.-Thurs. 9:30am-6:30pm, Fri.-Sat. 9:30am-9pm, Sun. 10am-6:30pm), functions as the depot for the **Galveston Island Trolley** running between the Strand and the Seawall and to most major attractions and hotels. (Tickets $2, seniors and children $1. Trains leave hourly Oct.-Apr., every 30 min. May-Sept.) Galveston's other visitors center is the **Convention and Visitors Bureau,** at 21st St. and Seawall (763-4311 or 800-351-4236; open Mon.-Fri. 8:30am-5pm, Sat.-Sun. 9am-5pm).

Seafood is abundant in Galveston, along with traditional Texas barbecue. Plenty of eateries line Seawall and the Strand. For seafood, go to **Benno's on the Beach,** 1200 Seawall (762-4621), and try a big bowl of the shrimp gumbo ($3.75) or one of their crab variations. (Open Sun.-Thurs. 11am-10pm, Fri.-Sat. 11am-11pm.)

Prices for accommodations in Galveston usually fluctuate with the seasons. The least expensive option is to make Galveston a daytrip from Houston. There are a few cheap motels along Seawall, but most are notoriously shabby and singles range from $25-60. Probably the best of the bunch is the **Treasure Isle Motor Hotel,** 1002 Seawall (763-8561). The first-floor rooms are decent, and new owners are making some attractive renovations for the 1990-1 season. (Singles from $34. Doubles from $45.) The familiar **Motel 6,** 7404 Broadway (740-3794), is about 1½ mi. from the beach, with decent rooms and a pool. (Singles $22. Doubles $26.) You can camp at **Galveston Island State Park,** on 13 Mile Rd. (737-1222), about 10 mi. southwest of the trolley-stop visitors center. (Sites $12.) The **Bayou Haven Travel Park,** 6310 Heards Ln. (744-2837), on Offatts Bayou, much more convenient to downtown, has laundry facilities and clean showers. (Full hookup $12 for 4, waterfront sites $15. Each additional person $2.) From the bus station, go left off 61st St., then ½ mi. to Heards Ln.

Texas Bus Lines, a **Greyhound** affiliate, operates out of the station at 4913 Broadway (765-7731), providing service to Houston (6 per day, 1½ hr., $9). **Emergency** is 911. Galveston's **time zone** is Central (1 hr. behind Eastern). Its main **post office** is at 601 25th St. (763-1527; open Mon.-Fri. 8:30am-1pm and 2-5pm, Sat. 9am-12:30pm). Galveston's **ZIP code** is 77550; the **area code** is 409.

East Texas

What is generally known as East Texas—the vast area north and east of Houston and east of Dallas—defies Texas's stereotype as flat, treeless ranch country. A swath of thick, hilly woods and lake country, it offers a shady alternative to the often sweltering city-scapes of Dallas and Houston.

The major cities of this region are **Beaumont** in the south and **Lufkin** in the north. In the area are four national forests. **Sam Houston National Forest,** about 50 mi. north of Houston, borders Lake Livingston in the northeast and Lake Conroe in the southwest. The 140-mi. **Lone Star Hiking Trail** winds through three different recreation areas. Double Lake offers campsites, picnic facilities, showers, and a swimming area with a beach. For more rustic hikers, primitive camping is also permitted along the trail. Lake Conroe and Lake Livingston offer both boating and excellent black bass fishing. Ranger offices are located in Cleveland (713-592-6462), off U.S. 59, and in New Waverly (409-344-6205), off I-45. On the outskirts of the forest off U.S. 75, the **Sam Houston Memorial Museum Complex,** 1836 Sam Houston Ave. (409-295-7824) in Huntsville, includes the general's two homes and his law office as well as a commemorative mini-model of the Eiffel tower and Taj Mahal rolled into one.

Davy Crockett National Forest and **Angelina National Forest** lie 10 mi. west and east of Lufkin, respectively. The Davy Crockett incorporates the scenic **Four C National Recreation Trail,** a 20-mi. pass from the Neches Overlook to Ratcliff Lake. The trail follows the old paths of the Central Coal and Coke Logging Company (the "Four-C"), traveling through pines, sloughs, and upland forests. Ratcliff Lake has 70 camping units, a swimming beach, picnic area, amphitheater, and showers. The Neches Overlook provides a panoramic view of the forest and is most beautiful during April when the redbuds are in bloom. **Ranger stations** are located in Crockett (409-544-2046) and Apple Springs (409-831-2246). The Angelina is split in two by the pristine **Sam Rayburn Reservoir,** in which catfish and bass are plentiful. The forest, home to both the endangered bald eagle and the red-cockaded woodpecker, also has a variety of recreation areas for camping, hiking, and boating. The **ranger station** is located at 1907 Atkinson Dr. (409-634-7709) in Lufkin. For more information, contact the Forest Supervisor, 701 N. First St., Lufkin 75901.

For those would-be naturalists who tire of the great outdoors, Lufkin offers a bit of civilized indoor relief. The obligatory **Motel 6** (409-637-7850; take bus #59), at the corner of 1st St., hosts lots of families and church groups. Its rather bare rooms are not exactly luxurious, but they are free of mosquitos. Enjoy free local calls and movie channel. Plenty of inexpensive restaurants within walking distance. (Singles $21. Doubles $27.) For help *with* the area, visit the **Lufkin Chamber of Commerce,** at 1615 S. Chestnut (634-6644); for help *in* the area, **emergency,** 634-6611, will put you in touch with the police.

The **Sabine National Forest** lies at the Louisiana border, 60 mi. south of Shreveport and just due east of the Angelina National Forest, on the other side of U.S. 96. The Sabine overlooks the **Toledo Bend Reservoir,** which teems with bluegill. Rangers can be reached in Hemphill (409-787-2791) and in San Augustine (409-275-

2632). Camping in designated areas of the national forests is usually free unless amenities (RV hookups, showers, etc.) are provided. There are also many private camping facilities in the area. Stop by the park service office in Lufkin for maps and permits.

Established to protect the rich biological diversity of the region, the **Big Thicket National Preserve,** just north of Beaumont, offers nature trails, canoeing, and undeveloped camping in designated areas. Stop by the **Big Thicket Visitors Center** on Rte. 420 off U.S. 287, 10 mi. north of Kountze and 35 mi. north of Beaumont. The **Sundew Trail,** located 10 mi. north of the visitors center off U.S. 287, is most scenic during the summer when the wildflowers bloom. Be sure to wear long pants and lots of bug spray. The trail is 1 mi. long, beginning on high sandy ground and then dipping into the savannah. There is also a wheelchair-accessible ½-mi. trail. The **Neches River, Village Creek,** and **Pine Island Bayou** are ideal for canoeing. Several local agencies rent canoes; the cheapest is **H&H Boat Dock and Marina** (409-283-3257), on Hwy. 190 near the junction with 92 at Steinhagen Reservoir. (Canoes $10 per day.) For more information, write or call the Superintendent, Big Thicket National Preserve, 8185 Eastex Freeway, Beaumont 77708 (409-839-2689). Permits are required for fishing and camping, and you should check in with the forest ranger at the visitors center before venturing out.

West Texas

On the far side of the Rio Pecos lies a region whose extremely stereotypical Texan character borders on self-parody. This land was colonized in the days of the Texan Republic, during an era when "Law West of the Pecos" meant a rough mix of vigilante violence, frontier gunslinger machismo, and lip service to the niceties of U.S. jurisprudence. However, this desolate region does not lack attractions, such as the so-called mountain ranges of Texas, and the border city of El Paso, and its Chihuahuan neighbor, Ciudad Juárez.

Guadalupe Mountains National Park

The Guadalupe Mountains saddle up as Texas's highest, carrying with them a legacy of unexplored grandeur. Early westbound pioneers avoided the area, fearful of the arid climate and the Mescalero Apaches who controlled the range. Even by the early 20th century, only a few homesteaders and guano miners inhabited this rugged region. Today the mountains maintain their primitive state and ensure challenging hikes in a mostly desert environment for those willing to journey to this remote part of the state. The passing tourist who hopes to catch only the most established sights will stop to see **El Capitan,** a 2000-ft. limestone cliff, and **Guadalupe Peak,** the highest point in Texas at 8749 ft. Less frantic travelers should hike to **McKittrick Canyon,** with its spring-fed stream and amazing variety of vegetation. Lush maples grow right next to desert yuccas, and thorny agaves circle stately pines. Mule deer and whiptail lizards sometimes greet visitors on the trails. The canyon and **The Bowl,** a high forest of Douglas fir and ponderosa pine, are both day hikes from the **Frijoles Information Center** (915-828-3251), right off U.S. 62/180. Here, you can pick up topographical maps, hiking guides, backcountry permits, and other information. (Open June-Aug. dialy 7am-6pm; Sept.-May daily 8am-4:30pm.)

Guadalupe National Park's lack of development may be a bonus for backpackers, but it makes daily existence tough. All water in the backcountry is reserved for wildlife and no food is available nearby. Bring water for even the shortest, most casual hike. The **Pine Springs Cafe** (915-828-3338), directly across from the campground, sells ready-made but reasonably priced sandwiches, sodas, and beer. You can get ice cream and hamburgers at **Nickel Creek Cafe** (915-828-3348), 5 mi. east. Or fill up on a pancake and coffee breakfast ($3-6) before visiting McKittrick Canyon, 3 mi. farther east.

Guadalupe Mountains Park Service conducts half- and full-day hikes from June to August, as well as evening programs. Information is available at the Frijoles Visitor Center or on radio station 1610 AM. An additional visitor contact station at McKittrick Canyon is staffed during the fall and sporadically throughout the year. Visit the park in the fall to marvel at the trees while avoiding the summer heat and spring winds.

The **Pine Springs Campgrounds** (915-828-3251), 1½ mi. west of the Frijoles station directly on the highway, has water and restrooms but no hookups. No fires are allowed. (Sites $5, Golden Age and Golden Access Passport holders receive a 50% discount.) **Dog Canyon Campground** (505-981-2418), just south of the state line at the north end of the park, can be reached only by a 70-mi. drive from Carlsbad, NM, on Rte. 137. Dog Canyon also lacks hookups, but provides water, restrooms, and charcoal grills. You can camp in the backcountry for free with a permit from the visitors center. When convenient material comforts take priority over close proximity, you should use White's City, NM, or Carlsbad, NM, as a base. They respectively lie 35 and 55 mi. northeast of the park along U.S. 62.

The park is less than 40 mi. west of Carlsbad Caverns in New Mexico (see Southern New Mexico), 110 mi. east of El Paso, and a 90-mi. drive from Kent. **TNM&O Coaches,** an affiliate of Greyhound, runs along U.S. 62/180 between Carlsbad, NM, and El Paso, passing Carlsbad Caverns National Park and Guadalupe National Park en route. This schedule makes flag stops at the park three times per day in each direction ($25, $47.50 round-trip). Guadalupe Mountains National Park is in the Mountain time zone (2 hr. behind Eastern).

For further information, write: Guadalupe Mountains National Park, HC60, P.O. Box 400, Salt Flat, TX 79847 (915-828-3251).

Big Bend National Park

Roadrunners, coyotes, wild pigs, mountain lions, and 350 species of birds make their home at Big Bend National Park, a 700,000-acre tract that lies within the great curve of the Rio Grande. The spectacular canyons of this river, the vast **Chihuahuan Desert,** and the cool **Chisos Mountains** have all witnessed the 100 million years necessary to mold the park's natural attractions. Although the Chihuahuan Desert covers most of the park, colorful wildflowers and plants abound.

You must get a free **wilderness permit** at the park headquarters to take an overnight hike. The park rangers will suggest places to visit and hikes to take according to time constraints and energy levels. It is possible to see much of the park by car since most roads are well paved, but many of the most scenic places are only accessible by foot. Do not use unpaved roads unless you have a sturdy, high clearance, four-wheel-drive vehicle. The **Lost Mine Peaks Trail,** an easy three-hour hike up a peak in the Chisos, leads to an amazing summit view of the desert and the Sierra de Carmen in Mexico. Another easy walk leads up the **Santa Elena Canyon** along the Rio Grande. The canyon walls rise up as much as 1000 ft. over the banks of the river. Three companies offer river trips down the 133-mi. stretch of the Rio Grande owned by the park. Information on rafting and canoeing is available at the park headquarters.

There are **grocery stores** in Panther Junction, Rio Grande Village, and the Chisos Basin at Castolon, but stock up before leaving urban areas for better prices and selections. Get damp at the park's only public shower (75¢ per 5 min.) at the Rio Grande Village store.

The only motel-style lodging is the expensive **Chisos Mountain Lodge** (915-477-2291) in the Chisos Basin. This lodge offers four types of service: a new hotel (singles $53, doubles $58); an older motel (singles $42.50, doubles $50); lodge units located ¼ mi. away from the lodge complex (singles $45, doubles $53); and stone cottages housing up to three people ($60). Reservations are a must, since the lodge is often booked up to a year in advance. The lodge also runs a restaurant and coffee shop, where entrees cost $5-12. (Open daily 7am-8pm; off-season daily 7am-7:30pm.) The entire complex is located in the **Chisos Basin,** 10 mi. from the park's visitor center.

Designated **campsites** within the park are allotted on a first come, first serve basis. Chisos Basin and **Rio Grande Village** have sites with running water ($5) while **Cottonwood** has toilets but no running water ($3). Free primitive sites pop up along the hiking trails, available with a required permit from any ranger station. Because of the relatively high temperatures at the river, you won't have to worry about getting a site at Rio Grande Village, though you may have to negotiate with the resident buzzards. The best (and coolest) campsites by far are those in Chisos Basin. Get here early, as the basin sites fill up fast; try to get a campsite near the perimeter. The **park headquarters** (915-477-2251) are at Panther Junction. (Open daily 8am-6pm. Vehicle pass $5 per week.) For information, write Superintendent, Big Bend National Park 79834. The other **ranger stations** are at Rio Grande Village, Persimmon Gap, Chisos Basin (open daily 8am-4pm), and Castolon (open daily 8am-6pm). In case of emergency, call 477-2251. After 6pm, call 477-2267 or any of the other numbers listed at each ranger station.

Big Bend may be the most isolated spot you'll ever encounter. El Paso is 300 mi. to the northwest, San Antonio 450 mi. to the east. The park is only accessible by car via I-118 or I-385. Rental cars are only available in Odessa, approximately 222 mi. north of the park. Amtrak serves Alpine three times per week. Hitching is a very problematic proposition; the roads to Big Bend are not well traveled, and you may wind up stranded.

El Paso

Over 400 years ago, Spanish refugees fleeing the Pueblo Revolt forded the Rio Grande to explore what is now New Mexico. Their passage, dubbed El Paso del Norte (passage of the north) gave this city its name as well as its impermanent character. Across the river from the Mexican city of Ciudad Juárez, El Paso forms half of a binational metropolis. Travel between the two requires neither passport nor special ID; cities on both sides of the border possess a transient population in an aura of flux that has persisted since the first Spanish settlers arrived here.

Although 33 million legal crossings happen each year, El Paso is embroiled in a long-running controversy over U.S. immigration policy, an issue which affects tourists (especially those of Hispanic origin) who cross the Mexican border or encounter a random INS checkpoint on the open road. Both sides of the fence still oppose the "open border" concept. Historically, immigrants have been used in this region to bust unions and keep wages low on the U.S. side.

Practical Information

Emergency: 911. Juárez Police, 248-35.

Visitor Information: Convention and Visitors Center, 5 Civic Center Plaza (534-0686), on the western edge of downtown within 1 block of the Greyhound station. Open Mon.-Fri. 8am-4:30pm, Sat.-Sun. 9am-noon and 1-5pm.

El Paso International Airport: in northeast El Paso (722-4271). Bus #50 stops about ½ mi. south of the terminal building, at the corner of Montana and Airway Blvd. **Sprint Airport Shuttle System** (833-8282) departs from the curb outside the Continental Airlines desk every 10 min. from 4am-1am. Door-to-door service offered. Advance 1-day reservations required for trips to the airport. Airport to downtown plaza $12.

Amtrak: 700 San Francisco Ave. (545-2247; 800-872-7245 for reservations), on the western side of the Civic Center, near Greyhound. Office open daily 11am-7pm. Three trains per week to San Antonio ($106, continues to Dallas) and Tucson ($69, continues to Phoenix and Los Angeles). Reservations required.

Greyhound: 111 San Francisco Ave. (544-7200), at Santa Fe across from the Civic Center. To: Albuquerque (4 per day, $29, $39 on TNM&O coaches); Dallas (7 per day, $75); San Antonio (5 per day, $72); Tucson (7 per day, $44, continues to Los Angeles); and Chihuahua in Mexico. Office open 24 hr.

Public Transport: Sun City Area Transit (SCAT), 533-3333. Extensive service. All routes begin downtown at San Jacinto Plaza (Main at Mesa). Fewer routes in the northwest. Connects with Juárez system. Maps and schedules posted in the Civic Center Park, at public libraries, and available at 700-A San Francisco Ave. Mon.-Fri. 8am-noon and 1-5pm. The visitors center puts out a pamphlet on sight-seeing by bus. Most buses stop around 5pm; limited service on Sun. Fare 75¢, seniors 15¢, students with ID 35¢.

Taxi: Yellow Cab, 533-3433. Base fare $1.20, $1.50 per mi. Airport to downtown $15.

Car Rental: Rent-a-Heap, 4305 Anapro (532-2170). Will deliver. $17.50 per day, unlimited free mi. 3-day min. rental. Cars must be kept within a 50-mi. radius of El Paso and are not allowed across the border. Must be 18 with a major credit card.

Help Lines: Crisis Hotline, 779-1800. **U.S. Customs Service,** 541-6794. Both open 24 hr.

Post Office: 5300 E. Paisano (775-7500), at Alameda about 5 mi. from downtown. Open Mon.-Fri. 8:30am-5pm. **ZIP code:** 79910.

Area Codes: El Paso, 915. International direct dialing to Ciudad Juárez is 011 + 52 (country code) + 161 (city code) + local number.

El Paso (pop. 520,000) is at the westernmost tip of Texas on I-10, 40 mi. south of Las Cruces, NM, and 570 mi. west of San Antonio. The geographical intrusion of the Rio Grande and the Franklin Mountains complicates the city's road plan. Split by the Franklins, the city roughly forms the letter "Y," angling northwest to southeast along the river.

Accommodations, Camping, and Food

The cheapest hotel rooms land across the border, but downtown El Paso has several good budget offerings within easy walking distance of San Jacinto Plaza. The **Gardner Hostel (AYH),** 311 E. Franklin (532-3661), at Stanton, lies one block northeast of the plaza. Bankrobber John Dillinger stayed at this historic landmark just before the Feds nabbed him in Tucson. Simple but sunny hostel rooms have four beds and a semi-private bath. ($10.50, nonmembers $12.80. Singles with private bath $17. Doubles $24.) Quality budget motels clump along **North Mesa Drive.** Among them, the surprisingly beautiful **Warren Inn,** 4748 N. Mesa Dr. (544-4494), 5 mi. north of downtown, stands out. Large clean rooms come with kitchenette and cable TV. Continental breakfast included. (Singles $27. Doubles $34. Discounts for military and AAA members.) Farther to the north is **Motel 6,** 7840 N. Mesa Dr. (584-2125), off I-10. While 8 mi. from downtown, it has simple and adequate rooms with free movies. (Singles $22. Doubles $32.)

Since no public transportation goes to campgrounds outside of town, **Hueco Tanks State Park** (857-1135) is a 32-mi. hike east of El Paso on U.S. 62/180. (Sites with utilities and showers $11.) **Desert Oasis Park** is at 12705 Montana (855-3366). (Sites $11 for 2 people , each additional person $1. Entrance $2.)

Forti's Mexican Elder, 321 Chelsea (772-0066), offers fantastic fajitas at a convenient location a few blocks south of I-10. (Entrees $5-7. Take-out available. Open Sun.-Thurs. 11am-10pm, Fri.-Sat. 11am-11pm. Take bus #22.) Rhyming **Chico's Tacos,** 4230 Alameda, offers cheap and filling burritos and burgers, along with its namesake. The beef stew burrito costs 95¢, 3 rolled beef tacos 90¢. Three other locations: 5305 Montana (772-7777), 3401 Dyer (565-5555), and 1235 McRae (592-8484). (Open daily 9am-1:30am.) Alonso's Cafe, 110 Franklin, two blocks from the hostel, serves tasty, cheap Mexican breakfasts ($2-3). **Arnold's Mexican Restaurant,** 315 Mills Ave. at Kansas, offers a substantial selection of Tex-Mex dishes. (Entrees $3-6. Open Mon.-Tues. 7am-3pm, Wed.-Fri. 7am-3pm and 5-8:30pm.) Near Fort Bliss, the **Brown Bag Deli,** 4319 Fred Wilson, offers 31 different blissful sandwiches ($3-5) and decent if less eclectic breakfasts. (Open Mon.-Sat. 7am-10pm, Sun. 9am-9pm.) Also located at 8001 N. Mesa Dr. (833-5251).

Sights and Entertainment

Northeast of downtown on Rim Rd. (which becomes Scenic Dr.), **Murchison Park,** at the base of the mountains, offers a fine view of El Paso, Juárez, and the Sierra Madre. The city center is a couple of miles to the south; the University of Texas at El Paso and the Sun Bowl are off to the west; Fort Bliss and the airport sprawl several miles to the east.

El Paso has a number of interesting museums focusing on local culture and history. The **El Paso Museum of Art,** 1211 Montana (541-4040), contains Western art, samples from the French, Venetian, and Sienese schools, and a plethora of Spanish religious paintings. (Docent tours Sun. at 1:30pm. Open Tues.-Sat. 10am-5pm, Sun. 1-5pm. Free.) The **Fort Bliss Replica Museum,** 5051 Pleasanton Rd. (568-4518), 7 mi. from downtown, re-creates the 1854 fort built to fight the Apache. (Open daily 9am-4:30pm. Free.) The small but ambitious **Americana Museum,** Civic Center Plaza (542-0394), downtown on Santa Fe between San Antonio and San Francisco, is dedicated to the display and study of pre-Columbian and historical art of the Americas. Exhibits include models of cliff houses, local and regional photography, and artifacts from the Hohoka and Anasazi cultures. (Open Tues.-Sat. 10am-5pm. Free.) El Paso's most controversial organization features prominently and often nostalgically in the **Border Patrol Museum of the Immigration and Naturalization Service,** 310 N. Mesa Dr. (533-1816), in the Merrill Lynch building. Exhibits focus on the colorful history and artifacts of the Border Patrol's three branches—Canadian, Mexican, and coastal. In 1924, the first group of Border Patrol officers received a badge, pistol, and rifle, but had to supply their own horse; today they receive 17 weeks of classes in Spanish and immigration law. The museum doesn't skimp on nostomania; at its hub stands a commemorative statue, "The Silent Sentinel." (Open Mon.-Fri. 10am-4pm, Sat. 9am-noon. Free.)

For a more thorough exploration of El Paso, try one of the visitors center's three tours. The **walking tour** directs you to the colorful relics of El Paso's "Wild West" phase, most of which are downtown. The **bus tour** transports you to the cultural highlights, such as the El Paso Museum of Art and the **Museo de Arte y Historia,** across the river in Juárez. The **car tour** covers the most territory, including a short drive up Alabama Rd. and McKelligon Rd. into **McKelligon Canyon,** high in the Franklins northeast of downtown.

To find nighttime doings in El Paso, talk to locals; a knowledge of Spanish is helpful. A few clubs cluster on Mesa St. next to the **University of Texas at El Paso (UTEP).** UTEP also sponsors art shows and dramatic performances during the school year (call 747-5481 for current events), while the student union runs a dinner theater year-round (call 747-5711 for ticket information). On weekends during the summer, the El Paso Arts Department (541-4481) sponsors free outdoor concerts at the Chamizal National Memorial. Music ranges from jazz to classical to Latin American; shows start at 8pm.

SOUTHWEST

Arizona, Nevada, New Mexico, and Utah offer a lot besides the lure of warm weather and a relaxed lifestyle. The Southwestern states claim some of the world's most awe-inspiring scenery, including the Grand Canyon and Carlsbad Caverns; the region also retains a rich history of cultural intermingling, unmatched elsewhere in the U.S.

The Anasazi of the 10th and 11th centuries first discovered that the arid lands of the Southwest, with proper management, could support an advanced agricultural civilization. The Navajo, Apache, and Pueblo people later migrated into the region, sharing the land with the Hopi descendants of the Anasazi. Spanish conquest in the early 17th century brought European and *mestizo* colonists to modern-day Texas and New Mexico. European American conquest of the region quickly followed the Mexican independence in 1821. Begun as a revolt by Mexican and U.S. settlers against Santa Ana's dictatorship, the Texan War of Independence in 1836 led to the Mexican-American War and an opportunity for the U.S. to influence the region. Santa Fe, Nuevo Mexico, became the first foreign capital ever to fall to the U.S.; by 1853, Mexico's beaten government sold the tract of land south of the Gila River that today forms a large part of Arizona and New Mexico.

The legacy of this cultural history still holds throughout the Southwest in the large Hispanic and Native American populations, Spanish and tribal place names, and numerous historical sites. But much of the land retains the tranquility of nature undisturbed by human hands. The lonely grandeur of the desert stretches for miles, and the water- and wind-scored landscape—the cliffs of the Guadalupe Mountains, the gorges of the Colorado and Rio Grande, the redstone arches and twisted spires of southern Utah and northern Arizona—stands as testament to past and present battles waged by erosion.

Travel

Travel in the Southwest involves extremes of temperature and distance unknown in other regions. **Amtrak** (800-872-7245) serves cross-country routes; lines from Dallas and Houston converge in San Antonio and continue through El Paso, Tucson, and Phoenix on the way to Los Angeles, while another line to L.A. passes through Santa Fe, Albuquerque, and Flagstaff. **Greyhound/Trailways** serves the major cities and towns along the interstates; **Texas, New Mexico, & Oklahoma Coaches (TNM&O),** a Greyhound affiliate, provides service in rural northern New Mexico.

Try to travel by car: there is no substitute when touring the Southwest. Public transportation serves a few of the cities, but cities are not the reason for venturing to this region. **Flying** to the Southwest costs relatively little. Phoenix is the hub of **America West Airlines,** which serves Los Angeles, Denver, and Chicago.

Since balmy winter weather in the lower elevations of the Southwest attracts many travelers, make reservations for accommodations if you plan to travel between December and April. Crowds understandably diminish in summer, when temperatures regularly top 100°F. **Youth hostels** are reproducing, particularly in New Mexico; call ahead or mail in reservations to stay in the more popular ones at the Grand Canyon, Phoenix, Taos, Salt Lake City, and Las Vegas. Many will require an advance deposit to reserve a space.

Outdoors

While predominantly arid, the landscapes of every Southwestern state include everything from hot, desolate flatlands to breezy mountain ridges; during one season, you can camp out under a desert sky, ski down powdered slopes, and hike through piñon forests. In southern Arizona, you'll find the barren sandy flats and

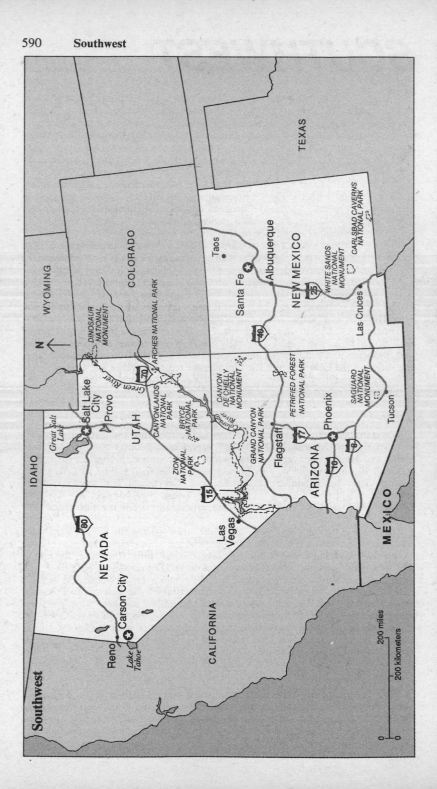

saguaro cacti of the Sonoran Desert, home of Wile E. Coyote and speedy roadrunners. Southern New Mexico shares the Chihuahuan Desert's tenacious, brilliant flowers and pine-covered mountains with West Texas and Northern Mexico. To the north, in southern Utah and northern Arizona, lies the slickrock country of the Painted Desert, where running water has gouged the sandstone bedrock into fantastic shapes and dramatic canyons. The southern Rockies tumble out of Colorado into the Sangre de Cristo, San Juan, Sandia, Manzano, Jicarilla, and Sacramento ranges of New Mexico. The Guadalupe range straddles the Texas-New Mexico border between El Paso and Carlsbad; farther south the Davis Mountains complete the picture. The desolate Llano Estacado plain covers much of eastern New Mexico and western Texas.

Travelers can access much of this incredible scenery cheaply and easily since the federal government owns a hefty portion of the region. Well-maintained park service campgrounds dot the region. By all means gawk at tourist magnets like the Grand Canyon, but also take advantage of the less publicized, less crowded, and more plentiful forest service and Bureau of Land Management (BLM) holdings. The forest service or BLM offices in most major towns are great places to ask about outdoor activities. Best of all, you can wander and camp at will throughout their property almost without cost. Get a free campfire permit at the nearest ranger station before starting out.

The **National Park Service** has two regional offices in the Southwest: the **Southwest Regional Office,** with jurisdiction over New Mexico, Utah, and eastern Arizona (P.O. Box 728, Santa Fe, NM 87504; visitor services at 1220 S. St. Francis Dr.; 505-988-6340); and the **Western Regional Office,** which covers Nevada and most of Arizona (450 Golden Gate Ave., P.O. Box 36063, San Francisco, CA 94102; 415-556-0560). The appropriate **National Forest Regional Offices** are the **Southwestern Office,** Federal Bldg., Albuquerque, NM 87102 (505-842-3292), and the **Intermountain Office,** Federal Bldg., 324 25th St., Ogden, UT 84401 (801-625-5182).

Desert Survival

The body loses a gallon or more of liquid per day in the heat, and water must be replaced. Whether you are driving or hiking, tote two gallons of water per person per day; less is adequate at higher altitudes and during winter months. Drink regularly, even when you're not thirsty: Do not merely drink huge quantities of water after you've become dehydrated—indeed, it may be dangerous. If you're drinking sweet beverages, dilute them with water to avoid a reaction to high sugar content. Alcohol and caffeine cause dehydration; if you indulge, compensate with more liquid. Avoid salt tablets, which shock your system.

Travelers should allow a couple of days to adjust to the climate, especially when planning a hike or other strenuous activity. This warning applies to activity at high altitudes as well as in low-lying deserts. Those new to high-altitude areas may feel drowsy, and one alcoholic beverage will have the same effect as three at a lower altitude. The desert is not the place to sunbathe. A hat, long-sleeved loose-fitting shirts of a light fabric, and long trousers actually keep you cooler and protect you from exposure to the sun.

In winter, nighttime temperatures can drop below freezing at high elevations, even though afternoon temperatures may be in the 60s or 70s. The desert is infamous for its flash floods, mostly during spring and fall. A dry gulch can turn into a violent river with astonishing speed; when camping, try to locate a site well back from moving water.

Those driving in the desert should carry water for the radiator. A two- to five-gallon container should suffice. Drivers should purchase a desert water bag (about $5-10) at a hardware or automotive store; once filled with water, this large canvas bag straps onto the front of the car. If you see the temperature gauge climbing, turn off the air-conditioning. If an overheating warning light comes on, stop immediately and wait about a half hour before trying again. Don't shut off the engine; the fan will help cool things down under the hood. Turning your car's heater on full force will help cool the engine. Never open the radiator until it has cooled, because internal pressure will cause scalding steam to erupt from it. And never pour water on the engine to cool it off; the temperature change may crack the engine block.

For any trips off major roads, a board and shovel are useful in case your car gets stuck in sand; the board can be shoved under a tire to gain traction and the shovel can take care of minor quagmires. Letting some air out of your tires can also help you drive free.

Reservations

Visiting Native American reservations can either prove an enlightening cultural experience or the imperialistic voyeurism. Avoid the latter by learning about the beliefs, customs, and politics of tribes before you blunder through their territories—considered sovereign areas by the U.S. government. The museums of Flagstaff, the **Pueblo Indian Cultural Center** in Albuquerque, the **University of New Mexico Museum of Anthropology,** Phoenix's **Heard Museum,** and the **Native American Folk Art Center** in Santa Fe each offer a general background of Southwest Native American life.

Books and museums, however, say little about contemporary tribal life. The overall picture can be bleak; unemployment on the reservations is well above 50%. Although federal law prohibits alcohol on the reservations, wet towns such as Gallup exist just outside their borders and fuel the rampant alcoholism among Native Americans, which combines with wandering livestock to make nighttime driving in these areas very dangerous. Realize as well that reservations are not strictly preservations—any Native Americans live in modern houses, drive trucks, and wear clothes that accord with the image of a Southwestern cowboy.

Despite these drawbacks, the reservations still provide fascinating places to visit. Talk to rangers at national parks and monuments near reservations, who are often unofficial experts on local customs and sights. General stores and gas stations in tribal capitals such as Window Rock are often the best places to find Native Americans who don't mind talking to outsiders. While you may wear shorts on the reservation, avoid tight-fitting or "provocative" clothing. Don't photograph anyone without permission—some residents believe that one's fate is tied up with the artificially produced likeness. Abide by laws intended to protect customs and rights of privacy; you may be arrested or fined by tribal police when you violate a village ordinance prohibiting non-Native American travel on local trails. Visitors may be deliberately ignored in stores and on roads, particularly by older residents.

Facilities for tourists on most reservations are minimal and overpriced. Camp and picnic if you can; primitive sites are usually free. Many back roads, usually unpaved, are passable only by four-wheel drive. Bus service is scarce, but Gray Line Tours runs to many reservations.

Arizona

The Cactus State has some of the world's most awe-inspiring natural scenery: the Grand Canyon's immense labyrinths, the four-story cliff-dwellings tucked into the striated walls of Canyon de Chelly, Monument Valley's fantastic sandstone formations, the streaked and arid landscape of the Painted Desert, and the *saguaro* cacti and old mining towns dotting the Sonoran Desert. Compared with these wonders, the state's cities often seem little more than massive, horizontal air-conditioners. Yet the cities and towns contain Arizona's many cultures, from retirees in search of sun to Native Americans preserving their heritage.

Practical Information

Capital: Phoenix.

Tourist Information: Arizona Office of Tourism, 3507 N. Central Ave. #506, Phoenix 85012 (255-3618). **Arizona State Parks,** 1688 W. Adams St., Phoenix 85007.

Time Zone: Mountain (2 hr. behind Eastern). Arizona (with the exception of the reservations) does not follow Daylight Savings Time; in summer it is 1 hr. behind the rest of the Mountain Time Zone. **Postal Abbreviation:** AZ.

Grand Canyon

As far as anyone knows, former U.S. President Richard Nixon never drove his RV up to Yavapai Point, took a deep breath, and exclaimed, "This is a *Grand* Canyon!" But well he might have. At 227 miles long, 13 miles wide, and over a mile deep, the canyon would merit a gander if only for its mind-boggling size. The canyon also looms unbelievably sublime with but a few trails and resthouses scratching the otherwise undisturbed combinations of ridges, gorges, and geological layers.

Until six million years ago, the Grand Canyon was just another hill. Then, according to both Havasupai and U.S. myth, the Colorado Rim began to flow right through it. Against the rushing might of the Colorado, the canyon's soft limestone, sandstone, and shale yielded quickly. Now the canyon serevs as an open textbook of the earth's history, making millions of years of strata accessible and easily viewed.

Grand Canyon National Park consists of three areas: the **South Rim,** which includes Grand Canyon Village; the **North Rim;** and the canyon gorge itself. The slightly lower, largely more accessible South Rim draws 10 times more visitors than the higher, more heavily forested North Rim.

The 13-mi. distance that traverses the canyon equals a two-day adventure for sturdy hikers, while the 214 miles of road prove a good 5-hour drive for those who would rather explore from above. Remember that, despite commercial exploitation, the Grand Canyon is still untamed; every year several careless hikers also take what locals morbidly refer to as "the 12-second tour."

South Rim

In summer, everything on two legs or four wheels converges from miles around on this side of the Grand Canyon. If you plan to visit during this mobfest, make reservations for lodging or campsites, and mules if you want them, and prepare to battle crowds. During the winter fewer tourists tour; however, many of the canyon's hotels and facilities close.

Practical Information

Nava-Hopi Bus Lines: 774-5003. Leaves Flagstaff Greyhound station daily at 7am, 9am, and 4pm. Leaves Bright Angel Lodge at Grand Canyon for Flagstaff daily at 9:45am and 5:45pm. Fare $23.60 round-trip, ages 5-12 $11.40, with Ameripass $12.90. $2 entrance fee not included.

Transportation Information Desk: In Bright Angel Lodge (638-2631). Reservations for mule rides, bus tours, Phantom Ranch, and taxi. Open daily 6am-6pm. **Visitor Activities Line,** 638-9304. 24-hr. recording.

Equipment Rental: Babbit's General Store, in Mather Center Grand Canyon Village (638-2262 or 638-2234), near Yavapai Lodge. Rents comfortable, adult-sized hiking boots ($5 for the first day), sleeping bags ($5-6), tents ($10), and camping gear. Open daily 8am-8pm. Deposit required.

Weather and Road Conditions: 638-2245. 24-hr. recording.

Post Office: (638-2512), next to Babbit's. Open Mon.-Fri. 9am-4:30pm, Sat. 10am-2pm. Lobby open Mon.-Sat. 5am-10pm. **ZIP code:** 86023.

Area Code: 602.

From Flagstaff, the fastest and most scenic route to the South Rim is Hwy. 93 south to I-40 east; Rte. 64 north then takes you to the Desert View entrance in the eastern part of the park. From Flagstaff, I-40 east to Rte. 64 provides the fastest path to the South Rim, Rte. 180 N. the shortest and most scenic (83 mi.). Admission to the Grand Canyon is $5 per car, $2 for travelers using other modes of transportation—even bus passengers must pay.

The National Park Service operates two free **shuttle buses**. The **West Rim Loop** runs between West Rim Junction and Hermit's Rest, with stops at all the scenic vistas along the way (operates Memorial Day-Labor Day every 15 min. 7:30am-sunset). The **Village Loop** covers Bright Angel Lodge, West Rim Junction, the visitors center, Grand Canyon Village, and Yavapai Point (operates year-round every 15 min. 6:30am-9:30pm).

Thanks to the efforts of the park service, the South Rim is quite accessible by wheelchair; pick up the free pamphlet "Access for Visitors" at the visitors center.

Accommodations and Camping

Think of it this way: compared with the six million years it took the Colorado River to cut the Grand Canyon, the six months it takes to get a room on the South Rim is the blink of an eye. Since the hostel closed in 1990, it is now nearly impossible to sleep indoors anywhere near the South Rim without reservations or gobs of cash, though you can check at the visitors center for vacancies.

Most accommodations on the South Rim other than those listed below are outrageously expensive. The campsites listed usually fill by 10am in summer. Campground overflow usually winds up in the **Kaibab National Forest,** adjacent to the park along the southern border, where you can pull off a dirt road and camp for free. Sleeping in cars is not permitted within the park, but is allowed and safe in the Kaibab Forest. The Nava-Hopi bus stops at Bright Angel Lodge, where you can check your luggage for 50¢ per day. Reservations for Bright Angel Lodge, Maswik Lodge, Trailer Village, and more expensive rooms can be made through Grand Canyon National Park lodges, P.O. Box 699, Grand Canyon AZ 86023 (602-638-2401). All rooms should be reserved six months in advance for summer, six weeks for winter.

Bright Angel Lodge, Grand Canyon Village. Scout-style rustic cabins with plumbing but no heat. Very convenient to Bright Angel Trail and both shuttle buses. Singles $32-44, depending on how much plumbing you want. A few rooms with no plumbing $27. Each additional person $6.

Maswik Lodge, Grand Canyon Village. Small, clean cabins with shower $44 (singles or doubles). Each additional person $8. Reservations required.

Mather Campground, Grand Canyon Village, ½ mi. from the visitors center. Shady, relatively isolated sites without hookups $6. Make reservations through Ticketron outlets 8 weeks in advance.

Trailer Village, next to Mather Campground. Clearly designed with the RV in mind. Campsites resemble driveways and lack seclusion. Sites with hookup $15 for 2 people. Each additional person 50¢.

Desert View Campsite, 25 mi. east of Grand Canyon Village. Sites $8. Open May 15-Oct. 30. No hookups. No reservations accepted; get there early.

Ten-X Campground in the Kaibab National Forest, (638-2443), 10 mi. south of Grand Canyon Village on Hwy. 64. Chemical toilets, water. Sites $7. Open April-Nov. No reservations, no hookups.

Phantom Ranch, on the canyon floor, a 4-hr. hike down the Kaibab Trail. Reservations required 6 months in advance for the April-Oct. season, but check at the Bright Angel Transportation Desk (see above) for last-minute cancellations. The ranch has a snack bar and serves expensive meals; bring your own food to conserve money. Don't show up without reservations—they'll send you back up the trail, on foot. Dorm beds $18. Cabins for 1 or 2 people $50, each additional person $10.

Food

You probably didn't come to the Grand Canyon in search of *haute cuisine,* and you certainly won't find it; on the other hand, eating inexpensively is not a hassle. **Babbit's General Store** (638-2262), in Mather Center, is the natural place to buy food for the trail, including sandwiches, dried fruit, and wine. (Open daily 8am-8pm; deli open 8am-7pm.) **The Maswik Cafeteria** in Maswik Lodge has a variety of inexpensive options, including made-to-order burgers ($3-4). (Open daily 6am-10pm). **Bright Angel Restaurant,** in Bright Angel Lodge (638-6389), has hot sandwiches from $4-6. (Open daily 6:30am-10pm.) The soda fountain at Bright Angel Lodge offers 16 flavors of ice cream ($1) to hikers emerging from the Bright Angel Trail. (Open daily 11am-9pm.)

Activities

Give yourself two days to see the Grand Canyon. Few experiences are as frustrating as climbing on the 5pm bus to Flagstaff just as shadows begin to lengthen and the hazy pinks and blues of midday give way to more dramatic sunset shades. Time permitting, the best way to see the canyon is to hike down into it. A funny thing often happens in the Grand Canyon, however: otherwise reasonable people, who would no sooner walk 8 mi. on flat ground than they would attempt to swim the Atlantic, suddenly think they can hike that distance straight up a cliff in 100° heat. Park rangers average over three rescues per day of hikers whose macho proves bigger than their muscles. Similarly, taking children more than a mile down the trail would be cruel and unusual.

The park service maintains two trails: **Bright Angel Trail,** which begins below the Bright Angel Lodge, and **South Kaibab Trail,** which begins at Yaki Point. The less strenuous Bright Angel trail has resthouses (with water during summer) 1½ mi. and 3 mi. from the rim, and water, shade, picnic tables, and toilets at **Indian Gardens,** 4½ mi. out. The much steeper, less shady Kaibab trail has better vistas but no water. For detailed descriptions of these trails, pick up copies of "Hiking the Bright Angel and Kaibab Trails" and "South Rim Day Hikes and Walks" at the visitors center.

If you have made arrangements to spend the night on the canyon floor, the best route is to hike down the Kaibab Trail (3-4 hr., depending on conditions) and back up the Bright Angel (7-8 hr.) the following day. The hikes down Bright Angel Trail to Indian Gardens and Plateau Point, 6 mi. out, where you can look down 1360 ft. to the river, make excellent daytrips. But start early (around 7am) to avoid as much heat as possible. One local rule: if you meet a mule train, stand quietly by the side of the trail and obey the wrangler's instructions in order not to spook the animals.

If you don't feel up to descending into the canyon, follow the **Rim Trail** east to Grandeur Point and the **Yavapai Museum,** or west to **Hermit's Rest,** using the shuttles as desired. There are no fences or railings between you and oblivion. The Eastern Rim Trail swarms at dusk with sunset-watchers, and the Yavapai Museum at the end of the trail has a sweeping view of the canyon during the day from a glassed-in observation deck. (Museum open daily 8am-8pm. Free.) The Western Rim Trail leads to several incredible vistas, notably **Hopi Point,** a favorite for sunsets, and the **Abyss,** where the canyon wall drops almost vertically to the Tonto plateau 3000 ft. below. To watch a sunset, show up at your chosen spot 45 minutes beforehand and face west instead of east, to see more than just shadow.

The park service rangers present a variety of free informative talks and hikes. Listings of each day's events are available at the visitors center or in the *Grand Canyon Guide* (10¢), available everywhere in the village. Every evening at 8:30pm, a free presentation highlights some aspect of the Grand Canyon in Mather Amphitheater, behind the visitors center.

The park also offers a variety of activities for younger visitors. *Grand Canyon's Young Adventurer,* available at the visitors center, includes entertaining stories, scavenger hunts, and puzzles.

In addition to the freebies offered by the National Park Service, a variety of commercial tours cover the South Rim. Tours by helicopter, airplane, inflatable raft, and mule soar beyond the reach of most budget travelers. Of the three bus tours, the Sunset and West Rim tours cover mostly places accessible by free shuttle buses. You may decide to take the tour to **West Desert View** (3¾ hr.; 2 per day in summer, 1 per day in winter; tickets $17, children $8.50). Unless you have a car, this tour provides the only access to Desert View, 26 mi. east of the village, with an even more commanding panorama of the canyon to the north and west, as well as the Painted Desert to the east. Contact the Bright Angel Transportation Desk (638-2401) for information on all commercial tours.

North Rim

Those arriving from Utah or Nevada, or want a more rugged, less crowded Grand Canyon experience, should consider the North Rim. Here things are a bit wilder, a bit cooler, and much more serene. The view from the North Rim is at least as spectacular as the view from the South Rim.

Unfortunately, getting to the North Rim without a car is difficult; there is virtually no public transportation. Canyon visitors seem wary of those on foot, making hitching a non-option.

The North Rim is a 200-mi.-plus, stunningly scenic drive from the South Rim. Take Rte. 64 east to 89 north; 64 south then hits Rte. 67, the road leading into the canyon. Rim to rim transportation is available from **Transcanyon**, P.O. Box 348, Grand Canyon, AZ 86023 (638-2820). late May to mid-Oct. ($50, $85 roundtrip). Between the first snows at the end of October and May 15, Rte. 67 is closed to traffic. Only a snowmobile can get you to the North Rim.

There is no visitors center on this side of the park, but you can direct questions to rangers at the entrance station and the information desk in **Grand Canyon Lodge** (638-2611; open daily 8am-5pm). The lodge lounges at the very end of Rte. 67. The front desk stays open 24 hours. The North Rim **emergency** phone (638-7805) is monitored around the clock.

Accommodations, Camping, and Food

As camping within the confines of the Grand Canyon National Park is limited to designated campgrounds, only a lucky minority of North Rim visitors get to spend the night "right there." If you can't get in-park lodgings, visit the **Kaibab National Forest,** which runs from north of Jacob Lake to the park entrance. Camp in an established site, or pull off the main road onto any forest road and camp for free. Another option is **Canyonlands International Youth Hostel,** 143 E. South, Kanab, UT 84741 (801-644-5554). It is 1½ hours north of the Grand Canyon, up Rte. 89, an equal distance south of Bryce Canyon in Utah. The hostel sleeps 40 in newly restored cabins. Guests also enjoy a large kitchen and free beverages. (Office open daily 8-10am and 5-10pm. Non-AYH, but all hostel cards honored; $8, nonmembers $10. Reservations recommended.)

Grand Canyon Lodge, on the edge of the rim. Rooms from $52.35 for 2 people. Write or call TW Recreational Services, P.O. Box 400, Cedar City, UT 84720 (801-586-7686).

Kaibab Lodge, on Rte. 67 (638-2389), 5 mi. north of the park entrance station. A quiet, secluded lodge with restaurant. Singles $43. Doubles $54. For reservations, contact Kaibab Lodge, North Rim, Rural Rte., Fredonia 85719. Reservations 526-0925 or 800-525-0924. Open late May-Sept.

North Rim Campground, on Rte. 67 near the rim. You can't really see into the canyon from the pine-covered site, but you know it's there. Near food store, recreation room, and showers. Sites $8. Reserve by writing to North Rim Campground, Grand Canyon National Park, Grand Canyon 86023.

Kaibab National Forest Sites: DeMotte Park Campground, 18 mi. north of the North Rim Entrance Station. 20 pleasant, shaded, and remote sites. Water and restrooms. **Jacob Lake Campground,** 32 mi. north of the park entrance, at the junction of U.S. 89A and Rte. 67 (643-7395). 48 sites. Both charge $6 and operate on a first come, first serve basis.

Activities

A ½-mi. paved trail takes you from the Grand Canyon Lodge to **Bright Angel Point**, which commands a fantastic view of the Canyon. **Point Imperial** overlooks Marble Canyon and the lesser known **Grand Canyon East Gorge** where thickets of whitebark aspen turn yellow in the autumn. Jutting out of the canyon in the east, the **Walhalla Plateau** obscures a full view of the canyon's sweep. **Point Sublime**, to the west, is accessible by Sublime Rd., recommended for rugged trucks and four-wheel drive vehicles only.

The North Rim offers nature walks and evening programs, both at the North Rim Campground and at Grand Canyon Lodge. Check at the information desk or campground bulletin boards for schedules. Half-day mule trips ($25) descend into the canyon from Grand Canyon Lodge (638-2292, in winter 801-679-8665; open daily 7:30am-9pm). Trips depart daily at 7:30am and 12:30pm. Ask at the desk in the lobby about the much more scenic full-day trips ($52).

On warm evenings, the Grand Canyon Lodge fills with an eclectic group of international travelers, U.S. families, and rugged adventurers. Some frequent the **Lodge Saloon** for drinks, jukebox disco, and the enthusiasm of a young crowd. Others look to the warm air rising from the canyon, a full moon, and the occasional shooting stars for their intoxication at day's end.

Northeastern Arizona

Navajo and Hopi Reservations

The capital of the Navajo Nation, **Window Rock**, lies near the edge of the largest reservation in the U.S. stretching from Lake Powell, UT, to south of Crownpoint, NM. The Navajo and their neighbors, the Hopi, also enclosed by the Navajo Reservation, have lived in this region for centuries—despite U.S. citizenship, most don't really consider themselves part of a national "melting pot." They, and not the U.S. government, have sovereignty over this large but agriculturally unproductive land. Over the years they have been treated brutally by Spanish, Mexican, and U.S. governments: don't expect too much hospitality.

A visit to these two reservations gives a unique glimpse of a land that most U.S. citizenss never see. Reservation politics are lively but obscure, written up only in the *Navajo Times* or in regional sections of Denver, Albuquerque, or Phoenix newspapers. In addition to the town and tribal government, Window Rock features the geological formation that gives the town its name.

The reservations have no central visitors centers. For information on the Hopis, visit their cultural center (see below). The Navajo Nation spreads out more; several tribal parks have their own small information booths. Pick up the excellent *Visitors Guide to the Navajo Nation* ($3), which includes a detailed map.

The "border towns" of **Gallup**, NM, and **Flagstaff**, AZ (see below), provide good entry points to the reservations; you can rent cars in one of these towns. Frequent **Greyhound/Trailways** routes along I-40 serve both. No public transportation goes into or runs within the reservations, with the notable exception of the **Navajo Transit Authority** (729-5457) in Fort Defiance, 6 mi. north of Window Rock. One bus per day leaves Tuba City, AZ, at 6am and travels along Rte. 264 through the Hopi mesa towns (flag stops) to Window Rock, arriving at 9:50am. (Leaves Window Rock heading west at 3pm, $13.)

The only reasonable way to see this part of the country is to rent a sturdy car and spend a few days. One good route is a loop along Rte. 264 from Tuba City east through Hopi land to Ganado, then north along U.S. 160 to Monument Valley and Navajo National Monument. The drive northwest along Rte. 98 to Lake Powell, near Page, AZ, on the Utah border (see Utah) makes a great detour. Plan to camp at the national monuments or Navajo campgrounds, and expect to pay dearly for the privilege.

On the Hopi Reservation, the **Hopi Cultural Center** (734-2401), on Rte. 264 in the community of **Second Mesa**, delineates the world of the tribe whose ancestors, the Anasazi, lived here centuries before the Navajo and their cousins the Apache arrived. The center consists of a museum of pottery, photography, and handicrafts, along with four gift shops, a motel, and a restaurant. The motel (734-2401) is expensive but decent and requires reservations two weeks to a month in advance. (Singles $50. Doubles $55.) The restaurant is surprisingly reasonable. Sandwiches cost $4-5, Native American dishes $3-6. (Open daily 6:30am-9pm.)

Inquire at the cultural center or at the Flagstaff Chamber of Commerce for the dates and sites of the **Hopi village dances**. Announced only a few days in advance, these religious ceremonies last from sunrise to sundown. The dances are highly formal occasions; tourists may come to watch, but should not wear shorts, tank tops, or other casual wear. Photography is strictly forbidden.

Monument Valley and Navajo National Monument

You may have seen the red rock towers of **Monument Valley Navajo Tribal Park** in one of the numerous westerns filmed here. Rather ironically, the 1000-ft. monoliths helped boost John Wayne to heights of movie heroism. The best and cheapest way to see the valley is via the Park's looping 17-mi. **Valley Drive**. This dirt road winds in and out of the most dramatic monuments, including the famous paired **Mittens** and the slender **Totem Pole**. The gaping ditches, large rocks, and mudholes on this road will do horrible things to your car: Drive at your own risk, and hold your breath. Much of the valley can be reached only in a sturdy four-wheel-drive vehicle or by a long hike. In winter, snow laces the rocky towers, and almost all the tourists flee. Inquire about snow and road conditions at the Flagstaff Chamber of Commerce.

The park entrance is 24 mi. north on U.S. 163 from the town of Kayenta and the intersection with U.S. 160. (Park open May-Sept. daily 8am-6:30pm; off-season 8am-5pm. Free.)

Twenty mi. past Kayenta on U.S. 160, Rte. 564 takes you 9 mi. to **Navajo National Monument**. This stunning site consists of three Anasazi cliff-dwellings, including **Keet Seel**, the best-preserved site in the Southwest. Inscription House has closed, and entrance into Keet Seel and **Betatakin**, a 135-room complex, is limited to 25 people per day in ranger-led groups. (Tours daily at 9am, noon, and 2pm; try to make reservations at least two months in advance. Write Navajo National Monument, Tanalea 86044.) For $50, Navajo guides will put you on a horse, lead you down the 8-mi. trail, and leave you with a ranger to explore the 400-year-old ruins left by the Anasazi. Allow a full day for the ride and the strenuous hike. Rangers also lead 5-mi. hikes. You can hike on your own, but you must obtain a permit. The **visitors center** (672-2366) has a craft shop as well as pottery and artifacts displays. (Open daily 8am-6pm; off-season 8am-5pm.)

The Navajo maintain a small campground with water next to the Monument Valley Tribal Park Visitors Center. (Sites $7.) The site at the National Monument has no showers or hookups, but it's free and has the added advantage of nightly ranger talks. If you need hookups, stop at **KOA** (801-727-3280), in Monument Valley, UT, 4 mi. west of Monument Valley Park off U.S. 163. (Sites $11 for 2 people, each additional person $2.)

Petrified Forest National Park

On a trip from Flagstaff to New Mexico, Petrified Forest National Park, 107 mi. east on I-40, makes an alluring detour off the Navajo/Hopi reservation circuit. The park includes some of the most scenic areas of the **Painted Desert**, named for the magnificent multicolored bands of rock that cut across its hills. Petrified logs of agate inlaid with quartz and amethyst crystals scatter across the desert floor, creating a stunning kaleidoscope of color.

Entrances are off I-40 to the north and U.S. 180 to the south (entrance fee $5 per vehicle). The **Painted Desert Visitors Center,** near the north entrance, shows a film explaining petrification every half hour. A 28-mi. park road through desert landscapes connects the two entrances, winding past piles of petrified logs and Native American ruins. Stop to look at oddly-named **Newspaper Rock,** covered not with newsprint, but with Native American petroglyphs. At **Blue Mesa,** a hiking trail winds through the desert. **Long Logs Crystal** and **Jasper Forest** contain some of the most exquisite fragments of petrified wood. It is illegal and traditionally unlucky to pick up fragments of petrified wood in the park; those who must take one home should buy one at a store along I-40. To camp overnight, make arrangements at the visitors center in the **Rainbow Forest Museum,** at the park's southern entrance (524-6228; open in summer daily 7am-8pm; in spring and fall 7am-6pm; in winter 8am-5pm). Public transport does not feed the Petrified Forest; several bus lines do stop in Holbrook, on I-40, 27 mi. away.

Canyon de Chelly National Monument

A narrow canyon traced by park roads rises eastward out of Beautiful Valley, with the sandstone walls rising 30 to 1000 ft. above the flat, sandy wash. The hollowed arcs of 12th-century adobe ruins, the remnants of Anasazi civilization, hide in the canyon walls. The caves and crevices created by seepage and erosion afforded the 19th-century Navajo protection from white attacks until frontiersman Kit Carson starved the tribe out. Since then the Navajo have returned to the lush valley as farmers, inhabiting modern-day hogans on the canyon floor.

Today the land constituting Canyon de Chelly National Monument is owned by the Navajo Nation and administered by the National Park Service. All but one of the park trails are closed to public travel unless Navajo escort hikers. Although the park service offers free short tours into the canyon, the only way to get far into the canyon or close to the Anasazi ruins is to hire a Navajo guide. Check with the **visitors center** (674-5436), 2 mi. east of Chinle on Navajo Rte. 64, off U.S. 191, which houses a small museum. The staff can arrange for guides and tours at any time of day, though guides usually arrive at the visitors center at about 9am. Guides generally charge $7 per hour to walk or drive into the canyon. Advance reservations are helpful, but you can try dropping in. (Open daily 8am-6pm; off-season 8am-5pm.) To drive into the canyon with a guide, you must provide your own four-wheel-drive vehicle. Horseback tours can be arranged through **Justin's Horse Rental** (674-5678), on South Rim Dr. at the mouth of the canyon. (Open daily approximately 8am-6pm. Horses $7 per hr.; mandatory guide $7 per hr.) **Twin Trail Tours** (674-3466) also rents horses.

Seven mi. from the visitors center, the 1-mi. trail to **White House Ruin,** off South Canyon Rd., winds down a 400-ft. face, past a Navajo farm and traditional hogan, through an orchard, and across the stream wash. The only one you can walk without a guide, this trail merits a trip, especially in the spring when you can hike in the canyon heat with the cool stream swirling about your ankles. Take one of the paved **Rim Drives** (North Rim 44 mi., South Rim 36 mi.), which skirt the edge of the 300- to 700-ft. cliffs. The South Rim is the more dramatic. Try to make it all the way to the **Spider Rock Overlook,** 20 mi. from the visitors center, a narrow sandstone monolith that towers hundreds of feet above the canyon floor. Native American lore has it that the whitish rock at the top of Spider Rock is actually composed of bleached bones of victims of the kachina spirit, Spider Woman. A written guide to the White House Ruins and the North or South Rim Drives costs 50¢ at the visitors center.

Camp for free in the park's **Cottonwood Campground,** ½ mi. from the visitors center. This giant campground in a pretty cottonwood grove rumbles at night with the din of a hungry army, and stray dogs tend to wander the site. Don't expect to find any budget accommodations in nearby Chinle or anywhere else in Navajo territory. Farmington, NM and Cortez, CO are the closest major cities with cheap lodging.

It's impossible to take an ugly approach to the park. The most common route is from Chambers, 75 mi. south of the park, at the intersection of I-40 and U.S. 191. The other approach is from the north, where U.S. 191 leaves U.S. 160 in Colorado near Four Corners, 50 mi. from the monument. There is no public transportation.

Flagstaff

Flagstaff is a mountain town with a split personality. Most of the year it graciously hosts a handful of skiers and the students of **Northern Arizona University.** Come May, however, the townspeople turn to the business of plundering tourists who use the town as a jumping-off point for journeys to the Grand Canyon and other local attractions. Flagstaff itself provides a good place to relax for a few days between photography binges. While the mountain elevation cools Flagstaff down during the day, local bands heat the town up at night.

Practical Information

Emergency: 911. **Police/Medical Assistance,** 774-1414.

Visitor Information: Flagstaff Chamber of Commerce, 101 W. Santa Fe Ave. (800-842-7293), across from the Amtrak station. Free city map, national forest map $2. Open Mon.-Sat. 8am-9pm, Sun. 8am-5pm. **Special Events Hotline,** 779-3733. 24-hr. recorded message.

Amtrak: 1 E. Sante Fe Ave. (774-8679 or 800-872-7245). One train per day to Los Angeles ($81) and Albuquerque ($76). Open daily 5:45-10am, 11am-2pm, 2:30-6pm, and 7-10:30pm.

Buses: Greyhound, 399 S. Malpais Lane (774-4573), across from NAU campus, 5 blocks southwest of the train station on U.S. 89A. To: Phoenix (5 per day, $21); Albuquerque (6 per day, $45); Los Angeles (5 per day, $75); and Las Vegas via Kingman, AZ (3 per day, $51). Terminal open 24 hr. **Gray Line/Nava-Hopi,** 774-5003; 800-892-8687 outside AZ. Shuttle buses to the Grand Canyon (3 per day, $25 round-trip, $12.90 with Greyhound Ameripass).

Public Transport: Pine County Transit, 970 Old Hwy. 66 (779-6624 or 779-6635). Three routes covering most of town. Fare 75¢, seniors, disabled, and children 60¢. Runs once per hour. In summer a free trolley runs to the mall Mon.-Sat.

Tours: Gray Line/Nava-Hopi, 774-5003; 800-892-8687 outside AZ. One-day sight-seeing tours to: the Grand Canyon ($32); Monument Valley and the Navajo Reservation and Monument ($72); the Hopi Reservation and Painted Desert ($62); and the Museum of N. Arizona, Sunset Crater, Wupatki, and Walnut Canyon (May-Oct.; $30). Kids under 13 ride ½-price on all tours. All tours except Grand Canyon run early April to mid-Nov. Grand Canyon runs year-round. Reservations required. Purchase tickets at the Amtrak and Greyhound stations. **Northern Arizona Wilderness Tours,** 284 Toho Trail (525-1028). To various national parks and monuments and Indian villages in vans and open four-wheel drive vehicles.

Camping Equipment Rental: Peace Surplus, 14 W. Santa Fe Ave. (779-4521), 1 block from the hostel. Daily rental of dome tents ($4-8), packs ($5), stoves ($3), plus a good stock of cheap outdoor gear. Open Mon.-Fri. 8:30am-9pm, Sat. 8:30am-7pm, Sun. 9am-6pm.

Bike Rental: Cosmic Cycles, 113 S. San Francisco St. (779-1092), downtown. Mountain bikes $5 per day, $20 on weekends. City bikes with wide tires $10 per day. Open Mon.-Fri 9am-6pm, Sun. 11am-4pm.

Taxi: Dream Taxi, (774-2934). Open 24 hr. You can dream anytime.

Car Rental: Allstar Rent-A-Car, 602 Mikes Pike (Hwy. 66) (774-7394 or 800-426-5243). $28 per day. 150 free mi., 19¢ each additional mi. Open Mon.-Sat. 7am-7pm, Sun. 9am-1pm. Must be 21 with major credit card or cash deposit.

Post Office: 104 N. Agassiz. Open Mon.-Fri. 9am-3pm. **ZIP code:** 86001.

Area Code: 602.

The center of Flagstaff is the intersection of **Beaver Street** and **Santa Fe Avenue** (U.S. 89A), where the train station rests. Within ½-mi. of this spot are both bus stations, the three youth hostels, the chamber of commerce, and several inexpensive restaurants. Other commercial establishments lie on **South Sitgreaves Street** (U.S. 89A), near the NAU campus.

Because Flagstaff is a mountain town, it stays cooler than much of the rest of the state, and receives frequent afternoon thundershowers. You can walk around most of downtown, but to get to anything worth seeing, rent a car, take a tour bus, or hitch.

Accommodations and Camping

Three competing hostels downtown, as well as other cheap motels on E. Santa Fe Ave., make sleeping in Flagstaff easily affordable. As the town can get rather chilly even in the summer, be sure to ask for a blanket. Don't expect to find budget lodgings in the vicinity of the the the Greyhound station or around the NAU campus. Camping in **Cocino National Forest** is a pleasant and inexpensive option.

Downtowner Independent Youth Hostel, 19 S. San Francisco (774-8461). Flexible management will send a Mercedes to shuttle between hostel and bus station. Very clean, well-maintained rooms with wooden floors and comfortable beds (not the other way around). Kitchen, hall baths. Open approximately 7am-9:30pm. Private rooms $10 per person, more crowded $8. Linens included. Open mid-May to mid-Aug.

The Weatherford Hotel (AYH), 23 N. Leroux (774-2731). Friendly management and convenient location. Rooms not as nice as the Downtowner, but more social. Dorm rooms, baths in rooms and halls, kitchen, and a cozy common area; ride board in lobby. Open daily 7am-3pm and 5-11pm; off-season 7am-1pm and 5-10pm. Curfew midnight. $9, nonmembers $12. Required sleepsheet $1. Private singles $22. Doubles $24. Guests receive ½-off cover at **Charly's,** downstairs, which has live music.

Hotel Du Beau, 19 W. Phoenix (774-6731), just behind the train station. This registered National Landmark hotel, built in 1929, once hosted L.A. film stars and Chicago gangsters. Kitchen, library, nightly videos, gift and necessities shop. No charge to borrow bikes. 4 campsites. $11. Breakfast included.

KOA, 5803 N. Hwy. 89 (526-9926), 6 mi. northeast of Flagstaff. Municipal bus routes stop nearby. Sites $16 for 2 people, with hookup $17. Each additional person $2.50.

You'll probably need a car to reach the public campgrounds that ring the city. Campgrounds at higher elevations close during the winter; many are small and fill up quickly during the summer, particularly on weekends when Phoenicians flock to these cool mountains. Stake out your site by 3pm, and you shouldn't encounter problems. National forest sites are usually $2 to 3 per night. Pick up a **Coconino National Forest** map ($2) in Flagstaff at the chamber of commerce. **Lake View,** 13 mi. southeast on Forest Hwy. 3 (U.S. 89A), has 30 sites ($5). **Bonito,** 2 mi. east on Forest Rd. 545, off U.S. 89, has 44 sites at Sunset Crater ($5). All have running water and flush toilets. Those (and only those) who can live without amenities can camp for free on any national forest land outside the designated campsites, unless there are signs to the contrary. For more information, call the Coconino Forest Service (527-7400; Mon.-Fri. 7:30am-4:30pm; 24-hr. emergency 526-0600).

Food

As befits a college town, cafés and coffeeshops liberally sprinkle Flagstaff, serving a variety of pastries, sandwiches, and hot drinks. Several typical Arizona steakhouses sizzle as well.

Macy's, 14 S. Beaver St. Superb fresh pasta ($3.25-5.25), plus a wide variety of vegetarian entrees, pastries, and espresso-based drinks. Open daily 7am-8pm, food served until 7pm.

Café Express, 16 N. San Francisco, near the Weatherford. Fine danishes ($1.50), plus various sandwiches and coffees. Open daily 7am-9pm.

Alpine Pizza, 7 Leroux St. (779-4109) and 2400 E. Santa Fe Ave. (779-4138). Excellent, huge *calzones* ($4.75) and *strombolis* ($5.50). Alpine with whole wheat crusts and a variety of toppings. Open Mon.-Thurs. 11am-11pm, Fri.-Sat. 11am-midnight, Sun. noon-11pm. Must be 21 Tues. and Thurs. after 3pm.

Main St. Bar and Grill, 4 S. San Francisco, (774-1519), across from the Downtowner. When the vegetarian meals and nonalcoholic drinks of the cafés get too healthy, try the delicious brabecued red meat ($2-11), the Buttery Texas Toast, and the calorie-laden but excellent selection of beers. Live music Fri.-Sat. Open Mon.-Sat. 11am-midnight, Sun. noon-10pm.

Near Flagstaff

Most of Flagstaff's legions of tourists are Grand Canyon-bound, but Flagstaff sits in the middle of six other "natural wonders," most not nearly as crowded. Seventeen mi. north on U.S. 89 lies **Sunset Crater National Monument** (527-7042). This volcanic crater erupted in 1065, forming cinder cones and lava beds; oxidized iron in the cinder gives the pre-nuclear crater its dramatic dusky color. Patronize the **visitors center.** (Open daily 7am-6pm; off-season 8am-5pm; in winter may close due to snow. Admission $3 per car or $1 per person.) Guided bus trips take off to **O'Leary Peak** three times per day (fare $2; make reservations at the visitors center). From the top you can look down the mouth of Sunset Crater (its treacherous terrain is closed to hiking). A ½-mi. self-guided tour wanders through the plain's surreal lava formations, 1½ mi. east of the visitors center. All interpretive materials along the trail are also available in Spanish, Dutch, French, and German. Guided tours of the lava tubes begin daily at noon and 3pm; aspiring spelunkers can rent a hard hat and light from the visitors center, don a coat, and explore as far as they dare.

Eighteen mi. north and several hundred feet down from Sunset Crater on a scenic loop road rests **Wupatki National Monument.** The ancestors of the Hopi moved here around 900 AD when they found the black-and-red soil ideal for agriculture. However, by 1215, droughts and overfarming precipitated the abandonment of their pueblos. Seven hundred seventy-six uneventful years later, Wupatki boasts some of the Southwest's most scenic ruins, perched on the sides of arroyos in view of Monument Valley and the San Francisco Peaks just for your vacation pleasure. Four major abandoned pueblos stretch along a 14-mi. park road from U.S. 89 to the visitors center. The largest and most accessible, **Wupatki Ruin,** rises three stories high. Below the ruin, you can see one of Arizona's two stone ballcourts, the sites of ancient games employing a rubber ball and a stone hoop in a circular court. Get information at the **Wupatki Ruin Visitors Center** (774-7000; open daily 7am-7pm; off-season 8am-5pm). When visiting Wupatki or Sunset Crater you can camp at the park's **Bonito Campground,** just across from the Sunset Crater Visitors Center. (Running water, no hookups. Sites $5. Overflow campers can pitch their tents for free in the national forest.)

Walnut Canyon National Monument lies 7 mi. east of Flagstaff off I-40. In the 13th century, the Sinagua people built more than 300 rooms under hanging ledges in the walls of this 400-ft.-deep canyon. From a glassed-in observation deck in the visitors center you can survey the whole canyon, out of whose striated gray walls sprout a stunning variety of plants. A trail snakes down from the visitors center past 25 cliff dwellings; markers along the trail describe aspects of Sinagua life, and identify the plants they used for food, dyes, medicine, and hunting.

Rangers lead hikes down a rugged trail to the original Ranger Cabin and many remote cliff dwellings. These strenuous two-and-a-half-hour hikes leave daily from the visitors center at 10am. Hiking boots and long pants are required. A walk along the main trail takes about 45 minutes. (Open daily 7am-6pm; Labor Day-Memorial Day 8am-5pm. Admission $1 perp person.)

The **San Francisco Peaks** are the huge, snow-capped mountains visible to the north of Flagstaff. Sacred to the Hopi, who believe that the Kachina spirits live there, **Humphrey's Peak** is the highest point in Arizona at 12,670 ft. Nearby **Mount Agassiz** has the area's best skiing. The **Fairfield Snow Bowl** operates four lifts from mid-December through mid-April; its 35 trails receive an average of 8 to 9 ft. of powder each winter. Lift tickets cost $18 on weekdays, $24 on weekends. Call the

Fairfield Resort switchboard (800-352-3524; 24 hr.) for information on ski conditions, transportation, and accommodations. During the summer, the peaks are perfect for **hiking**. When the air is clear, you can see the North Rim of the Grand Canyon, the Painted Desert, and countless square miles of Arizona and Utah from the top of Humphrey's Peak. Those not up to the hike should take the chairlift (20-30 min.) up the mountain (779-1951; runs Memorial Day-Labor Day; $7, seniors $5, ages 6-12 $3.50). The vista from the top of the lift proves almost as stunning. Picnic facilities and a cafeteria open from May to October. Since the mountains occupy national forest land, **camping** is free, although there are no organized campsites. To reach the peaks, take U.S. 180 about 7 mi. north to the Fairfield Snow Bowl turnoff. **Gray Line/Nava-Hopi** offers a tour of the Museum of Northern Arizona, Walnut Canyon, Sunset Crater, and Wupatki National Monument (see Flagstaff Practical Information). There is no other public transportation to these sights, nor, during the summer, to the San Francisco Peaks.

From Flagstaff to Phoenix

Although the traffic on I-17 to Sedona moves faster, 89A is more direct—in the end the two routes take about the same time, but 89A provides much better scenery. A few miles south of Flagstaff, U.S. 89A descends into **Oak Creek Canyon**, a trout-stocked creek bordered by trees and reddish canyon cliffs. You can pull over to swim or fish at several points along the route; look for **Slide Rock**, an algae-covered natural water chute. National forest campsites are scattered along 12 mi. of Oak Creek Canyon on the highway. Arrive early—sites fill quickly. Most of the campgrounds open from April to October. Call the forest service (282-4119) for information. **Manzanita** has a three-day limit, and **Cave Spring** and **Pine Flat** have seven-day limits. All have running water and toilets. (Sites $8.)

Twenty-seven mi. south of Flagstaff, the walls of Oak Creek Canyon open up to reveal the striking red rock formations surrounding **Sedona**, the setting for many western movies. The town itself, an incongruous blend of wealthy retirees and organic trend-followers, boasts a wide variety of restaurants and resort hotels.

Twenty mi. southwest of Sedona (take U.S. 89A to Rte. 279 and continue through the town of Cottonwood) lies **Tuzigoot National Monument**, which consists of a dramatic Sinaguan ruin overlooking the Verde Valley. (Open daily 8am-7pm. Entrance fee $3 per vehicle.)

From Sedona, Rte. 179 leads south to I-17. An amazing five-story cliff dwelling sits 10 mi. south back on I-17. **Montezuma Castle National Monument** (567-3322) is a 20-room adobe abode. Say that five times fast. The dwellings were constructed around 1100 AD, when overpopulation in the Flagstaff area forced the Sinagua south into the Verde Valley along Beaver Creek. Visitors can view the "castle" from a path below. (Path open daily 7am-7pm, visitors center daily 8am-6pm. Admission $3 per car.) Eleven mi. away is the little-known **Montezuma Well National Monument**. (Open daily 7am-7pm. Free.)

From Montezuma Castle, follow I-17: from the turnoff at Cordes Junction, 28 mi. south, a 3-mi. dirt road leads to **Arcosanti**. When completed around the turn of the century, Arcosanti will be a self-sufficient community embodying Italian architect Paolo Soleri's concept of **arcology**, somewhat mysteriously defined as "architecture and ecology working together as one integral process." Budgetarians will appreciate the architect's vision of a city where personal cars are obsolete. The complete city, with its subterranean parks, will surprise even the most imaginative Legoland architect. (Tours daily every hr. 10am-4pm. Open to the public daily 9am-5pm. $4 donation.) For more information, contact Arcosanti, HC 74, P.O. Box 4136, Mayer 86333 (632-7135). **Arizona Central** buses (see Phoenix Practical Information) can drop you off in Cordez Junction, 1½ mi. away from Arcosanti, but no tours go there.

Phoenix

Forget genetics—Phoenix is a product of its environment. Arizona's capital, and the 10th largest city in the U.S., may lie in the aptly named "Valley of the Sun," but it is more the pure heat that defines Phoenix. In the cooler (but still balmy) months, that warmth draws thousands of tourists for winter golf and Major League Baseball's spring training. But in the summer, the heat can turn downtown Phoenix into Arizona's largest ghost town. The heat from the town's burning namesake may make the beefiest of travelers or assistant editors feel like ectoplasm. And while the dryness keeps your skin sweat-free, it will also give you a thirst of such proportions you may vow never againt to forget watering your plants.

Phoenix was named in 1860 in hopes that a great city would rise from the ashes of the ancient Hohokam Empire. Certainly a *large* city has; the metropolitan area sprawls 60 mi. from the Mormon-dominated mesa to the retirement community of Sun City, continuing, cancer-like, to multiply past these boundaries. Avoid Phoenix year-round if you lack a car, and if you come in the summer, either have a swimming pool reserved and ready or expect to stay indoors.

Practical Information

Emergency: 911.

Visitor Information: Phoenix and Valley of the Sun Convention and Visitors Center, 505 N. 2nd St. (254-6500). Open Mon.-Fri. 8am-5pm. Convenient branch offices downtown on 2nd St. at Adams (open Mon.-Fri. 8am-4:30pm), and in Terminals 2 and 3 at Sky Harbor Airport (open Mon.-Fri. 9am-9pm, Sat.-Sun. 9am-5pm). Weekly Events Hotline, 252-5588. 24-hr. recorded information.

Amtrak: 401 W. Harrison (253-0121 or 800-872-7245), 2 blocks south of Jefferson St. at 4th Ave. Dangerous at night. Three per week to Los Angeles ($81) and El Paso ($81). Station open Sun.-Mon. and Thurs. 5:15am-12:45pm and 5:15-10:45pm, Tues.-Wed. 5:15-10:45pm, Fri.-Sat. 5:15am-12:45pm.

Greyhound: 5th and Washington St. (248-4040). To: Flagstaff (5 per day, $22.50); Tucson (10 per day, $18.45); Los Angeles (10 per day, $27.95). Open 24 hr.

Public Transport: Phoenix Transit, 253-5000. Most lines run to and from the City Bus Terminal, Central and Washington. Most routes operate Mon.-Fri. 5am-9:30pm, severely reduced service on Sat. Since many lines run only once every ½ hr., expect long, hot waits. Fares 75¢, disabled and seniors 35¢. To Mesa 85¢. 10-ride pass $7.50, all-day $2.50, disabled and seniors half-price. Pick up free time tables, maps of the bus system, and bus passes at the terminal. Buses running along Central Ave., Washington St., and Jefferson St. downtown cost only 25¢ within a limited zone Mon.-Fri. 9am-3pm. City bus #13 runs between the Sky Harbor International Airport and the city (buses leave the airport every ½ hr. Mon.-Fri. 6:20am-8:21pm, Sat. 5:17am-7:17pm, Sun. 7am-7pm; call Dial-A-Ride). Cab fare to downtown Phoenix costs about $6. Dial-A-Ride, 271-4545. Takes passengers anywhere in Phoenix only on Sun. and holidays 7am-7pm. Fare $1.50 plus 60¢ for each additional zone; seniors, disabled, and under 12 60¢, plus 30¢ each additonal zone. Call 258-9977 for weekday service in specified areas only. Some buses and Dial-a-ride vans have wheelchair lifts; call for details.

Car Rental: Rent-a-Wreck, 2422 E. Washington St. (254-1000). $20 per day with unlimited mi., 150 mi. radius. Open Mon.-Fri. 7am-7pm, Sat.-Sun. 9am-5pm. Must be 21 with credit card or cash deposit. Associated Rent-a-Car, 14 S. 22nd St. (275-6992). $22 per day with 100 free mi., 20¢ each additional mi. Open Mon.-Thurs. 7am-6pm, Fri. 7am-7pm, Sat. 8am-5pm, Sun. 9am-4pm. Must be 21 with credit card or cash deposit and Arizona driver's license.

Auto Transport Company: Auto Driveaway, 3530 E. Indian School Rd. (952-0339). First tank of gas free. Open Mon.-Fri. 9am-5pm. Must be 21 with $200 deposit.

Taxi: Ace Taxi, 254-1999. Yellow Cab, 252-5252.

Help Lines: Center Against Sexual Assault, 257-8095. Open 24 hr. Gay and Lesbian Hotline, 266-3733. Community Switchboard, 234-2752.

Post Office: General Delivery, 1543 E. Buckeye. Not downtown. Open Mon.-Fri. 8:30am-5:30pm. ZIP code: 85026; Area Code: 602.

The **city bus terminal** at Central Ave. and Washington St. idles in the heart of downtown Phoenix. **Central Avenue** runs north-south; "avenues" are numbered west from Central and "streets" are numbered east. **Washington Street** divides streets north-south.

Phoenix's sights scatter like sweat throughout the valley. Getting around with a car can be pleasant with air conditioning and a tape deck, but the summer heat and the city's limited bus service can turn an afternoon's recreation into an infernal ordeal.

Accommodations and Camping

Because Phoenix's hotel-owners keep a careful finger on the pulse of tourist activity, rates often change from week to week, peaking in late January and Febuary. Those without reservations, usually required in winter, should cruise the 25-mi. row of motels on occasionally decrepit, slightly dangerous East and West **Van Buren Street** or on **Main Street** (Apache Trail) in Tempe and Mesa. The city's notorious anti-vagabond ordinances make crashing in Phoenix parklands a bad idea. **Bed and Breakfast in Arizona,** P.O. Box 8628, Scottsdale 85252 (995-2831), can help visitors find accommodations in homes in Phoenix and throughout Arizona. (Preferred 2-night min. stay. Singles from $25. Doubles $35. Reservations recommended.) During the hot summer months, you can sleep in Phoenix in style by taking advantage of special packages offered by sun-battered resorts. Check for additional discounts for seniors and children.

Metcalf House (AYH), 1026 N. 9th St. (262-9439), a few blocks northeast of downtown. From the city bus terminal, take bus #7 down 7th St. to Roosevelt St., then walk 2 blocks east to 9th St. and turn left—the hostel is ½ block north. About a 20-min. walk from downtown. Dorm-style rooms, wooden bunks, and common showers. Kitchen, porch and common room, laundry. Check-in 7-9:30am and 5-11pm. $8, nonmembers $11. Linens $1. Bike rental $3 per day.

YMCA, 350 N. 1st Ave. (253-6181), downtown. From the city bus terminal, take bus #6 or walk 1 block west and 3½ blocks north. Mediocre rooms, hall bathroom. Men and women segregated by floor. Mostly retired people; rooms usually filled in winter. Singles $18, $60 per week. doubles $20. Weekly: singles $60; doubles $65. Key deposit $10.

Motel 6, 2323 E. Van Buren St. (267-7511), near the airport. Other locations north, east, and west of downtown, but this is the most central and, of course, they're all the same. Clean, comfortable rooms. A/C, pool, and TV with free movies. Singles $19. Doubles $25. Prices slightly higher in winter. Best to reserve a few days ahead.

Econolodge Airport Central, 2247 E. Van Buren St. (244-9341 or 800-492-2904). Nice, large rooms and a pool. Winter rates quite high; summer singles from $19.

Budget Lodge Motels, 402 W. Van Buren St. (254-7247), near downtown. A/C, and TV, plus a small pool in the parking lot. Singles $20, $85 per week in summer, but prices vary by season. Reserve a few weeks ahead in winter.

KOA, 2550 W. Louise (869-8189), 3 mi. north of Bell Rd. on I-17 at Black Canyon City. Sites $12.50 for 2 people. Each additional adult $2.

Food

Rarely will you find several restaurants together amid Phoenix's sprawl. Downtown is fed mainly by small coffeeshops, most of which close on weekends, though **The Mercado,** a faux-Mexican mall on E. Van Buren between 5th and 7th St. contains several inexpensive eateries, most open on weekends. For more variety, just drive down McDowell St.

Tacos de Juárez, 1017 N. 7th St. at Roosevelt (258-1744), near the hostel. Standard Mexican fare at rock-bottom prices. Specializes in tacos. A la carte items all under $3. Variable hours.

The Matador, 125 E. Adams St. downtown. Standard Mexican dinners $5-8. The deep-fried ice cream will never depose the banana split, but it's a novelty. Open daily 7am-11pm.

The Purple Cow, 200 N. Central (253-0861), in the San Carlos Hotel; also in the Park Central Mall. Great for lunch or fro-yo. A PC's delight. Open Mon.-Fri. 7am-4pm.

Sights

The **Heard Museum,** 22 E. Monte Vista (252-8848), 1 block east of Central Ave., has outstanding collections of Navajo handicrafts and promotes the work of contemporary Native American artists and craftspeople, many of whom give free demonstrations. Educate and prepare yourself for the journey into the Southwest's omnipresent Native American artifacts vending. (Guided tours daily. Open Mon.-Sat. 10am-5pm, Sun. 1-5pm. Admission $3, seniors $2.50, students and children $1.) The **Phoenix Art Museum,** 1625 N. Central Ave. (257-1222), 3 blocks south, has excellent exhibits of European, modern, and U.S. folk art. (Open Tues. and Thurs.-Sat. 10am-5pm, Wed. 10am-9pm, Sun. 1-5pm. Admission $3, seniors $2.50, students $1.50. Free Wed.)

The **Desert Botanical Gardens,** 1201 E. Galvin Way (941-1225), in Papago Park, 5 mi. east of the downtown area, grow a beautiful and colorful collection of cacti and other desert plants. Visit in the morning or late afternoon to avoid the midday heat. (Open daily 7am-sunset. Admission $3.50, seniors $3, children $1. Take bus #3 east to Papago Park.) Also in the park roars the **Phoenix Zoo,** 5810 E. Van Buren St. (273-7771), which includes special sections representing the Arizona desert and the African veldt. (Open daily 7am-4pm; winter 9am-5pm.)

Just south of Phoenix across the dry Salt River lies Tempe's **Arizona State University (ASU),** where you'll find the **Gammage Memorial Auditorium** (965-3434), at Mill Ave. and Apache Trail, one of the last major buildings designed by Frank Lloyd Wright. The pink-and-beige edifice draws both exclamations of amazement and snickers of derision. (20-min. guided tours every afternoon. Take bus #60 on weekdays, #22 on weekends.)

Unless you're in town for a convention, downtown Phoenix doesn't offer much. For an overview of the city and the mountains that poke out from among the houses, go to the Hyatt Regency at 2nd and E. Adams St. and take the glass elevator up 24 floors to the rotating **Compass Restaurant** (252-1234, ext. 7181). The restaurant itself is rather pricey, but if you dress nicely and order a coffee ($2 with free refills), drinks, or appetizers you should be able to sit in the "lounge" area for as much of the 55-minute period as you wish. (Open Mon.-Fri. 11am-2:30pm and 5:30-10pm, Sat. 5:30-10pm, Sun. 10am-2:30pm (brunch) and 5:30-10pm.)

Entertainment

Phoenix is the progressive rock and country capital of the Southwest, with an active (though awfully fashion-conscious) nightclub scene. New Music bands with names like Feedhog and Dead Hot Workshop blister the paint on the dark walls of the **Sun Club,** 1001 E. 8th St. (968-5802), in Tempe. (Music nightly at 8 or 9pm. Cover from $3.) **Char's Has the Blues,** 4631 N. 7th Ave. (230-0205), is self-explanatory. Dozens of junior John Lee Hookers rip it up nightly. (Music nightly at 9pm. Cover from $4.) Headbangers find their black leather, big guitar Eldorado in the bottom of the **Mäson Jar,** 2303 E. Indian School (956-6271). (*Heavy* jams nightly at 9 or 10pm. Cover from $2.) The free *New Times Weekly* (271-0040), on local magazine racks, lists club schedules. Pick up a copy of the **Cultural Calendar of Events,** a concise guide covering three months of area entertainment activities.

Near Phoenix

The drive along the **Apache Trail** to Tonto National Monument makes a great daytrip from Phoenix. Take Rte. 60-89 to Apache Junction, about 30 mi. east of Phoenix, then turn right onto Rte. 88, which follows the Apache Trail through the Superstition Mountains. Three mi. after Canyon Lake, the first of three artificial lakes along the trail, lies the good-humored town of **Tortilla Flat,** a way station for hot and dusty travelers. Five mi. east of Tortilla Flat begins a spectacular stretch of scenery. A well-maintained dirt road winds its way through 22 mi. of mountains and canyons to **Roosevelt Dam,** an enormous arc of masonry set between two huge red cliffs. Four mi. beyond the dam is the turn-off for **Tonto National Monument** (467-2241), where preserved dwellings of the Saledo tribe are tucked into sheltered caves in the cliffs. A one-hour self-guided hike up the mountainside, through the apartments and back, affords a lovely view of Roosevelt Lake. (Monument open daily 8am-5pm. Admission $3 per car or $1 per person.)

Tucson

In contrast to the mining towns of the 19th-century southwest and the sunny developments of the 20th, Tucson did not just appear out of nowhere. The city traces its roots centuries back to Hohokam and Pima settlements and the 1776 construction of a fortress wall by Spanish settlers. These early roots still affect Tucson's appearance; adobe and stucco are popular enough as building materials to make it difficult to distinguish a church from a saloon from more than 50 yards. In 1889, Tucson lost its position as capital of Arizona, but gained the University of Arizona as compensation. Today, the university's presence helps Tucson support a large number of galleries, museums, and performing-arts companies, while its status as a major research center has attracted high-tech industry. Air defense is as important to Tucson's growth today as land defense was to the original Spanish settlers, with the Davis-Monthan Air Force Base drawing new residents since World War II.

Practical Information

Emergency: 911.

Visitor Information: Metropolitan Tucson Convention and Visitors Bureau, 130 S. Scott Ave. (624-1889). Ask for a city bus map, the "Official Visitor's Guide," and the Arizona campground directory. Open Mon.-Fri. 8:30am-5pm; weekend times depend on season.

Tucson International Airport: On Valencia Rd., south of downtown. Bus #25 runs once per hr. to the Laos Transit Center, where bus #16 goes downtown. Last bus Mon.-Fri. at 7:50pm, Sat.-Sun. at 6:50pm. **Arizona Stagecoach** (889-9681) has a booth at the airport and will take you downtown for about $10.25 plus tip. Open 24 hr.

Amtrak: 400 E. Toole at 5th Ave. (623-4442 or 800-872-7245), in a large red-roofed building. Open Sun.-Wed. 7:45am-8:45pm, Thurs. 1:15-8:45pm., Sat. 7:45am-3:15pm. Three trains per week to: Phoenix ($26), Los Angeles ($97), and El Paso, TX ($68).

Greyhound: 2 S. 4th Ave. (792-0972), downtown between Congress St. and Broadway. To Phoenix (8 per day, $18.45).

Sun-Tran: 792-9222. Buses operate daily 5:30am-10pm. Fare 60¢, seniors 25¢. The "4th Avenue Trolley" (an eco-friendly, natural-gas burning, trolley-shaped van) runs from downtown, along 4th Ave., and to the university, 25¢. Racks containing maps and schedules at the Congress Hotel, the university visitors center, and elsewhere. "Rider's Information Guide" is particularly helpful.

Car Rental: Care Free (790-2655). $15 per day with 500 free mi.; within Tucson only. Open Mon.-Fri. 9am-5pm, Sat. 9am-3pm. Must be 21 with major credit card.

Bike Rental: The Bike Shack, 835 Park Ave. (624-3663), across from campus. $15 per day. Open Mon.-Thurs., (9:30am-6pm, Fri. 9:30am-5pm, Sat. 10am-5pm.

Help Line: Crisis Counseling/Suicide Prevention, 323-9373. Open 24 hr.

Post Office: 1501 S. Cherry Bell (620-5157). Open Mon.-Fri. 8:30am-5pm. **ZIP code:** 85726.

Area Code: 602.

Tucson catches the sun from the western flanks of the **Santa Catalina Mountains,** 65 mi. north of Nogales and the Mexican border on I-19 and 120 mi. southeast of Phoenix on I-10. The downtown area is just east of I-10, around the intersection of Broadway (running east-west) and Stone Ave., and includes the train and bus terminals. The **University of Arizona** studies 1 mi. northeast of downtown at the intersection of Park and Speedway Blvd.

Although surrounded by mountains, Tucson itself is quite flat, making most major streets (the downtown area a notable exception) perfectly straight. Streets are marked north, south, east, or west relative to Stone Ave. and Broadway. Avenues run north-south, streets east-west; because some of each are numbered intersections like "6th and 6th" are unfortunately possible.

Accommodations and Camping

Almost all of Tucson's hotels offer discounts in the summer, but they can't agree on when the summer begins and ends. The visitors bureau puts out a booklet of summer specials, most of which are available from mid-May through mid-September Tucson's motel row is along **South Freeway,** the frontage road along I-10 just north of the junction with I-19. The historic **Congress Hotel,** 311 E. Congress (622-8848), is conveniently located across from both Greyhound and Amtrak stations. The hotel also serves as a hostel, with bunk beds in a small room. Prices are higher in winter or for a beautifully renovated room. A café, a bar, and a club swing downstairs. (Hostel $12, nonmembers $15. Singles $25. Doubles $29.) **The Tucson Desert Inn,** I-10 and Congress (624-8151, 800-722-8458 outside AZ), could use new paint and carpeting, but has sunny rooms close to downtown. (Pool. Singles $24. Doubles $34. Winter $10 extra. Seniors 10% discount. Breakfast included.) **Travelodge,** 222 S. Freeway (791-7511, or 800-2555-3050), near downtown, has magnificent, towering palm trees, drab but bearable rooms. It also has a pool and movies. (Singles $25. Doubles $29. Winter $15 extra. AARP discount.) **Old Pueblo Homestays Bed and Breakfast,** P.O. Box 13603, Tucson 85732 (790-2399; open daily 8am-8pm), arranges overnight stays in private homes. (Singles from $25. Doubles $35-40. Reservations usually required 2 weeks in advance for winter.)

The best place to camp is the **Mount Lemmon Recreation Area** in the **Coronado National Forest.** Campgrounds and picnic areas are two minutes to two hours outside Tucson via the Catalina Hwy. The best unofficial camping in the forest is in Sabino Canyon, on the northeastern outskirts of Tucson. **Rose Canyon,** at 7000 ft., is heavily wooded, comfortably cool, and has a small lake. Sites at higher elevations fill quickly on weekends. (Sites $5 at Rose and Spencer Canyons; General Hitchcock Campground free, but no water available.) For more information, contact the **National Forest Service,** 300 W. Congress Ave. (670-6483), at Granada. 7 blocks west of Greyhound. (Open Mon.-Fri. 7:45am-4:30pm.) Among the commercial campgrounds near Tucson, try **Cactus Country RV Park** (574-3000), 10 mi. southeast of Tucson on I-10 off the Houghton Rd. exit. (Sites $10.50 for 1 or 2 people, with full hookup $17.50. Each additional person $2.)

Food

The dining scene in Tucson is dominated by "El" something Mexican restaurants, and for good reason: much farther north you begin to lose authenticity, while much farther south you have to worry about how the lettuce was irrigated.

El Charro, 311 N. Court Ave., 4 blocks north of the Civic Center. Flavorful but not fiery sun-dried *carne seca* in various forms (enchilada $4.75). Chips, salsa, and a pitcher of water free with every order. Open Sun.-Thurs. 11am-9pm, Fri.-Sat. 11am-10pm.

El Minuto, 354 S. Main Ave., just south of the community center. Voted Tucson's best in 1988. Largely local clientele. Cheese enchiladas $4.25, *chimichangas* $4.75-6. Open daily 11am-1am.

Café Magritte, 254 E. Congress, downtown. Bizarre culinary combinations (such as crabmeat, brie, sherry, and cashews) to match the unusual, even startling, decor. Interesting desserts as well. Open Mon. 11am-2am, Tues.-Thurs. 11am-11pm, Fri. 11am-midnight, Sat. 5pm-midnight.

Bentley's House of Coffee and Tea, 810 E. University Blvd., near the university. No smoking or styrofoam allowed in this crunchy joint. A wide variety of desserts and non-alcoholic drinks, plus more substantial meals. Part of the large bulletin board is reserved for upcoming events.

The Shanty, 401 9th St., off of 4th Ave. Pool tables, pleasant outdoor seating, and a wide variety of beers. Must be 21 with sleeves.

Entertainment

Tucsonites rock and roll near UA on Speedway Boulevard, and several country music lounges hunker down on North Oracle. The free "Tucson Weekly" (792-3630), comes out on Wednesdays and has arts listings.

Hotel Congress Historic Tap Room, 311 E. Congress (622-8848). Frozen in its 1938 incarnation. Eclectic, perhaps even weird, crowd, but very friendly. Open daily 11am-1am. Across the hall, a DJ plays "Mod . . . New Age . . . Alternative" dance music Thurs.-Sat. at **Club Congress.** Occasional live music. Drink specials $1.25.

Terry & Zeke's, 4376 E. Speedway Blvd. (325-3555). Longstanding institution of great live Texas blues and R&B. A hole-in-the wall with a great beer selection. Open daily noon-1am.

Berkey's, 5769 E. Speedway (722-0103). A slightly grungy, smoke-filled blues and rock club. Open daily noon-1am. Live music Tues.-Sun. at 9pm. Cover Fri.-Sat. $2.

The **Tucson Parks and Recreation Department** (791-4079) sponsors free concerts every Sunday evening in May, June, and September. Concerts begin at 7:30pm at the **De Meester Outdoor Performance Center.** Check the Thursday evening *Citizen* or call the office for information on other productions. The annual **Tucson Summer Arts Festival** runs from June through August, featuring dance, theater, music, and the visual arts. Pick up a schedule of events at the visitors center.

Sights

While most of Tucson's attractions lie some distance outside of town and are generally accessible only by car or tour bus, the city itself offers many diversions. The downtown is not "historic" by East Coast or European standards, with few buildings from before the Civil War; it lays a better claim as "artsy," with galleries and the **Tucson Museum of Art,** 140 N. Main Ave. (624-2333), whose impressive collection concentrates on the pre-Columbian. (Open Tues.-Sat. 10am-4pm, Sun. noon-4pm. Admission $2, seniors and students $1. Free Tues.)

The **University of Arizona,** whose "mall" sits where E. 3rd St. should be, parades another main concentration of in-town attractions. The mall itself is lovely, less for the architecture than the varied—and elaborately irrigated—vegetation. The **UA Visitor's Center,** at Cherry and the Mall (621-5130; events line 621-5784), stocks maps, event calendars, and information on current museum exhibits; the helpful staff answers questions both about the university and Tucson in general. (Open Mon.-Fri. 8am-5pm, Sat. 9am-2pm.) Across the Mall, the **Flandrau Planetarium** (621-7827) has a museum and a public telescope in addition to planetarium shows. (Museum open Mon. 1-4pm, Tue.-Thurs. 10am-4pm and 7-9pm, Fri. 7-9pm, Sat. 1-5pm and 7-9pm, Sun 1-5pm. Telescope open summer 8:30-10pm; winter Tues.-Sat 7-10pm. Free. Shows $3.75, seniors and children $3.) On the west side of campus lie several free museums. The **Arizona State Museum's** (621-6302) archeological displays offer little more than a nice break from the heat. (Open Mon.-Sat. 9am-5pm, Sun. 2-5pm. Free.) The **University of Arizona Museum of Art** (621-7567) displays lesser-known works ranging from 16th-century bronze sculpture to photographic prints. (Open summer Mon.-Fri. 10am-3:30pm, Sun. noon-4pm; school year Mon.-Fri. 9am-5pm, Sun. noon-4pm. Free.) Across from Park Ave. from the west end of campus, University Blvd. jams with shops catering to student needs—with clothing, records, and photocopies. **Campus Discount,** 9111 E. University Blvd. prices its fully-flavored sodas as low as 15¢, perhaps out of pure philanthropy. (Open Mon.-Fri. 7:30am-9pm, Sat. 9am-7pm, Sun. 10am-6pm.)

A vibrant local event, the **mariachi mass,** thrills at **St. Augustine,** 192 S. Stone Ave. downtown. The singing and dancing, which are not intended as tourist attractions, take place in Tucson's old white Spanish cathedral. (Sun. 8am mass in Spanish.)

Near Tucson

Attractions, both natural and artificial, surround Tucson. To the north, a tram takes visitors from the visitors center through **Sabino Canyon** (749-2861), where cliffs and waterfalls make an ideal spot for picnics and day hikes. (Tram daily every ½ hr. 9am-4:30pm.)

A forest of giant cacti grows in **Saguaro National Monument** (296-8576). The tall, forked *saguaro* cactus often lives 200 years and grows over 40 ft. tall. The monument divides into two areas; opinion splits over which is more interesting. To the west of the city, the **Tucson Mountain Unit,** on N. Kinney Rd. at Rte. 9 (883-6366), has limited hiking trails for day use only and an auto loop. (Visitors center open daily 8am-5pm. Free.) Just south of this unit is **The Arizona-Sonora Desert Museum,** 2021 N. Kinney Rd. (883-2702), where both the animals and plants of the southwest desert come up close. Cool morning hours are the best time to see the animals, who have the sense to rest during the afternoon. (Open winter daily 8:30am-5pm; summer 7:30am-6pm. Admission $6, ages 6-12 $1.) The way to and from the Tucson Mountain Unit and the Desert Museum goes through **Gates Pass,** whose vistas make it a favorite spot for watching sunrises and sunsets. To the east of the city, the **Rincon Mountain Unit** (296-8576), on the Old Spanish Trail east of Tucson, offers the same services as the Tucson Unit as well as overnight hikes. (Visitors center open daily 8am-5pm. Admission $3 per vehicle.)

Pima's **Titan II Missile Museum,** La Canada Dr. (791-2929), in Green Valley, 25 mi. south of Tucson, is a chilling monument built around a deactivated missile silo. (Open Wed.-Sun. 9am-5pm; Nov.-April daily 9am-5pm. Admission $4, seniors $3, ages 10-17 $2.) The Southwest is the desert graveyard for many an outmoded aircraft; low humidity and sparse rainfall preserve the relics. Over 20,000 warplanes, from WW II fighters to Vietnam War jets, are parked in ominous, silent rows on the **Davis-Monthan Air Force Base** (750-4570), 15 mi. southeast of Tucson. Take the Houghton exit off I-10, then travel west on Irvington to Wilmont. (Free tours Mon. and Wed. at 9am. Call ahead for reservations.) You can also view the 2-mi. long graveyard through the airfield fence.

Old Tucson, a preserved movie set, purports to convey the feel of the old cowboy-and-rustler Southwest, but the real thing exists in **Tombstone,** 71 mi. southeast of Tucson. An old silver mining town, Tombstone was the scene of the famous shootout at the O.K. Corral and the home of such legendary Western figures as Wyatt Earp, Bat Masterson, and Doc Holiday. The **O.K. Corral,** on Allen St. (457-3456), next to City Park, is open to visitors, and doubles as a general tourist information center. (Open daily 8:30am-5pm. Admission $1. Tickets $2.75; includes a movie screening, a copy of the *Epitaph,* and a cold *sarsparilla.*) Tombstone's sheriffs and outlaws, very few of whom died of natural causes, were laid to rot in the **Boothill Cemetery.** Try to catch the mock gunfights staged every Sunday at 2pm alternately between the O.K. Corral and the town streets. Come prepared to open your wallet; "the town too tough to die" touts an almost irresistible assortment of kitschy curios in several shops. For more information on Tombstone's sights, contact the O.K. Corral or the **Tombstone Tourism Association,** 9 S. 5th St. (457-2211; open Mon.-Fri. 9am-5pm, Sat.-Sun. 10am-5pm).

Nevada

Nevada once walked the straight and narrow path. Explored by Spanish missionaries and settled by Mormons, the Nevada Territory's searing, arid climate seemed a perfect place for ascetics to strive for moral uplift. But the discovery of gold in 1850 and silver in 1859 won the state over permanently to the worship of filthy lucre. When the boom-bust ferris wheel finally stalled during the Great Depression, Nevadans responded by shaking off even the last vestiges of traditional virtue. They made gambling and marriage-licensing the state industries, the twain meeting in the drive-through divorce. In a final break with the rest of the country, Silver Staters legalized prostitution—except in Reno and Las Vegas—and began paying Wayne Newton enormous amounts of cash for his concerts.

But a Nevada exists outside the gambling towns. The forested slopes of Lake Tahoe, shared with California, offer serenity in little resorts away from the casinos of the south shore. The rest of a mostly expansive and bone-dry Nevada is country-side, where the true West lingers in its barren glory.

Practical Information

Capital: Carson City.

Tourist Information: Nevada Commission on Tourism, #2075 Valley Bank Bldg., U.S. 50, Carson City 89710 (885-4322). Open Mon.-Fri. 8am-5pm. **Nevada Division of State Parks,** Nye Bldg., 201 S. Fall, Carson City 89701 (885-4384). Open Mon.-Fri. 8am-5pm.

Time Zone: Pacific (3 hr. behind Eastern). **Postal Abbreviation:** NV.

Area Code: 702.

Las Vegas

Only in Vegas could a major museum devote itself to Liberace. Forget Hollywood images of Las Vegas glamor; the city at base is nothing but a desert Disneyland. As a small, small world of mild, middle-aged debauchery, Vegas simply replaces Mickey and Minnie with overbright neon marquees, monolithic hotel/casinos, bese-quinned Ziegfieldesque entertainers, quickly marrying them in rococo wedding chapels.

And yet, amazingly, the city takes itself very seriously—employees literally wear poker faces, and fail to see anything amusing about a nightmarishly overdecorated casino lobby. What Vegas stays most serious about is making money. The city that models itself after L.A. gangster Bussy Siegel's Flamingo Hotel rakes in a substantial share of the annual $126 billion spent at U.S. gambling tables. Yet even if you wisely choose not to gamble, clever customers can take advantage of the inexpensive buffets and cheap drinks; the visiting voyeur may find that the best show in town is not an opulent "stage spectacular" but simply the bizarre and free spectacle of decadent Las Vegas itself.

Practical Information

Emergency: 911

Visitor Information: Las Vegas Convention and Visitors Authority, 3150 Paradise Rd. (733-2471), at the Convention Center, 4 blocks from the Strip, by the Hilton. Up to date info on hotel bargains and buffets. Open Mon.-Fri. 8am-5pm.

McCarran International Airport: (798-5410), at the southeast end of the Strip. Main terminal on Paradise Rd. Within walking distance of the University of Nevada campus and the south-ern casinos. Buses and taxis to downtown.

Amtrak: 1 N. Main St. (386-6896; fares and schedules 800-872-7245), in the Union Plaza Hotel. To: L.A. ($63, round trip $75; reservations required); San Francisco ($112, round trip $119); and Salt Lake City ($82, round trip $89). Open daily 6am-8:30pm.

Greyhound: 200 Main St. (382-2640), at Carson Ave. downtown. To: L.A. ($34), Reno ($38), Salt Lake City ($45), and Denver ($86). **Las Vegas-Tonopah-Reno Lines** provides service to Phoenix ($30). Open 24 hrs.

Las Vegas Transit: 384-3540. Common transfer point at 200 Casino Center downtown. Trol-ley shuttle runs downtown along Fremont St. (Fare 50¢, seniors and under 12 25¢.) Most buses 5:30am-9pm. Strip buses (#6) every 15 min. 7am-12:45am, every ½ hr 12:45-2:45am, every hr. 2:45-6:30am. Fare $1.10, ages 6-17 40¢, seniors and disabled people 10 rides for $4.20, transfers 15¢.

Tours: Gray Line Tours, 1550 S. Industrial Rd. (384-1234). Bus tours to Hoover Dam/Lake Mead (Mon.-Sat. at 9 and 11am, Sun. at 9am; 5 hr., $17); the Grand Canyon (2 days, $95 double occupancy, Mon. and Wed. at 7am; Oct.-April Mon., Wed., and Fri. at 7:30am); Old Nevada (7 hr., $27.75, daily at 10am). Reservations required. **Ray and Ross Tours,** 300 W. Owens St. (646-4661). Bus tours to Hoover Dam (6 hr., $17) and Hoover Dam/Lake Mead (7 hr., $24).

Taxi: Checker Cab, 873-2227. $1.70 first 1/7 mi., $1.40 each additional mi.

Car Rental: Avon, 800-621-2219 or 387-6717. $22 per day with unlimited mi. in Nevada. $25 for age 18. Free pickup from airport. Open Thurs.-Sat. 7am-midnight, Sun.-Wed. 7am-10pm. Must have credit card. **Fairway Rent-A-Car,** 5300 S. Paradise Rd. (736-1786 or 800-634-3476), near the airport. $17 per day. 100 free mi. per day, 35¢ each additional mile. Open daily 8am-9pm. Must be 21 and stick to local use only.

Help Lines: Crisis Line, 876-4357. **Rape Crisis,** 366-1640. **Gambler's Anonymous,** 385-7732. All open 24 hrs.

Post Office: 301 E. Stewart (385-8944), behind Lady Luck. Open Mon.-Fri. 9am-5pm. General delivery open Mon.-Fri. 10am-3pm. General delivery **ZIP code:** 89114.

Area Code: 702.

Las Vegas lurks in the southwest corner of Nevada, about 290 driving mi. northeast of Los Angeles and 589 mi. southeast of San Francisco. From L.A., the drive takes five to six hours, going east on I-10 and turning north on I-15 in San Bernardino. **Gambler's specials** number among the cheapest and most popular ways to reach Las Vegas. These bus tours leave early in the morning and return at night or on the next day; ask in L.A., San Francisco, or San Diego tourist offices. You can also call casinos for information. Prices include everything except food and gambling, though you are expected to stay with your group. Right.

Vegas has two major casino areas. The **downtown** area, around Fremont and 2nd St., is walker-friendly; casinos cluster close together, their big doors all-too-welcoming, and some of the sidewalks are even carpeted. The other main area, known as the **Strip,** is a collection of mammoth casinos on both sides of intimidatingly busy Las Vegas Blvd. S. Stay downtown during the day, unless you have a car or like long, hot, unshaded stretches of sidewalk. Except for the neighborhoods just north and west of downtown, Vegas is generally, and especially on the Strip, a safe place for late-night strolling. Security guards and lights reproduce in amoeba-like fashion; there is almost always pedestrian traffic.

Accommodations and Camping

You can easily find cheap food and lodging in Vegas, thanks to casino owners who make their money on gambling. Watch the travel and entertainment sections of local newspapers for ever-changing specials. Prices tend to rise on weekends and holidays, but with over 67,000 hotel rooms you can find some place to rest that slot-machine arm.

Las Vegas Independent Hostel, 1208 Las Vegas Blvd. S. (385-9955). Not AYH-affiliated, but gives members discounts. Spartan but airy rooms with foam mattresses. Free coffee, tea, and lemonade. Ride board in kitchen. Tours every Mon. to North Rim of the Grand Canyon. Office open daily 7-10am and 3-11pm, Nov.-March 8am-10pm and 5-11pm. Students and AYH members $8, nonmembers $10. Key deposit $2.

Las Vegas International Hostel (AYH), 1236 Las Vegas Blvd. South. (382-8119). Small kitchen. Rooms in separate cabins. Lots of common areas, even grass. Office open daily 7-10am and 5-11pm. $8.50, nonmembers $11.50. Key deposit $5.

Nevada Hotel, 235 S. Main St. (385-7311 or 800-637-5777). TV in large, pleasant rooms. Singles and doubles $18.

Crest Motel, 207 N. 6th St. (382-5642 or 800-777-1817), at Ogden St. Friendly management. TV, VCR, and refrigerators in room. Singles Sun.-Thurs. $25, Fri.-Sat. $35, kitchenettes $35. Breakfast at El Cortez included. Key deposit $3.

Motel 6, 195 E. Tropicana Ave. (798-0728), near the airport, 3 blocks from the Strip. Pool and jacuzzi. Even with 577 rooms, make reservations a day or two ahead for weekends. Singles $28. Doubles $34.

El Cortez, 600 E. Fremont (385-5200; 800-634-6703 for reservations). TV and A/C. Singles and doubles $23.

For all the luxuries of a hotel except room service, park your RV next door to a casino like: **Hacienda,** 3950 Las Vegas Blvd. S. (739-8214 or 800-634-6942), for $9.75; or **Circus Circus,** 500 Circus Circus Dr. (734-0410; 800-634-3450 for reservations), for $10.75, with free shuttle service to the Strip. Tent campers have to settle for the **KOA Campground,** 4315 Boulder Hwy. (451-5527), east of the Desert Inn. (Sites from $16 for 2 people. Each additional adult $4, each additional child $2.50. Pool, spa, recreation hall, and free shuttle to the Strip included.)

You'll need a car to reach any of the noncommercial campsites around Vegas. Twenty mi. west of the city on Rte. 159 rolls **Red Rock Canyon** (363-1921), where you can see an earthquake fault-line and other geological marvels. Camp here for free, but only in **Oak Creek Park.** Twenty-five mi. east, **Lake Mead National Park** (293-4041) has several campgrounds. Fifty-five mi. northeast via I-15 and Rte. 169, **Valley of Fire State Park** has campsites and spectacular sandstone formations.

Food

Astonishingly cheap prime rib dinners, all-you-can-eat buffets, and champagne brunches beckon high- and low-rollers alike into the casinos. In most cafeterias, buffet food is served nonstop from 11am to 10pm. Expect the "all-you-can-stomach" quality that comes from leaving food on a warming table for three hrs. Cruise the Strip or roam around downtown for advertised specials. The Visitors Authority (see Practical Information) keeps a reasonably up-to-date list of buffets. Aptly named **Circus Circus** looms the largest; pay $4, grab a 16-in. plate, and begin to chow in this three-ring crowd (4:30-11pm). Not as crowded as the bigger casinos, **El Rancho,** 2755 Las Vegas Blvd. S. (796-2222), serves a brunch buffet on weekends ($3.25; Sat.-Sun. 8am-3pm). The **Hacienda,** 3950 Las Vegas Blvd. S. (739-8911), lies a cut above comparably priced buffets, with champagne at breakfast and 12 entrees at lunch (breakfast Mon.-Fri. 7-11am, $4; lunch 11:30am-3pm, $5). **Caesar's Palace,** 3570 Las Vegas Blvd. S. (731-7110), is considerably more expensive than most; yet its comfortable chairs, friendly service, and especially appetizing display of fresh foodstuffs make it *the* place for a gastronomic orgy. Go for breakfast to get the most for your money. (Breakfast Mon.-Fri. 8:30-10:30am. $6.50. Lunch 11am-2:30pm; $8.)

Like inexpensive food, liquid meals come easy, operating on the same principle: casino operators figure that a tourist drawn in by cheap drinks will stay to spend tons more playing the slots or losing at cards. Drinks in most casinos cost 75¢-$1, free to those who look like they're playing. Look for 50¢ shrimp cocktail specials and offers of free champagne at casino entrances.

Restaurants not owned by casinos cannot match the buffet prices, but are a nice respite for those suffering from too much chipped beef and fish croquettes. Downtown holds a number of Thai, Chinese, and Italian restaurants; cutting across the Strip, Sahara Blvd. and Flamingo Rd. both scarify themselves with such places. Try the **Silver Dragon Restaurant,** 1510 E. Flamingo Rd., 1 block east of Maryland Pkwy., which serves great Cantonese and Szechuan meals. Their "graveyard menu" offers nocturnal nourishment. (Open daily 11:30am-5am.) Those who desire more typical Southwestern fare should visit **Mi Casa,** 2710 E. Desert Inn Rd., which offers enchiladas, strawberry *sopapillas,* and live Latin music nightly. (Open daily 11am-3am.)

Casino-Hopping and Nightlife

Casinos and their restaurants, nightclubs, and even wedding chapels stay open 24 hrs. You'll almost never see clocks or windows in a casino—the owners are afraid that players might realize it's past midnight, turn into pumpkins, and neglect to lose a nickel more. You'll quickly discern which games are suited for novices and which require more expertise, from **penny slots** in laundromats to **baccarat**, in which the stakes can rise as high as tens of thousands of dollars. The hotels and most casinos give first-timers "funbooks," with alluring gambling coupons that can stretch your puny $5 into $50 worth of wagering. But remember that casinos function on the basis of most tourists leaving considerably closer to the poverty line than when they arrived; don't bring more than you're prepared to lose cheerfully. Whether or not those under 21 can gamble is also a crapshoot. Keep your wallet in your front pocket, and beware of the thieves who prowl casinos to nab big winnings from unwary jubilants. You can get an escort from the casino security, or leave your winnings with the cashier, to be picked up later. Criminals often target seniors, who should be especially careful.

Visit several casinos if you can (entrance is always free) to survey the atmosphere, decor, and clientele. **Caesar's Palace**, 3570 Las Vegas Blvd. (731-7110), has taken the "theme" aspect of Vegas to the extreme; where other casinos have miniature, mechanized horse racing, Caesar's has chariot racing. Next door, the **Mirage**, 3400 Las Vegas Blvd. S. (791-7111), includes among its attractions Siberian white tigers and a "volcano" that erupts in fountains and flames every quarter hour, 8pm to 7am, excepting rain. **Circus Circus**, 2880 Las Vegas Blvd. S. (734-0410), attempts to cultivate a family atmosphere, embodied by the huge clown on its marquee. While parents run to the card tables and slot machines downstairs, their children can spend 50¢ tokens upstairs on the souped-up carnival midway. Two stories above the casino floor, tightrope-walkers, fire-eaters, and rather impressive acrobats perform from 11am to midnight.

Aside from gambling, every major casino has nightly shows. Some, like the **Union Plaza**, 1 Main St. (386-2110), feature free performances by live bands. Extra bucks will buy you a seat at a made-in-the-U.S.A. phenomenon—the Vegas spectacular. The overdone but stunning twice-nightly productions feature marvels such as waterfalls, explosions, fireworks, and casts of thousands. "Les Folies Bergère," a francophile musical farce at the **Tropicana**, 3801 Las Vegas Blvd. S. (739-2411), represents the genre well and offers an all-inclusive dinner for $27 ($20 Fri.-Wed. at 8pm, $14 at 11pm).

You can also see Broadway plays and musicals, ice revues, and individual entertainers in concert. Some "production shows" are topless, most tasteless. Musical stars, on the other limb, tend to be such libido-driven performers as Wayne Newton and Frank Sinatra, whose shows cost a small fortune. The lowest price for a cocktail show is $5. Dinner (steak is the norm) shows start at $10. To see someone such as Diana Ross or "Come aboard, we're expecting you" Charo, people fork over $35 or more. Far more reasonable are the many "revues" featuring imitations of (generally deceased) performers. In Vegas you can't turn around without bumping into an aspiring Elvis clone, or perhaps the *real* Elvis, impersonating the impersonator . . . in disguise.

Pick up a copy of *Las Vegas Today,* which has plenty of discount coupons, show information, and up-to-date special events listings, or *What's On,* distributed by the Visitors Authority (see Practical Information). Also good are *Entertainment Today, Vegas Visitor,* and *Fun and Gaming. The Games People Play,* distributed by the Golden Nugget Hotel, explains how each casino game is played. Many casinos also offer gambling classes for novices.

Nightlife in Vegas gets rolling around midnight, and keeps going until everyone drops. The casino lounge at the **Las Vegas Hilton**, 3000 Paradise Rd. (732-5111), has a disco every night (no cover, 1-drink min.). A popular disco, **Gipsy**, 4605 Paradise Rd. (731-1919), southeast of the Strip, may look deserted at 11pm, but by 1am the medium-sized dance floor packs a mixed crowd. **Carrow's**, 1290 E. Flamingo

Rd. (796-1314), has three outdoor patios, plus plenty of people and plants. During the 4-7pm Happy Hour, the filling hors d'oeuvres are free.

Reno

The chance for quick money lures most tourists to Reno; some desperate gamblers tug at the bank of slot-machines in the local supermarket (**J.J.'s Food Co. Market**, Virginia and 5th St.). Outnumbered only by pawn-shops and wedding chapels, casinos spill anxious crowds onto sidewalks and flower beds beneath their neon glow. The **Reno Arch** (on Virginia at Commercial), originally festooned across the road with its "Biggest little city in the world" slogan in 1926, gained 1600 bulbs a few years ago. Each casino claims fame and uniqueness for its "loosest slots" or accountant-certified "highest paybacks." The **Cal Neva**, 38 E. 2nd St. (323-1046), once held the world jackpot record ($6.8 million, made in February 1988). Most venues have live music in the evenings; the most famous and traditional **Bally's**, 2500 E. 2nd St (634-3450), hosts stars like Sinatra and Liza Minnelli. Check details in the weekly freebie *Showtime*. A free shuttle leaves the Cal Neva for Bally's every 40 minutes from 10am to 2am. **Circus Circus**, 500 N. Sierra (634-3450), has free "big-top" performances every night. Before you "stack 'em or rack 'em" (your chips, that is), you might try the "Behind the Scenes" gaming tour, which takes you to the other side of the one-way mirrors, and teaches you the rudiments of the games—the only time you'll be given chips for nothing (well, almost nothing: $5 tours Mon.-Fri. at 12:30 and 2pm; leaving from the visitors center, 135 N. Sierra, 348-7403).

If you plan to **gamble,** the best deals come up in the main casinos where expensive rooms are pro-rated for gaming packages. Usually, the casino welcome center can advise on discounts and specials. Ask a lot of questions and the prices may drop dramatically.

The casino buffets make a diner seem expensive: to bring gamblers in, or to prevent them wandering out in search of food, they provide a range of all-you-can-eat places. The dining room looks like the Starship Enterprise, but **Fitzgerald's** buffet is filling and good for breakfast (7:30-10:30am, $3), lunch (11am-3:30pm, $3.50), or dinner (4-10pm, $5). **Circus Circus**, 500 N. Sierra, offers enormous quantities on plastic plates. "Eat all you want, but eat all you take," they ask. Breakfast (6-11:30am, $2.29), brunch (11:30am-4pm, $2.69), dinner (4:30-11pm, $3.89). Friday seafood (4:30-11pm, $5.99). Be aware that price directly reflects quality, so have your Pepto ready and remember locals eat at only *some* of the buffets. Drinks are also cheap (beer nominally priced 75¢ or free) downstairs where the gaming takes place, either at the bar or on trays from sadly stereotypical bunny-girls.

For peaceful eating, outside the bustle of smoke-filled casinos, Reno has a varied selection of inexpensive restaurants. The large Basque population came to Nevada originally as sheepherders, bringing their fiery cooking which locals adore and wisely recommend. **Louis' Basque Corner**, 301 E. 4th St., is a local institution. A hefty $12.50 will buy you a full-course meal, including wine, soup, and salad; $6 for an a la carte entree. (Open Mon.-Sat. 10am-11pm, Sun. 4-11pm.) The **Santa Fe Hotel**, 235 Lake St., offers Basque dinners ($11) in a classic dining room with green-and-white checkered tablecloths. The real wood bar and ancient slots allow for pleasant 1950s time travel. (Open for lunch at 12:30pm and for dinner 6-9pm.) **Landrums's**, 1300 S. Virginia St., serves less spicy diner "cuisine." Great dinners with salad, vegetable, potatoes, and bread cost about $5. (Open 24 hr.) Vegetarians tiring of salad bars designed merely to round out the nutrition of a steak dinner will find refuge at **The Blue Heron**, 1091 S. Virginia, nesting place of natural foods in a large sunny room. Savory carrot cake costs $1.50. (Open Mon.-Sat. 11am-9pm.)

For the cheapest accommodations, head to the southern part of town. **Windsor Hotel**, 214 West St. (323-6171), 2 blocks from the Greyhound station toward Virginia, definitely merits a spin. The hall showers and rooms are wonderfully clean. Large fans wave lazily overhead to compensate for the lack of A/C. (Singles $22, with bath $26; Fri.-Sat. $26, with bath $28. Doubles $24; Fri.-Sat. $30.) **El Cortez,** 239 W. 2nd St. (322-9161), 1 block east of the Greyhound station, features pleasant management and great bargains. Ask for a private bath. The cheapest singles don't have A/C. (Singles and doubles $23-25, triples $33; in winter $16-17 and $19, respectively. Add $3 on weekends and holidays.) **Motel 6** has 3 locations in Reno, all about 1½ mi. from the downtown casinos: 866 N. Wells (786-9852), north of I-80 off Well Ave. exit; 1901 S. Virginia (827-0255), near Virginia Lake; 1400 Stardust St. (747-7390), north of I-80 off Keystone Ave. exit, then west on Stardust. (Singles $27. Each additional adult $6.) Families should try here first: kids under 18 stay free, and all three locations have pools.

You can park your RV overnight at **Bally's,** 2500 E. 2nd St. (789-2000), for $18. But the **Toiyabe National Forest** begins only a few mi. southwest of Reno, and you can try the woodland sites of **Davis Creek Park** (849-0684), 17 mi. south on U.S. 395, then ½ mi. west (follow the signs), with full service, including showers, but no hookups. (Sites $6.) The nearest Forest Service campground sits high atop **Mount Rose** (784-5030), 20 mi. southwest of Reno on Rte. 431. (No showers or hookups; sites $6.) **Boca Basin,** just over the California line, 23 mi. west on I-80, is a safe bet for campers heading on towards San Francisco or Sacramento. (2-week max. stay. No hookups. Free.)

Gay and lesbian travelers should be aware that public displays of affection are actively ticketed and can even lead to arrests in Nevada. Even,so, Reno has a fairly large community and 10 gay bars that complement its other nightlife. *The Reno Bugle* is a good monthly guide to local events. The **Chute No. 1,** 1278 S. Virginia St. (323-7825), provides the best floor to dance on, but **Ron's Piano Bar** (829-7667) proves a quieter place for beer and conversation.

Only 14 mi. from the California border, 443 mi. north of Las Vegas, Reno glitters at the intersection of I-80 and U.S. 395, which runs along the eastern slope of the Sierra Mountains. Scan West Coast big-city newspapers for **gambler's specials** on bus and plane fare excursion tickets. Some include rebates and casino credits. Although the city sprawls for miles, most of the major casinos are clustered downtown along **Virginia** and **Sierra Streets,** between 2nd and 4th St. The adjacent city of **Sparks** also has several casinos along I-80. The bus station and all the hotels listed are downtown or within a 10-minute walk. Downtown Reno is compact, and its wide streets and well-lit 24-hr. activity are heavily patrolled. However, only groups should walk in the outskirts of town, especially the northeast corner, after dark.

The **chamber of commerce,** 135 N. Sierra (329-3558), has a friendly staff and the usual deluge of maps and brochures. Pick up the excellent *Reno/Tahoe Travel Planner.* The weekly *Showtime* lists current events and performers. (Open Mon.-Fri. 9am-5pm, Sat. noon-5pm.) Adjacent to the chamber, **Ticket Station** sells tickets for shows (348-7403). **Cannon International Airport** (328-6499) is on East Plumb Lane and Terminal Way, on I-580 3 mi. southeast of downtown. Take bus #24 on Lake Ave. near 2nd St. Most major hotels have free shuttles for their guests. The **Amtrak** station, on E. Commercial Row and Lake St. (329-8638 or 800-872-7245), offers one train per day to San Francisco ($63), Salt Lake City ($103), and Chicago ($196). (Open daily 7:30am-6:30pm.) **Greyhound,** on 155 Stevenson St. (322-2970), ½ block from W. 2nd St., sports a nice, modern depot. Buses service San Francisco (15 per day, $42). **Gray Line Tours,** 2570 Tacchino St. (329-1147; outside NV 800-822-6009), offers bus tours to Virginia City (Tues., Thurs., Sat. at 11am; 4 hr.; $15) and Lake Tahoe/Virginia City (daily at 9am, 8½ hr., $30). **Reno Citifare** at Plaza and Center St. (348-7433; open 24 hr.) provides local bus service. (Fare 75¢, seniors and disabled 30¢, students 50¢.) Most routes operate from 5am to 7pm, some 24 hr.

The **post office** meters on 50 S. Virginia St. (786-5523; open Mon.-Fri. 7am-5pm; general delivery Mon.-Fri. 10am-3pm). The general delivery ZIP code is 89501. The **area code** is 702.

New Mexico

Vast, quiet spaces whisper New Mexico's story, from the mysterious ruins whose cliff-dwelling residents left 1000 years ago to the menacing silence of the world's first atomic testing ground. The first arrivals ambled into New Mexico during the Stone Age, setting up house in the area's many caves. Twenty thousand years later, the Anasazi elevated cliff-dwelling to an art form, constructing masterful buildings in the caves and valleys of this semi-arid landscape. A succession of residents followed in their tracks, including other Native American nations, Spanish conquistadors, Mexican settlers, and finally U.S. residents, who acquired the area after the Mexican-American War of 1848.

After 140 years of U.S. government domination, New Mexico still has a heterogeneous ethnic population. On the reservations, Navajo and Pueblo tribes preserve parts of their heritage in the face of poverty and dependence upon white tourism and government aid. In the cities, descendants of Spanish and Mexican Americans have incorporated elements of Native American culture into their own. Along with new immigrants from Latin America and Asia has come a sustained invasion of North American New Age devotees, seeking heightened spirituality in the ancient Native American religions and the jaw-dropping beauty of New Mexico.

Practical Information

Capital: Santa Fe.

Tourist Information: Dept. of Economic Development, 1100 St. Francis Dr., Santa Fe 87503 (827-0291 or 800-545-2040), **Park and Recreation Division,** Villagra Bldg., P.O. Box 1147, Santa Fe 87504 (827-7465). **U.S. Forest Service,** 517 Gold Ave. SW, Albuquerque 87102 (842-3292).

Time Zone: Mountain (2 hr. behind Eastern). **Postal Abbreviation:** NM.

Taos

Taos, a small town at the foot of the Sangre de Cristo range, has presented a cultural mosaic since the Spanish arrived in 1615. Despite both peaceful settlement and belligerent intrusion by the Spanish and other Europeans, the Taos Pueblos have managed to retain much of their own culture. Today, Taos provides the clearest example of the tricultural legacy of northern New Mexico: white, Hispanic, and Native Americans maintain their own identities and share the natural wonders of the area.

Practical Information

Emergency: Police, 758-2216. **Ambulance,** 758-1911.

Visitor Information: Chamber of Commerce, Paseo del Pueblo Sur (Rte. 68) (758-3873 or 800-732-8267), just south of McDonald's. Open Mon.-Fri. 9am-6pm, Sat.-Sun. 9am-5pm. **Information booth** (no phone) in the center of the plaza. Open Mon.-Sat. 9am-4pm. Pick up maps and tourist literature from either.

Taos Municiple Airport: 758-4995, northwest of town off Hwy. 64.

Greyhound/Trailways: Paseo del Pueblo Sur (Rte. 68) (758-1144), about 1 mi. south of Taos. To Albuquerque (4 per day, $21).

Public Transport: Pride of Taos Trolley, 758-8340. Serves several hotels and motels as well as the town plaza and Taos Pueblo. Schedules available in the plaza, the chamber of commerce, and most lodgings. Operates Mon.-Sat. 9:15am-5:30pm, Sun. 10am-5pm. Fare $1.

Taxi: Faust's Transportation, 758-3410. Operates 7am-10pm.

Bike Rental: Bicicletas Corp., (758-3522), next to Greyhound. Magnificent cycles $14 per day, including equipment. $2 discounts for hostel guests and Greyhound passengers. Open Mon.-Fri. 9am-6pm. Passport or major credit card required.

Bovine Rentals: Used Cow Dealer of New Mexico, 4124 Broadway Blvd. SE, Albuquerque (800-327-2697).

Help Line: Rape Crisis, 758-2910. Open 24 hr.

Post Office: 318 Paseo Del Pueblo Norte (Rte. 68) (758-2081), ¼ mi. north of the plaza. Open Mon.-Fri. 8:30am-5pm. **ZIP code:** 87571.

Area Code: 505.

Taos is 70 mi. north of Santa Fe. Drivers should park on **Placitas Road,** 1 block west of the plaza, or at the Park-and-Ride lots along Rte. 68 at Safeway and Fox Photo.

Accommodations and Camping

The gorgeous little **Plum Tree Hostel (AYH)** (758-4696 or 800-678-7586), on Rte. 68 15 mi. south of Taos in Pilar, hunkers down next to the Rio Grande. Though angling more for the B&B crowd (hot-tub and massage $45), the manager still organizes river rafting in summer and leads free hikes into the surrounding mountains every Monday when enough guests are interested. Because the hostel is a flag stop on the bus route between Santa Fe and Taos, getting in and out of town isn't a problem. (Office open daily 7:30am-10pm. $9.50, nonmembers $11.50. Breakfast included. Linen $2.) Named for its proximity to Taos Ski Valley, the **Abominable Snowmansion Hostel (AYH)** (776-8298) has been spotted in Arroyo Seco, a tiny town 10 mi. northeast of Taos on Rte. 150. The friendly, young hosts keep an exotic menagerie including a llama and a parrot. Guests may sleep in dorm rooms, bunk houses, or even a teepee. (Office open daily 8-10am and 4-11pm. Flexible 11pm curfew. $8.50, nonmembers $10.50; in winter $18.50 and $28. Breakfast included.) Hotel rooms are expensive in Taos. The cheapest rent at the **Taos Motel** (758-2524 or 800-323-6009), on Rte. 68 3 mi. south of the plaza. (Singles $28.75. Doubles $32.)

. **Camping** around Taos is easy for those who have a car. Up in the mountains on wooded Rte. 64, 20 mi. east of Taos, the **Kit Carson National Forest** operates three campgrounds. Two are free but have no hookups or running water; look for campers and tents and pull off the road at a designated site. **La Sombra,** also on this road, has running water. (Sites $5.) An additional six free campgrounds line the road to Taos Ski Valley. No permit is required for backcountry camping in the national forest. For more information, including maps of area campgrounds, contact the **forest service office** (758-6200; open Mon.-Fri. 8am-5pm, Sat. 8am-4:30pm). On Rte. 64 west of town, next to the awesome **Rio Grande Gorge Bridge** (758-8851), is a campground operated by the Bureau of Land Management. (Sites with water and porta-potty $6. Porta-visitors center open daily 8am-5pm.)

Food

The **Apple Tree Restaurant,** 123 Bent St., 2 blocks north of the plaza, serves up some of the best New Mexican and vegetarian food in the state. Dinner ($7-13) includes a huge entree (swimming in melted cheese and liberally garnished with chiles), homemade bread, and soup or salad. (Open daily 8am-9:30pm.) **Michael's Kitchen,** 304 N. Pueblo Rd., makes mainstream munchies such as doughnuts, sandwiches ($4), and great apple pie (95¢). (Open daily 7am-8:30pm.) Local sheriff's deputies and late night snackers frequent the **El Pueblo Cafe,** N. Pueblo. Their peak serving hour is often 2am. In the rear of **Amigo's Natural Foods,** 326 Pueblo Rd., across from Jack Donner's, sits a small but holistic deli serving such politically and nutritionally correct dishes like a not-so-spicy tofu on many-grained bread ($2.75). (Open daily 11am-5pm.) For other cheap eats, check out the pizza and fast-food places on the strip south of the plaza.

Sights and Activities

The spectacle of the Taos area has inspired artists since the days when the Pueblo exclusively inhabited this land. Many "early" Taos paintings hang at the **Harwood Foundation's Museum,** 238 Ledoux St. (758-3063), off Placitas Rd. (Open Mon.-Fri. noon-5pm, Sat. 10am-4pm. Free.) The plaza features other galleries with works by notable locals such as R.C. Gorman, as do **Kit Carson Road, Ledoux Street,** and El Prado, a village just north of Taos. Taos' galleries range from high-quality operations of international renown to upscale curio shops. In early October, the **Taos Arts Festival** celebrates local art.

Taos painters love rendering the **Mission of St. Francis of Assisi,** patron saint of New Mexico, trying to match its "miraculous" painting that changes into a shadowy figure of Christ when the lights go out. (Open Mon.-Sat. 10am-noon and 1-4pm.) Exhibits of Native American art, including a collection of beautiful black-on-black pottery, grace the **Millicent Rogers Museum** (758-2462), north of El Prado St., 4 mi. north of Taos off Hwy. 522. (Open daily 9am-5pm; Nov.-April Tues.-Sun. 10am-4pm. Admission $3, seniors $2, children $1, families $6.)

Remarkable for its five-story adobes, pink and white mission church, and striking silhouette, the vibrant community of **Taos Pueblo** unfortunately charges visitors dearly to look around. Much of the pueblo also remains off-limits to visitors; if this is the only one you will see, make the trip—otherwise, skip it. (Open daily 9am-5pm. Admission $5 per car, $2 per pedestrian. Camera permit $5, sketch permit $10, painting permit $15.) Feast days highlight beautiful tribal dances; San Gerónimo's Feast Days (Sept. 29-30), also feature a fair and races. Contact the tribal office (758-8626) for schedules of dances and other information. The less-visited **Picuris Pueblo** lies 20 mi. south of Taos on Rte. 75, near Peñasco. Smaller and somewhat friendlier to visitors, Picuris is best known for its sparkling pottery, molded from mica and clay.

The state's premier ski resort, **Taos Ski Valley,** about 5 mi. north of town on Rte. 150, has powder conditions on bowl sections and "short but steep" downhill runs rivaling Colorado's. Reserve a room well in advance if you plan to come during the winter holiday season. (Lift tickets $32, equipment rental $17. For information and ski conditions, call the Taos Valley Resort Association at 776-2233 or 800-992-7669.) In summer, the ski valley area offers great hikes.

After a day of strenuous sight-seeing, soak your weary bones in one of the natural **hot springs** near Taos. One of the most accessible bubbles 9 mi. north on Hwy. 522 near Arroyo Hondo; turn left onto a dirt road immediately after you cross the river. Following the dirt road for about 3 mi., turn left when it forks just after crossing the Rio Grande—the hot spring is just off the road at the first switchback. Though not very private, the spring's dramatic location part way up the Rio Grande Gorge more than compensates. Located 10 mi. west of Taos, the **U.S. 64 Bridge** over the Rio Grande Gorge is the nation's second-highest span, affording a spectacular view of the canyon and a New Mexico sunset (though you are not supposed to park).

Santa Fe

Santa Fe has always played a significant part in the Southwest's history. Capital of the region after the Spanish conquest in the early 17th century, the town reprised its role as a state capital in the Mexican Republic. After earning the dubious distinction during the Mexican-American War of first foreign capital to fall to the U.S. Army, Santa Fe lent its name to the Santa Fe Trail, one of the most important trade routes of the Old West.

City leaders have clung to this history, freezing (or baking) the past in adobe. By law all buildings near the downtown plaza—restaurants, rug shops, even parking ramps—must be 17th-century-style adobe, painted in one of 23 approved shades of brown. Such earth-toned beauty, as well as the mountains that fringe the city, has attracted a large artist community to Santa Fe. Hard on their heels have come yelping packs of well-to-do tourists. Nonetheless, the town remains a wonderful place to visit—manageably small, relaxed, and a nationwide center for bean-fueled New Mexican cuisine.

Practical Information

Emergency: 911.

Visitor Information: Chamber of Commerce, 333 Montezuma at Guadalupe (983-7317 or 800-528-5369). May relocate in 1991. Open Mon.-Fri. 8am-5pm, Sat. 9am-1pm; off-season closed Sat. **Information booth** in the First National Bank building on the west side of the plaza. Open daily June-Aug. Another booth inside the lobby of the **Santa Fe Convention Center,** 201 W. Marcy. Open Mon.-Fri. 8am-5pm. **National Park Service Southwest Regional Office,** 1100 Old Santa Fe Trail (988-6340). Information on camping and sights in the region. Open Mon.-Fri. 8am-4:30pm.

Greyhound/Trailways: 858 St. Michael's Dr. (471-0008). To: Denver (via Raton, NM, 4 per day, $55); Taos (4 per day, 1½ hr., $12.50); Albuquerque (7 per day, 1½ hr., $10.40).

Public Transport: Shuttlejack, 982-4311. Runs from the Albuquerque and Santa Fe airports; also goes to the opera.

Gray Line Tours: 471-9200 or 983-9491. Free pickup from downtown hotels. Tours Mon.-Sat. to: Taos and Taos Pueblo (at 9am, $38.50); Bandelier, Los Alamos, and San Ildefonso (at 1pm, $28.50); around Santa Fe (at 9:30am and 1pm, 3 hr., $12.75). Also operates the Roadrunner, a sight-seeing trolley around Old Santa Fe leaving from the plaza at Lincoln and Palace (5 per day, 1½ hr., $6, under 12 $3).

Taxi: Village Cab Co, 982-9990. Not exactly punctual, so leave yourself extra time. Coupons for a 45% discount on taxi fare available free from the public library, behind the Palace of the Governors.

New Age Referral Service: 984-0878. Information clearinghouse for holistic healing services and alternative modes of thought.

Post Office: in the Montoya Office Bldg. S. Federal Pl., (988-6351), next to the Federal Courthouse. Open Mon.-Fri. 8:30am-5:30pm, Sat. 8:30am-noon. **ZIP code:** 87501.

Area Code: 505.

Except for a cluster of museums southeast of the city center, most restaurants and important sights in Santa Fe cluster within a few blocks of the downtown plaza and inside the loop formed by the circular **Paseo de Peralta. Santa Fe Detours** (983-6565) offers two-and-a-half-hour walking tours of the city (daily at 9:30am and 1:30pm, $10) that leave from the La Fonda Hotel, on the corner of the plaza. Because the narrow streets make driving troublesome, park your car and hit the pavement. You'll find brown adobe parking lots behind Santa Fe Village, near Sena Plaza, and 1 block east of the Federal Courthouse near the plaza. Parking is available at two-hour meters on some streets.

Accommodations and Camping

Hotels become swamped with requests as early as May for **Fiesta de Santa Fe** week in early September and **Indian Market** the third week of August; make reservations or plan on sleeping in the street. At other times, look around the **Cerrillos Road** area for the best prices. At many of the less expensive adobe motels, bargaining is acceptable. The beautiful adobe **Santa Fe Hostel (AAIH),** 1412 Cerrillos Rd. (988-1153), 1 mi. from the adobe bus station, and 2 mi. from the adobe plaza, has a kitchen, library, and very large dorm-style adobe beds. ($9, nonmembers $10. Linen $2. $1 kitchen fee includes lots of free adobe. B&B rooms $24-35.)

To camp around Santa Fe, you'll probably need a car. Several miles out of town, **Santa Fe National Forest** (988-6940) has numerous campsites as well as free backcountry camping in the beautiful Sangre de Cristo Mountains. **New Mexico Parks and Recreation** (827-7465) operates the following free campgrounds on Rte. 475

northeast of Santa Fe from May through October (sites with hookup $4-6): **Black Canyon** (8 mi. away); **Big Tesuque** (12 mi.); and **Aspen Basin** (15 mi.).

Food and Nightlife

Santa Fe serves as a staple spicy Mexican food on blue corn tortillas. The few vegetarian restaurants are expensive, catering to an upscale crowd. The better restaurants near the plaza dish up their chilis to a mixture of government employees, well-heeled tourists, and local artistic types. Because many serve only breakfast and lunch, you should also look for inexpensive meals along **Cerrillos Road** and **St. Michael's Drive** south of downtown. One little-known fact: because it has served the local Native American vendors for decades, the **Woolworth's** on the plaza actually serves a mean bowl of chili ($2.75).

Tomasita's Santa Fe Station, 500 S. Guadalupe, near downtown. Locals and tourists line up for their blue corn tortillas and fiery green chili dishes ($4.50-5). Indoor and outdoor seating. Open Mon.-Sat. 11am-10pm.

Josie's, 225 E. Marcy St., in a converted house. Pronounce the "J" in the name like an "H." Family-run for 23 years. Incredible Mexican-style lunches and multifarious mouthwatering desserts worth the 20-min. wait. Open Mon.-Fri. 11am-4pm.

The Burrito Company, 111 Washington Ave. Excellent Mexican food at quite reasonable prices. Burrito plates $2.75-4. (Open Mon.-Sat. 7:30am-7pm.)

Tortilla Flats, 3139 Cerrillos Rd. (471-8685). Frighteningly bland family atmosphere belies the ineffably edible Mexican masterpieces ($6-8). Open daily 7am-10pm; winter Sun.-Thurs. 7am-9pm, Fri.-Sat. 7am-10pm.

Upper Crust Pizza, 329 E. Old Santa Fe Trail. Practically the only downtown restaurant open in the evening. Thick, chewy ten-incher with whole-wheat crust $7. Open Mon.-Thurs. 11am-11pm, Fri.-Sat. 11am-midnight, Sun. noon-11pm.

Sights

Since 1609, **Plaza de Santa Fe** has held Adrianistic religious ceremonies, military gatherings, markets, cockfights, and public punishments. The city also provided a stop on two important trails: the **Santa Fe Trail** from Independence, MO, and **El Camino Real** from Mexico City. The plaza is a good starting point for exploring the city's museums, sanctuaries, and galleries.

Since the following four museums are commonly owned, their hours are identical and a two-day pass bought at one admits you to all. (Open March-Dec. daily 10am-5pm; Jan.-Feb. Tues.-Sun. 10am-5pm. Admission $3.50, under 16 free. Two-day passes $6, children $2.50.) The **Palace of the Governors** (827-6483), the oldest public building in the U.S., on the north side of the plaza, was the seat of seven successive governments after its construction in 1610. The *hacienda*-style palace is now a museum with exhibits on Native American, Southwestern, and New Mexican history. To buy Native American crafts or jewelry, check out the displays spread out in front of the Governor's Palace each day by artists from the surrounding pueblos. Their wares are often cheaper and of better quality than those found in the "Indian Crafts" stores around town.

Across Lincoln St., on the northwest corner of the plaza, lies the **Museum of Fine Arts** (827-4455), a large, undulating, adobe building with thick, cool walls illuminated by sudden shafts of sunlight. Exhibits include works by major Southwestern artists, including Georgia O'Keeffe and Edward Weston, and an amazing collection of 20th-century Native American art.

Two other museums locate southeast of town on **Camiro Lejo,** just off Old Santa Fe Trail. The **Museum of International Folk Art,** 705 Camiro Lejo (827-8350), 2 mi. south of the plaza, houses the Girard Collection of over 100,000 works of folk art from around the world. Amazingly vibrant but unbelievably jumbled, the collection is incomprehensible without the gallery guide handout. In the nearby **Museum** of American Indian Arts and Culture, photographs and artifacts unveil a multifaceted Native American tradition.

Entertainment and Events

With numerous musical and theatrical productions, arts and crafts shows, and Native American ceremonies, Santa Fe offers rich entertainment year-round. Fairs, rodeos, and tennis tournaments complement the world-famous musicians who often play in Santa Fe's clubs and the active theater scene. For information, check *Pasatiempo* magazine, a supplement to the Friday issue of the *Santa Fe New Mexican*.

Don Diego De Vargas's peaceful reconquest of New Mexico in 1692 marked the end of the 12-year Pueblo Rebellion, now celebrated in the traditional three-day **Fiesta de Santa Fe** (988-7575). Held in early September, the celebration reaches its height with the burning of the 40-ft. *papier-mâché* **Zozobra** (Old Man Gloom). Festivities include street dancing, processions, and political satires. Most events are free. The *New Mexican* publishes a guide and schedule for the fiesta's events.

The **Santa Fe Chamber Music Festival** (983-2075) celebrates the works of great baroque, classical, and 20th-century composers. Tickets are not easily available. (Performances July to mid-Aug. Sun.-Mon. and Thurs.-Fri. in the St. Francis Auditorium of the Museum of Fine Arts. Tickets from $5 Sun. matinee to $25 some evenings.) The **Santa Fe Opera**, P.O. Box 2048 (982-3855), 7 mi. north of Santa Fe on Rte. 84, performs out in the open, so bring a blanket. The downtown box office is at Galisteo News and Ticket Center, 201 Calisteo St. (984-1316; open Mon.-Sat. 10am-4pm). Standing-room only tickets can be purchased for as little as $5. (Performances July-Aug. All shows begin at 9pm.) **Shuttlejack** (982-4311) runs a bus from downtown Santa Fe to the opera before each performance.

In August, the nation's largest and most impressive **Indian Market** floods the plaza. Native American tribes from all over the U.S. participate in dancing as well as over 500 exhibits of fine arts and crafts. The **Southwestern Association on Indian Affairs** (983-5220) has more information.

At night, gung-ho rock fans carouse at the always-hopping **Club West,** 213 W. Alameda (982-0099; cover $5). More subdued revelers relax at the **El Farol,** 808 Canyon Rd. (983-9912), which features excellent up-and-coming rock and R&B musicians. Gay nightlife centers at the **Cargo,** 519 Cerrillos Rd. (989-8790).

Near Santa Fe

Pecos National Monument, located in the hill country 25 mi. southeast of Santa Fe on I-25 and Rte. 63, features ruins of a pueblo and Spanish mission church. The small monument includes an easy 1-mi. hike through various archeological sites. Especially notable are Pecos's renovated kivas, underground ceremonial chambers used in Pueblo rituals, built after the Rebellion of 1680. Off-limits at other ruins, these kivas are open to the public. (Open daily sunrise-sunset. Admission $1.) The monument's **visitors center** has a small but informative museum and a 10-minute introductory film, shown every half hour. (Open daily 8am-6pm; Sept. 2-May 27 8am-5pm. Free.) Greyhound sends early-morning and late-evening buses daily from Santa Fe to the town of Pecos, 2 mi. north of the monument. Use the campsites, or simply pitch a tent in the backcountry of in the **Santa Fe National Forest,** 6 mi. north on Rte. 63 (see Santa Fe Accommodations above).

Bandelier National Monument, 40 mi. northwest of Santa Fe (take U.S. 285 to Rte. 4), features some of the most amazing pueblo and cliff dwellings in the state (accessible by 50 mi. of hiking trails), as well as 50 sq. mi. of dramatic mesas and tumbling canyons. The most accessible of these is **Frijoles Canyon,** site of the **visitors center** (672-3861; open daily 8am-6pm; fall and spring 9am-5:30pm; winter 8am-4:30pm). A 5-mi. hike from the parking lot to the Rio Grande descends 600 ft. to the mouth of the canyon, past two waterfalls and fascinating mountain scenery. The **Stone Lions Shrine** (12-mi., 8-hr. round-trip from the visitors center), sacred to the Anasazi, features two stone statues of crouching mountain lions. The trail also leads past the unexcavated Yapashi Pueblo. A two-day, 20-mi. hike leads from the visitors center past the stone lions to **Painted Cave**, decorated with over 50 Anasazi pictographs, and to the Rio Grande. Both hikes are quite strenuous. Free permits are required for backcountry hiking and camping; pick up a topographical map ($6) of the monument lands at the visitors center. A less taxing self-guided one-hour tour takes you through a pueblo and past some cliff dwellings near the visitors center. You can camp at **Juniper Campground**, ¼ mi. off Rte. 4 at the entrance to the monument. (Sites $6.) Park rangers conduct evening campfire programs at 8:45pm. (Park entrance fee $5 per vehicle.)

Los Alamos, 10 mi. north of Bandelier on NM Loop 4, stands in stark contrast to nearby towns such as Santa Fe, Taos, or Española. The U.S. government selected Los Alamos, a small mountain village at the outset of World War II, as the site of a top-secret nuclear weapons development program; today, nuclear research continues at the **Los Alamos Scientific Laboratory.** The facility perches eerily atop several mesas connected by highway bridges over deep gorges, supporting a community with more PhDs per capita than any other city in the U.S. The public may visit the **Bradbury Museum of Science**, Diamond Dr., for exhibits on the Manhattan Project, the strategic nuclear balance, and the technical processes of nuclear weapons testing and verification. (Open Tues.-Fri. 9am-5pm, Sat.-Mon. 1-5pm. Free.) The **Los Alamos County Historical Museum**, Central Ave. (662-6272), details life in the 1940s, when Los Alamos was a government-created "secret city." (Open in summer Mon.-Fri. 9am-6pm, Sat. 10am-4pm, Sun. 1-4pm.)

Albuquerque

I knew I should've turned left at Albuquerque.

—Bo Jackson

Approximately one third of New Mexico's population thrives amidst the youthful energy of the state's only "real" city. Against the dramatic backdrop of the Sandía Mountains, Albuquerque spreads across a desert plateau. Though the town's Spanish past gave rise to heavily touristy Old Town, the cheesy roadside architecture lining Route 66 ("I get my kicks," as the classic song goes) and the city's high-tech industry underlie Albuquerque's modern image. Despite understandable difficulty with spelling the city's name, Albuquerque's youthful residents (average age 29) view their home as a new and growing U.S. city.

Practical Information

Emergency: 911.

Albuquerque Convention and Visitors Bureau: 625 Silver SW (243-3696 or 800-284-2282). Willing to part with a free map and the useful *Official Albuquerque Travel Guide.* Open Mon.-Fri. 8am-5pm. After hours, call for recorded events information. **Old Town Visitors Center,** Romero St. at N. Plaza (243-3215). Open Mon.-Sat. 10am-5pm, Sun. 11am-5pm.

Albuquerque International Airport: Gibson St. (842-4366), south of downtown. Take bus #50 from Yale and Central downtown Mon.-Sat. 7:20am-6:20pm. Cab fare to downtown $7.25.

Amtrak, 314 1st St. SW (242-7816 or 800-872-7245). Open daily 10am-6:30pm. One train per day to Los Angeles ($84) and Kansas City ($142). Reservations required.

Buses: 300 2nd St. SW, 3 blocks south of Central Ave. **Greyhound/Trailways** (243-4435) and **TNM&O Coaches** go to: Oklahoma City (6 per day, $76); Denver (4 per day, $55); Phoenix (6 per day, $49); Los Angeles (6 per day, $70).

Public Transport: Sun-Tran Transit, 601 Yale Blvd. SE (843-9200 for schedule information Mon.-Fri. 7am-5pm, Sat. 8am-4:30pm). Most buses run Mon.-Sat. 6am-6pm. Pick up system maps at the transit office or the main library. Fare 60¢, ages 5-18 35¢. **Albuquerque Trolley,**

242-1407. Provides transportation with tour commentary. Stops at most major hotels. Operates Tues.-Thurs. and Sat. 10am-5:30pm, Fri. 10am-6:30pm, Sun. 11am-6:30pm. Fare $1, seniors and children 50¢.

Taxi: Albuquerque Cab Co., 883-4888. Fare $1.10 the first mi., $1.20 each additional mi.

Car Rental: Rent-a-Wreck, 500 Yale Blvd. SE (256-9693). Cars with A/C from $27 per day. 100 free mi., 15¢ each additional mi. Open Mon.-Sat. 8am-6:30pm, Sun. 10am-5:30pm. Must be 21 with credit card.

Bike Rental: The Wilderness Center, 4900 Lomas Blvd. NE (268-6767). Mountain bikes $18 per day, $35 per weekend, $75 per week. Open Mon., Wed., Fri. 9:30am-8pm, Tues., Thurs. 9:30am-6pm, Sat. 10am-6pm, Sun. 11am-5pm.

Help Lines: Rape Crisis Center, 266-7711. Open 24 hr. **Gay and Lesbian Information Line,** 266-8041. **Lesbian Information Support Line,** 255-7288.

Post Office: 1135 Broadway NE (247-2725). Open Mon.-Fri. 8am-6pm. **ZIP code:** 87101.

Area Code: 505.

Albuquerque (pop. 493,000) lies between the **Sandía Mountains** to the east and the **Rio Grande** to the west. **Central Avenue** and the **Santa Fe railroad tracks** create four quadrants sort of used in city addresses: Northeast Heights (NE), Southeast Heights (SE), North Valley (NW), and South Valley (SW). The all-adobe campus of the **University of New Mexico (UNM)** stretches scenically along Central Ave. NE from University Ave. to Carlisle St.

Accommodations and Camping

Central Ave., the old U.S. 66, contains the international hostel and at least three cheap motels per block. The **Albuquerque International Hostel,** 1012 W. Central Ave. (243-6101), at 10th St., is a large adobe house with stiff, even therapeutic mattresses and required morning chores. (Office open Mon.-Fri. 7am-11am and 4-11pm, Sat.-Sun. 7am-noon and 4-11pm. Check-out noon. $8, nonmembers $10. Linen $2. Kitchen fee of $1 includes plenty of free food. Most of Central Ave.'s cheap motels lie east of downtown around the university along with plenty of restaurants. The **De Anza Motor Lodge,** 4301 Central Ave. NE (255-1654), has bland decor but well-kept rooms with free movie channel and continental breakfast to boot. (Singles $19. Doubles $28.)

Named for the Spanish adventurer who burned some 250 Native Americans shortly after his arrival in 1540, the **Coronado State Park Campground** (867-5589), 1 mi. west of Bernalillo on Rte. 44, about 20 mi. north of Albuquerque on I-25, offers unique camping. Adobe shelters on the sites provide respite from the heat. The view of the Sandía Mountains is haunting, especially beneath a full moon. Sites have toilets, showers, and drinking water. (2-week max. stay. Open daily 7am-10pm. Sites $5, with hookup $8. No reservations.) Albuquerque's nearby **KOA,** 5739 Ouray Rd. NW (831-1911), has a swimming pool. Take I-40 west from downtown to the Coors Blvd. N. exit, or bus #15 from downtown. (Sites $10.50 for 2 people, each additional person $2.) Camping equipment and canoes can be rented from the friendly folks at **Mountains & Rivers,** 2320 Central Ave. SE (268-4876), across from the university. (Tents $15, backpacks $8-10 per weekend. Deposit required; reservations recommended. Open Mon.-Fri. 10am-6pm, Sat. 9am-6pm.)

Food and Nightlife

Downtown Albuquerque has great Mexican food. If you have one Mexican meal sitting in your stomach when you head into the desert, it should be the *carne adovada burrito* (marinated pork; $3.50) from **M and J Sanitary Tortilla Factory,** 403 2nd St. SW (242-4890), at Lead St. in the hot pink and blue building. Crowds appear at lunchtime. (Open Mon.-Sat. 10am-3:30pm.)

Tasty, inexpensive food eateries border the University of New Mexico, which stretches along Central Ave. NE. **Nunzio's Pizza,** 107 Cornell Dr. SE, has great, inexpensive 'za at $1 per huge slice. (Open Sun.-Thurs. 11am-10pm, Fri.-Sat. 11am-11pm.) "Feed your Body with Love, Light, and high VIBRATIONAL Food," advises **Twenty Carrots,** 2110 Central Ave. SE. Wheatgrass smoothies ($2.25) and bulk organic food are, apparently, sufficiently vibratory. (Open, relaxed, and shaking vigorously Mon.-Sat. 10am-8pm, Sun. noon-6pm.) Similarly laid back **E.J.'s Coffee and Tea Co.,** 2201 Silver SE, at Yale, has baked goods and a bewildering number of variations on the cup of coffee. (Open Mon.-Fri. 7am-11pm, Sat. 8am-midnight, Sun. 8am-2pm.) The cheap homemade ice cream (one scoop 75¢) and pastry at the nearby **Purple Hippo,** 120 Harvard Dr. SE, could turn you into one. (Open Mon.-Thurs. 7:30am-10:30pm, Fri.-Sat. 7:30am-11:30pm, Sun. 10am-9pm.)

Rub elbows with **Cowboys',** 3301 Juan Tabo Blvd. NE (296-1959), in this country-western bar and nightclub at the eastern end of town. Ranchers hang out here when they're not out on the range. You can also kick up your spurs at **Caravan East,** 7605 Central Ave. NE (265-7877), but mind your step around the tobacco-juice puddles. (Continuous live music every night 5pm-1:30am. Cover $2-3.) Less rurally inclined music lovers can hear rock, blues, and reggae bands over cheap beer ($1.50) at **El Ray,** 622 Central Ave. SW (242-9300), a spacious old theater transformed into a bar and nightclub. (Music usually Wed.-Sat. at 8:30pm. Cover $2-20.)

Sights

Old Town, on the western end of downtown, contains Albuquerque's Spanish plaza surrounded by restaurants and Native American art galleries. Located at the northeast corner of the intersection of Central Ave. and Rio Grande Blvd., 1 mi. south of I-40, Old Town providing the best place to hang out and watch tourists.

The **National Atomic Museum,** 20358 Wyoming Blvd., Kirkland Air Force Base (845-6670), tells the story of the development of the atomic bombs "Little Boy" and "Fat Man," and of the obliteration of Hiroshima and Nagasaki. *Ten Seconds that Shook the World,* an hour-long documentary on the development of the atomic bomb, is shown three times daily at 10:30am, 2pm, and 3:30pm. Access is controlled; ask at the Visitor Control Gate on Wyoming Blvd. for a pass to visit the museum. Be prepared to show several forms of ID. The Air Force base is several miles southeast of downtown, just east of I-25. (Open daily 9am-5pm. Free.)

For a much different feel for history, the **Indian Pueblo Cultural Center,** 2401 12th St. NW (843-7270), just north of I-40, provides a sensitive introduction to the nearby Pueblo reservations. The cafeteria serves authentic Pueblo food (fry-bread $1.50; open 7:30am-3:30pm) and hosts colorful Pueblo dance performances on weekends during the academic year at 11am and 2pm. (Open mid-May to Oct. Mon.-Sat. 7:30am-5:30pm, Sun. 9am-5:30pm; off-season Mon.-Sat. 7:30am-5:30pm. Admission $2.50, seniors $1.50, students $1. Take bus #36 from downtown.) The **New Mexico Museum of Natural History,** 1801 Mountain Rd. NW (841-8837), houses fascinating exhibits on biology, geology, and paleontology in a futuristic building. Take the "evolator" 70 million years into the past. (Open daily 9am-5pm. Admission $4, seniors and students $3, ages under 11 $1.)

Near Albuquerque

Located at the edge of suburbia on Albuquerque's west side, **Indian Petroglyphs State Park** (897-7201) includes a trail leading through lava rocks written on by Native Americans. Take the Coors exit on I-40 north to Atrisco Rd. to reach this free attraction, or take bus #15 to Coors and transfer to bus #93. (Open daily 8am-6pm; off-season 8am-5pm. Parking $1.)

On the east side of the city, the **Sandía Peaks** rise 10,000 ft., providing a pleasant escape from Albuquerque's heat and noise. Sandía means "watermelon" in Spanish, the peaks named for the color they turn at sunset. These peaks are convenient to Albuquerque by car. Take Tramway Rd. from either I-25 or I-40 to the **Sandía Peak Aerial Tramway** (298-8518) for a thrilling ride to the top of Sandía Crest that allows you to ascend the west face of Sandía Peak and gaze out over Albuquerque, the Rio Grande Valley, and western New Mexico. Try to make the ascent at sunset. (Operates daily 9am-10pm; Sept. 2-May 27 Thurs.-Tues. 9am-9pm, Wed. 5-9pm. Fare $9.50, seniors and students $7. 9-11am rates $8 and $6, respectively.)

A trip through the **Sandía Ski Area** makes a beautiful 58-mi., day-long driving loop. Take I-40 east up Tijeras Canyon 17 mi. and turn north onto Rte. 44, which winds through lovely piñon pine, oak, ponderosa pine, and spruce forests. Rte. 44 then descends 18 mi. to Bernalillo, through a gorgeous canyon. A 7-mi. toll-road (Rte. 536) leads to the summit of **Sandía Crest,** and a dazzling ridge hike covers the 1½ mi. separating the crest and **Sandía Peak.** Rangers offer guided hikes on Saturdays in both summer and winter. Reservations are recommended for the challenging winter snowshoe hikes (242-9052).

Right off I-25, 150 mi. south of Albequerque, **Truth or Consequences (T or C)** makes a delightful regional rest stop. Originally one of the many towns called Hot Springs, this tiny metropolis took up its bizarre name in response to a dare by "Truth or Consequences" game show host Ralph Edwards. In 1950 residents voted to rename the town for the TV show—in return for Edwards broadcasting his program here—giving the town national exposure. Since taking the dare, Edwards has returned to T or C every year for a fiesta in his honor, and outsiders have forgotten about the once-popular hot mineral baths.

You'll certainly remember the **Riverbend Hot Springs Hostel,** 205 S. Riverside Dr. (894-6183), right on the river. Just look at these fabulous prizes—the hostel has carpeting, a homey living room, and excellent kitchen facilities. ($9.50. Private rooms available.) But wait! There's more! Visit the **Geronimo Springs Museum,** 325 Main St. (894-6600), featuring artifacts from the Mimbres, ancient Native American tribes who wandered north through New Mexico. Directors Sylvia and Lee (who also run the hostel) will be happy to escort you around their glamorous showroom. (Open Mon.-Sat. 9am-5pm. Admission $1.50, students 75¢.)

Western New Mexico

West of Albuquerque lies a vast land of forests, lava beds, and desert mesas populated by Native Americans and boomtown coal and uranium miners. Though difficult to explore without a car, the region can prove very rewarding for the dedicated adventurer.

Chaco Culture National Historical Park

Sun-scorched and water-poor, Chaco Canyon seems an improbable setting for the first great flowering of the Anasazi. At a time when most farmers relied on risky dry farming, Chacoans created an oasis of irrigated fields. They also constructed sturdy five-story rock apartment buildings while Europeans still lived in squalid wooden hovels. By the 11th century, the canyon residents had set up a major trade network with dozens of small satellite towns in the surrounding desert. Around 1150 AD, however, the whole system collapsed: with no food and little water, the Chacoans simply abandoned the canyon for greener pastures.

Only the ruins remain, but these are the best-preserved sites in the Southwest. **Pueblo Bonito,** the canyon's largest town, demonstrates the skill of Anasazi masons. Among many other structures, one four-story wall still stands. Nearby **Chetro Ketl** houses one of the canyon's largest great kivas, used in Chacoan religious rituals. Bring water, since even the visitors center occasionally runs dry.

The **visitors center** (988-6727 or 988-6716; 24 hr.), at the eastern end of the canyon, houses an excellent museum that includes exhibits on Anasazi art and architecture, as well as a description of the sophisticated economic network by which the Chacoan Anasazi traded with smaller Anasazi tribes of modern Colorado and northern Mexico. (Museum open daily 8am-6pm; Sept. 2-May 27 daily 8am-5pm. Entrance fee $1 per person or $3 per carload.) **Camping** in Chaco costs $5; arrive by 3pm since space is limited to 46 sites. Registration is required. You can also make Chaco a daytrip from Gallup, NM, where cheap accommodations are plentiful.

Chaco Canyon, a 160-mi., 3½-hour drive northwest from Albuquerque, lies 90 mi. south of Durango, CO. When the first official archeologist left for the canyon at the turn of the century, it took him almost a year to get here from Washington, DC. Today's visitor faces unpaved Rte. 57, which reaches the park from paved Rte. 44 (turn off at the tiny town of Nageezi) on the north (29 mi.), and from I-40 on the south (about 60 mi., 20 mi. of it unpaved). **Greyhound's** I-40 run from Albuquerque to Gallup serves Thoreau, at the intersection of Rte. 57, five times per day.

El Morro National Monument and Gallup

Just west of the Continental Divide on Rte. 53, 4 mi. southeast of the Navajo town of **Ramah**, sits **Inscription Rock,** where Native Americans, Spanish conquistadors, and later European pioneers made their mark while traveling through the scenic valley. Today, self-guided trails allow access to the rock as well as to ruins farther into the park. (Open daily 8am-6:30pm.) The **visitors center** (open daily 8am-8pm) includes a small museum as well as several dire warnings against emulating the graffiti artists of old and marking the rocks. For those unable to resist the urge to inscribe, an alternate boulder is provided.

Southern New Mexico: Carlsbad Caverns National Park

East of the Sacramento Mountains lies the dusty plain named Llano Estacado. The lonely towns of southeastern New Mexico—Roswell, Artesia, and Carlsbad—would attract few visitors without the underground scenery that lurks in their basement. Dangling on the edge of nowhere, Carlsbad Caverns attract visitors from all over the world to their spectacular, often sublime formations. More unusually, the entire bat population of the caverns (currently 250,000) regularly makes a mass exodus at sunset, flying out of the caves' entrance in a long, twisting line on their way to feeding grounds. These bats gave explorers in this desolate region the first clue that another world lay underground. Indeed, before becoming a national park, Carlsbad Caverns supported the profitable mining of guano (bat dung, used as fertilizer), found in 100-ft. deep deposits in some of the caves.

Today the **visitors center** (785-2232 or 785-2233) has replaced dung-mining with a restaurant, gift shop, information desk, 24-hr. information recording, and lockers (25-50¢). For another 50¢ you can rent a small radio that transmits a guided tour. (Open May 27-Sept. 2 daily 8am-7pm; off-season daily 8am-5:30pm.) There are two ways to see the caverns. Those with strong knees and solid shoes can take the "blue tour," traveling by foot down a steep (but paved) 3-mi. descent. This tour instills the best sense of the depth and extent of the caverns. The "red tour" follows an easier, shorter route, descending from the visitors center by elevator. Most of the trail is wheelchair-accessible, and both tours are self-guided. Almost all visitors return to the surface by elevator, the last of which leaves a half-hour before the visitors center closes. After that it's just you, the bats, and the guano. (Tours June-Aug. 8:30am-5pm (red), 8:30am-3:30pm (blue); Sept.-May 8:30am-3:30pm (red), 8:30am-2pm (blue). Admission $4, over 62 and ages 6-15 $2.50.)

The undeveloped **New Cave** (785-2232) offers tours May 27 to September 2 daily at 9am and 12:30pm; in off-season weekends only. Two-hour, 1¼-mi. flashlight tours traverse difficult and slippery terrain; there are no paved trails or handrails. Even getting to the cave takes some energy, or better yet, a car, since the parking lot is 23 mi. on a dirt road from the Carlsbad Caverns Visitors Center (there is no transportation from the visitors center or from White's City) and the cave entrance is still a steep, strenuous ½ mi. from the lot. Reservations at least two weeks in advance and a flashlight are necessary for the cave tour, as the park limits the number of persons allowed to visit each day. (Tours $5, ages 6-15 $3. Children under 6 not admitted; Golden Eagle passes not valid.)

The nightly flight of the caverns' bats is also open to public viewing; the **Bat Flight Program** takes place in the amphitheater of the natural entrance to the cave just before sundown every night from May to October. Free guano samples.

No camping is permitted in Carlsbad Caverns National Park. The **Carlsbad Caverns International Hostel** (785-2291) in White's City is easily accesssible by bus (3 times per day from El Paso and Carlsbad). Spacious six-bed rooms include bathroom, access to kitchen, TV, pool and spa, and a nightly display of six-legged, nonpaying guests. Certain modern conveniences such as A/C, stove, and TV may not be functional; to stay overnight bring insect repellent and plan on eating out. Check in at the visitors lobby across the street. ($10. Linens $2. Open 24 hr.) The privately run (and usually overrun) **Park Entrance Campground** (785-2291; ask to be connected), in White's City, is just outside the park entrance. (Sites $15 for up to 6 people. Pay at the visitors lobby.) The campground provides water, showers, restrooms, and swimming. Find cheap beds at the Carlsbad **Motel 6**, 3824 National Parks Hwy. (885-0011). In summer, make reservations at least one month in advance. (Singles $25. Doubles $30.) Several more inexpensive motels lie farther down the road. Additional campsites are available at nearby Guadalupe Mountains National Park (see Texas).

The tiny, rather tacky town with the excessive title **White's City,** on U.S. 62/80, serves as the access point to the caverns. White's City is 20 mi. southeast of the town of Carlsbad, 7 mi. from the caverns along steep, winding mountain road. Because flash floods occasionally close the road, call ahead before making the trek. From Las Cruces on I-25, take U.S. 82 east to Alamogordo, crossing the Sacramento Mountains; then take U.S. 285 south to Carlsbad, a trip of 213 mi. in all. From El Paso, TX, also on I-25, take U.S. 62/180 east 150 mi., passing Guadalupe Mountains National Park, which is 40 mi. southwest of White's City. Greyhound, in cooperation with **TNM&O Coaches** (887-1108), runs three buses per day from El Paso ($25, $47.50 round-trip) or Carlsbad ($5.75 round-trip) to White's City. Two of these routes have White's City only as a flag stop. From White's City, you can take the overpriced **Carlsbad Cavern Coaches** to the visitors center ($14 round-trip for 1-4 people) buy tickets in the White's City Gift Shop where Greyhound drops you off.

Utah

Once home to dinosaurs, Utah now beckons human visitors to its rugged landscape, which ranges from a vast lake of salt water to a multitude of bizarre rock formations. Southern Utah is a weird wonderland of redstone canyons, deep river gorges, and naturally carved arches, spires, and columns. Northeastern and central Utah feature the Uinta mountains and national forests, dotted with lakes and covered with aspens and ponderosa pine.

Only the uniqueness of Mormon culture matches the oddity of Utah's terrain. Driven westward by religious persecution, the Latter Day Saints began settling Utah in 1848; today they make up over 80% of the state population. With its intensely family-oriented values, abstinence from alcohol, history of polygamy, and sheer prevalence, the Mormon culture can make Utah strange, and even a little intimidating, unless, like the skiers who flock to Park City and Alta, you only come for the snow.

Practical Information

Capital: Salt Lake City.

Population: 1,678,000.

Tourist Information: Utah Travel Council, Council Hall/Capitol Hill, 300 N. State St., Salt Lake City 84114 (530-1030), across the street from the capitol building. Information on national and state parks, campgrounds, and accommodations. Open summer, Mon.-Fri. 8am-5pm. Pick up a free copy of the *Utah Travel Guide*, with a complete listing of motels, national parks, and campgrounds. Utah Parks and Recreation, 1636 W. North Temple, Salt Lake City 86116 (538-7220). Open Mon.-Fri. 8am-5pm.

Time Zone: Mountain (2 hr. behind Eastern). Postal Abbreviation: UT.

Area Code: 801.

Salt Lake City

In a little town outside of Rochester, New York in 1830, 15-year-old avatar Joseph Smith had a vision that commanded him to start a new religion, the Church of Latter Day Saints. Known as Mormons because of the *Book of Mormon* which Smith supposedly translated from ancient tablets, the Latter Day Saints fled westward from persecution, stopping for periods in Ohio, Illinois, Missouri, Nebraska, and finally settling in Salt Lake City in 1847. Situated in a mountainous, desert terrain near the Great Salt Lake which resembles the Dead Sea, Salt Lake City bears a peculiar resemblance to another Holy Land even today. The city is graced by spiritual centers of the Church of Latter Day Saints, including the gargantuan Mormon Temple and the Mormon Tabernacle Choir, as well as the cultural and intellectual institutions of Utah.

Practical Information

Emergency: 911.

Salt Lake Valley Convention and Visitors Bureau, 180 S. West Temple (521-2868 or 800-831-4332), 2 blocks south of Temple Sq. Open Mon.-Fri. 8am-7pm, Sat. 9am-4pm, Sun. 10am-4pm; off-season Mon.-Fri. 8am-5:30pm, Sat. 9am-6pm, Sun. 10am-4pm. Other visitors centers at: Crossroads Mall, 50 S. Main St.; ZCMI Mall, 36 S. State St. (321-8745; open Mon.-Fri. 7:30am-9pm, Sat. 8am-6pm); and terminal 2 at the airport. The free *Salt Lake Visitors Guide* details a good self-guided tour.

Salt Lake City International Airport: 776 N. Terminal Dr. (539-2205), 4 mi. west of Temple Sq. UTA buses provide the best means of transport to and from the airport. Bus #50 serves the terminal directly. Delta/Western Airlines flies here from Los Angeles and San Francisco, and several airlines will take you to Denver for about $50.

Amtrak: 325 S. Rio Grande (364-8562 or 800-872-7245). Trains once daily to: Denver (13½ hr., $100); Las Vegas (8 hr., $82); Los Angeles (15 hr., $129); and San Francisco (17 hr., $133). Ticket office open Mon.-Sat. 5-9am, 10:30am-2pm, 4:15-7pm, 8pm-midnight; Sun. 4:15pm-1:20am.

Greyhound/Trailways: 160 W. South Temple (355-4684), 1 block west of Temple Sq. To: Cheyenne (3 per day, 9 hr., $52); Las Vegas (2 per day, 10 hr., $49); San Francisco (3 per day, 15 hr., $79); Boise (3 per day, 7 hr., $43); West Yellowstone (1 per day, 9 hr., $66); Denver (5 per day, 12 hr., $55). Ticket counter open daily 1:45am-10pm; off-season daily 7am-10pm. Terminal open 24 hr.

Public Transport: Utah Transit Authority, 600 S. 700 West (287-4636 until 7pm). Frequent service to University of Utah; buses to Ogden (#70/72 express), suburbs, airport, and east to the mountain canyons. Buses ½ hr. or more apart 6:30am-11pm; to Provo 5:30am-10pm. Fare 50¢, seniors 25¢, ages under 5 free; $1.25 to Provo. Maps available from libraries or the visitors bureau. Information desk at ZCMI Mall, 36 S. State St.

Tours: Gray Line, 553 W. 100 South (521-7060). 2½-hr. tours of the city focusing on Mormon historical sites. Departures in summer daily at 9am and 2pm. Fare $12, children $6.

Taxi: City Cab, 363-5014. Ute Cab, 359-7788. Yellow Cab, 521-2100. 95¢ base fare, $1.30 per mi. $9-10 from the airport to Temple Sq.

Car Rentals: Payless Car Rental, 1974 W. North Temple (596-2596). $22 per day with 200 free mi., or $110 per week with 1200 free mi.; 14¢ each additional mi. Open Mon.-Fri. 7am-10pm, Sat.-Sun. 8am-6pm. Must be 21 with a major credit card and may only drive in Utah.

Bike Rental: Wasatch Touring, 702 E. 100 South (359-9361). 21-speed mountain bikes $15 per day. Open Mon.-Sat. 9am-7pm.

Help Lines: Rape Crisis, 467-7273. 24-hr. hotline. **Gay Mormons,** 968-6885. Calls are screened; not exclusively for Mormons.

Post Office: 230 W. 200 South (530-5902), 1 block west of the visitors bureau. Open Mon.-Fri. 8am-5:30pm, Sat. 9am-2pm. **ZIP code:** 84101.

Area Code: 801.

Salt Lake is 750 mi. inland from San Francisco, 420 mi. northeast of Las Vegas, and 500 mountainous mi. west of Denver. I-80 and I-15 meet in the city. Hitchhiking out of Salt Lake City is easier going east-west than north-south because of major cities like San Francisco or Denver. The city's sprawl has been checked by the Wasatch Mountains to the north and east, and by the **Great Salt Lake,** 17 mi. west of downtown. Most of the built-up suburbs lie south in the **Salt Lake Valley.**

Salt Lake's grid system makes navigation quite simple. Brigham Young, the city's founder, designated **Temple Square,** in the heart of today's downtown, as the center. Street names define how many blocks east, west, north, or south they lie from Temple Square. **Main Street,** running north-south, and **Temple Street,** running east-west, are the "0" points. Smaller streets and streets that do not fit the grid pattern often have non-numerical names. Occasionally, a numbered street reaches a dead end, only to resume a few blocks farther on.

The city's main points of interest lie within the relatively small area bounded by the railroad tracks around 400 West, the **University of Utah** at 1300 East, the **State Capitol** at 300 North, and **Liberty Park** at 900 South. The downtown is equipped with audible traffic lights for the convenience of blind pedestrians. A "cuckoo" is a green light for east-west travel while "chirps" indicate a green light for north-south travel.

Accommodations and Camping

Avenues Youth Hostel (AYH), 107 F St. (363-8137), 5 blocks east of Temple Sq. Bright rooms with 4 bunks each or private singles and doubles. Popular with British and German students. Blankets provided: Bring sheets. Kitchen and laundry available. Drivers offer rides here, often flexible about destinations. No check-ins after 10pm. Dorm rooms $9.75, nonmembers $13. Singles $19. Doubles $30.

Austin Hall at the **University of Utah** (581-6331), 15 blocks east of downtown, off Wasatch Dr. Take bus 3 or #14. Must be "looking at" University of Utah. Quiet, grey carpeted rooms with phone, red bedspreads, desks. Tennis courts next door; golf course across street. Singles $18. Doubles $23. Reservations recommended. Rooms for rent mid-June to Aug.; at other times go next door to Baliff Hall for the same rooms and rates.

Colonial Village Motel, 1530 Main St. (486-8171). Take bus #36 or 42. Very nice rooms with thick carpet in a white building. Management flexible about extra beds. Singles $22. Doubles $25.

Kendell Motel, 667 N. 300 West (355-0293), 10 blocks northwest of Temple Sq. Enough room for you and your army. Spacious, well-kept rooms with kitchens, color TV, and A/C $25. Room with 4 double beds and kitchen, $50.

Motel 6, 3 locations: 176 W. 600 South (531-1252); 1990 W. North Temple (364-1053), 2½ mi. from the airport (take bus #50); and 496 N. Catalpa (561-0058), just off I-15 with white cockatoo in office. All fill quickly. Singles $23. Doubles $29. Catalpa and downtown locations $3 more.

The **Wasatch National Forest** (524-5030) skirts Salt Lake City on the east, proffering many established sites. The terrain by the city is quite steep, making the best sites those on the far side of the mountains. Three of the closest campgrounds lie near I-215, which runs along the mountain fronts off I-80. Between mile 11 and 18 out of Salt Lake City on I-80, there are four campgrounds with more than 100 sites altogether (no hookups). It's first come, first serve: Go early on weekends. Take "Fort Douglas" bus #4. (Sites $5.) The **Utah Travel Council** (538-1030) has detailed information on all campsites in the area, including the three near the ski areas off Rte. 152 and 210 to the south of Salt Lake. The **state parks** around Salt Lake also offer camping, though none on the lake itself. **East Canyon State Park,** 30 mi. from Pioneer State Park in Salt Lake, near the junction of Rte. 65 and 66, has sites by East Canyon Reservoir—a good place to go boating and fishing. (Open April-late Nov.) State parks normally charge $2 for day use and $6-9 for sites. For more information, contact **Utah Parks and Recreation** (see Utah Practical Information above). If you need a hookup, then the **KOA,** 1400 W. North Temple (355-1192; sites $13.75, with water and electricity $15, full hookup $18), and private campgrounds are your only alternatives.

Food

Affordable food abounds in Salt Lake City, but don't expect to find too many cheap eats downtown. Fill up on **scones,** a Utah specialty via England, and a popular fast-food staple throughout the area. Otherwise stick to ethnic food downtown and the cheap, slightly greasy eateries on the outer fringe.

Bill and Nada's Cafe, 479 S. 6th St. One of Salt Lake's oldest, most revered cafés. Patsy Cline's "I fall to pieces" on the jukebox, and paper placemats with U.S. presidents on the tables. Two eggs, hash browns, toast $2.75. Roast leg of lamb, salad, soup, vegetable, and potatoes $5. Open 24 hr.

Rio Grande Cafe, 270 Rio Grande, in the Rio Grande Railroad depot, 4 blocks west of the temple by Amtrak and the historical society. Take bus #16 or 17. Stylish, fun Mexican restaurant with neon-and-glass decor. Two tacos with rice and beans $4.50. Open Mon.-Thurs. 11:30am-2:30pm and 5-10pm, Fri.-Sat. 11:30am-2:30pm and 5-10:30pm, Sun. 5-10pm.

Union Cafeteria, at the university (581-7256). Serves the cheapest grub in town. Chat with students while you eat breakfast ($1-2), lunch, or dinner ($2-3). Open Mon.-Fri. 7am-9pm, Sat. 8am-7:30pm, Sun. 11am-7:30pm.

Bistro to Go, 271 S. Main St. (363-5300). Try the Scandinavian spinach torte ($3.75) and top it off with one of many exotic coffees ($1.25-2.50) Thursday night poetry readings, film series, and upstairs gallery along with cappucino and gourmet delicacies attract SLC's avant-garde. Open Mon.-Wed. 9am-3pm, Thurs.-Sat. 9am-3pm and 9pm-2am.

Salt Lake Roasting Company, 249 E. 400 South (363-7572). Classical or jazz music amid big burlap bags of coffee beans. Caters to the post-college set. Coffees and pastries; quiche complete with soup and French bread $3. Open Mon.-Sat. 7am-midnight.

The Sconecutter, 2040 S. State St. (485-9981). The king of sconemakers. Your favorite flavor of fluffy but stuffing scone only $1. Open 24 hr.

The Red Iguana, 736 North Temple (322-1489). Mexican food, with *moles* so spicy the tears will run down your face ($4-6). Open Mon.-Thurs. 11:30am-9pm, Fri.-Sat. 11:30am-10pm.

Mormon Sights

Salt Lake City is the world headquarters of the **Church of Jesus Christ of Latter-day Saints** whose followers hold the *Bible,* as well as the *Book of Mormon,* as the word of God. The highest authority in the Mormon church, and the largest and most important Mormon temple, reside here.

Temple Square (240-2534) is the symbolic center of the Mormon religion. Feel free to wander around the flowery and pleasant 10-acre square, but non-Mormons may not enter the sacred temple itself. Sitting atop the highest of the building's three towers, a golden statue of the angel Moroni watches over the city. The square has two **visitors centers** (north and south), each of which stocks information and armies of smiling guides. Those short of time should join in on the 30-minute **Pioneer Tour;** for more history and sight-seeing try the 45-minute **Historical Tour.** (From the flagpole, the Pioneer Tour leaves every 15 min., the Historical Tour every 30 min. Visitors centers open daily 8am-9pm; off-season daily 9am-8pm.) The pamphlet "Truth Restored" (75¢) is available at both centers and provides further explanation of the Mormon religious creed.

Visitors on any tour in Temple Square will visit the **Mormon Tabernacle,** the flying-sauceresque building that houses the Mormon Tabernacle Choir. Built in 1867, the structure is sensitive enough acoustically that a pin dropped at one end can be heard at the other end (175 ft. away). Rehearsals on Thursday evenings (8pm) and Sunday morning broadcasts from the tabernacle are open to the public (arrive by 9am). Though supremely impressive, the choir can't match the size and sound of the 10,814-pipe organ that accompanies them. (Recitals Mon.-Fri. at noon, Sat.-Sun. at 4pm.) **Assembly Hall,** next door, also host various concerts almost every summer evening.

Around the perimeter of Temple Square stand several other buildings commemorating Mormon history in Utah. The **Genealogical Library,** 35 N. West Temple (240-2231) provides the resources for Mormons and others to research their lineage, in accordance with Mormon belief that they must baptize their ancestors by proxy, thereby sealing them into an eternal family. If you've ever wanted to research your own family heritage, this is the place to do it; the library houses the largest collection of geneological documents in the world. (Tours every 15-20 min. Open Mon. 7:30am-6pm, Tues.-Fri. 7:30am-10pm, Sat. 7:30am-5pm. Free.)

The **Museum of Church History and Art,** 45 N. West Temple (240-3310) houses Mormon memorabilia from 1820 to the present. (Open Mon.-Fri. 9am-9pm, Sat.-Sun. and holidays 10am-7pm; off-season Mon. and Wed. 10am-9pm, Tues. and Thurs.-Sun. 10am-7pm. Free.) Once the official residence of Brigham Young while he served as governer of the territory and president of the church, the **Beehive House,** N. Temple at State St. (240-2671), 2 blocks east of Temple Sq. gives half-hour guided tours every 10 minutes. (Open Mon.-Sat. 9:30am-6:30pm, Sun. 9:30am-2pm; off-season Mon.-Sat. 9:30am-4:30pm, Sun. 9:30am-2pm. Free.)

The city of Salt Lake encompasses the **Pioneer Trail State Park,** (533-5881) in Emigration Canyon on the eastern end of town. Take bus #4 or follow 8th South St. until it becomes Sunnyside Ave., then take Monument Rd. The **"This is the Place" Monument,** 2601 Sunnyside Ave. (533-5920), commemorates Brigham Young's decision to settle in Salt Lake; a visitors center will tell you all about the Mormons' toilsome immigration through Ohio, Illinois, and Nebraska. Tour **Brigham Young's forest farmhouse,** where the dynamic leader held court with his numerous wives. (Park grounds open in summer daily 8am-8pm, but visit 9am-7:30pm for the best reception. entrance fee $1.)

Secular Sights and Activities

The grey-domed **capitol** lies behind the spires of Temple Square. Tours (521-2822) are offered daily from 9:30am to 3:30pm. For more information, contact the **Council Hall Visitors Center** (538-1030), across from the main entrance. (Open daily 9am-6pm; off-season Mon.-Fri. 8am-5pm.) While in the capitol area, hike up City Creek Canyon to **Memory Grove,** savoring the shade as you gaze out over the city. Or, better yet, stroll down to the **Church of Jesus Christ of Latter-Day Saints Office Building,** 50 E. North Temple, and take the elevator to the 26th-floor observation deck where you can see the Great Salt Lake to the west, and the Wasatch Mountain Range to the east.(Open Oct.-April Mon.-Fri. 9am-5pm; April-Oct. Mon.-Sat. 9am-5pm.) Also on capitol hill is the **Hansen Planetarium,** 15 S. State St. (538-2098). Even if you don't pay for a show, enjoy the fabulous free exhibits (Open daily 10am-8pm.) Head for the **Children's Museum,** 840 N. 300 West (328-3383), to pilot a 727 jet or implant a Jarvik artificial heart in a life-size "patient." (Open Tues.-Sat. 9:30am-5pm. Admission $2. Take bus #61.) You can also walk through the U. of Utah campus to the **Utah Museum of Natural History,** and marvel at the variety of life that has lived on the Salt Lake plain. (Open Mon.-Sat. 9:30am-5:30pm, Sun. noon-5pm. Admission $2, ages under 12 $1.) Next door is the yard-sale-like collection at the **Utah Museum of Fine Arts** (581-7332; open Mon.-Fri. 10am-5pm, Sat.-Sun. 2-5pm; free). For information on university happenings contact the Information Desk in the U. of Utah Park Administration Building

(581-6515; open Mon.-Fri. 8am-8pm), or the **Olpin Student Center,** (581-5888; open Mon.-Sat. 8am-9pm, Sun. 10:30am-9pm).

Next to the Amtrak station, the **Utah State Historical Society,** 300 Rio Grande (533-5755), hosts an interesting series of exhibits, including pre-Mormon photographs and quilts. (Open Mon.-Fri. 8am-5pm, summer Sat. 10am-2pm. Free.)

The **Utah Symphony Orchestra** (533-6407) performs in **Symphony Hall,** Salt Palace Center, 100 S. West Temple, one of the most spectacular auditoriums in the country. (Free tours Mon.-Fri. at 1, 1:30, 2, and 2:30pm; off-season Tues. and Thurs. only. Concert tickets $10-15, student rush $5.) Dance and opera performances occur at the neighboring **Salt Lake Art Center.** (Open Mon.-Sat. 10am-5pm. Donation.)

Alcohol and Nightlife

The Mormon Church's prohibitions against alcohol consumption among its members have led to a number of state restrictions. Utah law requires that all liquor sales be made through state-licensed stores; don't be surprised if you can't get more than a beer at most restaurants or bars. The drinking age of 21 is well-enforced. (State liquor stores open Mon.-Sat. 11am-7pm. Six sell within 3 mi. of downtown Salt Lake.) A number of hotels and restaurants have licenses to sell mini-bottles and splits of wine, but consumers must make the drinks themselves. Public bars serve only beer but you can bring your own liquor (and pay 75¢-$2.50) for a set-up. Private clubs requiring membership fees are allowed to serve mixed drinks. Some clubs have two-week trial memberships for $5; others will give a free, temporary membership to visitors in town for a night or two.

Even with the alcohol restrictions, there are several fun downtown bars and clubs. The **Dead Goat Saloon,** 165 S. West Temple (328-4628), attracts German and British tourists as well as locals. (Open Mon.-Sat. noon-2am, Sun. 6pm-2am. Beer served until 1am. Cannot BYOB. Cover $3, Fri.-Sun. $4.) The local pool bar, **X Wife's Place,** 465 South 700 East (532-2353), used to be "My Wife's Place," but the owner got divorced. (Open Mon.-Fri. 4pm-1am, Sat. 5pm-1am. Beer served; can BYOB. No cover.)

DV8, 115 S. West Temple (539-8400) is a hip industrial emporium. Friday is college night. (Open Mon.-Sat. 9pm-1am. Cover from $3.) The **Zephyr,** 79 W. 300 South (355-2582), hosts live rock and reggae bands nightly. (Open daily 7pm-2am; off-season daily 7pm-1am. Cover $3-10.) **Junior's Tavern,** 202 E. 500 South (322-0318), is the favorite local watering hole for jazz and blues afficionados. (Open Mon.-Sat. 4pm-1am. Music starts at 9pm. Cover varies.)

Near Salt Lake City

The **Great Salt Lake,** a remnant of primordial Lake Bonneville, contains a bowl of salt water where only blue-green algae and brine shrimp can survive. The salt content varies between 5 and 15%, and provides such buoyancy that it is almost impossible for the human body to sink; only the Dead Sea has a higher salt content. Unfortunately, flooding sometimes closes the state parks and beaches on the lakeshore, but you can still try Saltair Beach 17 mi. to the west, or head north 40 minutes to fresh-water **Willard Bay.** Bus #37 ("Magna") will take you only as close as four mi. from lake. Contact the visitors center or the state parks (538-7220) for up-to-date information on access to lake as it is fairly difficult to reach without a car.

In the summer, escape the heat with a drive or hike to the cool breezes and icy streams of Salt Lake City's beautiful mountains. One of the prettiest roads over the Wasatch Range is **Route 210.** Heading east from Sandy, 12 mi. southeast of the city, this road goes up **Little Cottonwood Canyon** to the Alta ski resort. The **Lone Peak Wilderness Area** stretches away southward from the road, around which the range's highest peaks (over 11,000 ft.) tower. **City Creek, Millcreek,** and **Big Cottonwood** also make good spots for a picnic or hike.

There are seven ski resorts within 40 minutes of downtown Salt Lake. **Snowbird** (521-6040; lift tickets $32) and **Park City** (649-8111; lift tickets $30) are two of the best and most expensive. For a more affordable alternative, try the nearby **Alta** (742-3333; lift tickets $22). The **Alta Peruvian Lodge** (328-8589) is a great place pass the night. (Bunks $12.50. Closed summer.) UTA runs buses from SLC to the resorts in winter, with pick-ups at downtown motels. You can rent equipment from **Breeze Ski Rentals** (800-525-0314), at Snowbird and Park City ($13-14; 10% discount if reserved over 2 weeks in advance; lower rates for rentals over 3 days). Call or write the Utah Travel Council (see Utah Practical Information above). Pick up the free *Ski Utah* for listings of ski packages and lodgings. The **Utah Handicapped Skiers Association**, P.O. Box 108, Roy 84067 (649-3991), provides information, specialized equipment, and instruction for disabled skiers. (Open Mon.-Fri. 9am-5pm.

Some resorts offer summer attractions as well. Snowbird's aerial tram climbs to 11,000 ft., offering a spectacular view of the Wasatch Mountains and the Salt Lake Valley below. (Open daily 11am-8pm. Fare $6, seniors and ages under 16 $3.50.) During the summer, Park City offers a comparable gondola ride. (Open Fri.-Mon. noon-6pm. $5, under 12 $4.) Their alpine slide provides the fastest transport down the mountain. (Open daily 10am-10pm. Fare $3.75, seniors and children $2.75. Take I-80 east 30 mi. from Salt Lake.)

Three Corners Area

In this little-known region where Utah, Colorado, and Wyoming meet, you'll find encapsulated the entire history and landscape of the west. The **Drive Through the Ages**, on U.S. 191 from the Wyoming border to Vernal, Utah, twists dramatically through a billion years of Earth history in just a couple hundred miles. The giant lizards that once lumbered through the long-vanished marshes are now neatly exhibited for lumbering automobiles at Dinosaur National Monument, while nearby spiny vertebrae of the snow-capped Uinta Mountain Range protrude from the desert plateau. This region is exceptional not only visually, but geologically as well; the Uinta (oo-IN-ta) mountains form the only range known to run east-west, while the Green River flows upwards, from flatlands into the mountains, creating an enormous expanse of water in a parched land.

In addition to U.S. 191, many other roads (U.S. 40, Rte. 150, Rte. 414, and Rte. 530) break away from mind-numbing I-80, facilitating exploration of the region. **Greyhound** sends its beasts of burden down I-80 four times per day as well as past the Uintas and Dinosaur Monument on the south, along U.S. 40. Even the farthest corners of the area are within a half-day's drive of Salt Lake City.

Vernal

Vernal is central to both Flaming Gorge and the Uinta Mountains, 16 mi. west of the Dinosaur National Monument on U.S. 40. The town is a perfect base for exploring the Three Corners Area; you'll find information about the whole region, including a list of 66 public campgrounds. Visit the Utah Travel Council's desk (789-4002), at the Natural History Museum, for many brochures on one-day drives in the area. (Open daily 8am-8pm; off-season hours shorter.) Or contact the **chamber of commerce**, 50 E. Main St., Vernal 84078 (789-1352; open Mon.-Fri. 8am-5pm). The **Ashley National Forest Service**, 355 N. Vernal Ave. (789-1181), has jurisdiction over much of this area, including most public campgrounds. (Open Mon.-Fri. 7:30am-5pm, Sat. 8am-4:30pm.)

Stop in at the **Utah Fieldhouse of Natural History and Dinosaur Garden,** 235 Main St. (789-3799). The full-scale dinosaur models strutting among garden plants somehow come off as less than grandiose, but the well-run museum has excellent displays on the natural and human history of the area, with special attention paid to the Ute and the region's geology. The fluorescent minerals make your shoelaces glow in the dark. (Open May 27-Sept.2 daily 8am-9pm; off-season daily 8am-4pm. Admission $1, children 50¢.)

Sleeping cheaply in Vernal is easy. The simple **Sage Motel**, 54 W. Main St. (789-1442), runs a coffee shop next door popular with truck drivers. (Singles $20-22. Doubles $28-34.) If you ask for rooms on the "old side" at the **Econolodge**, 311 E. Main St. (789-2000), you might be able to swing rates lower than those originally quoted. (Singles $25. Doubles $33.) The closest campground is **Campground Dina RV Park**, 930 N. Vernal Ave. (789-2148), about 1 mi. north of Main St. on Hwy. 46 and 191. (1-person sites $5, 2-person sites $10, with electricity and water $13, full hookup $14.)

Dinosaur National Monument

Dinosaur National Monument is more than just a pile of bones. The Green and Yampa Rivers have created vast, colorful gorges and canyons, and the harsh terrain still evokes eerie visions of the massive reptiles that roamed the continent 140 million years ago.

The park entrance fee is $5 per car, $2 for bikers, pedestrians, and those in tour buses. The more interesting western side lies along Rte. 149 off U.S. 40 just outside of **Jensen**, 30 mi. east of Vernal. Seven mi. from the intersection with U.S. 40 is the **Dinosaur Quarry Visitors Center** (789-2115), accessible from the road by free shuttle bus or a fairly strenuous ½-mi. walk (cars prohibited in summer). A hill inside the center has been partially excavated to reveal the gargantuan remains of dinosaurs; you can also see paleontologists chipping away at the rock, hear a brief lecture, and tour the excellent exhibits. (Open daily 8am-7pm; off-season daily 8am-4:30pm. You can drive your car in after closing.) Winter finds the park lonely and cold with no shuttle service and tours self-guided. A few miles farther along Rte. 149 you'll find the scenic but hot **Split Mountain Gorge Campground**, and the **Green River Campground**, with shady, green sites. Both have flush toilets, drinking water, and tent and RV sites. (Open late spring-early fall. Sites $5.) There are also several free primitive campsites in and around the park; call the visitors center for information. Split Mountain Gorge Campground has evening programs in its own amphitheater. Past the campgrounds on Rte. 149, just beyond the end of the road, you can see one of the best examples of the monument's many Native American petroglyphs, or paintings, on the rocks.

The eastern side of the park is accessible only from U.S. 40, outside **Dinosaur**, CO. The 25-mi.-long road (closed in winter) to majestic **Harper's Corner**, where the Green and Yampa River gorges meet, begins 2 mi. east of Dinosaur. From the road's terminus, a 2-mi. round-trip nature hike leaves for the corner itself. It's worth the sweat—from here you can view the river canyons of the Green and Yampa Rivers, thousands of feet below. The **Dinosaur National Monument Headquarters**, on U.S. 40 in Dinosaur, CO (303-374-2216), at the intersection with the park road, provides orientation for the canyonlands of the park and information on river rafting. (Open June-Aug. Mon.-Fri. 8am-7pm; Sept.-May 8am-4:30pm.) For more information on this side of the park, write to the Monument Superintendent, P.O. Box 210, Dinosaur, CO 81610.

In Dinosaur, CO, whose street names sound like those in Bedrock of Flintstones fame, the **Terrace Motel**, 301 Brontosaurus Blvd. (303-374-2241), has clean, beautiful rooms in mobile home units, which are fortunately not fueled by Fred's and Barney's feet. (Singles $22-24. Doubles $29-31.) The **Park Motel**, 105 E. Brontosaurus Blvd. (303-374-2267), offers kitchenettes without pterodactyl garbage disposals. (Singles $18. Doubles $24.)

Greyhound/Trailways makes a daily run both east and west along U.S. 40 (July-Aug. 2 per day), stopping in Vernal and Dinosaur en route from Denver and Salt Lake City. Jensen is a flag stop, as is the monument headquarters, 2 mi. west of Dinosaur (disembark only). The Vernal depot is at 45 E. Main St. (789-0404; open Mon.-Fri. 10am-1pm and 4:30-5:30pm, Sat. 11am-noon and 4:30-5:30pm). From Salt Lake City to Vernal (3½ hr., $30 and Dinosaur, CO (4 hr., $38.50). The Dinosaur, CO depot is at 103 W. Brontosaurus Blvd. (303-374-2711; open daily 8am-10pm).

Dinosaur, CO's **post office** is at 198 Stegasaurus Dr. (303-374-2353; open Mon.-Fri. 8:30am-12:30pm and 1-5pm). The **ZIP code** is 81610.

Flaming Gorge and Brown's Hole

Curiously, Flaming Gorge never suffered a firestorm and Brown's Hole is not a hole. The bright red canyons of northeastern Utah give the Flaming Gorge Recreation Area its name; "Brown's Hole" supposedly refers to the valley (in 1870 trapper-speak). However, a post-modern view affords the visitor/author a certain 19th-century displacement of sexuality, gender roles, and indeed, language itself, in the process delineating the tensions between recreation and re-creation. In other words, this peaceful retreat offers ample opportunities for hiking and water sports. **Flaming Gorge National Recreation Area** is part of the **Ashley National Forest,** spanning southwestern Wyoming and northeastern Utah. A towering army dam built on the Green River in the 60s created the 91-mi. Flaming Gorge Reservoir. Now the rocks of the canyon, red from iron oxides, are reflected with the Ponderosa pine and spruce in the green water.

From Wyoming, the most scenic route to the gorge is the amazing U.S. 191 south from I-80 (exit between Rock Springs and Green River). Route 530 closely parallels the reservoir's western shore, but the only scenery in sight here will be an occasional pronghorn antelope. Take this route only if you want to camp on the flat beaches of the lake's Wyoming portion. To reach Flaming Gorge from the south, take U.S. 191 north from Vernal, over the gorgeous flanks of the Uinta Mountains (see below), to **Dutch John,** UT. Much of the recreation area is in Wyoming, but Utah has the most scenic and best-developed area of the park, at the base of the Uinta Range.

The **Flaming Gorge Dam Visitors Center** (885-3135), off U.S. 191 just outside the government building complex in Dutch John, offers guided tours of the dam area along with maps of the area ($2) and relaxing coloring books. (Open daily 9:30am-4:30pm; off-season daily 8am-4pm). The **Red Canyon Visitors Center** (889-3713), a few miles off U.S. 191 on Hwy. 44 to Manila, perches a breathtaking 1360 ft. above Red Canyon and Flaming Gorge Lake. (Open daily 9:30am-4:30pm; closed winter.)

The diversity of activities in the recreation area parallels its startling variation in terrain. Watch the locals shoot carp with bow and arrow in the high desert of the Wyoming lakeshores, or try your own hand at fishing along the steep, forested slopes of the Green River gorge below the dam. The gorge has superb fishing (in 1989 a 51½-lb. Mackinaw was caught here), but you must have a license from Wyoming and a stamp of approval from Utah, or vice versa. Call the Utah Department of Wildlife Resources, 152 E. 100 North (789-3103; open Mon.-Fri. 8am-5pm). You can rent fishing rods and boats at **Cedar Springs Marina** (869-3795), 3 mi. before the dam in Dutch John, and at **Lucerne Valley Marina** (784-3483) in Manila. (Boats $6-12 per hr., with 8-hr. and full-day rates. Rod rentals $2-3 per day. Open April-Aug. daily 7am-8pm.) **Hatch River Expeditions** (789-4316 or 800-342-8243; 789-4715 after hours) offers a wide variety of summer float trips, including a one-day voyage for $36, ages under 12 $25.

Inexpensive, albeit primitive, campgrounds are plentiful in the Flaming Gorge Area. You can camp right next to the Red Canyon Visitors Center in the **Red Canyon Campground** (sites $5), or in one of the numerous national forest campgrounds along Rte. 191 and 44 in the Utah portion of the park. (2-week max. stay. Sites $5.) **Buckboard Crossing** (307-875-6927) and **Lucerne Valley** (801-784-3293), located farther north, tend to be drier and unshaded, but are close to marinas on the reservoir (sites $6-7). Either visitors center can provide information on campgrounds. If you'd rather sleep indoors, try the **Flaming Gorge Lodge** (801-889-3773), near the dam in Dutch John. The immaculate rooms have A/C and cable TV but prices you may not appreciate. (Singles $39. Doubles $45.)

For a hideout from tourists, visit **Brown's Park,** a large valley 23 partially paved mi. east of Flaming Gorge. The valley's incredible isolation attracted western outlaws, most notably local boy Butch Cassidy and his gang, the Wild Bunch. The outlaws also made creative use of the proximity of three state lines—great for getting out of a state posse's jurisdiction. There are primitive **campsites** ¼ mi. from the camp in either direction: just up the Green River lies **Indian Crossing,** while **Indian Hollow** is just downstream. The free sites here have no water. The Green River's shore is a beautiful place to camp or land your raft after a brisk ride downstream. To get to Brown's Park from Dutch John, head north about 10 mi. on U.S. 191 until you reach Minnie's Gap; from here follow the signs east to Clay Basin (13 mi.) and to the park (23 mi.).

For further information, contact the **Flaming Gorge National Recreation Area,** Dutch John 84023 (801-885-3315; open Mon.-Fri. 8am-4:30pm) or, if you're coming from Wyoming, stop by the **Green River Chamber of Commerce,** 1450 Uinta Dr., on Rte. 530, Green River 82936 (307-875-5711; open Mon.-Fri. 9am-4:30pm). **Rock Springs,** WY, has a well-marked **visitors center,** 1897 Dewar Dr., a few blocks south of I-80 (307-362-3771; open Mon.-Fri. 8am-5pm). This is the most convenient brochure stockpile for those planning to go south on U.S. 191.

Finally, you can write or call the **Ashley National Forest Service** in Vernal (see Vernal) or Manila. (P.O. Box 278, Manila, UT 84046; 801-784-3445).

Uinta Mountains

Descended from nomadic bands of hunters and gatherers, the Ute (Yoot) in the Three Corners region were first displaced by white men in the early 1800s. Fur trappers originally entered the area drawn by beaver, hoping eventually to establish a mountain rendezvous site; by the 1830s mountaineers like Jim Bridger and Jedediah Smith inundated the Uintas, clashing with the Ute. The trappers managed to hold on until the beaver ran out, even having a wild annual rendezvous in the area. Today, the Uintas' inscrutable peaks and silent valleys hold few Native Americans and attract more hikers than partying mountain folk.

The **Ashley** and **Wasatch National Forests** encompass most of the mountains; Utah's tallest peaks lie within the **High Uintas Wilderness Area,** a subsidiary of these two government territories. Here, even the most harassed city-dweller can find peace amid the tundra-covered meadows of the Uintas high country. The only major east-west range in the U.S., the Uintas have different environments on the shaded northern and exposed southern slopes. The mountains parallel U.S. 40, the main road connecting Vernal, UT, with Salt Lake City. While the southern slope is the more developed and accessible of the two, hiking connoisseurs claim that the northern slope is prettier. This slope is most accessible to I-80 via Rte. 414 or 530, or U.S. 191 out of southwestern Wyoming. Most trailheads on the northern side can be reached from Manila, UT, on Rte. 44, which goes to **Browne Lake** and **Deep Creek campgrounds** (pit toilets and water that should be boiled before drinking; sites free). From here, the well-equipped backpacker can plunge into the wilder regions to the south and west. For more information, contact Ashley National Forest's Flaming Gorge ranger station in Manila, at the intersection of Rte. 43 and 44 (801-784-3445; open May 27-Sept. 2 Mon.-Fri. 7:30am-5pm, Sat.-Sun. 8am-4:30pm). Several campgrounds line U.S. 191 as it winds through the aspen glens from Flaming Gorge south into Vernal and the arid Ashley Valley. Neither as remote nor as scenic as those near Manila, the campgrounds are bigger, however, and far more convenient. **Lodgepole,** 30 mi. north of Vernal on Hwy. 91, is the best of the bunch. (Sites $5. Open June-Sept.)

Some easy trails out of Vernal include the East Park and Oak Park Trails, but hardier backpackers will want to head straight for the wilderness area, where 13,000-ft. peaks tower over an unsullied wilderness (no vehicles allowed). The best departure points (Sat.-Sun. only) are on the southern slope, 12 mi. off U.S. 40. **Moon Lake** and **Yellow Pine campgrounds** in the **Rock Creek Canyon** are each just outside the primitive area boundary. Both are a few miles north of the tiny hamlet of **Moun-**

tain Home, 20 mi. north of U.S. 40 on Rte. 87. The High Uintas can also be approached from the west, through Wasatch National Forest off Rte. 150, which provides the quickest access to the range from Salt Lake City. For information on southern access to the primitive area, contact the **Duchesne Ranger District,** P.O. Box 1, Duchesne, UT 84021 (801-738-2482), or stop by their office in Duchesne, on U.S. 40. (Open Mon.-Fri. 8am-6pm, Sat. 8am-4:30pm.) For western access, contact the **Wasatch-Cache National Forest,** 125 S. State St., Salt Lake City 84138 (801-524-5030).

Southern Utah

All five of Utah's national parks and three of its six national monuments grace the southern half of the state with narrow canyons and broad swaths of desert. Although **Arches, Bryce,** and **Zion** have a tendency to become overcrowded during the summer months, **Capitol Reef, Natural Bridges** and **Cedar Breaks** offer refreshing reprieves from the mob scene. Traveling without a car here is difficult; renting one in Salt Lake City or Provo might well be worth the cost. Cars can double as campers in the extensive Dixie and Mani-La-Sal National Forests, or on the shores of Lake Powell and the Green and Colorado Rivers.

Bryce Canyon National Park

The fragile, slender spires of pink and red limestone that rise gracefully out of Bryce's canyons often seem more of an impressionist painting than the result of whimsical wind and water currents. But beautiful as they are, these barren canyons formed through erosion made life extremely difficult for both the Paiute and the white settlers. Ebenezer Bryce, the first white man to view the canyon, called it "one hell of a place to lose a cow," but it's also the perfect place to lose those big-city blues.

The park's **visitors center** (801-834-5322) is the place to begin any tour. Pick up a copy of the free Bryce Canyon *HooDoo,* which lists all park services, events, suggested hikes, and sight-seeing drives. (Open daily 8am-8pm; off-season daily 8am-4:30pm.)

23 designated hikes let you explore Bryce without guessing. The best scenery is concentrated within 2 mi. of the visitors center. Three spectacular lookouts—**Sunrise Point, Sunset Point,** and **Inspiration Point**—will refresh even the weariest traveler. Sunrises here are especially rewarding sights. The section between Sunrise and Sunset Points is suitable for wheelchairs. The 3-mi. loop of the **Navajo** and **Queen's Garden** trails takes you into the canyon itself. Escape the crowds by conquering the **Trail to the Hat Shop,** a strenuous 3.8 mi. down an extremely steep descent. From the bottom, you can see several pinnacles with stones perched on their peaks. The really strenuous part, of course, is climbing back.

If you don't want to hike, drive the 15 mi. from the visitors center to **Rainbow Point** and stop at the various lookouts along the way. Or take a day- long **TW Services** bus tour. ($16, ages under 12 $3, departs twice daily from Bryce Lodge). The corral across from the lodge gives two-hour horseback rides to the canyon bottom ($15).

Bryce has two campgrounds planted among the tall ponderosa pines: **North Campground** and **Sunset Campground.** (Sites at both $6.) Sunrise Point (834-5361), west of both campgrounds, has public showers and a small grocery store . (Open 8am-8pm. Showers $1.25 for 10 min., available 8am-10pm). **Backcountry camping** at designated sites is a lovely way to get intimate with the canyon's changing moods and wildlife. A free permit available at the visitors center, is required. Of the six **Dixie National Forest** campgrounds, most about an hour away just off Rte. 14, the best are **TE-AH Campground, Spruce Campground,** and the **Navajo Lake Campground.** (All $6 per night; no showers; running water and toilets.) The nearest forest service office is in Panguitch, 225 E. Center St. (676-8815; open Mon.-Fri. 8am-

4:30pm). Bryce has a **post office** at Ruby's Inn (open Mon.-Fri. 8am-5:15pm); the **ZIP code** is 84764.

Bryce Canyon lies five hours south of Salt Lake City and 45 minutes east of Cedar City on U.S. 89 in southwestern Utah. From U.S. 89 at Bryce Junction (7 mi. south of Panguitch), turn east on Rte. 12 and drive 17 mi. to the park entrance (entrance fee $5 per car, $2 per pedestrian). There is no public transportation within the park or from Cedar City; this is not the place to get stranded without a car anyway.

The **Cowboy Jubilee,** a Bryce summer institution at Ruby's Inn (834-5341), features singing, dancing, and rodeo rowdiness. Another popular annual event, the **Fiddler's Association Contest,** tunes up in early July.

Near Bryce

The recent paving of Rte. 12 has opened up some of the wilderness surrounding Bryce, including the beautiful towns of **Escalante** and **Boulder,** a reconstructed Anasazi village dating from about 1100 AD. The Anasazi ("ancient ones") disappeared almost completely around 1250 AD. The type of basket-weaving among present day Hopis indicates a relationship to the Anasazi, who anthropologists think left the area to assimilate with other tribes during a 23-year drought around 1150 AD. If you don't mind dodging cows and driving on dirt roads, head out 3 mi. to **Lower Bowns Reservoir Lake** (425-3702; no drinking water, pit toilets; no wonder its free). Near Escalante, try **Escalante State Park** (826-4466) where you may even find some petrified wood (showers, trailer space; sites $8). To hike into the unsullied desert environment of the ominously named **Phipps Death Hollow Outstanding Natural Area,** just north of Escalante, contact the Bureau of Land Management (826-4221), on Rte. 12, about 1 mile west of town (Escalante Ranger District, Escalante, UT 84726). (Open Mon.-Fri. 7am-4:30pm, Sat. 8am-4:30pm; off-season Mon.-Fri. 8am-4:30pm.)

Wandering out of Bryce in the opposite direction, on Rte. 14 to Cedar City, you'll come across the refreshing and surprisingly green **Cedar Breaks National Monument** (admission $3 per car). The rim of the giant amphitheater is a lofty 10,350 ft. above sea level; 2000 ft. of flowered slopes separate the rim from the chiseled depths (disabled access). At **Point Supreme** you'll find a 30-site **campground** (sites $5) and the **visitors center.** (Open summer Mon.-Thurs. 8am-6pm, Fri.-Sat. 8am-7pm.) For more information, contact the Superintendent, Cedar Breaks National Monument, P.O. Box 749, Cedar City 84720.

Cedar City's **Iron Mission State Park,** 585 N. Main St. (586-9290) has an amazing horse-drawn vehicle collection which merits a visit. (Open daily 9am-7pm; off-season daily 9am-5pm. Admission $1, ages under 6 free.) The cheapest place to stay, **Economy Motel,** 443 S. Main St. (586-4461), has very basic rooms; try to get one with a book-sized window. (Singles $19-24. Doubles $21-27.) For more information, contact the **Cedar City Visitors Center,** 100 E. Center St. (586-4484; open Mon.-Fri. 8am-5pm).

Zion National Park

Some 13 million years ago, the cliffs and canyons of Zion made up the sea floor. The sea has been reduced to the lone, powerful Virgin River, which today carves through the Navajo sandstone terrain fingers, turning it a fiery red. Cut into the Kolob Terrace, the walls of Zion now tower 2400 ft. above the river.

There are two visitors centers in the park. The main visitor center, **Zion Canyons Visitor Center** (722-3256), takes up the southeast corner of the park, ½ mi. off Rte. 9, which connects I-15 and Hwy. 89 along the southern border of the park. The **Kolob Canyons Visitor Center** (586-9548) lies in the northwest corner of the park, off I-15. (Both open daily 8am-8pm; off-season daily 8am-5pm.) The park entrance fee is $5 per car, $2 per pedestrian. Carry water wherever you go in the park. For emergency assistance, call 772-3256 or 800-624-9447.

Even if you wisely plan to visit **Kolob Canyon's** backcountry, be sure to make the pilgrimage to **Zion Canyon.** Drive along the 7-mi. dead-end road that follows the floor of the canyon, take the bus-tram (summer only; $4.50, children $2.25), or catch a ride at the visitors center. You'll ride through the giant formations of **Sentinel, Mountain of the Sun,** and the overwhelming symbol of Zion, the **Great White Throne.** Short hikes to the base of the cliffs may be made on foot as well as by wheelchair. A challenging trail takes you to **Observation Point,** where steep switchbacks let you explore an impossibly gouged canyon. Another difficult trail (5 mi.) ascends to **Angel's Landing,** a lonely monolith that offers a heart-stopping path along the ridge and an amazing view of the canyon. A great short hike (2 mi.) runs to the Upper Emerald Pool, passing the less spectacular lower and middle pools on the way. For fun without the sweat, rent an inner tube ($5) from the shop across from the Canyon supermarket and float down the Virgin River near the campgrounds at the southern entrance.

Try to stay in Springdale (at the southern entrance to the park) at the **Under the Eaves** 980 Zion Blvd. (772-3457). Kathleen and Dale can tell you about the Ute and Paiute tribes; a golden retriever will join you for breakfast. Four-poster beds, stained glass windows, and an old fashioned tub with feet. (Singles $30-35. Doubles $35-45. Room for larger groups includes full breakfast and great coffee.)

Forty mi. south of Zion in the town of **Kanab** is the **Canyonlands International Youth Hostel,** 143 East 100th South (801-644-5554). The hostel offers roomy bunks and a fun-loving management ($9, nonmembers $11).

For those who want to rough it, the park maintains two campgrounds at the south gate, **South Campground** and **Watchman Campground** (772-3402). Bathrooms and drinking water are available, but not showers. (Sites $6, 2-week max. stay. Open daily 9am-10pm.) Showers cost $2 at **Zion Canyon Campground** 8am-8pm. The visitors center rangers present campfire programs nightly at 9pm at these two locations. There is a grocery store and coin-op laundry just outside the south entrance, about a 10-minute walk from the campgrounds. The park's only other campground is a primitive area at **Lava Point,** accessible from a hiking trail in the midsection of the park or from the gravel road that turns off Rte. 9 in **Virgin.** You must obtain a free permit from the visitors center for **backcountry camping.** You cannot camp within Zion Canyon itself. Observation Point provides one of the only canyon rim spots where you can pitch a tent. Many backpackers spend a few nights on the 27-mi. **West Rim Trail** (too long for a day's hike) or in the Kolob Canyons, where crowds never converge. Zion Campground doesn't take reservations and often fills on holiday and summer weekends; if you don't get in, try one of the six campgrounds in Dixie National Forest (see Bryce Canyon).

Zion National Park can be reached from I-15, via Rte. 17 (Toqueville exit) or from U.S. 89, via Rte. 9 (at Mount Carmel Junction). The main entrance to the park is in **Springdale,** on Rte. 9, which bounds the park to the south, along the Virgin River.

Greyhound/Trailways runs along I-15, to the west of the park; ask to be let off, since the park is not a scheduled stop. In St. George (43 mi. southwest of the park on I-15), the bus station is located on 70 W. George Blvd. (677-2933), next to the Travelodge. Two buses run daily to Salt Lake City (6 hr., $49) and Provo (5 hr., $41); five buses daily to Los Angeles (15 hr., $78) and Las Vegas (2 hr., $27).

Capitol Reef National Park

Spiny and forbidding, like the backbone of an immense prehistoric sea creature, Capitol Reef's **Waterpocket Fold** dominates the terrain of south central Utah. This 100-mi.-long line of sheer cliffs cuts the state's southern region in half. To the west lie Zion and Bryce Canyon; to the east lie Arches and Canyonlands. Major bus lines don't serve the park itself.

You'll at least want to make a brief stop at the park's **visitors center** (801-425-3791), on Rte. 24, for information on the Capitol Reef and daily activities. (Open June-Sept. daily 8am-7pm; off-season daily 8am-4:30pm.) Waterproof maps here cost $6, guides to specific trails 10¢. The 25-mi. round-trip **scenic drive** is the best way to see the park by car. This 90-minute jaunt takes you out along the "reef" itself. Nearby **Capitol Dome,** which resembles the U.S. Capitol, explains the other half of the park's unusual name. If you have a few days to spare, explore the park's desert backcountry. Foot trails and four-wheel-drive roads crisscross the region, giving access to the area's most inspiring, remote scenery. Keep in mind that summer temperatures average 95°F and most water found in seep springs and rain-holding waterpockets is contaminated.

For **backcountry camping,** you must obtain a free permit from the visitors center. Sites at the pleasant, grassy *main campground* cost $5 and are available on a first come, first serve basis. Located just a mile from the visitors center, the campground lies in the heart of the old orchard town of **Fruita.** When the park service bought the land for Capitol Reef back in the 1960s, they suddenly found themselves with the town's extensive fruit orchards on their hands, with no one to pick the fruit. Tourists can now harvest fruit from late June (cherries) to mid-October (apples). In between fall bountiful harvests of apricots, peaches, and pears, all for ridiculously low prices.

For accommodations and restaurants in this region, try: **Torrey,** 11 mi. west of the visitors center on U.S. 24; **Boulder,** 50 mi. south of the visitors center on U.S. 12; or **Hanksville,** 37 mi. from the visitors center on U.S. 24. The **Redrock Restaurant and Campground** (542-3235), in Hanksville, is the main tourist service in the region. Meals at the restaurant go for $4-7, the daily special $4.75. (Open daily 7am-10pm.) Tent sites at the campground are $6, with electricity and water $7, full hookup $10.

If you've ever wanted to see real wild buffalo, not the mangy monsters they pen up at tourist traps, head for Hanksville and the **Henry Mountains,** 30 mi. east of the visitors center near the intersection of Rte. 24 and 95. The largest free-roaming buffalo herd in the continental U.S. chews its cud here. From an original group of 18 transplanted to the area in 1941, the herd has grown to its present size of about 100. In winter, the sturdy beasts graze in the mountains' lower meadows. The warmth of summer makes them more elusive: Look for them in high alpine valleys.

Moab

Dubbed "the mountain bike capital of the Known Universe," Moab's tongue-in-cheek title nevertheless evokes its dual populace—the hippie, new age, barefoot group whose universe is forever groovy and the die hard athletes who've hardly let the snow melt from their ski boots before they're either whitewater rafting, or mountain biking. With its proximity to Arches and Canyonlands, and its youthful, "crunchy" character, Moab provides a great base for exploring the region, either by car, mountain bike, or raft on the Green River.

Tex's River Ways (801-259-5101), N. Hwy. 191, organizes canoe trips to the confluence of the Green and Colorado Rivers. Trips are expensive, costing about $99 for four days, but you can rent a canoe for $11 per day. **Descent River Expeditions** (801-259-7252), 321 N. Main St., offers white and calm water rafting tours for $25-35 per day.

In summer Moab fills up fast, especially or weekends, so call ahead to guarantee your reservations if you can. The kind manager of the **Lazy Lizard International Hostel,** 1213 S. Hwy. 191 (259-6057), goes out of the way to be helpful, and will route your trip through Arches or elsewhere. The kitchen, VCR, laundry, and hot tub are at your beck and call. (Bunks $6. Singles $10, Doubles $15.) **Westwood Guest House,** 81 E. 100 South (259-7283), one block east of Main St., rents essentially one-bedroom apartments with quilts, a back deck, and pancake mix in the fridge. Ask for no breakfast, and they'll charge about $5 less. (Singles $30-35. Doubles $35-40.) **The Prospector Lodge,** 186 N. 1st West (259-5145), one block west of Main Street, offers cool, comfy rooms across the street from the local hippie co-op. (Singles $20. Doubles $26.)

Private campgrounds speckle the area surrounding Moab. The **Holiday Haven Mobile Home and RV Park,** 400 West (259-5834) charges $10 per site, with water

$11, with electricity and water $12, full hookup $13. The **Canyonland Campark,** 555 S. Main St. (259-6848) asks $10 per site, with electricity and water $14, full hookup $16, and has a laundry and a pool. The **Moab KOA,** 4 mi. south on U.S. 191 (259-6682) charges $12 for a tent site, with electricity and water $14, full hookup $16.

Moab sits 50 mi. southeast of I-70 on Hwy. 191, 15 mi. south of Arches. There is no public transportation to Moab, although buses will stop along I-70, in Crescent Junction, where you can hitch south along 191. (Note: in Crescent Junction offer no accommodations.) **Hitching** is tough only because of the heat—bring lots of water for summer afternoons.

The **Moab Visitors Center,** 805 N. Main St. (259-8825), can provide information on lodging and dining in Moab. (Open Mon.-Sat. 8am-7pm Sun. 8am-6pm; Sept. 2-May 27 Mon.-Sat. 8am-6pm, Sun. 8am-5pm.) The **Moab Post Office,** is at 39 S. Main St. (644-2760; open Mon.-Fri. 8:30am-4pm, Sat. 9am-noon);the **ZIP code** is 84741.

Arches National Park

In Arches National Park, nature has experimented with modern sculpture for millions of years. One hundred million years ago, the constant movement of a primordial sea deposited an uneven, unstable salt bed on the Colorado Plateau. The sea evaporated, but periodic washes, along with the tireless winds, deposited layer after layer of debris upon the new salt crust. Unable to bear the weight of the debris that was compacted into extremely heavy rock, the salt twisted, buckled, and crumbled. This process left behind some of the most fantastic natural shapes in the world: towering spires, pinnacles, and, of course, arches. Arches National Park has the highest density of arches in the world (more than 200); because of their nearly perfect form explorers thought the huge arches were, like Stonehenge in England, works of some lost culture or avatar.

The park **visitors center,** 27 mi. on U.S. 191 south of I-70, 3½ mi. north of Moab, provides 35¢ auto tour guides. (Open daily 8am-6pm; off-season daily 8am-4:30pm.) For additional information, contact the Superintendent, Arches National Park, P.O. Box 907, Moab 84532 (259-8161). An entrance pass ($5 per carload) remains valid for seven days at both Arches and nearby Canyonlands; pedestrians and bikers pay only $1. Water available in the park.

Plenty of scenic wonders glorify the 25-mi. road between the visitors center and Devil's Garden. No matter how short your stay, be sure to see the **Windows** section at **Panorama Point,** about ½ way along the road. Cyclists will also enjoy this ride in spring or fall, but the steep inclines make the trip unbearable in the summer heat. **Rim Cyclery,** 94 W. 100 North (259-5333), offers rimming bikes for $20 per day, including helmet and water bottle. (Open Mon.-Sat. 9am-9pm, Sun. 9am-6pm; off-season daily 9am-6pm.) At the end of the paved road by the campground, **Devil's Garden** boasts an astounding 64 arches. The climax of your visit should be **Delicate Arch,** the symbol of the monument. Take the Delicate Arch turn-off from the main road 2 mi. down a graded unpaved road (impassible after rainstorms). Once you reach Wolfe Ranch, go down a 1½-mi. foot trail to Delicate Arch. The freestanding arch spans 33 ft. and rises 45 ft. Beyond it you can get a glimpse of the Colorado River gorge and the La Sal Mountains. If you're lucky, you may come across petroglyphs—writings on the stone walls left by the Anasazi and Ute who wandered the area from 1000 to 100 years ago. Please don't touch: Preserve them for future wanderers.

Of course, arches aren't the only natural wonders here. Two of the most popular trails, the 1-mi. **Park Avenue** and the moderately strenuous 2-mi. **Fiery Furnace Trail** lead downward into the canyon bottoms, providing views of the cliffs and monoliths above. Only experienced hikers should attempt the Fiery Furnace trail alone; there are no guide markers and the ranger on duty will be more than happy to guide you safely through the labyrinth.

The park's only campground, **Devil's Garden,** has 53 sites; get there early since sites are often snatched up by 1pm. The campground is 18 mi. from the visitors center and has running water. (2-week max. stay. Sites $5. Open April-Oct.) **Dead Horse Point State Park,** perched on the rim of the Colorado Gorge south of Arches and 14 mi. south of U.S. 191, is accessible from Rte. 313. The campground has modern restrooms, water, hook-ups, and covered picnic tables. (Sites $6-8. Open April-Oct.) Winter camping is allowed on Dead Horse Point itself. For more information, contact the Park Superintendent, Dead Horse Point State Park, P.O. Box 609, Moab 84532 (259-6511). **Backcountry camping** in Arches National Park is a free adventure. Register at the visitors center first, and pick up a **USGS map** to avoid getting lost. Bring plenty of water and bread crumbs and avoid hiking on summer afternoons. Better than either the campground at Arches or Dead Horse Point in the summer, however, the **Manti-la-Sal National Forest** provides a means for escape from the heat, the crowds, and the biting gnats. These campgrounds are about 4000 ft. higher up, and about 20 to 25 mi. southeast of Moab off U.S. 191. All are free, except **Warner,** which charges $4. Three mi. down a dirt road is **Oowah Lake,** a rainbow trout heaven, at least from an angler's point of view (fishing permit $5 per day). Camping is free (no water, pit toilets). For more information on the forest, contact the Manti-la-Sal National Forest Service office in Moab, 125 W. 200 South (259-7155; open Mon.-Fri. 8am-4:30pm).

The entrance to the park is on a paved road that winds for 25 mi. into its interior. This road is accessible from U.S. 191 at the junction 5 mi. north of Moab. Arches is 230 mi. from Salt Lake City. There is no public transportaiton to Arches, but buses run along I-70, stopping in Crescent Junction.

Canyonlands National Park

The confluence of the Green and Colorado Rivers in **Canyonlands National Park** reveals that when these two mighty waterways joined, the coupling proved an uneventful one. The merging rivers gouged out rifts and gorges that sink into the desert's crust with a dizzying starkness. At those points in the park which the rivers bypassed, harsh desert prevails. The entire park, with its scenic but arid terrain, has remained remote and wild; Roads are unpaved, trails primitive, and the vistas some of the most breathtaking in the southwest.

Outside the park, there are two information centers. Monticello's **National Park Service Office,** 32 S. 1st E. (587-2737) sells maps ($2.50-6.) In Moab (see above), the **Park Service** resides at 125 W. 200 S. (259-7164) and has the same business hours. Both can provide information for French, German, and Spanish visitors.

The park contains three distinct areas. The most easily reached region, **Needles** (ranger station 259-6568), lies in the park's southeast corner. (Station open daily 8am-5pm.) To get there, take Rte. 211 west from U.S. 191, about 40 mi. south of Moab. Since this well-maintained paved road begins 34 mi. from the park entrance, be sure to have plenty of gas and water, and register with the park ranger before entering the area. Farther north, the **Island in the Sky** (ranger station 259-6568) sits deep within the "Y" formed by the two rivers, (Open Sun.-Wed. 8am-5pm, Thurs.-Sat. 8am-6pm.) Access to this dramatic mesa proves a little more difficult; take Rte. 313 west from U.S. 191 about 10 mi. north of Moab. The road becomes dirt before it enters the park, but well-groomed dirt. The most remote district of the park is the rugged **Maze** area (ranger station 259-6513; open daily 8am-4:30pm), to the west of the canyons, accessible only by four-wheel drive. Once you've entered a section of the park, you're committed: transferring from one area to another involves retracing your steps and re-entering the park, a tedious trip lasting from several hours to a full day.

Each ranger station has a booklet of possible hikes (including photos), so you can pick your own. Hiking options from the Needles area are probably the best. Cyclists should check at the visitors centers for lists of trails. If hiking in desert heat doesn't appeal to you, you can rent jeeps and mountain bikes at the **Needles Outpost,** or take an airplane ride ($25 for a 25-min. flight). **Lin Ottinger Tours,**

600 N. Main St., Moab (259-7312), leads all-day jeep and backpacking tours ($25-35) that teach you how to survive on local flora.

There are no food services in the park. Just outside the boundary in the Needles district, however, the **Needles Outpost** houses a limited, expensive grocery store and gas pumps. Hauling groceries in from Moab or Green River (for the Maze) is the best budget alternative.

Each region has its own official **campground.** In the Needles district, **Squaw Flat** is situated in a sandy plain surrounded by giant sandstone towers. Avoid this area in June, when flying insects swarm. Bring water, though it is usually available from April through September. A $5 fee is also charged during these months. **Willow Flat Campground,** in the Island in the Sky unit, sits high atop the mesa. You must bring your own water; sites are free. Willow Flat and Squaw Flat both have picnic tables, grills, and pit toilets, and both operate on a first come, first serve basis. The campground at the **Maze Overlook** has no amenities at all. Dead Horse Point State Park (adjacent to Island in the Sky) and Manti-la-Sal National Forest (adjacent to the Needles) provide alternative campsites. (See Arches National Park.) Before **backcountry camping** get a free permit from the ranger's office in the proper district and take along plenty of water (at least one gallon per person per day). Summer temperatures regularly climb to over 100°F.

CALIFORNIA

The Golden State has long lured herds of ambitious and desperate people. Spanish explorers, in search of a fabled strait between the Pacific and Atlantic Oceans, happened upon California and 200,000 Native Americans in the 1500s. Hoping to secure the land (and its not-so-imaginary treasure), they quickly named it "California" after an imaginary island kingdom inhabited by Amazons and located just around the corner from Paradise. Even after striking the real stuff in 1848 and subsequent statehood in 1854, Californians have kept trying to see around that corner.

What they saw is another matter. In the late 19th century, exploited Chinese workers constructed the railroads linking the West to the rest of the country. When severe droughts further reduced Depression-era Midwestern farmlands to lifeless "dust bowls," a flood of newcomers arrived to pick the grapes of wrath. Similar misplaced notions of opportunity drew African Americans westward during the great Southern exodus early in the 20th century. Along with California's longstanding Mexican population, many of these later "California Or Bust" groups met hostility, ironically from earlier fortune-seekers.

Yet no misfortune, not even severe earthquakes, could keep people away, either from the state, or from each other; since 1900, the state's population has doubled every 20 years. Today the accompanying naive industrial expansion has plagued a more mature California with pollution and water shortages. During the 1960s, frustrated and optimistic young Californians challenged the promise of paradise with Black Panther and Free Speech movements. By 1967, San Francisco's psychedelic Haight-Asbury neighborhood hosted the Summer of Love, spawning a Sexual Revolution. Most recently, such Californian zeal for "causes" has been replaced with mellow enthusiasm for a new ideal: the state itself. Urban renewal has met suburban expansion, all with concern for the environment. After all, Californians don't want to let their paradise, fool's gold or not, slip between their fingers.

For more comprehensive coverage of California than can be provided here, consult *Let's Go: California and Hawaii.*

Practical Information

Capital: Sacramento.

Visitor Information: California Office of Tourism, 1121 L St. #103, Sacramento 95814 (916-322-1396). **National Park Information,** 213-888-3770.

Time Zone: Pacific (3 hr. behind Eastern). **Postal Abbreviation:** CA.

San Diego

As rivers of tourists, streams of relocating Northeasterners, and a flood of Mexican immigrants arrive at the confluence that is San Diego, the question becomes not why so many, but why not more? Centuries after its founding on hills of chaparral, San Diego manages to maintain clean air and beaches, a sense of culture and history, and even lush greenery in the face of population growth and water shortages. A solid Navy "industry" cushions the economy, local architecture looks pleasant, not gaudy, and rain and winter are virtually unknown. But even "America's Finest City" has questions of water shortages and immigration surpluses for which there are few easy answers.

San Diego has ample tourist attractions—a world-famous zoo, Sea World, and Old Town—but your most enjoyable destination might simply be a patch of sand at one of the superb beaches. When exploring, don't neglect residential communities such as Hillcrest, La Jolla, and Ocean Beach. For relief from city noise and beach

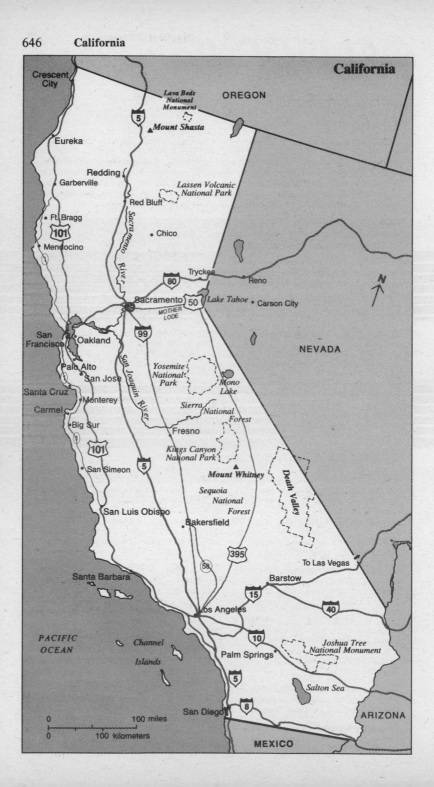

California

Crescent City

Lava Beds National Monument

OREGON

5

▲ *Mount Shasta*

Eureka

Redding
Garberville

Red Bluff

Lassen Volcanic National Park

Ft. Bragg

101

Mendocino

• Chico

Sacramento River

Tryckee

80

Reno

Sacramento

50

Lake Tahoe   • Carson City

MOTHER LODE

San Francisco

Oakland

99

NEVADA

Palo Alto

San Jose

Yosemite National Park

Mono Lake

Santa Cruz

Carmel

Monterey

San Joaquin River

Sierra

National Forest

• Big Sur

Fresno

101

Kings Canyon National Park

5

• San Simeon

▲ *Mount Whitney*

Death Valley

Sequoia National Forest

San Luis Obispo

• Bakersfield

395

58

To Las Vegas

Santa Barbara

Barstow

15

Los Angeles

40

PACIFIC OCEAN

Channel Islands

10

Palm Springs

Joshua Tree National Monument

5

Salton Sea

San Diego

8

ARIZONA

0   100 miles

0   100 kilometers

MEXICO

N

bumming, retreat to the nearby mountains and deserts, or head for Mexico, almost next door.

Practical Information

Emergency: 911.

Visitor Information: Visitor Information Center, 11 Horton Plaza (236-1212), downtown at 1st Ave. and F St. Like a Hoboken pizzeria, they don't display much, but have whatever you need under the counter. Open daily 8:30am-5:30pm. Old Town and State Park Information, 4002 Wallace Ave. (237-6770), in Old Town Square next to Burguesa. Take the Taylor St. exit off I-8, or bus #5. Historical brochures on the Old Town ($2). Open daily 10am-5pm. National Parks Information, 226-6311. Recorded information. Arts/Entertainment Hotline, 234-2787. Recorded calendar of performances, exhibitions, and other events.

San Diego Council American Youth Hostels: 1031 India St. 92101 (239-2644), between Broadway and C St. Student travel information, including full lists of hostels. Bike accessories, travel gear, and guides. Sponsors domestic and European trips. Open Mon.-Fri. 9:30am-5:30pm, Sat. 9:30am-4:30pm. After hours, you'll get a recorded listing of hostels in San Diego.

Travelers Aid: Airport, 231-7361. One station in each terminal. Directions for lost travelers. Open daily 9am-10pm. Downtown office, 1122 4th Ave. #201 (232-7991). Open Mon.-Fri. 8:30am-5pm.

San Diego International Airport (Lindbergh Field): at the northwestern edge of downtown, across from Harbor Island. Divided into east and west terminals. San Diego Transit "30th and Adams" bus #2 goes downtown. Buses run Mon.-Fri. 5am-11:30pm, Sat.-Sun. 5:50am-midnight.

Amtrak: Santa Fe Depot, 1050 Kettner Blvd. (239-9021, for schedules and information 800-872-7245), at Broadway. To L.A. (7-8 per day 5:20am-8:45pm; Mon.-Fri. $23, round-trip $30; Sat.-Sun. $28, round-trip $35). Information on bus, trolley, car, and boat transportation available at the station. Ticket office open daily 5:10am-9pm.

Greyhound: 120 W. Broadway (239-9171), at 1st Ave. To L.A. (12 per day 5:30am-midnight; Mon.-Thurs. $15, round-trip $23; Fri.-Sun. $17, round-trip $23).

Public Transport: see Getting Around below.

Taxi: Yellow Cab, 234-6161. Cab fare downtown around $7.

Car Rental: Six Ninety-Five A Day, 2975 Pacific Hwy. (260-1721). $6.95 per day, 12¢ per mi. Local use only. Ages 18-25 pay a 50% surcharge. Open Mon.-Fri. 8am-6pm, Sat. 8am-3pm, Sun. 9am-noon. Rent-A-Car-Cheep, 1747 Pacific Hwy. (238-1012). $18 per day with unlimited mi. Under 21 pay surcharge. Open daily 7am-10pm. Must be 18 with credit card. Aztec Rent-A-Car, 2401 Pacific Hwy. (232-6117). $20 per day, 150 free mi., 15¢ each additional mi. $115 per week with 1000 free mi. Cars may venture south of the border as far as Ensenada with purchase of Mexican insurance ($10). Open Mon.-Fri. 7am-8pm, Sat.-Sun. 8am-5pm. Must be 21 with major credit card.

Bike Rental: Pennyfarthing's, 520 5th Ave., in the Gaslamp Quarter. Bikes $2 per hr., $20 per day. Tandems twice as much. Open Tues.-Fri. 10am-5pm, Sat. 9am-4pm, Sun. 10am-2pm. Alexander's, 4315 Ocean Blvd. (273-0171), in Mission Beach. Bikes and skates $2 per hr., $8 per 6 hr. Boogie boards $3 per hr., $9 per 6 hr. Open daily 9am-9pm. La Jolla Cyclery, 7443 Girard (459-3141), in La Jolla. Limited rental bikes $2.50 per hr., $10 per day with a 2-hr. min. Tandems $3.50 per hr., $15 per day. Open Tues.-Fri. 9am-6pm, Sat. 9am-5pm.

Help Lines: Crisis Hotline, 800-479-3339 or 236-3339. Open 24 hr. Women's Center, 2467 E St. (233-8984). Open Mon.-Fri. 8:30am-4:30pm. Rape Crisis Hotline, 233-3088. Open 24 hr. Lesbian and Gay Men's Center, 3780 5th Ave. (692-2077). For counseling call 692-4297 Mon.-Sat. 6-10 pm.

Senior Citizen's Services: 202 C St. (236-5765), in the City Hall Bldg. Provides ID cards so that seniors can take advantage of senior discounts. Plans daytrips and sponsors "nutrition sites" (meals) at 8 locations. Open Mon.-Fri. 8am-5pm.

Community Service Center for the Disabled: 2864 University Ave. (293-3500), Hillcrest. Attendant referral, wheelchair repair and sales, emergency housing, motel/hotel accessibility referral, and TDY Line services for the deaf (293-7757). Open Mon.-Fri. 9am-5pm.

Post Office: 2535 Midway Dr. (547-0477), between downtown and Mission Beach. General Delivery. Open Mon.-Fri. 7am-1am, Sat. 8am-4pm. General Delivery ZIP code: 92138. Take bus #6, 9, or 35.

Area Code: 619.

Orientation

San Diego rests in the extreme southwestern corner of California, 127 mi. south of L.A. and only 15 mi. north of the Mexican border. Flights to the city often cost no more than those to Los Angeles or San Francisco. I-5 runs south from Los Angeles, skirting the eastern edge of downtown. Suburbanites spend many happy hours on this six-lane strip. I-8 runs east-west along downtown's northern boundary, connecting the desert in the east with Ocean Beach in the west. The major downtown thoroughfare, **Broadway,** also runs east-west.

A group of skyscrapers in the blocks between Broadway and I-5 makes up downtown San Diego. Streets running parallel to the bay (north-south) on the western end of downtown have proper names until they hit Horton Plaza in the east; then they become consecutively numbered avenues. Going east-west are lettered streets; "A" St. is the farthest north, L the farthest south. In their midst, Broadway replaces D St. and runs directly east from the bay. North of A, Ash St. begins a string of alphabetized streets named after plants that continues north all the way to Walnut. Other alphabetical schemes crop up throughout the metropolitan area, the most impressive being Point Loma's complete Addison to Zola literary system.

On the northeastern corner of downtown, **Balboa Park,** larger than the city center, is bounded by 6th Ave. on the west, I-5 and Russ Blvd. on the south, 28th St. on the east, and Upas St. on the north. To the north and east of Balboa Park are the main residential areas. **Hillcrest,** San Diego's most cosmopolitan district and a center for the gay community, lies at the park's northwestern corner, around the intersection of 5th and University Ave.; **University Heights** and **North Park** sit along the major east-west thoroughfares of University Ave., El Cajon Blvd., and Adams Ave.

Those Easterners accustomed to muscling their way across a street against the light will either be impressed or amused by the San Diegan habit of waiting obediently for the walk signal, no matter how clear the coast. Jaywalking is not in vogue, illegal (tickets are given out occasionally), and dangerous.

West of downtown is the bay, 17 mi. long and formed by the Coronado Peninsula (jutting northward from Imperial Beach) and Point Loma (dangling down from Ocean Beach). North of Ocean Beach lie Mission Beach (with neighboring Mission Bay), Pacific Beach, and La Jolla.

Getting Around

A car is extremely helpful in San Diego, but buses reach most areas of the city. The public transport systems (San Diego Transit, North County Transit, DART, FAST, and Dial-A-Ride) cover the area from Oceanside in the north to Tijuana in Mexico, and inland to Escondido, Julian, and other towns. Call for **public transit information** (233-3004; daily 5:30am-8:25pm) or stop by the **Transit Store,** 449 Broadway (234-1060), at 5th Ave. (open daily 8:30am-5:30pm). Pick up the *Transit Rider's Guide,* listing which routes to take to popular destinations. Fares vary: 80¢ for North County Transit routes, $1 for local routes, $1.25 for express routes, and about $2.25 for commuter routes. Transfers within San Diego are free; North County transfers cost 25¢. Exact change is required; most city buses accept dollar bills. At least one wheelchair-accessible bus travels per hour. Visitors age 60 and over receive discounts. Bike racks equip buses on some routes, especially those to the beaches. When you frequent buses, save money by using **Day Tripper** passes, which allow unlimited travel on buses, trolleys, and even the Bay Ferry ($4 for 1 day, $12 for 4 days). These and the various monthly passes are available at the Transit Store. Service is scanty after 9pm (check the schedule). Most urban routes originate, terminate, or pass through downtown.

The wheelchair-accessible **San Diego Trolley** runs on two lines from a starting point near the Santa Fe Depot on C St., at Kettner. One heads east for **El Cajon.** The other, popularly known as the Tijuana Trolley, runs 16 mi. south to **San Ysidro** at the Mexican border every 15 minutes from 5:30am to 9:15pm, then every 30 minutes until 12:15am. From the border, cabs to the oxymoronic Tijuana Cultural Center or shopping district cost less than $5. The trolley also provides access to local buses in National City, Chula Vista, and Imperial Beach. (Fare 50¢-$2 depending on distance, over 60 and disabled passengers 50¢. Transfers free.) You're on the honor system; purchase a ticket from machines at stations and board the trolley. There are no turnstiles or ticket takers, but occasionally an inspector will check for tickets.

Accommodations

Although San Diego attracts visitors throughout the year, both lodging rates and the number of tourists skyrocket in summer, particularly on weekends. Reservations can save you much time and disappointment. Many hostels and residential hotels offer weekly rates. Numerous, especially downtown, some resident hotels look modern and appealing. If you have a car, consider camping outside San Diego (see Camping). If not, staying downtown will give you access to bus routes that will take you most places.

There are many inexpensive, sterile hotels east of downtown along El Cajon Blvd., a large commercial strip devoted primarily to selling cars. Bus #15 offers a sweeping tour of the entire boulevard. Try **Lamplighter Inn Motel**, 6474 El Cajon Blvd. (582-3088 or 800-225-9610; singles $35, doubles $38) or **Aztec Motel**, 6050 El Cajon Blvd. (582-1414 or 800-225-9610; singles $31, doubles $33).

Downtown

Armed Services YMCA Hostel (AYH), 500 W. Broadway (232-1133), near train and bus stations. Hostel rooms offer all the comforts of a troop ship: gray walls, metal beds, communal showers. Check-out 9:30am. $8. Linen not included. Newly renovated singles $20. Doubles $30. Check-out noon. Key deposit $2. AYH membership required for dorm rooms only.

Downtown Inn Hotel, 660 G St. (238-4100), just east of the Gaslamp Quarter. Comfortable, tastefully furnished rooms with microwave/toaster oven, refrigerator, TV, and ceiling fan. Convenient to buses. Singles $24-39. Doubles $29-49. Weekly: singles $99-120; doubles $110-135.

YWCA Women's Hostel, 1012 C St. (239-0355), at 10th Ave. Women only. Often full, quite friendly. Dorm beds for ages 18-34 (no upper age-limit for AYH members) $8.25. Linen $5. Hall bathrooms. Nonmembers singles $18; doubles $30. Key deposit $5.

Jim's San Diego, 1425 C St. (235-8341), south of the park at City College trolley. Clean, hostel-type rooms. For international travelers only. Kitchen, laundry. $15. Weekly: $90. Breakfast included.

La Pensione on Second, 1546 2nd Ave. (236-9292), downtown. Close to I-5. Pretty rooms with microwave, refrigerator, and cable TV. Neat art on the walls. New building. Singles $24. Doubles $39-49. Weekly: singles $99; doubles $130-155.

Siesta Motor Inn, 1449 9th Ave. (239-9113 or 800-748-5604), at Beech St. close to Balboa Park. Comfortable, attractive rooms with A/C, pool, and satellite TV. Singles $35. Doubles $40. Key deposit $2.

Mission Hills, Hillcrest, Mission Valley

E-Z 8 Motels, 3 locations: 2484 Hotel Circle Pl., Mission Valley (291-8252); 4747 Pacific Hwy., Old Town (294-2512); 3333 Channel Way (223-9500), near the Sports Arena. Three clones, with TV, pool, and A/C. Singles $32. Doubles $37. Triples and quads $44.

Old Town Budget Inn, 4444 Pacific Hwy. (260-8024, for reservations 800-225-9610), near Old Town. Simple and reasonable. Singles $32. Doubles $34. Without A/C $2 less. Microwave and refrigerator $5 more.

South of Downtown and the Beaches

Imperial Beach Hostel (AYH), 170 Palm Ave. (423-8039). Take bus #910 from the Amtrak station or take the trolley on C St. to Palm St. Station (35 min.). Transfer to bus #33 westward-bound (every hr. on the ½ hr.). In a converted firehouse 2 blocks from the the beach, 5 mi. from Mexico. Quiet and fairly remote, with a well-equipped kitchen and large common area with a TV. Bunkbeds for 36 (more if people share). Open 7:30-9:30am and 4:30-11pm. Check-in 4:30-10pm. Curfew 11pm. $8, nonmembers $11. Key deposit $2. Make reservations by phone or by sending one night's payment.

Point Loma Hostel (AYH), 3790 Udall St., Point Loma (223-4778). Take bus #35 from downtown; get off at Elliott International shopping center at Voltaire and Worden St., and walk 1 block south to Udall St. An airy 2-story building 20 min. from Ocean Beach. 60 wooden bunk beds, common room, kitchen. Check-out 9:30am. Lockout 9:30am-4:30pm. Curfew 2am. $10, nonmembers $13. Bike rental $7 per day. Reserve by sending one night's payment.

Camping

All state campgrounds open to bikers for $2 nightly; state law requires that no cyclist be turned away because of overcrowding. Only Campland on the Bay lies within city limits. For information on state park camping, call the helpful people at San Elijo Beach (753-5091). MISTIX (800-444-7275) and not individual campgrounds handle reservations. Most parks completely fill in summer, and it's wise to make weekend reservations eight weeks in advance.

Campland on the Bay, 2211 Pacific Beach Dr. (274-6260). Take I-5 to Grand Ave. exit and follow the signs, or take bus #30 and get off on Grand at the sign on the left. Expensive and crowded as the only central place to pitch a tent or plug in an RV. Cheapest sites in a "dirt area" with nothing to block the wind coming off the water. Sites $20-43; in winter $19-30.

South Carlsbad Beach State Park, Rte. 21 (729-8947), near Leucadia, in north San Diego County. 225 sites, half for tents. On cliffs over the sea. Sites $12. Reservations necessary in summer.

San Elijo Beach State Park, Rte. 21 (753-5091), south of Cardiff-by-the-Sea. 271 sites (150 for tents) similar to South Carlsbad to the north. Good landscaping gives the illusion of seclusion. Hiker/biker campsites. Sites $12. Make reservations for summer.

Food

The bad news first: San Diego has over 70 Jack in the Boxes and hundreds of other fast-food joints, an achievement befitting the birthplace of the genre. The good news: the lunchtime business crowd has nurtured a multitude of restaurants specializing in good, cheap lunches. But in the land of the speedy burrito, **Robert's,** at 3202 Mission Blvd. and other locations, serves the best Mexican fast food. Pick up cheap, high-quality fruits and vegetables at the **Farmer's Bazaar,** 205 7th Ave. (233-0281), at L St., to complete the feast (open Tues.-Sat. 9am-5:30pm, Sun. 9am-5pm) or Ocean Beach's organic grocery stores on Voltaire Ave. For a wide selection of cheap meals downtown, the food court on the top floor of **Horton Plaza** offers far more than the standard 31 flavors of junk food.

Kansas City Barbeque, 610 W. Market St., south of Broadway near the bay. Enjoy decent non-KC barbecue in an atmospheric bar in San Diego where scenes from *Top Gun* were shot. Dinners with 2 side orders around $7. One-sided sandwiches $4.50 (served only after 10pm). Open daily 11am-1am.

Old Spaghetti Factory, 275 5th Ave., in the Gaslamp Quarter. An 1898 building that makes fresh spaghetti ($4.25-5.85), and well. Open Mon.-Thurs. 5-10pm, Fri.-Sat. 5-11pm, Sun. 4-10pm.

Filippi's Pizza Grotto, 1747 India St., on a block full of Italian restaurants. Other locations—all family-owned—around town. Subs big enough to threaten the Pacific fleet ($3.25-4.25). Try the homemade sausage. Open Sun.-Fri. 11am-10:45pm, Sat. 11am-11:45pm.

El Indio, 3695 India St., in India St. Colony. Lines all day long, but speedy service and high quality. Large portions; combination plates from $3. Buy a bag of fresh corn tortillas (12 for 55¢) or their "fantabulous" tortilla chips. Open daily 8am-9pm.

Chuey's Café, 1894 Main St., in Barrio Logan. Barrio Logan trolley stop; walk 1 block toward stoplight. A stretch out of downtown but easily reached by trolley. People go out of their way to reach this combination restaurant/cocktail bar/pool hall. Excellent Mexican entrees $4-6. Huge combination plates and *gringo* food too. Open Mon.-Wed. 11am-7:30pm, Thurs.-Sat. 11am-9pm.

Royal Bakery Thrift Store, 741 E St. (233-6704). The retail outlet of the Royal Pie Bakery, a commercial bakery in the Gaslamp Quarter. Fresh, big, fluffy, sticky, yummy things (45¢). A dozen day-old donuts $1. Open Mon.-Fri. 7:30am-5pm, Sat. 8am-5pm.

Conora's, 3715 India St. (291-5938), in India St. Colony. Sandwich shop extraordinaire. Over 60 varieties, almost all $3.50-4.50. Call ahead and Conora's will have your order ready when you arrive. Open Mon.-Sat. 8am-6pm.

Gelato Vero, 3753 India St., in India St. Colony. Taste the dark chocolate gelato. 11 other flavors ($1.35-3.50), plus pastries and coffees. Open Mon.-Thurs. 6:30am-midnight, Fri. 6:30am-1am, Sat.-Sun. 7:30am-1am.

Mandarin Dynasty, 1458 University Ave. As if the wonderful Yu Hsiang Beef and many vegetarian options were not varied enough, they "make anything on request." Most dishes $6-6.50. Open daily 11am-3pm and 5pm-midnight.

San Diego Chicken Pie Shop, 2633 El Cajon, at Oregon. A San Diego tradition for over 50 years, now at a new location. Namesake pie actually made with both chicken and turkey, smothered in gravy ($1.50; with potato, cole slaw, or vegetable, $2.25). Homemade fruit pies 75¢ per slice. Open daily 10am-8pm.

Point Loma Seafoods, 2805 Emerson, off Rosecrans by the bay. Take bus #29 from downtown. Fish come off the boats, go into the kitchen, and emerge ready to eat. Purchased seafood fresh, hickory smoked, or in sandwiches ($3-4). French fries $1. Open Mon.-Sat. 9am-6:30pm, Sun. noon-6:30pm.

John's Waffle Shop, 7906 Girard Ave. La Jolla. Basic golden waffles $2.50, up to $5.50 for whole grain banana nut waffles. Breakfast and sandwiches average $4.50. Open Mon.-Sat. 7am-3pm, Sun. 8am-3pm.

Nicolosi's Pizza, 4009 El Cajon Blvd. Family-owned pizza plaza and university tradition. Homemade baked lasagna $6.70 (including soup or salad and oven-fresh bread). Open Mon.-Sat. 11am-11pm, Sun. 11am-10pm.

Julio's, 4502 University Ave. Another of San Diego's dimly lit Mexican restaurants with good food; only its late weekend hours set it apart. Get away for less than a fiver by eating a la carte: big burritos with dressings $3.25 ($2.75 at lunch), 2 enchiladas $4.70. Open Mon.-Thurs. 11am-11pm, Fri.-Sat. 11am-3am, Sun. 9am-11pm.

Sights

In contrast to the rest of Southern California, where pre-fab houses and mobile homes resemble a package of instant, water-added city, San Diego's buildings form a tangible record of the city's history. The oldest buildings are the early 19th-century adobes of **Old Town**. Just up Juan St. from Old Town, **Heritage Park** displays old Victorian homes, carefully trimmed gingerbread houses. Extending south from Broadway to the railroad tracks and bounded by 4th and 6th Ave. on the west and east, the **Gaslamp Quarter** houses a notable concentration of pre-1910 commercial buildings now resurrected as upscale shops and restaurants. Well-preserved houses and apartment buildings from 1910 to the 1950s, in styles ranging from Mission Revival to zig-zag Moderne, are found on almost every block. For more relaxing pleasures, head toward the beaches, San Diego's biggest draw. Surfers catch tubular waves, sun-worshippers catch rays, and everybody gets caught up in sun-stimulated serenity. Or heatstroke.

Downtown

Horton Plaza, at Broadway and 4th Ave., centers San Diego's redevelopment. This pastel-colored, multi-fauceted, glass and steel shopping center encompasses seven city blocks; its complex architecture, top-floor views of the city, occasional live entertainment, and serious hyphenation set it apart from the average mall. (3-hr. parking free with validation at one of the shops.) Another noteworthy example of local architecture is the **Santa Fe Depot,** Kettner Blvd., a Mission Revival building whose grand arches welcomed visitors to the 1915 exposition. Standing just 3 blocks west of Horton Plaza, the building now serves as the San Diego Amtrak depot. On weekdays, Broadway bustles with professionals and panhandlers. At night and on weekends, only the latter remain.

Farther south past the Gaslamp Quarter, the **Coronado Bridge** stretches westward from Barrio Logan to the Coronado Peninsula. High enough to allow the Navy's biggest ships to pass underneath and to give a good view, the sleek, sky-blue arc executes a near-90° turn over the waters of San Diego Bay before touching down in Coronado. (Bridge toll $1. Bus #901 and other routes also cross.) When built in 1969, the bridge's eastern end cut a swath through San Diego's largest Chicano community. In response to the threatening division, the community created **Chicano Park,** taking legal possession of the land beneath the bridge and spiritual possession by painting splendid murals on the piers. The murals, visible from I-5 but fully appreciated only by walking around the park, are heroic in scale and theme, drawing on Hispanic American, Spanish, Mayan, and Aztec imagery. Take bus #11 or the San Ysidro trolley to Barrio Logan station.

The **Embarcadero,** a fancy Spanish name for a dock, sits at the foot of Broadway on the west side of downtown. Along with North Island's seaplanes, Point Loma's submarine base, and South Bay's mothball fleet, the vessels on the Embarcadero are reminders of San Diego's number-one industry as well as of the city's role as a major West Coast naval installation. **San Diego Harbor Excursion** (234-4111) offers cruises past the Navy ships and under the Coronado Bridge. (In summer, 1½-hr. cruises on the hr. 10am-5pm, $10; in winter, four 1-hr. cruises, $8.50, one 2-hr. cruise, $10.50. Ages 3-11 and over 55 half-price. Whale watching in winter twice daily.) Harbor Excursion also sells tickets for the ferry departing for Coronado (every hr. 7am-10pm, returning on the ½ hr. 7:30am-10:30pm, with one additional trip each way Fri.-Sat. evenings; $1.50). The ferry lands at the Olde Ferry Landing in Coronado on 1st and Orange St., a 10-block trolley ride from the Hotel del Coronado. **Invader Cruises** (234-8687) offers cruises similar to Harbor Excursion's, but also uses a sailing vessel for some of its tours.

Balboa Park

Balboa Park was established in 1868, when San Diego's population was about 2000. Now millions play at the 1000-plus acre park, which draws huge crowds with its concerts, theater, Spanish architecture, street entertainers, lush vegetation, and zoo. In 1915 it hosted the Panama-Pacific International Exposition and in 1935, the California-Pacific Exposition. The present buildings are mostly reconstructions of those temporary structures. Bus #7 runs through the park and near the museum and zoo entrances. Or take Laurel St. east from downtown and to one of the many parking lots.

With over 100 acres of exquisitely designed habitats, the **San Diego Zoo** (231-1515) deserves its reputation as one of the finest in the world. The zoo attracts more than animal-lovers though, as the flora excites as much as the fauna. They have recently moved to a system of "bioclimactic" areas, in which animals of all classes (as well as plants) are grouped together by habitat, rather than by taxonomy. The stunning **Tiger River** and **Sun Bear Forest** are among the first of these areas to be completed; in addition to the ususal elephants and zebras, the zoo houses such unusual creatures as Malay tapirs and everybody's favorite, the koala. Arrive as early as possible, sit on the left, and take the 40-minute open-air **double-decker bus tour,** which covers 70% of the park. (Bus tour $3, ages 3-15 $2.50.) You will avoid long lines and have the rest of the day to return to favorite animals or explore areas not covered by the bus. The **children's zoo** cockle-doodle-doos a barnyard delight (ages over 2 50¢). The Lettermania **"skyfari"** aerial tram will make you feel like you're suspended over a box of animal crackers. Most of the zoo is accessible by wheelchair (which can be rented), but steep hills make assistance necessary. (Main zoo entrance open July-Sept. 2 daily 8am-5:30pm, must exit by 7:30pm; Sept. 3-June 4 9am-4pm, exit by 6pm. Admission $10.75, ages 3-15 $4. Group rates available. Free on Oct. 1.)

Balboa Park also has the greatest concentration of museums in the U.S. outside of Washington DC. The park focuses at **Plaza de Panama**, on El Prado (a street running west to east through the plaza), where the Panama-Pacific International Exposition took place in 1915 and 1916. Designed by Bertram Goodhue in the florid Spanish colonial style, many of the buildings tried to stay temporary structures, but their elaborate ornamentation and colorfully tiled roofs kept them alert, hopeful, and too beautiful to demolish. Before exploring El Prado on your own, stop in the House of Hospitality's **information center** (239-0512) which sells simple maps (50¢), more elaborate guides ($1.50), and the **Passport to Balboa Park** ($9). The passport contains six coupons to gain entrance to the park's museums. (Passports also available at participating museums. Open daily 9:30am-4pm.)

The western axis of the plaza stars Goodhue's California State Building, now the **Museum of Man** (239-2001). Covered outside with shiny tiles in a Spanish design, inside the museum recaps millions of years of human evolution with permanent exhibits on primates, the Mayan and Hopi cultures, and other Native American societies. (Open daily 10am-4:30pm. Admission $3 or 2 passport coupons, ages 12-18 $1, 6-11 25¢, under 6 free. Free 3rd Tues. each month.)

Behind the museum dances the **Old Globe Theater** (239-2255), the oldest professional theater in California. The plays of Shakespeare and others go up nightly (Tues.-Sun.), with weekend matinees. (Matinee tickets from $22, seniors and students $14.) The **Spreckels Organ Pavilion** (236-5717; 236-5471 for info) at the south end of the Plaza de Panama opposite the Museum of Art, resounds with free evening concerts (Tues.-Thurs. at 6:30pm).

Ranging from ancient Asian to contemporary Californian, the **San Diego Museum of Art** (232-7931), across the plaza, possesses a comprehensive collection. (Open Tues.-Sun. 10am-4:30pm. Admission $5, seniors $4, ages 6-18 and college students with ID $2, under 6 free. Free 1st Tues. each month.) Nearby is the outdoor **Sculpture Court and Garden** (236-1725), with a typically rounded and sensuous Henry Moore presiding over other large abstract blocks of inspiration. (Open until 4:30pm. Pre-theater dinner 5:30-7pm on Old Globe performance days.)

Farther east along the plaza is the **Botanical Building** (236-5717), a wooden Quonset structure accented by tall palms threatening to burst through the slats of the roof. The scent of jasmine and the gentle play of fountains make this an oasis within an oasis. (Open Sat.-Thurs. 10am-4:30pm. Free.)

Next door, the **Casa de Balboa,** a recent reconstruction of the 1915 Electricity Building, contains four museums. **The Museum of Photographic Arts** (239-5262) features works of Southwestern masters and a bookstore that stocks one of the largest collections of photography books in San Diego. (Open Fri.-Wed. 10am-5pm, Thurs. 10am-9pm. Admission $2.50, under 12 free. Free 2nd Tues. each month.) The slick **San Diego Hall of Champions** (234-2544) has an astroturf carpet and the square footage of a baseball diamond. (Open Mon.-Sat. 10am-4:30pm, Sun. noon-5pm. Admission $2, seniors and college students $1, ages 6-17 50¢, under 6 free. Families $5. Free 2nd Tues. each month.) Downstairs, the **San Diego Model Railroad Museum** (696-0199), with its elaborate train sets, gives some idea of what Santa's basement would look like with a 10-year-old son. (Open Wed.-Fri. 11am-4pm, Sat.-Sun. 11am-5pm. Admission $1, children free. Free 1st Tues. each month.)

From the end of El Prado St., which is closed to cars, a left onto Village Place St. takes you to **Spanish Village**, a crafts center of 39 studios offering free demonstrations and exhibits for browsers and buyers alike. At the other end of Village Place lies the **Natural History Museum** (232-3821), with state-of-the-art exhibits on paleontology and ecology. (Open daily 10am-4:30pm. Admission $4, ages 6-18 $1, under 6 free. Free 1st Tues. each month.)

South of the Natural History Museum is the **Reuben H. Fleet Space Theater and Science Center** (238-1168), where two Omnimax projectors, 153 speakers, and a hemispheric planetarium whisk viewers inside the human body, up with the space shuttle, or 20,000 leagues under the sea. The world's largest motion pictures play here about 10 times per day. (Admission $5 or 3 passport coupons, seniors $3.50, ages 5-15 $3, under 5 free.) At night lasers dance on the ceiling of the **Laserium** in sync with musical accompaniment. (Admission $5.50, seniors $4, children $3.50, under 5 not admitted.) Tickets to the space theater also valid for the **Science Center**, where visitors can play with a cloud chamber, telegraph, light-mixing booth, and other gadgets. (Open 9:45am until the last show around 9:30pm. Science Center admission $2 or 1 coupon, ages 5-15 $1. Free 1st Tues. each month.)

For a bit of culture from south of the border follow Park Blvd. south to Pepper Grove, across from the Naval Hospital, to visit the **Centro Cultural de la Raza** (235-6135). The center offers changing exhibits of Chicano and Native American art, along with a permanent collection of murals. (Gallery open Wed.-Sun. noon-5pm. Free.)

Old Town, Mission Valley, and Mission Hills

The high prices and ubiquitous gift shops of **Sea World** (226-3901) won't let you forget it's a commercial venture; this is no San Diego Zoo. Though its famous animal shows range from educational to exploitative, once inside you shouldn't miss Shamu Stadium, unless seeing five-ton killer whales jump high above water makes up your weekly routine. Sea World also encompasses several impressive, well-lit state-of-the-art aquaria, plus open pools where you can touch and feed various wet creatures. (Open mid-June to early Sept. daily 9am-11pm; off-season 9am-dusk. Ticket sales end 1½ hr. earlier. Admission $22, ages 3-11 $16.)

The site of the original settlement of San Diego, **Old Town** remained the center of San Diego until the late 19th century. Take bus #4 or 5 from downtown. The Spanish *Presidio,* or military post, started here in 1769. Before becoming a museum, Old Town held the county courthouse, the town gallows, and a busy commercial district. Now the partially enclosed pedestrian mall is an overcrowded, overpriced tourist trap. The state park people offer free daily walking tours at 2pm, starting at the Casa de Machado y Silvas (237-6770). To appreciate Old Town's buildings on your own, pickup the indispensable visitor center's walking tour/history book ($2). **La Panaderia** serves coffee and Mexican pastries (75¢). The smell of mocha and sweet bread mixes well with the sweeter scent of fragrant flowers from across town.

Entertainment

San Diego is not renowned for its nightlife, but a certain amount of spelunking could turn up some action. To find out what's happening consult the *Reader* (235-3000), a free weekly newspaper listing places, dates, and prices. *Varieties,* a guide to UCSD events, proliferates on campus (try the front desk of any dorm or the campus bookstore). The monthly *San Diego Magazine* ($2) publishes a special annual issue focusing on restaurants and nightlife; this comprehensive guide, usually released in summer, is worth the trouble and cost. *Arts Tix,* 121 Broadway (238-3810), at 1st Ave., offers half-price tickets to shows on the day of performance.

Gorgeous weather and strong community spirit make San Diego an ideal place for local festivals, many of them annual affairs of over 30 years' standing. The visitors bureau (see Practical Information above) publishes a thorough yearly events brochure. A 24-hr. **Events Hot Line** (696-8700) lists the latest performances and activites in downtown San Diego.

Diego's, 860 Garnet Ave. (272-1241), Pacific Beach. The young and unattached come here en masse for the big dance floor and flood of videos. No dress code, but trendoids get decked out for the evening. Happy Hour Mon.-Fri. 3-6pm. Cover Sun.-Thurs. $2, Fri.-Sat. $5. Open Mon.-Sat. 11am-1:30am, Sun. 10am-10pm.

Confetti's, 5373 Mission Center Rd. (291-8635). A singles saturnalia. Lots of confetti and lots of comparison shopping. Drinks $1.75-3.75. Happy Hour (5-8pm) includes free buffet. Cover Mon.-Wed. $2, Thurs. and Sun. $3, Fri.-Sat. $5. No cover before 8pm. Open Mon.-Fri. 5pm-2am, Sat. 7pm-2am, Sun. 9pm-2am.

The Comedy Store, 916 Pearl St. (454-9176), in La Jolla. Well drinks $3. Potluck night Mon.-Tues. at 8pm; local comics air their schtick. (Call and sign up after 3pm.) Well-known comedians featured other evenings. Shows Wed.-Thurs. and Sun. at 8pm ($6), Fri.-Sat. at 8 and 10:30pm ($8-10). Wed.-Thurs. 2-for-1 admission with any college ID. Two-drink minimum enhance performances. Must be 21.

Near San Diego

With 70 mi. of beaches, San Diego has a place for "man's best friend" at Dog Beach and a resting ground for those wasted and indisposed at Garbage Beach. Sun-worshippers glaze the coast from Imperial Beach in the south to La Jolla in the north; it may take a little ingenuity to find room to bask. Chic places like Mission Beach and La Jolla will likely be as packed as funky Ocean Beach come prime sunning time on summer weekends. The coastal communities do have more to offer than waves and white sand; wander inland a few blocks and explore.

The Hotel del Coronado, Orange Ave. (435-6611), on the Coronado Peninsula, was built in 1888 as a remote resort. Take the Coronado Bridge from I-5 (toll $1) or bus #910 from downtown. Or take a ferry from San Diego Harbor Excursions for $1.50. (Every hr. on the hr. See Waterfront Sights.) One of the great hotels of the world, the "Del" has hosted twelve presidents and some lucky young editors. The 1959 classic *Some Like It Hot* showcased its white verandas and red, circular towers. Wander onto the white, seaweed-free beach in back, one of the prettiest in S.D.; it's seldom crowded, even on weekends.

Point Loma walks a fine line between residential community and naval outpost. The people of Point Loma range from Ocean Beach hippies to sedate and moneyed residents up the hill in the "wooded area." Dedicated to Portuguese explorer João Rodriguez Cabrillo, the first European to land in California, the Cabrillo National Monument (557-5450), at the tip of Point Loma, throws you views of San Diego and the herds of migrating whales from December through February. From downtown, take I-5 to Rosecrans Blvd. and follow the signs, or take bus #2 to 30th and Redwood and transfer to bus #6. The 2-mi. Bayside Trail winds through the brush along the coast on the harbor side; the trail exhibits describe the life of the Native Americans who lived here long before Cabrillo.

Mission Beach and Pacific Beach are more respectable wave-wise than Ocean Beach, codename O.B. Joggers, walkers, bicyclists, and the usual beachfront shops pack Ocean Front Walk. On San Jose Place, in one of the wind-beaten shacks, screams Keith's Klothing Kastle. The proprietor, Keith Nolan, sells his collection of silk Hawaiian shirts from the 40s and 50s at $100 apiece; the San Diego Museum of Art even featured some a few years ago. He also sells vintage Ocean Pacific and Hang Ten beachwear, at more conscionable prices. Hours, like Keith, are unpredictable—open most afternoons and evenings.

Situated on a small rocky promontory, La Jolla (pronounced la-HOY-a) in the 30s and 40s perched as the hideaway of wealthy Easterners who built luxurious houses and gardens atop the bluffs overlooking the ocean. Jags, Mercedes, and BMWs purr along Girard Ave. and Prospect St. past boutiques and financial institutions. At the summit of this runway sits the La Jolla Museum of Contemporary Art, 700 Prospect St. (454-3541), an impressive collection of post-1945 U.S. artwork in galleries overlooking the Pacific. (Open Tues. and Thurs.-Sun. 10am-5pm, Wed. 10am-9pm. Admission $3, seniors and students $1, under 12 50¢. Free Wed. 5-9pm.) Pick up a copy of the *South Coast Gallery Guide* from a sidewalk box for details on other galleries. La Jolla also claims some of the finest beaches in the city.

Grassy knolls run right down to the sea at **La Jolla Cove,** and surfers especially dig the waves at **Tourmaline Beach** and **Windansea Beach.** At **Black's Beach,** people run, sun, and play volleyball in the nude. It is a public beach, not *officially* a nude beach, but you wouldn't know it from the color of most beachcombers' buns. Take I-5 to Genesee Ave., go west and turn left on N. Torrey Pines Rd. until you reach the **Torrey Pines Glider Port** (where clothed hang gliders leap off the cliffs).

Take bus #30 or 34 to La Jolla from downtown San Diego; both the Veteran's Hospital here and the University Towne Centre are transfer points for North County buses.

The University of California at San Diego (UCSD; 452-2230 for the operator, or 534-8273 for information) studies above La Jolla, surrounded on three sides by Torrey Pines Rd., La Jolla Village Dr., and I-5. Despite the thousands of eucalyptus trees and varied architecture, the campus falls somewhere between bland and really bland. Buses #30 and 34 will get you to the campus, but once there a car or bike is invaluable in going from one of the five colleges to the next. An information pavilion on Gilman Dr., just north of La Jolla Village Dr., has campus maps (open daily 7am-8:30pm).

Los Angeles

Los Angeles is just a geographical expression. Born in 1781 as a small Spanish settlement on the banks of the Porciúncula, Los Angeles grew unconstrained by distinct geographical boundaries. You can best appreciate the city's layout by flying into Los Angeles International Airport on a clear night, with the lights of this massive city twinkling like a martini glass shattered over a vast urban carpet.

The popularity of the automobile in Los Angeles shows both a cause and an effect of the city's urban sprawl. The freeways and the great distances to various parts of the city initially made cars convenient and useful in the years after World War II; in turn, the proliferation of both cars and freeways made further expansion possible. However, L.A.'s lichenous relationship between city and machine has soured in recent years. Traffic jams have become ubiquitous, air pollution hovers hazardously over the city, and years of a different type of "auto-reliance" has created a public transportation crisis. Only in the 1990s has Los Angeles finally gotten around to building itself a rather expensive subway system.

All, however, is not gloom and doom in "La-La Land." The sun still shines, humidity is still low, and temperatures are still moderate (averaging 69°F in winter, 80°F in summer). Though the *L.A. Times* has run articles on the growing exodus of disgruntled residents, the beaches have stayed behind, keeping the other two great Southern California entertainers—movie studios and Disneyland—company. And while rumors of L.A. as a dying, hedonistic playland may be grossly exaggerated, a peculiar mix of frontier psychology, a population drawn from every corner of the globe, the image-making machine of Hollywood, and perhaps all those years on sucking of smog has combined to make life in L.A. quite different from anywhere else.

Practical Information

Emergency: 911.

Visitor Information: Los Angeles Convention and Visitors Bureau, 695 S. Figueroa St. 90015 (689-8822), between Wilshire and 7th St. in the heart of the Financial District. Trillions of brochures available. Staff speaks Spanish, Filipino, Japanese, French, and German. Good maps for downtown streets, sights, and buses. Publishes *Datelines* and *Artsline,* guides to Southern California events, 4 times per year. *Los Angeles Visitors Guide* and *Lodging Guide* are both free and available by mail—allow 3 weeks for delivery. Open Mon.-Sat. 8am-5pm. **Council Travel,** 1093 Broxton Ave., Westwood Village (208-3551), above the Wherehouse record store. Cheap flights, IYHF/AYH passes, ISICs. Open Mon.-Tues. 9:30am-5pm, Wed. 10am-5pm, Thurs.-Fri. 9:30am-5pm; April-June also Sat. 10am-2pm. **Los Angeles Council**

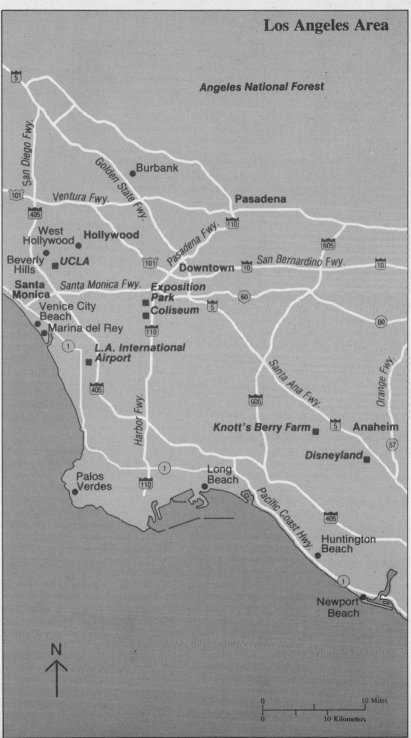

Los Angeles Area

Angeles National Forest

San Diego Fwy.

Burbank

Golden State Fwy.

Ventura Fwy.

101

405

Pasadena

Pasadena Fwy.

110

West Hollywood

Hollywood

Beverly Hills

UCLA

101

Downtown

San Bernardino Fwy.

605

10

10

Santa Monica

Santa Monica Fwy.

Exposition Park

Coliseum

60

5

60

Venice City Beach

Marina del Rey

110

1

Harbor Fwy.

Santa Ana Fwy.

Orange Fwy.

L.A. International Airport

405

605

Knott's Berry Farm

5

Anaheim

57

Disneyland

Palos Verdes

110

1

Long Beach

Pacific Coast Hwy.

405

Huntington Beach

Newport Beach

1

N

0   10 Miles

0   10 Kilometers

AYH, 335 W. 7th St., San Pedro (831-8846). Information and supplies for travelers. Guidebooks, low-cost flights, rail passes, and ISICs. Open Tues.-Sat. 10am-5pm.

National Park Service: 30401 Agoura Rd., Agoura Hills (818-597-9192 for local parks Info Center; 818-597-1036 for other offices), in the San Fernando Valley. Information on the Santa Monica Mountains and other parks. Open Mon.-Sat. 8am-5pm. **Los Angeles County Parks and Recreation,** 433 S. Vermont (738-2961). Open Mon.-Fri. 8am-5pm.

Consulates: U.K., 3701 Wilshire Blvd. (385-7381). Open 9am-5pm for calls, hours vary by department for visits. **Japan,** 250 E. 1st St. #1401, (624-8305). Open Mon.-Fri. 9:30-11:30am and 1-5pm for calls, until 4pm for visits.

Los Angeles International Airport: see Getting There, By Air below.

Amtrak: Union Station, 800 N. Alameda (624-0171), downtown. To San Francisco (1 per day, 11 hr., $71), and San Diego (8 per day, 3 hr., $23) with stops in San Juan Capistrano, San Clemente, Oceanside, and Del Mar.

Buses: Greyhound, 208 E. 6th St. (620-1200 for fares; 629-8400 for local ticket info), downtown terminal. To: San Diego (13 per day, 2½ hr., $16); Tijuana (15 per day, 3½ hr., $20); Santa Barbara (13 per day, 2-3½ hr., $13); San Francisco (20 per day, 8-14½ hr., $43-46). **Green Tortoise** (392-1990, 415-285-2441 in San Francisco). Northbound "hostels on wheels" leave L.A. every Sun. night with stops in Venice, Hollywood, and downtown. They arrive in San Francisco ($30) on Mon. morning, Eugene and Portland, OR ($69) on Tues. afternoon, and Seattle ($79) on Tues. night. Call for reservations and exact departure location and times.

Public Transport: RTD Bus Information Line, 626-4455. Customer Service Center at 5301 Wilshire Blvd. (972-6235; open Mon.-Fri. 8am-4:15pm). See Orientation, Public Transport below.

Taxi: Checker Cab, 482-3456.

Car Rental: Penny Rent-A-Car, 12425 Victory Blvd., N. Hollywood (818-786-1733). $14-17 per day with 75 free mi., 15¢ each additional mi. $98-111 per week with 500 free mi. Insurance $5 per day. Open Mon.-Fri. 7:30am-6pm, Sat. 9am-4:30pm. Must be 21 with major credit card or international driver's license. **Ugly Duckling,** 7415 Santa Monica Blvd. (874-0975). $20 per day with 150 free mi.; 2-day min. $105 per week with 500 free mi. Insurance $8.50 per day. Open Mon.-Fri. 8am-6:15pm, Sat. 8:30am-4:30pm. Must be 21 with major credit card or $600 cash deposit. **Avon Rent-A-Car,** 8459 Sunset Blvd. (654-5533). Also at LAX (322-4033) and Sherman Oaks (818-906-2277). From $17 per day with unlimited mi., from $102 per week. Insurance from $9 per day. Open Mon.-Fri. 7:30am-9pm, Sat.-Sun. 8am-8pm. Must be 18 with major credit card. Ages 18-22 a $15 per day surcharge, 22-25 $5 per day. **Budget Rent-A-Car** (645-4500), at LAX. Weekdays $30 per day, weekends $20 per day. 150 free mi. Insurance $10 per day. Open Mon.-Fri. 7:30am-7pm, Sat.-Sun. 8:30am-5pm. Must be 18 with credit card, 21 with someone else's credit card.

Auto Transport Companies: Dependable Car Travel Service, Inc., 8730 Wilshire Blvd. #414, Beverly Hills (659-2922). References from L.A. or destination. Most cars to the northeast, especially to New York, but also to Florida and Chicago. Call 1-2 days ahead to reserve. Open Mon.-Fri. 8:30am-5:30pm, Sat. 9am-noon. Must be 18 with $100 refundable deposit. **Auto Driveaway,** 3407 W. 6th St. (666-6100). Must be 21 and have references in both L.A. and your destination city. Foreign travelers don't need references, but must have passport, visa, and international driver's license. Application requires a photo. Most cars go to metropolitan areas nationwide. Open Mon.-Fri. 9am-5pm. Must have $250 cash, traveler's checks, or money order deposit. Call 1 week before you want to leave to inquire about availability.

Automobile Club of Southern California: 2601 S. Figueroa St. (741-3111), in a rough part of town. Lots of maps and information free to AAA members. *Westways* magazine a good source of inspiration for daytrips or vacations. Open Mon.-Fri. 9am-5pm.

Beach Information: 457-9701, recording for Malibu, Santa Monica, and South Bay. Most FM radio stations have a (you guessed it) surf report at noon.

Weather: 554-1212. An excruciatingly detailed region-by-region report.

Air Quality Info: 800-242-2022.

Gay and Lesbian Community Services Center: 1213 N. Highland Ave., Hollywood (464-7400), 1 block north of Santa Monica Blvd. Youth and senior groups, counseling, employment, housing, educational, and medical services. Open Mon.-Sat. 8:30am-10pm, but most offices close around 5pm.

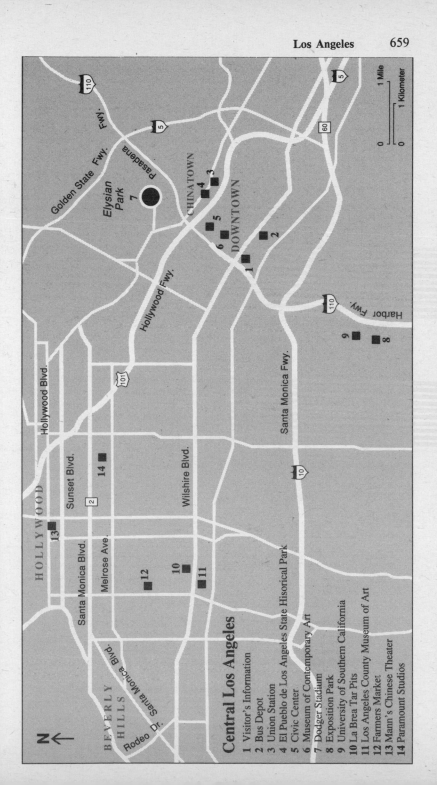

Central Los Angeles

1 Visitor's Information
2 Bus Depot
3 Union Station
4 El Pueblo de Los Angeles State Hisorical Park
5 Civic Center
6 Museum of Contemporary Art
7 Dodger Stadium
8 Exposition Park
9 University of Southern California
10 La Brea Tar Pits
11 Los Angeles County Museum of Art
12 Farmers Market
13 Mann's Chinese Theater
14 Paramount Studios

Help Lines: National Gay Advocates Hotline, 800-526-5050. AIDS Hotline, 800-922-2437.

AIDS Hotline: 800-922-2437. Suicide Prevention, 381-5111. Open 24 hr. hotline.

Rape Crisis, 392-8381. Open 24 hr. Response service, 855-3506. Committee for the Rights of the Disabled, 2487 W. Washington Blvd. (731-8591). Open Mon.-Fri. 8am-4:30pm. Call for appointment. Accommodations Crisis, 686-0950 or 800-242-4612. 24-hr. assistance. Be prepared to wait. Area Agency on Aging, 1102 S. Crenshaw Blvd. (857-6411). Open Mon.-Fri. 8am-5pm.

Post Office: Main office at Florence Station, 7001 S. Central Ave. (586-1723). Information on rates and schedules, 586-1467. ZIP Code information, 586-1737. General Delivery, 900 N. Alameda (617-4543), at 9th St. General Delivery ZIP code: 90055.

Area Codes: southern half of Los Angeles County (Downtown, Beverly Hills, Westside, Malibu, Santa Monica, Venice, South Bay, Long Beach) 213; northern half (including San Fernando Valley and Pasadena) 818; Orange County 714; San Diego County 619; Ventura County 805.

Check out the Monday *Daily News* "L.A. Life: section under "Helplines" for even more hotlines. Also useful are the *L.A. Times,* the *L.A. Weekly,* and *The Outlook,* a small Westside daily.

Hollywood

Police: 1358 N. Wilcox (485-4302).

Visitor Information: The Janes House, 6541 Hollywood Blvd. (461-4213), in Janes House Sq. Provides L.A. visitor guides. Open Mon.-Sat. 9am-5pm. Hollywood Chamber of Commerce, 6255 W. Sunset Blvd. #911 (469-8311).

Greyhound: 1409 N. Vine St. (466-6381), 1 block south of Sunset Blvd. To: Santa Barbara (8 per day, $12.25); San Diego (14 per day, $15.95); San Francisco (6 per day, $45.95). Terminal open daily 7:30am-11pm.

Public Transport: RTD Customer Service Center, 6249 Hollywood Blvd. (972-6000). Free information, maps, timetables, and passes. Open Mon.-Fri. 10am-6pm. Bus #1 goes along Hollywood Blvd., #2 and 3 along Sunset Blvd., #4 along Santa Monica Blvd., #10 along Melrose.

Post Office: 1615 Wilcox Ave. (464-2194). Open Mon.-Fri. 8am-5pm, Sat. 8am-1pm. General Delivery ZIP code: 90028.

Area Code: 213.

Santa Monica

Police: 1685 Main St. (395-9931).

Visitor Information: 1400 Ocean Ave. (393-7593), in Palisades Park. Local maps, brochures, and information on attractions and events. Open daily 10am-5pm; in winter 10am-4pm.

Greyhound: 1433 5th St. (395-1708), between Broadway and Santa Monica Blvd. Open Mon.-Fri. 10am-1pm and 4-6pm. To: Santa Barbara (4 per day, 2½ hr., $12); San Diego (3 per day, 4½ hr., $18.50); San Francisco (2 per day, 11 hr., $51.20).

Public Transport: Santa Monica Municipal Bus Lines (Big Blue), 1660 7th St. (451-5445), at Olympic. Open Mon.-Fri. 8am-5pm. Bus #10 provides express service between downtown L.A. and downtown Santa Monica for 80¢ (faster than RTD—but so is walking). Pick it up Flower St. between 3rd and 6th St., or on Grand Ave. down to the Santa Monica Fwy. (I-10). Buses #1 and 2 run between Santa Monica and Venice and are free with a transfer from the #10; otherwise fare 50¢.

Surfboard Rental: Natural Progression Surfboards, 22935½ W. Pacific Hwy., Malibu (456-6302). Boards $20 per day, plus $5 insurance. Wetsuits $8. Also windsurfer rental ($40 per day, plus $5 insurance), and lessons. Open daily 9am-6pm.

Post Office: 5th and Arizona (393-0716). Open Mon.-Fri. 9am-2pm and 3-5:30pm, Sat. 9am-12:30pm.

Area Code: 213.

Pasadena

Police: 142 N. Arroyo Parkway (405-4501), 2 blocks north of Colorado Blvd.

Visitor Information: Convention and Visitors Bureau, 171 S. Los Robles Ave. (795-9311), across from the Hilton Hotel. Open Mon.-Fri. 9am-5pm, Sat. 10am-4pm.

Greyhound: 645 E. Walnut (792-5116). Open Mon.-Fri. 6:45am-7:45pm, Sat. 6:30am-5pm, Sun. 8:30am-3pm. To: Santa Barbara (3 per day, 2½ hr., $11.75); San Diego (3 per day, 4 hr., $16); San Francisco (2 per day, 11 hr., $46).

Post Office: 600 N. Lincoln (304-7122), at Orange. Open Mon. and Fri. 8am-6pm, Tues.-Thurs. 8am-5pm, Sat. 9am-2pm. **ZIP code:** 91109.

Area Code: 818.

Getting There

Los Angeles sprawls along the coast of Southern California, 127 mi. north of San Diego and 403 mi. south of San Francisco. You can still be "in" L.A. even if you're 50 mi. from downtown. Greater L.A. encompasses the urbanized areas of Orange, Riverside, San Bernadino, and Ventura counties.

By Car

General approaches to Greater L.A. take I-5 from the south, I-1 or I-5 from the north, and I-10 or I-15 from the east. A dozen freeways crisscross the city itself. Driving into L.A. can be unnerving to those who've never before run the gauntlet of ramps, exits, and four-story directional signs.

By Train and Bus

Amtrak pulls into Union Station, 800 N. Alameda (624-0171), at the northwestern edge of the heart of downtown Los Angeles. Once the end of the line for westbound rail passengers from all over the U.S., this glorious building now stands sadly deserted. Buses travel out of the station to Pasadena and Long Beach; information about their schedules can be obtained upon arrival at the station.

Visitors arriving by **Greyhound** disembark at 208 E. 6th St. (620-1200), at Los Angeles St. downtown, in a rough neighborhood near skid row. Greyhound also stops in Hollywood, Santa Monica, Pasadena, and other parts of the metropolitan area. RTD buses #22 and 322 stop on 7th and Main St., 2 blocks southwest of the downtown station, and carry passengers westward along Wilshire Blvd. Bus #1 stops at 6th and Broadway, 4 blocks to the west, and travels westward along Hollywood Blvd.

By Plane

Once a nightmare of delays and disorganization, the **Los Angeles International Airport (LAX)** received the anointing power of $700 million worth of renovations. The result is an airport efficient enough to have processed 45 million passengers in 1989—the third largest passenger volume in the world. The airport complex soars in Westchester, about 15 mi. southwest of downtown, 10 mi. southeast of Santa Monica, and 1 mi. east of the coast.LAX divides into two levels, the upper serving departures and the lower arrivals. Nine contiguous terminals arrange themselves in a large horseshoe, with terminal two serving international carriers.

Many car rental agencies run shuttle buses directly from the airport to their lots (see Cars). Other ways to reach town include cabs and **public transportation.** All Rapid Transit District (RTD) service to and from the airport stops at the **transfer terminal** at Vicksburg Ave. and 96th St. To get downtown, take bus #439 (Mon.-Fri. rush hr. only) or #42 from the transfer terminal. Bus #42 operates daily from 5:30am to 11:15pm, from downtown daily from 5:45am to 12:10am. To get to UCLA, take express #560; to Long Beach, #232; to West Hollywood and Beverly

Hills, #220. From West Hollywood to Hollywood, take bus #1 (along Hollywood Blvd.), 2 (along Sunset Blvd.), or 4 (along Santa Monica Blvd.). **Metered cabs** are costly: $1.90 initially and $1.60 per each additional mi. Checker Cab (482-3456) fare from the airport to downtown is about $27, to Hollywood $25, and to Disneyland a goofy $90.

A final option—more expensive than the RTD but cheaper than a cab—is one of the many shuttle vans which offer door-to-door service from the terminal to different parts of L.A. for a flat rate. **Travelers Aid** (686-0950) offices grace terminals with extensive printed information, and a recording when stations are closed. (Open Mon.-Fri. 8:30am-5pm.) **Super Shuttle** (338-1111) services all parts of L.A. including: Santa Monica ($13), downtown ($10), and San Fernando Valley ($22). **Coast Shuttle** (417-3988) has service to Santa Monica ($12), downtown ($10), and San Fernando Valley ($30). For both, reservations deemed necessary only for trips to the airport; for trips from LAX, just pick up a terminal courtesy phone.

Getting Out

To reach LAX by car from downtown take I-10 west to I-405 south and get off at Century Blvd. heading west. Airport parking lots near the central terminal cost $2 for the first hour, $1 each hour thereafter, up to a maximum of $15. On busier days, eliminate hassle by parking in the aptly named "remote" lots at the airport's eastern edge and taking the free tram to the terminals. Lot C sits at Sepulveda and 96th St. ($6 per day), lot B at La Cienaga and 11th St. ($4 per day). These lots are also used for long-term parking. Disabled travelers needing assistance should park in Lot C and call 646-8021 for a van.

Reach LAX by bus from downtown on the #42, from UCLA express #560, from Long Beach #232, and from West Hollywood and Beverly Hills #220. At the airport, the "A" tram makes frequent free trips between terminals. Terminal two serves international carriers. Special flight bargains to San Francisco are offered by many airlines.

Those seeking or offering rides out of L.A. should consult the **rideboard** at UCLA's Ackerman Union. (For directions to the Union, see Getting Around, Cars.)

Getting Around

Before you even think about navigating Los Angeles's 6500 mi. of streets and 40,000 intersections, get yourself a good map; otherwise centerless Los Angeles defies all human comprehension. The repetitive *Thomas Guide Los Angeles County Street Guide and Directory,* maybe the best investment you can ever make. OK, at least it's worth the $14 for stays over a week.

A legitimate **downtown** Los Angeles does exist, but this small district is merely a conceptual construct to explain where all the "suburbs in search of a city" lie. Immediately east of downtown are the thriving Latino districts of Boyle Heights, Montebello, and El Monte; to the south is the University of Southern California (USC), Exposition Park, and Watts; farther south on Rte. 11 is Long Beach.

Los Angeles is a city of distinctive boulevards; its shopping areas and business centers distribute along these broad arteries. Streets throughout L.A. are designated east, west, north, and south from First and Main St. at the center of downtown. L.A.'s east-west thoroughfares are the most prominent; use them to get your bearings. Beginning with the northernmost, they are boutiqued Melrose Avenue and Beverly, Wilshire, residential Olympic, Pico, Venice, and Washington Boulevards. The important north-south streets of this huge grid, from downtown westward, are Vermont, Normandie, and Western Avenues, Vine Street, Highland, La Brea, and Fairfax Avenues, and La Cienaga and Robertson Boulevards.

The area west of downtown calls itself the **Wilshire District** after its main boulevard. Wilshire builds in a continuous wall of tall buildings (called the "Miracle Mile") with bungalows and duplexes huddled on either side. On the northeast portion of the district, **Hancock Park,** a green park and affluent residential area, harbors the Los Angeles County Museum of Art and the George C. Page Fossil Museum.

North of the Wilshire District paparazzis **Hollywood.** Santa Monica, the next major east-west boulevard, lies north of Melrose; north of that rises Sunset Boulevard, which runs from the ocean to downtown. Sunset presents a cross-section of virtually everything L.A. has to offer: beach communities, lavish wealth, famous nightclubs along "the strip," sleazy motels, the old elegance of Silver Lake, and Chicano murals. Farther north is Hollywood Boulevard, running just beneath Hollywood Hills, where homes to many screenwriters, actors, and producers perch precariously on hillsides.

Regal **Beverly Hills,** an independent city geographically swallowed by L.A., lies west of the Wilshire District and east of **Westwood,** which holds UCLA and its lively college village. Farther west, **Santa Monica** strings its wide and crowded beaches along the ocean. Just south is the wild beach community of **Venice.**

North of the Hollywood Hills and the Santa Monica Mountains stretches the San Fernando **Valley.** Like, one-and-a-quarter million people inhabit this "rad" basin bounded in the north and west by the Santa Susanna Mountains and the Simi Freeway, in the south by the Ventura Freeway, and in the east by the Golden State Freeway.

Eighty mi. of beach line L.A.'s coast. **Zuma** is northernmost, followed by **Malibu,** 15 mi. up the coast from Santa Monica. Comprising the area called the **South Bay,** Marina del Rey, El Segundo (with the airport and somebody's wallet just inland there), and Manhattan, Hermosa, and Redondo Beaches sit south of Santa Monica and Venice. The coast bulges south of Redondo Beach to form the **Palos Verdes Peninsula.** Beyond the peninsula the coast turns east again. **San Pedro** is both the terminus of the Harbor Freeway and the point of departure for **Catalina Island.** East of San Pedro is **Long Beach,** a port city of a half-million people. Finally, farthest south are the **Orange County** beach cities: Seal Beach, Sunset Beach, Huntington Beach, Newport Beach, and Laguna Beach. Confused yet? Invest in a good map, and sleep with it under your pillow.

Once the sun sets, those on foot should exercise caution outside West L.A. and off well-lit main drags. Women should not walk alone *anywhere* after dark. Crime rides Hollywood and the downtown area, east of Western Ave. at night. Women should exercise caution also in parking structures, even in such "safe" areas as UCLA.

Public Transportation

Nowhere in the U.S. does the great god of Automobile get held in greater reverence than in L.A. Although most Angelenos insist that it's impossible to live in or visit Los Angeles without a car, the **Southern California Rapid Transit District (RTD)** (800-243-7433) does work—sort of. With over 200 routes and several independent municipal transit systems complementing RTD, you may need an extra day just to study timetables. While RTD buses do carry 1.5 million passengers daily (but slowly), those determined to see *everything* in L.A. should somehow get behind the wheel of a car. If this is not possible, base yourself centrally, make daytrips, and have plenty of change for the bus.

To familiarize yourself with the RTD simply write for a **Tourist Kit,** RTD, Los Angeles 90001, or stop by one of the 10 **customer service centers.** Three serve downtown: in ARCO Plaza, 515 S. Flower St., Level B (open Mon.-Fri. 7:30am-3:30pm); at 419 S. Main St. (open Mon.-Fri. 8am-4:30pm); and at 1016 S. Main St. (open Mon.-Fri. 10am-7pm, Sat. 10am-6pm). The RTD prints route maps for the different sections of the city, as well as a brochure called *RTD Self-Guide Tours,* which details how to reach most important sights from downtown.

Bus service works best downtown and along the major thoroughfares west of downtown. Santa Monica and Wilshire Blvd. have 24-hr. service, for instance. The downtown **DASH shuttle** costs only 25¢, serving Chinatown, Union Station (use the DASH to get downtown from Union Station), Olvera Street, City Hall, Little

Tokyo, the Music Center, ARCO Plaza, and more. (DASH operates Mon.-Fri. 7am-6pm, Sat. 9am-4pm.) Bus service is dismal in the outer reaches of the city, and two-hour journeys are not unusual. Buses themselves are speedy, but transferring often involves interminable waits.

RTD's **basic fare** is $1.10, disabled passengers 55¢. Additional charges for express buses, buses taking the freeway, or special events sometimes raise total fare to $3 (exact change required). Transfers cost 25¢, whether you're changing from one RTD line to another or from RTD to another transit authority, such as Santa Monica Municipal Bus Lines, Culver City Municipal Bus Lines, Long Beach Transit, or Orange County Transit District. For information on other transit systems, see the appropriate city section below. All route numbers given are RTD unless otherwise designated. If you plan to use the buses extensively over a long visit, buy a **bus pass** with unlimited monthly use for $42, $25 for college students, $18 for students under 18, and $10 for disabled people.

Over 150 of RTD's lines offer **wheelchair-accessible buses,** outlined in their brochure *The New Mobility.* All bus stops with accessible service are marked with the international symbol of access.

If you don't want to spend hours on an RTD bus to get from one end of the basin to the other, consider paying a bit more to take Greyhound (620-1200) to such places as Long Beach, Huntington Beach, and Anaheim. **Gray Line Tours,** 6541 Hollywood Blvd., Hollywood (856-5900), is a more expensive (around $50) but easier way to reach distant attractions, with costs including transportation and admission.

The first stage of L.A.'s light-rail transit system, the Blue Line, which runs between Long Beach and the outskirts of downtown, became operational in July 1990 (call 800-252-7433 for information). The Red Line, running underground through downtown should begin running in 1991. Also in the works are lines to the San Fernando Valley and Pasadena. In June 1990, California voters passed an important ballot proposition which raised taxes to help pay for further light-rail construction.

Freeways

The *real* concrete jungle is not composed of the skyscrapers of New York, but the massive stretches of the Los Angeles freeways. Having acquired an almost mythological status in the American Imagination, the elephantine concrete haunches of these thoroughfares loom over the cityscape like grand aisles in an automotive cathedral. Riding the freeways is a phantasmagoria of speed, chrome, and concrete as well as a whirl of queer place names (Azusa, Cucamonga, Tarzana, Panorama City). The highway is without question one of the most curious, albeit unnerving, shows this city has to offer.

In a city the size of Los Angeles, freeways are a must for efficient travel. Traffic means, however, that the same freeways can also be a most *inefficient* way to get anywhere (or, perhaps more accurately, nowhere). For those who know the local streets (many residents don't), the major thoroughfares are often faster than freeways. It is best to avoid the freeways between 6 and 10am and between 3 and 7pm. In L.A., the decentered city, there is no "inbound" jam in the morning and an "outbound" one in the afternoon: traffic is snarled in all directions, in many places, and at all hours. Tie-ups are not limited to rush hours and can begin from something so simple as Caltrans (the Transportation Department) deciding to sweep the inside lane on a Sunday morning.

Perhaps to help them "get in touch with their freeway." Californians refer to the highways by names rather than by numbers. These names are little more than hints of a freeway's route—at best harmless, at worst misleading.

The most comprehensible **rideboard** is at UCLA's Ackerman Union, Floor B. Ackerman is in the center of campus, 2 blocks north of the Westwood Blvd. terminus. Also check the classified section of papers such as *The Chronicle.*

Bicycles

The best bike routes spoke along beaches. The most popular route is the **South Bay Bicycle Path,** running from Santa Monica to Torrance (19 mi.), winding over the sandy beaches of the South Bay past sunbathers, boardwalks, and roller skaters. Even the police ride bikes here. The path continues all the way to San Diego. For maps and advice, write to any **AAA office;** L.A. headquarters at 2601 S. Figueroa (741-3111), near Adams. It's worth calling just to talk to helpful and friendly **Norty Stewart,** "the Source" for bicycling information in Southern California.

Renting a bike in this age of rising insurance costs has become increasingly expensive. Most rental shops can be found near the piers of the various beaches, with an especially high concentration on Washington Blvd. near the beach in Venice/Marina Del Rey. Those planning extended stays should look into purchasing a used bicycle. Classified ads for such bikes may be found in all of the daily papers.

Walking

L.A. pedestrians are a lonely breed. The largely deserted streets of commercial centers will seem eerie to the first-time visitor; the long distances between sights will probably prove frustrating. However, traveling on foot allows you to see the city up close, and if you're not too ambitious about "doing" all the tourist spots in the area, you can enjoy a rewarding stroll through such colorful areas as Chinatown, Hollywood, or Westwood Village. Melrose Avenue is the best of the major boulevards for shopping on foot, and Venice Beach is perhaps the most enjoyable place to walk. Along Venice Beach, you'll be in the company of the thousands, and Venice's sights and shopping areas are all relatively close to one another. You may also wish to call **Walking Tours of Los Angeles** for tours of El Pueblo de Los Angeles State Historic Park (628-1274), City Hall (485-4423), or the Music Center (972-7483). Tours of historic theaters and a variety of other artistic sights are given by the **Los Angeles Conservancy** (623-2489).

Do not hitchhike, especially if a woman traveling alone—It is simply not safe. It is also illegal on all freeways and on streets unless on a sidewalk, out of traffic.

Accommodations

Many inexpensive lodgings in Los Angeles bear a frightening resemblance to the House of Usher. Dozens of flophouses around the Greyhound station charge between $10 and $20 per night, but those unnerved by skid-row street life should look elsewhere. Tolerable lodgings fall roughly into four categories: hostels and YMCAs, run-down but safe hotels, residential hotels offering weekly rates (these can save you a bundle), and budget motels located well off the beaten track but reasonably close by car. Reservations are a good idea year-round, though only summer is high tourist season. It never hurts to ask for off-season or student discounts, and occasionally managers will lower prices to snare a prospective but hesitating customer. Pick up the useful and comprehensive *L.A. Lodging Guide* from the Los Angeles Visitors Center. **Youth hostel passes** may be obtained from UCLA's Ackerman Union, #A-213 (825-0611).

YWCA lodgings open only to women, but their hotel will be closed for renovations until at least 1991 (see Downtown). YMCA lodgings (Hollywood branch 467-4161) open to men, women, and families.

Los Angeles has no **campgrounds** convenient to public transport. Even motorists face at least a 40-minute commute from campsites to downtown. The only safe, nearby place to camp in L.A. County is **Leo Carrillo State Beach** (818-706-1310) on PCH (Rte. 1), 28 mi. northwest of Santa Monica at the Ventura County line. The beach lays out 134 developed sites at $12 per night. In summer, make reservations through MISTIX (800-444-7275).

Downtown

Though busy and relatively safe by day, the downtown area empties and becomes dangerous when the workday ends. Both men and women should travel in groups after dark.

Hotel Stillwell, 828 S. Grand St. (627-1151). Recently refurbished, ultra clean hotel. The most sensible downtown. Bright and nicely decorated rooms. Indian restaurant and U.S. grill in hotel, Mexican restaurant next door. A/C, color TV. Singles $35. Doubles $40.

Park Plaza Hotel, 607 S. Park View St. (384-5281), on the west corner of 6th St. across from MacArthur Park. An eerily grandiose art deco monument built in 1927. 3-story marble-floored lobby and a monumental staircase. Once entertained Bing Crosby and Eleanor Roosevelt, but now caters to semi-permanent residents, especially students from the Otis Art Institute next door. A/C, color TV in clean but small rooms. Complete fitness center with Olympic-size pool and sauna. Singles $35. Doubles $45. Suites $60. Make reservations at least 1 week in advance.

Orchid Hotel, 819 S. Flower St. (624-5855). Central downtown location and cleanliness make up for the small, antiseptic rooms. A/C, color TV. Singles $33.75. Doubles $39.25. Weekly: singles $154; doubles $182. Reservations recommended.

Milner Hotel, 813 S. Flower St. (627-6981), next to the Orchid. As with its fraternal twin, central location and good upkeep compensate for dingy decor. Pub and grill in lobby. A/C, color TV. Singles $35. Doubles $45. No reservations.

Hotel Carver, 460 E. 4th St. (625-8015). Small, friendly hotel located in Little Tokyo. Color TV, 24-hr. security. Shared baths. Singles $24. Doubles $30.

Hollywood

Hollywood is an ideal base for tourists; budget motels line Hollywood Blvd., east of the main strip area. Despite its many charms, the place gets creepy at night and side streets can be dangerous, but caution should prevent any problems.

Hollywood Wilshire YMCA Hotel and Hostel, 1553 Hudson Ave. (467-4161) 1½ blocks south of Hollywood Blvd. Must be over 18. Far and away the best budget lodging in Hollywood. Clean and light hotel rooms. Gym and pool facilities. Very safe. Visitors allowed 7-10pm. Singles $29. Doubles $39. Hostel includes a kitchen, laundry, and lounge. 5-day max. stay. Curfew midnight. $10. No reservations.

Hotel Howard, 1738 N. Whitley Ave. (466-6943), ½ block north of Hollywood Blvd. Tastefully furnished, clean, cheerful rooms. A/C. Good security. Garage parking $4 per day. No visitors past 10pm. Singles $36. Doubles $45. Key deposit $10. Weekly: singles $200; doubles $250; key deposit $20. Reservations recommended.

Hastings Hotel, 6162 Hollywood Blvd. (464-4136). Youth-oriented hotel in the thick of Hollywood, near RTD bus lines. Color TV, 24-hr. security. Singles $35. Doubles $45.

Beverly Hills, Westside, Wilshire District

The Westside is an attractive and much safer part of town, but for the most part, room rates jump out of sight. Call the **UCLA Off-Campus Housing Office** (825-4491), 100 Sproul Hall, to see if they can put you in touch with students who have a spare room through their "roommate share board." UCLA is reorganizing its policies for off-campus visitors, but fraternities and sororities sometimes rent out rooms. Call the **Pan Hellenic Sorority Council** at 206-1285 or the **Inter-Fraternity Council** at 825-8409. The more intrepid may find success by going door-to-door down Sorority and Fraternity Rows and asking directly. Other options include consulting the *Daily Bruin* and kiosks on campus for sublets (a good bet for those planning a longer stay).

Hotel Del Flores, 409 N. Crescent Dr., Beverly Hills (274-5115), 3 blocks east of chic Rodeo Dr. and 1 block south of Santa Monica Blvd. Hard to believe you can stay in Beverly Hills this cheaply. Has seen better days but clean and well kept. Color TV. 2-day min. stay. Singles $39-43. Doubles $43-47. Weekly: singles $260; doubles $286. Call for reservations 2 weeks in advance.

Wilshire Orange Hotel, 6060 W. 8th St. (931-9533), in West L.A. near Wilshire Blvd. and Fairfax Ave. Buses #20, 21, 22, and 308 serve Wilshire Blvd. from downtown. One of L.A.'s best-located budget accommodations. Near many major sights, in a residential neighborhood. Most rooms have refrigerators, color TV, A/C; all but 2 have their own bath or a shared bath with one other room. Weekly housekeeping. Many semi-permanent residents. Singles $42. Doubles $48. Weekly: singles $210; doubles $275.

Santa Monica and Venice

To experience L.A. fully, stay at one of the cheap hostels in Venice. You may miss the Sunset Strip (and L.A. traffic), but in return you'll find dazzling beaches, kooky architecture, and a mellow and unpretentious community devoted to worshipping the sun and cultivating its own eccentricities. And when you do decide to venture into L.A.'s depths, the coast is just a fairly short bus ride or drive away. The hostels are a popular destination among foreign students.

Santa Monica International Hostel (AYH), 1436 2nd St., Santa Monica (393-9913), in the heart of downtown Santa Monica. Opened in June 1990 and immediately became the most popular hostel in town. Colossal kitchen, copious common rooms, and a casual, California-cool climate that must be seen. Lockout 10:30am-2pm. Curfew midnight. $2 late fee until 2:30am. Members only, $14. Linen $2.

Venice Beach Hostel, 701 Washington St. (306-5180), above Celebrity Cleaners. Relaxed, homey atmosphere with international travelers, large lounge, cable TV, and sunroof (bathing gear optional). Near nightclubs and bars. Free transportation from LAX. $17 per night, $70 per week. Doubles $15 per person. Open 24 hr.

Venice Beach Cotel, 25 Windward Ave., Venice (399-7649), on the boardwalk between Zephyr Court and 17th Ave. Close to beaches; shuttle from LAX. To stay here you must show your passport and not ask about the name. A friendly, lively hostel full of young international travelers. 3-6 people share each of the clean, functional rooms. No food allowed. Loud and animated bar and social area 7pm-1am. 5-day max. stay. No curfew. $12, with bath $15. Private rooms with ocean view $30-32 (no passport required).

Share-Tel International Hostel, 20 Brooks Ave., Venice (392-0325). Outstanding location ½ block off the boardwalk. Student ID or passport required. Family-style atmosphere; clean, pleasant rooms with kitchen facilities and bathroom sleep 4-12. LAX shuttle service, linen service, no curfew. $15.

Jim's at The Beach, 17 Brooks Ave., Venice (396-5138), ½ block off the boardwalk across from Share-Tel. Passport required. No more than 6 beds per clean, bright room. Kitchen, LAX shuttle service. No curfew. $15 per night, $90 per week.

Marina Hostel, 2915 Yale Ave., Marina Del Rey (301-3983), 3 blocks west from Lincoln Blvd. near Venice in a quiet residential neighborhood. A privately owned, friendly household with lockers, linen, laundry, and a microwave-equipped kitchen. Some bunks, some floor mattresses. Living room with cable TV. $12.

Interclub Hostel, 2221 Lincoln Blvd., Venice (305-0250), near Venice Blvd. Passport required. Festive after-hours common-room atmosphere as many nationalities bump elbows. Surfer murals on the walls. Rooms sleep 6, or you can sleep in the 30-bed dorm. Co-ed accommodations. Shuttle from LAX. 5-day max. stay. Lockout 11am-4pm; no lockout during summer. Curfew 4am. Grubby kitchen with stove and fridge. Laundry room. $12. Deposit $5. Linen included.

Food

L.A.'s culinary options approximate the city's ethnic diversity: Jewish and Eastern European food fills the Fairfax area; Mexican in East L.A.; Japanese, Chinese, Vietnamese, and Thai around Little Tokyo and Chinatown; seafood along the coast; and Hawaiian, Indian, and Ethiopian restaurants scattered throughout. The only cuisine indigenous to the area is fast food: McDonalds flipped its first quarter-pounder in Southern California in the 50s. Angelenos seem to have spent the intervening years trying to improve upon the fast food hamburger, creating burger joints on nearly every corner. For the optimal Southern Californian fast-food experience, try **In 'n Out Burger** (call 818-287-4377 for the one nearest you), a family-owned and operated chain that has steadfastly refused to expand beyond the L.A. area.

The rewards of such stubborness are evident in In 'n Out's burgers and fries, arguably the best in the business.

The best way to enjoy the fresh produce that made California famous is to find a health-food store or cooperative market that sells organic and small-farm produce. Visit one of the big public markets to appreciate the variety and sheer volume of foodstuffs. An inexpensive source of produce is the **Grand Central Public Market,** 317 S. Broadway (624-2378), a large baby-blue building downtown. The main market in the Hispanic shopping district, Grand Central has more than 50 stands selling not only produce, but also clothing, housewares, costume jewelry, vitamins, and fast food. (Open daily 9am-6pm.) The **Los Angeles Produce Market,** with one location at 9th and San Pedro and one at 7th and Central, serves as the central distribution center for many Southland supermarkets and restaurants. Starting at 3am, trucks roll in from the country to unload mountains of produce for sale to retailers and restaurant buyers (the public can buy here too, but only in quantities of a bushel or more). Nearby cafés keep the same hours as the markets. The most famous is **Vickman's** at 1228 E. 8th St. (Open Mon.-Fri. 3am-3pm, Sat. 3am-1pm, Sun. 7am-1pm.)

Downtown

Art's Chili Dogs, Florence Ave. at Normandie. Well worth the long trek from downtown. The best chili dogs in L.A. and the chance to watch Art in action. Pushing 90, Art has been serving customers out of the same small shack since the 30s. No burgers here. Chili dogs with cheese $2. Open Mon.-Sat. 9am-7pm, Sun. 9am-4pm.

Philippe's, The Original, 1001 N. Alameda, 2 blocks north of Union Station. Large portions, low prices, and tremendous variety of food. Claims to have originated the French-dipped sandwich; varieties include beef, pork, ham, turkey, or lamb ($3-4). Potato salad 65¢, glass of iced tea 40¢. Top it off with a large slice of pie ($1.80), and you've got a huge lunch. Open daily 6am-10pm.

The Pantry, 877 S. Figueroa St. Open since the 20s. You may have to share a table with someone you've never met before, and the waiter is as likely to insult you as to talk your ear off, but the patrons like it that way. Seats only 84 yet serves 2500-3000 people per day. Recently opened a deli/bakery next door (roast beef sandwich $3.85). Be prepared to wait for the huge breakfast specials ($6), especially on weekends. Open 24 hr.

Fortune Seafood Restaurant, 750 N. Hill St., in Chinatown. A new, small, late-night (by L.A. standards) restaurant with reasonable prices and excellent seafood. Lunch special includes entree, rice, and tea ($3.25). Open daily 11:30am-1am.

Hunan Restaurant, 980 N. Broadway, in Chinatown. Perhaps the best Mandarin food in L.A. Excellent 3 Flavors Sizzling Rice Soup and the Kung-Pao Chicken. Open Sun.-Thurs. 11:30am-2:30pm and 5-9pm, Fri.-Sat. 11:30am-2:30pm and 5-9:30pm.

Gorky's, 536 E. 8th St. (627-4060), on the southeast edge of downtown. One-of-a-kind restaurant, serving cafeteria-style Russian cuisine in an avant-garde setting. Entrees $5-7. Brewery on premises and live music Wed.-Sun. at 8:30pm. Open 24 hr.

Hollywood and West Hollywood

Some of L.A.'s best restaurants cook here, with an especially strong contingent of ethnic places on and around Hollywood Blvd. Most of the celebrity hangouts (such as the **Brown Derby,** 1628 Vine St.) are high-priced so that tourist riff-raff will stay away. But others do fish for visitors, who come peering in through the darkness for the invariably elusive stars.

Seafood Bay, 3916 Sunset Blvd., at Sanborn in Silver Lake, east of Hollywood. Modest eatery in a quiet residential area which substitutes a wide variety of seafood at great prices for decor. Filling "Light meals" like fettucine with clam sauce not more than $6. The accompaniments—garlicky sourdough bread, pungent rice pilaf, heaps of sauteed mushrooms—receive the same loving attention as the fish. Open Mon.-Thurs. 11:30am-10pm, Fri.-Sat. 11:30am-10:30pm, Sun. 4-10pm.

Lucy's El Adobe Café, 5536 Melrose Ave., 1 block east of Gower St. Family-run hole-in-the-wall. Favorite among politicians from downtown and executives from Paramount Studios across the street; some of the best Mexican food in town: tostadas ($5), burritos, and excellent enchiladas ($3-4). Full dinners (entree, soup or salad, rice, and beans) $8-10. Open Mon.-Sat. 11:30am-11pm.

Johnny Rocket's, 7507 Melrose Ave., away from the center of Hollywood in the trendy section of Melrose Ave. near Beverly Hills. The 30s Moderne architecture returns you to a lost era of U.S. diners. Always crowded, especially weekend nights. Excellent hamburgers (from $3.25), shakes ($2.85), and "real" flavored sodas, with syrup and everything (95¢). Open Sun.-Thurs. 11am-midnight, Fri.-Sat. 11am-2am.

Canter's Fairfax Restaurant, Delicatessen, and Bakery, 419 N. Fairfax Ave. An authentic Jewish deli with shelves of matzoh and gefilte fish. Sandwiches expensive ($7), but *gadol* enough to share. Stroll around the neighborhood and markets. Open 24 hr.

Beverly Hills, Westside, Wilshire District

Few restaurants in these upscale neighborhoods lie within budget range. Westwood keeps chic and convenient eateries perfect before a movie or while shopping, and you'll find everything from felafel to *gelato* in corner shops. Beverly Hills and the Wilshire District offer some of the finest dining in the country; don't expect any bargains here.

John O'Groat's, 10516 W. Pico Blvd. They lay the Scottish theme a wee bit thick, but John O'Groat is the genuine article. He's usually standing out front soothing those hungry for his mouth-watering biscuits, pancakes ($3.75), and omelettes (from $6.25). Popular on weekend mornings. Open Mon.-Fri. 7am-3pm, Sat.-Sun. 7am-2pm.

J.P. Throckmorton Grille, 255 S. Beverly Dr. Charming grill boasts an exquisite burger for $2.75 and a variety of hot and cold sandwiches at around $4. The milk shakes ($2) are thick and potent. Open Mon.-Sat. 11am-9pm, Sun. 11am-6pm.

Cassell's, 3300 W. 6th St., in the Wilshire District between Normandie and Vermont. From downtown, take bus #18 from 5th; from Hollywood, take bus #204 down Vermont, then walk 3 blocks west. Suspected of making the great L.A. burger ($4.35 including salad; garnish it yourself). They don't slaughter the cows out back but they do grind fresh beef daily. Homemade lemonade and potato salad, which has a horseradish aftershock. Popular during lunch hour. Open Mon.-Sat. 10:30am-4pm.

Sak's Teriyaki, 1121 Glendon Ave., in Westwood. Excellent, cheap Japanese plates including chicken and beef teriyaki ($3.50-4.75). Jams with students. Happy Hour special ($2.50) 3-6pm. Open Mon.-Thurs. 11am-10pm, Fri.-Sat. 11am-11pm, Sun. 11am-9pm.

Santa Monica and Venice

Ye Olde King's Head, 116 Santa Monica Blvd., in Santa Monica. Authentic British pub owned by an expatriate from Manchester. Fish and chips ($6.25) and a variety of other English entrees ($7-9). Large assortment of expensive English beers and ales, but there aren't that many publicans in Santa Monica who know the difference between Whitbread and Bud. Open Mon.-Sat. 11am-1:30am, Sun. noon-1:30am.

Tijuana Restaurant, 11785 W. Olympic Blvd. (473-9293), in West L.A. Menu looks like a Tijuana jai alai program but the food is first-rate. For an appetizer, try the *nopalitas,* young cactus served on a tortilla ($2.75). Dinner entrees and combination plates $6-7. Open Sun.-Thurs. 11am-10pm, Fri.-Sat. 11am-11pm.

Humphrey Yogart Café, 11677 San Vicente Blvd., in Brentwood. The place to come for dessert. Start with vanilla frozen yogurt (sweet or tart) and blend in whatever ingredients in whatever bizarre combinations you wish. A medium with 2 ingredients costs $2.10. Humphrey's also serves sandwiches, soups, and salads. Usually crowded. Open Sun. 11am-10:30pm, Mon.-Thurs. 9am-10:30pm, Fri. 9am-11:30pm, Sat. 10am-11:30pm.

San Fernando Valley

Chili John's, 2018 W. Burbank Blvd. (818-846-3611), in Burbank. Their chili recipe hasn't changed since 1900 ($3.85 per bowl). As your mouth burns you might want to check out the mountain landscape painted on one wall; it took the former owner/chef over 20 years to paint in-between serving customers. Take-out. Open Sept.-June Tues.-Fri. 11am-7pm, Sat. 11am-4pm.

Hampton's Kitchen, 4301 Riverside Dr. (818-845-3009), in Burbank. A gourmet hamburger parlor, with over 50 delectable combinations, including a Hawaiian burger with pineapple and barbecue sauce and a *Ménage à trois* burger with avocado, bacon, and Swiss cheese. Burgers with salad from $6. Open daily 11am-10pm.

Don Cuco's Mexican Food, 3911 Riverside Dr., in Burbank near the studios. Large outstanding Mexican meals. Combination dinners $6.50-7.50. Fajitas $9. Margarita as big as a soup bowl $4.25. Sunday brunch (10am-2pm) $6.50. Open Sun.-Thurs. 11am-11pm, Fri.-Sat. 11am-midnight.

Pasadena

Cafés and Mexican restaurants punctuate Fair Oaks Ave. and Colorado Blvd., in the Old Town section of Pasadena.

Rose City Diner, 45 S. Fair Oaks Ave., just south of Colorado Blvd. Another 50s-nostalgia restaurant with a jukebox and diner-style booths. Hardly authentic, but peppy enough that you can't fault it. Meatloaf, chicken-fried steak, and spaghetti and meatballs all $6-7. Extensive dessert selection (sundaes from $3.50). Bazooka gum presented with your check. Open daily 6:30am-2am.

Los Tacos, 1 W. California Blvd., enter around the corner of Fair Oaks Blvd. Good, inexpensive Mexican food in a fast-food setting. Soft tacos with your choice of filling ($1.25). Combination plates $4.75. Popular Fri.-Sat. night with local teenagers. Open Sun.-Mon. 10am-10pm, Tues.-Wed. 10am-midnight, Thurs.-Sat. 10am-2am.

The Espresso Bar, 34 S. Raymond (818-356-9095), in an alley to the left of the building marked 32 S. Raymond St. Just when you thought there were no hip cafés in Pasadena in which to pause and ponder Kafka, this bare, ratty little place rides to the rescue. Bagel with brie $2.75, steamed milk $1.25. Obligatory espresso ($1). Tues. open mike night for local bands, Wed. open poetry night, and Fri. night features a booked band. Open Sun.-Thurs. noon-1am, Fri. and Sat. noon-2am.

Sights

Downtown

The Los Angeles downtown area alone looms larger than most cities. An interesting mixture of neighborhoods, it beats the geographical drum of the city. The Financial District grows as a jungle of glass and steel, with huge corporate offices crowding the busy downtown center in an area bounded roughly by 3rd and 6th St., Figueroa St., and Grand Ave. Conspicuously perched atop Bunker Hill, the brand new I.M. Pei-designed **First Interstate World Center,** 633 W. 5th St. (955-8151), dominates the skyline; at 73 stories and 1017 ft., it stands as the tallest building west of the Mississippi River. The World Center's cylindrical shape and curved lines reflect the trend in recent years towards softer shapes in skyscraper architecture.

To the north of the Financial District, the **Civic Center,** a solid wall of bureaucratic architecture bounded by the Hollywood Fwy. (U.S. 101), Grand, 1st, and San Pedro St., runs east from the Music Center. It ends at Pei-influenced **City Hall,** 200 N. Spring St. Another of the best-known buildings in the Southland, the hall was the site of the *Daily Planet* in the *Superman* TV series. The building has an **observation deck** on the 27th floor.

Up, up, and away lies the historic birthplace of Los Angeles. Farther north, in the place where the original city center once stood, **El Pueblo de Los Angeles State Historic Park** (680-2525) preserves a number of historically important buildings from the Spanish and Mexican eras. Start out at the **docent center,** 130 Paseo de la Plaza, which offers free walking tours (Tues.-Sun. 10am-1pm on the hr.) and a free bus tour of L.A. (1st and 3rd Wed. of each month, make reservations as early as possible). (Open Mon.-Fri. 10am-3pm.) The **Old Plaza,** with its century-old Moreton Bay fig trees and huge bandstand, sprawls at the center of the pueblo. Tours start here and wind their way past the **Avila Adobe** (1818), 10 E. Olvera St., the oldest house in the city (the original adobe has been replaced with concrete in order to meet earthquake regulations), followed by **Pico House,** 500 N. Main St., once L.A.'s most luxurious hotel. Farther down, at 535 N. Main St., the **Plaza Church,** established in 1818, almost melts away from the street with its soft, rose adobe façade. Most tours also include the catacombs where Chinese immigrants ran gambling and opium dens. The **visitors center** occupies the **Sepulveda House** (1887), 622 N. Main St. (628-1274; open Mon.-Fri. 10am-3pm, Sat. 10am-4:30pm). One of L.A.'s original roads, **Olvera Street,** has miraculously survived as Tijuana North; and one tawdry stand after another sells schlocky Mexican handicrafts. Here L.A.'s large Chicano community celebrates Mexican Independence Day on **Cinco de Mayo.**

The grand old **Union Station,** across Alameda St. from El Pueblo, derails as a disused though beautiful monument to the bygone glory of the iron horse. The station has undergone revitalization for the new MetroRail system, scheduled to open in 1992.

Bustling **Chinatown** lies north of this area, roughly bordered by Yale, Spring, Ord, and Bernard St. From downtown, take the DASH shuttle. (See Getting Around, Public Transportation.) Wander about during the day and visit a market or sit and people-watch in the pedestrian plaza between Hill St. and Broadway north of College St. (the Food Mall). Excellent Chinese food simmers in this once vice-ridden neighborhood where Roman Polanski's Jake Giddis learned just what a tough, unforgiving world this is.

Little Tokyo centers on 2nd and San Pedro St., on the eastern edge of downtown. The **Japanese American Cultural and Community Center,** 244 S. San Pedro St. (628-2725), was designed by Buckminster Fuller and Isamu Noguchi, who created a monumental sculpture for the courtyard. (Administrative offices open Mon.-Fri. 9am-5pm.)

One of the predominantly Mexican sections of the city, **Broadway** south of 1st St., has all its billboards and store signs in Spanish. The **Grand Central Public Market** (see Food) takes a center seat. One of many Spanish-language cinemas housed in old movie palaces, the **Million Dollar Theater,** 307 S. Broadway (239-0939), boasts a baroque auditorium indoors, and stars in the sidewalk out front, each bearing the name of a Chicano celebrity—a *rambla de fama* to complement Hollywood's. Across the street, the **Bradbury Building,** 304 S. Broadway, stands as a relic of L.A.'s Victorian past. Unexciting from the street, this exquisite 1893 office building is mostly lobby. Its ornate staircases and elevators (wrought in iron, wood, and marble) are often bathed in sunlight, which pours in through the glass roof. Crews film period scenes with some regularity here. (Open Mon.-Sat. 10am-5pm. Self-guided tour $1.)

Undoubtedly the most striking and anagrammatic museum in the area, the **Museum of Contemporary Art (MOCA),** showcases art from 1940 to the present. The main museum at California Plaza, 250 S. Grand Ave. (626-6222), is a sleek and geometric architectural marvel, its collection focusing on abstract expressionism with works by Pollock, Calder, Miró, and Giacometti. Originally intended to house exhibits only while the main museum was under construction, the second MOCA facility is the **Temporary Contemporary,** 152 N. Central Ave. in Little Tokyo, now has become a permanent part of the MOCA package. The bare warehouse exterior conceals a wide collection of intriguing exhibits inside, showing the works of important younger avant-garde artists in a bold setting. The DASH shuttle provides transportation between the two MOCA locations; the admission price is good at both. (Open Tues.-Wed. and Fri.-Sun. 11am-6pm, Thurs. 11am-8pm. Admission $4, seniors and students with ID $2, under 12 free. Free Thurs. 5-8pm. Disabled access.)

Across from City Hall East, between the Santa Ana Fwy. and Temple in the L.A. Mall, is the **L.A. Children's Museum,** 310 N. Main St. (687-8800), where everything can be handled. One exhibit always focuses on a L.A. ethnic group, while children overcome the confusion of a hyper-technological society by participating in demonstrations of scientific principles. (Open Wed.-Thurs. 2-4pm, Sat.-Sun. 10am-5pm. Admission $4, under 2 free.)

The most intriguing but best-hidden of the downtown museums, the **Museum of Neon Art,** 704 Traction Ave. (617-1580), glows in the artist's neighborhood to the east of Little Tokyo. Exhibits range from neon artwork to other types of electric and kinetic sculpture. Traction runs east of Alameda St., between 2nd and 3rd St. (Open Tues.-Sat. 11am-5pm. Admission $2.50, seniors and students $1, under 17 free.)

The 1984 Summer Olympics revitalized the aging **Exposition Park** area, which assumed its present-day appearance when the Olympiad first came to town in 1932. Near downtown, the park has a number of important attractions clustered together. The park runs southwest of downtown, just off the Harbor Fwy., and is bounded by Exposition Blvd., Figueroa St., Vermont Ave., and Santa Barbara Ave. From downtown, take bus #40 or 42 (both from 1st and Broadway) to the park's southern edge. From Hollywood, take #204 down Vermont. From Santa Monica, take bus #20, 22, 320, or 322 on Wilshire, and transfer to #204 at Vermont.

Several large museums, including the **California Museum of Science and Industry**, 700 State Dr. (744-7400), dominate the park. Enter at the corner of Figueroa and Exposition next to the United DC-8 parked out front. Many of the exhibits are either corporate or governmental propaganda; those left to the MSI's own devices are rather amateurish. One exhibit re-creates an earthquake, complete with a shaking floor and mock news report, to acquaint Southern Californians with their future. The museum also includes the **Kinsey Hall of Health,** which uses interactive computer displays to educate visitors about their bodies and the effect of diet, alcohol, and drug use. The **Hall of Economics and Finance** does its best to enliven what even its practitioners call "the dismal science;" the **Aerospace Building,** as big as a hangar, exhibits $8 million worth of aircraft, including the Gemini 11 space capsule. (Open daily 10am-5pm. Free. Parking $1.)

In the same complex, but separate from the MSI is the **California Afro-American Museum,** 600 State Dr. (744-2060), with a permanent sculpture collection, a research library, and a changing assortment of exhibits. (Musuem open daily 10am-5pm. Free. Research library open Mon.-Fri. 10am-5pm.)

The park's other major museum, the **Los Angeles County Natural History Museum**, 900 Exposition Blvd. (744-3466), covers North American history from 1472-1914, pre-Columbian cultures, North American and African mammals, and dinosaurs. Befitting L.A., one hall showcases a dazzling array of precious rocks. (Open Tues.-Sun. 10am-5pm. Admission $3, seniors and students $1.50, ages 5-12 75¢, under 5 free.)

The large and beautiful **University of Southern California (USC)** campus sits opposite Exposition Park on Exposition Blvd. Though generally safe, women especially should exercise caution after dark. The **Fisher Gallery,** 823 Exposition Blvd. (743-2799), includes the Armand Hammer collection of 18th- and 19th-century Dutch paintings. (Open early Sept.-early May Tues.-Sat. noon-5pm. Free.)

To the south and east of the USC campus stretches **Watts,** a neighborhood made notorious by 1965 race riots. From the center of the Watts District rise the **Watts Towers,** 1765 E. 107th St. (569-8181), built singlehandedly over 33 years by resident Simon Rodia. The city now oversees these delicate towers of glistening fretwork, decorated with mosaics of broken glass, ceramic tile, and sea shells. Although a good 7-mi. drive from the nearest tourist attractions at Exposition Park and in a dangerous part of town, the towers are worth the trip. (By bus, take RTD #55 from Main St. downtown and get off at Compton Ave. and 108th St.; the towers rise 1 block to the east.) For a tour of the towers, which are undergoing restoration, call the Watts Towers Arts Center, 1727 E. 107th St. (569-8181; open Tues.-Sat. 9am-5pm).

Wilshire District and Hancock Park

Wilshire Boulevard, especially the "Miracle Mile" between Highland and Fairfax Ave., played a starring role in Los Angeles's westward suburban expansion. On what was then the end of the boulevard, the Bullocks Corporation gambled on attracting shoppers from downtown and in 1929 erected one of L.A.'s few architecturally significant buildings, the massive, bronze-colored **Bullocks Wilshire** at 3050 Wilshire Blvd., near Vermont Ave. Though now under a new name, docents of the

Los Angeles Conservancy (623-2489) offer tours of this art deco landmark. Also explore the nearby residential neighborhoods, with their 20s architecture. The streets south of Wilshire opposite Hancock Park are lined with Spanish-style bungalows and the occasional modernist manse.

A couple of miles farther down Wilshire, in **Hancock Park,** the acrid smell of tar pervades the vicinity of the aptly named **La Brea Tar Pits,** one of the most popular hangouts in the world for fossilized early mammals. Most of the one million bones recovered from the pits between 1913 and 1915 have found a new home in the **George C. Page Museum of La Brea Discoveries,** 5801 Wilshire Blvd. at Curzon and Wilshire (936-2230 recording, person 857-6311). Wilshire buses stop right in front. The museum includes reconstructed Ice Age animals and also murals of L.A. Ice Age life, a laboratory where paleontologists work behind plate-glass windows, and a display where you can feel what it's like to stick around in tar. (Open Tues.-Sun. 10am-5pm. Admission $3, seniors and students $1.50, children 75¢. Free 2nd Tues. each month. Museum tours Wed.-Fri. at 2pm, Sat.-Sun. at 11:30am and 2pm. Combined admission with L.A. County Museum of Art $4.50, seniors and students $2.25.)

The **Los Angeles County Museum of Art (LACMA),** 5905 Wilshire Blvd. (857-6000), at the west end of Hancock Park, has a distinguished, comprehensive collection that should rebut those who argue that L.A.'s only culture is yogurt-based. Opened in 1965, the LACMA is the largest museum in the West and still growing. Five major buildings cluster around the **Times Mirror Central Court:** a Japanese pavilion, the Ahmanson Building (the museum's original building and home to most of its non-modern permanent collection), the Hammer Building, the Bing Center, and the Robert O. Anderson Building, a spectacular 1986 addition to the museum of salmon-colored sandstone and glass. For tours and talks, check with the information desk in the Central Court or contact the Docent Council at 857-6108. (Open Tues.-Fri. 10am-5pm, Sat.-Sun. 10am-6pm. Admission $5, seniors and students $3.50, ages 6-17 $1. Free 2nd Tues. each month. Parking $3, with museum validation.)

Similar to Jerusalem's famous Yad VaShem Holocaust Memorial is the **Martyrs Memorial and Museum of the Holocaust** (852-1234, ext. 3200), located in the Jewish Community Building, 6505 Wilshire Blvd., just east of Beverly Hills. Chill photographs and prisoners' personal items are on display next to paintings and drawings made in the ghettos and death camps. The museum perches on the 12th floor; sign in at the security desk. (Open Mon.-Thurs. 9am-5pm, Fri. 9am-3pm, Sun. 1-5pm. Free. Call ahead for a tour.)

Hollywood

It's hard to believe that for decades, this tiny chunk of a massive city defined West Coast glamor. In the early days of silent movies, independent producers and directors, many of them Jewish, sought to escape the tight control and restrictions of the conservative Protestant Movie Trust based in New York. They began shooting films in the empty groves of Hollywood both to avoid the Trust's surveillance and to take advantage of the steady sunlight and infrequent rain (indoor lighting techniques were not employed at the time).

By the early 1920s, all the major studios had moved from the East Coast to this then-obscure suburb. Hollywood quickly became synonymous with the celluloid image. Home to the great stars (Garbo, Gable, Crawford, Dietrich) and the great studios (Metro-Goldwyn-Mayer, Paramount, Warner Bros., 20th Century Fox) and even its own governing bodies (The Motion Picture Academy of Arts and Sciences, the Screen Actors Guild), Hollywood became the arbiter of American mores and the official interpreter of the "American Dream." Hollywood today has lost much of its sparkle. The major studios have moved over the mountains into the San Fernando Valley, where they have more room to weave ever more elaborate fantasies; many blockbusters shoot "on location" on foreign soil. Hollywood has left behind pieces of filmdom's heyday as if on a cutting-room floor. Hollywood and Vine, once considered the quintessential California corner, now stands as just another corner. At night, prostitutes abound; women work Hollywood and Sunset Blvd., while boys ply their trade on Santa Monica Blvd. (also known as S&M Blvd.). Hollywood is still a fascinating place, but a far cry from the Emerald City it once thought itself to be.

The **Hollywood sign**—those 50-ft.-high, slightly erratic letters perched on Mt. Cahuenga north of Hollywood—stands with New York's Statue of Liberty and Paris's Eiffel Tower as a universally recognized symbol of its city. The original 1923 sign, which read HOLLYWOODLAND, advertised a new subdivision in the Hollywood Hills, with a caretaker living behind one of the Ls. Over the years, people came to think of it as a civic monument; acquiring the sign by 1978, the city reconstructed the crumbling letters, leaving off the last syllable. For a closer look at this legendary site, follow Beachwood Dr. up into the hills (bus #208; off Franklin Ave. between Vine St. and Western Ave.). Drive along the narrow twisting streets of the Hollywood Hills for glimpses of the bizarre homes of the Rich and Famous.

After this overview of Hollywood, fall back into the thick of things and explore Hollywood Boulevard itself. The street, lined with souvenir shops, porno houses, clubs, and theaters, keeps busy both day and night. The façade of **Mann's Chinese Theater** (formerly Grauman's), 6925 Hollywood Blvd. (464-8111), between Highland and La Brea, is a Polynesian interpretation of a Chinese temple. Hollywood hype at its finest, tourists crowd in the courtyard, worshipping cement impressions of the stars' anatomy and trademark possessions—Trigger's hooves, R2D2's wheels, Jimmy Durante's nose, George Burns's cigar, to name a few. To stroll among stars, have a look at the **Walk of Fame** along Hollywood Blvd. and Vine St. More than 2500 bronze-inlaid stars deface the sidewalk, inscribed with names and feats.

Two blocks east of Mann's melts the **Hollywood Wax Museum**, 6767 Hollywood Blvd. (462-8860), where you'll meet over 200 figures from Jesus to tiny restaurants. (Open Sun.-Thurs. 10am-midnight, Fri.-Sat. 10am-2am. Admission $6, senior discount, children $4.) Other Hollywood Blvd. attractions include the original **Frederick's of Hollywood**, 6608 Hollywood Blvd. (466-8506), that purple and pink bastion of tasteful teddies which now houses its own **museum of lingerie** in the back of the store. (Open Mon.-Thurs. 10am-6pm, Fri. 10am-9pm, Sat. 10am-6pm, Sun. noon-5pm. Museum same hours. Free.) Down the street, **Larry Edmund's Cinema and Theater Bookshop**, 6658 Hollywood Blvd. (463-3273), sells Ken Schessler's *This Is Hollywood: Guide to Hollywood Murders, Suicides, Graves, Etc.,* a guide to nondescript-places-made-famous by the fact that stars courted, married, fooled around, or made movies there. (Open Mon.-Sat. 10am-6pm.)

The **Hollywood Studio Museum**, 2100 N. Highland Ave. (874-2276), across from the Hollywood Bowl, provides a refreshingly un-Mannesque look at the history of early Hollywood film-making. Back in 1913, when it was a barn, famed director Cecil B. DeMille rented this building as a studio and shot Hollywood's first feature film, *The Squaw Man*. Antique cameras, costumes, props, and other memorabilia clutter the museum along with vintage film clips. (Open Sat.-Sun. 10am-4pm. Admission $2, seniors and students $1.50, children $1. Ample free parking.)

Music is another one of the industries that greases Hollywood's cash-register wheels. Designed to look like a stack of records, the 1954 **Capitol Records Tower**, 1750 Vine St., just north of Hollywood Blvd., encompasses a cylindrical building with fins sticking out at each floor (the "records") and a needle on top. More esoteric music and associated paraphernalia spin at **The Rock Shop**, 6666 Hollywood Blvd. (466-7276), which carries—in addition to records and tapes—posters, T-shirts, WWII artifacts, and leather and metal accessories.

Barnsdall Park, 4800 Hollywood Blvd., relatively small and discreet, contains the **Municipal Art Gallery**, 4804 Hollywood Blvd. (485-4581), a modern building showcasing the works of Southern California artists in a pleasant, low-key setting. (Open Tues.-Sun. 12:30-5pm. Admission $1, under 13 free.) Adjacent to the museum, on top of the hill, the **Hollyhock House**, 4808 Hollywood Blvd. (662-7272), commands a 360° view of Los Angeles and the mountains. Completed in 1922 for eccentric oil heiress Aline Barnsdall, the house remains one of Frank Lloyd

Wright's most important works, reflecting the influence of Mayan temples. (Tours Tues.-Thurs. on the hr. 10am-1pm; Sat. and all but the last Sun. each month noon-3pm. Admission $1.50, seniors $1, under 13 free. Buy tickets at the Municipal Art Gallery. Call for foreign-language tours.)

About 3 mi. northeast of downtown rests **Elysian Park**; with 525 acres of greenery, this paradise amid pomp is ideal for picnicking. The park largely surrounds and embraces the area of Chavez Ravine, home of well-run **Dodger Stadium** (224-1400) and the Los Angeles Dodgers baseball team. Purchase tickets ($4-8) in advance, if possible, you'd pay a premium from scalpers selling tickets illegally outside. Once in the ballpark, grab yourself a Dodger Dog, the hot dog that, according to David Letterman, tastes like vinyl.

Sprawling over a mammoth 4500 acres of hilly terrain is **Griffith Park**. This formidable recreational region stretches from the hills above Hollywood north to the intersection of the Ventura and Golden State Freeways, encompassing the L.A. Zoo, the Greek Theater, Griffith Observatory and Planetarium, Travel Town, a bird sanctuary, tennis courts, two golf courses, campgrounds Pick up a map at any of the entrance points. For information, stop by the **visitors center and ranger headquarters,** 4730 Crystal Spring Dr. (665-5188; open daily 5am-10pm).

A large bird sanctuary at the bottom of the observatory hill serves its function well, but if you want to see animals, you might as well go to the **L.A. Zoo,** at the park's northern end (666-4650). The zoo's 113 acres accommodate 2000 crazy critters, and the facility consistently ranks among the nation's 10 best. Take bus #97 from downtown. (Open daily 10am-6pm; winter 10am-5pm. Admission $4.50, seniors $3.50, ages 2-12 $2, under 2 free. Ticket office closes 1 hr. before zoo closing time.) On the southern side of the park, below the observatory, the 4500-seat **Greek Theater** (665-5857) hosts a number of concerts in its outdoor amphitheater virtually year-round. Check advertisements in the *Sunday Times* "Calendar" section for coming attractions. Take bus #203 from Hollywood.

Those with a hankerin' to relive those wild, wild days of yore will enjoy the recently opened **Gene Autry Western Heritage Museum,** 4700 Zoo Dr. (667-2000), also located within Griffith Park at the junction of Golden State (I-5) and Ventura Fwy. (Rte. 134). The museum's collection covers both fact and fiction of the Old West, with exhibits on pioneer life and on the history of western films. (Open Tues.-Sun. 10am-5pm. Admission $4.75, seniors $3.50, children $2.)

West Hollywood

Once considered a non-entity between Beverly Hills and Hollywood, West Hollywood incorporated in 1985. It has the distinction of being one of the first cities in the country governed by openly gay officials.

In the years before incorporation, lax zoning and other liberal laws gave rise to the decadent **Sunset Strip.** Posh nightclubs originally lined the Strip; these days, it jams with heavy metal clubs, drawing huge crowds and traffic jams on weekends (see Music).

Melrose Avenue, south of West Hollywood, is lined with unique restaurants, ultra-trendy boutiques, punk clothing pits, and art galleries. The choicest section stretches betweeen La Brea and Fairfax, but the *Repo Man*-like spectre of apocalyptic apathy haunts the whole 3-mi. distance between Highland and Doheny. At Beverly and La Cienega squats the massive, plate glass **Beverly Center,** an expensive shopping complex. At the corner of Beverly and San Vicente Blvd. is the Los Angeles **Hard Rock Café** (276-7605). A '57 pistachio-green Chevy juts out of the roof, unsuccessfully attempting to escape the crowds within. Be prepared for a wait every night of the week—over an hour on weekends. The line to buy T-shirts can grow just as long. (Open Sun.-Thurs. 11:30am-midnight, Fri.-Sat. 11:30am-1am.)

North of the Beverly Center, at Melrose and San Vicente, sits the **Pacific Design Center,** 8687 Melrose Ave. (657-0800), a huge, blue-and-green glass complex with a wave-like profile (nicknamed **The Blue Whale**). In addition to some design showrooms, the PDC houses a public plaza with a 350-seat amphitheater, used to stage free summer concerts. Call or inquire at the information desk in the entryway for details about such events. West Hollywood's **Gay Pride Weekend Celebration** (in late June) is usually held at the PDC plaza.

Beverly Hills

Though placed in the midst of Greater Los Angeles, about 2/3 of the way between downtown L.A. and the coast, Beverly Hills remains a steadfast enclave of wealth. Beverly Hills seceded from L.A. in 1914 and has remained distinct (physically and ideologically) from the city ever since. The liver of the city rests in the **Golden Triangle,** a wedge formed by Wilshire and Santa Monica Blvd., centering on **Rodeo Drive,** known for its many opulent clothing boutiques and jewelry shops. This famous street is one of the few places where you can feel underdressed simply window-shopping.

Some of the most luxurious homes in Beverly Hills locate north of the Rodeo Dr. area, up Benedict, Coldwater, and Laurel Canyons. Several sidewalk stands along Sunset Blvd. between Sunset Strip and the San Diego Fwy. sell "Star Maps" of the homes of celebrities. Stargazers be forewarned: these houses tend to be private and secure; driving tours often prove less than stellar.

Not actually in Beverly Hills, but close by, the **Simon Wiesenthal Center,** 9760 W. Pico Blvd. (553-9036), near Roxbury Dr., one of the largest U.S. institutions for Holocaust studies. Located in the **California Yeshiva University,** the Wiesenthal Center was named after the Mauthausen concentration-camp survivor and famous Nazi-hunter. The institute comprises both a museum and a library; the opening of **Beit Hashoah, The Museum of Tolerance** next door is projected for 1991. (Museum open Mon.-Fri. 9:30am-4:30pm; winter Fri. 9:30am-2:30pm. Library open Mon.-Thurs. 9am-6pm and 7-10pm, Fri. 9am-2pm, Sun. 1-4:30pm. Both free.)

Westwood and UCLA

With a total enrollment of 34,674, the **University of California at Los Angeles (UCLA)** is appropriately the largest of the nine UC campuses. Regarded as one of the top research universities in the United States. UCLA covers over 400 acres in the foothills of the Santa Monica Mountains, bounded by Sunset, Hilgard, Le Conte, and Gayley. The school is directly north of Westwood Village and west of Beverly Hills. You can park on campus by paying $4 at one of the campus information kiosks; you will receive a day permit that allows parking in the student garages.

The best place to start a tour of UCLA is at the **Visitors Center,** 10945 Le Conte Ave. #147 (206-8147), located in the Ueberroth Olympic Office Bldg. But the fun doesn't stop there: free 90-minute walking tours of the campus depart from the visitors center at 10:30am and 1:30pm Monday to Friday. Campus maps are also available at the information kiosks located at each of the streets leading into the campus. **Dickson Plaza,** also know as the **Quadrangle,** is the centerpiece of the campus. At the south end, **Powell Library** serves as the main undergraduate library and reflects an Islamic influence in its architectural design.

At the northernmost reach of the campus, the **Dickson Art Center** (825-1462) houses the Wight Art Gallery, which is home to the Grunwald Center for the Graphic Arts, as well as frequent internationally recognized exhibitions. (Open Sept.-June Tues. 11am-8pm, Wed.-Fri. 11am-5pm, Sat.-Sun. 1-5pm. Free.) The **Murphy Sculpture Garden,** with over 70 pieces spread over five acres, lies directly in front of the Art Center. The collection includes works by such major artists as Rodin, Matisse, and Miró. Another well-known piece of outdoor artwork, UCLA's **Inverted Fountain,** spumes between Knudsen Hall and Schoenberg Hall, directly south of Dickson Plaza. An innovation in the exciting world of fountain designs, water spouts from the fountain's perimeter and rushes down into the gaping hole in the middle. The **Botanical Gardens** (825-1260), in the southeast corner of the campus, encompass a subtropical canyon where redwoods and venerable palms mingle brook-side (open Mon.-Fri. 8am-5pm, Sat.-Sun. 8am-4pm); and the Zen Buddhist-inspired **Japanese Garden.** (Open Tues. 10am-1pm, Wed. noon-3pm, by appointment only. Call the visitors center at 825-4574 or 825-4338 to arrange tour.)

Before it attained national acclaim in research arenas, UCLA attained national acclaim in sporting arenas. UCLA has captured more National Collegiate Athletic Association (NCAA) titles over the last 20 years than any other university (62). The UCLA men's basketball team, which won seven consecutive NCAA championships in the 60s and 70s under legendary coach John Wooden, plays its home games at **Pauley Pavilion,** located to the west of Dickson Plaza, down Bruin Walk, next to the Bruin Bear Statue (depicting the school's mascot). The other athletic facilities cluster around Pauley.

Westwood Village, just south of the campus, with its myriad movie theaters, trendy boutiques, and upscale eateries, is geared more toward the residents of L.A.'s Westside than toward a collegiate coterie. Like most college neighborhoods, however, Westwood hums on Friday and Saturday nights when everyone (students, tourists, gang members, and police) show up to do their thing.

Santa Monica

To a resident of turn-of-the-century L.A., a trip to the beach resort of Santa Monica meant a long ride over poor-quality roads. The Red Car electric train shortened the trip considerably, and today, it takes about half an hour (with no traffic) on Big Blue express bus #10 or on the Santa Monica Freeway (I-10) from downtown. No longer far away, SaMo is still pretty far out, with an extremely liberal city council and the former Mr. Jane Fonda (Tom Hayden, one of the Chicago Seven) as one of its assemblymen. The beach is the closest to Los Angeles proper, and thus crowded and dirty. The magical lure of sun, surf, and sand causes nightmarish summer traffic jams on I-10 and I-405; much prettier and cleaner beaches shimmer to the north and south. Santa Monica, however, still demands a look for its seaside spectacle of luxurious condominiums and art deco hotels. The colorful **Santa Monica Pier** remains a nostalgic and popular, if a bit sleazy, spot. The prize of the pier is the magnificent turn-of the-century carousel featured in *The Sting.* **Palisades Park,** on the bluff overlooking the pier, provides a shaded home for numerous homeless people.

Venice

To the south of Santa Monica lies the dream, formidably enough, of bringing the Mediterranean to Southern California. In the beginning of this century, Abbot Kinney dug a series of canals throughout the town and filled them with water, intending to bring the romance and refinement of Venice, Italy to the sunny U.S. shores. But the water of the canals became dirty and oily, and instead of attracting society's upper crust, attracted a crust of their own. Venice became home to gamblers, bootleggers, and other assorted rogues; the canals were eventually forgotten and, for the most part, filled in and buried. Today, Venice is home to perhaps the most fully developed "beach culture" in the world. With everyone crowding the beachfront, trying either to see or to be seen, life in Venice is, as one hostel brochure aptly puts it, "spontaneous theater."

Ocean Front Walk, Venice's main beach front drag, marks a drastic demographic departure from Santa Monica's Promenade. Street people converge on shaded clusters of benches, revolting, healthy-types play paddle tennis, and bodybuilders of both sexes pump iron in skimpy outfits at the original **Muscle Beach** (1800 Ocean Front Walk, closest to 18th and Pacific Ave.). Here the roller-skating craze began, and here it will probably breathe its last. Even the police wear shorts while busting nude sunbathers with $55 fines. New Wavers, cyclists, joggers, groovy elders (such as the "skateboard grandma"), and bards in Birkenstocks make up the balance of this funky playground population.

Venice's **street murals** provide another free show. Don't miss the brilliant, graffiti-disfigured homage to Botticelli's *Birth of Venus* on the beach pavilion at the end of Windward Ave.: an angelically beautiful woman, wearing short shorts, a Band-aid top, and roller-skates, boogies out of her seashell. The side wall of a Japanese restaurant on Windward contains a perfect imitation of a Japanese Hokusai print of a turbulent sea. Large insect sculptures loom in the rafters of many of the city's posh restaurants.

To get to Venice from downtown L.A., take bus #33 or 333 (or 436 during rush hr.). From downtown Santa Monica, take Santa Monica bus #1 or 2.

The Pacific Coast Highway

From Santa Monica, where it temporarily merges with I-10, the **Pacific Coast Highway (PCH)** (Rte. 1) runs northward along the spectacular California coast. Some of the best beaches in L.A. County line this stretch of the PCH between Santa Monica and the Ventura County line.

Heading north from Santa Monica, the first major attraction is the **J. Paul Getty Museum,** 17985 PCH (458-2003), set back on a cliff above the ocean. Getty, an oil magnate, built this mansion as a re-creation of the first-century Villa dei Papiri in Herculaneum, with a beautiful main peristyle garden, a reflecting pool, and bush-lined paths. Because of the museum's operating agreement with its residential neighbors, access to the museum is more difficult than it could be. Because the parking lot is small, reservations are needed, a day in advance most of the time, weeks in advance in summer. You are not permitted to park outside the museum unless you do so at the county lot. Bicyclists and motorcyclists are admitted without reservations. Take RTD #434 (which you can board at Sunset and PCH in Malibu or Ocean and Colorado in Santa Monica) to the museum and ask for a free **museum pass** from the bus driver. The museum gate yawns ½ mi. from the bus stop; prepare to walk. (Open Tues.-Sun. 10am-5pm. Free.)

The celebrity colony of **Malibu** stretches along the low 20000 blocks of PCH. With their multi-million-dollar homes and celebrity neighbors, Malibu residents can afford to be hostile to nonlocals, especially to those from the Valley. The beach lies along the 23200 block of the PCH. You might want to walk onto the beach by the **Zonker Harris access way** at 22700 PCH, named after the quintessential Californian from Garry Trudeau's comic strip, *Doonesbury*. **Corral State Beach,** an uncrowded, windsurfing, swimming, and scuba diving retreat, lies on the 26000 block of PCH, followed by **Point Dume State Beach,** which is small and generally uncrowded.

North of Point Dume, along the 30000 block of PCH, is L.A. County's northernmost and largest county-owned sandbox, **Zuma;** with lifeguards, restrooms, and a $5 parking fee. The beach hosts a mixed bag of sun-worshippers: stations 8 to 12 belong to those looking for solitude; the Valley high schoolers have staked out 6 and 7, the most crowded and lively parts; Zuma 3, 4, and 5 hold families who keep things slightly more sedate. If you don't want to bring food, pick something up at **Trancas Market** (PCH and Trancas Canyon, around Station 12). Stay away from the beach stands unless you're willing to pay $2.75 for an insipid hamburger or hot dog.

Finally, visitors with cars should not miss **Mulholland Drive,** nature's answer to the roller coaster. Twisting and turning for 15 spectacular mi. along the crest of the Santa Monica Mountains, Mulholland Dr. stretches from PCH, near the Ventura County line, east to the Hollywood Fwy. and San Fernando Valley. Avoid Mulholland on late weekend nights, when the road fills with drag-racing teenagers and parked cars on Lover's Lane. Racers use both lanes; four headlights approaching at 70mph is a more arresting sight than all the panoramic lights of what Aldous Huxley called "the city of dreadful joy."

Pasadena

A quiet, placid suburb about 10 mi. northeast of downtown Los Angeles, Pasadena offers the perfect antidote to the hectic pace of Greater Los Angeles. Pleasant tree-lined streets and greenery coolly complement outstanding cultural facilities. Set in the gorge that forms the city's western boundary is Pasadena's most famous landmark, the **Rose Bowl,** 991 Rosemont Blvd. (818-793-7193). Home to the grandparent of the college football bowl games and the annual confrontation between the champions of the Big Ten and Pac 10 conferences, the Rose Bowl also houses to the UCLA Bruins football team. The New Year's Day Rose Bowl game follows the **Tournament of Roses Parade,** which runs along Colorado Blvd. through downtown Pasadena. Thousands line the Pasadena streets (often grabbing choice viewing spots days in advance) to watch the flower-covered floats go by. To reach the Rose Bowl, take the Pasadena Fwy. to its end and follow the signs of Arroyo Pkwy.

At the western end of the downtown area (also called Old Pasadena) lies Pasadena's sleek and modern answer to LACMA, the **Norton Simon Museum of Art,** 411 W. Colorado Blvd. (449-3730), at Orange Grove Blvd. Numerous Rodin and Brancusi bronzes frame the superb collection, which also includes Rembrandt, Picasso, impressionist, and Southeast Asian works. The presentation is flawless. Simon's eclectic, slightly idiosyncratic taste, as well as the well-written descriptions of the works, make this museum more interesting than similar assemblages elsewhere. (Open Thurs.-Sun. noon-6pm. Admission $4, seniors and students $2, under 13 free.) From downtown L.A. take bus #483 from Olive St., anywhere between Venice Blvd. and 1st St., to Colorado Blvd. and Fair Oaks Ave. in Pasadena. The museum preens 4 blocks west. The **Pasadena Civic Center** (818-449-7360), situated north of Colorado Blvd. at Garfield Ave., is the centerpiece of the city's Spanish-influenced architectural heritage. The City Hall, built in Spanish style around a beautiful open courtyard, comes complete with gardens and a fountain.

Some of the world's greatest scientific minds do their work at the West Coast rival to the Massachusetts Institute of Technology, the **California Institute of Technology,** 1201 E. California Blvd. (818-356-6811), about 2½ mi. southeast of downtown. The lush campus fills with bush- and olive tree-lined brick paths. Founded in 1891 as Throop University, Cal Tech has amassed a faculty which includes several Nobel prizewinners (Albert Einstein once taught here) and a student body which prides itself on its high I.Q., and elaborate and ingenious practical jokes. Whether unscrewing all the chairs in a lecture hall and bolting them in backwards, or altering the Rose Bowl scoreboard during the big game with the aid of computers, Techies truly do it well.

One ½-mi. to the south of Cal Tech lies the **Huntington Library, Art Gallery, and Botanical Gardens,** 1151 Oxford Rd., San Marino 91108 (213-792-6141, 818-405-2100; ticket information 818-405-2273). Despite the ban on picnics and sunbathing, families and tourists still flock here on Sundays to stroll around the grounds and visit the library and galleries. The stunning botanical gardens nurture 207 acres of plants, many of them rare. The library houses one of the world's most important collections of rare books and English and American manuscripts, including the requisite Gutenberg Bible and Benjamin Franklin's handwritten autobiography. The art gallery boasts 18th- and 19th-century British paintings: among the sentimental favorites on exhibit are Thomas Gainsborough's *Blue Boy* and its companion piece, Sir Thomas Lawrence's *Pinkie.* (Open Tues.-Sun. 1-4:30pm. Free. Parking donation $2.) To visit on a Sunday, write for tickets several weeks in advance (visitors from out of state don't need reservations). Include a self-addressed, stamped envelope. The museum sits between Huntington Dr. and California Blvd. in San Marino, just south of Pasadena. From downtown L.A., take bus #401 from Spring St. Get off at Colorado Blvd. and Allen Ave. Walk east to Sierra Madre Blvd. and catch #264 going south by the Huntington.

Entertainment

"Vast wasteland" mythology to the contrary, L.A.'s cultural scene is in fact active and diverse. The *L.A. Weekly,* available free in newspaper machines and stores all over the area, routinely runs 120 pages, trying to keep up with the city's film, music, art, theater, radio, television, and other entertainment events. The *L.A. Times* "Calendar" section provides accurate and up-to-date dope about what's going on where. Try the "L.A. Life" section of Friday's *Los Angeles Daily News* for planning a weekend.

Film and Television Studios

All of the major TV studios offer free tickets to show tapings. Some are available on a first come, first served basis from the Visitors Information Center of the Greater L.A. Visitor and Convention Bureau or by mail. Some of the networks won't send tickets to out-of-state addresses, but they will send a guest card or letter that can be redeemed for tickets. Be sure to enclose a self-addressed, stamped envelope. Write: Tickets, Capital City/ABC Inc., 4151 Prospect, Hollywood 90027 (557-4143); CBS Tickets, 7800 Beverly Blvd., Los Angeles 90036 (852-2624); NBC-TV, 3000 W. Alameda Ave., Burbank 91523 (840-3537); or FOX Tickets, 100 Universal City Plaza, Bldg. 153, Universal City 91608 (818-506-0043). Tickets are also available to shows produced by Paramount Television, 780 N. Gower St., Hollywood 90038 (468-5575). Tickets don't guarantee admittance; arrive a couple of hours early, as seating serves first-comers first.

Universal Studios, Universal City (818-508-9600). Hollywood Fwy. to Lankershim. Take bus #424 to Lankershim Blvd. For a hefty fee, the studio will take you for a ride; visit the Bates Hotel and other sets, see Conan the Barbarian flex his pecs, stare down Jaws, get caught in a flash flood, and witness a variety of special effects and other demonstrations of movie-making magic. Reservations for the tour not accepted; arrive early to secure a ticket—despite the price, the tour is quite popular. Allow 2½ hr. for the tour and at least 1 hr. to wander around. Tours in Spanish Sat.-Sun. Open summer and holidays daily 8:30am-11pm (last tram leaves at 5pm); Sept.-June Mon.-Fri. 10am-3:30pm, Sat.-Sun. 9:30am-3:30pm. Admission $22, seniors and ages 3-11 $16.50. Parking $5.

NBC Television Studios Tour, 3000 W. Alameda Ave. (818-840-3572), at Olive Ave. in Burbank, 2 mi. from Universal. Follow Hollywood Fwy. north, exit east on Barham Blvd., which becomes Olive Ave. Take bus #420 from Hill St. downtown. A cheaper, smaller, and in many ways, better tour than Universal's. A good chance to see shows being taped and to bump into a wandering star. Arrive early to avoid crowds and improve your chances of receiving free tickets to a live show taping. Tickets for shows including *The Tonight Show* available by mail or at the box office (off California St.) Mon.-Fri. 8am-5pm, Sat. 9:30am-4pm. Studios open Mon.-Fri. 8:30am-4pm, tours every ½ hr.; Sat. 10am-4pm and Sun. 10am-2pm, tours every hr. Tours $6.75, ages 5-14 $4.50.

Warner Bros. VIP Tour, 4000 Warner Blvd., Burbank (818-954-1744). Personalized, un-staged tours (max. 12 people) through the Warner Bros. studios. Technical, 2-hr. long tours show the detailed reality of the movie-making art. No children under 10. Tours daily at 10am and 2pm; additional tours in summer. Admission $22. Reservations required.

Cinema

In the technicolored heaven of Los Angeles, you'd expect to find as many theaters as stars on the Walk of Fame. You won't be disappointed; just about every major block of every major street has its own movie theater. A handful show films the way they were meant to be seen: in a big auditorium, on a big screen. Prices for adult admission to a first-run film in Greater L.A. has paused at $7.

Cineplex Odeon Universal City Cinemas, atop the hill at Universal Studios (818-508-0588). Take the Universal Center Dr. exit off the Hollywood Fwy. (U.S. 101). Opened in 1987 as the world's largest cinema complex. The 18 wide-screen theaters, 2 *Parisienne*-style cafés, and opulent decoration put all others to shame. Hooray for Hollywood.

Mann's Chinese, 6925 Hollywood Blvd. (464-8111). Hollywood hype to the hilt. For more details, see Hollywood Sights.

Village Theatre, 961 Broxton (208-5576), in Westwood. No multiplex nonsense here. One auditorium, one big screen, one great THX sound system, a balcony, and art deco design. Watch the back rows and balcony for late-arriving celebrities.

Devotees of second-run, foreign language, and experimental films are also rewarded. The following show **classics and cult films** all the time:

Nuart Theatre, 11272 Santa Monica Blvd. (478-6379), in L.A., at the San Diego Fwy. Perhaps the best known. The playbill changes nightly, so drop by for a copy of the monthly guide. Classics and documentaries.

Rialto Theater, 1023 Fair Oaks Ave. (799-9567), in S. Pasadena at Oxley. *Rocky Horror* mayhem every Sat. at midnight.

UCLA's Melnitz Theater, on the northeastern corner of campus near Sunset and Hilgard. An eclectic range of film festivals.

Foreign films can be found consistently at the six **Laemmle Theaters** in Beverly Hills, West L.A., Santa Monica, Pasadena, Encino, and downtown.

Though it's usually hard to get in without connections or, strangely enough, without lots of money, occasional free films are shown on weekday afternoons during the Los Angeles International Film Festival (469-9400). Popularly known as **Filmex,** the annual program runs from late June through early July.

A unique movie-going treat is the **Mitsubishi IMAX Theater,** at the California Museum of Science and Industry (744-2014; see Exposition Park). Movies burst onto a 54×70-foot screen. Seats are steeply raked and the films, of the entertainment-documentary variety, surround the viewer with brilliant sights and sounds. (Admission $5, seniors and children under 12 $3.50.)

Comedy

So you just flew into L.A. and boy are your arms tired: for a muscle relaxant catch the newest and wackiest stand-up comedians, or to watch famous veterans hone new material. Some clubs are open only a few nights per week. Call ahead to check age restrictions.

Comedy Store, 8433 Sunset Blvd. (656-6225). The shopping mall of comedy clubs, with 3 different rooms, each featuring a different type of comedy. (Each room charges its own cover.) Go to the Main Room for the big-name stuff and the most expensive cover charges (around $14). The Original Room features mid-range comics for $6-8. The Belly Room has the real grab-bag material, often for no cover charge. Must be 21; 2- drink minimum.

The Comedy Act Theater, 3339 W. 43rd St. (677-4101). A comedy club targeted at an African American audience, often featuring such nationally known comedians as Robert Townsend and Marsha Warfield. Open Thurs.-Sat. from 8:30pm. Cover $10.

The Improvisation, 8162 Melrose Ave. (651-2583). Offers L.A.'s best talent, including, on occasion, Robin Williams, Alex Tyler, and Robert Klein. Their restaurant serves good Italian fare. Open nightly; check *L.A. Weekly* for times. Cover $8-10; 2-drink minimum.

The Laugh Factory, 8001 W. Sunset Blvd. (656-8860), in West Hollywood. The Comedy Store's kid brother on the Sunset Strip. A high-tech complex complete with VIP gallery and well-known talent. Must be 18. Cover $6-10; 2-drink minimum.

Theater and Classical Music

Los Angeles has one of the most active theater circuits on the West Coast. One hundred and fifteen Equity Waiver theaters (under 100 seats) offer a dizzying choice for theater-goers, who can also enjoy small productions in museums, art galleries, universities, parks, and garages. During the summer hiatus, TV stars frequently return to their acting roots. Mainstream theater is often worth the high prices to see shows that are either Broadway-bound or beginning their national tour after a New York run. Most of the following double as sites for music concerts.

Hollywood Bowl, 2301 N. Highland Ave. (850-2000), in Hollywood. Perfect for a summer evening, the Bowl hosts a summer festival from early July to mid-Sept. Although sitting in the back of this outdoor, 18,000-seat amphitheater makes even the L.A. Philharmonic sound like AM radio, the bargain tickets ($1-3) and the sweeping views of L.A. from the Bowl's south rim compensates. Local restaurants, cafés, and the Bowl itself will pack a gourmet feast (wine, pâté, pasta salad) for about $10 per person and up. Or bring your own food, and buckets of Kentucky Fried Chicken are everywhere. Parking complicated and expensive ($8); use RTD's Park 'n' Ride service instead (get a brochure listing lots from which shuttle service is available). Or park away from the Bowl and hike up Highland. Bus #150 goes to the Bowl from the Valley; #420 runs from downtown.

Music Center, 135 N. Grand Ave., downtown (972-7475), at 1st in the heart of the city. Includes the **Mark Taper Forum** (972-7353) and the **Dorothy Chandler Pavilion** (972-7200).

Schubert Theatre, 2020 Ave. of the Stars, Century City (800-223-3123). Big Broadway shows.

Pantages, 6233 Hollywood Blvd. (410-1062). L.A.'s other place for big Broadway spectacles.

Nightclubs

Music in L.A. falls into two major categories: clubs and concerts. Clubs are crowded and intimate, concerts crowded and impersonal. Most clubs tend to be experimental, uneven in quality, and ephemeral. To find one to suit your taste, scan the *L.A. Weekly.*

Club Lingerie, 6507 Sunset Blvd., Hollywood (466-8557). Big college bands from 9pm. Rock, reggae, ska, and funk. They've got it, and they flaunt it. Two full bars. Must be 21.

China Club, 1600 N. Argyle Ave. (469-1600). A great sound system goes to work for some of the best local bands. Open nightly from 9pm. Full bar. Must be 21.

Coconut Teaszer, 8117 Sunset Blvd. (654-4773). The best place for weeknight rocking and weekend dancing (see Dance Clubs). Up to 10 different bands on Sun. nights, with free keg beer. Full bar. Must be 21 (except Fri.-Sat., when those over 18 are admitted).

Anti-Club, 4658 Melrose Ave. (661-3913). Avant-garde, smoky, and dim. Famous lair supporting innovative bands for years. Acts range from traditional to underground rock sounds. Full bar. Cover varies.

Roxy, 9009 Sunset Blvd. (276-2222). Among the best known along L.A.'s Sunset Strip. Fills with record company types and rockers waiting to get discovered. Many big acts at the height of their popularity play here. Cover varies.

Kingston 12, 814 Broadway (451-4423), Santa Monica. L.A.'s only full-time reggae club presents both local and foreign acts. Dance floor, 2 bars, Jamaican food. Open Tues.-Sun. 8:30pm-2am.

If you like mixing your food with your entertainment, you may want to sample L.A.'s flourishing **cabaret** scene.

Gardenia, 7066 Santa Monica Blvd. (467-7444), in Hollywood. A New York nightclub with "California Cuisine." Dinner starts at $8.50, cover charge $4. Open Mon.-Sat. evenings.

Café Largo, 432 N. Fairfax Ave. (852-1073). A nouveau bistro with steak, fish, crepes, and pastas. Jazz, poetry readings, performance art. No cover charge with dinner.

Sidewalk Café, 1401 Ocean Front Walk (399-5547), on Venice Beach. Acoustic and other cabaret performances, but the real show is out front, on the Venice Beach boardwalk. Dinner is American fare, burgers and sandwiches. Around $10.

The commonly used concert venues range from mouse-sized to massive. The Wiltern Theater (381-5005) has presented artists such as Suzanne Vega and The Church. The Hollywood Palladium (466-4311) is of comparable size. Mid-size acts head for the Universal Amphitheater (818-890-9421) and the Greek Theater (410-1062). Large indoor sports arenas, such as the Sports Arena (748-6131) or the Forum (419-3182), double as concert halls for large shows. Few performers dare to play at the over 100,000-seat L.A. Coliseum. In recent years, only U2, Bruce Springsteen, and the Rolling Stones have attempted this feat.

Dance Clubs

For excellent listings of both trendy and tried-and-true dance spots, try the *L.A. Weekly.* For more extensive listings of gay men's and women's bars contact the Gay and Lesbian Community Services Center (see Practical Information).

Coconut Teaszer, 8117 Sunset Blvd., W. Hollywood (654-4773). Big, popular club with DJs and live entertainment. One of L.A.'s best rock 'n' clubs. Must be 21; over 18 during weekend after-hours.

Rage, 8911 Santa Monica Blvd., W. Hollywood (652-7055). Dance and R&B sounds for a gay crowd. Full bar. Cover varies. Must be 21.

Obituary, 912 S. San Pedro St. (462-7442), downtown. For the gloom-and-doom, dress-in-black types. Alternative and industrial rock. Cover $10, before 11pm $5. Must be 18.

The Palms, 8572 Santa Monica Blvd. (652-6188), W. Hollywood's oldest women's bar. Top 40 dancing every night. Full bar. Low cover, if any. Must be 21.

Cover Girl, 9300 Jefferson Blvd. (870-1595). A big Westside bar with plenty of parking and room to dance. Open Sun.-Fri. 9pm-2am, Sat. 9pm-3am. Cover $5-10.

Code Blue L.A., 8450 W. 3rd St. (281-9903), W. Hollywood. Flashy upscale club for women who prefer women. Open Fri.-Sat. 9:30pm-3am. Cover $10.

Baxter's Underground, 1050 Gayley Ave., Westwood (208-3716). Hot spot with the UCLA crowd. Cover $5. Must be 21. Grill until 10pm.

Disneyland

The recent growth of Mike Eisner's Disney empire, with its exclusive Disney cable-TV channel, Touchstone movies, and new studio park in Florida, has breathed new life into the most famous, and still perhaps the best, amusement park in the world. Opened in 1955 through the vision of Walt Disney, "The Happiest Place On Earth" has delighted even the most hardened cynics. Nikita Khruschev was livid when true-blue Walt himself barred the Soviet premier from the park at the height of the Cold War. The attractions testify to the charm of child-like seduction, but the technological sophistication of the various amusements is no child's play. True, all this otherworldliness gets disturbing at times, especially with crowds of 75,000 per day jamming the park in search of artificial happiness, but one need only watch the kids in their euphoria to embrace Disney's magic.

Admission to the spotless, gleaming fantasy world is gained through the **Unlimited Use Passport** ($25.50, ages 3-11 $20.50). The A-E ticket system is now a relic, and visitors have unrestricted entrance to any attraction. (Park open summer daily 8am-1am; off-season, the park ordinarily closes at 5pm, though hours vary. Call 714-999-4000 for more information.)

Visitors enter the Magic Kingdom by way of **Main Street, U.S.A.** a collection of shops, arcades, and even a movie theater (showing continuous cartoons for free) that line a broad avenue leading to a replica of Sleeping Beauty's castle at the center of the park. There's also a bank, an information booth, lockers, and a first aid station. It is down Main Street that the **Main Street Electrical Parade** makes its way each summer night at 8:45pm and 11pm (earlier parade followed by fireworks). Floats and even humans wear thousands of multi-colored lights, making for a shocking nighttime display. This is one of Disneyland's most popular events; people begin lining the sidewalks on Main Street by 7pm for a front-row view.

Four "lands" branch off Main Street. **Tomorrowland,** to your immediate right at the top of Main Street, contains the park's best thrill rides, **Space Mountain** and the George Lucas-produced **Star Tours.** Moving counter-clockwise around the park, next comes **Fantasyland,** with the **Matterhorn** rollercoaster, some excellent rides for children, and the ever-popular if cloying **It's A Small World.** Next is Frontierland, with the **Thunder Mountain Railroad** coaster and **Tom Sawyer Island.** Last, but not least, swings **Adventureland,** with the **Jungle Cruise** and the **Swiss Family Robinson Treehouse.** In addition, tucked between Frontierland and Adventureland are two more areas that aren't official "lands." **New Orleans Square,** with **Pirates of the Caribbean** and the **Haunted Mansion,** offer some excellent dining. The other, **Critter Country,** claims Disneyland's newest super-attraction, **Splash Mountain,** a log ride that climaxes in a wet, 5-story drop.

Food services in the park range from sit-down establishments to decent fast-food eateries such as the Lunch Pad. Save much time and money by packing a picnic lunch and eating a big breakfast before you leave home. If you're looking for a martini, you'll be left high and dry: no alcohol is served in the park.

No matter when you go, you'll probably feel as if every Huey, Dewey, and Louie has picked the same day to visit. Fall months and weekdays are frequently less crowded than summer days and weekends. To avoid long waits, arrive shortly after the park opens. Lines for the most popular attractions are shorter just after opening and late at night; try midday and you'll see why some call it "Disneyline."

The Unofficial Guide to Disneyland ($8) is available from Simon and Schuster, Attn.: Mail Order Dept., 200 Old Tappan Rd., Old Tappan, NJ 07675 (201-767-5937). The authors have earned their mouska-ears by cramming the book with time-saving hints. The guide evaluates every attraction in the park, and the researchers suggest several specific itineraries for visitors, including adults with young children, senior citizens, and those pressed for time.

The park is located at one of the most famous addresses in the world: 1313 Harbor Blvd., in Anaheim in Orange County, bounded by Katella Ave., Harbor Blvd., Ball Rd., and West St. From L.A. take **bus** #460 from 6th and Flower St. downtown, about 1½ hours to the Disneyland hotel. (Service to the hotel from 4:53am, back to L.A. until 1:20am.) From the hotel take the free shuttle to Disneyland's portals. Also served by Airport Service, OCTD, Long Beach Transit, and Gray Line (see Public Transportation for prices). If you're **driving**, take the Santa Ana Fwy. to the Katella Ave. exit. Be forewarned: while parking in the morning should prove painless, leaving in the evening can hurt. In addition, when the park closes early, Disneygoers must contend with L.A.'s viscous, rush-hour traffic.

Other Amusement Parks

Six Flags Magic Mountain, 26101 Magic Mountain Pkwy. (818-367-5965), in Valencia, a 40-min. drive up I-5 from L.A. Magic Mountain. Not for novices. Home of the hairiest roller-coaster in Southern California. Other highlights include: The Revolution, a smooth metal coaster with a vertical 360° loop; Colossus, the world's largest wooden roller coaster; Free Fall, a simulated no-parachute fall out of the sky; Ninja, a coaster whose cars are suspended on a rail from above and are allowed to swing back and forth as they turn; and the park's newest coaster, the Viper, which is said to approach the limits of what coaster builders can do with G-forces without *really* hurting people. Coaster-o-phobes find peace at a crafts fair area and a children's playland with a Bugs Bunny theme. However, that few people over 48" tall come to Magic Mountain for the crafts fair or for the love of Bugs Bunny. This becomes especially apparent when you first encounter the lines for Colossus on a hot summer afternoon. Open Memorial Day to mid-September, and Christmas and Easter weeks Mon.-Fri. 10am-6pm, Sat. 10am-midnight, Sun. 10am-10pm; mid-September to Memorial Day (save Christmas and Easter holiday weeks) weekends only. Admission $22, seniors and children under 48" tall $11. Parking $4.

Knott's Berry Farm, 8039 Beach Blvd. (714-220-5200 for a recording), at La Palma Ave. in Buena Park just 5 mi. northeast of Disneyland. Take the Santa Ana Fwy. south, exit west on La Palma Ave. Bus #460 stops here on its way to Disneyland. An actual berry farm in its early days, Knott's now cultivates a country fair atmosphere with a recreated ghost town, Fiesta Village, Roaring Twenties Park, rides, and a replica of Independence Hall. The insane roller-coaster Montezuma's Revenge takes you through a backwards loop. A few summers back, Knott's unveiled a $12 million project featuring a Kingdom of the Dinosaurs ride through prehistory and 3 new thrill rides. The Chicken Dinner Restaurant has served good, inexpensive fowl since 1934. Open Sun.-Fri. 9am-midnight, Sat. 9am-1am; winter Mon.-Fri. 10am-6pm, Sat. 10am-10pm, Sun. 10am-7pm. Admission $21, seniors $15, ages 3-11 $7.

Raging Waters Park, 111 Raging Waters Dr. (714-592-6453 for recorded message, for directions 714-599-1251), in San Dimas. Near the intersection of the San Bernardino and Foothill Fwy. (I-10 and 210). Beat the heat with 44 acres and 5 million most excellent gallons of slides, pools, whitewater rafts, inner-tubes, fake waves, and a fake island. A cool but costly alternative to the beach. Hurl yourself over the 7-story water-slide "Drop Out" if you dare. Open Mon.-Thurs. 10am-6pm, Fri.-Sat. 10am-8pm, Sun. 10am-7pm. Admission $14.50, ages 3-5 $8.50, under 2 free.

The Desert

Mystics, misanthropes, and mescaline-users have long shared a fascination with the desert's vast spaces and austere scenery. California's desert region (and its sometimes brutal heat) has worked its spell on generations of passersby, from the Native Americans and pioneering fortune hunters of yesterday to today's city slickers disenchanted with smoggy L.A. The fascination stems partly from the desert's seasonal transformations: from a pleasantly warm refuge in winter to a technicolored floral landscape in spring to a blistering wasteland in summer. Considering that only six inches of rain trickle onto the parched sand each year, the desert supports an astonishing array of plant and animal life.

Southern California's desert is on the fringe of the North American Desert, a 500,000-sq.-mi. territory stretching east into Arizona and New Mexico, northeast into Nevada and Utah, and south into Mexico. The California portion claims desert parks, shabby towns around Death Valley, unlikely resorts such as Palm Springs, and dozens of ordinary highway settlements serving as pit stops for those speeding to points beyond.

Orientation

The desert divides roughly into two major regions with different climatic zones. The **Sonoran,** or **Low Desert** occupies southeastern California from the Mexican border north to Needles and west to the Borrego Desert; the **Mojave,** or **High Desert** spans the southcentral part of the state, bounded by the Sonoran Desert to the south, San Bernardino and the San Joaquin Valley to the west, the Sierra Nevada to the north, and Death Valley to the east.

The climate reflects the differences between the Low and High Desert, which stem essentially from the elevation. The Low Desert is flat, dry, and barren. The sparse vegetation makes shade-providing plants a necessary but scarce commodity, one that relies on an even rarer one, water. Humans and animals thrive in the oases in this area, the largest supporting the super-resort of Palm Springs. Despite the arid climate, much of this region has become agriculturally important. Water from the Colorado River irrigates Blythe, the Imperial Valley, and the Coachella Valley. Other points of interest are Anza-Borrego Desert State Park and the Salton Sea.

By contrast, the High Desert consists of foothills and plains nestled within mountain ranges approaching 5000 ft., making it cooler (by about 10°F in summer) and wetter. Though few resorts have sprung up, Joshua Tree National Monument remains a popular destination for campers. Barstow, the central city of the High Desert, often functions as a rest station on the way to Las Vegas or the Sierras.

Death Valley marks the eastern boundary of the Mojave but might best be considered a region unto itself, containing both high and low desert areas. Major highways cross the desert east-west: I-8 hugs the California-Mexico border, I-10 goes through Blythe and Indio on its way to Los Angeles, and I-40 crosses Needles to Barstow, where it joins I-15, which runs from Las Vegas and other points east to L.A.

Desert Survival

For special health and safety precautions in the desert, see Desert Survival in the Southwest regional introduction.

Palm Springs

On April 14, 1988, Palm Springs attracted national attention by electing Sonny Bono as its mayor. Although this event represented to most an example of democracy gone horribly, horribly awry, it was a perfectly logical political development in this desert resort town of 32,000. In fact, if anyone can epitomize the philosophy of Palm Springs, Mayor "Sunny" Bono can: nouveau riche, tan, relaxed, pleasantly superficial, and slightly detached from reality.

Palm Springs has long been a retreat from harsher climes. Centuries before any cigar-smoking developer arrived, the Agua Caliente (hot water) branch of the Cahuillian Indians tribe in the area enjoyed their winters bathing in the area's natural hot springs. Cahuillan wisdom in selecting a town site is still evident. The San Jacinto Mountains come grinding to a halt only blocks from Palm Canyon Drive, the city's main drag, providing a rugged backdrop to the downtown area. The San Gorgonio Pass weaves between Mt. San Jacinto and Mt. San Gorgonio, visible to the north. The smog that begrimes everything from L.A. to Banning (a town only minutes away from the Coachella Valley and Palm Springs) creeps through the pass rarely, and then only with its potency much diminished. The resulting clear, dry air makes even the summer heat bearable.

Sun and stars have long delineated Palm Springs. In the 1930s the fledgling resort began sending out publicity photos of Hollywood luminaries lounging poolside in the desert. The dateline PALM SPRINGS began to imply glamour, and the hotel business boomed. With things looking up, town leaders decided to get serious, incorporating in 1938. Since then, virtually every self-respecting multi-millionaire has purchased a home here.

Today the swimming pool reigns as the supreme emblem of Eden for the thousands who make their pilgrimage each year in unabashed worship of the sun. Spring vacation brings mobs of rowdy students, transforming Palm Springs into the Ft. Lauderdale of the West. Things turned ugly a few years ago when wild Spring Break partying erupted into a series of riots causing widespread mayhem and property destruction. "Cruising the strip" is now prohibited during Spring Break, with the police monitoring the streets.

The elevation changes over 5000 ft. from the base station to the terminal on Mt. San Jacinto at the **Palm Springs Aerial Tramway,** Tramway Dr., which intersects Rte. 111 just north of Palm Springs. Inside a quarter-hour, the gondolas glide from the arid foothills through five climate zones to snow and pine trees at 8516 ft., with a temperature change of as much as 50°F. Stairs from the deck lead up to a 360° viewing platform, which snow drifts cover except in high summer. (Round-trip tram $14, seniors $12, ages under 12 $9. Ride and dine service $4 extra.) The tramway station also provides the gateway to **Mt. San Jacinto State Park.** At the bottom of a lengthy concrete ramp lies the Long Valley Ranger Station (327-0222), which provides information on the park. Two short trails (under 1½ mi.) start here and introduce you to the sub-alpine ecology, with walks guided by volunteer naturalists. The Desert View Trail provides prettier peeks.

Local wealth has endowed Palm Springs with **The Desert Museum,** 101 Museum Dr. (325-7186), between Tahquitz-McCallum Way and Andreas Rd. a showcase of southwestern art that includes Native American and contemporary artists. The gorgeously posh museum also sponsors curator-led field trips ($3) to observe wildflowers or explore the canyons, leaving every Friday at 9am; some involve up to 9 mi. of hiking. (Open late Sept.-early June Tues.-Fri. 10am-4pm, Sat.-Sun. 10am-5pm. Admission $4, seniors $3, under 17 $2, accompanied children free. Free first Tues. of each month.)

The **Living Desert Reserve** in Palm Desert, 47900 Portola Ave. (346-5694), south of Rte. 111, contains tracts re-creating various desert environments, from Saharan to Sonoran, as well as slender-horned gazelles and bighorn sheep, both endangered species. Take bus #19 to Portola, and walk south 1 mi.; 6 mi. of nature trails await. (Open Sept. to mid-June daily 9am-5pm. Admission $3.50, ages 3-15 $1. Senior citizens $2.50 on Tues. Disabled access.)

The oases of **Indian Canyons** (325-5673) at the end of S. Palm Canyon Dr., feature large stands of Washingtonian palms, waterfalls, and gorgeous gorges popular with horseback riders and movie crews. (Open Sept.-July 4 daily 8:30am-5pm. Admission $3, ages 6-12 75¢, equestrians $3.50.)

But most visitors to Palm Springs have no intention of studying the desert or taking in high culture. Palm Springs means sunning and swimming, with no activity more demanding than drinking a gallon of iced tea each day to keep from dehydrating. When lazing about becomes tiresome, however, Palm Springs' ofther aquatic attractions should keep you occupied. Those not satisfied with the obligatory pool at their lodging should try the **Olympic-sized pool** at the Palm Springs Leisure Center, on Ramon Rd. just east of Sunrise Way (323-8278; open summer daily 11am-5pm, Tues. and Thurs. 7:30-9:30pm; off-season daily 11am-5pm; admission $3, ages 3-13 $2). For complete information about other recreactional facilities (including tennis and golf), call the Leisure Department at 323-8272. More aquatic excitement surfaces at **Oasis Water Park,** (325-7873) off Rte. 111 on Gene Autry Trail. The wave pool generates 5-ft. breakers, seven water slides generate screams. (Admission $15, ages 4-11 $10.)

For pure water-based pleasure, lounge in the naturally hot mineral pools of Desert Hot Springs, said to have curative properties. The **Desert Hot Springs Spa,**

10805 Palm Dr. (329-6495), has pools of different temperatures, a bar, saunas, and house masseurs. Unfortunately, on crowded days the decks are littered with cups and cigarette butts, and the pools awash in uninviting slicks of suntan oil. (Open daily 8am-10pm. Admission Mon.-Fri. $5, after 3pm $4; Sat.-Sun. $6, after 3pm $5; holidays $8. Refundable $3 lock deposit, $3 towel deposit, plus 50¢ rental.) The Hacienda Riviera Spa, 67375 Hacienda (329-7010), attracts younger bathers. (Open Sept.-June daily 9am-5pm; July Wed.-Mon. 9am-5pm. Admission $4, children $1.) Residents who want to hear good music invest in a high-tech stereo system or head to L.A. for the evening. Do what the locals do and catch a movie at Palms-to-Pines Theatre (346-3821), off Rte. 111 in Palm Desert, where a double feature costs $3. The behemoth disco with the ambience of a glitzy airplane hanger is Zelda's, 169 N. Indian Ave. (325-2375), Palm Springs' best S&M (Stand and Model, that is) bar. (Open daily 8pm-2am.) For a more elegant evening, Pernina's, 340 N. Palm Canyon Dr. (325-6544), offers lyrical piano music in a more intimate setting.

Palm Springs' accommodations and eateries cater to those with fat wallets. The cheapest lodgings are at nearby state parks and national forest campgrounds. The two best motel deals in Palm Springs are at the area Motel 6 locations: 595 E. Palm Canyon Dr. (325-6129; singles $24, doubles $30) or the more convenient 660 S. Palm Canyon Dr. (327-4700; singles $27, doubles $33). Both locations keep a big pool and A/C, and both fill quickly, sometimes up to six months in advance in winter. Some on-the-spot rooms are available around 9am; since no-shows are frequent, keep trying. The Mira Loma Hotel, 1420 N. Indian Ave. (320-1178), has 12 smartly decorated rooms in a one-story complex; all have refrigerators and color TV, and open onto the pool. (Singles Dec.-Sept. $33-48; winter $48-63. Children in summer only.) The Monte Vista Hotel, 414 N. Palm Canyon Dr. (325-5641), sits smack-dab downtown. (Rooms $45-50; June-Aug. $35-37.50. Suites with kitchens $60-65. Children in summer only.)

Before stocking up for a foray into the desert, head for one of the many supermarkets in Palm Springs. Ralph's, 1555 S. Palm Canyon Dr. (323-8446), and Vons, in the Palm Springs Mall on Tahquitz-McCallum (322-2192), are reliably low-priced. Palm Springs Leisure Center, on Sunrise at Ramon, and the Ruth Hardy Park, on Tamarisk, 4 blocks east of Indian Ave., make good picnic spots. For sit-down food and the best comida mexicana in Palm Springs, try the loud and busy El Gallito Cafe, 68820 Grove St., Cathedral City, 2 blocks west of Date Palm Dr.; look for the Mag Gas station on Rte. 111. The combinaciones (2 entrees, beans, rice, and tortillas; $6.25) are fit for a glutton. Take bus #20. (Open Sun.-Fri. 11am-9:30pm, Sat. 10am-9:30pm.) Cool Mexican mists pour out onto the sidewalk, inviting you into Las Casvelas Tennaza 222 S. Palm Canyon Dr. (325-2794). The nightly entertainment complements generous portions of south-of-the-border specialties ($6-12). (Open Mon.-Sat. 11am-10pm, Sun. 10am-10pm. The Sizzler, 725 S. Palm Canyon Dr., offers an all-you-can-eat tostada feast with fixings. (Open Sun.-Thurs. 11am-9:30pm, Fri.-Sat. 11am-10:30pm.) The Hamburger Hamlet, 105 N. Palm Canyon Dr. (325-3231), alases even the Poorest Yorick with scores of southern California burger specialties for around $6.

Palm Springs lies off I-10, 120 mi. east of L.A., just beyond a low pass that marks the edge of the Colorado Desert. The chamber of commerce is at 190 W. Amado (325-1577). Ask for a map ($1) and a free copy of The Desert Guide. (Open Mon.-Fri. 8am-5pm, Sat. 10am-2pm.) Amtrak, on Jackson St. in Indio, 25 mi. southeast of Palm Springs (connect to Greyhound in Indio) sends 3 trains per week to and from L.A. ($29). Greyhound, 311 N. Indian Ave. (325-2053) is much more convenient. Five buses per day run to and from L.A. ($16). Desert Stage Lines (367-3581) serves Twenty-nine Palms and Joshua Tree National Monument (3 buses per day, $8.50), with Friday service to L.A. ($20) and San Diego ($23.50). Sun Bus (343-3451) is the local bus system, serving all Coachella Valley cities (50¢, plus 25¢ per zone and 25¢ per transfer). Rent a car at Rent-a-Wreck, 67501 Rte. 111 (324-1766), for $25 per day, or $149 per week; 700 free mi., 10¢ each additional mi. (Must be 21 with major credit card.)

The Palm Springs **post office** sorts at 333 E. Amado Rd. (325-9631; open Mon.-Fri. 8:30am-5pm). Palm Springs' **ZIP code** is 92262; the **area code** is 619.

Joshua Tree National Monument

The low, scorching Sonoran Desert and the higher, cooler Mojave Desert meet here, resulting in over a half-million acres of extraordinarily varied scenery. The monument stars the Joshua Tree, a member of the lily and U2 family whose erratic limbs sometimes reach 50 ft. in height. The Mormons who came through here in the 19th century thought the crooked branches resembled the arms of Joshua leading them to the promised land. Spare forests of gangly Joshuas extend for miles in the high central and eastern portions of the monument, punctuated by great piles of quartz monzonite boulders, some over 100 ft. high. This bizarre landscape emerged over millenia as hot magma pushed to the surface and erosion exposed the rocks to the elements. Together, the two forces have created fantastic textures, shapes, and rock albums. Alongside the natural environment appear vestiges of human existence: ancient rock pictographs, dams built in the 19th century in order to catch the meager rainfall for livestock, and the ruins of gold mines that operated as late as the 1940s.

Over 80% of the monument is designated wilderness area; for those experienced in **backcountry desert hiking and camping,** Joshua Tree provides a fantastic opportunity to explore truly remote territory. Hikers should go to one of the visitors centers for the rules and recommendations on use of isolated areas of the monument, and for a topographic map ($2.50). The wilderness lacks water except when a flash flood comes roaring down a wash, and even this evaporates quickly. Carry at least a gallon of water per person per day; two during the summer months. You must register at roadside boxes before setting out (see maps), to let the monument staff know your location, and to prevent your car from being towed from a roadside parking lot.

Less hardy desert rats can also enjoy Joshua Tree for a day or a weekend in relative comfort. The most popular time, as with other desert parks, is **wildflower season** (mid-March to mid-May), when the floor of the desert explodes in yucca, verbena, cottonwood, mesquite, and dozens of other floral variations. Summer is the hottest and slowest season. Bear in mind that no off-road driving is permitted.

A drive along the winding road from Twenty-nine Palms to the town of Joshua Tree (34 mi.) passes by the **Wonderland of Rocks,** a spectacular concentration of rock formations. The slightly longer drive between Twenty-nine Palms and I-10 through the monument offers a sampling of both desert landscapes. Along the way on both of these tours, explore as many of the side roads as time allows—some are paved, some dirt, and some suitable only for four-wheel-drive vehicles; signs indicate which vehicles are safe. One site not to miss, **Key's View,** off the park road just west of Ryan Campground, offers a stupendous vista. You can see as far as Palm Springs and the Salton Sea on a clear day. The **palm oases** (Twenty-nine Palms, Forty-nine Palms, Cottonwood Spring, Lost Palms) also merit a side trip, as does the **Cholla Cactus Garden,** off Pinto Basin Rd.

A number of hiking trails lead to the most interesting features of Joshua Tree: five oases, mine ruins, and fine vantage points. Short trails run near picnic areas and campsites. Visitors center brochures describe these trails, which range from a mere 200 yd. (the Cholla Cactus Garden) to 35 mi. (a section of the California Riding and Hiking Trail). The degree of difficulty varies almost as widely; the staff at the visitors center can help you choose a trail. Plan on at least one hour per mi. on even relatively short trails.

Campgrounds in the monument accept no reservations, except for group sites at **Cottonwood, Sheep Pass,** and **Indian Cove,** where Ticketron handles reservations (mandatory at these 3 sites). Sites are also available at **White Tank** (closed in summer), **Belle, Black Rock Canyon, Hidden Valley, Ryan,** and **Jumbo Rocks.** All campsites have tables, fireplaces, and pit toilets; all are free except Cottonwood ($6) and Black Rock Canyon ($8), which have the only available water. You must bring your own firewood. If your trip to Joshua Tree is an educational activity contributing to a degree, you can secure a fee waiver at one of the group sites; write to the monument on your best official stationery and explain your "bona fide educational/study group" purposes. There is unlimited **backcountry camping.** Pitch your tent more than 500 ft. from a trail, 1 mi. from a road. (14-day max. stay Oct.-May; 30 days max. in summer. Entrance fee $2 per individual or $5 per vehicle, good for a one-week stay at any California state park.)

Joshua Tree National Monument occupies a vast area northeast of Palm Springs, about 160 mi. (3-3½ hr. by car) from west L.A. The monument is ringed by three highways: I-10 to the south, Rte. 62 (Twenty-nine Palms Hwy.) to the west and north, and Rte. 177 to the east. From I-10, the best approaches are via Rte. 62 from the west, leading to the towns of Joshua Tree and **Twenty-nine Palms** on the northern side of the monument, and via an unnumbered road that exits the interstate about 25 mi. east of Indio. **Desert Stage Lines** (367-3581), based in Palm Springs, stops in Twenty-nine Palms.

The monument's main **visitors center** offers displays, lectures, and maps at 74485 National Monument Dr., Twenty-nine Palms 92277 (367-7511), ¼ mi. off Rte. 62. (Open daily 8am-5pm.) Another visitors center sits at the southern gateway approximately 7 mi. north of I-10 (exit 4 mi. west of the town of Chiriaco Summit); an information kiosk adjoins the west entrance on Park Blvd., several mi. southeast of the town of Joshua Tree.

Barstow

Barstow is an adequate place to prepare for forays into the desert. Once a booming mining town, this desert oasis (pop. 20,000) now thrives on business from local military bases, tourists, and truckers. Stop in at the **California Desert Information Center,** 831 Barstow Rd. (256-3591), for free maps and information on hiking, camping, and exploring.

What Barstow lacks in charm (and it truly lacks) is made up for by its abundant supply of inexpensive motels and eateries. To prevent a Big Mac attack in this fast-food town, head for the **Barstow Station McDonald's,** on E. Main St. Constructed from old locomotive cars, this Mickey D's serves more burgers per annum than any other U.S. outfit. **Vons** on E. Main St., has a variety of supermarket specialties but no Filets-O-Fish.

The **El Rancho Motel,** 112 E. Main St. (256-2401), convenient to the Greyhound and Amtrak stations, has clean, bright rooms with TV, A/C, pool. (Singles and doubles $27-37.) The **Economy Motel,** 1590 Coolwater Lane (256-1737), has singles for $22, doubles for $29. The **Calico KOA,** I-15 and Ghost Town Rd. (254-2311), is ironically crowded with Ghost Town devotees. (Sites $13, with electricity $15, full hookup $16. Each additional person $2.50.)

Barstow, the western terminus of I-40, orders drinks midway between Los Angeles and Las Vegas on I-15. At the **Amtrak** station, N. 1st St. (800-872-7245), you can get on or off a train—that's all. Two trains per day go to L.A. ($31) and San Diego ($50); one per day ventures to Las Vegas ($42). **Greyhound,** 120 S. 1st St. (256-8757), at W. Main St., sees 12 buses per day to L.A. ($16.50) and Vegas ($27). (Open daily 8am-6pm.)

Death Valley

Though Milton and Dante couldn't write to save their hell-bound lives, they could have received some inspiration, or perhaps a hint of their fate by visiting Death Valley. Nowhere in England, Italy, Paradise or Purgatory even begins to approach the searing everyday temperatures here in the summer.

The *average* high temperature in July is 116°, with a nighttime low of 88°. Ground temperatures hover near an egg-frying 200°.

Much of the lanscape resembles the Viking photographs of the surface of Mars, with its reddish crags and canyons, immobile and stark. The strangeness of the landscape lends it a certain beauty. The earth-hues of the sands and rocks change hourly in the variable sunlight. The elevation ranges from 11,049-ft. Telescope Peak down to Badwater, the lowest point in the hemisphere at 282 ft. below sea level. The region features pure white salt flats on the valley floor, impassable mountain slopes, and huge, shifting sand dunes. As in the best of Milton's work, nature appears to have focused all of its extremes and varieties here at a single location.

The region sustains a surprisingly intricate web of Dantean life. Casual tourists and naturalists alike may observe a tremendous variety of desert dwellers, such as the great horned owl, roadrunner, coyote, and kit fox, gecko, chuckwalla, and raven.

Practical Information

Emergency: 911.

Visitor Information: Furnace Creek Visitor Center (786-2331), on Rte. 190 in the east-central section of the valley. For information by mail, write the Superintendent, Death Valley National Monument, Death Valley 92328. Simple and informative museum. Slide show every ½ hr., nightly lecture. Office open daily 8am-5pm. Center open daily 8am-5pm; Nov.-Easter 8am-8pm.

Entrance Fee: $5 per car. Good for 7 days.

Ranger Stations: Grapevine, junction of Rte. 190 and 267 near Scotty's Castle; Stove Pipe Wells on Rte. 190; Wildrose, Rte. 178, 20 mi. south of Emigrant via Emigrant Canyon Dr.; and Shoshone, outside the southeast border of the valley at the junction of Rte. 178 and 127. Weather report, weekly naturalist program, and park information posted at each station. Emergency help too. All open year-round.

Gasoline: Fill up outside Death Valley at Olancha, Shoshone, or Beatty, NV. Otherwise, you'll pay about 20¢ per gallon more at the stations across from the Furnace Creek Visitors Center, in Stove Pipe Wells Village, and at Scotty's Castle (all Chevron). Don't play chicken with the fuel gauge: Death Valley takes no prisoners. Propane gas available at the Furnace Creek Chevron; white gas at the Furnace Creek Ranch and Stove Pipe Wells Village stores; diesel fuel pumped in Las Vegas, Pahrump, and Beatty, NV, and in Lone Pine, Olancha, Ridgecrest, and Trona, CA.

Groceries and Supplies: Furnace Creek Ranch Store. Expensive and well-stocked. Open daily 7am-9pm. Stove Pipe Wells Village Store. Same price range. Open daily 7am-8pm. Both sell charcoal and firewood. Ice available at the Furnace Creek Chevron and the Stove Pipe Wells Village Store.

Post Office: Furnace Creek Ranch (786-2223). Open Mon.-Fri. 7am-7pm. ZIP code: 92328.

Area Code: 619.

Quite isolated, Death Valley spans over 2 million acres (1½ times the size of Delaware). However, visitors from the south will find it only a small detour on the road to Sierra Nevada's Eastern slope; those from the north will find it reasonably convenient to Las Vegas. The monument lies about 300 mi. from Los Angeles, 500 mi. from San Francisco, and 140 mi. from Las Vegas.

There is no regularly scheduled public transportation into Death Valley, only charter buses make the run. Las Vegas-Tonopah-Reno Stage Lines (702-384-1230) sends an occasional charter between Las Vegas and Furnace Creek. Bus tours within Death Valley are monopolized by Fred Harvey's Death Valley Tours, the same organization that runs Grand Canyon tours. Excursions begin at Furnace Creek Ranch, which also handles reservations (786-2345, ext. 61; $15-25).

The best way to get into and around Death Valley is by car. With two or more Death Valley pilgrims to share gas expenses, renting a car will prove far cheaper and more flexible than any unreliable bus tour. The nearest agencies rent in Las Vegas, Barstow, and Bishop. Be sure to rent a reliable car: this is emphatically not the place to cut corners.

Of the 13 monument entrances, most visitors choose Rte. 190 from the east. The road is well-maintained, the pass much less steep, and you arrive more quickly at the visitors center, located at the approximate midpoint of the 130-mi. north-south route through the valley. But since most of the major sights adjoin not Rte. 190 but the north/south road, the daytripper at the helm of a trusty vehicle should enter from the southeast (Rte. 178 west from Rte. 127 at Shoshone) or the north (direct to Scotty's Castle via NV Rte. 267 from U.S. 95) in order to see more of the monument. Unskilled mountain drivers should probably not attempt to enter via the smaller roads Titus Canyon or Emigrant Canyon Dr., since no guard rails prevent cars from sailing over the canyon's precipitous cliffs.

Eighteen-wheelers have replaced 18-mule teams, but transportation around Death Valley still takes stubborn determination. Radiator water (*not* for drinking) is avaliable at critical points on Rte. 178 and 190 and NV Rte. 374, but not on any unpaved roads. Obey the signs that advise "four-wheel-drive only." Those who do bound along the backcountry trails by four-wheel-drive should carry extra tires, gas, oil, water (both to drink and for the radiator), and spare parts; also leave an itinerary with the visitors center. Be sure to check which roads are closed—especially in summer.

Hitching is suicidal. Don't do it.

Death Valley has **hiking** trails to challenge the mountain lover, the desert daredevil, the backcountry camper, and the fair-weather dayhiker. Ask a ranger for advice (see Sights below). Backpackers and dayhikers alike should inform the visitors center of their trip, and take appropriate topographic maps. During the summer the National Park Service recommends that valley floor hikers spend several days prior to the hike acclimating to the heat and low humidity, plan a route along roads where assistance is readily available, and outfit a hiking party of at least two people with another person following in a vehicle to monitor the hikers' progress. Wearing **thick socks** and carrying salve to treat feet parched by the nearly 200° earth also makes good sense.

Check the weather forecasts before setting out—all roads and trails can disappear during a winter rainstorm. The dryness of the area, plus the lack of any root and soil system to retain moisture, transforms canyon and valley floors into deadly torrents during heavy rains. For other important tips, see Desert Survival in the introduction to the Southwest.

Accommodations

Fred Harvey's Amfac Consortium retains its vise-like grip on the trendy, resort-style, incredibly overpriced concessions in Death Valley. Look for cheaper accommodations in the towns near Death Valley: Olancha (west), Shoshone (southwest), Tecopa (south), and Beatty, NV (northwest).

The National Park Service maintains nine **campgrounds,** none of which accepts reservations. Call the visitors center to check availability and prepare for a battle if you come during peak periods (see below). Park Service campgrounds include **Mesquite Springs** ($5), **Stove Pipe Wells** ($4), **Emigrant** (free), **Furnace Creek** ($8), **Sunset** (tent sites $8, RV sites $4), **Texas Springs** ($5), **Wildrose** (free), but camping fees are not pursued with vigor in the summer. All campsites have toilets; all except Thorndike and Mahogany Flat have water; all except Sunset and Stove Pipe Wells have tables. Open fires are prohibited at Stove Pipe Wells and Sunset; bring a stove and fuel or eat raw meat. Fires are permitted at Thorndike and Mahogany Flat, though there are no fireplaces; collecting wood, alive or dead, is *verboten* anywhere in the monument. **Backcountry camping** is free and legal, as long as you check in at the visitors center and pitch tents at least 1 mi. from main roads and 5 mi. from any established campsite.

Sights

When doing Death Valley in one day, adopt a north-south or south-north route, rather than head directly to the Furnace Creek Visitors Center via Rte. 190, which connects east with west.

The visitors center and museum (see Practical Information) offers information on tours, hikes, and special programs. The nearby museums amuse as well. If you're interested in astronomy, speak to one of the rangers; some set up telescopes at Zabriskie Point and offer freelance shows. In **wildflower season** (Feb. to mid-April), tours run to some of the best places for viewing the display. **Hells Gate** and **Jubilee Pass** are especially beautiful, **Hidden Valley** even more so, though it is accessible only by a difficult, 7-mi. four-wheel-drive route from Teakettle Junction (itself 25 mi. south of Ubehebe Crater).

Artist's Drive is a one-way loop off Rte. 178, beginning 10 mi. south of the visitors center. The road twists and winds through rock and dirt canyons on the way to **Artist's Palette,** a rainbow of green, yellow, and red mineral deposits in the hillside. The dizzying 9 mi. turn back upon themselves again and again, ending up on the main road only 4 mi. north of the drive's entrance. About 5 mi. south of this exit, you'll reach **Devil's Golf Course,** a huge plane of spiny salt crust, the precipitate left from the evaporation of ancient Lake Manly. Amble across this gigantic sponge; the salt underfoot sounds like crunching snow.

Immortalized by Antonioni's film of the same name, **Zabriskie Point** is a marvelous place, particularly at sunrise, from which to view Death Valley's corrugated badlands. The trip up to **Dante's View**, 15 mi. by paved road south off Rte. 190 (take the turn-off beyond Twenty Mule Team Canyon exit) will reward you with views of Badwater, Furnace Creek Ranch, the Panamint Range, and, on a clear day, the Sierra Nevadas. Faintly visible are the tracks of the 20-mule-team wagons across Devil's Golf Course, itself intricately patterned. Common here are snows in mid-winter and low temperatures anytime but mid-summer.

Late November through February are the coolest (40-70° in the valley, freezing temperatures and snow in the mountains) and also the wettest months, with infrequent but violent rainstorms which can flood the canyons. Desert wildflowers bloom in March and April, accompanied by moderate temperatures and tempestuous winds that can whip sand and dust into an obscuring mess for hours or even days. Over 50,000 people vie for Death Valley's facilities and sights during the **49ers Encampment** festival, held the last week of October and the first two weeks of November. Other times that bring traffic jams, congested trails and campsites, hour-long lines for gasoline, and four-hour waits at Scotty's Castle include three-day winter holiday weekends, Thanksgiving, Christmas through New Year's Day, and Easter.

Central Coast

San Franciscans and Los Angelenos rarely agree. However, both northerners and southerners beam proudly at the mention of the Central Coast, proclaiming it the most dramatic coastline in California—if not the world. This coast combines the best of southern and northern California: wide beaches on swimmable waters without the pollution and frenetic autoculture of the southland plus lush, breathtaking scenery—from rocky cliffs to glorious parks—and cozy watering holes without northern pretensions to urbanity.

Big Sur

Big Sur simultaneously welcomes and shuns visitors. Its dramatic beaches, swirling waters, and acres of moist redwood forest—populated by an abundance of wildlife—invite all, while the fickle weather can prove unsettling. Powerful winter storms in 1983 carried much of the coastal highway into the Pacific. Even as the sun shines, Big Sur's winds can rock buses, tip cows, and make even the bravest hippie very uncomfortable. At the same time, the human residents of Big Sur do little to make strangers feel at home. This "non-town" has no banks, no theaters, no mini-golf, in keeping with its history as an artistic and beatnik hideaway. While perfectly willing to sell tourists sandwiches and souvenirs, residents hide their houses in the woods and religiously remove the sign giving directions to their favorite beach.

The Big Sur area state parks and wilderness areas provide exquisite natural settings for dozens of outdoor activities, including tremendous hiking. The northern end of **Los Padres National Forest** has been designated the **Ventana Wilderness,** which contains the popular 12-mi. **Pine Ridge Trail.** Pick up a map and a required permit at the USFS **ranger station** (667-2423), ½ mi. south of Pfeiffer Big Sur State Park, 2 mi. north of the post office. **Pfeiffer Big Sur State Park** keeps six trails of varying lengths; pick up a map (25¢) at the park entrance. Try the short but steep **Valley View Trail;** its apex offers a remarkable view of redwood country. Big Sur jealously guards USFS-operated **Pfeiffer Beach,** reached by an unmarked narrow road roughly 100 yd. south of the ranger station. Take the road 2 mi. to the parking area, then follow the footpath to the beach. The small cove, partially protected from the Pacific by a huge offshore rock formation, is safe for wading, but riptides make swimming risky. For the uninhibited, a nude beach lies bare just to the north of the cove.

Big Sur is not *all* nature and no civilization, however. The **Coast Gallery** (667-2301), on Rte. 1 just above the Pfeiffer Big Sur State Park, has long showcased works by local artists, with a collection of paintings and lithographs by *Tropic of Cancer* author Henry Miller, who lived near here for 17 years. Miller's casual reminiscences and prophetic ecstasies made scores of readers aware of Big Sur, and his more explicit works drew many to Big Sur seeking the sex cult he purportedly led. (Open daily 9am-6pm.)

The **Fernwood Motel** (see below) includes a bar, a grocery store, a cheap gas pump, and the **Fernwood Burger Bar,** Rte. 1 (667-2422). Fish and chips or chicken cost $5.50-6.50; hamburgers start at $3. (Open daily 11:30am-midnight.) The **Center Deli,** right beside the Big Sur post office, serves the cheapest sandwiches ($2.50-5) in the area. (Open daily 8am-9pm; winter 8am-8pm.) At the Monterey-Salinas Transit bus stop, **Café Amphora** (667-2660), in **Nepenthe Restaurant,** serves coffee and liquor on an outdoor patio spectacularly situated on the edge of a Big Sur cliff. (Open daily 11:30am-4pm and 5-9:30pm.)

Campgrounds are abundant, beautiful, and cheap. The **Fernwood Motel,** Rte. 1 (667-2422), 2 mi. north of the post office, offers friendly management, 65 campsites, and cabins for the tentless. (Registration 8am-midnight. Sites $14, with hookup $16. Cabin doubles $47.) The **Pfeiffer Big Sur State Park** (667-2315), just south of Fernwood and 26 mi. south of Carmel, is a popular inland spot; sometimes all 218 developed campsites (no hookups) are full. (Hot showers. Sites $10. Reservations 800-444-7275.) **Limekiln,** south of Big Sur (667-2403), runs a private campground with grocery, showers, and beach access. (60 sites. $9 per vehicle, $4 per person. $3 reservation fee.) Los Padres National Forest includes two USFS campgrounds: **Plaskett Creek** (927-4211), south of Limekiln near Jade Cove, and **Kirk Creek,** about 5 mi. north of Jade Cove. (Toilets and cold running water. Sites $8, hikers $2. No reservations.)

Big Sur stretches between Salmon Cove in the south (17 mi. from San Simeon's Hearst Castle) and Carmel in the north, two groovy hours by car south of the cultivated Monterey Peninsula. For a guide to the area, send a stamped, self-addressed envelope to the **Chamber of Commerce,** P.O. Box 87, Big Sur 93920 (667-2100). The **post office** mails on Rte. 1 (667-2305), next to the Center Deli. Big Sur's **ZIP code** is 93290; the **area code** is 408.

Near Big Sur: Hearst Castle

In San Simeon did William Hearst a stately pleasure dome decree. Popularly known as Hearst Castle (927-2020), the Hearst San Simeon Historic Monument perches high on a hill 5 mi. east of Rte. 1 near San Simeon. Satirized as Charles Foster Kane's "Xanadu" in Orson Welles' *Citizen Kane,* the castle lives up to every adjective ever applied to the state of California itself: opulent, plastic, beautiful, fake, dazzling, and overreading. William Randolph Hearst, tycoon of yellow journalism, began building this Spanish-Moorish indulgence in 1919, but abandoned the project during the Depression. The three houses and two pools are undeniably grand, yet simultaneously unsettling. Once a weekend getaway for Hearst's celebrity friends, today the castle has an air of blighted bloom. On one side of the hill the remains of Hearst's miniature zoo rot peacefully, long abandoned.

Visitors have a choice of four **tours,** each an hour and 45 minutes long. You can take all four in one day, but each costs $10 (ages 6-12 $5, under 6 free, if well-behaved—otherwise they meet the fate of Kane's Rosebud). Groups are taken up the hill in old school buses, shepherded around, then taken back down. Tours are given at least once per hour October through March from 8am until 3pm (except tour #4, which runs April-Nov. only), later and more frequently according to demand in summer. To see the Castle in summer, make MISTIX reservations (800-444-7275) since tours sell out quickly. The gates to the visitors center open in summer at 6am, in winter at 7am; tickets go on sale daily at 8am.

Monterey

In the 1940s, John Steinbeck's Monterey swam as a crusty coastal town geared to sardine fishing and canning. When Steinbeck revisited his beloved Cannery Row around 1960, he scornfully wrote that the area had sea-changed into a tourist trap. He was right. Cannery Row and Fisherman's Wharf have converted their packing plants to souvenir malls and wax museums. Because residents treat with dignity at least some of the area's history—both as a canning town and former capital of Spanish and Mexican Alta California—and because the sun hasn't left the area, visitors should forgive Monterey's crasser side.

The annual **Monterey Jazz Festival** (373-3366) during the third week in September comprises five concerts over three days, attracting crowds from all over California. Season tickets ($80-90) sell out by the end of May. The **Blues Festival** (394-2652) occurs in late June, the annual **county fair** in mid-August. All three events take place at the fairgrounds, south of Fremont St.

The **Monterey Bay Aquarium,** 866 Cannery Row (648-4888), lives in glorious symbiosis with its namesake bay. Both exposed to ocean currents and free of major industry, the bay remains an incredibly unpolluted body of water. The aquarium pumps in raw, unfiltered seawater, making the tanks an almost exact duplicate of the environment in the bay—right down to the dozens of species of algae and the simulated waves. In addition to standards like enormous octopi and docile starfish, the aquarium contains 30-ft. tall kelps, diving birds, and a clever exhibit that allows otters to be seen from both above and below the water's surface. A special show of sharks from around the world will run from January 13 to October 21, 1991. The aquarium packs tourists like sardines on holidays and can clog in the mornings, but after 3pm things calm down. (Open daily 10am-6pm. Admission $9, seniors and students $6.50, ages 3-12 $4.)

On the waterfront lies **Cannery Row** to the southeast of the aquarium. It could have been a contender. Once a depressed center for languishing sardine-packing plants, this ¾-mi. street has magically converted into glitzy mini-malls, bars, and discos. To make your visit more endurable, visit one of the **winetasting** rooms for a free sample of California's Lethe. Designed as a temporary mask for some ugly construction, the **Great Cannery Row Mural** stretches along the 700 block of the row; each of the 50 large panels makes a local artist's statement about Monterey's history and lore. The sum effect is quite moving. Unfortunately, the mural will come down when the construction is complete.

At the south end of the row floats yet another **Fisherman's Wharf,** built in 1846. The fishermen have left, and the wharf now lures tourists with expensive restaurants and shops selling seashells and Steinbeck novels. The best thing about the wharf, and maybe Monterey in general, is the **smoked salmon sandwiches** ($5-5.50) sold by local vendors. Made with fresh sourdough bread, cream cheese, and plenty of the local salmon (smoked right on the pier), these sandwiches make a great breakfast or lunch.

Ungreen **Monterey State Historic Park** holds a group of historic adobe buildings maintained by the state, headquarted at the **Cooper-Molera complex,** 525 Polk St. (649-7118). Two of the park's buildings are museums near Fisherman's Wharf. In 1846, Commodore John Sloat raised the Stars and Stripes over the **Custom House,** claiming all of California for the U.S. Today, goods typical of the days when Monterey was the busiest port in Mexican Alta California clutter the place. Next door, the **Pacific House** has a less impressive display of costumes and artifacts. (Both open daily 10am-5pm; winter 10am-4pm. Custom House free. Pacific House admission $1, ages 6-17 50¢.) Farther from the water, the park's four **adobe houses** are accessible only by tours, given six times per day, five in the winter; check at any of the houses for exact times and addresses. The abodes' 19th-century owners include Thomas Larkin, the U.S. consul in Monterey who helped persuade Commodore Sloat to annex the territory, and Robert Louis Stevenson, who stayed in Monterey in 1879. (Admission $1 per house, ages 6-17 50¢; all 4 $3.50.) For the hardcore history fan, a 90-minute tour of ten buildings and five gardens departs from Colton Hall on weekends at 11am and 2pm ($3.50, under 18 $2). Better yet, buy *The Path of History,* a walking tour book, from Colton Hall and the Pacific House ($2). In the same neighborhood as the adobes lies the **Monterey Peninsula Museum of Art,** 559 Pacific St. (372-5477), with a downstairs exhibit of monochrome works from across the centuries in both Europe and the U.S., an upstairs collection of Western art, including works by Charlie Russell, and another gallery for temporary shows. (Open Tues.-Sat. 10am-4pm, Sun. 1-4pm. Suggested donation $2.)

The **Casa de Gutierrez,** 590 Calle Principal, an 1841 structure now serving as a Mexican restaurant, offers a more intimate adobe experience. Many entrees ($7-8) take their names from figures in Monterey's history; try the heaping Cooper's tostada, a wonderful chicken creation. (Open Mon.-Thurs. 11am-9pm, Fri.-Sun. 10am-10pm.) For a decadent breakfast, head to **Belleci's,** 470 Alvarado, where the specialty is the *speengie,* a hunk of dough fried before your eyes until crisp outside and fluffy inside, then topped with cinnamon and sugar (75¢) or fruit and whipped cream ($1.50). (Open Mon.-Wed. 8am-4pm, Thurs.-Fri. 7am-4pm.) The clean bay has plenty of squid, crab, red snapper, and salmon. Aside from the snacks on the wharf, seafood dinners usually run high; however, many restaurants have money-saving early bird specials between 4pm and 6:30pm. You also don't have to eat at a specifically fish-oriented joint; Thai and Japanese places have access to the same fresh delicacies.

The rates at Monterey's hotels and motels vary by day, month, and proximity to an important event, such as the Jazz Festival. The visitors bureau's free *Monterey Peninsula Hotel and Motel Guide* has prices for all accommodations in the area. Generally, hotels along **Fremont Street** in Monterey and **Lighthouse Avenue** in nearby Pacific Grove are the most reasonable. The **Monterey Peninsula Youth Hostel (AYH)** (649-0375) theoretically has no fixed location, but has stayed in the gym of the Monterey High School on Larkin St. for the past few summers. The hostel lacks a kitchen and mattresses lie directly on the floor, but the friendly staff tries to make up for the deficiencies by providing cheap food, free games, and lots of information. (Lockout 9am-6pm. Curfew 11pm. Open mid-June to mid-Aug.) **Motel 6,** 2124 N. Fremont St. (646-8585), offers a rare phenomenon: prices that remain constant year-round. (Singles $36. Doubles $42.) As a result, the motel often fills long in advance—make reservations as early as possible. The **Vagabond Motel,** 2120 N. Fremont St. (372-6066), has prices that go as low as $36 for a single, but fluctuate widely. Reserve two weeks ahead. The **Veterans Memorial Park Campgroud,** Via del Rey (646-3865), is 1½ mi. from the town center. Take Skyline Dr. off W.R. Holman Hwy. (Rte. 68). From downtown, take Pacific St. south, turn right on Jefferson, and follow the signs; or take bus #3. First come, first camped—arrive before 3pm in summer and on winter weekends. (Showers. Sites $10, hikers $2.)

Monterey shares the Monterey Peninsula with Pacific Grove to the west, Ft. Ord and Salinas to the east, and **Carmel-by-the-Sea,** to the south. Depending on your view, Carmel is either an undersized town or an oversized shopping mall, though it has a very pleasant, sparkling-white beach, plus a restored Spanish mission. Just south of Carmel on Rte. 1 is the **Point Lobos Reserve** (624-4909), a state-run, 1276-acre wildlife sanctuary, popular with skindivers, dayhikers, and naturalists. On weekends a line of cars frequently waits to get in by 8am; park outside the tollbooth and walk or bike in for free. (Open daily 9am-7pm; winter 9am-5pm. Admission $3 per car. Map 50¢. No dogs allowed.)

The **Monterey Peninsula Chamber of Commerce,** 380 Alvarado St. (649-1770), sits on Monterey's main commercial street. Get advance information by writing to P.O. Box 1770, Monterey 93942. (Open Mon.-Fri. 8:30am-5pm.) The **post office** sorts at 565 Hartnell (372-5803; open Mon.-Fri. 9am-5pm). Monterey's **ZIP code** is 93940; the **area code** is 408.

Santa Cruz

Santa Cruz sports an uncalculated hipness that other coastal towns can only envy. Often seen as the epitome of California cool, the town's beaches and bookstores even lure visitors from San Francisco, 75 mi. to the north. Santa Cruz's location is crucial to its identity. Without a beach, it would be Berkeley; with a better one, it would be Coney Island. The 7.1 richter earthquake of 1989 had its epicenter only 10 mi. away from this mellow town, doing serious damage to Santa Cruz's center. Tremors destroyed the pleasant Pacific Garden Mall and forced many shops to relocate in euphemistic "pavilions" (tents) until they could find new homes. Though by no means a pile of rubble, the city's condemned, fenced-off buildings provide a dramatic counterpoint to the youthful cheerfulness of the campus and boardwalk.

A 3-block arcade of ice cream, caramel apples, games, rides, and taco restaurants, the **Boardwalk** (432-5590) dominates the Santa Cruz beach area. The classiest rides are two old veterans: the 1929 **Giant Dipper** roller coaster, one of the largest wooden coasters in the country ($2) and the 1911 Looff Carousel, accompanied by an 1894 organ ($1.25). (Boardwalk open May 27-Sept. 2 daily; weekends the rest of the year. Call for hours.)

The broad and sandy **Santa Cruz beach** generally jams with high school students from San Jose during summer weekends. When looking for solitude, try the banks of the San Lorenzo River immediately east of the boardwalk. To just hang out, nude sunbathers should head for the **Red White and Blue Beach.** Take Rte. 1 north to just before Davenport and look for the line of cars to your right; women should not go alone. ($5 per car.) Those who don't feel like paying for the privilege of an all-over tan should try the **Bonny Doon Beach,** 11 mi. north of Santa Cruz on Bonny Doon Rd. off Rte. 1, a free but somewhat untamed surfer hangout.

A pleasant 10-minute walk along the beach to the southwest will take you to two madcap and mayhem-filled Santa Cruz museums. The first is the unintentionally amusing **Shroud of Turin Museum,** 544 Cliff Dr. (423-7658), at St. Joseph's shrine. Earnest curators shepherd you through many exhibits, including one of only two replicas of Jesus' alleged burial shroud, "casting doubt" on recent Carbon-14 tests that suggest it dates back only to the Renaissance. (Open Sat.-Sun. noon-5pm. Call to visit during the week.) Just south lies Lighthouse Point, home to the **Santa Cruz Surfing Museum** (429-3429), the first of its kind in the world. The cheerful, one-room museum features vintage boards and surfing videos which show little sign of the tragedy that inspired its creation; the lighthouse and gallery were given in memory of a local boy who drowned in a surfing accident. (Open Wed.-Mon. noon-4pm. Donation.) You can still watch people challenge the sea right below the museum's cliff. The stretch of Pacific along the eastern side of the point offers famous **Steamer Lane,** a hotspot for local surfers for over 50 years. A recent rash of drownings has inspired a sign there asking "lame tourists" not to surf; novices should stick to the city beach.

The 2000-acre **University of California at Santa Cruz (UCSC)** hangs out, in its entirety, 5 mi. northwest of downtown. Take bus #1 or ride your bike along a scenic path to the campus. Then-governor Ronald Reagan's attempt to make it a "riot-proof campus" without a central point where radicals could inflame a crowd resulted in beautiful, sprawling grounds. University buildings appear intermittently, like startled wildlife, amid spectacular rolling hills and redwood groves. The school itself remains more Berkeley than Berkeley; extracurricular leftist politics supplement a curriculum offering such unique programs as the "History of Consciousness." Guided tours start from the **visitors center** at the base of campus. Make sure you have a parking permit when driving on weekdays. (Parking permits and maps available at the police station, 429-2231.)

Directly south of UCSC, the **Natural Bridges State Beach** (423-4609), at the end of W. Cliff Dr., offers a nice beach, tidepools, and tours twice per day during Monarch butterfly season from October to February. "Welcome Back Monarch Day" flies on October 9, but it's best to visit from November to December, when thousands of the little buggers swarm along the shore. (Open daily 8am-sunset. Parking $3 per day.)

Santa Cruz innkeepers double or triple rates for the summer season, rendering $20 winter singles $60-100 summer retreats. The **Santa Cruz Youth Hostel**, 511 Broadway (423-8304), offers 16 beds. Reservations are almost always necessary; send ½ of the $10 fee to P.O. Box 1241, Santa Cruz 95601 (AYH/IYHF members only). A 10-minute walk north of the boardwalk sits **The Best Inn**, 370 Ocean St. (458-9220), at Broadway. Cross the bridge east from the boardwalk, take Edge Cliff Dr. north until it intersects Ocean St., and follow Ocean north. A bit more tasteful than average, The Best promises A/C, color TV, and pretty quilts. (Singles mid-Sept. to early June $20; mid-June to early Aug. $30; early Aug. to mid-Sept. $40. $10 extra Fri. and Sat. nights. $5 extra for two. $500 for an accountant to figure out the room rates. No reservations—show up between 11am-2pm.) The **American Country Inn**, 645 7th (476-6424), 5 blocks from the beach just north of Eaton St., is small, pleasant, and off the main drag. (Weekdays $20, with bath $30; weekends $40, with bath $50. Weekly: $150, with bath $170.) The small RV camp in back has full hookup. (Sites $18; weekly $95. Reservations with deposit recommended.)

Reservations for state campgrounds can be made by calling 800-444-7275 at least two weeks in advance. The **New Brighton State Beach** (688-3241), 4 mi. south of Santa Cruz off Rte. 1 near Capitola, offers 115 lovely campsites on a high bluff overlooking the beach. (1-week max. stay. No hookups. Weekdays $12, weekends $14. Reservations highly recommended. Take SCMDT "Park Avenue" bus #58.) No relation to loyal PCC Chris, the **Henry Cowell Redwoods State Park**, off Rte. 9 (335-9145), computes 3 mi. south of Felton. Take Graham Hill Rd., or SCMDT bus #34, 35, or 36. (1-week max. stay. Sites $10.) **Big Basin Redwoods State Park**, north of Boulder Creek (338-6132), merits the 45-minute trip from downtown. Take Rte. 9 north to Rte. 236 north, or the infrequent SCMDT bus #37, for the best camping south of Point Reyes and north of Big Sur. Rent mountain bikes and horses nearby. (Showers. 15-day max. stay. Sites $10. Backpackers $1 at special backcountry campsites. Security parking $3 per night. Reservations recommended.)

Santa Cruz cultivates two distinct types of eateries. On the boardwalk, it's hard to get past arm's length from a corndog, dipped ice cream cone, or slushie. Farther inland, it can prove equally difficult to get out of earshot of a hissing espresso machine. The **Food Pavillion**, at Lincoln and Cedar, houses a collection of eateries rendered homeless by the quake. (Open daily 8am-9pm.) The manic **India Joze**, 1001 Cinter St., serves three different cuisines per week and offers up to five different meals in a day. Monday to Wednesday it's Middle Eastern, Thursday to Friday Indian, and Saturday to Sunday Southeast Asian; some dishes from each offered every day. Monterey Bay Snapper costs $9.25, while vegetarian options, such as the delicious *kota kari* (Indian pea and cashew dumplings with yogurt and rice) run around $7.75. (Open Mon.-Thurs. 8am-2:30pm and 5:30-10pm, Fri. 8am-2:30pm and 5:30-11pm, Sat. 10am-2:30pm and 5:30-11pm, Sun. 10am-2:30pm and 5:30-10pm. Coffee available between lunch and dinner daily; desserts until midnight Fri. and Sun.) Dylan's inspiration, the hip and friendly **Positively Front St.**, 44 Front St. (426-1944), has over 40 beers and a lit model train that runs around the ceiling. Good burgers and sandwich dinners are $4.50-6. (Open daily 11:30am-10pm.) At **Zachary's**, 819 Pacific Ave., locals crowd in for Breakfast Number 1: 2 eggs, great cottage fries, and toast for $2.75. (Open Tues.-Sun. 7am-2:30pm. Arrive before 9am to avoid long waits.) The **Saturn Cafe**, 1230 Mission St., cooks up vegetarian meals at their Santa Cruz best (generally for under $4). Cracked wheat is positively right-wing around here. (Open Mon.-Fri. 11:30am-12:30am, Sat.-Sun. noon-12:30am.) **Zoccoli's Delicatessen**, Cedar and Center, has great food at great prices. The lunch special of lasagna, salad, garlic bread, salami and cheese slices, and an Italian cookie goes for $4. (Open Mon.-Sat. 9am-5:30pm.)

Santa Cruz thinks of itself as a high-class operation, and most bars frown on backpacks and sleeping bags. Carding at local bars is stringent. The restored ballroom at the boardwalk makes a lovely spot for a drink in the evening, and the boardwalk bandstand also offers free Friday night concerts. The **Kuumbwa Jazz Center,** 320-322 E. Cedar St. (427-2227), has regionally renowned jazz, and music lovers under 21 are welcome. (Tickets $5-11.50. Most shows at 8pm.) The **Blue Lagoon,** 923 Pacific Ave. (423-7117), a relaxed gay bar, swims with a giant aquarium in back, taped music, videos, and dancing. (No cover. Drinks about $1.50. Open daily 4pm-2am.) **The Catalyst,** 1011 Pacific Garden Mall (423-1336), a 700-seat concert hall, draws second-string national acts such as Guadalcanal Diary, along with good local music. Boisterous and beachy, the bar serves lots of brightly colored sugar drinks, as well as pizza ($1.60) and sandwiches ($4.25). (Open daily 9am-2am. Shows at 9:15pm. Cover varies.)

Call the **Live Theatre Hotline** (476-2166) for the latest shows. The **Barn Theatre,** Bay and High St. (429-2159), on the UCSC campus, presents student theatrical productions in winter. In summer, local repertory companies perform. (Tickets Thurs. and Sun. $7, Fri.-Sat. $8; $2 discount for the self-described "low income.") **Shakespeare Santa Cruz,** Performing Arts Building Complex, UCSC campus (429-2121), features outdoor and indoor modern interpretations of the Bard (July-Aug.; tickets for regular performances in the Performing Arts Theatre $10-15.) Watch for occasional, free outdoor performances.

Santa Cruz relaxes about one hour south of San Francisco on the northern lip of Monterey Bay. Hitching to or from the city is fairly easy. **Greyhound/Peerless Stages,** 425 Front St. (423-1800), offers service to San Francisco (4 per day, $10) and L.A. via Salinas (2 per day, $45) or via San Jose (2 per day, $50). (Open daily 7:30am-8pm.) **Santa Cruz Metropolitan District Transit (SCMDT),** 920 Pacific Ave. (425-8600 or 688-8993), serves the city and environs. Pick up a free copy of *Headways* here for route information. (Open Mon.-Fri. 7am-6pm, Sat.-Sun. 9am-1pm and 2-5:30pm.) The **Santa Cruz Conference and Visitor's Council,** counsels at 701 Front St. (425-1234 or 800-833-3494). The **post office** dates at 850 Front St. (426-5200; open Mon.-Fri. 9am-5pm). Santa Cruz's **ZIP code** is 95060; the **area code** is 408.

Sierra Nevada

The Sierra Nevada crouches as the highest, steepest, and most physically stunning mountain range in the contiguous United States. The heart-stopping sheerness of Yosemite's rock walls, the craggy alpine scenery of Kings Canyon and Sequoia National Parks, and the abrupt drop from the eastern slope into Owens Valley produce little breath and less oxygen. At 14,495 ft., Mt. Whitney mounts all other points in the U.S. outside Alaska.

The **Sequoia National Forest** encompasses the southern tip of the Sierras as they march from Kings Canyon and Sequoia down to the low ranges of the Mojave Desert. The forest includes both popular recreational areas and isolated wilderness regions. **Forest headquarters** sit in Porterville, 900 W. Grand Ave. (209-784-1500), 15 mi. east of Rte. 99 between Fresno and Bakersfield. The **Sierra National Forest** fills the area between Yosemite, Sequoia, and Kings Canyon. Yet the forest is not exactly the "undiscovered" Sierras; droves of Californians jam the busier spots at lower elevations, and even the wilderness areas overpopulate in the summer. The main **information office** counsels at the Federal Bldg., 1130 O St. #3017, Fresno (209-487-5155; 209-487-5456 for 24-hr. recorded information). Pick up an excellent map ($2.10) of the forests here or in Porterville, or order one from the Three Forest Interpretive Association (3FIA), 13098 E. Wire Grass Lane, Clovis 93612.

Yosemite

Three million tourists pour into Yosemite every year for a glimpse of stunning waterfalls, rushing rivers, alpine meadows, and granite cliffs. The resulting congestion poses a knotty question to the overtaxed park service—whose park is it anyway? Purists bemoan Yosemite's accessibility and the snack shops, delis, photo galleries, and grocery stores that pamper the droves of tourists. Casual visitors counter that the valley's unique splendor belongs to everyone, not just to backpackers. Fortunately, the embattled valley occupies only a handful of the nearly 1200 square miles encompassed by this national park. Yosemite graciously manages to accommodate all its suitors.

Yosemite National Park divides into several areas. **Yosemite Valley,** the most spectacular, consequently receives the most traffic. Bus tours operate throughout the valley, as well as up to **Glacier Point** and the giant sequoias in the **Mariposa Grove.** Day-hikers often venture up the falls' trails and into **Little Yosemite Valley.** For a moderate hike with varying landscapes, water of all speeds, and an optional ridge or two, head toward **Lake Merced** from Glacier Point and then down toward the **Clark Range.** Hiking during the week almost guarantees privacy. The two main backcountry trailhead areas, **Tuolumne Meadows** and **Happy Isles Nature Center,** are accessible from Yosemite Valley by hitching along Tioga Rd. or by bus (372-1240) after July 1; ask to be let off at the trailhead. Buy both a topographical and a trail route map from a visitors center, namely the *Guide to Yosemite High Sierra Trails* ($2.50). A map of valley trails is also available (50¢). Acquire a wilderness permit from the Backcountry office, the Tuolumne Permit Kiosk (both open daily 7:30am-7:30pm), Big Oak Flat Station (open daily 7am-6pm), or the Wawona Ranger Station (open daily 8am-5pm).

Practical Information

Visitor Information: General Park Information, 372-0265; 372-0264 for 24-hr. recorded information. Advice about accommodations, activities, and weather conditions. TTY users call 372-4726. Open Mon.-Fri. 8am-5pm. **Yosemite Valley Visitors Center,** Yosemite Village (372-4461, ext. 333). Open daily 8am-8pm. **Tuolumne Meadows Visitors Center,** Tioga Rd. (372-0263), 55 mi. from Yosemite Village. Headquarters of high-country activity, with trail information, maps, and special programs. Open summer daily 8am-7:30pm. **Big Oak Flat Information Station,** Rte. 120 W. (379-2445), in the Crane Flat/Tuolumne Sequoia Grove Area. Open summer daily 7am-6pm. **Wawona Ranger Station,** Rte. 141 (375-6391), at the southern entrance near the Mariposa Grove. Open daily 8am-5pm; winter Mon.-Fri. 8am-5pm. **Backcountry Office,** P.O. Box 577, Yosemite National Park 95389 (372-0308; 372-0307 for 24-hr. recorded information), next to Yosemite Valley Visitors Center. Backcountry and trail information. Open daily 7:30am-7:30pm. Free map of the park and informative free *Yosemite Guide* both available at visitors centers. Information folders and maps available also in French, German, Japanese, and Spanish. Wilderness permits available at all visitors centers.

Yosemite Park and Curry Co. Room Reservations: 5410 E. Home, Fresno 93727 (252-4848; TTY users 255-8345). Except for campgrounds, Y.P.&C. has a monopoly on all the facilities of what has become a full-fledged resort within the park. Contact for information and reservations.

Tour Information: Yosemite Lodge Tour Desk (372-1240), in Yosemite Lodge lobby. Open daily 7:30am-8pm, or contact any other lodge in the park.

Bus Tours: Yosemite Via, 300 Grogan Ave., Merced 95340 (384-1315 or 722-0366). 2 trips per day from the Merced Greyhound station to Yosemite ($15; discount for seniors). **California Yosemite Tours,** P.O. Box 2472, Merced 95344 (383-1563 or 383-1570). Meets the morning train arriving in Merced from San Francisco and takes passengers to Yosemite. Returns to Merced in time to catch return train to San Francisco ($15). Also runs to and from Fresno ($18). **Yosemite Transportation System** (372-1240) connects the park with Greyhound in Lee Vining ($32.50). Reservations required; runs July-Labor Day. **Green Tortoise** (415-285-2441) based in San Francisco. Two- or 3-day trip. Buses leave San Francisco at 9pm. "Sleep-aboard" bus arrives at popular sites before the crowds. 2-day trip $79, 3-day trip $99, food $8 per day. Reservations required.

Equipment Rental: Yosemite Mountaineering School, Rte. 120 at Tuolumne Meadows (372-1335; Sept.-May 372-1244). Sleeping bags $4 per day, backpacks $3.50 per day, snow shoes $5 per day. License or credit card required.

Post Offices: Yosemite Village, next to the visitors center. Open Mon.-Fri. 8:30am-5pm; Sept.-May Mon.-Fri. 8:30am-12:30pm and 1:30-5pm. **Curry Village,** near Registration Office. Open June-Sept. Mon.-Fri. 9am-3pm. **Yosemite Lodge,** open Mon.-Fri. 9am-4pm. General Delivery **ZIP** code: 95389.

Area Code: 209.

Yosemite crowns the central Sierra Nevada, 180 mi. due east of San Francisco and 320 mi. north of Los Angeles. It can be reached by taking Rte. 140 from Merced, Rte. 41 north from Fresno, and Rte. 120 east from Sonoma and west from Lee Vining. Park admission costs $2 on foot, $5 for a 7-day vehicle pass.

Drivers planning to visit the high-country in spring or fall should have snow tires, also sometimes required in early and late summer. Of the five major approaches to the park, Rte. 120 to the Big Oak Flat entrance is particularly brutal. The easiest route from the west is Rte. 140 into Yosemite Valley. The eastern entrance, Tioga Pass, closes during snow season. The road to Mirror Lake and Happy Isles is forbidden to private auto traffic; free shuttle buses serve the road during the summer. In winter, snow closes the road to Glacier Point and sections of Tioga Road.

Accommodations and Camping

Those who prefer some kind of roof over their heads can shell out for a small, clean, sparsely furnished cabin at Yosemite Lodge. (Singles or doubles $40, with bath $50.) Southeast of Yosemite Village, Curry Village offers noisy but clean cabins close to pizza and ice cream spots. (Cabins $40, with bath $50. Canvas-sided cabins $26.50.) Reservations are necessary for all hotels, lodges, and cabin tents in the park; send one night's rent to Yosemite Park & Curry Co. Reservations (see Practical Information). Off-season mid-week rates may drop as much as $15 per night. **Housekeeping Camp** has canvas and concrete units that accommodate up to six people. Bring your own utensils, warm clothes, and industrial-strength insect repellent. (1-4 people $30.50. Each additional person $4.) **Tuolumne Meadows,** on Tioga Rd. in the northeast corner of the park, has canvas-sided tent cabins. (2 people $29. Each additional person $5.) **White Wolf,** west of Tuolumne Meadows on Tioga Rd., has similar cabins ($29) and cabins with bath ($49).

For the at-one-with-nature set, Yosemite provides many options. Most of the park's campgrounds are crowded, many with trailers and RVs. In Yosemite Valley's drive-in campgrounds, reservations are required from April to November and can be made through Ticketron (900-370-5566) up to eight weeks ahead. Sleeping in cars is emphatically prohibited. With the exception of major holidays, you should be able to camp in one of the first come, first serve campgrounds provided you arrive at a reasonable hour. In summer, a 14-day limit applies to campers outside Yosemite Valley and a seven-day limit to those in the valley, except at **Backpacker's Camp** (2-day limit in the valley, 1-day for the sites at Tuolumne). This camp is for backpackers with wilderness permits and without vehicles; "walk-in" camps do not require reservations.

Backcountry camping (for general information 372-0307) is prohibited in the valley (you'll get slapped with a stiff fine if caught), but it's unrestricted along the highcountry trails with a free wilderness permit. Reserve specific sites by mail February through May (write Backcountry Office, P.O. Box 577, Yosemite National Park 95389), or take your chances with the remaining 50% quota held on 24-hr. notice at the Yosemite Valley Visitors Center, the Wawona Ranger Station, or Big Oak Flat Station. Popular trails like **Little Yosemite Valley** and **Clouds Rest** fill up regularly. To receive a permit, you must show a planned itinerary (though you needn't follow it exactly). Most hikers stay at the undeveloped mountain campgrounds in the high country for the company and for the **bear lockers,** used for storing food (not bears). These campgrounds often have chemical toilets.

Kings Canyon and Sequoia National Parks

If your impression of national parks has been formed by the touristy Grand Canyon and Yosemite, you'll thrill to the lack of sightseers in most of Sequoia and Kings Canyon, two separate and enormous parks administered jointly by the National Park Service. Glacier-covered Kings Canyon displays a beautiful array of imposing cliffs and sparkling waterfalls. Home to the deepest canyon walls in the country, turn-outs along the roads offer vistas breathtakingly similar to aerial photographs. In Sequoia, the Sierra Crest lifts itself to its greatest heights. Several 14,000-ft. peaks scrape the clouds along the park's eastern border, including Mt. Whitney, the tallest mountain in the contiguous U.S. (14,495 ft.) Both parks contain impressive groves of massive sequoia trees in addition to a large and troublesome bear population, and both afford an ever-rarer opportunity to view natural beauty free from transistor radios and tourist traps. Visitors like to cluster around the largest sequoias, which loom near the entrances to the parks; vast stretches of backcountry remain relatively empty. The "summer season" usually runs from Memorial Day through Labor Day, "snow season" from November through March.

Kings Canyon's **Grant Grove Visitors Center,** 2 mi. east of the Big Stump Entrance by Rte. 180 (335-2315), has books, maps, and exhibits. (Open daily 8am-6pm; winter 8am-5pm.) Sequoia's **Ash Mountain Visitors Center,** Three Rivers 93271 (565-3456), on Rte. 198 out of Visalia, has information on both parks; the **Lodgepole Visitors Center** (565-3341, ext. 631), climbs in the heart of Sequoia, near the big trees and the tourists.

The two parks are accessible to vehicles from the west only. You can reach trailheads into the John Muir Wilderness and Inyo National Forest on the eastern side from spur roads off U.S. 395, but no roads traverse the Sierras here. From Fresno follow Rte. 180 through the foothills; a 60-mi. sojourn takes you to the entrance of the **Grant Grove** section of Kings Canyon. Rte. 180 ends 28 mi. later in the **Cedar Grove,** an island of park land enveloped within Sequoia National Forest. The road into this region closes in winter. From **Visalia,** take Rte. 198 to Sequoia National Park. Both roads are maintained by snow plows in winter. **Generals Highway** (Rte. 198) connects the Ash Mountain entrance to Sequoia with the **Giant Forest,** and continues to Grant Grove in Kings Canyon.

In summer (June-Nov.), the treacherous road to **Mineral King** opens up the southern parts of Sequoia. From Visalia, take Rte. 198; the turnoff to Mineral King is 3 mi. past Three Rivers, and the **Lookout Point Ranger Station** lies 10 mi. along the Mineral King Rd. Take a break from driving here: Atwell Springs Campground and the nearby town of Silver City are 10 mi. (but 45 min.) farther along. Cold Springs Campground, Mineral King Ranger Station, and several trailheads lie near the end of Mineral King Rd. in a valley framed by 12,000-ft. peaks on the north and east. The route to Mineral King includes stunning scenery—that is, if you can tear your eyes away from the tortuous road while making 698 turns between Rte. 198 and the Mineral King complex. Allow two hours for the trip from Three Rivers.

Roads can't touch the northern two-thirds of Kings Canyon and the eastern two-thirds of Sequoia; here the backpacker and packhorse have free rein. Check at a ranger station or visitors center for more detailed information.

Sequoia Guest Services, Inc., P.O. Box 789, Three Rivers 93271 (561-3314), has a monopoly on indoor accommodations and food in the parks. Their rustic **cabins** cluster in a little village in Sequoia's Giant Forest, as well as at Grant Grove. (Cabins available May-Oct., $25.50 per person, $3.50 per each additional person up to 8.) Most park service **campgrounds** open from mid-May to October (2-week limit year-round). For information about campgrounds, contact a ranger station or call 565-3351 for a 24-hr. recording. Kings Canyon offers sites for $8 at **Sunset, Azalea,** and **Crystal Springs,** all within spitting distance of Grant Grove Village, and at **Sheep Creek, Sentinel, Canyon View,** and **Moraine,** at the Kings River near Cedar Grove. Sequoia has sites without hookups at **Lodgepole** (565-3338), 4 mi. northeast of Giant Forest Village in the heart of Sequoia National Park. (Sites $8-10; free in winter.) Reserve up to eight weeks in advance through Ticketron (900-370-5566) from mid-May to mid-September. Other options are **Atwell Mill** and **Cold Springs,** about 20 mi. along the Mineral King Rd., in the Mineral King area. (Sites \$4.)

Lake Tahoe

A few million years ago, an area of land between two geological faults sank as the Sierra Mountains rose by uplift on either side. Lava flows sealed the depression, which filled with water and formed the third deepest lake in North America—Tahoe. Today the clear blue lake, surrounded by evergreens and mountains, draws millions of tourists to its edenic shores. For decades, wealthy families from San Francisco came to Lake Tahoe on vacation and built houses along the water. The crowds return each year, heading for the beaches in summer and the ski slopes in winter. Adjacent Stateline, a modest extension of the town into Nevada, accommodates a few casinos. However, the healthy proliferation of mini-malls and fast-food chains inclines many to use the area simply as a base for the many activities involving the lake.

To see the lake in style, board a boat: the glass bottoms of the *Tahoe Queen* (541-3664) leave the Ski Run Marina three times daily, and the *M.S. Dixie* (588-3508) leaves Zephyr Cove five times daily for tours of Emerald Bay (fare \$9-30). In the summer, **Windsurf Tahoe** rents sailboards for \$12 per hour. You may want to hire a wet-suit, too, since the base temperature of the lake remains a chilling 39°F. Several marinas rent out fishing boats, and you can get paddle boats for under \$10 per hour. Or share the cost with several people, and rent a motorboat and waterskis for \$49 per hour, or a jet-ski for \$45 per hour at **Zephyr Cove,** on U.S. 50 (702-588-3833), 4 mi. north of the casino. You're more likely, incidentally, to bump into the friendly green monster "Tahoe Tessie" in gift shops than in the water.

Incline Village, just into Nevada north of Tahoe, owes its name to an incline-railway which supplied local mines in the late 19th century. The famed *Bonanza* **Ponderosa Ranch** (702-831-0691) makes its home in the village on Tahoe Blvd. Consider the Haywagon Breakfast for a scenic buffet and hayride (daily at 8am). (Open daily 10am-5pm. Admission \$6.50, ages 5-11 \$5.50, under 5 free.) Both the **Forest Service Fire Lookout** and the **Mount Rose Scenic Overlook** (Rte. 431 from Incline to Reno) afford excellent views of the lake. The **Heavenly Mountain** chairlift (541-1330) will carry you up 2000 ft. for a birds-eye view (open Mon.-Sat. 10am-10pm, Sun. 9am-10pm).

For those who prefer to earn their views with boot leather, the U.S. Forest Service (573-2674) produces a series of leaflets and can advise on many different trails. The western side of Tahoe offers the **Tahoe State Recreation Area** (583-3074), **Sugar Pine Point Park** (525-7982), and the **D.L. Bliss** and **Emerald Bay State Parks** (both 525-7277). Magnificent **Emerald Bay** contains Tahoe's only island. Off U.S. 50 away from the shore lie **Fallen Leaf Lake** and **Cascade Lake.** A ¼ mi. from the road at Emerald Bay sits **Vikingsholm** (540-3030), a Scandinavian-style castle built in the 1920s. (Open June-Sept. daily 10am-4pm. Admission \$1.) The ultimate hike, along the 150-mi. **Tahoe Rim Trail,** loops around the entire lake and takes about 15 days (call 576-0676 for information).

Winter finds Lake Tahoe as tourist-filled as in summer. Sixteen ski resorts, nine cross-country areas, and snowmobile routes draw many to the mountains surrounding the lake. **Squaw Valley** (800-545-4350), home of the 1960 Winter Olympics, **Alpine Meadows** (800-824-6348), and **Diamond Peak** own the biggest reputations, but the smaller, less crowded **Homewood** draws rave reviews.

The recent decision to level smaller budget motels in order to build luxury high-rise establishments makes budget accommodation scarce. Realize that the dump charging \$15 on Tuesday may become a rich and regal chamber on Friday. Most hotels sell out on weekends year-round. Try to book ahead and get written confirmation of the price. Scout around for discount coupons: some offer up to a \$10 discount off weekday rates. The cheapest deals cluster near Stateline on U.S. 50 and may display prices. Others reside on less noisy Park Ave. The standard-issue **Motel 6,**

2375 Lake Tahoe Blvd., 95731 (542-1400), fills very quickly, especially on week-ends. (Singles $30. Each additional adult $6. Make reservations in advance or hope someone cancels.) At **Midway Motel,** 3876 U.S. 50 (544-4397), try to bargain gently for weekday rates. Clean, comfortable rooms include A/C and TV. (Singles $20, weekends $30. Doubles $30, weekends $40.) The Bliss family's **Pine Ridge Inn,** 3772 U.S. 50 (541-5839), has a pool, spa, and blissful rooms. (Singles $20, weekends $35. Doubles $24, weekends $40. Reservations strongly recommended.)

The forest service at the visitors bureau provides up-to-date information on the numerous (over 30) campgrounds around Lake Tahoe. Make reservations for state park campgrounds by calling MISTIX at 800-444-7275. Call the Forest Service (573-2600) for more details. Free campsites include **Bayview** (573-2600; 1-night max. stay; open June-Sept.), **Granite Flat** (587-3558; open April-Oct.), and **Alpine Meadow** (639-2342; tents only; open May-Oct.). Most sites cost $10.

The **Visitors Bureau and Chamber of Commerce,** 3066 U.S. 50 (541-5255 or 800-822-5922), at San Francisco Ave., has gallons of helpful brochures and maps, nota-bly free copies of *101 Things to Do in Lake Tahoe.* Disabled visitors should pick up the complimentary *Handbook for the Handicapped,* an extensive directory of facilities and information. (Open Mon.-Fri. 8:30am-5pm, Sat.-Sun. 9am-4pm.) The U.S. **Forest Service,** 870 Emerald Bay Rd., S. Lake Tahoe (573-2600), publishes the free, informative *Lake of the Sky Journal* and supervises campgrounds. (Open Mon.-Fri. 8am-4:30pm.) **Greyhound,** 1099 Park Ave. (544-2351), on the state line, has service to San Francisco (10 per day, $28.50) and Sacramento (6 per day, $16). The **Showboat Lines** Reno Airporter sends eight buses per day ($12.50; daily 8:30am-5pm). **Tahoe Area Regional Transport** (581-6365) connects to the western and northern shores from Tahoma to Incline Village. (Operates daily every hr. 6:30am-6:30pm. Fare $1, unlimited travel day pass $2.50.) **South Tahoe Area Ground Express** (573-2080) offers 24-hr. bus service around town, and daily service to the beach (1 per hr. for 7 hr.). (Fare $1.25, under 8 free.) For those traveling without luggage, the major hotels all offer free shuttle service along U.S. 50 to and from their casinos. **Harvey's** (588-2411) runs their bus daily from 8am to 2am. Rent bikes at **Anderson's Bicycle Rental,** 645 Emerald Bay Rd. (541-0500), convenient to the well-maintained west shore bike trail. (Full day $14, half-day $10. Open daily 8:30am-6pm. License required for deposit.) **Sierra Cycleworks,** 3430 U.S. 50 (541-7505), has lightweight mountain bikes from $4 per hour, $15 per day. (Open daily 9am-6pm.) Mopeds are available from **Country Moped,** Rte. 89 S. at 10th St. (544-3500; $10 1st hr., rates decrease over time; helmets available).

The **post office** registers at 1085 Park Ave. (544-6162), next to the Greyhound station. (Open Mon.-Fri. 8:30am-5pm.) Lake Tahoe's **ZIP code** is 95729; the **area code** is 916 in California, 702 in Nevada.

San Francisco

Occupying only 47 square miles at one end of an enormous urban horseshoe, San Francisco proper appears tiny and isolated. Yet that lttle plot holds a manic city, whose name cannot help but conjure images of gold, cable cars, LSD, and gay libera-tion. San Fran's many meanings have inspired hope, scorn, and immigration for a century and a half.

Originally inhabited by the Miwok people, the Bay area remained peaceful for hundreds of years. In 1776, Father Junipero Serra arrived and planted the northern-moet of his long string of missions, naming it *San Francisco de Asis.* A settlement grew up around the mission, remaining small and unimportant under Spanish and Mexican rule. Then in 1848, two years after the United States took over California, gold was discovered in the Sierras, just a short river trip from San Francisco's mag-nificent natural harbor. Within two more years San Francisco loomed, not just as a city, but as a center of trade and transportation. Most of San Fran emerged from the massive earthquake of 1906 shaken (but not stirred) like a James Bond martini. Three days of fire and looting ensued; many saw the quake as retribution for the

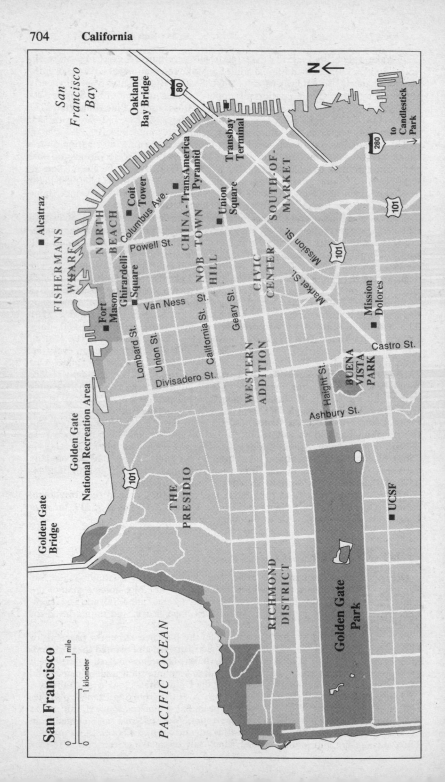

San Francisco

PACIFIC OCEAN

Golden Gate
Bridge

Golden Gate
National Recreation Area

THE
PRESIDIO

RICHMOND
DISTRICT

Golden Gate
Park

UCSF

San Francisco
Bay

Oakland
Bay Bridge

80

Alcatraz

FISHERMANS
WHARF

NORTH
BEACH

Coit
Tower

Columbus Ave.

Fort
Mason

Ghirardelli
Square

Powell St.

Van Ness

Lombard St.

Union St.

Divisadero St.

CHINA-
TOWN

NOB
HILL

California St.

Geary St.

WESTERN
ADDITION

Haight St.

Ashbury St.

BUENA
VISTA
PARK

TransAmerica
Pyramid

Union
Square

CIVIC
CENTER

Market St.

Mission St.

Transbay
Terminal

SOUTH-OF-
MARKET

280

to
Candlestick
Park

101

101

101

Castro St.

Mission
Dolores

N

1 mile

1 kilometer

0

0

town's "sinful ways." Sinful or not, San Fran had rebuilt better than ever by the late 1930s when the openings of the Oakland and Golden Gate Bridges ended the city's long isolation.

Always receptive to the unorthodox, the Beat Generation moved here in the 1950s; the 60s saw Haight-Ashbury blossom into the hippie capital of the world; and in the 70s, the gay population emerged as one of the most powerful and visible groups in the city. Though hit hard by the continuing AIDS epidemic, the gay community has fought back, comforting victims while increasing public awareness of the disease. Today everything from bus shelters to radio spots advocate safe sex and condoms. San Francisco's latest tragedy came when the biggest quake since 1906 killed 62 people, knocked out the Bay Bridge, and cracked Candlestick Park during a World Series game against Oakland on October 17, 1989. Bay residents once more came to each other's aid, gracefully unifying in the face of uncertainty.

San Francisco remains very much a confederation of neighborhoods; the average San Franciscan thinks in terms of the Mission District, Chinatown, and Nob Hill rather than the city as a whole. Subdivisions follow no discernible logic: a few blocks will take you from ritzy Pacific Heights to the impoverished Western Addition; the crime-ridden Tenderloin abuts the steel-and-glass wonders in the Financial District. Quaint small-scale streets, superb restaurants, and extensive parks afford a European air, and turreted houses line the avenues. The people are friendly, the food unbeatable, and the atmosphere tolerant. Everyone leaves inhibitions behind in San Francisco; you'll have to fight against the odds not to leave your heart.

Practical Information

Emergency: 911.

Visitor Information: Visitor Information Center, Hallidie Plaza (391-2000), at Market and Powell St. beneath street level. Free street maps, events calendars, and the helpful *San Francisco Book.* Open Mon.-Fri. 9am-5:30pm, Sat. 9am-3pm, Sun. 10am-2pm. 24-hr. event and information recordings in English (391-2001), French (391-2003), German (391-2004), Japanese (391-2101), and Spanish (391-2122). **Center for International Educational Exchange (CIEE),** 312 Sutter St. (421-3473), between Stockton St. and Grant Ave. downtown. Student-flight, discount, and lodgings information. ISIC cards. Open Mon.-Fri. 10am-5pm. **Redwood Empire Association,** 1 Market Plaza (543-8334), Spear St. Tower, 10th floor. Maps and brochures on the area from San Francisco to Oregon. Open Mon.-Fri. 9am-4:30pm. **Sierra Club Store,** 730 Polk St. (923-5600), just north of the Civic Center. Tremendous resource for those planning wilderness trips. They prefer and encourage visitors to join the club. Open Mon.-Fri. 10am-5:30pm. **San Francisco Ticket Box Office Service (STBS),** 251 Stockton St. (433-7827), near Post St. Tix to concerts, clubs, and sports events. Half-price tickets on day of show. Cash only. Open Tues.-Thurs. noon-7:30pm, Fri.-Sat. noon-8pm. Also sells BASS tickets to sports events, concerts, and clubs.

San Francisco International Airport (SFO): See Getting There below.

Trains: Amtrak, 425 Mission St. (for ticket information 800-872-7245), 1st floor of Transbay Terminal. Really just a boarding area for the free shuttle bus to the actual train station in Oakland on 16th St. (982-8512). Shuttle trip takes 30 min. Open daily 6:30am-10pm. **Southern Pacific Transportation Company,** 4th St. (495-4546), between Townsend and Key St., nearly 1 mi. south of Market St. Regional daily train service between San Francisco and San Jose 4:50am-10pm. Fare $4. **CalTrain,** 4th and Townsend St. (557-8661), 6 blocks south of Market St. Trains between San Francisco and San Jose along the peninsula. Open Mon.-Fri. 7am-7pm, Sat. 8am-5pm, Sun. 8am-3pm.

Buses: Greyhound, 50 7th St. (558-6616), between Mission and Market St. downtown. Coin-operated storage lockers ($1 per day) frequently full. Baggage check $1.50 per day per bag. Security lounge for ticketed passengers. Unsafe neighborhood at night. Open daily 5am-midnight. Also serves Transbay Terminal (425 Mission St. downtown; open 24 hr.) **Green Tortoise,** 285-2441. Friendly bus trips up and down the coast to L.A. ($30) and to Seattle ($59). Also to New York and Boston (both 14 days, $279). Organized tours of Yosemite ($69-89) and other national parks. Make reservations in advance. Bus pick up at 1st and Natoma St., behind the Transbay Terminal. Open Mon.-Fri. 8am-8pm.

Gray Line Tours: (558-9400). 3½-hr. bus tours of the city $21.50, ages 5-11 $10.75, plus a variety of other tours departing from Union Square or the Transbay Terminal. Reservations required.

Public Transport: See Getting Around below.

Taxi: Yellow Cab, 626-2345. **Luxor Cabs,** 282-4141. **DeSoto Cab Co.,** 673-1414. First mi. $1.40, $1.50 each additional mi.

Car Rental: Rent-A-Wreck, 555 Ellis St. (776-8700), between Hyde and Leavenworth St. Used, mid-sized cars $22 per day with 150 free mi., $119 per week with 700 free mi. 20¢ each additional mi. Under 25 $3 extra per day. Open Mon.-Fri. 8am-7pm, Sat.-Sun. 9am-4pm. Must be 21 with major credit card. **Bob Leech's Auto Rental,** 435 S. Airport Blvd. (583-3844), South San Francisco. New Toyotas $20 per day with 150 free mi., 10¢ each additional mi. Travelers coming into SFO should call for a ride to the shop. Open Mon.-Fri. 8am-9pm, Sat.-Sun. 8am-6pm. Must be 25 with major credit card.

Auto Transport: Auto Driveaway Company, 330 Townsend (777-3740). Many destinations. Open Mon.-Fri. 9am-5pm. Must be 21 with valid license and references. Cash deposit $250. **A-1 Auto,** 1300 Old Bayshore Rd., Burlingame (342-9611). Call 10 days in advance. Open Mon.-Fri. 8am-5:30pm. Must be 21 with major credit card. Cash deposit $150.

Bike Rental: Lincoln Cyclery, 772 Stanyan St. (221-2415), on the east edge of Golden Gate Park. 3-speeds $2 per hr., 10-speeds $3 per hr. Open Mon. and Wed.-Sat. 9am-5pm, Sun. 11:30am-5pm. Driver's license or major credit card required. **Presidion Bicycle Shop,** 5335 Geary (752-2453), between 17th and 18th Ave. 10-speed or mountain bike $25 per day. Open Mon. and Sat. 10am-6pm, Tues.-Fri. 10am-7pm, Sun. 11am-4pm.

Help Lines: Drug Line, 752-3400. **Suicide Prevention,** 221-1423. **Rape Crisis Center,** 647-7273. Operated by San Francisco Women Against Rape. **Gay Switchboard and Counseling Services,** 841-6224. Information on gay community events, local clubs, etc., as well as counseling. Open Mon.-Fri. 10am-10pm, Sat.-Sun. noon-4pm.

Post Office: 7th and Mission St. (621-6838), opposite the Greyhound station. Open Mon.-Fri. 9am-5:30pm, Sat. 9am-1pm. **ZIP code:** 94101. **Rincon Annex,** 99 Mission St. Open Mon.-Fri. 8am-10pm, Sat. 9am-5pm.

Area Code: 415.

Getting There

San Francisco, the cultural capital of Northern California and third largest city in the state (pop. 727,400), lies 548 mi. north of San Diego, 403 mi. north of Los Angeles, about 390 mi. south of the Oregon border, and about 6900 mi. from Guangzhou, China. The city proper lies at the northern tip of a peninsula separating San Francisco Bay from the Pacific Ocean.

San Francisco International Airport (SFO) (761-0800) runways on a small nub of land in San Francisco Bay about 15 mi. south of the city center on U.S. 101. There are two ways to commute from SFO to the city by public transportation. **San Mateo County Transit (samTrans)** (761-7000), runs two buses from SFO to downtown San Francisco. The express (#7F) takes 30 minutes, but you can only bring carry-on luggage (every ½ hr. 6am-1am; $1.25, seniors and under 17 75¢). Bus #7B takes a little longer (45 min.), but you can carry all the luggage you want (every ½ hr. 5:40am-1:30am; seniors and under 17 75¢). An **Airporter** bus runs a shuttle route from all three terminals to major hotels and a downtown terminal at 301 Ellis St. (every 15 min. 5:30am-9:15pm, after 9:15pm every 30-40 min., $6). Taxi rides to downtown from SFO cost about $20.

Lorrie's Travel and Tour (334-9000), on the upper level at the west end of all three terminals, provides convenient door-to-door van service to and from the airport. Reserve at least six hours in advance for service to the airport. No reservations are needed for travel from the airport. (Vans run daily 4:25am-10:25pm. Fare $8, ages 2-12 $5, under 2 free.) **Franciscus Adventures** (821-0903) runs a small bus between San Francisco and SFO (fare $7, $5 per person for groups of five or more). Call ahead to arrange a time.

The San Francisco airport is out of the way. Give yourself plenty of time as traffic can get very bad, especially during the evening commute.

CalTrain (557-8661 or 800-558-8661 for voice or TDD) is a regional commuter train that runs south to Palo Alto ($3 one way, $1.50 elderly/handicapped) and San Jose ($3.50 one way, $1.75 elderly/handicapped) with additional bus service to Santa Cruz. The depot sits at 4th and Townsend St., served by MUNI buses #15 and 42.

From the south, the city can be reached by car via U.S. 101 to I-280, via I-5 to I-580, or via Rte. 1. From the east take I-580 or I-80 to the Bay Bridge. From the north, U.S. 101 leads directly into the city over the Golden Gate Bridge.

If you're a driver who needs a passenger or vice versa, call the **Berkeley Ride Board** (527-0352) for free, 24-hr. listings. The San Francisco International Hostel and San Francisco State University (469-1842, in the student union; open Mon.-Fri. 7am-10pm, Sat. 10am-4pm) also have ride boards. KALX radio (642-5259), on the Berkeley campus, broadcasts a ride list Monday through Saturday at 10am and 10pm. Call them to put your name and number on the air for free. KSAN radio (986-2825) provides a similar service.

Getting Around

The hilly city of San Francisco, surrounded by water on three sides, is an amalgam of distinct neighborhoods organized along a few central arteries. Each neighborhood is compact enough to explore comfortably on foot.

San Francisco once radiated outward from its docks, on the northeast edge of the peninsula just inside the lip of the bay. Most visitors' attention still gravitates to this area, although the city now extends south and west from this point. Many of San Francisco's attractions cluster here, within a wedge formed by **Van Ness Avenue** running north-south, **Market Street** running northeast-southwest, and the **Embarcadero** (waterfront road) curving along the coast. Taking the diagonal course, Market St. disrupts the regular grid of streets and accounts for an exceptionally confusing street-numbering system. Streets radiating north from Market and west from Market and the Embarcadero are numbered from these thoroughfares, although you should keep in mind that parallel streets do not bear the same block numbers.

At the top of this wedge lies **Fisherman's Wharf**, an area frequented mainly by tourists, and **North Beach**, a district shared by Italian Americans, artists, and professionals. The focal point of North Beach is Telegraph Hill, topped by Coit Tower and fringed counterclockwise from the northwest to the southeast by Columbus Ave. Across Columbus begin the **Nob Hill** and **Russian Hill** areas, resting places of the city's old money. This fan-shaped area is confined by Columbus along its northeast side, Van Ness along the west, and (roughly) Geary and Bush St. on the south. Below Nob Hill and North Beach, and still north of Market, **Chinatown** covers around 24 square blocks between Broadway in the north, Bush St. in the south, Powell St. in the west, and Kearny St. in the east. The heavily-developed **Financial District** lies between Washington St. in the north and Market in the south, east of Chinatown and south of North Beach. Going down Market from the Financial District, heading toward the bottom of the wedge, you pass through the core downtown area centered on **Union Square** and then, beyond Jones St., the **Civic Center,** an impressive collection of municipal buildings including City Hall, the Opera House, and Symphony Hall. The Civic Center occupies the base of the wedge and spills out over Van Ness to Gough St., 2 blocks west.

Also within this wedge is the **Tenderloin,** which still qualifies as a somewhat seedy region to avoid at night, despite the sprouting high-rises. The Tenderloin is roughly bounded by Larkin St. to the west and to the east by Taylor St. extending from Market St. north to Geary. Some of the area's seediness, however, seeps across Market to the area near the Greyhound station (6th and 7th St.).

Below Market St. lies the aptly named **South-of-Market-Area (SOMA),** home to much of the city's nightlife. The South-of-Market extends inland from the bay to 10th St., at which point the Hispanic **Mission District** begins and spreads south.

The **Castro** area, center of the gay community, adjoins the Mission District at 17th and also extends south, centered upon Castro St.

West of Van Ness Ave., the city distends all the way to the ocean side of the peninsula. At the top of Van Ness, the commercially developed **Marina** area embraces a yacht harbor, Fort Mason, and the youth hostel. Fisherman's Wharf lies immediately east. Above the marina rise the wealthy hills of **Pacific Heights.** South of Pacific Heights, across Van Ness from the Civic Center, is the somewhat seedy **Western Addition,** extending west to Masonic Ave. **Japantown** locates within the Western Addition. Farther west is the rectangular **Golden Gate Park,** extending to the Pacific and bounded by Fulton St. in the north and Lincoln St. in the south. At its eastern end juts a skinny Panhandle bordered by the **Haight-Ashbury** district. North of **Golden State Park** nods San Francisco's token suburb within the city, the **Richmond District.**

It seems only fitting that S.F.'s cable cars are well-known, even if only from Rice-a-Roni ads, for they represent a truly marvelous mass transit network. Quiet, clean, electric buses run promptly and frequently, while covering the entire city well. Furthermore, despite its location in a state of automobile worshipers, San Francisco has not neglected rail transportation. Connections to neighboring cities are well-coordinated and speedy. See San Francisco Bay Area for information on transportation beyond San Francisco. A *Comprehensive Regional Transit Guide,* covering all of the regional bus and subway services, sells for $4 at most bookstores.

San Francisco Municipal Railway (MUNI) (673-6864) operates buses, cable cars, and a combined subway/trolley system. Fares for both buses and trolleys is 85¢, ages 5-17 25¢, seniors and disabled passengers 15¢. Exact coins required. Ask for a free transfer, valid in any direction for several hours, when boarding. A month pass costs $28. In addition, MUNI Metro runs **streetcars** beneath Market St. and above ground along points south and west of downtown. The Metro and bus lines along a few major streets run all night; most buses run daily 6am to midnight. When using the system briefly, the MUNI's *San Francisco Street and Transit Map,* available at most bookstores, makes a good $1.50 investment. The map contains not only information on frequencies, wheelchair accessibility, and late-night service, but also a complete street index—it doubles as a necessary general street map, especially since the maps on bus shelters are unreadable. Started in 1873, San Francisco's **Cable cars** were named a national historic landmark in 1964 and received an overhaul from 1982 to 1984. Though novel, cars are noisy, slow (9½ mph), and often full. Try them anyway, especially if you have a MUNI pass. Of the three lines, the California St. line from the Financial District up Nob Hill is by far the least crowded. (Fare $2, ages 5-17 75¢, seniors 15¢, under 5 free. Unlimited transfers allowed within a given three-hour period. Cars run daily 7am-1am.)

Bay Area Rapid Transit (BART) (778-2278) does not (alas) really serve the entire Bay Area. It does operate modern, fully carpeted trains along four lines connecting San Francisco with the East Bay, including Oakland, Berkeley, Concord, and Fremont. BART does not operate within the city of San Francisco; use MUNI for local transport. One-way fares range from 80¢ to $3. A special excursion deal for $2.60 is designed for tours of the system: you must begin and end at the same station, and your trip must not take more than three hrs. (Trains run Mon.-Sat. 6am-midnight, Sun. 9am-midnight.) Maps and schedules are available at the visitor information center and all BART stations. All BART stations and trains are wheelchair accessible.

A car is not the necessity it is in Los Angeles. Furthermore, parking spots are scarce and very expensive. A car, however, is definitely the best way to explore the outer reaches of the Bay Area. In the city, contending with the hills is the first task; those in a standard-shift car will need to develop a fast clutch foot, since all the hills have stop signs at the crests. When renting, get an automatic. And remember, in San Francisco, cable cars have the right of way.

The street signs admonishing you to "PREVENT RUNAWAYS" refer not to wayward youths but rather to cars improperly parked on hills. When parking facing uphill, turn the wheels toward the center of the street; when facing downhill, turn the wheels toward the curb; and *always* park in gear with the brake set.

Accommodations

Unlike most cities, San Francisco has a wide selection of conveniently located, relatively satisfying budget accommodations. But don't expect miracles for these prices. Note that a rather hefty 11% bed tax is not included in the prices given below. Most hotels listed here are in areas such as the Tenderloin, the Mission District, Union Square, and downtown, where caution is advised both on the streets and within the buildings, particularly at night. Self-described "European-style" hotels are often charming, but you may have to look elsewhere for a private bath and an ultra-firm mattress. Women, especially, should go elsewhere and pay more if suspicious about a particular neighborhood or establishment.

The International Network Globe Hostel, 10 Hallam Pl. (431-0540), near the Greyhound station, just off Folsom St. in the South-of-Market district. Clean and convenient. 4 beds per room with chairs and tables. No kitchen. Friendly, lively atmosphere. Continental breakfast, sauna, and jacuzzi. Over 100 beds. Community lounge and laundry room good places to meet international student travelers. Open 24 hr. No curfew. $15. Key deposit $5.

San Francisco International Hostel (AYH), Bldg. 240, Fort Mason (771-7277). Entrance at Bay and Franklin St., 1 block west of Van Ness Ave. at the northern end of the peninsula. From Greyhound, walk to 9th and Market St., then take MUNI bus #19 ("Polk") to Polk and Bay St. Turn left, and walk 2 blocks to Franklin St.; follow signs to hostel. One of the largest AYH-affiliated hostels in the nation, with about 160 beds. The General Motors of hosteling: clean, well-run, and efficient. Chore-a-day rule enforced. Extensive lounges, large kitchen, spic-and-span food-storage areas, and pay lockers for valuables. Good ride board. Frequented by students, families, and seniors. Crowded in summer. Arrive around 7am or send a night's fee three weeks ahead to reserve a place. 3-day max. stay in summer, 5-day in winter. Open 7am-2pm and 4:30pm-midnight. Lockout 10am-4:30pm. Curfew midnight. Members and nonmembers $10.

San Francisco Summer Hostel (AYH), 100 McAllister St. (621-5809), near civic center subway and many bus routes. Not a great area at night. Laundry facilities and small kitchen. 3-day max. stay. Open 7:30am-noon and 4:30pm-midnight. Lockout 10am-4:30pm. Curfew midnight. $10, nonmembers $13. Open summer only.

International Guest House, 2976 23rd St. (641-1411), at Harrison St. in the Mission District. Somewhat rough neighborhood, away from the most touristy areas, but 24th St. fairly busy. Strictly adheres to a foreign-travelers-only rule. 2 fully equipped kitchens for 28 guests. Common room, TV, and stereo. 5-day min., no max. stay. No curfew. Bunks $12 for each of the first 10 nights, $10 thereafter in 2- or 4-person rooms. Rooms for couples $20. No reservations.

European Guest House, 761 Minna St. (861-6634), near 8th St., 8 blocks south of Greyhound and west on Minna in a quiet but run-down neighborhood. Free-wheeling, relaxed, improvised, friendly; people sleep on sofas, mats, cushions. Co-ed rooms. TV room, laundry facilities, kitchen, small information board. Open 7:30am-2pm and 6pm-midnight. No curfew. Huge hot dorm $10. Bunks $12.

YMCA, 166 Embarcadero (392-2191), between Mission and Howard St. in the Financial District. Men and women. 269 rooms. Best of the city's YMCAs: conveniently located, attractive lobby, friendly people. Unfortunately, its future uncertain; call before rushing over. Use of pool, sauna, and gym. No curfew. No membership required. Singles $24. Bunks $33. Doubles $35, with TV $37.

YMCA Hotel, 220 Golden Gate Ave. (885-0460), at Leavenworth St., 2 blocks north of Market St. Men and women. One of the largest lodgings in the city. Impressive post-modern façade belies spartan rooms. Has the only indoor track in the city; just as well given the uninviting surroundings. Double locks on all doors. Pool and gym. No curfew. Hostel beds $15. Singles $29. Doubles $39. Breakfast included.

YMCA Chinatown, 855 Sacramento St. (982-4412), between Stockton St. and Grant Ave. Good location near the city center. Men over 18 only. Friendly young staff, pool, and gym. Bare, somewhat shabby rooms. Registration Mon.-Fri. 6:30am-10pm, Sat. 9am-5pm, Sun. 9am-1pm. No curfew. Singles $22-24. Doubles $29. 7th day free.

El Capitan, 2361 Mission St. (695-1597), north of 20th St. in the Mission District. Rooms clean but not as impressive as the façade. How symbolic. Bit of a rough neighborhood but busy street and two locked gates. Singles $18. Doubles $20.

Sam Wong Hotel, 615 Broadway (781-6836), bewteen Grant Ave. And Stockton St. in Chinatown. Extremely convenient location. Rooms could use more maintenance, but secure and clean. Singles with toilet $19, with bath $25. Doubles $21 and $27, respectively. Triples with bath $32.

Gum Moon Women's Residence, 940 Washington (421-8827), at Stockton in Chinatown. Women only. Bright, spacious rooms with shared bath. Kitchen and laundry facilities. Primarily a boarding house—call ahead for availability. Registration 9am-6pm. Singles $22. Doubles $36. Weekly: singles $91; doubles $152.

Olympic Hotel, 140 Mason St. (982-5010) at Ellis St., a few blocks from Union. Caters mostly to Japanese students and Europeans. Clean and comfortable with atrocious wallpaper. Tends to fill during summer. Singles or doubles $28, with bath $35.

Pensione International, 875 Post St. (775-3344), east of Hyde St., 4½ blocks west of Union Sq. Very nice rooms with interesting art. Singles $30, with bath $50. Doubles $40, with bath $60.

Adelaide Inn, 35 Isadora Duncan (441-2261), off Taylor near Post St., 2 blocks west of Union Sq. Warm hosts and jumbled paintings. Does not answer door after 11pm. Steep stairs, no elevator. All rooms with a bright outside exposure. Kitchenette and microwave available. Hall baths. Singles $32. Twin bed or doubles $42, 3rd bed $10. Continental breakfast included. Reservations required.

Grant Plaza, 465 Grant Ave. (434-3883 or 800-472-6899; in CA 800-472-6805), at Pine St. near the Chinatown gate. Excellent location. Recently renovated like a chain motel, but more colorful. Rooms with bath, phones, and color TV. Check-in after 2:30pm. Singles $34. Doubles $39. Twin beds $44. Reservations recommended 2-3 weeks in advance.

The Ansonia, 711 Post St. (673-2670), 3 blocks west of Union Sq. in a nice area. Pretty nice rooms with firm mattresses. Nice laundry facilities. Breakfast and dinner nicely included Mon.-Sat. Singles $35, with bath $52. Doubles $47, with bath $60. Weekly: singles $213, with bath $300; doubles $280, $360. Student weekly rates: singles $150, with bath $180; $125 per student for a shared room. Legend has it Nicely Nicely Johnson slept here.

Sheehan Hotel, 620 Sutter St. (775-6500 or 800-848-1529), near Mason St. Excellent location near public transport and trendy art galleries. Busy, elegant lobby something of a scene on warm summer evenings. Many international students. Worn, very English rooms; doubles have tea settings. Olympic-sized swimming pool. Economy singles $35, with bath $45. Economy doubles $35, with bath $50.

Obrero Hotel and Basque Restaurant, 1208 Stockton (989-3960), between Pacific Ave. and Broadway in Chinatown. 12 comfortable, cheerful rooms with fluffy comforters. Hall baths. Family-style basque dinners at 6:30pm cost $13. Check-in 8am-noon and 5-10pm. Singles $35. Doubles $42. Full breakfast included. Reservations required.

Pacific Bay Inn, 520 Jones St. (673-0234 or 800-445-2631, within CA 800-343-0880), 3 blocks west of Union Sq. Entirely renovated after fire. Pleasant rooms with TV. Singles and doubles $55-65; only $45 if you bring your copy of *Let's Go.* Continental breakfast included.

All Season's Hotel, 417 Stockton St. (986-8737 or 800-628-6456), between Sutter and Bush St., 1 block north of Union Sq. Thin walls and some peeling paint but big brass beds with firm mattresses. Singles $45. Doubles $49. Reservations required in summer.

The Red Victorian Bed and Breakfast Inn, 1665 Haight St. (864-1978), 2 blocks east of Golden Gate Park in Haight-Ashbury. 3 mi. from downtown, but close to buses and the "N" trolley. Barely describable—more a state of mind than a hotel. 14 individually and exquisitely decorated rooms honor butterflies, the nearby Golden Gate Park, and the equally proximate 1960s. Even the 4 hall baths, shared by some of the rooms, have their own names and motifs. If canopied and teddy-bear festooned beds aren't enough to soothe your mind, try the meditation room, the therapeutic massage ($40 per hr.), or a talk with the hotel cat. Downstairs, a newly opened global family network center promotes planetary consciousness with a café, market, and computers. A non-smoking, angst-free environment that you won't want to miss if your wallet can deal. Stop by for a tour regardless. Summer rates $55-125 depending on room size and karma, weekends $5 more; winter $55-120. Extra futon $10. Breakfast of freshly baked bread, pastry, and requisite granola included. Complimentary tea, coffee, and cheese in the evenings. Make reservations well in advance for summer months.

Food

For quality and variety, it's hard to beat the range of cuisines offered by one of the great port cities in the U.S. As in NYC, immigrants have transformed the joys of the palate beyond the simple utensil-to-mouth-to-sea Americanism. The city feasts on Chinatown's tantalizing *dim sum*, the *cilantro*-spiced burritos of the Mission, and the freshest seafood. The pizzas that emerge from the wood ovens of the Bay Area range from North Beach Neapolitan to the trendy but tasty goat cheese and *pancetta*. Sourdough is a city landmark and San Franciscans are as serious about their coffee as they are about the wines of Napa Valley.

The urban professionals of San Fran may have sold their souls for the earthly pleasures of great food, but money need not be a limiting factor for gourmet dining. Ethnic food will consistently get you the very best value and often outdoes the most expensive meals. Head to the Mission or Chinatown for excellent, inexpensive cuisine. The Haight has a fabulous selection of bakeries and Columbus Ave. in North Beach lures visitors to café after café.

Downtown

Tommy's Joynt, 1101 Geary Blvd., at Van Ness Ave. Outrageously painted establishment with a stunning selection of beers brewed from Finland to Peru. Famous thick pastrami sandwich ($3.50) goes with 2 types of mustard plus horseradish on each table. Rich, lean buffalo stew ($3.50). Open daily 10am-2am.

Pasta Bella, 30 Fremont St., between Mission and Market. Elegant fast food, served cafeteria-style. Lunch options around $6. Open Mon.-Fri. 6:30am-8pm.

Gelato Classico, 448 Post St., 1 block west of Union Sq. The *gelati* against which all others in the city measure themselves (small $1.75). Open Mon.-Thurs. 7:30am-11pm, Fri. 7:30am-midnight, Sat. 8:30am-11pm, Sun. 9am-9pm.

Chinatown

The Hunan, 924 Sansome St. Called the best Chinese restaurant in the world. Originally a joint on Kearny St. where devotees sat and stared into the enormous, blackened woks lost in the '89 quake. The menu lives on here. Get up from your table to see the woks. Fiery entrees around $7. Open daily 11:30am-9:30pm.

Brandy Ho's, 217 Columbus Ave. at Pacific and 450-452 Broadway. Very classy interior. Great Hunan-smoked and fried meats $8-10. Flavor-filled dumpling soup $2. Open Sun.-Thurs. 11:30am-11pm, Fri.-Sat. 11:30am-midnight.

Yuet Lee, 1300 Stockton St. at Broadway. Locals know: this ugly lime-green restaurant with evil fluorescent lighting equals your best choice for Chinese seafood. Try the tasty clams with pepper and black bean sauce. Open daily 11am-3am.

North Beach

Tommaso's, 1042 Kearny St., just below Van Ness Ave. For a break from *nouvelle pizza* try some of the very best traditional Italian pizza anywhere. The super deluxe, piled high with mushrooms, peppers, ham, and Italian sausage sates 2 ($12). Francis Ford Coppola known to occasionally toss pizza dough in front of Tommaso's huge wood burning ovens. Wait sometimes long but always worth it. Open Tues.-Sat. 5-10:45pm, Sun. 4-9:45pm.

Café Sport, 574 Green St. (981-1251), near Columbus Ave. Terrific food served in an oddly decorated, claustrophobic dining room. Order the garlicky *pesto* over pasta ($8). Dinner can cost over $15. Tues.-Sat. noon-2pm; dinner sittings at 6:30, 8:30, and 10:30pm. Reservations essential.

Bohemian Cigar Store, 566 Columbus Ave., corner of Union Sq. Excellent espresso ($1) and agreeable Italian food. Try their Italian sandwiches ($4-5). Open Mon. 10am-11pm, Tues.-Sat. 10am-midnight, Sun. 10am-6pm.

U.S. Restaurant, 431 Columbus Ave., at Stockton St. Popular with young San Franciscans (a patriotic lot). Long wait at dinner. Large, tasty portions. Garlicky pot roast $7.50. *Calamari* ($7.50) their most popular dish. Most meals under $10. Open Tues.-Sat. 6am-9pm.

Caffe Trieste, 609 Vallejo St. (392-6739), at Grant. Only a few beatniks now; sip coffee and remember the exciting Eisenhower years when Ginsberg and Ferlinghetti hung out here. Loud live music Sat. noon-4pm. Otherwise settle for a tune from the opera jukebox. Coffees $2.25. Open Sun.-Thurs. 7am-11:30pm, Fri.-Sat. 7am-12:30am.

Marina and Pacific Heights

Bepple's Pies, 1934 Union St. A bit expensive, but perfect pies. Fruit pie slices $3. Another 95¢ for a solid slab of excellent vanilla ice cream. Whole pies $11. Meat pies $6. Pies pies. Open Mon.-Wed. 9am-11:30pm, Thurs. 7am-midnight, Fri. 7am-1am, Sat. 9am-1am, Sun. 9am-10am.

Jackson Fillmore, 2506 Fillmore St. Usually a long wait at this popular and hip *trattoria*, with great southern Italian cuisine and a lively atmosphere. Put your name down and browse the Fillmore scene while you wait. Large portions; you can maybe sneak out for less than $10 per person. Eat lots of tasty breadsticks to fill up. Open Tues.-Thurs. 5:30-10:30pm, Fri.-Sat. 5:30-11pm, Sun. 5-10pm.

Mai's Vietnamese, 1838 Union St. Sidewalk dining on Union St. The crab claws get good marks ($6.75) as does the vegetarian imperial roll($5). Crabmeat soup with flavor and clarity $4. Entrees around $7.50. A romantic spot on warm summer city nights. Open Mon.-Fri. 11am-10pm, Sat. noon-11pm, Sun. noon-10pm.

Mission District and Castro Street

La Cumbre, 515 Valencia St. The top. Ample superlative burrito ($2.35, large $3.75). Open Mon.-Sat. 11am-10pm, Sun. noon-9pm.

Taqueria San Jose, 2830 Mission St., at 24th. Don't be put off by the fast-food-style menu; real care goes into the cooking. Soft, articulate tacos with your choice of meat—a full house of 3 brain and 2 tongue tacos for $3.50. Free chips and guacamole. Open Mon.-Thurs. 8am-1am, Fri.-Sat. 8am-4am.

Malai Lao, 3189 16th, at Guerrero. Lao specialties such as *ping nok,* delicately barbecued quail served with vinagrette. Open Sun.-Mon. 5-10:30pm, Tues.-Sat. 11am-2pm and 5-10:30pm.

Manora, 3226 Mission. Attractive Thai restaurant with delicious cuisine at reasonable prices. Especially light with its sauces—food not smothered in peanut butter. The red beef curry ($5.25) gets good reviews. Most dishes under $8. Open daily 5-10pm.

Yuet Lee, 3601 26th St. Same horrendous green paint, blinding fluorescent lighting, and good seafood as the Chinatown location. Open Mon. and Wed.-Thurs. 11am-10pm, Fri.-Sat. 11am-11pm, Sun. 4-10pm.

Haight-Ashbury and Richmond

Ganges, 755 Frederick St. Not exactly in the Haight, but close enough. Delicious though slightly xeroxed vegetarian Indian food draws health-conscious students from the nearby medical school. Traditional, low Indian seating in back. Dinners $7.50-11.50. Open Mon.-Sat. 5-9:30pm.

Cambodian House, 5625 Geary Blvd., near 20th Ave. Attractive restaurant with interesting menu. Remarkably complex and tasty lunch specials $4. Dinner entrees about $6, seafood $7.50-8. Open Sun.-Thurs. 11am-3pm and 5-10pm, Fri.-Sat. 11am-3pm and 5-10:30pm.

Cha Cha Cha, 1805 Haight St. Love children fighting against the stream of late capitalist society join hands with the yuppies who urge it on. Trendy but best Latin restaurant in the Haight. Try the *tapas*. Entrees $5-8. Open Mon.-Wed. 11:30am-3pm and 5-11:30pm, Thurs. 11:30am-3pm and 5-midnight, Fri. 11:30am-3pm and 5:30pm-midnight, Sat. noon-3pm and 5:30pm-midnight, Sun. noon-3pm and 5-11pm.

Tassajara Bread Bakery, 1000 Cole St. at Parnassus, 5 blocks south of Haight St. One of the best bakeries in the city. A branch at Fort Mason, but the purist will want to make the pilgrimage to Haight-Ashbury for the original. Open Mon.-Thurs. 7am-7pm, Fri. 7am-10pm, Sat. 8am-10pm, Sun. 8am-2pm.

Sights

San Francisco has its share of tall structures. But the Golden Gate Bridge, the TransAmerica Pyramid, and Colt Tower don't just make good plastic ash-trays, they also prevent the fog from completely submerging the city. Some delightful open spaces also bless San Fran, from the sprawling Golden Gate Park to the smaller, but equally lovely assistants Union and Washington Squares. Yet San Francisco's essence remains its neighborhoods. Whether defined by ethnicity, income, topography, or simply a shared spirit, these communities and their buildings, bookstores, and activities present the visitor with constant contrasts and the city with a unique unpurchasable identity.

Downtown

Union Square is the center of San Francisco. Now an established shopping area, the square has a rich and somewhat checkered history. During the Civil War, at a large public meeting here, citizens decided whether San Francisco should secede. The square became the rallying ground of the Unionists, who bore placards reading "The Union, the whole Union, and nothing but the Union." At the Sheraton Palace Hotel, a few blocks away on Market at New Montgomery St., Warren Harding died in 1923. And on the square itself, by a side entrance of the St. Francis Hotel, Sara Jane Moore failed to assassinate President Gerald Ford, who was touring the country to promote the World Court, on September 23, 1975.

Even when the Barbary Coast (now the Financial District) stayed down and dirty, Union Square stayed cheaper. Morton Alley, in particular, offered off-brand alternatives to the high-priced prostitutes and stiff drinks of the coast; the prices were low, but the action sizzled just as hot. At the turn of the century, murders averaged one per week on Morton Alley, and prostitutes with shirts unbuttoned waved to their favorite customers from second-story windows. After the 1906 earthquake and fire destroyed most of the flophouses, a group of proper merchants moved in and renamed the area Maiden Lane in hopes of changing the street's image. The switch worked. Today Maiden Lane, extending 2 blocks from Union Square's eastern side, boasts smart shops and classy boutiques. Traces of the old street live on, however, in words like "hoodlum," "shanghaied," and "Mickey Finn," all added to the U.S. vocabulary by the people who frequented the area.

The best free ride in town is on the outside elevators of the St. Francis Hotel. As you glide up the building, the entire Bay Area stretches out before you. The "elevator tours" offer an unparalleled view of Coit Tower and the Golden Gate Bridge. The Powell St. cable cars also grant an excellent view of the square.

Financial District

North of Market and east of Kearny, snug against the bay, beats the West's financial heart, or at least one of its ventricles. Try to catch Montgomery Street, the Wall Street of the West, before the workday ends. After 7:30pm, the heart stops, to be resuscitated the next morning.

San Francisco's most distinctive structure, totally out-of-scale with the surrounding buildings, is the 853-ft. TransAmerica Pyramid, at Montgomery St. between Clay and Washington St. Designed mainly to show off the talents of its architects, the building's pyramidal shape and subterranean concrete "anchor" base make it one of the city's most stable, earthquake-resistant buildings. A disappointing observation deck faces north on the 27th floor. (Open Mon.-Fri. 9am-4pm. Free.)

Diagonally across from the pyramid is the Old TransAmerica Building, 701 Montgomery St., at Washington St., the opulent showpiece of the corporation and a gem of older commercial architecture. Among the best of banking mini-museums in the area, the Wells Fargo Museum, 420 Montgomery St. (396-2619), at California St., contains an impressive display of Gold Rush exhibits, including gold nuggets and a nineteenth-century stagecoach. The affable guide possesses the sort of quiet yet unfathomable knowledgability usually found only in National Park Service rangers. (Open Mon.-Fri. 9am-5pm.) Nearby the Chinese Historical Society, 650 Commercial St. (391-1188), tells the history of the Chinese in California. Gawk at the 1909 parade dragon head and a queue once worn in loyalty to the Manchu Emperor. (Open Wed.-Sun. noon-4pm.)

Chinatown

The largest Chinese community outside of Asia, Chinatown also stays the most densely populated of San Francisco's neighborhoods. Chinatown was founded in the 1880s when, the gold dug and the tracks laid, bigotry fueled by unemployment engendered a racist outbreak against the "Yellow Peril." To protect themselves Chinese residents banded together in a small section of the downtown area. As the city grew, speculators tried to take over the increasingly valuable land, especially after the 1906 earthquake leveled the area. Yet not to be moved, Chinatown has gradually grown beyond its original borders, remaining almost exclusively Chinese. **Grant Avenue,** the street Rodgers and Hammerstein wrote a song about, stays the most picturesque part of Chinatown. From the monumental **Chinatown Café,** which straddles Grant at Bush St., and for a few blocks north, Grant cultivates a forest of Chinese banners, signs, and architecture. The less famous streets, such as Jackson, Stockton, and Pacific give a better feel for this neighborhood where Chinese-newspaper vendors eat their morning noodles out of thermoses. The **Chinese Culture Center,** 750 Kearny St., 3rd floor (986-1822), houses exhibits of Chinese American art and sponsors two walking tours of Chinatown. (For reservations call Tues.-Sat. 9am-5pm.) **Chinese New Year** celebrations involve massive fireworks displays, parades, and feasting.

North Beach

As one walks north along Stockton St. or Columbus Ave., supermarkets displaying ginseng give way to those selling provolone; restaurants start luring customers with biscotti instead of roast duck. Lying north of Broadway and east of Columbus, North Beach splits personalities between the bohemian Beats who made it their home—Kerouac, Ginsberg, Ferlinghetti—and the residents of a traditional Italian neighborhood. North Beach bohemianism flourished in the 1950s when the artists and brawlers nicknamed the Beats (short for "beatitude" according to Kerouac) first moved in. Drawn to the area by low rents and cheap bars, the group came to national attention when Ferlinghetti's **City Lights Bookstore** (see Entertainment) published Ginsberg's anguished and ecstatic dream poem *Howl.* More than one poet still tinkers with the language of Blake and Whitman, but the Beats have left. Through the middle of North Beach runs Broadway, the neon netherworld of pornography purveyors. Above it all stands the pleasant old residential district of Telegraph Hill, topped by appropriately named Coit Tower. North Beach is most fun to visit at night as the after-dinner, after-show crowd flocks to the area's numerous cafés for relaxing, ever-present cappuccino.

Between Stockton and Powell lies **Washington Square,** a lush lawn edged by trees. Across Filbert to the north of the square the **Church of St. Peter and St. Paul** beckons tired sight-seers to an island of quiet in its dark, wooden nave. In the square itself sits the **Volunteer Firemen Memorial,** donated by Mrs. Lillie Hitchcock Coit, once rescued from a fire in childhood. Coit's more famous gift to the city, **Coit Tower,** looms a few blocks east on Telegraph Hill, the steep mound from which a semaphore signalled the arrival of ships in Gold Rush days. An elevator will take you to the top for a spectacular 360° view. (Open June-Sept. daily 10am-6pm; Oct.-May daily 9am-5pm. Elevator fare $3, seniors $2, ages 6-12 $1, under 6 free. Last tickets sold ½ hr. before closing.) Sponsored by the Public Works Arts Project in the 30s, the murals inside depict scenes of manual labor. Since parking is limited, leave your car on Washington St. and walk up the Filbert Steps, which rise from the Embarcadero to the eastern base of the tower. The short walk allows excellent views, passing by many gorgeous art deco buildings.

Fisherman's Wharf

Continuing northward, toward the water, one leaves San Francisco proper and enters tourist limbo. "Fisherman's Wharf" maintains 4/5 mi. of gifts for lefties, porcelain figurines, and enough T-shirts to have kept even *Let's Go* staff meetings argument-free. Or not. Crowded, very expensive, and quite bland, the wharf manages to provide something to offend almost anyone. The area basically consists of a strip of boutiques flanked by shopping malls on each end; on the west end sits **Ghirardelli Square** (GEAR-a-deli), 900 N. Point St. (Information booth, 775-5500; open daily 10am-9pm). The only remains of Ghirardelli's chocolate factory now lie in the back of the **Chocolate Factory,** a soda fountain (open daily 11am-midnight). Drool over the huge vats of melted chocolate before purchasing one of the "factory's" disappointing desserts. Pricey boutiques now fill the rest of the old factory's red brick buildings, and local musicians and magicians entertain the masses. If you must, take MUNI bus #19 ("Polk"), #30 ("Stockton"), or #42 ("Downtown Loop").

To escape from this chocolate morass, take one of the **tour boats** or ferries from the wharf. Because times may very, call for schedules. The **Blue & Gold Fleet's** 75-minute tours cruise under both the Golden Gate and Bay Bridges, and past the Marin Hills, Angel, Alcatraz, and Treasure Islands, and the San Francisco Skyline (781-7877; adults $14, seniors and ages 5-18 $7). On the **Red & White Fleet** (456-2628) at Pier 41, a 45-minute Bay Cruise goes under the Golden Gate Bridge and past Alcatraz ($14, over 55 and ages 12-18 $10, 5-11 $7) while another 45-minute tour goes around the island, narrated by a former guard there. (Summer only. $7.50, seniors $7, ages 5-11 $4.) Ferries from pier 43½ to Sausilito are $4, ages 5-11 $2. Red & White boats also discharge passengers at Alcatraz (see below). For a really pleasant escape, try one of the **sailboat charters** that line the wharf: run by an experienced sailor, the *Rondo* (421-8353) sails two to six people on one- to three-hour voyages ($10 per person per hr.; March-Nov. Mon.-Fri. 1-5pm, Sat.-Sun. noon-6pm). Depending on tides and winds, voyages head for Angel Island, Sausalito, and the Golden Gate Bridge. The *Ruby* (861-2165) sails at lunchtime (with sandwiches) daily from May to October, departing from the China Basin building at 12:30pm and returning by 2pm, but call as the schedule often changes (tickets $25, under 10 $12.50). The *Ruby* also takes a turn in the bay on Friday and Saturday at 6pm. Reservations are required for sailboat charters. Bring a heavy sweater in summer and a jacket in winter.

Easily visible from boats, the Waterfront, and Powell St., no one who tried to escape **Alcatraz Island** has been heard from again. Except Clint Eastwood. A former federal prison, the island looms over the San Francisco Bay, 1½ mi. from Fisherman's Wharf. The island was named in 1775 for the *alcatraces* (pelicans) that flocked there. During the Civil War Union soldiers fortified "the Rock," then little more than barren stone, with a massive cannon and a garrison of several hundred to protect San Francisco from a possible Confederate attack. After the war the army took advantage of the island's isolation and resident police force to incarcerate troublemakers from across the country. In 1934, Alcatraz became a prison within the prison system, designed to hold those who had made too much trouble within other jails. Life for prisoners was extremely harsh and security tight—of the 23 escape attempts all were recaptured or killed, save the five "presumed drowned." The prison closed in 1962 and is now administered by the National Park Service. Ask about the Native American civil rights takeover in the late 60s. The Red & White Fleet (546-2805) runs boats to Alcatraz from Pier 41. Once on Alcatraz, you can wander by yourself or take an audiotape-guided two-hour tour. (Departures from Pier 41 in summer every ½ hr. 9:15am-4:15pm, in winter 9:45am-2:45pm. Fare $5, with tape tour $7.50; seniors $4.50, with tape $7; ages 5-11 $3, with tape $4.) Reserve tickets in advance through Ticketron (392-7469) for $1 extra or suffer long lines and risk not getting a ride.

Those unsure of their sea legs can inspect docked vessels along the wharf. **Maritime State Historic Park,** at Jefferson and Hyde St., harbors five boats, two of which are open to the public. The nearby museum displaying related memorabilia is worth popping into just to stand on the terrace overlooking the bay. (Boats and museum open daily 10am-6pm; off-season 10am-5pm. Free.) At the Haight St. Pier floats the famous windjammer the *Balclutha* (929-0202), a swift trading vessel that plied the Cape Horn route in the 1880s and 90s and was featured in the first Hollywood version of *Mutiny on the Bounty*. (Open Wed.-Sun. 10am-5pm. Admission

$2, under 16 free.) At Pier 45 you can board a WWII submarine—the *U.S.S. Pampanito*. (Open daily 9am-9pm; off-season Sun.-Thurs. 9am-6pm, Fri.-Sat. 9am-9pm. Admission $3, seniors and ages 6-12 $1, ages 13-18 $2, under 6 free.)

Nob Hill and Russian Hill

Until the earthquake and fire of 1906, railroad magnates occupied the mansions of Nob Hill. Even today, Nob Hill remains one of the nation's most prestigious addresses. Fine buildings line the streets with a certain settled wealth. Sitting atop a hill and peering down upon the masses can prove a pleasant afternoon diversion. Nearby Russian Hill is named after Russian sailors who died during an expedition in the early 1800s and were buried on the southeast crest.

The notorious **Lombard Street Curves,** on Lombard between Hyde and Leavenworth St. at the top of Russian Hill, afford a fantastic view of the city and harbor—if you can keep your eyes open down this terrifying plunge. The switchbacks were installed in the 1920s to allow horse-drawn carriages to negotiate the extremely steep hill. Devising transportation on the city's steep streets also inspired the vehicles celebrated at the **Cable Car Museum,** at the corner of Washington and Mason St. (474-1887). The building houses the cable-winding terminus for the picturesque cable cars, the working center of the system. (Open daily 10am-6pm; Nov.-March 10am-5pm. Free.)

Grace Cathedral, 1051 Taylor St. (776-6611), crowns Nob Hill. The castings for its portals imitate Ghiberti's on the Baptistry in Florence exactly enough that they used them to restore the originals. Inside, modern murals mix San Franciscan and national historic events with scenes from the lives of the saints.

Marina and Pacific Heights

The Marina, Pacific Heights, and the adjoining Presidio Heights are the most sought-after residential addresses in San Francisco. Centered about Union and Sacramento St., Pacific Heights boasts the greatest number of Victorian buildings in the city. The 1906 earthquake and fire destroyed most of the northeast part of San Francisco, but left the Heights area west of Van Ness Ave. unscathed; in contrast, the 1989 quake hit this area the hardest. Victorian restoration has become a full-fledged enterprise; consultants try to determine the original form of fretwork, friezes, fans, columns, corbels, cartouches, rosettes, rococo plaster, and so on. The **Octagon House,** 2645 Gough St. (885-9796), and **Haas-Lilienthal House,** 2007 Franklin St. (441-3004), allow the public a look inside. Rather sedate free tours of the impeccably preserved Octagon House are given on the first Sunday and second and fourth Thursdays of each month between 1 and 4pm. The Haas-Lilienthal House has more regular hours (open Wed. noon-3:15pm, Sun. 11am-4pm; admission $4, seniors and under 18 $2).

For those who prefer shopping to Victoriana, however, **Union Street** is your salvation. Between Scott and Webster St., Union St. is chock-full of upscale shops, bars, restaurants, and bakeries. Try to catch the Union Street Spring Festival, one weekend in late May or early June.

Down from Pacific Heights toward the bay, sits the **Marina** district. **Marina Green** by the water seethes with joggers and walkers and is well-known for spectacularly flown two-line kites. To the west lies the **Palace of Fine Arts,** on Baker St. between Jefferson and Bay St. The strange, domed structure and two curving colonnades are reconstructed remnants of the 1915 Panama Pacific Exposition, which commemorated the opening of the Panama Canal and symbolized San Francisco's completed recovery from the great earthquake. In 1959, a wealthy citizen, dismayed by the erosion, paid to have it rebuilt in stone. On summer days performances of Shakespeare sometimes grace the colonnade section.

The domed building houses the **Exploratorium** (561-0360), whose hundreds of interactive exhibits may teach even poets a thing or two about the sciences. (Open Wed. 11am-9:30pm, Thurs.-Fri. 11am-5pm, Sat.-Sun. 10am-5pm. Admission $5, seniors $2.50, ages 6-17 $1.50. Tickets valid 6 months.) Inside sits the **Tactile Dome** (561-0362), a pitch-dark maze of tunnels, slides, nooks, and crannies designed to help refine your sense of touch—a wonderful place to bring the kids. (Admission $5. Reservations required 2 weeks in advance.)

Western Addition and Japantown (Nihonmachi)

Japan Center (922-6776) is a popular, modern complex of shops and light manufacturing located near the corner of Webster and Geary St. Built in 1968, the center was intended as a gathering place for San Francisco's large Japanese American population. Instead, it now exists mainly for tourists, many of them from Japan. The Peace Pagoda, a memorial to the victims of Hiroshima and Nagasaki, stands in the center of Peace Plaza. Japanese folk festivals animate the plaza in April (Cherry Blossom Festival), early July (Star Festival), mid-September (Fall Festival), and December (Mochi, or rice loaf, Pounding Festival). Free outdoor entertainment enlivens summer Saturdays.

Civic Center

There are two ways to see the Civic Center: by day, for the architecture and museums, and by night, for performing arts. Although the San Francisco Museum of Modern Art, Van Ness Ave. (863-8800), at McAllister St. in the Veterans Bldg., plans to move to a larger home, the current site displays an impressive collection of 20th-century European and U.S. works. (Open Tues.-Wed. and Fri. 10am-5pm, Thurs. 10am-9pm, Sat.-Sun. 11am-5pm. Admission $4, seniors and under 16 $1.50. Free Tues. 10am-5pm. $2 Thurs. 5-9pm, seniors and under 16 $1.)

In the evening, Louise M. Davies Symphony Hall, 201 Van Ness Ave. (431-5400), at Grove St., rings with the sounds of the San Francisco Symphony. Next door, the War Memorial Opera House, 301 Van Ness Ave. (864-3330), hosts the well-regarded San Francisco Opera Company and the San Francisco Ballet. The Civic Center has two other theaters: the Orpheum, 1192 Market St. (474-3800), tends to draw flashy overblown shows, while the smaller Herbst Auditorium, 401 Van Ness Ave. (552-3656), at McAllister St., hosts string quartets, solo singers, and ensembles. Tours of the symphany hall, opera house, and Herbst Auditorium leave on the hour and half-hour from the Grove St. entrance of the Davies Hall. (½ hr., Mon. 10am-2:30pm. Admission $3, seniors and students $2. For more information, call 552-8338).

Mission District and Castro Street

Castro Street and the Mission District lie far enough south that both areas may still enjoy sunshine when fog blankets Nob Hill. Two thriving cultures make their home in this area: the gay community around Castro St. and the Hispanic community to the east. Although the scene has mellowed considerably from the wild days of the 70s, Castro St. still remains a proud and assertive emblem of gay liberation. In the Hispanic Mission District, the colorful murals along 24th St. reflect the rich cultural influences here of Latin America.

The best way to see Castro St. is to wander, peering into shops or stepping into bars. Two popular hangouts are Café Flor, 2298 Market St. (621-8579), and Café San Marco, 2367 Market St. (861-3846).

Down the street, The Names Project, 2362 Castro (863-1966), sounds a more somber note. This organization has accumulated 12,000 panels for an AIDS memorial quilt, each 3 ft. by 6 ft. section bearing the name and memory of a person who has died of AIDS. In addition to housing the project's administration, the building contains a workshop where a victim's friends and relatives can create panels; several are on display. (Open Mon.-Fri. 10am-10pm, Sat.-Sun. noon-8pm.)

At 16th and Dolores St. lies the old heart of San Francisco, Mission Dolores. The building, said to be the oldest in the city, turns 200 in 1991. Father Junípero Serra founded the Mission in 1776, and named it, like San Francisco itself, in honor of St. Francis of Assisi. However, the Mission sat close to a marsh known as Laguna de Nuestra Señora de los Dolores (Lagoon of Our Lady of Sorrows) and, despite Serra's wishes, it gradually became known as Misión de los Dolores. Exotic bougainvillea, poppies, and birds of paradise bloom in the cemetery, which was featured in Alfred Hitchcock's *Vertigo*.

Haight-Ashbury

The 60s live on in Haight-Ashbury, though more self-consciously than 20 years ago. The Haight willfully preserves an era that many seek to forget. Originally a quiet lower-middle-class neighborhood, the Haight's large Victorian houses—perfect for communal living—and the district's proximity to the University of San Francisco drew a large hippie population in the mid- and late-1960s. LSD, possession of which was not a felony at the time, flooded the neighborhood. The hippie scene reached its apogee in 1966-67 when Janis Joplin, the Grateful Dead, and the Jefferson Airplane all lived or played in the neighborhood. During 1967's "Summer of Love," young people from across the country converged on the grassy Panhandle of Golden Gate Park for the celebrated "be-ins." Despite recent gentrification, Haight-Ashbury remains cheap and exciting. Many of the bars and restaurants are remnants of a past era, with faded auras, games in the back rooms, and live-in regulars.

Walk down Haight St. and stick your head in as many stores as you like. **Aardvark's Odd Ark,** 1501 Haight St. (621-3141), at Ashbury, has an immense selection of used new wave jackets, good music in the background, and prices that will take you back in time. (Open Sat.-Mon. 11am-9pm, Wed. 11am-7pm, Thurs. 11am-9pm, Fri. 11am-8pm.) Another used clothing store, **Wasteland,** 1660 Haight St., is worth chcking out if only for its great façade, window displays, and shantih. (Open Mon.-Fri. 11am-6pm, Sat. 11am-7pm, Sun. noon-6pm.) The **Global Family Networking Center,** 1665 Haight St. (864-1978) contains a café, market, and global awareness. The rooms at the Red Vic, upstairs, could be a museum but for the lack of velvet rope and "Do Not Touch" signs (see Accommodations). The offbeat **Holo Gallery,** 1792 Haight St. (668-4656), glows with an amazing collection of holograms, the closest today's USF students come to the visions of the 60s LSD users. (Open Mon.-Sat. 11am-6pm, Sun. noon-6pm. Free.)

Resembling a dense green mountain in the middle of the Haight, **Buena Vista Park** has a predictably bad reputation. Enter at your own risk, and once inside, be prepared for those doing their own thing.

MUNI buses #6, 7, 33, 37, 66, 71, and 73 all serve the area, while Metro line N runs along Carl St., 4 blocks south.

Golden Gate Park

No visit to San Francisco is complete without a picnic in Golden Gate Park. Frederick Law Olmsted, designer of New York's Central Park, said it couldn't be done when San Francisco's 19th-century leaders asked him to build a park to rival Paris's Bois de Boulogne. But engineer William Hammond Hall and Scottish gardener John McLaren proved him wrong. Hall designed the 1000-acre park—gardens and all—when the land on the city's western side was still shifting sand dunes, and then constructed a mammoth breakwater along the oceanfront to protect the seedling trees and bushes from the sea's burning spray.

Fulton St. bounds most of the park to the north, Stanyan Street to the east, Lincoln Way to the south, and the Pacific Ocean to the west. The major north-south route through the park is named Park Presidio By-Pass Drive in the north and Cross Over Drive in the south. The **Panhandle,** a thin strip of land bordered by Fell and Oak Street on the north and south respectively, is the oldest part of the park; originally the "carriage entrance," it contains the oldest trees in the park, surrounded by the intriguing Haight-Ashbury. **Park headquarters,** home of information and maps, advises at Fell and Stanyan St. (558-3706), in McLaren Lodge on the eastern edge of the park. (Open Mon.-Fri. 8am-5pm.)

Three museums invigorate the park, all in one large complex on the eastern side between South and John F. Kennedy Dr., where 9th Ave. meets the park. The **California Academy of Sciences** (221-5100; 750-7145 for a recording; 750-7138 for Laserium), the West Coast's oldest institution of its kind, contains several smaller museums. The **Steinhart Aquarium** is more lively than the natural history exhibits. The engaging alligator and crocodile pool pales in comparison with the unique Fish Roundabout, a large tank shaped like a doughnut where the fish swim around the visitors. (Seals and dolphins fed Fri.-Wed. every 2 hr. 10:30am-4:30pm; penguins fed daily at 11:30am and 4pm.) The "Far Side of Science" gallery shows dozens of Gary Larson's best cartoons about nature and scientists. The academy also includes the **Morrison Planetarium** with its shows about white dwarves and black holes. (Additional charge of $2.50, seniors and students $1.25. Schedule changes; call 750-7141.) The Laserium orients its argon laser show to such robust themes as the Summer of '69 and Pink Floyd's *Dark Side of the Moon.* (Tickets $6, 5pm matinee $5, seniors and ages 6-12 $4.) Call 750-7138 for the current schedule. The synesthetic spectacle may be too intense for children under six. (Academy open daily 10am-7pm; Sept. 2-July 3 10am-5pm. Admission $4, $3 with MUNI Fast Pass or transfer, seniors and ages 12-17 $2, 6-11 $1, under 6 free. Free first Wed. each month until 8:45pm.)

The **M. H. de Young Museum** (750-3600) takes visitors through a 21-room survey of U.S. painting, from the colonial period to the early 20th century, including several works by John Singer Sargent. Mixed in with the survey are some sculptures and pieces of furniture, which include Shaker chairs and a redwood and maple bed made in San Francisco in 1885. Also noteworthy is the museum's glass collection. The **Asian Art Museum** (668-8921), occupies the west wing of the building, boasting a collection of rare jade and fine porcelain plus bronze works over 3000 years old. Most pieces were donated by Avery Brundage in 1966 in a gift that inaugurated the museum. (Both museums open Wed.-Sun. 10am-4:45pm. Admission $4, $3 with MUNI Fast Pass or transfer, seniors and ages 12-17 $2, under 12 free. One admission fee covers the de Young, Asian, and Palace of the Legion of Honor (see Richmond) museums for one day; save your receipt. All 3 free first Wed. each month and 10am-noon on the first Sat.)

Despite its sandy past, the soil of Golden Gate Park appears rich enough today to rival the black earth of the Midwest. Flowers blossom everywhere, particularly in spring and summer. The **Conservatory of Flowers** (386-3150), the oldest building in the park, allegedly was constructed in Ireland and shipped from Dublin via Cape Horn. The delicate and luminescent structure, modeled after Palm House in London's Kew Gardens, houses brilliant displays of tropical plants. (Open daily 9am-6pm; Nov.-March 9am-5pm. Admission $1.50, seniors and ages 6-12 $1, under 6 free.) The **Strybing Arboretum**, on Lincoln Way at 9th Ave. (661-1316), southwest of the academy, shows 5000 varieties of plants. Walk through the Garden of Fragrance for the vision-impaired, with labels in braille and plants chosen especially for their texture and scent. (Tours daily at 1:30pm and at 10:30am Thurs.-Sun. Open Mon.-Fri. 8am-4:30pm, Sat.-Sun. 10am-5pm. Free.) Near the Music Concourse on a path off South Dr., the **Shakespeare Garden** contains almost every flower and plant ever mentioned by the herbalist of Avon. Plaques with the relevant quotations are hung on the back wall; a map helps you find your favorite hyacinths, cowslips, and gillyvors. (Open daily 9am-dusk; winter Tues.-Sun. 9am-dusk. Free.)

A relic of the 1894 California Midwinter Exposition, the **Japanese Tea Garden** is a serene, if overpriced, collection of dark wooden buildings, small pools, graceful footbridges, carefully pruned trees and plants, and tons of tourists. Buy some tea and cookies for $1 and watch the giant goldfish swim placidly in the central pond. (Open daily 9am-6:30pm; Oct.-April 8:30am-5:30pm. Admission $2, seniors and ages 6-12 $1, under 6 free. Free first and last ½ hr. of operation, and all national holidays.)

At the extreme northwestern corner, the **Dutch Windmill** turns and turns again. Rounding out the days of old is the **Carousel** (c. 1912), accompanied by a $50,000 Gebruder band organ. (Open daily 10am-4pm; Oct.-May Wed.-Sun. 10am-4pm. Tickets $1, ages 6-12 25¢, under 6 free.)

The multinational collection of gardens and museums in Golden Gate Park would not be complete without something expressly American: a herd of buffalo.

A dozen of the shaggy beasts roam a spacious paddock at the western end of John F. Kennedy Dr., near 39th Ave. To get to the park, hop on bus #5 or 21. On Sundays traffic is banned from park roads, and bicycles and roller skates come out in full force. Bike rental shops are plentiful: skates, though harder to come by, are also available. Numerous MUNI buses cover the streets that surround Golden Gate Park and the north-south Park Presidio By-Pass/Cross Over Dr.

The Richmond District

The **Golden Gate Bridge**, the rust-colored symbol of the West's bounding confidence, sways above the entrance to San Francisco Bay. Built in 1937 under the directions of chief engineer Joseph Strauss, the bridge exudes almost indescribable beauty from any angle on or around it.

Lincoln Park, the Richmond district's biggest attraction, grows at the northwest extreme of the city. To get there, follow Clement St. west to 34th Ave., or Geary Blvd. to Point Lobos Ave. The park's **California Palace of the Legion of Honor** (750-3659), modeled after the Collonade Hôtel de Salm in Paris, houses San Francisco's major collection of European art. The gallery's particularly strong French collection includes one of the best Rodin inventories in the country, both in plaster and bronze, plus many impressionist works and two unusual Davids. Downstairs you'll find portions of the Achenbach Foundation's extensive graphic arts holdings. (Open Wed.-Sun. 10am-5pm. Admission $4, $3 with MUNI pass or transfer, seniors and ages 12-17 $2, under 12 free. Price includes same-day admission to the de Young and Asian Art Museums in Golden Gate Park. Free first Wed. and Sat. of each month 10am-noon.) Take the **Land's End Path**, running northwest of the cliff edge, for a romantic view of the Golden Gate Bridge.

Entertainment

San Francisco abounds with free publications listing the events in the Bay Area. The two that natives rely on most are the *San Francisco Bay Guardian* (824-7660) and the *East Bay Express.* The *Guardian,* filled with reviews, some news, and a detailed weekly calendar, lives by Wilbur Storey's statement that "It is a newspaper's duty to print the new and raise hell." For a more detailed listing of Berkeley theater and the Oakland jazz scene, try the *Express* (652-4610). For listings of the visual and performing arts, try the monthly *CenterVoice* (398-1854). The *Bay Times* (626-8121), the gay and lesbian paper, also appears monthly. While it has an entertainment section, it is mostly articles.

Two newspapers worth loose change are the daily *San Francisco Chronicle* (25¢), particularly the Sunday edition ($1) with its ample, pink-paged entertainment listings; and the weekly *Advocate,* whose own pink pages are another thing entirely. This national newsmagazine for gay people offers a large amount of information on San Francisco's gay community.

Publications are distributed in record stores, bookshops, and street corner distribution boxes. When you can't find a magazine, call the publication itself for the nearest distribution point. Or call the **Entertainment Hotline,** 391-2001 or 391-2002.

Clubs

Firehouse, 3160 16th St. (621-1617). Hip Mission District habitat with excellent rap and underground music. Live bands on Sun. Open Mon.-Sat. 9pm-until the crowd tires. Cover Fri.-Sat. $5.

Southside, 1190 Folsom St. (431-3332). Popular danceteria can accommodate upwards of 2000 upwardly mobile singles. Food served. Open daily 5pm-4am. Cover $5.

Channel's, #1 Embarcadero Center (956-8768). Financial District watering hole. A bustling reservoir of eligible young people. Open daily 4pm-2am.

Kimballs', 300 Grove St. (861-5555), at Franklin St. Great jazz musicians scare off the New Age/fusion frauds at this popular club/restaurant. Shows Wed.-Thurs. at 9pm, Sat.-Sun. at 11pm. Cover usually $8-12.

The I-Beam, 1748 Haight St. (668-6086), Haight-Ashbury. Specializes in post-Branca bands and DJs playing high-tech rock. Decor includes shooting light beams and 2 screens full o' clips from cartoons, golden oldies, and Japanese monster flicks. Often free student night Wed. or Thurs. Carding fairly stringent. Open daily from 9pm. Cover $5-10. Must be 21.

The Fillmore, 1805 Geary St. (567-2060, 474-2995 for recording), opposite Japantown. Big name bands for the younger set. All ages welcome. You pay dearly to recall the times when everyone from Janis Joplin to Herbert Marcuse entertained here. Box office open day of show only, generally around 7pm. Advance tickets available from BASS. Call for show times.

Wolfgang's, 901 Columbus Ave. (441-4334, 474-2995 for recording), at Lombard St. Rock, video, vinyl, acoustic—you name it, they'll have it. Bands or DJ every night after 9pm. Cover $15 plus 2-drink minimum ($5).

Gay and Lesbian Clubs

While less visible than in recent years, gay nightlife in San Francisco still flourishes. Most popular bars thrive in the city's two traditionally gay areas—the Castro (around the intersection of Castro St. and Market St.) and Polk St. (for several blocks north of Geary St.). In the Castro, stop for a drink at the **Metro Bar and Restaurant,** 3600 16th St. (431-1655), near Market St. or at **Castro Station,** 456 Castro (626-7220). **The Stallion,** 749 Polk (775-2213), provides a convenient, central starting point for a survey of Polk folk. For something more elegant, try **Imo's,** 1351 Polk (885-4535). Although the gay stronghold on the South-of-Market has given way to the invasion of straight clubs, one landmark remains: **Trocadero Transfer,** 520 4th St. (495-0185), reputedly the largest gay disco in the union. **Amelia's,** 647 Valencia St. (552-7788), is a popular lesbian bar and dance club.

San Francisco Bay Area

Berkeley

A quarter-century ago Mario Salvo climbed a top a police car and launched Berkeley's free speech movement. Berkeley today remains a national symbol of political activism and social iconoclasm. In the 1980 presidential election Ronald Reagan finished fourth. Even as today's students prefer climbing corporate ladders to digging ditches in underdeveloped countries, the Berkeley City Council eagerly considers an initiative to curb "excess profits" in real estate. Berkeley's rent control law, now in its tenth year, has served as a model to the rest of the country.

The site of one of the country's best public universities, Berkeley is as renowned for its academics and chefs as for its political cadres and street people. Chez Panisse is regarded as having originated California Cuisine, now imitated in almost every major city. Northwest of campus, residents call the shopping area around Chez Panisse the "Gourmet Ghetto." Stylish clothing boutiques and gourmet specialty stores blanket the city. Miraculously, Berkeley revels in these bourgeois accoutrements while maintaining its idealistic rhetoric. By purchasing free-range chickens and avoiding styrofoam, citizens contentedly strike their blows against mechanized farming and the destruction of the environment. In Berkeley when you consume, you "shop for peace."

Practical Information

Visitor Information: Chamber of Commerce, 1834 University Ave. (549-7000). Open Mon.-Fri. 9am-5pm. **Council on International Educational Exchange (CIEE) Travel Center,** 2511 Channing Way (848-8604), at Telegraph Ave. Open Mon.-Fri. 10am-5pm. **Recorded Event Calendar,** 835-3849. **U.C. Berkeley Switchboard,** 1901 8th St. (642-6000). Information on community events. Irregular hours.

Public Transport: Bay Area Rapid Transit (BART), 465-2278. Berkeley Station at Shattuck Ave. and Center St., close to the west edge of the university. The free university **Humphrey-Go-BART shuttle** (642-5149) connects the BART station with the central and eastern portions of campus. During the school year, the shuttle leaves the station every 5-10 min. 7am-5:45pm, and every 15 min. after that until 7pm Mon.-Fri.—not on university holidays. **Alameda County Transit (AC Transit),** 839-2882. Buses leave from Transbay Terminal for Berkeley every 15 min. 6am-11pm, less frequently at other times. City buses operated by AC Transit run frequently. Fare 75¢, seniors 15¢, under 18 50¢.

Ride Boards: Berkeley Ride Board, ASUC building near the bookstore, on the 1st floor. Or call KALX-FM at 642-1111.

Transportation Information: Berkeley TRIP, 644-7665. Information on public transport, biking, and carpooling. Mostly local transportation, but not confined to daily commuting.

Help Lines: Rape Hotline, 845-7273. **Suicide Prevention,** 849-2212. Both open 24 hr.

Post Office: 2000 Allston Way (845-1100). Open Mon.-Fri. 8:30am-5pm, Sat. 10am-2pm. **ZIP code:** 94704.

Area Code: 415.

Berkeley lies across the bay northeast of San Francisco, just north of Oakland. There are two efficient ways to reach the city: by car (I-80 or Rte. 24) or by public transportation from downtown San Francisco. Crossing the bay by **BART** ($1.85) is quick and easy, and both the university and Telegraph Ave. are a short, 5-minute walk from the station. The **University of California** campus stretches into the hills, but most of its buildings reside in the westernmost section, near the BART.

Lined with bookstores and cafés, **Telegraph Avenue,** which runs south from the student union, is the spiritual center of the town. The mostly residential north side of campus has a few places to grab a snack. The **downtown** area, around the BART station, contains what few businesses Berkeley will allow. The public library and central post office shelf and sort there. The **Gourmet Ghetto** encompasses the area along Shattuck Ave. and Walnut St. between Virginia and Rose St. West of campus and by the bay lies the **Fourth St. Center,** home to great eating and window shopping. To the northwest of campus, **Solano Avenue** offers countless ethnic restaurants (the best Chinese food in the city), bookstores, and movie theaters as well as more shopping.

Accommodations

Sleeping cheaply in Berkeley remains surprisingly difficult. The town has no good hostels, and clean, cheap motels are few. Most of the city's hotels are flophouses. You might try renting a **fraternity room** for the night: Check the classified ads in the *Daily Californian* for possibilities.

YMCA, 2001 Allston Way (848-6800), at Milvia St. Men over 17 only. No membership required. Registration 8am-10pm. Small rooms $21. Medium rooms $22. Pool and basic fitness facilities included. Key deposit $2.

University of California Housing Office, 2700 Hearst Ave. (642-5925), in Stern Hall at the northern end of campus. Rents rooms in summer to anyone who claims connection with the school (e.g. thinking of transferring). Open daily 8am-11pm. Singles $30. Doubles $38. Call ahead.

Berkeley Capri Motel, 1512 University Ave. (845-7090), about 1 mi. west of campus near the North Berkeley BART. Otherwise decent rooms scream for paint and decoration. HBO. Singles and doubles $35.

The Berkeley Motel, 2001 Bancroft Way (843-4043), at Milvia St. Close to campus but poorly maintained—check the mattress before you check in. Single and doubles $33.

Food

Eating takes on an existential significance in Berkeley. Choosing between radicchio or endive for a lunchtime salad is an anxiety-filled act of self-creation. The free Berkeley monthly *Bayfood* (652-6115) devotes articles, ads, and recipes to cooking and dining. Because of its devotion, Berkeley supports several exceptional restaurants, many of them budget-busters. Fret not: an inexpensive alternative or two do exist.

Plearn Thai Cuisine, 2050 University Ave., between Shattuck and Milvia. Elegant decor. One of the best Thai places in the Bay Area. Some lines at peak hours. Entrees $5-8.50. Try the Gai-Young chicken ($6.75). Open Mon.-Sat. 11:30am-3pm and 5-10pm, Sun. 5-10pm.

Flint's Barbecue, 6609 Shattuck Ave., in Oakland. Just over the city line near the Ashby bars, and worth the trip. Considered the best barbecue around. Even fiery Duncanic eaters should stick to "medium" or "mild." No seating. Beef or pork ribs $6. Open Sun.-Thurs. 11am-2am, Fri.-Sat. 11am-4am.

Fat Apple's, 1346 Martin Luther King Dr., northwest of campus. Natural foods and hamburgers piled high with cheese and fixings ($5.50) make this restaurant popular. Don't miss the fresh apple pie ($2), baked here daily, or the cream puffs. Allow plenty of time; the line to get in often goes out the door. Open Mon.-Fri. 6am-11pm, Sat.-Sun. 7am-11pm.

Shin Shin, 1715 Solano Ave. Noteworthy, cheap, and varied Chinese lunch specials (daily 11:30am-3:30pm). Small bowl of hot and sour soup, 2 wontons, and rice topped with your choice of 34 different entrees, plus half an orange and a fortune cookie $2.85. Open Sun.-Thurs. 11:30am-9:30pm, Fri.-Sat. 11:30am-10pm.

Zachary's Chicago Pizza, 1853 Solano Ave. Flaky crusts—thick or thin—with interesting toppings, such as pesto and zucchini. Slices with toppings $1.75, pizzas $5-17. One wall displays works by talented local artists. Open Sun.-Thurs. 11am-9:30pm, Fri.-Sat. 11am-10:30pm.

Mario's La Fiesta, 2444 Telegraph Ave., at Haste St. Great Mexican food and a friendly atmosphere. Large chicken *flauta* combination plates, with rice, beans, guacamole, and chips $5.40. Open daily 10:30am-10:30pm.

Saul's, 1475 Shattuck. Honorable deli which flies in its smoked fish from New York, has a special weekend brunch menu, and serves excellent "Noah's Bagels." Sandwiches $4-7.25, bagels 50¢ (plain)-$6.50 (with cream cheese and lox). Open Mon.-Fri. 10:30am-9pm, Sat.-Sun. 9am-9pm.

The Cheese Board Collective, 1504 Shattuck Ave. A pillar of the Gourmet Ghetto. A few hundred fantastic cheese selection—but no Venezuelan Beaver cheese. Add a few hundred to the excellent french bread for a great picnic. Very generous about giving samples. 10% discount for customers over 60, 15% for ages over 70, and so on. If you reach 150, they'll pay to eat the cheese. Open Tues.-Fri. 10am-6pm, Sat. 10am-5pm.

Espresso Strada, 2300 College Ave., at Bancroft. Philosophy and art grad students throng this glittering jewel of a culinary-intellectual complex. Get your cappucino cold when the sun's hot, and enjoy the beautiful outdoor terrace. Coffees 85¢-$1.25. Open Mon.-Fri. 7:30am-11pm, Sat.-Sun. 8:30am-11pm.

Jade Villa, 800 Broadway (839-1688), a serious challenge to SF's *dim sum*. Sit down to a traditional *dim sum* lunch or order individual items from a take-out counter. Incomparable 3 pork buns ($1.50). Open daily 9am-5:30pm.

Sights

Pass through Sather Gate into **Sproul Plaza** and enter the university's world of gracious buildings, grass-covered hills, and sparkling streams that give the impression of an intellectual Arcadia. The **information center** (642-4636), in the student union building at Telegraph and Bancroft, has maps, information, and booklets for self-guided tours. (Open Mon.-Fri. 8am-6pm, Sat. 10am-6pm.) Guided tours start at the **visitors center** (642-5215), room 101, University Hall, Oxford St. and University Ave. The Berkeley campus swallows 160 acres, bounded on the south by Bancroft Way, on the west by Oxford St., by Hearst Ave. to the north, and by extensive parkland to the east. Founded in 1868 and moved to Berkeley in 1873, the school has an enrollment of over 30,000 and more than 1000 full professors. Imposing **Bancroft Library,** with nearly six million volumes, is among the nation's largest. Located in the center of campus, the library contains exhibits ranging from California arcana to folio editions of Shakespeare's plays. You can see the tattered bronze plaque left by Sir Francis Drake in the 16th century, vainly claiming California for England. (Open Mon.-Fri. 9am-5pm, Sat. 1-5pm. Free.)

The most dramatic on-campus attraction is **Sather Tower**, the 1914 monument to Berkeley benefactor Jane K. Sather. For 50¢, you can ride to the top of the tower, known affectionately as the *Campanile* because it's modeled after the clock tower in Venice's St. Mark's Square. (Open daily 10am-4:15pm.) The tower's 61 bells are played manually most weekdays at 8am, noon, and 6pm.

The **University Art Museum**, 2626 Bancroft Way (642-1124; 24-hr. events hotline 642-0808), holds a diverse and interesting permanent collection. Innovative directors have put together a number of memorable shows over the years on everything from cubism to the interaction of U.S. painting and popular 50s culture. (Open Wed.-Sun. 11am-5pm. Admission $4, seniors and ages 6-17 $3. Free Thurs. 11am-noon.)

The **Lawrence Hall of Science** (642-5132), standing above the northeast corner of the campus in a concrete building, shares honors with San Francisco's Exploratorium for finest science museum in the Bay Area. Take the free express shuttle from the BART station weekdays during museum hours. Exhibits stress learning science through hands-on use of everyday objects. (Open Mon.-Fri. 10am-4:30pm, Sat. 10am-5pm. Admission $3.50; seniors, students, and ages 7-18 $2.50; under 7 free.)

Back in the campus center, the **Worth Ryder Art Gallery** (642-2582), in Kroeber Hall room 116, displays works of wildly varying quality by students and local artists. (Open Tues.-Thurs. 11am-4pm. Free.)

The **Botanical Gardens** (642-3343) spread over 30 acres in Strawberry Canyon, contain over 10,000 species of plant life. (Open daily 9am-5pm. Free.) The **Berkeley Rose Garden**, on Euclid Ave. at Eunice St. north of the campus, spills from one terrace to another in a vast semi-circular amphitheater. You can see Marin County and the Golden Gate Bridge from the far end. While in bloom, from May through September, the gardens are always open.

Outside of campus stand more museums and noteworthy architecture. The **Judah Magnes Museum**, 2911 Russell St. (849-2710), displays one of the West Coast's leading collection of Judaica. (Open Sun.-Fri. 10am-4pm.) The **Julia Morgan Theater**, 2640 College Ave. (548-7234), is housed in a beautiful former church designed by its namesake and constructed of dark redwood and Douglas fir.

People's Park, on Haste St. 1 block off Telegraph Ave., is an unofficial museum of sorts, featuring a mural that depicts the 60s struggle between the city and local activists over whether to leave the meager block a park or to develop it commercially. During that struggle, then-governor Ronald Reagan sent in state police to break a blockade, resulting in the death of one student. In 1989, a rally was held to protest the university's renewed threats to convert the park. The demonstrators quickly forgot their noble purpose and began turning over cars, looting stores, and setting fires. Presently, crack dealers and the homeless have claimed this dismal site. Avoid it at night.

Go for an off-beat experience at the **Takara Sake Tasting Room**, 708 Addison St. (540-8250), at 4th St. You can request a sample of several varieties, all made with California rice. A narrated slide presentation on *sake* brewing is shown on request. (Open daily noon-6pm.)

A short drive or BART ride (to the Lake Merrit stop) into Oakland will take you to the **Oakland Museum**, 1000 Oak St. (834-2413); a well-designed complex of three galleries devoted to California's artistic, historical, and natural heritage. The top floor houses the **Gallery of California Art** where everything from traditional 19th-century portraits to contemporary works using car doors finds a wall. Besides rotating photography exhibits, the gallery also has some splendid Currier cartoons about the Gold Rush. One floor down, the fantastic **Cowell Hall of California History**, takes visitors through California's boom-like social and economic history, using artifacts, costumes, Chris, and even vehicles. On the lowest level, the **Hall of California Ecology** uses state-of-the-art fish-simulation technology in its new Aquatic California gallery. (Open Wed.-Sat. 10am-5pm, Sun. noon-7pm. Tours daily at 2pm. Free.)

Entertainment

Hang out with procrastinating students in front of or inside the **student union** (642-5215). The ticket office, arcade, bowling alleys, and pool tables are all run from a central desk. (Open Mon.-Fri. 8am-6pm, Sat. 10am-6pm; off-season Mon.-Fri. 8am-10pm, Sat. 10am-6pm.) Next door the **Bear's Lair** (486-0143), a student pub, sells pitchers of Bud for $3.50. (Open Mon.-Thurs. noon-midnight, Fri. 11am-8pm.) **CAL Performance,** 101 Zellerbach Hall (642-7477), is a university-wide concert and lecture organizer. Information on all the rock, classical, and jazz concerts, lectures, and movies on campus finds a home here. Big concerts are usually held in the Greek Theatre (642-5550) or Zellerbach Hall. (Open Mon.-Fri. 10am-5:30pm, Sat. noon-4pm.)

Berkeley is awash with free publications explaining where to go and what to do. Most reliable and interesting is *The Berkeley Monthly* (848-7900), with comprehensive listings; delivered free to local residents, the paper costs $1 on the stands. For information on university happenings, find the *Daily Californian* (548-8300), published by Berkeley students, available in Sproul Plaza daily during the term (on Tues. and Thurs. in summer). The *Express* (652-4610) and its vast listings section is widely available at book and record stores.

Ashkenaz, 1317 San Pablo Ave. (525-5054), between Gilman St. and Camelia. A folk-dance co-op that often swings with reggae bands. Children welcome. Cover depends on performer; usually $4-7. Open some afternoons and most evenings from 9:30pm-1am.

The Griffin, Virginia St. at Shattuck Ave. Lively jazz club popular with students. Top-line acts. Cover $3-5.

Brennan's, 4th St. and University Ave. (841-0960), down by the waterfront in nonstudent Berkeley. Cheap liquor and large crowds from every part of the city combine for the perfect Bacchanalian budget-obliteration. Steam tables at one end offer cheap food for the fearless. Great Irish coffee $2.25. Open Tues.-Sat. 11am-1am, Sun.-Mon. 11am-midnight. Food served until 9pm.

Starry Plough, 3101 Shattuck Ave. (841-2082). Pub with Irish bands and Anchor Steam on tap. Posters espouse the pro-Irish, anti-nuclear, and U.S.-out-of-Nicaragua points of view. Open daily 4pm-2am.

Larry Blake's Downstairs, 2367 Telegraph (848-0886), at Durant Ave., through the college's upstairs dining room and down a flight. An excellent drinking and meeting spot. Sawdust on the floor and live jazz. Drinks from $2. Cover $3-6. Bar open until 1am. Food served until midnight.

Bertola's, Telegraph Ave. and 41st St. (547-9301), in Oakland. The student's place to get smashed. Well drinks $1.50, double bourbons $1.75, triples $2. Open daily 4-10pm.

Triple Rock Brewery, 1920 Shattuck Ave. (843-2739). Micro-brewery producing 3 delicious regular beers (2 pale ales and 1 porter) and occasional specialties. A bargain at $2.25 per pint. Old beer logos grace the walls. Roof garden, too. After 7pm, you can only stand in the crowded barroom, but in the afternoon, come to meet friendly noncollegiates who really enjoy their beer. Open daily 11:30am-1:30am.

Spats, Shattuck Ave. (841-7225), in the Gourmet Ghetto. Looks like Adrian's aunt's attic except for the taxidermy victims standing here and there. Have a drink on a ramshackle sofa amid parasols, and a sign reading "Bachelor Officers Quarters." Hors d'oeuvres served 2-7pm. 8-page drink menu (drinks from $1.75). Open Mon.-Sat. 11:30am-1am, Sun. 4pm-1am.

U.C. Theater, 2036 University Ave. (843-6267), west of Shattuck Ave. Standard reruns, film noir series, studio classics; nicely-matched double feature. Schedules available throughout Berkeley or at the theater. Creative film festivals. Admission $3.50 before 6pm, $6 after 6pm, seniors and children $3.50.

Marin County

The wealthiest county in the United States, Marin (pronounced ma-RIN) is also by some reports the most vapid. An unmistakably Californian conflation of hedonism and mysticism has produced a sort of New Age opulence; residents confer in hot tubs, worship crystals, consume macrobiotic food, and accumulate obscene heaps of wealth.

The undeveloped hills just west of the Golden Gate Bridge comprise the **Marin Headlands,** part of the Golden Gate National Recreation Area which sprawls across the Bay Area. The view from the Headlands back over the bridge to San Francisco arguably has the most spectacular vista in the Bay Area. You can get to the Headlands (and the viewpoints) easily by car; simply take the Alexander Ave. exit off U.S. 101 and take your first left. You'll go through an underpass and up a hill on your right. You should consider hiking the ¾-mi. trail that leads from the parking area down to the sheltered (and usually deserted) beach at **Kirby Cove.**

About 5 mi. west along the Panoramic Hwy. off U.S. 101 stands **Muir Woods National Monument,** a congregation of primeval coastal redwoods. A loop road takes you through the most outstanding area. (Open daily 8am-sunset.) The **visitors center** (388-2595), near the entrance, keeps the same hours as the monument. West of Muir Woods lies **Muir Beach,** which offers a tremendous view of San Francisco from its surrounding hills.

North of Muir Woods lies the isolated, largely undiscovered, and utterly beautiful **Mount Tamalpais State Park.** The heavily forested park has a number of challenging trails that lead: to the top of the peak, to a natural stone amphitheater, and to **Stinson Beach,** a local favorite for sunbathing. **Park headquarters** is at 810 Panoramic Hwy. (388-2070). The park opens a half-hour before sunrise and closes a half-hour before sunset.

Encompassing 100 mi. of coastline along most of the western side of Marin, the **Point Reyes National Seashore** juts audaciously into the Pacific from the eastern end of the submerged Pacific Plate. Here the infamous San Andreas Fault comes to an end. The remote position of the point brings heavy fog and strong winds in winter, a special flora and fauna, and crowds of tourist to gawk at it all.

Limantour Beach, at the end of Limantour Rd. west of the seashore headquarters, and **McClures Beach,** at the extreme north of the seashore near the end of Pierce Point Rd., are two of the nicest area beaches. Both have high, grassy dunes and long stretches of sandy beach. In summer a free shuttle bus runs to Limantour Beach from seashore headquarters. Strong ocean currents along the point make swimming suicidal. To reach the dramatic **Point Reyes Lighthouse** at the very tip of the point, follow Sir Francis Drake Blvd. to its end and then head right along the long stairway to Sea Lion overlook. From December to February, gray whales can occasionally be spotted off the coast from the overlook.

Marvelous Marin, to its credit, has managed to avoid the cheap motel plague that can ruin lovely areas overnight. The **Golden Gate Youth Hostel (AYH)** (331-2777), a few miles south of Sausalito, sits close to a waterbird sanctuary and houses 60 beds in an old, spacious building that is part of deserted Fort Barry. (Check-in 8-9:30am and 4:30-9pm. From 9:30am-4:30pm, leave your name on a sign-up sheet and return at 4:30pm to claim a bed. Curfew 11pm. $7. Linen 50¢. Reservations recommended in summer.) By car from San Francisco, take the Alexander Ave. exit off U.S. 101; take the second Sausalito exit if going toward San Francisco. Follow the signs into the Golden Gate National Recreation Area, then follow the hostel signs through the park (about 3 mi.). Golden Gate Transit buses #2, 10, and 20 stop at Alexander Ave. From there, you'll have to hitch. A taxi from San Francisco costs $11-12.

Farther north, the spectacularly situated **Point Reyes Hostel (AYH),** Limantour Rd. (663-881), opens nightly for groups and individuals. You're more likely to get a late-notice room here than in the Golden Gate Hostel, although reservations are advised on weekends. Hiking, wildlife, birdwatching, and Limantour Beach are all within walking distance. Plan ahead to use the well-equipped kitchen since the nearest market hawks its waves 8 mi. away. (Registration 4:30-9pm. $7.) By car take the Seashore exit west from Rte. 1, then follow Bear Valley Rd. to Limantour, 6 mi. from the hostel. For public transportation information, contact Golden Gate Transit (332-6600) or call the hostel.

Rabbit-like campsites on Pt. Reyes reproduce more than in more populated areas. The campground closest to Sausalito hunkers down in **Samuel Taylor State Park** (488-9897), on Sir Francis Drake Blvd. 15 mi. west of San Rafael (itself 10 mi. north of Sausalito on U.S. 101). The park's 60 sites ($10, $12 Sat.-Sun.) with hot showers stay open year-round. A hiker/biker camp costs $2 per person (2-night max. stay). Make reservations one week in advance from April to September (800-444-7275). Four campgrounds (accessible only by foot) line the national seashore in the south, inner cape portion of Pt. Reyes. All are fairly primitive, with pit toilets, firepits, and tap water; all require permits from the **Point Reyes National Seashore Headquarters,** Bear Valley Rd. (663-1092; open Mon.-Fri. 9am-5pm, Sat.-Sun. 8am-5pm). All camps command exquisite views of the ocean and surrounding hills.

The **Sausalito Chamber of Commerce** answers the call at 332-0505. **Point Reyes National Seashore Headquarters,** on Bear Valley Rd. (663-1092), ½ mi. west of Olema, offers wilderness permits, maps, and campsite reservations. (Open Mon.-Fri. 9am-5pm, Sat.-Sun. 8am-5pm.) There is little public transportation in Marin. **Golden Gate Transit** (453-2100; 332-6600 in San Francisco) provides daily bus service between San Francisco and Marin County via the Golden Gate Bridge, as well as local service within the county. Buses #10, 20, 30, and 50 run from the Transbay Terminal at 1st and Mission St. in San Francisco ($1.85). The **Golden Gate Ferry** (453-2100, in San Francisco 332-6600) serves Sausalito, departing from the ferry building at the end of Market St. for a 25-minute crossing (Mon.-Fri. 7:50am-8pm, Sat.-Sun. 11:30am-6:55pm; in winter last ferry at 4:50pm). Boats return from Sausalito roughly one hour later than departures. (Fare $5; off-season $3.)

The **area code** for Marin County is 415.

Northern California

Wine Country

Although **Napa Valley** holds the most well-known U.S. vineyards, northern California houses no less than five valleys which produce award-winning bottles of the grape year after year. Beginning in Napa Valley, transplated Europeans recognized the Dionysian virtues of this area (75 mi. northeast of San Francisco) when California was still a part of Mexico. Prohibition, however, turned the vineyards into fig plantations; only in the last 20 years have vintners recovered lost ground. Today, the wine-tasting carnival lasts from sunup to sundown, dominating the life of small towns in Napa, Sonoma, Dry Creek, Alexander, and Russian River Valley. Closest to San Francisco (75 mi. northeast), Napa also remains the most heavily trafficked. Learn to tolerate bus tours gulping from plastic glasses in overcrowded tasting rooms, or try visiting Napa Valley on weekdays and heading farther north and west to the other valleys.

Sonoma offers slightly less crowded wineries than Napa, as well as more exciting local history. The Sonoma mission, General Vallejo's home, and Jack London's Beauty Ranch all may interestthe wine-weary traveler. Farther north, the **Russian River** flows lazily between small towns and smaller wineries. The **visitors center,** 14034 Armstrong Woods Rd. (869-9009 or 800-253-8800) has an energetic staff that will help plan your trip around this area.

Nevertheless, Napa Valley is home to wine country's heavyweights; vineyards include national names such as Inglenook, Christian Brothers, and Mondavi. Neophytes should especially enjoy large vineyards' well-organized tours; there's no pressure to spout obscure adjectives at the tastings. After dipping your feet in the proverbial wine bucket, head to the smaller wineries of Sonoma Valley (Kenwood and Château St. Jean are especially good) or Oregon to discuss vintages with the growers themselves.

Of the more than 250 wineries in Napa County, and nearly two-thirds reside in Napa Valley; almost all give free tours and tastings. The vineyards listed below are some of the valley's larger operations. To reach the smaller places, pick up a list of vineyards from the chamber of commerce in Napa or look for signs along the roadside.

Robert Mondavi Winery, 7801 St. Helena Hwy. (963-9611), in Oakville. Spirited tours through marvelous catacombs and past towering stacks of oaken barrels with mellowing wine. The best free tour and tasting for the completely unknowledgeable. Fairly decent wine. Open daily 9am-5pm; Nov.-April 10am-4:30pm. Reservations required. Tours fill fast in summer: Call before 10am.

Domaine Chandon, California Dr. (944-2280), next to the Veteran's Home in Yountville. One of the finest tours in the valley; available in several languages by prior arrangement. Owned by Moët Chandon of France (makers of Dom Perignon), and not surprisingly most capable of divulging the secrets of champagne making. Champagne tastings $2 per glass at the restaurant attached to the winery. Open daily 11am-6pm; Nov.-April Wed.-Sun. 11am-6pm.

RMS Vineyards, 1250 Cuttings Wharf Rd. (253-9055). For yet another type of Napa grape-based alcohol. New and unique brandy distillery. Tours Mon.-Fri. at 10:30am and 2:30pm. Sales room open until 4pm.

Hanns Kornell Champagne Cellars, 1091 Larkmead Lane (963-2334), 4 mi. north of St. Helena. A 1-room testing area with excellent dry champagne (try the Sehr Trocken). Entertaining, informative tours until 3:45pm. Open daily 10am-4pm.

Beaulieu Vineyard, 1960 St. Helena Hwy. (963-2411), in Rutherford. Tour includes a brief, imaginative audio-visual presentation. First tour at 11am, last at 3pm. Tasting daily 10am-4pm.

Clos Du Val Wine Company Ltd., 5330 Silverado Trail (252-6711), in Napa. Outdoor picnic area with whimsical drawings by Ronald Searle. Tours by appointment at 10am and 2pm. Tasting room open all day. Open daily 10am-4pm.

Budget motels amid the valleys are scarce and inaccessible to those without cars. Everpresent **Motel 6,** 3380 Solano Ave. (257-6111), in Napa at Redwood Rd. off Rte. 29, has rooms with TV and A/C, plus a small pool. (Usually full by 6pm in summer. Singles $32. Each additional adult $6.) For the valley's best deal ssslip into the all-wood cabinsss at the **Triple S Ranch,** 4600 Mountain Home Ranch Rd. (942-6730), in Calistoga. (Take Rte. 29 north to Calistoga, turn left on Petrified Forest Rd., and then right on Mountain Home Ranch Rd. Singles $30. Doubles $40. Open April-Oct.) Campers can camp at the **Bothe-Napa Valley State Park,** 3601 St. Helena Hwy. (942-4575; 800-444-7275 for reservations), north of St. Helena on Rte. 29. (Open daily 8am-10:30pm; Oct.-April 9am-5pm. Sites with hot showers $10. Reservations recommended.)

Though sit-down meals may squeeze your wallet, Napa and its neighboring communities support numerous delis where you can pick up inexpensive picnic supplies. Off the beaten tourist track in Yountville, **The Diner,** 6476 Washington St., serves huge, delicious white-bread Mexican dinners. (*Chile relleno* with rice, beans, and salad $7. (Open Tues.-Sun. 8am-3pm and 5:30pm-closing.) Should you tire of the valley's delicate slices of brie on baguette, try the **Hi-Way 29 Diner,** 101 Kelly Rd., for hearty greasy spoon fare. Fluffy frisbee-sized hotcakes cost $2.80. (Open Mon.-Sat. 6am-3pm, Sun. 7am-4pm.)

Route 29 runs through the middle of the valley with the main town of **Napa** at its southern end and **Calistoga** to the north. Cycling in the area yields the best results; the valley is dead level and no more than 30 mi. long. The **tourist information office,** 4076 Byway E. (257-1112), in Napa, recommends that bicyclists use the Silverado Trail rather than jammed Rte. 29, which runs parallel. Rent a bike at **Napa Valley Cyclery,** 4080 Byway E. (255-3377). ($4 per hr., $15 per day. Open Mon.-Sat. 9am-6pm, Sun. 10am-5pm. Major credit card required.) **Greyhound** stops in Napa, Yountville, St. Helena, and Calistoga. (Yountville office on California Dr., 944-8377; open Mon.-Fri. 7am-5pm, Sat.-Sun. 7-11am and 1-5pm. Napa office 1620 Main St., 226-1856; open Mon.-Fri. 7:45am-noon and 1:15-6pm, Sat. 9:15-10:15am.)

Napa's **post office** cancels at 1625 Trancas St. (255-1621; open Mon.-Fri. 8:30am-5pm). The **ZIP code** is 94558; the **area code** in the valley is 707.

Redwood National Park

Redwood National Park flaunts an astonishing variety of flora and fauna in addition to the burly, abundant, 500-year-old trees themselves. The region's fishing is famous, with variegated terrain ideal for hikers and backpackers. The park begins just south of the Oregon border and extends 50 mi. south, hugging the coast for about 40 mi., and encompassing three state parks. The lack of public transportation within the park, however, demands of the car-less both perseverance and well-honed hitchhiking skills. Beaches line the coastal trail which marches most of the length of the park; the heavy rains, created by moisture off the Pacific, foster a lush environment of elk, bear, birds, and marine life. Day use of state parks costs $3 per car.

Campsites are numerous, ranging from the well equipped (flush toilets and free hot showers; sites $10, hikers $1) to the primitive (outhouses at best; free). Peak season begins in the third week of June and concludes in early September. Try to visit from mid-April to mid-June or September to mid-October, when the park's summer crowds and fogs dissipate. Call MISTIX (800-444-7275) for reservations ($3.75; highly recommended in the peak season).

The most pleasant roost in this neck of the woods, the **Redwood Youth Hostel (AYH)**, 14480 U.S. 101, Klamath 95548 (482-8265), features modern amenities and rugged coastal outlooks. Housed in the historic De Martin House, the hostel has a kitchen, dining room, and laundry facilities, as well as disabled access. (Family rooms available by reservation. $7, under 18 with parent $3.50. Linen $1.)

Practical Information

Visitor Information: Redwood Information Center (488-3461), 2 mi. south of Orick on U.S. 101. **Orick Chamber of Commerce**, at the same station. Open late June-Sept. 2 daily 8am-6pm; off-season 9am-5pm. **Prairie Creek Ranger Station**, on U.S. 101 (488-2171), in Prairie Creek State Park. Open daily 8am-5pm; mid-Sept. to mid-June hours subject to change. **Hiouchi Ranger Station**, on U.S. 199 (458-3134), across from Jedediah Smith Redwoods State Park. Open daily 8am-5pm. **Redwood National Park Headquarters and Information Center**, 1111 2nd St., Crescent City 95531 (464-6101). Open daily 8am-5pm. **Crescent City Chamber of Commerce**, 1001 Front St. (464-3174), at J St. Open Mon.-Fri. 9am-5pm.

Park Activity Information: 464-6101. Open 24 hr.

Greyhound: 1125 Northcrest Dr. (464-2807), in Crescent City. Supposedly travelers can flag down buses at 3 places within the park: Shoreline Deli (488-5761), 1 mi. south of Orick on U.S. 101; Paul's Cannery in Klamath on U.S. 101; and the Redwood Hostel. Capricious bus drivers may ignore you. Call the Greyhound station directly preceding your stop to alert the driver of your presence. Lockers $1 per 24 hr. Beware of sporadic hours which keep your pack locked away from you, as well as from thieves.

Public Transport: Del Norte Senior Center (464-3069) offers a very limited service connecting Klamath and Crescent City. **Dial-A-Ride** (464-9314) operates in the immediate Crescent City area as well. Fare 75¢, seniors and children 50¢. Open Mon.-Sat. 7am-7pm.

Bike Rentals: Escape Hatch Sport and Cycle, 960 3rd St. (464-2614). Town bikes $4 per hr. Open Mon.-Sat. 9am-5pm.

Post Office: 751 2nd St. (464-2151), in Crescent City. Open Mon.-Fri. 8:30am-5pm. **ZIP code:** 95531.

Area Code: 707.

The park divides naturally into five segments (Orick, Prairie Creek, Klamath, Crescent City, and Hiouchi) stacked from south to north along Rte. 101—except for Klamath, each has its own ranger station. Though the scenery varies widely, always present are the imposing *Sequoia sempervirens.*

Accommodations, Food, and Sights

The Orick region, which includes the southernmost section of the park, contains a new ranger station, about 2 mi. south of Orick on U.S. 101 and 1 mi. south of the Shoreline Deli (the Greyhound stop). The area's main attraction is the **tall trees grove,** an 8-mi. hike from the ranger station. In peak season, a shuttle bus (fare

$3, seniors $1.50, children $1) runs twice per day from the station to the tall trees trail. From there, you can hike 1.3 mi. to the tallest known tree in the world (367.8 ft.). Be sure to leave extra time, since the strenuous return hike is mostly uphill. Backpackers may camp anywhere along the way after obtaining a permit at the ranger station.

Orick, (pop. 400) a narcoleptic and uninteresting town, brims over with souvenir stores selling "burl" (tacky, expensive wood carvings). Nevertheless, the town provides some amenities. A post office, the reasonably priced **Orick Market** (488-3225), and some motels line U.S. 101. The market delivers groceries to Prairie Creek Campground daily at 7:30pm. Call in your order in before 6pm (minimum order $10; delivery free). Two mi. north of Orick on U.S. 101 (Fern Canyon exit) lies the area's only gourmet restaurant, the **Prairie Creek Park Cafe** (488-3841). The adventurous menu ranges from elk steak to wild boar roast, but prices are rather steep, with dinner entrees about $10. (Open Mon. noon-8:30pm, Wed.-Sat. 8am-9pm.)

The **Prairie Creek** Area, equipped with a ranger station and state park campgrounds, is perfect for hikers. Starting at the Prairie Creek Visitors Center (see Practical Information), the 10-mi. **James Irvine Trail** winds through magnificent redwoods, around clear and cold creeks, through **Fern Canyon** (famed for its 50-ft. fern walls and mossy bottom), and by a stretch of the Pacific Ocean.

To the north, the **Klamath** Area comprises a thin stretch of park land connecting Prairie Creek with Del Norte State Park. Klamath River, the main attraction here besides the rugged coastline, draws stares and lures for its salmon. (Fishing permit required.) There is no ranger station in this area. Check out the home cooking at the **Klamath Café** (482-7245), south of town.

Crescent City is the place to refuel—but not much else. Seven mi. south of the city lies the **Del Norte Coast Redwoods State Park,** an extension of the Redwood Forest. The park's magnificent ocean views—along with picnic areas, hiking trails, and nearby fishing—lure enough campers to keep the sites full during peak season. (RV and tent sites $6, day-use fee $2.) Crescent City itself, technically not part of the park, was largely destroyed by a 1964 *tsunami*. The town struck back, rebounding uglier than ever. South of the city, across the highway from the beach picnic area, the **El Captain Motel,** 100 Elk Valley Rd. (464-5313), provides the park's loudest, cheapest motel lodging. (Singles $20. Doubles $24.) Consider the **Bon Dormé Motel,** 731 9th St. (464-5611), but see your room before paying. (Singles $25. Doubles $29.) In winter, all motel prices drop $15 to 20. One die-hard cyclist swears by the authentic Mexical fare at **Los Campadres,** Hwy. 101 S. (464-7871; open daily 11am-9pm).

The **Hiouchi** region sits in the northern part of the park inland along Rte. 199 and offers several excellent trails. The **Stout Grove Trail,** an easy ½-mi. walk, boasts the park's widest redwood, 16 ft. in diameter. The path is also accessible to the disabled; call 458-3310 for arrangements. **Kayak** trips on the Smith River leave from the ranger station.

Sacramento

Sacramento is so unexceptional, say rival San Franciscans, that market researchers often use it to test new brands of soap. But the 99 44/100 city turns a deaf ear to its maligners, confident that its several excellent museums and interesting historical sights, all nestled among leafy, quiet streets, will continue to attract a steady stream of visitors. Recent high-class hotel development has sparked architectural flair and sophistication downtown, with the city growing into its role as the cultural center of the Sacramento Valley.

A hobo-hangout in the 1960s, **Old Sacramento** has undergone restoration, now attracting money-drunk tourists with many up-market shops. A pleasant atmosphere pervades a number of historically interesting structures, among them the **B.F. Hastings** building at the corner of 2nd and J St. Dating from 1852, the building houses Wells Fargo's offices, a museum, and the reconstructed chambers of the California Supreme Court. Pick up a self-guided walking tour at the Old Sacramento Visitors Center, or join a tour beginning at the center (442-7644).

Before overdosing on souvenir stores and cutesy-pie potpourri gift shops, try one or two of the excellent historical museums in Old Sacramento's northern end. The **California State Railroad Museum,** 111 I St. (448-4466), at 2nd St., will delight even those who don't know the difference between a cowcatcher and a caboose. The museum houses a fascinating collection of historical locomotives in its enormous exhibition space. The same ticket admits you to the **Central Pacific Depot and Passenger Station,** at 1st and J St., a reconstruction of a station that once stood here. (Both open daily 10am-5pm. Admission $3, ages 6-17 $1.)

The **Sacramento History Museum,** 101 I St. (449-2057), at Front St., educates with lively, informative exhibits set in a two-story glass-and-chrome extravaganza. The interactive videos complimenting most exhibits provide a more engaging look at California history. (Open daily 10am-5pm. Guided tours upon request. Adults $2.50, seniors $1.50, ages 6-17 $1.)

Art connoisseurs should pop into the small but elegant **Crocker Art Museum,** 216 O St. (449-5423), at 3rd St., which shows mainly 19th-century European and U.S. oil paintings. One large gallery showcases photography, another contemporary works by California artists. (Open Tues. 1-9pm, Wed.-Sun. 10am-5pm. Admission $2, seniors and ages 7-18 $1.)

Two modern twin towers very nearly replaced the **state capitol,** at 10th St. and Capitol Mall (324-0333), in Capitol Park, when the old and abused structure began to crumble like everything else in the 1970s. Fortunately, the generous collective Californian taxpayer forked out $68 million, and the building was finally restored in 1982 to its glorious 1906 finery: pink and green decor, oak staircases, gilt, and all-too-flattering oil paintings of forgotten governors. The "Restoration" tour covers the chambers; the "Historic" delves into the re-created office spaces, decorated as they were decades ago. (Both hour-long tours daily on the hour 9am-4pm. Free.) Another tour explores the gardens, including the elaborate Vietnam Memorial (daily at 10am). For information, self-guided walking tour brochures, and an excellent free 10-minute film, go to Room B-27 in the basement.

Before the arrival of a certain Ronald Reagan, who demanded more spacious surroundings, the **Old Governor's Mansion,** 16th and H St. (323-3047), fit the bill. This 15-room Victorian masterpiece (c. 1877) housed 13 of California's governors. The building practically bursts with gables and attics, displaying the architectural subtlety of a three-tiered wedding cake. (Open daily 10am-5pm. ½-hr. tours on the hour. Last tour at 4pm. Admission $1, under 18 50¢.)

Across town at 27th and L St., stands **Sutter's Fort** (445-4422), a reconstruction of the 1839 military settlement that launched Sacramento. All supplies had to be dragged overland from the river to build the settlement, which now contains the **State Indian Museum** (349-0971). Rangers fire the fort's cannon at 11am and 2pm. (Both open daily 10am-5pm. Admission to each $1, under 18 50¢.)

Though perhaps a bit disheartened by the dominance of compact discs, vintage vinyl collectors will still enjoy a trip to the original **Tower Records,** at the corner of Landpark Dr. and Broadway (444-3000). Tower started out with a small shelf of records in the back of his dad's drugstore in the 40s, and now owns a national chain of stores. The store's overwhelmingly large selection and late hours are replicated in the adjacent Tower Books, Drugs, Theater, Tobacco, *ad nauseum.* Prices have moved into the 90s, however. (Record store open daily 9am-midnight.)

The kid in you (or with you) will enjoy the **Sacramento Zoo,** 3930 W. Land Park Dr. (449-5885). When mere animals don't suffice, get off your tuffet and head for the zoo's **Fairytale Town,** a 6-acre theme park with puppet shows throughout the day. (Open daily 9am-5pm. Admission $2.50, seniors and ages 3-12 $1. Take bus #5 or 6 to William Land Park, 3 mi. south of the capitol.) Another kids' place is the **Visionarium,** 2901 K St. (443-7476), on the 2nd level of the Sutter square galleria, an aggressively interactive children's museum billed as "Kids on Kampus." (Open Mon.-Sat. 10am-6pm, Sun. noon-5pm. Admission $4.)

Downtown Sacramento supports a bunch of breakfast and lunch spots; unfortunately, many close by 3 or 4pm and most close for a few hours in the afternoon (2-5pm). The restaurateurs go home once the government does. Old Sacramento is the place to go for ice cream, light snacks, and classier wining and dining. But the best meals appear in the blocks between 19th St. and 22nd St., concentrated around Capitol St. **Zelda's Original Gourmet Pizza**, 1415 21st St. (447-1400), has the best deep-dish pizza (medium $7.50) in Sacramento—ask any passerby. This dark, cool retreat from Sacramento's heat lies distant from the center of town. (Open Mon.-Thurs. 11:30am-2pm and 5-10pm, Fri. 11:30am-2pm and 5-11:30pm, Sat. 5-11:30pm, Sun. 5-9pm.) **Rubicon Brewing Company**, 2004 Capitol Ave. (448-7032), home of India Pale Ale, the number one beer at the American Beer Fest (pints $1.75), serves food that measures up to the brew. Filling sandwiches ($4-5) served on fresh sourdough. In Old Sacramento, **Annabelle's**, 200 J St. (448-6239), boasts an all-you-can-eat lunch buffet ($3.75) which includes pasta, lasagna, pizza, and salad bar. (Buffet served daily 11am-4pm.)

Sacramento's extraordinary supply of motel rooms wanes when one of the city's frequent large conventions is in progress: all but the sleaziest dives are booked full by midweek. Try to reserve a month in advance. The cheapest places lie near the Greyhound station across from Capitol Park but provide questionable cleanliness and security. Several motels east of Capitol Park, along 15th and 16th St., also average $30 for singles. For even cheaper rates go to West Sacramento, a 10- to 30-minute walk along W. Capitol Ave. from Old Sacramento. Call the **West Sacramento Motel & Hotel Association** (372-5378 or 800-962-9800) or the **West Sacramento Chamber of Commerce** (372-5378; open Mon.-Fri. 8am-5pm). Yolo buses #40, 41, or 42 go to West Sacramento from the L St. terminal. Like many cities, the quality of rooms ranges extremely, even within some of the motels. See your room before paying.

With nine comfortable beds, the **Gold Rush Home Hostel (AYH)**, 1421 Tiverton Ave. (421-5954), on the outskirts of town near the zoo, is like visiting your favorite relatives, except they charge you. (Lockout 9am-6pm. $7, nonmembers $10. Reservations required.) Primarily apartments for the elderly, **Capitol Park Hotel**, 1125 9th St. (441-5361), at L St. 2 blocks from Greyhound, rents some well-worn rooms nightly. The ancient hotel, with a fabulous downtown location, keeps cool with large windows. (Singles $25. Doubles $39.) The **Americana Lodge**, 818 15th St. (444-3980), the nicest in the range, features a small pool, A/C, and TV. (Singles from $33. Doubles $44. Confirm reservations with advance payment.)

Sacramento not coincidentally commands the center of the Sacramento Valley. No fewer than seven major highways converge on the city from various directions. As in many other cities, each block represents one hundred numbers. These numbers also correspond to the lettered cross-streets, so 200 3rd St. intersects B St., 1700 C St. is on 17th St., 300 3rd St. intersects C, and so on. The capitol and endless state government buildings occupy the rectilinear downtown area. The **Broadway** area, home of the original Tower Records, lies beyond Z St. The 40 avenues north of Broadway, known as the "fabulous forty," contain the mansions of Sacramento's industrial barons. One housed Ronald Reagan during his term as governor. **West Sacramento** lies, strangely enough, west of downtown, on the other side of the river. With well-marked lanes, the city is a good biker's town. Rent at the **American River Bike Shop**, 9203 Folsom Blvd. (363-6271), for $3 per hour or $15 per day.

The small, congenial **Sacramento Convention and Visitors Bureau**, 1421 K St. (442-5542), between 14th and 15th St. presents a tidy discreet stand of brochures on the corner table. Find the only accommodations guide in the free "Sacramento" produced by the city. (Open Mon.-Sat. 8am-5pm.) The **Old Sacramento Visitors Center**, 1104 Front St. (442-7644), also has a modest handful of brochures. The **Discover Sacramento Hotline** (449-5566) offers 24-hr. recorded information on arts, sports, and special events.

Amtrak, at 4th and I St. (444-9131), has a huge terminal (open daily 5:15am-11:15pm). Daily trains roll to Reno ($50), Chicago ($196), L.A. ($71), Seattle ($137), and San Francisco ($16). Reservations must be made months in advance for all eastbound and most westbound trains. The **Greyhound** station idles at 715 L St., (444-7270), between 7th and 8th St. in a relatively safe if unpleasant neighborhood. Buses run to Reno (gambler's special round-trip $19; one way $28), L.A. ($47), and San Francisco ($10). (Open 24 hr.) **Sacramento Regional Bus Transportation** (321-2877) offers service in downtown Sacramento. (Fare 85¢. $1 express buses run Mon.-Fri. 6:30-9am and 3:30-6pm.) A trolley connects downtown with Old Sacramento via the I-5 underpass on K St. (Mon.-Fri. 11am-4pm). Though cheap (25¢), the trolley covers a walkable distance—don't wait around for it. An 18.3-mi. **light rail** transit line connects the central business district with the eastern regions of the city. (Trains run every 15 min. 6am-8:30pm. Fare 85¢.) The **Yolo Bus Commuter Lines** (371-2877) connect downtown with Old Sacramento, West Sacramento, Davis, and Woodland. (Fare 60¢, rush hour 75¢; 50¢ surcharge for some routes.)

The **post office** stamps at 2000 Royal Oak Dr. (921-0280; open Mon.-Fri. 8:30am-5pm). **General Delivery** mail can be picked up at Metro Station, 801 I St. (442-0764), at 8th. (Open Mon.-Fri. 8am-5pm.) The General Delivery **ZIP code** is 95814. The **area code** is 916.

THE PACIFIC NORTHWEST

The drive of "manifest destiny" brought 19th-century pioneers to the Pacific Northwest, some of the most beautiful and awe-inspiring territory in the United States. Lush rainforests, snow-covered mountains, and the deepest lake on the continent all reside in this corner of the country. Oregon's Dunes, Washington's Cascades, miles and miles of the Pacific Crest Trail, and a long, stormy coast inhabited by giant redwoods and sequoias draw the mountaintop-born and bred and the adventurous city-slicker alike.

Settled amidst the wildlands of the Pacific Northwest dance cities with all the urban flair of their northeastern counterparts. But unlike New York, Washington, DC, or Boston, the cosmopolitan cities of Seattle and Portland have mountain ranges at their back doors. The northwestern traveler can hike the Cascade Range by day and club-hop by night, ride Seattle's monorail or raft down southern Oregon's wild river rapids.

For more comprehensive coverage of the Pacific Northwest than can be provided here, please consult *Let's Go: Pacific Northwest, Western Canada, & Alaska.*

Travel

Perhaps the best strategy for getting to the Pacific Northwest by air requires flying by budget airline to San Francisco, and then traveling by land. **Amtrak** also transports passengers from the East Coast or Midwest to Seattle: the "Pioneer" and the "Empire Builder" trains ramble from Chicago to Seattle along two slightly different routes. The "Coast Starlight" train runs along the western beaches between Seattle and Los Angeles, stopping at numerous points in between.

Gee, the accommodations in this region smell terrific. Well-established **hostels** throng Oregon's coast, Willamette Valley, and Washington's Puget Sound; most seldom fill. Inexpensive **bed & breakfasts** proliferate in the area.

Outdoors

The Northwest coastal region remains cool and misty year-round. The densely populated central valleys enjoy a mild climate, with warm summers and rainy winters. The Cascade Range keeps moisture and cool air from reaching eastern Washington and Oregon, where the arid climate resembles that of the Rocky Mountain states.

In addition to camping and hiking, a variety of unusual activities invite you to explore the Coast. Whitewater rafting does a huge business in the Pacific Northwest, offering the adventurous a chance to view otherwise inaccessible areas. Canoeing and kayaking are two other perenially popular water sports. Mountain schools at Mt. Rainier and elsewhere offer instruction in rock-climbing and mountaineering. The Pacific Crest Trail stretches from the Mexico/California border all the way into Canada. This rugged, challenging trail suits one- or two-week hiking trips particularly well.

For information on national parks, contact the **Pacific Northwest Regional Office,** National Park Service, 2001 6th Ave., Seattle, WA 98121 (206-442-0170). The national forest system manages huge expanses of land, including the West Coast's least spoiled natural landscapes, the designated wilderness areas. Reach the **Pacific Northwest Region** at U.S. Forest Service, P.O. Box 3723, Portland, OR 97212. State parks are rarely fully booked even on popular summer weekends. Sites are about $8. All along the West Coast, state parks and forests, especially those by the ocean, offer hiker/biker campsites, where those on two feet or two wheels can camp for $1.

Oregon

Although their shoreline, inland forests, and parks share all the lush drama of those in California, Oregon residents for years disdained the gaggles of tourists that overran their southern neighbor. The 1980s brought hard times for Oregonians, however, and with them a reconsideration of this once-widespread disdain. Bumper stickers that read "Don't Californicate Oregon" disappeared, replaced by giant "welcome" signs in every backwater town. Cities that once thrived on Oregon's now dwindling mining and foresting industries resurrected as tourist towns.

But tourism fuels much of the state's history. Lewis and Clark rented canoes and slipped quietly down the Columbia River when their *Let's Go* research brought them to Oregon; later, waves of settlers surged along the Oregon Trail. Long after Native Americans began trails in this region, the narrow coastal route along U.S. 101 provides the best-worn corridor of travel. Visitors should, however, venture off the highway to reach Oregon's more natural glories.

Practical Information

Capital: Salem.

Tourist Information: State Tourist Office, 595 Cottage St. NE, Salem 97310 (800-547-7842). Oregon State Parks, 525 Trade St. SE, Salem 97310 (378-6305). Department of Fish and Wildlife, 506 SW Mill St., Portland 97208 (229-5403). Oregon Council American Youth Hostels, 99 W. 10th St. #205, Eugene 97402 (683-3685).

Time Zone: Pacific (3 hr. behind Eastern) and Mountain (2 hr. behind Eastern). Postal Abbreviation: OR.

Portland

On the afternoon of May 18, 1980, Washington's Mt. St. Helens erupted in a jealous attempt to smother the beauty of its southern neighbor, Portland, under a layer of volcanic ash. Fortunately for the largest city in Oregon, the area's frequent spring showers cleansed the streets of their dusty blanket, letting the natural endowments of the area shine through once again.

The impressive surroundings draw people as rugged, or at least as green, as the surrounding locale; consummate grape-nuts kind of folk flock to the largest park enclosed by a U.S. city, as well as one of the two parks in the world located on a dormant volcano. The mighty Columbia River rolls majestically onward north of the city, while the Willamette River flows through the heart of the city, providing downtown denizens with a range of aquatic leisure possibilities. Five minutes west of the center, dense forests hide miles of well-maintained hiking trails. Along with a thriving arts community, even Portland's mayor has taken inspiration from the city—he swept into office shortly after he posed as a flasher revealing himself to a sidewalk sculpture for an "Expose Yourself to Art" poster.

Practical Information

Emergency: 911.

Visitor Information: Portland/Oregon Visitors Association, 26 SW Salmon St. (275-9750), at Front St. Free *Portland Book* contains maps, general information, and historical trivia. Open Mon.-Fri. 8:30am-5pm, Sat. 9am-3pm.

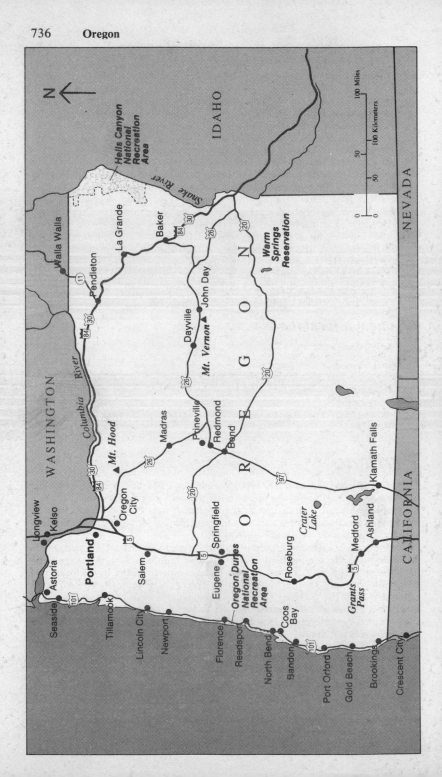

Portland International Airport: north of the city on the banks of the Columbia. Served by I-205. To get downtown, take Tri-Met bus #12, which will arrive on SW 5th Ave. (fare 85¢). **Raz Tranz** (recorded information 246-4676) provides an airport shuttle (Fare $5, under 12 $1) that leaves every 20 min. and takes 35 min. to reach major downtown hotels and the Greyhound station.

Amtrak: 800 NW 6th Ave. (800-872-7245), at Hoyt St. Open daily 7:30am-5:30pm.

Buses: Greyhound/Trailways, 550 NW 6th St. (243-2323). Buses almost every hr. to Seattle ($20-24). Ticket window open daily 5:30am-12:30am. **Green Tortoise,** 205 SE Grand Ave. (225-0310). To Seattle (Tues. and Sat. at 4pm, $15) and San Francisco (Sun. and Thurs. at noon, $49).

Public Transport: Tri-Met, Customer Service Center, #1 Pioneer Courthouse Sq., 701 SW 6th Ave. (233-3511). Open Mon.-Fri. 9am-5pm. Seven regional service routes, each with its own color totem. A few buses with black and white totems cross color-coded boundaries. Crux at the **mall,** with covered bus stops and information centers. Fare 85¢-$1.15. All rides free within *fareless square,* bounded by the Willamette River, NW Hoyt St., and I-405. Service generally 7am-midnight, reduced Sat.-Sun. Tri-Met's light rail system **MAX** only serves one line (running between downtown and the city of Gresham), but uses the same fare system as the buses.

Taxi: Broadway Cab, 227-1234. **New Rose City Cab Co.,** 282-7707. Both charge $1.30 for the first mi., $1.40 each additional mi.

Car Rental: Rent-A-Wreck, 2838 NE Sandy St. (231-1640). $14 per day. 50 free mi., 15¢ each additional mi. Must be 25. **Thrifty Car Rental,** 632 SW Pine (227-6587). $34 per day, unlimited mileage. Must be 21 with credit card.

Help Lines: Crisis Line, 223-6161. Open 24 hrs. **Senior Citizens Crisis Line,** 223-6161. **Gay and Lesbian Services,** 223-8299.

Time Zone: Pacific (3 hr. behind Eastern).

Post Office: 715 NW Hoyt St. (294-2300). Open Mon.-Fri. 7:30am-6:30pm, Sat. 8:30am-5pm. **ZIP code:** 97208.

Area Code: 503.

Portland sits just south of the Columbia River about 75 mi. inland from the Oregon coast. The city blazes 637 mi. north of San Francisco and 172 mi. south of Seattle. The primary east-west highway, I-84 (U.S. 30), follows the route of the Oregon Trail through the Columbia River Gorge. West of Portland, U.S. 30 follows the Columbia downstream to Astoria. I-405 curves around the west side of the business district to link I-5 with U.S. 30.

Portland can be divided into five districts. **Burnside Street** divides the city into north and south, while east and west are separated by the Willamette River. **Williams Avenue** slices off a corner of the northeast sector, simply called "North." The **Southwest district** is the city's hub, encompassing the downtown area, historical Old Town in the northern end, and a slice of ritzy West Hills. The very core of the hub lies at the downtown mall area between SW 5th and 6th Ave. Car traffic is prohibited here; don't mess with the transit system's turf. The **Northwest district** contains the southern end of Old Town, an industrial area to the north, and a residential area, culminating in the posh Northwestern hills area to the west. Most students enrolled in Portland's several colleges and universities live in the Northwest. The **Southeast district** keeps less well-to-do residential neighborhood. Anomalous amidst its surroundings, **Laurelhurst Park** is a collection of posh houses around E. Burnside St. and SE 39th St. The **North** and **Northeast** districts are chiefly residential, punctuated by a few quiet, small parks.

Accommodations and Camping

With Portland's increasing gentrification, finding cheap lodgings has become more challenging. **Northwest Bed and Breakfast,** 610 SW Broadway, Portland 97205 (243-7616), extensively lists member homes in the Portland area and throughout the Northwest. You must become a member ($10 per year) to use their lists and reservation services. They promise singles from $25-40 and doubles from $30-60.

The remaining cheap downtown hotels are generally unsafe; the hostel undoubtedly provides the best option. Barbur Ave. hosts a comely and accessible motelstrip; N. Interstate Ave. and Motel 6.

Portland International AYH Hostel (AYH), 3031 SE Hawthorne Blvd. (236-3380), at 31st Ave. Take bus #5. Cheerful, clean, and crowded. Sleep inside or on the porch. Kitchen facilities; laundromat across the street. Open 8-9:30am and 5-11pm. $8.75, nonmembers $11.75. Reserve in summer.

Youth Hostel Portland International, 1024 SW 3rd St. (241-2513). Accessible, but neighborhood would make Mr. Rogers cringe. Laundromat. Open 24 hrs. $8.75, nonmembers $13-18; with private bath $18.

YWCA, 1111 SW 10th St. (223-6281). Women only. Close to major sights, clean, and safe. Small rooms. Shared double $12. Singles $20, with bath $25.

Bel D'air Motel, 8355 N. Interstate Ave. (289-4800), just off I-5. Take bus #5 from SW 6th Ave. Pretentious in name, not in decor. Very small; call 1 week in advance. Singles $25. Doubles $30.

Aladdin Motor Inn, 8905 SW 30th (246-8241), at Barbur Blvd. about 10 min. from downtown by bus #12 from SW 5th Ave. Clean and comfortable. A/C and kitchens available. Singles $29. Doubles $32.

Mel's Motor Inn, 5205 N. Interstate Ave. (285-2556). Take bus #5 from 6th Ave. No aspirations to elegance, but clean and comfortable with A/C and cable TV. No comedic diner attached. Singles $28. Doubles $32.

Ainsworth State Park, 37 mi. east of Portland on I-84, along the Columbia River Gorge. Hot showers, flush toilets, and hiking trails. Sites $9, with electicity $10, with full hookup $12.

Milo Molver State Park, 25 mi. southwest of Portland, off Oregon Rte. 211, 5 mi. west of the town of Estacada. Fish, boat, and bicycle along the nearby Clackamas River. Hot showers and flush toilets. Sites $9, with electricity $10, with full hookup $12.

Food

Portland's restaurants reflect the health-conscious attitude of the people; you can more easily find a tofu burger on an oatbran bun than a simple chilidog. Some of the best fresh produce in town sells at the **Corno Foods,** 711 SE Union St. (232-3157), under the Morrison Bridge, a labyrinthine market offering mainly fruits and veggies.

The Original Pancake House, 8600 SW Barbur Blvd. Take green bus #12, 41, or 43. Great place for breakfast ($3.50-5). Hour-long lines on Sat. and Sun. morning. Open Wed.-Sun. 7am-3pm.

Escape from New York Pizza, 913 SW Alder St. Also at 622 NW 23rd St. The best pizza in town; look for the daily message on the menuboard. Hefty cheese slices $1. Large cheese pie $8 Open Mon.-Thurs. 11:30am-9pm, Fri.-Sat. 11:30am-10pm.

Chang's Mongolian Grill, 1 SW 3rd St. at Burnside. Also at 2700 NW 185th and 1600 NE 122nd. All-you-can-eat lunches ($6) and dinners ($9). Select your meal from a buffet (fresh vegetables, meats, and fish), mix your own sauce to taste, and then watch your chef make a wild show of cooking it on a grill the size of a Volkswagen. Rice and hot-and-sour soup included. Open daily 11:30am-2:30pm and 5-10pm.

Foothill Broiler, 33 NW 23rd Pl., in the Uptown Shopping Center (223-0287). Take bus #20 up Burnside. Fantastic food served by enterprising survivors of the 60s. Tasteful art on the walls, greenery dangles from the ceiling. Best burgers in the Northwest from $3. Come off-hours or prepare to wait. Open Mon.-Fri. 7:30am-7pm, Sat. 7:30am-4pm.

Macheesmo Mouse, 715 SW Salmon St. Also at 811 NW 23rd St. and 3553 SE Hawthorne Blvd. (5 blocks from the AYH hostel). Fast, authentic Mexican food for the health-conscious, in part Hard Rock Café, part Pompidou Center. The $3 veggie burrito stands out. Open Mon.-Sat. 11am-10pm, Sun. noon-9pm.

Hamburger Mary's, 840 SW Park St. at Taylor. Good food near the museums and theaters, with a relaxed atmosphere and eclectic decor: floor lamps hang upside down from the ceiling. Mixed straight and gay clientele. Burgers with everything and fries $5. Excellent vegetarian fare. Open daily 7am-midnight.

Maya's Tacqueria, 1000 SW Morrison St. at 10th. Genuinely Mexican, complete with wall-sized murals of Mayans doing Mayan things. Mongo Mayan burrito $4.50-5.50. Open Mon.-Sat. 10:30am-10pm, Sun. noon-8pm.

Saigon Express, 309 W. Burnside St. Exquisite Vietnamese food; not at all the cheesy place the name may suggest. Entrees $5-8, unusual combinations (such as shrimp and sugarcane) add that extra *je ne sais quoi.* Open Mon.-Sat. 11am-9pm.

Jarra's Ethiopian Restaurant, 607 SE Morrison St. (230-8990). Take bus #15. Authentic and hot cuisine served by a friendly staff. Scoop up the spicy morsels with spongy *injera* bread. *Doro wat* (chicken in a hot sauce) $6.50. Open Mon.-Tues. and Thurs.-Fri. 5-10pm, Wed. 11:30am-2pm and 5-10pm, Sat. 4-10pm.

Sights

Since some of the best things to do in Portland frolic outside, visit Portland in late spring and early summer when the city blooms after the dismal winter weather. This also proves the best season in which to appreciate Portland's fountains, all of which seem to have long, intricate histories; the best include the 20 bronze drinking fountains located on street corners throughout Portland, donated by Simon Benson, a wealthy Prohibition-era Portlander, ostensibly to ease the thirst of loggers. Other objets d'art dot the downtown area, the products of a city law requiring that one percent of the costs of all construction and renovation work be devoted to public art projects.

Almost all the major sights are grouped **downtown** in the southwest district. Portland's downtown area centers on the **mall,** running north-south between 5th and 6th Ave. and closed to all traffic except city buses. At 5th Ave. and Morrison St. stands the **Pioneer Courthouse,** the elder of downtown landmarks. The monument now houses the U.S. Ninth Circuit Court of Appeals, overlooking the **Pioneer Courthouse Square,** 701 SW 6th Ave. (223-1613), opened in 1983. Forty-eight thousand citizens supported its construction by purchasing personalized bricks; it seems as though all 48,000 make a daily pilgrimage to their gift to the city. Live jazz, folk, and ethnic music draws the rest of Portland to the square for the **Peanut Butter and Jam Sessions,** held every Tuesday and Thursday from noon to 1pm.

The most controversial building in the downtown area, Michael Graves's postmodern **Portland Building** struts on the mall. This amazing confection of pastel tile and concrete has received praise to the stars, condemnation as an overgrown jukebox, and even once had a full-sized inflatable King Kong placed on its roof. Make sure to visit the interior as well, which looks like something out of *Blade Runner.*

West of the mall extend the **South Park Blocks,** a series of shady, rose-laden enclosures running down the middle of Park Ave. A number of museums open onto the parks, including the **Portland Art Museum,** 1219 SW Park Ave. (226-2811), at Jefferson St. Dote on the museum's especially fine exhibit of Pacific Northwest Native American art, including masks, textiles, and sacred objects, or the interspersed international exhibits and local artists' works. (Open Tues.-Sat. 11am-5pm, Sun. noon-4pm. Admission $3.50, seniors and students $1.50, under 12 50¢. Seniors free Thurs.) The **Northwest Film and Video Center** (221-1156), in the same building, screens classics and off-beat flicks.

Rowdy sailors fresh off their ocean-going trawlers filled **Old Town,** to the north of the mall, a century ago. Large-scale refurbished store fronts, new "old" brick, and a bevy of recently-owned shops and restaurants has revived the district. A popular people-watching vantage point, the **Skidmore Fountain,** at SW 1st Ave. and SW Ankeny St., marks the entrance to the quarter. Had the city accepted resident draftsman Henry Weinhard's offer to run draft beer through the fountain, it would have been a truly cordial watering hole indeed. Old Town marks the start of **Tom McCall Waterfront Park,** an enormous expanse of grass and flowers that offers little shade but provides great views of the Willamette River.

From March until Christmas, the area under the Burnside Bridge turns into the **Saturday Market** (222-6072), 108 W. Burnside St. Saturdays from 10am to 5pm and Sundays from 11am to 4:30pm, street musicians, artists, craftspeople, chefs, and produce sellers clog the area.

Portland's finest galleries shack up downtown. The **Image Gallery,** 1026 SW Morrison St. (224-9629), presents an international potpourri of Canadian Inuit sculpture and Mexican and Japanese folk art. (Open Mon.-Fri. 10:30am-6pm, Sat. 11am-5pm.)

Less than 2 mi. west of downtown, in the posh **West Hills,** looping trails for day hiking, running, and picnic-laden expeditions crisscross **Washington Park.** Obtain trail maps at the information stand near the parking lot of the arboretum, or refer to the maps posted on the windows. **Hoyt Arboretum,** 4000 SW Fairview Blvd. (228-8732), at the crest of the hill above the other gardens, features transplendent conifers and "200 acres of trails." (Free nature walks April-Oct. Sat.-Sun. at 2pm, and June-Aug. Tues. at 9:30am.) The five-acre **Japanese Garden** (223-1321) holds a formal arrangement of idyllic ponds and bridges. Cherry blossoms ornament the park in summer, thanks to sibling city Sapporo, Japan. (Open daily 10am-6pm; mid-Sept. to mid-April daily 10am-4pm. Admission $3.50, seniors and students with ID $2.) Roses galore and spectacular views of the city await a few steps away at the **International Rose Test Garden,** 400 SW Kingston St. (248-4302).

Below the Hoyt Arboretum circumnavigates Portland's favorite tourist-attracting triad: the **Washington Park Zoo,** 4001 SW Canyon Rd. (226-1561 for a person; 226-7627 for a tape; open daily 9:30am-7pm, gates close at 6pm; call for winter hours; admission $3.50, seniors and children $2, Tues. after 3pm free); the **World Forestry Center,** 4033 SW Canyon Rd. (228-1367; open daily 9am-5pm; admission $3, seniors and children $2); and the **Oregon Museum of Science and Industry,** (better known as **OMSI),** 4015 SW Canyon Rd. (228-6674; open Sat.-Thurs. 9am-7pm, Fri. 9am-8pm; admission $5.25, seniors and under 17 $3.50). Bus #63 "Zoo" connects the park with Morrison St. in the downtown mall, and a miniature railway also connects the Washington Park gardens with the zoo (fare $1.75). Beginning in late June, the zoo sponsors **Your Zoo and All That Jazz,** a nine-week series of open-air jazz concerts (Wed. 6:30-8:30pm), free with regular zoo admission. Bring a picnic dinner. **Zoograss Concerts** features a 10-week series of bluegrass concerts (Thurs. 6:30-8:30pm). The World Forestry Center specializes in exhibits of Northwestern forestry and logging, but may broaden its scope. OMSI will occupy children and adults with do-it-yourself science, computer, and medical exhibits. Within OMSI, the **Kendall Planeterium** (228-7827) gives daily shows (50¢) and also puts on "laser fantasy" rock shows most evenings (schedule of shows 242-0723; admission $4.50). The new, tastefully done **Vietnam Memorial** rests a few steps up the hill. From Washington Park, you have easy access to sprawling **Forest Park,** jampacked with hiking trails and picnic areas affording spectacular views of Portland.

Southeast Portland, largely a residential district, nourishes an enclave of progressive politics and regressive 60s hairdos at **Reed College,** SE 28th and Woodstock, a small liberal arts school founded in 1909. Reed sponsors numerous cultural events and in 1968 became the first undergraduate college to open a nuclear reactor. Tours of the campus leave Eliot Hall twice per day during the school year. (Call 771-7511 for hours.)

Farther southeast sleeps **Mt. Tabor Park,** one of two city parks in the world on the site of an extinct volcano. More of a molehill than a mountain, the park serves as the Southeast's lone hill. Take bus #15 from downtown, or drive down Hawthorne to SE 60th Ave.

Entertainment

Portland no longer swims as the hard-drinking, carousing port town of yore; ships still unload sea-weary sailors daily, but their favorite waterfront pubs have evolved into upscale bistros and slambanging nightclubs. Current listings abound in the Friday edition of the *Oregonian* and a number of free handouts: *Willamette Week,* the *Main Event, Clinton St. Quarterly,* and the *Downtowner.* The first of these caters to students, the last to the yuppwardly mobile. Find each in restaurants downtown and in boxes on street corners.

The **Oregon Symphony Orchestra** (228-1353) plays in the Arlene Schnitzer Concert Hall, on the corner of SW Broadway and SW Main St. (Tickets $10-28. "Symphony Sunday" afternoon concerts $5-8. Performances Sept.-April.) **Chamber Music Northwest** performs summer concerts at Reed College Commons, 3203 SE Woodstock Ave. (223-3202). (Classical music Mon., Thurs., and Sat. at 8pm. Admission $13, under 15 $9.)

Portland's many fine theaters produce everything from off-Broadway shows to experimental drama. At

Portland Civic Theatre, 1530 SW Yamhill St. (226-3048), the mainstage often presents musical comedy, while the smaller theater-in-the-round puts on less traditional shows. (Tickets $6.50 and $9.50.) **Oregon Shakespeare Festival/Portland,** at the Intermediate Theatre of PCPA, corner of SW Broadway and SW Main St. (248-6309), has a five-play season running from November to February. **New Rose Theatre,** 904 SW Main St. in the Park Blocks (222-2487), offers an even mix of classical and contemporary shows. (Tickets $9-14.)

The best clubs in Portland are the hardest to find. Neighborhood taverns and pubs often tuck away on backroads. Those with happy feet should bop down the length of 6th Ave. to find most of the dancing clubs. The under-21 crowd heads to the **Confetti Club,** 126 SW 2nd St. (274-0627), for new wave music, or the **Warehouse,** 320 SE 2nd St. (232-9645), for Top-40 tunes. **Produce Row Cafe,** 204 SE Oak St. (232-8355), has 21 beers on tap ($1), 72 bottled domestic and imported beers, and a lovely outdoor beer garden. (Open Mon.-Fri. 11am-1am, Sat. noon-1am, Sun. 2pm-midnight.) The **Mission Theater and Pub,** 1624 NW Glisan St. (223-4031), serves excellent home-brewed ales as well as delicious and unusual sandwiches. Relax in the balcony of this old moviehouse with a pitcher of Ruby, a fragrant raspberry ale ($1.25 glass, $6.50 pitcher). (Open daily 5pm-1am.) **Key Largo,** 31 NW 1st Ave. (223-9919), has an airy, tropical atmosphere. Dance to rock, R&B, or jazz on the patio weather permitting. (Cover $2-8. Open Mon.-Fri. 11am-2:30am, Sat.-Sun. noon-2:30am.) Tavern-owner-turned-mayor "Bud" Clark's **Goose Hollow Inn,** 1927 SW Jefferson (228-7010; bus #57 or 59), acts as a meeting spot for aspiring progressive politicos as well as a popular tavern. (Sandwiches $3-6.50. Open daily 11:30am-1am.) **Harrington's,** 1001 SW 6th Ave. (243-2933), on Main St., is a sight unto itself. Actually a little gazebo, the front door leads to an underground stairway in the middle of a downtown sidewalk. It's been listed as one of the nation's "top-10" bars by *Esquire,* which gives you an idea of the clientele—schmooz with the likes of Zanley Phränqué Galton the Third. (Cover Thurs.-Sat. $1-5; live music all week. Open Mon.-Fri. 11:30am-9pm. Take-out breakfast window opens at 7:30am.)

Oregon Coast

The "Pacific" hurls itself at the Oregon Coast with abandon, amidst impressive explosions of spray. Only the most daring swim in this ice-cold surf; others stay satisfied by the matchless views and huge stretches of unspoiled beach.

Possessively hugging the shore, **U.S. 101,** the renowned coastal highway, edges by a series of high-perched viewpoints. From northernmost Astoria to Brookings in the south, it laces together the resorts and historic fishing villages clustered around the mouths of rivers feeding into the Pacific. Still, it appears most beautiful between the coastal towns, where hundreds of miles of state and national park allow direct access to the beach. Whenever the highway leaves the coast, look for a beach loop road—these quieter ways afford some of the finest scenery on the western seaboard.

Drive or bike for the best encounter with the coast. Most traffic flows south. Portlanders, like spawning salmon, head down-road to vacation. While biking works well, the long days also stay wet. Write the Oregon Dept. of Transportation, Salem 97310 or virtually any visitors center on the coast for the free *Oregon Coast Bike Route Map;* it provides invaluable information on campsites, hostels, bike repair facilities, temperatures, wind speed, etc. For those without a car or bike, transportation becomes a bit tricky.

Greyhound's coastal routes from Portland run only twice per day, with half of the routes running in the middle of the night. Local public transport goes from Tillamook to Astoria, but no public transport links Tillamook and Lincoln City.

Gasoline and grocery prices en route to the coast cost about 20% more than in inland cities. Motorists may want to stock up and fill up before reaching the coastbound highways.

Reedsport and the Dunes

For 42 mi. between Florence and Coos Bay, the beach widens to form the **Oregon Dunes National Recreation Area.** Shifting hills of sand rise to 300 ft. and extend inland up to 3 mi. (often to the brink of U.S. 101), clogging mountain streams and forming numerous small lakes. Glaciation created the dunes 15,000 years ago, sponsoring their maximum development 9000 years later. A constant, unidirectional, wind maintains their shape. Hiking trails wind around the lakes, through the coastal forests, and up to the dunes themselves. In many places, no grasses or shrubs grow, and you can see only bare sand and sky; in others you might feel more like you're in the Gator Bowl parking lot rather than in the Gobi. Campgrounds fill up early and loudly with dunebuggy and motorcycle junkies, especially on summer weekends. The blaring radios, thrumming engines, and swarms of tipsy tourists might drive you like Lawrence of Arabia into the sands seeking eternal truth—or at least a quiet place to crash.

Visit the **Oregon Dunes National Recreation Area Information Center,** 855 U.S. 101, Reedsport (271-3611), just south of the Umpqua River Bridge, to pick up their free guide with details on camping, hiking, fishing, boating, wildlife observation, environmental exploration, and dune-buggy access for each side the NRA maintains. (Open Mon.-Fri. 8am-4:30pm, Sat.-Sun. 9am-5pm; Labor Day-Memorial Day Mon.-Fri. 8am-4:30pm.) The **Reedsport Chamber of Commerce,** U.S. 101 and Rte. 38 (271-3495), sits across the street from the NRA office. (Open Mon.-Fri. 9am-5pm, Sat.-Sun. 10am-5pm.)

Sand Dunes Frontier, 83960 U.S. 101 S. (997-3544), 4 mi. south of Florence, gives 25-minute **dune buggy rides** ($6, under 11 $3, under 5 free). But if you really want to rock and roll around the dunes, shell out $25 for an hour ($15 each additional hr.) on your own dune buggy; **Dunes Odyssey,** on U.S. 101 in Winchester Bay (271-4011), and **Spinreel Park,** Wildwood Dr., 8 mi. south on U.S. 101 (759-3313; open daily 8am-6pm), both offer rentals. The best access to the dunes is at **Eel Creek Campground,** 11 mi. south of Reedsport. Leave your car in the parking lot of the day-use area and hike a short and easy distance through scrubby pines and grasses until suddenly, the dunes tower above you. Many travelers get lost wandering from one identical, stark rise to the next. The ocean dips another 2 mi. to the west.

Inside **Umpqua Lighthouse State Park,** 6 mi. south of Reedsport, the Douglas County Park Department operates the **coastal visitor center** (440-4500), in the old Coast Guard administration building. The center has small exhibits on the shipping and timber industries at the turn of the century. (Open May-Sept. Wed.-Sat. 10am-5pm, Sun. 1-5pm. Free.)

Restaurateurs of Winchester Bay (3 mi. south of Reedsport) pride themselves on their seafood, especially salmon. The **Seven Seas Cafe,** Dock A, Winchester Bay, at the end of Broadway at 4th St., sails a small diner crowded with marine memorabilia and navigational charts. The local fishing crowd gathers here to trade big fish stories in this self-proclaimed "haunt of the liars." (Fish and chips $4, deep-fried prawns $6, coffee 40¢. Open Fri.-Tues. 8am-2pm.) The **Seafood Grotto and Restaurant**, 8th St. and Broadway, Winchester Bay, serves unexpectedly excellent seafood around a large Victorian doll house. Lunches go for $5-7, a large salmon steak $10. (Open Sun.-Thurs. 8am-9pm.) **Sugar Shack Bakery and Restaurant**, 145 N. 3rd, Reedsport (271-3514) won't win any Mr. Clean certificates of merit, but does have delicious sweets and fast meals. Try the large apple fritters (65¢ after your sandwich ($3). (Open daily 5am-dusk, depending on the weather.)

Whether you prefer motels or campsites, head to peaceful Winchester Bay. The **Harbor View Motel**, on Beach Blvd. (271-3352), across from the waterfront, may look a little shabby, but harbors fairly clean rooms with color TV and some kitchenettes. (Singles $21. Doubles $30. Mid-Sept. to April: singles $18.50; doubles $23.) You may want to blow dough in the **Winchester Bay Motel**, at the end of Broadway (271-4871), at 4th St. past dock A, after weeks of grumgy camping. (Color TV and free coffee. Singles $30. Doubles $35. Labor Day-Memorial Day: singles $25; doubles $30.) The rather small rooms in the **Fir Grove Motel**, 2178 Winchester Ave., Reedsport (271-4848) come with color TV, free coffee, and a pool. (Singles $34. Doubles $42. In winter: singles $25; doubles $28.)

The National Forest Service's pamphlet *Campgrounds in the Siuslaw National Forest* covers campgrounds in the dunes. The sites closest to Reedsport lie in Winchester Bay. The campgrounds that allow dune-buggy access—South Jetty, Lagoon, Waxmyrtle, Driftwood II, Horsfall, and Bluebill—generally start loud and stay rowdy. The **Surfwood Campground**, ½ mi. north of Winchester Bay on U.S. 101 (271-4020), has all the luxuries of home—including a laundromat, heated pool, grocery store, sauna, tennis court, and hot showers. (Sites $9, full hookup $11.50. Call at least 1 week in advance in the summer.) The county's **Windy Cove Campground** (271-5634), adjacent to Salmon Harbor in Winchester Bay, has rather steep rates for tent camping. (Drinking water, hot showers, flush toilets, and beach access. Sites $7.)

Reedsport's **post office** licks and affixes at 301 Fir St. (271-2521; open Mon.-Fri. 9am-5pm). General Delivery **ZIP code** is 97467. The **area code** is 503.

Klamath Falls and Crater Lake National Park

Native American shamans forbade people to view mirror-blue Crater Lake, now desecrated as Oregon's only National Park. Iceless in winter and flawlessly circular, the lake (at an elevation of over 6000 ft.) plunges to an astonishing depth of 2000 ft., making it the nation's deepest lake (and second deepest in the hemisphere). **Route 62** through Crater Lake National Park circumnavigates the lake and then heads west to Medford or southeast to Klamath Falls. To get to the park from Portland, take I-5 to Eugene, then Rte. 58 east to U.S. 97 south. Call ahead for road conditions during winter (238-8400). Park admission (charged only in summer) costs $5 for cars, $3 for hikers and bikers. The tiny **visitors center** (594-2211) on the lake shore at **Rim Village**, distributes books and maps on hiking and camping. (Open daily 8am-7pm.) Rangers conduct nightly talks in the **Rim Center** across the street starting at 8pm.

The **Rim Drive**, open only in summer, runs a 33-mi. route high above the lake. Points along the drive offer views and trailheads for hiking. Among the most spectacular are **Discovery Point Trail** (from which the first pioneer saw the lake in 1853), **Garfield Peak Trail**, and **Watchman Lookout**.

The hike up **Scott Peak**, the park's highest (9000 ft.), begins from the drive near the lake's eastern edge. Although steep, the 7½-mi. trail to the top gives persevering hikers a unique overhead view of the lake. Also, steep **Cleetwood Trail**, a 1-mi.

switchback, provides the only trail that leads down to the water's edge. From here a boat tours the lake (fare $10, under 13 $5.50; check with the lodge for times). Both **Wizard Island,** a cinder cone 760 ft. above lake level, and **Phantom Ship Rock** resemble fragile and tiny specks from above, yet prove surprisingly large from the surface of the water. Picnics and fishing are allowed, as is swimming, providing you can stand the frigid 50° temperature. Park rangers lead free walking tours daily in the summer and periodically in winter (on snowshoes). Call the ranger station for exact times.

When pressed for time, walk the easy 100 yd. from the visitors center down to the **Sinnott Memorial Overlook** for the area's best and most accessible view. For a short lecture on the area's history, attend a ranger talk at Rim Village.

Eating inexpensively in Crater Lake may prove a tad more difficult. Crater Lake Lodge has a small dining room, and Rim Village has several groceries that charge high prices for a skimpy selection of foodstuffs. As in most national parks, the intrepid *Let's Go* reader should buy supplies at nearby towns and cook meals once inside. From the south, **Fort Klamath** is the final food frontier before the park. Stock up here at the **Old Fort Store** (381-2345; open daily 8am-8pm). In **Klamath Falls,** try **McPherson's Old Town Pizza,** 722 Main St., for some of the tastiest and cheapest food in the area. (Small pizzas from $2.55. Open daily 11am-11pm.)

The only hotel in the park, **Crater Lake Lodge,** Rim Village (594-2511), stays open from June to September. Call far in advance for reservations; renovations because of safety hazards have closed parts of the lodge for extended periods of time. Staying here will put a crater in your wallet; cottages cost $36, and rooms with views of the lakes start at $47.

Nearby Klamath Falls, however, features several affordable hotels; you may be wise to sack out in the town and base your visits to Crater Lake from there. The **Pony Pass Motel,** 75 Main St. (884-7735), offers clean, comfortable rooms at the edge of town with A/C and TV. (Singles $25. Doubles $35.) The **Maverick Motel,** 1220 Main St. (882-6688), down the street from the Greyhound station in the center of town. (TV, A/C, and a handkerchief-sized pool. Singles $25. Doubles $27.50.) **Molatore's Motel,** 100 Main St. (882-4666), across the street from the Pony Pass, caters mostly to business travelers. All 104 immense rooms have A/C. (Singles from $32. Doubles $40.)

For camping with the ambiance of a parking lot, try **Mazama Campground** (594-2211), a monster facility usually usurped by equally mammoth RVs in summer. (Sites $7.) **Lost Creek Campground** (594-2211), is hidden at the southwest corner of the park. (12 sites. Arrive by morning to secure a spot.)

Washington

Washington has two personalities, clearly split by the Cascade Range. The western ridge of the range blocks Pacific moisture heading east and hurls it back toward the ocean, bathing the Olympic Peninsula with a certain liberalism and an average annual rainfall of 135 inches. Always drawn to moisture, most inhabitants cluster here with the seafood around Puget Sound. But pity not comparatively arid eastern Washington; 10 fewer feet of water per annum isn't everything, especially with the miracle of modern refrigeration. Residents can use time otherwise devoted to cracking crabs savoring fresh fruit in Yakima. In Washington's less congested side, residents and tourists can enjoy the rolling countryside without jostling for space.

Yet unifying this study in geopsychology, Washington runs the textbook of terrain: deserts, volcanoes, untouched Pacific Ocean beaches, and the world's only non-tropical rain forest all await exploration. Mount Rainier has fantastic hiking, while the Cascades keep perfect conditions for nearly any winter activity. Seattle and Spokane drape themselves in equally beautiful green landscapes, showing that

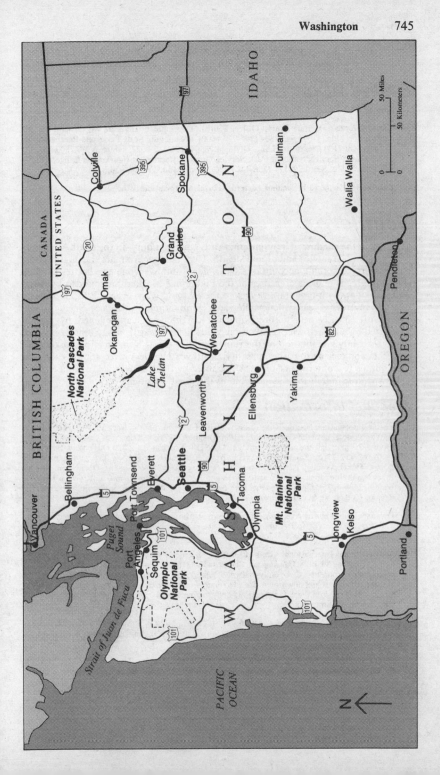

botany and exhibitionism can still intersect. Best of all, Washington is a compact state by West Coast standards—everything remains less than a daytrip away.

Practical Information

Capital: Olympia.

Visitor Information: State Tourist Office, Tourism Development Division, 101 General Administration Bldg., Olympia 98504 (206-753-5600). **Washington State Parks and Recreation Commission,** 7150 Clearwater Lane, Olympia 98504 (206-753-2027; summers WA 800-562-0990). **Forest Service/National Park Service Outdoor Recreation Information Office,** 915 2nd Ave. #442, Seattle 98174 (206-442-0170). Open Mon.-Fri. 8am-5pm.

Time Zone: Pacific (3 hr. behind Eastern). **Postal Abbreviation:** WA.

Seattle

A city in the shadow of a mountain, Seattle dukes it out—to the death—between big city guerrilla tactics and alpine stealth. Here octogenarian architects tote backpacks, thirtysomething accountants wear clogs, and everyone else battles through the fresh greens and sea creatures at the Pike Place Market. Surrounded by water on three sides, with mountain ranges to the east and west, every hilltop in the city offers an impressive, easily defensible view, culminating in the Space Needle. Luckily, Seattle spends nearly three quarters of the year camouflaged by clouds. Prompted by a hometown organization called Lesser Seattle, many inhabitants ballyhoo their city's reputation as the rain capital of the U.S. in an effort to keep the city from conquering tourists; in reality, Seattle catches less precipitation each year than quite a few other major cities. Undaunted by the wet, warlike conditions, residents spend as much time as possible in the great outdoors.

Practical Information

Visitor Information: Seattle-King County Visitors Bureau, 666 Stewart St. (461-5840), in the Vance Hotel near the Greyhound station. Open Mon.-Fri. 8:30am-5pm, Sat. 10am-4pm. From 5-7:30pm, call the airport branch at 433-5218. **Tourism B.C.,** 720 Olive Way, Seattle 98101 (623-5937). Information on travel to British Columbia. Open Mon.-Fri. 9am-1pm and 2-5pm. **Ticket Agency: Ticket Master,** 201 S. King St. #38 (628-0888). Open Mon.-Sat. 10am-10pm, Sun. 10am-6pm. **Seattle Parks and Recreation Department,** 5201 Green Lake Way N. (684-4075). Open Mon.-Fri. 8am-6pm. **National Park Service, Pacific Northwest Region,** 83 S. King St., 3rd floor (442-4830).

Travelers Aid: 909 4th Ave. #630 (461-3888), at Marion in the YMCA. Free services to stranded travelers with lost wallets, grandparents, or their marbles. Open Mon.-Fri. 8:30am-9pm, Sat.-Sun. and holidays 1-5pm.

Seattle-Tacoma International Airport (Sea-Tac), on Federal Way (433-5217), south of Seattle proper. **Sea-Tac Visitors Information Center** (433-5218), in the central baggage claim area across from carousel 10. Open daily 9:30am-7:30pm. **Gray Line** coaches and limousines operate between airport and downtown. $6, $11 round-trip. Metro buses #174 and 194 run daily every ½ hr. 6am-1am. Peak fare $1.25, 85¢ off-peak; under 18 75¢ during peak, 55¢ off-peak. Taxi downtown around $22.

Amtrak: King St. Station, 3rd and Jackson St. (800-872-7245). Trains to: Portland (3 per day, $27), Tacoma ($9), and San Francisco ($146). Station open daily 6am-10pm; ticket office 6am-5:30pm.

Buses: Greyhound, 8th Ave. and Stewart St. (624-3456). To: Sea-Tac Airport (4 per day, $2.50); Vancouver, BC ($30); Spokane ($33); and Portland (2 per day, $25). Open daily 5:30am-9:30pm and midnight-2am. **Green Tortoise Alternative Travel,** 324-7433 or 800-227-4766. Buses leave from 9th and Stewart. Trips leave Thurs. and Sun. at 8am to: Portland (5 hr., $15); Berkeley, CA (26 hr., $49); and San Francisco (27 hr., $59). Reservations required 3-4 days in advance.

Metro Transit: Customer Assistance Office, 821 2nd Ave. (447-4800; TTY service 447-4826), in the Exchange Bldg. downtown. Open Mon. 8am-5:30pm, Tues.-Fri. 8am-5pm. Buses run

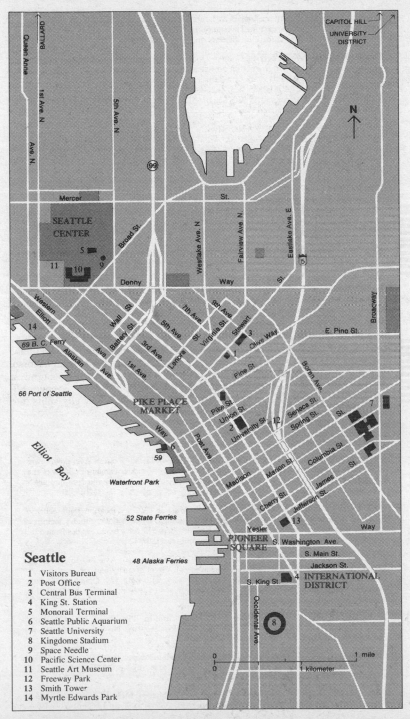

Seattle

1 Visitors Bureau
2 Post Office
3 Central Bus Terminal
4 King St. Station
5 Monorail Terminal
6 Seattle Public Aquarium
7 Seattle University
8 Kingdome Stadium
9 Space Needle
10 Pacific Science Center
11 Seattle Art Museum
12 Freeway Park
13 Smith Tower
14 Myrtle Edwards Park

6am-1am. Fare 55¢, during weekday peak hours 65¢. One-day pass $2.50, $1 weekend day. Ride free in the daytime area from Jackson St. to Battery St. and between 6th Ave. and the waterfront. Transfers valid for 2 hr. Seniors and ages 5-17 discounts.

Ferries: Washington State Ferries, Colman Dock, Pier 52 (464-6400; in WA 800-542-0810 or 800-542-7052). Service to Bremerton on Kitsap Peninsula and Winslow on Bainbridge Island. Ferries leave frequently daily 6am-2am. Fares from $3.30, car and driver $5.55. **B.C. Stena Line,** Pier 48, 2700 Alaskan Way (624-6663). Daily cruises on the *Crown Princess* to Victoria, BC. Fare $30, round-trip $40. Seniors $10 discount, ages 5-11 half-price. Bikes $4, motorcycles $9. Car and driver $40.

Car Rental: Five & Ten, 14120 Pacific Hwy. S. (246-4434). $17 per day. 100 free mi., 5¢ each additional mi. Airport pickup. Open Mon.-Sat. 8am-6pm, Sun. 12:30-6pm. Must be 21 with credit card or $120 deposit. **A-19.95-Rent-A-Car,** 804 N. 145th St. (364-1995). $20 per day, under 21 $25. 100 free mi., 15¢ each additional mi. Free delivery. Must have credit card. Drivers under 21 must have auto insurance.

Bike Rental: Gregg's, 7007 Woodlawn Ave. NE (523-1822). 10-speeds and mountain bikes $25 per day; other bikes $3.50 per hr. Open Mon.-Fri. 9:30am-9pm, Sat.-Sun. 9:30am-6pm. Must have credit card. **Alki Bikes,** 2722 Alki Ave. SW (938-3322). Mountain bikes $7 per hr., $17 per day; 10-speeds $4 per hr., $13 per day. Open Mon.-Thurs. 10am-7pm, Fri. 10am-8pm, Sat. 10am-6pm, Sun. 10am-5pm. Credit card or license required as deposit.

Help Lines: Crisis Clinic, 461-3222. **Senior Citizen Information and Referral,** 1601 2nd St. #800 (448-3110). Open Mon.-Fri. 9am-5pm. **Gay Counseling,** 329-8707. Open Mon.-Fri. noon-9pm.

Post Office: Union St. and 3rd Ave. (442-6300), downtown. Open Mon.-Fri. 8am-5:30pm. **ZIP code:** 98101.

Area Code: 206.

Seattle is a long, skinny city stretched out north to south between long, skinny **Puget Sound** on the west and long, skinny **Lake Washington** on the east. Lake Union and a string of locks, canals, and bays cut the head of the city from its torso. In the downtown area, avenues run northwest to southeast and streets southwest to northeast. Outside the downtown area everything simplifies vastly: avenues run north to south and streets east to west, with few exceptions. The city splits into quadrants: 1000 1st Ave. NW is a far cry from 1000 1st Ave. S.

Accommodations

Seattle International Hostel (AYH), 84 Union St. (622-5443), at Western Ave. downtown. 125 beds in sterile rooms, immaculate facilities, and plenty of modern amenities. View of the bay helps combat loud traffic. Sleep sacks required. Open daily 7-10am and 5pm-midnight. $10, nonmembers $13.

YMCA, 909 4th Ave. (382-5000), near Madison St. Must be 17. Good location, tight security. Small but well-kept rooms; worse dorm bunks. TV lounge on each floor, laundry facilities, use of swimming pool and fitness facilities. AYH members $17 for a bunk. Singles from $38. Doubles from $44. Weekly: singles from $158, doubles $180.

YWCA, 1118 5th Ave. (461-4888), near the YMCA. Take any 4th Ave. bus to Seneca St. Women only, under 18 require advance arrangement. Great security and location, but an older facility than the YMCA. Open 24 hr. Singles $24, with bath $29. Doubles $35, with bath $39. Weekly: singles $143, with bath $173. Key deposit $2. Additional charge for health center use.

St. Regis Hotel, 116 Stewart St. (448-6366), 2 blocks from the Pike Place Market. Not the safest neighborhood. Pleasant management and excellent security. No visitors after 10pm. Singles $25, with bath $31. Doubles $31, with bath $37.

Commodore Hotel, 2013 2nd Ave. (448-8868), at Virginia. Downtown. Not as well-kept but clean and safe. AYH members can get a dorm bed for $11. Singles $19.50, with color TV and bath $35. Doubles $24, with 2 beds and bath $42.

Moore Motel, 2nd and Virginia (448-4852), next to the historic Moore Theater. Big rooms include 2 beds, bath, and TV. Singles or doubles $39.

Park Plaza Hotel, 4401 Aurora Ave. N. (632-2101). Another option along an endless strip of car dealerships and fast-food joints. Clean rooms, in-room coffee, cable TV. Singles $25. Doubles $27.

Hillside Motel, 2451 Aurora N. (285-7860). Take bus #6 or 16. One of a number of relatively inexpensive motels along noisy Aurora. 11 units with hot plates. Singles $23, doubles $27.

Nites Inn, 11746 Aurora Ave. N. (365-3216). Large rooms. Movie channel. Singles $30. Doubles $32.

Motel 6, 18900 47th Ave. S. (241-1648), exit 152 off I-5. Take bus #194. Near Sea-Tac but inconvenient to downtown. Singles $30. Doubles $37. Make reservations.

The College Inn, 4000 University Way NE (633-4441). European-style B&B in the University District. Breakfast served in a lovely refinished attic; ask for quieter rooms facing 40th. Singles from $37. Doubles from $46.

Food

By a Sound full of fish and in a state tacked in place by orchards, Seattle rivals San Francisco in culinary excitement and eclecticism. Seafood and produce here always stay fresh in season. To eat in, buy fish right off the boats at **Fisherman's Wharf**, at NW 54th St. and 30th Ave. NW in Ballard, along bus route #43. The wharf usually opens from 8am to 3 or 4 pm.

Farmers have been selling their produce at the **Pike Place Market** since 1907, when angry Seattle citizens demanded an alternative to the middle merchant. Crazy fishmongers and produce sellers yell at customers and at each other, while street performers do their thing—meanwhile tourists wonder what they've walked into. Seattlites sail through at day's end in search of something special for dinner. (Market open Mon.-Sat. 9am-6pm; many stands also open Sun.)

El Puerco Llorón, 1501 Western Ave., at the 2nd level of the Hillclimb overlooking the waterfront. Some of the best Mexican food in Seattle—no nachos here. Entire place transported from Tijuana. Unfortunately, portions fall short of hearty. *Tacos de carne asada* (charcoal-broiled flank steak in soft tortillas) $4. Open Mon.-Sat. 11:30am-9pm, Sun. noon-7pm.

World Class Chili, 1411 1st Ave., in the South Arcade. Texas-sized portions of Seattle's best chili ($3.50). Four different kinds to choose from; California-style contains chicken instead of beef. Open Mon.-Sat. 11am-6pm.

Phnom Penh Noodle Soup House, 414 Maynard Ave. S. Excellent Cambodian cuisine. Head to the upstairs dining room for a good view of the park and a spicy, steaming bowl of #1, the Phnom Penh noodle special ($3.50). Open Mon.-Tues. and Thurs. 8:30am-6pm, Fri.-Sat. 8:30am-7pm, Sun. 8:30am-6pm.

Ivar's Fish Bar, Pier 54, on the waterfront. One of a string of seafood restaurants named for Seattle celebrity Ivar Haglund. This locals' favorite charges $3 for fish and chips, serving definitive Seattle clam chowder. Dine with the gulls and pigeons in covered booths outside. Open daily 11am-2am.

Fran-Glor's Creole Cafe, 547 1st Ave. S., near the viaduct. Genuine gumbo with crabmeat, sausage, and who knows what else. The bric-a-brac and the jazz are classic New Orleans. Lunches from $4.50. Open Mon.-Sat. noon-9:30pm.

Kokeb Restaurant, 926 12th Ave. (322-0485). Behind Seattle University at the far south end of Capitol Hill, near the First Hill neighborhood. An intriguing Ethiopian restaurant offering hot and spicy meat stews served on *injera,* a soft bread. Very purple. Entrees $8-9. Open Mon.-Thurs. 11:30am-9pm, Fri.-Sat. 4-10pm, Sun. 11:30am-3pm and 6-9pm.

The Cause Célèbre, 524 E. 15th Ave., at Mercer St., at one end of Capitol Hill. The special province of Seattle's well-fed left. Stay away if you don't like feminist music or discussions on the struggle for Chinese succession. Sublime ice cream and baked goods. Free evening entertainment. Lunch $3-6. Open Mon. and Wed.-Sat. 9am-9pm, Tues. and Sun. 9am-5:30pm.

Copacabana, 1520½ Pike Pl. Music and passion are always in fashion. The outdoor tables probably the best place in the market to watch the harried crowds pass. Try the Bolivian *salteñas,* the house specialty (meat and raisin pastries, $3). Open Mon.-Thurs. 11:30am-4pm, Fri.-Sat. 11:30am-9pm.

Ho Ho Seafood Restaurant, 653 S. Weller St. Santa's favorite. Elegant yet laid-back. Generous portions, great seafood. Check the blackboard for daily specials. Entrees $4.50-10. Open Sun.-Thurs. 11am-1pm, Fri.-Sat. 11am-3am.

Asia Deli, 4235 University Way NE. No corned beef here—this atypical deli offers quick service and generous portions of delicious Vietnamese and Thai food (mostly of the noodle persuasion). Try the saute chicken and onions ($3.45), and don't forget the banana with tapioca in coconut milk (90¢), a superb palate cleanser. Open Mon.-Sat. 11am-9pm, Sun. noon-8pm.

The Unicorn Restaurant, 4550 University Way. Renowned for its large collection of obscure English ales ($2.50-3), the Unicorn also cooks up a mean steak-and-kidney pie ($6). Try their afternoon special—tea and scones ($2.50), of course. Open Mon.-Sat. 11:30am-10pm, Sun. 5-9pm.

Sights and Activities

If you only have a day to spare in Seattle, despair not. In one day of dedicated sight-seeing you can cover a good deal of the city. If you've got a little more time, head out to Seward Park for a late afternoon dip in Lake Washington, or cycle along the lake's western bank.

The **Pike Place Market,** at the bottom of Pike St. between 1st and Western Ave., somehow crowds produce stands, fish vendors, bakeries, craft sellers, restaurants, and boutiques into a 3-block indoor/outdoor area. An information table at the corner of Pike St. and Pike Place (in front of the bakery) provides information about market history and shop (and rest room) locations. **Freeway Park,** on Seneca St. at 7th Ave., is a smashing place for picnicking in the midst of Seattle's high-rises. At the south end of the market begins the **Pike Place Hillclimb,** a set of staircases leading down past more chic shops and ethnic restaurants to Alaskan Way and the **waterfront.** (An elevator is also available.)

The waterfront docks once played Ellis Island to shiploads of gold coming in from the 1897 Klondike gold rush. Today, on a pier full of shops and restaurants, the credit card is firmly established as standard currency. On Pier 59 at the base of the hillclimb, the **Seattle Aquarium** (625-4357) explains the history of marine life in Puget Sound and the effects of tidal action. (Open daily 10am-7pm; Labor Day-Memorial Day 10am-5pm. Admission $4.50, seniors and ages 13-18 $2.50, ages 6-12 $1.75.)

Four blocks inland from Pier 70 you'll find **Seattle Center,** a 74-acre, pedestrians-only park originally constructed for the 1962 World's Fair. Thousands of sightseers still visit each day. Take the monorail from Pine St. and 5th Ave. downtown. (Fare 60¢, seniors and children 25¢.) The **Pacific Science Center** (443-2001), within the park, houses a laserium and IMAX theater. (Science Center open daily 10am-6pm; Labor Day-June Mon.-Fri. 10am-5pm, Sat.-Sun. 10am-6pm. Admission $5, seniors and ages 6-13 $4, ages 2-5 $3. Laser shows $1 extra.) The **Space Needle** (443-2100), sometimes known as "the world's tackiest monument," has an observation tower and restaurant. On clear days, the view from atop has no peer. (Admission $4.75, ages 5-12 $2.75.) After working up an appetite in the Center's amusement park, head next door to the **Center House,** home to dozens of shops and restaurants serving everything from Mongolian to Mexican. (Open summer daily 11am-9pm; spring 11am-7pm; fall and winter Sun.-Thurs. 11am-6pm, Fri.-Sat. 11am-9pm.) The Center has an **information desk** (625-4234) on the court level in the Center House which can inform you of events. (Open daily 1-4pm.)

Pier 57 holds Seattle's new maritime museum, **The Water Link** (624-4975). Wallow in the city's waterfront history or probe the geological mysteries of the ocean floor. (Open May 17-Sept. 30 Tues.-Sun. noon-6pm. Admission $1.) From Pier 56, **Harbor Tours** (623-1445) leaves for a one-hour cruise south to the Coast Guard outposts around Harbor Island (June-Sept. 5 per day; May and Oct. 3 per day. Fare $6.50, seniors $6, children $3.)

Two blocks from the waterfront sits historic **Pioneer Square,** where 19th-century warehouses and office buildings were restored in a spasm of prosperity during the

70s. The *Compleat Browser's Guide to Pioneer Square,* available in area bookstores, provides a short history and walking tour.

When Seattle nearly burned to the ground in 1889, an ordinance was passed to raise the city 35 ft. At first, shops below the elevated streets remained open for business and were moored to the upper city by an elaborate network of stairs. In 1907 the city moved upstairs permanently, and the underground city was sealed off. The vast **Bill Speidel's Underground Tours** (682-4646) does exactly that. Speidel spearheaded the movement to save Pioneer Square from the apocalypse of renewal. The tours are informative and irreverent glimpses at Seattle's beginnings; just ignore the rats that infest the tunnels. Tours (1½ hr.) leave from Doc Maynard's Pub at 610 1st Ave. (March-Sept. 6-8 per day 10am-6pm. Reservations strongly recommended. Admission $4, seniors $2, students $3.25, ages 6-12 $2.75.)

Once back above ground, learn about eating shoes at the **Klondike Gold Rush National Historic Park,** 117 S. Main St. (442-7220). The "interpretive center" depicts the lives and fortunes of the miners. Saturday and Sunday at 3pm, the park screens Charlie Chaplin's 1925 classic, *The Gold Rush.* (Open daily 9am-5pm. Free.)

Three blocks east of Pioneer Square, up Jackson on King St., is Seattle's **International District.** Though sometimes still called Chinatown by Seattlites, this area has peoples from all over Asia. The 45-minute slideshow *Seattle's Other History,* presented at the Nippon Kan Theater, 628 Washington St. (624-8801), reveals the years of discrimination that Asians in Seattle experienced and the strength with which they met hardship. (Presentation given whenever large enough groups accumulate; call ahead. Admission $2.) Whether or not you see the show, be sure to pick up the free brochure *Chinatown Tour: Seattle's Other History* from the **Nippon Kan Theater,** itself a good place to start your tour of the district. Built in 1909 to house weddings and cultural events, the Nippon Kan fell into disrepair during World War II as the U.S. government put Japanese Americans in concentration camps, only getting restored and reopened in 1981.

Capitol Hill inspires extreme reactions from both its residents and neighbors. The former wouldn't live anywhere else, while the latter never go near the place. The district's leftist and gay communities set the tone for its nightspots (see Entertainment), while the retail outlets include a large number of collectives and radical bookstores. Saunter down Broadway or its cross streets to window-shop, or walk a few blocks east and north for a stroll down the hill's lovely residential streets, lined with beautiful Victorian homes. Bus #10 runs along 15th St. and #7 along Broadway.

Volunteer Park, between 11th and 17th Ave. at E. Ward St., north of the main Broadway activity, beckons tourists to travel east of the city center. Named for the "brave volunteers who gave their lives to liberate the oppressed people of Cuba and the Philippines," the park boasts lovely lawns and an outdoor running track. Climb the water tower at the 14th Ave. entrance for stunning 360° views of the city and the Olympic Range, rivalling the views from the Space Needle. The **Seattle Art Museum,** 14th St. E. and Prospect (625-8901), houses an excellent permanent collection of Asian art. Pick up a program listing or call 443-4670 for information about special exhibits. (Open Tues.-Wed. and Fri.-Sat. 10am-5pm, Thurs. 10am-9pm, Sun. noon-5pm. Admission $2; seniors, students, and under 12 $1. Free Thurs.)

The **University of Washington Arboretum** (325-4510), 10 blocks east of Volunteer Park, has great cycling and running trails. The tranquil **Japanese Garden** (625-4725) soothes in the southern end of the arboretum at East Helen St. Take bus #43 from downtown. The nine acres of sculpted gardens include fruit trees, a reflecting pool, and a traditional tea house. (Open March-Nov. daily 10am-8pm. Admission $1.50; seniors, under 19, and disabled 75¢. Arboretum open daily dawn-dusk; greenhouse open Mon.-Fri. 10am-4pm.)

With 35,000 students, the **University of Washington** is the state's cultural and educational center of gravity. The "U district" swarms with bookstores, shops, taverns, and restaurants. Stop by the friendly and helpful **visitors information center,** 4014 University Way NE (543-9198), to pick up a map of the campus and to obtain information on the university. (Open Mon.-Fri. 8am-5pm.)

On the campus, visit the **Thomas Burke Memorial Washington State Museum,** NE 45th St. and 17th Ave. NE (543-5590), in the northwest corner of the campus. The museum houses artifacts of the Pacific Northwest Native American tribes. It will be closed for renovation until March 1991. Especially good is the scrimshaw display. (Open daily 10am-5pm, Thurs. 10am-8pm.) The **Henry Art Gallery,** 15th Ave. NE and NE 41st St. (543-2256), houses a collection of 18th- to 20th-century European and American art. (Open Tues.-Wed. and Fri. 10am-5pm, Thurs. 10am-7pm, Sat.-Sun. 11-5pm. Admission $2, students and seniors $1.) The **UW Arts Ticket Office,** 4001 University Way NE, has information and tickets for all events. (Open Mon.-Fri. 10:30am-4:30pm.) To reach the U district, take buses #71-74 from downtown, #7 or 43 from Capitol Hill.

Waterways and Parks

A string of attractions stud the waterways linking Lake Washington and Puget Sound. House and sailboats fill **Lake Union.** Here, the **Center for Wooden Boats,** 1010 Valley St. (382-2628), maintains a moored flotilla of new and restored small craft for rental. (Sailboats $8-25 per hr., rowboats $7 per hr. Open Wed.-Sun. noon-6pm.) **Kelly's Landing,** 1401 NE Boat St. (547-9909), below the UW campus, rents canoes for outings on Lake Union. (Sailboats $10-34 per hr. Usually open Mon.-Fri. 10am-dusk.) Tour the houseboat moorings along Lake Union's shores or go through the Montlake Cut to Lake Washington.

Mock and ridicule trout and salmon as they struggle up 21 concrete steps at the **Fish Ladder** (783-7059) on the south side of the locks. Take bus #43 from the U District or #17 from downtown. Farther north, on the northwestern shore of the city, lies the **Golden Gardens Park** in the Loyal Heights neighborhood, between NW 80th and NW 95th. The frigid beach is for the brave. Several expensive restaurants line the piers to the south, and the unobstructed views of the Olympics almost make their uniformly excellent seafood worth the price.

Directly north of Lake Union, the beautiful people run, roller skate, and skateboard around **Green Lake.** Take bus #16 from downtown. The lake also draws windsurfers, but woe to those who lose their balance. Whoever named Green Lake wasn't kidding; even a quick dunk results in gobs of green algae clinging to body and hair. Next door grows Woodland Park and the **Woodland Park Zoo,** 5500 Phinney Ave. N. (789-7919), best reached from Rte. 99 or N. 50th St. Take bus #5 from downtown. The park itself looks shaggy, but this makes the animals' habitats seem all the more realistic. (Open daily 10am-6pm; winter daily 8:30am-4pm. Admission $4, ages 6-17 $2, seniors, disabled, and ages 6-12 50¢.)

Entertainment

Obtain a copy of *The Weekly* (75¢) at newsstands and in boxes on the street, for a complete calendar of music, theater, exhibits, and special events. The free *Rocket,* available in music stores throughout the city, is a monthly off-beat guide to the popular music scene around the Puget Sound area, and *Seattle Gay News* (25¢) lists events and musical happenings relevant to the gay community. The "What's Happening" Friday insert of the *Seattle Post-Intelligencer* has more music listings.

During summertime lunch hours downtown, city-sponsored free entertainment of the **"Out to Lunch"** series (623-0340) brings everything from reggae to folk dancing to the parks and squares of Seattle.

One of the joys of living in Seattle is the abundance of community taverns dedicated to providing a relaxed environment for dancing and spending time with friends. In Washington a tavern serves only beer and wine; a fully licensed bar or cocktail lounge must adjoin a restaurant. You must be 21 to enter bars and taverns. The Northwest produces a variety of local beers (none bottled): Grant's, Imperial Russian Stout, India Pale Ale, Red Hook, Ballard Bitter, and Black Hook.

For $4 or so, catch an evening of live stand-up comedy in one of Seattle's comedy clubs, such as Pioneer Square's **Swannie's Comedy Underground,** 222 S. Main St. (628-0303; acts daily at 9pm and 11pm).

The University Bistro, 4315 University Way NE (547-8010). Live music (everything from blues to reggae) nightly. Happy Hour (4-7pm) finds pints of Bud for $1.25, pitchers $4. Cover Tues. $2, Wed.-Sat. $3-5, no cover Sun.-Mon. Open Sun.-Fri. 11am-2am, Sat. 6pm-2am.

Murphy's Pub, 2110 N. 45th St. (634-2110), in Wallingford, west of the U district. Take bus #43. A classic Irish pub with a mile-long beer list. Popular with the young folks, Murphy's has live Irish and folk music nightly. Open daily 2pm-2am. Cover $1-2.

Squid Row Tavern, 518 E. Pine (322-2031). Bizarre paintings, black booths, a bar, and earfuls of melodious punk rock. Pint of Bud $1.50. Open Mon.-Fri. noon-2am, Sat. 4pm-2am, Sun. 6pm-2am. Cover $4.

The Borderline, 608 1st Ave. (624-3316), in the heart of Pioneer Sq. Under 25 crowd dances to a mix of music from Motown to new-wave. Occasional live bands. Happy Hour (8-10pm) features 50¢ pints of Bud and free snacks. Fri.-Sat. cover $2 for men, $1 for women. Open Thurs.-Sat. 8pm-2am.

The Double Header, 407 2nd Ave. (464-9918), in Pioneer Sq. Claims to be the oldest gay bar in the country. An oom-pah band plays nightly to a mostly middle-aged crowd of gay men and women. A Seattle institution. Open daily 10am-2pm. No cover.

San Juan Islands

The San Juan Islands hold an uncorrupted treasure. Bald eagles circle above ragged hillsides dotted with family farms, pods of killer whales spout offshore, and the sun shines perpetually. To travelers approaching from summer resorts infested with vacationers, the islands will seem blissfully quiet. Even in mid-summer, you can drive the back roads and pass another car just once per hour. For this reason, islanders don't begrudge admission to their towns and campsites. Although tension has built between the locals and the Seattle vacationers who are buying up huge chunks of the islands, quiet well-behaved tourists and their dollars are still very welcome on the San Juans.

Pick up *The San Juan Islands Afoot and Afloat* by Marge Mueller ($10), an excellent guide to the area, available at book and outfitting stores on the islands and in Seattle. The *Islands Sounder,* the local paper, annually publishes *The San Juans Beckon* to provide up-to-date information on island recreation. When no one's looking, you can pick it and the *San Juanderer* up for free on the ferries and in island stores.

Washington State Ferries serve the islands daily from **Anacortes** on the mainland. To reach Anacortes, take I-5 north from Seattle to Mt. Vernon. From there, Rte. 20 heads west; the way to the ferry is well marked. **Evergreen Trailways** buses to Anacortes depart Seattle from the **Greyhound depot** at 8th Ave. and Stewart St. twice per day. Call Evergreen Trailways (728-5955) for exact times.

In Anacortes, you can purchase a ticket to Lopez, Shaw, Orcas, or San Juan Island. You pay only on westbound trips to or between the islands; no charge is levied on eastbound traffic. (In effect, any ticket to the islands is a round-trip ticket.) Therefore, you can save money by traveling directly to the westernmost island on your itinerary, and then making your way back island by island. The ferry unloads first at Lopez Island, followed by Shaw, Orcas, and finally San Juan. You can also purchase one-way tickets to Sidney, BC, or from Sidney to the islands. Foot passengers travel in either direction between the islands free of charge. Fares from Anacortes to San Juan Island are $4.75 for pedestrians ($2.50 for seniors and ages 5-11), $6.25 for bikes, and $9.50 for motorcycles; cars cost $19. Fares to the other islands en route generally run a few dollars cheaper. Inter-island fares average $2.25 for bikes and motorcycles, $7.75 for cars. The one-way fare to Sidney, BC costs $6.25 for pedestrians, $8.75 for bikes, $13.25 for motorcycles, and $31.25 for cars in summer ($26.05 in winter). Some car spaces are available from the islands to Sidney; make reservations. Call Washington State Ferries (206-464-6400; in WA 800-542-0810) before noon on the day before your trip to ensure a space. They're also the people to call for specific departure times and rates. The ferry authorities only accept cash or in-state checks as payment. You may park your vehicle for free at the Anacortes parking lot on the corner of 30th and T St. A free, reliable shuttle then whisks you 4 mi. to the terminal.

San Juan Island

Although the ferry makes its last stop in San Juan, it is the most frequently visited island, home to the largest town in the group, **Friday Harbor.** Since the ferry docks right in town, the island proves the easiest to explore.

The **National Park Service Information Center** and **Chamber of Commerce Information Center,** 1st and Spring (378-2240), will answer questions about the British and American camps (see below). (Open Mon.-Fri. 8am-4:30pm, Sat.-Sun. 10:30am-3:30pm.) **San Juan Tours and Transit Co.,** 470 Hillcrest Dr. (378-5545), runs two sight-seeing tours of the island every afternoon (June-Sept.). The two-hour tours circle the island, stopping at Roche Harbor, English and American Camps, and Limekiln Lighthouse ($8, ages 5-11 $5). The company also runs hourly shuttle buses from the ferry to Lakedale campground ($3) and Roche Harbor ($4).

To begin a loop of the island, head south out of Friday Harbor on Argyle Rd., which merges into Cattle Point Rd. on the way to **American Camp** (378-2240), 5 mi. south of Friday Harbor. The camp dates to the infamous Pig War of 1859, when the U.S. and England remained at loggerheads over possession of the islands. An interpretive shelter near the entrance to the park explains the history of the war; a self-guided historic trail leads from the shelter through the buildings and past the site of the English sheep farm.

Returning north on Cattle Point Rd., consider taking the gravel False Bay Rd. to the west. The road leads to **False Bay,** true home to a large number of nesting bald eagles. As a University of Washington biology preserve, the bay's student projects are all indicated by markers. Farther north on False Bay Rd., you'll run into **Bailer Hill Road,** which turns into West Side Rd. when it reaches Haro Straight. (You can also reach Bailer Hill Rd. by taking Cattle Point Rd. to Little Rd.) Along the road, sloping hills blanketed with wildflowers rise to one side, and rocky shores fall to the other. **San Juan County Park** on Smallpox Bay provides a convenient opportunity to park your bike or car and examine this scenery more closely.

English Camp, the second half of San Juan National Historical Park, rests on West Valley Rd. amid the forest surrounding Garrison Bay. From West Side Rd., take Mitchell Bay Rd. east to West Valley Rd. Here, four preserved original buildings, including the barracks, now function as an interpretive center, which explains the history of the "war" and sells guides to the island. (Park open year-round; buildings open Memorial Day-Labor Day daily 9am-6pm. Free.)

Friday Harbor loses much of its charm when the tourists arrive in full force, but remains quite appealing in the winter. Take the time to poke around the galleries, craft shops, and bookstores. The **Whale Museum,** 62 1st St. (378-4710), will teach you everything you ever wanted to know about the giant cetaceans, starring skeletons, sculptures, and information on new research. The museum even has a **whale hotline** (800-562-8832) for you to report sightings and strandings. (Open daily 10am-5pm; winter 11am-4pm. Admission $2.50, seniors and students $2, children under 12 $1.)

Walking south a block will take you to the **Friday Harbor Youth Hostel (AYH),** 35 1st St. (378-5555), in the Elite Hotel. It has a clean, well-lit women's dorm and a slightly more cramped men's dorm. Check-in 8-11 pm. ($9, nonmembers $14.) **San Juan County Park,** 380 Westside Rd. (378-2992), 10 mi. west of Friday Harbor on Smallpox and Andrews Bays, provides a public alternative. (Cold water and flush toilets. Bikers and hikers $3; cars, campers, and trailers $12.50.) The parks and shoreline drives beg you to pack a picnic lunch and leave Friday Harbor behind. Stock up on bread and cheese at **King's Market,** 160 Spring St. (Open daily 8am-10pm.)

The **post office** stamps at Blair and Reed St. (378-4511; open Mon.-Fri. 8:30am-4:30pm); the **ZIP code** is 98250. San Juan Island's **area code** is 206.

Whidbey Island

This 50-mi.-long, telephone-receiver-shaped island sits in the rain shadow of the Olympic Mountains. Clouds, wrung dry by the time they pass over Whidbey, release a mere 25 in. of rain per year and a luxurious ration of sunshine. This leaves visitors free to enjoy rocky beaches bounded by bluffs blooming with wild roses and crawling with blackberry brambles.

Whoever named **Useless Bay** certainly did not use aesthetic criteria. On the west side of the bay, uninterrupted beach stretches from Bayview Beach along **Double Bluff Park** to the tip of the peninsula of Double Bluff. Comb the 1½-mi. beach, explore the bluffs, or just gaze across the water at Seattle and Mt. Rainier. Another ideal spot for the wanderer, **South Whidbey State Park,** 4128 S. Smuggler's Cove Rd. (321-4559), blushes about 7 mi. north of Freeland. The park wraps around the west coast of the island, covering 87 acres of forest. Park by the tiny outdoor amphitheater and walk down the bluff to the beach (10 min.). Wander along the pebbly beach approximately 1½ mi. in either direction—to Lagoon Point in the north or to a lighthouse on Bush Point in the south.

Around the bend to the north, **Fort Casey State Park,** 1280 S. Fort Casey Rd. (678-4519), stands right next to the Keystone ferry terminal, 3 mi. south of Coupeville. The park occupies the site of a late 1890s fort designed to defend against a long-anticipated attack from the west. (Interpretive center open in winter for large groups by appointment. Park open year-round.) Reach **Fort Ebey State Park,** 395 N. Fort Ebey Rd. (678-4636), from Libbey Rd. off Rte. 20 north of Coupeville, by Valley Drive's park entrance. As the driest spot on the island, prickly pear cacti grow right up next to the beach.

Federally established for the "preservation and protection of a rural community," **Ebey's Landing National Historical Reserve** contains both parks and the town of **Coupeville.** Many of Coupeville's homes and commercial establishments date from the 19th century, and the city also maintains the **Island County Historical Museum** at Alexander and Coveland St. (Open May-Sept. daily noon-4pm; April Sat.-Sun. noon-4pm. Free.) The town extends along E. Front St. between two 1855 blockhouses meant to withstand an anticipated Skagit tribe uprising that never occurred. Of the zealously fortified buildings, the **John Alexander Blockhouse,** at the west end of town, and the **Davis Blockhouse,** at the edge of the town's cemetery, still stand at attention. A few miles north of Oak Harbor on Rte. 20, fruit fiends and aviation aficionados peacefully coexist at the **U-pick Strawberry Farms,** where the roar from low-flying Navy "Prowler" jets virtually rattles the fruit from the plants.

When the Skagit tribe lived and fished in the area, the Haida tribe from the north often raided at Deception Pass. A bear totem of the Haidas now stands on the north end of West Beach in **Deception Pass State Park,** 5175 N. Rte. 20 (675-2417). The most heavily used of Whidbey's state parks, its views will amaze. Camping facilities, a saltwater boat launch, 8½ mi. of trails, and a freshwater lake for swimming, fishing, and boating, allow for a closer look at the tidal pools, beaches, and natural life of the area. A fishing license, available at most hardware stores, is required for fishing in the lake; fishing season runs from mid-April to October. (Park open year-round.)

Whidbey swims in smoked salmon; every town (and every milepost along the highway) has its share of salmon shacks. In Langley, **Mike's Place,** 215 1st St. (321-6575), serves the best clam chowder on the island ($2.25). The all-you-can-eat nightly specials also come highly recommended. (Breakfast $5, lunch $4-6, dinner under $10. Open Mon.-Fri. 7am-10pm, Sat.-Sun. 8am-10pm.) The **Doghouse Tavern,** 230 1st St., on the main drag of this 1-block town, serves 10¢ 6-oz. beers with lunch (limit 2). Eat $4 sandwiches and $4.55 corn soup out of an edible bread bowl, either in the tavern or around the back in the "family restaurant." (Open Mon.-Sat. 11am-1am, Sun. noon-1am.) In Oak Harbor, locals swear by the Mazzone mushroom burger ($4.50) at **Jason's,** 5355 Hwy. 20, at Goldie Rd. (Lunch $3-4, dinner $5-8. Open 24 hr.)

Inexpensive motels are few and far between on Whidbey; those that do exist are frequently in need of repairs. A number of B&Bs offer elegant rooms for a few more dollars. Contact **Whidbey Island Bed and Breakfast Association,** P.O. Box 259, Langley 98260 (321-6272), for a full listing; reservations are necessary. The **Tyee Motel and Cafe,** 405 S. Main St., Coupeville (678-6616), offers clean, straightforward rooms with showers. The location is within walking distance of Coupeville center and the water makes up for the bleak setting. (Cafe open daily 6:30am-9pm. Singles $30, each additional person $4.) On the northern edge of Oak Harbor lies the **Crossroads Motel,** 5622 Hwy. 20 (675-3145). The cinderblock construction looks like a fort, but the immaculate rooms compensate. Fully equipped kitchens are available. (Singles $32. Doubles $39, with kitchens $43. Each additional person $5.)

Four state park campgrounds service the island, each with sites for $7.50. **South Whidbey State Park,** 4128 S. Smuggler's Cove Rd. (321-4559), 7 mi. northwest of Freeland via Bush Point Rd. and Smuggler's Cove Rd., perches on a cliff in a stand of Douglas firs. A steep ¼-mi. trail leads down to a rocky beach. (Open year-round.) **Fort Casey State Park,** 1280 S. Fort Casey Rd. (678-4519), right next to the Keystone ferry terminal, has 35 sites interspersed with turn-of-the-century military memorabilia. Arrive early in summer. **Fort Ebey State Park** (678-4636) does what forts do on N. Fort Ebey Rd., north of Fort Casey and just west of Coupeville. Miles of hiking trails and easy access to a pebbly beach make this, the island's newest campground, also the island's best. (50 sites for cars and RVs. 3 for hikers and bikers $3.) **Deception Pass State Park,** 5175 N. Hwy. 525 (675-2417), 8 mi. north of Oak Harbor, has 8½ mi. of hiking trails and Cranberry Lake, for good freshwater fishing and swimming. (4 rustic sites for hikers and bikers $3.)

Unfortunately, **Island Transit** (678-7771 or 321-6688) only runs one intra-island bus line—the automobile still reigns. Yet only one main road runs: "Rte. 525" on the southern half of the island and "Rte. 20" at Coupeville and beyond.

The southern tip of Whidbey Island lies 40 mi. directly north of Seattle. The 20-minute **ferry** to Clinton leaves from Mukilteo (pronounced mu-kul-TEE-o), a small community just south of Everett. Take I-5 north from Seattle and follow the large signs to the ferry. (Ferries leave Mukilteo every ½-hr. 6am-11pm, and return ferries leave Clinton every ½-hr. 5:30am-11:30pm. Call Washington State Ferries at 800-542-7052 for exact times. Car and driver $3.75, bicycle and rider $3, walk-on $1.65, each additional passenger $1; seniors, ages 5-12, and disabled travelers 50¢, under 5 free. Small surcharges added in the summer.) Avoid commuter traffic eastbound in the morning and westbound at night.

You can also reach Whidbey Island from Port Townsend on the Olympic Peninsula. Ferries leave the terminal in downtown Port Townsend for Keystone, on the west side of the island, 8 times per day between 7am and 5:45pm. Ferries return from Keystone to Port Townsend 8 times per day between 7am and 6:30pm. More ferries ply the waters on weekends; extra daily ferries run in August. (35 min. Car and passenger $5.75. Bicycle riders $3.50. Walk-on $1.75; over 64, ages 5-12, and disabled 80¢; under 5 free. For more information, call 800-542-7052.)

To reach Whidbey from the north, take exit 189 off I-5 and head west toward Anacortes. Stay on Rte. 20 when it heads south through the stunning Deception Pass State Park (signs will direct you); otherwise you will fly on to Anacortes. **Evergreen Trailways** runs a bus to Whidbey from Seattle.

The **post office** in Langley registers at 115 2nd St. (321-4113), **ZIP code** 98260; in Coupeville at 201 NW Coveland (678-5353), **ZIP code** 98239; in Oak Harbor at 7035 70th NW (675-6621), **ZIP code** 98277. The **area code** for Whidbey is 206.

The Olympic Peninsula

In the fishing villages and logging towns of the Olympic Peninsula, locals joke about having webbed feet and using Rustoleum instead of suntan oil. The Olympic Mountains wrench out the area's heavy rainfall (up to 200 in. per year on Mt. Olympus) from the moist Pacific. While this torrent supports bona fide rain forests in the western peninsula's river valleys, towns such as Sequim in the range's rain shadow are the driest in all of Washington, with as little as 17 in. of rain in a typical year.

The peninsula's geography matches its extremes of climate. The beaches along the Pacific strip provide a hiker's paradise—isolated, windy, and beautiful. The glaciated peaks of the Olympic range sport spectacular alpine scenery; the network of trails covers an area the size of Rhode Island. These wild, woody mountains resisted exploration well into the 20th century.

Because it compresses such variety into a relatively small area, the Olympic Peninsula attracts those seeking accessible wilderness and outdoor recreation. U.S. 101 loops around the peninsula, stringing together scattered towns and sights around the nape of the mountains. The numerous secondary roads departing from 101 were specially designed with exploration in mind, although some are gravel-covered, making bicycling into the heart of the park difficult. Heart o' the Hills Rd. to Hurricane Ridge makes a particularly good detour, offering an unbeatable panorama. Route 112 follows the Strait of Juan de Fuca out to Neah Bay, the driftwood-laden coastal town near Cape Flattery. Greyhound provides service only as far as Port Angeles to the north and Aberdeen/Hoquiam to the south. Although local transit systems extend public transportation a little farther, the western portion of the peninsula and the southern portion of Hood Canal do not receive regular service.

Hitchhiking is illegal on U.S. 101 southwest of Olympia. Where it is legal, hitching can often prove slow, and you may stay stranded in the rain for hours. Bicycling is dangerous in some spots, particularly along Crescent Lake just west of Port Angeles, as the shoulders are narrow or nonexistent, the curves sharp, and the roads ridden with rapid logging trucks. Motoring suits the peninsula best, although some of the beaches and mountain wilds can be reached only on foot. Extended backpacking trips offer spectacular rewards.

Camping

Although many towns on the peninsula cater to tourists with motels and resorts, the beautiful outdoors make camping the more attractive option. **Olympic National Park** maintains a number of campgrounds. (Sites $5.) The numerous **state parks** along Hood Canal and the eastern rim charge $4 per night, with an occasional site for tenters at only $1-3 per night. The **national forest** and the park services welcome backcountry camping (free everywhere), but a permit, available at any ranger station, is required within the park. Camping on the beaches comes especially easy, although you should pack a supply of water. The beaches in the westernmost corner of Neah Bay and from the town of Queets to Moclips farther south fall within Native American reserve land, which is private property: travelers are welcome, but respect local regulations prohibiting alcohol, fishing without a tribal permit, and beachcombing. The Quinault Reservation gained fame 20 years ago by forcibly ousting vandals trespassing on their beaches.

Washington's **Department of Natural Resources (DNR)** manages huge tracts of land on the Kitsap Peninsula and along the Hoh and Clearwater Rivers near the western shore, as well as smaller, individual campsites sprinkled around the peninsula. In DNR areas, camping is free and uncrowded; no reservations are required. DNR areas, however, can prove hard to find. For maps, contact the Department of Natural Resources, Olympic Area, Rte. 1, Box 1375, Forks, WA 98331 (206-374-6131).

Hood Canal and the Kitsap Peninsula

The long ribbon of the Hood Canal reaches down from Puget Sound, nearly separating the Kitsap Peninsula from its parent Olympic Peninsula. The Canal's structure invites comparison with Scandinavia's famous fjords—the same narrow, steeply banked waterway, the same jagged peaks for backdrops, the same little towns tucked in the crevices of the coastline. U.S. 101 adheres to the western shore of the canal from Potlatch State Park on its southern tip to Quilcene in the north. Here, the **Olympic National Forest** rims the eastern edge of the national park. Much of the forest is more developed and more accessible than the park and gives those with little time or small appetites for the outdoors a taste of the peninsula's wildlife. Stop by one of the forest's **ranger stations** along the canal to pick up information on camping and trails in the forest. The two stations are in **Hoodsport,** P.O. Box 68 (877-5254; open early May-late Sept. daily 8am-4:30pm) and **Quilcene,** U.S. 101 S. (765-3368; open Mon.-Fri. 8am-5pm, Sat.-Sun. 8:30am-5pm). Adjacent to the Hoodsport Ranger Station stands a **post office** (877-5552; open Mon.-Fri. 8am-12:30pm and 1:30-5pm, Sat. 8:30-11:30am; ZIP Code: 98548.). Many of the forest service **campgrounds** cost only $4, including **Hamma Hamma,** on Forest Service Rd. 25, 7 mi. northwest of Eldon; **Lena Creek,** 2 mi. beyond Hamma Hamma; **Elkhorn,** on Forest Service Rd. 2610, 11 mi. northwest of Brinnon; and **Collins,** on Forest Service Rd. 2515, 8 mi. west of Brinnon. All have drinking water, as well as good fishing, hiking, and gorgeous scenery. Unfortunately, many of these require travel along gravel roads, which bicyclists may find difficult to navigate.

Lake Cushman State Park (877-5491), 7 mi. west of Hoodsport on Lake Cushman Rd., stretches by a beautiful lake with good swimming beaches. Many use it as a base camp for extended backpacking trips into the national forest and park. Lake Cushman has 10 sites ($7.50, $10 with full hookup) with flush toilets and pay showers (25¢). Clinging to a quiet cove just north of Eldon, **Mike's Beach Resort and Hostel,** N. 38470 U.S. 101 (877-5324) lacks a kitchen, and too many bunks crowd its tiny rooms, but it does have a small grocery store. ($5, nonmembers $7.50. Open April 15-Nov. 1.) The **Hungry Bear Cafe,** in Eldon, serves the Hood Canal specialty: geoduck (GOO-ee-duck) steak ($8). The geoduck, a giant mollusk which lives 2½ to 7 ft. below the surface of Hood Canal's beaches, has a taste somewhere between that of a razor clam and a scallop; the Bear serves it with mounds of great french fries and homemade tartar sauce. Burgers ($1.50-5) cater to less daring diners. (Open Mon.-Thurs. 9am-7pm, Fri. 9am-8pm, Sat. 8am-8pm, Sun. 8am-7pm.)

Topologically, the amorphous **Kitsap Peninsula** resembles a half-completed landfill project jutting into Puget Sound. The new bridge over the northern end of Hood Canal links the Kitsap Peninsula with the towns along the Strait of Juan de Fuca; no pedestrian traffic is allowed. Kitsap can also be reached by ferry: from Seattle to Bremerton or Winslow on connected Bainbridge Island, or from Edmonds, north of Seattle, to Kingston on the northern end of the peninsula.

In **Bremerton** you'll swear that you have stepped into the setting of a Tom Clancy novel; every third person has a Navy security pass swinging officially from their neck. The city is basically an overgrown repair shop for U.S. Naval ships. Chain hotels cluster along Kitsap Way in Bremerton, but you might prefer **Scenic Beach State Park,** near the village of Seabeck, featuring 50 campsites with water and bathrooms. (Sites $7, walk-in sites $3.) From Silverdale, take Anderson Hill Rd. or Newberry Hill Rd. west to Seabeck Hwy., then follow the highway 7 mi. south to the Scenic Beach turn-off. Cyclists beware of the staggering hills along this route. The Department of Natural Resources' **Tahuya Multiple Use Area** encompasses eight free campgrounds, each with drinking water, and many with good swimming beaches and boat launches. These are hard to find, however, and require travel along difficult gravel roads.

The Kitsap's most appealing attraction is the **Suquamish Museum** (598-3311), 6 mi. north of Winslow, just over the Agate Pass Bridge on Rte. 305. Run by the Port Madison Indian Reservation, this small but well-presented museum (pronounced sue-QUAH-mish) focuses entirely on the history and culture of the Puget Sound Salish Native Americans. (Open daily 10am-5pm. Admission $2.50, seniors $2, under 12 $1.)

Olympic National Park

Lodged among the august Olympic mountains, Olympic National Park covers 900,000 acres of velvet rainforest, jagged snowcovered peaks, and dense evergreen forest. This enormous region at the center of the peninsula affords limited access to four-wheeled traffic. No scenic loops or roads cross the park, and only a handful of secondary roads make insignificant attempts to penetrate the interior. The roads that do exist serve mainly as trailheads for over 600 mi. of hiking trails. Come prepared for rain; a parka, good boots, and a waterproof tent are essential in this area. Stop at the **Park Service Visitors Center**, 3002 Mt. Angeles Rd., Port Angeles (452-4501, ext. 230), for backcountry camping permits and a map of the locations of other park ranger stations. (Open daily 8am-6pm; off-season reduced hours.) The park service runs interpretive programs such as guided forest walks, tidal pool walks, and campfire programs from its various ranger stations (all free). For a full schedule of events everywhere in the park, obtain a copy of the park newspaper, available at ranger stations and the visitors center. More popular entrances, such as the Hoh, Heart O' the Hills, and Elwaha, charge $3 entrance fee per car . The fee buys an entrance permit good for 7 days. A similar pass for hiker/bikers costs $1.

July, August, and September work well for visiting Olympic National Park, since much of the backcountry often remains snowed-in until late June, and only the summer has a good number of rainless days. **Backcountry camping** requires a free wilderness permit, available at ranger stations and trailheads. The park service's shelters are for emergencies only; large concentrations of people attract bears.

Never drink untreated water in the park. *Giardia,* a very nasty microscopic parasite, lives in all these waters and causes severe diarrhea, gas, and abdominal cramps; symptoms often don't appear for weeks after ingestion. Bring your own water supply, or boil local water for five minutes before drinking it. Dogs are not allowed in the backcountry, and must be restrained at all times within the park.

Berry picking ranks high on the list of summer activities on the peninsula. Newly cleared regions and roadside areas yield the best crops; raspberries, strawberries, blueberries, and huckleberries abound. Bears also seem fond of this fruit; if one stumbles onto your favorite berry patch, don't argue. **Fishing** within park boundaries is allowed without a permit, but you must obtain a state game department punch card for salmon and steelhead trout at outfitting and hardware stores locally, or at the game department in Olympia.

The **Eastern Rim** of the park is accessible through the Olympic National Forest from U.S. 101 along Hood Canal. For information on camping in the forest see Hood Canal and the Kitsap Peninsula above. The car-accessible campgrounds lure hikers who use them as trailheads to the interior of the park. **Staircase Campground** (877-5569), 19 mi. northwest of Hoodsport at the head of Lake Cushman, has 59 sites and a ranger station with interpretive programs on weekends. (Open year-round. Sites $5.) **Dosewallips** (pronounced doh-see-WALL-ups), on a road that leaves U.S. 101 3 mi. north of Brinnon (27 mi. north of Hoodsport) offers free but less developed sites. (Open June-Sept.)

On the park's **Northern Rim, Heart o' the Hills** (452-2713) and **Elwha Valley** (452-9191) campgrounds both have interpretive programs and ranger stations, as does **Fairholm Campground** (928-3380), 30 mi. west of Port Angeles at the western tip of Lake Crescent. (Sites $5.) The **Lake Crescent** station (928-3380) has an extensive interpretive program but no camping. The **information booth** here opens Memorial Day to Labor Day daily from 11:30am to 4:30pm. **Soleduck Hotsprings Campground** (327-3534), to the southeast of Lake Crescent, 13 mi. off U.S. 101, adjoins the hot springs resort. (Sites $5.)

The main attraction of the northern area for those not planning backcountry trips, **Hurricane Ridge** affords magnificent views of Mt. Olympus, the Bailey Range, and even Canada on clear days.

Down the Hoh River Rd. (19 mi.) sits the park service's **Hoh Rain Forest Campground and Visitors Center** (374-6925). The center is wheelchair-accessible, as are trails leading from the center into the only temperate (as opposed to tropical) rain forest in the world. Camping costs $5. (Visitors center open summer daily 9am-5pm.) Farther south, after U.S. 101 rejoins the coast, the park's boundaries extend southwest to edge the banks of the **Queets River.** The unpaved road here leads to free campsites at the top. (Open June-Sept.) The park and forest services share the land surrounding **Quinault Lake** and **Quinault River.** The park service land is accessible only by foot. The forest service operates a day-use beach and an information center in the **Quinault Ranger Station,** South Shore Rd. (288-2444; open daily 7:30am-5pm; winter Mon.-Fri. 7:30am-5pm).

Mora (374-5460) and **Kalaloch** (962-2283), have campgrounds (sites $5) and ranger stations. The Kalaloch (kuh-LAY-lok) Center, including lodge, general store, and gas station, stays more scenic with 195 sites near the ocean.

Cascade Range

Formed by centuries of volcanic activity, the relatively young Cascade Range is still evolving—as the 1980 eruption of Mt. St. Helens attests. While a handful of white-domed beauties attract the most interest, the bulk of the range consists of smaller systems that together form a natural barrier from the Columbia Gorge to Canada. The mountain wall intercepts moist Pacific air, creating both Seattle's cloudy weather and the 300 rainless days per year in the plains of eastern Washington.

Although much of the heavily forested range is accessible only to hikers, horseback riders, and the Sasquatch, four major roads cut through the mountains along river valleys, each offering good trailheads and impressive scenery. **Route 12** through White Pass goes nearest Mt. Rainier National Park; **Interstate 90** sends four lanes past the major ski resorts of Snoqualmie Pass; scenic **Route 2** leaves Everett for Stevens Pass and descends along the Wenatchee River, a favorite of whitewater rafters; and **Route 20, the North Cascades Highway,** provides access to North Cascades National Park from April to November, weather permitting. These last two roads are often traveled in sequence as the **Cascade Loop.**

Greyhound travels the routes over Stevens and Snoqualmie Passes to and from Seattle, while **Amtrak** cuts between Ellensburg and Puget Sound. Locals warn against thumbing across Rte. 20, where a few hapless hitchers have apparently "vanished" over the last decade. The mountains are most accessible in the clear months of July, August, and September; many high mountain passes are snowed in the rest of the year. For general information on the Cascades contact the **National Park/National Forest Information Service,** 915 2nd Ave., Seattle 98174 (442-0181 or 442-0170).

North Cascades

A number of different agencies administer the North Cascades, an aggregation of dramatic peaks north of Stevens Pass on Rte. 2. Pasayten and Glacier Peak are designated wilderness areas, each attracting large numbers of hardy backpackers and mountain climbers. Ross Lake Recreation Area surrounds the Rte. 20 corridor, and **North Cascades National Park,** 2105 Hwy. 20, Sedro Wooley 98284 (206-856-5700; open Sun.-Thurs. 8am-4:30pm, Fri.-Sat. 8am-6pm), extends north and south of Rte. 20. The **Mt. Baker/Snoqualmie National Forest,** 915 2nd Ave., Seattle 98174 (206-442-0170), borders the park to the west; the **Okanogan National Forest,** 1240 2nd Ave. S., P.O. Box 950, Okanogan 98840 (509-422-2704) to the east; and **Wenatchee National Forest,** 301 Yakima St., P.O. Box 811, Wenatchee 98801 (509-662-4335) to the south. For snow avalanche information on all these jurisdictions call 206-526-6677. Rte. 20, the North Cascades Hwy., provides the major access to the area, as well as astounding views past each new curve in the road.

Rte. 20 from Burlington (exit 230 on I-5) across the mountains gives the best first impression of the North Cascades. A feat of modern engineering, Rte. 20 follows the Skagit River to the Skagit Dams and lakes, whose hydroelectric energy powers Seattle, then crosses the Cascade Crest at Rainy Pass (4860 ft.) and Washington Pass (5477 ft.), finally descending to the Methow River and the dry Okanogan rangeland of eastern Washington. The road forks at Baker Lake Rd., which in turn dead-ends for some unknown reason 25 mi. later at **Baker Lake.** Only two campsites along the way provide water: **Horseshoe Cove** (sites $7.50) and **Panorama Point** (sites $7.50). All other sites are free.

Rte. 9 leads north from the rich farmland of **Skagit Valley** through inspiring forested countryside, with roundabout access to **Mount Baker** via the forks at the Nooksack River and Rte. 542. Mt. Baker (10,778 ft.) has been belching since 1975, and in winter, jets of steam often rise from its dome. The nerve. Sneeze four times in succession and you miss the town of **Concrete** and its three neighbors—and you may want to reach for the pepper. If you drive through at lunchtime, stop at the **Mount Baker Café,** 119 E. Main St. (853-8200; open daily 6am-8pm). The road from Concrete to Mt. Baker runs past the lakes created by the Upper and Lower Baker Dams. Solid facts are available from the **Concrete Chamber of Commerce** (853-8400), in the old depot, tucked between Main St. and Hwy. 20—follow the railroad tracks upon entering town. (Open Sat.-Sun. 9am-4pm.)

Neighboring **Rockport** borders **Rockport State Park,** featuring magnificent Douglas-firs, a trail that accommodates wheelchairs, and 50 campsites that rank among the nicest in the state ($7.50). The surrounding **Mount Baker National Forest** permits free camping closer to the high peaks. From Rockport, Hwy. 530 stems south to **Darrington,** home to a large population of displaced North Carolinians, and therefore host to a rapidly growing **Bluegrass Festival** on the third weekend of July. Darrington's **ranger station** (436-1155) presides on Hwy. 530 at the north end of town. (Open Mon.-Fri. 6:45am-4:30pm, Sat.-Sun. 8am-5pm; off-season weekends only.)

Pitch your tent at the free sites at the **Cascade Islands Campground,** on the south side of the Cascade River. Ask for careful directions in town, and bring heavy-duty repellent to ward off the swarms of mosquitoes.

From Marblemount, head 22 mi. up Cascade Rd. for a 9-mi. hike to **Cascade Pass** and the **Cottonwood Trailhead.** For $4 the park service's **shuttle** will take you the 26 mi. to the isolated town of **Stehekin.** Always confirm at the **Marblemount Ranger Station** (873-4590), 1 mi. north of Marblemount on a well-marked road west of town, that the thrice-daily shuttle is in operation. (Open daily 8am-4:30pm.)

Newhalem, a buffer zone between Rte. 20 and North Cascade National Park, is the first town in the **Ross Lake National Recreation Area.** A small grocery store and hiking trails to the dams and lakes nearby make up the town's largest attractions. Information emanates from the **visitors center,** on Rte. 20. (Open late June-early Sept. Thurs.-Mon. 8am-4pm.) At other times, stop at the general store (open daily 8am-8pm; call 206-386-4489).

Plugged up by Ross Dam, the artificial expanse of **Ross Lake** extends back into the mountains as far as the Canadian border. Fifteen campgrounds ring the lake, some accessible only by boat, others by trail. The trail along Big Beaver Creek, a few mi. north of Rte. 20, leads from Ross Lake into the Picket Range and eventually to Mt. Baker and the **Northern Unit** of North Cascades National Park. The **Sourdough Mountain** and **Desolation Peak** lookout towers near Ross Lake have eagle's-eye views of the range.

The National Park's **Goodell Creek Campground,** just south of Newhalem, has 22 sites ($3) suitable for tents and trailers, and a launching site for white-water rafting along the Skagit River. (Open year-round. Drinking water and pit toilets.) **Colonial Creek Campground,** 10 mi. to the east, is a fully developed, vehicle-accessible campground with flush toilets, a dump station, and campfire programs every evening. (Open mid-May to Nov. Sites $5.)

Diablo Lake fumes directly to the west of Ross Lake, the foot of Ross Dam acting as its eastern shore and the top of the Diablo Dam stopping it up on the west. The town of Diablo Lake, on the northeastern shore, is the main trailhead for hikes into the southern portion of the North Cascades National Park. The Thunder Creek

Trail traverses Park Creek Pass to the Stehekin River Rd. in Lake Chelan National Recreation Area. Diablo Lake has a boathouse and a lodge that sells groceries and gas.

The **Pacific Coast Trail** crosses **Rainy Pass** (alt. 4860 ft.) 30 mi. farther on Rte. 20, on one of the most scenic and challenging legs of its 2500-mi. Canada-to-Mexico span. The trail leads up to **Pasayten Wilderness** in the north and down to **Glacier Peak** (10,541 ft.), which dominates the central portion of the range. Glacier Peak can also be approached from the secondary roads extending northward from the Lake Wenatchee area near Coles Corner on U.S. 2, or from Rte. 530 to Darrington. **Washington Pass**, at mile 163 of Rte. 20, has a well-maintained scenic turn-out. A 5-minute walk up paved wheelchair-accessible trails leads to a view of the Early Winters Creek's Copper Basin, validating the whole drive.

Despite the Puritan namesake, the town of **Winthrop** now capitalizes on a Wild West theme. The one row of restaurants, stores, and hotels along the main street—all made of weather-beaten wood with corrugated tin roofs—features creaky wooden sidewalks and painted signs. Though slightly ludicrous, the whole scene will certainly impress the kids.

The great billows of hickory-scented smoke draw customers to the **Riverside Rib Co. Bar B-Q**, 207 Riverside, which serves fantastic Winthropian ribs in a convertible prairie schooner (i.e. covered wagon); satisfying vegetarian dinners ($7) are also available. (Open daily 11am-9pm.) Across the street sits the **Winthrop Information Station** (996-2125), on the corner of Rte. 20 and Riverside. (Open Memorial Day-Labor Day 9am-5pm.)

While in Winthrop, mark time at the **Shafer Museum**, 285 Castle Ave. (996-2712), up the hill overlooking the town, 1 block west of Riverside Ave. The museum features all sorts of bizarre pioneer paraphernalia in a log cabin built in 1897. (Open daily 10am-5pm. Free.) You can rent horses at the **Rocking Horse Ranch** (996-2768), 9 mi. north of Winthrop on the North Cascade Hwy. (996-2768; $10 per hr.), and mountain bikes at **The Virginian Hotel** just east of town on Rte. 20 ($4.50 for the 1st hr., then $3 per hr; full day $20).

The **Winthrop Ranger Station**, P.O. Box 158 (996-2266), up a marked dirt road west of town, has information on camping in the National Forest. (Open Mon.-Fri. 7:45am-5pm, Sat. 8:30am-5pm.) North of Winthrop, the **Early Winters Visitor Center**, outside Mazama, stocks information about the Pasayten Wilderness, an area whose relatively gentle terrain and mild climate endear it to hikers and equestrians (996-2534; open Sun.-Thurs. 9am-5pm, Fri.-Sat. 9am-6pm; off-season weekends only).

Early Winters has 15 simple campsites ($5) 14 mi. west of Winthrop on Rte. 20, and **Klipchuk**, 1 mi. farther west, has 39 better developed sites ($5). Cool off at **Pearrygin Lake State Park** beach. From Riverside west of town, take Pearrygin Lake Rd. for 4 mi. Sites ($6) by the lake have flush toilets and pay showers. Arrive early, since the campground fills up in the early afternoon.

Leave Winthrop's prohibitively expensive hotel scene and stay in **Twisp**, the town that should have been a breakfast cereal. Nine mi. south of Winthrop on Rte. 20, this peaceful town offers low prices and few tourists. Stay at **The Sportsman Motel**, 1010 E. Rte. 20 (997-2911), whose barracks-like exterior belies the tasteful rooms, decor, and kitchens. (Singles $25, doubles $30; Nov. to mid-June singles $18, doubles $23.) The **Blue Spruce Motel** (997-8852) offers more spartan accommodations just a ½ block away. (Singles $24. Doubles $36.) The **Twisp Ranger Station**, 502 Glover St. (997-2131), has an extremely helpful staff ready to load you down with trail and campground guides. (Open Mon.-Fri. 7:45am-4:30pm, Sat. 10am-2pm.) The **Methow Valley Tourist Information Office**, at the corner of Rte. 20 and 3rd St., slings area brochures. (Open Mon.-Fri. 8am-noon and 1-5pm.)

The **Methow Valley Farmer's Market** sells produce from 9am to noon on Saturdays (April-Oct.) in front of the community center. Join local workers and their families at **Rosey's Branding Iron**, 123 Glover St., where the wonderfully droll staff serves all-you-can-keep-down soup and salad for $6. (Open daily 5am-9pm.)

Five mi. east of Twisp stands a training station for **Smoke Jumpers,** folks who get their kicks by parachuting into the middle of blazing forest fires and taking a more offensive approach to firefighting. Occasionally they give tours or have training sessions for public viewing. Call the base (997-2031) for details.

Gray Line Tours (343-2000) runs buses to North Cascades National Park from Seattle ($20, under 12 $10). Take the 12-hr. tour or stay in the park for the week. Buses depart Sundays at 7:45am from the Space Needle (June 5-Sept. 26). **Greyhound** stops in Burlington once per day on its Portland-Seattle route, and **Empire Lines** (affiliated with Greyhound), serves Okanogan, Pateros, and Chelan on the eastern slope. Avoid hitching in this area.

Mount Rainier National Park

Mt. Rainier rises grandly above the tops of the other Cascade mountains, 2 mi. taller than many of the surrounding foothills. Residents of Washington refer to it simply as "The Mountain;" Pete Seeger called it "that great strawberry ice cream cone in the sky."

Unfortunately, Rainier meteorologically drenches all that lies in its shadow. Warm ocean air condenses when it reaches Rainier and falls on the mountain at least 200 days of the year. When the sun does shine, you may understand why Native Americans called Mt. Rainier "Tahoma" (Mountain of God).

First-time visitors will appreciate Mt. Rainier more from lower elevations than from the 14,410-ft. summit. Many experiences available at slightly lower elevations—midnight views of the mountain silhouetted against the moon, inner-tube rides down the slick sides in winter, romps in alpine meadows full of unparalleled wildflower displays—approach the same intensity at much less cost and personal risk. Nevertheless, 2500 determined climbers ascend to Rainier's peak each year.

For visitor information stop in at the **Longmire Museum and Hiker's Center** (open mid-June to Sept. daily 8am-5:30pm; mid-Sept. to mid-June daily 9am-5pm); **Paradise Visitors Center** (open mid-June to mid-Sept. daily 9am-6pm; off-season hours vary); **Ohanapecosh Visitor Center** (same hours as Paradise); or **Sunrise Visitors Center,** (same hours as Paradise). All centers can be contacted c/o Superintendent, Mt. Rainier National Park, Ashford, WA 98304, or through the park central operator (569-2211). Admission to the park costs $5 per car or $2 per hiker. Gates stay open 24 hr.

Much of the activity in Rainier occurs in these centers, each of which has displays, a wealth of literature on everything from hiking to natural history, postings on trail and road conditions, and a smiling ranger to fill in any gaps. Naturalist-guided trips and talks, campfire programs, and slide presentations take place at the visitors centers and vehicle campgrounds throughout the park. Check at a visitors center or pick up a copy of the free annual newsletter, *Tahoma,* for details.

A car tour provides a good introduction to the park. All major roads offer scenic views of the mountain and have numerous roadside sites for camera-clicking and general gawking. The roads to Paradise and Sunrise prove especially picturesque. **Stevens Canyon Road** connects the southeast corner of the national park with Paradise, Longmire, and the Nisqually entrance, and affords truly spectacular vistas of Rainier and the rugged Tatoosh Range that would put the Swiss Alps to shame.

Several less-developed roads provide access to more isolated regions. These roads often abut trailheads that crisscross the park or lead to the summit. Cross-country hiking and camping outside designated campsites is permissible through most regions of the park, but overnight backpacking trips always require a permit. The **Hikers Center** at Longmire has information on day and backcountry hikes through the park. You can also obtain permits there. (Open mid-June to late Sept. daily 7am-7pm.)

A segment of the **Pacific Crest Trail (PCT),** running between the Columbia River and the Canadian border, crosses through the southeast corner of the park. The U.S. Forest Service maintains the PCT for both hikers and horse riders. Primitive campsites and shelters line the trail; camping requires no permit, although you should contact the nearest ranger station for information on site and trail conditions. The trail, sometimes overlooking the snow-covered peaks of the Cascades, snakes through delightful scenery where wildlife abounds.

Hardcore campers will thrill to the **Wonderland Trail,** a 95-mi. loop around the entire mountain. Because it includes some brutal ascents and descents, rangers recommend that even experts plan on covering only 7-10 mi. per day. Rangers can provide information on weather and trail conditions, and can even help with food caches at stations along the trail. Specific dangers to be aware of along Wonderland include snow-blocked passes in June, muddy trails in July, and early snowstorms in September. Expert climbers can discuss options for reaching the summit itself with rangers.

Less-ambitious, ranger-led **interpretive hikes** feature themes from local wildflowers to area history. Each visitors center conducts its own hikes and each has a different schedule. The hikes, lasting anywhere from 20 minutes to all day, especially suit families with young children. These free hikes complement evening campfire programs, also conducted by each visitors center.

The towns of **Packwood** and **Ashford** have a few motels near the park. For general lodging information and reservations at the two inns within the park, call 569-2275. Camping at the auto campsite costs $6 between mid-June and late September. Subject to certain restrictions, alpine and cross-country camping require free permits. Pick up a copy of the *Backcountry Trip Planner* at any ranger station or hiker's center before you set off. Alpine and cross-country permits are strictly controlled to prevent enviromental damage, but auto camping permits are easy to come by. The best developed campgrounds sit at **Sunshine Point** near the Nisqually entrance, at **Cougar Rock** near Longmire, at **Ohanapecosh,** at **White River** in the northeast corner, and at **Carbon River.** Open on a first come, first camp basis, they fill up only on the busiest summer weekends. Only Sunshine Point, however, remains open throughout the year. With a permit, cross-country hikers can use any of the free, well-established **trailside camps** scattered throughout the park's backcountry. Most camps have toilet facilities and a nearby water source; some have shelters. Fires are prohibited and there are limits on the number of members in a party. Mountain and glacier climbers must always register in person at ranger stations in order to be granted permits.

To reach Mt. Rainier from the west, drive south on I-5 to Tacoma, then go east on Rte. 512, south on Rte. 7, and east on Rte. 706. This scenic road meanders through the town of Ashford and into the park by the Nisqually entrance. Rte. 706 is the only access road kept open throughout the year; snow usually closes all other park roads from November through May. The city of Yakima provides the eastern gateway to the park. Take I-82 from the center of town to U.S. 12 heading west. At the junction of the Naches and Tieton Rivers, go either left on U.S. 12 or continue straight up Rte. 410. U.S. 12 runs past Rimrock Lake, over White Pass to Rte. 123, where a right turn leads to the Stevens Canyon entrance to Rainier. **Gray Line Bus Service,** 2411 4th Ave., Seattle (343-2000), runs excursions from Seattle to Rainier daily from May 15 to October 15. (Round-trip $25, under 13 $15.) **Hitchhiking** along the mountain roads is exceptionally good, though cars may be few and far between.

Mount St. Helens

Once thought to be extinct, Mt. St. Helens started rumbling on May 18, 1980, 69 years to the day after the death of Gustav Mahler. In the three days that followed, a hole 2 mi. long and 1 mi. wide opened in the mountain. Ash from the crater blackened the sky for hundreds of miles and blanketed the streets of towns as far as Yakima, 80 mi. away. Debris spewed from the volcano flooded Spirit Lake, choked rivers with mud, and descended to the towns via river and glacier. The blast leveled entire forests, leaving a stubble of trunks on the hills and millions of trees pointing like arrows away from the crater. Because the blast was lateral, not vertical, it destroyed much more since no energy dissipated in fighting gravity. Almost a decade later, the Mt. St. Helens National Monument still looks like a disaster area. The vast expanses of downed timber resemble an immense graveyard, an eternal monument to a blast of an intensity many times greater than that of any manmade atomic detonation. As Mahler would have wanted it, signs of returning life dot the spectacle of disaster. Saplings push their way up past their fallen brethren, insects flourish near newly formed waterfalls, and a beaver has been spotted in Spirit Lake.

Start any trip to the mountain at the **Mount St. Helens National Volcanic Monument Visitor Center** (247-5473), on Rte. 504, west of Toutle (take exit 49 off I-5, and follow the signs). The **Gifford Pinochet National Forest Headquarters**, 500 W. 12th St., Vancouver, WA (696-7500), has camping and hiking information. For 24-hr. recorded information on current volcanic activity, call 696-7848.

Gray Line, 400 NW Broadway, Portland, OR (503-226-6755) runs buses from Portland to Mt. St. Helens. (Round-trip $26, under 13 $14.)

Mount St. Helens' **area code** is 206.

Spokane

The first pioneer settlement in the Pacific Northwest, Spokane started out with the name Spokan Falls, a rather backhanded reference to the Spokan-ee, the area's original residents. After the Great Fire of 1889, Spokane quickly rerooted in industries spawned by local natural resources. Today, with an economy still based on lumber, mining, and agriculture, the spunkiest city in eastern Washington remains one of the Northwest's major trade centers. And its most successful native son, Representative Thomas Foley, now has a steady job as Speaker of the House in the other Washington (DC, that is).

In its own unwilling way, Spokane achieves urban sophistication without typical big-city hassles. The downtown thrives, though the pace remains slow. The Expo '74 legacy includes Riverfront Park's museum and theater, as well as a number of elegant restaurants and hotels. Arboretums, gardens, abundant outdoor activities, and a cpectacular series of bridges spanning the Spokane River and Falls celebrate wonders more ancient than concrete.

Practical Information

Visitor Information: Spokane Area Convention and Visitors Bureau, W. 926 Sprague Ave. (747-3230). Open Mon.-Fri. 8:30am-5pm, and most summer weekends 9am-3pm. **Spokane Area Chamber of Commerce**, W. 1020 Riverside, P.O. Box 2147 (624-1393). Open Mon.-Fri. 8am-5pm.

Travelers Aid: W. 1017 1st Ave. (456-7169), near the bus depot. Helps stranded travelers find lodgings. Open Mon.-Fri. 1-5pm.

Amtrak: W. 221 1st Ave. (624-5144), at Bernard St. downtown. One per day to: Chicago ($196); Seattle ($60); Portland ($60). Depot open Mon.-Fri. 11am-3:30am, Sat.-Sun. 7:15pm-3:30am.

Buses: Greyhound, W. 1125 Sprague (624-5251), at 1st Ave. and Jefferson St. downtown. To Seattle (5 per day, $33). **Empire Lines** (624-4116) and **Northwest Stage Lines** (838-4029 or 800-826-4058) share the terminal with Greyhound, serving Eastern Washington, Northern Idaho, and British Columbia. Station open daily 6am-8pm and 1-3am.

Public Transport: Spokane Transit System, W. 1229 Boone Ave. (328-7433). Serves all Spokane areas, including Eastern Washington University in Cheney. Operates until 12:15am downtown, 9:15pm in the valley along E. Sprague Ave. Fare 60¢, seniors and disabled 30¢. Coupon booklets, available at midday, give discounts in local shops and restaurants.

Taxi: Checker Cab, 624-4171. Open 24 hr.

Car Rental: U-Save Auto Rental, W. 918 3rd St. (455-8018), at Monroe. From $19 per day. 100 free mi., 20¢ each additional mi. Open Mon.-Fri. 8am-6pm, Sat. 8am-5pm. Must be 21 with $250 deposit or major credit card.

Help Line: Crisis Hotline, 838-4428. Open 24 hr.

Post Office: W. 904 Riverside (459-0230), at Lincoln. Open Mon.-Fri. 8:30am-5pm. **ZIP code:** 99210.

Area Code: 509.

Spokane lies 280 mi. east of Seattle by I-90. Downtown wedges between I-90 and the Spokane River. Exits 279 to 282 serve the area. Avenues run east-west parallel to the river, streets north-south, and both alternate one-way. The city is divided into north and south by **Sprague Avenue,** east and west by aptly named **Division Street.** **Riverfront Park** abuts Spokane Falls at the heart of the city. Downtown lies north of Sprague and west of Division. Street addresses list with the compass point first, the number second, and the street name third (e.g., W. 1200 Division). No one knows why.

Accommodations and Camping

Let's face it: you have few options. A handful of hotels south of downtown are cheap but sleazy. Most camping areas throw down at least 20 mi. away. Don't try to sleep in Riverfront Park; the police won't take kindly. No one knows why.

Brown Squirrel Hostel (AYH), W. 1807 Pacific Ave. (838-5968), in Browne's Addition. Near a supermarket and Elks Drug, an old-fashioned pharmacy with real fountain sodas. Cozy rooms, unmatched hospitality. 20 beds. Officially open 8-10am and 5-10pm but stop in just about anytime. Linens, towels, and transportation to the airport or bus station. $8, nonmembers $11.

Town Centre Motor Inn, W. 901 1st St. (747-1041), at Lincoln St. Large, comfortable rooms with phones and wonderfully garish oil paintings. Some rooms also have refrigerators at no extra charge. Complimentary coffee served with the morning paper. Singles $30. Doubles $38. Canadian dollars accepted at par. Call for reservations.

El Rancho Motel, W. 3000 Sunset Blvd. (455-9400). Take 2nd Ave. west to Maple St., where Sunset cuts diagonally across the intersection; follow Sunset approximately 15 blocks. On the edge of town, with easy access to freeway. Rooms with cable, free coffee, A/C. Laundromat and pool. Singles $27.50. Doubles $40.

Eastern Washington University (359-7022), 18 mi. from Spokane in Cheney. Take bus #24 from Howard and Riverside St. downtown. By car, take I-90 southwest 8 mi. to exit 270, then Hwy. 904 south; turn right on Elm St. and continue to 10th. Inquire at Morrison Hall in the summer, or Anderson Hall during the school year. Pleasant dorm rooms. Linen included. Singles $9.70, students $7. Doubles $19.40, students $14. Rarely full.

Riverside State Park (456-3964), 6 mi. northwest of downtown on Rifle Club Rd., off Hwy. 291 or Nine Mile Rd. Take Division north and turn left on Francis. 101 standard sites in an urban setting. Kitchen and small museum in the park. Facilities for the disabled. Shower and bath. Sites $7.50.

Mt. Spokane State Park (456-4169), 35 mi. northeast of the city. Take U.S. 395 5 mi. north to U.S. 2, then go 7 mi. north to Hwy. 206, which leads into the park. Popular for its cross-country ski and snowmobiling trails. From the Vista House, views of 4 states and Canada. Flush toilets, cold water only. Sites $7.

Food

For a variety of interesting restaurants downtown, head to **The Atrium,** on Wall St. near 1st Ave. **Europa Pizzeria,** one of the eateries in this small brick building, bakes the best pizza in town. May through October, Wednesdays and Saturdays in Riverfront Park, the **Spokane County Market** (456-5512) sells fresh fruit, vegetables, and baked goods. Twenty-odd fruit and vegetable farms make up the **Green Bluff Growers Cooperative,** 16 mi. northwest of town off Day-Mountain Spokane Rd. Many of the farms have "U-pick" arrangements, with nearby free panoramic picnic areas. Peak season for most crops is from August to October. No one knows why.

Dick's, E. 10 3rd Ave., at Division. Look for the pink panda near I-90. A takeout burger phenomenon whose fame grows as its prices stay the same. Burgers 93¢, fries 39¢, soft drinks

39¢, pies 89¢, sundaes 58¢, etc. Always crowded, but lines move quickly. Open daily 9am-1:30am.

Cyrus O'Leary's, W. 516 Main St., in the Bennetts Block complex at Howard St. A Spokane legend. Devour delicious food from a creative 25-page menu. Proper attire—crazy 1890s Wild West. Costumed staff serves enormous $6-12 meals. Sandwiches $3-5. Happy Hour 4-6pm. Open Mon.-Thurs. 11:30am-11pm, Fri.-Sat. 11:30am-midnight, Sun. 11:30am-10pm.

Auntie's Bookstore and Café, W. 313 Riverside. Browse through the excellent selection of books, including extensive collections on regional history, gender studies, and religion, then compose your own sandwich from $3. Lunch specials $4. Open Mon.-Sat. 9am-9pm, Sun. noon-5pm.

Knight's Diner, N. 2442 Division. Take bus #6. A long red-and-black diner in an old train car. Western down-home cooking and hospitality. Hearty breakfasts and lunches $2-4. Open Tues.-Sun. 6:30am-2pm.

Coyote Café, W. 702 3rd Ave. Jazzy Mexican joint with *cerveza* (beer) signs on the walls, cacti in the windows, and $2.25 margaritas all day. Specialties include the Coyote Chimichanga ($6) and *fajitas* ($8). Open Mon.-Thurs. 11am-11pm, Fri. 11am-midnight, Sat. noon-midnight, Sun. noon-10pm.

Sights and Entertainment

Spokane has few aspirations to flashy exhibits or high-flown architecture. The city's best attractions focus on local history and culture. A few blocks east of Riverfront Park, the unusually shaped **Museum of Native American Cultures (MONAC),** E. 200 Cataldo St. (326-4550), stands on a hill to the northeast of downtown, off Division St. The four-story museum houses a collection of art and artifacts from North and South American. (Open Tues.-Sat. 10am-5pm, Sun. 11am-5pm. Admission $3, seniors and students $2, families $7.)

The **Cheney Cowles Memorial Museum, W.** 2316 1st Ave. (456-3931), also has exhibits on Native American culture and history in addition to well-explicated displays on the natural history and pioneer settlement of eastern Washington. The **Grace Campbell House** (456-3931) next door is affiliated with the museum. Built in the Tudor revival style with a fortune extracted from the Coeur d'Alene gold mines in Idaho, this elegant Victorian museum describes Spokane's high-society life during the 1890s boom era. (Museum open Tues.-Sat. 10am-5pm, Sun. 2-5pm. Admission $2, seniors and students with ID $1. House open Tues.-Sat. 10am-4pm, Sun. 2-5pm. Free.)

Built for the 1974 World's Fair, **Riverfront Park, N.** 507 Howard St. (456-5512), still hangs on just north of downtown. As Spokane's center of gravity, here the populace strolls on leisurely weekend afternoons. Ride the beautifully hand-carved **Looff Carousel** (open daily 11am-9pm; admission 60¢). The **IMAX Theatre** (456-5511) shows 3D films on a 5½-story screen. (Shows run noon-9pm and start on the hr. Admission Tues.-Sun. $4, seniors $3.50, under 18 $3.) The **Gondola Skyride Over the Falls** travels from the park over Spokane Falls and over to the north side of the river. (Open summer daily 11am-9pm. Fare $2.50, children $1.50.)

Hard-core Bingsters will be drawn to the **Crosby Library, E.** 502 Boone St. (328-4220), at Gonzaga University. Here, the faithful display the crooner's relics: gold records, awards, photographs and even a piece of his right index finger bone. (Open Mon.-Thurs. 8am-midnight, Fri. 8am-5pm, Sat. 9am-5pm, Sun. 1pm-midnight. Free.)

Spokane's collection of two dozen parks includes tranquil, well-groomed **Finch Arboretum, W.** 3404 Woodland Blvd. Over 2000 species of trees, flowers, and shrubs allow viewing 24-hr. **Manito Park,** on S. Grand Ave. between 17th and 25th Ave. (856-4331), south of downtown, features flower gardens, tennis courts, a duck pond, and the Graiser Conservatory which houses many tropical and local plant species. (Open daily 8am-dusk; off-season 8am-3:30pm. Free.) Adjacent to the Manito Park is the **Nishinomiya Garden,** a lush Japanese garden symbolizing the friendship between Spokane and its Japanese sibling city, Nishinomiya. (Same hours as Manito Park.)

The state runs two parks near Spokane; both merit a trip. **Riverside State Park** (456-3964 or 456-2499) embroiders the Spokane River with 7655 acres of volcanic outcroppings, rushing water, hiking (especially good in Deep Greek Canyon), and equestrian trails (horse rental $9 per hr. in nearby Trail Town; 456-8249). The park also weaves prime cross-country ski territory in the winter. **Mount Spokane State Park** (456-4169) stands 35 mi. to the northeast of the city with a road extending to the summit. Clear days afford views of the Spokane Valley and the distant peaks of the Rockies and Cascades. Mt. Spokane is a skiing center with free cross-country trails and $15-20 downhill ski packages.

Don't leave Spokane without sampling one of the fine Eastern Washington wines. The **Arbor Cliff House**, N. 4705 Fruithill Rd. (927-9463), offers a tour of a national historical house, a view of the city, and free wine (daily noon-5pm). Take I-90 to the Argonne north exit, travel north on Argonne over the Spokane River, turn right on Upriver Dr., proceed 1 mi., and then bear left onto Fruithill Rd.

Spokane's more traditional tastes are reflected in the large number of bowling alleys and movie theaters gracing the city. However, the variety of live music here keeps the populace boppin' until they're droppin'. No one cares why. The *Spokane Spokesman-Review's* Friday Weekend section and the *Spokane Chronicle's* Friday Empire section give the low-down on area happenings. During the summer, the city parks present a free **Out-to-Lunch** concert series at noon on weekdays. (Call 624-1393 or check in the Weekend for schedule information.)

Henry's Pub, W. 230 Riverside Ave. (624-9828), is the place for live rock Wednesday through Saturday nights. Local favorites such as the Peace Frogs and Final Exam cram here. Draft beer costs $1.75. (Open Mon.-Fri. 11am-2am, Sat.-Sun. 4pm-2am.) At that bastion of yuppiedom, **The Onion Bar and Grill,** W. 302 Riverside (747-3852), men in European suits act tough. Nurse your frozen margaritas while playing pool in the back room. Peer Gynt would love it. Friendly faces serve nightly drink specials. (Dinners under $7, frozen margaritas $3.50, drafts $1.85. Open Sun.-Thurs. 11:15am-1am, Fri.-Sat. 11:15am-2am.)

HAWAII

"Hawaii is what is known as a hot spot."
—James Rosen, esq.

Aside from its meteorological and slang implications, Mr. Rosen's expert statement helps to describe how Hawaii became an island "chain." Geologically, a "hot spot" means the stream of lava (or magma) originating deep beneath and rising through the earth's surface to create a volcano. Such searing activity occurred 25 to 40 million years ago in Hawaii, but plate tectonics prevented Hawaii from remaining an enormous erupting island. As the Pacific Plate shifted to the northwest, the underlying source of the eruptions remained stationary; the original island volcanoes moved beyond the active zone of volcanic intrusion while new eruptive fissures progressively surfaced farther southeast. In this conveyer-belt fashion, the 1600-mile archipelago known as the Hawaiian Islands formed. The oldest islands in the northwest have been worn away to tiny coral atolls by the erosion of the sea, while at the other end of the chain fiery eruptions reclaim new land from the ocean's depths. In actuality, Mr. Rosen advises, the "Islands" are only the highest peaks of a whole ridge of hot spots, the rest of which lies below the ocean's surface. Mauna Kea claims the highest mountain in the world award if measured from the sea floor (not sea level).

Long before plate tectonics were in vogue, the ancient Hawaiians grasped the volcanic mechanism at work. Their legends told of the Fire Goddess, Pele, who fled from island to island, moving southeast down the chain to escape the watery intrusions of her older sister, the ocean. These early Polynesian settlers arrived long after Pele's voyage to her current abode on the Big Island in a no less remarkable odyssey. Traveling across thousands of miles of unbroken ocean as early as the 6th century AD, the first Hawaiian inhabitants carried with them roots, seeds, dogs, chickens, and a pig or two in their double-hulled canoes.

In 1778, Captain Cook sailed through Hawaii while searching for the Northwest Passage. He was received as a god but eight months later was accidently killed in a skirmish. His inadvertent discovery propelled Hawaii into the modern world. Revered today as the man who united the islands and created modern Hawaii, King Kamehameha I of the Big Island exploited the force of European arms and conquered all of the other islands escept Kauai within 20 years of Cook's arrival. Yet the European trade ships Kamehameha welcomed brought more than he could handle: the washing away of Hawaiian culture by an inexorable tide of Western influence paralleled the physical decimation of the Hawaiian people by an influx of Western disease.

Following the arrival of Calvinist missionaries from Boston in 1820, the *haole* (pronounced HOW-lee) or Caucasian presence in island life became entrenched; by 1853, 30% of Hawaiians belonged to Christian churches. An expanding sugar (and later pineapple) industry supplanted the original whaling and sandalwood trade which brought in Chinese, Japanese, and Filipinos as indentured plantation laborers to replace the dying Hawaiians. U.S. sugar magnates, leery of a strong monarchy and desirous of ensuring a market for their product, overthrew King Kalakaua in 1887. In 1898, the U.S. government, having acquired Spain's interests in the Pacific and desiring Hawaii as a military base, annexed the islands as a formal U.S. territory. Many white plantation owners viewed the annexation warily, fearing that their laborers might gain new rights. Hawaiian commerce developed peacefully until the Japanese attack on Pearl Harbor, half a century later, dramatically summoned the U.S. into WWII. In 1959, Hawaii became the fiftieth state.

Today, very little racial tension affects the many ethnic groups. Instead, residents have merged parts of each ethnic heritage to form a "local" culture—more of a melange than a melting pot. This culture manifests itself everywhere from the menus

Hawaii

Oahu

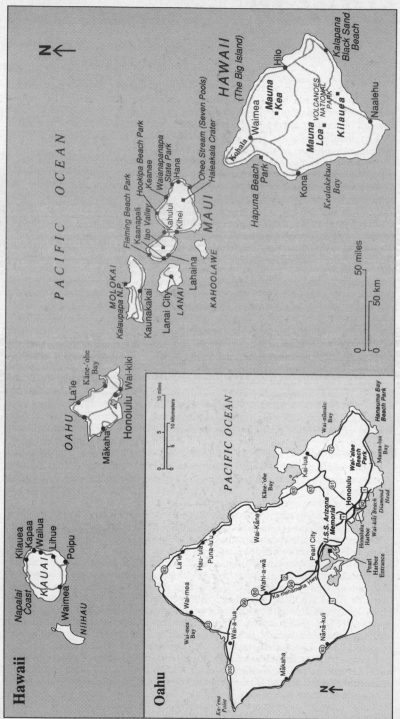

of the island lunchwagons to the linguistic pot-pourri of Pidgin (the islands' dialect of bastardized English).

For more comprehensive coverage of Hawaii than can be provided here, consult *Let's Go: California & Hawaii.*

Practical Information

Capital: Honolulu.

Visitor Information: Hawaii Visitors Bureau, 2270 Kalakaua Ave. #1108, Honolulu 96815 (923-1811). Open Mon.-Fri. 8am-4:30pm. The prime source. Neighboring islands staff offices at major towns, as listed in the appropriate sections. **Department of Land and Natural Resources,** 1151 Punchbowl St., Honolulu 96813 (548-7455). Information, trail maps, and permits for camping in state parks. Open Mon.-Fri. 8am-4pm. **National Park Service,** Prince Kuhio Federal Bldg. #6305, 300 Ala Moana Blvd., Honolulu 96813 (541-2693). No permits available here; given instead at individual park headquarters. Open Mon.-Fri. 7:30am-4pm.

Time Zone: Hawaii (6 hr. behind Eastern in spring and summer; 5 hr. otherwise).

Postal Abbreviation: HI.

Area Code: 808.

Getting There

Reaching paradise isn't as expensive as you might think. Good deals can be made even in winter (Feb.-April), when rates rise. Investigate the Sunday *L.A. Times* or the *New York Times* Travel section for discount packages, which usually include airfare from major mainland cities, accommodations, and a bevy of fringe benefits. Learn the nitty gritty details: tour packages often list sights without including admission fees, and rates are almost always listed per person based on double occupancy. An individual traveling solo may wind up paying more.

If you need only a plane ticket, purchasing a frequent flyer award coupon may prove the best bet. Look for these in the newspaper. Along more traditional lines, seek out special advance purchase fares or bulk rates from cut-rate travel agencies. From Los Angeles and San Francisco, many major carriers fly round-trip for $200.

Getting Around

Island Hopping

While Oahu is the hub of much of Hawaii's activities, the "neighbor" islands offer equal excitement, especially for those wanting to escape the trappings of civilization. Airplanes provide the fastest and most convenient means of transport between the islands. The major inter-island carriers—**Hawaiian** (537-5100) and **Aloha** (836-1111)—can take you quickly (about 40 min., $50) from Honolulu to any of the islands. Travel agents, such as **Pali Tour and Travel, Inc.,** 1304 Pali Hwy. (533-3608), in Honolulu, sell Hawaiian Air inter-island coupon books (6 flights for $220). Check the miscellaneous section of the classified ads in the *Star-Bulletin* or *Advertiser* for individuals selling these coupons at cut-rate prices. Most carriers offer the same fare to each island they serve. **Air Molokai** (831-2000) and **Aloha Island Air** (831-3219) are minor airlines with small planes and bumpy rides. A new eager-to-please airline, **Discover Air,** (946-1500 on Oahu; 800-733-2525 from neighbor islands) flies to Maui, Kauai and Honolulu with possibly more flights to come. Cheaper than Hawaiian or Aloha, Discover usually has deals; call to find out about specials. Many regularly scheduled flights cost about $30.

Aloha and Hawaiian often cooperate with resorts and car rental agencies to create economical **package tours.** Ask a local travel or reservations agent about deals best suited to your needs, and keep an eye out for ads in pamphlets and newspapers. **Associated Travel, Inc.,** 947 Keeaumoku, Honolulu 96813 (949-1033), about 3 blocks inland of the Ala Moana Shopping Center, offers cheerful help in finding the least expensive excursions. Be explicit in your requests. Air transport, room, and rental car can be had for $120 ($43 each additional day) for two. (Open Mon.-Fri. 8:30am-5pm, Sat. 8:30am-noon.) **Student Travel Network,** 1831 S. King St. #202, Honolulu (942-7755), has information on student discounts, student tours, and group rates, as well as AYH referral. (Open Mon.-Fri. 9am-5pm.)

On the Islands

While the **bus** system is fairly reliable and extensive on Oahu and patchy on the Big Island, public transport is virtually non-existent on the other islands (see individual island listings). You might want to rent your own set of wheels for a neighbor island sojourn.

Car rental agencies fill major island airports and tourist areas in towns. If you have not booked a rental through an airline or other package deal, check local weekly and monthly travel guides for specials and ask about weekly rates. Because car rental agencies are not state-regulated, an automatic, air-conditioned compact car can rent from $10 to $37 per day. Since Hawaii is a no-fault insurance state, insurance coverage is optional, but most companies do not honor individual coverage even if you already own a car. **Budget** will rent to those ages 18 to 21, but only with a major credit card. Renting upon arrival at an airport, you will surely pay exorbitant rates. Whenever possible, use the phone to hunt down cars, and make reservations at least 24 hr. in advance.

Bicycle and **moped rentals,** based in tourist centers, offer competitive rates, and are a great way to see Hawaii in an easy-going, close-up manner. Congestion in Honolulu, however, may be too much for two wheels—better used on the other side of Oahu, or on the neighbor islands. If you bring your own bicycle, register it (for $3.50) at the **Pawaa Police Station,** 1455 S. Beretania St., Honolulu (943-3324; open Mon.-Fri. 7:45am-4:15pm). Also pick up the free *Bicycle Regulations Pamphlet* here. More information emanates from **The Bike Shop,** 1149 S. King St. (531-7071) in Honolulu (open Mon.-Thurs. and Sat. 9am-5:30pm, Fri. 9am-8pm, Sun. 10am-5pm), or the **Hawaii Bicycling League,** P.O. Box 4403, Honolulu 96813 (732-5806). Inter-island airlines charge about $20 to transport bikes; continental flights about $15.

Accommodations and Camping

Despite rumors to the contrary, reasonable room rates do exist on the islands. In general, high tourist season runs from mid-December to late April. Look for special deals that often include rental car and air transportation. **Hukilau, Sands, and Seaside Hotels** (922-5737 or 922-1228 on Oahu; 800-451-6754 from the outer islands; 800-367-7000 from the mainland) manage some of the cheapest resort hotels ($32-55 per night).

Hostels and the **YMCA** provide cheap shelter on most islands. Another alternative is the growing number of bed and breakfast organizations which offer doubles in private homes for $35 to $55. **B&B Hawaii,** P.O. Box 449, Kapaa 96746 (536-8421 on Oahu; 822-7771 on Kauai; toll-free on neighboring islands 1-367-8047, ext. 339) and **B&B Honolulu,** 5242 Keehinani Dr., Honolulu 96817 (595-7533), operate statewide.

Camping in state parks is popular and rigidly regulated. Free camping permits are required; applicants must be at least 18 years old to receive a permit for an individual or group. Camping is limited to five nights per thirty days. Sites open Friday through Tuesday on Oahu, daily on the other islands. Two sorts of shelters also grace state parks, but usually require reservations at least one month in advance: **A-Frames** are single rooms with wooden sleeping platforms, cooking facilities, and bathrooms with shower ($7 per night, 4-person max.); **housekeeping cabins** come with kitchen, living room, and one or two bedrooms, as well as utensils, linen, and heating or fireplace wood ($15 per night for 1 person, max. 6 persons). For information, reservations, and permits, write or visit one of the **State Parks Division** offices (also called the Department of Land and Natural Resources). (All open Mon.-Fri. 8am-4:15pm.) The **national** and **county parks** on each island also maintain campsites. Free camping outside of designated parks is widely practiced throughout the state by locals; visitors may be harrassed by the police or locals if they are too obvious or too permanent, especially on Oahu and Maui. Nevertheless, with some discretion and enough sense to avoid four-wheel-drive tire tracks and empty beer cans, many travelers find own quiet beach. Camping on Oahu is less convenient and less safe than on the other islands, especially the Big Island.

Outdoors

The Hawaiian Islands are punctuated with hidden treasures: rare birds, tropical fish, botanical delights, and sandy beaches with glassy waves. Surfing originated here, and the 20-footers breaking off Oahu's North Shore continue to beckon a die-hard faithful, while the new hybrid sport of windsurfing dominates Maui beaches. Hiking, snorkeling, swimming, bird- and whale-watching, and fishing also number among the outdoor activities visitors can enjoy with little or no expense. However, because inland valleys of Maui, the Big Island, and Oahu—prime spots for illegal marijuana cultivation—can put hikers in danger of trespassing, stay on defined trails. Exercise even more caution when wandering in sugar cane fields.

Hawaiian Trail and Mountain Club, P.O. Box 2238, Honolulu 96804. Watch for listing of free hikes in the weekly "Pulse of Paradise" column of the *Honolulu Star-Bulletin.*

Sierra Club Hawaii Chapter, 1212 University Ave., Honolulu 96826 (946-8494), behind the Church of the Cross Roads. Call for recorded message, an update of hikes on Oahu. Hiking information and organized weekend hikes. Open Mon.-Sat. 8-11am.

State Forestry Division, 1179 Punchbowl St. #325, Honolulu 96813 (548-8856). Free maps of its 24 trails. Open Mon.-Fri. 7:45am-4:30pm.

Oahu

Since witnessing the arrival of missionaries in the 1820s, Oahu and its principal city of Honolulu have constituted the cultural, commercial, and political focal point of modern Hawaii. Tourism, the island's major industry, centers at the famous ¾-mile stretch of Waikiki Beach. The nearby downtown area serves as a major business and economic center for the Pacific basin.

Oahu can be roughly divided into four sections: **Honolulu,** the **Windward Coast,** the **North Shore,** and the **Leeward Coast.** The slopes of two now-extinct volcanic mountain ridges (to whom the island owes its existence), **Waianae** in the east and **Koolau** in the west, make up the bulk of Oahu's 600 square miles. The narrow inlets of **Pearl Harbor** push in from the sea at the southern end of the valley between the two ridges. Honolulu spreads along 6 miles of oceanfront southeast of Pearl Harbor, hemmed in by the Koolau Range in the northeast. **Waikiki Beach** lies near Diamond Head, the island's southernmost extremity; the downtown area clusters 3 miles west. With the exception of the Leeward Coast and Kaena Point, well-maintained highways circle the rest of the coast and navigate the central valley.

Honolulu

Like any other metropolis, Hawaii's capital city is overcrowded and plagued by traffic. Unlike other cities, however, the trade winds keep Honolulu free of stagnant pollution, and the pleasant climate brightens the environment. Further, zoning rules prohibit large, flashy billboards and signs.

Waikiki, Hawaii's famed concrete jungle on the coast, revolves around the high-rise hotels that line Kalakaua and Kuhio Ave. Soak in the tackiness while soaking in the rays or skip this "Las Vegas on the Beach" altogether. Wander through downtown at lunchtime for more Aloha shirts than you had ever hoped to see, or tour the ethnic communities of Chinatown, Kalihi, and Kapahulu. Here, away from the tourist towers lining the beach, lies the *real* Honolulu—the city that most visitors never see.

Practical Information

Emergency: 911.

Visitor Information: Hawaii Visitors Bureau, 2270 Kalakaua Ave. #804, Honolulu 96815 (923-1811). Information on Oahu and the rest of the state. Pick up the member *Accommodation Guide* and the member *Restaurant Guide,* a map of points of interest, and a walking tour of downtown Honolulu. Travel guide for the disabled, too. All publications free. Open Mon.-Fri. 8am-4:30pm. Information centers in both the overseas and inter-island air terminals and at the Ala Moana Shopping Center. **Department of Parks and Recreation,** 650 S. King St., Honolulu 96817 (523-4525). Information and permits for county parks. Open Mon.-Fri. 7:45am-4pm. Permits available no earlier than 2 weeks in advance. **Department of State Parks,** 1151 Punchbowl St., Honolulu 96813 (548-7455). Information and permits for camping in state parks, and trail maps. Open Mon.-Fri. 8am-4pm.

Honolulu International Airport, 20 min. west of downtown, off the Lunalilo Freeway (H-1). Several companies will tote you and your luggage between the airport and Waikiki or downtown for $5. **Grayline** (834-1033) operates from 5am to 11:30pm. **Waikiki Express** (942-2177) operates from 7am to 9pm; **Airport Motor Coach** (926-4747) operates from 6:30am to 10pm. Both require reservations.

Public Transport: 531-1611. Very frequent and reliable bus srvice for the entire island, especially in downtown Honolulu and Waikiki. Operates daily 5:30am-midnight. Runs less frequently to North Shore and Waianae than to downtown. Fare 60¢.

Transit for Disabled: Handi-Van, 905 Ahuh St. (833-2222). Curb-to-curb service if reservations made at least a day in advance. Service Mon.-Fri. 8am-4pm. Disabled travelers can obtain a bus pass from the City Department of Transportation Services. Write in advance to **Handicapped Bus Pass,** 650 S. King St., Honolulu 96813 (523-4083). **Handi-Cabs of the Pacific,** P.O. Box 22428 (524-3866), a private taxi company with van ramps for wheelchairs. Airport-to-Waikiki service $28. Call for reservations.

Taxi: Sida, 439 Kalewa St. (836-0011). All cabs charge 20¢ per 1/6 mi. Base rate about $1.50. Airport to Waikiki $15-18.

Car Rental: Honolulu Rentacar, 1856 Kalekaua Ave. #105 (941-9099 or 942-7187). **Maxi Rentals,** 413 Seaside Ave. (923-7381). Both have used cars from $10 per day; mandatory $7 insurance if under 25.

Moped and Bike Rentals: Aloha Funway Rentals, 2025 Kalakaua Ave. (942-9696) and 2976 Koapakapaka St. (834-1016), near the airport. Mopeds $20 per day, $75 per week; bikes $12 per day. Open daily 8am-5pm. **Inter-Island Rentals,** 353 Royal Hawaiian Ave. (946-0013). Mopeds $20 per day, $96 per week; bikes $12 per day. Open daily 8am-6pm. Must be 18 with cash or credit card deposit.

Water Equipment Rentals: Ohana Rentals, near the breakers at Queen's Beach. Boogie boards $8 per day, fins $8 per day. Cash only. Open daily 8am-6pm. **Star Beachboys,** Kuhio Beach, to the left of the pavilion. Canoe rides $5, surfboard lessons $10 per hr., boogie boards $5 per hr. **South Sea Aquatics,** 870 Kapahulu (735-0437). Snorkeling gear $8 per day. Open Mon.-Fri. 8am-6pm, Sat.-Sun. 8am-5pm.

Help Lines: Sex Abuse Treatment Center, 524-7237. **Coast Guard Search/Rescue,** 536-4336. **Suicide and Crisis Center,** 521-4555. **Gay Information Services,** 926-2910. Lists gay-supported community programs and businesses.

Post Offices: Main Office, 3600 Aoleilei Ave. (423-3990). Open daily 8am-4:30pm. **ZIP code:** 96813. **Waikiki Branch,** Royal Hawaiian Shopping Center, 2nd floor, Bldg. B. Open Mon.-Fri. 8:15am-11:45am and 1pm-3:30pm. **ZIP code:** 96815.

Area Code: 808.

The **H-1 Freeway** stretches the length of Honolulu. Downtown Honolulu, about 6 blocks long and 4 blocks wide, wedges between Honolulu Harbor and Punchbowl. In Waikiki, Ala Wai Blvd., Kuhio Ave., and Kalakaua Ave. run parallel to the ocean and provide the main routes of transportation. **Hitchhiking** is illegal on Oahu.

Besides *mauka* (inland) and *makai* (seaward), you are also likely to hear directions given as *ewa* (west) and *diamondhead* (east).

Accommodations

Finding a reasonably priced room in Honolulu is a surmountable challenge. Page through the *Honolulu Advertiser* for deals when you can't land a spot at a hostel or a Y. Make reservations as soon as possible for any of the following—bargains go fast in Hawaii.

Manoa Hostel (AYH), 2323-A Seaview Ave., Honolulu 96822 (946-0591), 1 block west of University Ave., 1½ mi. north of Waikiki near U. of H. at Manoa. By car, take University Ave. exit off H-1. Take bus #6 at Ala Moana Shopping Center to Metcalf and University Ave. Clean facilities. Kitchen, bike storage, lockers, recreation room. Office open daily 7:30-9:30am and 5-11pm. Lockout 9:30am-5pm. $9, nonmembers $11.50. Linen $1.50. Busy Aug.-March—write early and include one night's deposit.

Hale Aloha (AYH), 2417 Prince Edward St. (926-8313), 2 blocks from the beach in Waikiki. Members only. Spots guaranteed for 3 nights. Open daily 8-10am and 5-9pm. Dorm bunks $10. Studio doubles $23.50. Reservations required 1 month in advance.

Inter-Club Hostel Waikiki, 2413 Kuhio Ave. (942-2636). Standard hostel facilities. Weekend BBQs. Bunks $16. Open 8am-11pm.

YWCA and YMCA: Fernhust Residence, 1566 Wilder Ave. (941-2231), near the university. Take bus #4 to Punahou School. For single women over 18. 2 rooms per bath; 2 persons per room. Office open daily 8:30am-8:30pm. $20, nonmembers $25. 3-day max. stay for non-members. Breakfast and dinner included Mon.-Sat. **Central Branch,** 401 Atkinson Dr. (941-3344), across from Ala Moana Shopping Center downtown. Men over 18 only. Open 24 hr. Singles $25, with bath $30.50. Doubles $35. Key deposit $5. **Nuuanu Branch,** 1441 Pali Hwy. (536-3556), downtown. Singles $23. Key deposit $5.

Edmunds Hotel Apartments, 2411 Ala Wai Blvd. (923-8381), across from the Ala Wai Canal. Plain, printed rooms with fans and good views; no phone. Laundry facilities, small TV, refrigerator, and ancient stove. Singles $25. Doubles $30.

Waikiki Prince, 2431 Prince Edward St. (922-1544). Functional rooms all with A/C $30, with kitchenette $35, with full kitchen $37.

Camping

The prospects for camping on Oahu aren't quite as bright as on other islands. Oahu's campgrounds are located in the more rural Hawaiian communities, and locals often consider the campgrounds their domain, especially on the island's western shore. Four state parks and 13 county parks allow camping. For free required **permits,** contact the Department of Parks and Recreation (see Practical Information). In Honolulu, tent camping is available at two state parks, **Sand Island** and **Keaiwa Heiau State Recreation Area.** (5-day max. stay.) Apply at the Division of Land and Natural Resources (see Practical Information). Sand Island offers flat camping outside Honolulu Harbor (take Sand Island Access Rd. from Rte. 92). Keaiwa Heiau State Recreation Area, at end of Aiea Heights Dr. (488-6626), has forest sites—hike over to the ruins of the **heiau hoosola** (temple of healing).

Food

Honolulu dining can be a truly international extravaganza, so "grind to da max, no shame, just scahf out." Don't miss Ala Moana's **Food Market** for a true cornucopia of cornucopias. Small Chinese counters serve excellent lunch snacks downtown; try the area around **Hotel Street,** in the red-light district. Down some *dim sum,* served daily at most counters from 11am to 2pm. A variety of ethnic restaurants, including Hawaiian, Japanese, Thai, and French, thrive between the 500 and 1000 blocks of **Kapahulu Avenue** and in the surrounding area. Catch bus #2 going *mauka* up Kapahulu Ave. from the Diamond Head area of Waikiki.

Travelers to Waikiki will be deluged with ads and flyers recommending *luaus,* often hokey Hawaiian-style dinners with Polynesian dancing that rake in the big tourist bucks. Some, however, prove fun and belly-filling (and a few even reasonably priced). The **Queen Kapiolani,** 150 Kapahulu Ave. (922-1941), offers a $9.50 unlimited *luau* luncheon buffet with entertainment (Mon.-Wed. and Fri.-Sat. 11am-2pm).

Patti's Kitchen, Ala Moana Shopping Center, also in the Windward Mall in Kaneohe. Build your own buffet-style Chinese plate lunches ($3.35-5). An incredible bargain. Open Mon.-Sat. 10am-8pm, Sun. 10am-4:30pm.

Ted's Drive Inn, 2820 S. King St., 1 block south of University Ave. Tongue-tingling Korean plate lunches $3-5. Open Mon.-Wed. 9:30am-9:30pm, Thurs.-Sat. 9:30am-10pm, Sun. 9:30am-9pm.

Leonard's Bakery, 933 Kapahulu Ave. Indulge in the hot *malasadas,* an island tradition (40¢).

Kings Bakery and Coffe Shop, 1936 S. King St., Moiliili. Also at Kaimuki shopping center and Eaton Square. Renowned for their Portuguese sweet bread. Great for a late night treat. Try the banana cream or *lilikoi* pie (about $1.50). Filling breakfast specials $3-5. Lunch and dinner specials $3.50-6.50. Kaimuki branch open 24 hr.

Perry's Smorgy, 2335 Kalakaua Ave., in the Outrigger Waikiki Hotel. Extensive all-you-can-eat buffet of local treats, chicken spaghetti, roast beef, and tasty breads. Breakfast $4. Lunch $5.45. Dinner $8. Open daily 7-10:30am, 11am-2:30pm, and 5-9pm.

Sights and Activities   .

As with most capital cities, Honolulu holds museums, palaces, parks, historic houses, shops and ethnic neighborhoods; some enhance and some detract from the surrounding paradise. The one-hour loop around the #14 bus route provides a colorful cross section of Honolulu's neighborhoods from Waikiki to St. Louis Heights.

In the wake of World War II, the dramatic crescent of Waikiki's white sand beach backdropped by the profile of Diamond Head lured growing crowds of vacationers. Today more savvy visitors spend time on the less crowded neighbor isles. However, as an unrelenting spectacle of glitz commercialism, Waikiki itself provides a show.

Actually comprised of several smaller beaches, Waikiki Beach puts Hawaii's tourists on exhibit. Farthest to the east lies the **Sans Souci Beach,** in front of the Kaimona Otani Hotel. Site of an old natatorium built as a war memorial, Sans Souci has shower facilities but no public restrooms. The **Queen's Surf Beach,** closer to downtown, attracts swimmers and roller skaters. The area to the left of the snack bar is a popular tanning spot for gay people. On Sunday evenings, bongo players gather under the banyan tree to cut a tropical tattoo through the serenity of an unforgettable sunset.

For a break from the beach, hike the 1 mi. into and up to the top of the **Diamond Head Crater,** at Queen's Surf. To reach Diamond Head, take bus #58 from Waikiki. The **Clean Air Team** (944-0804) leads a four-hour guided hike ($3) from the zoo parking lot to the top of the crater every summer Saturday and Sunday at 9am. (No reservations necessary.) The lookout area along Diamond Head Rd. affords a breathtaking view of the windsurfers below. Conspicuous estates cover the slopes of Diamond Head, some belonging to scions of Hawaii's original missionaries. It has been said that the missionaries came to do good, and did very well indeed.

Several cultural and historical attractions dot the downtown area. Get a seagull's eye view of all Oahu from the **Aloha Tower** (537-9260), on the 10th floor of Pier 9. (Free.) The **Iolani Palace,** King and Richard St. (538-1471), was first the residence of King Kalakaua and Queen Liliuokalani and later nerve center to *Hawaii Five-0.* Now the fabulous museum, in the process of multi-million dollar reconstruction, features sumptuous carved *Koa* furniture and elegant European decor. (Palace open Wed.-Sat. 9am-2:15pm. 45-min. tours by reservation only at the barracks in the palace grounds. Tours $4, ages 5-12 $1, under 5 not admitted.)

At the corner of Beretania and Richard St. stands Hawaii's modern **State Capitol,** an architectural montage reflecting all facets of the state's geography. The pillars represent palm trees, while the inverted dome of the house chambers stands resembles a volcano. Reflecting pools recall the blue Pacific nearby. (Open Mon.-Fri. 9am-4pm. Free.)

The collection of Asian art at the **Honolulu Academy of Arts,** 900 S. Beretania St. (538-1006), is one of the finest in the U.S. Thirty galleries and six garden courts also display 17th-century samurai armor, African art, and temporary exhibits.

(Open Tues.-Sat. 10am-4:30pm, Sun. 1-5pm. Free. Tours Tues.-Wed. and Fri.-Sat. at 11am, Thurs. at 2pm, and Sun. at 1pm.) Island history comes alive at the **Honolulu Mission House Museum,** 553 S. King St. (531-0481), near the Iolani Palace. Using Hawaii's oldest western buildings as their backdrop, museum actors escort visitors back to the missionary 1830s. (Open Tues.-Sun. noon-4pm. Admission $3.50, under 15 $1.) The **Bishop Museum,** 1525 Bernice St. (848-4129 or 848-4106), in Kalihi, offers the best collection of Hawaiiana in the world and daily craft demonstrations. (Open Mon.-Sat. 9am-5pm. Admission $4.75, ages 6-16 $2.50. Take "School St." bus #2 from Waikiki.)

Nearly 50 years ago, a stunned nation listened to the reports of the Japanese obliteration of **Pearl Harbor.** The **U.S.S. Arizona National Memorial** (422-2771) is an austere, three-part structure built over the sunken hull in which over a thousand servicemen perished. (Free tours 7:45am-3pm, including ½-hr. film. Launches out to the hull every 15 min. No children under 6 years of age or under 45 in. in height admitted on the launch. Visitors center open Tues.-Sun. 7:30am-5pm. Take bus #20 from Waikiki or the #50, 51, or 52 from Ala Moana or the $2 shuttle (926-4747) from major Waikiki hotels.

Looking *mauka* (inland) from downtown you'll see the lush Nuuanu Valley; the next valley to the east is the **Manoa Valley.** At the mouth of the Manoa Valley lies the **University of Hawaii,** a sanctuary for those unfortunate academics who must contend with tropical weather 12 months per year. The highlight of the entire valley is a 1-mi. trail through tropical plants to **Manoa Falls** leading from the end of Manoa Rd. behind Paradise Park. Don't hike after a hard rainfall or you may unwittingly discover the popular sport of mudsliding. Bus #5 serves all of Manoa's attractions.

Parallel to the Manoa Valley, the **Pali Highway** (Rte. 61) winds its way through **Nuuanu Valley** and over into Kailua, on the windward side of the island. As you near the top of the Pali, pull into the **Pali Lookout.** The view overlooking the windward side is one of the finest in all of the islands. But hang onto your hat—the wind can gust hard. Kamehameha the Great consolidated his kingdom by defeating Oahu's soldiers and driving them over this dramatic cliff.

Entertainment

Honolulu enjoys its symphony and opera season at the **N. Blaisdell Center** (527-5400); theater is staged at the **Honolulu Community Theater** (734-0274) near Diamond Head, and the **Manoa Valley Theater** (988-6131). Waikiki's active nightlife challenges the liver and the feet.

The Wave, 1877 Kalakaua Ave. (941-0424), on the edge of Waikiki. Videos and special events every weekend. Local bands, such as Sonia and Revolución, perform all kinds of live music (Wed.-Sun.). The building sports a huge *ukiyoe* wave. Cover $3. Free 9-10pm.

Masquerades, 224 McCully (949-6337). The place for gold chains and shirts open to the navel. Hey, babe—what's your sign? Open daily 8pm-1am. Cover $5, $3 for residents; ages 18-21 $10, $6 for residents.

Hamburger Mary's, 2109 Kuhio Ave. (922-6722). A popular gay bar, organic and co-ed. Open daily 11:30am-2am. No cover.

Moose McGillycuddy's Pub & Cafe, 1035 University Ave. (944-5525), near the university. A real student hangout serving huge sandwiches ($3-6) for lunch and dinner. Special promotion each night. Must be 21 for the disco after 9pm. Open Mon.-Sat. 11:30am-2am, Sun. 10am-2am. Happy Hour 4-8pm. No cover.

Seagull Bar and Restaurant, 2463 Kuhio Ave. (924-7911), in Waikiki. A hostel hang-out. Drink 75¢ beers with the international crowd. Open daily 4:30pm-2am.

The Other Side of the Island

The part of Oahu outside Honolulu is considered "the other side." Windward and Leeward Oahu are walled off by the islands' two mountain chains to the east and west, while Central Oahu and the North Shore lie north of Honolulu. Boundaries have blurred in recent years as Honolulu has pushed west into the city of Ewa and north into Central Oahu's plantation land.

Separated from Honolulu by the Koolau Mountains, the **Windward Coast** thrives on its picture-postcard scenery and isolated serenity. Miles of beaches and rural towns span the 40-mi. coast running from Laie, in the north, to Makapuu Point, in the south, where the highway wraps around a rugged 4-mi. stretch to Koko Head. From Waikiki, take **Kalanianaole Highway** (Rte. 72) east to **Koko Head Crater** whose eastern wall has fallen victim to the ocean to form spectacular Hanauma Bay. The bay remains a snorkler's Arcadia; its federally protected waters contain some of the tamest, most beautiful fish in the Pacific. Bring some bread or peas and the fish will eat right out of your hand. You might attract the small *humuhumunukunukuapuaa* ("fish with a pig-like nose"). Walk around the bay to the left to the wave-flushed **"Toilet Bowl."** Climb into the "bowl" when it's full and get flushed up and down by the natural lava plumbing.

A mile farther on, a similar mechanism drives the **Halona Blow Hole** to spout its spray. The secret beach to the right of Halona Blow Hole was the designated site for the famous "kiss in the sand" scene in *From Here to Eternity*. Couples may feel inclined to indulge in a reenactment in this tiny romantic cove.

Kalanianaole ends by intersecting **Kailua Road**. Follow this road toward **Kailua town** and the **Ulupo Heiau** (1200 Kailua Rd.), next to the YMCA. The temple still stands as a platform of black lava rock overlooking the Keanui swamp. Swimmers and windsurfers should adore **Kailua Beach Park** (450 Kawailoa Rd.) and **Lanikai Beach** (Mokulua Dr.)

Farther up the coast, the Mormon-dominated city of Laie hosts the **Polynesian Cultural Center**, 55-3700 Kamehameha Hwy. (293-3333), an authentically recreated village representing the indigenous cultures of New Zealand, Samoa, Tonga, Fiji, Hawaii, Tahiti, and the Marquesas. Special performances throughout the center include *hula* dancers on canoes and coconut-husking. Walk through the park at your leisure or take a guided tour at no extra cost. (Open Mon.-Sat. from noon. Dinner served 4:30-7pm, followed by spectacular evening show at 7:30pm. Admission to the grounds $25, with dinner and show $35.)

The surfer's mecca on the North Shore, **Haleiwa,** once a plantation town, now teems with boutiques and art galleries. The central supplier of water sport equipment on Oahu's "other side," Haleiwa also buzzes with surf shops and rental agencies. **Surf-N-Sea, Inc.,** 62-595 Kamehameha Hwy. (637-9887), rents windsurfers ($18 per day), surfboards, boogie boards, scuba and snorkeling equipment ($10.50 per day). They also offer instruction and organize fishing, sailing, and dive charters.

Places to stay on the "other side" include the **Vacation Inn & Hostel,** 59-788 Kamehameha Hwy. (638-7838), ¼ mi. north of Waimea Bay. (Beachside bunks $15; doubles $30-35; beach apartments for 4-6 persons $55-60. Reserve 2 weeks in advance, especially during winter by writing P.O. Box 716, Haleiwa, HI 96712.) Also look into **Countryside Cabins,** 53-224 Kamehameha Hwy. Panaluu 96717 (237-8169), across the highway on the Kanoehe end of Panaluu Beach Park (2-person studios $25, 2-person cottages $30, 4-person houses $45).

State and county beach parks with camping possibilities ring the island (permit required, see Practical Information). Unfortunately, escalating violence from locals makes many unsafe. Those on the Windward Coast are probably the best bet. **Malaekahana State Recreation Area** (293-1736), north of Lanea, is ranger patrolled for safety. Wade across at low tide to Mokuauia Island, a bird refuge. (Showers, toilets, picnic tables, barbecue pits. Permit required.)

Hawaii (Big Island)

Hawaiian legend has it that Pele, the Polynesian goddess of volcanoes, lives here; if so, she has been a busy deity in this last decade. In the spring of 1984, the volcanoes Kilauea and Mauna Loa erupted simultaneously. Geological history takes place here daily; you can inspect the steam vents, lava tubes, and the still-bubbling molten mess by visiting Volcanoes National Park.

The island of Hawaii anchors the Hawaiian archipelago on its southeasternmost end. Twice the size of all the other Hawaiian Islands combined, the Big Island encompasses a multitude of climates—from the hot, desert-like North Kona coast to the cold 13,000-ft. peaks of Mauna Kea and Mauna Loa, to the rain forest valleys and waterfalls of the Hamauka Coast.

Highways circle both Mauna Kea and Mauna Loa along the coast. Both the old Saddle Road (Rte. 200) cutting between the mountains, and the Chain of Craters Road in Kilauea Crater offer a closer view of the volcanoes at Volcanoes National Park. The main arrival points for tourists are Hilo on the windward, eastern side and the resort town of Kailua-Kona on the leeward, western side. The sun-drenched white sand beaches of the Kona coast are more suitable for snorkeling and swimming than those in rainier Hilo. The most striking scenery grows in the island's northern Kohala peninsula, highlighted by lush Waipio Valley.

Hilo

After Honolulu, Hilo is the largest city in the state. The center of the Hawaiian orchid and anthurium industry, the city is primarily residential, and travelers will find both hotels and food inexpensive. You can cover Hilo in just a day, but the city provides a convenient base to visit the island's other attractions such as Volcanoes National Park or Kaimu Black Sand Beach (see the Volcano Area).

Hilo and its environs are a nature-lover's dream. Take a morning stroll, or drive, down **Banyan Court,** around **Liliuokalani Garden** (a Japanese-style garden), and out to **Coconut Island** for a view of Mauna Kea before the clouds roll in. From Hilo, take Waianuenue Ave. up to **Rainbow Falls,** the legendary home of the goddess Hina. When Hina's rebuffed suitor trapped her behind Rainbow Falls with dammed-up waters, Hina's demigod son Maui rescued her by breaking the dam with his canoe paddle. One mile farther inland is **Peepee Falls** and the **Boiling Pots;** walk down from the observatory to the falls by following the trail which starts at the left of the stone wall. Swimming is prohibited, but locals do anyway. Fifteen mi. north on Rte. 220, off Rte. 19, **Akaka Falls** plummets a spectacular 420 ft. Route 130 winds down to **Kaimu Black Sand Beach.** Past **Kalapana,** the daring will want to walk out on the still-warm lava flows which have cut across the highway as they pour into the sea.

Remember that this soggy town averages about 125 in. of rain per year. You'll get discouraged if you try to wait out a storm more than a day or two—for best results go to the sunny Kona-Kohala coast and roast a while.

Be sure to try the island specialties—macadamia nuts and Kona coffee. Get free samples of the nuts at the **Hawaiian Holiday Macadamia Nut Company** in Haina, off Rte. 19 near Honokaa. Downtown Hilo is loaded with cheap restaurants, sushi counters, and *okazu-ya.*

Outstanding local cuisine cooks at **Cafe 100,** 969 Kilauea St. Try the *loco mocos,* big island specialties with rice, meat, gravy, and a fried egg ($1-2), and wash it down with guava juice (80¢). (Open Mon.-Thurs. 6:45am-8:30pm, Fri.-Sat. 6:45am-9:30pm.) Local favorite **Lanky's Pastries and Deli,** at Kilauea and Kekuanaoa in the Hilo Shopping Center, under the Mall Entrance sign, gets back to basics with a Hawaiian twist. Most items cost $3-5. (Open Mon.-Sat. 7am-10pm, Sun. 7am-10:30pm.) **Tomi Zushi,** 68 Mamo St., has fantastic special *teishoku:* Japanese appetizers, soup, rice, tea, and 2 entrees for $5.50. (Open Mon.-Tues. and Thurs.-Sat. 10:30am-2pm and 4:30-8:30pm, Sun. 4:30-8:30pm.) Outside of Kona, tourism on the Big Island has lagged behind its neighbors. Even the hotels clustered on Banyan Dr. by the bay are often quiet, cheap, and empty. Rooms become scarce only during spectacular volcanic eruptions. Booking rooms locally, rather than from the mainland, can save you $5-10 per day.

Dolphin Bay Hotel, 333 Iliahi St., Hilo 96720 (935-1466), in the Puueo section of town across the river, has 18 units, some plush with fans, TV, and kitchens. Cool, tropical gardens supply rooms with daily flower arrangements. (Singles from $31. Doubles from $42. Pre-payment required; make deposit 10 days prior to stay to confirm reservations.) **Hilo Hotel**, P.O. Box 726, Hilo 96720 (961-3733), at 142 Kinoole St. downtown across from Kalakaua Park, is old, yet neat and clean offering A/C, refrigerators, free coffee and sweet rolls in the morning. (Singles and doubles $39.) **Onekahakaha Beach Park** and **Kealoha Beach Park** are both within 3 mi. of Hilo. The tent sites feature toilets and showers. ($1 permit required.)

Visitor information is available from: **Hawaii Visitors Bureau**, 180 Kinoole St. (961-5797; free bus schedules, island guides, and maps; open Mon.-Fri. 8am-noon and 1-4pm); **Wailoa Center**, P.O. Box 936, Hilo 96720, Kamehameha Ave. and Pauahi St., on the seaward side of the State Bldg. (961-7360; open Mon.-Fri. 8am-4:30pm); **State Visitor Information Center**, Hilo Airport (935-1018); and the **Big Island Center for Independent Living**, 1190 Wainuenue (935-3777; assistance for disabled visitors).

For outdoors information, contact: **Department of Parks and Recreation**, 25 Aupuni St. #210, Hilo 96720 (961-8311; information on county parks; open camping permits $1 per night per person; open Mon.-Fri. 7:45am-4:30pm); **Division of State Parks**, 75 Aupuni St., Hilo 96720 (961-7200; information on state parks; free permits with a 5-day max.; open Mon.-Fri. 7:45am-4pm); **Hawaii District Forester**, 1643 Kilauea Ave., Hilo 96720 (961-7221; open Mon.-Fri. 7:45am-4pm); **Division of Forestry and Wildlife**, Dept. of Enforcement (next to the State Parks Office), P.O. Box 936, Hilo 96720 (961-7291; information on hunting, fishing, hiking, and forest regulations; open Mon.-Fri. 7:45am-4pm).

The airport, **General Lyman Field**, 3 mi. from town, is served by inter-island and mainland flights and sits a $10 taxi ride from the hotel district or downtown. **Hele-On-Bus**, 25 Aupuni St. (935-8241) provides public transport. (Buses operate Mon.-Sat. 6:30am-6pm. Fare 50¢-$6. Luggage and backpacks $1, plus additional charge per piece.) Pick up schedules at the office or the Hawaii visitors bureau. The company also runs a bus between Kona and Hilo at least once per day, making a convenient circuit of the island ($5.25). Disabled travelers can take advantage of curb-to-curb service on a day's notice: Call 323-2085. All national and state car rental chains reside at Hilo aiport. **Budget** (800-935-7293) charges $25 per day. You must be 18 with a major credit card. Rent a moped from **Ciao**, 71 Banyan Dr. (969-1717). Mopeds are $25 per day, cruiser bikes $15. (Open daily 8am-7pm.) Water equipment rentals swim at **Nautilus Dive Center**, 382 Kamehameha Ave. (935-6939). Mask and snorkel are $3 per day, an underwater camera $15 per day. The center also offers beginner and certified dive charters for $45. (Open Mon.-Sat. 8:30am-5pm. Deposit required.)

The **post office** zips at Waianuenue Ave. (935-6685), in the Federal Bldg. (Open Mon.-Fri. 8:30am-4:30pm, Sat. 9am-noon.) Hilo's **ZIP code** is 96720; the **area code** is 808.

The Volcano Area

The volcanoes of the Big Island are unique in the world for their size, frequency of eruptions, and accessibility. Resting on the current center of the geological hot spot whose volcanic upthrusts fashioned each of the Hawaiian islands in turn, the two mountains in **Volcanoes National Park** continue to heave and grow, adding acres of new land each year. **Kilauea Crater**, with its steaming vents, sulfur fumes, and periodically spectacular "drive-in" eruptions, dominates the park. However, the less active **Mauna Loa** and its dormant northern neighbor, **Mauna Kea,** are in some respects more amazing fire breathers. Each towers nearly 14,000 ft. above sea level and drops 30,000 ft. to the ocean floor. Mauna Loa is the largest volcano in the world, while Mauna Kea, if measured from its base on the ocean floor, would hold the title of tallest mountain on earth. (Park entrance $5; good for 7 days.) An 11-mi. scenic drive around the Kilauea Celdera on **Crater Rim Drive** is accessible via Rte. 11 from the east and west, or via the Chain of Craters Rd. from the south. Well-marked trails and lookouts dot the road; you can stop frequently to explore. You can also hike the 11 mi. along the vista-filled **Crater Rim Trail,** which traverses *ohia* and giant fern forests, *aa* (rough) and *pahoehoe* (smooth) lava flows, and smoldering steam and sulfur vents. Walk through the **Thurston Lava Tube,** formed by lava that cooled around a hot core which continued to move, leaving the inside of the flow hollow.

The free **Jaggar Museum,** next to the closed volcano observatory, explains the volcano's history, and contains displays on many Hawaiian legends. (Open daily 8:30am-5pm.)

Four-mi. **Kilauea Iki Trail** starts at the Kilauea Iki overlook on Crater Rim Rd. The trail leads around the north rim of Kilauea Iki, through a forest of tree ferns, down the wall of the little crater, past the vent of the '59 eruption, over steaming lava, and back to Crater Rim Rd., passing *ohelo* bushes laden with red berries on the way. Legend has it that you must offer some berries to Pele, or you'll incur her wrath. The 3.6-mi. **Mauna Iki Trail** begins 9 mi. southwest of park headquarters on Rte. 11 and leads to footprints made in 1790 ash. From here you can hike down into the coastal area.

The Chain of Craters Rd. leads down the slopes of Kilauea to the Puna Coast, where the current eruption meets the sea. In June 1989, a new phase of the lava flows blocked off the connection to Rte. 130 from the north. Park rangers can inform you of the current status of the eruption, and the safety of lava-watching. The crashing white ocean sprays against black rock, providing a spectacle as powerful as its volcanic antithesis nearby. The famous **Kaimu Black Sand Beach** to the north on Rte. 130 formed in this way, a sparkling gem born of nature's torment.

At the visitors centers at **Kilauea,** Crater Rim Rd. (967-7311; open 7:45am-5pm), you can see 10-minute films shown hourly from 9am to 4pm and catch the bulletins on the latest volcanic activity. Trails of varying difficulty lead around Kilauea and to the summit of Mauna Loa; speak to a ranger before setting out. Picnic in the park, since prices at the only restaurant and snackbar are outrageous.

Volcano House, P.O. Box 53, Hawaii Volcanoes National Park 96718 (967-7321), offers 37 units overlooking Kilauea Crater from a 1220-ft. vantage point. (Rooms from $59. 4-person cabins $25.) **Morse Volcano B&B,** P.O. Box 100, Volcano 96785 (967-7216), in Volcano Village just outside the park, offers roomy common areas and single rooms for $25, with bath $30. (Doubles $40, with bath $45.) Volcanoes National Park (967-7311) has free sites at **Kipukanene, Namakanipaio** (near Kilauea Crater), and **Kamoamoa** (on the coast)—each with shelters and fireplaces, but no wood. **Kalopa State Recreation Area** kicks back at the end of Kalopa Rd. (775-7114), 3 mi. inland from Mamalahoa Hwy. 19. Surrounded by a wonderful *ohia* forest, sites feature camping, group lodging, picnicking, and nature trails.

Kona

Kona, on the western side of Hawaii, is home to the town of Kailua (officially hyphenated as Kailua-Kona), a resort center whose shops, nightlife, and perfect weather cater to tourists. Hot and gorgeous, the white sand beaches of Kona and the coves of the major hotels (all hotels must have public access paths to the beach) make for perfect tanning. The calm deep waters along the entire coast are ideal for novice scuba divers and prized for giant billfish.

Kailua-Kona is small enough to see in a short walk. Historic sites and white sand beaches abound, the latter dotted with cheap fast-food restaurants and some nightclubs. Visit **Hulihee Palace,** 75-5718 Alli Dr. (329-1877), King Kalakaua's beautifully restored summer home. (Open daily 9am-4pm. Admission $4, ages 12-18 $1, under 12 50¢.) The nearby **Mokuaikaua** was Hawaii's first church (1838). Still used for sermons and as a museum, the building has been lovingly maintained; the chimes ring every afternoon at 4pm. (Open daily sunrise-sunset.)

To the south on Rte. 11 lies **Kealakekua Bay.** From Rte. 11 turn right onto Napoopoo Dr., which leads down to the small bay (about 15 min.), steeped in history. In 1778, Captain Cook tried to restock his ship here during the **Makahiki**—a holy season honoring the god Lono. The Hawaiians thought Cook's white sails and masts signified the return of Lono, and they proclaimed Cook a god at the **Hikiau Heiau** on the bay. A year later Cook was killed on the far side of the bay when he tried to end a fight between his men and the islanders; a white monument marks the site. **Captain Bean's Glass Bottom Cruises** (329-2955) can take you across the bay to the monument where colorful fish frolic in this protected marine life preserve. (Tickets $22, under 12 $11. Includes equipment and food. Departs Kailua Pier daily at 8:30am.)

The beaches are Kona's main attraction. **Magic Sands** (also called "Disappearing Sands") at the Kona Magic Sands Hotel, 77-6452 Alii Dr. (329-9177), is a good place to park your towel and wade in the surf. Or, travel up Rte. 19 to prime **Hapuna Beach** and **Spencer Beach** parks, 35 mi. north. Both parks have disabled access.

Food can be expensive; take advantage of the 24-hr. **Food-4-Less** on Pawai St. and the early bird specials (5-6pm) at most hotels. For breakfast, try **Stan's,** 75-5646 Palani Rd., in the Kona Hukilau. (All-you-can-eat hotcakes and 1 egg for $4. Complete dinners $6.25-7. Open daily 7-9:30am and 5:30-8:30pm.) The popular **Ocean View Inn,** 75-5683 Alii Dr., across from the boat dock, serves seafood, U.S., Chinese, and Hawaiian fare in a diner setting at diner prices. (Lunch $3-6, dinner $6-9. Open Tues.-Sun. 6:30am-2:45pm and 5:15-9pm.) **Poki's Pasta,** 75-5699F Alii Dr., a traditional Italian place, spotlights delicious pasta made fresh daily. (Lunch $5-6, dinner $8-10. Open daily 11am-3pm and 4-9pm.)

Staying overnight in Kailua-Kona can be an expensive proposition; hotels here cater to the affluent traveler. Other nearby towns provide more reasonable lodgings. The nearest camping is at Kohala. **Kona Lodge and Hostel,** 8 mi. south of Kailua-Kona on Rte. 11 (322-9056 or 322-8136), offers a kitchen and fruit from the gardens. (Office open daily 7am-9:30pm. Primitive coed dorm bunks $12, nonmembers $14. Private rooms $24.) **Manago Hotel,** P.O. Box 145, Captain Cook 96704 (323-2642), has comfy and clean, but austere rooms. (Singles $18. Doubles $21. Larger rooms with bath and ocean view in newer wing from $29.) A darling hotel near a snorkeling beach, the **Kona Tiki Hotel,** P.O. Box 1567, Kailua-Kona 96740 (329-1425), relaxes at 75-5968 Alii Dr. on the southern side of town. (Singles and doubles $35, with kitchen $40. Reservation deposit $50.)

For visitor information and maps, contact the **Hawaii Visitors Bureau,** 75-5719 Alii Dr. (329-7787), across from the Kona Inn Shopping Center. (Open Mon.-Fri. 8am-noon and 1-4pm.) **Department of Parks and Recreation,** Yano Stall, Captain Cook (323-3046 or 323-3060), by the police station, has information on county parks, camping, and permits. (Open Mon.-Fri. 7:45am-4:30pm.)

Keahole Airport soars 9 mi. (15 min.) north of town. Taxi rides into town cost about $16, plus 30¢ per bag. The public transport system, **Hele-on-Bus** (935-8241), provides infrequent service up and down the west coast out of Kona (6:15am-4:30pm; 3 per day via Alii Dr., one via Hulualoa). **Honolulu Rent-a-Car,** 74-5588 Pawaii Pl. (329-7328), rents used cars for as little as $15 per day (3-day min. rental). For bikes, check out **B&L Bike & Sports,** 74-5576B Pawaii Pl. (329-3309), at Kaiwi St. (Open Mon.-Fri. 9am-5:30pm, Sat. 9am-3pm.) For water equipment rentals, stop in at **Big Island Divers,** Kona Market Pl. (329-6068; open daily 8am-9pm).

The **post office** licks at Palani Rd. (329-1927; open Mon.-Fri. 9am-4pm, Sat. 9am-noon). Kona's **ZIP code** is 96740; the **area code** is 808.

Maui

Long before college athletes televised the slogan, "We're number one," Maui's warlike chieftans sounded their defiant equivalent "Maui No Ka Oi." Even after the islands' consolidation under the Kamehameha dynasty from the Big Island, Maui's transcendence was upheld in its selection for a time as the capital of a new kingdom. Although the commercial preeminence of Honolulu eventually forced a royal relocation to Oahu, most visitors choose Maui over the other islands. With a recent rise in tourism has come traffic, elevated prices, commercial hype, and crime and drug problems. Increasing resort development also means, however, that rent-a-car outfits, restaurants, and an active nightlife flourish.

Named for the demi-god Maui, who pulled all the islands from the sea-bottom with his fish hooks, the island rose up around the slopes of two mightly volcanoes and a narrow isthmus in between. "The Valley Island," as it is known, features clapboard cane towns, concrete condos, sunny beaches, and a sometimes snowcapped volcano. Maui's popularity will seem justified once you've toured mountainous, sleepy West Maui; the windy central isthmus that holds Wailuku, Kahului, and acre upon acre of sugar cane; the spiritual Haleakala volcano, which dominates East Maui; and the remote splendor of the Hana Coast.

Practical Information

Visitor Information: Hawaii Visitors Bureau, 380 Dairy Rd., Kahului (871-8691). Information on Molokai and Lanai. Open Mon.-Fri. 8am-4:30pm. **Haleakala National Park,** P.O. Box 369, Makawao 96768 (572-9306). Information and permits for national park camping (572-9177). **Visitors Center,** 65 Hana Hwy., Paia (579-8000). Open Mon.-Sat. 9am-noon and 5-6pm. **Department of Parks and Recreation,** War Memorial Gym, 1580 Kaahumanu Ave., between Kahului and Wailuku (244-9018). Information and permits ($4) for county parks. Open Mon.-Fri. 8-11am and noon-4:15pm. **Division of State Parks,** 54 High St. (244-4354), in Wailuku. Information on state parks on Maui and Molokai. Open Mon.-Fri. 8-11am and noon-4:15pm.

Kahului Airport, on the northern coast of the isthmus. Regular flights from the mainland and other islands. Visitors information booth in front of the terminal's entrance provides free maps, information, and directions. Taxi to hotels costs $5-8, but renting a car here might save you time later (see Car Rental below). Gray Line (from Oahu 833-8000, on Maui 877-5507, from mainland 800-367-2420) runs between Kahului Airport and the Lahaina-Kaanapali area. Fare $8; reservations required.

Tours: Gray Line (phone above). Tours to Iao Valley, Lahaina ($15-25), and Hana ($35-48). Operates daily 7am-9pm.

Boats: Maalaea Activities Center (242-6982), at Maalaea Harbor. Daily ferries to Kaunakakai, Molokai ($32); 4 trips per week to Kaumalapau Harbor, Lanai ($22). From Lahaina, **Expeditions** (661-3756) boats twice daily to Manele Harbor, Lanai ($25), while the **Maui Princess** (661-8397) runs between Molikai, Oahu, and Maui for $21.

Taxi: Yellow Cab, Kahului Airport (877-7000). Fare $6 into town.

Car Rental: Trans Maui, Kahului Airport (877-5222). $20 per day, $115 per week. Insurance $6 per day. Must be 21 with major credit card. 24-hr. advance reservation required. **Avis,** Kahului Airport (871-7575). $78 per week, $10 per day insurance. $5 extra per day for ages 18-25; major credit card required. 24-hr. advance reservation.

Bike Rental: The Island Biker, Kahului Shopping Center (877-7744). High-quality 18-speed mountain bikes $20 per day. Open Mon.-Fri. 9am-5pm, Sat. 9am-3pm. Discount with student ID. **Gogo Bikes Hawaii,** 30b Halawai Dr. (661-3063), ¼ mi. north of Kaanapali off Rte. 30. 1-speeds $10 per day, 12-speeds $20. Open daily 9am-5pm. Discount with student ID.

Moped and Scooter Rentals: Gogo Bikes Hawaii, Kaanapali (661-3063). Mopeds $5 per hr., $20 per day, $95 per week. Scooters $25 per day, $125 per week. Open daily 9am-5pm. Must be 18 with cash deposit or major credit card. Free pick-up in the Kaanapali area. 10% discount with student ID. **Paradise Scooters,** 102 Halawai Dr. (661-0300), next to Gogo Bikes.

Free snorkeling equipment with each rental. Delivery to Kihei, Wailea, and Kahului $23.
Open Mon.-Sat. 8am-5pm, Sun. 8am-noon.

Water Equipment Rentals: Maui Dive Shop, Azeka Place, Kihei (879-3388), and Wakea
Ave., Kahalui (661-5388). Free scuba and snorkeling lessons with equipment rental. Per day:
mask $3, snorkel $2, boogie board $8, wetsuit $6, underwater camera $20. Open Mon.-Fri.
8am-9pm, Sat.-Sun. 8am-6pm. **Hunt Hawaii,** 120 Hana Hwy. (579-8129), Paia. Surfboards
$15 per 2 hr., $25 per day. Windsurfers $30 per day, $150 per week. Surf or sailboard lessons
$35 per 2 hr. Open daily 9am-6pm.

Help Lines: Sexual Assault Crisis Center, 242-4357. **Coast Guard,** 244-5256. **Gay and Bi
Information,** 572-1884 (serves Maui, Molokai, Lanai). All 3 open 24 hr.

Post Office: Lahaina. Open Mon.-Fri. 8:15am-4:15pm. ZIP code: 96761. In Paia, on Baldwin
Ave. Open Mon.-Fri. 8am-4:30pm, Sat. 10:30am-12:30pm. Mail collection Mon.-Sat. 1:15-
3:45pm. ZIP code: 96799. In Wailuku, next to the State Office Bldg. on High St. Open Mon.-
Fri. 8:30am-4:30pm, Sat. 9-11am. ZIP code: 96793. In Kihei, 1254 S. Kihei Rd., in Azeka
Market Place. Open Mon.-Fri. 9am-4:30pm, Sat. 9-11am. ZIP code: 96753.

Maui is shaped like a bowling pin, around which the highways wind like a broken
figure eight. To the west lie **Kahului** and **Wailuku,** business and residential communities offering less expensive food and supplies than the resort towns. From Kahului,
Rte. 30 will lead you clockwise around the small, western loop of the figure eight
to hot and dry **Lahaina,** the former whaling village, and **Kaanapali,** the major resort
area.

Most roads are fairly well-marked but poorly lit. Heed the warnings on roads
recommended for four-wheel-drive vehicles only; a passing rainstorm can quickly
drain your funds, since most rental car contracts stipulate that dirt road driving
is at the driver's risk. **Hitchhiking** is troublesome and illegal.

Accommodations and Camping

Abandon all desire to stay in the resort areas. Stay in Honokowai instead of
Kaanapali, or in Kahului instead of Kihei. Groups of two or more can profit from
car/room packages. Larger groups should investigate condominium rentals. **Bed
and breakfasts** usually run $35-50. In East Maui camping is the watchword.

Maui YMCA (AYH), Keanae (248-8355), about 32 mi. and a 2-hr. drive east of Kahului
Airport, midway along Hana Hwy. to Hana. Inaccessible by public transportation. 100 beds,
6-8 persons per room. 3 dormitory cabins, kitchen, public hot showers. Extensive sports facilities. Cafeteria. 3-day max. stay. Curfew 9pm. Check-in 4-6pm. $5, nonmembers $6. Call 244-
3253 for reservations.

Northshore Inn, 2080 Vineyard St. (800-242-8999), above Hazel's in Wailuku. A recently
renovated bargain hotel. Excellent facilities and friendly management. Attracts an international windsurfing and MTV kind of crowd. Bunks $15. Singles $29. Doubles $39.

Valley Isle Lodge, 310 N. Market Street. (808-244-6880), Weiluku. Caters to surfing and
windsurfing dudes. Board room for equipment, barbecue grill in back. Lounge with TV and
refrigerator. Rooms have different bumper stickers on the doors for the lost or inebriated.
Singles $26. Doubles $34.

Pioneer Inn, 658 Wharf St. (836-1411), Lahaina. Directly in front of the boat harbor and
next to the famous giant banyan tree. Two buildings—the "original" and the "Mauka." The
Old Whaler's Saloon spouts liquor long into the night, spraying part of the inn with noise.
Pool. Ask for a room with a harbor view. Singles and doubles $25, with bath $30. Mauka
building $60.

Nani Kai Hale, 73 N. Kihei Rd. (879-9120 or 800-367-6032 from the mainland), Kihei. Condominium on a sandy beach. Double with bath April 16-Dec. 15 $32.50, 3-day min. stay;
Dec. 16-April 15 $42.50, 1-week min. stay. Call for reservations.

The county maintains two campsites in Paia, **H.A. Baldwin Park** and **Rainbow
Park,** both about 5 mi. east of the Kahului Airport. Neither are safe for solitary
travelers. (Tent and permit required. 3-day max. stay. Sites $3, under 18 50¢.) The
Baldwin offers restrooms, showers, and a beautiful, windy white-sand beach; unfortunately, the fenced-in camping area lies on the edge of busy Hwy. 36. Rainbow

Park lies along Baldwin Ave., 3 mi. upcountry from Paia. For more information contact the Department of Parks and Recreation (see Practical Information above).

On West Maui, the only recognized camping is at **Camp Pecusa**, ¼ mi. north of the 14-mi. marker on Hwy. 30. (661-4303). This less-than-glamorous camp-ground offers little shade. (Shower, washbasin, pit toilets, and tables. $3 per person on a walk-in basis.)

You can camp in any of the three state parks (5-day max. stay) after obtaining a free permit at the Department of Parks and Recreation. **Waianapanapa State Wayside** in Hana, about 52 mi. east of Kahului Airport, offers by far the best state camping facilities on the island. Sites include restrooms, picnic tables, barbecue grills, and outdoor showers. (12 cabins available: $5 per person for groups larger than 6; $10 for a single bed. Reservations recommended.)

Maui's two federal parks require no permit. Diminutive **Hosmer Grove**, 7000 ft. up Haleakala's slope, provides drinking water, toilet, grills, and firewood. On a weekend night, you'll have to squeeze your tent in with a crowbar. (Groups limited to 15 people and 3 nights.) **Oheo** is at sea level, about 67 mi. from Kahului Airport, ¼ mi. south of **Oheo Stream** near the Seven Pools. (No drinking water or firewood. 3-day max. stay.)

Camping at the **national campsites** within the crater requires a permit and a hike to the site. (2-day max. stay per campground.) Permits are available from the **Haleakala National Park Headquarters**, P.O. Box 369, Makawao, Maui 96768 (572-9306).

Food

Guava trees line the road to Hana. Other fruits sell for a song at stands along the Hana Hwy. and Rte. 35 in Kihei. Maui specialties such as sweet kula onions and Maui potato chips (try them chocolate-covered) populate most supermarkets. *Guri Guri,* a local-made sherbet that comes in pineapple and strawberry, has pleased islanders for years from its main outlet **Tasaka Guri Guri,** in the Maui Mall (871-4512; open daily Hawaiian time, i.e. whenever).

Delicious fish can be found everywhere on the island. Restaurants serve seafood fresh from the sea; add some indigenous sauces, and the result is *ono* (delicious). The cheapest places to eat lie away from the resorts, especially in Wailuku.

The Maui Boy, 2102 Vineyard St. at Church St., in Wailuku. Curtains and potted plants give this diner an edge over the competition. Large New York-style deli menu featuring sandwiches and Asian dishes ($4-5). Open Tues.-Fri. 10am-2pm and 5-9pm, Sat.-Sun. 7am-2pm and 5-9pm.

Siam Thai Cuisine, 123 N. Market St., Wailuku. Trendy but popular. Large Thai menu: good vegetarian selections, excellent curries. Combination plates $4-5. A la carte entrees $6. Open Mon.-Fri. 11am-2:30pm and 5-9:30pm, Sat. and Sun. 5-9:30pm.

Hazel's Café, 2080 Vineyard St., Wailuku. Simple and unadorned. Inexpensive local food, untainted by tourist dollars. A huge selection of daily homestyle specials; pigs' feet soup served Fri. Open Mon.-Fri. 6am-9pm, Sat. 6am-8pm.

Sheik's Restaurant, 97 W. Wakea Ave., Kahului. Home of the year-round Christmas tree. A favorite late-night eatery. Try *saimin* ($2.25), a hearty soup with noodles, bits of pork, and scallions. Reasonably priced sandwiches $2-4. Open Sun.-Thurs. 5:30am-10pm, Fri.-Sat. 5:30am-11pm.

Ichiban the Restaurant, Kahului Shopping Center. Japanese cuisine with an Hawaiian flair. Lunch $4.25. Dinner $5.50-7. Open Mon.-Sat. 7am-2pm and 5-9pm.

Picnics, 30 Baldwin Ave. (597-8021), Paia. Quite a concept. Big, delicious sandwiches around $4.25. Lots of take-out pasta salads, fit for a picnic. Accepts phone-ins. Open daily 7:30am-3:30pm.

Sights and Activities

Haleakala Crater, the "House of the Sun," dominates the eastern end of the island from its perch 10,000 ft. above the sea. According to Polynesian legend, the demi-god Maui ascended Haleakala to slow the sun's trip across the sky, letting his mother have more of the sun's rays to dry her *tapa* cloth. When the sun arose from his house at the end of the sky, Maui lassoed him by his **genitals;** the sun agreed to cruise across the sky more slowly. The House of the Sun is still a moving place from which to watch the sun rise. **Haleakala National Park** stays open 24 hr. (Entrance $3 per car.) Be sure to stop your **loins** at the **park headquarters** (572-9306), about a mile from the Rte. 378 entrance.

Haleakala Visitors Center (572-9172), near the summit, has exhibits on the geology, archeology, and ecology of the region. (Free ranger talks at 9:30, 10:30, and 11:30am. Open daily 6:30am-4pm.) The **Puuulaula Center,** at Haleakala's summit, offers shelter to those who forgot a sweater or jacket. (Open 24 hr.) An 11-mi. descent into the crater via Sliding Sands Trail and out again via Halemauu Trail could prove the seven most impressive hours of your trip to Hawaii. Along it you'll encounter the **Kaluuokaoo Pit,** also called the Bottomless Pit, one of several exposed lava tubes in the crater. Early Hawaiians threw the **umbilical cords** of their newborns into the pit to ensure that the sacred cords would not be eaten by the valley's **evil rodents.** Drive farther south on Rte. 37 to **Tedeschi Winery** (878-6058), to taste their "Maui Blanc" pineapple wine for free. (Open Mon.-Fri. 9am-5pm, Sat.-Sun. 10am-5pm.)

Try to spend a full day touring the **Hana Coast.** The northern route (H-36) through **Paia** and **Keanae** is incredibly tough on the **internal organs,** but the scenery rewards. Make sure you start out from Paia with a full tank of gas, and don't venture out if the road is wet—it's a long way down. Paia itself has flourished with nearby **Hookipa Beach Park,** an international windsurfing mecca.

Wailuku, a tranquil plantation town, merits an afternoon stroll. The government buildings on High St. and vintage shops on Market St. reveal urban life "local style," unaltered by the ravages of resort development to the south.

You can visit a reconstructed ancient native place of worship at the **Hale Kii** (House of Images), atop a nearby hill near Rte. 32 between Wailuku and Iao Valley. The temple affords the island's most idyllic views, and the locals know it well (high school sweethearts make the trek uphill every Thurs. evening). Follow Main St. (Rte. 32) to the traffic light at Rte. 330. Turn left, pass the macadamia grove, and turn right on Rte. 340. Continue to Kuhio Place, and follow the tortuous route to the right.

Lahaina, an old whaling port, was the capital of the islands during the time of Kamehameha the Great. Whale-watching in spring and fall remains popular today all along the coast. Lahaina itself, remains a sunny, dry town, immediately infects everyone with laid-back syndrome. When Mark Twain visited, he planned to stay one week and work; he stayed a month and didn't write a thing. In Lahaina's town square grows a 114-year-old East Indian **banyan tree.** Take pictures if you must but please, keep your chainsaw away from the branches. Obtain a free copy of the *Lahaina Historical Guide* from one of the many tourist activities centers that crowd the town.

Kihei and **Wailea,** on the southwest coast, have begun to merge into the Kaanapali-Lahaina-Kapalua resort area. Some good swimming beaches and parks cluster around Kihei's condominiums. **Kamaole Sands Beach Parks** (numbered 1 to 3) have the best facilities. Check the *Maui News* to rent unsold condo units at bargain prices. **Kalama Beach Park,** a 36 sandy acres with volleyball and basketball courts, is a reliable standby if Kamaole is crowded. Rte. 31 continues past Wailea to some fabulously quiet beaches.

West Maui hosts most of the Rosenesque hot spots on Spuds Mackenzie's top-ten list of island party pads. Go dancing at **Partners,** 118 Makawao Ave. (572-6611), in Makawao; **Spats,** in the Hyatt Regency Maui (667-7474); or **Banana Moon,** in the Maui Marriott (667-1200). The free *Maui Beach Press* provides decent listings of both local and tourist resort happenings.

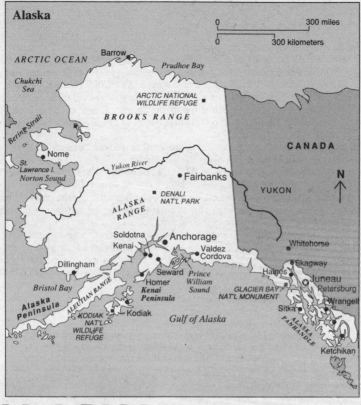

ALASKA

Called "Alashka" ("The Great Land") by the Aleuts and "The Last Frontier" by adventurous settlers, Alaska is large and unspoiled enough to accommodate even the most rugged individualist. Misty fjords, mountain lakes, forests, glaciers, and tundra complement a population as varied as the Great Land itself. The term "Alaskan" encompasses everything from Native American to lifetime resident to *cheechako* (outsider) lured by homesteading opportunities. But virtually all Alaskans possess a strong sense of community and statehood; ask any local to tell you about the state, and you'll see someone get more excited than a polar bear contemplating a fat seal dinner.

Though broad enough to accommodate England, France, Spain, and Italy within its borders, Alaska did not host a European visitor until 1741 when the czar of Russia hired Dutch navigator Victor Bering to map out the region near the Kenai Peninsula. Bering died in the effort, but his crew brought home such an abundance of valuable furs that Russian traders soon overran Kodiak Island with traps in hand and rubles in mind. The fur harvest dried up in less than a century, and the czar, dead broke from the Crimean War, decided to sell what he considered to be a territory sucked dry of its natural resources. In 1867 the U.S. bought the vast wasteland for less than 2¢ per acre—quite a bargain until you do some quick multiplication to get the total price of $7,200,000. Alaska soon became known as "Seward's Icebox," a jab at Secretary of State William Seward who negotiated the purchase. But within 20 years, U.S. prospectors unearthed enough gold to turn Seward's folly into a billion-dollar profit.

787

The modern development of Alaska began with World War II. In response to the 1941 Japanese occupation of the Aleutian islands, the U.S. military connected Alaska to the lower 48 states by the Alaskan Highway, also building ports and airfields. Many GIs liked what they saw, and stayed. The Cold War with Russia led to an increase in military development in Alaska. In the 60s, oil discovered on the Kenai Peninsula and on the north slope of the Brooks Range catalyzed Alaska's growth. The Alaska pipeline pumped its first barrel of crude 800 miles from Prudhoe Bay to Valdez in July of 1978.

The considerable uproar surrounding the spill of Exxon *Valdez's* oil cargo obscures the fact that it damaged only 1% of Alaska's coastline. The area covered by the leak makes up just a speck in Alaska's enormity. Despite the pipeline, the Alcan highway, and the still-secret Nucleon Early Warning System access roads, only one-fifth of the land is accessible by roads—the float plane is the primary mode of transportation. Native Alaskans still live with privacy and autonomy unknown to most other Native Americans; Athabascans, Aleuts, Eskimos, Tlingits, and Haidas still subsist on the land's abundant resources. The rivers teem with salmon; the rocky shores harbor seals while whales sing offshore; bears of all kinds compete with wolves, lynx, and other carnivores for food and territory; and moose, bighorn sheep, and bald eagles coexist in numbers unheard of elsewhere in the United States.

Practical Information

Capital: Juneau.

Tourist Information: Alaska Division of Tourism, Pouch E-101, Juneau 99811 (465-2010). Open Mon.-Fri. 8am-4:30pm. **Alaskan Public Lands Information Center,** Old Federal Building (271-2737), 4th Ave., Anchorage 99510. Tips on all federal, state, and local parks, refuges, and forests. Will refer you to the appropriate office such as: **Alaska State Division of Parks,** Pouch 7-001, Anchorage 99510 (561-2020). Open Mon.-Fri. 8am-4:30pm. **United States Forest Service,** Box 1628-ATD, Juneau 99802 (586-7282). General information regarding national parks and reserves. Open Mon.-Fri. 8am-4:30pm. **National Park Service,** Parks and Forests Information Center, 2525 Gampbell, Anchorage 99503 (261-2643). Open Mon.-Fri. 8am-5pm. **State Department of Fish and Game,** P.O. Box 3-2000, Juneau 99802. Information on hunting and fishing regulations.

Time Zones: Alaska (4 hr. behind Eastern); Aleutian-Hawaii (5 hr. behind Eastern). **Postal Abbreviation:** AK.

Travel

Anyone who has ever ventured onto Alaska's roads owns a copy of *The Milepost,* published by the Alaska Northwest Publishing Company, 130 2nd Ave. S., Edmond, WA 98020 (907-563-1141; open Mon.-Fri. 8:30am-4:30pm). Each thick volume ($15) packs information about Alaskan and Canadian communities as well as up-to-date ferry schedules and maps of the highways and roads.

Travel in Alaska is easy but expensive. Most Alaskans use air travel, often piloting themselves; one in 36 has a pilot's license. Several airlines run frequent scheduled flights to most places any visitor might be inclined to go: **Alaska Air** (larger towns—contact your local Delta desk); **Markair** (to larger Bush towns, Kodiak, and the Aleutians; 800-426-6784); **ERA Aviation** (southcentral; 243-3300); and **Ryan Air Service** (practically anywhere in the Bush; 248-0695). Many other charters and flight-seeking services are available. Check *The Milepost* (see above) or write **Ketchum Air Service Inc.,** North Shore Lake Hood, Anchorage 99503 (243-5525), to ask about their charters.

Trains along the **Alaskan Highway** connect Seward and Whittier in the south to Fairbanks in the north via Anchorage and Denali. Though beautiful, both the train itself and the view it affords may not be entirely worth the fare ($98 from Anchorage to Fairbanks). The train will stop to drop off passengers anywhere with advance notice. It also provides semi-local service from Anchorage to Portage Glacier ($47.50). All trains run daily. Advance reservations are required for all except

Whittier trips. Write **Alaska Railroad Corporation,** Passenger Services, P.O. Box 7-2111, Anchorage 99510. (Call 265-2623 for schedules, fares, and reservations.)

Scheduled **bus service** connects Whitehorse, British Columbia, and Haines with Central Alaska, including Anchorage. **Alaska Sightseeing Company,** 327 F St., Anchorage 99510 (276-1305), provides service to Anchorage from Haines, which is on the Alaska Marine Highway. **Whitepass-Yukon Motorcoaches,** P.O. Box 100479, Anchorage 99510 (279-0761), has two buses per week from Whitehorse, YT to Anchorage; service to Haines is also available twice per week. Bus rides to Anchorage from the Lower 48 are expensive. **Greyhound** charges well over $300 from Seattle, slightly less from Vancouver. **Bus tours** that often include meals, lodging, and sights otherwise difficult to get to can be a good deal. For example, **Gray Line Tours,** 547 W. 4th Ave., Anchorage 99501 (277-5581), offers a three-day excursion from Whitehorse to Anchorage that includes a sail across Prince William Sound, a train ride from Whittier, and two nights of accommodations, all for under $500.

Driving in Alaska is not for the faint at heart. To the embarrassment of most residents, many major roads in Alaska remain in deplorable condition. Dust and flying rocks are a major hazard in the summer, as are miserable 10- to 30-mi. patches of gravel. Radiators and headlights should be protected from flying rocks with a wire screen, and a fully functioning spare tire is essential. Winter can actually offer a smoother ride. Active snow crews keep roads as clear as possible, and the packed surface and thinned traffic permit easy driving without summer's mechanical troubles. At the same time, the danger of avalanches and ice is cause for major concern. Check the road conditions before traveling; in Anchorage call 333-1013, or simply tune in to local radio stations. Both winter and summer travelers are advised to let a friend or relative know of their position along the highway several times in the course of a trip. Drivers should also take into account the cost of gas, which varies significantly from station to station.

Physical Characteristics and Climate

Alaska spans 586,412 sq. mi., one-fifth the area of the continental United States, stretching west to a longitude that coincides with New Zealand. It has 33,904 mi. of shoreline (about 1½ times the combined coastlines of the Lower 48), and the highest mountain in North America (20,320-ft. Mt. Denali). No single temperate zone covers the whole region; Prudhoe Bay differs from Ketchikan as much as Minneapolis does from Atlanta. In general, summer and early fall (June-Sept.) are the best times to visit. Visitors can expect daylight from 6am to 2am in many areas during these months.

Fairbanks, Tok, and the Bush frequently enjoy 95°F hot spells, receiving less than eight in. of precipitation annually. The Interior freezes in its −60° to −80°F temperatures in winter. Farther south, the climate is milder, but also rainier. Cordova "rusts" with 167 in. of precipitation annually. Anchorage and other coastal towns in the southcentral are blessed with the Japanese Current, which has a moderating effect on the climate. Average temperatures for Anchorage are 13°F in January (the coldest month) to 57°F in July (the warmest).

Travelers should prepare for wet, wind, and cold year-round. In summer, those staying below the Arctic Circle probably won't need anything heavier than a light parka or jacket and sweater. For forays into the "Bush" (Alaskans' term for the wilderness), be absolutely certain to bring waterproof boots and sturdy raingear. Wool and polypropylene are staples for socks, underwear, pants, shirts, and hats. The warmest coats and snowsuits are hollofil, not down-filled, garments.

Winter travelers should always expect the chilly unexpected. The National Park Service advises that visitors learn to recognize the symptoms of hypothermia, the gradual lowering of the body temperature; also carry extra dry clothing, blankets, and food. Read Jack London's *To Build a Fire* to learn what a drag it is freezing to death.

Camping

Just setting up a tent or igloo in a scenic spot is an ancient Alaskan tradition kept up by land-bridging, roving Athabascans to homesteading ex-GIs. "Squatting" has long been an Alaskan right—and now institutions have stepped in to make it possible for tourists.

The U.S. Forest Service maintains more than 178 wilderness log cabins for public use—142 in Tongass National Forest in Southeastern Alaska and 36 in Chugach National Forest in Southcentral Alaska. The cabins are beautifully located and well maintained. User permits are required along with a fee of $10 per party per night. Reserve several months in advance. Most cabins have seven-day use limits, except hike-in cabins (3-day max. stay May-Aug.). Cabins sleep six, and are usually accessible only by air, boat, or hiking trail. Facilities at these sites rarely include more than a wood stove and pit toilets. Some cabins provide skiffs (small boats). For maps or further information write to the U.S. Forest Service. For information about free cabins within wildlife ranges, contact the U.S. Fish and Wildlife Service (see Practical Information above).

Alaskan state-run campgrounds are always free. Often they have toilets and drinking water, but no showers. For information on state campgrounds and waysides, contact the Alaska State Division of Parks (see Practical Information above). Four federal agencies control and manage park lands in Alaska: the U.S. Forest Service (USFS), the Bureau of Land Management (BLM), the National Park Service, and the U.S. Fish and Wildlife Service (see Practical Information above). The USFS maintains numerous campgrounds within the Chugach and Tongass National Forests (sites $4-5; 14-day max. stay). The BLM runs about 20 campgrounds throughout the state, all free except the Delta BLM campground on the Alaska Hwy. The National Park Service maintains campgrounds in Mt. Denali National Park, Glacier Bay National Park, and Katmai National Park and Preserve. (Sites $4-6.) The several campgrounds managed by the U.S. Fish and Wildlife Service are confined to the Kenai National Wildlife Refuge, Box 2139, Soldotna 99669. Government campgrounds in Alaska rarely have dump stations or electrical hookups.

Most towns, and all those with canneries, have tent cities for seasonal workers. These will cost you a few dollars a night to bunk down, and generally have poor facilities but interesting if fishy communities of student workers.

Remember to leave an itinerary at the offices of parks, hotels, state troopers, guides, and other authorities. This important safety measure takes little time to execute. Alaska looms bigger and more rugged than you can possibly imagine, with weather unpredictable at best.

For additional information about hiking and camping in Alaska, consult one of the following books: *55 Ways of Wilderness* or *Alaska's Parklands,* both published by the Mountaineer Press, or *Adventuring in Alaska,* published by the Sierra Club.

Southeastern Alaska (The Panhandle)

The Panhandle flings 500 mi. from the Gulf of Alaska to Prince Rupert, BC. The Tlingit (pronounced KLING-kit) and Haida (pronounced HI-duh) tribes have left a deep mark on the region, formed by a loose network of islands, inlets, and deep saltwater fjords, surrounded by deep valleys and rugged mountains. Temperate rain forest conditions, 60-odd major glaciers, and 15,000 bald eagles distinguish the Panhandle.

Southeastern Alaska is one of the few places in the world where the blast of a ferry boat heralds the day's important event. The 1000 islands and 10,000 mi. of coastline in the Alexander Archipelago are connected to each other and to Seattle by ferries run by the Alaska Marine Hwy. While the Interior and the Southcentral regions of Alaska have experienced great urban sprawl (by Alaskan standards), the communities of Southeastern Alaska cling to the coast. Gold Rush days haunt such towns as Juneau; others like Sitka hearken back to the era of the Russian occupation. The Alaska Marine Hwy. system provides the cheapest, most exciting way to explore the area. The state-run ferries connect Seattle, Ketchikan, Sitka, Juneau, and Haines, as well as some smaller Native American and fishing communities. You can avoid the high price of accommodations in smaller communities by planning your ferry trip at night and sleeping on the deck.

Ketchikan

A Ketchikan proverb claims, "if you can't see the top of Deer Mountain, it's raining, if you *can* see the top, it's about to rain." About 164 in. per year marinate this good-sized fishing and lumber town of 14,600, cradled at the watery base of the mountain; locals have to ignore the rain, or nothing would ever get done. The southernmost city in Alaska, Ketchikan is also the first port for ferries and cruise ships visiting the state. Elevated walkways and numerous staircases between multi-leveled streets keep tourists—the most important source of the town's income—high and dry.

The **Ketchikan Visitors Bureau,** 131 Front St. (225-6166), across from the cruise ship docks downtown, offers maps of a good walking tour. (Open daily 9am-6pm.) **Creek Street,** the red-light district that thrived until 1954, preserves Ketchikan's mining boomtown history. This is the only creek where both sailors and salmon went upstream to spawn. Revel in the sordid past of **Dolly's House,** 24 Creek St. (225-6329), a brothel-turned-museum. Hours vary; call ahead. (Admission $2.) Also on the walking tour is the **Totem Heritage Center,** 601 Deermount St., which houses 33 well-preserved totem poles from Tlingit and Haida villages. (Open Mon.-Sat. 8am-5pm, Sun. 9am-5pm. Admission $2, under 18 free. Free Sun. afternoon.) The **Tongass Historical Society Museum,** on Dock St., explains the region's past. (Open mid-May to Sept. Mon.-Sat. 8:30am-5pm, Sun. 1-5pm. Admission $1, under 18 free. Free Sun.) Ketchikan currently has the highest population of Native Alaskans in the southeastern portion of the state. **Saxman Native Village,** 2½ mi. south of town, displays 24 totems, including the world's largest, from original sites at villages in the Inland Passage. (Open daily 9am-5pm and on weekends when cruise ships in.) The reconstructed Tlinget community house and the 13 totems of the **Totem Bight** lies 13½ mi. north of town. Without wheels it is difficult to reach the park; taxis charge $7 each way to Saxman.

The **Ketchikan Youth Hostel (AYH)** (225-3319), kneels in the United Methodist Church on the corner of Grant and Main St. Kitchen is available; no beds, just comfortable mats on the floor. (Lockout 8:30am-6pm. Lights out 11pm. $4, nonmembers $7. Open June-Aug. No reservations.) Anne Rothrock, at the **Ketchikan Bed and Breakfast Network,** P.O. Box 3213 (225-8550), can find you slightly more glamorous accommodations. (Singles $35-65.) Camp on the shores of Ward Lake at the **Signal Creek Campground,** 6 mi. north on Tongass Hwy. from the ferry terminal. (Sites $5. Open in summer.) Privately run **Last Chance Campground,** 2.2 mi. from Signal Creek down Ward Lake, caters mostly to RVs. (Water, pit toilets. Sites $5.)

The most convenient supermarket to downtown is **Tatsuda's,** 633 Stedman, at Deermount St. just beyond the Thomas Basin. (Open daily 7am-11pm.) **Pioneer Pantry,** 124 Front St. (225-3337), across from the visitors bureau, offers clean-cut decor with a few tables and a long bar. Sandwiches ($4.25-7) include salad, fries, or soup. (Open daily 8am-6pm.)

Frequented by fishermen, the **Anchor Inn,** 834 Water St., a few hundred yards past the tunnel from downtown, will buoy your spirits with their big breakfast (eggs, hashbrowns, bacon, and toast) for $4.95. The **Ketchikan Café,** 314 Front St., shines with superb views of the Tongass Narrows, tasteful decor and melodious classical music filling full dinners ($15). (Open daily 8am-9pm.)

Ketchikan sits on an island 235 mi. south of Juneau, 90 mi. north of Prince Rupert, BC, and 600 mi. north of Seattle, WA. The town stretches for 12 mi. but rarely exceeds 7 blocks in width.

The magical **Misty Fjords National Monument** lies 30 mi. east of Ketchikan, accessible by boat or float plane. This 2.2-million-acre park offers great camping, guided tours in summer, and workshops year round. Call the Ketchikan Visitors Bureau or the **Misty Fjords Visitor Center,** on Mill St., for information about tours to the park (over $120). In town, the **Frontier Saloon,** 127 Main St. (225-4707), has live music Tuesday though Sunday in summer. (Open daily 10am-2am.) The **Arctic Bar** (225-4709), on the other side of the tunnel, is a more earthy fishers' haunt. (Open Sun.-Wed. 9am-midnight, Thurs.-Sat. 9am-2am.)

Ketchikan **buses** run about every ½ hour from Monday to Saturday 6:45am-6:45pm. (Fare $1, seniors and under 11 75¢.) Ketchikan's **ZIP code** is 99901; the **area code** is 907.

Sitka

Dominated by the snow-capped volcano of Mt. Edgecumbe, Sitka centered Alaskan history until the early 20th century. Russian explorer Vitus Bering made the first European landfall in Alaska in 1741, beginning decades of bloody fighting between Russian settlers and Tlingits. After defeating the Native Americans, the Russian company established "New Archangel" as the capital of Russian Alaska in 1804. The settlement stayed Russia's "Paris of the Pacific" for the next 63 years; visitors came here for the lure of money from sea otter pelts and the trappings of glittering society life. After the U.S. purchased Alaska in 1867, Sitka remained the territory's capital from 1884 until 1906.

The beautiful, onion-domed **Saint Michael's Cathedral** shows much of the earlier colonial influence. Decimated by fire in 1964 but rebuilt in accordance with the original, this Russian Orthodox Church still displays precious icons and vestments. (Open daily noon-4pm; 9am-4pm when cruise ships in. Donation required.) Historic **Castle Hill,** site of Baranof's Castle and Tlingit forts, offers an incredible view of Mt. Edgecumbe, an inactive volcano known as the "Mt. Fuji of Alaska." The U.S. bought Alaska here in October of 1867.

Stroll down the enchanting, manicured trails of the **Sitka National Historic Park** (Totem Park, as locals call it), at the end of Lincoln St. (747-6281), 1 mi. east of St. Michael's. The trails pass by many restored totems on the way to the side of the **Tlingit Fort,** where hammer-wielding chieftain Katlian almost held off the Russians in the battle for Alaska in 1804. The park **visitors center** offers audiovisual presentations and the opportunity to watch native artists in action in the Native American Cultural Center. (Open daily 8am-5pm.) The park service recently restored the **Russian Bishop's House,** across from Crescent Boat Harbor, to duplicate its 1842 appearance when built for its first resident, Bishop Ivan Veniaminor—though it probably didn't cost him $9 million. Unlike St. Mike's, you can even photograph the beautiful gold and silver icons. (Open daily 9am-5pm. Tours every ½ hr.)

The Sitka area offers excellent **hiking** opportunities—make sure to pick up the thick booklet *Sitka Trails* ($1) at the **USFS information booth,** in front of the Centennial Bldg. at Lincoln St. Several outstanding trails include the **Indian River Trail,** an easy 5.5-mi. trek up the valley to the base of **Indian River Falls,** and the 3-mi. uphill trail to the top of **Gavan Hill.** From downtown across the runway at the Japonski Island airport to the old WWII causeway, a fine 3-mi. trek heads past abandoned fortifications all the way to **Makhanati Island.**

Sitka has about eight bed-and-breakfast homes priced from $30 to $50 per person. The **visitors bureau,** Centennial Bldg., 330 Harbor Dr. (747-8601 or 747-5940; open Mon.-Sat. 8am-5pm), has a complete list. The small **Sitka Youth Hostel (AYH),** P.O. Box 2645 (747-8356), has army cots in the United Methodist Church on Edgecumbe and Kimsham St. Find the McDonald's, 1 mi. out of town on Halibut Pt. Rd., and walk 100 ft. up Peterson St. to Kimsham. (Kitchen facilities; 1 chore required. Lockout 9am-6pm. Curfew 11pm. $5, nonmembers $8.) **Sitka Hotel,** 118 Lincoln (747-3288) has cheap, clean rooms but the building itself is a little dingy. (Singles $38, with bath $43. Doubles $43, with bath $49. Senior discounts available.)

The USFS runs the **Starrigaven Creek Campground,** at the end of Halibut Pt. Rd., 1 mi. from the ferry terminal, 8 mi. from town. (Pit toilets. 14-day max. stay. Sites $5.)

Pick up your groceries at the **Market Center Grocery** at Sawmill Creek and Baranof St., uphill from the Bishop's House (open Mon.-Sat. 10am-8pm, Sun. noon-6pm), or close to the hostel at **Lakeside Grocery,** 705 Halibut Pt. Rd. (Open Mon.-Sat. 9am-9pm, Sun. 11am-7pm.) Fresh seafood is available from fishers along the docks or at **Sitka Sound Seafood** on Katlian St., which occasionally offers surplus fish for retail sale. **The Bayview Restaurant,** upstairs in the Bayview Trading Company at 407 Lincoln St. (747-5440), cooks up everything from *russkia ribnia blyood* ($7.25) to a Mousetrap sandwich (grilled cheese, $4), as well as great burgers. (Open Mon.-Fri. 11am-7pm.) **Staton's Steak House,** 228 Harbor Dr., across from the Centennial Bldg., alliterates delicious lunch specials of halibut and french fries ($7). (Open Mon.-Thurs. 11:30am, Sat. 8am-5pm, Sun. 8am-2pm.)

Sitka sits on the western side of Baranof Island, 95 mi. southwest of Juneau and 185 mi. northwest of Ketchikan. The O'Connell Bridge connects downtown to Japonski Island and the airport. **Sitka Tours** (747-8443) offers a shuttle bus and tour guide service from the ferry terminal (ride into town $2.50; tours $8). Sitka's **post office,** 1207 Sawmill Creek Rd. (747-3381), lies outside of downtown. (Open Mon.-Fri. 9am-5pm.) The **ZIP code** is 99835; the **area code** is 907.

Juneau

Built on a tiny strip of land at the base of noble Mt. Juneau, Alaska's capital city is the only one in the nation inaccessible by highway. This "Little San Francisco" mixes and matches Victorian mansions, log cabins, Russian Orthodox churches, "Federal" style *quonset* huts, and simple frame houses with shutters painted in Norwegian *rosemaling.* The potpourri of styles only hints at the richness of Juneau's history.

Tlingit Chief Kowee led Joe Juneau and Richard Harris up Gold Creek to the "mother lode" of gold in October, 1880. By the next summer, boatloads of prospectors found themselves at work in the already claimed mines. Twenty-five years later Juneau superseded Sitka as capital of the territory of Alaska. Poor Sitka. Mining ended in Juneau in 1941, but by then fishing, lumber, and the government had filled in to support the city's economy. Today, Juneau may exist for the government and tourists, but it remains a city of energy and grandeur.

Practical Information

Emergency: 911.

Visitors Information: Davis Log Cabin, 134 3rd St. (586-2284), at Seward St. Open Mon.-Fri. 8:30am-5pm, Sat. 10am-5pm; Oct.-May Mon.-Fri. 8:30am-4pm. **Marine Park Kiosk,** Marine Way at Ferry Way, right by the cruise ship unloading dock. Open May-Sept. daily 9am-6pm. **U.S. Forest and National Park Services,** 101 Egan Dr. (586-8751), in Centennial Hall. Makes reservations for USFS cabins in Tongass Forest. Write for application packet (see Camping under Ketchikan). Open daily 9am-6pm; late May-early Sept. Mon.-Fri. 8am-5pm.

Juneau International Airport: 9 mi. north of town on Glacier Hwy. **Alaska Air,** in the Baranof Hotel, Franklin at 2nd St. (789-0600 or 800-426-0333). To: Anchorage ($195), Sitka ($71), and Ketchican ($103).

Public Transport: Capital Transit (789-6901). Runs from downtown to Douglas, the airport, and Mendenhall Glacier. Leaves Marine Park for airport and glacier 5 min. after the hr. every hr. 7am-3pm. From 3-10pm, leaves Marine Park 35 min. after the hr. Fare to all points 75¢. **Eagle Express Line** (789-5460) runs vans to the airport ($5); also has an cheap tour of Juneau and Mendenhall Glacier (2½ hr., $19, children $9.50) or the glacier alone (1½ hr., $8). Departs 10:30am and 2:30pm from the Marine Park.

Alaska Marine Highway: P.O. Box R, Juneau 99811 (465-3940 or 800-642-0066). Ferries dock at the Auke Bay terminal at mile 13.8 Glacier Hwy. To: Bellingham, WA ($200, car and driver $680), Ketchikan ($66, car and driver $221), and Sitka ($22, car and driver $70).

Taxis: Capital Cab, 586-2772. Taku Taxi, 586-2121. Both conduct city tours and run to Mendenhall ($50 per 1½ hr.).

Car Rental: Rent-a-Wreck, Airport Blvd. (789-4111). $28 per day, 100 free mi., 15¢ each additional mi.

Help Lines: Crisis Line, 586-4337. Open daily 7-11pm.

Post Office: 709 W. 9th St. (586-7138). Open Mon.-Fri. 9:30am-5:30pm. General Delivery ZIP code: 99801.

Area Code: 907.

Juneau stands on the Gastineau Channel opposite Douglas Island, 650 mi. southeast of Anchorage and 900 mi. north of Seattle. The **Glacier Highway** connects downtown, the airport, the residential area of the Mendenhall Valley, and the ferry terminal.

Accommodations and Camping

For those not interested in Juneau's wonderful hostel, the **Alaska Bed and Breakfast Association**, P.O. Box 3/6500, #169 Juneau 99802 (586-2959), will provide information on rooms in local homes year-round. Most Juneau B&Bs lie uphill, beyond 6th St., offering singles from $40 and doubles from $45. Reservations are recommended.

Juneau Youth Hostel, 614 Harris St. (586-9559), at 6th. Clean, friendly, and properly managed. 24 bunk beds. Showers ($1), laundry, and kitchen facilities. Lockout 9am-5pm. $7, nonmembers $10. Make reservations well in advance for July and Aug.

Alaska Hotel, 167 S. Franklin St. (586-1000 or 800-327-9347), in the center of downtown. Handsome hotel made of dark wood restored to its 1913 Victorian decor. Singles $40, with bath $55. Doubles $45, with bath $61. Hot tubs noon-4pm $10.50, after 4pm $21.

Driftwood Lodge, 435 Willoughby Ave. (586-2280), behind the state office bldg. Courtesy van will whisk you to and from the airport, and sometimes out to Mendenhall Glacier. Singles $49. Doubles $62. With kitchen $59-62.

Campgrounds: Run by the forest service (see Practical Information above). 14-day max. stay. Mendenhall Lake Campground, Montana Creek Rd. Take Glacier Hwy. north 9 mi. to Mendenhall Loop Rd.; continue 3½ mi. and take the right fork. Nice view of and trails leading to the glacier. 61 sites. Fireplaces, water, pit toilets. Sites $5. Auke Village Campground, 15 mi. from Juneau on Glacier Hwy. 11 sites. Fireplaces, water, pit toilets. Sites $5.

Food

Travelers on a shoestring should head to the **Foodland Supermarket**, 631 Willoughby Ave., past the Federal Bldg. and near Gold Creek. (Open Mon.-Sat. 9am-7pm, Sun. 10am-6pm.) Seafood lovers should haunt **Merchants Wharf**, next to Marine Park. Always packed with tourists and locals, **Armadillo Tex-Mex Cafe**, 431 Franklin St., has fantastic "BBQ Hot Link Sausages" ($7) and heaping platefuls of T. Terry's nachos ($4.50). (Open Mon.-Sat. 11am-10pm, Sun. 4-10pm.) Complete with ferns and formica, the upscale **Heritage Cafe And Coffee Co.**, Franklin St., across from the Senate Bldg., is the best place in town for vegetarians, with excellent bottomless coffee ($1) and large sandwiches ($5). (Open Mon.-Wed. and Fri. 7am-11pm, Thurs. 7am-7pm, Sat. 8am-11pm, Sun. 9am-11pm.) Try **Silverbow Inn**, 120 2nd St. (586-4146), downtown, for budget-busting. French and U.S. cuisine served on antique oak tables. Lunch costs $7-13, dinner $12-24. Reservations are recommended. (Open Mon.-Fri. 11:30am-2pm, Sat.-Sun. 9am-2pm; off-season daily 5:30-9:30pm.

Sights

Juneau's greatest attraction is undoubtedly the **Mendenhall Glacier,** about 10 mi. north of downtown. The glacier, descending from the 1500-sq.-mi. Juneau Ice Field to the east, glowers over the valley where most downtown workers reside. At the glacier **visitors center,** rangers explain the relation of the glacier to the ice field and why the glacier is now retreating. Apparently the two have been quarreling of late. (Open daily 9am-6:30pm.) The rangers give good ecology walks everyday at 10:30am. The best view of the glacier without a helicopter is from the 3½-mi.-long East Trail. To reach the glacier, take the local public bus down Glacier Hwy. and up Mendenhall Loop Rd. until it connects with Glacier Spur Rd. From here it's less than a half-hr. walk to the visitors center. **Eagle Express Lines** runs excellent tours (see Practical Information), but you can see this hulk on your own.

In Juneau itself, the **Alaska State Museum,** 395 Whittier St. (495-2901), provides a good introduction to the history, ecology, and Native American cultures of "The Great Land." The museum's exhibits cover Alaska's four main Native American cultures: Tlingit, Athabaskan, Eskimo, and Aleut. (Open May 15-Sept. 15 Mon.-Fri. 9am-6pm, Sat.-Sun. 10am-6pm; off-season Tues.-Sat. 10am-4pm. Admission $1, students free.)

The unimpressive **state capitol** building, 4th and Main, offers summer tours daily from 9am to 5pm. Your time is better spent wandering uphill to **St. Nicholas Russian Orthodox Church** on 5th St. between North Franklin and Gold St. Built in 1894, the church is the oldest of its kind in southeastern Alaska. Services, conducted in English, Slavonic, and Tlingit are open to the public. One block farther uphill on 6th St. stands a 45-ft. **totem pole** carved in 1940.

Finding the best view of downtown is simply a matter of walking to the end of 6th St. and then up a steep 4-mi. trail to the summit of **Mt. Roberts** (3576 ft.). Miners flocked to "them thar hills" in the 1880s after Joe Juneau and Dick Harris found treasure in Gold Creek. Though no longer active in Juneau, the mines are active tourist sights which frequently host salmon bakes. The **Alaska-Juneau Mine** was the largest in its heyday. **Last Chance Basin,** at the end of Basin Rd., now holds Gold Creek's mining museum.

Juneau stalks one of the best hiking centers in the southeast. In addition to the ascent of Mt. Roberts, one popular daytrek is along the first section of the **Perseverance Trail,** which leads past the ruins of the historic **Silverbowl Basin Mine** behind Mt. Roberts. For more details on this as well as several other area hikes, drop by the state museum bookstore, the park service center, or any local bookstore to pick up *Juneau Trails,* published by the Alaska Natural History Association ($2). The rangers will provide copies of particular maps in this book at the park service center. (See U.S. Forest and National Park Service under Practical Information.)

During winter the slopes of the **Eaglecrest Ski Area** on Douglas Island (contact 155 S. Seward St., Juneau 99801, 586-5284), offer good skiing. ($19 per day, ages 12-18 $14, under 12 $10.) In summer, the Eaglecrest "Alpine Summer" self-guided nature trail soaks in the mountain scenery of untouched Douglas Island.

At night, tourists head to the **Red Dog Saloon** (463-3777) on S. Franklin. With imported sawdust on the floor and folksy frontier sayings on the wall, its live music on weekends beats the authenticity. Locals hang out farther up Franklin: the **Triangle Club** (586-3140), at Front St., attracts a hard-drinking set, while young people and the cruise ship crowd congregate at the **Penthouse,** on the fourth floor of the Senate Bldg. The **Lady Lou Revue** (586-3686), a revival of Gold Rush days, plays multiple shows daily at the Elks Lodge on Franklin. (Admission $14, Children $7.)

Northern Panhandle

North of Juneau, the inside passage grows in magnificence; the mountains become bigger and snowier, the whales and eagles friendlier. The **Alaska Marine Highway** can take you up to Haines ($14 from Juneau, ages 6-11 $8; vehicle up to 15 ft. $35).

Sleep on the ferry or stay up all night traveling through this land of many glaciers and soaring peaks.

Haines and the Haines Highway

In the early 1890s, adventurer Jack Dalton improved an old Native American trail from Pyramid Harbor up to the Yukon. During the Gold Rush from 1897 to 1899, thousands of stampeders paid outlandish rates for a quick trip into the Klondike. Thanks to the army's improvements on the road during World War II, the **Haines Highway** is now the most traveled overland route into the Yukon and the Interior from southeastern Alaska.

The area's main attraction is the convergence of over 3000 bald eagles (more than double the town's population) on the "Council Grounds" on the Chilkat Peninsula from November to January each year. Although both the federal and state government protect our national bird here in its national preserve, the land originally belonged to the Tlingit tribes, whose contemporary solvency relies on a mass production of winged totem poles. White trolling boats from the local harbor now replace talons in capturing salmon from the frigid waters.

Gentlemen prefer **Haines** as one of the only southeastern ports connecting with the Interior; not exactly a thrill a minute, but it provides shelter and sustenance. Backpackers can stay at the exquisitely trimmed **Portage Cove State Park,** ¾ mi. outside of town along Beach Rd., behind the clump of trees. (Pit toilets, water. Sites $5.) For indoor accommodations, the **Hotel Halsingland,** Box 1589 MP, Haines 99827 (766-2525), on the parade grounds south of town, is Haines's luxury address. (Singles from $30. Doubles $63.) Less luxurious, the **Bear Creek Camp & Hostel (AYH),** Box 1158, Haines 99827 (907-766-2202), on Small Tract Rd. almost 3 mi. outside of town. From downtown, follow 3rd Ave. out Mud Bay Rd. to Small Tract Rd.; call ahead for ferry pickup. (Kitchen. No curfew. $8, nonmembers $12. Cabins $30. Showers $2.)

Those wishing to forgo restaurant fare can hit **Howser's Supermarket** on Main St. (open Mon.-Sat. 9am-8pm, Sun. 10am-7pm). The store has a great deli bar, a salad bar with a large pasta selection ($2.50 per lb.), and chicken dinners ($5). At **Porcupine Pete's,** Main and 2nd Ave., a slice of pizza and soup ($3) prefaces good 95¢ ice cream. (Open daily 11am-10pm.) The **Bamboo Room,** 2nd Ave. near Main St. next to the Pioneer Bar, is a great breakfast spot, always crowded with fishermen on their way out to the nets. (Hot cakes and coffee $3.75, omelettes $4. Open daily 6am-10pm.)

The town maintains a **visitor information center,** 2nd Ave. near Willard St. (766-2234 or 800-458-3574), with information on accommodations and nearby parks. Pick up the *Haines is for Hikers* pamphlet. (Open June-Sept. Mon.-Sat. 8am-8pm, Sun. 10am-7pm.) The **Alaska Marine Highway Terminal,** 5 Mile Lutake Rd. (766-2111), is 4 mi. (a $7 cab ride) from downtown.

The **Haines Highway,** one of the most beautiful in the state, winds 40 mi. from Haines through the **Chilkat Range** past bright-blue glaciers, ice-cold waterfalls, and up through the Yukon Territory in Canada. **Chilkat State Park,** a 19-mi. drive up the highway, protects the largest population of bald eagles in North America—3500 all told. From November through January, travelers can see great numbers of eagles perched on birchwoods in the rivers or flying overhead. **Chilkat Guides** (766-2409), P.O. Box 170, leads four-hour raft trips down the Chilkat River when the eagles are flocking. ($70, rubber boots and ponchos provided.)

Haines even has a **post office** at the corner of 2nd Ave. and Haines Hwy. (open Mon.-Fri. 9am-5:30pm). General Delivery **ZIP code** is 99827; the **area code** is 907.

Anchorage

Anchorage, or "Los Anchorage," as some rural residents prefer to call it, is "big city" Alaska. Only 70 years ago, it remained wilderness area. But in 1914, railroads began bringing a steady flow of trains, pioneers, and oil, transforming Anchorage into the state's commercial center. Today half the state's population—more than 250,000 people—live here. Its international airport is among the world's busiest, serving passengers en route to East Asia. Perhaps the most remarkable fact about Anchorage is that everything—the glass and steel for the buildings, the food and merchandise the supermarkets and department stores—arrives here the same way people do. Everything travels 1500 miles of tortuous road or an expensive air journey, or by barge or container ship across one of the roughest seas in the world, giving Anchorage an aroma of prefabrication.

Practical Information

Visitor Information: Anchorage Convention and Visitors Bureau, 201 E. 3rd Ave. (274-3531). **Log Cabin Visitor Information Center,** W. 4th Ave. at F St. (274-3531). Open May-Sept. daily 7:30am-7pm; Oct.-April 8:30am-6pm. The **All About Anchorage Line** (276-3200) runs a recorded listing of each day's events. For information on fine arts and dramatic performances, call the **Artsline** (276-2787). Smaller visitor information outlets located in the airport near the baggage claim in the domestic terminal; in the overseas terminal in the central atrium; and in the Valley River Mall, first level.

Alaska Public Lands Information Center, Old Federal Bldg. (271-2737), 4th Ave. between F and G. An astounding conglomeration of 8 state and federal offices (including the **National Park Service, U.S. Forest Service, Division of State Parks,** and **U.S. Fish and Wildlife Service**) under one roof providing the latest information on the entire state. Open daily 9am-7pm.

Anchorage International Airport: a few miles southwest of downtown off International Airport Rd. The People Mover Bus runs 3 times per day to downtown, but the visitors center near the baggage claim can direct you to more frequent routes. **Dynair Charter Service** (243-3310) shuttles to downtown for $5; a cab costs about $13.

Alaska Railroad: 2nd Ave. (265-2494), at the head of town. To: Denali ($68), Fairbanks ($98), and Seward ($35). For more information write to Passenger Service, P.O. Box 107500, Anchorage 99510. Office open daily 8am-8pm; may close if no trains are arriving.

Public Transit: People Mover Bus (343-6543), in the Transit Center on 6th St. between G and H. Most buses from here to all points in the Anchorage Bowl. Buses run 5am-midnight. Cash fare 85¢, tokens 75¢; from hostel 60¢. Office open Mon.-Fri. 9am-5pm.

Taxi: Yellow Cab, 272-2422. **Checker Cab,** 276-1234.

Car Rental: Rent-a-Dent, 512 W. International Airport Rd. (561-0350), at the airport. $25 per day with 50 free mi., 20¢ each additional mi. Open daily 7am-11pm.

Alaska Marine Highway: 333 W. 4th St. (272-4482), in the Post Office Mall. No terminal, but ferry tickets and reservations. Open Mon.-Fri. 8am-5pm.

Time Zone: Alaska (4 hr. behind Eastern).

Post Office: W. 4th Ave. and C St. (277-6568), on the lower level in the mall. Open Mon.-Fri. 10:30am-5pm, Sat. 9am-3pm. **ZIP code:** 99510.

Area Code: 907.

Anchorage dominates the southcentral region of Alaska, 114 mi. north of Seward on the Seward Hwy., 304 mi. west of Valdez on the Glenn and Richardson Hwy., and 358 mi. south of Fairbanks on the George Parks Hwy. Due north of Honolulu, and equidistant from Atlanta and Tokyo, Anchorage can be reached by road, rail, or air.

The downtown area of Anchorage follows a grid. Numbered avenues run east-west, with addresses designated East or West from **C Street.** North-south streets letter alphabetically west of **A Street,** and name alphabetically east of A St. The rest of Anchorage spreads out along the major highways. The **University of Alaska-Anchorage** campus lies on 36th Ave. off Northern Lights Blvd.

Accommodations and Camping

Several bed and breakfast referral agencies operate out of Anchorage. Try **Alaska Private Lodgings,** 1236 W. 10th Ave., Anchorage 99511 (258-1717), or **Stay With a Friend,** Box 173, 3605 Arctic Blvd., Anchorage 99503 (344-4006). Both can refer you to singles from $45 and doubles from $55.

There are several free campgrounds outside the city limits; for information contact the **Alaska Division of Parks,** 3601 C St., 10th Floor, Pouch 7-001 Anchorage 99510, or the **Anchorage Parks and Recreation Dept.,** 2525 Campbell St. #404 (271-2500).

Anchorage Youth Hostel (AYH), 700 H St., (276-3635), 1 block south of the Transit Center downtown. Excellent location. Clean rooms with common areas, kitchens, showers, and laundry. Often family rooms. Lockout 9am-5pm. $10, nonmembers $13. Hardly ever full.

Qupquqiag Bed and Breakfast, 3801 Lois Dr. (562-4636) at Spanish Rd. 5 min. from the airport. Clean, comfortable rooms with a full breakfast share 2 baths. Singles $18, with king-sized bed $28.

Heart of Anchorage Bed and Breakfast, 4025 Hillcourt Dr. (279-7066 or 279-7703), off Diamond St. near June Lake. Convenient to downtown and close to the airport. Dorm beds $15. Singles $45. Doubles $55. Call ahead for reservations.

Northern Lights Thrift Apartments, 606 Northern Lights (561-3005). Clean rooms, but not much bigger than the queen-sized bed. Singles $35.

Centennial Park, 8300 Glenn Hwy. (333-9711), north of town off Muldoon Rd.; look for the park sign. Take bus #3 or 75 from downtown. Facilities for tents and RVs. Showers, dumpsters, fireplaces, pay phones, and water. 7-day max. stay. Check-in before 6pm in summer. Sites $12, seniors $8.

Lions' Camper Park, 5800 Boniface Pkwy. (333-1495), south of the Glenn Hwy. In Russian Jack Springs Park next to the Municipal Greenhouse. Take bus #12 or 45 to the Boniface Mall and walk 4 blocks. Connected to the city's bike trail system. 10 primitive campsites with water station, fire rings, and showers. Self-contained vehicles only. 7-day max. stay. Open daily 10am-10pm. Sites $12. Open May-Sept.

Food

By virtue of its size and largely imported population, Anchorage wears a culinary coat of many fabrics. Within blocks of each other stand greasy spoons, Chinese restaurants, and classy hotel-top French eateries. You will also find huge portions of Alaskan sourdough and seafood—halibut, salmon, clams, crab, and snapper. The city's finer restaurants line the hills overlooking Cook Inlet and the Alaska Range.

Skipper's, at 5 locations: 3960 W. Dimond Blvd., 702 E. Benson Blvd., 5668 DeBarr Rd., 601 E. Dimond Blvd., and 3611 Minnesota Dr. Good enough to make you think you're on Gilligan's Isle. Only $5.50 for all the fishfries, chowder, and cole slaw you can fit (with shrimp $8). Open daily 11am-11pm.

Burger Jim's, 704 4th St., at Gampbell. Jim takes his work seriously. Burger, fries and a Coke $3. Open Mon.-Sat. 10am-8:30pm.

Wing and Things, 529 I St. (277-9464), at 5th. Unbelievably delicious BBQ chicken wings. Decorated with wing memorabilia and inspirational poetry. 10 wings, celery, and sauce $6. Open daily 10am-9pm.

Downtown Deli, 525 W. 4th Ave., across from Log Cabin Visitors Center. Elegant deli owned by former mayor Tony Knowles. Try the delicious fried Monte Crisco ($7). Open daily 6am-11pm.

Simon and Seafort's Saloon and Grill, 420 L St. (274-3502). Down a few beers and a bowl of great clam chowder ($3.50) while taking in the view of Cook Inlet. Open Mon.-Fri. 11:15am-2:30pm and 5-10:30pm, Sat. noon-2pm and 5-10:30pm, Sun. 5-10:30pm. Saloon open daily 11:30am-11:30pm. Reservations recommended.

Sights and Entertainment

Mount Susitna, known to locals as the "Sleeping Lady," watches over Anchorage from Cook Inlet. For a fabulous view of Susitna, as well as the rest of the mountains that form a magnificent backdrop for Anchorage's ever-growing skyline, drive out to Earthquake Park at the end of Northern Lights Blvd. Once a fashionable neighborhood, the park now memorializes the disastrous effects of the Good Friday earthquake in 1964, a day Alaskans refer to as "Black Friday." Registering at 9.2 on the current Richter scale, this was the strongest earthquake ever recorded in North America. On a clear day, you can even see Mount McKinley far to the north.

The visitors center can set you up with a self-guided walking tour (3-4 hr.) of downtown. For guided walking tours, contact Historic Anchorage Inc., 542 W. 4th Ave. (562-6100, ext. 338), on the second floor of the Old City Hall. (Tours Mon.-Fri. at 10am. $2, seniors $1.) The People Mover sponsors less strenuous jaunts. Hop on one of the double-decker buses downtown for a $1 ride through the area. Gray Line Tours (277-5581) offers a 3½ hr. tour of Anchorage City, leaving daily at 8am and 3pm. ($20, under 12 $7.)

The Anchorage Museum of History and Art, 121 W. 7th Ave. (264-4326), at A St., features permanent exhibits of Alaska Native artifacts and art, as well as a Thursday night Alaska wilderness film series (at 7pm). (Open June-Aug. Mon.-Sat. 10am-6pm, Sun. 1-5pm; Sept.-May Tues.-Sat. 10am-6pm, Sun. 1-5pm. Admission $3.) To see real, honest-to-goodness Alaskan wildlife in the comfort of urbania, visit the Alaska Zoo, mile 2 on O'Malley Rd. (346-3242; open daily 10am-6pm; admission $3.50, seniors and ages 13-18 $2.50, under 13 $1.50).

For a tad more authenticity, head to the close confines of the nonprofit gift shop at the Alaska Native Medical Center at 3rd and Gampbell. Because many Native Americans pay for medical services with their own arts and handicrafts, the Alaska State Museum in Juneau sent its buyers here last year to outfit its exhibitions. Walrus bone ulus (knives, $15-60), fur moccasins and Eskimo parkas, and dolls highlight the selection. (Open Mon.-Fri. 10am-2pm.) Craftworks from Alaska's bush country, similar to those on display at the Museum of History and Art, are sold at the Alaska Native Arts and Crafts Showroom, 333 W. 4th Ave. (274-2932; open Mon.-Fri. 10am-6pm, Sat. 10am-5pm).

Anchorageans of all types and incomes party at Chilkoot Charlie's, 2435 Spenard Rd. (272-1010), at Fireweed. The bar has a rocking dance floor and a quiet, "share-my-space" lounge. Regular patrons always ask about the nightly drink specials. (Take bus #7 or 60.) Less crowded and more interesting is Mr. Whitekey's Fly-by-Night Club, 3300 Spenard Rd. (279-7726), a "sleazy bar serving everything from the world's finest champagnes to a damn fine plate of Spam." The house special gives you anything with Spam at half-price when you order champagne (free with Dom Perignon). Try Spam nachos or Spam and cream cheese on a bagel ($2-6). Monty Python would have loved it. Nightly entertainment ranges from rock to jazz to blues. (Open daily 3pm-2:30am.)

Denali National Park

Established in 1917 to protect its abundant wildlife, Denali National Park just happened to include Mt. Denali, "The Great One" in Athabascan. Denali looms as the tallest mountain in North America and the greatest vertical relief in the world base to summit. 20,320 ft. above sea level and 18,000 ft. above the meadows below, Denali is so big it makes its own weather; it is only visible about 20% of the summer. Missing the mountain doesn't ruin a Denali trip—the park's tundra, taiga, wildlife, and lesser mountains are also worthwhile.

The park is accessible by Alaska Railroad (see Anchorage Practical Information) or by car. Some vans and buses run from Anchorage to the park. Try Alaska Denali Transit (561-1078 or 273-3331) for $35. All visitors should check in at the Visitor Access Center (683-1266) less than a mile from Rte. 3. Permits are issued here to stay in the park's **campgrounds** ($10), ride the park's **shuttles** ($3), and for free **back-country camping.**

Kenai Peninsula

The Kenai (KEY-nigh) Peninsula sounds like Alaska in miniature. Like parts of Alaska's interior, Kenai's interior is flat; like the state itself, mountains ring the peninsula. Kenai relies on all three big sectors of Alaska's economy: oil, tourism, and fishing. The Russian influence on the Panhandle can be seen on the town of Kenai, the first Russian settlement in Alaska, and the urban sprawl of Anchorage and Fairbanks mimics road-side towns like Soldotna.

The Peninsula is the place Alaskans, especially those from Anchorage and Fairbanks, go for vacation when they don't go to the towns. Take a hint from the Native Alaskans: find an isolated campsite and fish. Every town can set you up cheaply with the requisite permits and gear. Stay in **USFS Campgrounds**, located every 8 or 10 mi. on Seward and Sterling Highways. There are also great spots in between—ask the locals. For more information on hiking, hunting, fishing, camping, and other recreational opportunities as well as regulations, contact the following: **Kenai Fjords National Park** (see Seward); **Alaska Maritime national Wildlife Refuge** (see Homer); **Kenai National Wildlife Refuge** (see Soldotna); **Chugach National Forest,** 201 E. 9th Ave. #206, Anchorage 99501 (261-2500); **State of Alaska, Division of Parks and Outdoor Recreations,** P.O. Box 1247, Soldotna 99669 (262-5581); and **State of Alaska, Department of Fish & Game,** P.O. Box 3150, Soldotna 99669 (262-9368). If you're unclear about which of these offices to contact, check out the **Alaska Public Lands Information Center** (see Anchorage Practical Information) for a referral.

The Kenai Peninsula is serviced by the **Seward** and **Sterling Highways,** as well as the **Alaska Marine Highway,** which runs between Homer, Seward, and Whittier, and extends out to Kodiak Island and Prince William Sound. To reach the peninsula from Anchorage, simply take any of the buses that run onto the New Seward Hwy. (such as the #2 or #9) as far south as possible and hitch. Hitching is common, safe, and easy.

Kenai

Kenai, the second-oldest white settlement in Alaska, is the largest (pop. 6546) and fastest growing city on the peninsula. First a Native Alaskan community, it became a Russian village when Fort St. Nicholas was built in 1791, then was established as an American settlement in 1889 when the U.S. Army built Fort Kenay. Kenai finally became known as the "Oil Capital of Alaska" with the 1957 discovery of oil in Cook Inlet. Vestiges of each era scatter throughout town: Native American artifacts, a Russian Orthodox church, a U.S. military installation, and oil rigs stationed in the inlet. Kenai remains one of the most beautiful cities on the Kenai Peninsula, with imperial Mt. Iliamna and the still-active volcano of Mt. Augustine looming nearby.

In the spring and early summer, be on the lookout for migrating white beluga whales in **Cook Inlet,** where they feed on sockeye salmon. The top of the bluff at Alaska and Mission Ave. and the overlook at the end of Forest Dr. are good spots to see these monstrous mammals, as well as Mt. Augustine and Mt. Iliamna, which come out on clear days.

The sights in town are comparatively uninspiring. The **Kenai Historical Museum** and **Fort Kenai** (283-7294 for both) lie next to one another on Overland and Mission St. The museum is threadbare and the fort a cheap replica of the 1868 original. (Both open Mon.-Sat. 10am-5pm.) Across from the fort is the **Holy Assumption Russian Orthodox Church,** the oldest building in Kenai and the oldest standing church in Alaska (1896). This national historic landmark contains a 200-year-old Bible. Call the priest at the rectory (283-4122) for a tour. (Donation $2.)

Recreational opportunities in the Kenai area abound. Check at the chamber of commerce for fishing charter information (prices are comparable to those in Soldotna); check with the forest service for canoeing and hiking opportunities. The **Captain Cook State Recreation Area,** 30 mi. north of Nikiski at the end of Kenai Spur Rd., offers swimming, canoe landing points on the Swanson River, superb fishing, and free camping. Contact the Kenai Chamber of Commerce for rules and regulations.

For a quick fix, hit **Pizza Paradiso** on Kenai Spur Rd. (283-7008) across from the Kenai Mall, for thick pizza with plenty of toppings (from $11 for large) and other Italian food. (Open daily 11am-7pm. Free delivery.) In the Kenai Mall **Harry Gaines Bar-B-Q Express** serves "the cowpoke" (sandwich, beans, and drink) for $4, with ribs and bread $6. (Open Mon.-Thurs. 9am-7pm, Fri.-Sat. 9am-8pm, Sun. noon-5pm.)

To save money, head for the city **campground** on Forest Dr. off Kenai Spur Rd., where you can spend three happy days camping for free. Near the beach not far from the center of town, the campground has fireplaces and covered picnic tables. Unfortunately, the noise from motorcycling patrons and other campers may annoy at night. Hard-sided campers can head for the **Kenai Riverbend Campground,** Porter Rd. (283-9489, 262-5715, or 262-1068); take Kalifonsy Beach Rd. off Spur Hwy. Every summer fishers descend to the Kenai Riverbend, one of the best salmon fishing holes in the world. The campground has everything you need: boat launching and rentals, rods and tackle, bait, laundry, and showers. Reservations are often necessary, though not required. (Singles $60. Doubles $65. Camping sites $12, RVs $18, with hookup $20.) The town itself also has two RV parks with full hookups: **Overland RV Park** (283-4648) and **Kenai RV Park** (283-4646), both in Old Kenai near Overland St.

Kenai, on the western Kenai Peninsula, preens 148 mi. from Anchorage and 81 mi. north of Homer. It can be reached via Kalifonsky Beach Rd., which joins Sterling Hwy. from Anchorage just south of Soldotna, or Kenai Spur Rd., which runs north through the Nikiski area and east to Soldotna. Both roads boast superb views of the peninsula's lakes and snow-capped peaks.

The town's **chamber of commerce** and **visitors center,** 401 Overland St. (283-7989), counsel in the log cabin on Main St. and Kenai Spur Hwy. (Open Mon.-Fri. 9am-5pm, Sat. 10am-4pm; winter Mon.-Fri. 9am-5pm.) Write to P.O. Box 497. Kenai's **ZIP code** is 99611; the **area code** is 907.

Soldotna

Once merely a fork in the road which people passed on their way to Homer, Kenai, or Seward, Soldotna has just now become the center of the Kenai Peninsula's government and recreation. Soldotna leads its neighbors on Kenai as the peninsula's premier fishing spot. World record salmon are consistently caught in the Kenai River, a few minutes from downtown. Kenai Riverbend Campground, halfway between Soldotna and Kenai (see Kenai) offers a $10,000 reward to the person who catches a salmon over the record 97 pounds. (Ten thousand dollars will go a long way toward paying for a budget vacation.)

Visitors to Soldotna come to fish. Pink, silver, and king salmon, as well as steelhead and dolly varden, swim in the waters all summer long. Numerous **fishing charters** run the river, usually $100-125 for a half-day of halibut or salmon fishing, or $150 for both (contact the visitors center for more information). There is no reason to spend so much, however. The downtown area is loaded with equipment rental shops that will fully outfit you with everything from bait to licenses for under $25 per day. Just wade into the Kenai and plunk in your line.

When fishing gets too slow-paced, you might participate in river sports at the **Kenai National Wildlife Refuge.** Dozens of **canoe routes** wind their way through the forest on one- to four-day journeys. A few places in town, including the Riverbend Campground and **The Sports Den,** will rent you boats (canoes $25 per day, $50 per weekend day). Otherwise, a drive along the highway from downtown will bring you into the wild depths just as quickly; more than one resident puts their boat in the front yard and hangs a "for rent" sign on it. Boat rentals are far from inexpensive, but the experience of gliding through some of the nation's most remote waterways merits the dip into your wallet. For free canoe route maps, write the Refuge Manager, Kenai National Wildlife Refuge, P.O. Box 2139, Soldotna 99669 (262-7021).

So you didn't come just for the fish. The **Damon Memorial Historical Museum,** at mile 3 on Kalifonsky Beach Rd., holds artifacts from Native Alaskan burial grounds and a large diorama. The **Kenai National Wildlife Refuge Visitors Center** (262-7021), off Funny River Rd. at the top of Ski Hill Rd. directly across from the visitors center, is a great source of information on the 197-million-acre refuge for moose, Dall sheep, and other wild game. It also has dioramas, victims of taxidermy, and a ½-mi. nature trail nearby. (Open Mon.-Fri. 8am-6pm, Sat.-Sun. 10am-6pm; Sept. 3-May 26 Mon.-Fri. 8am-4pm, Sun.-Sat. 10am-5:30pm.)

Because Soldotna began as a highway crossroads, there's plenty of fast food along the road downtown. Burger-chain prices are slightly higher than in the Lower 48, but budget-oriented visitors may still have to opt for the Big Mac over sit-down dining. **Sal's Klondike Diner,** Sterling Hwy. a ½-mi. from the river, cooks the best dinner in town. Try the "fisherman's buffet" breakfast ($5) or a sandwich with salad and fries ($4-6). Caffeine addicts will appreciate $1-per-hr. unlimited coffee. (Open daily 4am-10pm.) **Four Seasons,** 43960 Sterling Hwy., just north of the "Y," has some of the best homestyle food in Alaska from $5-11. (Open Mon.-Sat. 11am-3pm and 5:30-10pm.)

Backpackers can stay at nearby campgrounds and shell out $2 for hot, clean showers at the **River Terrace RV Park** at the river. **Swiftwater Park Municipal Campground** south of Sterling Hwy. at mile 94, and **Centennial Park Municipal Campground,** off Kalifonsky Beach Rd. near the visitors center, hunker down in the woods and have boat launches. Conveniently located on the river, the campgrounds feature excellent fishing and tables set aside for cleaning fish. (1-week max. stay. Sites $6.) Indoor accommodations are available at **Duck Inn,** mile 3 on Kalifonsky Beach Rd. (262-5041; write P.O. Box 3634, Soldotna 99669), by the Red Diamond Mall. All rooms have a private bath. (No reservations. Singles $49.50.)

Soldotna has a sizeable **visitors center,** P.O. Box 236 (262-1337), on the Sterling Hwy. and Kalifonsky Beach Rd., with a sizeable world record king salmon, serving Soldotna and the less-inhabited regions of the peninsula, such as Winilchik, Clam Gulch, and the Interior.

Homer

At first glance, Homer would appear no different from any other college town, complete with health food grocery stores and foreign films. Yet with no major university, Homer's lively progressive atmosphere results from the more sincere combination of a large artist's enclave, a hearty fishing community, and traditional Alaskan individualism.

Not only one of Alaska's most cherished towns, Homer also has the best museum and art gallery on the peninsula. **Pratt Museum,** 3779 Bartlett St. (235-8635), has exhibits by local artists and a feature on the Valdez oil spill. (Open daily 10am-6pm. Admission $3.)

Colorful, 3½-mi.-long **Homer Spit,** a long walk or a short drive from downtown, is the second-longest spit in the world. And they don't mean watermelon seeds. Boardwalks line its beaches, and shops perched on pilings hawk souvenirs and snacks.

Townsfolk gather at **Smoky Bay Cooperative,** 248 Pioneer Ave. (235-7242), where getting groceries makes a good excuse to hear town gossip. (Open Mon.-Sat. 8am-8pm, Sun. 10am-6pm.) Fresh seafood is available at **Icicle Seafood Market,** 842 Fish Dock Rd. at the base of the spit near the mouth of the Harbor.

The name of the **Sourdough Express Bakery and Coffee Shop,** 1316 Ocean Dr., says it all, except for the "delicious" added by the clientele. The all-you-can-eat breakfast buffet costs $8. (Open Tues.-Sun. 6am-10pm.) **Boardwalk Fish & Chips,** at the end of Cannery Row Boardwalk across from the harbormaster's office, is a local favorite. A big hunk of halibut with chips costs $5.75. (Open daily 11:30am-10pm.) As gathering ground for artists and young travelers, **Café Cups,** 162 Pioneer Ave., serves tasty unusual sandwiches ($4-5) and excellent coffee for a buck. (Open Mon.-Fri. 7am-11pm, Sat. 8am-midnight, Sun. 9am-4pm.)

Nightlife in Homer ranges from beachcombing at low tide in the midnight sun to discovering whether the **Salty Dawg Saloon,** under the log lighthouse at the end of the spit, ever really closes (open 11am-whenever, as the sign says). More adventurous readers should try finding the 1991 researcher/writer's blood donor card, located across the bar. For country fare head to **Alice's Champagne Palace,** 196 Pioneer Ave. (235-7650), a wooden barn with honkytonk music as well as nickel beers and dollar tacos on Monday nights. For more cultured types, the **Pier One Theater,** P.O. Box 894, Homer 99603 (235-7333 or 235-7951), performs classic plays on weekend nights from Memorial Day to Labor Day at their theater halfway down the spit. (Admission $7, seniors and children $5, families $20.)

Homer has two **municipal campgrounds,** one in town, one on the spit. In town, take Pioneer to Bartlett St., go uphill and take a left onto Fairview. The city allows camping on the edges of the spit, 2 mi. out. Sites ($5) have neither showers nor hookups. For these amenities, head to the **Homer Spit Campground** (275-8206), at the spit's tip (sites $6, with full hookup $13).

The visitors center has a list of **bed and breakfasts,** with rooms starting at $40. **Heritage Hotel,** 147 W. Pioneer (235-7787 or 800-478-7789), has rooms with shared baths, with private baths, and smiles. (Rooms $55-65.) The **Ocean Shores Motel,** 300 TAB Crittendon (235-7775), ebbs close to downtown, and has excellent views of the ocean on one side. (Singles from $45.)

Half-way down the spit is Homer's **visitors center** (235-7740; open Mon.-Sat. 7am-10pm). Beverly Wood literally wrote the book on Homer—*250 Ways to Enjoy Homer* ($3.50). She can set you up with everything from walking tours to expensive halibut charters to stories of Trojan horses.

Homer sits cozily on the southwestern Kenai Peninsula on the north shore of Kachemak Bay. The Sterling Hwy. links Bart's dad to Anchorage (225.8 mi. away) and the rest of the Kenai Peninsula. To reach the downtown area, bear left off the highway onto Pioneer Ave.; bear right onto Homer Bypass to venture onto the spit via the imaginatively named Spit Rd. The town and the spit are small enough to be crossed on foot, but the long walk from the far end of the spit to downtown covers 6 mi. Take a $3 bus ride if you must.

To reach Homer from Anchorage, drive along Seward Hwy. to Sterling Hwy. south. **Alaska Intercity Line** (800-478-2877 or 235-4235) will take you from one to the other for $37.50. The **Alaska Marine Highway** serves Homer from Valdez or Cordova ($126), Seward ($86) and Kodiak ($42).

Seward

History-hungry Seward stretches its origins to a small Russian shipyard built nearby by ubiquitous explorer Alexander Baranof in the 1830s. Not until 1903 was a new town built by U.S. railway workers as a supply center and shipping terminal. Today, the two blocks that comprise most of downtown Seward are strictly "middle America," with souvenir shops, gas stations, and pleasant, homey cafés. But only one glance up toward the peaks of Mt. Alice and Mt. Marathon or over to lovely Resurrection Bay will remind you that you're still amid Alaska's untamed and astonishing natural beauty. Recently Seward has become enshrined in state consciousness as the beginning of the Iditarod dog-sled trail.

The chamber of commerce's walking tour map of Seward passes many homes and businesses dating back to the early 1900s. A complete tour takes two to three hours. The **Resurrection Bay Historical Society Museum,** in the basement of City Hall (corner of 5th and Adams), features exhibits of Native Alaskan artifacts and implements used by pioneers. (Open June 15-Sept. 2 daily 11am-4pm. Admission

50¢, children 25¢.) The **K.M. Rae Educational Bldg.**, on 3rd Ave. between Washington and Railway, part of the Seward Marine Science Institute, contains marine life displays and results of institute research. (Open late May-Aug. Mon.-Fri. 1-5pm, Sat. 9am-5pm. Movie daily at 4pm. Free.)

Seward gives good day hike. Each fall locals run up nearby **Mt. Marathon,** which offers a great view of the city and ocean. You may walk. The trail begins at the end of Cowell St. **Exit Glacier,** billed as Alaska's most accessible glacier, chills 9 mi. west on the road that starts at Seward Hwy. mile 3.7. From the **ranger station** (no phone; open Mon.-Fri. 9am-5pm) only the intrepid should take the 4-mi. steep and slippery trail to the magnificent **Harding Ice Field.**

Known as the gateway to Alaska because of its position as the southern terminus of the railroad, Seward also serves as the point of entry to the **Kenai Fjords National Park.** Much of the park consists of a coastal-mountain system with an abundance of wildlife. The best way to see this area involves a boat on the bay; pick up the list of charters at the Park Service visitors center or from companies along the boardwalk next to the harbormaster's office. Most run $70-100 per day, $45-50 per half-day. For more information, contact **Kenai Fjord Tours** (224-8068 or 224-8069), **Kendi Coastal Tours** (224-7114), **Mariah Charters** (243-1238), or **Quest Charters** (224-3025; open in summer daily 6am-10pm).

Fishing tastes heavenly in the Seward area. Salmon and halibut thrive in the bay, grayling and dolly varden right outside of town. Some people just fish off the docks. For a less luck-oriented approach, try a fishing charter, available for both halibut and salmon throughout the summer. Prices run from $90-100, with all gear provided. Call Quest Charters or Mariah Charters.

Downtown Seward has seafood restaurants, hamburger joints, and pizza parlors galore. Pick up groceries at **Bob's Market,** 207 4th Ave. (Open Mon.-Sat. 9am-7pm, Sun. noon-6pm.) **Bob's Kitchen,** at 4th Ave. and Washington St., serves up the biggest Alaskan breakfast ever—2 eggs, 2 bacon, 2 sausage, toast, hash browns, biscuit with gravy, and coffee ($5). Bob's a busy guy. (Open daily 6am-8pm.) The **Breeze Inn,** Small Boat Harbor, is not your average hotel restaurant. Breeze in for the huge all-you-can-eat buffet (lunch $8, dinner $11). Breakfasts include the "2-2-2" (2 eggs, 2 bacon, and 2 pancakes, for $5). (Open Mon.-Fri. 7am-10pm, Sat.-Sun. 8am-10pm.) Also look for Bob at **Seward Salmon Bake and Bar-B-Q** in the municipal boat harbor, across from the national park center. Serves great salmon ($10) and by far the best barbecue in Alaska ($5-6.75). (Open daily 11am-9pm.)

Seward's three municipal campgrounds are typical: no showers, pleasant view, grassy sites. The best, **City Greenbelt Camping Area,** sits off 7th Ave. (Sites $4.25.) The nearest full-hookup RV park is **Kenai Fjords** on 4th Ave. (Sites $9, with full hookup $13.50.) Bob runs a beautifully restored hotel, the **Van Gilder,** at 308 Adams St. (224-3525), with clean, frontier-style rooms. (Singles $50, with baths $60. Doubles $60, with bath $85.) One step down in price, quality, and Bob is **Tony's Hotel and Bar** (224-3045), on Railway at 4th St. Above the bar are surprisingly clean rooms for $38 per night, $100 per week.

Seward bobsleds on the southeast side of the Kenai Peninsula, in Resurrection Bay. It connects to Anchorage due north on the 127-mi. Seward Hwy. Seward, NE lies 4135 mi. southeast. Downtown cross streets are numbered, while the longer north-south avenues are named after U.S. presidents, sequentially, starting with Washington. **Visitor Information** (224-3094) in the streetcar Seward on 3rd and Jefferson, offers an interesting walking tour. (Open Mon.-Fri. 9am-5pm.) The **Seward Ranger Station,** 334 4th Ave., has information on local hikes and trails, while the **National Park Visitor's Center,** 1212 4th Ave. (224-3375), near the harbor, has information, films, and exhibits on the Kenai Fjords and western Prince William Sound. (Open daily 8am-7pm.)

Seward's **post office** swears by 5th and Madison. (Open Mon.-Fri. 9:30am-4:30pm, Sat. 10am-2pm.) The **ZIP code** is 99664; the **area code** is 907.

CANADA

Canada is the second largest country in the world (after the USSR), but one of the most sparsely populated. Ten provinces and two territories sprawl over more than 9,000,000 square kilometers of land, spanning seven time zones. But numbers don't tell Canada's story. Framed by the rugged Atlantic coastline to the east and the Rockies to the west, Canada spreads north from fertile farmland and urbanized lakeshores to barren, frozen tundra. Cities range from cosmopolitan Montréal and Toronto to the leisurely, Old-World Québec City, to bold and youthful Calgary.

The name Canada derives from the Huron-Iroquois world "kanata," meaning "village" or "community." The diversity of Canadian backgrounds and the geographic segregation of the French- and English-speaking peoples make labeling Canada today difficult. As the offical languages of Canada, both French and English share equal status in federal government; nonetheless, only about 15% of Canadians are bilingual French-English. Indeed, the country's population ranges from the Inuit of northern Canada and other Native American peoples, to the French of Québec province, to the very-British British Columbia. Though such separate and distinct cultures may all call for recognition and question the existence of a Canada at all, they also make it a vibrant, welcoming place.

Travel

Canada's only international border, with the U.S., is easily accessible from Boston, New York City, Detroit, Chicago, Minneapolis/St. Paul, and Seattle. Canada's highway system makes driving easy, even in remote areas of the country, though gas is twice as expensive as in the U.S. (50-60¢ per liter). Because of excellent public transportation both within urban centers and throughout the country, even budget travelers can manage without a car. Canada is bilingual, but communication should not pose a problem if you speak only English, and people are generally tolerant of visitors from all over the world.

Student Travel

The **Canadian Federation of Student Services** sponsors a number of student travel assistance organizations. The **Studentsaver National Student Discount Program** provides 10-25% discounts on food, clothing, books, and other goods at some Canadian retail stores with the International Student Identity Card (ISIC), available at most travel agencies. A list of outlets that give discounts, details on the program, and a great deal more advice for student and budget travelers are available at **Travel CUTS** (Canadian Universities Travel Service Ltd.). A fully licensed national travel agency, CUTS will help you plan trips within Canada or to other countries. The federation also publishes *Canadian Student Traveler,* available free at Canadian universities.

Headquarters for CFS Services and Travel CUTS are at 187 College St., Toronto, Ont. M5T 1P7 (416-979-2406). Other Travel CUTS locations (all open regular business hours) include:

Montréal: Université McGill, 3480 McTavish, Montréal, Québec H3A 1X9 (514-398-0647).

Toronto: 74 Gerrard St. E., Toronto, Ont. M5B 1G6 (416-977-0441).

Vancouver: Student Union Building, University of British Columbia, Vancouver, B.C. V6T 1W5 (604-228-6890).

Victoria: Student Union Building, University of Victoria, Victoria, B.C. V8W 2Y2 (604-721-8352).

Money

During the past several years, the Canadian dollar has been worth 80-85% of (or 20-25% less than) a U.S. dollar. Symbols for dollars ($) and cents (¢) are the same with Canadian currency—all prices in the Canada section of this book are for Canadian dollars unless otherwise noted. Banks provide a reasonable exchange rate, but often charge a handling fee and shave off several percentage points. Exchange houses have the best rates and hours, with most open on weekends when banks close. U.S. currency is accepted by vending machines, parking meters (not a good habit to pick up), and most businesses. Though they are under no legal obligation to give you any back, let alone all of the difference, most businesses do.

Customs

The U.S.-Canadian border is the longest undefended border in the world; to cross it, U.S. visitors need only proof of citizenship. If you are under 18 and unaccompanied by an adult, you must have written consent from your parent or guardian. Non-U.S. citizens must have a Canadian visa for entry. Visitors from other countries should have their papers in good order, as customs officials on both sides of the border often act tough with anyone with a foreign accent. Those wishing to bring pets into Canada must bring certification of the animals' vaccination against rabies. Visitors who spend at least 48 hr. in Canada may take back to the U.S. up to US$400 worth of goods duty-free, including up to 100 non-Cuban cigars, one carton of cigarettes, and 32 oz. of liquor. U.S. residents who stay in Canada for less than 48 hr. may return with US$25 worth of duty-free merchandise (40 oz. of alcohol, no tobacco). There are several helpful customs offices located throughout Canada. Write for their helpful pamphlet *I declare/Je declare* at Revenue Canada Customs and Excise Department, Communications Branch, Mackenzie Ave., Ottawa, Ont. K1A UL5 (613-957-0275).

Telephones and Mail

Telephone numbers in Canada have seven digits, and are preceded by a three-digit area code as in the U.S. Direct phone calls may be made from one country to the other without the need for operator assistance. Long-distance calls within Canada and to the U.S. are 35-65% cheaper in the evening or on weekends. Local calls cost 25¢ throughout Canada. **Canada Post** requires a 39¢ Canadian postage stamp for all domestic first class mail. Letters or postcards sent to the U.S. cost 45¢. Since postage prices increase yearly, expect to pay a bit more in 1991. When sending mail to destinations within Canada, be sure to note the six-character **postal code** (of numbers and letters). Even with the postal code, expect items passing through the Canadian mail system to take 1-2 days longer than they would south of the border.

Measurements

Canadians use the metric system (as do all but two nations in the world). For residents of those 2 nations, simple conversions are as follows:

Distance: 1 centimeter (cm) — .394 inches, 1 meter (m) — 3.281 feet (ft.) and 1.094 yards, 1 kilometer (km) — .621 miles (mi.).

Volume: 1 liter (l) — .2642 gallons;

Mass or Weight: 1 gram (g) — .0353 ounces, 1 kilogram (kg) — 2.2046 pounds.

Holidays

Canadians celebrate both national and provincial holidays. All government offices and most businesses close on national holidays, except on Easter Monday and Remembrance Day. Check in local newspapers for a list of what is and isn't open. The following is a list of the major national holidays in 1991: New Year's Day (Jan. 1); Good Friday (April 13); Easter Monday (April 16); Victoria Day (May 21); Canada Day (July 1); Simcoe Day (first Monday in August); Labor Day (Sept. 3);

Thanksgiving (Oct. 8); Remembrance Day (Nov. 11); Christmas Day (Dec. 25); and Boxing Day (Dec. 26).

Alcohol

The drinking age, while lower than in the U.S., is still neither as token nor as low as in many countries. The age in Alberta, Manitoba, Québec, and Prince Edward Island is 18; in all other provinces and territories 19. You can import 40 oz. liqour or wine, 288 oz. beer or ale into Canada only if you can document the above ages.

Accommodations

The price of Canadian hotels, combined with the lack of budget motel chains, may force budget travelers toward the wilderness. Almost every city has families that take travelers into their **Bed and Breakfasts** for $25-60. A similar but more structured lodging option is the **farm vacation**. With a minimum duration of one week (average rate about $250 per person), the family-oriented farm vacation system integrates guests into the daily life of farm families in the Maritimes (New Brunswick, Nova Scotia, and Prince Edward Island), Québec, and Ontario. Guests eat with the family and are encouraged to help with the chores. For travelers who prefer urban lodgings, the network of **YMCAs** and **YWCAs** among the larger cities offers clean and affordable rooms, generally in downtown areas. In summer, other budget choices include university dorms, open for travelers early to mid-May and closing mid- to late August.

The **Canadian Hostelling Association (CHA)**, founded in 1933, maintains over 70 hostels nationwide. Graded "basic," "simple," "standard," or "superior," hostels ($4-14) have kitchens, laundries, and often meal service. Open to members and non-members, most hostels allow a maximum stay of three nights. For hostels in busy locations, reservations are recommended. In addition, hostelers must have a sleeping bag or "sleepsheet;" rentals are usually available for $1. The CHA, affiliated with the International Youth Hostel Federation, generally upholds the same rules and rates as American Youth Hostels. For information, the write Canadian Hostelling Association, 1600 James Naismith Dr., Gloucester, Ont. K1B 5N4 (613-748-5638).

Members of CHA receive a $1-4 reduction in room rates and the opportunity to take advantage of concessions at many local businesses. Furthermore, CHA membership includes membership in IYHF, which allows for discounts at hostels around the world. Likewise, IYHF memberships purchased in any country are valid in Canada. Memberships are valid from October 1 of the year purchased until December 31 of the following year.

Canada's **national** and **provincial parks** entice travelers with vast expanses of excellent campgrounds. National parks sprinkle Canada: 12 in western Canada, six in the central provinces, seven in the Atlantic Provinces, and four in the Yukon and Northwest Territories (all free). Both provincial and national parks prohibit campfires on the beach, and no camping is allowed in picnic parks.

Transportation

Train Travel

VIA Rail handles all of Canada's passenger rail service. VIA Rail's routes are as scenic as Amtrak's and its fares are often more affordable. Fares vary according to season: in off-season, from September 15 to June 15, **Advance Purchase Excursion (APEX)** tickets, may shave as much as 40% off the fare for destinations within Ontario and Québec. Best for transcontinental travel in summer is the **Canrailpass** (for non-Canadian citizens only) which is valid for 45 days and allows unlimited travel and unlimited stops. (Students $449. Non-students, $499.) **Amtrak** links with VIA Rail in Toronto and Montréal. For more information, contact VIA Rail Canada, P.O. Box 8116, Montréal, PQ H3C 3N3 (in Québec 800-361-5390; in Ontario 800-665-8630; outside Canada 800-561-3949).

Bus and Car Travel

The major inter-provincial bus carriers are **Gray Coach, Greyhound, Voyageur,** and **Charterways.** Greyhound makes the most convenient links between the Canadian and U.S. bus networks. The **Trans-Canada Highway,** the world's longest national highway, stretches 8000 mi. from St. John's, Newfoundland to Victoria, British Columbia. Drivers in Canada must have proof of insurance coverage; because the minimum required is higher than in the U.S., check with your insurance company to ensure sufficient coverage. Drivers entering Canada from the U.S. must also carry their vehicle registration certificate. If the car is borrowed, have on hand a letter of permission from the owner; if rented, keep a copy of the rental contract for use when crossing the border. In addition, radar detectors are illegal in Canada. British Columbia, Ontario, and Québec law requires that auto travelers wear seatbelts.

A valid driver's license from any country (including the U.S.) is good in Canada for three months. Although international bridges, tunnels, and ferries charge a fee, highways are toll-free. Along the Trans-Canada Hwy., some toll-free ferries are part of the highway system and operate during daylight hours. In summer, cross early in the morning or late in the afternoon to avoid traffic.

If you plan to rent a car in Canada, investigate the discount **White-Corp** rate, offered to Canadian Hostelling Association members over 21. In addition, agencies dealing in late-model automobiles rent cars throughout Canada for significantly less than their U.S. counterparts. Finally, you can contact one of the numerous auto-transport agencies. If you are 21, have a valid driver's license, and agree to travel at least 400 mi. per day on a reasonably direct route to the destination, you could have an entire car for the price of the gasoline.

Québec

Home to more than 90% of the country's citizens of French origin, Québec is also Canada's largest province at over 900,000 square kilometers. Most *québecois* feel a primary allegiance and sense of identity with their province rather than with their country. Culture-shocking or not, a trip to Québec cuts to the heart of French-Canadian tradition; its language, culture, and institutions set the region and people apart from the rest of Canada which, like much of the U.S., evolved from British colonization. Few *québecois* greet you with a robust hello but almost all will converse in English if asked. Street signs may confuse monolinguists since provincial law requires that they be in French, but Québec, like any other distinct culture, should be understood as well as experienced. Even though the province's separate identity is expressed in every level of society, it continues to fight a political and legal battle as the leaders of Canada take on those of Québec. Citizens of the province rejected splitting off from their fellow Canadians in a 1980 referendum, but 1990 activity in Québec and in smaller provinces seeking their own independence now favors establishing a sovereign nation of Québec. "If you can't sleep together," quipped former Québec Premier René Lévesque, "you might as well have separate beds."

Yet Prime Minister Brian Mulroney still wants to cozy up at night; business leaders prefer an economically healthy and vital Québec as a trading partner in the day. Fearing national calamity if Québec secedes, Mulroney has scrambled to incorporate the *québecois* smoothly into Canada's 1982 Constitution, which the province refused to sign until granted recognition as a "distinct" though not necessarily separate society within Canada. The 1987 Meech Lake Accords granted that distinction, but a brawl over ratification makes Québec's future as part of Canada uncertain

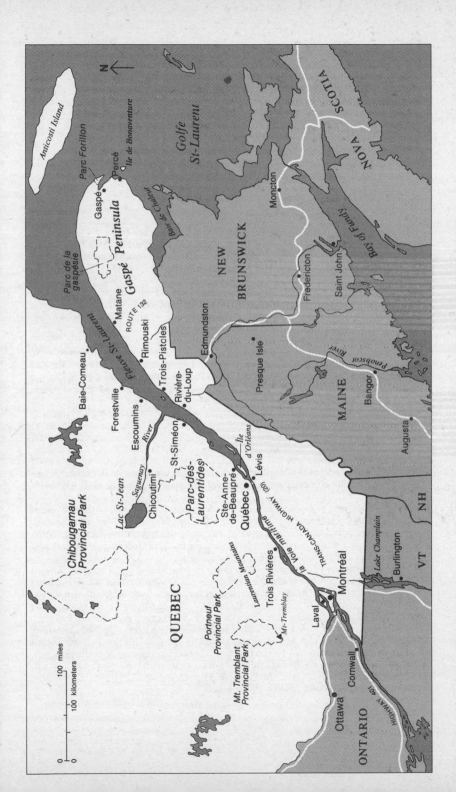

if not unlikely. Yet behind all the hubbub, the people of Québec have engaged in a struggle to maintain their identity; the provincial motto *Je me souviens* not only serves as a way of life but as a sign of the prosperous future awaiting a people who refuse to forget their past.

Practical Information

Capital: Québec City.

Tourist Information: Tourisme Québec, c.p. 20,000, Québec G1K 7X2 (Montréal 514-873-2015; Québec, elsewhere in Canada, and the U.S. 800-363-7777.).

Time Zone: Eastern.

Alcohol: Legal drinking age 18.

In almost every town **tourist information offices** are easy to find. Look for the square brown signs with a question mark. Excellent transportation by train or bus covers the entire province. The one bus line in Québec, **Voyageur,** also serves Ontario. Besides its regular fares, Voyageur offers a **Tour Pass** ($115) in summer for unlimited travel. Call for dates (Montréal 514-842-2281, Québec City 418-524-4692). **VIA Rail** of Canada provides the main railroad for passenger and tourist service, with frequent runs between major urban centers. VIA Rail also offers a fixed-cost travel card for unlimited travel for non-Canadian citizens only (45 days $499, students $449).

Traveling by **car** in Québec can be expensive, since gas is heavily taxed. You'll pay about 50-60¢ per liter (3.8 liters—1 gallon). Québec requires that you have enough liability coverage to meet the insurance requirement of your home state or country. For more information, call the **Régie de l'assurance automobile du Québec** (Québec Automobile Insurance Board; 418-643-7620). Parking and traffic violation fines vary from city to city in Québec. Call 418-643-4134 for more information.

Most of Québec is rural and sparsely populated. Just outside the major cities you can visit magnificent lakes, mountains, forests, cliffs, waterfalls, and beaches in regions like la Gaspésie and les Laurentides. Popular provincial activities include fishing, canoeing, hunting, and skiing. Shimmering summer and brilliant fall encourage people to bike, camp, windsurf, and waterski. Fishers and hunters must obtain a Québec permit. Contact the Ministère du Loisir, de la Chasse et de la Pêche, Service de la Réglementation et des Permis, 150, blvd. St-Cyrille E., Québec G1R 4Y3 (418-890-5349).

In addition to the many private campgrounds, look for camping in the **provincial parks** and **forest reserves** (sites $10-21.50; call Tourisme Québec for information). The latter are primarily wilderness areas but some offer primitive camping. More typical campgrounds abound in the provincial parks. The Québec government also arranges **farm accommodations** ($35, ages 10-14 $30, 6-9 $20, 1-5 $17; meals included). Experience rural Québec hospitality first-hand and practice your French in a family setting by writing about a week in advance to Fédération des Agricoteurs du Québec/Vacances-Familles, Stade Olympique, 4545, ave. Pierre-de-Coubertin, c.p. 1000, Succursale "M", Montréal P.Q., H1V 3R2 (514-252-3138). Québec also has at least 26 youth hostels. Many provide access to excellent recreational facilities. For information, contact **La Fédération Québécoise de l'Ajisme** (Québec Hostelling Federation), 3541 Aylmer St., Montréal H2X 2B9 (514-843-3317). For short stays try one of the many **Gîtes du Passant** (bed and breakfasts) throughout the province. Check accommodations listings for networks that will place you in a B&B. **Vacances-Familles,** 1661, ave. du Parc, Ste-Foy, Qc. G1W 3Z3 (514-282-9580), a travel agency in Québec, locates cheap hotels.

Montréal

Easily the largest city in Québec, Montréal contains the largest community of French speakers in the world, outside of France. Montréal's size at once represents the essence of and allows a diverse challenge to French-Canadian traditions. Almost 350 years after the French founded the original colony of Ville-Marie de Montréal (that anniversary will be celebrated in 1992), old European cultures merge with the influx of recent immigrants to form modern Montréal. The first French settlement in 1647 aimed at Christianizing the Native Americans in the village of Hochelaga. By the 19th century, the influx of rich British and Scottish merchants, the development of the continent's railroad, and strategic use of Montréal's two rivers, the Saint-Laurent and the Ottawa, all combined to make the city the center of trade for the New World.

This sometimes forced melange of distinct peoples gives this Canadian city a worldly atmosphere, combining a strong sense of tradition and a healthy alternative lifestyle. Downtown has moved north from **Vieux Montréal** (Old Montréal), which has the greatest concentration of 17th-, 18th-, and 19th-century buildings in North America. Today, the city stretches out from the river and burrows underground in a network called, fittingly, the Underground City.

Practical Information

Emergency: 911.

Visitor Information: Infotouriste, 1001, rue du Square-Dorchester (873-2015; outside Montréal 800-363-7777), on Dorchester Sq. between rue Peel and rue Metcalfe. Métro: Peel. Free city maps and guides, plus extensive restaurant and accommodations listings. Open daily April 15-May 20 9am-6pm; May 21-June 10 8am-6pm; June 11-Sept. 2 8am-7:30pm; Sept. 3-Oct. 7 9am-6pm; Oct. 8-March 31 9:30am-6pm. Branch offices in **Old Montréal,** 174, rue Notre-Dame est. Open early June-Sept. 2 daily 9am-7pm; fall and winter Mon.-Fri. 9am-1pm and 2:15-5pm, Sat.-Sun. 9am-5pm. Also at **Dorval International Airport.** Open daily 1-8pm.

Tourisme Jeunesse (youth tourist information), 4545, Pierre de Coubertin (252-3119), right on the Olympic site. Métro: Pie-IX. Free maps; youth hostel information and memberships available. Open Mon.-Fri. 9am-5pm. Mailing address: c.p. 1000, Succursale "M," Montréal P.Q., H1V 3R2. More convenient to the center of town is **Travel CUTS,** at the McGill Student Union, 3480, rue McTavish (849-9201). Métro: McGill. They also sell the ISIC and provide budget travel information. Open Mon.-Fri. 9am-5pm.

Language: The population of Montréal is 80-85% French-speaking. Most citizens are bilingual, but prefer to avoid English. If you know French, speak it. You're less likely to be dismissed as a mere tourist.

Consulates: U.S., 1155, rue St-Alexander (398-9695). Open Mon.-Fri 8:30am-2pm. **U.K.,** 1155, rue de l'Université (866-5863). Open Mon.-Fri. 9am-12:30pm and 2-4:30pm. **Germany,** 3455, Mountain (286-1820). Open Mon.-Fri. 9am-noon.

Currency Exchange: Bank of America Canada, 1230, rue Peel (393-1855). Métro: Peel. Open Mon.-Fri. 8:30am-5:30pm, Sat. 9am-5pm, Sun. 10am-4pm. **Deak International Exchange,** 625, blvd. René-Lévesque ouest (397-4029). Open daily 9am-5pm. Dorval Airport location (636-3582) open daily 6am-9pm for all currencies, 6am-11pm for U.S. dollars. **National Commercial-Foreign Currency,** 1250, rue Peel (879-1300). Métro: Peel. Another office at 390, rue St-Jacques (879-1300). Métro: Square-Victoria. Open Mon.-Fri. 8am-5pm, Sat. 8am-3pm. Most cafés will take U.S. dollars and give you Canadian change, but at a worse exchange rate than the banks. Some banks charge $2 to cash traveler's checks. Many instant teller machines in Montréal will accept a cash card from a bank.

American Express: 1141, blvd. de Maisonneuve ouest (284-3300). Métro: Peel. Open Mon.-Fri. 9am-5pm.

Airports: Dorval (633-3105), 10 mi. from downtown. From the Lionel Grioulx Métro stop, take bus #211 to Dorval Shopping Center, then transfer to bus #204. **Aerocar** (397-9999) runs buses from the airport to the Queen Elizabeth Hotel, the Sheraton Center, Terminus Voyageur (the stop closest to St-Denis), and the Bonaventure Hotel (Mon.-Fri. every 20 min., Sat.-Sun. every ½ hr.; $7). **Mirabel International** (476-3040), 35 mi. from downtown. Aerocar buses connect this airport to the city's central train station (daily 11am-11pm departures from Mirabel, 11am-10pm departures from Montréal; $12).

Trains: Central Station, 800, rue de la Gauchetière. Métro: Bonaventure. Served by **VIA Rail** (871-1331) and **Amtrak** (800-426-8725). Direct service to: Québec City (3 per day, 3 hr., $32); Toronto (5 per day, 5 hr., $65); Vancouver (3 per week, $397); New York City (2 per day, US$72). Inconvenient connections to Boston (US$90, change trains in New London). Ticket counters open daily 7am-11:30pm.

Buses: Terminus Voyageur, 505, blvd. de Maisonneuve est (842-2281). Métro: Berri de Montigny. Voyageur offers 10-day unlimited tour passes for $115 in summer, which will take you all over Québec and Ontario. **Greyhound** serves New York City (5 per day, US$80.50). **Vermont Transit** serves Boston (2 per day, US$72); Burlington, VT (3 per day, US$18); and Québec (US$27.50). Open 24 hr.

Public Transport: CTCUM Métro and Bus, 288-6287. A safe and efficient network, with Métro subway service to the city core only. The 4 Métro lines and most buses operate daily 5:30am-12:30am; some have night schedules as well. Get network maps at the tourist office, or at any Métro station toll booth. Fare for trains or bus $1.25, under 18 55¢, 6 tickets $6, unlimited monthly passes $32.75.

Car Rental: Beau Bazou, 295, rue de la Montagne (939-2330). Métro: Lucien l'Allier. $22.75 per day plus 9¢ per km; insurance included. Open Mon.-Fri. 9am-9pm. Must be 25 with credit card. Reserve in advance. **Via Route** (formerly Rent-a-Wreck), 1255, rue MacKay (871-1166; collect calls accepted). From $40 per day; 100km free, 12¢ each additional km. Insurance $13 per day. Collect calls accepted. Open Mon.-Fri. 8am-7pm, Sat. 8am-5pm, Sun. 9am-5pm. **Avis** (800-367-7600), **Budget** (800-268-8900), and **Hertz** (800-263-0678) also serve Montréal.

Driver/Rider Service: Allo Stop, 4317, rue St-Denis (282-0121 or 849-1626). Will match you with a driver heading for Québec City ($11), Ottawa ($8), Toronto ($18), Sherbrooke ($8), New York City ($30), or Boston ($37). Fees for Vancouver vary.

Canadian Automobile Association (CAA), 1180, rue Drummond at blvd. René-Lévesque (information 861-7111; emergencies 861-1313). Métro: Bonaventure. Affiliated with American Automobile Association (AAA). Members have access to tourist information and emergency road service. Open Mon.-Fri. 8:30am-5pm.

Bike Rental: Cycle Peel, 6665, St-Jacques (486-1148). Take bus #90 West from Vendome Métro stop. First day $13, $7 thereafter. $40 per week. Open Mon.-Wed. 9:30am-6pm, Thurs.-Fri. 9:30am-9pm, Sat.-Sun. 9:30am-5pm. Credit card or $200 cash deposit required.

Ticket Agencies: Call the tourist office (875-0300) for tickets, reservations, and information on cultural events. Open May-July daily 9am-7pm; Aug.-April 9am-5pm. **Billet Plus,** 2021, rue St-Denis (845-3535), offers tickets to Montréal events. **Teletron** (288-2525) is the phone branch of Ticketron. Credit card number required.

Help Lines: Distress Centre, 935-1101. Open 24 hr. **Gay Switchboard,** 933-2395. Open Thurs.-Sat. 7-10:30pm.

Pharmacy: Jean Contu Drug Store, 1370, ave. Mont-Royal est (527-8827). Open 24 hr.

Post Office: Succursale "A," 1025, St-Jacques (283-2567). Open Mon.-Fri. 8am-5:45pm. **Postal code:** H3C 1T1.

Area Code: 514.

Montréal lies 554km (334 mi.) down Rte. 401 and the St-Laurent from Toronto, 250km upstream (southwest) of Québec City, 615km (382 mi.) north of New York City, and 500km (310 mi.) northwest of Boston. Québec autoroutes link directly with I-87 in New York and I-91 in Vermont.

Convenient for orientation two major streets divide the city. The **boulevard St-Laurent** (also called "The Main") runs north-south, dividing the city and streets east-west. The Main also serves as the unofficial French/English divider: English **McGill University** lies to the west of St-Laurent, while St-Denis, the **French student quarter** (also called the *"Quartier Latin"*) is slightly east. **Rue Sherbrooke** runs almost the entire length of Montréal, perpendicular to boulevard St-Laurent and parallel to the St. Laurent River.

Parking is often difficult in the city, particularly in winter when snowbanks narrow the streets and slow down traffic. Take the **Métro** instead.

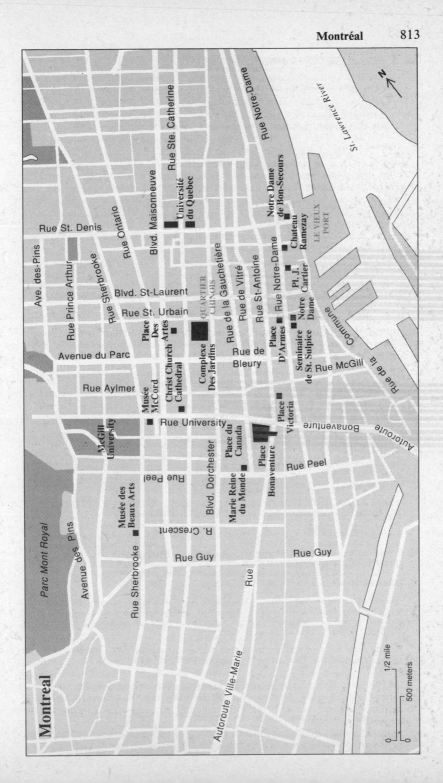

Montreal

St. Lawrence River

LE VIEUX PORT

Rue Notre-Dame

Rue Ste. Catherine

Université du Quebec

Blvd. Maisonneuve

Rue St. Denis

Rue Ontario

Ave. des Pins

Rue Prince Arthur

Rue Sherbrooke

Notre Dame de Bon-Secours

Chateau Ramezay

Pl. J. Cartier

Rue Notre-Dame

Rue de Vitré

Rue St-Antoine

Rue de la Gauchetière

QUARTIER CHINOIS

Blvd. St-Laurent

Rue St. Urbain

Place Des Arts

Complexe Des Jardins

Rue de Bleury

Place D'Armes

Notre Dame

Seminaire de St. Sulpice

Rue McGill

Commune

Avenue du Parc

Christ Church Cathedral

Rue Aylmer

Musée McCord

Rue University

Place Victoria

McGill University

Place du Canada

Place Bonaventure

Autoroute Bonaventure

Rue Peel

Rue Peel

Blvd. Dorchester

Marie Reine du Monde

Musée des Beaux Arts

R. Crescent

Rue Guy

Rue Guy

Parc Mont Royal

Avenue des Pins

Rue Sherbrooke

Rue

Autoroute Ville-Marie

1/2 mile

500 meters

0

0

Accommodations and Camping

The Québec Tourist Office is the best resource for information about hostels, hotels, and **chambres touristiques** (rooms in private homes or small guest houses). Universities offer inexpensive accommodations, although availability during the school term is unlikely. Bed and breakfast singles cost $25-40, doubles $35-75. The most extensive B&B network is **Bed & Breakfast à Montréal,** 4912, ave. Victoria, H3W 2N1 (738-9410), which lists about 50 homes but recommends that you reserve by mail ($25-40 deposit required for reservations). B&B à Montréal also provides 15% discounts on Gray Line city tours and some restaurant coupons. (Singles from $30, doubles from $45. Open daily 9am-7pm.) The **Downtown Bed and Breakfast Network,** 3458, ave. Laval, Montréal H2X 3C8 (289-9749), at Sherbrooke, works with about 40 homes. (Singles $25-40. Doubles $35-55. Open spring and summer daily 8:30am-8pm; fall and winter 8:30am-6pm.) For cheaper B&B listings check with Antonio Costa at **Antonio's B&B,** 101, ave. Northview, H4X 1C9 (486-6910; credit cards not accepted) or **Marbel Guest House,** 3507, blvd. Décarie, H4A 3J4 (486-0232). Both have doubles starting at $35.

Many of the least expensive *maisons touristiques* (tourist homes) and hotels are around rue St-Denis, which ranges from quaint to seedy. Convenient to the bus station, the area flaunts lively nightclubs and abuts Vieux Montréal. Before choosing a place to stay, pick up a **Tourist Guide** at the Tourist Office; it lists and maps out the location of hundreds of accommodations.

The area's university dorm rooms are all clean and similarly priced. Though slightly more expensive, these rooms offer a great deal more privacy than the hostels. All have desks and free linen and towels. The main consideration is location; check a map before you plan to stay at any of the three.

Dorms: Université de Montréal, Residences, 2350, Edouard-Montpetit H2X 2B9 (343-6531). Métro: Edouard-Montpetit. Modern building on the edge of a beautiful campus. Singles $18, non-students $28. Open May-Aug. 21. **McGill University,** Bishop Mountain Hall, 3935, rue de l'Université, H3A 2B4 (398-6367). Métro: McGill. Follow Université through campus, up the hill until it ends. Over 1100 beds. Singles only. Desk open Mon.-Fri. 7am-11pm, Sat.-Sun. 8am-10pm, but a guard will check you in late at night. $22, non-students $30. Weekly: $95. Open May 15-Aug. 15. Reservations (one night deposit) recommended for July and Aug. **Concordia University** (848-4755), Hingston Hall in the northeast corner of Concordia. Take Sherbrooke west, turn right on Broadway, take your first right and Hingston is on your left. Far from downtown. Métro: Vendôme and bus #155. Large rooms with phones in the hall. Don't be confused; summer residence in the Loyola Campus, not the Sir George William Campus downtown. Singles $16, non-students $22. Open May 11-Aug. 27.

Montréal Youth Hostel (IYHF), 3541, rue Aylmer, Montréal H3A 2W6 (843-3317), in the McGill campus area, 10 min. from downtown. Métro: McGill. Rooms with 3 bunks. Recently renovated, great location. Fills up quickly, especially in summer, so arrive before noon. Large kitchen available until midnight. Coffee (60¢) and croissants ($1) sold in morning. $12, non-members $14. Deposit $5. Hot showers and linen included. Open daily 8am-2pm. Reservations 3 weeks in advance. Overflow youth hostel at **Collège Français,** 5155, de Gaspé, Montréal H3G 1M8 (495-2581 or 270-9260 after 5pm and on holidays). Métro: Laurier, then walk west and north. Over 1200 beds. A bed in a double $14.50, quad $9.50, 8-10 bed dorm $8.50. Breakfast in summer $2.50. Open daily 8am-2am.

Maison André Tourist Rooms, 3511, rue Université (849-4092). Métro: McGill. Mrs. Zanko will rent you a room (singles $25-35, doubles $38-40) and spin great stories, but only if you don't smoke. Her dog Max doesn't care for smokers either. Nice-sized and clean rooms with German-style decor. Reservations recommended.

YWCA, 1355, rue René-Lévesque ouest (866-9941). Métro: Lucien l'Allier. Women only. Clean, safe rooms in the heart of downtown. Building newly renovated. Singles $42-47. Doubles $49-58.

YMCA, 1450, rue Stanley (849-8393), downtown. Métro: Peel. 331 rooms. Singles $30-44. Doubles $48-54. Over 65 $3 off. Students with ID $2 off. Usually fills up June-Aug. No reservations.

Hotel Le Breton, 1609, rue St. Hubert (524-7273). Métro: Berri-UQAM. Lobby and some rooms recently renovated. All 12 rooms have TV. Singles $30-45. Doubles $40-55. Fills up quickly—make reservations.

Hotel Louisburg, 1649, rue St. Hubert (523-0053). Métro: Berri-UQAM. Owner promises renovations for 1991. Clean rooms with TV. June-Sept. singles $30-45, doubles $35-54; Oct.-May singles $25-35, doubles $28-42. Connected with Hotel Jay, 1655, rue St. Hubert.

Hotel Manoir-Sherbrooke, 157, Sherbrooke est (845-0915 or 285-0894). Métro: Sherbrooke. Extremely small but inexpensive rooms. Don't bring too much baggage. Most have TV and showers on the hall or in the room but some only have tubs. Cheapest rooms pretty dingy—try to avoid the basement. Singles from $29. Doubles from $35.

Those with a car and some time to drive it can camp at **Camping Parc Paul Sauvé** (347-2417), on Rte. 344 45 minutes from downtown. Take 20 west to 13 north to 640 west to Rte. 334 west and follow the signs to the park. 873 beautiful sites on the **Lac des Deux Montagnes.** (Sites $11, with electricity $16.25.) For private sites, try **KOA Montréal-South,** 130, blvd. Monette, St-Phillipe J0L 2K0 (659-8626), a 15-minute drive from the city. Follow Rte. 15 south, take exit 38, turn left at the stop sign, and go straight about 1 mi.—it's on your left. (Sites $14.50, with hookup $21.50.) Or try **Camping Pointe-des-Cascades,** Exclusé Ste.-Catherine (632-1510). Like KOA, Cascades is on the south shore, southwest of Montréal. Take 20 west to rue Ile-Tereot and Ste-Ame de Bellevue. Look for signs for the town of Doreon. (Sites $11, with hookup $15.)

Food

French-Canadian cuisine is unique but generally expensive. When on a tight budget, look for *tourtière,* a traditional meat pie with vegetables and a thick crust, or *québecois crêpes,* stuffed with everything from scrambled eggs to asparagus with *béchamel.* Wash it down with *cidre* (hard cider) and *caribou* (a heady combination of Bordeaux and hard stuff). Other Montréal specialties include French bread (the best on the continent), smoked meat, Gaspé salmon, Matane shrimp, and lobster from the Maydalen Islands.

Montréal's ethnic restaurants offer a variety of cuisine from curry to pirogi at reasonable prices. Look for Greek *souvlaki* or Vietnamese asparagus and crab soup. A small **Chinatown** lies along rue de la Gauchetière, near old Montréal's Place d'Armes. A Jewish neighborhood complete with Hebrew neon signs, delis (see Schwartz's and Wilensky's below), and bagel bakeries lies north of downtown around blvd. St-Laurent. Don't miss the best bagels in town (30-50¢)—baked before your eyes in brick ovens 24 hr.—at **La Maison de Original Fairmount Bagel,** 74, rue Fairmount ouest (272-0667), or the **Bagel Bakery,** 263, rue St-Viateur ouest (276-8044). From the St-Laurent Métro stop, take bus #55 north to Fairmount or St-Viateur and turn left. For a quick sampling of Montréal's international cuisine, stop by the **Feaubourg Center,** 1606, rue Ste-Catherine ouest at rue Guy. (Métro: Guy.) The food is diverse (crêpes, falafel, Szechuan) and fresh, despite the fast-food atmosphere. Markets here sell seafood, meats, bread, and produce. (Open daily 11am-9pm.)

The drinking age in Montréal is 18. You can save money by buying your own wine and bringing it to **unlicensed restaurants.** These are concentrated on the blvd. St-Laurent, north of Sherbrooke, and on the pedestrian precincts of rue Prince Arthur and rue Duluth. When preparing your own grub, look for produce at the **Atwater Market** (872-2009; Métro: Lionel-Groulx); the **Marché Maisonneuve,** 4375, rue Ontario est (256-4974); or the **Marché Jean-Talon** (Métro: Jean Talon). (All open Mon.-Wed. 7am-6pm, Thurs.-Fri. 7am-9pm.)

Rue St-Denis, the main thoroughfare in the French student quarter, has many small restaurants and cafés, most of which cater to student pocketbooks. **Da Giovanni,** 572, Ste-Catherine est, serves generous portions of fine Italian food; don't be put off by the lines or the diner atmosphere. The sauce and noodles cook up right in the window. (Open Mon.-Thurs. 7-11am and 2pm-2am, Fri.-Sat. 7-11am and 3pm-3am, Sun. 7:30-11am and 1pm-1am.)

Since law requires all restaurants to post their menus outside, shop around. You'll be charged 10% tax for meals totalling more than $3.25. For more information, consult the free "Shopping, Restaurant, and Nightlife" guide, available at the tourist office.

Café Santropol, 3990, St-Urbain at Duluth. Métro: Sherbrooke, then walk north and west. Student hangout filled with young voices and bizarre decor. Depending on where you sit, a plaster cow or a mannequin with ski-goggles may watch you eat. Huge vegetarian sandwiches (chicken also available) served with piles of fruit ($5-7). Open Tues.-Thurs. 11:30am-midnight, Fri. 11:30am-2am, Sat. 2pm-2am, Sun. noon-midnight.

Terasse Lafayette, 250, rue Villeneuve ouest at rue Jeanne Mance (288-3415), west of the Mont-Royal Métro. Pizzas, pastas, souvlaki, and salad $6-10. One of the better Greek restaurants in this neighborhood with a huge outdoor terrace. BYOB. Open daily 11am-1am. Free delivery.

Etoile des Indes, 1806, Ste-Catherine ouest. Métro: Guy. Split-level dining room with tapestries covering the walls. The best Indian fare in town. Dinner entrees $6.50-12. The very brave should try their bang-up *bangalore phal* dishes. Open Mon.-Fri. 11:30am-2:30pm and 5-11pm, Sat. noon-3pm and 5-11pm, Sun. 5-11pm.

Restaurant Jam-Can, 5518, Sherbrooke ouest. Honest Jamaican cuisine served in an intimidating atmosphere with wire mesh separating the lunch counter from the employees. Don't come here for conversation—the reggae would drown it out anyway. Curried goat $6.50, meat or vegetable patty $1. Open daily 11am-10pm.

Kam Fung, 1008, ave. Clark, in Chinatown. Métro: Place d'Armes. Huge dining room more suited to a banquet than an intimate meal, but the inexpensive *dim sum* dishes are excellent ($2-6; served daily 11am-3pm). Regular Cantonese entrees more expensive ($9-15). Open Mon.-Thurs. 11am-midnight, Fri.-Sat. 11am-1am, Sun. 10am-midnight.

Schwartz's Deli, 3895, St-Laurent, near Napoléon. Métro: St-Laurent. The best smoked meat in town piled on thick (sandwiches $3.20, larger meat plates $6-8). Often jam-packed, but you'll get your food in 5 min. Open Mon.-Fri. 9am-12:45am, Sat. 9am-1:45am, Sun. 9am-2:45am.

Wilensky's, 34, rue Fairmount ouest. A great place for quick lunch in the heart of the old Jewish neighborhood. Lunches $2.50-5. Open Mon.-Fri. 9am-4pm.

Binerie Mont-Royal, 367, rue Mont-Royal est. Métro: Mont-Royal. Classic lunch-counter joint—they'll look at you funny if you ask for a menu. Breakfast special (eggs, bacon, toast, and coffee) $2.75. Sandwiches $2.20. Open Mon.-Fri. 6am-10:30pm, Sat. 6am-2am.

McGill Student Union, 3480, rue McTavish, 5 min. from IYH. Métro: McGill. Cheap cafeteria food with surprisingly friendly service. Breakfast special (toast, hash browns, and coffee) $2. Sandwiches ($2-3) and burgers ($1.75) for lunch. Beer to boot. Open May-Aug. Mon.-Thurs. 8am-3pm, Fri. 8am-2:30pm; also open during academic year.

Sights

An island city, Montréal has burgeoned from a riverside settlement of French colonists to a metropolis internationally acclaimed for its cultural traditions and economic power. The city's ethnic and architectural diversity can hold your attention for days on end. Museums, Old Montréal, and the new downtown may be fascinating but don't forget that the island's greatest asset is the sheer amount of life packed into such a small area. Wander aimlessly and often—and not through the high-priced shops and boutiques that the tourist office touts. Many attractions between Mont-Royal and the St. Laurent River are free, from parks (Mont-Royal and Lafontaine) and universities (McGill, Montréal, Concordia, Québec at Montréal) to ethnic neighborhoods.

Walk or ride a bike (available free from the IYH if you stay there) down **boulevard St-Laurent** north of Sherbrooke. Originally settled by Jewish immigrants, this area now functions as a sort of multi-cultural center after an influx of Greek, Slavic, Latin American, and Portuguese immigrants. **Rue St-Denis,** home of the French language elite around the turn of the century, still serves as the mainline of Montréal's **Latin Quarter** (Métro: Berri-UQAM). Jazz fiends command the street the first week of July during the **International Jazz Festival** (288-5653) with over 200 outdoor shows. **Carré St-Louis,** or Saint Louis Square, (Métro: Sherbrooke), with its fountain and sculptures, **rue Prince-Arthur,** packed with street performers in the summer, and **Le Village,** a gay village in Montréal from rue St-Denis est to Papineau along rue Ste-Catherine est, are also worth visiting.

Students will feel at home on the **McGill University** campus (main gate at the corner of McGill and Sherbrooke St.; Métro: McGill). The campus stretches up Mont-Royal, offering Victorian buildings and a pleasant spot of green grass and oak trees in the midst of downtown. The estate of James McGill, a Canadian merchant and politician, founded McGill, the oldest university in Québec, in 1821. More than any other sight in Montréal, the university manifests the British tradition and continuing English presence in the city. The campus also contains the site of the Native American village of Hochelaga in the 1500s and the **Redpath Museum of Natural Science,** with rare fossils and two genuine Egyptian mummies. (Open June-Sept. Mon-Thurs. 9am-5pm; Oct.-May Fri. 9am-5pm. Free.) Guided tours of the campus are available with 24-hr. notice (398-6555).

The Underground City

Montréalers aren't speaking metaphorically of a sub-culture or a particularly hip part of town when they boast of their Underground City. They mean *underground:* 22km of underground passages tunneling between Métro stops form a subterranean village of climate-controlled restaurants and shops. The ever-expanding network now connects railway stations, a bus terminal, restaurants, banks, cinemas, theaters, hotels, 1200 businesses, 1250 housing units, 2 universities, 2 department stores, and 1400 boutiques. Enter the city from any of the Métro stops, or start your exploration at the **Place Bonaventure,** 901 rue de la Gauchetière ouest (397-2205; Métro: Bonaventure), Canada's largest commercial building. The **Viaduc** shopping center inside contains a cluster of shops that each sell products of a different country. The tourist office's guide to the city contains maps of the tunnels and underground attractions. (Shops open Mon.-Wed. 9am-6pm, Thurs.-Fri. 9am-9pm, Sat. 9am-5pm.)

Parks and Museums

The finest of Montréal's parks, **Parc du Mont-Royal** (872-6211), swirls in a vast green expanse up the mountain from which the city took its name. Visitors from New York may recognize the omnipresent hand of Frederick Law Olmstead, the architect who planned Central Park and half the U.S. From rue Peel, hardy hikers can take a foot path and stairs to the top, where a fantastic view of the city awaits. In 1643, De Maisonneuve promised to climb Mont-Royal bearing a cross if the flood waters of the St-Laurent would recede. The existing 30-ft. cross, built in 1924, commemorates this climb. When illuminated at night, you can see the cross for miles. In winter, *Montréalais* congregate here to ice-skate and cross-country ski.

Parc Lafontaine contains the Jardin de Merveilles (Garden of Wonders), and a **children's zoo** (872-2815; Métro: Sherbrooke). There are also picnic facilities, an outdoor puppet theater, 17 public tennis courts, ice-skating in the winter, and an international festival of public theater in June. (Zoo open mid-May to late Sept. daily 10am-7pm; off-season 10am-6pm. Admission $2.50, under 18 $1.50. Free parking.)

For a beautiful view of Montréal and the St-Laurent, head up rue Belvedere to **Westmount Summit.** This small wooded park crowns **Westmount,** one of the wealthiest neighborhoods in the city. Subdued, green, and very English, Westmount is an enclave of stately mansions. (Take bus #66.) On the northern edge of Westmount stands **Oratoire St-Joseph** (St. Joseph's Oratory), 3800, rue Queen Mary (Métro: Snowdon, Guy, and bus #165), a mammoth monument of *québecois* Catholicism built in honor of the healing monk Frère André. Aside from an impressive basilica, the complex includes the **Musée de Frère André** and the **Musée de l'Oratoire** (both 733-8211), a spacious art gallery. (Oratory open daily 6am-10pm. Museums open daily 10am-5pm. Donation.)

Musée des beaux-arts de Montréal (Fine Arts Museum), 1379, Sherbrooke ouest (285-1600; Métro: Guy), houses a small permanent collection that touches upon all major historical periods, including Canadian and Inuit work. (Open daily 7am-10pm. Admission $10, seniors and students $5, under 12 $1.) **Musée d'art contem-**

818   Québec

porain (Museum of Contemporary Art), Cité du Havre (873-2878), has the latest
by *québecois* artists, as well as textile, photography, and avant-garde exhibits. (Open
Tues.-Sun. 10am-6pm. Free. Métro: McGill, then bus #168 Tues.-Fri. On weekends take bus #125 from rue de l'Université and rue Ste-Jacques.)
Opened in May 1989, the **Centre Canadien d'Architecture,** 1920 Baile St. (939-
7000; Métro: Guy), houses one of the most important collections of architectural
prints, drawings, photographs, and books in the world. (Open Wed. and Sat.-Sun.
11am-5pm, Thurs. 11am-8pm, Fri. 11am-6pm. Admission $3, students $2, under
13 free.) The **Olympic Park,** 4545, ave. Pierre-de-Coubertin (252-4737; Métro: Pie-
IX or Viau), hosted the 1976 Summer Olympic Games. Its daring architecture includes the world's tallest inclined tower and a stadium with one of the world's only
fully retractable roofs. (Guided tours daily at 12:40 and 3:40pm; more often May-
Sept. Admission $5, ages 5-17 $3.50, under 5 free.) Trains, leaving every 20-30 minutes from 10am to 6pm, will take you throughout the park for $2. Or try taking
a ride in a cable car. (Leaves daily every 10 min. 10am-7pm. Fare $5, ages 5-17
$3.50, under 5 free; cable car and tour $8.50, ages 5-17 $6.)

Vieux Montréal

An exploration of Montréal's French heritage should begin where the first settlement began; Vieux-Montréal (Old Montréal) lies on the stretch of riverbank. between rue McGill, Notre-Dame, and Berri. The fortified walls that once protected
the quarter have crumbled, but the beautiful 17th- and 18th-century mansions of
politicos and merchants have maintained their full splendor. (Métro: Place
d'Armes.)
The 19th-century church **Notre-Dame-de-Montréal** towers above the Place
d'Armes and the memorial to de Maisonneuve, Montréal's founder. A historic center for the city's Catholic population, the neo-Gothic church once hosted French
Canadian separatist rallies, and, more recently, a tradition-breaking ecumenical
gathering. Seating 4000, Notre-Dame is one of the largest and most magnificent
churches in North America. Destroyed in a fire, the Wedding Chapel behind the
altar re-opened in 1982 with a tremendous bronze altar.
From Notre-Dame walk next door to the **Sulpician Seminary,** Montréal's oldest
remaining building (built in 1685) and still a functioning seminary. The clock over
the facade (built in 1700) is the oldest public timepiece in North America. A stroll
down rue Saint-Sulpice will bring you to **rue de la Commune** on the banks of the
St. Lawrence River. Here the old docks of the city compete with the new. Proceed
east along rue de la Commune to **rue Bonsecours.** At the corner of Bonsecours and
rue St-Paul (the busiest and most commercial street in Old Montréal) stands the
18th-century **Notre-Dame-de-Bonsecours.** Marguerite Bourgeoys (1620-1700),
leader of the first congregation of non-cloistered nuns, founded the church (older
and less ornate than Notre-Dame-de-Montréal) on the port as a sailor's refuge. Sailors thankful to have arrived safely on their pilgrimage presented the nuns and
priests with the wooden boat-shaped ceiling lamps in the chapel. The church also
has a museum in the basement and a bell tower with a nice view of Vieux Montréal
and the St. Lawrence River. (Chapel open May-Nov. daily 9am-5pm; Dec.-April
10am-5pm. Tower and museum open May-Nov. Tues.-Sat. 9am-4:30pm, Sun.
11:30am-4:30pm; Dec.-April Tues.-Fri. 10:30am-4:30pm, Sat. 10am-4:30pm, Sun.
11:30am-4:30pm. Admission $2, children 50¢.)
Opening onto rue St-Paul is **Place Jacques Cartier,** site of Montréal's oldest market. Here the modern European character of Montréal is most evident; cafés line
the square and in summer, street artists strut their stuff. Visit the grand **Château
Ramezay,** 280, Notre-Dame est (861-3708), built in 1705 to house the French vice-
roy, and its museum of québecois, British, and American 18th-century artifacts.
(Open Tues.-Sun. 10am-4:30pm. Admission $2, seniors and students $1.) Nearby,
in the square of Place Vauquelin, is the Vieux Palais de Justice, built in 1856; across
from it stands City Hall. **Rue St-Jacques** in the Old City, inaugurated in 1687, is
Montréal's answer to Wall Street.

There are three good reasons to venture out to **Ile Ste-Hélène,** an island in the St. Lawrence River, just off the coast of Vieux Montréal. The first is **La Ronde** (872-6222), Montréal's popular amusement park. Since La Ronde fills at night, it's best to go in the afternoon, buy an unlimited pass ($17, children $10), and stay until the evening crowds overtake the place. (Open June 20-Sept. 2 daily noon-2am.) The second reason is the **Terre des Hommes** (World of People) exhibit, from the 1967 World's Fair. A few pavilions remain open, and outdoor concerts, educational exhibits, and films are featured here in summer. (Open late June-Sept. daily 8am-midnight. Buildings open daily 11am-8pm.) Finally, there's **Le Vieux Fort** (The Old Fort; 861-6701), built in the 1820s to defend Canada's inland waterways. Now primarily a military museum, the fort displays artifacts and costumes detailing Canadian colonial history. Three military parades take place daily from late June to the end of August. (Museum open May-Aug. Wed.-Mon. 10am-5pm; off-season Wed.-Mon. 10am-6pm. Admission $7, seniors, students, and children $4, under 6 free. Take the Métro under the St. Lawrence to the Ile Ste-Hélène stop.

Whether swollen with spring run-off or frozen over during the winter, the **St. Lawrence River** can be one of Montréal's most thrilling attractions. The whirlpools and 15-ft. waves of the **Lachine Rapids** once barred river travelers. Now St. Lawrence and Montréal harbor cruises depart from Victoria Pier (842-3871) in Vieux Montréal (May 15-Sept. 30 4 per day; 1½ hr.; fare $7.50, seniors $6, children $4). My, how far Montréal has come!

Nightlife and Entertainment

After looking beyond the massive neon lights flashing "films érotiques" and in one case "Château du sexe," you should find quality nightlife in Québec's largest city—either in **brasseries** (with food as well as beer, wine, and music) or in **pubs** (with more hanging out and less eating). You may even have to look underground.

Downstairs at 1107, rue Ste-Catherine ouest is **Peel Pub** (844-6769), with live rock bands nightly and good, cheap food. Here waiters rush about with three pitchers of beer in each hand to keep up with the crowd of Montréal's university students. (Small pitchers $6, large $7.50.) Other locations: 1106, rue Maison neuve (844-6769), 3461, rue Parc (845-9002). (Open Mon.-Thurs. 7-11am, 2pm-2am; Fri.-Sat. 7am-11am, 3pm-3am; Sun. 9:30am-11am, 1pm-1am.) For a slightly older and more subdued crowd search the side streets of rue Ste-Catherine ouest—away from the glitz. Try the English strongholds around **rue Crescent** and **rue Bishop** (Métro: Guy), where bar-hopping is a must. **Déjà-Vu,** 1224, Bishop (866-0512), has live bands nightly. **Charlie's** just down the street at 1204, Bishop (871-1709) also has bands each night. Set aside Thursday for a night at **D.J.'s Pub,** 1443, Crescent (845-1813), when $15 gets you into an open bar. (All three open daily noon-3am. No cover.) You can boogie at **Tangerine,** 2125, rue de la Montagne (845-3607; no jeans; open daily 6pm-3am; cover $8), the **Club Scaramouche** across the street, or at countless other danceterias in this area. Reggae fans should go to **Rising Sun,** 286, Ste-Catherine ouest (861-0657; Métro: Place des Arts or McGill; open daily 8pm-3am; no cover). Jazz enthusiasts should stop by **Biddles,** 2060, rue Aylmer (842-8656), for ribs and live jazz nightly. Métro: McGill. (Open Mon.-Tues. 11:30am-1am, Wed.-Thurs. 11:30am-2am, Fri. 11:30am-3am, Sat. 5pm-3am, Sun. 5:30pm-1am. $6 minimum Fri.-Sat.)

French nightlife parleys on **rue St-Denis** (Métro: Berri de Montigny). Stop in for live jazz at **Le Grand Café,** 1720, rue St-Denis (849-6955; open daily 11am-2:30am; cover in the evening $4). Also in the Latin Quarter, young, lively **rue Prince Arthur** densely packs Greek, Polish, and Italian restaurants. Street performers and colorful wall murals further enliven this ethnic neighborhood. The accent changes slightly at **ave. Duluth,** where Greek and Vietnamese establishments prevail. Vieux Montréal, too, is best seen at night. Street performers, artists, and *chansonniers* in various *brasseries* set the tone for lively summer evenings of clapping, stomping, and singing along. Walk down St-Paul, and try the *brasseries* near the corner of St-Vincent.

Montréal has long been the cultural capital of Québec. The city bubbles with a wide variety of theatrical groups: the Théâtre du Nouveau Monde, 84, Ste-Catherine ouest (861-0563), and the Rideau Vert, 4664, St-Denis (844-1793), stage québecois works. For English language plays, try the Centaur Theatre, 453, rue St-François-Xavier (288-3161). The city's exciting Place des Arts, 175, Ste-Catherine ouest (842-2112 for tickets; 285-4200 for information), houses the Opéra de Montréal, the Montréal Symphony Orchestra, and Les Grands Ballets Canadiens. Check the *Calendar of Events* (available at the tourist office and reprinted in daily newspapers), and call Ticketron (288-3651) for tickets.

Québec City

Canada's oldest city, Québec City not only is the capital of Québec province but has been the country's capital under both French and English regimes. Built on the rocky heights of Cape Diamond, where the St. Lawrence River narrows and joins the St. Charles River in northeast Canada, the city has been called "Gibraltar of America" because of the stone walls and military fortifications protecting the port.

French explorer Jacques Cartier visited the Algonquin village of Stadcona in 1535; on July 3, 1608, Samuel de Champlain founded Québec City on the same site. It served as the capital of French North America until September 1759, when the British scaled the city's cliffs. Fighting continued until 1763, when Canada became a British colony under the Treaty of Paris. But, despite the past British control of the area, the French have shaped Québec City with their heritage and language. At least 95% French-speaking, Québec City offers traditional French-Canadian cuisine, music, and ambiance. Visitors who can speak French certainly should do so, but since much of the population is bilingual, Anglophones will have little difficulty getting by. In summer, tourists and students crowd the narrow streets of the city, the warm air filling with music from the rows of nightclubs and cafés. For those who can't afford a trip to Europe, Québec City offers an Old World charm nearly unparalleled in North America. The best times to visit are during the summer arts festival in mid-July and February's winter carnival, a raucous French-Canadian Mardi Gras.

Practical Information

Emergency: Police, 691-6123 (city); 623-6262 (provincial). **Télémedic:** 687-9915. Open 24 hr.

Visitor Information: Maison du Tourisme de Québec (Québec Province Information), 12, rue Ste-Anne (873-2015; outside Québec City 800-363-7777). Visit here before touring Québec City or before you plan forays into the Québec countryside. Accommodation listings for the entire province and free road and city maps. English also. Open May-Sept. daily 8am-7pm; off-season 9am-5pm. **Ste-Foy Tourist Information Office,** Ministère de l'Industrie, du Commerce et du Tourisme et Communauté Urbaine de Québec, 3005, blvd. Laurier, Ste-Foy (651-2882), at rue Lavigerie, 4 mi. southwest of the old city. Open June 1-Sept. 2 daily 8:30am-8pm; Sept. 3-Oct. 8:30am-5pm; Nov. to mid-April 9am-5pm; mid-April to late May 8:30am-5:30pm.

Youth Tourist Information: 19, Ste-Ursule (694-0755), in the lobby of the Centre International de Séjour (see Accommodations and Camping below). Most literature in French, but the office plans to offer tours of the city in 1991. Open Mon.-Fri. 10am-6pm; also Sat. from July-Aug.

U.S. Consulate: 1, Ste-Geneviève (692-2095). Open Mon.-Fri. 9am-5pm.

Airlines: Air Canada (692-0770) and **Inter-Canadian** (692-1031). Special deals available for students under 21 (with ID) willing to go standby.

Trains: VIA Rail Canada, 3255, chemin de la Gare (692-3940), in Ste-Foy (658-8792), and 1, ave. Laurier, in Lévis (833-8056). Call 800-361-5390 anywhere in Canada or the U.S. for reservations and information. To Montréal (5 per day, 2½ hr., $32, students $29; $19 and $16 respectively Fri. or Sun. with reservations 5 days in advance).

Buses: Voyageur Bus, 225, blvd. Charest est (524-4692). Open daily 5:20am-1:20am. Also outlying stations at 2700, ave. Laurier, in Ste-Foy (651-7015; open daily 5:45am-1:15am) and 63, rte. Trans-Canada ouest (Rte. 132), in Lévis (837-5805; open 24 hr). To Montréal (every hr. 6am-11pm, 3 hr., $27.50) and Ste-Anne-de-Beaupré (5 per day, $3.50). Connections to U.S. cities via Montréal or Sherbrooke.

Public Transport: Commission de transport de la Communauté Urbaine de Québec (CTCUQ), 270, rue des Rocailles (627-2511). Buses operate daily 5:30am-12:30am. Fare $1.40, seniors with ID free.

Taxis: Taxi Québec, 529-0003. **Coop Taxis Québec,** 525-5191.

Car Rental: Though often expensive, agencies abound in Québec City. Check the yellow pages for a full listing.

Moped and Bike Rental: Location Petit Champlain, 94, rue Petit-Champlain (692-2817). Cycles expensive. Bikes $10 per hr., $25 per day; mopeds $20 per hr., $5 each additional hr. A guide will lead you around the city at no extra charge.

Help Line: Tel Aide, 683-2153. Open Sun.-Thurs. noon-midnight Fri.-Sat. noon-2am.

Canada Post: 3, rue Buade (648-4682). Open Mon.-Fri. 8am-5:45pm. **Postal Code:** G1R 2J0. **Post Office** in the city at 300 rue St-Paul (648-3340). **Postal code:** G1K 3W0.

Area Code: 418.

Québec jumps 253km (160 mi.) from Montréal, 700km (426 mi.) from Gaspé, and 620km (400 mi.) from Boston. From Montréal, take Autoroute 20. Autoroute 23 and Rte. 173 join U.S. 201 in a deserted corner of northwestern Maine.

Accommodations and Camping

Québec City now has two B&B referral services. Contact Denise or Raymond Blancher at **B&B Bonjour Québec,** 3765, blvd. Monaco, Québec G1P 3J3 (527-1465) for lodgings throughout the city, city maps, and descriptions of houses. Singles usually cost $35-45, doubles $45-55. **Gîte Québec** offers similar services. Contact Thérèse Tellier, 3729, ave. Le Corbusier, Ste-Foy, Québec G1W 4R8 (651-1860). (Singles $30-40. Doubles from $60.) Hosts are usually bilingual; these services inspect the houses for cleanliness and convenience of location.

You can obtain a list of nearby campgrounds from the Maison du Tourisme de Québec, or by writing Ministère du Tourisme, Direction de l'hôtellerie, 710, place D'Youville, 3e étage, Québec G1R 4Y4 (800-363-7777).

Centre international de séjour, 19, Ste-Ursule (694-0755), between rue St-Jean and Dauphine. A renovated convent in the heart of the old city. No kitchen, but breakfast or lunch costs about $2 in the hostel's basement cafeteria. Microwave. No curfew. Lights out 11pm-7am. One bed in a 4-person room $12, nonmembers $14. Linen included. Key deposit $5. Bunks in a large dorm room $9. Doubles $30-32. Reservations accepted.

Auberge de la Paix, 31, rue Couillard (694-0735). Yellow peeling paint, cramped lobby and beds—but clean. Stay here when Centre is full: both have great access to the restaurants and bars on rue St-Jean. Predominantly 8-10 bed dorms, some doubles. Curfew 2am. $12. Breakfast of toast, cereal, coffee and juice included. Make reservations July and Aug.

Campus de l'université Laval, Pavillion Parent (656-2921), Ste-Foy. Take bus #11. Modern building with dorm rooms. Rooms clean and big enough, but stay in Vieux Québec if possible. Singles with sink and desk $15. Doubles $20. Non-students extra $5. Cafeteria breakfast $2. Reserve in advance if you plan to stay more than 2 nights. Open May 10-Aug. 20.

Montmartre canadien, 1679, chemin St-Louis, Sillery (681-7357), on the outskirts of the city. Take bus #25 and look for the big painting of Jesus on the wall. Run by a group of monks associated with a college in the U.S.; Father François particularly friendly. Common showers. Dorm-style singles $14. Doubles $24. Breakfast (eggs, cereal, bacon, and pancakes) $2.25.

Manoir La Salle, 18, rue Ste-Ursule (647-9361), opposite the youth hostel. Clean private rooms fill up quickly, especially in the summer. Cat haters beware: several felines stalk the halls. Singles $23. Doubles $40, with shower $45.

Camping Canadien, Ancienne-Lorette (872-7801). Follow Rte. 360 4-5km east of town. Ask at the tourist office for the municipal bus to nearby Beauport. 50 sites. Try for the site on the Rivière Montmorency, just above the falls. Sites $14.50, with hookup $16.50. Open May 11-Oct. 27.

Municipal de Beauport, Beauport (666-2228). Take Autoroute 40 east, exit at rue Labelle onto 369, turn left, and follow signs marked "camping." 137 sites. $10, with hookup $15. Weekly: $60, with hookup $95. Open June 1-Sept. 5.

Food and Nightlife

In general, rue Buade, St-Jean, avenue Grande Allée, and Cartier, as well as the **Place Royale** and **Petit Champlain** areas offer the widest selection of food and drink. One of the most filling yet inexpensive meals is a *croque monsieur,* a large, open-faced sandwich with ham and melted cheese ($5), usually served with salad. Québecois French onion soup always serves well, loaded with onions, slathered with melted cheese, and usually served with bats of French bread. Other specialties include the French crêpe, stuffed differently for either main course or dessert, and the French-Canadian "sugar pie," made with brown sugar and butter. For basic home-cooked meals, dine at the clean and cheap cafeteria in the basement of the Centre internationale de séjour (see Accommodations and Camping above).

Casse Crêpe Breton, 1136, rue St-Jean. Great, inexpensive crêpes ($2.50-4.50) with friendly service in a bohemian-chic atmosphere. Breakfast special (2 eggs, bacon, toast, and coffee) $3. Lunch specials (served 11am-2pm) an even better bargain. Suck on a strawberry milkshake ($2.25) for dessert. Open Sun.-Thurs. 8am-1am, Fri.-Sat. 8am-2am.

La Vieille Maison du Spaghetti, 625, Grand Allé est or 40, rue Marché Champlain. Both in the Petit-Champlain quarter near Place Royale. Great, fresh Italian food in a perfect setting—red tablecloths and wine glasses at each seat. Spaghetti with tangy sauces, a skimpy salad bar, and bread $6.25-8.25. Pizza $7-9. open Sun.-Thurs. 9:30am-11pm, Fri.-Sat. 9:30am-11:30pm.

Les Couventines, 1124, rue St-Jean. Buckwheat crêpes in a quiet, elegant dining room. Crystal glasses and nicely finished wood tables and chairs. Great spot for serious conversation or a mellow night out. Butter crêpes $1.50, smoked salmon $7.50. Open Tues.-Sun. 11am-9:30pm.

Restaurant Liban, 23, rue d'Auteuil, off rue St-Jean. Great café for lunch or a late-night bite. Tabouli and hummus plates $2.75, both with pita bread. Fantastic variety of baklava. Open daily 11am-4am.

Café Ste-Julie, 865, rue des Zouaves off St-Jean. Lunch-counter joint with specials scrawled on the walls—breakfast (2 eggs, bacon, coffee, toast, beans) $3; lunch (good-sized cheeseburger, fries, and a Coke) $4.50. Open Sun.-Tues. 7am-9pm, Wed.-Sat. 7am-midnight.

L'Entrecôte St-Jean, 1011, rue St-Jean. Nice dining room with bar. Five-oz. steak, soup, vegetables, and salad $10. Open Sun.-Thurs. 11:30am-10:30pm, Fri.-Sat. 11:30am-11pm.

La Fleur de Lotus, 38, Côte de la Fabrique, across from the Hôtel de Ville. Cheerful and unpretentious. A local favorite. Thai dishes $2.75-8.75. Open Mon.-Fri. 11:30am-10:30pm, Sat.-Sun. 5-10:30pm.

Croissant Plus, 50, rue Garneau, off Côte de la Fabrique. Around the corner from the Auberge hostel. A real tourist trap—English is a requirement for employment—but for a trap it's friendly and quick. Chocolate croissants $1.55. Ham and cheese $3.05. Open Mon.-Fri. 7:30am-10 or 11pm, Sat.-Sun. 7:30am-3am.

Le Kismet, 780, rue St-Jean. Indian cuisine with atmosphere to match. Tandoori chicken $6. Beef Tikka $5.50. Open Mon.-Fri. 11:30am-2:30pm and 5:30-11pm. Sat.-Sun. 5:30-11pm.

Numerous boisterous nightspots line rue St-Jean. Duck into any of these establishments and linger over a glass of wine or listen to some *québecois* folk music. Most balk at cover charges and close around 3am. **L'Apropo,** 596, rue St-Jean, frequently has live music. (Open daily noon-whenever.) The **Bar en Bar,** 58, Côte du Palais, fills with locals and pool tables. (Half-price drinks daily noon-8pm.) In summer, musicians, magicians, and other performers take their act to the street. Call 529-5511 for a recorded message (in French) of cultural events.

Sights

Confined within walls built by the English, *le vieux Québec* (old Québec City) holds most of the city's historic attractions. Though monuments are clearly marked and explained, you'll get more out of the town with the tourist office's *Québec Walking Tour Guide*, available from the Maison du Tourisme (see Practical Information above). It takes one or two days to explore old Québec by foot, but you'll learn more than on the many guided bus tours.

La Haute-Ville

Begin your walking tour of Québec City by climbing uphill, to the top of **Cap Diamant** (Cape Diamond), just south of the **Citadelle**. From here take Promenade des Gouverneurs downhill to **Terrasse Dufferin**. Built in 1838 by Lord Durham, this popular promenade offers excellent views of the St. Lawrence River, the Côte de Beaupré (the "Avenue Royale" Highway), and Ile d'Orléans across the Channel. The promenade passes the landing spot of the European settlers, marked by the **Samuel de Champlain Monument**, where Champlain built Fort St-Louis in 1620, securing the new French settlement. A *funiculaire* (cable car; 692-1132; Mon.-Sat. 7:30am-11:30pm, Sun. 8:30am-11:30pm; 75¢) connects Lower Town and Place Royale. The western end of the terrace has **la grande glissade** (a long public toboggan run) in winter, frequented by drunk revelers during the Winter Carnival.

At the bottom of the promenade, towering above the *terrasse*, near rue St-Louis, you'll find **le Château Frontenac**, built on the ruins of two previous *châteaux*. The immense, baroque Frontenac was built in 1893 by the Canadian Pacific Company and has developed into a world-renowned luxury hotel. Although budget travelers will have to forgo staying here, the public can enter the grand hall which contains a small shopping mall.

Near Château Frontenac, between rue St-Louis and rue Buade, lies the **Place d'Armes**. The *calèches* (horse-drawn buggies) that congregate here in summer provide a nice atmosphere, but can smell strong in muggy weather; carriage tours also cost $40. Also on rue Buade, right next to Place d'Armes, is the **Notre-Dame Basilica**. The clock and outer walls date back to 1647; the rest of the church has been rebuilt twice (most recently after a fire in 1922). Notre-Dame, with its odd mix of architectural styles, contrasts sharply with the adjacent **Seminary of Québec**, founded in 1663, which stands as an excellent example of 17th-century *québecois* architecture. At first a Jesuit training school, the seminary became the University of Laval in 1852. The **Musée du Séminaire**, 9, rue de l'Université (642-2843), tonsures nearby. (Open June-Sept. Tues.-Sun. 10:30am-5:30pm; Oct.-May Tues.-Sun. 11am-5pm. Admission $2, seniors and students $1, children 50¢.)

The **Musée du Fort**, 10, rue Ste-Anne (692-2175), presents a sound-and-light show that narrates (in French and English) the history of Quebec City and the series of six battles fought to control it. (Open April-Aug. Mon.-Fri. 10am-6pm, Sat.-Sun. 10am-5pm; in fall Mon.-Fri. 10am-5pm; in winter Mon.-Fri. 11am-5pm, Sat. 10am-5pm, Sun. 1-5pm; closed Dec. 1-20. Admission $3.50, seniors and students $2.)

Walk along rue St-Louis to see its 17th- and 18th-century homes. Of historic note, the surrender of Québec to the British occurred in 1759 at **Maison Kent**, 25, rue St-Louis, built in 1648. The Québec government now uses and operates the house. Touché. At the end of rue St-Louis is **porte St-Louis**, one of the oldest entrances to the fortified city.

La Basse-Ville

You can take a *funiculaire* (75¢) from Terrasse Dufferin to **La Basse-Ville**, the oldest section of Québec, or walk down the steps from Côte de la Montagne. Either way leads to **rue Petit-Champlain**, the oldest road in North America. Many of the old buildings that line the street have been restored or renovated and now house coy craft shops, boutiques, cafés, and restaurants. The **Café-Théâtre Le Petit Champlain**, 68, rue Petit-Champlain, presents québecois music, singing, and theater. The **Poste de taite**, 79, rue Petit-Champlain, sells and displays high-quality local art.

From the bottom of the *funiculaire* you can also take rue Sous-le-Fort and then turn left to reach **Place Royale**, built in 1608, where you'll find the small but beautiful **l'Eglise Notre-Dame-des-Victoires** (692-1650), the oldest church in Canada dating from 1688. A sign asks visitors to observe a respectful silence yet cash registers incessantly ring up tourists buying pictures of the church. (Open daily 9am-5pm; Oct.-May Mon.-Sat. 9am-noon and 2-3:30pm, Sun. 8am-1pm.) The houses surrounding the square have undergone restoration to late 18th-century styles. Considered one of the birthplaces of French civilization in North America, the Place Royale now provides one of the best spots in the city to see outdoor summer theater and concerts. Also along the river stands the recently opened **Musée de la Civilisation**, 85, rue Dalhousie (643-2158). A celebration of Québec culture of past, present, and future, this thematic museum targets French-speaking Canadians, though English tours and exhibit notes are available. One permanent collection follows Québec history from its beginning with life-sized models of old-style houses through the 20th into a projection of the 21st century (with famous hockey players' uniforms). (Open late June-early Sept. daily 10am-7pm; off-season Tues.-Sun. 10am-5pm, Wed. 10am-9pm. Admission $4, seniors $2, students $3, under 17 free. Free Tues.)

The boardwalk on the shore of the St. Lawrence River provides access to Québec's active marina. The "lock" still maintains the safety of the boats docked in the city's Bassin Louise.

Outside the Walls

From the old city, the **promenade des Gouverneurs** leads to the **Plains of Abraham** (otherwise known as the Parc des Champs-de-Bataille) and the **Citadelle** (694-3563). On the Plains of Abraham you'll find the **Musée du Québec**, 1, ave. Wolfe-Montcalm, parc des Champs-de-Bataille (643-4103), which contains a collection of *québecois* paintings, sculptures, decorative arts, and prints. (Open Tues. and Thurs.-Sun. 10am-6pm, Wed. 10am-9:45pm.) The final battle between French and British troops in 1759 before the French surrendered occurred here. A magnificent fortification, the Citadelle still protects Québec City. Visitors can witness the **changing of the guard** daily at 10am from mid-June through Labor Day. (Tours daily every 50 min. from 9am-7pm. Admission $3, children $1.)

Exit the Citadelle along Côte de la Citadelle, which leads back to Porte St-Louis and the Grande Allée. At the corner of la Grande Allée and rue Georges VI, right outside Porte St-Louis, stands **l'Assemblée Nationale** (643-7239). Completed in 1886 and built in the style of French King Louis XIII, the hall merits a visit. You can view debates from the visitors gallery; Anglophones have recourse to simultaneous translation earphones. (Free 30-min. tours Mon.-Fri. 9am-9pm, Sat.-Sun. 9am-5pm; Sept.-May Mon.-Fri. 9am-5pm. Call ahead since large groups can book all the tours.)

Locals follow the **Nordiques,** Québec's hockey team, with near-religious fanaticism; they play from October through April in the Coliseum (691-7211). The raucous **Winter Carnival** happens the second week in February; call 626-3716 for more information. Québec's **Summer Festival** (692-4540), in the second week in July, also proves spectacular.

Near Québec City

Québec City's public transport system leaves St. Lawrence's **Ile-d'Orléans** untouched. The island's proximity to Québec (about 10km or 6 mi. downstream), however, makes an ideal short side trip by car or bicycle; take Autoroute Montmorency (440 est), and cross over at the only bridge leading to the island (Pont de l'Ile). Originally called *Ile de Bacchus* because of the number of wild grapes growing here, the Ile-d'Orléans still remains a sparsely populated retreat of several small villages, with strawberries as its main crop. The **Manoir Mauvide-Genest,** 1451, chemin Royal (829-2915), dates from 1734. A private museum inside has a collection of crafts as well as traditional French and Anglo-Saxon furniture. (Open daily 10am-5pm; Oct.-May Sat.-Sun. 10am-5pm. Admission $1.50.)

Exiting Ile-d'Orléans, turn right (east) onto Rte. 138 (blvd. Ste-Anne) to view the splendid **Chute Montmórency** (Montmorency Falls), substantially taller than Niagara Falls. In winter the falls freeze completely and look even more beautiful. About 20km (13 mi.) along 138 lies **Ste-Anne-de-Beaupré** (Voyageur buses link it to Québec City, $3.50). This small town's entire *raison d'être* seems to be the famous **Basilique Ste-Anne-de Beaupré**, 10018, ave. Royale (827-3781). Since 1658, this double-spired basilica containing the Miraculous Statue and the forearm bone of Ste-Anne (the mother of the Virgin Mary) has supposedly effected miraculous cures. Every year over one million pilgrims come here to pray. (Open daily 8am-9:30pm.) Ask the tourist office about bike rentals in this scenic area.

Ontario

First claimed by French explorer Samuel de Champlain in 1613, Ontario now serves as the stronghold of British influence in Canada. The British first asserted their control with a takeover of Ontario in 1763; a flood of U.S. residents loyal to the crown streamed in when revolution broke out across the border in 1776. Fifteen years later, Ontario officially split with Québec to become Upper Canada. These two provinces, sites of the original French-English conflict, have now become the focal point of the country's struggle to retain a national identity. If Québec has been the Canadian rebel with a cause—threatening independence unless the constitution recognizes it as a distinct society—Ottawa remains true to its motto *Ut Incepit Fidelis Sic Permanent* (Loyal she began, loyal she remains).

Ontario sits in the middle of Canada, stretching from the Great Lakes northward. Home to the nation's capital (Ottawa) and its most populous city (Toronto), Ontario's varied terrain also includes miles of parkland and lakes.

Practical Information

Capital: Toronto.

Tourist Information: Ontario Travel, 77 Bloor St. W., 9th floor, Toronto M7A 2R9 (800-268-3735). Free maps.

Alcohol: Legal drinking age 19.

Time Zone: Eastern. Postal Abbreviation: Ont.

Toronto

For a city that had less than a million residents as recently as the 1950s, playing the role of Canada's most populous city (2.3 million), and unrivalled financial leader takes some getting used to. Next to Montréal's sophisticated lifestyle, Toronto once seemed as bland as suet pudding. Charles Dickens claimed that the townspeople's idea of a Saturday night consisted of wrapping themselves in Union Jacks and singing "God Save the Queen."

The city's reverence for royalty still shows—every other street not named "Queen" or "King St." seems to be named for a specific monarch—but the waves of immigrants following WWII have recognizably altered the city's character. The United Nations dubbed Toronto the world's most multi-cultural city in 1988. And since the late 70s, when the perceived threat of *québecois* nationalism caused a number of companies' head offices to move from Montréal to Toronto, the city donned the crown as Canada's financial capital. Today, the Toronto Stock Exchange handles over 70% of the country's stock trade while most of the city's inhabitants enjoy gainful employment.

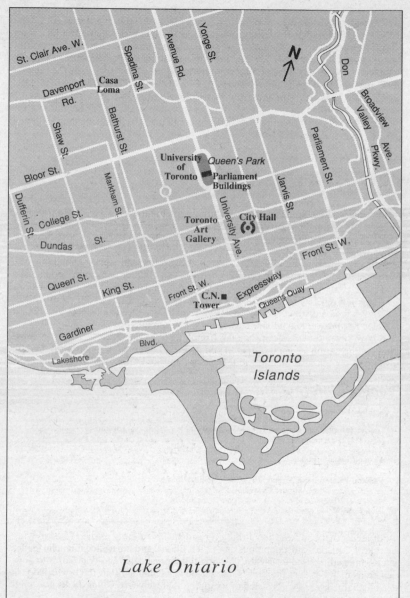

Toronto

0 |———————| 1 Mile

0 |———————| 1 Kilometer

Torontonians have loosened their collars quite a bit (sending starch sales down dramatically) but the staid, flag-clad contingent still clearly influences this town. Shopkeepers sweep the street in front of their businesses, the public transportation is both squeaky clean and efficient, and Toronto hones the cutting edge of environmental consciousness. Recyclables are collected with the trash and even the subways have collection boxes for old newspapers. Do your part to keep Toronto clean, but don't brush aside the ethnic neighborhoods, cultural events, and bar scene of the still-growing city.

Practical Information

Emergency: 911.

Visitor Information: Metropolitan Toronto Convention and Visitor's Association, 207 Queen's Quay Terminal at Harborfront, P.O. Box 126, M5J 1A7. (Infoline 368-9821 in Toronto; 387-3058 in Montréal; 800-387-2999 in Ontario and U.S.). Open daily 8:30am-5pm; mid-May to early Sept. 8:30am-6pm. Two permanent information booths in front of the **Skydome** and **Eaton Centre** at Yonge and Dundas; 3 booths open mid-May to early Sept. at the **Harborfront**, at **Mel Lassman's Square** at Yonge and Shephard, and on **Front St.** across from the Convention Center; 2 booths open mid-June to early Sept. at **Nathan Phillips Square** and **Avenue Rd. and Bloor.** All booths open Mon.-Sat. 9am-7pm, Sun. 9:30am-6:30pm.

Student Travel Agency: Travel CUTS, 187 College St. (979-2406), just west of University Ave. Subway: Queen's Park. Smaller office at 74 Gerrard St. E. (977-0441). Subway: College. Open Mon.-Fri. 9am-5pm. **YHA Travel/Canadian Hostelling Association,** 219 Church St. (862-0226), 2 doors down from the hostel. Subway: Dundas. Excellent for advice and cheap flights. Open Mon.-Wed. and Fri. 10am-5:30pm, Thurs. 10am-7pm, Sat. 10am-4pm.

Canada Customs: locations at 1 Front St. #1514 (973-8022; open Mon.-Fri. 8:30am-4:30pm) and Pearson Airport (676-3643; open daily 7:30am-11pm).

Consulates: U.S., 360 University Ave. (595-0228). Subway: St. Patrick. Open Mon.-Fri. 8:30am-4pm; for visas Mon.-Fri. 8:15-10:30am; for passports Mon.-Fri. 9am-1pm. **Australia,** 175 Bloor St. E. #314-6 (323-1155). Subway: Bloor St. Open Mon.-Fri. 10am-1pm. **U.K.,** 777 Bay St. #1910 (593-1267 or 593-1290). Subway: College. Open Mon.-Fri. 8:30am-5pm. **Germany,** 77 Admiral St. (925-2813). Subway: St. George. Open Mon.-Fri. 9am-noon.

Currency Exchange: Toronto Currency Exchange, 389 Yonge St.; 313 Yonge St. at Dundas; and 727 Yonge St. (598-3769). Open daily 9am-9pm. **Royal Bank of Canada** has exchange centers at Pearson Airport (676-3220). Open daily 6am-11pm.

American Express: 50 Bloor St. W. (967-3411; 474-9280 for lost or stolen travelers' checks). Subway: Bloor-Yonge. Open Mon.-Wed. and Sat. 10am-6pm, Thurs.-Fri. 10am-7pm.

Pearson International Airport: (676-3506) about 20km west of Toronto via Hwy. 427, 401, or 409. **Gray Coach Airport Express** (393-7911) bus service runs each day directly to downtown hotels every 20 min. 6:50am-12:50am. Last bus from downtown at 11:10pm. Fare $8.75, round-trip $15. Buses also serve the Yorkdale ($5.25), York Mills ($6), and Islington subway stations. **Air Canada,** 925-2311. To: Montréal ($175); Calgary ($495); New York City ($184); and Vancouver ($592). All flights 50% less for "student standby;" max. age 21. 50% off round-trip fare if you book 21 days in advance.

Trains: VIA Rail Union Station, 61 Front St. at Bay (366-8411). Subway: Union. To: Montréal (5 per day, $65); Windsor (5 per day, $49); Vancouver (3 per week, $363); New York City (1 per day, $107); Chicago (1 per day, $106). Seniors 10% discount on all fares, seniors and students 40% off tickets purchased 5 days in advance for Sat. and Mon.-Thurs. trips within Québec or Ontario, under 12 50% off all fares. Ticket office open daily 6:45am-7:30pm.

Buses: Voyageur/Greyhound Bus Terminal, 610 Bay St. (Voyageur 393-7911; Greyhound 367-8747), just north of Dundas. Subway: St. Patrick or Dundas. Service to: Montréal ($40), Calgary ($141), Vancouver ($141), New York City ($96). Seniors 10% discount. 14-day advance purchase for most trips. Ticket office open daily 5am-1am.

Public Transport: Toronto Transit Commission (TTC), 393-4636. Network includes 2 subway lines and numerous bus and streetcar routes. Free maps at all stations. Some routes 24 hr. Free transfers among subway, buses, and streetcars, but only within stations. Fare $1.20, 8 tokens $8, seniors 50% off with ID, ages 2-12 55¢. Unlimited travel day pass $5. Monthly pass $53.

Toronto Island Ferry Service: 392-8193 or 392-8194. Numerous ferries to Toronto Islands Park on Centre Island leave daily from Queen's Quay at foot of Yonge St., or Bay St. Ferry Dock at foot of Bay St. Service approximately every ½ hr. (during daytime). Fare $2.25 round-trip; seniors and students 80¢, under 15 45¢.

Taxi: Co-op Cabs, 364-7111. $2 plus distance and waiting.

Car Rental: Downtown Car and Truck, 72 Lippincott St. (947-0212). Subway: Bloor St. $39 per day; 200km free, 12¢ each additional km. Insurance $10-15 per day, depending on age. Open Mon.-Fri. 8am-6pm, Sat. 9am-3pm. Must be over 21 with major credit card. **Hertz** (800-263-0600), **Tilden** (925-4551), **Budget** (961-8006), and **Thrifty** (868-0350) also serve Toronto.

Auto Transport Company: Toronto Driveaway, 5803 Yonge St. (225-7754 or 225-7759), just north of the Finch subway stop, north of Hwy. 401. Most rides to western Canada. In summer, pay gas plus $50-100 to western Canada. **Allostop,** 63 Yonge St. (323-0874), at Bloor. Matches riders with drivers. To: Ottawa ($15), Montréal ($18), Québec City ($30), and New York ($36). Open Tues. and Thurs. 9am-7pm, Wed. 9am-5pm, Sat.-Sun. 10am-5pm.

Bike Rental: Brown's Sports and Cycle Bike Rental, 2447 Bloor St. W. (763-4176). $14 per day. Open Mon.-Wed. 9:30am-6pm, Thurs.-Fri. 9:30am-8pm, Sat. 9:30am-5pm. $100 deposit required.

Help Lines: Rape Crisis, 964-8080. **Services for the Disabled,** Ontario Travel, 965-4008. **Toronto Area Gays (TAG),** 964-6600. Open Mon.-Fri. 7-10pm.

Post Office: Toronto Dominion Centre (973-3120), at King and Bay St. General Delivery at Station K, 2384 Yonge St. at Eglington (483-1334). Open Mon.-Fri. 8am-5:45pm. **Postal Code:** M4P 2E0.

Area Code: 416.

Toronto hunkers down on the northwestern shore of Lake Ontario, across the lake from Niagara Falls, about 175km from Buffalo, NY, along the Queen Elizabeth Way (QEW). From Detroit/Windsor, take Hwy. 401 E. (about 380km); from Montréal, take Hwy. 401 W. (about 540km).

The intersection of **Yonge** (pronounced young) **Street** and **Bloor Street,** at the Bloor-Yonge subway stop, makes up the city center. The streets of Toronto form a grid pattern. Yonge divides the city east-west. "North" addresses start from Lake Ontario.

Traffic feels quite heavy in Toronto—avoid rush hour (7-10am and 3-7pm) at all costs. Parking spots are hard to find and the police ticket zealously. Parking garage rates are generally steep (75¢-$2.50 for the first ½ hr. or less). The parking lot on Church St. just south of Dundas across from the hostel (see Accommodations and Camping below) charges a flat rate of $4 from 6pm-7am and $8 from 7am-6pm. The lot on Dundas just west of Sherbourne charges $6 per day, $3 per night. Save money by leaving your car in the street at night (meters stop at 6pm, start again at 8am) or by parking at an outlying subway station (often free) and taking trains downtown.

The bus and train stations are both in the downtown area; the train station (Union Station) is also a subway stop. From the main bus terminal, walk along Dundas in either direction to reach the St. Patrick or Dundas subway stop.

Accommodations and Camping

Cheap hotels and motels, concentrated around Jarvis St., tend to be of dubious character. However, several guest houses keep their rates low and standards high, despite the rugged clientele that low prices tend to attract. For relatively inexpensive accommodations in a private home, reserve ahead through **Toronto Bed and Breakfast,** P.O. Box 269, 253 College St. M5T, 1R5 (461-3676 or 588-8800) for 23 homes, all with access to subway. (Singles from $40. Doubles from $50. Call Mon.-Fri. 9am-7pm.) Also of great assistance is the **University of Toronto Housing and Residence Service,** Koffler Center, 214 College St. (978-8045). Excellent, up-to-date hotel, hostel, B&B, and U of T Residence listings developed for U of T students. Ask nicely and they'll give you the list, too. Comprehensive sublet listings available for college students or graduates with ID for $5. (Open July-Aug. Mon.-Tues. 8am-7:30pm, Wed.-Fri. 8am-4:30pm, Sat. 10am-4pm; off-season Mon.-Fri. 8am-5pm.) Camping alternatives are uninspiring and far-removed from the city center.

Toronto International Hostel (IYHF), 223 Church St. (368-1848 or 368-0207), just south of Dundas, a 5-min. walk from Eaton Centre. Subway: Dundas. Three separate buildings with clean but varied rooms. One has a single toilet and shower for 21 beds; another perches directly above Dundas and Church where streetcars pound by 24 hrs. Staff could act much friendlier. Huge lounge with TV and excellent kitchen. 3-night max. stay enforced. Check-in 7am-2am. Check-out 10am. $14, nonmembers $18. Linen $1.50.

Knox College, 59 Saint George St. (478-2793). Huge rooms with wood floors in a theological college around a Utopian coutyard. Common rooms and baths on each floor, but no kitchen. Great location in the heart of U of T campus. Singles $25. Two-single suites $35. Call for reservations Mon.-Fri. 9am-4pm.

Neill-Wycik College Hotel, 96 Gerrard St. E. (977-2320). From College subway stop, walk 1 block east on Carleton to Church St., turn right, walk to Gerrard and make a left. Rooms impeccably clean, some with beautiful views of the city. Kitchen on every floor. Breakfast included. Singles $34. Doubles $40. Family room $45-47 (extra beds $8, under 17 free). 10% discount for 7-night stay if you pay up front; 20% off for IYHF members with no reservations after 8pm. Open early May-late Aug.

Victoria College Residence, Margaret Addison Hall, 140 Charles St. W. (585-4524), just east of Avenue Rd. 1 block south of Bloor St. Subway: Museum. 150 modern dorms with shared baths. Great location near trendy shopping areas and museum. Comfortable lounge on each floor, but no kitchen. Singles $37-49. Doubles $54-60. Seniors and students: singles $25, doubles $42. Huge breakfast included. Open mid-May to late Aug.

Trinity College Residence, 6 Hoskin Ave. (978-2523), on Queen's Park Crescent close to the Royale Ontario Museum and shopping on Bloor St. Subway: Museum. Dorms in one of U of T's 6 colleges. Beautiful Gothic quadrangle. Shared bath and kitchen. Library available. Huge rooms. Singles $36. Doubles $48. Reservations recommended. Office hours Mon.-Fri. 9am-4pm.

Karabanow Guest House and Tourist Home, 9 Spadina Rd. (923-4004), at Bloor St. 6 blocks west of Yonge. Subway: Spadina. Centrally located. Small and intimate. 18 rooms (mostly doubles) in a mixture of old-fashioned and renovated modern styles. TV and parking. Singles $35. Doubles $45, with private bath $60. Add $5 July-Aug.

Janvary Guest House, 314 Saint George St. (923-8186), at Dupont St. in the University student district. Subway: St. George. 2-day min. stay. Huge rooms covered with oriental rugs in an old house. Owner takes care of all 5 rooms personally. Singles $30. Doubles $50. Call for reservations.

Indian Line Tourist Campground, Finch Ave. W. (678-1233), at Darcel Ave. Follow Hwy. 427 north to Finch and go west. Sites $12, with hookup $15. Open mid-May to mid-Oct.

Food

The best and least expensive fare in Toronto simmers in ethnic restaurants and open-air markets. You can find just about any kind of food here; check the yellow pages, which lists restaurants by ethnic category. To best sample the numerous cuisines of Toronto, walk all of the ethnic neighborhoods of the city. These include an immense China and Vietnam Town, Little Italy, Greek Island, Hungarian Village, and Little India.

In **Chinatown,** around Dundas St. east and west of University Ave., you'll find delicious and cheap Chinese food of every variety. In recent years Chinatown has been expanding north onto Spadina Ave. (Subway: St. Patrick.) From the heart of Chinatown, walk across Spadina Ave. and up 1 block for the freshest and cheapest meat, produce, and cheese in **Kensington Market,** at Augusta and Baldwin St. west of Spadina, south of College St. The market, originally the old Jewish ghetto of the city, is now predominantly Portuguese, Chinese, and West Indian. Visit the Portuguese bakeries on Augusta St. for sweet bread and pastries and the West Indian shops for *roti* and spicy meat patties. The **St. Lawrence Market,** 95 Front St. E. at Jarvis, a few blocks east of the King subway stop, is a huge two-story warehouse where farmers, fishers, and butchers sell their produce.

Little Italy, mostly on St. Clair Ave. W. (take the St. Clair streetcar west from Yonge subway), but also west of University Ave. on College St. (College streetcar), helps to imbue Toronto with its distinctly European flavor. Cafés, social clubs, bakeries, and sandwich shops stay open until very late, and the *gelati* and espresso rival Italy's best. **Greek Island,** on Danforth Ave. E. (take Bloor subway eastbound), has miles of shish-kebab houses and bakeries brimming with flaky *baklava* and sugary Turkish delight. **Little India** mainly makes up a 2-block area on Gerrard St. E. (Take the Gerrard or College St. streetcar.) Many cheap *tandoori* places provide buffets for under $6; shops selling *paan* (a dessert of nuts, seeds, and honey wrapped in paan leaf) line the streets.

Blue Cellar Room, 469 Bloor St. W., west of Spadina near Brunswick Ave., part of L'Europa Restaurant. Subway: Spadina. Walk down a long, blue hallway to this Hungarian haunt of students. Heaps of *goulash* or a plateful of *wienerschnitzel* less than $6.75. Sandwiches $5-6. Open Mon.-Sat. 11am-1am, Sun. 11am-midnight.

House of Noodles, 457 Dundas St. W. Take the streetcar west on Dundas. Enormous mounds of noodles cooked in every conceivable Asian way, topped with the meats and vegetables of your choice. At the center of bustling Chinatown. Noodles $5.25-9. Open daily 11am-midnight.

Café Diplomatic and Restaurant, 594 College St. Take the College streetcar west to Clinton St. Wonderful European-style café, with colorful clientele and relaxed outdoor seating. Excellent *gelati* ($2.50), expresso ($1.50), and cappuccino ($2). Pasta $6-8. Open daily 9am-2am.

Astoria Shish Kebab House, 390 Danforth Ave. Subway: Chester Ave. Traditional Greek cuisine—tasty shish kebab (platter $10) and *baklava* ($2). Comfortable patio in summer. Open Mon.-Sat. 11am-1am, Sun. 11am-midnight.

Antonio's Mostly Pasta, 99½ Dundas St. E. at Church, around the corner from the hostel. Eager to succor weary travelers. 15% discount for IYHF members. Fresh pasta dishes $4. Open Mon.-Sat. 11:30am-9pm.

Renaissance Café, 509 Bloor St. W. Subway: Spadina. Fun for tofu lovers and other hip health eccentrics. Funky decor plastered with original modern art. Moon burger (tofu, spices and *tahini* sauce) $6. Pasta $9-10. Open Mon.-Thurs. and Sun. noon-midnight, Fri.-Sat. noon-1am.

Yung Sing Pastry Shop, 22 Baldwin St. Take the Dundas streetcar to McCaul St. and walk 2 blocks north. Lines file outside Chu Ko's tiny bakery for the city's best pork *bao* and *don* tart. Crowds eat the delicacies right outside the shop on an exciting street of student-filled cafés and bars. Fried pork dumplings (4 for $2.60), cookies and tarts (65-85¢). Open daily 11am-6pm.

Bahamian Kitchen, 14 Baldwin St., 2 blocks north of Dundas, off McCaul St. Take the Dundas streetcar. Lively café/restaurant with cheap and spicy Bahamian treats. Try the *conch* shells. Lunch entrees $6-7.25. Dinners from $9.50. Open daily noon-10pm.

Sights

Urban **Yonge Street** is Toronto's main shopping street, intersecting with Bloor in the ritzy, three-piece-suited city center. Bloor Street W., between Yonge St. and Avenue Rd., will remind many of New York's Fifth Ave. Just north of this area lies **Yorkville,** which attracted the hippie counterculture during the 60s when Joni Mitchell and James Taylor used to strum here. Today it's a chic shopping and dining neighborhood: come to window-shop at expensive boutiques, people-watch from outdoor cafés, or have your fortune told.

The vast, ultra-modern **Eaton Centre,** a glass-domed, four-tiered shopping mall, preens on Yonge St., spanning the distance between Queen and Dundas St. several blocks north. The underground shops stretch all the way to Union Station. While in the area, visit the trendy strip of **Queen Street West,** at its funkiest between University Ave. and Spadina Rd. (Subway: Osgoode.) Catch the bohemian, punk, and new wave clubs and bizarre second-hand clothing stores. The newest fads start here, at the "cutting edge of the wedge" hangouts.

Slightly north of the Queen St. W. strip lies Canada's largest and most exciting **Chinatown.** Centered at Dundas and Spadina, this neighborhood offers authentic

Chinese cuisine, grocery stores, bakeries, boutiques, and theater. Visit the famous **China Court,** 208 Spadina, just south of Dundas, a colorful Chinese shopping plaza modeled on the Imperial Palace in Peking.

The **Art Gallery of Ontario (AGO),** 317 Dundas St. W. (977-0414), 2 blocks west of University Ave. in the heart of Chinatown, houses an enormous collection of Western art from the Renaissance up through the past decade, with particular concentration on famous Canadian artists. (Open mid-May to early Sept. daily 11am-5:30pm, Wed. 11am-9pm. Admission $4.50, seniors and students $2.50, under 12 free, families $9. Free Wed. 5-9pm. Seniors free Fri. Subway: St. Patrick.) Reach Chinatown on a streetcar going west from Dundas subway stop. Bilingual street signs let you know when you're there.

Members of Toronto's various ethnic groups meet and sell their wares at famous **Kensington Market,** a frenetic multilingual bazaar located south of College on Baldwin, Augusta, and Kensington St. (Open Mon.-Sat. from dawn, but the area really jumps Fri. afternoons and Sat.) Other neighborhoods worth a gander include Greek Town on Danforth, east of the Don Valley Pkwy. (extension of Bloor St. E.; subway: Broadview), and Little Italy on College, west of Bathurst, and along St. Clair Ave. W. The **Beaches** neighborhood, named for Kew Beach, merits a visit on a warm day. The **Kew Gardens** face Queen St. E. (take the streetcar as far as it will go), making it easy to skip between sunbathing and the shops on Queen. The neighborhood of Bloor St. W., next to the University, features the Hungarian Village, Peruvian craft shops, bookstores, student bars, and various lively cafés.

The building that most travelers associate with the city is the **CN Tower,** at 301 Front St. W. (360-8500). Visible from almost everywhere in Toronto, the tower is the tallest free-standing structure in the world at 553m. Three observation decks offer panoramic views of the vast metropolitan area. Choose a clear, dry day and you might even see Niagara Falls, 160km distant. Unfortunately, the view isn't free—you must shell out $10 to take the glass-fronted elevator to the first observation deck, 346m up (seniors and ages 5-16 $3, under 5 $2). Traveling farther up to the "space pod," the highest observation level, costs an extra $1. This leg of the journey is not really necessary—but who would stop three-fourths of the way up Everest? (Open Mon.-Sat. 9am-midnight, Sun. 10am-10pm.) From the top of the CN Tower during good weather, you can look down at the **Skydome** (341-3663), home field of the Toronto Blue Jays baseball team. Opened in 1989, the Dome has a fully retractable roof and an occasionally lewd luxury hotel among the stands. A huge shopping network containing North America's largest McDonald's adjoins the dome.

Another classic tourist attraction is the 98-room **Casa Loma,** Davenport Rd. at 1 Austin Terrace (923-1172), near Spadina a few blocks north of the Dupont subway stop. Though the outside of the only real turreted castle in North America belongs in a fairy tale, the inside's dusty old exhibits can be skipped. (Open daily 10am-4pm. Admission $7, seniors and under 16 $4.)

The pink sandstone **Provincial Parliament Buildings** of the Ontario government preside over beautiful **Queen's Park** right in the city's center. (Subway: Queen's Park.) Begin a tour of the area with these Romanesque 19th-century edifices. Stroll through the marble halls, or take a free guided tour (965-4028; daily every hr. on the hr. or ½ hr. 9am-4pm, Sept. 8 to mid-May Mon.-Fri. only). To see the legislative assembly in action, ask for free visitors gallery passes at the information desk in the main lobby (Oct.-Dec. and Feb.-June Mon.-Thurs. 1:30-6pm). Just west of Queen's Park is **King's College Circle,** the focal point of the **University of Toronto** **(U of T),** established in 1827. The university stretches miles across the city, but most of the older buildings lie near this circular grass playing field. The U of T divides into colleges, each with a distinctive architectural style. Look for Romanesque **University College** (1859) and adjacent Gothic **Hart House** (1919). Student guides conduct free hour-long walking tours of the campus in English and French, beginning in the Map Room of Hart House. (978-5000; June-Aug. Mon.-Fri. at 10:30am, 12:30pm, and 2:30pm; Sept.-May 978-4111; ask for Susan Grant.) Groups of fewer than five people can get a tour any time during the summer. Call to arrange group tours.

From here, head back toward Queen's Park and walk north to visit the **McLaughlin Planetarium**, 100 Queen's Park Crescent (586-5736), the neighboring **Royal Ontario Museum (ROM)**, just south of Bloor (586-5549), and the **George M. Gardiner Museum of Ceramic Art**, 111 Queen's Park (593-9300), opposite the ROM. The planetarium's cozy reclining seats allow you to lie back as you take in the excellent evening laser light shows. You can also catch an audiovisual presentation on astronomy in the afternoon or evening. (Open Tues.-Sun. Laser shows $6.50, regular shows $4.50, seniors, students, and children $2.50.) The ROM is one of the best natural history museums on the continent, and also contains a superb collection of Chinese art and archeology; the Gardiner has an impressive display of European and South American ceramics. (Both open Fri.-Mon. and Wed. 10am-6pm, Tues. and Thurs. 10am-8pm. Admission for both $5; seniors, students, and children $3; family $12. Free Thurs. after 4:30pm.)

Modern architecture aficionados should visit the **City Hall** at the corner of Queen and Bay St. (392-9111) between the Osgoode and Queen subway stops, with curved twin towers and a rotunda considered quite avant-garde when completed in 1965. **Nathan Phillips Square,** in front of City Hall, a forum for art shows, rock concerts, and multi-cultural festivals also hosts more mellow events such as sunbathing, picnicking, and people-watching.

The **Ontario Science Centre,** 770 Don Mills Rd. at Eglinton Ave. E. (429-0193 or 429-4100), lies one hour from downtown; take the subway to Eglinton, then the eastbound bus to Don Mills Rd. Part museum, part hands-on fun-fair, the centre entertains with great gadgets and displays. (Open Mon.-Thurs. and Sat. 10am-6pm, Fri. 10am-9pm, Sun. noon-6pm; Sept.-June daily 10am-6pm. Admission $5.50, seniors free, ages 13-17 $4.50, under 13 $1.50, families $9. Free Fri. 5-9pm.)

Metro Toronto Zoo (284-8181), about 25km northeast of downtown, 5km north of Hwy. 401 on Meadowvale Rd., has 700 acres of huge, climate-controlled pavilions representing the world's geographic regions. (Open May-Aug. daily 9:30am-7pm, ticket office closes at 6pm; Sept.-April daily 9:30am-4:30pm, ticket office closes at 3:30pm. Admission $8, seniors and ages 12-17 $5, 5-11 $3; cheaper off-season. Take subway to Kennedy station, then take bus #86A.) **Canada's Wonderland** (832-2205 or 800-668-2756), 30km north of downtown, rocks with 33 rides, seven theme areas, and five roller coasters. (Open mid-June to early Sept. daily 10am-10pm; early May to mid-June and early Sept. to mid-Oct. Sat.-Sun. 10am-8pm. One-day pass $23, seniors and ages 3-6 $11. Buses ($3) run every ½ hour as long as the park is open, from York Mills and York Dale subway.) **Toronto Islands Park** (392-8193 for ferry information), a 4-mi. strip of connected islands just opposite the downtown area (15-min. ferry trip), is a popular "vacationland," with a boardwalk, bathing beaches, canoe and bike rentals, a Frisbee golf course, and a children's farm and amusement park. Ferries leave from the Bay Street Ferry Dock at the foot of Bay St. (the Bay St. bus stops there), and from Queen's Quay at the foot of Yonge St.

The **Harbourfront** development, 2½ mi. of renovated lakeshore piers, encompasses malls, craft shops, and stages for cultural events. (Take the subway to Union, then the streetcar south.) Famous landmarks figure prominently in Toronto. You'll need more than a weekend to explore and appreciate them thoroughly. The sprawl of the city makes it impossible to construct a single walking tour that covers the important spots. If you'll only be in Toronto briefly, a bus tour is a good idea. **Gray Line Sight-Seeing** (393-7911) offers tours of the principal sights (2½-hr. "Inside Toronto" tour leaves the main bus terminal at Bay and Dundas daily at 10am and 2pm. $15. From late June-late Aug. buses will end tour at either the Casa Loma or CN Tower for $5 extra.)

Entertainment

Nightlife

Many of Toronto's clubs and pubs remain closed on Sundays because of antiquated liquor laws. Otherwise, the city's Victorian stiffness has vanished, though some of the more formal clubs uphold dress codes. Toronto has bars and nightclubs to suit every mood and lifestyle. Infiltrating the university crowd can be somewhat difficult since most campus pubs restrict admission to their own students. But you can mingle with students dedicated to several classic bars near U of T, Ryerson, and York including **The Brunswick House, Lee's Palace,** (see below) and the **All-Star Eatery,** 277 Victoria (977-7619), at Dundas 1 block east of the Dundas subway stop. The most interesting new clubs are on trendy **Queen Street West.** The gay scene centers around Wellesley and Church, although there's also some gay activity on Queen and Yonge St. *Now* magazine, published every Thursday, is the city's comprehensive entertainment guide, available in restaurants and record stores all over Toronto. The Friday edition of the *Toronto Star* has a section called "What's On" filled with information on clubs, danceterias, pubs, restaurants, concerts, and movies.

Bamboo, 312 Queen St. W. (593-5771), 3 blocks west of the Osgoode subway stop. Popular with students. Live reggae, jazz, rock, and funk daily. Great dancing. Caribbean/Thai menu. Dinner entrees from $8.50. Patio upstairs. Open Mon.-Sat. noon-1am. Hefty cover varies from band to band.

El Mocambo, 464 Spadina Ave. at College St. (324-9591; 324-9667 for recording), at the edge of the U of T campus. Neon palm tree façade. Loud rock 'n' roll club, with dancing and live performances. The Rolling Stones recorded "Love You Live" here in 1977 before an audience that included Margaret Trudeau. Doors open at 8pm. The music upstairs and show downstairs start at 9:30pm. Open Mon.-Sat. 11am-1am, Sun. 5pm-1am. No cover downstairs; upstairs varies with band.

Brunswick House, 481 Bloor St. W. (964-2242), at Brunswick between the Bathurst and Spadina subway stops. Rowdy dive reeling with students. Beer $1.10. Upstairs is **Albert's Hall,** famous for its blues. Open Mon.-Sat. noon-1am.

George's Spaghetti House, 290 Dundas St. E. at Sherbourne St. (923-9887). Subway: Dundas; take the streetcar east to Sherbourne. The city's best jazz club attracts the nation's top ensembles. Dinner entrees from $8.50. Restaurant open Mon.-Thurs. 11am-11pm, Fri. 11am-midnight, Sat. 5pm-midnight. Jazz Mon.-Sat. 6pm-1am. Cover Sun.-Thurs. $4, Fri.-Sat. $5. No cover at bar.

Lee's Palace, 529 Bloor St. W. (532-7383), just east of the Bathurst subway stop. Amazing art depicting rock 'n' roll frenzy. Live music nightly. Pick up a calendar of bands.

Second City, in The Old Firehall, 110 Lombard St. at Jarvis (863-1111), 2 blocks east and 2 short blocks south of Queen's Park subway stop. One of North America's craziest and most creative comedy clubs. Spawned comics Dan Aykroyd, John Candy, Gilda Radner, and Dave Thomas; a hit TV show (SCTV); and the legendary "Great White North." Dinner and theater $23-25. Theater without dinner $10.50-12, students $6.50. Free improv sessions (Mon.-Thurs. at 10:30pm)—students welcome. Shows Mon.-Thurs. at 8:30pm, Fri.-Sat. at 8 and 11pm. Reservations recommended, especially for weekends.

Nuts and Bolts, 277 Victoria St. (977-1356), at Dundas. Underground dance club and bar popular with Ryerson students. Tri-level dance floor packed on weekends. Open Mon.-Wed. and Sun. 9pm-1am, Thurs. 9pm-3am, Fri.-Sat. 9pm-4am. Cover Thurs. $2, Fri.-Sat. $5.

The Copa, Yorkville Ave. at Yonge St. (922-5107); entrance off Yorkville. Subway: Bloor St. Huge warehouse dance emporium. No need to pack a bread box: great hot/cold buffet included. Cover Wed.-Thurs. $5.50, Fri.-Sat. $6, Sun. $5. Open Wed.-Thurs. 7pm-1am, Fri.-Sat. 6pm-4am, Sun. 6:30pm-1am.

Festivals and Cultural Events

Toronto flaunts some lively ethnic festivals and special events. In late June, at the **Metro International Caravan** (977-0466), dancers, singers, musicians, and chefs representing more than 50 nations demonstrate their skills in pavilions around the city (single day $6, 9-day passes $12). **Caribana,** an enormous celebration led in early August by Canada's West Indian community, excuses a massive open-air party in the streets with a parade and plenty of *soca* music. Devotees of the big screen should catch the **Festival of Festivals** (967-7371), a movie marathon offering 300 screenings of 250 innovative new films over 10 days in early September. The city also offers a few first-class freebies. Enjoy superb performances of Shakespeare by **Toronto Free Theater** (392-7251) amid the greenery of High Park, Bloor St. W. at Parkside Dr. (Subway: High Park). Bring something to sit on or wedge yourself on the 45° slope to the stage. Call for performance schedules. Every Thursday night in July and August between 7:30 and 9:30pm, the **Toronto Summer Music Festival** presents free jazz concerts on the grounds of Queen's Park (Subway: Queen's Park). The **du Maurier Ltd. Downtown Jazz Festival** also offers some free shows. Call Harbourfront Information (973-3000) or Roy Thomson Hall (872-4255) for details.

Ontario Place, 955 Lakeshore Blvd. W. (965-7917; 965-7711 recording), features first-class cheap entertainment in summer—the Toronto Symphony, National Ballet Company, Ontario Place Pops, and top pop artists perform here free with admission to the park. Kids should love the slides and water games of Children's Village (waterslide and log ride $2 each; 4 tickets $6). Admission also includes a six-story Cinesphere with a psychedelic simulation of flight and free-fall. (Open mid-May to early Sept. Mon.-Sat. 10am-1am, Sun. 10am-11pm. Admission $7, seniors and children $3. $2 after 9:30pm. Seniors free Wed.) **Roy Thomson Hall,** 60 Simcoe St. at King St. W. (872-4255), is the home of the Toronto Symphony Orchestra. Tickets are expensive ($15-30), but $7.50 rush tickets go on sale at 6pm the day of the concert at the box office (592-4828; order by phone Mon.-Fri. 9am-8pm, Sat. noon-5pm; office opens 2 hr. before Sun. performance). The same office serves **Massey Hall,** 178 Victoria St., near Eaton Centre (Subway: Dundas), a great hall for rock and folk concerts. The opera and ballet companies perform at **O'Keefe Centre,** 1 Front St. E. at Yonge (393-7469; tickets from $30). Rush hour tickets (for the last row of orchestra seats) on sale daily at 11am for $9. Seniors and students can line up one hour before performances for the best seats available ($9). (Box office open daily 11am-9pm.) Next door, **St. Lawrence Centre,** 27 Front St. E. (366-7723), presents excellent classic and Canadian drama and chamber music recitals in two different theaters. Student rush tickets for theater are available half an hour before showtime ($6). Call for schedules and prices—some shows free. (Box office open Mon.-Sat. 10am-8pm.)

Pick up monthly *Key to Toronto* and *Toronto Life* magazines for cultural events and restaurants; *Now* magazine for comprehensive theater listings. All three are free. You can often beat the high cost of culture by seeking out standby or student discount options. **Five Star Tickets** (596-8211) sells half-price tickets for theater, music, dance, and opera on the day of performance: Visit their booth at Dundas and Yonge in front of Eaton Centre. (Subway: Dundas. Open Mon.-Sat. noon-7:30pm, Sun. 11am-3pm.) **Ticketron** (872-1212) and **Ticketmaster** (872-2262) also carry tickets in Toronto. For **Blue Jays** seats ($4-15), call 341-1000.

Near Toronto: Algonquin Provincial Park

The wilder Canada of endless rushing rivers and shimmering lakes awaits in Algonquin Provincial Park, about 300km north of Toronto. There are two ways to experience Algonquin: the Hwy. 60 Corridor, where tents and trailers crowd the roadside; and the park interior, the "essence of Algonquin." You can rent gear for a backcountry adventure at several outfitting stores around and inside the park. Try **Algonquin Outfitters,** RR#1-Oxtongue Lake, Dwight P0A 1H0 (April-Nov. 705-635-2243), just off Hwy. 60 about 10km west of the park's west gate. To enter the park, you need an Interior Camping Permit ($2.50 per person per night), available at the main gate or from any outfitter.

Ottawa

Diplomacy could be Ottawa's middle name. Each of the provinces send representatives to Ottawa, their nation's capital, with the tricky task of simultaneously creating national unity and preserving local identity. Though neighbors Toronto and Montréal win far more acclaim for their modern, cosmopolitan communities, Ottawa remains perhaps the only truly bilingual city in the confederation. French and English share time both in theory and in practice; the federal government insists on it, and Ottawa's border with Québec allows residents genuine access to both tongues. In a country this size, such strategic location is invaluable—Queen Victoria chose this remote lumbering settlement to house the nation's government in 1857 as a compromise between French and English interests. The site's distance from the border of a hostile United States also favored her decision.

City planning spurred by tension with the U.S. continued for Ottawa around the turn of the century, when Prime Minister Sir Wilfred Laurier lamented the unsavory appearance of the town and called on urban planners to create a "Washington of the North." Today, close to a century of work manifests itself in Ottawa's museums, parks, and artistic communities, which give it the look of a bigger, older city. Ottawa also bears the marks of a young city still trying desperately to expand. Rush-hour headaches have prompted some citizens to propose banning cars from downtown—the city would be cleaner, and the nation's leaders could probably benefit from the exercise.

Practical Information

Emergency: 911. **Ottawa Provincial Police:** 821-9171. **Hull Police,** 770-4444.

Visitor Information: National Capital Commission Information Center, 14 Metcalfe St. (239-5000), at Wellington opposite Parliament Buildings. **Ottawa/Hull Inc.,** 65 Elgin St. (237-5158). Both provide free maps and a visitors guide to restaurants, hotels, and sights. Both open summer daily 8:30am-9pm; early Sept.-early May Mon.-Sat. 9am-5pm, Sun. 10am-4pm.

Embassies: U.S., 100 Wellington St. (238-5335). Open for information Mon.-Fri. 10am-4pm; for visas Mon.-Fri. 8:30am-1pm. **U.K.,** 80 Elgin St. (237-1530). Open for information Mon.-Fri. 10am-4:30pm; for visas Mon.-Fri. 10am-1pm. **Australia,** 500 O'Connor St. (236-0841). Open Mon.-Fri. 9am-noon and 2-4pm.

Student Travel Agencies: Travel CUTS, 1 Stewart St. #203 at Waller (238-8222), just west of Nicholas. Experts in student travel—youth hostel cards, cheap flights. Open 9am-5pm. July-Aug. 9am-4pm. **Canadian Hostelling Association (CHA),** 18 Bywood St. (230-1200). Eurail and youth hostel passes. Travel information. Open Mon.-Sat. 9am-5pm.

American Express: 220 Laurier W. (563-0231), between Metcalfe and O'Connor in the heart of the business district. Open Mon.-Fri. 8am-5pm.

Airport: Ottawa International Airport, 20 min. south of the city off Bronson Ave. Take bus #96 from Le Breton station, Albert St. at Booth, or Slater St. for regular fare. Express airport buses from **Lord Elgin Hotel,** 100 Elgin Blvd. at Slater (235-3333) cost $6. (Daily every ½ hr. 6:30am-10:30pm.)

VIA Rail Station: 200 Tremblay Rd. (reservations 238-8289; recorded departure information 238-4706), off Alta Vista Rd. To: Montréal (3 per day, 2 hr., $26); Toronto (3 per day, 4 hr., $57); Québec City (1 per day, $53). Poor U.S. connections. To New York ($107, spend the night in Toronto). 40% discount for reservations 5 days in advance and travel Sat. or Mon.-Thurs. Ticket office open Mon.-Sat. 6am-5:30pm, Sun. 7am-7:20pm.

Voyageur Bus: 265 Catherine St. (238-5900), between Kent and Lyon. Service throughout Canada and the U.S. To: Montréal ($18), Toronto ($36), Québec City ($46), Boston ($97), and New York ($98). Open daily 7am-11pm.

Public Transport: OC Transport, 294 Albert St. (741-4390), at Kent. Excellent bus system. Buses congregate on either side of Rideau Centre; Mackenzie Bridge and the corner of Nicholas and Rideau. Fare 90¢, rush hour $1.80. Seniors 90¢. **Visibus** pass for a day of unlimited travel $3, family of 4 $7, ages under 6 free.

Taxi: Blue Line Taxi, 238-1111. Rates fixed by law ($1.70 plus distance and waiting).

Car Rental: Tilden, 199 Slater St. at Bank (232-3536). cheapest car $52 per day with 200km free, 10¢ each additional km. Insurance $12 per day. Open daily 7am-11pm. Must have credit card. **Budget,** 443 Somerset W. at Kent (232-1526). $52 per day with 200km free, 12¢ each additional km. Insurance $11 per day. Open Mon.-Fri. 7am-8pm, Sat.-Sun. 8am-8pm. **Hertz,** 881 St. Laurent (746-9969) and **Myers,** 1200 Baseline St. (225-8006) also serve Ottawa/Hull.

Rider/Driver Matching Agency: Allostop, 246 Maisonneuve (778-8877). To: Toronto ($15), Québec City ($19), Montréal ($8), and New York ($40). Open Mon.-Wed. and Sat. 9am-5pm, Thurs.-Fri. 9am-7pm, Sun. noon-7pm.

Bike Rental: Rent-A-Bike-Location Velo, 1 Rideau St. (233-0268), behind the Château Laurier Hotel. $3-7 per hr., $11-25 per day. Maps and locks free. Open mid-May to mid-Oct. daily 9am-7pm.

Help Line: Gayline-Telegai, 238-1717. Information and special events and meetings, as well as counseling services. Open Mon.-Fri. 7:30-10:30pm, Sat.-Sun. 6-9pm.

Alcohol: Legal ages 19 (Ottawa) and 18 (Hull). Bars stay open in Ottawa until 1am, in Hull until 3am.

Post Office: Postal Station "A," 347 Dalhousie St. at George St. (992-4760). Open Mon.-Fri. 8am-6pm. **Postal Code: T1N 8T9.**

Area Codes: 613 (Ottawa); 819 (Hull).

Ottawa is 195km west of Montreal, 170km north of Kingston, and 395km northeast of Toronto. Driving from Montréal, take Hwy. 40 west to Hwy. 417, which leads to Ottawa. Drivers with an extra half-hour to spare might prefer to take scenic Hwy. 17 or Hwy. 148, which follow the banks of the Ottawa River. Highway 17 is accessible from Hwy. 417 just after the end of Hwy. 40 from Québec. Drivers from Toronto and Kingston should take Hwy. 401 east to Hwy. 16 north, and then follow Hwy. 16 to Ottawa.

The **Rideau Canal** divides Ontario into eastern and western sections. West of the canal, Parliament buildings and government offices line **Wellington Street,** the main east-west artery. East of the canal, Wellington St. becomes Rideau St., surrounded by a fashionable new shopping district. To the north of Rideau St. lies the **Byward Market,** a recently renovated shopping area and the focus for Ottawa's nightlife. **Bank Street,** which traverses the entire city and services the other, older shopping area, is the primary north-south street. **Elgin Street,** the other major north-south artery, stretches from the **Queensway (Hwy. 417)** to the War Memorial in the heart of the city in front of **Parliament Hill.** The canal itself is a major access route: in winter, thousands of Ottawa residents skate to work on the world's longest skating rink; in summer, power boats breeze by. Bike paths and pedestrian walkways border the canals, allowing a pleasant alternative to transit by car or bus. Parking is difficult downtown. Meters cost 25¢ for 15 min. with a one-hour limit. Residential neighborhoods east of the canal have one-hour and three-hour limits but the police ticket less often than on main streets.

Across the Ottawa River lies **Hull,** Québec, most notable for its proximity to Gatineau Provincial Park and the many bars and discos that rock nightly until 3am. Hull is accessible by several bridges and the blue Hull buses from downtown Ottawa.

Accommodations and Camping

Clean, inexpensive rooms are not difficult to find in Ottawa, except during May and early June, when droves of high school students studying politics make a pilgrimage to the capital and fill budget lodgings to the brim. **Ottawa Bed and Breakfast,** 488 Cooper St. (563-0161) will place you in one of 10 homes. Some lodgings are downtown, others in outlying areas of Ottawa. Reservations recommended; call between 10am and 9pm. (Singles $34. Doubles $44.)

Nicholas Gaol International Hostel (IYHF), 75 Nicholas St. (235-2595), near Daly St. in the heart of downtown Ottawa. Take bus #4 from the inter-city bus terminal or bus #95 west from the train station. Site of Canada's last hanging, this intriguing hostel now houses 4-8 guests in former Carleton County jail cells. 160 rooms. Hot showers and kitchen, as well as extensive lounge facilities. Lockout 10am-5pm.Curfew 1am. $10, nonmembers $14. Open daily 7am-midnight.

University of Ottawa Residences, University St. (564-5400), in the center of campus. Clean dorm rooms within easy walking distance of downtown. Shared hall showers. Lounges with kitchen and microwave. Linen and towels free. Singles $28.50. Doubles $38. Students with ID: singles $12.50, doubles $25. Open early May-late Aug.

YM/YWCA, 180 Argyle St. at Bank (237-1320). Nice-sized rooms in a modern high-rise. Phones and refrigerators in every room. Kitchen with microwave available until midnight. Singles $30. Doubles $37. Children under 12 with adult free. Cafeteria (breakfast $2.25) open Mon.-Fri. 7am-7:30pm, Sat.-Sun. 8am-2:30pm.

Centre Town Guest House Ltd., 502 Kent St. (233-0681), just north of the bus station. A 5-10 min. walk from downtown. Impeccably clean rooms in a warm, comfortable house. Free breakfast (eggs, cereal, bacon, toast) in a cozy dining room. Singles $25. Doubles $35. Rooms are available in nearby houses at lower rates for stays of a week or more. Reservations recommended.

Camp Le Breton, in a field at the corner of Fleet and Booth (239-5000 or 800-267-0450 for information). Urban camping within sight of the Parliament Buildings. More of a well-groomed football field with trees than a campsite. Washrooms, showers, and drinking water. 5-day max. stay. Check-in 24 hr. Sites $6 per person, seniors $3. Reservations not necessary—they'll squeeze you in.

Gatineau Park, northwest of Hull (reservations 456-3016; information 822-2020). Map available at visitors center. Three rustic campgrounds within ½ hr. of Ottawa: **Lac Philippe Campground,** with facilities for family camping, trailers, and campers; **Lac Taylor Campground,** with 35 "semi-wilderness" sites; and **Lac la Pêche,** with 39 campsites accessible only by canoe. (Canoeing equipment $16 per day, $9 per ½ day, $3 per hr. Call 456-4015 for info.) Each campground off Hwy. 366 northwest of Hull—look for signs. From Ottawa, take the Cartier-MacDonald Bridge, follow Hwy. 5 north to Scott Rd., turn right onto Hwy. 105 and follow it to 366. To get access to La Pêche continue on 366 to Eardley Rd. on your left. Camping permits for Taylor and Philippe available just off the highway in the information center. Pay for a site at La Pêche on Eardley Rd. All sites $13. Open May 18-Oct. 8; some sites Dec.-March.

Food and Nightlife

A huge number of restaurants and pubs pack into downtown Ottawa. While the food isn't necessarily unique (save the Beaver Tail, Ottawa's jazzed-up fried dough served with toppings), it's cheap enough. Look for restaurant/bars in Ottawa serving food dirt-cheap to lure you into their den of high-priced beer. **Coasters,** 54 York St. (563-4954) dishes out all the mussels you can eat for $6 on Monday. **Tramps,** 53 William St. (238-5523) and **On Tap,** 160 Rideau St. (236-6827) both serve 15¢chicken wings on Mon. Tap's dinner specials ($6) are also tasty. **Chichi's** gives away free wings and curly fries on Wednesdays. (All open Mon.-Sat. 11:30am-1am, Sun. until 11pm). Fresh fruit, vegetables, and flower stands cluster at **Byward Market** on Byward between York and Rideau. (Open daily 8am-6pm.) Inside, you can buy fresh food at **Zunder's Fruitland,** 60 Byward St. (233-7773; open Mon.-Thurs. and Sat. 8am-6pm, Fri. 8am-8:30pm, Sun. 10am-5pm).

The International Cheese and Deli, 40 Byward St. Deli and middle eastern sandwiches. Turkey on rye $3, felafel on pita $2.25, hummus and tabouli $2. Open Sat.-Thurs. 8am-6pm, Fri. 8am-8pm.

Mexicali Rosa's, 207 Rideau St., at Waller St. A colorful Mexican restaurant featuring the standards (taco and enchilada dinners $8.25-11) as well as barbecue items grilled in Ottawa's only "Texas wood-burning smoker." 20% discount for youth hostel members. Open Mon.-Tues. 11:30am-10:30pm, Wed.-Thurs. 11:30am-11pm, Fri.-Sat. 11:30am-midnight, Sun. 4-10pm.

Café Crêpe de France, 76 Murray St. (235-2858). A cozy spot in the heart of the market area. Meat, vegetable, and fruit crêpes $8-13. Salads $4.50-7.25. Open Mon. 5:30-10pm, Tues.-Thurs. 11:30am-11pm, Fri.-Sat. 11:30am-midnight, Sun. 11am-10pm.

Malibu Jack's California Food Epic, 47 Clarence St., at Parent St. in the Byward Market area. Jack, former hippie and current owner of this jazzed-up burger and barbecue joint, recounts the origins of each of his dishes on the menu—most involve hanging out with James

Dean and Jimi Hendrix. Huge outdoor terrace. Haight Ashbury pizza (sprouts, guacamole, cheese, and tomato) $6.50. Open Mon.-Sat. 11:30am-1am, Sun. 11:30am-11pm.

Hitsman's Restaurant and Bakery, 1242 Bank, at Chesley St. south of Hwy. 417. Take one of several buses that travel down Bank from downtown. An incredibly cheap sandwich shop and bakery. Sandwiches $2-4. Great burgers $2.25. Chocolate lovers should sample the high-pitched 50¢ rumballs. Open Mon.-Thurs. 7:30am-5:30pm, Fri. 7:30am-7pm, Sat. 7:30am-5pm, Sun. 7:30am-3pm.

The dedicated bar-hopper or disco devotee should follow the locals across the river to Hull, where most establishments grind until 3am every day of the week and the legal drinking age is 18. In Ottawa, the Byward Market area contains most of the action. Ottawa clubs close at 1am (11pm on Sunday), but most, in an effort to keep people from going to Hull, offer free admission. **Stoney Monday's,** 62 York St. (236-5548), just west of William, is a trendy bar for people in their early to mid-20s. **Chateau Lafayette,** 42 York St. (233-3304), the oldest tavern in Ottawa, is the neighborhood watering-hole for local artists, merchants, and general riff-raff. Lures the budgeteer with $1.20 draft beer and $3.60 quarts.

Over 20 popular nightspots populate the *promenade du Portage* in Hull, just west of Place Portage, the huge government office complex. **Helium,** 75, promenade du Portage (771-0396), has it all: huge video screens, lights, a balcony for surveying the scene, good loud dance music, and plenty of people. **Chez Henri,** 179, prome-nade du Portage (777-2741), is a classier dance club with six bars and an older clien-tele. A tougher crowd congregates at **Le Zinc,** 191, promenade du Portage (778-0462), to enjoy the large dance floor, loud music, and $2 schnapps, the house special. **Le Coquetier,** 147, promenade du Portage (771-6560), is a more peaceful place to treat a friend to a brewski.

Sights

The food tastes about the same in Ottawa as in any Canadian city, but when it comes to tourist and cultural attractions, its status as Canada's capital dominates. Since the national museums and political action are packed in tightly, most sights can be reached on foot. **Parliament Hill** on Wellington St. at Metcalfe, towers over downtown as the city's focal point, while its architecture sets it apart. The **Centen-nial Flame,** lit in 1967 to mark the 100th anniversary of the Dominion of Canada's inaugural session of Parliament, burns at the south gate. The central parliament structure, **Centre Block,** contains the House of Commons, the Senate and the Li-brary of Parliament. Free, worthwhile tours in English and French depart every 10 minutes from the Infotent. (Reservations 996-0896. Tours late May-Aug. Mon.-Fri. 9am-8:30pm, Sat.-Sun. and holidays 9am-5:30pm; Sept.-mid-May 21 daily 9am-4:30pm.) Politicophiles accustomed to the reserved and formal manner of debate in the U.S. Congress shouldn't miss Canada's Prime Minister and representatives duking it out (usually only verbally) during the official **Question Period** in the House of Commons chamber (Mon.-Thurs. 2:15-3pm, Fri. 11:15am-noon; free). After the tour, climb the 293-ft. **Peace Tower,** Canada's most phallic political sym-bol. Lovers of pageantry will adore the **Changing of the Guard,** ceremoniously pre-sented on the broad lawns in front of Centre Block (June 23-Aug. 27 daily at 10am). At dusk, Centre Block and lawns transform into the set for *Sound and Light,* which relates the history of the Parliament Buildings and the development of the nation. A five-minute walk west along Wellington St. is the **Supreme Court of Canada** (995-4330), where nine justices preside. One block south of Wellington, Sparks St. greets one of North America's first pedestrian malls, hailed as an innovative experiment in 1960. The **Sparks Street Mall** recently received a $5-million facelift, rejuvenating many of Ottawa's banks and upscale retail stores.

East of the Parliament Buildings at the junction of Sparks, Wellington, and Elgin stands **Confederation Square** and in its center the enormous **National War Memo-rial,** dedicated by King George VI in 1939. The towering structure symbolizes the triumph of peace over war, a rather ironic message considering the state of world affairs in 1939. The **Rideau Centre,** south of Rideau St. at Sussex Dr., is the city's primary shopping mall as well as the main bus depot.

Nepean Point, several blocks northwest of Rideau Centre and the Byward Market by the Alexandra Bridge, provides a panoramic view of the capital. An open-air theater, **The Astrolabe,** was constructed on Nepean Point in 1967 and is one of the sites of **Cultures Canada** (239-5000), a festival of song and dance from July to August.

Parks and Museums

Ottawa boasts a multitude of parks and recreational areas. The green spaces, walkways, and bike paths surrounding the canal are the city's largest and longest parklands. Those near the mouth of the canal, near the Parliament Buildings, provide incredible views. **Major Hill's Park,** behind the Château Laurier Hotel on the banks of the Ottawa, is the city's oldest park. Within it stands a relic from the Crimean War, the **Noon Day Gun,** which fires daily at noon, except on Sunday when it resounds at 10am. **Dow's Lake** (232-1001), accessible by means of the Queen Elizabeth Driveway, is an artificial lake on the Rideau Canal, 15 minutes south of Ottawa. A popular recreation area year-round, Dow's Lake blazes with color in spring when 150,000 tulips bloom along its shore. Pedal boats, canoes, and bikes are available at the Dow's Lake Pavilion, just off Queen Elizabeth Driveway.

Ottawa headquarters many of Canada's huge national museums. **The National Gallery** (990-1985), in a spectacular glass-towered building at 380 Sussex Dr., adjacent to Nepean Point, contains the world's most comprehensive collection of Canadian art, as well as outstanding European, American and Asian works. The building's exterior is a postmodern avatar of the facing neo-Gothic buttresses of the Parliament Library. Inside, you'll find (Open May-early Sept.-Tues. 10am-6pm, Wed.-Fri. 10am-8pm; early Sept.-April 30 Tues.-Sun. 10am-5pm, Thurs. 10am-8pm. Public tours daily at 11am and 2pm. Admission $4, seniors and students $3, under 16 free.) The gallery is free Thursday, as are all of Ottawa's public museums and galleries. A spaceship-like structure across the river in Hull houses the **Canadian Museum of Civilization** at 100 Laurier St. (776-7006). Exhibits from totem poles to the **Ciné Plus,** the first cinema in the world capable of projecting both Imax and Omnimax, offer a perspective on 10,000 years of human history in Canada. (Open May-early Sept. Fri.-Wed. 9am-5pm; early Sept.-April closed Mon. and holidays. Admission for museum $4, seniors and students $3, under 15 free. Ciné Plus $6, seniors and students $4, under 15 free.) The **Canadian Museum of Nature** (996-3102) introduces newcomers to the natural world with multi-media displays. (Open Fri.-Wed. 9:30am-5pm, Thurs. 9:30am-8pm; early Sept.-April Fri.-Wed. 10am-5pm, Thurs. 10am-8pm. Admission $2, seniors and students $1.50, ages 6-16 $1, under 6 free.)

The **Canadian War Museum,** 330 Sussex Dr. (992-2774), just north of St. Patrick, houses a fine collection of war art, medals, and weaponry. (Open daily 9:30am-5pm. Admission $2, seniors and students $1, under 6 free. Call 996-1420 for group tours.) The **Royal Canadian Mint,** 320 Sussex Dr. (992-2348), beside the War Museum, the plant that manufactures Canada's currency, gives tours by appointment only. (Open Mon.-Fri. 8:30-11am and 12:30-2:30pm.) History enthusiasts could easily disappear in the **National Library and Public Archives,** 395 Wellington St. (992-3052 or 995-5138), which houses enormous quantities of Canadian publications, old maps, photographs, and letters, as well as historical exhibits. (Library open Mon.-Fri. 8:30am-5pm. Exhibit area open daily 9am-9pm.)

Farther out of town, the **National Museum of Science and Technology,** 1867 St. Laurent Blvd. (998-4566), lets visitors explore the developing world of mechanics, transportation, and high technology with hands-on exhibits. Huge locomotives and train cars enliven the transportation exhibits with a raw, often sizzling sexuality. The museum entrance is on Lancaster, 200m east of St. Laurent. The **National Aviation Museum** (993-2010), at the Rockcliffe Airport off St. Laurent Blvd. north of Montreal St., illustrates the history of flying with more than 100 aircraft. (Both open Wed.-Fri. 9am-8pm, Sat.-Tues. 9am-6pm; early Sept.-April Tues.-Sun. 9am-5pm,

Thurs. 9am-8pm. Admission to each $4, seniors and students $3, ages 6-15 $1, under 6 free.)

Entertainment

Unlike the U.S., Ottawa's government fuels the "serious" artistic community with large grants, and visitors can reap the reward. The **National Arts Centre,** 65 Elgin St. (tickets 755-1111; information 996-5051), home of an excellent small orchestra and theater company, frequently hosts international soloists and performing groups. **Odyssey Theatre** (232-8407) holds open-air shows at **Strathcona Park,** at the intersection of Laurier Ave. and Range Rd. well east of the canal. (Shows late July to mid-Aug. Admission $8, students and seniors $6, under 12 $4.) In summer on Parliament Hill, roving groups of actors present historical vignettes at fairly random times and locations; dancers and musicians often add flair. Don't be surprised when you're suddenly entangled in a wild political rally or an emotional legal case—you've merely stumbled into one of these intriguing skits.

Alberta

The icy peaks and torquoise lakes of Banff and Jasper National Parks preside as Alberta's most sought-after landscapes. Alberta has much more—plenty more farmlands, prairie, and oil fields, that is. Rural Alberta features kilometer after kilometer of untraveled roads, thousands of prime fishing holes, and world-renowned dinosaur fossil fields. Most intriguing perhaps are Native American cultures, many of which still thrive in this western province.

Practical Information

Emergency: 911.

Capital: Edmonton.

Visitor Information: Travel Alberta, 15th floor, 10025 Jasper Ave., Edmonton T5J 3Z3 (800-661-8888, in AB 800-222-6501). Recreation and Parks, Standard Life Centre #1660, 10405 Jasper Ave., Edmonton T5J 3N4 (427-9429). Information on Alberta's provincial parks. Parks Canada, Box 2989, Station M, Calgary T2P 3H8 (292-4440). Information on the province's national parks (Waterton Lakes, Jasper, Banff, and Wood Buffalo). Alberta Wilderness Association, P.O. Box 6389, Station D, Calgary T2P 2E1. Information on off-highway adventures.

Time Zone: Mountain (2 hr. behind Eastern). Postal Abbreviation: AB.

Area Code: 403.

Highway 16 connects Jasper with Edmonton, while the **Trans-Canada Highway** (Hwy. 1) runs right through Banff and then continues 120km (75 mi.) east to Calgary. The extensive highway system facilitates bus connections; use Calgary as a travel hub. **Greyhound** and **VIA Rail** run from Calgary to Edmonton to Jasper, as well as from Calgary to Banff. **Brewster** has an express bus running between Banff and Jasper, while Calgary and Edmonton house Alberta's two major airports. You should leave the Trans-Canada Hwy. to explore rural Alberta—a feat easier said than done. To reach out-of-the-way sights, consider renting a car from **Rent-A-Wreck,** a Canadian-based company that rents cars that aren't really wrecks for very reasonable rates.

From the glaciers of Jasper National Park to the huge lakes of northern Alberta, the Ice Age designed the province with the hiker, ice climber, canoeist, and bicyclist firmly in mind. Virtually every region of Alberta provides the setting for any outdoor activity; however, each has some Rozen-like "hot spots." Hikers, mountaineers, and ice climbers will find the most and best terrain in the mountains surrounding Banff and in Jasper National Park. Canoeing centers dot the lakes of northern

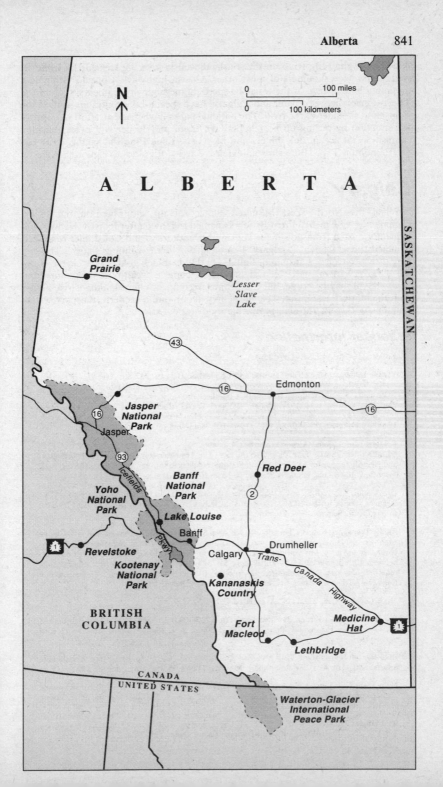

Alberta and the Milk River in the south. Bicyclists love the Icefields Parkway, as well as the wide shoulders of most other Alberta highways. Consider bringing a mountain bike instead of the usual 10-speed. Some highway segments, such as the Trans-Canada between Banff and Calgary, have special bike routes marked on the right-hand shoulder of the road. The national parks have made an effort to improve the situation by setting up hostels between Banff and Jasper and by establishing campsites that accept only hikers and bicyclists. **Lone Pine Publishing, 9704 106 St., Edmonton T5K 1B6,** prints an extensive array of guides to exploring Alberta.

Calgary

When the North West Mounted Police set up shop here in the 1860s, Commander-in-Chief Ephrem Brisebois named the town after himself. He was subsequently ousted from power for abusing his authority, and Col. James MacLeod renamed the settlement "Calgary"—Scottish for "clear running water." The city now thrives on a less transparent liquid. Oil that is. Black gold, Texas cheese. Since the discovery of oil in 1947, Calgary has become a wealthy and cosmopolitan city—the oil may be crude, but the people are refined. Office buildings rise higher than the oil derricks, businesspeople scurry about, and a modern transport system soundlessly threads through immaculate downtown streets.

Practical Information

Police: 316 7th Ave. SE (266-1234).

Visitor Information: Calgary Tourist and Convention Bureau, 237 8th Ave. SE (263-8510), on the 2nd floor. Will help locate accommodations, especially around Stampede time in July. Open daily 8:30am-4:30pm. **Information booth** at the same address open June-Sept. daily 8am-7pm; Oct.-May Mon.-Fri. 8:30am-4:30pm. **Travel Alberta,** 455 6th St. SW (297-6574; in AB 800-222-6501), on the main floor. Open Mon.-Fri. 8:15am-4:30pm. **Trans-Canada Highway Office,** 6220 16th St. NE. Open daily 8am-9pm; Sept.-June 10am-5pm.

Calgary International Airport: (292-8477), is about 5km northwest of the city center. Free but infrequent shuttle buses service to the city. The **Airporter Bus** (291-3848) offers frequent and friendly service for $6.50. Greyhound drops off close to the city center (about ½-hr. walk from downtown) and offers $1.25 shuttle buses to the C-Train.

Greyhound: 850 16th St. SW (265-9111 or 800-661-8747). To Edmonton (10 per day, $22); frequent service to Banff ($10.50). Free shuttle bus from C-train at 7th Ave. and 10th St. to bus depot. Seniors 10% discount.

Public Transport: Calgary Transit, 206 7th Ave. SW. Bus schedules, passes, and maps. Open Mon.-Fri. 8:30am-5pm. Buses and streetcars (C-Trains). Buses run all over the city; C-Trains cover less territory, but you can ride them free in the downtown area (along 7th Ave. S.; between 10th St. SW and City Hall). Fare $1.25, ages 6-14 75¢, under 6 free; exact change required. Day pass $3.50, children $2. Book of 10 tickets $10, children $6.50. **Information line** (276-7801) open Mon.-Fri. 6am-11pm, Sat.-Sun. 8am-9:30pm.

Taxi: Checker Cab, 272-1111. **Associated Cab,** 276-5312.

Car Rental: Rent-a-Wreck, 2339 Macleod Trail (237-7093). From $33 per day with unlimited mi. Open Mon.-Fri. 8am-7:30pm, Sat. 9am-5:30pm, Sun. 10am-5:30pm. Must be 21 with major credit card.

Bike Rental: Sports Rent, 7218 Macleod Trail SW (252-2055). $15-20 per day. **Abominable Sports,** 640 11th Ave. SW (266-0899). Mountain bikes $15 per day; mopeds $20 per day.

Help Line: Gay Lines Calgary, 223 12th Ave. SW (234-8973), 3rd floor. Recorded phone message provides gay community information; peer counseling available at the office. Phone and office open Mon.-Sat. 7am-10pm.

Post Office: 220 4th Ave. SE (292-5512). Label mail General Delivery, Station M, Calgary, AB T2P 2G8. Open Mon.-Fri. 8am-5:45pm. **Postal Code:** T2P 2G8.

Area Code: 403.

An extremely well-planned city, Calgary is a cinch for back-seat navigators. The city partitions into quadrants. **Centre Street** divides it east-west, and the **Bow River** (with the adjacent Memorial Dr., where the Bow starts bowing) divides the north from the south; address numbers increase as you move away from these thoroughfares. You can always determine the cross-street from an avenue address by disregarding the last 2 digits: thus 206 7th Ave. is at 2nd St., and 2339 Macleod Trail is at 23rd St. Avenues run east-west, streets north-south.

Hitchhiking is illegal within the Calgary city limits; the law is enforced and punishable by a large fine.

Accommodations

Cheap rooms in Calgary come easy except during the Stampede. While most of the places listed below don't raise their prices seasonally, reserve ahead for July.

Calgary International Hostel (IYHF), 520 7th Ave. SE (269-8239). Conveniently located several blocks south of downtown with access to C-Train and public buses. Complete with snack bar, meeting rooms, cooking and barbecue facilities, laundry, and a cycle workshop. Disabled access. Lockout 10am-4:30pm. Curfew Tues.-Wed. midnight, Thurs.-Mon. 2am. $10, nonmembers $15.

University of Calgary, 3330 24th Ave. (220-3203), in the NW quadrant of the city. A little out of the way, but very accessible via bus #9 or the C-Train. Olympian-sized (literally) rooms for competitive prices. Cafeteria and a pub on campus. Room rental office, in the Kananaskis Building, open 24 hr. Singles $22. Doubles $30. Student rate: singles $15.75; shared rooms $10.50. Breakfast included. Fewer rooms available in winter.

YWCA, 320 5th Ave. SE (263-1550). A deluxe place for women only, in a fine quiet neighborhood. A range of rooms. The security makes for a somewhat lifeless lodging. Cafeteria. Dorm beds $15. Singles $22, with bath $29.50.

St. Louis Hotel, 430 8th Ave. SE (262-6341), above the St. Louis Tavern. Depending on your point of view, the location means either excitement or danger. Not suggested for women. The few grim-looking long-term residents generally keep to themselves. Friendly management. Singles $16, with TV and bath $21. Doubles with bath and TV $26.

Food

You can easily find good, inexpensive eating in Calgary. Ethnic and cafeteria-style dining spots line the **Stephen Ave. Mall,** 8th Ave. S. between 1st St. SE and 3rd St. SW, and the indoor mini-malls nearby. Look for more good, cheap food in the **"Plus 15" skyway system.** Designed to provide indoor passageways during bitter winter days, this bizarre mall connects the second floors of dozens of buildings throughout the city. You can join the system at any "participating" building; just look for the blue-and-white "Plus 15" signs on street level. For more expensive, trendy restaurants, go to the **Kensington District,** along Kensington Rd. between 10th and 11th St. NW.

Hang Fung Foods Ltd., 119 3rd Ave. SE, located in the rear of a Chinese market with the same name. Enormous bowl of plain *congee* (rice broth) $1, with abalone and chicken $3. A heaping plateful of BBQ duck and steamed chicken on rice both $4.25. Bring your own silverware if you haven't mastered chopsticks. Open Mon.-Fri. 8:30am-9pm.

4th Street Rose, 2116 4th St. SW. Take bus #3 or 53 and avoid the hike. California cool pervades this fashionable restaurant on the outskirts of town: high ceilings, tile floors, and servers sporting jeans and short-sleeved shirts. Gourmet pizzas, homemade pasta, and fresh salads ($2.75-6). Open Mon.-Thurs. 8am-1am, Fri. 8am-2am, Sat. 10am-2am, Sun. 10am-midnight.

Take Ten Cafe, 304 10th St. NW. Light dining in Kensington with a German accent. The wiener schnitzel ($4.50) includes gravy, vegetable, and fries. Hungarian ghoulash $4. Homemade cakes and muffins. Open Mon. and Thurs.-Sat. 8am-5pm, Tues.-Wed. 8am-4pm, Sun. 10am-4pm.

Bohemia Bistro, 124 10th St. NW, near Kensington Rd. (on the 2nd floor). Bohemia in the original sense of the word—the region around Prague. Perhaps the most unusual of the Kensington district restaurants. An eclectic menu features unkosher kosher sandwiches ($6-7) and pastas ($7-8.50). Pick up a chocolate truffle ($1) on the way out. Open Tues.-Thurs. 11:30am-midnight, Fri.-Sat. 11:30am-1am.

Sights

The **Calgary Tower** (266-7171), 101 9th Ave. SW, presides over the city. Rather than simply gaze up at the spire, ride an elevator to the top ($3 round-trip, children $1.25) for a spectacular view of the Rockies on clear days. The 190m tower also affords a 360° view of the city.

A nexus of boomtown cultural pride, the **Glenbow Museum,** 130 9th Ave. SE (264-8300), just across the street from the tower, keeps an odd mix of modern art, military artifacts, and mineral samples. At the entrance stand five cases of Olympic pins, the most extensive collection in town. (Open daily 10am-6pm. Admission $3, seniors $1, students and children $2. Free Sat.) Less than a block northeast of the museum, the **Olympic Plaza** still attracts crowds on sunny days. The site of the medal presentations during the Winter Games, this open-air park now hosts a variety of special events including Kids' Fest and the Calgary Jazz Festival (both in June). For an update on Olympic Plaza programming, call 268-5207 during business hours.

A short walk down 8th Ave. to the west will bring you to the home of **Devonian Gardens,** 4th floor Toronto Dominion Sq., 8th Ave. and 3rd St. SW. This 2.5-acre indoor garden contains fountains, waterfalls, bridges, and over 20,000 plants, including 138 different local and tropical varieties. (Open daily 9am-9pm. Free.) A few blocks to the northwest, the **Energeum,** 640 5th Av. SW (297-4293), in the lobby of the Energy Resources Building, is Calgary's shrine to fossil fuel. A film in the upstairs theater effectively re-creates the mania of Alberta's first oil find 1947. In an interactive display, you can run your gloved hand through a pile of the oozing glop. (Open Sun.-Fri. 10:30am-4:30pm; Sept.-May Mon.-Fri. 10:30am-4:30pm. Free.)

Farther west, about 4.3 light-years from Alpha Centauri, warps the **Alberta Science Centre and Centennial Planetarium,** 11 St. and 7th Ave. SW (221-3700). (Open Wed.-Sun. 1-9pm. Hands-on experiments here test the law of physics, and planetarium shows give you a close look at Jupiter (Open Wed.-Sun. 1-9pm. Most planetarium shows after 6pm. Admission to planetarium and Science Centre $5, children $2.50; Science Centre only $2, children $1.50.)

Reach **St. George's Island** by the river walkway to the east; the island houses the **Calgary Zoo.** Try to visit in the late spring when many of the animals give birth to new attractions—the Australian couples seem to be especially prolific. The zoo also features a prehistoric park, which takes you back in time some 65 million years, a botanical garden, and a children's zoo. (Open daily at 9am; closing time seasonally adjusted. For more information, call Zooline, 232-9300. Admission $6, seniors and ages 12-17 $3.50, under 12 $2.50. On Tues. $3, seniors free.)

The nearby **Fort Calgary Interpretive Centre** (290-1875) maps out Calgary's evolution from cowtown to oiltown with an exhibit hall and a comprehensive film. (Open daily 9am-5pm. Free.) The center interprets on 9th Ave. SE, just east of downtown; grab bus #1 ("Forest Lawn") eastbound.

Although the actual Olympic flame has long since extinguished in Calgary, retailers still carry the torch, offering hundreds of different forms of official Olympic merchandise at reduced prices. The more substantial and important legacies of the Games are several newly built, world-class athletic facilities—not only great arenas for recreation but also fascinating architectural sights. The two most impressive are the **Olympic Oval,** an indoor speed-skating track on the University of Calgary campus (hours vary from season to season; call 220-7890 for more information), and **Canada Olympic Park,** the site of the bobsled, luge, and ski jumping competitions. A guided tour of Olympic Park costs $6 (seniors and children $3), but take the plunge—the one-hour trip around includes a chance to stand in the bobsled track and to glance down the slope from atop the 90km ski jump tower. The **Olympic Hall of Fame,** (268-2632), also located in Olympic Park, reinforces the Olympic ideology with displays, artifacts, and videos. (Open daily 10am-5pm. Admission $3, seniors, students, and children $2.)

The Stampede

Even people who find rodeo grotesque still have trouble saying "Calgary" without letting a quick "Stampede" slip out. Calgarians themselves are perhaps the most guilty of perpetuating this relationship. Every year around Stampede time, the locals throw free pancake breakfasts and paint every ground-level window downtown with cartoon cowboy figures offering misspelled greetings ("Welcum, y'all"). Capped by ten-gallons, locals command tour groups to yell "Yahoo" in the least likely of circumstances. Simply put, at Stampede time the entire city of Calgary wigs out.

And why not? Any event that draws millions from across the province, the country, and the world deserves the hoopla. Make the short trip out to **Stampede Park,** just southeast of downtown; those smart enough to arrive in July will get a glimpse of steer wrestling, bull riding, wild cow milking, and the famous chuckwagon races, where canvas-covered, box-shaped buggies whiz by in a chariot race that defies the laws of aerodynamics. (Tickets $9-31.) The Stampede also features a **midway,** where you can perch yourself atop the wild, thrashing back of a roller coaster.

Parking is ample, but since the crowd swells in July, take the C-Train from downtown to the Stampede stop. In 1991, the Stampede will run from July 5-14. For official information and ticket order forms, write Calgary Exhibition and Stampede, Box 1060, Station M, Calgary T2P 2K8, or call 800-661-1260. If you're in Calgary, visit **Stampede Headquarters,** 1410 Olympic Way, or call 261-0101 for more information.

Entertainment

After a long, hard day of counting barrels of crude, Calgarians knock down bottles of local brew along **"Electric Avenue,"** the stretch of 11th Ave. SW between 5th and 6th St. SW. Here several look-alike clubs swim in neon, all spinning the same Top-40 music. Last call in Calgary is at 1:45am.

Bandito's, 620 11th Ave. (266-6441). The current favorite, but any of the joints along 11th Ave. will do. Drinks $3-4. Most open for lunch around 11am and stay open until somewhere past 2am.

Ranchman's Steak House, 9615 Macleod Trail S. (253-1100). One of Canada's greatest honkytonks. Experience Calgary's Wild West tradition firsthand, on the dance floor to the tune of live C&W tunes or in the not-so-subtle flavor of Calgary Stampede beer. Open Mon.-Sat. 7pm-2am.

The Stadium Keg, 1923 Uxbridge Dr. NW (282-0020). Where the "Dinos" from nearby University of Calgary eat, drink, and be merry. On Thurs. nights from 6-10pm, devour chicken wings (25¢ each) and wash them down with a mug of Big Rock ($1.50), the dark, delicious local brew. Open daily 4:30pm-1am or 2am.

Banff National Park

For natural splendor, you really can't do better than Banff. Snowcapped mountains and turquoise lakes make up only two of the park's gorgeous physical features. Free-roaming moose rule the marshes of Bow River Valley and bighorn sheep reign on the rocky slopes.

Unfortunately, scores of tourists seem to have discovered this national treasure and overrun the park. The townsite resembles resort towns such as Vail or St. Moritz; a deluxe suite at the Banff Springs Hotel costs $735 per night, plus $15 per pet. This does not mean a less jet-set crowd doesn't exist as well. Bicyclists from around the world come to enjoy Banff's facilities. The Trans-Canada Hwy. has a large shoulder built as a bike path, while the older Hwy. 1A has less traffic and better access to campgrounds and hostels.

Practical Information

Emergency: in Banff 762-4333, at Lake Louise 522-3811.

Visitor Information: Banff Information Centre, 224 Banff Ave. (762-3777). Open daily 8am-10pm; Oct.-May 10am-6pm. **Lake Louise Information Centre** (522-3833). Open mid-May to mid-June daily 10am-6pm; mid-June to Aug. 8am-10pm; Sept.-Oct. 10am-6pm. **Park Headquarters,** Superintendent, Banff National Park, P.O. Box 900, Banff T0L 0C0 (762-3324).

Greyhound: operates out of the Brewster terminal. To: Lake Louise (5 per day, $5.25) and Calgary (6 per day, $10.50). The Lake Louise buses continue to Vancouver ($67).

Brewster Transportation: 100 Gopher St. (762-6767), near the train depot. Specializes in tours of the area, but runs 1 express daily to Jasper ($29). Depot open daily 7am-midnight.

Car Rental: Banff Used Car Rentals, corner of Wolf and Lynx (726-3352). $34 per day. 150km free, 10¢ each additional km. Must be over 21 with credit card. Also, **Avis,** 209 Bear St. (762-3222). $50 per day. 100km free, 19¢ each additional km. Ask about IYHF member discount.

Other Rentals: Mountain Mopeds, in the Sundance Mall (762-5611). $8.50 per hr., $30 per 4 hr., $45 per day. Open daily 10am-8pm. Must have ID and $100 deposit. **Spoke 'n' Edge,** 315 Banff Ave. (762-2854). 3-, 5-, and 10-speed bicycles $2.50 per hr., $10 per day; mountain bikes $4 per hr., $16 per day.

Post Office: Buffalo and Bear St. (762-2586). Open Mon.-Fri. 9am-5:30pm. **Postal Code:** T0L 0C0.

Area Code: 403.

Banff National Park adjoins the Alberta-British Columbia border, 120km west of Calgary. The **Trans-Canada Highway** (Hwy. 1) runs east-west through the park. Greyhound connects the park with major points in British Columbia and Alberta. Civilization in the park centers around the twin townsites of Lake Louise and Banff, 55km to the southeast. Buses and the daily train are expensive.

Accommodations, Camping, and Food

Over 20 residents of the townsite offer rooms in their own homes—many year-round, and the majority in the $20-40 range. Just ask for the *Banff Private Home Accommodation* list at the Banff Townsite Information Centre. The local **YWCA,** (762-3560) also opens its doors and hospital-style rooms to travelers, both male and female. (Singles $38. Doubles $46. Bunk rooms from $14.)

Banff International Hostel (IYHF), Box 1358, Banff T0L 0C0 (762-4122), 3km from Banff Townsite on Tunnel Mountain Rd., among a nest of condominiums and lodges. The look and setting of a chalet, but when full, the feel of an overstuffed warehouse. A hike from the center of the townsite, but worth it for the modern amenities and friendly staff. Ski and cycle workshop, laundry facilities, disabled access. Clean quads with 2 bunk beds; linen provided. $12, nonmembers $17. Open 6-10am and 4pm-midnight.

Hilda Creek Hostel (IYHF), 8.5km south of the Icefield Centre on the Icefields Parkway. Features a tiny primitive sauna. In the morning, guests must replenish the water supply with a shoulder-bucket contraption that will give you an appreciation for the agility of the peasant farmer. Closed Thurs. night. Accommodates 21. $7, nonmembers $12.

Rampart Creek Hostel (IYHF), 34km south of the Icefield Centre. Wood-heated sauna. Closed Wed. night. Accommodates 30. $7, nonmembers $12.

Mosquito Creek Hostel (IYHF), 103km south of the Icefield Centre and 26km north of Lake Louise. Fireplace and sauna. Closed Tues. night. Accommodates 38. $7, nonmembers $12.

Corral Creek Hostel (IYHF), 5km east of Lake Louise on Hwy. 1A. The hostel nearest Lake Louise. Closed Mon. night. Accommodates 50. $7, nonmembers $12.

Castle Mountain Hostel (IYHF), on Hwy. 1A (762-2637), 1.5km east of the junction of Hwy. 1 and Hwy. 93. Recently renovated. Closed Wed. night. Accommodates 36. $8, nonmembers $13.

Banff's popularity keeps "campgrounds full" signs up; because none of the park sites accept reservations, arrive early. Many campgrounds reserve sites for bicyclists and hikers; inquire at the office. Some campgrounds raise rates during the "premium period" (late June-Labor Day). Rates range from $7.50 to $11.50. Park facilities include (listed from north to south): Waterfowl Lake (116 sites), Lake Louise (221 sites), Protection Mountain (89 sites), Two Jack Main (381 sites), Two Jack Lakeside (80 sites), and Tunnel Mountain Village (622 sites).

Bring along your favorite recipes for campfire cooking, and you'll eat well here. Otherwise, you'll pay high prices for mediocre food. The International Hostel and the YWCA, however, serve affordable meals. The hostel's cafeteria serves up a great breakfast special (egg, cheese, and bacon on a kaiser roll with coffee, $2.50; served 7-9am), as well as decent dinners (5-7pm). The **Spray Café**, at the Y, boasts an even bigger breakfast deal: two eggs, bacon, hashbrowns, and toast for $3.25. (Open Thurs.-Tues. 8am-3pm.)

Coriander Nature Food, on the upper level of the Sundance Mall on Banff Ave., even smells healthful thanks to freshly-cut lilacs at each table. Take a break from that burger diet with Mexican beans and rice in a pita ($3, with tofu $4.50). Pick up some vitamins and trail mix on your way out. (Open Mon.-Sat. 10am-6pm, Sun. 11:30am-5:30pm.) At **Joe Btfsplk's Diner,** 221 Banff Ave. (762-5529), the meatloaf blue plate special with all the fixin's ($8.50) will keep your stomach happy well into tomorrow. Dubbed after a *L'il Abner* character, the name of this diner may be hard to pronounce (bi-TIF-spliks), but you'll be speechless when you see the sandwiches on fresh-baked bread ($5-7). (Open daily 8am-11pm.)

Sights and Activities

Hike to the **backcountry** for privacy, beauty, and trout that bite anything. The pamphlet *Drives and Walks* covers both the Lake Louise and Banff areas, describing both day and overnight hikes. In order to stay overnight in the backcountry, you need a permit, available free from park information centers and park warden offices. All litter must be taken out of the backcountry with you; in addition, no wood may be chopped in the parks. Both the International Hostel and the Park Information Centre have copies of the *Canadian Rockies Trail Guide,* an excellent, in-depth source of information and maps.

Canada's first national park (and the world's third), Banff began in 1885 as Hot Springs Reserve, featuring the **Cave and Basin Hot Springs** nearby. In 1914, a resort went up at the springs. The refurbished resort, now called the **Cave and Basin Centennial Centre** (762-4900), screens documentaries and stages exhibits. Relax in the hot springs pool, watched over by lifeguards in pre-World War I bathing costumes, or explore the original cave. The center lies southwest of the city on Cave and Basin Rd. (Center open early June-Sept. daily 10am-8pm; Oct.-early June 10am-5pm. Pool open early June-Sept. only. Admission to pool $2, ages 3-16 $1.25.) If you find Cave and Basin's 32°C (90°F) water too cool, try the **Upper Hot Springs pool,** a 40°C (104°F) cauldron up the hill on Mountain Ave. (Cooler in spring during snow run-off. Open June-Sept. daily 8:30am-11pm. Admission $2, under 12 $1.25.) Bathing suit rental at either spring ($1), towel rental (75¢), and locker rental (25¢) available.

Taking a gondola to the top of a peak saves your legs for hiking at the summit. The **Sulphur Mountain Gondola** (762-5438), located right next to the Upper Hot Springs pool, affords a good view of Banff Townsite, and offers a $3 "early bird" breakfast special. (Open Nov. 15-Dec. 15 and in summer daily 9am-8pm. Fare $7.50, under 12 $3.) The **Sunshine Village Gondola** (762-6555) climbs to the resort village, at 7200 ft. (Open June 27-Sept. 7 Mon.-Thurs. 8:30am-7:30pm, Fri.-Sun. 8:30am-10:30pm. Fare $12, under 12 $5.) If that's not high enough for you, jump on the **Standish Chairlift,** which will carry you to the peak, almost 7900 ft. up.

When you'd prefer to look up at the mountains rather than down from them, all the nearby lakes will provide a serene vantage point. **Moraine** (near Lake Louise) and **Two Jack** (near Banff) Lakes can be explored by boat and canoe. On Two Jack

Lake, rowboats cost $8.50 per hour, $42.50 per day; canoes $8 per hour, $40 per day, with a $20 deposit. (Open July-Aug. daily; June Sat.-Sun. only.) On Moraine Lake, rent a canoe for $10 per hour with a $20 deposit (522-3733; open daily summer 8am-sundown). Fishing is legal virtually anywhere you can find water, but you must hold a national parks fishing permit, available at the information center ($5 for a 7-day permit, $10 for an annual one). And after you catch your 10-pound trout, many restaurants will cook it up for about $10.

The hilly road leading to Lake Minnewanka provides cyclists with an exhilarating trip, as do many other small paths throughout the park. Bicycling is also allowed on most trails in the Banff Townsite areas. Remember, however, to dismount your bike and stand to the downhill side if a horse approaches. Also be forewarned that the quick and quiet bicycle is more likely to surprise bears than hikers' tromping. Since horseback riding rates are almost identical throughout the park, pick your favorite location.

North American filmmakers often use Lake Louise's crystal waters framed by snow-capped peaks as a substitute for Swiss alpine scenes. Rent a canoe from Chateau Lake Louise Boat House (522-3511) for $15 per hour; also rent binoculars to scan the hills for wildlife. Several hiking trails begin at the lake. If you aim for one of the two teahouses (at the end of the 3.4km Lake Agnes Trail and the 5.3km Plain of Six Glaciers Trail), be prepared to pay dearly for your meal, since all the food climbs up the mountain on horseback. (Teahouses open summer daily 9am-6pm.) The Lake Louise Gondola (522-3555), which runs up Mt. Whitehorn across the Trans-Canada Hwy. from the lake, provides another chance to ooh and aah at the landscape. (Open mid-June to late Sept. daily 9am-6pm. Fare $7, ages 5-11 $3.50. "One-way hiker's special" $5.)

After a long day of hiking and biking, knock back a few at one of Banff's boisterous bars. Each night, a different place hosts "Locals Night" with drinks for $1.75. For culture aficionados, Banff offers the Banff Festival of the Arts, a summer-long event featuring drama, ballet, opera, and jazz. Pick up a brochure at the Visitor Information Center or call 762-6300 for details.

Icefields Parkway

A glacier-lined, 230km road connecting Lake Louise with Jasper Townsite, the Icefields Parkway (Hwy. 93) snakes past dozens of ominous peaks and glacial lakes. Wise drivers and cyclists set aside at least three days for the parkway. The challenging hikes and endless vistas just get better and better. All points on the parkway lie within 30km of at least one place where you can roll out your sleeping bag.

Before setting your wheels on the road, pick up a free map of the Parkway, available at park information centers in Jasper and Banff. The pamphlet is also available at the Icefield Centre, to the side of the parkway at the boundary between the two parks. The center sits in sight of the Athabasca Glacier, the most prominent of the eight glaciers that stem from the 325-sq.-km Columbia Icefield.

Jasper National Park

Jasper boasts the same natural wonders and outdoor opportunities as Banff, minus the ritz and glitz of its southern neighbor. The town is small, the locals are friendly and down-to-earth, and the surroundings consist of 10,000 square kilometers of breathtaking nature.

Practical Information

Emergency: 852-4848.

Visitor Information: Park Information Centre, 500 Connaught Dr. (852-6176). Trail maps and information on all aspects of the park. Open June 14-Labor Day daily 8am-8pm; spring and fall daily 9am-5pm. **Alberta Tourism,** 632 Connaught Dr. (in AB 800-222-6501). Open June-Sept. daily 8am-8pm; May Sun.-Thurs. 9am-6pm, Fri.-Sat. 9am-7:30pm. **Jasper Chamber of Commerce,** 634 Connaught Dr. (852-3858). Open Mon.-Fri. 9am-noon and 1-5pm. **Park Headquarters,** Superintendent, Jasper National Park, 632 Patricia St., Box 10, Jasper T0E 1E0 (852-6161).

VIA Rail: 314 Connaught Dr. (800-561-8630 or 852-4102). To: Vancouver (1 per day, 16 hr., $98); Edmonton ($57); and Winnipeg ($166). Seniors and students with ID 33% off. Station open daily 8am-10:30pm; shorter hours off-season.

Greyhound: 314 Connaught Dr. (852-3926), in the VIA station. To: Edmonton (14 per day, $32.25) and Kamloops ($34.25).

Brewster Transportation and Tours: Also in the VIA station (852-3332). To Banff (full-day tour $49, daily 5½-hr. express $29) and Calgary (1 per day, 8 hr., $38).

Car Rental: Jasper Car Rental, 626 Connaught Dr. (852-3373). $40 per day. 50 free km, 22¢ each additional km. Reduced rates for multi-day rental. Must be 21 with credit card.

Bike Rental: Free Wheel Cycle, 600 Patricia St. (852-5380). Enter through the alley behind Patricia St. Mountain bikes (preferable for this terrain) $4 per hr., $10 per ½ day, $17 per day. Also 10- and 15-speeds. Open Mon.-Sat. 9am-9pm, Sun. 10am-8pm; April-June and Labour Day-Oct. 9am-6pm. Must have valid ID, and place a deposit. **Whistler's Youth Hostel** also rents mountain bikes. IYHF members $16 per day. Nonmembers $25 per day.

Post Office: 502 Patricia St. (852-3041), across Patricia St. from the townsite green. Open July-Aug. Mon.-Fri. 9am-5pm, Sat. 9am-3pm; Sept.-June Mon.-Fri. 9am-5pm. **Postal Code:** T0E 1E0.

Area Code: 403.

All of the above addresses are in Jasper Townsite, which sits near the middle of the park, 362km southwest of Edmonton and 287km north of Banff. **Highway 16** conducts travelers through the park north of the townsite, while the **Icefields Parkway** (Hwy. 93) connects to Banff National Park in the south. Buses run to the townsite daily from Edmonton, Calgary, and Vancouver. Trains arrive from Edmonton and Vancouver. Renting a bike is the most practical option for short jaunts within the park.

Accommodations, Camping, and Food

Ask for the **Approved Accommodations List** at the Park Information Center if you wish to sleep cheaply in Jasper (singles $20-25, doubles $25-35, triples $35-40). If you prefer mingling with the youthful set, head to a hostel (listed below from north to south). Reservations, as well as information on closing days and on the winter "key system," channel through the Edmonton-based Southern Alberta Hostel Association (439-3089).

Maligne Canyon Hostel (IYHF), on Maligne Canyon Rd. (852-3584), 15km northeast of the townsite. Closed Wed. Accommodates 24. $4, nonmembers $6.

Whistlers Mountain Hostel (IYHF), on Sky Tram Rd. (852-3215), 7km south of the townsite. Closest to the townsite and the park's most modern (and crowded) hostel. A hike from town, mostly uphill. The management shuts off the lights at 11pm sharp and flicks them on again at 7am. You may have to sweep out the fireplace before you leave in the morning, but at least it works. Accommodates 50. $10, nonmembers $14.

Mount Edith Cavell Hostel (IYHF), on Edith Cavell Rd. off Hwy. 93A. Closed Thurs. Accommodates 32. Road closes in winter, but the hostel welcomes anyone willing to ski or snowmobile the 11km from Hwy. 93A. Closed Thurs. $6, nonmembers $10. Open mid-June to Oct.

Athabasca Falls Hostel (IYHF), on Hwy. 93, 30km south of Jasper Townsite near the namesake falls. Closed Tues. $7, nonmembers $11.

Beauty Creek Hostel (IYHF), on Hwy. 93, 78km south of Jasper Townsite. Beautifully situated next to a brook. Closed Tues. Accommodates 20. Accessible through a "key system" in winter. $6, nonmembers $10. Open May to mid-Sept.

For campground updates, tune in to 1450 AM on your radio near Jasper Townsite. The park maintains sites at 10 campgrounds, including (north to south): Whistlers (781 sites), Wapiti (345 sites), Wabasso (238 sites), Columbia Icefield (33 sites), and Wilcox Creek (46 sites). Rates range from $6 to $14.

For cheap eats, stock up at a local market or bulk foods store and head for the backcountry. For around-the-clock grocery supplies, stop at **Wink's Food Store,** 605 Patricia St. **Nutter's,** also on Patricia St., offers grains, nuts, dried fruits, and (if you're sick of healthful food) candy, all in bulk form. They also sell deli meats, canned goods, and fresh-ground coffee. (Open Mon.-Sat. 9am-10pm, Sun. 10am-9pm.) For a sit-down meal, try **Mountain Foods and Cafe,** 606 Connaught Dr. The menu features sandwiches, soups, and desserts. (Open daily 8am-10pm.) **Jasper Bakery,** on Patricia St., a small, café-style bakery, serves a delicious variety of baked goods (75¢-$2). (Open daily 7am-11pm.)

Sights and Activities

An extensive trail network connects most parts of Jasper, with many paths starting at the townsite. Information centers distribute free copies of *Day Hikes in Jasper National Park* and a summary of the longer hikes.

Mt. Edith Cavell, named after a WWI hero, often thunders with the sound of avalanches off the Angel Glacier. Take the ½km loop trail or the 8km return **Path of the Glacier.** Mt. Edith Cavell rears 30km south of the townsite on Cavell Rd. **Maligne Lake,** the largest glacier-fed lake in the Canadian Rockies, has vivid turquoise water. One special feature of Jasper National Park is **Medicine Lake,** 30km east of Jasper Townsite. Water flows into the lake, but there is no visible outlet. The trick? The water flows out through a series of underground caves, and emerges in such areas as **Maligne Canyon,** 11km east of the townsite on Maligne Canyon Rd. Another natural phenomenon, this canyon drops over 46m, and squirrels can jump across the narrow gorge. Humans cannot, though; several squirrel-wannabees have proven this by falling to their deaths.

Joining the Banff tradition, Jasper has a **gondola** of its own. Rising 2½km up the side of Whistlers Mountain, the Jasper Tramway affords majestic views of the park, as well as an opportunity to spend money at its gift shops and restaurant. (Fare $8, under 12 $3.75. Open mid-April to Oct. 8am-9:30pm; Sept. to mid-Oct. 9am-4:30pm. Call 852-3093 for more information.) A trail starting from the Whistlers Mountain Hostel also leads up the slope, but it's a steep 10km; to spare your quadriceps you'll want to take the tram ride down ($3.50). But no matter which way you go, be sure to bring along a warm coat and sunglasses to combat the rapidly-changing climate at the peak.

British Columbia

Larger than California, Oregon, and Washington combined, British Columbia attracts enough visitors year-round to rank tourism the province's second largest industry (after timber). The million flowers of Victoria and the million people of Vancouver draw city slickers, while the graceful lakes of the nearby Okanagan Valley lure those intent on escaping civilization. B.C., Canada's westernmost province, covers over 350,000 square miles, bordering four U.S. states and three other Canadian provinces. The difficulty of road travel throughout the province varies with the immensely diverse terrain. When taking your own vehicle, be sure to avoid potential hassles by obtaining a Canadian non-resident Interprovince motor vehicle **liability card** from your insurance company before leaving; border police may turn you away for not being properly insured. In the south, roads are plentiful and well paved, but farther north, the asphalt (and the towns) seems to have been blown away by the arctic winds.

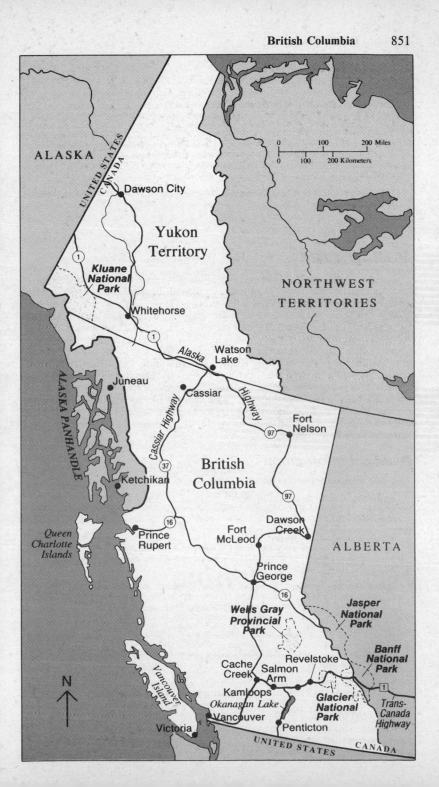

Practical Information

Capital: Victoria.

Visitor Information: Ministry of Tourism and Provincial Secretary, Parliament Bldg., Victoria V8V 1X4 (604-387-1642). Write for the accommodations guide, which lists prices and services for virtually every hotel, motel, and campground in the province. In the U.S., write **Tourism BC,** P.O. Box C-34971, Seattle, WA 98124. Branches also in **San Francisco,** 100 Bush St. #400, San Francisco, CA 94104 (415-981-4780); and **Irvine,** 2600 Michelson Dr. #1050, Irvine, CA 92715 (714-852-1054). **Canadian Parks Service,** Senior Communications Officer, 220 4th Ave. SE, P.O. Box 2989, Station M, Calgary, AB T2P 3H8, or call **BC Parks** at 604-387-5002.

Time Zone: Pacific (3 hr. behind Eastern) and Mountain (2 hr. behind Eastern). **Postal Abbreviation:** BC.

Alcohol: Drinking age 19.

Vancouver

Canada's third largest city comes as a pleasant surprise to the jaded metropolis-hopping traveler. Vancouver's 1.4 million residents display big-city sophistication, while escaping most conventional urban traumas. Tune out the language, and Vancouver could be a North American Switzerland, with immaculate and efficient public transport, spotless sidewalks, and even safe seedy areas. Fast joining the post-industrial age, Vancouver's electronics and international finance have largely replaced timber and mining as the city's economic base. A growing wave of Chinese immigration, largely from Hong Kong, has significantly broadened this British-settled city into a modern multi-cultural metropolis. Denying cynical predictions of racial tension, Mayor Gordon Campbell has promised that his city will "not become like a city in the United States." With nature walks among 1000-year-old timber stands, wind-surfing, and getting wrapped up in a film at the most technologically advanced movie theatre in the world all right downtown, Vancouver will certainly keep that promise.

Practical Information

Police: Main and Powell St. (665-3321).

Visitor Information: Travel Infocentre, 1055 Dunsmuir (683-2000), near Burrard in the West End. Buy the larger-scale street map ($2). Open daily 8:30am-6:30pm. **B.C. Transit Information Centre:** 261-5100.

Vancouver International Airport: on Sea Island 11km south of the city center. Connections to major cities. To reach downtown from the airport, take Metro Transit bus #100 to 70th Ave., transfer there to bus #20, which arrives downtown heading north on the Granville Mall.

Trains: VIA Rail Canada, 1150 Station St. (800-665-8630 or 669-3050), off Rte. 99 (Main St.) at 1st Ave. Three per week to Jasper ($64) and Edmonton ($136). Open Mon. and Sat. 7:30am-9:30pm, Tues.-Wed. and Sun. 7:30am-3pm, Thurs. 3-9:30pm, Fri. 10am-5:30pm. **B.C. Rail,** 1311 W. 1st St. (984-5246), just over the Lions Gate Bridge in North Vancouver. Take the SeaBus downtown to North Vancouver, then bus #239 west. One way daily to: Whistler ($11), Prince George ($61), and Squamish and points north. Open daily 7am-9pm.

Buses: Greyhound, 150 Dunsmuir (662-3222), downtown on Beatty St. Service to the south and across Canada. To: Calgary (4 per day, $73); Banff (4 per day, $67.50); Jasper (3 per day, $64); and Seattle (7 per day, US$20). Open daily 5:30am-midnight. **Pacific Coach Lines,** 150 Dunsmuir (662-3222). Serves southern B.C., including Vancouver Island, in cooperation with Greyhound. To Victoria ($16.50, including ferry).

B.C. Ferries: (general information 669-1211; recorded information 685-1021; Tsawwassen ferry terminal 943-9331). Ferries to Victoria, Prince Rupert, Queen Charlotte and surrounding islands. Mainland to Vancouver Island ($4.75, car and driver $22, motorcycle and driver $12.75, bicycle and rider $7; ages 5-11 ½-price). Terminal serving Victoria actually located in Swartz Bay, north of Victoria. (See Victoria below.)

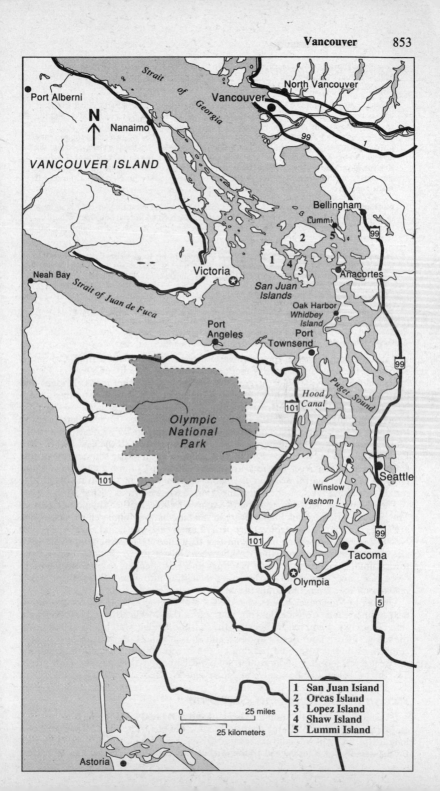

Gray Line Tours: 900 W. Georgia St. (681-8687), in Hotel Vancouver. Expensive but worthwhile city tours with a number of package options. Basic tours leave daily and last 3½ hr. (fare $29.50, children $15). Reservations required.

Public Transport: Metro Transit covers most of the city and suburbs, with direct transport or easy connections to the city's points of departure: Tsawwassen, Horseshoe Bay, and the airport. One-way ride in central zone $1.25, seniors and ages 5-11 65¢. Two-zone peak hour (6:30-9:30am and 3-6:30pm), fare $1.75, seniors and ages 5-11 90¢; off-peak fares for one-zone price. Day-passes $3.50, transfers free. Single fares, passes, and transfers are good for the SeaBus and SkyTrain, as well as the bus. Schedules available at Vancouver Travel. The **Sea-Bus** runs from the Granville Waterfront Station, at the foot of Granville St. in downtown Vancouver, to the Lonsdale Quay at the foot of Lonsdale Ave. in North Vancouver. All single-zone fares, all transfers and passes accepted.

Car Rental: Rent-A-Wreck, 180 W. Georgia (688-0001), in the West End, or 1085 Kingsway (876-5629) at Glen. From $35 per day. 150km free, 15¢ each additional km. Open Mon.-Fri. 8am-9pm, Sat. 8am-6pm, Sun. 9am-5pm. Kingsway location open Mon.-Fri. 8am-7pm, Sat. 9am-5pm. Must be 19 with credit card.

Help Lines: Vancouver Crisis Center, 733-4111. Open 24 hr. **Rape Crisis Center,** 875-6011. Open 24 hr. **Gay and Lesbian Switchboard,** 1-1170 Bute St. (684-6869). Open Mon.-Fri. 7-10pm, Sat.-Sun. 4-10pm. **Seniors Information and Support,** 531-2320 or 531-2425.

Time Zone: Pacific (3 hr. behind Eastern).

Post Office: 349 W. Georgia St. (662-5725). Open Mon.-Fri. 8am-5:30pm. **Postal Code:** V6B 3P7.

Area Code: 604.

Vancouver crounches in the southwestern corner of mainland British Columbia, across the Georgia Strait from Vancouver Island and the city of Victoria. Rivers, inlets, and bays divide Vancouver into regions and neighborhoods. Bridges and boats abound—the profusion of waterways can confuse even the most diligent map-reader. Most of the city's attractions attract on the city center peninsula and the larger rhino snout to the south. Many neighborhoods, as the residents perceive them, are not labeled on the city maps issued by Tourism B.C. Locals refer to the center peninsula's residential area, bounded by downtown to the east and Stanley Park to the west, as the **West End.** The western portion of the southern peninsula from around Alma Ave. to the University of British Columbia campus is **Point Grey,** while the central area on the same peninsula, from the Granville Bridge roughly to Alma Ave., is the Kitsilano, (familiarly known as **"Kits").**

The distinction between streets and avenues follows neither rhyme nor reason. The one exception to this Shakespearean madness is the numbered streets, which are always avenues in Vancouver proper (running east-west), and always streets in North Vancouver (running whichever way they choose). Downtown, private vehicles cannot run on the **Granville Mall,**between Nelson and W. Pender. Both **China-town,** running east-west between Hastings and East Pender, from Garrel Ave. to Gore Ave., and **Gastown,** on Alexander as it runs into Water St., you can easily reached on foot from the Granville Mall.

Driving in Vancouver is a serious hassle, and finding parking spaces downtown next to impossible. Consider leaving your car at the **Park'n'Ride** in New Westminster. (Exit Hwy. 1 and follow signs for the Pattullo Bridge; watch for signs just over the bridge.) Rush hour begins at dawn and ends at sunset. Beware of the 3 to 6pm restrictions on left turns and parking on the streets. When you can't find parking at street level, look for underground lots, but be prepared to pay sky-high prices. Try the lot below Pacific Centre at Howe and W. Georgia.

Accommodations and Camping

Greater Vancouver is a rabbit warren of bed and breakfast accommodations; average rates run about $25 for singles, $35 for doubles. The visitors bureau has a long list of B&Bs in Vancouver. Several private agencies also match travelers with B&Bs, usually for a fee; get in touch with **Town and Country Bed and Breakfast** at 731-5942 or **Best Canadian** at 738-7207. Always call for reservations at least two days in advance.

Vancouver International Hostel (IYHF), 1515 Discovery St. (224-3208), in Point Grey on Jericho Beach. Turn north off 4th Ave., following signs for Marine Dr., or take bus #4 from Granville St. downtown. Comely location on beach and park, with a superlative view of the city from False Creek. Over 350 beds, massive dorm rooms, good cooking facilities, chore opportunities, and TV room. 8 family rooms. In summer, 3-day max. stay. Strictly enforced midnight curfew. $10, nonmembers $12. Linen $10.

Globetrotter's Inn, 170 W. Esplanade in North Vancouver (988-5141). Take the SeaBus to Lonsdale Quay, then walk 1 block east to W. Esplanade and Chesterfield. Needs vacuuming, but close to downtown. Kitchen facilities and shared baths. $12. Private singles $25. Doubles $30.

Vincent's Backpackers Hostel, 927 Main (682-2441), right next to the VIA train station, under a big green store called "The Source." Take "Main St." bus #3 or "Fraser" #8. Not quite as clean or as structured as the IYHF hostel, but more colorful, cheaper, and walking distance from downtown. Kitchen, fridge, TV, stereo, and the music of revving Greyhound engines. Office open 8am-midnight. Check-in before noon for the best shot at a bed. Shared rooms $8. Singles with shared bath $16. Doubles with shared bath $20.

YWCA, 580 Burrard St. (662-8188 or 800-633-1424), downtown at Dunsmuir, 7 blocks from the bus depot. Women, male-female couples, and families; men when there's extra room. Recently remodeled and clean. High-quality sports facilities for female guests over 15 years old (free). Kitchens on every other floor, and cafeteria in basement. Some singles smaller than others; ask to see a few before choosing. 4-week max. stay. Singles $34. Doubles $49. Extra bed $10. YWCA members, seniors, and groups 10% discount. Weekly and monthly rates available from Sept.-June.

YMCA, 955 Burrard (681-0221), between Smithe and Nelson, 4 blocks south of the YWCA. Newly renovated. Concerned staff on duty 24 hr. Shared washrooms and showers. Pool, gymnasiums, ball courts, and weight rooms (free). Cafeteria open Mon.-Fri. 7am-4pm, Sat. 8am-2pm. Singles $27. Doubles $46. Weekly and monthly rates available Oct.-April.

Richmond RV Park, 6200 River Rd. (270-7878), near Holly Bridge in Richmond. Take Hwy. 99 to Westminster Hwy., then follow the signs. Sites offer little privacy, but great showers and friendly staff soothe your woes. Sites $13, with hookup $16-18. Open April-Oct.

ParkCanada 4799 Hwy. 17 (943-5811), in Delta, about 30km south of downtown Vancouver. Take Hwy. 99 south to Tsawwassen Ferry Terminal Rd., then go east for 2.5km. Located next to a giant waterslide park; flush toilets, free showers, and tidal pool, though the lines may be long. Sites $11.50.

Food

Steer clear of places specializing in "authentic Canadian cuisine"—nobody really knows what Canadian cuisine is. Seek out the city's best offerings in the diverse ethnic restaurants and the older natural-foods eateries. The East Indian neighborhoods along Main, Fraser, and 49th St. offer spicy dishes of the subcontinent. Vancouver's Chinatown (see Sights below) is the second largest in North America, after San Francisco's. Here groceries, shops, and restaurants cluster around East Pender and Gore St.

The **Granville Island Market,** under the Granville Bridge, off W. 4th Ave. and across False Creek from downtown, intersperses trendy shops, art galleries, and restaurants with produce stands selling local and imported fruits and vegetables. Take one of the many buses that run south on Granville and cross the Granville Bridge; get off at W. 4th St. and walk back 6 blocks down the hill. Otherwise, stay on the bus to Broadway and Granville Exchange and change to bus #51; it will take you directly to the island. (Market open daily 9am-6pm, Labour Day-Victoria Day Tues.-Sun. 9am-6pm.)

The Naam, 2724 W. 4th Ave., in the Kits area. Take bus #4 or 7 from Granville. Vancouver's oldest natural-foods restaurant. Don't let the name's homonyms scare you; Naam delights both the fanatic and the indifferent. Very good tofu-nut-beet burgers ($5), spinach enchiladas ($8), and salad bar ($1.25 per 100g). Open 24 hr.

Isadora's Cooperative Restaurant, 1540 Old Bridge Rd., on Granville Island, 1 block to your right immediately after entering the shopping area. Natural-foods restaurant which sends profits to community service organizations. Sandwiches $7, dinner entrees $10, Bamfield burger made with filet of rock sole $6.25. Open Mon.-Thurs. 7am-10pm, Fri. 7am-11pm, Sat. 9am-10pm. Closed Mon. evenings in winter.

Did's Pizza, 622 Davie St. (681-7368), near Seymour. The graffiti and loud music belie a tame clientele. Excellent east-coast style pizza, with just the right amount of semi-coagulated grease. $3 per slice. Open Mon.-Sat. 11am-3:30am, Sun. 5pm-1am.

The Souvlaki Place, 1807 Mortan St., at Denman near Stanley Park. Greek establishment with an inspiring view of English Bay. *Souvlaki* $4.25; yogurt, honey, and pita $2.75. Open daily 11:30am-11pm.

The Only Seafood Cafe, 20 E. Hastings St., at Carrall St. on the edge of Chinatown, within walking distance of downtown. Large portions of great seafood at decent prices. Cooking since 1912, and they *still* don't have a rest room. Fried halibut steak $9. Open Mon.-Thurs. 11am-9:30pm, Fri.-Sat. 11am-10pm.

The Green Door, 111 E. Pender, in central Chinatown, 3 blocks from The Only. Follow the alley off Columbia St. to find the hidden entrance. This wildly green establishment plays a prominent role in the annals of Vancouver hippie lore. Huge servings of slightly greasy Chinese seafood ($5.50). Open daily noon-10:30pm; Oct.-May Wed.-Mon. noon-10pm.

A Taste of Jamaica, 941 Davie St. (683-3464), downtown. Reggae, Jamaica posters, and red, green, and yellow seat covers. Filling and authentic food. Ox-tail stew $6, goat or lamb curry $6. Open Mon.-Sat. 11am-11pm, Sun. 5-11pm.

Sights

The landmark of the Expo '86 World's Fair is a 17-story, metallic, geodesic sphere which houses **Science World,** 1455 Quebec St. (687-7832), at Terminal Ave. Science World features hands-on exhibits for children and the **Omnimax Theatre** (875-6664), a high-tech hemispheric screenhouse. Featured film subjects range from dinosaurs to asteroids. (Admission both $10, to Science World only $6.50. Call for show times.) The second expo site is the Canada Pavilion, now called **Canada Place,** about ½km away. You can reach it by SkyTrain from the main Expo site. Visitors who make this four-minute journey can view Canadian arts and crafts as well as films in the CN IMAX Theatre (682-4629). Ranging in price ($5.50-8), the not-so-cheap movie thrills from the flat, five-story screen do not look as stunning as the domed screens of other IMAX theatres. (Open daily noon-9pm.)

Newly renovated, the **Lookout!** 555 W. Hastings St. (683-5684), offers fantastic 360° views of the city and surrounding areas. Though expensive, your ticket lasts the whole day; you can take in the skyline later to see if any of the buildings move. (Admission $5, seniors $3. Open daily 9am-10pm.) The **Vancouver Art Gallery,** 750 Hornby St. (682-5621), in Robson Sq., has a small but well-presented collection of classical, contemporary, and Canadian art and photography. Free tours for large groups are frequently given; just tag along. (Open Mon.-Wed. and Fri.-Sat. 10am-5pm, Thurs. 10am-9pm, Sun. noon-5pm. Admission $2.75, seniors and students $1.25. Free Thurs. 5-9pm.)

Most Vancouverites view **Gastown,** a revitalized turn-of-the-century district, as an expensive tourist trap (unlike other, cheaper tourist traps). The area is named for "Gassy Jack" Deighton, the glib con man who opened Vancouver's first saloon here in 1867. Today it overflows with craft shops, boutiques, nightclubs, and restaurants. Many cater exclusively to tourists, but the whole area can still be fun, especially along **Water Street.** Listen for the continent's only steam-powered clock on the corner of Cambie and Water St.—it chimes every 15 minutes. Bordered by Richards St. to the west, Columbia St. to the east, Hastings St. to the south, and the waterfront to the north, Gastown takes a fair walk from downtown or a short ride on bus #22 along Burrard St. to Carrall St.

Just east of Gastown, **Chinatown** also lies within walking distance of downtown. You can also take bus #22 on Burrard St. northbound to Pender St. at Carrall St., and return by bus #22 westbound on Pender St. Vancouver's Chinatown spreads out along Pender St. and both sides of Main St., replete with restaurants and shops. The area is rundown and somewhat unsafe; at night, women traveling alone should exercise caution. Gray Line Tours (see Practical Information) provides a safer but more expensive way to see Chinatown.

Probably the most popular of the city's attractions, **Stanley Park** (681-1141), on the westernmost end of the city center peninsula, testifies to urban foresight. (Take bus #19.) The watery perimeter is followed by a **seawall promenade**, with more views, and more company to the walker or cyclist. Within the park's boundaries lie various restaurants and tennis courts, hiking and biking trails, the Malkin Bowl (an outdoor theater), and equipped beaches. Nature walks leave May to September on Tuesday at 10am, from July to August at 7pm. Call the park for departure points. Rent practically new bikes from **Bayshore**, 745 Denman (688-2453) for $5.75 per hour, $20 per day. Strange aquatic species lurk at the **Vancouver Aquarium** (682-1118), on the eastern side of the park, not far from the entrance. (Open daily 9:30am-8pm; off-season 10am-5:30pm. Admission $5.75, seniors and ages 13-18 $4.75, under 12 $3.25.) Visit Stanley Park's small, free **zoo** next door, if only to see the green monkeys pelt the neighboring harbor seals with apple cores. (Open daily 10am-5pm.)

Follow the western side of the seawall south to **Sunset Beach Park** (738-8535), a strip of grass and beach that extends south all the way to the Burrard Bridge. All of Vancouver's beaches have lifeguards from Victoria Day to Labour Day daily from 11:30am to 9pm. At the southern end of Sunset Beach flounders the **Aquatic Centre**, 1050 Beach Ave. (689-7156), a public facility with a 50m indoor saltwater pool, sauna, gymnasium, and diving tank. (Open Mon.-Thurs. 7am-10pm, Sat. 8am-9pm, Sun. 11am-9pm. Pool opens Mon.-Thurs. at 7am. Gym use $3, pool use $2.50.)

Vancounverites frequent Kitsilano Beach, known to locals as **"Kits,"** on the other side of Arbutus Ave. from Vanier. Its heated salt water outdoor pool (731-0011; open summer only) has changing rooms, lockers, and a snack bar. (Beach open daily 7am-8:45pm; Oct.-May Mon.-Fri. noon-8:45pm, Sat.-Sun. and holidays 10am-8:45pm. Pool admission $1.50, seniors and children 70¢, families $2.75.)

Jericho Beach, to the west, tends to be used less heavily than Kits Beach. Jericho begins a border of beaches and park lands that lines Point Grey and the University of British Columbia. Old-growth forest covers much of the extensive UBC campus in a delightfully untailored fashion. Bike and hiking trails cut through the campus and around the edges. The university rests on a hill, providing lovely views of the city and the surrounding mountains.

Scramble down the cliffs to the southwest of the **University of British Columbia** (UBC) campus to **Wreck Beach**, an unofficial, unsanctioned, unlifeguarded beach for the unclothed. Any UBC student can point you toward one of the semi-hidden access paths.

Entertainment and Events

To keep abreast of the entertainment scene, pick up a copy of the weekly *Georgia Straight*—an allusion to the body of water between mainland B.C. and Vancouver Island—or the new bi-monthly *Boulevard,* both free at newsstands and record stores. The 25¢ *Westender* lists entertainment in that lively neighborhood and also reports on community issues, while the free *Angles* serves the city's gay community.

Basin St. Cabaret, 23 W. Corova St. (688-5351). Hip new club. Local blues and jazz aficionados jam from 9pm-2am. Cheap beer (pint $3, glass $1.50), dance floor, and terrace. No cover.

Blarney Stone Inn, 216 Carrall St. (687-4322). Live Irish music, restaurant, and dance floor. Lunch $5, dinner around $12. Open Mon. 11:30am-5pm, Tues.-Fri. 11:30am-2am, Sat. 5pm-2am. Cover $3.

Town Pump, 66 Water St. (683-6695), a few blocks away from the Blarney Stone in the center of Gastown. Clientele ranges from college students to business people. Snack menu available all day, burgers $6. Live music from jazz to reggae nightly. Open Mon.-Sat. 11:30am-2am, Sun. 11:30am-midnight. Tickets for big names $10-15.

The Gandy Dancer, 1222 Hamilton St. (684-7321), in the warehouse district. Enter facing Pacific Blvd. The city's most innovative gay and lesbian club. Contests Tues. and Wed., men only Fri. Open daily 7:30pm-2am.

Robson Square Media Centre, 800 Robson St. (660-2487), sponsors events almost daily during the summer and weekly the rest of the year, either on the plaza at the square or in the center itself. Their concerts, theater productions, exhibits, lectures, symposia, and films are all free or at low cost. Pick up the center's monthly brochure *What's Happening at Robson Square* from the visitors bureau or businesses in the square.

Vancouver also has an active theater community. The Arts Club Theatre, Granville Island (687-1644), hosts big-name theater and musicals, while the Theatre in the Park program (687-0174) in Stanley Park's Malkin Bowl, has a summer season of musical comedy. The annual Vancouver Shakespeare Festival (734-0194), from June to August in Vanier Park, often needs volunteer ushers and program-sellers, who get to watch the critically acclaimed shows for free.

Vancouver's universities have dance cards filled with cultural activities. At Simon Fraser University, the SFU Centre for the Arts (291-3514) offers both student and guest-professional theater, primarily from September to May. For UBC activities, call (228-3131) or pick up a free copy of *Ubissey*. UBC's film series screens high-quality movies Thursday and Friday nights for $1.50.

Vancouver's Chinese community celebrates its heritage on Chinese New Year (usually in early to mid-Feb.) with fireworks, music, parades, and dragons. The famed Vancouver Folk Music Festival takes place in mid-July in Jericho Park, when North America's best big- and little-name performers give concerts and workshops for three days. You can purchase tickets by the event, or for the whole weekend; buy a whole-weekend ticket before June 1 to receive a $5 discount. For more details, contact the festival at 3271 Main St., Vancouver V6V 3M6 (879-2931). Hotels fill months in advance for the First People's Cultural Festival, which holds a full day of traditional dance and crafts at a different venue each June. Call the information center for details. (Admission $10. Proceeds to charity.)

Near Vancouver

Puff along on the Royal Hudson Steam Locomotive, operated by 1st Tours (688-7246). After a two-hour tour along the coast from Vancouver to Squamish (the gateway to Garibaldi Provincial Park), passengers on the "Love Train" get 90 minutes to browse in town before they head back. (Excursions May 21-July 16 Wed.-Sun.; July 19-Sept. 4 daily; Sept. 6-Sept. 24 Wed.-Sun. Fare $24, seniors and youths $20, children $14.) The train departs from the B.C. Rail terminal, 1311 W. 1st St., across the Lions Gate Bridge in North Vancouver. Call 1st Tours for required reservations.

To the east, the town of Deep Cove maintains that *je ne sais quoi* of a fishing village. Sea otters and seals gather on the pleasant Indian Arm beaches. Take bus #210 from Pender to the Phibbs Exchange on the north side of Second Narrows Bridge; from there, take bus #211 or 212. Cates Park, at the end of Dollarton Hwy. on the way to Deep Cove, has popular swimming and scuba waters. A good biking daytrip out of Vancouver. Bus #211 also leads to beautiful Mount Seymour Provincial Park. Trails leave from Mt. Seymour Rd., and a paved road winds the 8km to the top. One hundred campsites ($7) are available, and the skiing is superb.

For a less vigorous hike that still offers fantastic views of the city, head for Lynn Canyon Park. The suspension bridge here is free and uncrowded, unlike its more publicized look-alike in Capilano Canyon. Take bus #228 from the North Vancouver Seabus terminal and walk the ½km to the bridge.

A classic trip farther outside Vancouver is the two-hour drive up Rte. 99 to the town of Whistler and nearby Garibaldi Provincial Park. Follow Rte. 99 north from Horseshoe Bay, or take local Maverick Coach Lines (255-1171). B.C. Rail (see Practical Information above) also serves Whistler from Vancouver; their run stops directly behind the local youth hostel. Check the ride board at the IYHF hostel in Vancouver, since people frequently trek between the two. Whistler Mountain has top skiing, with the highest accessible vertical drop in North America. Slopes for the beginner and intermediate are also available. For more information contact Whistler Resort Association, Whistler V0N 1B0 (932-4222). The park also offers some fine wilderness hiking but vehicle access is out of the question. On the western shore of Alta Lake in Whistler, that North American giant, the **Whistler Youth Hostel (CYHA)** (932-5492), has 35 beds, laundry, and extensive kitchen facilities. ($10, nonmembers $12.) In cahoots with Vincent's in Vancouver, a **Backpackers Hostel**, 2124 Lake Placid Rd. (932-1177), lies near the train station. With nice but cramped rooms ($12), the hostel also has a kitchen, TV, and VCR.

Victoria

Much like its imperious namesake, British Columbia's capital city should convince even the most revisionist of travelers and travel guides that Britain was a crucial founding nation of Canada. Victoria's Inner Harbour, where most action occurs, fills with double-decker buses adorned with the Union Jack and British accents, from Cockney to the Queen's English, are never far away. Even afternoon tea remains a daily ritual here, especially behind the Tweed Curtain in Oak Bay. Queen Victoria herself would have been amused.

Practical Information

Police: 625 Fisgard (384-4111), at Government St. Open 24 hr.

Visitor Information: Tourism Victoria, 812 Wharf St. (382-2127), in the Inner Harbour. More pamphlets than you'll ever read, and an omniscient staff.

Buses: Greyhound, 710 Douglas St. (385-5248) behind the Empress Hotel. No service on the island or to Vancouver. **Pacific Coach Lines** and **Island Coach Lines,** 700 Douglas St. (385-4411), in the same building. Service to most island cities.

Ferries: BC Ferry, 656-0757 or 386-3431. Service to Vancouver or the mainland. **Washington State Ferries,** 381-1551. To the San Juans. **Black Ball Transport,** 286-2202. Port Angeles connection.

Public Transport: Victoria Regional Transit, 382-6161. Buses to most major attractions stop along Douglas St. Two-zone fare $1.25. Day passes $3.

Help Lines: Crisis Line, 386-6323. **Handicapped Services,** 382-4488 or 727-7811.

Time Zone: Pacific (3 hr. behind Eastern).

Post Office: Postal Station E, 1230 Government St. (388-3575), at Yates. Open Mon.-Fri. 8:30am-5pm. **Postal Code:** V8W 2L9.

Accommodations and Camping

Victoria Youth Hostel (IYHF), 516 Yates St. (385-4511), at Wharf. Big, modern, and clean. 102 beds. Kitchen and laundry. $10, nonmembers $12.

Salvation Army Men's Hostel, 525 Johnson St. at Wharf, around the corner from the youth hostel. Immaculate and well-run. Dorms $6. Private rooms $10. Meals $1.50.

YWCA, 880 Courtney St. (386-7511), at Quadra. Women only. Private rooms with shared bath. Singles $29. Doubles $43. Breakfast included.

James Bay Inn, 270 Government St. (384-7151), at Toronto St. Rooms with shared bath above the pub. Don't get your liquids confused. Singles $29. Doubles $37. Reservations required July-Sept.

McDonald Park Campground, 655-9020. 30km north of downtown on Hwy. 17. Sites $6.

Thetis Lake Campground (478-3845), 10km north of the city center. Sites $10, with hookup $12.50.

Food

Victoria's predilection for the old ways is perhaps best evidenced by the way its citizens eat. Victorians actually do take tea—some only on occasion, others every day. Other foods exist, of course, but to indulge in the romanticism of the city, you must partake of the ceremony at least once. To experience some of the city's ethnic and gastronomic diversity, head into **Chinatown**, west of Fisgard and Government. To create your own culinary delight, pick up the day's catch at **Fisherman's Wharf** between Superior and St. Lawrence. Other essentials sell at the **Ideal Food Market**, 640 Wharf at Broad (open daily 9am-11:30pm).

The Blethering Place, 2250 Oak Bay Ave. at Monterey St. Take bus #11. Behind the Tweed Curtain. Afternoon tea ($5.50) or a "Ploughman's Lunch" ($6). Open daily 8am-10pm.

Flying Rhino Diner, 1219 Wharf St., close to the youth hostel. No pachyderms, just great nut burgers and homemade soup combos for $6. Open Mon.-Fri. 8am-8pm, Sat. 10am-6pm, Sun. 10am-4pm.

Eugene's, 1280 Broad St., off View. Wonderful variety of Greek foods; breakfast selections other than eggs and OJ. Open Mon.-Fri. 8am-10pm, Sat. 10am-9pm.

Las Flores, 536 Yates St. Difficult-to-decipher newsprint menus, but the food compensates. Filling burrito-enchilada combos $8. Terrific hot sauce. Open daily noon-10pm.

James Bay Tearoom, 332 Manzies St., at Superior. Another simply smashing tea room—so smashingly busy that the service suffers. Tea daily 1-4:30pm, but don't arrive any earlier than 2:30pm. Open Mon.-Sat. 7am-9pm, Sun. 8am-9pm.

Sights and Activities

After your bus schedule wears out, Victoria restores your faith in traveling on foot. Almost everything lies within walking distance in the **Inner Harbour,** and you never have to venture more than a couple of kilometers ("clicks" in local parlance) to reach the city's parks and beaches. Every visitor should take time to visit the **Royal British Columbian Museum,** 675 Belleville St. (387-3014 for a tape, 387-3701 for a person). Considered by most the best museum in Canada, it chronicles the geological and cultural histories of the province while displaying detailed exhibits on logging, mining, and fishing. The extensive exhibits of Native American art, culture, and history include full-scale replicas of various forms of shelter used centuries ago. The gallery of Haida totem art is particularly moving; "open ocean" provides a wonderfully tongue-in-cheek re-creation of the first desert in a bathysphere. (Open daily 9:30am-7pm; Oct.-April daily 10am-5:30pm. Two-day admission $5, seniors, disabled, students with ID, and ages 13-18 $3, children 6-12 $1. Free Mon. Oct.-April.) Fascinating free films about British Columbia's heritage run in the summer from 11am to 3:30pm in the museum's Newcombe Theatre. Behind the museum, **Thunderbird Park** displays a striking bevy of totems and longhouses, backed by the intricate towers of the Empress Hotel.

Across the street from the museum stand the imposing **Parliament Buildings,** 501 Belleville St. (387-6121), home of the provincial government since 1859. Almost 50 taels (an anachronistic British measure slightly more than an ounce) of gold grace the 10-story dome and Renaissance-inspired vestibule. Free tours leave the steps every 20 minutes (daily 9am-5pm).

Surrounding the Parliament buildings along Belleville and Menzies St. are a number of less-than-unique attractions. **Undersea Gardens** (382-5717) takes you underwater in a plexiglass corridor to view denizens of the deep and not-so-deep. (Open daily 9am-9pm. Admission $5.50.) Just next door, the **Royal London Wax Museum** (338-4461) ironically casts Mme. Tussaud in wax. (Open daily 8:30am-10:30pm.)

Around the corner on Wharf St., the **Emily Carr Gallery,** 1107 Wharf St. (387-3080), features original work of this turn-of-the-century BC artist who synthesized British landscape conventions and Native American style. The collection includes many of her paintings of totems, conscious attempts to preserve what she saw as "art treasures of a passing race." Also on display are photographs and manuscripts of other period artists, politicians, and prominent citizens. Free films on Carr's life and work show at 2:30pm. (Open Mon.-Sat. 10am-5pm. Free.)

South of the Inner Harbour, **Beacon Hill Park** (take bus #5) has arresting views over the Strait of Juan de Fuca. The park's flower gardens, 350-year-old garry oaks, and network of paths make for a perfect picnic spot. One mi. east of the Inner Harbour, **Craigdarroch Castle,** 1050 Joan Crescent (592-5323), embodies Victoria's wealth. Take bus #11 or 14 to Oak St. and transfer to #1 or 2. The house was built in 1890 by Robert Dunsmuir, a BC coal and railroad tycoon, in order to tempt his wife away from their native Scotland. (Open daily 9am-7:30pm; winter 10am-5pm. Admission $4, seniors and students $3.50.)

The museum that's never the same, the **Art Gallery of Greater Victoria,** 1040 Moss (384-4101), shifts 1 block back towards the Inner Harbour on Fort St. Save a wooden Shinto shrine, the gallery has no permanent collection, instead housing an endless succession of temporary exhibits culled from local and international sources. (Open Mon.-Sat. 10am-5pm, Thurs. 10am-9pm, Sun. 1-5pm. Admission $3, seniors $1.50.)

Almost worth the exorbitant entrance fee are the stunning **Butchart Gardens,** 800 Benvennto, 22km north of Victoria (652-4422 Mon.-Fri. 9am-5pm; 652-5256 recording). Jennie Butchart begun the rose, Japanese, and Italian gardens in 1904 in an attempt to reclaim the wasteland that was her husband's quarry and cement plant. From mid-May to September, the whole area is lit at dusk, and the gardens, still administered by the Butchart family, host variety shows and cartoons; Saturday nights in July and August, the skies shimmer with fireworks displays. (Gardens open May-June and Sept. daily 9am-9pm; July-Aug. 9am-11pm; March-April and Oct. 9am-5pm; Jan.-Feb. and Nov. 9am-4pm; Dec. 9am-8pm. Summer admission $9.50, ages 13-17 $5, ages 5-12 $1; otherwise, the more flowers, the more you pay. Take bus #74.) Motorists should consider an approach to Butchart Gardens via the **Scenic Marine Drive,** following the coastline along Dalles and other roads for a spectacular 45 minutes. The route passes through sedate suburban neighborhoods and offers a memorable view of the Olympic Mountains across the Strait of Juan de Fuca.

Pick up the misnamed weekly *Monday Magazine,* available around the city. The mag is published, logically enough, every Thursday; listings include jazz, blues, rock, and more jazz. The **Victoria Symphony Society,** 846 Broughton St. (385-6515), performs regularly under conductor Peter McCoppin, and the **University of Victoria Auditorium,** Finnerty Rd. (721-8480), stages a variety of student productions. The **Pacific Opera** performs at the McPherson Playhouse, 3 Centennial Sq. (386-6121), at the corner of Pandora and Government St. During the summer, they undertake a popular musical comedy series.

The **Folkfest** in late June celebrates Canada's birthday (July 1) and the country's "unity in diversity" with performances by politically correct and culturally diverse musicians. The **JazzFest,** sponsored by the Victoria Jazz Society (381-4142), also culminates on Canada Day. The **Classic Boat Festival** sets sail on Labor Day weekend and displays pre-1955 wooden boats in the Inner Harbour. Free entertainment accompanies the show. Contact the visitor and convention bureau (382-2127) for more information on all Inner Harbour events.

INDEX